1850 CENSUS, EAST CENTRAL KENTUCKY

Counties of Clark, Estill, Fayette, Garrard, Jessamine, Madison, Montgomery and Owsley

VOLUME 8

By

BYRON SISTLER, BARBARA SISTLER,
and SAMUEL SISTLER

JANAWAY PUBLISHING, INC.
Santa Maria, California
2012

Notice

In many older books, foxing (or discoloration) occurs and, in some instances, print lightens with wear and age. Reprinted books, such as this, often duplicate these flaws, notwithstanding efforts to reduce or eliminate them. The pages of this reprint have been digitally enhanced and, where possible, the flaws eliminated in order to provide clarity of content and a pleasant reading experience.

Copyright © 1995, Byron Sistler & Associates, Inc.

Originally published:
Nashville, Tennessee 1995

Reprinted by:

Janaway Publishing, Inc.
732 Kelsey Ct.
Santa Maria, California 93454
(805) 925-1038
www.janawaygenealogy.com
2012

ISBN: 978-1-59641-171-5

Made in the United States of America

INTRODUCTION

The entries appear in the same order as on the original schedules. In general an entry comprises all members of a given household, except that any individuals whose surname differed from that of the household head are shown as a separate unit.

An asterisk (*) identifies each entry which does not consist of an entire household.

The symbol (B) identified black or mulatto individuals or families. If the (B) follows the first name in the entry it means the entire household is black. Where the household is mixed, each black person is separately identified with the (B).

The symbol (I) was supposed to identify Indians, but actually was used by the enumerators to represent various racial mixtures.

The number after each name is the person's age. The "Schedule Page" number is the stamped number in the upper right hand corner of every other page of the original schedules. The page following the numbered one assumes the same number.

Transcription for the six counties is followed by a full name index listing the first name of each entry—usually the household head. Page numbers referred to in the index are the Schedule page numbers, not the page numbers of this book.

County of residence is identified in the index by appropriate county symbols. They are as follows:

Clark	CL	Jessamine*	JE
Estill	ES	Madison	MA
Fayette	F	Montgomery	MT
Garrard	GD	Owsley	OS

*IMPORTANT NOTE: the scribe for the Jessamine County schedules consistently cut off any names extending beyond the last line of each page. Many individuals, especially young children, are consequently missing.

As always, we urge the researcher to refer back to the original schedules where possible, as there is important information on those schedules not contained in this book. Data such as occupation, real estate value and state of birth are all very meaningful, and a full genealogical search is not obtainable without this additional information.

The Sistlers

TABLE OF CONTENTS

Clark County 1

Estill County 53

Fayette County 87

Garrard County 181

Jessamine County 227

Madison County 271

Montgomery County 335

Owsley County 381

Index 403

1850 Census Clark County Kentucky

Schedule Page 1

GRIGSBY, Charlott 75*, Nathanil 35
JENKINS, Ann M. 13*
GRIGSBY, John V. 24*, Amanda M. 26, Lewis B. 13
BUSH, Sarah 69*, Amanda F. 40
HILL, James 32, Mary 25, William 11, Peter 8, James 6, Mary J.? 4, Georg 1
MAPLES, Shadrack 60*, Susan 55, John 22, Abram D. 16, Abslom F. 14, Sarah A. 12
STRODE, James 56*, Mary 58
LINGINFELTER, Philip 18*
MCDONALD, Mary 37*, Frederick 10
BOWREN, Cornelius 65*
SHRITES, William P. 16*, Mary E. 14
WEATHERS, James 48*, Eliza 49, Mary 22, James E. 17, Elizabeth 5/12
QUISENBERY, C. P. 20 (m)*
SMITH, Joseph? 60* (B)
FERGUSON, Lucy 49*
MCKINNEY, William 26*, Sarah 24, Lucy 1, Virginia 5/12
TAYLOR, Tom 66*
SAVARY, Henry 43*, Ellen 32, John 10, Susan 7, Mary 3, Henrietta 2, Milley 8/12
TAYLOR, Henry S. 25*
ROBENSON, Peyton 21*
SMITH, Willis R. 60*, Elizabeth 55, John 33, Minon 23 (m), Lucy 18, Knox 16, Allice 14, Mary 11
STONESTREET, Edmond 46* (B)
HENSLEY, George W. 32*, Mary J. 23, John W. 5, Nancy E. 4, Melissa 2, Mildrid 8/12, Nathan 78
DONLEY, Benj. D. 16*
LOWE, William 34*, Louisa 23
JOHNSON, Stephen 27*
TAYLOR, Dorotha 37, Reuben 17, Robt. W. 16, Lucy C. 12, Mary F. 10, James E. 5, Charles M. 3, Francis A. 9/12
RAINEY, James sr. 81, Elizabeth 73, James jr. 15
TAYLOR, John P. 51, Rachel P. 50, Charles M. 17, Martty? G. 14, Edward 11, Mildred R. 9

Schedule Page 2

TAYLOR, H. M. H. 42 (m), Catharine 40, Colby H. 14, Mary R. 12, Richard 5, Sarah H. 4, Robert M. 1, Reuben S. 72, Colby H. 71, Mary T. 30, John W. 27, Malinda M. 30
SUTHERLAND, George 23, Margarett A. 18, Mary H. 1
SUTHERLAND, Mary 40, Ann 16, Rolley 13, David 10, Lucinda 7
GRIGSBY, John 51*, Sarah P.? 54, James S. 18, Wm. B. F. 15
PALMER, William 24*
BENNING, James 22* (B)
GARNER, John C. 39*
CAMPBELL, Sudieth? 82 (f)*
CLARK, Harriett 41*, Richard 14
THOMAS, Pohma? 45 (m), Permelia 40, Sarah 21, Eliz. 17, Elizabeth 15, Almanzer 12 (m), Eliza 10, John 9, James 7, Alonzo 5
ELKIN, Zach 21, Mary E. 20, Frances A. 1

1850 Census Clark County Kentucky

MORTON, John 50*, Lean B. 40 (f), Susan 17, John W. 15, Tabitha A. 13, Elizabeth 11, Jeremiah 8, Mary J. 3, Sarah A. 1, Lewis 25 (B)
WILLIAMS, Abram 25*
DIDLAKE, Edmond H. 52, Mildred G. 43, Robert 23, Lucy W. 18, John T. 16, Sally 14, George H. 11, Clifton F. 9, Madison T. 7, Edmond H. 5
RASH, William 67, Elizabeth 62, A. D. 27 (m), A. B. 28 (f), Elizabeth A. 4, Wallin 1
CAPPS, Caleb 72, Marth 66, Charles W. 24, Nancy J. 18, Anna 8/12
SMITH, Daniel 47*, Drusilla 43, Thomas C. 19, Mary E. 17, John D. 15, Evaline 13, Sarah A. 11, Louisa P. 9, Benjam. H. 7, William F. 7/12, Elizabeth 88

Schedule Page 3

CLARK, Charity 70* (B)
LONG, George 50, Mary 42, Robert 20, William 20, Henry 13, James 7, Mariam 12, Catharine 7, Ellen 5
SPENCER, John 37, Louisa 26, Jesse 6, John W. 4, James 2
COUCHMAN, William 43*, Mary J. 33, John 7, Mary 5, Peter 4, Sarah 9/12
WILLIAMS, James 22*
TAYLOR, Thomas M. 49*, Ann C. 47, James H. 24, Mary 20, William W. 20, Knox P. 15
WOODFORD, John 12?*
DUVALL, Daniel 34*, Mary A. 31, John D. 11, Rachel F. 1
CRIM, Albien 23*
SPHAR, James M. _7*, Isabella 31, Amanda C. 23
SPHAR, Willis 36, Mary 26, James M. 1
KENDALL, Bailey 40, Elizabeth 20, Frances 2
MARTIN, Robert E. 55*, Elizabeth B. 40, Willis 21, Sarah M. 15, Robert E. jr. 10, Rachel R. 6, Freeman T. 2
LEWIS, Asa K. 4*
FREEMAN, William 27*
NOE, Nimrod 19*
ALLEN, John S. 63, Rebecca 63
MORGAN, Van 59*, Margarett 49
THORNSBERG, Mary 15*
WILLIAMS, Charles B. 24*
CRIM, Benjamin Y. 45*, Ann E. 39, Joseph H. 21
COONS?, Nancy 27*
WILSON, George S. 32, Mary E. 23, Benjamin H. 5/12
DUVALL, Perry 64 (B), Polly 60
MCMILLAN, James 42*, Rachel P. 33
PRICE, Ida 1*
BUSH, William 40*
BROOKING, Robert E. 69*, Mariane 33?, Roger R. 26
CHILES, Laura 12*
BATTAILE, James E. 28*, Dorothea 28, George N. 4, John W. 2, William 29

1850 Census Clark County Kentucky

Schedule Page 4

PRICE, Anna 73, William 32
NICHOLAS, Primus 55 (B)
PRESTON, Letitia 77, Alfred 35, Gertrude 11
PRESTON, Lucy 63 (B)
GREEN, Thomas 34* (B), Tina 66
COLEMAN, Rosetta 5* (B)
ELLIS, Dick 67 (B), Lenny 60 (f)
LEWIS, Evaline 45 (B), Edward 15, Lucy 11, William 10, John 4
SPURR, William H. 41*, Rebecca 22, Edward 3, William 1, Mary 83?
KETTLE, Henry 23*
MARTIN, Samuel D. 59, Elizabeth 55, Samuel T. 31, Ann E. 28, Francis M. 19, Rachel D. 15, Helen B. 12, George T. 9, Samuel D. 7, Fanny S. 5, Charles G. 3, Betty F. 1, Peggy _8 (B)
TAYLOR, Hubbard sr. 61, Mary Ann T. 51, Sarah M. 20, Jones M. 17, George W. 14, Pendleton 11
STONESTREET, James 62*, Jacob 28, Amelia 21, James 22, Henry 17, Lucy 1
MARTIN, Willis 25* (B)
WAYMAN, James 34, Sarah 34, Mary 73?, James 14, William O. 13, Fielding T. 11, Joseph M. 9, Mary E. 7, Richard W. 4, Sarah E. 1
PARRISH, Dickerson 65
GRAVETT, Ellis jr. 27, Martha 22, Sarah E. 2, Susan F. 8/12
FLYNT, Margarett 36, Josanna 12 (f), Mary D. 10, John R. 9, William H. 8, Martha E. 6, Ella J. 4
FISHBACK, George T. 37, Louisa H. 30, William P. 12, George W. 10, Anna M. 7
FISHBACK, Samuel _. 30, Mary A. 28, James L. 8, Cramel H. 15 (m)
TAYLOR, Robert S. 30*, Elizabeth 21, Sary E. 4 (f), Ann 3, Robert S. 10/12

Schedule Page 5

MORRISON, Harriet 50*, Harrill 14 (f)
CROW, Nathanel 21*
JONES, Roger 31, Elizabeth 24
TAYLOR, James F. 41*, Susan M. 34, John W. 16, Mary W. 13, Fracis 35 (m)
BALLARD?, Byrd W. 28*
TALIAFERRO, Thomas 22*
MORGAN, Raleigh 25, A. A. 19 (f), Thomas 27
SHARP, Benjamin 40, Mary 35, Martha A. 14, Bossell 9, Mary J. 6, Lethia Ann 3, John 5
BURBRIDGE, Thomas 53, Elizabeth 48, Benjamin 28, Sally 21, Thomas 3
BOSWELL, James M. 35, Susan 29, Ann M. 8, Thomas 6, Joseph 4, Elizabeth 2
SCHOOLER, Lewis 39*, Louisa 42
RIDEN, Nancy 61*, Mary F. 8, Thomas 5, Samuel 1
STRAFFORD, Samuel 38, H. 32 (f), William S. F. 14, Rebecca F. 8, Nancy J. 6, Matilda J. 4, Oliver A. 1
SHARP, Benjamin jr. 25*, Mahala 17, Mary A. 50, Diana 27, Eliza 30, Calvin D. 12
MCCORD, Samuel 6*
SPURR, Jasper N. 22*, Susana 28
ANDERSON, John 12*
NELSON, James? 50*, Rebecca 37, Robert 23, James 21, Elizabeth 16, Theodocia A. 15, Sarah M. 5, John W. 3, George B. 4/12

1850 Census Clark County Kentucky

ROGERS, James 35*
HOLLADAY, Waller 53*, Sarah A. 29, Cordelia 5, Gemima 4, Ann E. 2
WHITTINGTON, James H. 10*
LAFAYETT, James 21*
SPURR, James 48*
BROOKING, Caroline 37* (B), John E. 3, Armasinda 7/12
GARTON, Henry 35* (B)
SPURR, John C. 46*, America 36, Martha 19, Mahala 17, Bluford 15, Dudley 12, Susan 11, James 9, Milly P. 6, William H. 5, Nancy 3, Sarah A. 1
LAUGHLIN, John W. 23*

Schedule Page 6

HOLLADAY, Joseph 59*, Sarah 55, Milton 25, Stepher 23 (m), Joesph 21, David 19, Benjamin 17, Lewis 16, Mary E. 9
MCCALLA, James D. 25*
HICKMAN, Joel 88*, Adaline P. 50, Edwin C. 35, R. B. 9 (m), P. A.? D. 7 (m)
ELLIOTT, Priscilla F. 23*, E. F. 27 (m)
SHACKELFORD, T. M. 23 (m)*
HALTON, Tho. 60 (m), Sophia 55, Adaline 23, Tho. jr. 21, Charles 7, Thomas jr. 2
BARBEE, George 27, Eleanor F. 22, Clara 4, Catharine 7/12, Junius 30
JONES, Fauntleroy 33*, Martha J. 25, Mary 7, Francis 6, William 2, Lewis 6/12
SHORT, John 58*
ROGERS, Robert C. 41, Elizabeth 32, Robert C. 6, William H. 4, John C. 2
BROWNING, E. C. 31 (m), Lucy W. 25, Jane 72, Eilzabeth 5, JAmes 4, Blaydes 11/12
CHRISTIAN, Lucinda 25, Elizabeth 6/12
GIBSON, Anna 68*
WILSON, Dillard 23*, Jarred? P. 12
BERKLEY, Samuel 34
GIBSON, Henry 37*
WILLIFORD, Mary 65*, James 21
SMITHEA, Granvith 25*
SUTHERLAND, Lewis 25, Mary 19, Ann E. 1, Thomas 7
WILSON, William H. 39, Sarah H. 36, James L. 11, Ann E. 10, Lucinda 6, China M. 5 (f), William B. 3
BERKLER, Reuben 57
MORTON, Jonathan 70*, China 62 (f), Shelbey 30, Telitha 28, David 26
GRIMES, Sally 32*, Mary P. 4

Schedule Page 7

SIMPSON, Eleanor 41, Elizabeth 18, Jonathan 15, Mary 10, Sally A. 7
GRIMES, Carla 40 (m), Louisa 33, Aria P. 9 (f), Willis T. 7, Albert 4, Telitha 2, Charles 1, Charles O. 22
PARRISH, Temple 43, Diana 39, Emily 17, Ryal? 14, John 12, Henry 9, Joseph 7, Robert 5, Samuel 2
PETTICORD, William 37, Harlippa 41, Ruscius? 77 (f), Harriet A. 15, Arabella F. 13, Thomas J. 11, Sarah M. 9, Mary M. 7, Henrietta 4
BERKLEY, Daniel 89, Kutty 46 (f), John 44, Nancy 42
SHARP, Nancy 54, Lewellen 19 (m)

- 4 -

1850 Census Clark County Kentucky

BERKLEY, Leven 35, Rachel 27, Willis P. 4, Sarah F. 1
BUSH, Ambrose 72*, Jutia? 23 (f)
BERRY, Robert 23*
BUSH, Pleasant 25, Polly Ann 25, Buford A. 6, Williar O. 4
TINSLEY, Ransom 37, Mary J. 34, Mary A. 73, Jane 13, Thomas G. 10, William M. 9, Rebecca L. 7, Susan W. 5, EEliza 2, Emily 11/12
BOONE, George 68, Jane 30, William 11, Henry 10, James M. 7, Mary C. 5, Martha J. 3, Juliann 1
MORTON, George G. 32, Elizabeth 38, Mary 10, John W. 8, James S. 6, Prescius P. 4 (f), David 1
HILL, Moses 36*, Grandison 26, Moses jr. 21
DAY, John 35*
THOMPSON, Allen 45, Catharine 35, Zerilda 15, Ephraim 13, Lawrence 11, Maria 9, Tandy 7 (m), Elizabeth 5, Shelby 1

Schedule Page 8

POINDEXTER, Zach 55, Matilda 43, John W. 26, Jones M. 24, Richard 21
GREEN, Jesse P. 61, Nancy 56, James 22, Edmona 21, Leroy 17, David 13, Corind 15 (f), Samuel 10
GREEN, Thomas C. 65*, Catharine 65
BRANDENBERG, Ruth 60*
BEASLEY, America 29*, Sarah A. 5, Minerva F. 1, Thomas J. 3
MCCROSKY, W. Jim? 11 (f)*
HILL, George W. 29*, Angeline 30, Serilla 2, Grandison 6/12
ROGERS, Rachel 75*
HAMPTON, John 38, Sarah M. 28, Sarah M. 6, Ezekiel J. 30
THOMPSON, William 23, Sarah 21, Elizabeth 1
BUSH, Thomas G. 35, Susan 32
GREEN, John H. 30, Martha Ann 25, Alcinda 8, Emily F. 4, Mary E. 2, Margarett 1
GREEN, Thomas P. 27, Betha A. 20, Frances M. 3, James H. 1
CALINES?, Henry B. 46*, Margarett N. 38, Thomas G. 14, Henry 14, Jane 11, Mary 10, Can 9 (m), Cyrus 7, Waller 6, George 4, Margarett A 11/12
MCMILLAN, James W. 18*
MARSHALL, William N. 43*, Sally 50, Robert 19, William 16
FLETCHER, Rufus 16*
STONE, Frances 25*
COUCHMEN, Frederick 49, Lucy 53, Elizabeth 43
WELLS, Mary 38, William F. 17, James Robert 13
BROWN, Francis G. 45, Frances _. 34, Amanda 12, Joseph L. 8, Mary H. 6, James Y. 4, Benjann F. 2 (m)
HAYS, David B. 53, Rachel 56, Charity 88, Sarah 45, Elizabeth 23, Colby H. T. 21, Araminta 17, Sarah F. 15

Schedule Page 9

RADENS, Thomas 38, Harriett 29, Phebe 14, William A. 12, Lewellen 9, Nancy E. 6, Maria L. 3, Sarah M. 6/12
YOUNG, James 31, Gabrella 21, Rebecca 70
BUSH, Barbara 59*, John W. 26, Robert T. 5

1850 Census Clark County Kentucky

HENDERSON, Samuel 27*, Mary F. 22, Fanny A. 1
BUSH, Philip W. 38, Mary J. 27, Owen 7, Maria J. 5, Barbara 4, Mary S. 1
SUTHERLAND, David 29, Caroline 21, Mary E. 2?, John T. 3/12
PARRISH, Calib 49*, Priscilla B. 33, James W. 19, Thomas M. 15, Lucy V. 10, Calib W. 8, Henry C. 3
WEBB, Windfield D. 23*
CHILES, Samuel W. 47*, Susan Q. 22, Tarlton 16
HOPKINS, P. T. 42 (m)*
BLAYDES, Hugh T. 27*
WEBB, Susan 53*, Richard 26, Jane 14
ROY, Sarah 35*
MOORE, Mary 32*, John W. 7, Reuben 3
LOWE, James R. 28*
COMBS, Allen 40* (B)
CARTWRIGHT, James L. 25, Nancy E. 19, James L. 2, George L. 3/12
HOCKADAY, Edmond W. 46, Margarett 42, Isaac 24, Amelia J. 19, Edmond J. 16, Newton T. 14, Mary W. 12, Margarett 10, Sarah F. 3
GREEN, Edmond 60*, Mary 61, Elizabeth 80
MARTIN, Fanny 17*, William 26, John 21
MARTIN, Peggy 55*, Willis 15, James T. 13
ARNOLD, Richard 40*, Martha J. 19, John 8
WOODFORD, Samuel A. B. 35*, Martha 27, Mildrid 9, Elizabeth 3
HAGGARD, James 18*

Schedule Page 10

MARTIN, Hudson 52, Martha 51, Richard 22, Adelaide 19
DEACON, John 33, Elizabeth 24, William 1
JONES, Elizabeth 60*, Thomas A. 35, Joseph F. 16
THOMSEN, Maria 17*
EXEM, Benjamin 42, Emily 36, Margarett 12, Minerva 10, Kincher 9 (m), Robert 5, Edwin 2
HIERONYMUS, Benjamin 77, Susan 53, Benjamin 23 (B?), Clifton 19, Albert 9, Qudwell? 53 (m)
HILL, Thomas 25 (B?), Paulia? 19, Mary F. 3
MARTIN, Robert 28*, Mary 36, Eliza Jane 6, William L. 5, James B. 4, Judith F. 2, Ann E. 6/12
ARNOLD, Adaline A. 23*
RICHARDS, Bartlett 30*
JOHNSON, N. B. 30, Editha 24, Sarah E. 2, Joseph F. 6/12
OLDS, Micajah 51, Lavina 39, Benjamin F. 19, John T. 16, Margarett A. 14, James 12, Mary M. 9
COMBS, Stephen D. 25, Kitty Ann 23, William S. 3, Benjamin 1
HOOTON, William 74, Catharine 78
HICKS, William 24*, Mary 34, Margarett E. 7
FAULKNER, Margarett 22*
BUSH, Richard G. 37, Mary Ann 23, Richard R. 10
DYKES, Benjamin 60*, Lydia 54
PATTON, William 16*
BUSH, Colby 38, Sarah 33, Enoch W. 15, Sariah M. 9, Pleasant L. 7, Susan J. 3, Julia C. 2, Elizabeth A. 2/12
ARNOLD, Henry 59*, Jane 49, Jackson 30, Louisa 27, Mary Jane 18, Smalwood 10, John H. 8, Samuel 3/12

1850 Census Clark County Kentucky

COMBS, Wallace 26*, Fielding 1
RIGSBY, Betsey 70*
COMBS, Edward 22, Mary Ann 22, Maria J. 2, Sarah Ann 4/12

Schedule Page 11

BRINK, John A. 25, Elizabeth 20, Samuel C. 3, Francis M. 2
DEACON, Joseph 37, Elizabeth 39
CONNELL, James 31, Mary Ann 25, David H. 5/12
ELKIN, Ezekiel P. M. 26*, Polly A. E. 21, Winfield S. 10/12
QUISENBERRY, Cloe 61*
BUSH, Jonathan 70, F. A. J. 36 (m), Angiline 28, Filman 8, Nancy A. 5, Alexander G. 3, John R. 43 (B?)
SEARCEY, Anderson 49, Hannah 49, William H. 24, Mary 24, Hannah 2, Mary J. 18
MARTIN, Valentine 76*, Hannah 74
RYON, Polly 56*, Mary S. 15
TAYLOR, Edmond T. 35*, Mary Ann 33, Mary H. 13, William G. 10, D. W. 8 (m), Elizabeth A. 6
PICKETT, Alfred 14*
JORDAN, Sarah 25, Martha 12, Elizabeth 10, Joseph 7, Nancy 1
SMITH, William L. 50, Mary 48, William W. 15, John S. 12, Isabella D. 8
SMITH, Joseph S. 20, Emma 17, George E. 8/12
TATE, Zachariah 37, Maria 30, Sarah E. 9, John W. 7, Robert S. 6, Rachel S. 4, Mary S. 2, Zachariah D. 1
ELKIN, Smalwood A. 44*, Lucinda G. 41, William F. 21, Nancy G. B. 19, Philip B. 17, Julia D. 9, Ezekiel F. 3, Lucy G. 11/12
BUSH, Nancy G. 65*
TATE, John 48, Elizabeth 46, Mary Ann 20, George 24, Nancy 18, John 14, Zachariah T. 1, Richard 47
TATE, William sr. 76, Patsey 65
COUCHMAN, John 61*, Sarah 54, Nathaniel D. 21, William A. 29, George F. 18, Sarah 15, John A. 12, James H. 10
RAGLAND, Amand 25*, Thomas A. 3

Schedule Page 12

QUISENBERRY, Fielding 31*, Rebecca P. 28, Ezekiel C. 10, Claudius V. 7, Ann T. 6, Bluford A. 4, Frace L. 2 (f)
FISHER, Rebecca 65*
FLETCHER, William 22*
QUISENBERRY, James F. 26, Emma 17, Alice 1
QUISENBERRY, Roger 57*, Polly 54, Roger S. 18
BROCKMAN, Roger P. 6*
DARNABY, George E. 18*
EUBANK, Stephen 60*, Nancy 55, Henry Louis 30, Benjamin B. 25, Thomas J. 23, John C. 21, Ann M. 17, Catharine B. 15, Charles S. 13, James A. 11
BERKLEY, Ludwell 53*
VIVION, Thomas 73, Ann 55, Marina 45, Willis 30, Albert 34, John 22, Benjamin 20, James H. 15, Marth F. 17, William 7
DAVIS, John 57, Matilda 48, John 20, Benjamin 19, Sarah E. 17, Richard 15, Mary 12

- 7 -

1850 Census Clark County Kentucky

MURRAY, Joseph 53 (B), Joseph 24, Newton 20, Squire W. 13, Henry 11, Lucinda 17
WINN, Nancy 65*, William P. 26, Susan Ann 19, Emeline 17
REYNOLDS, Lucy 40*
SHAMBLIN, Ambrose 80* (B)
EVANS, Peter 42, Letitia 35, James E. 14, Peter 12, Mary C. 10, George W. 7
MILLER, David 66, Persena 67
OLIVER, Raney 69 (f)*
OLDS, John T. 15*
BERKLEY, Daniel 65, Jones 33
LYSLE, John E. 54, Mary 52, Francis 28, Maria 19, Margarett 17, Mary 15, Marcus 16, John B. 11, Lydia W. 9, Washington 41

Schedule Page 13

QUISENBERRY, Thacker 32, Permelia 22, William P. 13, Corilia 10, Elizabeth 5, Susan 3, Johnson 1
QUISENBERRY, P. J. B. 38 (m)*, Ann E. 30, William F. 18, Thomas T. 8, Elmore 6, Niel 4, Ailen 4, Adelaid 4/12
BUSH, Susan 18*
DUNBAR, Peter 25*
QUISENBERRY, Mills 22*, Mary 17, Florinda 10/12
OLDS, Benjamin 20*
KING, David A. 32, Jane E. 27, John W. 8, Harriett R. 7, Margarett A. 5, Jane E. C. 3, Susan B. 11/12
ELKIN, Reuben H. 35*, Glevenna 34, Ann S. 62, Nancy J. R. 14, Ezekiel 12, Sinonia? 7
BUSH, Nancy J. 13*
HAMPTON, Andrew H. 11/12*
ELKIN, Mildred 32, Isaiah 15, Lucy B. 13
BUSH, Nancy H. 55, William M. 23, Nancy G. 19, Valentine 19, Jeremiah P. 13
RAGLAND, William 37, Sally 34, Louisa 16, Catharine 14, Patsey E. 12, Colby 10, Lucy A. 9, Nathaniel 7, Elkanah 6, Milton 4, Mary M. 2, Sary F. 3/12
BUSH, Oliver E. 25*, Dorinda 22, Mary M. 4, William R. 3, Henry S. 2, Sarah T. 7/12
CRIM, John W. 20*, Lewis P. 18, John 50
MATTHEWS, Pleasant 36, Jane 52, Ann M. C. 13
ELKIN, Willis 39*, Jane 38, Frances A. 18, William M. 17, Tandy 16, Mary M. 14, Napoleon B. 12, Zachariah T. 10, Armasinda 7, Nancy G. 4, Lydia 1
BUSH, Sally T. 6*
DAVIS, William C. 25, Minerva H. 23, Mary B. 1, James C. 22

Schedule Page 14

RAGLAND, Nathaniel sr. 74, Martha 74
GEORGE, John 43, Elizabeth 24, Mildrid 6, Frances 4 (f), John N. 2
WRIGHT, William T. 27, Amanda 25, Zepora 4, Sarah F. 11/12
HAGGARD, Bartlett 22*, Mary H. 20
BUSH, Barbara S. 13*
HAGGARD, Fraces 44, George W. 20, James A. 19, Martin 16, Enoch 13, Elizabeth 10
LITRALL, John 59*, Catharine 58, Janie 17, Stephen 15
HILL, Leonard 33*, Sally D. 31, Thomas 7, James R. 4, Alexander 2

1850 Census Clark County Kentucky

BROCKMAN, James T. 29*, Frances 26 (f), Mary J. 9, ann E. 7, Tandy Q. 5, JAcob M. 3, Asa T. 26
BURROWS, William P. 23*
BROCKMAN, Jacob B. 23*, Narcissa 17, James T. 4/12
QUISENBURY, Jane 6*
RAGLAND, Thomas S. 46, Mary M. 32, Martha 14, Agnes 10, Gabrilla 7, Mary A. T. 6
BUSH, Jeremial 42*, Ann E. 40, Mary Ann 20, Jenie 18, william M. 16, Ransom jr. 14, Sarah T. 12
EATON, Jonta 62 (m)*
ELKIN, Enoch 41, Ann P. 36, Jones R. 16, Frances F. 9, Eleanosa 7, Polly A. 4, William F. 9/12
BUSH, Anbose G. 27 (m), Martha J. 18, Minerva 5
ELKIN, Robert M. 24, Malinda 22, William F. 1
BUSH, Landen 56*
BERRY, Williar C. 59*, Lucy 53, Mary T. 19, Williar 28, Margarett 20, A. J. 21 (m), Pleasant 15, Margarett P.H. 11
QUISENBERRY, P. J. 37 (m), Ann 32, Richard 12, Silas 8, Susan 6, Sarah 4, Laura 3, John 11/12

Schedule Page 15

WRIGHT, McArthur 32, Hannarh 30 (f), Washington 11, William H. 9, Mary E. 6, Silas T. 2
PAYNE, Colby 24, Fanny 22, Isaac M. 1
HAGGARD, Nathaniel 74, Elizabeth 70
LOTT, Elizabeth 55, Fountain P. 22, James W. sr. 19, James W. jr. 8
KING, Robert D. 25, Elizabeth 22, Jefferson 2, Benjamin 1
QUISENBERRY, Colby B. 61*, Lucy 60, Tandy 24, Elkanah 19, John M. 17
RUPELL, Samuel 22*
CRIM, Peter 39, Jane 43, James 11, John 9, Rebecca 7, Charles 6, Margarett 4, David 1
QUISENBERRY, Tandy 59 (m), Margarett 55, Skip? 22, Brastle? 14 (m), Margarett 11, Roger 9, Rodes 7, Jackson 32, Sarah F. 11, Philip T. 5, Lucinda 2, Cuthbert 8
BUSH, Joseph 78, Sarah 71, Robert 28, Eliza 17
REED, George 67, Jane 54, Ezekiel 33, Josep 24, William 17, Polly Ann 19, Elza 17
OGDEN, Thomas 31*, Tabitha 45, James 17
MENIR, Robert 22*
LISLE, James 64*, Nancy 55, John 28, Joseph 19, James C. 14
GEORGE, Lucy 80*
BARY, Mercer 29, Mildrid 24, Landen 1
DYCKES, James 59*, Susan 45, Luther 24, Milly 19, Gerbuide 20 (f), Hantippa 18 (f), James 15, Thendas 12 (m), Catharine 9, Mary 7, Matthias 3, Susan 25, Polly 32
ARNOLD, James 29*, Eliza 23

Schedule Page 16

DYCKE, Henry 33*, Sarah 38, Robert P. 4, Colby 2
ARNOLD, Frances 40*
EPPERSON, Francis 30, Anna 38, John 18, Achilles 16, Tandy 10, Catharine 8, Lydia 3, Thomas 6/12
HOOTON, Nicholas 50, Scythea 48, Mary J. 19, Lydia 12, Johnson 9, Allen 4
LITRALL, Richard 25, Rachel 23, James T. 3, William 1, Stephen 4/12
WALLER, John 35, Amanda 35, Archa 15 (m), Fielding 13, Margarett 11, Robert 9, Sally 3, Susanna 4/12

1850 Census Clark County Kentucky

WALLER, Elizabeth 65*, Thomas 20
JOHNSON, Mary 18*
HATON, John 23, Marilda 17
JOHNSON, William 69, Elizabeth 68, Lawrence 28, Polly Ann 25
BUSH, Moses 54, Kelly 45, William J. 17, Elizabeth J. 15, Joseph 8, Elizabeth 30
EUBANK, Achilles W. 26, Leanna 25, Sarah F. 5, John W. 1
ELKIN, Lewellen 40, Sarah 39, William A. 16, Nancy M. 14, Sarah F. 3
JOHNSON, Martin 47, Lucy 49, Mary C. 25, William 23, Nancy 18, Henry M. 15, George 12, Claiborn 11, James H. 9
ADAMS, Lewis 29, Sally A. 23, Isaac W. 2, James 27
KENNEDARY, James 47, Ascena 43, George 28, Nancy 22, Thomas 19, Eusebia 17, William 15, Martha 7, James E. 2
EUBANK, Stephen B. 37*, Lucy 29, Richard C. 14, Ambrose B. 5, Mary E. 4, Westley H. 1

Schedule Page 17

WRIGHT, Patsey 38*
FIELDER, Harvey 42*, Amanda 35, William W. 14, James H. 12, Frances Ann 10, Thomas J. 9, Minerva 7, Rufus 5, John B. 3, Doctor 10/12
EMERSON, Henry H. 38, Mary Ann 32, William T. 10, Frances M. 8, Rufus S. 3
HAMPTON, George 73, Catharine 60, John 36, Minerva 31, Lewis 12, Mary C. 11, Martha J. 4, John D. 4
BERKEY, John W. 39, Sarah Ann 26, Charles 6, Thomas F. 4, Mary 1
OWENS, Milton 27*, Mahala 43, John S. 6, Malinda 4, Benjamin F. 6/12
DAVIDSON, Polly A. 19*, William L. 12
BUSH, Howard 36, Synthia 35, James W. 5, Sarah F. 1
JOHNSON, William 40, Martha 37, Jane 14, George 12, William 11, James 9, Sarah 7, Mary D. 5, Catharine 5, Robert 2
ACTON, Francis 40, Amanda 34, Sallay 16, Nancy 14, James S. 12, Zephora 10, Rufus 7, Winfield 4
CRIM, James 34, Lucy 29, Elias 1
HAMPTON, Jonathan 82*, Sally 49, Elizabeth 35, Nancy 46, Martin 33, Lucinda 28
VESSER, Melissa 16*, Mary 12
HODGKINS, Samuel 64, Peggy 62, Mary 19, William 15
QUISENBERRY, Thomas P. 27, Frances 18, Elizabeth 65, Mary J. 1
CLEM, John W. 31, Martha A. 25, Mary J. 12, Wesley 10, Pamelia 8, Francis 6, A. T. 4 (m), John 1

Schedule Page 18

ROBERSON, Emily 48, John 24, Payton 21, Elizabeth 19, Sarah 17
HAPTON, Polly 75*
JONES, Edmond 63*
ANDERSON, Alexaner 46, Martha 29, Sarah 12, Martha 10, William 6, Julia 4, Archer 1
RUBER?, Stanley 36, Frances 28, Martha 5, James W. 4, George W. 2
ARMSTRONG, Allen 30*, Susan 49
RANKIN, John 31*, Martha J. 25, Allen R. 8, Susan F. 3
DOYLE, Dennis 47, Eliza 47, Caleb 18, Mary 16, Nancy 14, John 12, Sally 10, Eliza 9, Allen 7, George 1

1850 Census Clark County Kentucky

OWENS, Horatio 65*, Martha 58, William 36, Elizabeth 35, Amanda 31, Mildred 26, Sarah 24, Frances 23, Martin 21, Henry S.? 19, Zachry W. 15
CULLIM, Jack 70* (B)
TUGGLE, Nancy 93*
WELCH, Garrett 28*, Sally A. 21
HAMPTON, A. H. 42 (m), Polly 31, David R. 38, Henry A. 8, Jesse M. 5, Nancy 3, David B. 5/12
RYAN, John B. 51*, Lucy 42, Marcia J. 17, Alvien 15, Mildred 13, William 11, Ann 8, Susan 9/12, Marcia 78
HARRIS, Eliza 9*
GAINES, Martha P. 6*
CURTIS, Ranson O. 38, Lucy 35, Nancy 5, Sarah 2
MULLINS, James 49, Elizabeth 83
BROWN, Anderson 28, Lucy 23, Jesse T. 8, Sally 6, Nancy 4, John 2, William P. 4/12, Nancy 22

Schedule Page 19

HALL, James 27*, Marthe 25, Nancy J. 4, Lucy A. 2, Polly H. 5/12
WILCOXEN, Margarett E. 8*, Sarah 6
BROWN, Henry 32, Nancy 28, Mary 8, James H. 6, Sarah C. 4, Nancy 2, Milly 10/12
TUGGLE, Achillis 44, Catharine 40, Nancy 21, Elizabeth 17, William 15, George 12, James 6, Milly 4
MOORE, Mashall? 41, Catharine 28, Marian 3, James M. 8/12
RYAN, Elisha 42*, Mary S. 38, James W. 18, John B. 15, David S. 12, Mary F. 10, Edward 7, Ann C. 4, Sally 2
REED, Sarah C. 12*
GORDON, David M. 48, Narcissa 20, John? D. 18, Mary 15, James 14, Sarah A. 11
RUTLEDGE, Catharine 38, Joicey 30, Isaac A. 19
LAWRENCE, Merideth 64, Nancy 62, Robert 24, Elizabeth 25, Lucinda 21, Andrew 19
EMBRE, Tarlton 42, Martha 42, John M. 16, James W. 14, Margarett 11, Thomas P. 9, Henry C. 4
STOUT, Samuel 40*, Polly 32
FARMER, Sarah 29*, Peggy 25, Thomas 16
HULSE, William 29, Martha A. 29, Margarett 4
GARNER, Landford 32, Sarah 28, James F. 7, John W. 6, Joseph 4, Milton 1
SHARP, Stephen 28, Sally 49, Harriett 13, Mary 13, George W. 9
OWEN, Hezakiah 42*, Martha 43, Zerilda 30, Alvin A. 19, Salvisa 17, Cassandra 13, James 11
SHANK, Greenbury 30*

Schedule Page 20

OWEN, William 45*, Eleanor 44, John W. 23, Richard F. 21, Mahala 19, Wilson 19, Sarah P. 16, George W. 14, Mary A. 13, Pamelia 11, William P. 10, Francis N. 7, Margarett 1
CREED, Julian 22*, John 23
FARMER, Irvine 39, Milly 30, John W. 6, Josephine 4, Robert S. 3, Howard 1, William 19
BABER, James 34, Mary 40, David 17, Francis M. 15, Mary 13, Louisa 11, Thomas E. 5, Malinda 3, Manley 1, Jonathan 1
HENKILL, Eda 27*, Sarah E. 9, Johnson R. 8, Nancy M. 5, John N. 3
BROOKSHIRE, Elizabeth 60*
BUSH, Christopher C. 26, Sarah 25, Narcissa 3, Nancy 1, Albert 10, Tandy 23

1850 Census Clark County Kentucky

QUISENBERRY, Jas. H. 30, Margarett 25, Thodocius 5, Enoch 2
SIMPSON, Edward 32, Caroline 21, John F. 1, Sally A. 74, Rezin 34
HODGKIN, Philip B. 40*, Sally 32
HAMPTON, Nancy P. 14*, Congrave 9, Rebecca 10/12
QUISENBERRY, William F. 52*, Rachel 50, William F. 27, Roger 19, Shelton L. 15, Gelina 21, Emily R. 13, Marcia S. 10
BUSH, William S. 2*, Sally A. 9/12
HODGKINS, James 29, Ormazinda 29, Samuel 6, Susan 3, Sandy 2 (m), James 4/12
BRYANT, James H. 40, Nancy J. 7, Lucy A. 5, Elizabeth 3, Lydia 1, Jane 30
HARRIS, Richard F. 35*, Nancy 27, Eliza C. 7, John W. 4, Luan 2

Schedule Page 21

MOBLEY, Tandy 18*
BALLARD, John 65, Nancy 58, Margaretta A. 21, Milly J. 19, Jackson 18, Lucy 13
MILLER, Isaac 27, Sally 24, Theodocia 4, Junius 2, Alpheus 11/12, Nancy 75
BUSH, Fielding 35, Adelaid 43, John 24, Rachel 17, Luann 14, Fielding M. 11, Lucy 8, Virginia A. 4
JENKINS, Thomas 45, Rachel 34, Lucy J. 12, Maria S. 10, Sally A. 8, Colby M. 6, James 3, Leslie S. 7/12, Sally 64
BLACKWELL, Armstead 45*, Sally J. 20, Roger J. 1
STOKELEY, William 28*
HART, Jesse G. 33*, Lucy A. 23, Belam 9, William F. 1
SMITH, Thomas 32*, Beleva 54
EVANS, James 45*
DAVIS, George S. 30*, Eliza 35, Augusta 5, James 1
CUMMINS, John S. 12*, Francis M. 10
SHANKS, David 38, Verlinder 25, Maregarett P. 5
LISLE, Claiborn 30*, Esther 28, James D. 9, Susan 7, Zipphorah 4, George R. 2
JORDAN, Betsey 60*
EATON, Wm. J. 29, Cynthia A. 29, George 7, James W. 5, Mary E. 3
RAILSBACK, David 29, Catharine 28, William E. 7, David H. 5, Mahala J. 3, Wm. S.? H. 10/12
EUBANK, Philip C. 41*, Emily 31, John A. 9, William 7, Christopher 5, Philip C. 2
PANE, Elizabeth 8/12*
RUTLEDGE, James 40*, Nancy 32, John 17, Martha 15, Philip 11, Mary 9, James 7, Samuel 4, William 1

Schedule Page 22

VANCE, Thomas 23*
QUISENBERRY, Wm. J. 26*, Emerine E. 21, Benjamin F. 4, Mary S. 2
CRIM, John 20*
HAMPTON, Jesse 65, Nancy 53, James 33, Joseph 18
QUISENBERRY, Loyed? 25*, Mary A. 25, James R. 1
BUSH, Dillard 19*
TOLEN, Morgan 67, Elizabeth 61, Frances 33, Milly 24, Richard H. 22, Thomas J. 18
WILCOXEN, Sarah 66

1850 Census Clark County Kentucky

HICKS, Hendley 49, Nancy R. 46, Caleb 21, Rebecca J. 23, William T. 19, Philip H. 16, John F. 11, Sally Ann 8, Fielden Q. 6
MCMILLAN, James 56, Nancy 49, James W. 19, John 13, Elizabeth 10, Colby S. 4
LISLE, Manson 26, Martha Ann 27, Sarah V. 4, James 2, Achillis 7/12
BYBEE, James 49, Jane 48, Mary J. 15, Colby 16, Emily M. 13, James A. 11, Ryland D. 6
KING, Robert S. 63, Sarah 38, Margarett 22, Isabella R. 19, Frances 3, Samuel 3, Thomas D. 6/12
HALL, Ambros 33, Elizabeth 22, William T. K. 7, Nancy 5, Mary 3, James T. 1
EMERSON, Francis M. 30*, Elizabeth M. 24
LAINE, William H. 9*
MAPPIN, Elizabeth 23, David 8, James 7, John 4, Jane 2
HAGAN, David 78*
CARNER, Sally 50*, John 13, Nancy 7
ATKINSON, Washington 20, Julian 16
HAGAN, John 40, Dolly 40
SHARP, William R. 29*, Eliza 28
WILCOXEN, Rachel 57*, Tarlton 60, William 25

Schedule Page 23

BROWN, David 39, Rachel 37, Sally A. 18, Jane 14, James B. 12, Elizabeth 8, John A. 6, Henrietta 4, Mary F. 1
BUSH, William T. 31, Mildrid 26, Sally G. 9, Jonathan 7, Diana 5, Arthusa 3, Mariam 10/12
RAILSBACK, Daniel 26*, Frances 50
BYBEE, Araminta 32*, Elizabeth 6, Napoleon J. 2
MESIR?, John 59, Nancy 51, James 27, Ellen 24, Minerva 20, John 17
THOMPSON, Alfred 48, Jane 36, Sally A. 18, Susan 17, Schuyler 15, Rebecca 10, Richard 5, Nathaniel 3, Theodore 1
CHISM, James 62, Frances 30, Julian 16, Minerva 11, James M. 10, Benjamin F. 7, Emily 6, Amanda 2
WHITE, Richard 57, Elizabeth 40
EMERSON, Francis 58*, Mary 60, James 40, Benjamin 15
ELKINS, Elizabeth 18*, Enoch 18
KNIGHT, Sarah F. 3*
CRIM?, John 40*
SIMPSON, Gabriel 40*
THOMAS, Fielder 64*, Obidiah 25, Lewis 22, Charles 14, Mary A. 16
DEWITT, Smalwood 18*
EATON, Sarah S. 10*
ATKINSON, Joseph 25, Elizabeth 22, Samuel 2, George 4/12
WILCOXEN, Israel 27, Elizabeth 27, Salley A. 11, John W. 9, Eliza J. 7, Mary B. 5, Elizabeth 2
EVANS, John 60*
TUCKER, John 23*
MITTON, William 25*
THOMAS, Fielder jr. 34, Polly 26, Violet 3, George 24
EATON, Zachariah 65, John 23, Lydia 19

1850 Census Clark County Kentucky

Schedule Page 24

WOOSLEY, Peter 27, Adaline 29, Henry S. 8, John 6, Mary E. 5, George W. 3, Margarett 1
LAINE, James 62*, Elizabeth 44
HENRY, Polly A. 15*
JONES, John 29, Lavina 15, Margarett E. 8/12
BROOKSHIRE, Hampton 30, Nancy 29, Feriby E. 4, Sarah E. 2
SHEARER, S. B. 40 (m)*, Joicy 28, Elizabeth 8, Martha 6, Hanna 4, Simeon 2, Abslom 1
SHEPHERD, Martin 22*
HEISLE, Christipher 22*
BALDWIN, John W. 19*
JORDAN, Thomas 35*
ATKINSON, William 32, Elizabeth 37, Nancy J. 9, Elizabeth 7, Lucy A. 5, Richard 3
MULLINS, Gordon C. 31, Nancy 28, James H. 6, Luan 5 (f), William T. 3, Milly A. 1, Augustus L. 5/12
BURGESS, John 42, Cynthia 38, John T. 18, Eliza A. 16, Nancy E. 11, William L. 8, Howard M. 6, Mary F. 3
HAMILTON, William 26, Rachel 30, David T. 3, William S. 2, Sarah E. 11/12
WOOSLEY, Thomas 68*, Minerva 19, Serilda 15, Catharine 11, Henry 26, Margarett 5, Elvina 3, Evan 1, Abby 3/12, David 17
PARKER, Margarett 53*
ALDRIDGE, Richard 48, Frances 46, Thomas J. 18, George W. 16, Mary C. 13, William B. 11, Martha J. 9
WOOSLEY, William 42, Martha 36, Susan F. 9, William 5, Woodford 1
JACKSON, Francis F. 73*, Ann C. 39, John H. 11, Lucy L. 9, Mary V. 6

Schedule Page 25

SNYDER, David 10*
LAUGHLIN, Simeon 73*
WINN, John A. 31*
GROOMS, Dorothea 18*
MOORE, Leander 20, Eliza 17
NICHOLAS, William C. 43*, Sarah 35, Martha L. 5, Fanny L. 2, Mary C. 4/12
WINN, Robert N. 33*
ROUT, Benjamin 50, Polly 48, James 18, Martha J. 17, Sally 14, Rebecca 12, Catharine 12, Lewis 9, Ann 6, Temperance 4
MUNDAY, James 63*, Joicy 52, William 25, Sally 31, Arsrylia 15
SCOTT, Thomas R. 9*
CRUTCHFIELD, Martin 53, Nancy 52, Frances 22, Synthia 20, Woodson 16, Thomas 13, David 7
WELCH, James 63, Elizabeth 53, William 32, James 22, Jesse 20, Elizabeth 22, John 17, Henry 15
WINN, Minor H. 59, Polly 52, James 28, Martin S. 21
HAGGARD, David D. 43, Eliza 40, Pleasant 18, Jane 16, Lewis T. 14, Elizabeth 12, Augustin L. 9, Nancy 5, Sally 3
GRAVETT, John 34, Elizabeth 26, Mary A. 9, Nancy J. 7, Telitha E. 3, John W. 4, Thomas J. 2
GRAVETT, Elizabeth 60, Mary 38
WHITE, Francis 65, Phebe 48, Nancy 16, Frances 15, Robert 12, Cynthia 7, Eliza 10
BROOKSHIRE, Judieth 35, Elizabeth 15, P. M. O. 13 (m), Marthe 11, Mary J. 10

1850 Census Clark County Kentucky

HAGGARD, Pleasant 72, Mary 61, Garrett 24, James 21
RUTLEDGE, Thomas 23*, Louisa 24, Elijah H. 2, Isaac 8/12

Schedule Page 26

REECE, Susanna 61*
GRAVETT, George S. 34, Catharine 34, Eliza 8, Ellen 7, Libby 5, Isaiah 3, Melville 2
GRAVETT, Ellis 60*, Elizabeth 60, James S. 22, Isabella 24, Nancy 50, Francis M. 2
OLIVER, Catharine 19*, Isaac W. 11/12
BROWN, Joseph 13*
CUMMINS, Harriett 2*
WARE, Harvey 30, Elizabeth 30, Henry 10, Mary 8, James 7, John 5, Martha 3, Samuel 2
HAGGART, John S. 38, Martha 23, Pleasant 7, Edward 5, Winfield 1
HALL, Achilles 37, Malinda 25, Briant 15, Itson? 13 (m), Rebecca 11, Thomas 9, Nancy 7, Martha 5
HAGGARD, James H. 27*, Mary E. 19
TWYMAN, George 18*
HAGGARD, Martin 60*, Woodson 19, Allen S. 16, Eliza A. 13
HAMPTON, Sally 52*
BROOKSHIRE, Feriby 21*
ROUT, Daniel 82
HAMPTON, Jesse 77, William 46
HALL, Nancy 58, Milly 21, Lewis 18, George W. 15
JONES, Abslom 42, Rutha Ann 38, Mary E. 18, Martha A. 16, Elizabeth M. 14, Amelia C. 12, William H. 10, Lucy E. 9, Benjamin F. 7, Jarah J. 5 (f), John R. 4, Milly T. 1
BABER, Thomas W. 26, Mary J. 26, Jonathan L. 4, James A. 1
MCINTOSH, Frederick 58, Rebecca 47, Syllney 17, Sarah 15, Lewis H. 13, Ann R. 11, James J. 8, Mary C. 6
HAGGARD, John 55, Lewis 28, Clifton 23, Julia 19, Clinton S. 11

Schedule Page 27

MANOR, Marcus 25, Lucy 24, Emerine M. 2
BABER, Jonathan 55, Malinda 55, Cynthia A. 22, Mary J. 21, Pleasant 19, Elizabeth 18, Sally A. 16, Frances M. 15, Jonathan M. 12
LIPSCOMB, Nathan 33, Mary F. 25, Patsey Ann 7, David L. 5, Flavius J. 2
HAGGARD, David S. 22, Mary E. 20, Leslie 1 (m)
HAGARD, Augustin L. 30*, Luan 25 (f), Rodney 5, Martha M. 3
MULLINS, Mary A. 16*, Colby 23
CULLUM, Charles 60* (B)
LEWIS, George W. 34*, Lydia C. 24, Richard E. 3, James H. 1
DARNABY, Sydnia S. 17 (m)*
GUINN, James 27, Lucy A. 21, Augustin L. 3, Ann E. 1
BALLARD, John 23, Harriett M. 22, Mary J. 2, Catharine F. 8/12
SEWELL, Sandford 37*, Margarett 37, Mary C. 12, James 10, Elizabeth 8, John 6, William 4, Sarah 1
CULBERTSON, David 60*
CAST, Dudley S. 28, Sophia 30, William H. 8, Amon O. 1
CHISM, William 27, Frances 19, James W. 2, John Richard 6/12

1850 Census Clark County Kentucky

FITZPATRICK, James 24*, Telitha A. 14, Lewis E. 1/12
HARLOW, Mary A. 32*
OWEN, Francis T. 34*, Catharine 25, Martha A. 4, John T. 2, George L. 1
WILLIAMS, Rachel 12* (B)
ADAMS, Stephen 33*, Mary 25, William F. 6, John F. 3, Mary E. 11/12
CRUTCHFIELD, John 28*
WEBB, Jefferson 45*, Edefledd 24 (f), Sandford 5, Francis A. 4, Nancy 1
HAGGARD, Lewis 33*
JONES, John 27, Mary A. 22, William 1
ALDRIDGE, James 41, Martha 38, Nancy V. 16, Susan R. 15, John N. 12, Honor K. 10 (f), Margarett E. 8, Mary A. 4, Sarah M. 1, James M. 7/12

Schedule Page 28

MILLER, Washington 52*, Maria D. 37, Harriet 13, Washington 11
LEVINGSTON, R. W. 33 (m)*
ADAMS, William H. 20*
BEAL, Burgess 27 (m)*, Luan 29 (f), Allison 42, Maria 40, Catharine 15, Stephen 12, Elizabeth 12
CRIM, Elizabeth 65*
CRIM, George W. 34*, Lavina 34, Sarah E. 1
JONES, John T. 11*
RUTLEDGE, Nancy 5*
HOUSE, Thomas B. 47*, Martha 44, Louisa F. 18
MERRILL, Chilton A. 28*, Martha A. 9/12
BRUCE, Eli 55, Temperence 49, John H. 14
WATTS, Johnson 43*, Nancy J. 18, John W. 16, Mary A. 14, Martha C. 12, Sarah E. 10, James W. 4
BALLARD, Jane 60*
REESE, William 39*, Martha 31, Amanda E. 10, Lucy C. 6, James W. 3, Mary F. 1, Lucy 61, Margarett 42
MASSIE, William R. 65*, Margarett 65, Edward 24, Isaac N. 23
FORD, Amanda 25*
NICHOLAS, William 13*, Fanny 8
HAGGARD, William 43, Philadelphia 46, Margarett E. 14, Milly F. 12, William S. 8
GREENING, Henry 50*, Catharine 47
LAWRENCE, Frances M. 26*
HAGGARD, David D. 38, Temperance 38, Margarett E. 14, Barbara J. 12, Samuel 9, James P. 7, Dillard A. 2, Mary M. 4/12, Charles P. 4/12
PRESTON, Benjamin R. 33, Orpha 35
OGDON, Aquilla 32, Rosaline 27, Dillard 8, Mary E. 6, John W. 3, Pamelia 2

Schedule Page 29

HERKILL, David 40, Elizabeth 40, Thomas 16, Benjamin 14, John P. 12, Richard 9, Martha 6, Zachariah 2
LAWRENCE, Frances 60*, Thomas B. 21, Frances A. 18, Dolly A. 18
JEWELL, Thomas S. 34*, Elizabeth A. 25
HOGAN, William 33, Mary 33, James W. 9, Stephen L. 8, Robert N. 6, John T. 4, Sarah E. 1

1850 Census Clark County Kentucky

MOBERLY, Lucinda 40, Elizabeth 22, Matilda 11, Catharine 9, Sydey A. 5 (m), Mary F. 3, William 16
ALDRIGE, Noah 34, Mary 30, Angeline 16, William H. 8, James 7, Rebecca 7, Squire 5, Cynthia A. 3, May E. 2, Noah 11/12
BROOKSHIRE, Johnson 26, Alla 38, Polly A. 6, Catharine 4, John F. 2, Temperance B 5/12, Hanor 19
RAINEY, John 28, Sarah 24, Richard F. 4, William T. 2, Milly J. 1
RAINEY, Thomas 68*, Susanna 51, Thomas C. 16, James C. 13
ALDRIDGE, Fanny 45*
RANEY, Benjamin L. 24, Rebecca 38, Isabinda 4, William S. 2, Ambrose D. 1, George W. 21, James H. 17
JONES, Thomas 54, Sally 46, Nancy A. 19, Amanda 15, Benjamin H. 12, Sarah 9, Allen R. 5
RAINEY, Lewis 56, Mary 55, Sarah C. 17, Henry G. 15
RANEY, John H. 29, Cynthia A. 30, Mary E. 4/12, Ctaharine W. 4
ALDRIDGE, Squire 45, Sally 38, Nancy A. 20, John W. 19, Mary F. 17, James R. 16, Elizabeth 14, Josiah 11, Lucinda 9, Martha 7, Catharine 3

Schedule Page 30

ADAMS, Tandy 23, Lucy A. 22, Mary E. 3, Martha J. 1
PARRISH, Greenberry 26, Sarah A. 26, Sarah M. 5, Nancy C. 4, Mary E. 3, David A. 7/12
GORDON, Sarah 75*
COOPER, Milly 13*
COOPER, Eleanor 40, Megowen 17, Frances 11, John W. 8, Catharine 3
LOCKNANE, Charles S. 37, Catharine 28, William J. 8, Manda A. 6, Milton P. 4, Elizabeth 5/12, Miles B. 2, Nancy 74
WATTS, John S. 63*, Nancy 60
GRIGGS, Martin 19*
GORDON, Jackson 36, Sarah 33, John W. 10, David N. 8, Eli 5, Henry P. 3
MCCARTY, Tandy 30, Clarissa 29, Sally A. 9
GASPER, Thomas 36*, Rebecca 36, Mary E. 8
GRIGGS, Susan R. 16*
RIPPEY, Sarah 67, Elizabeth 40, John J. 5
BLACK, James W. 45, Mary 35, Sally 17, Elizabeth 14, James H. 13, Milly 7
MOON, Smalwood 47, Nancy 36, John 21 (B?), George H. 15, Squire D. 12, Susan C. 9, Louisa F. 5
RUTLEDGE, John P. 26*, Hanor 33, Henry N. 2, Sally A. 11/12
ALDRIDGE, Honor 66 (f)*
EPPERSON, Ambrose 12*
GAMBOE, Eda 49, Clifton 20, Samuel N. 19, Catharine 16, Polly A. 14, Honor E. 11 (f), John S. 9
HOUSE, Squire B. 32, Sally Ann 31, John S. 11, Sarah E. 9, Louisa F. 7, George W. M. 4, Samuel B. 3, Nancy M. S. 6/12
BLEDSOE, William 60*, Polly 40, Mincy M. 14 (f)

Schedule Page 31

GAMBOE, Greenberry 24*
ADAMS, William 61*, Sally 61, John W. 17
JONES, William C. 23*, Eliza 21
FRANKLIN, Sarah M. 17*

1850 Census Clark County Kentucky

HOUSE, George W. 34*, Nancy 34, Mary A. 13, Margarett 12, Frances C. 1
FARMER, Milton 12*
HAGGARD, Dewitt? 38, Mary 38, Nathaniel 9, Michael 7, Sarah E. 6, James M. 2
ELGIN, Dick 60* (B)
CROW, Polly 55* (B)
WILLIAMS, Delila 45* (B), James 16
BRADLEY, Samuel 40*, Elizabeth 36, Stephen 16, Sally 13, Mary E. 11, John D. 9, Nancy J. 7, Lewis 5, Robert 2
BRADLEY, William N. 6*
BRADLEY, Sarah 58, Delila 21, Milly M. 18, Dennis W. 15, John H. 18, Sarah M. 8, Hannah B. 26
LOCKNANE, John M. 49, Cecillia 45, Virginia 22, Samuel H. 19, James T. 11
RICHIE, William 55, Clarissa 46, Mildred E. 22, W. L. 21 (m), Alexander H. 19, Mary A. 16, Sarah N. 14, Madison F. 10, Rebecca C. 7
COOPER, James M. 43, Rachel 39, Mary E. 12, John H. 3
GROVES, Sally 74*, Anna 70
RISEN, Clorah 10*
BROOKSHIRE, Wiley 33, Mary E. 20, John H. 3, Henry A. 1
RAGGANA, Nathaniel 49, Sarah B. 44, Joel J. 13, Jackson W. 11, Christopher C. 9, James O. 2, William F. 20
RAGLAND, Nathaniel T. 25*, Nancy 28, Sarah F. 1
EDWARDS, Cynthia A. 2*
RAINEY, James 50, Polly 54, Mary 18, Nancy A. 15
PARADORE, George 36, Polly 20, John W. 9, Calpana 6/12

Schedule Page 32

QUISENBERRY, Achillis 32*, Mary F. 33
EMMERSON, Tilly 33*, William 8
BRISH, Pleasant 58*, Jane 49, Thomas J. 22, Jane 18, Elkanah 16, Eilzabeth 12, Nelson 11
CONKRIGHT, John M. 13*
BROOKSHIRE, Martin 42, Amand M. 40, William 17, Martin A. 15, Elias 13, Wiley 11, Overton 9, John N. 7, Amanda 4, Achillis 2, James 11/12
BRINIGAR, Sam 75 (B)
CONKRIGHT, Ketura 68 (f)
TRUSSELL, John 40, Sally 42
BAXTER, John 65*, Nancy 35, Caroline 10, Ellis 8, Elzine 6 (f), Elliot 4, Clifton 2
CURTIS, Sally 22*, Maria 24
RUCKER, William 20*
TAYLOR, Calvin C. 30*
HARPER, Matheas 25*
BUSH, Heyman G. 29*, Hannah W. 22
CONKRIGHT, Pleasant P. 11*
OLDHAM, Abner 11*, Mary E. 7
HENRY, Evan 39, James W. 17, Polly A. 14, John 13
RISEN, James 33, Elizabeth 31, Mary 9, Nancy 4, James 2
HAGGARD, Martin 24, Courtney A. 20, James N. 3, Garrett 1
TROYMAN, Pleasant B. 21, Doicey A. 23 (f)
GRIGGS, Nancy 41, Martin 19, James S. 18, Allen P. 15

1850 Census Clark County Kentucky

CURTIS, John J. 32, Anna 32, Nancy 16, Elizabeth 7, James 5, Noah 4, Taylor 2
CURTIS, James J. 32, Martha 17
BROOKSHIRE, Ann 55*
KISEN, Thomas 28*, Eliza J. 26, Susan 3, Mary F. 1
EPPERSON, Nancy 38, Louisa 34, Patsey 24, Fanney 11, John F. 9, W. P. H. 9 (m), Athacaswell 5, Lyrana 4

Schedule Page 33

DUNCAN, William 55, Gemima 55, John 20, Isabella 23, Gemima 19, Ann 23, Catharine E. 16, Isaiah 17
JONES, John 70, Margarett 50, William 30, Thomas 32, Nancy 20, Lucinda 18, Mary 14
SMITH, Elizabeth 77, Susan 43, Lydia 35, Clarinda 21
SMITH, Francis 53, Clarissa 58, Reuben 22, Asa 17
NOEL, Richard 22, Matilda 15
LOWE, William 50, Virginia 46, Nancy 22, Elizabeth 20, James 18, Sicily 16, Frances 14, John 10, William J. 9, Newton 6, Zachry T. 4
CRUTCHFIELD, John 48, Jenetta 42, Sally 21, Amanda 19, Harriett 17, Anna E. 15, George N. 13, Hesther 11, Delphia 9, William W. 8, John R. 6, Thomas F. 3, Mary E. 10/12
CUMMINGS, William H. 35, Susan 29, Melissa 13, Milda 11, George 7
WATTS, Howard 29, Lucinda E. 23, John J. 4, Wiley J. 3, Margarett T. 1
GRIGGS, Allen 21*, Telitha A. 18
ALBY, Fanny 9*
LAURENCE, Robert 48, Lucy A. 25, Thomas V. 16, Sabina A. 13, Mary L. 11, Robert W. 8
GLOVER, James 32*, Mahala 44, Peter 20, James 19, Eliza 17, Thomas 14, John 12, Sally 10, Catharine 6
GASPER, Lucy A. 1*
SMILEY, John __, Nancy 41, George W. 17, Mary E. 11

Schedule Page 34

CURTIS, William 20, Mary 22
WATTS, William 25, Sally Ann 25, James O. 3, John W. 2, Mary E. 4/12
JOHNSON, Elijah 54, Elvina 40, Catharine 26, Ryland 21, Martha J. 17, Eli J. 14, Rebecca 14, John W. 13, Francis 11, Henry 9, Perry W. 6, Sarah E. 6/12
GRIGGS, John 71, Rebecca 71, Cynthia A. 23, Elizabeth 10
CURTIS, Benjamin 20, Nancy A. 19
THOMAS, Robert H. 50, Sally 44, Eliza 20, Strauder 17, Sarah 12, Leroy 9, Louisa 6, Moses 2, William 9/12
ALLEN, Francis S. 29*, Elizabeth 27, James L. 6, Pleasant 4, Sophia A. 2, Mary M. 5/12
BUSH, Pleasant 27*
ALLEN, Patsey 80
BROCK, John jr. 45, Polly 43, Henry 20, John W. 17, Mary O. 14, Julia A. 12, Charles W. 9, Allen H. 6, Elizabeth F. 4, Thomas 1
HAMPTON, Parnetha 33*, Esther 4, James W. 3, Frances M. 8/12
WALLER, John T. 16*, William H. 13, Mary A. 9, Sarah w. 7
HAMPTON, Esther 4*, James W. 3, Frances M. 8/12

1850 Census Clark County Kentucky

MORGERSON, Elijah 52, John F. 30, Pamelia 14, William 17, Armilda 12, Otheniel 11, James T. 9, Susan M. 7
RICHARDSON, Solomon 34, Sarah 37, Harrison B. 8, Robert F. 5, O. H. P. 3 (m), Henry A. 10/12
CRUTCHFIELD, Sutton 45, Jane 35, Martha J. 21, Elizabeth 16, Westley 13
MCCHRISTY, Jesse 45, Milly 42, James O. 18, Susan O. 17, Josephine 15, Nancy 12, Sarah 6, John W. 4

Schedule Page 35

THOMAS, Augustus 24*, Justina 18, Nancy E. 1, James 67, Frances 70
WOODFORD, Edwin T. 33*, Mary J. 25, Sarah L. 4, Lucy a. 2, James W. 9/12
REED, Martha L. 56*
MARTIN, John W. 26, Martha F. 26, Zachry T. 3, Elizabeth F. 1
WRIGHT, Jeptha 37, Sally S. 27, Hetha 8, Sarah 6, Polly A. 4, Martha 1
BROCK, James S. M. 23, Catharine 16, Mary E. 8/12
BLAKEMORE, Ellen 44, Thomas H. 23, George N. 15, John E. 18, Lucy E. 14
AUSBURN, William T. 35, Nancy 27, Elizabeth 8, Eda 6, Marshall E. 3, Mary 5/12
STEVENS, William 23*, Susan 24, Lucinda 1
WRIGHT, Mary 65*
LAWRENCE, James M. 35*, Rebecca 35, Luan 11 (f), Matha 8, Mary 7, Wilson 5, Milly 3
BROCK, Amanda 16* (B)
ROBINSON, John 69*, Ritty 55, Butler 22, Enoch 18
CURTIS, Kitty 24*
PIGG, Briston 70 (B), Judy 75
BUSH, Thomas J. 31*, Cynthia 58
ELKIN, Frances 16*
RICKET, Thomas J. 12*
ELKIN, Ezekiel 33, Sydney 34, William 13, Zachry 11, Robert 10, John A. 8, Shelby W. 6, Jane 4, Pleasant 2, Ezekiel L. 10/12
MUDAY, David 27, Sally 16
OLIVER, Joel 50, Polly 40, James 27, Richard 25, John 24, Henry M. 18, Lunea A. 16, Polly A. 15, William A. 6
JOHNSON, Armstead 30*, Elizabeth 23, James W. 5, Nancy 3, Jane 5/12
OLIVER, Joel S. 21*

Schedule Page 36

BROCK, John sr. 74, Frances 76, Rebecca 25
BROCK, Simpson W. 22*, Elizabeth 20, Nancy J. 2, Emily 12
SPRY, Lucy 50*
CURTIS, Levi 50, Harriett S. 50, Caroline M. 23, Evan M. 21
PATRICK, Bryant 48, Lucy 46
PATRICK, John W. 21*, Sarah F. 23, William D. 4, Achillis B. 3/12
DUVALL, Thomas D. 7*
SHEPHERD, James 38*, Susan R. 40, Mary E. 12, John 10, Samatha 8
LANGLEY, Eliza 20*
ROBINSON, Arrin 42, Margaret 43, William 19, Susan 13, Tipton S. 8

1850 Census Clark County Kentucky

POWELL, Jesse 56*, Judieth 44, Eilzabeth 22, James M. 21, Mary J. 17, Jasper N. 11, Ansil D. 9, William H. 6, Mary G. 2
ALDRIDGE, James 18*
ROBERTS, George 66*, Elizabeth 63
DOUGHERTY, George 23*, Nancy 21
RICHARDSON, Nancy 17*
STEVENS, Asa 48*, Martha 43, Zachariah 19, John 17, David 15, Milly 13, Wilson 10, Octavius 7, Thomas 3, Melinda 1
GRAVETT, Nicholas 33*
GRAVETT, Nancy 27, Isaac 8, Ellis T. 5, James N. 2
CONNER, Moses 25, Margarett F. 17, John W. 1
LANGLEY, Robert W. 30*, Mewitha F. 21, Ann 3, Wallace 1
PATTON, Sampson 21*
KENT, John W. 14*
WALLACE, Enfield 18 (f)*
GRAVITT, John S. 22, Frances 22, Luan 3
GRIGGS, Minor 31*, Frances 29
RAINY, John W. 19*
CONKRIGHT, John 42*, Sarah 42, Sallan 13, Harriett 3, Sarah 4/12
TUTTLE, Cynthia 27*

Schedule Page 37

CLANCY, Lewis 56, Elizabeth 53, Rebecca 11, James 10
DEBARA, Treobe 48 (m), Lucinda 36, Mary J. 16, Marcus D. 14, Napoleon B. 13, Matilda E. 12, Sarah 10, William C. 9, John R. 6, Benjamin T. 2, Pleasant 6/12
TRUSSELL, Roberta 40, Simpson A. 17, Mary A. 14, Silas W. 11, Armstead A. 9, Martha J. 7, Caroline 5
ROBERTSON, William 77*, Susan 67
ROBINSON, Calvin C. 40*, Elizabeth 36, Lucy A. 15, Martha 14, Mary J. 12, John N. 8, James H. 6, William G. 4, David L. 6/12
TUTTLER, Nelson C. 25, Mary 24, Susan 2
DUMFORD, Solomon 60, Sarah 62
GLOVER, Owen 45, Nancy 55, Milly 14, James 13
STEVENS, John 40, Polly 40, Rachel 5
MORELAND, Elijah 40, Sarah A. 34, William 12, George 10, James 9, Martha 8, Alexander 7, Nancy 6, Harmon 4
MONROE, William 27, Sally A. 27, Thomas J. 8, John 6, George W. 4, Chilton 1
FINNELL, Jones 26, Mary 26, Susan 8, John 5, Catharine 1
MOPPIN, Jane 28, Westley 9, Lucy 7, Nancy 3, Mary E. 1
LAWRENCE, William H. 29, Mary J. 26, Polly A. 8, John M. 5, Frances 2, Achillis 8/12
PALMER, Robert S. 25, Mary F. 21, Elizabeth C.11/12
TROBRIDGE, Jonathan 40*, Mary Ann 37
PATTON, Indina? 18*

1850 Census Clark County Kentucky

Schedule Page 38

LAWRENCE, Andrew J. 23, Eliza J. 18, James P. 7/12
BERRYMAN, Alexander 28, Jane 26, Mary A. 6, Fielding 4, George 3, Thomas J. 1
MERRITT, Abram 38*, Sophia 31, Thomas P. 10, Mary E. 8, Sernera 4, John 7/12
MERIDITH, David 19*
BROCK, James 22* (B), Henry 20, Noah 14, Maria 12
PIGG, Thomas 24
KEAS, Aurelius 31, Pamelia 31, Francis M. 8, Milly 5, William T. 3, George W. 2
WILLIAMS, John W. 60, Rebecca 60, Washington 23, Charlotte 21, Sarah A. 17, Martillas 15, Jerene 12
DOUGHERTY, William 60, Mirian 44, Simeon 18, Van Buren 16, Angeline 13, Isaac 11, Susannah 10, Vienna 7, Lucinda 4, John W. 2
FARNEY, Benjamin F. 28, Rebecca B. 26, Greenberry C. 5, Milly A. 3, Jas. H. 9/12
RICE, James H. 37, Sarah 8, Catharine 7, Meruth 1 (m)
RICE, Catharine 66
RUCKER, John 39*, Arthusa J. 31, Lucy J. 15, Juliett 13, William R. 11, Mary 9, Susan 7, Martha 5, Irvine C. 2
WILLIAMS, Alfred 30*
WITT, John M. 25*
THOMAS, William N. 25*
FARNEY, Hudson 64, Milly 30
CROW, John 76, Martha 35
FRITTS, Isaac 36, Eliza 33, Susan 12, Sabrina 10, Martha C. 6, John T. 2, Isaac 10/12
WILLIAMS, Joseph 26, Mary 26
HUGHS, Thomas 36*, John M. 5, Sarah C. 4, Polly A. 1
FRITTS, Elizabeth 37*, William P. 7
FARNEY, Polly A. 9/12*
RICE, Nancy 8*

Schedule Page 39

HUGHES, John 41*, Ann 34, James 12, John W. 9, Caroline 7, Benjamin F. 5, Mary E. 3, Sarah 6/12
MCFARRIN, William 46*
MABERY, Sally 23*
FARNEY, Green E. 35*, Elizabeth 35, John 14
MABERRY, Elizabeth 20*
SNOWDEN, James 10*
LANGLEY, James W. 38*, Elizabeth 27, Susan 7, Martha 6, John 5, Nancy 4, Eliza 2
CHISM, Calvin 27*
CLEM, Leroy 30, Allice 33, Nancy 14, Albert 6, Martha 5, Henry 2
HUGHES, Matthew 43, Milly 35, Louisa 14, Mary J. 12, Amanda 10, Sarah 7, John W. 1
HUGHES, George W. 32, Nancy 28, Algin 9 (m), Augustin 7, Armstead 5, William 3, Lucy 6/12, Sally 78
STEVENS, Hiram 47, Zilpha 40, Hannah 20, Elizabeth 18, Simpson 15, William 13, Solomon 11, Benjamin 9, Mary J. 7, Mickelberry 5, Sally 2
BUSH, George W. 51, Eliza 31, Lucy A. 6, Mary E. 4, Frances P. 3, Sarah E. 1
MARTIN, Hudson 45, Cynthia 39, Nancy 17, James 16, John W. 14, Azariah 12, Polly 12?, Hudson 8?, William 6?, Milly 4, Elizabeth 2

1850 Census Clark County Kentucky

KEAS, William B. 48*, Nancy 49
CLANAHAN, Sarah 30*
BUSH, Nacy J. 6*
RANKIN, Robert 39?, Matilda 38, Sarah 18, Nancy 16, John 14, Solomon 12, Robert W. 10, Evaline 8, Albert 6, Abbott 6, Amanda 4, Mary 1

Schedule Page 40

HAGGARD, David T. 54*, Sarah 31, Thomas P. 9, Martha E. 16
RAKER, Sarah E. 13*
BLAKEMORE, James S. 25, Mahala 22, Thomas J. 3, William 9/12
THOMPSON, Thomas 37, Margarett 32, Elizabeth J. 13, Nathan M. 11, Orville B. 9, Rebecca 16
BRONAUGH, James H. 32*, Susan 24, John 4, Amelia 2
ALLEN, Charles 50*
HURONYMUS, Franklin 25*
QUISENBERRY, Stephen Q. 28, Cloah 24, Lucy A. 2, Julia E. 11/12
LOCKNANE, James T. 39, Frances 36, John 16, Eliza A. 14, Samuel 5, Thomas 50
SYMPSON, William C. 51*, Mary J. 44, James 20, Frances E. 14, William C. 8, Allan H. 3
NEELLY, Ann B. 65*
GASPER, Peter 63*, Catharine 30
GROVER, Elizabeth 15*
HOBBS, Susan 22*
CARTER, James 45*
CASKY, Frederick 24*, Sarah 28, Robert A. 6/12
BEALL, Durrett 27, Elizabeth 35, Mary J. 3
EPPERSON, James 39, Louisa 30
DANDY, William C. 29*, Mary Ann 24, James C. 1
MCCLURE, Mary 62*, Mary E. 14
HICKMAN, William 61*, Susan 28, Nancy 20, William L. 24
TALIAFERRO, John 35*, Lucy 25, Sally 6, Charles 4, Elizabeth 2
TRAMMELL, John 57*, Ann P. 59
GLOVER, Daniel 70* (B), Dirah 75
WHEELER, Samuel 48*, Caroline 40, Eliza A. 19, Caroline 10, Martha 6
MASON, James 80*
DEARBON, John 24*
SPURGIN, D. M. 37 (m), Amana 33, William F. 12, James S. 6

Schedule Page 41

TAYLOR, Hubbard jr. 30*, Sarah B. 17, George M. 25, Thomas A. 20
JORIETT?, Edward S. 20*
NAHM, Leopold 31*, Joseph 19, Hannah 17, Lewis 10/12
OPENHEIMER, Simon 29*
LISLE, Rufus 32*, Mary A. 20
WATTS, Oschar F. 24*
HAMPTON, Lewis 36*
JONES, Cadwallader 30*

1850 Census Clark County Kentucky

CART, O. R. 27 (m)*
WEBSTER, Leslie 27 (m)*
MILLS, John 69*, Lucy 67, John 20, William 2
HOCKADAY, Elizabeth 18*
BUCKNER, A. H. 40 (m)*
WINN, William 33*
VANMETER, Lucy 1*
CLAY, John W. 28*, Mary E. 23, Albert 3, Mary 1
WARD, Amalza 36 (m)*, Eliza C. 23
BRUNER, John W. 34, Margarett P. 22, Mary E. 4, Ann 2
CATHERWOOD, John 44, Mary J. 12, Albert W. 10, Martha W. 8, Lucy M. 6, Samuel 1
BOUREN, Alfred F. 31*, Ann H. 30
MITCHEN, Mary 12*
MEFFORD, Leonard 23*
SAMUELS, Sarah 19*
HOUSTON, John B. 37*, Mary J. 33
ALLEN, Chilton 64*, Ann 53, Ann jr. 12, Daniel W. 21, Henry C. 28, Bittie 24, Barbara 3
FUMY, Henry 35*
SNYDER, Andrew 18*, George 15
EGENTON, Charles 35, Sarah L. 33, Mary 5, Thomas M. 3
DOWNEY, William S. 27*, Lucy 23, Mary E. 2, Catharine 50, Martha 24
STOCKTON, Mary 24*, John D. 10, Catharine 8, William 6, Caroline 4, George W. 1
COX, David H. 28*, Louisa 20, Sarah 1
WEBB, Isaiah 47*, Martha 40, John 11, Augusten 10, Caroline 8

Schedule Page 42

WEBB, John T. 37, Mildrid 28, Nancy 6, Martha 4
MCCALLISTER, Patrick 35*, Catharine 29, Betta 10, Patrick 1, Susannah 13
MCWILLIAMS, Patrick 26*
WHITE, Richard 28*
HENNESSY, Richard 26*
DONYHESS?, Thomus 26*
DONELLE, Robert 25*
DAVIS, Patrick 25*
GARLEND, Patrick 20*
FORAN, John 22*
DUNIEN, Bryant 25*
TAYLOR, Samuel M. 65*, Mildred 57, Hetty H. 17, George E. 16, Clarah H. 13
MITCHELL, F. T. 28 (m)*, Susan A. 21
HAWES, Mildred 13*
HANSEN, Samuel 64*, Minerva 43, Sarah 26, Samuel jr. 18, Thomas 16, Lydia 14, Mary R. 14, Ellen 10, Isaac S. 6
HOCKADAY, Ametia 22*, Martha 18, Serena 10, Hailman 1
SMITH, George 47*, Penelope 30
KELLY, Charles S. 12*, John 10, Cassandra 8, Mary S. 3
OWENS, Fielding 43, Ann 45, Mary C. 10, Augustus W. 5
STRINGFELLEN, Elizabeth 53*, Sarah 34

1850 Census Clark County Kentucky

PETTICORD, Susan 17*
CLARK, Gemima 75* (B)
SIMPSON, Delpha 50* (E)
WARD, Peggy 80* (B)
DUNCAN, Jesse 49 (B)
KARRICK, Samuel 26*, Martha 22, Mary 5/12
BROUGHTON, Ruth 62*
HUTCHINGS, Africa 51 (m) (B)
HARDING, James W. 26", Mary E. 20, James A. 2
MCDONALD, Lucy 13*
WEST, Wright N. S. 25*, Mary 19, Sarah 2
SWINNY, Nancy 40*, John 13, George 10
ANDERSON, William 41, Sarah 35, Joseph 13, Abnor 10, Thomas 7, Charles 3
GARNER, William 39, Rachel R. 31, James T. 11, Orra V. 9, Ann C. 7, America 5, Cana 4 (f), Emma 3, William 11/12, Sarah 50, Louisa 40, Clementine 35

Schedule Page 43

DONALDSON, Thomas F. 45, Matilda 43, Julian 16 (f), Amanda 15, Ruth E. 14, Milly 13, Walter 10, William 8, Catharine 6, David 4, Mary 2
POOL, Philip 60, Polly 59, William 28
BERRY, Thomas J. 33*, Caroline 32, Mary E. 10, Martha A. 8, Amon A. 6, James F. 4
BELL, John H. 24*
DOWREN, Elizabeth 38, Susan 17, John 14, Melissa F. 11, Henry 8
FOLEY, Rebecca 50, Eleanor 24, Susan 22, Elizabeth 20
COLLINS, James 40*, Jare 40
BURNES, Catharine J. 10', Mary C. 13
COLE, Jerry 27* (B), Henrietta 28, William 2
JOHNSON, Charles 4/12* (B)
FOSTER, Nancy 35 (B), Andrew 12
DAVIS, Richard 54, Catharine 44, Richard 12, Lucinda 6
HARRIS, Elijah 68, Ellen 56, James P. 25, Louisa 22, Sarah A. 18
NELSON, Warner 45 (B), Peggy 57
STUBBLEFIELD, John P. 59, Elizabeth 44, Robert B. 24, William 22, John 19, Elijah 16, Susan 14, Catharine 12, Benjamin B. 8, Elizabeth 6, Sarah 6
WARD, Maria 54 (B)
STORM, Joel 35, Catharine 25, William W. 14, Allen R. 7
MASSIE, A. W. 41 (m)*, Nancy C. 29, Mary E. 8, Charles E. 4
MCMAHAN, Julia 30*
POSTON, Edwin 37*, Mary F. 22, Edmond 1
PARISH, Edwin 18*
WEBSTER, David 33*, Narcissa 31, James W. 7, Ann E. 6, Winfield S. 3

Schedule Page 44

MATTHEWS, Thomas 84*, Ann 48
OLIVER, Robert 27, Isabinda 18, James 4, George 1

- 25 -

1850 Census Clark County Kentucky

MOSS, Francis B. 46*, Eliza A. 43, Elias 18
JAMES, Hezakiah J. 22*
ALGAIER, Charles A. 28*, Mary F. 25, George E. 3
CLINKENBEARD, Lewis 17*
WEBSTER, Eli 21*
MARDEN, John 19*
DUNCAN, Joseph 53*
WEBSTER, James W. 26, Mary 67
OWSLEY, Wyatt 47, Nancy 47, Elizabeth 17
WALDRIDGE, John 37, Lititia 32, Matha F. 7, James 5, Lucy E. 2, Allice 11/12
HERNDON, William 80*, Catharine 75, George 50
FEEMSTER?, Sarah 40*, Mary 19
BURBERRY, David 28*, Emily M. 22, James M. 6, Catharine R. 4, David jr. 2
KENNEDAY, Robert sr. 65*, Robert jr. 24
RIFFE, John M. 27, Mary A. 21, Cordelia 2
WEBSTER, George 30, Amand 31, Oschar 6, Roger 4, Castilla 1, Leroy F. 25
BLUNT, Margarett 34, Elizabeth 20, Arabella 14
OWSLEY, John D. 56, Elizabeth 45, Amanda 18, Mary 14, Henry 12, Margarett A. 10, Emily 7, Edward 5
SKINNER, Cato 40 (B), Ann 37, Richard 8, Lucy 1, Sarah 10/12
ADAMS, William 64*, Catharine 64
CAHILL, Margarett 31*, William 12, Margarett 2
MCCALLA, John 15*
ADAMS, Thomas 38*, Sarah 40
THOMPSON, George 20*, Eliza 11
BENTHALL, Seth 54, Elizabeth 45, John 22, Joseph 21, Nelson 17, Mary 19, Elliott 12, Samuel 11

Schedule Page 45

BALL, John 57*, Thomas 27, Elizabeth 21, George S. 19
TRUE, Elijah 20*
LUBA, Henry 43*, Catharine 35, George 11, Charles 5, Fanny 3
WOODS, Frances E. 29*, Fanny 5
FAULKNER, Thomas 50* (B), Winney 50, William 12, Amanda 8
CAREY, Harry 30* (B)
SIMPSON, James 53*, Mary L. 45, Caro 11 (m), James D. 4
BRASFIELD, Eliza 55*, Mary J. 24
DEAN, William H. 23, Mary E. 19, Addison F. 2
COLE, James W. 44, Elizabeth 41, Lucy J. 20, Martha 18, William 16, James 14, Rebecca 9, John 6, Augustus 3, Robert 11/12
JEFFRIES, Smith 50, Magdalene 45, John 22, Mary 16, Harriett 12
WINN, Ruth 70
ADAMS, John Q. 26, Harriett 24, Ellen 5, Frances 2
HOLHASS, Henry jr. 30, Catharine M. 26, Mary J. 5, William 3, Emma P. 1
WHITEHEAD, James N. 45, John W. 16, George 14, Peter 12, William 4
FRAZIER, Warren 45*, Laura 35, Robert 11, John 8, Amanda 5, Anna A. 3
WILLIAMS, Oscar 27*
DIDLAKE, Robert Q. 39*, Elizabeth C. 36, George W. 15, Susan F. 12, Amanda F. 10, Ellen W. 4

1850 Census Clark County Kentucky

SCRUGGS, E. O.? 25 (m)*
HARROW, Thomas A. 29*
BALLARD, James 38, Catharine S. 22, Eliza A. 4, Martha E. 2, Nancy J. 3/12, Linville 29
PARRISH, James G. 29*, Eliza 22, James W. 31, Christopher H. 23
FOWLER, Sally A. 14*
PRESTON, Alexander M. 36*, Elizabeth 43, Mary 14, Ann 12, Elizabeth 11, Samuel 9, Lucy 6, Ellen 4, Alexander 2
BRUNER, Jackson 26*
HINDE, Anna 24*

Schedule Page 46

BERRY, David 45, Lorilla 35, John H. 17, Mary C. 16, Louisa 14, George W. 9, America 6, Amanda 3, James 1
TURNBULL, James R. 51*, Eliza 46, Sarah J. 23, Susan 18, Margarett 16, Julia 14, Ellen 9, Prudence 7
DILLS, Proctor 30*
BENTLEY, John 16*
ASHBURN, Ambrose 15"
WILLIAMS, John 51*, Parthenia 53, Charles 24, Julia 21, Jesse 20, Mary 18, E. Ann E. 21
KERR, Parthenia 11*, Mary 9
SPILMAN, James 57, William 15, James R. 13, Elizabeth P. 8, Richard H. 6, Robert S. 4
ALLEN, A. S. 26 (m)*, Susan T. 22
YOUNG, Margarett 39*
VANMETER, Elizabeth 5*
FOSTER, Mary 13*
HOOD, Andrew 54, Ellen 41, Nancy 16, Lucas 13, John 11, Josiphat 8 (m), Richard T. 6
FLANAGAN, William 45, Laura 20, James 29
TURNER, Benjamin 56*, Catharine 44, Elizabeth 13, Benjamin F. 11, Nathaniel L. 9
COUCHMAN, Nathaniel 32*
BERRY, Grant 45, Rebecca 38, Mildred M. 11, James T. 9, William G. 6, Alice B. 3
DANIEL, Jackson M. 38*, Frances 33, John H. 4, Madison T. 1
QUISENBERRY, Philip 12*, Ann 10
PATRICK, Alexander 36", Susannah 25, Isaac 7, Albert 2, James 1
HENIP, Joshua 20*

Schedule Page 47 (Page 48 has no entries)

WOOD, William H. 33, Amelia 20, Mary E. 12, Richard B. 8, William H. 7, Robert B. 3, James T. 8/12
ALLEN, James 41*, Amanda 24, Bryant 15, John 13, Thomas 11, Robert 5, Lucy 2
OWSLEY, James R. 21*
ANDERSON, William 18*
ANDERSON, Maria 45 (B)
ALLEN, Thomas B. 37*, Sarah A. 27
CRIM, Sally 13*
KOHLHASS, Theodore 37, Henry W. 10, McElroy 8, Julia 6, Theodore 4, Henry 74, Prudence 62
YEATES, Benjamin 25*, Elizabeth 22, Mary F. 5, Nancy M. 2, Sarah E. 7/12
HICKEY, James 27*

1850 Census Clark County Kentucky

CUFF, John 30*
GLEASON, Joset 33 (m)*
HOLLY, Patrick 33*
WELCH, Patrick 25*
PROVINCE?, Wiley 21*
DOWNER, Peggy 58 (B)
MCCRUNE, James 38*
GARLAND, Peter 20*
LAUGHLIN, Lucy W. 65*, Mary 27, Bettie 20, Lucy 25, Sarah V. 4, Ann T. 1, Virginia 35, Charles W. 3
NICHOLAS, Robert C. 35*
KEMP, Henry 35*, Henry T. 1
HERNDON, P. J. 48 (f)*
FOWLER, Martha 26*, Mary R. 3
BERRY, John 8*
HOOD, James M. 30*, Louisa 23, Nancy 2
HAMPTON, Catharine 2*
OWSLEY, Ellen 28, Eliza A. 9, Joseph 7, Richard 6, William 5, Rutha E. 2, James 6/12
KEITH, Andrew M. 49, Mary J. 36, Sarah 17, James A. 16, Marshall 11, Mary B. 8
BUCKNER, Charlotte 34*, Benjamin 14, Susan 11, Daniel 8, Garrett D. 4
FORSYTH, Ann 65*
SHEPHERD, Mary F. 13*
KEITH, James W. 61, Asa 14, Lucy 17

Schedule Page 49

WEAVER, John D. 51, Absalom 26, John 32, Amanda 24, Elizabeth 16, Joel 12, Robert 10, Duan 8 (f), Atha 4 (m)
ELSBERRY, John R. 47, Elizabeth 37, Ann 14, Sarah 6, Jane 5, Benjamin 3, Joseph 2, Nancy 9/12
KENNON, Robert 55, Mary 33, Banks? W. 18, John W. 12, Christopher C. 10, William W. 7, Mary E. 5, Andrew J. 6/12
FOSTER, John 66, Nancy 60, Thomas 22, John 18
TANNER, David 64, Lydia 64, Julia 19
FRANKLIN, Lydia J. 14
TANNER, Branch M. 32*, Rebecca 33, Reuben 6, Harriet 8, Sarah 4, David 1
REED, Thomas 30*
FRANKLIN, Elizabeth 25*
ADAMS, William R. 19*, Susan? 28
BRADLY, William 8*
BURK, James H. 31, Julia A. 27, Richard H. 7, Lucy K. 4
LOCKNANE, Jane 30, John 19, Charles 18, Miles 15, Jane 10, Nancy 5
RIPPEY, Gelkerson 32, Sarah 26, Mary 7, William 5, Julia F. 3
TAPP, Major 56*, Malinda 50, Andrew F. 20, Benjamin 18, Marium 21 (f), Emily 15, Mildred 13
HAMILTON, Huldah 50*, Nancy 20
LOWRY, James 57, Jane 56
HOUS, James C. 23, Mary A. 18, James T. 1

1850 Census Clark County Kentucky

HAGGARD, Nathaniel 70, Elizabeth 67, Mason 26
OGDEN, Smalwood 39, Sabina A. 30, Amanda 10, Eliza 9, Mary C. 7, Harvey S. 5, Ezekiel 4, Minerva S. 2, Thomas M. 10/12

Schedule Page 50

BARNES, Israel 36, Eliza A. 25, Mary J. 5, Sarah M. 2, James C. 7/12
BIRCH, George 38*, Mary 37, James 13, Thomas 11, George 7, Heny 5 (m), Amanda 3, William 1
GROEN, Sarah 19*
JONES, Ducon 62, Nancy 49, Thomas 32, Ann 30, Elizabeth 23, Mary 18, William 21, Elizabeth 5
ECTON, Theodore 59, Malinda 56, Dillard 19, Nancy A. 16, William 13, Horatio 10
ECTON, James S. 22, Mary E. 17
BENNING, Sarah 79
ECTON, Horatio 56*, Margaret 50, Lydia 20, William F. 18, John C. 14, Martha 13, Amanda 12
ROBINSON, Thomas 70*
STUART, James 59*, Susan 49
THOMPSON, William 24', Mary 23, Frances 18, Thomas 15, William 13, Charles 10
WILLS, Cyrus S. 5*, Sarah A. 11, Mary J. 9, Luvina 7, George 6
PARIDO, Colby 17*
EVANS, John S. 44*, Sarah 43
PARIDO, John 30*
BAXTER, Richard 38*, Mary A. 29, William 4, Sarah E. 2
ELSBERRY, Mary 15*
EVANS, Marcus C. 43*, Nancy 40, Susan A. 6, Mary H. 5, Louisa S. 3, D. H. 2 (m)
STUART, William M. 23*
EVANS, Oliver P. 29, Mary 75, James H. 6
HAMPTON, Wade 45*, Rebecca 43, David S. 16, Margaret J. 8, Philip J. 3
CLAMPET, Henry 90*
JONES, Linney 90 (f)*
BOWMAN, Polly 80*, Jane 75
JACKSON, Sally 78*
IMFREL?, Darly 60 (f)*

Schedule Page 51

BAKER, Jerry 60*, Ann 55
WOODS, Sarah 36*
JONES, Hiram 45*, Amica 40, John S. 13, Mary A. 6, Margaret 6/12
CHISM, Thomas 82*
GWYNN, Addison 31, Lucy E. 30, Nancy A. 4, Mary E. 2
RUPARD, Joseph 58, Samuel 21, Sarah 15, Harrison 10
PARIDO, William 75, Elizabeth 69, Mary A. 31, Charles 6, Robert 4
DUNN, Stephen 57, Agness 48, Stephen 24, Agness 20, Samuel 19, Fielding 16, William 12, Thomas 9, Mary 8, Amanda 6
TIPTON, Robert L. 24, Eve 22, James 4, Sally 2, Jane 4/12
HUNT, Jon_ 75 (m)*, Nancy 42, Jesse P. 34, Cynthia 30, Catharine 26
HAGGARD, Mary 32*

1850 Census Clark County Kentucky

POTTS, Smith V. 35, Elizabeth 38, Edward D. 5, Jonathan H. 3, Sarah F. 1, Martha 14
HAYDEN, Andrew 34, Mary A. 22, Sarah A. 5, Robert 3, Rebecca 3/12, Samuel 26
HUNT, James 47, Jon_ W. 18 (m), William 10, Martha 7, James H. 5, Dand? R. 3 (m), Mary K. 1
BAILY, Eliza 39, Mary Ann 38, Sidney 19 (m), Mary E. 17, Sarah Ann 15, William S. 12, Peter E. 10, Thornton 8, Julia A. 6, Robert 4, Margaret F. 1
CLEM, James 40, Cyntha 17, Jackson 12, William H. 10, Nancy 6, James 4/12
HUNT, Jeptha 45*, Frances 41, Mary 19, Simeon P. 17, Sally Ann 15, John D. 12, James W. 11, Martha B. 10, George 6

Schedule Page 52

CHRISTY, Hannah 73*
TIPTON, John 41, Sally 40, Orifa 17 (f), Eliza 15, William 14, Samuel 13, Armena 11, Solomon 7, Henry C. 6, Smith P. 3
FRANKLIN, John W. 59*, Mary 47
DUGAN, Hugh 12*, Virginia 17
ECTON, John 31*, Susan S. 27, Francis M. 8, Sally 7, James C. 4, John S. 1
QUISENBERRY, Margaret 9*
QUISENBURY, Nicholas 35, Susan 35, Mary E. 7, Lucy A. 5
ECTON, Theodore jr. 35, Arthusa 20, James 5, Martha D. 1
HAMPTON, Leonard 36, Nancy 23, Mary J. 4/12
ECTON, James S. 27, Susan 22, John S. 2
SUTHERLAND, Frederick 58*, Santy 57 (m), Susan 58
AYERS, Martin 35*, Mary 21, Catharine 3, Peter 1
RAKER, Jacob 37, Sarah 29, David 12, Mary 10, Richard 8, Sarah Ann 2
RAKER, William 30, Elizabeth 25
HAMPTON, Sarah 60, Sally Ann 20, George W. 24
FARIS, Granville 27, Elizabeth 28
SKINNER, Alfred 41*, Lucretia 28, John 5, James 3, Alfred 2, no name 6/12 (m)
JONES, William 27*
GREEN, John 42, Polly 38, Sarah 17, Eliza 15, Mary E. 12, Jane N. 10, Patsey 6, Susan 3, Amanda 11/12
WILES, Leroy 39, Amanda 37, Eli T. 17, John C. 13
EVANS, Silas 38, Susan 38, Nancy 16, Garland 13, Marcus 10, Polly 8, Sarah 6, Edwin 5, Peter 4, Newton 4/12

Schedule Page 53

ELLAGE, John 49*
METCALFE, Thomas 48*, Patsey 22
WARREN, Thompson 41*, Lucy 31
BENNETT, Elizabeth 20*
HALLY, James H. 41*, Lucinda 30, William H. 8, Emily 6, James 4, Elizabeth 1
EDGERTON, Judith 64*, Louisa 24
TALBOTT, Augustus 12*
FRANKLIN, Reuben S. 55*, Mary 46, William J. 27, Joel 21
GRANT, Hannah 70*

1850 Census Clark County Kentucky

FOX, George 44, Rhoda 30, Dillard 12, Clinton 10, Amanda 8, Marey K. 6, William T. 3
NOE, William F. 46*, Mary H. 35, Elizabeth C. 15, Sally ANn 14, Thomas T. 12
GARRETT, Ezekiel E. 30*
RAMEY, Franklin H. 30, Mary Ann 25, William R. 6, John A. 4, John M. 2
GORDON, Richardson 46*, Nancy 44, John E. 23, Jesse E. 22, Lewis A. 19, William J. 13, Frances M. 11, Augustus R. 5, Nancy M. 7, Ryland D. 2, Mary 89
DUNN, Pleasant 46*
DUCKWORTH, Thomas 47*, Delilah 45, John D. 16, James 14, Alvin 12, Thomas 10, Alfred 7, Mary Jane 20
EATON, Thomas 24*
BRADLEY, Dennis 92*
RUCKER, Reuben 46, Margaret 48, Eliza Jane 18, Mary Ann 16, Isaac 12, Sally Ann 8
COOPER, Mary 74, Mary 38, Mary E. 21, Eliza F. 17, Sidney 14, Susan E. 12, Amanda 10, Benjamin F. 7, Maria J. 4
PARISH, William M. 27*, Fanny N. 30, Amanda 2
FANK?, Frances 2*, John W. 1/12, John 47, Rachel 42, Zaida 21, Nancy 19, Martin 16, Elizabeth 13, John A. 10, James 7, Sally 4, Milam 2

Schedule Page 54

EMBREE, Sophia 40, Elvina 35, Fanny 4
GAINES, Thomas 40, Harriet 27, Martha J. 6, John P. 3, James T. 8/12
FARIS, Harvey 40*, Ann O. 45, Mary J. 2
CUMMINS, Saml. 21*
FARIS, John 84, Margaret 72, Rennes? 30 (f)
BAXTER, Green 43*, Luan 40
LAWRENCE, Nancy J. 12*
LAWRENCE, Will H. 33, Eliza Jane 28, Mary Frances 7, James W. 6, Jefferson G. 3, Nancy M. 10/12
LAWRENCE, William 45, Mavin? 45 (f), Zadock 8, James H. 4, Nancy A. 2
TUTTLE, William 53*, Sarah 39, Polly 22, John H. 19, John W. 12, Jane 14, Isaac N. 12, Talitha 9, Sarah 8, Thomas J. 5, Winfred S. 3 (m), Adaline 4/12
DEBARD, Joseph 21*
FOX, Beaufred 38, Sabrina 32, Adeline 9, Margaret 7, James 5, Benja. C. 4, Martha 1
VIVION, Elizabeth 74, Herman 40, Elizabeth 38, Nancy 36, Juliet 13, Sarah 11, Ann 5, Margaret 34
BROWN, Perry 27, Elizabeth 26, Peyton J. 7, John W. 4, Ephraim T. 3, Jas. B. 4/12
OLIVER, Elizabeth 48, Katy 37, Isaac 19, Eveline 16, Mary 12
DRURY, Hensfro? 37, Luan 39, Sabrina 13, John S. 11, Thomas C. 8, Frances A. 5, Julia M. 2

Schedule Page 55

TWYMAN, David R. 55, Matilda 47, Lucy B. 28, Pleasant H. 26, Franky 24 (f), Mary 22, Elizabeth 20, Martha 19, John G. 13
PARISH, Barnett 59*, Tacy 60, Hetty 24, Tacy 22, Catharine 19, Barnett 16
KENNER, Willis 7*
CUMMINS, Hester 81*
RAGLAND, John 55, Jane R. 59
BUSH, Allen N. 30*, Polly 24, Edith 7, Nancy 5, Allen N. 3, Jonas 8/12

1850 Census Clark County Kentucky

RICHARDSON, John 22*
NEAL, Edgar 39, Eliza Jane 32, Sally Jane 12, Robert 11, Williamson 10, Elizabeth 8, James S. 6, Lucy? 4, Nancy 2
FRANKLIN, Harrison 39, Angeline 24, James C. 6, Reuben H. 4, Fanny J. 2, Lydia M. 11/12
TWYMAN, Simeon 50, Milly 45, Allen H. 25, John A. 14, Sarah E. 12
PARISH, William 30, Catharine 29, James N. 10, Milton J. 6, Elizabeth 4, Hester 2, William 8/12
FOX, Benjamin 70, Margaret 60, Benjiman 33, Catharine 60
FOX, William 75*, Jane 26
GROOMS, James 35*, Almira 30
HOPWOOD, Smith 15*
POWELL, Mary H. 43, Harvy L. 13, Wm. H. 10, Elizabeth F. 8, Mary K. 5
WILLIAMS, William 81*, Willis 31, Dulcena 33, Sarah M. 11, William W. 9, James B. 7, Mary E. 4, Mildred A. 2
WEST, Mary 17*
STUART, William 76*, Susan 78, Susan 36
MCCAFFRY, Margaret 93*

Schedule Page 56

CROW, Nicholas 36, Catharine 38, John 10, Hezekiah 8, James B. 6, Edward M. 4, Nicholas 1
BOONE, Thomas 64, Sally 64, Milton 28, Frank 19
NOE, Harvey 40, Paulina 34, Augustus W. 9, William L. 6, George H. 2
THOMAS, Ennis 30, America 25, William E. 9, James S. 7, Mary J. 4, John M. 2
WILLIAMS, Ongmore? R. 47, Mildred 33, John W. 19, James T. 15, Dennis 13, Marion 12, Lucinda M. 11, George 8, Willis F. 6, Joseph 4, Dudly 2, Nancy M. 1
JEWELL, Ewell 60, Lucinda 48, John W. 20, Peter M. 13, Mary C. 12, Sarah M. 10, Armilda 8, Ewell 4
LOWE, Frederick 32*, Mary 48, Fanny 9
TUTTLE, John W. 25*, Nancy N. 24, Amanda 20, Milton W. 18, Mary W. 16
PARKER, Sarah 75, Nancy 50, Mahala 35, William 25, John 21, James 20, Henry 13, Sarah 13, Amanda 10, Elizabeth 8
PALMER, Elizabeth 48, Mary E. 19, Sarah T. 15
CLAWSON, Jesse 32, Catharine 27, Almelda 10, Isabel 7, Martha J. 3, John W. 2, Richd. H. 11/12
PARISH, Meredith 27, Margaret 23, William J. 2, Landon N. 4/12
RICE, Benja. C. 26, Sally 22, Mary Jane 4, John W. 2
DUNCAN, Charles 27*, Sally 25, James A. 6, John 4, David 6/12
SNOWDEN, David 21*

Schedule Page 57

STUART, Margaret 62, James 24, Francis 22
CHRISTY, Julius 43, Margaret 35, Mary F. 10, William C. 8, Simon C. 6, Hannah J. 4, Elizabeth A. 2
CAMPBELL, Chilton 27*, Eliza J. 27, Joseph C. 7, Margaret J. 4, Martha P. 2
CLEM, Joseph 50*, Polly 38, Polly A. 18, Nancy A. 10, Nancy J. 7
ALLEN, Richard 32*, Emily A. 23, Rebecca 3, Mary C. 1
PETTY, James 17*
COOPER, William C. 45, Marium 30, John 10, Richard F. 7, Henry 5, Mary E. 2
STUART, Joseph 32*, Lucinda 37, Elizabeth 10, Caroline 8, Nancy 5, James 3, Mary 4/12

1850 Census Clark County Kentucky

SNOWDEN, Charles C. 25*
ALLEN, William 43, Maria 30, James 12, Richard 10, Frances 8, Miner 6, Benjamin 3
ALLEN, John 45, Polly 27, William 65
ALLEN, Thomas 52*, Arkadile 42 (f)
WHITE, John J. 14*
ALLEN, John E. 45, Nancy M. 26
GARRETT, John 52, Therisa 49, Alvina A. 22, Columbus 16
JONES, William 32*, Elizabeth 25, Cleopatra 10, Thomas 6, Sutella 5
RHOMBURG, John 18*
STUART, Edward W. 44, Sarah M. 50
NOE, Landon 71
PREWITT, William F. 25, Mary E. 17
QUISENBERRY, James 44, Elizabeth 30, Amanda 14, Sally 10, Franklin 8, Hiram 6, Ellen 7/12
BRUCE, Eli 27, Elizabeth 18, Mary E. 6/12
DEORE, Joseph 66
MILLER, Elijah 28, Eliza L. 23, Elizabeth 2
IRVINE, William 47, Nancy 50, James 23, Angeline 21, Hezekiah 16, Mary E. 12, Martha T. 10

Schedule Page 58

ECTON, Smalwood 63, Sally A. 27
STANHOPE, Arthur 38, Polly 40, Clarke 19, William ann 17, James 15, Nancy E. 13, Ellen 6, Mary 10/12
BAKERS, Susan 50*
BUTLER, Lucy 30*, David 22
CURRY, Elias 47, Adeline 37, Charles 11, Adam 9, Elizabeth 7, Ann 5, Mary J. 3, Amanda 1
CURRY, Abed 39 (m), Clarissa 35
FLYNN, Michael 50, Mary 52, Lucy Ann 22, Susan 20, Elizabeth 18, Martha 17, Mahlon 15
WATKINS, Marion S. 30 (m), Morrison H. 26, Charles M. 7, John W. 5, Sarah F. 4, Benjamin F. 2
HULSE, Joshua 39, Polly 30
TRACY, George 32*, Julia 24
RANKINS, Bluford 39*
GREY, John 35, Martha J. 9, Charles 30, Eliza 25, Rose 4, Sarah E. 3
GOOSEY, William C. 54*, Elizabeth 23, William 21, George 19, Milly 16
ADAMS, Frankey 26 (f)*, Reuben 26, Nancy 3, Mary 6/12
VIVION, Flavel 45, Isabel C. 40, William H. 15, Mary F. 14, Milton H. 12, Margaret 9, Ann 5, John 4
VIVION, Milton 45, Julia 35, Mary F. 9, Thacker 7, Sabrina 5, Ann 3
MONTGOMERY, Sarah 65, Gillum 24 (m)
DAWSON, Lydia 84*
NEWKIRK, Sytha 23*, Benjamin 20, John W. 2
PARISH, Milton J. 28, Talitha 25

Schedule Page 59

RINGO, Philip 43, Sophia 36, John C. 12, William H. 8
RICE, Clarke 45*, Charlotte 45, Margaret J. 17, Nancy 15, Mary A. 14, James C. 12, Narcissa 8, Gelina 7 (f), John W. 5, Telford 3

- 33 -

1850 Census Clark County Kentucky

PARKERS, William 23*
GOOLMAN, Mary 60*, Elizabeth 30, James 28, Eliza J. 26
WISE, David 15*
WHITE, David 50, Jane 45, Nancy 18, John S. 16, Amanda 15, Elizabeth 13, James 12, William 10,
   Sidney 8 (m), Chilton 6, Tandy 4 (m), Taylor 2
HOLBROOK, John 26, Sally Ann 32, Sophia 6, Margaret 4, James 3, William 8/12
BUSH, Nelson 60, Nancy 69, Mary Jane 21, Robert 19, William N. 17, Napoleon B. 15, Narcissa 13,
   Lucy 11, Hanrah 9
OSBORN, Canterberry 24, Catharine 21, Paulina 6/12
OSBORN, George 70, Garrett 40, Peter 28, Margaret 25, Arkadile 22 (f)
RICHARDSON, Robert 50*, Lucinda 38, Garret 18, VanBuren 15, Robert 12, Mary 9, William 6,
   Benjamin 3, Weeden 4/12
PAYNE, Nelly 70*
OSBORN, Greenup 40, Margaret 35, Sarah A. 22, Flournoy 20, Dillard 14, James H. 12
BYBEE, Fielding L. 25, Elizabeth 24, Nancy J. 4, James L. 3, William H. 8/12
BULLARD, Heny 35 (m), Eliza 30, James W. 3, John 1
PATRICK, Weeden 25, Elizabeth 24, Lucy C. 3, Moses F. 7/12

Schedule Page 60

JOHNSTON, William 30, Mary 25, John R. 4, James 1
RICHARDSON, Peyton 58*, Letty 50, William 25, John 23, Andrew 18, Jefferson 15, Nancy 12
RAINEY, Squire 22*, Polly 22
OSBORN, Willis 32, Isabella 30, Amanda 10, George 8, Tuttle 6, Peter 4, Nancy 2
RICE, John C. 40, Minerva 33, Angeline 16, Harrison 14, Isaac F. 13, Emeline 10, John S. 8, Enoch 6,
   Rebecca 4, Julia 1
COMBS, Cuthbert 67, Fanny G. 63
WILSON, Mary 32, Minerva A. 8, Sarah E. 6
PRICE, Andrew B. 45, Eveline E. 33, Dillard 19, Mary C. 17, John 16, Absalom 12, Lucy A. 6, Sarah 3
OSBORN, George W. 38, Mary Ann 34, Narcissa A. 9, Daniel B. 6, John T. 4, Sarah 2
OGDEN, John 48, Minerva 42, Mary F. 21, James 19, Catharine 16, Washington 13, William 10,
   Thomas 8, Benjamin 6, Minerva 4
WILSON, Jacob 32, Lucinda 25, James E. 2
STUART, Hezekiah 47, Elizabeth 40?, William 22, Elizabeth 20, Minerva 18, Nancy W. 16, Susan M.
   15, Maria 12, Polly J. 10
EUBANKS, Achilles 26*, Mary 20, Susan V. 4, Peyton A. 1
PARIS, John 30*
WARE, John E. 28, Isabella _. 23, Robert D. 3, Christopher 2, Sarah J. 6/12
MOORE, John M. 50, Fanny 30, Hetuniss? 8 (f), Mary 6, Teliatha W. 4

Schedule Page 61

DEBARD, Marcus 45, Elizabeth 32, Joseph H. 21, Mary 18, Sarah 16, Susan 14, Milly J. 12, Trebo 9,
   Solomon 7
VICE, Margaret 60, Rhoda 43, Sarah 25, Susan 12, Elizabeth 8, Margaret 2
VICE, John 25, Nancy 21, Mary E. 3, William M. 1

- 34 -

1850 Census Clark County Kentucky

CHISM, Nathaniel 62, Elizabeth 55, Mary 20, James T. 19, Sarah 18, Eliza 14, Silas 12, Amanda 8, Dump? 5 (f)
GOODE, Walter R. 47, Amanda 40, Mary 18, Albert 17, George 15, Ann 12, John 6, William 2
FARNEY, Robert 33, Milly 31, Martha 8/12
CARR, Edmund 34, Nancy 32, Nancy 14, Louisa 12, Martha 9, Delia A. 8, Mary 6, Julia 3, Bluford 5/12
LOWRY, William 27, Nancy 26, Nancy 70
MENELL, Polly 65, Lydia 28
CARR, Simeon 43, Frances J. 39, Malinda 18, Eliza J. 16, Sidney 14 (m), John B. 12, Cynthia 10, William F. 6, Simeon B. 4, James S. 10/12
BISHOP, William 50, Jane 40, Sarah 20, David 15, Richard 7, Eliza 4, Elizabeth 4/12
FISHER, John 53, Sarah 50, Simpson 21, Samantha 19, Ealener 13, Susan 10, John H. 6
FISHER, Matthias 33, Milly J. 30, Mary E. 7, William 5, Sarah A. 2

Schedule Page 62

COTMAN, Tubman 50, Marion 13 (m), Joseph 26, Paulina 23
ELKIN, James 50, Lucinda 46, Thomas B. 18, Martha 17, Benjamin C. 14, Zachariah 13, John 11, Solomon 9, Silas 7, Cinderella 5
ELKIN, William 26*, Meranda 20, John 1
POOR, Mary 14*
OSBORN, Hezikiah? 64* John 30, Dulcena 28
MANIFREED, Sally 26*, Keziah 3
BONNY, Nathaniel 26, Jane 30, James W. 6, Sarah A. 4, Susan C. 2, Phebe E. 6/12
ADAMS, Thomas 37, Patsey 31, Nancy 14, William L. 12, Custer 10, Anderson 8, Nathan 6, Mary E. 4, Owen 3, John 2
EADS, Jourdan 44, Polly 44, Dillard 18, James 17, Robert M. 15, Leander 13, Samantha 11, Willis W. 9, Bethenia 7, Jourdan 5, Ann 3
ADAMS, John 60, Elizabeth 55, James H. 15
ADAMS, Fielding 24, Sarah A. 21, Leana 11/12
LOWRY, Garnett 45, Matilda 33, Nancy 16, Margaret 14, Louisa 12, William 11, Philip 7, Nelson 4, Robert 2
WILLIAMS, George 56, Sally 50, Jane S. 26, Sally 24, James 21, Matilda 20, Margaret 18, Polly A. 12, John N. 10
SANDRUM, Silas 25, Amanda 21, Sally M. 5, Mary A. 3, Martha J. 2, William Y. 11/12
WOOD, Charles 30*, Frances 30, Elizabeth 16, James 15, Nancy 12, Fielding 10, John 8, Marion S. 6 (m)
Polly A. 4, Franky 2 (f)

Schedule Page 63

POOR, William 18*
LOMAS, Elizabeth 48, Lavina 21, Lotty A. 17, Elizabeth 16
EWELL, William 64, Sytha 50, Susan 24, Nancy M. 22, Cuthbert B. 18, Narcissa 16, Peter E. 13
CROW, William 22, Nelly 30, Mary 1
HATTER, James 72, Susanna 65, Minerva 20, John 18
CAMPBELL, Sarah 50*
WATTS, Elizabeth 22*, John M. 19, Wallace 18, William H. 16, Samuel W. 14, Nancy 12

1850 Census Clark County Kentucky

WATTS, Beverly B. _, Josephine 28, John W. 8, Simpson D. 5, James H. 4, Wallace T. 11/12
NEBLACK, William 71*, William H. 29, Sarah A. 20
SNOWDEN, David 14*
CLEM, Joseph 22, Evaline 20
BROUGHTON, James G. 37, Rachel 33, William 16, James 14, John 12, Mary 10, Zerilda 8, Julia 3, Samuel 10/12
KING, Francis 25, Eilzabeth 21, Thomas 3, John 2
RANKINS, Hiram B. 36, Julia 26, James 17, Nancy 9, Ruth 7, Catharine 5, Serena 3
POTTS, Alfred 26, Elvira 26, Thomas J. 4, Martha 2, David D. 17
ANDERSON, William M. 29, Delilah 30, Caroline 6, Eilzabeth 5, Thomas J. 3, Thomas M. 2, Adeline 1
EWELL, John W. 33, Fanny 25, Mary J. 5, William A. 3, Elizabeth C. 1
PARLEY, Lewis G. 26, Mary A. 25, Almanza 3 (m), Samantha 10/12

Schedule Page 64

HARRISON, John C. 49, Martha 44, Martha E. 20, Washington 18, Angeline 15, Eliza J. 14, Mary C. 9, John 6, Margaret 4, Francis M. 11/12
FREEMAN, Thomas 50, Alice 35, William 17, Mary 14, Sarah 11, Welbourn 7, Edward 5, Lucy 4, Cynthia 2
SEE, Nancy 55, James 15
EATON, John 60, Viney 47, Sally A. 20, Jane 16, James 12, Jonathan 10, Susan 6, William 3
LAUGHLIN, Benjamin 56
LAUGHLIN, John W. 28, Lurena 22, Margaret E. 3, Jemima 2
FISHER, William 35, Lavina 26, Mary E. 8, Joseph F. 6, Charles B. 4, Martha 20
CURRY, Joseph 26, America 18, Sarah 1
LYLE, George 20*, Elizabeth 19, Martin 14
JOHNSTON, Polly 18*
AKEBY, Lott 38*, Rosanna 36, Elizabeth 16, Martha 14, Daniel 12, Joseph 10, Brady 8 (f), Sarah A. 6, Thomas 5, Mary A. 6/12
MCKELLIPS, Daniel 30*
HUGHS, Daniel 40, Mary 32, Emerine 9, Oscar 3, Edwin 2
WILLIAMS, Samuel 62, Sarah 53, Rebecca 30, Elizabeth 22, Matilda 21, John S. 21
CURTIS, Thomas 53, Elizabeth 50, John 22, Thomas 20, Theodocius 19, William 16, Eady 14, David 12
GRIFFITH, William 50, Sarah 39, Mary 18, Catharine 15, David 12, Ann 10, George 7, Maria 5, Sarah 8/12

Schedule Page 65

ALEXANDERS, James 45, Elizabeth 36, John 17, Hiram 15, William H. 13, Sarah J. 12, Achilles 10, Matilda 5, Lorenda 2
ALEXANDER, John 70*, Sarah 65
HOWARD, Isabella 100*
WILLIAMS, Henry 25, Sarah J. 22, Samuel 1
ALEXANDER, Hiram 48, Ann 40, John H. 18, James M. 15, Malvina 13, Eliza 12, Hiram 4, William 3, Martha A. 6/12
BURRISS, Thomas 50, Elizabeth 49, James 23, Nancy 16, Martha J. 12, Thomas J. 14
BALLARD, Eliza 60, Frankey 60, Polly J. 18, Samuel 15, William 13, Chilton 11

1850 Census Clark County Kentucky

BALLARD, Wiley 29, Nancy 22, Catharine 6, Adeline 4, Benjamin D. 1
EDWARDS, James 26, Nancy 26, Sarah E. 3, Frances A. 2, no name 8/12 (f)
MARTIN, Jane 23, Sarah 4, James H. 1
KIMBRELL, James 45, Sally 41, Andrew J. 21, Jane 18, Glendy 17 (f), David B. 15, Emerine 13, George W. 9, Delilah 7, Luvina 5, James M. 2
KEAS, James 74*, Milly 68, Lucy 21, Wesly 31
GOOSEY, Nancy 15*
VANCE, Eliza 30, Hannah 5, French 3, Betty 1
EVERMAN, Presly 30, Elizabeth 22
POTTS, Jefferson 27
FISHER, Elizabeth 60, Louisa 25, Catharine 22, John 20
FISHER, Thomas 30, Martha 25, Mary E. 11, John W. 4, James 2

Schedule Page 66

KIMBRELL, Wiley 41, Lavina 46, Elizabeth 21, Phoebe 20, Presley 18, Newman 15, Malinda 14, Wiley 11, Malvina 8, Henry 6, Diantha 3
EVERMAN, Samuel 63, Mary 33, William 30, Garrett 25, Gibson 22, Sarah 20, Samuel 17
EVERMAN, Arthur 36*, Susan 35, Samuel 8, William 5, Sally A.? 7, Allen 4, Farnes 3, George 1
CURTIS, Mary A. 20*
SCOTT, Edward 48*, Elizabeth 56, Josiah 22, Charlotte 17
HOLDER, Francis M. 10*
DAWSON, Jonathan 40, Susan 25, Lewis 13, John W. 11, Catharine 9, Lucy Ann 1
COMBS, Marem 44, Susan 28, William E. 10, Robert 7, Benjamin H. 6, Sarah E. 1
RANKINS, John 80, Nancy 75
ABBOTT, Eveline 42, John 22, William 19, Daniel 16, Washington 14, Nancy 8, Mary 6
ANDERSON, John 24, Mary J. 23, Fanny 3, Martha 1, John W. 4/12
ANDERSON, Archibald 48, Dorcas 46, Sally 22, Julia 21, James 15, Benjamin J. 14, Elizabeth 11, Isaac 5, Cyrus 3, Lucretia 1
WARES, Robert 28, Emily 24, Marietta 1, Richard 32
ABBOTT, Aaron 44 (B), Charity 36, Lewis 22, Henry 19, Martha 4, Margaret 11/12
PEDDICORD, Nathaniel 50, Nancy 55, William G. 30, James 28, Polly 25, John 20, Elizabeth 18, Thomas 16, Nancy 11

Schedule Page 67

PEDDICORD, Dawson 23, Frances 23
WATTS, Winceton 30, Mary 25, Amelia 13, John A. 12, Lucinda 7, Mary E. 6, Ruthy 5, Melissa 2
BRANDENBURG, Peter 54 (B), Marcena 23, James 3, Lucy 9/12
BOONE, Nancy 30, Mary A. 26, William M. 5, Squire 4/12, Noah M. 4/12
ANDERSON, James 35, Ann 24, James W. 9, Sarah A. 7, Pleasant 5, Martha 1
ANDERSON, Wingate 50, Patsey 46, Nancy 17, Elizabeth 15, William J. 5, Elizabeth 10/12
THOMPSON, Louisa 25, William 13, Mary Jane 5, America 10/12
HULSE, Richard 23, Elizabeth 22
MOTZBAUGH, David 42*, Hannah 32, Mary J. 15, Rebecca 11, Henrietta 4, Elizabeth A. 2
WILDER, Ebenezer 39*, Mary E. 21, John 1
SEWELL, James 53, Dolley 48, Joseph 11, Martha 11, Maria 9, Robert 6, William 26

- 37 -

1850 Census Clark County Kentucky

TOLIN, Jourdan 27, Mary 22, Sarah J. 5, Martha 6/12
SKINNER, Henry 54, Frances 47, William 23, Clifton 21, Olivia 16, Julia 14, Milly A. 12, Mary 10, Amanda 8
EVANS, Paul J. 57*, Polly 57, Elizabeth 24, Rebecca 22, Ann 20, Mary 18, Catharine 16
COMBS, Paul __ *
CALMES, John W. 28, Ann 24, Paul 9, Henry 7, Richard 3, Edward P. 8/12
KARRICK, James V. 45*, Harriet 31, John 16, Camilla 8, Rebecca 5, Harriet 3, Drusilla 2

Schedule Page 68

WARE, Madison 28*, Drusilla 19, Frances 6/12
SKINNER, Willis 43*
PATTON, Charles 22*
JONETT, Lou 50 (f)*, Elizabeth 16, William 14, Sally Ann 12
CLEM, Josiah 34, Martha 23, Mary 4, William H. 2
PATTON, William 39, Elizabeth 37, George W. 16, James S. 14, William T. 12, Dillard 8, Green 6, Caroline 5, Mary C. 4/12, James 22
PATTON, Rachel 63, Nathaniel 37
BERRY, Isaac N. 30, Abigail 36, Peter 29
BERRY, Thomas 55*, Sarah 45, Louisa 16, Joseph 13, Amanda 11, Joicy 8
HULSE, James 21*, Margaret 17, Martha 1
MILLER, Green K. 30, Caroline V. 20, Horace D. 7/12
DOWEN, John S. 46, Indiana 43, Margaret 15, William 12, James 8, Mary 6, Charles 4, Lusette 2
BERRY, Washington 35*, Mary 22, Martha W. 11/12
TRIPLETT, William 40*
PATTON, William M. 20*
CROW, John 52, Nancy 55, Margaret 23, Susanna 21, Eveline 17, Simeon 16, Nanney? A. 12, John B. 29, Julia M. 27, Josephine 4, William M. 3, Sarah A. 1, George N. 27, Sarah A. 25
JONES, William 26, Eveline 20, Nancy M. 6/12, John W. 1/12
MACHEAD, John 44, Lucy 44, Albert 17, Martha 12, Frances 10, Lucy 8
THOMAS, Ennis? 21

Schedule Page 69

TREDAWAY, Peter 54, Margaret 44, Simeon 22, Margaret 19, John 17, Sarah A. 16, Albert G. 14, Louisa 10, Bluford 7, Charles D. 2
HAMBLETON, Hezekiah 39, Catharine 36, Mary E. 18, John 16, Margaret 14, Joseph 12, James 10, Rebecca 8, Charles 1
WESTBROOK, Thomas 60, Mary 56, Eliza 30, John 26, Susan 24
HUNTON, John C. 40, Alice 32, Mary A. 10, Nancy M. 9, Frances E. 6, Sarah C. 3, Laura 1
COMBS, James P. 40, Polly J. 26, John E. 1, Leslie 3/12 (m)
EUBANKS, Price 50, Rebecca 60, John 20, Mary J. 18, Thomas J. 5/12
WHITE, James 50, Elizabeth 45, Lavina 16, John J. 14, Lucretia 12, James R. 10, Chilton 8
ELKIN, James M. 24, Sally A. 18, Lucinda 11?/12
SMITH, Daniel 50 (B), Margaret 45, Phillis 21, Alice 19, George W. 29, Jesse 21
LANGSTON, Joab 26*, Mary E. 17, James M. 1
TRACY, Sally 48*

1850 Census Clark County Kentucky

PACE, William 33, Elizabeth 29, Robert 10, John 8, Mary 6, Joseph 4, Zachy T. 2 (m), Mary E. 3/12
WHITE, William 39, Elizabeth 30, John 18, Martha 16, Frances 12, Sarah 8, Milly J. 6, Allen 4, Catharine 2
ABBOTT, Isabella 70 (E)
PEGG, Lewis 56, Lucy 52, Elkanah 17
PEGG, Martin 23, Amanda 18, Elkanah 8/12

Schedule Page 70

GROVES, Nelson 35, Permela 24, James W. 10, Elizabeth A. 10, John D. 9, Lucinda 8, Nelly 5, Eliza 1
GROVES, Travis 60, Casey 65 (f), William 29, Henry D. 21, Annfield 18, Elizabeth 9
CURTIS, Harrison 28, Malinda 28, Dillard 5, Jane 3, Jemima 1
ALLEN, John Will 24, Nancy 18, Benjamin 45
JOHNSTON, Alexander M. 60, Eliza 55, Silas S. 21, James C. 19, Yonworkie? 16 (f), Eli 12, William 9, John M. 24, Elizabeth 23
GRAY, Matthew 60, Jeanette 60, Martin 28, William 21, Sally A. 22, Mary 18, Alfred 16
GOOLMAN, Martin 40, Susan 38, Cynthia 12, Thomas 10, William 9, Josiah 7, Martha 2
WILLIAMS, Heram S. 39, Sally 35
BRUNER, Joseph 27
COX, Sarah 50, Jeremiah 25, Allen 22, Eliza 22, George 21, Lydia 19, Milly 10/12
SNOWDEN, Mary 52, Mary 18, Andrew 14
CURTIS, Jacob 42 (B?), Jane 42, William J. 17
EVERMAN, James 56, Polly Ann 24, William 21, Jacob 18, Sally Ann 14, Daniel B. 6
EVERMAN, Elijah 48, Elizabeth 44, Mahala 18, John 15, Jacob 14, Samuel 11, Mary 9, Algin 7, Martha 4, Elijah 3/12, Elsey 24
CROW, David 26, Lucy 20, John H. 3/12
WILLIAMS, Susan 50, Lydia 35, Martin 24

Schedule Page 71

JOHNSON, Mahala 39, Samuel 22, Ann Eliza 5
ARTIS, Robert 52, Fanny 46, Robert 23, Parker 20, William 18, Harriett 15, Nancy 13, John 11, Henry 9
VIVION, John 50, Nancy 40, Sally 19, Mary J. 17, Luann 15, John S. 12, Telitha 10, Nancy 6, Martha 2
CROW, Zachariah 25, Rachel 24, Harriet 9, Rhoda 7, Mary J. 5, Susan 3, John W. 9/12
NIBLACK, Luallen 51, Elizabeth 50, Willis V. 20, America 18, Eliza Jane 16, Harmon 15, John M. 12, Elvila 8
RICHARDSON, John 38, Paulina 26, Rhoda 7, Zachariah 5, Mary 3
CROW, Rhoda 57, Daniel 20
SCOTT, McEbeny 25, Martha 18, Rhoda E. 6/12
SCHOLL, Joseph 58, Malinda 57, Dillard 17, Isaiah 15, Joseph 13, Caroline 19
SCHOLL, William 25, Orma 22, Elizabeth 5, Winney 3, James N. 6/12
STEVENSON, William 55*, Milly 47, John 22, Mary 22, James 12
STONE, John D. 14*, Thomas 8, Nancy 6
WILLIAMS, John W. 31*, Nancy 40, John 15, Margaret 13, Mary E. 11, Thomas J. 8, Pauline 4
GOODRICH, Elizabeth 8:1*
SNOWDEN, William 35, Patsey 30, Franklin 10, Thomas 8, Melissa 6, Louisa 5, William 3, Mary 6/12
CALMES, William 66, Matilda 34, Nancy 13, Mary 9

1850 Census Clark County Kentucky

Schedule Page 72

DUNCAN, Jesse 85 (B), Suky 70 (f)
DANIEL, Robert 51, Eliza 47, Robert 25, Eliza 21, Margaret 19, Christopher 17, Oscar 15, Mary 12, Ethlin 10 (f)
TRACY, Asa 54, Elizabeth 50, Sarah 15, Naomi 12
GOFF, David 75 (B), Nelly 48
POSTON, Charles 29*, Mary 25
WHITEHEAD, Charles P. 2*
SCOBEE, James 29, Mary J. 22
WELLS, Fielding 49, Mary 46, Isaac 19, Elizabeth 17, George T. 15, Rebecca A. 12
HUMPSTON, William 36, Ann E. 20, Ann 12, Miner 9, Nancy M. 7, William _. 5
LAWRENCE, John B. 65, Elizabeth 62, Eliza 30
EMBREE, William 44, Elizabeth 25, John 3, Elizabeth 6/12
GIBSON, F. B. 37 (m), Ruthy 30, Martha 15, Nancy 14, Sarah 8, Benjamin 5, Lucy 2
KIDD, Zadick 46, Jane 40, Bird 18 (m), Sarah 16, Oswell 14, James 10, Elizabeth 8, Ann 6
SHULTZ, Samuel 45, Angeline 35, John 15, Thomas 9, Mary M. 7
RAIBORN, James 34, Mary 26, Nancy 13, Leand 11 (f), Thomas 9, Samuel 6, James T. 3, Sarah E. 5
ANDERSON, Alexander 27, Mary Ann 26
CLEVELAND, John H. 30, Margaret 22, James 1
BALLANCE, William 47, Lavina 30, Willis P. 23, William J. 18, Susan 14, John 10, Elizabeth 7, Oliver 5, Charles? 4, James C. 3, Mary 1, Lavina 8/12

Schedule Page 73

SHOUSE, Robert 41, Martha A. 35, Green 17, Franklin T. 10, Benjamin 8, Mary E. 6, Susan 5, Cordelia 3, Martin W. 2
FISHER, william 39, Sarah A. 28, James 11, John G. 9, Clifton 7, Ann 5
PACE, James 37*, Minerva 30, Robert 12, Mary E. 5, John W. 3, Murray 3/12
BRANDENBURG, Samuel 24*
WALKER, Nancy 60, Abel 60, Joshua 28
HISLE, Margaret 56, William A. 24, George W. 22, Mann H. 15, Hambleton 13, Leonard 44
GOFF, Nancy 51*, Thomas 29
TRACY, William 22*
GOFF, John 29*, Martha 20, Thomas 2, Therane? 3/12 (m)
TRACY, James 30*
KIDD, Robert 42, Elizabeth 33, Sally Ann 15, Albert C. 10, Mildred J. 8, Nancy J. 6, Robert 3, Louisa E. 10/12
EASTIN, Thomas 60, Marium 48 (f), Prucilla 23, A. Frazeris 22, Columbus C. 21, Thomas H. 18
HOOTREL?, Matthias 45, Frances 35, Eliza 17, Elizabeth 15, Gibson 13, Robert 14, Mary 11, Matthius 3
NOEL, Robert 35, Nancy 30
BRUSH, William 50, Joicy 23, Albert 17, Washington 14, John M. 4/12
HULETT, Jesse 33, Elizabeth 30, Benjamin 8
HULETT, Silas 26*, Paulina 25, Richard 7, Alfred 5, William 3
FARLEY, Richard 16*
ADAMS, Peyton 52*, Polly 45
WALLACE, Susan 35*, Stephen P. 7, James W. 6

1850 Census Clark County Kentucky

Schedule Page 74

MIZE, Martin W. 27*, Elizabeth 20, DeWitt 1, Henry H. 31
JONES, Cleopatra 10*
DANIEL, Venon 32 (m)*, Lucy A. 26, Clarinda 6, Clifton 1, Zadock 21
BELL, Edward 24*
MOREHEAD, William 30*
SEWELL, John 28, Sarah A. 28, Amanda E. 5, James L. 4, Clarinda T. 2, John T. 1
SHEPHERD, Azariah 24, Elizabeth A. 21
ELLIOTT, Joel 60, Margaret 60, Catharine 30, Lucy 26, James 24
ELLIOTT, Joel T. 30, Mary 24
PACE, Joseph 32, Rosaline 26, Mary 60, Elizabeth 26
HULETT, Wyatt 66, Margaret 60, Alfred 30, Margaret 24
JORDAN, Shurshall? 49 (m.), Louisa 31, Effaulea 11 (f), Jonah 9, William C. 6
HENSLY, John W. 41, Mary 30, Orlando 15, Fulton 11, Eudora 7, James 3, Elizabeth 3/12
RISK, William 76*, Polly 55
REYNOLDS, Isom 32*, Sally A. 34, Louisa J. 7, Mary A. 4, Malinda 2
ANDERSON, William H. 14*
HANDY, Orla 47 (m), Sylva 48, Manleus 16, Miller F. 15, Eliza 14, Eunice 12, Eldah 10, Isaiah 8
RUPURD, William 56, Patsey 50, Daniel 20, Cyrus 19, Martha 16, Samuel 13, Thomas 11, Allen 8
RUPEND, William 25, Nancy 17
RISK, Cynthia 34, william 10, Jessamine 8 (m), Boone 6, Martha A. 4, Mary E. 2
FLYNN, Mary 58*, John J. 28, Elizabeth 18, James 22, William F. 21, Andrew J. 20

Schedule Page 75

MILLER, Lucinda 13*
COMBS, Edward M. 32, Louisa 27, Mary 8, Ennis 6, Sarah 4, Levi 1
RISK, Joseph 52, Sarah 45, Malinda 18, Susan 10, Rachel 8, Louisa 5
ANDERSON, Preston M. 27, Eliza 26, Ruthy A. 10, Elizabeth 9, Mary 7, Daniel 5, William 2
HINDE, James O. 40, John 25
RUPARD, Samuel 45, Asenath 39, Luallen 17, Laban 13, Rachel 12, Ellen 9, Asenath 6, Drusilla 4, no name 8/12 (f)
COMBS, Glenmore 36*, Mary J. 33, Leslie 9 (m), Elizabeth W. 7, Thomas S. 5, Glenmore 2
HARRIS, Lindsey 22 (m)*
HARMON, John S. 3, Mary 32, Sarah H. 11, George A. 9, William T. 6, Alpheus L. 4, Mary K. 1
HARROW, Joseph 30*, Elizabeth 25, Luella J. 4, Daniel P. 25
WILES, Eli 17*
BOONE, Thomas N. 23, Mildred J. 22, Enoch 3, Mary E. 1
PEANALL?, John 42, Matilda 40, William 20, John 17, Jane 15, George 13, Martha 11, Samuel 7, Eli 6, Susan 3
STAGGS, Ulfred 50, Elizabeth 40, Margaret C. 16, Sarah K. 14, John J. 4, Benjamin F. 1
RUPARD, Willis 44, Martha D. 36, Silas 21, Sarah W. 19, Seth 17, Chilton A. 15, John H. 11, Willis 5, Eliza J. 7, Edward F. 3, Millard J. 4/12
JONETT, Lynch 44, Mary 37, Benjamin A. 5, Malinda E. 4

1850 Census Clark County Kentucky

Schedule Page 76

REED, William 34, Mary 32, Samuel 13, John W. 11, Rebecca 7, Edmond A. 5, Martha M. 2
BOONE, Jeptha 28, Sarah 23, Caroline E. 3, William J. 1
SHOLL, James 34, Telitha 23, Clayton 3, Mary 6/12
CAYWOOD, William D. 37*, Jerusha 35 (f), Margaret E. 10, Levi 8, Martha 5
LANE, Jon. N. 15 (m)*
ROBERTSON, Mary E. 2*
HULSE, John 71
REDMAN, John W. 50*, Lucinda 43, Eliza 16, Thomas 15, Edmund 13, James 4
BUSH, John 26*, Mary 20
LEWIS, Thornton 56, Emma 35, Thomas 15, Amelia 14, Frances 9, Ann W. 2
RAMSEY, Rachel 58*, James 44, Samuel W. 35
STAPLES, Richard 14*
SPINGEN, David 71, Margaret 71
DUCKSON, Richard 59, Polly 40, Henry 17, Eldred 14 (m), Maria 13, Charles 11, Mildred 9, Catharine 7, Lucy 4, Richard 2
TANNESY, William 38, Susan 35, Branch D. 16, Martha J. 17, William A. 9
PALMER, William 65*, Mintha 62, John 26
KENT, Jane 36*
STUART, Roy 64, Elizabeth 64, Thaddeus 26, Elizabeth 24, Louisa 9, George 7
STUART, John G. 67, Sarah 52, Laura 16, Charles E. 13, Maria 11, Amanda 9
CHILES, Ambrose 70 (B), Lucy 61
WOODALL, James R. 37, Ann E. 26, Thomas B. 7, Eliza W. 5, Emma 3

Schedule Page 77

WELLS, Thomas J. 40, Maria 30, Isaiah 14, Joana 12, Joseph D. 10, William 9, Nancy 7, Elizabeth 4, Dudly J. 3/12
CHORN, Samuel 63, Nancy 57, Jonah 20, James 16
THOMPSON, Sandford 35*, Susan 26, Ellen 7, Matthew 5, Harriet S. _. 3, Mary E. 9/12
CLAY, Sarah 20*
WELCH, James 21*
CLINKENBUND?, John 57, Sally 52, Jonathan 23, Stephen 22, James 21, Elmore 16, Thomas 15, Simeon 14, Ruth E. 13, Andrew 11, Allen 10, Sally 7
AUDDRETH?, Thomas 44, Elizabeth 37, William L. 11, Mary A. 10
SUTHERLAND, William 27, Eliza 20
WALLACE, James H. 37, Margaret 39, Mary Ann 12, William H. 11, George 9, Isabella 7, John 3, Nancy 5/12
SMITH, Robert W. 54, Fanny 31, Mary 21, Eliza 10, William 7, Susan 6, Lewis 4, Elizabeth 1
JUDY, David B. 34, Eliza 28, John K. 7, Mary E. 4, Isabella 1
ECTON, Burgess 44, Lucinda 32, Joseph 18, James 11, Martha 8, Charles 6, Jefferson 4, Nancy 1
GAITSKILL, William 60, Mary 50, Q. Ann 12
ASHLEY, Josiah J. 31*, Olivia 29, Josiah 9/12, Eliza 32, Elizabeth 29, Sally 26, Amanda 23, Cyntha 20, James M. 22
HILL, Herndon 54*
HULSE, Paul 48, Clarke 44 (f), J. W. C. 19 (m), Sarah 17, John 15, Martha 10, James 5

1850 Census Clark County Kentucky

Schedule Page 78

MARTIN, John 52, Mary 40, Creth 18 (f), Sally 16, Samuel 14, Newton 13, Nannie 11, Rebecca 9, Rachel 8, Kate 6, Laura 4, Susan 10/12
FOX, Alfred 40*
DAWSON, Patsey 30*, no name 1 (m)
WELLS, John P. 47, Nancy 47, John 14, Benjamin 12, Elizabeth 8, John 1
DEAN, Ellis 62, Nancy 60, John W. 26, Sidney 25 (m), Elizabeth 23, Nancy 17, Stephen 19, Ellis 14, Polly 12, Elizabeth 85
LINDSEY, Charles 53, Malinda 47, William 24, Thomas 22, Elizabeth A. 20, Mary M. 15
LEWIS, Alpheus 51, Theodocia A. 40, Alpheus 23, William 16, Elizabeth 14, Theodocia 12, Nancy 10, Asa K. 7, Sophia 6, James N. 5, Hector P. 2
BRYANT, Harvey 38, Sarah A. 37, James R. 11, William T. 9, Zerilda 4, Charles E. 3, Nancy 10/12
DEAN, Simpson M. 35, Martha 33, William E. 7
SCOTT, James 46*, Martha 41, William 20, Robert 13, Thomas J. 11, Daniel 8, Ann E. 5
HOGAN, James 29*
LINDSEY, Thomas 60, Elizabeth 50, Jacob 70
LANDRUM, Stephen H. 28*, Patsey 72
WARE, Richard 11*
QUISENBERY, John H. 36, Martha 35, Rebecca 9, Mary E. 7, Joel 5, Robert 4, Thomas J. 3, George W. 2, Martha 1

Schedule Page 79

LENVILLE, Goon 53*, Lucinda 43, Catharine 15, Sabrina E. 12, Mary M. 10, Caroline E. 8
BRYANT, Keziah 63*
CURRY, William E. 30, Mary 24, Willis 2, John 10/12, John 22
MORRIS, Mason 45, Calpurnia 24, Henry N. 3
RAMSEY, Samuel A. 37, Sarah A. 32, Mary F. 10, Hannah E. 4/12
FOX, Boaz 41, Sarah 39, Hiram 16, Richard 14, Julia 13, James 8, Edward 6, George 4, Boaz 2
BUCKNERS, william S. 40, Caroline 38, Lucy 15, Thomas M. 11, Jane E. 8, Sarah L. 5, Mary 2, William T. 5/12
ECTON, Nancy 76
HISLE, Younger 51*, Martha 44, William 20, Catharine 20, Martha 16, Chilton 15, William 12, Thomas 10, James 8, Younger 6, Coleman 4, Mary 2
GARNERS, Laura 80*
COTMAN, Benjamin 45, Katey 40, Elizabeth 16, Eliza 15, Amanda 12, John 8, Nancy 6, Eveline 4
WATTS, Richard 45, Rebecca 35, Sarah 15
WILKERSON, Charles 30, Mary M. 26, Catharine 7, John 5
HORNBACK, Anthony 64, Sally 45, Margaret 22, Mary 20, Sally A. 19, George 17, Amanda 13, James 11, Solomon 6
MORRIS, Prucilla 46, James 24, Jane E. 20, John T. 18, Martha 17, Margaret 13, Sarah M. 11, Rosanna 8, Mary A. 5

- 43 -

1850 Census Clark County Kentucky

Schedule Page 80

HOUSE, Samuel 40, Maria 40, Nancy 19, John W. 18, Sarah 14, Mahala E. 8
RASH, Thomas W. 44, Mary 40, William 18, Thomas 14, Marietta 12, James 9, Dillard 7, Clay 5, Mildred W. 2, Nelson B. 6/12
SEWELL, Samuel 74*, Caroline 20
LAWRENCE, J. M. 30 (m)*, Mary 23, Charity A. 3, Zachy T. 2 (m)
HULSE, Elizabeth 61, Margaret 32, Thomas 22, Mary A. 19, Stephen 10/12
STRODE, Nelson 36*, Susan 39, William 13, John 12, Ann E. 10, James 8, Edward 6/12
WELDEN, William D. 18*
GROOMS, Jesse 37, Sally A. 27, Sarah E. 10, Samuel 8, Caroline 5, Rebecca J. 2, James 6/12
BUNCH, Benjamin W. 40, Catharine 36, Sarah A. 15, James C. 13, William 11, Silas 8, Julia 5, Mary 3
BUNCH, Elijah 45, Julia 40, Sarah M. 15, Mary M. 13, David H. 11, Nancy E. 7, William 3
BOONE, Squire 45, Lucy 43, James T. 20, Cyrus W. 19, Sidney 17 (m), Simeon M. 15, Henry W. 13, Levi 11, Squire 8
HOLLY, Jefferson 23*, Maria 20
STUART, Samuel 28*, Mariah L. 24
HOLLY, James 65, Barbara 50, Elizabeth 17, Mary J. 15
HAGGARD, Zachy 48 (m), Zelpha 42, Alvin 20, Columbus 18, Adeline 16, Elizabeth 12, James H. 10, Jane 8, Miranda 5, William 3

Schedule Page 81

BAKER, James 35, Lucinda 36, William 15, James T. 13, Joseph 11, Lucinda J. 11, Allen A. 10, Mary J. 8, Nathan 5, Catharine 2
RUPARD, Daniel 28*, Parmela 24, Nancy M. 2, Mary A. 15
RITCHIE, Samuel 37*
RUPARD, Eveline 36, Wesley 13, Joseph 12, Isaac 8
EDMONSON, James 65, Polly 37, Thomas 24, John 19, Mary 17, Susan 8, Robert E. 7, Harriet 4, Milton 3, Emily 7/12
EDMONSON, Nathan 29, Dolly 30, Sarah C. 4
EDMONSON, James 27, Elizabeth 27, Sarah R. 1
BOONE, Samuel 33, Edna J. 34, William T. 10, John F. 8, George M. 7, Manleno T. 5, Robert E. 4, Ira 1
JONES, Hiram 30, Susan 25, Mary 5, William 3, Chilton 1
BOONE, George 44, Rachel 45, Samuel 14, Thomas 14, William 7, Clifton C. 5, Andrew 3, Sarah T. 6/12
WELLS, Tilman T. 37, Polly 27, Nancy 11, Martha C. 9, Mary E. 7, Amanda J. 5, John T. 2
TRIBBLE, Austin 55, Nancy 30, Buonaparte 15, LaFayette 4, Rachel B. 2, George W. 3/12
WELLS, Isaac 66, Agness 57
WELLS, Austin B. 37, Mary J. 30, Isabella 13, Marcus 10, Lucretia 8, Agness 5, William 2
CLAWSON, Pleasant 35*, Agness 41, Nancy 7, Martha 3, David B. 5/12
MAGOWAN, Sarah 21*, Thomas 20

Schedule Page 82

WELLS, Thornton 69, Nancy 65, Catharine 36, Simpson 33, James 12, Thomas 8, Margaret 23
BELL, Otha 46 (m), Nancy J. 8, Mary Wells 16

1850 Census Clark County Kentucky

BATTENSHELL?, William 38, Elizabeth 34, James 16, Sally A. 13, Mary E. 12, Sandford A. 10, Amanda 8, Simpson 5, Nancy 5, Lucilla 2, Nancy 83
WELLS, Benjamin 24*, Sally A. 18
ROBINSON, Thomas A. 25*
GREEN, Daniel 29, Polly 25, Major E. 6, Richard 3, Andrew J. 2
SCOTT, William 46, Eliza 46, Rebecca 21, James 15, Joseph 11, Maletta 6, Mathew 3
BAXTER, Abner 40*, Jane 38, Martha L. 4
PALMERS, William 22*
BAILEY, John 42, Mary a. 37, Eva 20, Sarah T. 18, Marium 16 (f), Nancy 14, Martha 12, Mary C. 8, William T. 5, Jacob 2
WATTS, John 59, Drusilla 51, Franklin 22, Mary J. 20
FLYNN, Mason 25*, Lucinda 70, John 12, Rebecca 10
GREEN, Thomas 22*
JAMES, John M. 41, Mary 32, Sarah E. 11, James W. 10, William 5, James A. 3, John 10/12
BENNING, James 50 (B), Iberiah 48 (f), Easter 20, Alfred 16, Henry 12, Mary 9, James 25
RAMSEY, Frances 51*, Andrew 28, Alexander 23, Lisey 15 (f), James T. 5
CLARKE, James A. 5*
FRY, Green B. 45*, Dulcena 43, John L. 22, Susan 17, George F. 15, Catharine 11

Schedule Page 83

BUTLER, David 25*, Mary M. 22, John L. 10/12
FRY, Julia 80*
RAMSEY, Varner 28*, Mary E. 6
STAPLES, Thomas 26, Elizabeth 18, Mary C. 2, David B. 1, Elizabeth 54
BARROW, Asa 33, Mary 26, Elizabeth 2, William H. 4/12, Rebecca 7
TRACY, Obed 50, Martha 43, Virginia 17, Branford 15, Sarah B. 14, Gurta A. 12, Malinda E. 8, John 7, Tayler 5
THOMPSON, William 30*, Catharine 25, Benjamin 9, Joel 7, Nancy 2, Matthew 4/12
TOLEN, Frances 30*
BAKER, William H. 34, Sarah 40, Mary E. 10, Elizabeth 8, Minerva 7, Armelda 4
GARDNER, Thomas 38, Mary A. 35, William 14, James 10, Margaret 6, Rachel 5, Mary C. 3
RAMSEY, Joseph 32, Cynthia 29, William N. 10, Maria E. 8, Mary C. 6, Preston 4, Sarah T. 2, Lydia 5/12
STEVENSON, Samuel 51*, Mary A. 44, George W. 22, Julia A. 20, Susan M. 19, Peter 14, Mary E. 12, James W. 10, Christopher 7
CLARKE, Mary E. 2*, Edward 4/12
PERKINS, John 36, Elizabeth 30, William 16, George 14, Elizabeth 11, John 10, James 8, Meners? 6 (m), Elijah 2
HEDGES, Preston 42, Patsey M. 32, Abram T. 16, Elizabeth 14, Charles G. 12, Bula C. 8, John E. 4, Francis E. 2

Schedule Page 84

CLARKE, Mary 53*, William M. 26, John T. 24
FRY, John 22*, Sally M. 20
SMITHSON, Wesley 38*, Mary E. 26, Sarah E. 6, Haney 4 (m), Lucy E. 2

1850 Census Clark County Kentucky

MARTIN, Job 73*
CHORN, Samuel S. 25, Mary 21, Nancy 4, Elvira 3, Sarah 1
RAMSEY, Andrew 70*, Jane 64, Alexander 29, Andy 25, John 19
MILLERS, Alice 30*, James 4, Eliza 2, Mildred 8/12
WATTS, Fielding 24, Sarah J. 17
FLYNN, Dudly 27*, Martha A. 21, Martha E. 5, Rebecca 1
MILLERS, Eilzabeth 15*
GREEN, Edward 60, Mary 48, Mary C. 17, Naomi 15, Peter 13, Edward 8
FLYNN, John 30, Elizabeth 28, John 8, James 6, Mason 3, Fielding 4/12
WILLS, Eli B. 38, Mary 38, Simpson 3, Melissa T. 1
STEVENSON, William 55, Jane 53, Archey 25, William 14, Mary 18
STEVENSON, Joseph 27, Mary E. 20, James 6/12
ANDERSON, Jesse 37, Elizabeth 32
ALLEN, William P. 40, Phoebe 43, Nancy E. 15, Mary M. 12, John W. P. 10, Sarah H. 7, Benjamin T. 2
PERSALL, Isaac 44, Melissa 40, John W. 20, Thomas B. 18, Mantha A. 15 (f), Jesse R. 14, Mary J. 11, Archy C. 6, Lucy J. 4, Nancy 2, Cyntha 33
TANNER, Branch 65, John 22, Jane 22
TANNER, Archy 28*, Zerilda 22, Lucien 3
TRUMAN?, Charles W. 6/12*
CLARKE, John 52, Paulina 46, Samuel W. 22, Sally A. 19, Margaret 17, Martha J. 14, Jemima 11

Schedule Page 85

HAYDEN, George 40, Lucy A. 29, Robert S. 12, John W. 10, Dorinda G. 8, Thomas R. 1
SKINNERS, Isaac C. 45, Frances 30, Phineas 4 (m), Isaac 2
SAMMONS, Aquilla 25*, Sidney 32, Nancy J. 7/12
BYRD, Mitchel 74*, Elizabeth 62
PACE, Nancy 49, William 23, Amanda 19, Hannah 17, Nancy 13, Sarah 11
JUDY, Martin 40, Evaline 33, Jane 72
MILLER, Noah 54, Maria 42, Elizabeth 6, Emily 5, Rachel 3, Martha _. 16
RAMSEY, James 61, Frances 55, John 19, Preston 17, Thomas 14, George 6, Sarah 21, Eliza 13, Martha 7
WILSON, Nancy 80
REDMAN, Robert 55, Mary 48, Agness 18, William 17, Robert 14, Charles 12, Squire 8
RAMSEY, Nancy 30, Mary 13, Martha 11, Robert 8, Lucinda 4
REDMON, William 24, Martha A. 16, Emily A. 5/12
FORMAN, Dana W. 36 (m), Eliza A. 35, James 9, William 6, Nancy J. 3, Elm 21
HALL, James 60, Nancy 58, James E. 22
POSTON, Mildred 58, Mary 18, Helen 17
SUDDUTH, John 41, Sarah W. 23, Mary 65
MIRGUN?, Thomas 28*
ANDERSON, William 40*, Mary 30, Aaron 14, Jane 10, William 7, Oscar 4
MCDANIEL, John 78, Ellen 28, Chilton 23, Malinda 22, Nancy 18, Amanda 17, George W. 17

Schedule Page 86

LOVELY, John V. 36, Mary 32, Jesse 14, Mary 8, Susan 3, Andrew J. 26
JUDY, John A. 30, Elizabeth J. 25, John D. 4, Martha E. 2, Richard 6/12

1850 Census Clark County Kentucky

JUDY, John 63, Susan 57, Clementine 28, Mary 18, Susan 12, Thomas 10, Mary J. 8, John 6, Zachary T. 3, George W. 1
SHANKS, Joseph A. 34, Nancy 35, Elizabeth A. 11, David 9, John S. 7, William _. 5, Many? C. 3 (f), Sarah 2
SCOBEE, Robert 33, Lucy W. 23, Elizabeth A. 12, Reason A. 9, Rice P. 3, Mary C. 1
PENDLETON, Rice 56 Catharine 52
HARDMAN, George 39, Elizabeth 33, Sarah A. 13, John R. 11, Elizabeth S. 9, David P. 7, Lucy C. 5, Nancy H. 3, Eliza H. 1
BENTON, Norval 47, Elizabeth B. 37, Hezekiah J. 18, Susan A. 14, William H. 12, Norval T. 9, Frances E. 7, Horace 3, Mary C. 8/12
YOST, Sarah 60, Philip 30, America 24
GAITSKILL, John 33, Frances 22, Charles 2
GAITSKILL, Jon. 50 (m)*, Jopseph 24, Mary 18, Harvey 16
THOMPSON, Nancy 28*, Martha J. 5
ODEN, John 51, Sarah 48, Maria 14, Hezekiah 13, Samuel 10, Armstead 5
KING, John 33, Mary E. 24, Sarah R. 6, Martha W. A. 4, Mary B. 3, Benjamin C. 10/12

Schedule Page 87

THOMPSON, David 78*
EDMONSON, Archy 24*
COFER, David T. 23*
THOMPSON, James 54, Elizabeth 54, Martha 28, William 25, James 23, Henrietta 12
THOMPSON, John 25, Levi 23
THOMPSON, John 76*, Sarah 70
HODGE, Cretea T. 45 (f)*, Edward W. 20, James 18
MILLER, Rebecca 76, Melova 38, Susan 31, Hampton 28
THOMPSON, Nancy 38, Columbus 17, Martha J. 15, Mary G. 14
WILLIAMS, Sally 25*, Anne 6, Fanny 4, Mary 2
GARY?, David 22*
SCOBEE, Catharine 66*, John 27
KENADEY, Dolly 56*
PATTON, Elizabeth 81*
GARY, James 57*, Ann 49, Asa 18, Eliza 14
DUFFEE, Thomas 46*
HALL, John W. 27*, Mary J. 23, Mary E. 5, Martha J. 3, Emma L. 1
ELSBERRY, Jackson 18*
SMITH, Isaac 38 (B)
FORDS, Malinda 40, Jane 20, David 18, Franklin 14, James 11, Martin 10, Thomas 8, Doctor 5
LEWIS, William 32, Elizabeth 32, James T. 4
GARY, John Dunlap 46, Catharine 40, Elizabeth 20, Jonathan S. G. 18, John D. 16, Watson M. 14, Nancy 9, Catharine E. 7
GARY, Robert 23, Martha A. 19, Nancy C. 1, William 6/12
SALMONS, Gilson 33, Hannah 35, James 12, John 10, Jeremiah 8, Joseph 6, Jabez 4, Sarah F. 10/12
JUDY, Hetty 65, Boone 26, Henry 25, Philip 20, John 14
GARDNER, John 80, Nancy 71

1850 Census Clark County Kentucky

Schedule Page 88

ELSBERRY, Benjn. 72, Ann 55, Benjamin 12
WILES, Washington 74*, Mary 68
GARDNER, Mary 13*
PERKINS, Henry 46, Spicy 49, Richard 14
FLYNN, Sarah 65*, Nancy 30, Elizabeth 28, Martha 21
RAMSEY, Eliza A. 6*
BUSH, Ambrose E. 24*, Delila 25
HUME, Matthew D. 46*, Elizabeth 19, Ann 15, Laura 12
HORNBACK, Hany 25 (m)*
LYNG, Dennis 26*
GAY, Jacob W. 49, James 20
BEAN, Eli 55, Sarah W. 48, John 26, James 25, Edwin 22, Asa 20, Mary 17, Sarah W. 14, Eliza 12, Susan 7, Bennett 9
BEAN, Peter 47, Ann 37, John 16, Marcella 14, Silas 12, Marcus 10, Lewis H. 4, Martha R. 3
THOMPSON, Andrew 29, Amelia A. 26, Dudley H. 4
WINN, Joshua N. 28, Emily 22, William 4, Philip 6/12
WINN, Philip B. 64*, Martha 56, Catharine J. 36
NICHOLAS, George A. 38*
MARTIN, Pleasant 35, Jemima 37, John 12, Alfred 10, George W. 8, Thomas 2
DIXON, John 38, Sarah 40, Mary A. 14, Sarah E. 12, William 10, Margaret A. 8, Nancy 6, Martha 4, John 2
MCCONNELL, Elizabeth 45, William 26, Amanda 17
WRIGHT, Thomas 84, Mary 70
WRIGHT, W. H. H. 38 (m)*, Sarah 35, Lewis C. 11, Mary E. 9, Thomas 7, William H. 1
RIDGEWAY, Mary 22*
VANMETER, Isaac 55, Rebecca 50, Benjamin 16, Thomas 14, Abram 12, Lewis M. 10, John M. 8

Schedule Page 89

DOYLE, James 21
RENNOCK, Abram 47, Maglin 78 (f)
ROBINSON, Jonas 32, Elizabeth 18
DANIEL, Esther 65
CLARK, John 28*
DUFFY, Barny 32*
ONIEL, Parlor 29*, Rosey 26, Hugh 4, Eliza 2, Arthur 6/12, Eliza 20
GALLAGHER, John 30*
OBRADY, Dennis 30*, Daniel 27
SWEENY, Timothy 25*
RAGAN, Dennis 27*
SHAY, Patrick 35*
WELCH, James 25*
DOOLIN, Thomas 40*
GAMUNDY?, Thomas 20*
DONIVAN, Archy 36*
SULLIVAN, Daniel 40*

1850 Census Clark County Kentucky

NOLAN, Thomas 38*
GAY, Benjamin P. 60, Mary 53, Benjamin 24, Elizabeth 19, Mary 16, George 12, Lewis 10, James P. 26, Mary 25
ANDERSON, George 58, Susan 36, George M. 7, Mary E. 4, Susan 2
SPHARS, Daniel 77*, Trabella 73, William 35, Elizabeth 19
FOSTER, Jane 38*, Mary 13
ROY, John 24, Mary 21
LEWIS, Asa K. 69, Margaret 51, Hector 24, Sarah 21, Henry 17, Sidney 15 (m)
WOODALL, Sarah 73*
HIRST, Doctor 25*, Fanny 17
RANDOLPH, Judith 52 (B), William D. 37, John 24, America 23, Frank 15
LONG, Thomas? 35*, Celia 30, Thomas 3, no name 1
MCCRUM, Junius 45*
WELLS, Joshua 48*, Mary 28, Mary 4, Susan 2, no name 1 (f), James 35, Elizabeth 20
WEBSTER, Peter 60*
BRIGHTON, William 43, Martha J. 21, William 14, Christee 13, Charles 9, Margaret A. 7, Jacob 5, Sally 1, Lucy 1

Schedule Page 90

NESBIT, Mary 68*
STEELE, Albert R. 24*
SIDENER, Martin 68, Nancy 53, William 26, Benjamin 21, George 19, Susan 16, Amanda 14, Thomas 12, Emily 8
CLINKENBEARD, Harriet 30 (B), Maria 13, Daniel 12, Eliza 10, Perry 4, Cella 1
WADE, John 60*
WELLS, Washington 24*, Rebecca 20, Polly A. 1
WADE, Dudly 30, Eliza 26, James 7, William D. 5, Joseph 3, Robert 1
SHORT, Nat 50 (B), Tabby 45, George 2
WADE, Daniel 62, Sally 60, William 37, Susan 18
EVANS, John 56, Demarius 45, John 23, Thomas 18
MCDANIEL, Albert 30, Sally 22
BRATTON, David 40, Sally 25, Loretta 5, John 2
MORRIS, Washington 46, Evila 39, Martha J. 17, Evaline M. 15, Mary E. 13, Samuel 11, George Ann 9, James G. 7, William T. 5, John 10/12
HYMER, Andrew P. 42*, Matilda 32
DOOLY, Henry 21*
MORRIS, Samuel 85, Martha 71, Polly 50
BIGGERS, Landie 63 (m)*, Nancy 50
GATSON, William 17*
BIGGERS, Nancy 60
BIGGERS, Mary 30 (B), Sylva 10
GARTSKELL, Albert G. 28, Ann 23, Thomas 4, Richard 1, Ann 83
GARTSKELL, William 25, Elizabeth 18
DOOLEY, Obediah 34, Isabella 28
DOOLEY, Ann __
DOOLY, William 46, Minerva 38, Henry 22, James M. 20, Martha A. 18, William 16, Elkanah 14, Obediah G. 13, Mary E. 11, Samuel 10, Matilda C. 8, Demaris 6

1850 Census Clark County Kentucky

Schedule Page 91

STEVENSON, George 42, Susan 32, Charles 11, Mary 7, Ellen 5, Sarah 4, Warren T. 3
DORNIGAN?, Thomas 45, Mary 44, Elizabeth 22, Thomas 19, Nancy 17, Letitia 15, William 14, Mary 12, Henry 6
TINCHER, William*, William R. S. 27, Sarah 22, Jemima 3
BAYES, Elizabeth 31*, Catharine 20, William 7, Mary A. 5
LEWIS, Stephen D. 58, Catharine 35
BEAN, Eve 74, Asa 42
PRICE, James 50*, Charlotte 39, John W. 16, D. Webster 15, Austin H. 13, James R. 11, Cornellus H. 5, Oliver 2
HART, Camillus J. 25*
DONALDSON, Patrick H. 50, Sarah 49, Joseph 24, Lucy A. 23, Rebecca 18, David 15, James 9
DUNCAN, William R. 32, Mary 23
DUNCAN, Margaret 72, Sally 40, Thomas 30
CUNNINGHAM, Abner 48*, Parmelia 43, Jesse 24, William 20, Elizabeth 18, Mary C. 16, Sidney 14 (m), Benjamin B. 12, Parmelia 10, James C. 8, Charles 5, Nannie W. 2, Wellington 22, Sarah J. 23
BAILEY, Elizabeth J. 28*
CUNNINGHAM, Polly 75*, Jemima 35
ROBINSON, Joab 70*
WOOD, Mary 24*
CUNNINGHAM, Jesse 53, George 16, Abner 14, Robert 12, William 10
PEEBLES, Margaret 50, Polly 45, William 56

Schedule Page 92

HUME, Robert 40, Letitia 20
HUME, Esther 81
KIMES, William 40, Mary 30, Mary 5, Jane 2
MOORE, Thomas H. 29*, Maria 26, Anna 6, Thomas 4, Martha 2, Mary 3/12
HUNTER, Peter 33*
BOGGENS?, Cyntha 45, Elizabeth 13, William 11, Jane 9, Thomas 7
GOFF, Strawder 48, Sarah 33, Benjamin 13, Margaret 9, Mary E. 2
SCOTT, Martin 25*, Martha A. 24, Margaret A. 4, Rebecca J. 2, Sarah C. 5/12
VANMETER, Solomon 32*
KELLY, Griffin 80, Sally 78
WHITESIDES, John 80*, William 59, John jr. 53
YOUNG, Catharine 29*, Ephraim 25
ALLEN, Thomas 74
PENDLETON, Edmond 60*, Mary 31, Edmond 23, Virgil 29, Mary 20, William 4/12
MCCONNELL, Lucinda 33*
HUNT, Reuben 43, Mary 71, Elizabeth 30
TRIMBLE, William 48, Margaret 46, John 21, James 17, Caroline 7, Benjamin 5, Margaret 19
HULETT, Robert 56
MCDANIEL, Hugh 35, Eliza 29, Milton J. 4, Junis W. 2 (m)
HULETT, Jesse 53, Rebecca 49
MCDANIEL, Nathan 38, Zerilda 30, William J. 11, Hugh B. 9, Mary E. 7, Susan F. 1

1850 Census Clark County Kentucky

LYON, Eligah 55, Elizabeth 50, Emily C. 30, Sally A. 22
ESTES, Bulah 70, John 28
MCCANN, John 34, Polly 74, Marium? 43
BARKLEY, Hiram 25, Marium 18, Nancy 56
CHEVIS, John G. 50
NICHOLS, Frederick B. 63, Polly 60, Jefferson 30, Nancy 26, Frederick 21, Elizabeth 104

Schedule Page 93

CLARKSON, Jas. M. 37, Rebecca 23, Millard F. 6, Mary 4, Rebecca A. 3, Ada V.? 11/12
MOORE, Eveline 51, Isaac 24, John 21, Margaret 18, Patsey 15, Sally 13, Charles 10
WORNALL?, Matilda 40 (B), Silas 17, Harriett 14, James 13, Jerry 8, Emma 7, Mary 6, Fanny 5, Henrietta 3
MCDANIEL, Francis 60, Elizabeth 60, Thomas 24
LACKEY, Thomas 61
LACKEY, Mildred 38, Robert 22
GROOMS, Benja. 26*, Elizabeth C. 19, Rachel 49
KENNER, Jane L. 80*, Mary 35
THOMPSON, Harrison 39, Josey 38, Emma 17, Albert W. 15, Ann M. 10, Sandford J. 8, Harrison 5, Manlius V. 2
HART, Thomas 54, Lucy 42, Mary 24, Tona? J. 22, John 20, Judith E. 18, Andrew H. 15, Henry 12, Lucy A. 10, James R. 4
DANIEL, Willis 36, Sarah 27, Beverly 11 (m), John H. 9, Thaisa? 7, Lucy 6, Francis F. 3, Thomas J. 2
PENDLETON, Dana J. 26, Elizabeth R.? 20, John T. J. 3, Charles L. 10/12
THOMPSON, Haynie 48*, Polly 48, Matthew 25, Samuel 23, Mary E. 15
TRIBBLE, John 17*, Haynie 10
WARREN, Thomas 57*, Malinda 52, Mary 17, Thomas 14, Annetta 12, William 24, Jane 17
TRIBBLE, Alfred 14*
JACOBS, Isaac 37, Polly 32

Schedule Page 94

BIGGERS, Kitty 46, Sabra 23, Emily 20, Sarah 15
SMITH, John 34*, Drusella 38, Catharine 21
JENKINS, Benjamin 18*, Elizabeth 23
RASH, Lewis 33, Martha J. 21, Mary E. 4, Laura J. 2, Susan A. 6/12
SMITH, John 60*, Jane 56, Jonathan 27, Elizabeth 25, Isaac 23, Louisa 14, John L. 12, Drucilla 10
BIGGERS, Mary 10*
CUNNINGHAM, Isaac 45, Milly 40, Isaac 16, Robert 14, Sally 18
DAVISS, D. M. 32 (m), Martha 25, James 6, Sally A. 3
ROBINSON, Moses 60 (B)
JACOBS, David 65 (B)
STEPP, Frederick 73, Mary 67, Mary? 23, James 22
WHITESIDES, Louisa 53*
ROWZES, Samuel 41*, Albina 28, Mary L. 3, Henry S. 1
MCMAHAN, James 30*, Traviana? 30, Daniel 2, Michael 6/12
KERNS, Patrick 38*, Elizabeth 12, Mary 7

- 51 -

1850 Census Clark County Kentucky

ANDERSON, John 26*, Ann 33, Elizabeth C. 4
GOLIN, Michael 30*
CONNER, Patrick 30*
BARKLEY, Silas 33, Ann 20, William 2
BUSH, James 51*, Nancy 52, Ambrose 23, Lucy E. 18, Harmon? 11, Thomas 9, Nancy 7
PEMBERTON, James 20*
TAUL?, Andrew J. 35*, Cassina J.? 34, Jonathan R. 14, Benja. H. 12, Mary J. 10
CROW, John 28*
SCOTT, Robert 52, Elizabeth 46, Catharine 15, James H. 11, Rebecca 9, Patsey D. 7, Robert B. 3
BEALL, Leonard 53, Polly 52, William 29, Edmond Y. 26, Thomas G. 23, Martin L. 20, Elizabeth W. 17, Sarah A. 12, Ambrose D. 10

Schedule Page 95

POSTON, Henry G. 38, Ann M. 34, Martha 11
BARROW, Hencher G. 59, Rachel 60, Ann 21, David 18
HULSE?, Stephen 40, Margaret 33, Elisha G. 14, John J. 12, Richard A. M. 10, Waller D. 8, Mary A. S. 6, Ennis C. 4
CURRY, Charles 50, Elizabeth 45, Provy 21 (f), John 20, Elias 14, Charles 12
WILLIAMS, John S. 31*, Mary E. 7
HARRISON, Polly 46*
SUTHERLAND, John T. 23*
LYON, Hezekiah 67*
BRANEGAR, Sally 35*, John 17
SCRUGGS, Ann 4*

1850 Census Estill County Kentucky

Schedule Page 47

SWOPE, William 43, Nancy 41, Marcus 22, Serena Jane 18, Cyntha An 16, Nancy 14, Carey 12 (f), William 10, Joseph 8, Sarah 4
FRAZIER, John M. 36, Sally Ann 28, Augustus 8, Martha J. 5, Elizabeth 3, S. G. T. 1 (f)
GRIGGS, David 52, Elizabeth 24, Sally Ann 28, Elisha A. 20, John L. 3
BULEY, Samuel M. 36, Elizabeth C. 36, Mary E. 11, Stilly Jane 1
BARNETT, James 34, Eliza Ann 26, John 12, Angeline 10, Fanny 8, Nancy 6, Moses 3/12
VAUGHN, Elijah 31*, Nancy 24, Stephen 9, John 6, Samuel 4, Mary E. 1
SAILS, Anderson 23*
MCKINNEY, Wilda E. 24 (m)*, Nancy A. 21, Anna 1
THURMAN, James 36, Pop? 33 (f), Josephine 8, Oliver G. D. 6, Amanda J. 4
ABNEY, Elijah 41, Patsy 40, John 15, William M. 13, Allen 9, Mary 4
LYLE, William H. 24, Drusilla 23, Mary S. 2
BRINEGAR, John S. 26, Lucy 19
KING, Presley 22, Mary 21, James W. 9/12
CHARLES, Joseph 40, Maria 33, James 18, Wilda 15 (m), William 13, Henry 9, Joshua 5, Elizabeth 11/12
PUCKETT, James 26, Malinda J. 19, Josiah 10/12
PUCKETT, Nelson 34, Lucretia 34, William 10, Mahalia 7, Ann E. 3, James 3/12
BAYLE, Henry 66, Patience 56
STRANGE, Edward 33, Sarah 22, Margarett 3, John W. 1

Schedule Page 48

PUCKETT, William 26, Manerva 25, Achilles 5, Bluford 3, Sarah 2
CONNER, Ezekial 35, William 16, Rebecca 14, Elizabeth 11, James 8, John 6, Susan 4, Sally J. 1
HILL, Jefferson A. 27, Emely 24, A. J. 1 (f)
STRANGE, James 28
LAW, Jackson 22, Mary 20, Syntha A. 2, Isom 3/12, Daniel 60
COX, Lewis 38, Elizabeth 21, Ansil D. 11, Isaac 1
FOWLER, Jeremiah 48, Polly 38, Rachael 14, Jane 11, Lucy 3, Polly Ann 1
MUNEY?, Isaac S. 29*, Elizabeth 38, James W. 9, Jordan 7, Sidney 5 (m)
WOOLEY, Roberet 14 (m)*, Nancy 14
NORTON, Amos 42, Amanda J. 22, William S. 1
REYNOLDS, Tobias 57*, Nancy 48, William C. 4
OWINGS, Elizabeth 80*
JOHNSON, Isaac 32, Sarah J. 21, James 7, Gideon 4, George W. 3
TUCKER, David 45, Anna R. 26, William 12, Minerva A. 10, Polly 7, Nancy 5, Merrill 2
TUBBS, Bartlett 29, Jane 29, William 8, Elizabeth 7, Bartlett 5, Thomas 4, Hiram 2
ABNEY, Daniel 28, Elizabeth 20, Luvisa 2, Nelson L. 9/12
ROGERS, Berry 29, Emly 20, Hiram 2, Malinda F. 1
WHITE, James 42, Isabell 40, Larkin 19, Jefferson 17, Stephen 15, Sarah 13, Isabell 11, James 9, Armilda 7, Mary F. 5
SHEPHERD, John 26, Mary E. 24, William 28, Henry 16

- 53 -

1850 Census Estill County Kentucky

Schedule Page 49

BARNES, William 37, Elvira 24, Rachael 5, Speed 4 (m), Weeden 8/12
ABNEY, Tucker 50, Rachael 50
NEAL, Richard 26, Patsy 24, Sally Ann 6, Middleton 2, Andy 63, Nancy 61, Fanny 17
NEAL, Samuel 33, Elizabeth 29, Martha J. 13, Sally Ann 11, William H. 9, Nancy J. 7, James R. 5, Samuel 3, John A. 2
JOHNSON, James 30, Mary 23, Elizabeth 4, Lucy 2, Martha 6/12
WALDIN, Elisha 45, Elender 30 (f), Rebecca J. 16, Anna 14, John 13, Mathew 9, Milly 7
SKINNER, William 22, Martha J. 19, Sarah A. 1
EASTIS, Jackson 32, Milly 27, Mary J. 7, John H. 4, William 1
BARNES, Richard 36, Dianah 36, George W. 14, Delany 4, Lucy Ann 9, Susan J. 7, Joseph 4, Henry 1
ABNEY, Allen 36, Syntha 38, Elizabeth 14, Martha A. 12, David 8, Benjamin 6, Liza J. 3, Levina J. 3
ABNEY, Clem 31 (m), Mary 31, Sarah A. 9, John T. 8, Sandford 6, Rebecca 5, Nancy 9/12
BARNETT, William 50, Susan 47, Susan 18, Sarah 16, Martha A. 14, Malinda 12, Samuel 6, David 5 (twin), George 5 (twin)
THOMAS, Isaac 24*, Mary A. 23, Milly 5
BARNETT, James 27*
HOWARD, William 31, Elizabeth 28, Nancy 7, Francis 6, Lucy Ann 4, Jackson 1

Schedule Page 50

LARRISON, David 45, Rutha 20, Matilda 13, David 11
WATTERS, James 47, Hannah 51, Bailey 21, Andrew 17, Samuel 16, Juniper 13 (m)
WALDIN, Stephen 50, John 41, Mathew 39, Milly 36
HENRY, Elizabeth 43*, Aquilla 18, America 16 (f), Joseph 15, Sally Ann 12, Daniel 10, Catharine 9, Nancy 7, Elizabeth 4
RIDDELL, Sally 88*
SHEARER, James 50*, Julia 24, Edward T. 7/12
LAND, Sarah M. 7*
DUNAWAY, William G. 30*, Ally 29, Eliza J. 8, John N. 1, Benjamin N. 35
CONNER, Nancy 19*
HENRY, Absolom 56, Margarett 42, Lydia 16, Absolom 12, Moses 10, Simon 7, William J. 6, Evaline 2
BARNES, James 23, Elizabeth 22, Mary A. 5, John W. 2
MOORE, Harrison 35*, Mary D. 21, Amanda F. 3, Eliza J. 1
SHEPHERD, Ansil D. 24*
THOMAS, Henry C. 27, Sally A. 20, Martin W. 7/12
THOMAS, Henry H. 68, Margarett 63, M. L. 25 (m), Temperance 18, Henry F. 1, Neomy 2/12
ELLIOTT, Sarah 35*, Mitton 13, Nathan 11, Burgess 8 (m), William H. 5, Martha J. 3
HARRIS, John P. 29*
TATE, Waddy 51 (m), Rutha 45, Richard S. 16, Rutha A. 14, Martha 12, Elizabeth 8, Euphram? 5 (m)
STEWART, Martin 45, Elizabeth 40, Harvey 17, John H. 15, Martin W. 13, Margarett L. 11, Wesley 9, Cordella 7, Caroline 5, Elizabeth 2

Schedule Page 51

TYRE, Satterwhite 23, Sally J. 18, Murrill 9/12
EASTIS, John 33, Eda 22, Elizabeth M. 13, Martha J. 10, Milly Ann 3, Pernetta 1

1850 Census Estill County Kentucky

SAILS, Samuel 61, Mildred 48, Webber H. 25, Robert 21, Elizabeth 18, Bowles 14
HARRIS, Webber 70
REED, Thomas 52, Nancy 46, Chilton 18, Webber 17, Mary 15, Frances 11, Joel F. 8, Sarah J. 5
CRAWFORD, Volentine 73 (m), Armiria 28, Armilda 26, Hardin 16
SMYTH, William 29, Eliza 25, John M. 3, Levina 1
FINNEY, Bailey 33*, Luraney 26, Louisa 5, Lewis 3, John 10/12, Joseph 10/12
CALINNIS?, Eveline 16*
ROGERS, James 25, Rachael 25, Elizabeth 6, Margarett 5, Nancy 1
RUSSELL, William H. 28, Eliza 24, Martha J. 3, Leonidas 1
CRAWFORD, Oliver 45*, Delina 36
LAND, James 21*
DUGAN, John W. 24, Mary 21, James W. 3, Hugh 2, Mary E. 11/12
EASTIS, Milton 27, Sally 27, Jackson 9, James 7, Rutha 5, William M. 4, Sarilda 3, Lewis T. 1
EASTIS, James 23, Jane 24, John H. 11/12
CRABTREE, John T. 26, Matilda 25, Job 5, William 4, Abraham 2, America 6/12
CRAWFORD, R. Lee 45
EASTIS, Henry 21*, Nancy 30, Samuel 6/12
WALDEN, William 13*, Dillard 9
WEST, Tinsley 42, Eliza 38, Anderson 19, Evaline 17, Elihu 12, Columbus 5, Amanda 1

Schedule Page 52

HALL, Thomas 64, Martha 64
PENNINGTON, Pealy? 31 (m), Martha 26
SMYTH, Tobias 47, Matilda 34, John 14, Polly P. 12, Sally 10, Rebecca 8, Edward 6, Elizabeth 4, Jeptha 2
SMYTH, Edward 39, Prudence 38, Robert W. 17, Hannah 15, Didama 14, Emily 12, Thomas 10, Tobias 8, Edward 6, James 4, Castira 2, James 26
CURRY, William 33, Ellen 25, Andrew M. 4, George 3, David A. 1
CRABTREE, Jacob 52, Polly 48, Elizabeth 20, William 18, Abraham 16, Mary 14, George 12, Simpson 10, Edwin 8
THACKER, William 44, Sarah 44, John 19, Abraham 18, Elisha 16, Elizabeth 13, James 12, William 10, America 6 (f), Wesley 2, George 3
JOHNSON, Robert 40, Susan 35, William 16, Elcanah 14, Sally E. 13, John 11, Alfred 9, James H. 7, Richard 5, Moses 3 Gilly Ann 6/12
TOWNSEND, Garrett 33, Sarah 21, William 6, James L. 4, Morton P. 2, Newton 1/12
TOWNSEND, Rueben 34, Kesiah 39, Julia 10, Reuben 4, Susan 1
TOWNSEND, James 57, Susan 53, Robert 19, Eada? 17 (f), Nancy 14, William 12

Schedule Page 53

POWELL, John 36*, Elizabeth 34, Sarah Ann 14, Demarcus 12, Hannah 10, John 6, William 3, Morton 1
LEE, Elizabeth 60*
LEE, Benjamin 38, Amy 39, William 19, Manda M. T. 14, Nimrod 13, George W. 9, Francis M. 6, Benjamin F. 4, Andrew J. 1
TOWNSEND, Eli 26*, Lucy 20

- 55 -

1850 Census Estill County Kentucky

TACKETT, Mahalah 14*
MEADOWS, Green 43, Frances 36, George 18, Henry 14, Delina 13, Harrison 6, Mary 4
EVANS, James 57, Hannah 46, Louisa 19, John F. 16, Elizabeth 13, Delina 9
WELLS, John 35, Kitty 34, Henry B. 14, William A. 13, Sally A. 11, Edmund 8, Jalia 7 (f), Elizabeth 5, Margarett J. 2, Catharine 9/12
CENTERS, William 29, Larcena? 28 (f), John 11, William E. 9, Achilles D. 5, Martha E. 3
TOWNSEND, James 29, Emily 26, Sally Ann 8, Arthur 6, Elizabeth 5, William 3, James 9/12
HALL, Green 24, Nancy 18, Green 9/12
CENTERS, Joshua 25, Julia Ann 21, Elizabeth J. 2, Arthur 1
ADAMS, Jesse 68, Mary 66
REED, Nathan 26, Elizabeth 41
ROGERS, Nelson 30, Judy 24, Barthena 2, Susan Jane 6/12
REED, William 28, Nancy 26, Elijah 12, Sally 2
REED, William 62, Easter 44, John 18, Evaline 16, Manerva 14, Jesse 11, Easter 9, George M. 7, Miranda 2

Schedule Page 54

REED, Thomas 44, Nelly 45, Polly A. 16, Eliza 13 (twin), Susan 13 (twin), Peggy 10, Enoch 7, Noah 2
ROGERS, Isaac 24, Ally 18, John H. 11/12
ROGERS, Milly 51, Hiram 21, John 18, Pernetta 16, Milly Ann 9, Josephus 8
ROGERS, John 36, Mary 36, Abigill Jane 13, Elizabeth 12, William 11, James G. 8, Eliza E. 6, Isaac T. 3, Elcanah 9/12
ADAMS, David 38*, Arrilda 26, Mary 16, Sarah M. 6, Weeden L. 2 (m), Susan 3/12
PATRICK, Thomas 52*
LOWRY, Ludwell 53, Margarett 50, Lavina P. 19, Elizabeth 16, William 14
JACKSON, Samuel 27*, Mariah 19, George 6/12
FRANKLIN, Josephine 11*
BRYANT, James 30, Elizabeth 34, William 9, Elizabeth 6, James 5, John 2
LOWERY, James 28, Ellen 23, Sarah C. 7, Moses J. 5, Margarett S. 3, Francis M. 8/12
MCCREARY, Jincy 43 (f)*
WISEMAN, Mary Jane 12*
BENNETT, Thomas 47*, Nancy 44, Catharine 21, Elizabeth 20, Margarett 18, Page 16 (m), Joseph 14, Fanny 12, Mary A. 10, Peter 8, Caleb 5, Cristina 3
TREADWAY, Catharine 75*
MCINTOSH, Bayless 27, Elizabeth 28, Silas 7, Luvisa 5, William F. 3, James 1/12
MCINTOSH, Francis 32, Agila? 23 (f), Martha E. 5, JAmes T. 6/12
TIPTON, Paul 35, Louisa J. 33, James W. 6, William H. 5, Castira E. 3, Jacob 1

Schedule Page 55

THORNSBURG, John 32, Sarah A. 31, Mary F. 11, Andrew 9, Isaac 7, Elizabeth 5, Naomai 2, Temperance 6/12
MCKINNEY, Thomas S. 29, Mary 25, Jane 9, Dillard 5, James 2, Toby 2/12 (m)
ADAMS, Berryman 56, Cyntha A. 25, Eady 17 (f), George W. 16, Enoch 15, Thomas 13, Elizabeth C. 11, Mary A. 5, Nancy M. 4, Susan J. 1
HARRIS, Josiah 34, Nancy 28, Patsy 12, John B. 9, Robert D. 7, Sarah 5, Bowles 3, Mahalia 2, Mary 5/12

1850 Census Estill County Kentucky

JUDY, Henry M. 34*, Milly 27, Milton B. 3, Boone 8/12, Thomas C. 22
CLARK, Thomas 12*
CHRISMAN, Isaac 52, Sophia 42, John H. 11, William H. 9, Marilda J. 8, Sarah E. 5, Thomas J. 2
WITT, James 32*, Levina J. 26, John W. 5, George R. 2, Sarah E. 1/12
DUNAWAY, Easter 54*
GRUBBS, John O. 26*, Jane 22, Thomas W. 1
WHITE, Mary Jane 16*
NEAL, Jourdan 23, Bertha 23
TIPTON, Jesse P. 29*, Patsy 27, Robert L. 6, Nancy J. 4, Mary E. 2, Thomas 1
LAND, Sylvester 11*
RANKINS, A. G. 48 (m), Catharine 38, Nancy 20, John 18, Sophia 15, Catharine 12, Elizabeth 10, H. H. R. 4 (m), Lucy Ann 1
WILLIAMS, James 47, Matilda 52, Elizabeth J. 20, George S. 18
POWELL, F. M. sr. 31 (m)*, M. E. 30 (f), John H. 6, A. G. 4 (m), Harriett A. 1

Schedule Page 56

HAMPTON, James 9*
ADAMS, David C. 32, Elizabeth 28, Sarah A. 11, Polly A. 10, Lucinda 6
MOORE, Thomas 46, Jane 32, Greenberry 16, Elizabeth 12, Jane 11, Samuel 9, Robert 8, Lewis 5, Elihu 2, James H. 6/12
JONES, L. B. W. 51 (m), Amanda 26, Bryaldra 14 (f), John A. 6, Sarah A. 4, James R. 2
ELLIOTT, Sandford 28, Martha A. 26, Mary P. 7, Levi P. 4, Ann Taylor 1
REED, James 27, Lydia 21, William 7, Delina 4, Susan 2
MCKINNEY, Richard 65, Ann 60, Catharine 21, F. M. 15 (m), Martha J. 12
MCKINNEY, James B. 26, Sally A. 16, Elizabeth F. 8/12
WATTON, Mily G. 39 (m), Margarett 36, Nancy E. 14, Susan J. 13, Lewis F. 11, Elihu G. 9, Lucinda 8 (m?), Marcus L. 6, Madison 5, ARmilda 3, Armanda G. 3/12
DOSIER, Joseph 27, Barthana 22, John P. M. 5, William B. 2
BAKER, John William 23*, Elizabeth 19, Nancy J. 6, Milly A. 3, Andrew J. 6/12
SKINNER, Mary Ann 17*, John W. 2
MCDOWELL, Elizabeth 40, Elizabeth 12, Samuel 10, John 8, Milly Ann 3, Mun? 9/12 (m)
ELLISON, Mary A. 40, Malinda 16, Artamissa 15, Charles 5
BAKER, Moses 49, Sally 40, Henry 18, James 16, Jacob 14, Polly Ann 10, Tarleton 6, William H. 1
BUSH, Mahal 25*, Lavina 23, Elizabeth 8, Mary Ann 4, Margarett 1

Schedule Page 57

HALL, Rebecca 60*
SHINFESTLE?, Peter 65*, Betsy 65, Augustus 26, Rebecca 21, Francis 20
HARRISON, William 7*
FRAZIER, William 5*
TARBER, William 50*, Elizabeth 29, Louisa 10
HATTON, Lucinda 14*, John 13
VANCE, John 65, Mildred 65, Thomas 23
POTTS, John F. 32, Mary A. 30, Martha E. 10, Sabrina 8, John T. 6, David D. 4, Francis M. 2/12
MOUNTS, Adam 44, Jane 24, William 9, Rebecca 7, John T. 4, Josiah 2

1850 Census Estill County Kentucky

CARMICLE, George 45, Elizabeth 42, John 22, Martha 20, William 18, Nancy 15, Mary 12, Amanda 10
MOUNTS, George 42, Mary 39, Peter 20, Elizabeth 17, Justina 15, Susan 13, Augustus 9, Sarah J. 7, Mary Ann 3
BALLARD, Mordica 21 (m), Elizabeth F. 18, Susan J. 1 (m?)
SNOWDEN, James H. 51, Matilda S. L. 46, James M. 21, Martha A. 15, Jeremiah J. 12, Lemuel 6, Elizabeth A. 11, Margaret M. 3
HOSKINS, John 43, Sarah 41, Theresa E. 16, William A. 14, Lydia C. 12, Charles M. 10, Daniel D. 9, John B. 7, Sarah M. 6, Nancy A. 4, Termethus W. 2, Ansil D. 8/12
BALLARD, Byrom 25*, Elizabeth 28, Christopher C. 4, Benjamin 3, Winzy 8/12 (f)
BRANDENBURG, Sarah B. 10*, James H. 8
HOSKINS, Nancy 64*, Martha A. 23
CURRY, Andy 4*
WELLS, John J. 55*, Jennett 55, William 29, James S. 21, Daniel S. 18, Elizabeth F. 13

Schedule Page 58

KANNON, Robert C. 24*, Amanda M. S. 22, Ann E. 3
CONNER, George 24, Elizabeth 17
BUSH, Anderson 44, Frances 36, William 12, Elizabeth 10, Mary 8, George 5, Josiah 2, Tandy 5/12 (m)
TYRE, George 44, Elenor 54, William T. 13, Simms? D. 11 (m), Mary C. 7
ALLEN, Stephen 28*, Ellen 20, Pheba J. 1
WRIGHT, William 35*
LEE, Turner 37, Lucy 17, William 1/12, David 12
VAUGHN, Elijah 74
WARSON, William W. 22, Catharine 22, Sidney 1 (m), Elizabeth 56
VAUGHN, Samuel J. 43*, Polly 41, Sarah F. 14, John W. 12, Phebe 8, Joshua 4
LOW, Isom 27*
JOHNSON, Moses 60, Lucy 54, Amy 20, Moses 18, John 14, Margarett J. 4
VAUGHN, Doretha 68, Nancy 38, James M. 19, Malinda 11
CHANEY, Joseph 37, Nancy 29, Frances 5, John W. 3, Ruben 1
NOLAND, Joshua 38, Frances 37, John N. 11, Angeline 9, Amanda 5, Daniel 2, Samuel 8/12
BRINEGAR, Jacob 56*, Elizabeth 52, Martha A. 20, Wesley 16, Perlina E. 14, William H. 11, Elizabeth 10
HENRY, Angeline 24*, Elizabeth F. 3, Speed S. 1 (m)
TIPTON, Jonathan T. 39, Kitty J. 33, Samuel 13, Jacob J. 11, Emeline 9, Demarious 7 (f), Susan 5
BARNES, John 54, Margaret 47, Sarilda 22, William 20, Brinsley 19 (m), Mary 17, Isabella J. 15, Jesse 13, Joseph 11, Louvisa 9, Jacob 7

Schedule Page 59

TIPTON, Samuel 75*
HINDS, James B. 31*, Sarah P. 34, Samuel F. 5, Mary E. 2, Jesse T. 11/12
CUNNINGHAM, William 42, Elizabeth 32, John F. 10, Marshal 8, Marklin 5, Owen 3, Eliza 4/12
FOX, Samuel 29, Rutha 18, William 6/12
WARREN, John T. 24, America 21, Josiah 3, Marium A. 1 (f)
PARK, John 32, Louisa 30, Thomas E. 8, Mary A. 6, William O. 4, John 1
ALLCORN, James 39, Nancy 32, William 15, Sally A. 13, Leroy 11, Joel 9, Deby 7 (f), Polly 5, James 2

1850 Census Estill County Kentucky

WHITE, James 24*, Sally 27, Syrus 3, William G. 1
PEARSON, Malinda 14*
MOSELY, Martin B. 35*, Emily J. 28, Olivia P. 12, John W. 6, Charles H. 4, Alice J. 11/12
BELL, James H. 24*, Delila 23
SNOWDEN, Archibald 27, Eliza J. 26, Maria 3, Hiram 2
SCHOLL, Daniel B. 31, Mary L. 24, A. W. 7 (m), Mary C. 5, Elizabeth A. 1
RAWLINGS, Robert 26, Susan 22, Susan 1, Benjamin H. 1/12
ROBERTS, John 23, Telitha 19, N. B. 1 (m)
SCHOLL, Peter D. 29, Goodwin 29, Edward A. 4, Elizabeth A. 3, Mary E. 1/12
NORTON, James H. 38, Patsy A. B. 27, Henry C. 5, Ansil D. 4, George M. 2, Sylomious? 2/12
CLARK, William J. 37*, Matilda 34, Joseph 13, John S. 9, Mary Jane 6, George H. 2

Schedule Page 60

PARK, Polly 75*
HERNDON, Elijah 39, Ann P. 34, Fanny 9, William 7, John 5, James 3, Henry Clay 10/12
WALTERS, Sampson 58, Nancy A. 58, Elizabeth 22, Simeon 21, Josephine 17
BONTA?, Abraham 48*, Elizabeth 28, Sarah A. 6, William G. 4
CHAMBERS, James 14*, Jeremiah 12
REYNOLDS, Williamson 30, Susan 22, Pleasant H. 7, John W. 5, George E. 1, Mary J. 3/12
POWELL, John B. 58*, NAncy 58, Ansil D. 24, Newton 21, Elizabeth 22, James H. 18, Sarah 13
SHEPPHERD, Aquilla 13*, Robert 11, Adam 21
WAGLE, Lewis 50*, Charlottee 42, John 21, Emily J. 16, Martha A. 14, Mary E. 11, Henry C. 9,
    Charlotte B. 6
KELLEY, Alexander C. 10*
ELLISON, Travis 48, Sally 52, Polly 22, John 18, Nancy 10
CURTIS, A. A. 32 (m)*, M. M. 24 (f), Ann E. 3, William 1
STOCKTON, E. D. 31 (m)*, Mary 21, Matt. H. 1/12 (m)
PIGG, M. H. 17 (m)*
MARTIN, William 38, Amelia 34, Mary A. 12, Azanah 10 (m), Singleton 8, Sarah 6, Elizabeth 4, Lucy 1
CHILES, Thomas D. 36*, Maranda 26, S. H. 5 (f), M. W. 3 (f), M. D. 1 (f), John 33
WYLIE, James B. 23*
STEWART, Eli 33, Susan 32, William M. 13, James A. 11, Polly A. 9, Louisa J. 7, Levi 4, Emily 1

Schedule Page 61

STEPHENS, William 64, Nelly 48, James A. 15
PARKS, Mary 37*, Eliza 17, Thomas W. 8, Henry Clay 6
DANIEL, A. C. 28 (m)*
UTLEY, Jordan N. 23*
WATTS, John W. 21*
BELLIS, Hiram 27, Mary 25, William 25
BENTON, William 38, Martha 37
MOORE, evan 42, Margarett 35, Patsy A. 15, John 10, William H. 8, Pertina 7, Sidney 1 (m)
FINNEY, John 50, Susan 38, William 15, Nancy R. 13, John D. 12, Sarah M. 4
EASTIS, Lott 44, Patsy 36, Catharine 10, Moses 6, Andy S. 2
KERLEY, George S. 34, Milly 28, Elihu P. 4, Sarah E. 2

1850 Census Estill County Kentucky

SPARKS, Thomas 45, Patsy 41, Sally A. 22, John 20, Polly 18, William 16, Fanny J. 12, Thomas C. 10, Elihu P. 6, F. M. 4 (m), Taylor 2

EASTIS, David 46, Sally 30, Charlotte 20, Wilmoth 13 (f), Lora 11, David S. 10, Nancy 9, Jeremiah 5, Sally A. 1

CAMPBELL, Andly 41 (m), Maria 36, Eliza J. 17, Armilda 14, William J. 11, John S. 7, Andly 4

LANE, John C. 29*, Emily 21, Arbell 2 (f), M. F. 3/12 (f)

CHAMBERS, Sarah 10*

ARAINE, Joseph 28, Mahala 32, Lucinda 6, Susan 5, Mahala J. 1

WAGES, James 49, Gilford 20, William H. 18, Ebenezer 16, Josiah 14, John B. 12, Sarilda 10, Armilda 8, Amanda 6, Eliza 4

Schedule Page 62

KING, Celia 82, Lucy 38, Mary 18 (B)

MCINTOSH, John 56, Ellenor 35, Madison 19, Azariah 15, Martha 11, William C. 9, Eliza 6, B. F. 4 (m), Mary T. 1

MCINTOSH, Peter 48, Malinda 37, Nashville 19, Sytha 17 (f), Fanny 15, Major 13, Mary A. 11

WINBURN, William 42, Mary 36, Elizabeth 15, Henry 12, Emily 10, Jason 9, Syntha A. 6, Polly A. 4, William O. B. 1

SHERMAN, Daniel 58, Rebecca 42, Polly A. 22, Anderson 18, Evaline 16, Emily E. 14, Eliza J. 12, Thomas 9, Gilla A. 7, John 4

SAMS, Edward 32, John 11, Martha J. 6

BEST, Jackson 33, Winey 38 (f), Zachary 11, Elizabeth 9, Garland 6, George W. 4

KING, Zackary 76*, Lucretia 68

CAMPBELL, Sally A. 14*

KING, Garland 34, Mahala 38

RAINEY, John 46, Judy 48, Thomas W. 19, Clerissa 14, Mary F. 7

PITCHER, Joshua 50, Clerissa 35, William H. 14, John T. 5

COBB, Henry 48, Sarah 44, Martha 14, Mary 13, Sarah M. 4, Henry 1

STONE, Francis E. 49, Lucy 47, Lewis D. 19, Franklin 13, Thomas D. 6

PATTON, Polly Ann 32, A. J. 14 (m), F. M. 12 (m), G. W. 10 (m), J. H. 8 (m), R. S. 6 (m)

RHODES, Isaac 43, Patsy 44, Lucinda J. 22, Albert 18, Sally A. 16, Thomas 14, James 12, William 10, Louisa 9, Martha F. 6, Cassander 5 (f)

Schedule Page 63

WARNER, Edward 20, Martha A. 17

COBB, Richard 32, Manerva 28, Sarah 7, Elizabeth 5, Eliza 1

COBB, Jesse 34, Tabitha 19, Mary E. 7, Rhoda 5, Milly 3, Eliza B. 2

OLDHAM, Mary 56*, R. K. 32 (m), Absolom 22

STONE, John 25*, Milly A. 27, Mary Ann 4, Margarett J 11/12

HALL, James 46, Mary 37, Arzela 13, Garrett 12, Elizabeth 9, Emily 4, Mary H. 2

WARNER, John 53*, Nancy 50, Aaron 20, Zachary 9

VAUGHN, Mary 7*

HALL, Bryant 48, Elizabeth 25, America 6, Milly 4, Emarine 3, William H. 1, Milly 82

BYRD, John S. 37, Polly 25, Nancy 7, Catharine 5, Orthonile? 2 (m), Richard 75, Cassandra 60

HAMPTON, Willis 40*, Sally 28, Mary E. 7, Nancy J. 4, Lucinda 3, John S. 3/12

1850 Census Estill County Kentucky

VISSER?, Samuel 16*
WITT, George 39, Louisa 29, Amand J. 11, William H. 9, James H. 8, Rebecca J. 6, Pheba A. 2
HALL, Morton 51, Elizabeth 50, John P. 22, Evaline 21, Thomas F. 20, Martin 17, Frances 15, William 14, James 11
ADAMS, Robert 60, Delila 39, Elizabeth 10, Eliza 9, Mary J. 7, John Q. 5, Matilda 2
WALTERS, Eliza 64*
HOLEMAN, Margarett 30*, James 12, Polly J. 10, Washington 2

Schedule Page 64

WILLIAMS, Original 52, Jane 40, Joseph 21, Elizabeth A. 19, Polly J. 17, Margarett 14, Julia A. 11, Sarah 5, John W. 2
ALEXANDER, Joseph 34, Emarine N. 23
TUTTLE, Benjamin 52, Elizabeth 44, Elizabeth 23, Emily 21, Nancy 19, James W. 16, William 14, Clarke J. 12, John 10, Benjamin 8, Richard 5, John 1
WALTERS, William 32, Nancy 28, Richard P. 12, Sarah E. 10, Henry 6
ALLEN, Celia 39, George W. 16, Malinda R. 14, Rachael 13, Polly Ann 10, Eliza J. 6, William H. D. 1
WILLS, Malinda 67, A. J. 21 (m)
WILLS, Alexander 31, Sarilda 24, William F. 7, Elizabeth 5, Milly A. 2, John N. 2, Andrew A. 9/12
FINNELL, John 50*, Susan 45, Fountain 17
WHITE, Catharine 70*, Margaret 27
FLIRTY, John 27, Catharine 20
STONE, Francis 56, Sarah 50, William 33, Eliza 18, John 17, Nancy 15, Eada 12, Francis M. 10
TODD, Jasper R. 31, Mary W. 30, Josephine 10, Augusta Ann 8, Mourning E. 6, Mary 4, Christopher C. 1
FLIRTY, John 58, Catharine 57, Ranson 19, David 16, Margarett A. 12
WOOD, Fielden 29, Martha 21, James T. 9, John N. 7, Francis M. 1
BERRY, Levi 41, Kitty A. 34, Martha Ann 18, Mary 17, John Berry 13, Abner 11, Nancy 8

Schedule Page 65

WEBB, William 28, Eada 27, Sarah 9, Fountin 7, JEsse 4, Doretha 1
HARRIS, Sarah 58, Polly Ann 17, Bowles 15
HARRIS, Henry 26, Elizabeth 25, Sarah F. 1, Daniel 22
CONNER, James 50*, Syntha 38, James 19, Polly Jane 17, George 9, Susan 7, John 6, Sarah 5, William T. 4, Casius 10/12
BARNES, Catharine 16*
MARTIN, Joel 48, Mary 47, Eada 24, Robert 20, William 19, Azanah 17 (m), James 16, Josiah 14, Jack 12, David 9, George 8, Susan Jane 6, Eliza J. 4
WEBBER, Jones 68*, Sarah 66
EASTIS, Sarah 22*
WEBBER, Jones 37, Elizabeth 50, Doretha 16, Sarah 14, Simpson 12, Mary 10, John 8, Sandford 6, Eada 4, Martha 2
WEBBER, Sandford 39, Julia 37, Eliza 18, Elihu 17, Polly 15, Lewis 13, Phillip 11, Irvine 9, Jane 7, Sarilda 5, Jones 4, Austin 2, William S. 1
FIELDER, Tarleton 50, Elizabeth 50, Franklin 25, Robert 21, Tarleton 12
FIELDER, William 27, Perlina 24, Emily C. 10/12

1850 Census Estill County Kentucky

HARRIS, Leland 29, Nancy 23, William 6, Elizabeth 4, Josiah 2, Sarah F. 6/12
HARRIS, Thomas 27, Perlina 22, Lucinda 5/12, Sarah 21, Matilda 18
SKINNER, William 58*, Marium 39 (f), James 17, John 15, Henry 13, Nathan 10, Elizabeth 7, Amanda 4

Schedule Page 66

MCINTOSH, Nancy 30*
HELMSTINE?, John P. 38, Mary A. 26, James L. 9, Margaret A. 7
PADON, James 29, Manerva 23, Lucy F. 1, Lucy 57
ADAMS, Robert 27, Elizabeth 18, Sarah E. 2, William F. 1
HISLE, Willis 39, Sarilda 33, Eada 10, Mary 8, Simpson 7, Francis 5, Elvira 3, Amanda 1, Mary J. 16
NOLAND, Abraham 38, Elizabeth 39, Syntha Ann 10, Nancy Jane 8, Elizabeth 4, John 3, Thomas 1
WILSON, Anderson 33
ALEXANDER, Joshua 28*
WINBURN, Sidney 21*
WILLS, Michael 32, Ann 33, Malinda 13, Elizabeth 11, Mary J. 9, Phillip 7, John 5, Michael 1
WILSON, William H. 58, Elizabeth 23, Pleasant 21, Edith 21, Deborah 17, William 15, Francis M. 10
BARNES, John 49, Lucinda 45, Jemima 24, Lydia 22, Catharine 19, Rebecca 17, William 13, Alice 10
WILSON, Elihu 24, Nancy 20, Michael 2
NOLAND, John 42, Patsy 43, Mary A. 17, John 14, Lorinda 12, Syntha 10
CHRISTOPHER, Wily M. 44, Eliza A. 29, Malvina C. 20, Chatus H. 18 (m), Hawell 17 (m), Wily J. 14, Haden 8, David 6
WOOD, John 48*, Phebe 49
SKINNER, Joseph 88*
CAMPBELL, John 15*
LEWIS, William 75, William 27, George 16

Schedule Page 67

HOPPER, John 25, Julia A. 19, John 2, Lewis 8/12
DICKERSON, Susan 62, Anderson 29
WADE, George 33, Tabitha 33, Thomas A. 6, Susan 4, Elizabeth 2, William A. 10/12
SAMS, Wilson 44, Susan 35, Edmund 15, Eliza 12, Elizabeth 9, Temperance 6, Leroy 4, Chesley 1
RICHARDSON, Dudley 28, Eliza 22, Mary L. 1
PARK, Isom 38, Dianna 34, Josiah 8, Louisa 6, Asa 1
WALTON, David H. 46, Elizabeth 54, Elizabeth J. 24, Polly A. 22, Susan J. 20, William J. 17, Nancy P. 15, John C. 8
INGRAM, William 26, Mary A. 23, Elizabeth 4, Daniel 2, Dianah 8/12
LYNCH, John D. 21, Eada A. 21, Daniel 1
HUGHES, Turner 40, Sarina 30, Elizabeth 12, William 9, Dudley 7, Edward 4, Kisiah 3, Samuel 6/12
CAMPBELL, A. D. 51 (m)*, Elizabeth 37, Thomas J. 23, Mary 18, John S. 16, William F. 15, Amanda 13, Silas S. 11, Nancy L. 9, Margaret 7, Ansil D. 5
SCRIVNER, Silas 35*, John 22
MEBREARY?, James 41, Lucinda 26, John 10, William J. 6, James C. 4, Paulina 2
MCKINNEY, Curtis 23, Elizabeth 18, Richard 6/12
DURBIN, Pias 30 (m), Margaret 27, William 9, John 7, Jimma A. 5 (m), Mary F. 3, Margarett A. 8/12

1850 Census Estill County Kentucky

MCCAY, William 50, Margaret 33, Alexander 17, Nancy 15, Sarah 13, Jesse 11, Daniel 10, Bartlett 9, Thomas 6, James R. 3, Margaret 5

Schedule Page 68

ALLEY, William 58, Jane 43, Clem 16, Rachael 14, Payton 12, Fielden 6, Francis M. 4
KING, William 50, Rebecca 47, James R. 19, William M. 17, Samuel 14, Lucy 9
ABNEY, Coleby 23, Elizabeth 28, Newton T. 2, Sarah 11/12
WISE, John 28, Drucilla 27, John W. 6, Rebecca J. 3, Docia A. 1, Ellender 100, Docia 65
EMMS, Moses 50, Rachael 52, Susan 14, Polly A. 12, William 11, Augustin 10, Greenup 6 (m), Margaret 5
LARRISON, George 24, Elizabeth 18
BLANTON, G. D. 36 (m)*, Margaret E. 26, James R. 6, Mary F. 4, Hiram D. 2
BAXTER, Mary 59*
WILLIAMS, James C. 30*
BATTERTON, Henry T. 20*
SMITH, Reuben 28, Cyntha Ann 21, James H. 2
KING, William 48, Lucy 38, Ipson O. 17 (m), Frederick 15, William R. 12, A. J. 6 (m)
ADAMS, William 29*, Sibia A. 24, Eliza 6, Polly 5, Sarah 4, Samuel 3, Elizabeth 1
HOPPER, Hiram 22*, William 18
BERRYMAN, John 60, Elizabeth 66
BARNES, Hannah 68, Cassa 37, Dulcena 9, James D. 6, MAhala J. 3
HAWKINS, William 70, Nancy 60, William 17
SMITH, Elizabeth 39, Isaac S. 17, William 14, Thomas 11, Sally 5, Boone 3

Schedule Page 69

HAWKINS, Moses 25, Joica A. 23 (f), Nancy 3, Polly 1/12, Polly 44, William 11, Juniper 3
CLEMM?, George 70*, Patsy 20, John 18, Kelly 14 (m), Lodriska? 13 (f), Elizabeth 11, James 9, Simpson 6, Eliza 4, Mary F. 2, Patsy 65
BEST, John 15*
HENDERSON, William 28, Sarah A. 24, Abram 7, Mahalia 5, Mary E. 2, James W. 4/12
HENDERSON, Robert 29, Marium 27 (f), Mary E. 6, Harvey 4, Malinda 2, Levi 4/12
STEPHENS, John 27, Rhoda 21, Polly 13
CREED, Robert B. 51, Luvisa 39, Cobb D. 16, Paulina 13, Marium 11 (f), Elizabeth 9, William H. H. 8
BERRYMAN, Samuel 38, Ann 38, America 14, Amanda 13, Irvine 11, James 9, William 9, Jackson 7, Mary E. 5, Samuel T. 2, Ann 6/12
FINNELL, John 20, Elizabeth 18, Fountin 1
SPARKS, Samuel 37, Kitty 27, Julia A. 12, John W. 9, Susan J. 5, Phillip 4, Nathan 1
SPARKS, William 26, Susan 18, Catharine 3, Litty 7/12
STEPHENS, Richard 82, Sarah 47, Alvan 19, Mary J. 16, Shipton 13, Richard M. 11, Marium 9 (f), Lucinda 7, Isabella 4
HENDERSON, Ellenor 59, John 23, David 22, Eliza J. 21, Elizabeth 16, Artaminta 3
HENDERSON, Carcus 40, William 18, Mary J. 15, Syntha A. 14, John T. 12, James H. 10, Catharine 8, Abram 6

1850 Census Estill County Kentucky

Schedule Page 70

GREEN, Eli 25, Syntha A. 28
STONE, Catharine 72*
FINNELL, Nelly A. N. 40*
STEPHENS, Jane 52*
FINNELL, Simpson 22, Frances 18, William 2/12
FINNELL, Fountain 47, Mary 47, Catharine 15, Susan 12, Jones 8
WEBBER, Sally 42, Augustin 22, William 20, Manerva 18, Absalom 15, Eada 14, Jones 12, Martha 10, Thomas 8
WILLIAMS, William 50, Charlotte 46, Catharine 22, Elizabeth 21, Sally A. 18, John 16, Fanny 13, Nelly 10, Francis 8
WOOD, James 41, Elizabeth 41, John M. 18, James W. 13, Manerva A. 9, Marilda 7, Charles T. 3
BONNEY, Mary Ann 55, John 20, Catharine 17
KING, Samuel 52, Polly 50, Samuel 18, Uriah 15, Eleanor 13, Armilda 11, Greenbury 28
MONROE, Matilda 42, George 20, John 17, Matilda 15, Francis 8, Maria 6, Alfred D. 4
MONROE, Martha 23*
JOHNSON, Mahalia 3*
RICE, Isaac J. 35, Elizabeth 24, James H. 1, Benjamin T. 2/12
STONE, James 53, Susan 40, Syntha 15, James 13, John 12
HUDSON, Thomas 40, Malinda 39, Benjamin 14, Wesley 12, Meranda 11, Amanda 10, John W. 9, Milton 7, Thomas 5, James 3, Polly 6/12

Schedule Page 71

MORELAND, Enoch 35, Irena 36, Richard 10, James F. 8, Ira 4, Lucy A. 2, Rhoda 61, Rhoda A. 9
WLILLS, Elijah 43, Rutha 50, Alvin T. 22, Nancy 15, Cora W. 13, James T. 12
JOHNSON, Martin 39, Uphin? 35 (f), John T. 12, Susan 11, James W. 9, Nancy 7, Hannah S. 5, Mary J. 3, Sarah F. 1
RIYM?, William 42, Mima 39, Josiah 16, Jane A. 15, Isabella 13, Clora 10, John S. 9, Mary E. 8, Thomas M. 6, Sarah M. 4, James C. 1
CROW, Job B. 45, Nancy 43, Jesse 17, James 16, William 14, John 11, MArtin 5, Hannah 2
WILLCOX, James 23, Ann 19, Benjamin F. 3, Thomas J. 7/12
MOORE, Moses 31*, Julia A. 37, William P. 5, Mary J. 3, Henry 2
CROW, Thomas 13*
RUBLES, George 60, Nancy 48, Nancy A. 18, Susan J. 16
MILLION, Richard 34, Harriett 26, Nancy J. 9, Rodney 7, Moob 5 (m), Hannah A. 3, James T. 2
BURTON, Isom 32, Permelia 27, Irvine 9, Henry 6, William 4, Eliza 2
HOWARD, William D. 27*, Mary J. 24, Susan F. 4, Leannah 2
RUBLES, John 26*
KELLY, John 46, Sally 43, William A. 20, Nancy A. 17, Susan 15, Milly T. 12
GUM?, John P. 27, Ann 28, Thomas M. 4, Stephen J. 3, Susan Ann 4/12, Susan 52

Schedule Page 72

MCSWINE, William 49, Elizabeth 44, Thomas 22, Mary 18, Josephus 16, Sarah 15, Susan 10, Hannah M. 5, Elzira 4, Nancy E. 2

1850 Census Estill County Kentucky

DALTON, Thomas 36, Julia A. 36, Margina A. 9, Harriett R. 8, Nelson 5, Audley 3 (m), Clorien 2 (m)
BECKNELL, Perry 34*, Lucy 40
PEARSON, Jemima 2*
BLANTON, William 42, Elizabeth 39, Alexander 18, John 16, Mary 13, George 11, Thomas 9, Elizabeth 7, William 5, Scott 3, Ann E. 1
PHILLIPS, Beverly 33 (m), Martha 30, John P. 10, Jemima 9, Emanuel 8, Elizabeth 7, Mimory 6, Ryon 4, Aaron 2
COYLE, Tilford 33, Malvina 33, Mary A. 15, Lucinda 12, James M. 10, Newton J. 8, Jaila? 4 (f), Isaac T. 3, Parylla 1
WILLIS, Edward 28, Mourning 26, Thomas J. 7, Pacena A. 5 (f), McKinze 2
PHILLIPS, Memory 26 (m), Elizabeth 20, America J. 4, George W. 2
BECKWELL, Hiram 28, Mourning 28 (f), William H. 6, Sandford 4, John A. 1
ASHCROFT, Amos 50, Rebecca 45, James 16, Elias 14, Angeline 12, Louisa 10, John C. C. 8, Francis M. 6, Rebecca 2
RICHARDSON, Dudley P. 26, Anna 26, Lucy Ryon 4, Samuel 2, William 10/12
BECKWELL, Linfield 65 (m), Polly 50, Hudson 24, Tyre 21 (m), Nancy 15, Elizabeth 11, William R. 4

Schedule Page 73

ROSE, John 31, Sumira 26 (f), Lorenzo 12, Elzira 11, Lucinda 9, Polly 5, Milly 3, Calvin 2, Manerva 1
DURBIN, Joseph 28, Sabina 28, Marcus L. 6, Edmund F. 3
DALTON, Timothy 39, Susan 39, William B. 19, Nancy A. 15, Reuben T. 5
ADAMS, John T. 34, Polly A. 32, Thomas W. 9, William F. 7, Susan A. 5, Joseph H. 3, Frances 4/12
ASDELL, Joseph 60, Polly 43, Louisa 14, Cinder R. 12 (f), Charlotte 10, Wilson D. 7
RICHARDSON, John 22, Martha 19
WALTON, William 34, Mary 25, Andrew J. 8, Richmond W. 6, Thomas J. 4, Malinda J. 3, William B. 6/12
ASBELL, Levi 23, Rhoda 21, John P. 3/12
VAUGHN, Nancy 63, Harrison 22
ABNEY, Littlebury 62, Elizabeth 64
ABNEY, Madison 24, Narcissa 21, Sarah E. 8/12, Joshua 45, Sarah 45, Singleton 20, Syntha A. 18, Asa 17, Rebecca J. 14, Martha 12, Silas 6, Speed S. 1, John King 20
THORNSBURGH, Isaac 64, Frances 63
BARNETT, Berry 38, Elizabeth 30, Martha A. 13, William J. 10, Elizabeth 2
GRAVITT, Thomas 37, Angeline 30, James 16, John W. 14, Daniel 10, George 8, Harriett 7, Ellis 5, Susan 4, Frances 6/12
HALL, David E. 33, Sally 33, Caty 8 (f), John D. 6, Susan F. 4, Harmon S. 1

Schedule Page 74

HALL, Mayse 22 (m)*, Sally A. 20, Mary C. 2
SAMS, David 22*
HALL, Evan 21, Julia A. 19, Syntha A. 1
HALL, Samuel 59, Catharine 49, Chilton 19, Syntha A. 14
THURMAN, Henry 30, Martha 30, James 9, William 8, David 7, Mary 6, Fountain 5, Nathan 2, Eliza 8/12
HARRIS, John V. 36, Martha A. 23, Nancy D. 6, Richard J. 4, Elizabeth 3, Daniel 11/12

1850 Census Estill County Kentucky

BURTON, Samuel 42*, Eliza 42, Martin 15, Susan 13, Agnes 11, Eliza 4
GRIGGS, Samuel 1*
GREEN, Zachary 31*, Sally 34, James S. 11, Sarilda 3, John 7/12
HOWARD, Nancy 13*, Sarena 11
SPRY, Enoch 19, Polly 17
GRAVITT, George 62, Hannah 59
DAUGHETER, Andrew J. 27*, Malinda 23, Mary E. 2/12
HATTON, Mary 20*
CROW, Samuel 28, Nancy 30, Kitty J. 1/12, Martha S. 19, Nancy A. 17, Rebecca 14, Nickolas 12, Mathew 9, Hannah 8, Syntha A. 6, Louvisa F. 3
PATRICK, Hickman 40, Syntha A. 35, Tillitha 15, Frances 13, Louvisa 11, Elizabeth 9, Hester A. 6
RICHARDSON, Levi 22, Eliza 19, Mary J. 2/12
POOR, Benjamin 48, Eliza 38, Berry 19, Thomas 11, Nancy 9, Richard 6, Milly J. 3
STONE, Berry 46, Sarah 42, Catharine 18, William 17, Mary J. 15, George 14, America 12, Francis M. 10, Benjamin F. 9, John 7, Eliza 5, Sarah 3, Berry 7/12

Schedule Page 75

KING, Benjamin 38, Elizabeth 39, Susan 17, Henry 15, George 13, Sally 11, Joseph 10, Francis 8, Eliza 7, Stephen 4, John 2/12
SPRY, John 45, Malvina 42, Mary 17, Joseph 15, Green 12, Sally Ann 9, John 4
OSBORN, Mathew 42, Polly 42, William 15, Miranda 13, Sarilda 9, Caroline 7, Solomon 4
LILLY, James 51*, Louvisa 30, William 26, Henry 20, Nancy 19
SMOTHERS, Daniel 8*
JENKINS, Daniel 36, Louisa 29, Eliza A. 1
PASLEY, James 27, Margarett E. 26, Evan 4, Levina J. 2
EVANS, Rainey 51 (f)*, John 11
PASLEY, Thomas 18*
KIMBRELL, Elizabeth 78*
LILLY, James 22, Elizabeth 21
WITT, Sandy 37 (m), Mary B. 29, John P. 10, Lewis G. 7, Ailsy J. 5 (f), Simon K. 3, Francis S. 1
BARNETT, John W. 35, Jemima A. 24, Mahala J. 7, Emily C. 5, Sarah A. 4, Ambrose M. 2, James W. 4/12
POOR, Pricilla 35*, William 19, Augustin 16, Arsula 11, Mary 9, Milly A. 7, Elizabeth 1
EVANS, Sally 65*
HARRIS, Archibald 21, Elizabeth 22, Martin 2, Mary J. 1
COOPER, George 46, Sarah 30, Sarilda J. 19, John W. 17, Florinda 15, Rachael G. 13, Robert H. 4, James S. 3, Sarah A. 2, Susan A. 6/12

Schedule Page 76

HARRIS, Josiah 42, Sally 39, John 14, James 12, William J. 10, Thomas J. 8, Susan J. 6, Lewis F. 4, Mary E. 1 (twin), Sarah F. 1 (twin)
RICHARDSON, Elcanah 32, Matilda 32, William 10, Mahalia E. 8, Manuel 6, Sarilda 4
SNOWDEN, John 57, Elizabeth 40, John 21, William 15, Sarah 14, Sarilda 12
HAMILTON, Andrew 75, Sally Ann 15
MCKINNEY, Wilda 67 (m)*, Mary 64

1850 Census Estill County Kentucky

CURTIS, Dudley 12*
CURTIS, Addison 44, Mary 23, Jeremiah 14, Delila 12, Thomas C. 3
DAUGHETEE, William 52, Rosannah 40, Margaret A. 17, James 15, Eliza 14, Samuel 12, John W. 9, Francis M. 4
BARNETT, Celia A. 35*, Matilda 16, Augustin 4
HIGHLY, William 22*, Docia A. 23
BARNETT, Franklin 21, Nancy 23, William 2
HIGHLY, John M. 31, Jane 35, William T. 12, Wilda 10 (m), Nancy 9, James F. 8, Henry H. 6, Edward 4, Lucy A. 1
CRAIG, Jacob 42, Nancy 42, Syntha A. 15, John 13, Mary J. 12, David 10, Barthena 7, Susan 6, Amanda 4, Alfred 1
BURTON, William 29*, Eliza A. 24, William H. 8, Isom 3, Benjamin F. 6/12, Allen 21, Samuel 19
GRIGGS, Wade H. 21*, Elisha A. 19
MCKINNEY, Joseph 29, Eada 28, Nancy J. 5, James F. 3, Joel 2
DICKERSON, William 27, Nancy 23, John 4, Honor 2 (f), Julia A. 10/12

Schedule Page 77

CURTIS, William F. 37, Elizabeth 35, Angeline 15, Mary J. 13, James A. 10, Patsy 8, William 6, Amelia 5, John 4, Solomon 2
HARRIS, Jane 60*
SHEARER, Zackariah 24*, Syntha 20, John C. 1
CURTIS, William 62, Patsy 60, Elijah 22
CURTIS, William 64, Matilda 45
BENNETT, Malinda 41, John 20, Richard 18, William 14, Thomas 10, Sally 8, Major 4, Dewit C. 1
MCKINNEY, Wilda 19 (m), Susan B. 23
BURGHER, Manson 59, Maria 33, Elvila 17, David 14, Marcus 12, Fanny 8, Cornelius 2
BURGHER, John 24, Mary V. 17, Benjamin S. 3
WALTERS, Henry 57, Nancy 49, John S. 21, James F. 16, Nancy J. 14, Jeptha M. 10, Henry G. 8
TODD, Moses G. 47, Esau? 45 (f?), Shelby 9, Isaac 8, Sally A. 6, Newton 4
GRIGGS, Roland 27*, Manerva 21, John L. 1
HOWARD, Nancy 14*
BURGHER, Nicholas 33, Mary 25, Pleasant 2
BROCK, Joshua 50, Polly 39, James 13, John W. 11, Nancy J. 9, Allen 7, David 5, Elijah 1
SEE, John 25, Nancy 25, Margaret A. 2, Elvila 3/12
CURTIS, Jeremiah J. 35, Rachael 29, Margaret A. 13, Nelly J. 5, Thomas D. 2, Israel B. 4/12
CURTIS, John 58, Sidney 35 (f), Clendenna 13 (m), Nancy 12, Mary 11, Marium 9 (f), Elisha 8, Martha 5, Rachael 2, Maria 1

Schedule Page 78

MASTIN, Curtis 26, Eliza A. 24, James F. 2, William T. 9/12, William 24, Polly 20
CURTIS, Jesse 49, Eada 60, John H. F. 18
CURTIS, George 26, Polly 26, Thomas B. 5, Mahalia J. 3, James T. 8/12
SPENCER, Samuel 34, Lucy 27, Nancy 4, Lewis 2, Hiram 4/12
KING, Samuel 42, Rachael 29, Catharine 10, Elizabeth 9, Joseph 6, Major 5, John W. 1
PRICE, David 29, Rebecca 29, Ann E. 9, James 7

1850 Census Estill County Kentucky

DOUGLASS, William 45, Mahalia 42, Julia A. 14, George 12, Amanda 10, Adaline 7, Caroline 4, Nancy J. 2, Paulina 8/12
PRICE, Jacob 41, Louvina 37, John W. 19, Hiram 18, Mary E. 15, Charles 11, Louvina 9, Jacob 5/12
MAYBERRY, John 55, Betsy 40, Polly 18
SELBY, Charles 40, Manerva 35, Sarah 13, John 5, Charles C. 3, James J. 1
JOHNSON, Edward 30*, Jane 26, William 1
MAYBERRY, Mary 19*
MUNCEY, James 44, Isabella 47
SHARP, Tilman B. 41*, Demarious 36 (f), Elizabeth 13, Justena 11, Jane B. 9, Lucy 7, Moses 4, William F. 1
BREWER, Thomas 17*
MCKINNEY, Mathew 37, Elizabeth 28, Daniel L. 12, Louisa 9 (twin), Louisa 9 (twin), Anna J. 7, Sarah F. 7/12

Schedule Page 79

SHARP, Moses 62
STEWART, Archibald 39*, Cindrella 42, James 14, Tilman 12, Thomas D. 10, Mary J. E. 9, Bluford A. 6, Zackary T. 3, Justina P. 6/12
MCKINNEY, William A. 22*, Francis M. 21, John R. 19
MCKINNEY, David R. 46, Louanna 46, Elizabeth J. 22, Justina 20, John 18, Louanna 14, Lucy 12, Ann 9, Moses 7, Mildred C. 4, Sarah F. 2
COMBS, Cuthbert 49, Lydice 36 (f), Joseph 16, Sylvester 11, Davis 8, Gideon 5, Eugine 3, Sarah A. 1
BALLARD, John 57, Charity 52, Jinsey 21 (f), Julia A. 17, Augustus 14, Paulina 12, Mary Ann 10, Sally Ann 10
CROUCH, James 53, Francis 23, Sally 20
BARNES, Catty 48 (f)*, Rebecca J. 15, Sarilda 13
CROUCH, Mima 30*, Nancy 2
ADAMS, Jackson 29, Julia Ann 25, Nancy A. 7, Fielden 6, Leanah 4, Virgin 3, Lucretia 1
BAKER, William 34, Lucretia 33, John S. 17, James H. 15, Ann E. 13, Jackson 10, Mary J. 5, Curtis 3, Martha E. 2/12
MILLER, Tunstall Q. 32, Precella 20, Margaret 6/12
TIPTON, Samuel 42, Margaret 35, Tirza 12, Wallace 10, Nelson 8, Albert 6, Hannah 5
KIRK, William G. 24, Julia 20
BELLIS, Thomas 54, Elizabeth 60, Thomas J. 22, Elizabeth 15
BRINEGAR, Israel 58, Catharine 55, Ansil D. 24, William 22, Turner 19, Hudson 16, Delina 12, Israel 7

Schedule Page 80

CRAIG, Sarah M. 32, William T. 10, Eliza J. 9, Amanda F. 8, John T. 5, Mary E. 3, Sarah E. 1
WALLACE, Jane 55*, Susan 29, John A. 27, William R. 21, Thomas K. 18, Sarah 14, Andrew 12
BUSLEY, N. B. 35 (m)*
SWOPE, Henry 22*
CRAIG, Herman T. 21*
MEARICK, William 28*
JONES, Lucy 17* (B)
BRINEGAR, David S. 32, Sally A. 21, Sally A. 10, John P. 7, Mary L. 1

1850 Census Estill County Kentucky

OWINGS, John R. 32, Amanda 28, Winston 11, Elizabeth 10, Nancy J. 5, Milly A. 4, James 2, John P. 5/12, William D. 5/12
ALEXANDER, James 38, Rhoda 30, Elizabeth 11, Syntha A. 10, Andrew 9, Mary A. 7, Silas 3, James W. 1
MATHERLY, James C. 36, Aelia 42, Amanda 11, Sarilda 9
CROW, Randall 37, Martha A. 30, Sally A. 10, Savilla 8, William 6, Lavina 4, Mary E. 4/12
BERRYMAN, James 49, Docia 42, Francis 18, Dudley 16, Dillard 16, Syntha A. 13, Mary 11, Samuel 9, William 7, Thomas 5, Sarilda 2, Armilda 2
MCKINNEY, Pleasant 30, Paulina 25, Elizabeth F. 6, Susan 5, Richard T. 3, Eliza J. 6/12
KIMBRELL, John 48, Caroline 46, Marion B. 15, Celia J. 13, George W. 11, Syntha A. 9, John W. 6, Z. Taylor 3
ADAMS, Jesse 37*, Mary A. 32, Armilda 14, Maryilla 12, Mary A. 10, Thomas J. 8, Green A. 6, Henry C. 4

Schedule Page 81

PATRICK, Samuel 25*
WYATT, William 37, Nancy 24, Phillip 7/12
MIZE, Joshua 68*, Elizabeth 67
SHEPHERD, Nancy 12*
HOWELL, A. J. 32 (m), Caroline 31, Achilles 5, Weeden J. 2
BENTON, Merrill P. 22, Lourinda 23, Owen 1
WINBURN, Jeptha 45*, Rebecca 38, Rhodes 20, Polly A. 15, Doratha 10, Jesse 6, Thomas 2
STONE, Lerona 25*
PHELPS, Jonathan 39, Mary 30, Willia W. 8, Amanda V. 7, Mary E. 5, John D. 4, James R. 2, W. S. 3/12 (m)
HOLEMAN, George W. 35*, Eliza J. 34, Timothy 5, Sidney 2 (m)
WITT, Mary J. 16*, Jeremiah 8
ABNEY, Paulina 16*
KING, Scuyler 50 (m), Malinda 56, Elihu 18, George 16, Elijah 13
ROGERS, Julius 49, Catharine 48, Elizabeth 21, Granville 17, John P. 15, Simpson 11, Emaline 8
BAILEY, A. M. 29 (m)*, Mary C. 26, George H. 1
BOND, Preston 26*, Belinda 26
DAWS, Joseph 30*, Eliza J. 30, Abram 16
RATLIFF, William 21*
TAYLOR, John W. 49, Ann 48, Martha A. 4, Robert 15, Mary F. 13, Amanda F. G. 11
TUDDER, Samuel J. 35, Jemima 36, Tillitha J. 16, Judith 13, Daniel F. 9, Sarah E. 4, John B. 1
MCKINNEY, William 40*, Nancy 38, Nicholas 17, Polly J. 15, Julia A. 12, Marium 10 (f), Sally A. 8, Elizabeth 6, Lucy 4, David R. 6/12

Schedule Page 82

MCPHERSON, Rachael 65*
PUCKETT, Leroy 37, Matilda 29, Ansil D. 11, Elihu 11, Eliza J. 6, Owen 2
KELLEY, Green B. 39, Nancy A. 34, Achilles 11, Susan 10, Andrew V. 8, Sarilda 6, William O. B. 5, Mary J. 4, Armina 2, Green 4/12

1850 Census Estill County Kentucky

NOLAND, Joseph P. 48, Frances A. 38, Henderson M. 19, Joseph 17, Mary J. 15, George B. 11, Sarah 9, Paulina 6, Almira 3, John R. 1
MOORE, Eli 54, Polly 51, Rebecca 23, Charles 22, Paulina 16, Daniel 12, Archibald 10, Loucinda 7
TODD, Daniel P. 41, Evaline 36, William H. 17, John P. 16, Isaac 14, Stanton 12, Sarah C. 10, Tarleton 8, Manerva 6, Sarna 2 (f)
RICHARDSON, Kesiah 56, Amos 30, Nancy 25, Kesiah 22, David 16
BERRY, Thomas J. 26, William P. 22, Nancy 20, Mary 3, Martha 1
MARTIN, Milton 27*, Elizabeth 21, Nancy E. 6, Albert 1/12
WILLIAMS, Shadrack 32*, John 27, William 25, Charles 19
ASBELL, Joseph 30, Nanny 26, Amanda 6, Elizabeth 5, Sarilda 2, Mary E. 6/12
TURPIN, Martin 30*, Louisa 23, Owen 5, Milo 3
KERFOOT, Elizabeth 40*
BRANDENBURG, Joseph 35, Sarah 29, George W. 12, Sandford 10, Senica 8 (m), Elizabeth 5, Eliza J. 4, Joseph E. 1

Schedule Page 83

BRANDENBURG, John 20, Mary 22
RICHARDSON, Absolom 28, Patsy 27, Eada 5, William S. 2, Zackary 9/12
WAKEFIELD, Enoch 43, Angeline 41, James M. 14, Margaret A. 12, Lucy J. 10
KELLEY, James 37, Lycina 26, Polly J. 4, Thomas M. 2, Elenor 4/12
LAY, Carter 58, Eada 52, William 20, Merrill 18, LEannah 16, John 12, Armilda 11
FORDING, Zachariah 29*, Sally A. 30
JOHNSON, Manerva 12*, Amanda 10, Coleman 6
JOHNSON, Mordica 50 (m), Sally 27, Irvine 20, William 16, Patsy 14, Eada 12, Elizabeth 10, Beuford 8, Martha 6, Susan 4, Rhoda 2, Morgan 3/12
AMBROSE, Joseph 52*, Hannah 50, James H. 17, Clemmons R. 20, Joseph S. 15, Nancy H. 13, Hannah M. 9
DUNBAR, John P. 22*, Amelia 18
MARTIN, Thomas 65, Sarah A. 59, Jefferson 22, John W. 14
MARTIN, Lilburn B. 28, Ann 26, Green 3, Joseph 1, Jerome 7/12
MOORE, Sidney 26 (m), Nancy 26
FORDING, Hezekiah 35, Malinda 35, George 16, Samuel 14, Elizabeth 12, Harrison 10, Mary A. 9, Rutha J. 7, Nancy 5, Joseph 1
WINKLER, William 52, Margaret 34, Sally A. 12, Susan 9, Elizabeth 7, James K. 5, Polly A. 3, Elzira 8/12
FORDING, Dudley 59, Elizabeth 67, William 16

Schedule Page 84

MCMAHUN, William 40, Betsy A. 30
PINKSTON, Thomas M. 33, Elizabeth M. 23, Cyrene V. 6 (f), Joseph W. 4, Dillard E. 1
OSBORN, Thomas 25, Emily 22, Eada D. 1
CROW, James 47, Nancy 50, John 21, Dillard 15, Morton 13
RICHARDSON, Jesse 39, Patsy 25, Pearson 14, Asa 12, Nancy 9
CROW, Robert 43, Elizabeth 39, John S. 11, Robert A. 9, James A. 7, Zackary D. 4, Elizabeth 2
RICHARDSON, James 40, Elizabeth 42, George W. 13, Armilda 12, James T. 6, Lucy A. 4

1850 Census Estill County Kentucky

COLLINS, Eli C. 49*, Polly 29
BERRYMAN, Richard 5*
BLEVINS, Joseph 45, Mary 46, Absolom R. 18, Eli 17, Nancy 15, Joseph 13
WEBB, Jesse 27, Lotty 21 (f), Elizabeth A. 2, Sidney 5/12 (m)
FRENCH, James 34*, Elizabeth 32, George W. 10, Sophia 4, Angeline 2
PEARSON, Green 18*
PRICE, Thomas S. 42, Elizabeth 32, Thomas E. 18, Frances 11, Ansil D. 9, Catharine B. 8, Nancy 5, William O. B. 2
COMBS, R. K. 39 (m), Sarah 33, Hugh L. 12, Owen T. 10, Windmer 7 (m), Henrietta 5, Frances 3, Sarah A. 1
BRADEY, George 49, Susan 44, Flemon 17 (m), Lydia A. 15, William 14, Jerome 13, Horace 11, George 8, Mary 6, James 3, Elizabeth 1
DIMMETT, John B. 43, Elizabeth 37, Stacy A. 13 (f), Mary 10, Lucy J. 8, Thomas J. 6, James M. 6, Martha A. 4, John R. 2

Schedule Page 85

COVINGTON, Charles 20, Samyra 21
CLOWERS, James M. 32, Elizabeth 31, David 10, Joseph 7, James 5, Rutha 48
TAYLOR, Thomas 33, Samyra 24, John G. 8, Lucy A. 6, Nancy 5, Elizabeth 3, Amanda 1
WHITE, Stephen 32, Sally A. 19, Mary F. 8
WEBB, Elisha 39, Elizabeth 37, Joseph 16, Eliza A. 14, Dorotha 13, William 10, Sally A. 8, Henry 6, Nancy 4, Lucy 3, Richard 4/12
KING, Daniel 24, Sally 29, Elzira 5, Reason 4, Alla 2 (f), Sarilda 4/12
CARSON, Thomas H. 42, Sarah 27, Isabella 2, Mary E. 1
NEWMAN, David J. B. 24, Nancy J. 25, Mary F. 2, Robert 1
WITT, Allen 35, Polly 29, Syntha A. 11, William 10, Claborn 8, Thomas J. 6, Isom 4, David 3, Nancy 3/12
KEARSEY, Silas 59, Hannah 40, Thomas 16, Frances 14, James 11, George 10, Richard 8
NOLAND, Obed 46*, Julia A. 24, James P. 8/12
FREEMAN, Edna J. 4*, Sabrina 2
MOORE, Nathan 37, Martha A. 32, Margarett A. 11, Sarah A. 9, Mary J. 7, William H. 5
MOORE, Joshua 52*, Sally 50, Robert B. 19, Jaila W. 17
BENTON, B. G. 15 (m)*, Hulda 13
PEARSON, Joseph 25, Elizabeth 30, Robert 1
RICHARDSON, Conrad 21, Susan 22

Schedule Page 86

RICHARDSON, Henry 32, Rebecca 29, David 12, Edward 10, John 8, Elizabeth 6, Milly A. 4, William H. 2, Levi 11/12
ABNEY, William 22, Nancy 24, Amos 7, Liley 3, William 1
ASBELL, John 31, Sarah E. 21, Samuel C. 5
WHITE, Abner 27, Lydia 22, William 1
PEARSON, Eli 38, Elizabeth 29, Manerva 13, Margaret F. 11, Milly J. 9, William 7, Joseph 6, Lucy 4, Susan A. 2
LOWELL, Andrew 49*, Mary A. 52

1850 Census Estill County Kentucky

MCCAY, Mary 24*
STEVENSON, William 17*
WARD, John B. 19*
GRIFFITH, Mary 18*
BOSTICK, L. B. D. 57 (m)*
FOLEY, William 24*
CUNNINGHAM, David 19*
JACKSON, W. G. 29 (m)*, Mary E. 23, Julia A. 5, Andrew F. 3, Mary V. 6/12
CADWALADER, Andrew 6*
ARVINE, James 31, Josephine 26, N. B. 6 (m), Nancy 3
HUDGENS, Thomas 44, Elizabeth 36, Francis M. 12, Rebecca J. 10, Amos F. 8, Perry 6, Nancy A. 4, Samuel 1
RICHARDSON, James 34, Nancy 26, Armilda 11, Littlebury 5, Sarah A. 1
COX, Charles 69*, Frances 57, William 19, Ansil D. 11
FOX, Elizabeth 21*
HYMER, William 25, Anna 23
PARK, Asa 70, Susan 70, Elizabeth 37, Rebecca 35
PARK, Ebenezer 31, Spicy 30 (f), Franklin 10, Amanda 8, Rhoda A. 6, Eliza J. 3, Gentry 1
ROSE, Nathaniel 36, Amelia 29, Sally A. 13, Susan 10, Elihu 8, Eli 5, Amelia 2

Schedule Page 87

WALTON, Edward 74, Susan 63
WITT, Elisha 56, Paulina 47, James 25, John 19, Milly A. 15, Robert 14, George 13, Harrison 11
RAWLINS, Andrew 30, Venetta 25, James 4, Sally 2, Eliza 3/12
HOWARD, Henry H. 53, Nancy 51, Henry 25, America 19, Jackson 18, Irvine 16
MARTIN, Jack H. 39, Mary 32, Ann E. 5, Sidney 3 (m), MArtha 1, Robert 68
DANIEL, Pleasant 54, Elizabeth A. 56, Carrītiny? 24 (f)
AMES, S. F. 39 (m)*, Esther 38, George 8, Franklin 3, Mary 5/12
EASTIS, Berry 15*
DANIEL, Ansil 49, Sarah 39, Dillard C. 21, Jane 10, Moses P. 8, Isabella W. 3
THOMSON, John M. 27, Gabriella 17
SMITH, Robert W. 32, Mary 21, Thomas M. 5, Bettie 3, Ellen 6/12
NORTON, Benjamin 46, Narcissa 39, Henrietta 11, Sarah M. 9, Henry J. 6, Jesse T. 5
DERICKSON, Jesse 29, Mary J. 22, Henry 3, George M. 2, William M. 6/12
MAPEL?, George W. 28*, Susan 21, William 2, Sidney M. B. 6/12
MIZE, R. S. 24 (m)*
BARNES, Sidney M. 29, Elizabeth 28, Thomas H. 8, Elizabeth 4, James K. 2, Kate 10/12
NOLAND, Stephen 32, Amanda F. 29, Samuel 9, William 7
RIDDELL, John H. 42, Elizabeth 42, Robert 16, Lucy A. 14, N. J. 12 (f), Frances 10, Susan J. 8, John M. 6, Kitty 2

Schedule Page 88

MCKINNEY, James F. 31*, Ann 28, Elizabeth 2
DUNAWAY, Joseph 22*
STACY, James 24, Mary J. 19, John W. 2, James W. 1, Auldin 22 (m)

- 72 -

1850 Census Estill County Kentucky

CLARK, Robert 57*, Elizabeth 50, Frances 47, Robert B. 18, Francis E. 12
ELLIDGE, Sarah 69*
KIRBY, Elizabeth 30*
PRICE, Morton M. 45, Frances 30, Emma D. 5, Zachary T. 3, Edwin B. 9/12, Moses M. 73, John M. 20
WILSON, Catharine 48, Joseph 19, Mary Jane 15, Elizabeth 13, Syntha 9
CHANEY, Thomas 20, Isabella 17
NOLAND, William P. 45*, Mary A. 74, Thomas J. 19
HEATHER, Mary Ann 17*, Thomas J. 7/12
GRUNT, Jesse 40, Amanda 35
SPARKS, Elizabeth 55
HARRIS, Bowles 41*, Mary J. 31, Thomas J. 12, Sarah 10, Elizabeth 4, Mary J. 1
DICKEN, Sarah 59*
FROMAN?, Daniel C. 36*, Sarah E. 13, Frances 9
COATNEY, William 16*
WHITE, Aquilla 35*
JACOBS, Nathan 52*, Berilla 46, Henry W. 21, George 17, Isaac 13, Emaline A. 11, Benjamin F. 8, Francis C. 5
WITT, Mitchael 14*
WITT, Silas 47, Lucinda 48, James M. 25, John M. 24, Weeden M. 19, Jincy 16 (f), Wallis M. 11
WILSON, Lewis M. 32, Malvina F. 26, Patterson W. 2
GREEN, Bayless M. 50, Ann 51, Francis M. 17, ARabella C. 14, John W. 12, Nancy A. 10, James M. 8
WYLIE, Tuman? 23 (m)*, Mary J. 19, Nancy J. 1
JOHNSON, Hannah 13*
RAINEY, Andrew J. 33, Mary A. 25, Mary F. 8, Sandford W. 7, James M. 5, Rebecca J. 3, Sarah E. 10/12

Schedule Page 89

MOORE, Lewis 68, Tobitha 50, Elizabeth S. 3
TIPTON, William L. 51, Lycortye? 18 (m), Hicuba 16
WISEMAN, Abner 47*, Sophia 33, Amanda 10, Westley M. 9, Maranda F. 7, Nancy M. 5, Eun. E. 3/12 (f)
BROWN, Elizabeth 58*
MOORE, Thomas 46, Susan 43, Josiah 22, Mary J. 21, Caleb 19, Morton P. 17, Susan 15, Thomas J. 13, Nancy R. 11, Sarah G. 9
WRIGHT, Joseph P. 30, MArtha A. 27, Nancy V. 2
WARD, Voluntine 38*, Lockey 6, William H. 12, Allen 10, Elizabeth 7, Emily 4, Mary 1
BURTON, Agnes 68*
WITT, Charles 64*, Isabella 62
CARR, David 13*
WHITE, America 5*
KING, Samuel 19, Eliza J. 22
WINBURN, Rhodes 27, Martha 19
WITT, Garland 35, Louisa 32, Louvina J. 11, Barthena 9, Armilda 7, Joseph L. 5, Mary F. 4, Sarah E. 1
KING, Merida 27, Louisa 22, Franklin 4, Silas 2
WITT, Lucy 63, Malinda 31, Delany 29, Mary A. 27, Emaline 17, Francis M. 13

1850 Census Estill County Kentucky

LOCKEY, Elias 60, Nancy 52, Agnes 33, Docia 31, Elizabeth 30, Simpson 26, Susanna 24, Andrew 21, Elias 18, James 16, Nancy 14, Mary 12, Dillard 7, Delany W. 2
FLOYD, Mary 32*, Andrew 13, Aaron 11, Elizabeth 9, Patsy 5, Sally 3

Schedule Page 90

HENDERSON, John 80*
JOURDON, James R. 44, Eliza 35, John J. 16, Lance 14, Joseph 12, Susannah 10, James F. 8, Squire 4, Hannah E. 4/12
ELLISON, Travis 21, Margret 21
LANE, William N. 30*, Tobitha 31, Mary E. N. 7, James A. N. 3
LOCKEY, Mary 62*
WINBURN, Thomas 22, Temple 17, John 15, William 14, John V. 54
BOWMAN, Andrew 42, Sarina 38, Lorenzo D. 17, Elizabeth 14, Washington 8, William 1
HATTON, William H. 38, William 78, Tobitha 65
RONAN, James 50, Nancy 42, Robert 11, Mary R. 10, Joseph 8, Sarah 7, James 6, Coleman A. 4
WEBB, William 69, Doratha 71
RICHARDSON, Benjamin 37, Sally 36, Martha A. 13, Edward 11, David 9, Sarilda 7, Amos 6, Julia A. 3, Kisiah 1
EVANS, John 33*, Elizabeth 30, Diza 12 (f), William 9, Nancy 7, Angeline 5, JAmes 3, Stephen 3/12
BENTON, Hiram 16*
HENDRICKS, Julia 79*, William 50, Fanny 45, David 27, Elijah 19, Thomas J. 15, Roland 13, Syntha A. 8
ABNEY, Liley 9*
OLDHAM, John C. 30, Nancy 25, Clifton 7, William 5, Rufus 4, America 2
RICHARDSON, Sally 26, James 10, Sally A. 8, Mary F. 6, Amanda J. 4, Sarah D. 2
HENDRICKS, Cislia 36 (f), Susan A. 15, Mildred A. 16, William R. 10

Schedule Page 91

FRIEND, Samuel K. 28*, Elizabeth 28, Mary A. 5, Amanda J. 2, Nathan 5/12
THORP, Lear 8 (f)*
FRIEND, George 55*, Elizabeth 52, Charles L. 32, Nancy 34, Elizabeth 5, George W. 4, William C. 1
HARRIS, Elizabeth 71*
ABNEY, William 22, Nancy 25, Amos 7, Liley 3 (f), William 1
BOWMAN, Hezekiah 37*, Elizabeth 40, Sarilda 16, Mary J. 15, Sarah 12, Angeline 10, Hezekiah 8, Elizabeth 8, Jones 6, Armilda 1, Elizabeth 66
LOCKEY, James 19*
COVINGTON, Rachael 55, Elizabeth 22
RILEY, Emaline 28, Baylie 9 (m), William 3, Mary E. 5/12
JONES, Ansil D. 24, Elizabeth 20, Loukitty 2 (f), Humphrey 2/12
NEWMAN, Samuel W. 50, Sally 36, Josephine 7, Martha A. 5, William 4, John 2, Jonathan 17
WEATHERS, James 41, Eliza J. 28, Thomas O. 11, Loucinda A. 9, Mary E. 5, William H. 2, Louvisa Edge 60
ROSE, William 29, Sally A. 28, Mary A. 8, John 5
WHITE, Edward 51, Polly 48, Lucy 15, William 14, Polly 12, Joel 10, Henry 6, Arnold 74

1850 Census Estill County Kentucky

TUDDER, Samuel D. 48, Judith 45, Jemima 22, James M. C. D. 20, Sidney H. 18 (m), Elizabeth 16, Tobitha S. 14, David P. 12, Mary S. 10, Samuel L. 8
LAWSON, John 25, Nancy A. 16, Martha F. 5/12
GUM, Stephen B. 30, Elizabeth 26, Ann E. 12, John D. 8, Nancy J. 6, Susan F. 5, Mary A. 2

Schedule Page 92

LOGSDEN, John B. 47, Nancy 43, Edward 21, William 18, Rufus J. 16, Elizabeth 11, Ambrose 9, Francis 7, James 5
BURTON, Jackson 35*, Elzira 35
FREEMAN, Delila 14*
MEGOTHLIN, Wylie 14*
PEARSON, Robert 34, Emily 33, Henry J. 5, Sarah E. 2
SPARKS, John 23, Mary J. 17, Catharine 3/12
COLLINS, Joseph 39, Elizabeth 28, Narcissa 13, James 11, Joseph 9, Mary F. 5, Sally A. 3, John 1/12
KINDRED, Anderson 29, Sally A. 27, William G. 5, James M. 3, Lewis D. 3/12
WALTON, John 41, Rosanah 39, Elizabeth F. 17, Dulcena 15, Sarilda J. 14, Susan 12, John 10, Thomas C. 8, Martha 6 (twin), Mary 6 (twin), Zackary T. 4, James W. 4, Jefferson 8/12
RICHARDSON, James 30, Sarilda 20, Syntha A. 1
COYLE, Alfred 51, Martha 46, William 16, Oliver 14, Margaret 11, Armilda 5 (twin), Sarilda 5 (twin), Jesse 1/12
KELLEY, Emanuel 43, Harvey 21, Josiah 19, Loucinda 17, Nathaniel 16, Mary E. 13, Morton P. 11, John P. 9, Curtis 7, Emanuel 3
ROSE, Edward 33, Sarilda 33, Hayden 12, Perry 11, Louisa 9, Mahalia 7, Delina 5, John 4, William T. 3, Cassa A. 1
CATES, Alexander 42, Mary A. 35, Elizabeth 16, William 11, James 9, Mary 9, Martha 7, Franklin 6, Jacob 5/12

Schedule Page 93

MURPHEY, William 38, Nancy 32, Sally A. 12, Simpson 11, Elizabeth 9, Hannah F. 7, Madison 6, Mary 5, Stephen 4
RICHARDSON, William 34, Martha 27, Mary 11, Elizabeth 8, Sarah 6, John W. 3, Elmyra 1
HARRISON, Elisha 28, Delila 24, Mary J. 8/12
MILLER, Thomas 62, Patience 53, Margaret 35, Sally 22, Martha 18, Ezekial M. 16, Thomas J. 14
RICHARDSON, Aaron 30, Eada 30, Ann E. 9
SAMS, Lervy? 43 (m), Neoma 40, Isaac 19, John 16, Allen E. 15, Benjamin N. 13
MCINTOSH, Jesse 57, Rebecca 50, William 20, Rebecca J. 18, Neoma 13, Pleasant B. 11, John 38, Simpson 7, Dudley 5
HUGHS, Loucinda 44, Madison 24, Francis 21, Thomas 17, Margaret 16, Elender 11, Martin V. B. 9
VAUGHN, Gabriel 26, Eliza J. 22, Cassins 3, Rhoda A. 2, Middleton 9/12
PIGG, Johnson 34, Nancy 35, William 16, Joshua M. 15, John A. 14, Mortin 12, Lewis 10, Richard 6, Mary C. 2
FREEMAN, William 28, Patsy 24, Efford 8 (m), Edford 6, Thomas E. 4, Martha J. 1
TRIGGLE, James 45, Jane 41, John 19, George 17, Margaret J. 14, Jesse 12, Mary 9, Nancy 3

1850 Census Estill County Kentucky

Schedule Page 94

KING, Joshua D. 38, Sally 33, Thomas J. 13, Nancy A. 10, John A. 8, Samuel 7, Joshua 6, Margaret 3
HALL, Jefferson 40, Nancy 35, John R. 14, Allen B. 12, Mary J. 8, W. O. B. 2 (m)
MOORE, Morton P. 32*, Paulina 25, Mary F. 6, Theodore 4, Sarah A. 2
HAMILTON, Andrew 24*
LAND, B. Jackson 32, Mary A. 32, Sally A. 9, John 7, William J. 4, James T. 2, Emily 6/12
MOORE, William J. 38*, Milly 35, John A. 15, James A. 13, Archibald 11, Josiah 9, Simeon 8, Coleman 6, Candis 9/12 (f)
SCRIVNER, Jemima 13*, Jefferson 11, William M. 9, Amrose M. 8, Wesley 6
WILSON, John 28*, Sarah A. 24, Theadore 3, Mary E. 2
KERBY, Rebecca 21*
HARRISON, Thomas 35, Loucinda 32, Mary A. 12, Nancy A. 10, John W. 8, William H. 6, Eada 5, Elizabeth 3, Elisha 2/12
SCRIVNER, James 73, Susanah 78, James D. 43, Sarah C. 39, Mourning 14 (B,f)
WAGES, Simpson M. 23, Martha A. 24, Coleman D. 4/12
QUINN, A. W. 57 (m)*, Nancy 47, Andrew J. 18, Green W. 16, Richard J. 14, James S. 13, Sidney K. 10 (m)
VAUGHN, William 32*
HENDRICKS, William 59, Mary 43, Sally A. 23, Marium 21, James 19, Mahaney 16 (f), Louisa 14, Rebecca J. 12, Elihu 9, Narcena 7, William 5, John 3, Woodson 4/12

Schedule Page 95

LYNCH, Sidney 27 (m), Aria C. 21, Calatius 2, Benjamin H. H. 1
ROBERTS, George 42, Polly 37, Abram 16, William B. 14, Lucy A. 11, Richard 9, Mary A. J. 8, Letha A. 6, Maria L. 4, John P. M. 3, Sarah F. 1
BARKER, William 42, Sally A. 34, Angeline 17, Abram 15, Susanah 10, William 9, Margaret A. 7, Emarine F. 5, John C. 3
COX, Perry 25, Elizabeth 24, John H. 5, Simpson 2, Martha A. 2/12
HENDERSON, Elenor 37, Orthervile D. 20, Joshua T. 17, Martha J. 15, Abram 11, William D. 9
REYNOLDS, Lewis 28, Susan 17, William D. 10/12
COFFEE, Coleby 50, Mary 46, John 19, Susan 14, Theresa A. 12, Matilda 10, William 8, Osborn 4, Mary J. 2, Elizabeth 5
ADAMS, William 79, Elizabeth 76
RICE, Frances 44, John 25, Thomas J. 23, William L. 19, Elizabeth E. 15, Henry C. 11, Charles 9, Mary L. G. 7, Silas T. 3
KELLEY, Harrison 36, Paulina 33, Manerva 16, Samuel 14, Nancy M. 9, William H. 1
ROGERS, William 53, Abegail 50, Marcus 19, Nancy 17, Hiram 15, Hezekiah 14, Alley J. 13 (f), Isaac 11, Sarah 8
RUBLES, William 28, Mary J. 22, John W. 7, Joshua 5, George 3, James O. 8
GENTRY, Jaila 51 (f), Bailey 18, David W. 15, Ann E. 11

Schedule Page 96

ASBELL, James 28, Paulina 19, Hardin 3, Mary E. 2, Josephine 8/12
COYLE, Jesse 69*, Jane 49, Barley 18 (f), Armilda 16, Salena J. 14, Tabitha A. 12, Marthane A. 8

1850 Census Estill County Kentucky

HUNT, Arthusan 40 (f)*, James E. 3
HARRIS, Jeremiah V. 39, Frances 31, Lucy A. 12, Byston 10, Mary 9, Milly 7, Elizira 5, Sarah E. 2, Emily 1/12
COYLE, Francis M. 26, Tillitha 22, Sally A. 3, Pleasant M. 9/12
BENTON, Cyrus 27, Nancy 20, James L. 3, Walter J. 2
KELLEY, Rachael 43, Hiram 18, Robert 15, Amelia 13, Sidney 11 (m), Elbridge 8
NICKERSON, William 45, Polly 45, F. J. 20 (m), Frances J. 19, Cassius 16, Mary 14, Samuel 13, Archibald 11, William 9, Martha A. 7, Elizabeth 4
ALLCORN, John 35, Sally A. 32, Manerva 13, Lousinda 11, Albert 9, Sandford 7, Martha 5, Jemima 4/12
RICHARDSON, John H. 34, Fanney 27, Nancy A. 5
NEAL, William 35, Paulina 30, Nancy J. 8, Isaac 6, Joseph A. 4, Sally 2, Joshua 6/12
CLEMENTS, Jonathan 42, Nancy 42, Sally B. 18, John R. 16, Elizabeth A. 15, James M. 13, William T. 10, David H. 8, Jasper N. 7, Zackary T. 3, Gustavus H. 10/12
WILSON, Ebenezer 55*, Rhoda 63, Andelina 23, Lydia 78

Schedule Page 97

WINKLER, Anderson 22*
WILSON, William D. 30*, Marium 25, Abner 4, John 2, Rhoda 2/12
JAMISON, Irvine 20*
BENTON, Joseph 28, Lydia J. 25, Albert D. 5
FRY, Catharine 61, John 20, Valentine 17
SCRIVNER, John L. 37, Louanna 29, Volentine H. 9, Hickman 7, Hulda 5, Mary E. 1
WHITE, Thomas 35, Polly 34, Michael F. 13, Sarah C. 11, Maria J. 6, William T. 4, James H. 9/12
ARVINE, William 35*, Sally A. 25, John W. 4, Sarah F. 2, Edwin T. 9/12
PRATHER, Carroll 30 (m)*
WRIGHT, Thomas J. 20*, Grunt? 21 (f)
SPARKS, Joseph 24, Malinda J. 22, James J. 4, Michael J. 3
WHITE, Jonathan 47, Sarah 31, Rhoda E. 13, Joseph D. 10, William M. 8, Jonathan C. 6, Margaret F. 4
PARK, Solomon D. 36, Lucy 29, Cassius M. 10, Turner 2, Mardrida 5/12
PARK, Winney 38, Solomon D. 16, Emaline 14, David 12, Louisa 10, Armilda 8, Mary T. 6
DURBIN, James 25, Fanny 19, Emaline 2, Mary E. 1
ROBINSON, Hugh L. 37, Rebecca 22, Hannah J. 6/12
WINKLER, John 31*, Louvinia 40, Benjamin 11, John R. 8, William R. 7, Curtis 4, David 3, Jefferson 3/12
HENDRICKS, Milly E. 16*
ELLISON, William 45, Peggy 47, Elizabeth 22, Andy 21, Elias 18, Thomas 16, Sally A. 12
HISLE, Daniel 28, Nancy 27, Walker 9, Broaddus 7, Simpson 4, Emily J. 1

Schedule Page 98

TIPTON, Jacob 49, Hannah 40, Laura G. 20, Rebecca A. 17, America E. 13, Hubanks 10, William 78
RICHARDSON, John 58, Barbary 52, Elizabeth 26, Chilton 24, Matilda 20, Paulina 19, William 17, Simpson 14, Ann E. 12
SCRIVNER, Morgan J. 35, Sarah A. 29, Elizabeth F. 6, Syntha A. 5, Lewis M. 2
PLOWMAN, James 27, Syntha 25, Theopholus 9/12

1850 Census Estill County Kentucky

TIPTON, Jesse 53, Frances 49, Delila 25, Samuel W. 23, Joseph 21, Elizabeth 19, Mary 15, John 13, James 6

ALEXANDER, John 29, Abbey 26, Polly A. 8, Nancy E. 3, Elizabeth F. 2, Morton 1/12

BURTON, Allen 47, Lydia 44, John N. 16, Tempey J. 13, Sarah 12, Lockey H. N. 10, Greenberry 6, Emaline 4, Uriah 2

PARK, Jonah 44*, Malinda 39, John 22, Sarah Ann 20, Mary E. 16, Susan 14, William W. 12, Eliza F. 8, Marrinda 6

CRAWFORD, Mary 25* (B), Ann M. 4

NOLAND, Hayard P. 27, Mary A. 18

ARVINE, John 45, Sally 43, Martha A. 19, William 17, Joseph 13, John 11, Jamison 9, Demarious 7 (f), Samuel 5, Zackary T. 2, Emily F. 7/12

ELKINS, Anna 43, John 17, Louvina 15, Louvisa 12, Tillitha 10, Amanda 7

BARNETT, Mathew 30, Elizabeth 21, Mary J. 5, Nancy 2

Schedule Page 99

KING, Margaret 71*, Susan 45, Lourana 29

FOX, John 6*

ARVINE, Sally 35, Jesse 14, Jamison 12, William B. 9

TUBBS, Mary 70*

WATSON, Elizabeth 38*, William 17

CROUCH, Mary 5*

WOOSLEY, Thomas 30, Elizabeth 26, James J. 7, Mary 6, George W. 4, Dillard 3, Margaret 8/12

LAY, Willis 31, Elizabeth 32, Archy 13, William 10, Thomas J. 8, Ellen 6, Elijah 4, Rossy? 1 (m)

WILLIAMS, Dennis 49, Mildred 51, Margaret 19, William T. 17, Ann E. 15, James R. 13, John D. B. 9, Morton P. 6

RAWLINS, Benjamin H. 54, Sally 53, Benjamin 21, D. Breck 20 (m), Lucy Ann 17, Owen 15

SCRIVNER, Amelia 46, Elizabeth 17, Anderson 16, Joseph C. 14, Hannah 11, Mary B. 9, David N. 2

SCRIVNER, Joseph 63, Rebecca 50

SCRIVNER, William 31*, Elizabeth 22, Elizabeth A. 3/12

PLOWMAN, Ambrose 16*

ABNER, Arzela 13*

SCRIVNER, Joseph jr. 34, Polly 28, Julia A. 8, Mary J. 6, Sylvester 4, John 2, Martin 10/12

GRAY, Marcus 68, Barsheba 41, Jasper 13, Jackson 12, Marcus 9, Morgan 7, George 5, Loucinda 1

PARK, Ebenezer 74

SCRIVNER, John 68, Mary 59, Mary 24, Martha A. 19, Benjamin F. 17

RICHARDSON, Joseph 39, Polly 34, Julia A. 17, America 15, Nancy 13, John 11, William 8, Emily J. 6, Marcus 4, George W. 2, James M. P. 2/12

Schedule Page 100

SCRIVNER, Joseph Q. 29, Ann E. 19, John T. 11/12

FLINN, Levi 47, Loucinda 21, Syntha A. 19, John 13, George W. 11, Jefferson 9, Westley 7, Louisa J. 3, Stephen 92, Anna 13

LOGAN, William S. 34, Ellen 24, William 7, Mary 5, James 3, Jane 1

HOOVER, Daniel 44, Dianah 48, Rachael 20, Rebecca 17, Arcidney 13 (f), John A. J. 12

RICHARDSON, Bradley 68, Martha 55, Elizabeth 18, George W. 17

1850 Census Estill County Kentucky

RICHARDSON, Bradley 24, Susan 21, Cassino 1
RICHARDSON, Zachary 22, Catharine 18
FOX, Catharine 60, John 27, Elmyra 18, William R. 16
RICHARDSON, John 32, Nancy 26, Coleman D. 5, Harriet A. 4, Michel 2 (m), George W. 2/12
FREEMAN, Moab 56, Tennessee 43 (f), Mary J. 22, Thomas 20, Michel 18 (m), Tontroy? R. 16(m), Elizabeth A. 14, Samuel 11, Sandford 9, Sarah F. 6, Sally A. 4, Chaney 2 (f), Madleton 2 (f)
SPARKS, Frances 49, Daniel 22, Susanah 19, Caty 17 (f), Mary 14, Nancy 14, Isaac T. 12, Solomon 7
HILL, James 58
COX, John 37, Syntha A. 29, Sarilda 9, Mary F. 8, Charles 4
STEPHENS, Emily 18, Humphrey 3, John 1
STEPHENS, Mary 38, Mary J. 13, Elizabeth 1
FOWLER, Isaac 23, Eada 23, Jeremiah 3, Carter 2, Lewis 4/12

Schedule Page 101

MCQUEEN, John 47, Rachael 37, Robert 15, Polly 13, Barnett 11, Joseph 9, John 8, Daniel 6, Sally A. 1
MOORE, William 22, Alice 18
SPARKS, William 38, Sally A. 22
FLINN, William 23, Susan E. 17, Jesse 14
SPARKS, Barnett 35, Polly 33, Elizabeth 11, Eliza 9, Thomas 7, George 5, Agnes 3, Robert 3/12
MUCK, Joseph 34, Elizabeth 22, William J. 8, Mary J. 6, Stephen 4, Azaniah 3 (m), Patsy 1
MUCK, Joseph 60, Elizabeth 54, Humphrey 23, Elizabeth 15, Solomon 19, James 17, Louisa 13, Francis M. 11, Stephen 7
JOHNSON, Louvisa 22, Nancy J. 7, Eada 4, Jackson 2
ISAACS, Ficlden 34, Susan 34, Cornelius 14, Wilbourn 11, Darius 7, Jasper 4, Alfred 2
PHILLIPS, Bright 36, Polly 27, Sarah F. 7, Franklin 5, Andrew J. 4, Sylvana 2
GREEN, Elias 57, Susan 47, Samuel 16, Abram 13, Abner 11, Celia 7, Eada 5, Agnes 4, Stephen 1
HUGHES, Margaret 69, Caleb 24
CAIN, James 45, Martha 55, James M. 16, William 13, John 10
GABBARD, Phillip 50, Jane 50, Wiatt? 18, Mary 14, Matilda 12, George 8
COLLINS, Levi 36, Matilda 26, Sarah 18, William 17, Syntha 9, Elizabeth 8, Nancy J. 2

Schedule Page 102

HARRISON, Iva 60, Sally 20, Rachael 15, Nathan 2
HARRISON, William 23, Elizabeth 17
LAY, Green 29, Nancy 28, Mary J. 11, Sally A. 9, Delila 7, Elenor 5, William R. 3, Armilda 4/12
MURPHY, John 84, Lucy 20, Harrison 10, Pearson 7, Eliza 5, Elhannon 2
MURPHY, John 41, Catharine 37, Jesse 13, Nancy A. 10, William B. 7, Elihu 4, Malinda 9/12
COX, Benjamin 56, Elizabeth 46, John 19, Hardin 17, Milton 13, Julia A. 11, Hannah F. 7, Ann E. 4
COX, Benjamin 30, Elizabeth 38, Eliza J. 8, Sally A. 6, Louana 3, Liberty 9/12 (m)
COX, James 33, Sally A. 27, Frances 3
LAKES, Rebecca 48*, Octava 16
ALEXANDER, James 69*
COLLINS, William 27, Mary J. 23, Timothy 4, Margaret 3, Francis M. 1
COLLINS, James 67*, Nancy 61
BARKER, Polly 34*, Nancy A. 7, Nathan 5

- 79 -

1850 Census Estill County Kentucky

LYNCH, Calvin 29, Lucy 27, William W. 7, Lavina C. 5, Loucinda 3, Joseph 1
FOWLER, Perdilla 35, Andrew J. 7, Patience 5
PARK, Hiram 45*, Malinda 43, Susan 18, Marium 16, Winna 14, Angeline 12, Elizabeth J. 10, Drucilla 7, Mercy 5 (f), Spicey 3 (f)
EASTIS, Elisha 52*
RICHARDSON, Woodson P. 33, MArium 34, John 12, Mary E. 10, Barbara A. 8, Susan F. 6, Paulina 4, Sally 2

Schedule Page 103

PARK, Hezekiah 43, Mercy 47, Mary 17, Angeline 15, Francis M. 14, Martha 12, George 9, Stephen 5
CHILES, William 72*, Olivia 45, Susan M. 14, Benjamin M. 12, James M. 10, Emily M. 8, Henry C. 32, William H. 9, George P. 7
BRADLEY, Richard N. 35*
BOONE, M. R. D. 28 (m)*
CURD, Nancy J. 21*
BRUCE, Benjamin G. 23*, Louisa 22
REYNOLDS, William 29, Rachael 26, Amanda J. 8, William H. 5, Sarah M. 4, James H. 1
MORTON, Asa W. 32, Frances A. 31, Mary E. 10, Frances A. 8, Ann T. 5, James R. 4, Charlett 1
WISEMAN, Isaac 40, John 20, Robert 18, Isaac M. 13, Mary J. 12
VAUGHN, Thomas H. 42, Patsy 40, James W. 19, Fielden 17, Kitty A. 16, Nancy 13, Harriet 11, Elizabeth 9, Milton 2
BARNETT, Stanten 24, Polly 24
JONES, Thomas 34, Elizabeth M. 29, Thompson P. 11, William 9, America 8, Ann 6, Henry 5, Zackary 3, Luther B. 2
BOWMAN, M. M. 33 (m), Mary J. 26, Sarah F. 8, Theopholus 6, George T. 3, William 10/12
BOWMAN, Thomas 28, Margaret 28, Elizabeth 7, Martin 5, Harrison 4, Joseph 2
MCDOWELL, Thomas 57, Jane 58, Elcanah 23, Hugh Allen 12, Thomas 27, Sally 23, Elcanah 4, Nancy J. 3

Schedule Page 104

PEIRATT, James 30*, Mary 35, James 4, Albert W. 2, William B. 10/12
TIPTON, Ellen 45*
BARNETT, Robert 31*, Mary A. 28, John D. 10, Amanda 9, Jonathan 6, Eliza J. 3
DUNAWAY, James 22*
BROWN, James 65*, Philadelphia 60
TIPTON, Philadelphia 12*
BARNES, John 23*
TIPTON, Joseph 40, Margaret 42, Malvina 14, Cyrus 12, Mary F. 11, Susan 10, Elizabeth 9, Sarah M. 5, James T. 3
TIPTON, Reuben S. 54, Betsy 53, Louvisa 30, Samuel W. 28, Paulina 24, Loucinda 22, Mary A. 20, Reuben S. 13
TIPTON, William H. 26, Malinda 26, Elizabeth 6, Reuben S. 4, Louvisa 2, John W. 6/12
JACKSON, Josiah A. 42*, Elizabeth L. 32, S. M. G. 12 (m), George M. 10, Elizabeth G. 8, Mary S. 5, Sarah S. 3
HUNTER, Thomas C. 35*, Sarah F. 24

1850 Census Estill County Kentucky

JONES, Danford D. 69*, Jesse W. 25
ADAMS, Nathan 33*
BIRCH, Abel 36, Mahalia 34, Berry 9, William 8, Andrew J. 7, John 6, Hannah 2
HOWELL, Lucy 66, Anna 28
WATSON, Jeptha 29 (m), Susan 30, Sarah A. 10, William M. 9, Thomas G. 7, Riley W. 2/12, Matilda V. 21, William J. 19, Alexander 17, Samuel R. D. 16
WALDEN, James 56*, Rutha 50, Easter 20, Jefferson 17, Milly A. 15, Lucy A. 13, Elizabeth 11
BLYTHE, Samuel 4*
ADAMS, Richard 33, Martha 46, Elizabeth 13
WATSON, Isaac T. 31, Elizabeth 30, Susan 12, Abigail 10, William T. 8, Matilda V. 7, John D. 6, Sarah 4, Mary A. M. 2

Schedule Page 105

GILLASPIE, Thomas J. 33, Syntha 24, Abba J. 7, William R. 4, Nancy A. 1
MOORE, James 64, Margaret 64
MOORE, Samuel 25, Loucinda 25, Martin 6, James 4, Thomas 2
RAINEY, Elihu 26, Anjamima 19, Christo. D. 10/12
RAILSBACK, David 42*, Martha E. 38, James 22, NAncy 20, Mary 8, Mahalia 5, Richard 1
SMITH, Sarah J. 18*, Martha E. 16, John P. 14, William H. H. 10
HARRIS, Anderson 36, Elizabeth 24, Candis 3/12 (f)
LYLE, John 25, Rachael 30, Anderson 16, Daniel 12, Frances 10, Amanda 8
BENTON, Jesse 62, Phebe 56, Elihu 18, Jesse 16, James 12, Mitchael 30
JUDY, Henry M. 31*, Milly 31, Milton B. 3, Boone 8/12
CLARK, Thomas 11*
HAWKINS, Thomas 62, Sally 62
EASTER, James D. 28, Ailsey 24, Jesse 3, Albert 11/12
CRAFFORD, Harvey 43, Nelly 40, Sanders 15, William 13, Jane 11, Susan 8, James H. 4, John M. 2, John 1/12
BOWMAN, Sarah 54*, Seldon F. 28, Constantine 25
HUNT, Armina 18*
COCKRILL, E. L. 28 (m)*, Rebecca 26, Mary P. 2
MCMONIGAL, Aaron 18*
ELLIOTT, Thomas 36, Martha J. 28, Amelia 11, Phillip J. 8, William D. 6, Elizabeth 4, Martha J. 2, Dorson D. 2/12

Schedule Page 106

HAMILTON, Lewis D. 45, Elizabeth 34, Thomas J. 11, Emaline 9, John F. 7, Malinda 5, Elizabeth 3, James L. 1
JOHNSON, Alexander 29, Elizabeth 22
HAMILTON, Anderson 39, Malinda 40, William J. 14, Delina 11, Nancy 9, Robert L. 6, Henry C. 2
ARVINE, Nancy 69*, Jesse 27
JOHNSON, Nancy 22*
WINKLES, Levi 23, Patsy 20, James 4, Josiah 2
WINKLES, William 26, Polly 19, William 2, Elizabeth 6/12
MOORE, William 41*, Elizabeth 29, Rachael 7, Margaret 5, Nancy 2

1850 Census Estill County Kentucky

WYATT, Margaret 70*
EASTIS, Charles 56, Sally 52, Debba 22, Hiram 12, Charles 11, Polly 10, Asbury 8
HORN, Elizabeth 44, Emaline 17, Malinda 14, John 12, Susan 9, William 5, Rebecca A. 5
HORN, Simpson 22, Louisa J. 18, Nancy A. 1
ASHCROFT, Gideon 49, Nancy 47, William 26, John 14, Gilrad? 12 (m)
EASTIS, Elisha 49, Rachael 46, Gilford 22, Merryweather 20, Dulcena 17, Martin V. 14, Artitus 11 (m), Luther 10, Bluford 10, Hambleton 8, Glenmore 6, Winfield S. 3
KELLY, Dolly 66
BARKER, Jincey 29 (f), Elias 12, Polly A. 10, William 9, Peggy 7, John 3
KINCAID, John 45, Emily 35, Margaret P. 16, Edward D. 14, Patience A. 12, Nancy A. 10, James S. 8, John F. 6, George B. 4

Schedule Page 107

DURBIN, Francis 30, Margaret 24, John P. 1
DURBIN, William H. 21, Mary 21, Nancy A. 3/12
DURBIN, Edward 32, Elvina 32, Arvina 11, Nancy 10, Armina 9, William F. 8, John S. 7, Melvina 5, Loucinda 4, Thomas E. 3, Sarah A. 1
ARVINE, Nathaniel 43*, Loucinda 32, Nancy M. 2
SPARKS, Sally A. 13*
FRANKLIN, John L. 25*
WALLACE, John 52*, Louanna 37, Joseph 11, Mary J. 4, Louvisa 2
WEST, William W. 14*
SPARKS, William 17*, James 15
HORN, Warren 36, Syntha A. 31, Uriah 16, Littleton 13, Polly A. 10, Sally A. 6, Jackson 4, Jerusha 2 (f)
WARNER, Anderson 26, Maria 20, Dillard 2, John 1
GRIFFITH, Benjamin F. 33, Malvina 34, Charles 8, Armilda A. 6, Jesse 5, William K. 1
WARNER, Daniel 29, Nancy 27, Armilda 10, Elizabeth 7, Nancy A. 5, John W. 3, Wesley 9/12
TODD, Harvey 32, Nancy 6
HORN, Jackson 30, Polly 28, Sarilda 9, Vina 7, Wesley 5, John 3, Aaron 1
HORN, Aaron 51, Elizabeth 50, William 25, Woodson 20, Mitchell 16, Rebecca 13, Susan J. 9, Thomas 7
WATSON, Daniel 20
INGRAM, Hardin 29, Debba 23, William S. 3, James M. 1
HORN, Susan 76, Jerusha 40
WOOSLEY, Chilton A. 21, Sarah A. 20
POYNTER, James 34*, Narcyssa L. 24, Mary C. 2

Schedule Page 108

CHAMBERS, Evaline 7*
WINKLES, JAmes 46, Polly 47, Emaly J. 15, Mary Jane 13, Elizabeth 7, Edward S. 2, Amanda J. 1
REYNOLDS, John W. 56*, Lucy 48
PLOWMAN, Sally 21*
BENTON, Milton 35, Angeline 33, Coleman D. 11, Curtis M. 9, Amanda J. 7, Delina F. 4, Henry J. 2/12
MIZE, Isaac 56*, Nancy 51, Robert 17, Frances 14, Isaac 12
MOORE, Sarah 18*

1850 Census Estill County Kentucky

TIPTON, John J. 50, Martha 43, Mockafee 22 (m), Sally 19, Jonathan 18, Ally 17, Samuel 15, John 11, Martha F. 5
HAMILTON, Alexander D. 38, Nancy 33, Rufus 10, Elizabeth A. 8, Malvina 6, Louisa 4, Albert 2
BROADDUS?, Edward J. 36, Sarah 35, Frances 6, Elizabeth 4, Pleasant 4, Ann 3, Bemsly 1 (m)
WITT, David 50, Nancy 46, William M. 12, Henry G. 9, David 5
WEBB, Richard 45, Clemency 45 (f), William J. 23, Elijah P. 22, Julia A. 21
HINDS, Samuel 29, Mary 33, Albert F. 8, Howard W. 5
MORRIS, Jacob E. 33, Polly 33, Sylvester 11, Mary E. 9, John W. 7, Mason 6, David 3, Eliza A. 1/12
WINKLER, Lewis 56, Sally 59, Henry 16, Bethel 12
HARRIS, Milton V. 30, Ann T. 22, Ann E. 2, Eliza J. 6/12
PRITCHETT, Edward 65, Kisiah 53, Isaac 22
HAMILTON, Elizabeth 60, Granville D. 25, Julia Ann 17
BURTON, John 44*, Milly 40, Irvine 19, Richard 17, Vanburen 13, Owen 11, Ann E. 9, Amaline 7, William 5, Thomas H. 2

Schedule Page 109

ROBINSON, John F. 68*
PARK, Solomon B. 47*, Eliza 37, Mortimore 17, Jefferson 15, Thomas 13, Elihu 11, Samuel 9, William C. 1/12
CHILES, William P. 28*, Amanda M. 19
GARRETT, Andrew 32, Deborah 33, Robert H. 20, Benton 18, John 17, Thomas J. 13, Rinton 4, David 2, Malinda 18, MArtha A. 15, Manerva 11, B. M. 9 (f), Nancy E. 7, Mary 5
RIDDELL, Sally 42, Eliza J. 18, Amilda C. 14, Aquillan E. 10
RICHARDSON, William 65, Mary 63, John T. 14
RICHARDSON, William 35, Mahal 30, Harvey 7, Artemissa J. 5, Mary E. 1
KIRBY, Elisha 22, Lavina 20, William H. 2/12
KIRBEY, Elisha 56, Nelly 44, Robert 21, Permelia 19, Frances 17, John H. 14, Mary E. 12, Eptharine 10 (f), William 8, Joel 6, Asenath 3 (f), James J. 1
RIDDELL, Robert 36, Celna? 26 (f), John 8, William 4, Roland 1, Alice 55
RIDDELL, Adam 47, Angeline 16, William J. 15, John 12, Robert L. 9, Sarah E. 7, Cyrus G. 4, Elizabeth 3
WHITE, Henry F. 22, Elizabeth 17, William H. 1/12
BENTON, Richard T. 40, Esther 38, Mary A. 14, William G. B. 12, Jesse 9, Elihu 6, Amanda 4, Emaline 1

Schedule Page 110

THOMSON, Jesse 32, Mary J. 27, Elzady 5 (f), Polly A. 4, Sally A. 3, Squire 1
BOWEN, William 44*, Maria 40, Martha 18, John 16, Nancy 14, Mary A. 13, James 11, Emily 10, Sarah 6, William 4, Rhoda 2, Thomas 6/12
LANE, William 28*
WINKLER, Jackson 29, Maria 26, Lewis 7, Willis 6, Delina 5, Andrew J. 1
PEARSON, Lucy 65
WINKLER, Lewis 25, Emily J. 18
GARRISON, Morgan 30*, Rachael A. 26, Sarah E. 5, George W. 4, Nicholas R. 2, William G. 11/12
STEPHENS, Emily 25*

1850 Census Estill County Kentucky

JONES, Tarleton 31, Luan 30, William C. 10, Eli 8, Sally A. 7, James 3
LANE, James B. 21, Rebecca 17, Nancy E. 8/12
DILLINGHAM, Henry H. 59, Elihu 19
FARDING, Jeremiah 33, Rachael 33, Elizabeth 12, Joel 10, Dudley 8, Sally A. 5, Nathan 1
JOHNSON, Joseph 27, Anna 30, William 3, James 1
WOODSON, Ayrael? 37 (m)*, Jane 36, Paulina 3, Henry T. 1
BUSH, Nancy 78*
WILLIS, McKinsey 51, Polly 50, William 16, Marium 14, Loucinda 10
SHUCK, David 50*, Louisa 30
PEARSON, Lourena 6*
LAWSON, Theresa 38, Gabriel G. 17
SKINNER, Elizabeth 60*
LAWSON, Patsy 32*, Sally 28
WOODSON, Elizabeth 39, William J. 13, Anna A. 11, Sally A. J. 7, Dethridge B. 2
WOODSON, Tarleton 70, Sally 59, Polly 37, Elizabeth A. 15, George W. 10

Schedule Page 111

BAXTER, Mary 75
WARFORD, Joel 50, Nancy 49, Susan 25, James 24, John 21, Benjamin 16, Eliza 13, Elizabeth 13, Silas J. 11, Levi H. 9, Joel A. 6
WARFORD, Mitchell 22, Elizabeth 21, William H. 8/12
WARFORD, Abraham 77, Rebecca 81
BENTON, Eli 39*, Sally A. 24, Riston 3 (m), William B. 1
WAGES, Judy 85* (B)
FINNEY, Squire 51, Nancy 43, June 22, Samyra 17, Julia 15, Nancy 13, Filman 11, Eliza 9, William 5, Thomas R. 2
WHITE, Rutha 46, Catharine 16, Nancy 14, Emaline 7, Richard 27, Elizabeth 24, William J. 4, Nancy 3, Susan J. 3/12
FINNEY, Amos 42, Elizabeth 43, Elizabeth 14, Susan 12
CALIHAN, Mary 59, Rebecca 24, Lucy E. 5
JESSEE, Thomas J. 24, Ann 22, William 4, Mary A. 2
RICHARDSON, Ryon 50, Jemima 49, Elizabeth 17, William 15
NEAL, Creath 36 (m), Sally 35, Andy 12, Rebecca J. 11, William H. 5, Samuel 3, James R. 7/12
TOWNSEND, John 52, Betsy 45, Armilda 15, Elizabeth 13, John 10, Ambrose 2
CHANEY, John 65, Jemima 62, Daniel 24
CHANEY, Hiram 23, Rebecca 26, Nancy 3, John W. 1
COLE, James 40, Louvisa 42, Sally A. 18, Nancy G. 17, William S. 15, John H. 13, Emily J. 11, B. B. 9 (m), Armina 7, Mary 5, Elizabeth E. 1

Schedule Page 112

PEARSON, Henry 29, Catharine 25, Thomas G. 6, James L. 4, Lucy F. 2
CHAMBERLIN, William 36, Nancy 26, Richard 6, John 4, David 1
PRATHER, John M. 42, Eliza J. 25, Margaret A. 20, Thomas 14, Annis 10, James W. 7, John 5, William 2

1850 Census Estill County Kentucky

FLIRTY, Ezekial 31, Laure 22 (f), Ransom 5/12
WISEMAN, JAcob B. 39, Sarah A. 30, James D. 9, Ann E. 7, Louisa 5, Sarah E. 2
COX, William 25, Polly A. 20, Edwin R. 2
HENRY, Peggy 48, Eada 18, Joseph 13, Ivan 11, John W. 7
POWERS, John K. 49, Emely 30, Joshua F. 22, Edmund R. 17, Frances C. 13, Simon 10, Josephine 6, John W. 4
CROUCH?, Thomas 46*, Nancy 32, Loucinda 16, Loucinda 14, Audley 12, William H. 10, Milly 6, Silvester 4, Nancy L. 1, David 40
PRATHER, William 30*
BLACKWELL, Nancy 51*, Samuel 21, Joseph 19, Susan 17, Elizabeth 15
SPARKS, Nancy M. 7*
ANEME?, Thomas G. 35, Nancy 30, Nathaniel 10, Jane 8, Mary A. 6, William J. 3, Christopher N. 1
KING, Simon P. 29, Evaline 23, John H. 6, Joseph N. 5, Margaret E. 4, Samuel W. 1
WILLIS, Merrill 21, Mahalia 20, Lucy A. 1
PLOWMAN, Henry 37, Jane 40, Sally A. 17, Nancy 15, Mary J. 12, Barnett 8, Thomas J. 7, William S. 3

Schedule Page 113

GRIGGS, Fielden 55, Milly 55, Polly 18, Milly A. 16, Martha J. 15, Fielden 11
SHARP, William A.L.B. 32, Elizabeth 27, Mary Ann 5, Aaron A. 3, Elizabeth 1, A. Low 18 (m)
HACKETT, Granville 28, Sarah Ann 23, Sarah Ann 3, Benjamin F. 2
PARK, William 68, Sally 64
WILSON, Jesse C. 30*, Sarilda 27, Nathan 9, Milly 8, Jesse 2
BENTON, Judy 18*

Page 86 Blank

1850 Census Fayette County Kentucky

Schedule Page 114

MILTON?, Wm. E. 39*, James __, _____ 12 (m), Martha J. 9, Elizabeth 6?, Mary W. 9 3?
TAYLOR, George 85?* (B)
PINDELL, Henry C. 27*, J. A. 24 (f)
VICK, Henry C.? 14*, Ann R. 12, Mary B. 9, George R. C. 3?
BAYLISS, Jesse 47?, Mary 31, Sarah 25, Rebecca 9, Edward O. 7, Ann S. 5, Lucy 3, Jesse 1
SHARP, Robert M. 40*, Matilda 39, Mary F. 11, Charles 6, Sarah A. 5
HINTON?, Mary R. 6/12*
GEORGE, Melurath 30, Elizabeth 23, Lucinda 10, Elizabeth 3
LANGHORN, Levi 36, Martha 36, Isaac 17, Malinda 15, Sarah Ann 14, Caraline 12, Jefferson 10, Milton 4
KNOBLE, David 34, Sharlotte 30, Edward 6, Henry 4, Mary 2, John 1
BAWZER?, Robert 35*, John 6
CALELAZER?, Sarah 28*
SPEGLE, George Ann 24*, Cilestine 7, Charlton 5
RICHARDSON, Elenor 17*
HARRISON, Saml. 29*
CHINN, Rachael 60 (B), Wm. 60
PARKE, Margaret 57*
HUDY, Hester J. 24*
HALDEN, Josephine 12*
BURNELL?, Anthony 55 (B), Martha 10
JOHNSON, Sarah 40 (B), Frances 9, Alfred 3, Martha 1
ROGERS, Dorithy 53*
RATHBURN, James? 25*, Ellen W. 20, Benj. F. 5/12
CAMPBELL, Enos 32*, Mary E. 23, Ernest 5
WOODFORD, Eliza B. 15*
TEPPER, Mary L. 15*
DARR, Sarah M. 15*
ALLEN, Sarah 15*
ROBERTS, Emma 13*
FORSYTH, J. M. 30 (m)*, Rachael M. 28, Orenlea? 32, Alex. T. 5, Robert B. 3, Joel H. 1
BARNETT, Eliza 63*, Joseph G. 22

Schedule Page 115

COGGSHELL, John B. 29, Mary Ann 26, George 63, Sarah 3
COLELAZER, James 40*, Elizabeth 27, Robert 5, Catharine 3
TYRA, William 47*, Permelia 47, Susan 25
WATTS, John B. 39*, Harriet 38, William B. 4
RYAN, George W. 13*
GUSS?, Jane S. 10*
RHODES, Elizabeth 30*
NICKSON, James 15*, thomas 13
BOWYER?, Ezra 36*
AUSTIN, H.? P. 25, Lucinda 21, Mary A. 3

1850 Census Fayette County Kentucky

HOWELL, H. R. 30 (m)*, Mary F. 30, Robert A. 11
KITTMAN?, Ann 71*
DALEY, Benjamin 44, Sarah a38, Evan 11, Ann 9, Sarah E. 7, David M. 4, Josephine 2
MCCONNELL, Herbert 22*, Ann A 18, Susan E. 3/12
BROCK, Isaac 17*
SCOTT, Matilda 45*
GRAVES, John 48*, Margaret 37, Levi 14
KIBLER, Susan 7*
AUSTIN, William 32, Martha J. 30, Rosea Ann 12, Mary M. 10, Leonidas B. 8, Frances O. 6, Sidney E. 4, Davidella 2
BABCOCK, George W. 28, Sabina 27, Mary E. 3, Dillila 11/12
STILFIELD, John 38, Elizabeth 42, Margaret A. 10?, Thomas R. 14, John K. 12, James F. 9, William H. 8, Sarah E. 7, Martha J. 6, Mary L. 2
MYRES, John 40, Emily 40, Margaret F. 25, John 12, Virginia 8, James K. P. 6
SELF, William Jr. 24, Margaret 47, Sarah 18, Elizabeth 12, William Jr. 24
SELF, Henry A. 27, Virginia 22, William D. 3, Margaret A. 1
SAXTON, Henry A. 30*, Ann E. 24, Mariam E. 8, Oswald O. 6, Henry A. 4, Ann E. 2, Julia M. 2/12

Schedule Page 116

PARKER, Elizabeth 45*, Oswald 45, Cassus C. 40
MERCHANT, John 40*, Ann 29
BELERT?, George 44*, Septua 16, Catharine 68
HANIM?, David D. 20*
TRAVIS, John 26, America 23, Frances 21, John Jr. 24, William 4, John F. 2
MCCARTY, Jerimiah 48*, Cynthia 50
ADAMS, Mary 27*
BRECKENRIDGE, Mary E. 32 (B), Smith 9, J. A. 7, Chas. W. 4
SIKES, Jane 50* (B)
ROGERS, Edward 75* (B)
JACKSON, Peter 64 (B), Amanda 45
HALL, Elizabeth 54*, Ellen J. 16
CALLOWAY, William 33*
JENKINS, Charles 32*, Julia 25, Mary A. 9, Chas. K. 7, Lewis 4, Sarah 3/12
GEORGE, Harrison 26*
HOGAN, Martha 59*
WILLIAMS, James 25* (B), Alsey 24, John 35, William E. 4, James H. 1
DAVIS, George 11* (B)
RUTHERFORD, Zerilda 28*
WHITNEY, Emily 13, Mary 10*, Laura 8, Henry Clay 6, Joseph 4, Julia 1
THOMAS, Charles B. 25, Sarah 40, Sarah A. 21, Barrack G. 23
PLUNKETT, William F. 43*, Jane 28, Martha 11, Nannie 8/12
PILCHER, Frances 27*
WINSLOW, Hallitt? M. 76*, Sarah 65, Ann 20
SANDERS, Sarah 39*, Sarah W. 11
WADDLE, Septimus 76, Elizabeth 65, Zacharia 23, William 17
CARTER, Saml. 60 (B), Mary 60

1850 Census Fayette County Kentucky

ACKMAN, John 38, Pamelia 38, John 16, George M. 12, Wm. H. H. 9, Sarah E. 6, Wiley F. 4, Samuel T. 2
LANGDON, Ann 73, Harriet 44

Schedule Page 117

ROGERS, Lazarus M. 41, Mildred 26, Julia 11, Emma G. 6, George Ann 4, John W. B. 1
LAWRENCE, Ann 55, Mary 30, Thomas 9, Mary C. 8, Theadore 4, Lewis 2
MCKENNON, John 30*, Charlott 20
GRUNDELL?, John 33*
CLABOURN, John 35 (B), Lucy 70, William 28, Fanny 30, Agnus 10, Preston 7
LETCHER, William 70*, Mary B.? 41, Barthenia 6, George E. 9, Mary P. 1
PIANT, Cornelia 13*
ATKINS, R. J. 48 (m), Margaret 47, Robert 21, E. A. 14 (f), Sarah G. 12
STEEL, Thomas 47*, Prissille 34, Mary J. 11, Silas 8, Nancy 7
WEBSTER, Spencer 34*, Jane 65
SPARKS, Polly 39, Robert 13
ENNIS, Elijah 39*, America C. 23, Saml. 13, Charles 1
LALEY, Dennis 48*
HUBER, Joseph 40*
GOFFNEY, Thomas 41*
BARKER, Ann 37*
HANKER, Elizabeth 90*
JUDD, Sarah 84*
SOLOMON, William 69*
STEPHENS, Mary 64*, Nora 64, Ann 44
STAIRS?, Robert N. 1/12*
BARKER, Lewellin 3*
ITCHER?, Wrily 62? (f)* (B), Rachael 84, Jonah 52 (f)
GREEN, Frances __ * (B), John 4
GRIMES, Mary 1* (B)
BLAIR, Malinda 16* (B)
WHITAKER, Vincent 39*
MCCLURE, Thomas 29*
TALBOT, Chas. 30*
DILLEN, Michael 25*
MCGEE, Thomas J. 50 (B), Hulda 32, Mary 13, Nora 11, Margaret 12, Saml. 10, Elizabeth 8, Thomas J. 4, Malinda J. 1
SHUMAKE, Mary 47, William 20
JONES, John H. 37, Mary A. 31, Mary H. 13
STEPHENS, Susan 33*, Hadden 32, Thomas 14, William 13, Jackson 12, Arah J. 6, Mary E. 5

Schedule Page 118

GEORGE, Reuben 23*
METCALF, George 35*, Nancy 35, Henry 16, William 9, George 8, Cisora 6 (m), Charles 1, Mary 70, Margaret 19?

1850 Census Fayette County Kentucky

COLEMAN, Paul 35* (B)
BUFORD, Jeremiah 47 (B)
GRAY, Henry 33*, Eliza A. 31, Martha J. 14, Saml. 11, Robert H. 6, Mary E. 3
SMITH, Benjamin 80*, Joel 50, Paulina 18, Joel 17
CRISSEL, Margaret 37, Margaret 17, Elizabeth 14
MURRAY, David 43, Rachael 42, Olander 20, Edward B. 13, Lucretia 10, David 2
TOLL, Jonathan 35*, Martha 28, Jonathan T. 9, Charles R. 8, J. K. P. 6 (m), Hunseta 4, Andrew J. 2
TOMLINSON, Hethy 57*, Elijah 33
DRAKE, William M. 35, Mary A. 24, Drucila 10, George W. 8, Edward S. 6, Madison S. 8/12
JOHNSON, Peter 34*, Ellen 32, James W. 18, Mary C. 16, John E. 14, B. H. 9 (m), Lavina 8, Chas. C. 5, Robert D. 1
PARKER, Catherine 58*
TANDY, John 45 (B), Susan 35, George H. 16, John L. 15, Charlton H. 14, Susan A. 12, Robert S. 10, Martha E. 8, Elizabeth D. 6, Ann M. 5, Joseph 1
STALEY, John 40, Malinda 40, William 19, John 13, Harrison 10, James H. 8, Catharine 4, Julia 3
WILLIS, John A. 40, Catharine 29, Octavia 10, Orilius 1 (f), John M. 4, Mary E. 1, Elizabeth 68

Schedule Page 119

BUSSARD, Nancy 74?*
ERWIN, Mary 67*
MISSMER?, M. A. 16 (f)*, W. H. 14 (m)
TRAVIS, Nancy 65* (B)
DIXON, Isabella 60* (B)
NICHOLAS, Laura 42 (B), Margaret 14?, Naomi 7, M. J. 3 (m)
HARBERT, Mary 45 (B), Hilra 40
SMITH, Sally 60 (B)
BRICE, Henry 40 (B), Emily 30, Anna 8, M. L. 7 (f), Rebeca 5, Joseph 3, Julia 1
STIFLER, James M. 38*, Susan 30, J. W. 13 (m), J. H. 11 (m)
THOMAS, Samuel 44*
FILLAYSON?, James 28*
BRUIN, James 25, Mary 22, Francis 4, Susan 2
VAUGHN, George W. 30, George Ann 25, Francis 11, Richard 9, Julia 2
LEWIS, S. B. 49 (m), Luvina 16, John W. 13, Stephen G. 12
HARRISON, Thomas J. 39, Margaret B. 17, Fabius? A. 13
SINCLAIR, William 31*, Susan 30, Ann M. 8, M. J. 6 (f), Elsey 55, William 27
MOFFUTT, M. M. 18 (f)*
MCMAINS, robert 32, Elzia 26, John 8, Sarah 6, Mary 4, Robert 2
CONLEY, Louisa 36, Jane 13, Mary 11, Ann M. 10, William 8, Martha 3
WHITT, Mason 34, Mary 31, Louisa 13, Mary A. 11, John 10, Sarah 8
VAUGHTER, Sarah 70*
MARDAC?, Anna 16*
DRAKE, Catharine 30 (B), William 17, Robert 9, J. K. P. 3 (m)
COTTON, John 45* (B)
ALLEN, Celia 28* (B)
MURPHY, Jack 28 (B), Mary 24, John 7/12
YOUNG, John C. 30, Mary E. 20, Charles 3/12

1850 Census Fayette County Kentucky

Schedule Page 120

BLAIR, Caroline 40 (B), David 22, Nancy 18, Malinda 16, Matilda 14
DOYLE, John 45, Bridget 23, Patrick 3, Thomas 2
ALEXANDER, David 46*, Martha 32, M. E. 22 (f), M. J. 17 (f), W. F. 6 (m)
HUTCHINSON, Margaret 68*
LAUDEMAN?, Margaret 16*
HOLMES, James 33*, M. A. 32 (f), Josephine 11, Mary 6, Anna 2, Silas 4
MERRILL, Isabella 65*, Margaret 15, A. 19 (m)
KELLY, Robert 36*, Evaline 28, Nannie 2
WIGART, Alex 27*, Martha 23
PIGG, Lewis 29, Mary 25, Emma 7, Virginia 5, David 1
WEIGART?, William 26, Ann 24, Ann M. 1/12
BORHITE, John A. 28, E. 36 (f)
FORMAN, Saml. 29*, Margaret 34
FONNER, Warren 5*, M. E. 2/12 (f)
PAYNE, Richard 30*, M. S. 30 (f), John 2
PRICE, Ellen 24*, Douglas 10
COONY, James 28, Mary 28, Sarah 30, John 8, Henry 6, Thomas 4, Florence 2
AKEN, Gryza 74*, Jane 35
CAMPBELL, William 20*, Grisseld 20, M. J. 1 (f)
KINKEAD, H.? 46 (m), Jane 46, John J. 22, M. J. 18 (f)
JENNINGS, Pascal 39, Maria 33
INGLES, William 30*, M. B. 23 (f), Frnaklin 3, Gurtrude? 3/12, Hiram 23
VERMONT, Elizabeth 15*
FLEMING, Mary Susan 38*, Mary E. 19, William 17, Susan 15 (m)
CASS, Abba 40* (B)
TAYLOR, Venie 80* (B)
BRUIN, M. 50 (f), Sarah 20
KING, Isaah 36, Catharine 34, Ellen 13, Isaah 5

Schedule Page 121

KYLE, John 39*, Sarah 29, William 9, David 6, John 3
GIBBON, Nancy A. 60*
BROWNSTON, Susan A. 34*
MAGEE, Mary 14* (B)
HAMILTON, Mary 31, John 9, M. E. 7 (f)
ATKINS, Margaret 57, Lewis 36, James 34, Liny 25, Barbara 23
PIGG, James H. 25, George Ann 21, Isam 3, John M. 2
VAUGHN, Ellen 34*
CHRISTIAN, James 32*, John 2
ADAMS, Elizabeth 52*, Andrew 19, Amanda 18, William 15, Mary E. 11
FRY, Chrystopher 25*
DEARMOND, Hester A. 40*
HOOVER, Pelina 15*
HANES, Jefferson 30 (B), Ann 30, Madison 6, Virginia 3, Nancy E. 9
MONTAGUE, Elijah 32, Mary 28, M. A. 8 (f), John 6, George T. 3, Mary F. 3

1850 Census Fayette County Kentucky

MOORE, Harvey 47, Polly 47, Kelly 15, Fanny 13, Alfred 10, Malinda 7
JOHNSTON, James 30*, Mary __
WHITE, Elizabeth __ *
MOORE, Richard 58, Catharine 57, Thomas J. 23, Lucretia 21, Mary 10
HAW?, Alexander 60, Sarah 46, Isabella H. 23, Harriet 20, John 16, Thomas 14, Mary 11, George 9, William 6
RICHARDSON, Margaret 50*, Hannah 21, John 25
MOORE, Catahrine 9*
SMITH, W. M. 44 (m), S. A. 26 (f), J. W. 6 (m), M. E. 4 (f), John C. 2
GARBER, Frederick 41
DUCKIMER?, Catharine 66*, John 34, Harriet 32, Maria 14, Bilsoret? 9 (f), Rosa 2
ROBINSON, Henry 14*, Sarah 13, Thomas 9, Elizabeth 7, George 5

Schedule Page 122

TAYLOR, A. 39 (m)*, Lutitia 40, Luly A. 14, William 11, Lewis 7, Lizzette 1
HOWARD, Mary A. 19*, Gabriel 17
HUKILL, Robbert 30*, Sarah F. 30, James T. 4, C. E. 2 (m), Hulda 10
CONALL, M. A. 11 (f)*, Joseph S. 10, John W. 8
TUTTLE, J. C. 25 (m)*, Elizabeth 27
TANKERSLEY, Danl. 43, Luann 42, A. J. 20 (m), C. A. 18 (m), Danl. 14, Francis 9, C. R. 7 (f)
STEPHENS, Sarah 30, Mary S. 11, Isaac S. 10, David 7, Alvin 5
LEWIS, John 24*, Ellent 23 (f), John R. A. 1, Fielding 80
TEMPY, Elvira 26*
HUGHES, Ferdinand 35*
MEDERS?, John 60*
MILLER, Sophia 45*, Jane 11, Mahala 8, C. 4 (f)
SHARP, William 19*
HUGHES, Mary 22*, Thomas 24, Margaret 7
BUNNELL, Jessee 44
PENNY, S. 26 (m), Sarah A. 25
RICE?, Ta? A. 48 (f)*
RATHNAY, John A. 30*
SPENCER, E. R. 37 (f)*, A. A. 33 (m), Charles 11, William 7, Ellen 5, Edward 2
SHEPPARD, David 26*
WILLSON, Joseph 25*, Elizabeth 18, Frank 4/12
ADAMS, Mary 61*
COOK, Thomas B. 50
HENNASSY, J. R. 29 (m)*, John 60, A. W. 31 (f)
WILLIAMS, A. W. 16 (f)*
ROBERTS, H. S. 14 (m)*
CLEAVELAND, Mary 60*
FRANKLIN, Lucy 56, Margaret 22, Benjamin 5/12
OWENS, W. T. 25 (m)*, Catharine 48
CONNER, M. A. 29 (f)*, Catharine 7
ELDER, David L. 36*, S. A. 35 (f), C.? E. L. 10 (f), George L. C. 8, Julia 6, E. H. C. 2 (f)

1850 Census Fayette County Kentucky

Schedule Page 123

BROWN, A. 41 (f) (B)
COOK, William 47, Margaret 48, S. S. 23 (f), W. P. 19 (m), Darkas T. 16, M. C. 10 (f)
STILFIELD, Elizabeth 73
LANCASTER, Henry 40*, Emaline 36, Mary 12, William 7, Ann J. 3
GURS?, James 26*, Emma 18
DUNHAM, Susan 76*
REED, Mary B. 45*
MERIDETH, Jane 60*
GREENHOW, Sarah 35*
CROSS, A. A. 44 (f)*
FLOURNOY, S. C. 50 (m)*, Crasie 5 (m)
HAWKINS, Elizabeth 66*, Catharine 42, W. H. 26 (m)
BRIDGES, E. A. 8 (f)*
SIMPSON, John 29, E. J. 26 (f), George W. 2
HALL, John 38, Mary 37, John W. 15, S. J. 14 (f), M. C. 13 (f), R. S. 12 (m), Chas. E. 10, M. S. 5 (f), Eliza 4, Julia 2, Louisa 3/12
STONE, George W. 45*, Mary 33
DAVIS, Elizabeth 42*
MARITT, Joseph 32, M. S. 24 (f), M. R. 2 (f)
HAYS, Henetta 33*, William 17, R. A. 13 (f), Martha 10, Andrew 4
HUDSON, Isabella 9*, John 7
ALLEN?, Simeon 18*
PARKER, R. B. 54 (m)*, Eliza 38, M. E. 13 (f), L. J. 10 (f)
RICE, Labina 70*
CORDREY, John L. 29*, Sarah 24, A. E. 7 (f), Dudley 5, James B. 3, Mary 66
RUSSELL, J. C. 14 (m)*, W. H. 12 (m)
SHUMAKE, Thomas 28*, Susan 20
MCMEEKIN, William 55, Sarah 50, Julia 18, Rebecca 20
MCMANIS, James 23, Ann E. 19, Andrew 20
DULAND, Terry 39 (m), Martha 32, Eliza L. 2, Wila A. 1
HAMBROUGH, F. C. 50 (f)*, John C. 20, M. E. 14 (f)

Schedule Page 124

GRAVES, B. F. 45 (m)*
OLIVER, Funky? 50 (f)* (B)
DICKSON, E. 28 (m)* (B)
TURNER, James 33* (B)
WEST, Dolly 70* (B)
WEBB, Lucy 70* (B)
GROOMS, Jane 65*, Emily 33, Malinda 28
SULEY?, A. 16 (m)*
SIOMAY?, Mary J. 8*
GORE, Lewis 5*
BERK, Laura 6*
PAYNE, Matilda 61*, Caroline 35

- 93 -

1850 Census Fayette County Kentucky

HICKS, M. A. 26 (f)*, Amanda 13, Hugh 2, Sanford 3
PRICE, Harrell 29* (B)
MARKER, Malinda 60* (B), Lucy 26, Medoe 29 (m)
CROMWELL, W. B. 33 (m)*, PEYCDPBS 1/12 (M)
SCOTT, Saml. 24*, Caroline 16
ZEISER?, R. E. 40 (m)*, M. 42 (f)
PINKARD, M. 17 (f)*, Ferdinand 14
SHIVEL?, Edwin 24*
JENKINS, James 27*
CHAMBERS, Fayett 32*
KIRKPATRICK, R. 50 (m)*, N. 47 (f)
SHULEY, H. J. 3 (f)*
LONEY, Peter 23*
BONEY, Edward 30*
BYRNES, John 23*
FINNEY, Peter 34*
HARDESTY, Sarah 33, Hincey 29, Magdalena 9, J. H. 7 (m), C. C. 4 (f), George A. 2
MOORE, Henry 33*, Ann 25, Robt. 43
DAVIS, Catharine 11*
FINNELL, Mary 30*, Amanda 2
THOMPSON, Thomas 20*, Saml. 13, Alinder? 45 (m)
SLUTHER, M. 30 (m)*
GENKINS, Esther 50 (B), Nancy 16, Austin 9
LONEY, Hugh 56*, Nancy 31, Morgen? 26 (f), Catharine 22, William 19, Thomas 12, Hugh 17, Edward 11, James 9, Elizabeth 7, J. K. P. 5 (f), H. A. D. 5 (m), Rebecca 3
CAMPBELL, Catharine 3*
CHANCELLOR, Julius 51*
DRIVER, A. 53 (m) (B)
GURS, James 66, Sarah 60

Schedule Page 125

GURS, William 40, Amelia F. 18, Isaac 13, N. J. 11 (f), Amanda B. 3
RAWLINS, James 43, America 24, Mary 22
STAFFORD, Mary 40, Ellen 21
FRAZER, Martha 35, Virginia 25
FINLAY, John 38, R. D. 36 (f)
STEPHENS, William 31*, Isabella 20, M. M. 5 (m), Harriet 1
GURS, Thomas 17*
COLLINS, Asa 45, Sarah 54, M. E. 19 (f)
SHULER, Tabitha 27, Charles 14, J. J. 12 (m), Tobitha 10, M. C. 9 (m), William S. 6, E. B. 1 (m)
CANLIN, James 28, Sarah 24
MORRIS, Saml. 40, M. A. 37 (f)
MCCULLOUGH, S. D. 47 (m)*, H. C. 38 (f)
REED, A. J. 33 (m)*, M. J. 30 (f), Lucretius 10, Rebecca 5, Elinora? 3, Edward 2, John J. 21, Henry S. 12
GRUCON?, William 35*
TRIMBLE, William 35*

1850 Census Fayette County Kentucky

REED, W. L. 32 (m), Josephine 30, Mary 3, Andrew 1
BAXTER, Thomas B. 50, Mary 30
STEPHENS, Allain? 30
SHIDDELL, Susana 54*, A. 41 (m), Catharine 36, Banud? 32 (f), Robert D. 20, A. J. 18 (m), Mary 15
DUCKE?, Susan 29*, D. C. 2 (m)
PETTIT, George 11*
MURPHY, M. A. 50 (f), Henry 15, Frank 13
CALDWELL, Andrew 52, Mary 50
SANDERS, C. 60 (f)* (B)
BELL, E. 50 (f)* (B)
CARTER, Jane 70* (B)
MASON, Rodd 30 (f)* (B), Jacob 3, M. A. 6/12 (f), Gabriel 34, Hudson 21
LEWIS, Danl. 30 (f)* (B)
WILLIAMS, Judy 70* (B)
HILL, James 27*, H. A. 26 (f), E. 9 (f), M. A. T. 7 (f), Susan 6, S. L. 5 (f), Margaret 3, Virginia 3/12
MOORE, M. 45 (m)*

Schedule Page 126

WOOLEY, John 62, George 31, J. A. 21 (f), C. H. 16 (m), Margaret 21
ODONALD, John 24
PRICE, Henry 52 (B)
ELLIS, H. C. 35 (m), M. J. 22 (f), C. W. 9 (m)
MESSICK, C. T. 34 (m)*, Martha H. 32, Margaret 56, B. M. 13 (m)
WILLIAMS, J. B. 32 (m)*
MCCONNELL, J. E. 36 (m), Frances 14, J. J. 12 (m), M. T. 10 (f), Sarah 8, M. H. 6 (f), James 7/12, Alonso 23
HALL, Jessee A. 23, George 22, Maria 1
STEUBAN, Baron 67 (B), William 18, A. 13 (f), H. 7 (f)
SHARP, K. P. 44 (m)*, Emaline 36
TRUMAN, James 28*, F. T. 19 (f)
CANNON, Whitney 32?*, Mary A. 20, M. W. 1 (m)
DOWDEN, E. W. 41 (m)*, Mary 10, Ann 12, William 16, M. S. 14 (m)
VANPELT, J. S. 38 (m)*, Jane 40, S. M. 14 (f), M. S. 12 (f), Emily F. 10, W. V. 8 (m), M. E. 6 (f)
YOUNG, E. S. 23 (m)*
MARTIN, C. 60 (f)* (B)
COONEY, Thomas V. 36*, Julia 30, Ann 8, Thomas 6, M. T. 1 (f)
RYAN, E. 18 (f)*
SHERMAN, Ann 16*
MAYLONE, Maria 30, Whitney 12, Mary 11
REECE, Sarah 44, Hiram 15, Nancy 10
MEDIGATE, C. 39 (f)
HICKEY, Willis 43, Catharine 40, Mary 17, D. N. 10 (m), L. O. 8 (m)
SCHOOLY, Joseph 24, Minea? 22, Mary O. 3
WARNOCK, John R. 28*, M. A. 25 (f), M. C. 10 (f), L. S. 7 (f), Amabell 5, John C. 2
WILLIAMS, E. 19 (m)* (B)
SMITH, Joshua 38, Nancy A. 26, A. V. 9 (f), Pleasant 7, Lesander 5 (f)

1850 Census Fayette County Kentucky

Schedule Page 127

LEWIS, Saml. 44, Albina 16, John 14, Stephen 13
HUMPHREY, Mahala 22* (B)
HENDERSON, M. E. 2 (m)* (B)
CROTH, S. 49 (f)* (B)
BATEMAN, William 31 (B), Maria 24, W. 1 (m)
WILLIAMS, Caleb 74, Nancy 37, E. 13 (m), N. 8 (m), Mary 6, Henry C. 3
MULOCK, M. 30 (m), B. 28 (f), John 13, Mary 11, James 9, Thomas 9, Edward 7, Ellen 6, Margaret 1
SILLMAN, S. 32 (m), W. 31 (f), L. 7 (f), George 3, Mary 1
WHEELER, L. 50 (m) (B), C. 45 (m), Ellen 8/12
DAVIS, Mary 31*, Joseph 13, M. C. 12 (f), M. J. 8 (f), Rhody 6, Thomas 2
PETTY, C. 56 (f)*, Joel 56
GROOMS, Sarah 60*, E. A. 29 (f)
JENNINGS, M. 28 (f)*
BODLEY, C. S. 27 (m), Fanny C. 25, Elenor H. 5, Catharine S. 3, Ann R. 1
ROBERTS, D. 43 (m)*, S. 22 (f), B. G. 21 (f), Nancy 17
WORSHAM, Mary 5*
EARP, Joshua 55, Elizabeth 51, Ellen 16, Joseph 14, M. A. 12 (f)
BROWN, Caleb 46, Nancy 39, Edward 16, Margaret 10
KUGER?, James 22*, Mary 66
HIGGENBOTTOM, A. 70 (m)*
STEPHENS, L. 7 (f)*
MILLER, M. 66 (m)*, Frances 48
DAVIS, E. 35 (f)*
WALKER, A. B. 4 (m)*, E. C. O. 2 (f)
WRIGHT, George T. 22*, R. J. 20 (m)
JETER, Hugh 45*, L. B. 40 (f), M. E. 22 (f), M. E. 16 (f), Sarah 12, Mamontil 8?, Florence 2
MANSHIP, Jane 20*, Mary 6/12

Schedule Page 128

CROMWELL, Vincent 24, Harriet 21, B. H. 4 (m), A. A. 1 (f)
MILBOURN, John D. 36*, Elizabeth 30, John W. 6, E. A. 4 (f), Mary A. 1
SHREWSBERRY, W. S. 23 (m)*
FOURSLER, M. C. 22 (m)*
KINNEY, Ellen 51
ANDERSON, George 25* (B), Louisa 22, Douglas 2, H. C.? 4/12 (f)
WASHINGTON, C. 30 (f)* (B)
GOHAGAN, E. 55 (f)*, Fanny 32, Saml. 21, Ellen 17, Ann 15
COFFIELD, Margaret 33*, Isabella 8
HOPKINS, William 30*
GREEN, M. 40 (m)*
KEISER, Benj. 56*, M. A. 48 (f), E. M. 18 (f), M. A. 12 (m), Isaac B. 8, A. J.? 8 (f)
REECE, Ann 25*
HOLLAND, John 49*, Margaret 39, Elizabeth 9, Amanda 6, Andrew J. 4, Sophia? 66
PATRICK, Benj. 64*
BENNETT, Joseph 45*

1850 Census Fayette County Kentucky

CANOVER, Chas. 40*
LAWLESS, Richard 50*, Elizabeth 43, Jemima 16, Susana 14, M. J. 11 (f), S. R.? 9 (m), Thomas P. 7, Walker 5, Taylor 3, Elizabeth 1
DODD, Richard 17*
HUNT, Washington 17?*
BRADFORD, Thomas T.? 52, Thomas J. 7
AKIN, Elizabeth 59*, Elizebeth 18
DEVLIN, Frances 25*, Margaret 24
HAGGINS, Patrick 26*, Mary 3
CUMER?, John 27*
COLLINS, John 27*
CLARY, John 40, M. A. 38 (f), William W. 17
PAPPUL?, Lewis 38*, D. 38 (f)
GRUNDID?, Louisa 25*
DARLINGTON, C. 22 (m)*, R. 25 (m)
MARSH, David 32, Malinda 28, James W. 9, Julia A. 8, Thomas D. 6, S. D. 3 (m), Chas. A. 8/12
BLAIN, David 38, Rebecca 36, Mary 6?, Jane 3, Alex 6/12

Schedule Page 129

OUTON, Warren 31*, M. J. 26 (f), W. B. 5 (m)
HIGGINS, L. A. 7 (f)*
MCLAUGHLIN, J. H. 38 (m)*, E. 25 (f)
WARREN, J. F. 28 (m)*, M. J. 19 (f), Julia 3
GILLMAN, Martin 28*
DEVINE, David 20*
HOUGHTON, W. F. 31 (m)*
HARDING, P. 21 (m)*
REMINGTON, B. F. 19 (m)*
WEST, Herman 18*
MCMURRAY, Edwin 39*, M. J. 36 (f), E. R. 6 (f)
REED, Rebecca 60*
BUTLER, Mary 2*
BRIDGES, Isaac 15*
WILKINS, Cison? 64 (m)* (B)
ADAMS, Thomas 44, Susan 38
JACKSON, W. T. 17 (m), Ann 14, A. 13 (m), S. A. 10 (f), L. 6 (f), M. 1 (f), S. 36 (f), M. E. 30 (f)
CORDWELL, E. C. 36 (m), M. 30 (f), W. 14 (m), M. 12 (f), H. 10 (m), Sarah 7
CORDWELL, James 37*, Rosana 23
MCGARVEY, John 6*, Mary 4, James 1
MALAND, Patrick 40*
DOURGHTY?, Danl. 50*
COCHRAN, M. 40 (m)*
DRAKE, James 27*
DONAH, M. 23 (m)*
GORGAN, Patrick 30*
MCBRIDE, M. 22 (m)*
RICHARDS, Edwin 26*, Mary 44, John 14, C. 12 (f), E. 10 (f), Mary 8, C. 6 (f), Emma 4

1850 Census Fayette County Kentucky

MOONY, F. 20 (m)*
PILKINGTON, J. M. 23 (m)*, M. C. 22 (f), M. C. 5/12 (f)
HUGGINS, Thomas 50*
HANLEY, W. J. 20 (m)*
DALY, John G. 28*, Catharine 24, Edward 6, Ellen 4, Mary 2
COFFIELD, B. G. 22 (m)*
WHITE, Thomas 26*
WHITE, George W. 28
NICHOLS, Geo. 28*, Mary J. 23, Virginia 2
RUCKELL, Henry 52*, Catharine 35
WILLSON, Rebecca 12*
GARRETT, William 23*
SMITH, J. B. 25 (m)*
FINCH, John 25*
STOCKDELL, James 19*

Schedule Page 130

HOGAN, D. F. 33 (m), M. B. 32 (f), Harriet 7, William 5, Charles 2?
FUDGER, E. 50 (f)*
CHADWICK, S. S. 30 (f)*, Mary 22, Elizabeth 6, S. B. 4 (f), F. R. 3 (m), W. H. 2 (m)
ABBOTT, Eliza 26*
FINNELL, Mary 16*
MCCARTY, Zerelda 19*
TURNER, Nelson 68*, N. W. 34 (m)
HIGBEE, S. E. 37 (f)*
POSTLETHWAIT, John 17?*
MASON, Saml. 28* (B)
KINKEAD, John 21
TILFORD, Edward 24, Anna M. 23
TILFORD, J. B. 38 (m)*, C. 27 (f), Richard 5, John 3, M. 2 (m)
TROTTER, Alex 47*
WATT, Henry 64?*
SAUSEY?, Saml. 75?* (B)
HUGHES, Betsey 45* (B)
GRUNT?, A. 30 (f)* (B)
RIORDAN, William 39*, Mary 3, Eliza 8, Saml. 5
JOHNSTON, Henry 25*
READEN, Margaret 18*
TODD, L. O. 32 (m), L. A. 25 (f), R. S. 6 (m), E. L. 3 (f), J. S. 1 (m)
MEDER?, Saml. 33*
QUISON?, Patric 16*
TAYLOR, Thomas 29*, Eliza J. 26
SHARP, Frances 61*, Jane 36
PILCHER, Sarah 36*
_____, Caroline 17* (B)
MILWARD, Joseph 47*, E. A. 44 (f), H. K. 15 (m), Chas. Y. 13, N. R. 8 (m), Bettie 5
CROUCH, N. 24 (m)*

1850 Census Fayette County Kentucky

WILLSON, John 44*
MILWARD, Henry F. 23, Emili 20, K. S. 1/12 (f)
SHAW, Emma 37*, Hiram 15, Catharine 13, Julia 9, Emma 11, Ann 6, Margaret 3
LIGHTFOOT?, John 24*
MARSH, Catharine 63*, Tho. A. J. 39
ENNIS, Josiah 42*, Catharine 33, J. W. 15 (m), W. H. 11 (m), Mary C.? 9, Josiah 5, Gustavus 1, Dolly 1/12
COOLIDGE, Loonrisla? 11*, Hannah 10, Anna 8

Schedule Page 131

BABCOCKE, John 23*
CAMPBELL, Stephen 17*
SPENCER, Masus 44 (B)
HARRIS?, Madison 27 (B)
TWEEDIE, William 47, Briddie 34, John 19, George 8, Albert 6, Mary 16
CLARK, Manuel 57 (B)
WEIGART, George 32, Catharine 26
ERD, Francis 25*, Mary 24, William 5, Harriet 2
MAUVER?, Albert 19*
DOUGLAS, Robert 19?*
WRIGHT, James 52*
LAMBERT, Barnes? 33*
NORDMAN, Fredrick 1*
BUNERD?, K. A.. 22 (m)*
WARREN, Elizabeth 26
LOCKHART, Henry 47*, Sarah 38, Henarita 12, W. H. 10 (f), E. 8 (m), M. 6 (f), George C. 4
CHAMBLIN, Isabella 17*
LAUDEMAN, David 38, Sarah A. 31, Mary 10, W. H. 8 (m), A. 5 (m)
BURDEN, William 31, Martha 27, J. H. 6 (m), H. F. 3 (f), W. B. 4/12 (m), Harriet? R. 16, L. E. 23 (m)
SNEEDER, H. 44 (m)
ANDERSON, R. 33 (m)*, M. 28 (m)
LEWIS, M. 16 (f)*
LUSBY, W. H. 33 (m), Matilda 32, Thomas 10, Letcher 6, William 4, Henry 9/12
TRUE, Robert 35, M. J. 25 (f), James 5, Mary 3, Sarah 3, P. 1 (f)
WEATHERHEAD, P.? 47 (f)*, M. E. 11 (f)
KITTS, Polly 54*
VANAKEN, A. 41 (m)*, G. H. 34 (f), Caleb 11, Ann 8, Robert 6, Archibald 4, Mary 1
HENRY, Ann 75*
BAKER, R. 53 (f)*, M. 52 (f), P. 30 (f), W. 25 (m), Martha 21, Clayborn 18, John J. 17, Patewell? 14 (f), George W. 11, J. E. 2 (f)
SHACKIN, M. 13 (f)*

Schedule Page 132

RICHARDSON, Isaac 23
WEAVER, E. L. 27 (m), M. A. 29 (f), W. 7 (m), Eliza 4, Thomas 1

1850 Census Fayette County Kentucky

JETER, Benjamin 32?, A. 33 (f), Isabella 73, R. A. 9 (f), H. E. 2 (f)
DUNCAN, Michael 32*, Mary 31
TUTTELL?, Mary 54*, Charles E. 14
TOOL, Michael 48*
CROWLEY, David 47*
SULIVANT, John 33*
CALLIN, Ellen 28*, Thomas M. 10
CANLIN, James 5*, J. R. 3 (m)
BRISCO, Catharine 52, William 23, George 17, Mary 14, James 12
SHINDLEBOUR?, Thomas 50, M. 40 (f), John 14, William 23, M. 20 (f), Charles 10, R. 7 (m), Mary 5
BELL, Chas. S. 28, Margaret 28, George 3, John M. 2, Ellen 6/12
WRIGHT, M. A. 23 (f), M. J. 23 (f), Lewis 21, John 14, Destimony 13, Cynthia 9, R. A. 7 (m), Nancy 6, James T. 4
LEE, Mary F. 23*
EATON, Mary 5*
STONE, William D. 4*
SHUMAKE, Elizabeth 23*
THOMPSON, Emma 20*
HUTCHINS, E. 18 (f)*
WINTER, John 37, Jane 9, Emma 7, Anna 5, Julia 3
VENABLE, George 33*, Elizabeth 27, W. S. 4 (m)
LONEGAN, James 1/12*, Lucy 55
KIDD, P.? H. 37 (m)*, Sarah 37, F. M. 9 (f), Henry 7, James W. 3
NORTON, Malinda 27*
MONTGOMERY, Sarah 27*
BRYANT, Benjamin 20*
MILTON, A. 17 (m)*
THWAITS, Nancy 55, Hannah 46, James 17, Walter 14, J. H. 12 (m)
STOUT, J. B. 40 (m), R. A. 35 (f), A. M. 20 (f), A. H. 15 (f), E. 12 (f)

Schedule Page 133

NAGHEL, E. J. 23 (m)
COGWELL, George 47*, Matilda 43
COWELL, C. 24 (f)*, Danl. 21, Catharine 16, Lucy 10, S. J. 12 (f), Eliza 8, Martha 6
TAYLOR, Stark 64, Elizabeth 61, Andrew 26, H.? L. 24 (m), B. F. 22 (m), Susan 23, Julia 19, Catharine 20, Frances 16
BARKLEY, C. H. 29 (m), E. C. 22 (f), R. B. 2 (m)
BRYAN, Thomas 50, Mary 44, Phebe 11, Thomas 8, Mary 5
SIDNER, John 38, Jane 73, Mary 45
LAID, Saml. 69, Catharine C. 55
WARE, Abraham 64*, Nancy 52, John 7
TARLTON, William Ware 37*
KEYS, John L. 34*, M. A. 34 (f), M. L. 3 (f), N. R. 1 (m)
ROGERS, Joseph M. 10*, Susan C. 8, C. 6 (m)
HEATHMAN, Elias 44, Mariah 38, George 15, Charlott 13, William E. 11, Joseph M. 10, Mahaila 6, Margaret 2, K. L. 1/12
HALEY, Johnson 54, Sarah J. 22, B. F. 16 (m)

1850 Census Fayette County Kentucky

PULLEN, William 47, Sarah 34, Ellen 12, John W. 14, Ida 9, H. B. 5 (m), Lucy 2, James 6/12
CALVIN, A. H. 37 (m)*, E. L. 48 (f), John Will 14, Robert Preston 6
MCCARTY, ____ 23 (m)*
COONS, John 37*
BRECKENRIDGE, Robt. H. 52*, Elizabeth M. 54, E. L. P. 25 (m), R.H.B.R.C. 11 (m)
RUTOFF, John 65, Mary Ann 62, Harriett 22, Margt. 17
THOMISON, John T. 30, E. M. 22 (f), V. T. 5 (m)
LINCOLN, John K. 28*, Elmira 20, Geo. A. 3, Collins M. 5/12, George T. 13, Fanny 70, Fanny 20, Peter 8

Schedule Page 134

HOWARD, Lucy Jane 7*
PARKER, W. O. 30 (f), R. E. 23 (m), W. M. 4 (f), Ann E. 2
BUSBY, William 56, Elizabeth 38, Elizabeth 6, Will 3, Galeda 1
TALBOT, Courtney 46*, Elizabeth 37, Nicholas 19, Elizabeth 17, Emily 15, Margaret 13, Rebecca 11, H. H. 9 (m), Nancy 6, J. W. 1 (m), Rufus 29
HILL, Lorenzo 20*
SHOMAN, Patric 30, M. J. 29 (f)
LOGAN, William 45*, Saml. 48, Jsames 21, A. M. 19 (f), Saml. 17, Laura 14, William 17, Dudly 9, John B. 7, Ether 21 (f)
PERRY?, Ann 22*
MOORE, Marcus 23, E. J. 22 (f), Julius A. 1/3
BROWN, John 52*, Eliza 50, Patrick 58
BEARDEN, Cyrus 32*
VAUGHN, Causby 38*, L. A. 28 (f), Laura 9, Ausburn 7, Francis B. 5, Cosby 4, R. 2 (f), Zachariah 5/12?
COWELL, Julian 31 (f)*, Malissa 4
POULTER?, John 23*
COOPER, William 38*, Susan 33, James 19, John 14, Bill 7, William 5, Albert 4
FRAZIER, George 28*
HALEY, Randolph 47, Lucy 32, Jerburn? 14, Mary J. 12, Henry A. 10, James K. 8, Jordian? 5
STEPHENS, H. H. 53 (m)*, Chas. J. 25
SHEPPARD, M. A. 17 (f)*, W. H. 16 (m), L. W. 14 (m), J. 9 (f), R. M. 6 (m)
BEARD, Martha 30*
ROSS, Danl. 30, William 30, Louisa 23, M. M. 22 (f), E. E. 21 (f)

Schedule Page 135

SMITH, Thomas 53, Mary 48, James? R. 22, Nancy 18, C. M. 16 (f), John A. 14, N. G. 12 (m), Joseph 10
HUNT, Thompson 43, Elizabeth 29, NSancy 13, Ellen 5, Bryan 3
HOUGHTON, F. R. 33 (m), Rachael 6, M. R. 28 (m), James W. 28, Amanda 21, Senison? 59
HOUGHTON, Reuben 59, John 32, Sarah 22, W. C. 21 (m), Reuben 19, Mary E. 11?, W. F. 27 (m)
LAUCENT?, Joseph 59*, Mary 54, George 22
DEVINE, David 22*
KRAUSE, Martha 27*, John 19

1850 Census Fayette County Kentucky

ZIEGLER, John 30*, Martin C. 18
MASON, Frances 46*, Mary 41?
CHAMBERS, George 35*
JENKINS, Lewis 60, Sarah 41, John 14, Lucia? 7
GREEN, Rebecca 77*
HARWOOD, A. 53 (f)*
LOWRY, Prudence 62
LOWRY, W. R.? 38 (m), Julia A. 29, Cynthia 9, Gresham 35
LOWRY, Nathaniel 39, Harriet 11, R. M. 9 (f), M. L. 5 (m), George N. 3, A. J. 1 (m), J. G. 50 (f)
LOWRY, Flora 24*, Rebecca 30, Mary 21, Hulda 16, B. 23 (f), Margaret 60 (B), C. Ross 70 (f)(B)
ROSS, Stortling? 12* (B)
EVANS, William 7* (B), James 2, J. W. 56 (m)
REYNOLDS, Jeremiah? 25, S. W. 17 (m), S. A. 50 (m)
HAWKINS, Lawson 60 (B), Fanny 13, E.? J. 70 (m)
CONNELL, Catharine 70
WILGUS, J. B. 26 (m), L. T. 22 (f)
HEMMINGWAY, Thomas 49, Jane 44, H. C. 18 (m)
DEGARRIS?, John 36, M. A. E. 24 (f)
HUTCHINSON, Sarah 49*, Chas. 30
MCMEEKINS, L. 14 (f)*

Schedule Page 136

HARRIS, Edward 43, Elizabeth 40, A. F. 16 (f), Margaret 13, Martha 11, Rebecca 9, Thomas 7, Pelina 5, Ellen 3
NORRIS, Thomas 42*, Margaret 39, Thomas 12, William 10, Margaret 11, Mary 5, Chas. 4, James 2, Hannah 21
LAMKIN, V. 16 (f)*
YOUNG, Edward 19*
AKIN, Richard 17*
BAKER, John 54, Cynthia 53, C. 30 (f), James 18, Henry 16, Ellen 15, Pelina 11
GILMORE, Andrew? 38, N. A. 34 (f), John 15, M. T. 13 (f), W. D. 10 (m), A. F. 8 (m), R. F. 5 (m)
SHERALL, Charles 25, Lucinda 25, Sarah 4, Catharine 2, Mary 34
ESTICE, John 37*, Frances 37
MILLER, A. F. 21 (m)*, C. 16 (f)
SHEPPARD, Ann 28*
CLARK, John W. 39*, Maria 35, W. S. 8 (m), S. M. 6 (f), M. E. 4 (f), A. M. 3 (f), Darcas 38
COLLINS, Lewis 24*
NUTLER?, Henry 30*
FAIRHEAD, Robert 25, Mary Jane 23
MCMEEKIN, William 47*, Elizabeth 45, Nancy 18, Samuel 14, William 9, Elizabeth 8
GRIGGS, Noah 21*
RYAN, Sarah S. 28*
VAUGHN, Rhoda 70*, Preston 42
GENKINS?, Margaret 14*
SALMONDS?, Louisa 25*
ABERNATHY, George W. 40*, Fenita 37, John B. 12, George H. 10, E. A. A. 74 (f)
BAXTER, Simeon? 26*

1850 Census Fayette County Kentucky

ESTHAM, Malinda 30, William 28, Geo. B. 23, Edwin 21, John 19, S. A. 14 (f), Milton 12, Sallie 56
WORSHAM, W. S. 25 (m)*, Frances 23

Schedule Page 137

ESTIS, J. D. 13 (m)*, M. A. 10 (f), L. A. 8 (m), L. F. 3 (f)
WILSON, W. 27 (m)*
WILSON, Carolina 18*
SHEDELL, John J. 35, Sytha 28, H. B. 8 (m), L. C. 4 (m)
OATS, Sampson 50, Mary 53, E. H. 34 (f), Jackson 20, Mary 16, Charles 14, Emma 12, Virginia 10, Henry C. 8
TAYLOR, Henry 40 (B), Sally 71
ANDERSON, Charlott 30* (B)
JOHNSON, Isaah 27* (B)
CHIPLEY, W. S. 39 (m)*, Elizabeth 30, Stephen F. 12, Milliun? 10, Emily C. 8, Charlie 5, Stephen 65, Amelia 61
MITCHELL, Mary 25*, Margaret 4, Elizabeth 1
ELIATH, Nancy 63, A. G. W. 33 (m)
AUSTIN, Robert 51 (B), Rosana 55, Sophia 75, Ellen 13
THOMPSON, Nelson 40, Catharine 34
WORSHAM, Elizabeth 6/12*, E. L. 23 (m)
LANCART, William 29, Mary Jane 21, W. H. 7 (f), Mary 4
LASWELL, James 43*, M. A. 39 (f), A. 18 (f), Eliza A. 17, James W. 14, E. J. 13 (f), John M. 12, Rebecca 8
HAYS, Thomas 20*
FEENEY, Peter 20*
NICHOLAS, Judy 10*
MASON, William 26*, Billy 28, Henry 34
HARTHEY, Thomas 28*
HAYNE?, John 25*
WETHINGTON, Richard 25, Ellen 24, Joseph 1
VAUGERSON?, C. 39 (m)*, K. 37 (f), M. 17 (m), Mary 14, Pyason? 11 (m), Jane 8
HAPPS, George 30*, Charlotte 27
GREAT HOUSE, Fanny 30* (B), William 7, Thomas 1
TANDY, Mary 43* (B)
HARLIN, Mary 17* (B), Sarah 8, Lura 6, Robt. 1
TAYLOR, Leara 50* (B)

Schedule Page 138

WHEELER, Basil 51* (B)
ROBINSON, Isaac 39 (B), Eliza 38, Jane 9, George A. 2, Amanda 1/12
HEWETT, John M. __*, Ann __
RICHARDS, C. N. 13 (f)*
HARRIS, Eliza 30* (B), C. 6 (m), M. 5 (f), Henry 40
WILLIAMS, Martha 14* (B)
SHEPHARD, J. N. 35 (m)*, Sarah 25, Mary L. 1

- 103 -

1850 Census Fayette County Kentucky

KERSEY, K. A. 28 (m)*, Nancy 23
SHREWSBERRY?, Cynthia 60*, Emily 17
MCCLURE, W. 18 (m)*
HOLMES, John 41*, Sarah 37, Warner 13, W. H. 3 (m), Isaac 3/12
DEGARRIS, Isaac 32*
KIDD, George W. 40*, Nancy 36, Robert 15, John 13, Georgetha 2
DESMOND?, George 21*
KEISER?, John __*, Jane __, James __
WILMOT, S. T.? __ (m)*
DULSEM?, W. Van __ (m)*
ROBB, J. H. __ (m)*, Ann __, N. __ (m), Louisa 10, Joseph 7, Patsey 5, Frank 4, Worthington 2
PILCHER, David 40 (B), L. 40 (f), Dennis 14, Charles 11, Jacob 5, Isaac 3, Sarah 2, Jane 1
RAINEY, W. H. 56 (m)*, Matilda 48
MILLER, John 45*, Elizabeth 44, Robert 17, Alada 16, John 10, Charles 8?, Elizabeth 17
JOHNSON, Ramsey 70*
ROBINSON, Priscilla 45*
WATSON, John C. 27*, F. P. 20 (f), John P. 1
TAYLOR, Milky 8 (f)*
DARBY, J. C. 38 (m)*, A.? D.? 27 (f), S. R. 9 (f), L. L.? 7 (f), Ann 5
KOPPUKUS, A. 38 (m)*, A. 33 (f), A. F. 12 (m), J. R. 10 (f), M. E. 8 (f), C. F. 6 (f), J. F. 3 (m), A. D. 3/12 (m)
BERNARKE?, John 27*

Schedule Page 139

DARBY, M. R. 3 (m)*, Thomas L. 7/12
SHIELDS, Mary A. 46, Joanna 22, John 19
MORGAN, Nicholas 32*, Nancy 30
NICHOLAS, S. A. 14 (f)*, Nicholas 6 (f), George 5, James 2
ROBERTS, Sidney 16 ()*
ROSS, Julian 38 (B), ---- Moss 13 (m), Prissella 11, Molly 9, William 8, Susan 2
FORD, Margaret 57*, Benj. 21, Thomas R. 17
ZONNY, Danl. Y. 28*, E. A. 24 (f)
OFFUT, Mary A. 37, Caroline 18
BURINGER, Henry 24, Catharine 20, Augustus 5/12
THOMPSON, Chas. R. 26, Julia 24, A. E. 14 (f), Malcome 8, M. H. 5 (f)
HALLER, Benjamin 70*, Hannah 50, A. 26 (f)
RICHARDS, M. H. 7 (f)*
HARRIS, Ed. 52*, Elizabeth 51, E. A. 24(f), Sarah 19, Susana 15, Martha 12, Catharine 10, Louisa 6
WHENEY, Elizabeth 14*
N. 29 (M),
SHOOMAN, F. 22 (m), Rebecca 26
ROGERS, C. W. 43 (f), Augustin 21
TAYLOR, C. D. 30 (m), Emily M. 24, Chas. W. 3
SHRYOCK, S. 32 (m), Olivia 22, Eliza 4, John 1
GRAZER, Davel 23, Sopha 19, Anna 15, Frank 21, Henry 17
FORD, C. W. 33 (m), J. S. 34 (f), Benjamin 9, R. W. 7 (m), Mary C. 3

1850 Census Fayette County Kentucky

TRUMBULL, Jane 43, Henry C. 23, Amanda 20, M. J. 17 (f), M. C. 15 (f), John 12, Rebecca 10, William 8, Saml. 6
HOW, Mary 34*, Ann 10
RAYEN, Eli How 16*
WASHINGTON, Jane 25*, Amanda 4/12
JENKINS, Josephine 56*
HUKILL, Robt. 51, Louisa 50, Juliana 17, W. 14 (m), A. J. 12 (m), Henry 9, Thomas 7

Schedule Page 140

CAMPBELL, Robert 57, Elizabeth 46, E. S. 18 (f), W. J. 14 (f), Stephen 17, George A. 10, C. A. 8 (f)
WILLIAMS, Caleb jr 24*, J. A. 20 (m), Joseph E. 1/12
BAXTER, B. 24 (m)*, Elizabeth 19, S. A. 1 (f)
MANLEY, Allen 34, George A. 27, John A. 1/12
JONES, Alfred F. 38*, Mary 63
PECK, A. D. 40 (f)*, Thomas 13
HEADINGTON, W. 58 (m)*, Mary 49
KING, John 15*, A. C. 8 (f)
JONES, Wm. 40*
HARDING, Blaney? 20*
MAXLEY, John M. 50*
BOGGS, mary 26*, Thomas 30, John 7
BRUCE, James M. 27, Elizabeth 26, Elizabeth 1
KINNARD, John 40, Rebecca 38, John 13, S. M. 9 (m)
HOLLENKEMP, H. 30 (m)*, Mary 23, M. 1 (f)
KUHLMAN, B. 24 (m)*
JOHNSTON, H. 23 (m)
DALLINGHOUSE, G. H. 35 (m)*, M. A. 33 (f), M. A. 6 (f), Isabella 3, J. H. 26 (m)
KUNTY, Chas. 26*
WASHBUK, A. H. 26 (m)*
MOSBAK, Furnudad 26*
SWIFT, William 56, Sarah 21, Mary 20, William 15, Charles 13, Gertrude 7, Henry 4
TAYLOR, Leonard 56*, Ann 50, Sarah 25, Saul Ellen 16, Lucretia 13, Virginia 11
SCHOEMAKER, Anna 3*, Lawra 1
GRANT, G. W. 28 (m), A. M. 24 (f), George M. 6, M. L. 4 (f), R. L. 3 (m)
GRANT, Thomas 64*, Margaret 60
BOSWORTH, Eliza 50*
WILLIAMS, M. 50 (f)* (B)
TAYLOR, Luoisa 29* (B), P. A. 4 (f), A. M. 1/12 (f)
RAINS, W. 21 (m)* (B)
THOMAS, E. A. 3/12 (f)* (B)

Schedule Page 141

HUNT, John 114? (44?) (B)
GILLETT, L. 19 (m) (B), Margaret 5, Charles 3, Wesley Ann 29
WOOD, James 54, Mary 54, m. J. 21 (f), M. E. 19 (f), W. S. 11 (m), Lucy 58 (f)

1850 Census Fayette County Kentucky

TAYLOR, Jackson 22, Catharin 19
BROWNING, M. C. 40 (m), R. C. 40 (f), H. M. 16 (f), E. K? 8(f)
HARPER, J. 31 (m)*, Mary E. 25, James P? 4, Catharine R. 3, Ann J. 23
HART, A. M. 35 (f)*
MILTON, B. F. 42 (m), mary Ann 37, Rebecca C. 15, Ann M. 11, Wm. A. 7, John B. 3
PAYNE, Danl. M. D. 52, Zelinda 41, John B. 19, W. S. 17 (m), W. 15 (m), R. 13 (m), Mary T. 14, Edward 8, D. W. G. 5 (m)
GRAVES, Thomas P. 51, M. A. 46 (f), Squire 22, Evalina 22, M. A. 2 (f), Thomas 1
HIGGINS, W. K. 35 (m)*, P. A. 334 (f), M. H. 12 (f), Henry 8, W. K. 5 (m), A. L. 6/12 (f)
WILMOT, Mary T. 56*
WEBB, S. W. 19 (m)
WALLS, Richard 38*, mary 38, A. M. 23 (f), Margaret 21
GRUK?, Ann 9*
COX, T. M. 25 (m)*, Sallie 19, T. S. 6/12 (m)
ANDERSON, A. T. 17 (m)*
SHELBY, Joseph C. 19
STEWART, George W. 30, A. E. 30 (f), Abba 7, Henry 5, Austin 3, Mary 1
COLBERT, Thomas 17
SKILLMAN, A. T. 60 (m)*, Elizabeth 50, E. S. 6 (f)
BENNETT, M. B. 50 (f)*
CRISTY, W. 45 (m)*
BROWNING, M. E. 42 (m), A. 34 (f)
SCOTT, M. T. 45? (m)*, E. T. 45 (f), M. 25 (m), L. C. 24 (f), Joseph 21, M. T. 17 (m), Joseph P. 12?

Schedule Page 142

GALAGER, M. T. 5 (m)*
DRAKE, B. P. 41 (m), Ana B. 36, David 17, M. H. 16 (f), L. J. 13 (f), R. J. 5 (m)
WATSON, Joseph 56*, Ann O. 46, John S. 23
WALLACE, Davidella 20*
HUTCHINSON, Betty 13*
WALLACE, H. B. 44 (m), Elizabeth 33, A. P. 7 (m), Nancy A. 5, Infant 1/12 (f)
BOWMAN, R. P. 37 (m), Elizabeth E. 35, P. T. H. 12 (m), J. P. 9 (m), W. B. 6 (m), E. M. 1 (f)
CRITENDEN, Nancy 35?*
WINCHESTER, Martha 25*, Frank 32
REECE, Sidney 17 (f)*
WIEGART, Mary A. 15*
ALTON, Mildred 15*
TINGLE, Amanda 21*, A. M. 19 (f)
WHITE, Mary 19*
APPLETON, Philadelphia 21*
NEEL, M. H. 16 (f)*
WINCHESTER, Josephine 6*, Thomas 4, Ireene 1
BACCUS?, L. A. 12 (m)*
TROUDER?, John 19*
MITCHELL, Kitty 39
KLINGER, Danl. 24*, Rosea 23

1850 Census Fayette County Kentucky

FROST, John M. 48*, Elizabeth 44, Fayette 20 (f), James 18, Mary 16, Sarah 13, John 10, Elizabeth 6, Joshua 46
DAY, Sarah 61*, Joseph 5
HICKENBOTTOM, Mary 26*
CONNAH?, Margaret 58*, Caroline 39
MCFADDEN, A. 44 (m), R. 28 (f), R. F. 8 (f), John 6, Ellen 3, C. 1 (f)
WHEELOCK, Sarah J. 47*, Sarah A. 19
JONES, M. A. 27 (f)*, R. A. 8 (f)
GUNKLE, John 32*, A. 23 (f)
NILES, Isaac 34*
YOUNG?, William 54, Sarah 53, Edwin 24, Sarah 15, Mary 11, Elizabeth 9
SCOTT, Tillis 19 (B), Annis 3 (f)
LEMON, Beverly 60 (m) (B), Becky 60
JONES, L. D. 46 (m)*, Pelina 43, Lloyd 19, Wm. 11, Sarah 6, Martha 2, Laura 29, Cordelia 15

Schedule Page 143

TOLL, M. E. 5 (f)*
YOUNG?, Susan 87
FRANCIS, Danl. 91* (B), Lewis 18
WHEELER, Danl. 18* (B), Mary 17, Martha 15
LEWIS, R. A. 13 (f)* (B)
MILLER, Andrew 32*, Martha 22, Fountain 3, Alex 1
BUNNELL, Martha 18*
YATES, Sarah 19*
TANKERSLEY, F. 61 (m), N. 50 (f), George 21, Cassius 17
PRATT, W. M. 33 (m), M. E. 25 (f), Laura 1
BARTLETT, J. C. 34 (m)*, Chas. M. 6
TANKERSLEY, M. 60 (f)*, C. 62 (f), George 58
ROBERTS, Jane 65, Luthy 50 (f)
BRENNAN, John 62*, Mary 42, John 12, James 10, Ernest 8, Henry 7, M. M. 5 (f), W. M. 2 (m)
MORTON, Gabriella 32*
ALLENDER?, Thomas 25, S. A. 23 (f), L. A. 23 (f), W. E. 10/12 (m)
MILIGON, W. 47 (m)*, Manerva 39, E. A. 18 (f), J. H. 17 (m), E. A. 13 (f), L. E. 10 (f), M. J. 8 (f), George T. 6, D. C. 4 (m)
HOWARD, E. 74 (f)*, E. 30 (f)
SPROWL, Alex 47, C. 37 (f), Susan 5, E. 6 (f), W. A. 4 (m), A. E. 2 (f), Mary 19
FRY, Thomas J. 28, S. 26 (f)
TAYLOR, M. 55 (f)*, E. 36 (f), Caroline 21, Jessamine 7 (m), C. C. 3 (m)
SINGLETON, C. 7 (f)*
RANDALL, W. R. 58 (m), Caroline 40, M. T. 27 (f), W. R. 25 (m), Margaret 17, R. S. 16 (m), A. E. 11 (f), James E. 11, James E. 10, John S. 7, Virginia 2
BRISBY, David 43, Margaret 55, M. A. 19 (f)
FOGLE, W. E. 39, Mary 38, Thomas B. 18, Virginia 8?, Gertrude 5, W. W. 4 (m), F. N. 1 (m)

1850 Census Fayette County Kentucky

Schedule Page 144

RUTER?, P. J. 33 (m), M. S. 28 (f), J. M. 8 (f), T. A. 5 (m)
MCLEAR?, Francis 61, Sarah 49, M. L. 17 (f), Ann M. 14
LONG, Robert 40*, A. M. 30 (f), Emma 7
BLUNT, Ann 7*
PEARSON, Susan P.? 31*
SKINNER, Joseph D. 19*
BUSH, J. M. 40 (m)*, Charlotte 28, Ann 14, Dudley 11, Thomas 9
TAYLOR, M. A. 35 (m)* (B)
DUDLEY, E. L. 32 (m)*, Mary S. 32, M. T. 6 (m), Louisa 1
CUNNINGHAM, T. 21 (m)*
PARKER, Mary 82*
CRITENDEN, Mary W.? 57*, R. 19 (m)
JUCHO?, William 46, Julia 45, Wm. 18, Julia A. 17, Luella 15, Thomas 14, E. C. 12 (f), Adaline 10, M. L. 8 (f), Caroline 6
SCOTT, Docia 1* (B), Elizabeth 31, W. M. 3 (m), John C. 11, Henry 10
WORSHAM, Susan 40* (B), Washington 20
DODD, James B. 43*, Eliza J. 28, M. E. 17 (m), James W. 16, Thomas H. 12, Virginia 8, A. F. 7 (m)
TUFTS, William 26*
RANSOM, R. R. 22 (m)*
JONES?, Lucy 56* (B)
BRIENT, S. O. 9 (m)* (B)
OWENS, Eliza 2* (B), Eliza 27
LEGRAND?, Abner 75*, Jane R. 63, Julin 24 (f), Catharine 22
ELLIOTT, James L. 35*, Legrand 7/12, C. L. 5 (f)
KEEN, E. L. 10 (f)*, M. J. 7 (f), Richard 5
CLARK, John 63
CURD, Eleanor 46, Ellen 18, Henry 16, Nanny 15, Thurston 14
PETER, R. 39 (m), Frances R. 35, L. D. 14 (m), Benj.? D. 10, L. D. 7 (f), John M. 5, Robert 3, Sarah H. 6/12

Schedule Page 145

PIGG, Saml. 37, Adalaid 26, Isabella 9, Cordelia 8, James 7, Horrace 4, Vetula 2/12
LANGDON, Harriet C. 45, W. C. 18 (m)
KINSEY, James 38, Catharine 23, Thomas 12
GRAVES, Richard 40* (B), Hannah 37, Louisa 33
MORTON, Clowry 70 (f)* (B)
KEELER, Lucy 65* (B)
CHINN, William 30* (B)
SNOWDEN, Thomas W. 23
WELGUS, Garrard 23*, Agnus 19
LANCART?, Lewis 20*
DOWNING, Benj. 17*, Sarah 65
TOLL, M. E. 7 (f)*
MONKS?, Ellen 12*
DUDLEY, John J. 33, E. J. 29 (f), Florence G. 5, Georgia Ann 41

1850 Census Fayette County Kentucky

MCCONNELL, A. W. 46 (f)*, Mary C. 11
VAUGHN, James A. 16*
BONFILES, Luvenia 51*, Cornelia 21
SLOAN, J. R. 31 (m)*, E. S. 31 (f), P. H. 13 (f), Elizabeth 11, Theadore 8, Anna 5, Briget 59
BONFILES, Cunard? 17*
BRADLEY, Thomas 29*, Isabella 31, O. L. 10 (m), M. B. 4 (f), Chas. W. 1
WOODROUGH, James 24*
DUDLEY, E. A. 43 (m), Sarah M. 29, Jetha? 11 (m), Thomas 6
KEITH, M. L. 24 (m)*, Susana 21, B. W. 2 (m)
WICKLIFFE, Fanny W. 45*, Elizabeth 47
FONNARD?, J. E. 42 (m), J. E. 30 (f), Chas. E. 17, Thomas 2, Martha 4/12
PINDELL, R. 37*, Anna 34, Thomas H. 58, J. M. 31? (m)
EDMONDSON?, J. E. 51 (f)*
FOX, H. P. 24 (m)*, Margaret 22, H. T. 1 (m)
BENNETT, Lucy 16*
HOLLAND, M. A. 18 (f)*
JOHNSON, M. C. 41 (m)
LAMB, Harry 45*, Mary 40, R. A. 13 (m), S. B. 8 (f), M. A. 4 (f)
COOK, Nancy 63* (B)

Schedule Page 146

HUNTER, J. J. 38 (m), Margaret 32, Julia 5, Kate 2
MILLER, J. F. 48 (m)*, Matilda 46, John T. 25, M. H. 21 (f), D. V. 21 (f?), Christianna 16, Moseph T. 14, Charles H. 12, Florida 9, Davidella 6, Erma K. 4/12
CUDLESS, George 24*
THOMPSON, M. G. 23 (m)*
PAGE, James 18*
CURSEY, M. 17 (m)*
EDGE, B. F. 31 (m)*, Mary 18
HARNEY, Charels 16*, Christopher 11, Margaret 10
BISHOP, P. 54 (m)*, Sarah 40, Robert C. 16, Josephine 10, H. C. 8 (m), George 6, Ellen 4, Allen 3, Chas. 1
COLLIN, Randolph 29*
SEARLES, James 63*, E. G. 40 (f), M. E. 9 (f), James I. 11
EDGE, Saran A. 27*, R. R. 32 (m)
BARNS?, William 15*, A. W. 12 (f)
KINNY, W. 28 (m)*
YOUNG, L. K. 37 (m), Nancy 29, B. F. 12 (m), L. R. 4, Alles 2
SMITH, L. B. 63 (m), Margaret 62
CLOUD, Harriet 35*, Mary B. 66, John 14, C. W. 12 (m), Mary E. 10
RAGSDALE, Ann E. 21*
BRUCE, Margaret 60*, J. T. 34 (m)
MORGAN, Jno. H. 25*, Rebecca 20
BROWNING, Mary 39, Sarah 56, J. H. 22 (f), M. A. 20 (f), H. 17 (f), Thomas C. 16
MERRECK, Wright 50
MCMILLON, F. 23 (m) (B), John 30, L. 2 (f), H. 2 (f), F. 70 (f)
JACKSON, W. 65 (m)*, E. 55 (f), E. 35 (f), E. 30 (f), L. 28 (f), Polly 24, Mary 18, Thomas 16

1850 Census Fayette County Kentucky

EDDY, Clara J. 27*
BABB, J. M. 18 (f)*
MOORE, William 47*, Julia 44, John 18, Francis 16, Sarah 14, Richard 10

Schedule Page 147

LEWIS, A. E. 7 (f)*
EVANS, John 39*, E. 67 (f), Mary 19
RUBITHON, W. 31 (m)*, William 9, Elizabeth 8, M. 6 (f)
VIGUS, Susana W. 35, A. E. 13 (f), S. M. 11
WEST, John 64, Eve 62, W. W. 37 (m), Elziabeth 21, Hiram 17, Richard 7, Virginia 5, Louisa 3
WHITT, E. A. 38 (f)*
NAPPER, Sallie 27*
WHITE, Corella 18*
ROBERT, Jane V. 60*, B. J. 25 (f)
CONDA, Thomas J. 14, L. J. 8 (f), Adolph R. 7, E. J. B. 3 (m)
BERKLEY, E. F. 36 (m), Sarah L. 33, F. M. 7(f), M. F. 4 (f), M. F. 1 (f)
SHARES, William I? 51*, B. A. 52 (f), William 20, Jane 18, Thomas 17, Lalml. 10, Andrew 6
SMEADLEY, Mary 62*
LONG, Hannah 39, Caroline 14
HAMILTON, James 53, Jane P. 46, W. C. 25 (m), John W. 20, Thomas M. 15, George W. 13
HAMILTON, E. W. 11 (m)*, Julia 9, Robt. S. 6, Thornton 3
ALEXANDER, Edmund 45* (B)
WILLIAMS, Patrick 30 (B)
CHRISLY, John 45
LILLY, Ervin 34*, M. A. 26 (f), Elizabeth 7, M. M. 5 (f)
MILES?, Charles 41 (B)
SCOTT, R. 40 (m), M. A. 25 (f), James F. 11, Jane 6, Walter 4, Hamelton 8/12
EVANS, Joseph 40*, W. J. 33 (f), W. R. 11 (m), Cathar 10, Mary L. 7
CHAMBERS, Jane 45*
HAMILTON, R. B. (m)*, A. E. (f), M. L. (f), Robt. H., A. E. (f), Thos. L., [ages not given], Turner 5, John 2

Schedule Page 148

SMITH, Thomas 65*, Mary 60
ANDERSON, George 27* (B)
MCMURRAY, James 68, Rebecca 68, George A. 36, Frances 15, O. 12 (f), Alonso 17
CAMPBELL, A. L. 11 (m)*
BAIN, M. L. 57 (f)*, George C. 27, Catharine 19, Paterson 4/12
HARDESTUN, H. E. 30 (f), H. E. 3 (f), A. Otto 4, Roselle 2
WOODS, Mary 25*
SAYRE, Lucy 50*
JOHNSON, Verbeda 50, L. T. 32 (m), J. J. 30 (m), J. T. 27 (m), C. R. 17 (m), J. M. 26 (f), Lidia 26, Mary 1
CLARK, A. H. 40 (m)*, M. P. 40 (f), P. R. 9 (f), C. R. 7 (m), Wiley 4
RAIN?, James K. 19*

1850 Census Fayette County Kentucky

MCMURTRY, Mary J. 27*, David 22
HARRIS, Joseph 37*, Kate 39, Edward 14, E. H. 3 (m), James 1
ELLIS, Saml. 14*
FISHER, John 50*, Ellen 42
LILLY?, Louisa 8*
WALKER, John 77*
WILLIAMS, W. W. 50 (m), Asenoth 32
WEAVER, Thomas 49, Ann 43
FREDRICK, L. 33 (m), E. 26 (f), L. 4 (m), Chas. 3, E. 1 (f), Anna 1
MONKS, Thomas 56*, M. A. 30 (f), Adalaid 9, W. W. 5 (m), M. A. 3 (f), M. A. 1 (f), R. 21 (m)
DELHOUSE, John 45* (B)
BROWN, John H. 44*, Clara 42, Dwight 20
MCCONNAT, V? 30 (m)*
RODES, Waller 50, Lurerya 47, Nancy 24, Mary 22, James 20, John 18, Sarah 15, Joseph 12, Clifton 9, Anna 6
ROSS, George N. 53 (f), Cashia 44 (m)
ALLEN, Richd. 39, Hellen 30, Sallie 10, Ann C. 7, John 5, Henry 3, J. L. 1 (m), Elizabeth 13

Schedule Page 149

LAYNE, James 66
HENDERSON, James 35, M. D. 30 (f), E. M. 9 (f), R. R. 8 (m), James W. 6, Sarah J. 4, W. S. 3 (m), John T. 4/12
WALLACE, W. K. 32 :(m)*, SArah A. 29, L. D. 6 (m), W. A. 4 (m), John H. 2 (f), Mary 6/12, Ann 52
HOOKER, Nancy 65*
MCLANE, Thos. 17*
WALLACE, James T. 21
BUTLER, James D. 24*
MCLANE, W. 24 (m)*
SEDNER?, W. 22 (m)*
RAYNTS?, W. R. 3 (m)*
LENNESSEE?, James 21*
RUNSDALL, W. R. 24 (m)*
WALLACE, J. H. 43 (m)*, M. A. 44 (f), Jane 19, M. 17 (f), W. K. 13 (m), M. E. 11 (f), George H. 7, A. R. 5 (m), John H. 3, C. K. 1 (m), James 79
---, Fanny 65* (B)
MCDOWELL, S. P. 61 (m)*, T. 80 (m)
SIBASTIAN, L. 17 (m)*, Hellen 53
---, Hanah 22* (B), Luk 6, John 3
STEEL, John 66*, Jane 56, William 18
MCAFEE, James 47*
STEEL, Andrew 30*, Sallie 20, Jane 4, Maria 1
SANFORD, Frances 45*
HARRIS, Thomas 45, Nancy 46, William 22, Simeon 21, James 19, Thomas 15, E. F. 7 (f), Thomas 3
STONE, John 71*, Polly 66
MONZ, Maria 45*, S. B. 47 (m)
JENKINS, James 22*
NEAL, Chas. 55, Frances 58

1850 Census Fayette County Kentucky

MCMEEKIN, A. 53 (m), Maria 53, Catharine 20, M. A. 18 (f), J. E. 15 (f), James 58
PARKER, John 53*, Sarah 36
LOUDENSUN, R. H. 10 (m)*, J. A. 17 (f)

Schedule Page 150

CAUSEY, Robert 43*, Susan 36, Rebecca A. 13, Thomas A. 11, John W. 9
HOLLAND, Eliza 7*
PRICE, Sanford 28, Sarah A. 16
ELBERT, Pollard 37, Sarah 31, M. A. 13 (f), Elizabeth 11, James 9, H. D. 7 (m), C. Ann 11, M. J. 2 (f)
EDGE, Mary 70, W. W. 43 (m), E. J. 10 (f), Sanford 47
LINGENFELTER, John 40*, Mary 35, F. E. 14 (f), John D. 13, Mc. C. 11 (f), J. C. 24
MCDONALD, Chas. 30*
COFFMAN, Saml. 30*
LINGENFELTER, John jr 85*, Mary 80
WATTY, D. H. 41 (m)*
YOUNG, E. A. 35 (f)*, B. W. 5 (f), C. D. 3 (m)
SULEVAN, F. 23 (m)*
FRAZER, Mary 72*, Joseph 32
STEWART, Mary E. 19*
KINKEAD, E. 35 (m)*
STEWART, G. W. 15 (m)*
BYRNES, Morgan 48, Susan M. 10, Robert D. 18
MURE, E. 57 (m), E. S. 19 (m)
BYRNES, Felix 47*, A. M. 42 (f), W. S. 20 (m)
LOGAN, Robt. B. 31*, E. V? 22 (f), Anna A. 3/12
MADOX, Samuel 32, J. A. 32 (f), Ellenurd 10 (f)
ELBERT, J. L. 42 (m), F. 40 (f), Martha A. 17, Mary J. 17, Henry J. 18, E. H. 8 (f), M. C. 5 (m), J. R. 3 (f), Catharun 1
WATSON, Joseph 55*, Sarah 53, Evalilne 29, Sarah M. 18
ADAMS, Sarah L. 11*, K? V. 9 (f), Nancy M. 7, Milley Ann 5, Josephine J. 4
RICE, James L. 36*, Martha H. 33, Mary D. 10, Patsy 65
ALLISON, George S. 20*
HOFFUTT, Richard 20*
ALLEN, A. M. 21 (m)*
HENSHALL, Jenney 15*
MCCANN, Virginia 10/12*
WARD, John 70*
BROWN, Edgar A. 37*, Andelusia 37, Wm. W. 5

Schedule Page 151

DAVIDSON, A. 23 (m)
JACKSON, M. 41 (m)* (B), L. A. 36 (f)
CLARK, M. B. 23 (f)* (B)
TALBOTT, Hampton 33* (B), Martha 30
PHILLIPS, Sallie 16* (B)

1850 Census Fayette County Kentucky

STEVENSON, Sam 18* (B)
GIBSON, Chas. 39*, V. H. 16 (f)
TETER, John 64*, W. 28 (m), R.H. 31 (m)
GIBSON, M. J. 37 (f)*
PAYNE, Isaac 29 (B), Katy 70
PU, Parker 51 (B)
MCILROY, Thos. 58, Cornelia 37, J. T. 10 (m), W. D. 6 (m), M. E. 3 (f), Mary 61
BARKELY, James 58, Rebecca 52, James C. 18, D. M. 16 (m), John 14, J. H. 12 (m)
SMITH, G. A. 40 (m)*, L. C. 35 (f), Gabriella 12, Lucinda 14, Octavia K. F. 8, Wm. 5, Clayton 7/12
FICKLEN, Joseph 75*
BASSITT, Squire 27*
MITCHELL, D. W. 18 (m)*
TWYMAN, Laura 4*
ROBINS, James 33*, Ann M. 29, Virginia 10, M. W. 9 (f), Sarah 6, James M. 4, Matilda 3, Jane 1
WINTER, Julia 2*
SCULLY, James 39*, Elizabeth 28, Julia 9, Emily 9, M. E. 7 (f), Thos. P. 5, James
MORLIN, James 1*
MCCRACKIN, H. 28 (m)*
MORLIN, Isaac 36*
BALL, Charles 30*
JENKINS, Charles 28*
HARVEY, Joseph 27*
MCINTIRE, Berry 47*
OWENS, Wm. 24*
STEEL, Henry 16*
SCOOLEY, James 58*, Elizabeth 20, Wm. 14, Edward 12
LACY, Thos. 39*, Adaline 34
WOLVERTON, Silas 39*, Angeline 34, W. R. 16 (m), Joanna 14
WOODS, James 39* (B)
BROWNING, W. P. 36 (m)*, Emaline 30, A. E. 9 (f), Betty 6, Charlotte A. 4
ARMSTRONG, Thos. 21*
HOLLADAY, Benj? 19*

Schedule Page 152

BLEDSOE, Thomas C. 48*, Frances 37, Margarett 16, Hiram M. 15, John W. 11, Thos. C. jr 9
ELLEY, Thos. 23*, Mary J. 19
BROCKWAY, Mary E. 34*
ELLIS, Hegekeah 30*
HINSHALL, Mary 55*, Anna 20
REID, James 30*
HUGGINS, Thos. 17*
BROCKWAY, Abby S. 34*
MARCH, James 45* (B)
WARFIELD, Wm. 53* (B), Celey 46
PAYTON, Amanda 17* (B)
JACKSON, Wm. 19* (B), M. V. 3 (f), Virginia 1
WALLER, Wm. 65, Catharine 62, Jas. B. 32, Lucy 25, M. E. 2 (f)

1850 Census Fayette County Kentucky

ELLIS, Sarah 24* (B), Maud 8, Jas. W. 3, Ann 18
MCMULLEN, Ann 26* (B), Sarah 4
JOHNSTON, Tamie 70* (B)
EPPERSON, Jane 36*, Mary 16, Thos. 12, Wm. 8
FOLEY, Jane 74*
FISHBACK, Susan 58*
SHELLY, Susan P. 20*
WHEELER, Leonard 61
BRECKENRIDGE, Wilcher 64 (B)
LUTZ, John 48*, Josephene 29, Fielding 9, Margaret 5, Oscar 2
TURNER, Lucinda 19*, M. E. 16 (f)
KASE, A. 35 (f)*
HARRIS, H. 15 (f)*
NEAL, M. O. 44 (f)*
STEVENSON, Lucy 10* (B)
SMITH, Geo. W. 40, M. J. 23 (f), Rob A. 7, D. W. 8 (m), M. A. 1 (f)
SHAW, Hiram 41*, Nancy 41, Joshua 12, Agness 9, Joseph 7, Kate 5, Thos. 3, Margaret 75
PILCHER, Margaret 13*
MCCONETHY, H. 40 (m), E. 36 (f), N. J. 9 (m), J. H. 7 (m), Milton 5, M. S. 2 (f)
BRITTEN, Thos. 74 (B)
CENICK, Wm. 33*, M. A. 26 (f), John T. 9, Nancy A. 6, E. J. 3 (f)
FOSTER, S. E. 19 (f)*
GROOMS, James 38*, Matilda 42, Joseph L. 1/12

Schedule Page 153

RETHERFORD, W. 19 (m)*
MASONER, James 21, M. J. 20 (f), J. E. 7/12 (f)
ADAMS, Frances 37*, A. 15 (m)
MASTERSON, Mary 40*
SMITH, J. Y. 40 (m)*
ATKINS, W. 30 (m)*, Betsey 22
LAFOE, M. 19 (f)*, Susan 12
MERRYMAN, Betsey 50*
KELLEY, John 36, Mary 36, Thos. 7, Allice 5, Robt. 2, Wm. 1/12
LLOYD, W. H. 28 (m), Ann M. 22, James B. 6/12
WEBSTER, Elizabeth 40*, A. J. 19 (m)
LOYD, Stephen 25*
NOBLE, D. E. 39 (m), Sarah 25, J. A. M. 7 (f)
CARR, Eliza 44
GORE, Sophia 24, Lewis 35, Sallie 4, Mary 1
HANIKER, M. 38 (m), Casander 29, J. A. 13 (f), Mary 9, Rob 8, C. J. 5 (f), J. W. 2 (m)
CLIMES, M. Q.? 32 (m), Livica 28, Hiram 11, H. A. 7 (f), Geo. 5, L. F. 3 (f)
LEE, Eliza 37* (B)
ELLIS, Ira 35* (B)
MORRISON, Dick 40* (B), Mary 23, Dick 3, Ellen 5, Jim 1
YELMAN, John Geo. 29*, Sophia 24, John H. 6/12
INGLEHEART, Joseph 22*

1850 Census Fayette County Kentucky

BOYD, Robt. 38, Ann E. 39 (f)
TUDER, S. 54 (m), Casandra 50, Martin 31, Sarah 30, Mary 27, Eliza 25, John T. 23, Matilda 18, W. H. 11 (m), R. E. 6 (f)
HOAGLAND, Thos. 64, Wm. 45, Zabenid? 39 (f), Ann L. 12, Martin 9, C. 7 (f), Jesse T. 1, Cornelia 45, Rebecca 18
WILSON, Susan 35*, Catherine E. 14, S. M. 11 (f), Isabella S. 7
HOAGLAND, L. 83 (f)*

Schedule Page 154

DAVIS, W. P. 32 (m), Elizabeth 26, E. S. 5 (m), L. J. 2/12 (f)
PARKER, John T. 50, A. M. 21 (f), M. E. 18 (f), Corilla M. 18, Jas. P. 12
TAPP, Wilson 56*, J. W. 44 (f), W. 23 (m), E. S. 5 (f)
FRELEY, Thos. 20*
ELLIOTT, Uriah 28*
JEFFERS, Affd? 29 (f)*, Stephen 35, Jas. M. 14, L. A. 12 (f), E. F. 6 (f)
ELLIS, M. S. 15 (f)*
MURPHY, Susana 29*
TUDER, Josephene 14*
DUNN, Nancy 58*
RYAL, Frances 30*
CRAIG, Sharlott 15*
GILTNER, David 15*
SHREWSBERRY, Amelia 14*
NEWCANT, James 12*, Cyrus 8
WILSON, M. J. 11 (f)*, Lucy 9
CAMPBELL, Betty 8*
HUNT, Wilson S. 40, M. J. 25 (f), S. E. 17 (f), Jasper 9, C. M. 3 (m), E. J. 1 (f)
SELF, James 21*, Mary 18, James 2/12
HULL, John C. 30*
WARFIELD, Elisha 39*, C. A. 34 (f), N. W. 16 (m), E. P. 13 (f), T. P. 11 (m), M. R. 8 (f), Catharine 6, Lloyd 4
WARE, N. W. 69 (m)*
SHORTRIDGE, W. J. 27 (m), Thomasella V. 20, Lucy F. 2/12
VANCE, James D. 40, A. 25 (m), M. 25 (m)
RICHARDSON, Ann 50, Marcus 25
DOYLE, James 39, Martha 27, Mary 2/12
KIDD, S. A. 32 (m)*, Martha 26, Phillip 7, Augustus 5, Samuel 3, E. C. 1, James W. 17, Robert 19
LOWERY, W. G. 35 (m)*
_____, Bryant 45* (B), Blackmore 25, Basel 40
SAYRE, James 33*, Elizabeth 30, D. W. 12 (m), H. C. 9 (m), J. P. 5 (m), R. P. 2 (m)
MEYRES, W. C. 25 (m)*
COOK, John 56, Harriett 41, Louisa 19, Henry 14, David L. 12, Wm. 9, John E. 7, Garret D. 4, Chas. H. 1

1850 Census Fayette County Kentucky

Schedule Page 155

MONTAGUE, Jas. C. 30, Nancy 27, Sarah J. 7, Thos. W. 5, M. E. 3 (f), Alice 3/12
OLDHAM, Ed 57*, Mary 27
PARKER, Nancy 29*
GOHAM, Nancy 60*, G. M. 34 (m), W. 27 (m), T. G. 25 (m), B. C. 21 (m), Hamlin 14, Andrew 17, B. 14 (m), L. A. 23 (f), Prissilla 20
PETRY, Wm. 70*
WILLIAMS, J. H. 36 (m), Pelina 27, Mary 7, A. E. 6 (f), Wm. 2, Mary 1/12
HARP, Geo. 30, Susan A. 23
HOSTETTER, Jacob 33*, Adaline 27, Mary 9, Ann 7, Frances 4, John 2/12
RANDELL, Mary 80*
PAYTON, E. 70 (f)*
UNDERWOOD, N. 22 (m)*
SMITH, Obadiah 26, Lucinda 21, Geo. W. 3, W. H. 8/12
CARBIN, John 43, M. A. 36 (f), M. E. 9 (f), M. A. 7 (f), W. A. 4 (f), A. C. 2/12 (f)
ROSE, J. W. 31 (m), E. 25 (f), Thos. M. 5, J. W. 3 (m), T. M. 1 (m)
HAGGIN, Samuel 67, Jane 58, Nancy 28, Margaret 26, Saml. 22
TOMLINSON, Chas. 63*, Julia A. 51, Wm. 23, M. J. 19 (f), Chas. 17, S. E. 16 (f)
WINT, Susan 4*
APPLETON, Joseph 7*
CROMWELL, Benj. 6y7, Jane 67, M. H. 20 (m)
CHEW, S. H. 30 (m)*, Emily 21, Saml. H. 3, Sam. 63, Ann 50
MARTIN, M. T. 23 (m)*, M. 21 (f), Robt. 3, Geo. Ann 4/12

Schedule Page 156

DEVORE, R. H. 27 (m), Mary 23, Robt. 4, Martha 1
WEBSTER, Weall? 36 (m), Eliza 33, Mary 14, John 12, Lafayette 10, F. A. 7 (f), Almead 5, Allen 3, Chas. 5/12
MCMEEKIN, A. F. 29 (m)*, Eliza 21
GREGG, R. 20 (m)*
MCMEEKIN, Jeremiah 31, Sarah 29, John 7
COLCLOZURE?, John 44, L. E. 36 (f), Jacob 16, J. H. 10 (m), H. 12 (f), N. H. 10 (m), F. 8 (f), Susan 5
BRECKENRIDGE, A. 70 (m)*, A. R. 4 (m)
LEWIS, Malinda 44*, Thos. 23, Margaret 24, Susan M. 3, Elmira 9/12
DOWNS, Benj. 62, J. B. 27 (m), E. 24 (f)
ROSELL, F. 50 (m), Polly 47, Joann 18, Elizabeth 19, John 17, F. Ann 7
HUTCHISON, D. 70 (f)
GREEN, D. 54 (m), L. 47 (f), Ann M. 23, James 20, Sarah 18, E. 16 (m), A. 13 (m), Wm. 10, Lowra 8, Mary 6
MCMINNEY, W. 61 (m)*, C. 47 (f), Sarah 17, E. 15 (m), A. 12 (m), Nancy 9, A. J. 8 (m), Thos. 6, A. P. 10/12 (m)
MCCAY, Mary 23*, J. H. 23 (m)
BASTON, Polly 100*
MCCOY, Jas. 57*, Nancy 56, Sarah 24, Susan 19, Rosana 17, Frank 14, Sanford 13, Spurr 7, James 14
JOHNSON, Hamson 22*

1850 Census Fayette County Kentucky

GORTNEY, J. F. 30 (m), Sarah 27, M. T. 9 (f), M. A. 7 (f), Rebecca 1
WEBB, John 31, Margaret 25, James 1

Schedule Page 157

LEWIS, Isaac 43, Maud 38, Louisa 20, Saml. 18, M. T. 17 (f), Sarah 14, Wm. 11, S. A. 9 (f), Albert 8, Caroline 7, James 5, Bowles 3, Robt. 1
GRIGGS, Vergis 47, D. C. 14 (m), Elizabeth 13, Saml. 12, Wiley 18
GRIGGS, Rice 22, Martha 20
READMAN, Loyd 45, Susan 38, Ann 16, Elizabeth 13, M. F. 10 (f), James 8, Julia 6, Joseph 3
ROACH, F. 52 (m), Wm. 17, Caroline 19, John 14, Ann 12, Sarah 10, Geo. 7
GRIGGS, Hannah 44, Lucrecia 16, E. 14 (f), S. E. 12 (f), H. H. 7 (m), W. H. 19 (m)
WILLIAMSON, Eunice 49, Mary 27, Lucious 18, Francis 15, C. E. 12 (f), H. J. T. 10 (m)
NOLAN, Wm. 53, Jane 51, Joshua 23, Ruth 19, Nancy 17, Sidney 14 (f)
WRIGHT, John 27, Emily 26, S. A. 6 (f), J. B. 3 (m)
WRIGHT, Alsey 45, Maria 17, Dorethy 15, Wm. 13, Mird 11 (f), Henry 17
SABASTIAN, Saml. 21*, Elizabeth 23, M. E. 7/12
EADS, Isaac 21*, Mary 19
SALLYERS, Mary 52, Ann M. 24, Laura 22, Wm. 18
SALLYERS, Mitcher 27, Eliza 25, Chas. 1
MARTIN, Hezekiah 37*, Catharine 39, W. F. 3 (m))
JACOBY, Andrew 42*
SCOTT, Robt. 70 (B), May 40, Robt. 22
MORROW, James 60, Rachael 41, Mary E. 21, Ellen 16, James 7, Isabella 4

Schedule Page 158

HENDERSON, J. C. 34 (m), Frances 23, C. R. 1/12 (f), David 28
LINN, Mary 50*
JONES, Mary 7*, Robt. 6, Theophilus 3
SAWYERS, Wiley 60* (B)
HUNT, Agness 8* (B)
MCCANTRY, F. T. 41 (m)*, Rebecca 30, James 3
REED, James 70*
WASON, Elizabeth 60*
HARDING, Wm. 30*, M. E. 23 (f)
VAUGHAN, Cornilius 28, Mary 33, S. E. 10 (f), F. H. 7 (f), T. C. 6 (m), J. F. 5 (m), David 1, M. C. 1/12 (f)
ALLEN, Jerry 73 (B)
MOORE, Butler 77, M. A. 70 (f)
KEEN, Oliver 30, Sallie 26, Sidney Clay 6, M. O. 3 (f)
MOORE, Yelley 74, Elizabeth 76, James 33, Wm. 30, Harrison 25
FITZPATRICK, Emily 52, Dennis 27, William 25, E. J. 17 (f)
VAUGHAN, Cornelius 63*
CAWGILL, James 27*
BRUEN, Wm. 24, Polly 25, Wm. 3, M. J. 1 (f)
CRAIG, Mary 70*

1850 Census Fayette County Kentucky

BLAKEMORE, Eliza 34*, Joseph C. 4
MULDER, S. J. 23 (f)*
HARRIS, James 63 (B), Florida J. 57, J. M. 10, F. A. J. 4, Sallie J. 2, J. R. 6/12 (m), Fanney 70
FOLEY, James 37*, Richard 9, Pheby 7, C. P. 5 (m), Arabella 3, S. C. 2 (f), Jas. W. 4/12, M. J. 37 (f)
WYMORE, Martin 77*, John 54
WHITE, Elijah 24*
HILL, Geo. W. 31, Josephene 27, Rodolph 7, clara 5, Geo. A. 3
MCPHETERS, Andrew 51, Susan A. 32, D. S. 22 (m), M. E. 19 (f), A. N. 16 (m), Ranken 16, Mary R. 2, Jas. S. 7/12

Schedule Page 159

RICHARDSON, W. H. 56 (m), J. C. 24 (m), Saml. C. 26, Isabella 19, W. P. 18 (f)
CLOUD, R. T. S. 34 (m)*, Ann A. 29, Ana L. 6, Mary J. 4, Sallie R. 2
JONES, W. C. 12 (m)*
KING, Nancy 69*
WHITE, Phillip 60* (B)
KEENE, Mary 66*, John 19, May 11
BELL, Betty 60* (B)
KEEN, Geo. F. 42, Ethelinda 38, Sandford 16, Nancy C. 14, Jos. O. 9, Patsy 7, Geo. F. 5, Martha 55, Horrace 33
MAIDLOW, James 74*
FINLEY, Martha 72*
----, Mary 23* (B), John 2
WORLEY, Jane 52*, harvey 23, Joshua 20, Nanney 17
WALKER, Jinney? 13*, Mariem 10, Saml. 8
NOVE, Daniel 47, Sarah 38, Mary J. 16, A. E. 14 (f), S. C. 9 (f), Amelia 17, J. J. 5 (m), F. M. 2 (m), John 3/12
SPENCER, Geo. G. 50, Amelia 51, Harlow 26, Martha 25, Geo. 24, Franklin 16, Charles 2
YATES, Wm. 23*, Margaret 22, Lucy C. 4/12
SIMMS, Solomon 21*, Alfred 19
NONLEY, A. 45 (m), M. A. 39 (f), Benj. 16, Sarah A. 1
COOK, Jas. D. 43, Mary 19, Robt. F. 20, Jas. N. 11, Alexander W. 9, Fanny A. 6, Sarah C. 4, Emily 2, May E. 4/12
STIPE, Henry 23, Elizabeth 18
CUNN, Batris 51 (f)*, Nancy A. 13, M. C. 10 (f), Wm. 7
VALENTINE, Elizabeth 19*
CLARK, Rody 70 (B)
CLARK, Richard 75 (B)
JONES, Joseph 44, Harriot 43, Lucy A. 19, M. J. 14 (m), Mancy C. 12, E. H. 7 (f), John R. 5, W. J. 17 (f)

Schedule Page 160

PARSONS, Geo. W. 42*, Isabella 48, Louisa 14, Lucy A. 11
HANES, Lucinda 52*
YATES, John 15*

1850 Census Fayette County Kentucky

BERRYMAN, J. S. 61 (m), E. M. 57 (f), John G? 19, Charles H. 17
THRASHLEY, M. R. 37 (f)*
JACKSON, John H. 21*
DUGLASS, Hesekiah 24, S. A. 23 (f), A. M. 3 (f), John J. 2
MILTON, Eben 54*, Emely B. 47, S. C. 26 (f), John 24, Mary 17, Sarah 16, Teaball 15 (m), Eben 14, Benj. 10, Jas. B. 8, Griffin T. 4, Louisa 1
BAYLESS, S. M. 40 (m)*, Elizabeth 22
CASTLEMAN, M. P. 66 (f)*
TAYLOR, A. B. 37 (m)*, Ellen 24
VALENTINE, John 27*, Catherine 24, A. 1
HANEY, Robt. 23*
DAWES, John 21*
WILLIAMSON, Dudley 21*
DAWES, James 20*
CLARK, Robt. 40* (B)
GRAVES, W. W. 62 (m)*, Polly 53, Arabella 27, Geo. W. 23, L. C. 18 (m), James 15, Robt. 11
SPRINGATE, Almoore 22*
SMEDLEY, Morgan 53, Ann 43, Geo. 23, Mary J. 17, John 18, Nancy 16, Frances 12, Elizabeth 10, Jacob 8, Sallie 5
ALEXANDER, Isabella 68, Elzia 40
CRUMBAUGH, Ezra 53, David 42
MUNEY, Dudley 53*, Elizabeth 54, Wm. 22, Mary 25, Elizabeth 23, Margaret 20, Rachael 18, C. 16 (m)
SMITH, Jas. 4*
ALLEN, Elizabeth 50*, Margaret 27, Geo. Ann 18, S. F. 14 (f), John 10/12
BERTON, John 20*

Schedule Page 161

SULLIVAN, Jas. W. 43*, M. S. 32 (f), A. M. 3 (m)
BULLOCK, Elizabeth 8*
PECK, A. F. 22 (m)*
SULLIVAN, Mary 62*, Martha 21, Wm. 28
DOWNING, Saml. 22*
BOWMAN, Wm. 60*, Nancy T. 57
HENRY, Sarah 56*
TODD, Robt. 34, Mary 14, Alice 1
TODD, W. L. 60 (m), Nelly 60, Jane 28, Margaret 23, Isabell 17
CRUMBAUGH, John 41, Sharlott 38, M. L. 18 (f), Geo. W. 8, Emely 6, Charles 4, D. H. 1 (m)
FOLEY, Almira 46, Darcus 16, Frances 13, Nepolion 12, Luther 9, Mary B. 8, Ann 7, Jas. W. 4
WALTZ?, Frank 81, Elizabeth 30, Mary 19, Benj. 14
BERRY, H. K. 42 (m), M. C. 39 (f), Lucy 17, Laura B. 15, Anderson 11, S. E. 9 (f), F. W. 6 (f), L. B. 4 (f), M. B. 2 (f), Jane 69
BERRY, Eliza 13, Henry C. 27
BERRY, Benj. 36, Camild 22 (f), Nora 2
HOGAN, John 60, Margaret 41, Isham T. 17, John H. 15, Lucey Ann 13, Wm. 10, Samuel 8, Jas. 5, M. J. 3 (f), Martha H. 1/12
DEDMAN, Richmond 27, Martha 47, Dudley 19, James 14, Lucy Ann 11, Martha 8

1850 Census Fayette County Kentucky

CASTLEMAN, Charles W. 39*, S. E. 39 (f), M. P. 14 (f), B. T. 12 (m), Milton 10, Chas. H. 8, Mary L. 7, David 5, Anna 3, Jacob 2/12
HULL, Henry 16*
BELL, Billy 80* (B)
YOUNG, E. A. 34 (f)*, Betty 5, John 3

Schedule Page 162

KINKEAD, Chunn 38, Susan 14, James 10, Elizabeth 8, F. M. 6 (m), Robt. 4, Barton 6/12, Catherine 31
STANHOPE, W. F. 36 (m)*, Nancy C. 25, Alfred 7, J. B. 5 (m)
POAG, J. G. 40 (m)*
CUNNINGHAM, Nancy 39*, John P. 12, W. H. 8 (m), Jacob H. 6, Nancy 3
SMITHER, E. W. 18 (f)*
CLARK, Zachariah 23*
SRELEY?, B. W. D. 26 (m)*
DAVIS, Jesse 43*, Zerilda 35, Wm. 22, Mary 18, Susan 18, Hamilton 14, Henry 12, Jesse 10, Harrison 8, Milly 1
SANDERS, Allen 14*, John 12
DAVIS, Geo. 35, Nancy 32, Margaret 14, Julia A. 12, Wm. 11, Mary 9, Nancy 4, Ann 7/12, John 20, Hannah 22
CRAVENS, Geo. 58, Frances 50, John 27, C. W. 24 (m), Wm. 22, Mary 16, Elizabeth 8
CRAVENS, James C. 21*, Catherine 18, Josephene 4/12, Jesse 16
BLACKFORD, Benj. 9*
HENRY, Charles 10* (B)
JAMES, John G. 50*, A. E. 13 (f), R. S. 12 (m), D. H. 6 (m), Jas. P. 4, W. H. 2 (m)
EASLEY, Sallie 60*
TAYLOR, Geo. W. 31*
HOWARD, J. L. 45 (m), J. C. 22 (f), Peter T. 8, Julia 4, Joseph 3, Leland 2, Robt. 4/12
BOWMAN, Joseph 56, C. R. 20 (f), A. 29 (m), Amanda 17
WOLFORK, Sawyel D. 60, Sarah H. 54
TURNER, John 56, Elizabeth 50, M. J. 21 (f), Georgeana 20, Edward 19, Charles 17

Schedule Page 163

FOLEY, Thos. 28*, Lucinda 23, John W. 1
HEFNER, Peter 22*
ALFORD, John 34, J. M. 25 (f), M. E. 4 (f), S. J. 2 (f), Stephen 29
ELGIN, H. S. 60 (m)*, Sarah W. 48, Jas. H. 28, Margaret 20, John S. 18, Elizabeth 16, Catherine 15
SINGLETON, E. S. 19 (m)*, John W. 15
BUTLER, Thompson 23*, Susan 50, M. A. 19 (f), Martha 17, Wm. 10?, Sarah 12, Robt. 8
RUMSEY, Martha 54*, Jas. 35
GRAW, Levi 22*
CHRISMAN, Joseph H. 50*, Pelina 45, Matilda 20, Florida 17, Joanna 16, Catherine 7
HIGBEE, Alex 21*, S. M. 18 (f), Henry 16, C. H. 14 (m)
MIMMS, M. A. 18 (f)*
_____, Jane 75* (B)
HITER, C. M. Y. 33 (m)*, Mary 33, Sarah 12, Jas. F. 9, Nancy 7, Thos. 5, Mary 3, Kitty 3

1850 Census Fayette County Kentucky

BUTLER, Thomson 21*
EASTON, Elizabeth 22*
CLEMMONS, Madison 22*, Catherine 19, N. E. 2 (f)
JENKINS, James 25*
FAULCONER, Joseph 49, Julia 47, Frances Ann 21, Thos. M. 19, M. E. 6 (f), Joseph 8, Nancy 7, Elijah 6, M. J. 11 (f)
BRYAN, Elijah 26, Lucy 19
SALLER, Geo. M. 25, M. A. 25 (f), A. E. 4 (f), M. J. 2 (f), John B. 5/12
BOWMAN, H. C. 24 (m), Sallie 20, Annabell 1
BRYAN, Wm. 43, Eliza 33, John J. 12, Mary 3/12, Margaret 64
WILMOT, John L. 32, S. D. 22 (f), Mansfield 7, Sarah N.? 5, Geo. H. 5/12

Schedule Page 164

BOWMAN, Geo. H. 57*, Isabella 29, Thunniethis? 18, George Ann 13, Eliza T. 4, Bell 2
GITON, W. H. 12 (m)*
KIDD, Frances 30*
LATHAM, Robt. T. 42*, Sarah Ann 35, Ann 11, Laura 9, Robt. T. 4, Augusta 2
CHRISMAN, John 24*
HAYSE, R. A. 37 (m), Mary 23, Elizabeth 4, Joseph 1
CURD, John 51, Elizabeth 48, John C. 9
MCCANN, John 27, Mary 22, M. E. 3 (f), Francis 2
TURNER, James H. 26, R. E. 24 (f), R. D. 4 (f), Betsy 1
SAYRE, James 49, Sallie 52, M. 11 (f), Zenophan 6
SAYRE, A. 20 (f), Orelius 6/12
INGELS, H. B. 35 (m)*, Elizabeth 25, Maria L. 9, Joseph B. 7, E. A. 5 (f), Florance L. 3, E. S. 4/12 (m)
SAYRE, James 29*
_____, Isaac 17* (B)
JONSON, Joseph 50, Lidia 37, Jas. 19, M. J. 18 (f), S. A. 15 (f), M. A. 13 (f), Joseph 11, Helen 10, Geo. T.? 8, Lidia 6, John E. 3, Eliza 10/12
DUNCAN?, James 30*
KIDWELL, Mary 37*, Harriet 14
GAMLEY, Patrick 50
KAY, Mary B. 44, Daniel B. 22, Elizabeth J. 16, John 25, Sarah A. 16, Lewis B. 12
TARLTON, L. B. 34 (m), Caroline B. 33, Elisha W. 9, L. P. 4 (m)
LAUDERMAN, J. H. 26 (m)*, Martha 20, C. E. 1 (f)
MONTAGUE, Wm. 24*
STONE, Jacob 65, Martha 62, Wm. 32
SALLER, Daniel 53, Margaret 38, Livonia 20, Wm. 25, M. C. 2 (f), Joseph 4/12

Schedule Page 165

GIST, John 58*
ELLY, John W. 45*, Martha A. 40
MOORE, Nancy 60, Mary 60
SALLER, Joseph 48, Nancy 48, N. J. 23 (m), Amanda 17, Elizabeth 15, W. F. 13, Joseph H. 11, Polly J. 9, John E. 7, Daniel B. 4

1850 Census Fayette County Kentucky

SALLER, Jas. 50, Permelia 29, Joseph 24, D. A. 15 (m), P. F. 8 (f), Julia A. 7, John T. 5, Geo. D. 3, Jennetta 1
CLEMMONS, Thos. C. 28, M. A. 21 (f)
JENKINS, Willis 45, Nancy 43, Jas. 27, Levi 25, Tilford 23, Alice 18, Wm. 16, Sallie 14, John 12, Mariam 10 (m), Mary 8, Lucinda 6, Columbus 4
GRADY, John 26*, M. A. 38, Ellen 4, Nancy 4, Mary 3, Kitty 4/12, Catherine 70
ADAMS, Wm. 14*, Elisha 12, Nathaniel 9, Newton 7
SMITH, Grandison 20*
FAULCONER, Lewis 74*, Harriet 56
STEPHENS, Sarah 47*
CRAVENS, Milton 31, Rebeca 35, Elisha 16, Andrew 14, Wm. 11, Frances 4
FOLEY, Elizabeth 67, Sanford 42
FOLEY, Margaret 24*, Alexander 8/12
SANDERS, Wm. 16*
MCLEAN, Isabella 55*, Mary 23, Francis 27
CROMWELL, Mary 1*, Isabella 7
DOWNING, Wm. 55, Sharlotte 52, Willis 28, Jas. 23, Saml. 50, E. 5 (f), Elizabeth 44
DOWNING, Saml. 29*, Margaret 22, Kate A. 2
HUNT, Sarah 48*

Schedule Page 166

SECRET?, Jacob 39*, Sarah 45, Shedrick 16, David 9, Jacob 3, Thos. 70?
VAUGHN, Benj. 12*
BRYAN, Joseph 53, Margaret 45, Mary C. 20, Joseph 14
DALEY, Lawrence 57, A. M. 55 (f), Joseph 28, Isabella 17, Manetha? 16
FRANKLIN, H. B. 36 (m)*, O. C. 36 (f), M. E. 13 (f), A. E. 11 (f), H. F. 6 (m), Emma 2
AKIN, W. A. 37 (m)*
KELLEY, Patrick 30*
PETTIL?, W. B. 37 (m), A. D. 30 (f), N. J. 5 (f), John N. 1
AKIN, Saml. 27*, Pulina 22, Emely 2
FITZPATRICK, C. 19 (m)*
NUNLY, Sarah 63*, Jane A. 29
TURNER, F. L. 23 (m)*
DIAMOND, Jas. 20*
DAVIS, W. R. 31 (m), M. A. 24 (f), E. R. 3 (m), Garrard 76
WARE, Jas. H. 35*, Dyanitia 30, Sarah V. 9, John A. 7, Rassellas 5 (m), Leonidus 4, Nasessa 3, Geo. W. 6/12
VAUGHN, Mary J. 36*, James 1
BOSWELL, Thos. E. 55, Harriet R. 36, H. E. 15 (f), Ellen 13, Anna S.? 12, Alice F. 10, Edward C. 7, L. W. 6 (m), Geo. 5
COLEMAN, David S. 26*, Judith 18, Mary 1/12
JONES, Richard 25*
SUTTON, Julliet 60*
DELPH, J. 48 (m)*, Mary A. 28, A. E. 22 (f), S. J. 19 (f), Pelina 17, Edward 14, Martha 11, M. E. 5, Nancy 3
CAMPBELL, John B. 37*
FORD, W. H. 41 (m)*, Elenor 30

- 122 -

1850 Census Fayette County Kentucky

MCINTIRE, Mary 75*, Martha 16, Benj. 48
CARRICK, Robt. 55*, Nancy 55, John 26, N. R. 18 (f), M. E. 1 (f)

Schedule Page 167

COCHRAN, R. E. 4 (f)*, N. A. 2 (f)
HENDERSON, S. G. 36 (m)
MARTIN, Thos. B. 55, Susan 50, Wm. 24, Lavisia 18, Thos. 16, Edwin 9
SIDNER, G. P. 41 (m), Ann 35, M. A. 20 (f), Geo. P. 16, John F. 14, Josephine 11, Rebecca J. 9, Jas. H. 7, Zacheriah T. 1
GRINSTEAD, Jas. A. 36*, Robt. 77, Elizabeth 70, Julia A. 37
HERT, Julia F. 22*
ALLEN, Jas. H. 45*, Patty B. 60, Wm. 20, L. W. 16 (f), M. D. 13 (f), Elizabeth 11, Sarah 9, Robt. B. 7
PHILLIPS, Richard 21*
OBANNON, E. 45 (m)*, T. A. 48 (m), O. 17 (m), A. P. 14 (f), E. C. 13 (f), S. C. 10 (f), M. E. 4 (m)
LEACH, Jas. B. 71*
BROWNING, Sally 69*, Ann 27
HARP, Henry 32, Elizabeth 29, Chas. P. 4, Lucy B. 3, Henry C. 6/12
BRECKENRIDGE, R. J. 50 (m), Virginia 41, Sallie C. 17, R. J. 15 (m), Maria P. 13, W. P. C. 12 (m), Sophy P. 10, Jos. C. 8, Virginia 2, N. H. 10/12 (m)
INGELS, Andrew 32
READ, Thomas S. 42*
DUDLEY, C. W. 28 (m)*
MOORE, Alexander 45*, Mary 43
ANDERSON, Nancy 47*
RUNYON, S. A. 7 (f)*
WICKLIFF, Robt. 76, Mary C. 28
WICKLIFF, Robt. 30, Josephene 30
ANNAN, Saml. 50, A. M. F. 35 (f), Emely 7, Robt. K. 5
LOGAN, Jas. H. 50, M. V. 40 (f), Jas. V. 15, E. J. S. 13 (f), M. F. 11 (f), M. V. 9 (f), Sarah A. 7, M. A. 5 (f), Joseph A. 2
ANDREWS, A. M. 57 (m), M. J. 20 (f), C. J. 17 (m), Sarah A. 16, A. M. 14 (f), M. E. 12 (f), Thos. D. 23

Schedule Page 168

DOWNING, Richard 60, Mary 53, Richard 17, Pressilla 12
FARRER, John M. 50*, Martha 36, Ellen 8, Lannie? 5, M. J. 3 (f), Elizabeth 2, Catherine 4/12
GILL, Therissa 17*
WILSON, R. J. 33 (m), F. R. 27 (f), Elizabeth 4, Robt. E. 2
WOOD, John J. 32, Nancy A. 70?, Margaret B. 36, Wm. G. 30
SKILMAN, W. G. 51 (m)*, C. A. 40 (f), E. J. 16 (f), M. W. 13 (f), Charles G. 8, Sarah C. 5
COX, Joshua 25*
ALLEN, W. W. 24 (m)*
EADS, Thos. 46, Elizabeth 47, W. A. 22, Charles H. 19
COLEMAN, Eliza 70*
IRWIN, M. E. 20 (f)*
CROMWELL, Aben W. 36

1850 Census Fayette County Kentucky

MOORE, Robt. 49, Jane 21, Anna 16, Grandison 14, James 12, Patsy 10, Cathrine 9, Elizabeth 77
CROMWELL, Benj. 67, Jane 67, Marcus 20, Wm. 3
CALCLOYER?, Livina 27, May J. 23
TUCKER, Robt. 44*, Julia 34, Robt. 13, Sarah 11, Thoms W.? 10, Mary 4, Julia 2
HALSTEAD, Sarah 16*
BOSWORTH, Benj. 28, Sarah 26, Henry 20, David 14
LEAKER?, Jestes 56*
LIMFORST?, Francis 75*
SHIDDELL, W. F. 27 (m)
WEBB, Hugh 28*, Jane 22, E. M. 3 (f), Anna 7/12, Catherine 54, H. H. 16 (f)
SPRINKLE, Mary 52*
BOSWORTH, Geo. 19*
FOREMAN, John 28, Harriet E. 30, W. T. 7 (m), John R. 5, Joseph 3
PAYNE, Henry C. 56, Thos. H. 26, Lidia 23, Sallie 21

Schedule Page 169

MARTIN, Thos. B. 55, Susan 50, W. H. 24 (m), L. L. 18 (f), Thos. 16, Edwin 7
LEWIS, Thos. M. A. 23, Margaret 25, S. M. 2 (f), Almira J. 7/12, Malinda 44
PAYNE, William 65, May J. 32, E. M. 12 (m), W. S. 23 (m)
READ, A. O. 42 (m), Julia A. 35, Harriet 16, Elizabeth M. 14, Virginia 12, Thos. H. 10, Mary A. 6, Maria 4, Agatha 2
NAVE, John 36*, Elizabeth 33, Julia F. 5, W. R. 2 (m)
CAMPBELL, Julia A. 22*
WILEY, Adam 27*
WILLIAMS, Hanson 78*, Nancy 66, Wm. G. 46, Harvey 31, Sallie 20, Margaret 17, Nancy 15, Louisa 13, Livina 11?, Geo. W. 29
BROMBOYER, John 65*, Sarah 54
DOWNES, Wm. H. 35*
STONE, James 37, Nancy E. 36, Elizabeth 14, John 12, M. E. 10 (f), Wm. 8, B. W. 5 (m), Martha 1
PRICE, D. L. 36 (m)*, Elizabeth 29, John 12, Elizabeth 10
RUSK, W. J. 22 (m)*
BAUCHAMP, Jesse 47*, Louisa 44, M. E. 14 (f), M. F. 12 (f), M. C. 10 (f), Theophilus 8, L. J. 5 (f)
WILLIAMS, M. L. 3 (f)*, A. E. 21 (f)
BAUCHAMP, H. 27 (m)*, Rose A. 25
BROCKMAN, Wm. 37*, Catharine 30, Isaac N. 17, W. W. 15 (m), Nancy 11, Louisa 9, Osker 5, Geo. 2
EDWARDS, Martha 60*
NAVE, Robt. 35*
OFFUTT, Sandford 35, Mary 40, Thos. 19, Wm. 17, J. S. 14 (m), Casius M. 7, Caroline 17, Susan 13, Maria 10, Elizabeth 11, Nancy 6, J. E. 4 (f)

Schedule Page 170

HICKS, John D. 31, Ellen 28, John E. 6, Davis H. 4, Paulina 2
CAWBY, David 35, N. A. 30 (f), Moses 10, Joshua 8, Mary E. 5, Martin 4, David 2
MCAFEE, Wm. 47*
HICKS, Hager 14*, H. H. 11 (m), Wm. 26

1850 Census Fayette County Kentucky

READ, Peter 38?* (B)
ALLEN, John 29*
MITCHELL, Maryman 24*
HAGER, Sarah 48, Caroline 18, Wm. 18
ALLEN, Albert 26, A. E. 21 (f), Francis 5, James 3, Polly 1
BLANCHARD, Hester 60
WILLIAMS, Malinda 50 (B)
HIRONEMUS, W. T. 44 (f)*, Elvira 50, Edwin 8, Wm. 6, Benj. 5, James A. 2
LANDRETH, A. E. 50 (f)*, Robert 47, O. D. 16 (m)
MARTIN, Manlius 21*, Minerva 21, Robt. 2, Geo. Ann 4/12
VAUGHN, Ricd. 8*
STONE, Joseph 23, Susan 53, Enoch 21, Jacob L. 17, John B. 13
RITCHEY, Saml. 73, Jane 62, Robt. 31, Saml. 22
STONE, Uriah 34, Margaret 21, Geo. W. 2, John H. 1/12
PRICE, Cosby 67, Mary J. 32, T. B. 10 (f), Virginia E. 7, W. C. 4 (m), S. F. 2 (m)
GRADY, Wm. 80*
MITCHELL, Sallie 60*, Edward 25, Meryman 21
SMITH, John T. 44*, Henry 11, Wm. 9
FOLEY, Elijah 19*, Catherine 15
WHEELER, Geo. 57, Ann 56, Charles N. 33, Warren 29, Ann E. 2

Schedule Page 171

TUCKER, F. A. 30 (f)*, Leona 12, Nancy T. 9, Mary C. 7, James 5
GOINES, Americus 43*, Caleb 17
BRAGG, Grace 38, Susan C. 6, Ann H. 3, Frances J. 3
BOSWORTH, Ann W. 51, Charles C. 26, Ann E. 21, Benj. E. 16, Harriet E. 10
HEADLEY, Saml. 52*, Mary 40, Mary J. 20, James A. 10, Maria 7
LAMME?, Jane 33*
TUCKER, Abraham 70 (B), Lucy 65, Abraham 4
DUVALL, Geo. H. 75, Elizabeth 69, Willis P. 29, Geo. D. 27, John H. 4
BAXTER, Reuben 27*, Irenia C. 21, M. E. 3 (f), J. J. 1 (f)
ADAMS, Sarah J. 17*
JONSON, Joseph M. 50, Adaline 36, C. E. 15 (f), John H. 18, Robt. B. 12, Joseph W. 9, M. A. 6 (f), W. E. 3 (m), C. C. 1 (m)
TUCKER, Ann 50*, Jane 19, Margaret 16, W. W. 12 (m), Henry C. 7
DONAVAN, Sallie A. 26*, Peter W. 11/12
TUCKER, John 40, Elenor 27, Mary J. 16, Elizabeth 14, Andrew 10, Josephine 7, Margaret 5, Chas. 4, Geo. 2
FRY, Thos. C. 54*, Sharlotte 44, Elizabeth 75, C. A. 12 (f), Henry C. 9, Virgil 7, Geo. W. 5, Joseph A. 3
PRICE, John 17*
CRANDELL, J. B. 22 (m), Cathrine 24, D. V. 2 (m)
UNDERWOOD, L. 52 (f), Sarah 26, Nelson 21, Thos. 20, E. J. 16 (f)
BAXTER, Geo. 30, Deborah 25, Cathrine 7, Mary 4, Mary E. 2

1850 Census Fayette County Kentucky

Schedule Page 172

DOLEN, Wm. 70, Elizabeth 58
KIRKPATRICK, W. 22 (m), Sallie 19
KIRKPATRICK, David 25, Louisa 21, A. 5 (m), L. 3 (m)
BYRNS, Wm. 66*, Margaret 58
EVANS, Isabella 17*
ELLIOTT, J. W. J. 14 (m)*
VANMETER, Abraham 45*, E. A. 40 (f), Jacob 21, James 17, Saml. 16, W. 14 (m), H. J. 9 (f), David 4, E. A. 7/12?
HULL, Rebecca 34*
INSKEP?, A. 78 (m)*
NOLAND, John 31, Sarah 20, Nathan 10, Palina 7
HENDERSON, James W. 70, Elizabeth 62, D. B. 26 (m), Sarah 54
PERKINS, Wm. 31*, Margaret 25, W. H. 6 (m), M. J. 3 (f), R. E. 4/12 (m)
HERKEL?, Thos. 54*
GRINSTEAD, Robt. 26, Lurana 17, Wm. 1/12
RAMSEY, Lewis 32*, Sarah A. 26, Andrew 7, Henry 5, Wm. 2, Margaret 63
HUKELL?, John 22*
CLESER, Elizabeth 13*
JOHNSON, David 60, Susana 56, Joseph 18, Amanda 16
MARTIN, David 22*, C. E. 20 (f), A. E. 1/12
HUKEL, Leslie 7*
TYLER, Benj. 65*, Susan 62
HIGGINS, Charles 11*
GLASS, David 68, Sarah 60, Thompson 27, Davidella 18
JAMES, M. R. 58 (m), Almira 22
SPURR, R. J. 42 (m)*, Susan 38, Estill 17 (f), Mary 11, Martha 9, Sarah 6, Elizabeth 2/12, Baty 23, Richard 73, Barbary 62
MORRIS, W. P. 35 (m)*, M. A. 32 (f), Baty 4, Ella G. 4/12
PATTERSON, Isaac 22*
FITZGERALD, S. F. 42 (m), H. J.? 33 (f), Susan E. 13, R. H. 11 (m), Sarah E. 9, M. T.? 5 (f), E. J.? 3 (m), R. L. 7 (m)

Schedule Page 173

HIGGINS, Eliza 60*, John 27, Mary E. 14, W. W. 39 (m)
SPURR, Sarah E. 50?*, E. A. 7 (f), R. L. 4 (m), W. J. 8/12 (f)
KISE, Harriet 49*, Mary B. 30
ROBERTS, Amanda 19*, Joab 10, L. N. 8 (f)
JOHNSON, Jacob 28*
CANNON, James 40*, Calvin 36, Michel 4, Ellen 2
LINCH, Mary 13*, Thos. 11, John 9, Sarah 7
MCGARVEY, Peter 30, Isabella 30, Matilda 6, John 4, Jas. 1
OHERRIN, Dennis 37*, Ellin 40, John 4, John 38
SULLIVAN, Garrett 39*
QUARLES, Roger 78*, Jane 71
FARNSWORTH, B. F. 53 (m)*, Maria 55
THOMPSON, P. H. 29 (m)*, Julia F. 25, A. E. 10 (f), J. M. 8 (f), Rodes 6, B. F. 5 (f), Wm. G. 3

1850 Census Fayette County Kentucky

HENRY, Charles 35*
PEARSON, Molly 65, Eliza 45, James T. 31
COOK, Prissilla G. 43, Geo. 17, Charles 11, Wm. 8, Jirene 6 (f), Prissilla 4
LAUDMAN, Malinda 47*, L. W. 7 (m), Thos. 6
GRAVES, Lidia 52*
MORRIS, Hannah 69, David 35, Julia Ann 34, Willey M. 33, Robt. A. 30, Elizabeth H. 17
PROUT?, Dyna 65* (B)
BROWN, Katy 50* (B)
LANKHART, Edward 38, E. 26 (f), Thos. 4
YARNALL, Isaac W. 31*
BROWN, Geo. 33*
DELONY, Andrew 30*
BREWER, John 38*
SHAY, Murtey 22 (m)*
PRICE, Willis 72*, Margaret 63, Nancy 24, Willis 27, John 16

Schedule Page 174

DAVENPORT, Louiser 7*
STONE, Oliver 33*, M. 41 (f), Wm. 11, Deborah 6, Ellen 6, Martha 4, Malissa 2
KIRKPATRICK, Mary 18*, Ann 16, Alx. 14
HILLICKS, Wm. 19*
TABOUR, Geo. 33, Martha 33
HARP, David 34, Nancy 33, Martha A. 11, E. C. 9 (f), Henry C. 7, Jas. W. 5, Nancy J. 4, Charles C. 2, Sarah E. 2/12, Susan 30
HOLMAN, Edward 30*
PARKER, Oswell*, Jane 50 (B)
DOLAN, Patrick 27, Susan 29, Thos. 35
ERWIN, John M. C. 64, Martha 60, M. A. J. 22 (f), G. E. 21 (m), E. M. 17 (f), M. C. 11 (m)
MARSHALL, Glass 40*, Mary A. 40, M. W. 13 (f), Robt. 11, Elizabeth G. 10, M. A. 9 (f), Saml. W. 7, Joseph C. 5, A. W. 3 (m)
ROGERS, Madison 24*
LOGAN, Wm. 60*, James 35, Jane 30, Hester 28, Zilla 24, Margaret 22
SMITH, Eli O. 40*, Abigal 27
WILLIAMS, John 37, Paulina 27, Mary E. 6, Ann E. 4, Wm. S. 1, Nancy 1/12
BAXTER, Geo. 32, Deborah 29, Sarah C. 7, May E. 6, Margaret E. 4
DOWNS, Jackson P. 33, Virlenda 22, Leslie 3, Benj. 8/12
SMEE, James 25, Jane 52, Emeline 20, Margaret 16
MURPHREE, John 42, Mary A. 38, Mary J. 13
PAYNE, Augustus 34*, Thos. 4, Nancy E. 2
SMITH, Morison A. 8*
HALMON, Cornelius 62, Mary 25, Richard 13, Frances 10, Rebecca 15

Schedule Page 175

COLE, L. W. B. 30 (m), Catherine 22, Sarah A. T. 4, James W. 3, T. A. G. 2 (m), Octavie 43
PATRICK, Charles 77, Christian 45, James 30

1850 Census Fayette County Kentucky

FRY, Benj. 50, Eliza 44, Sharlotte 20, John 18, Elizabeth 16, Rachael 14, B. F. 12 (m), Wm. 9, Marietta 7, Amanda 6, Artemetia 5, Marian S. 3 (m)
GIBSON, John 72, Nancy 45, Susana 34, Elonor 25
WILLIAMS, John 40*, Rachael 30, Jane 6, John 4, James 1
JOHNSON, Wm. 22*
SALYERS, S. P. 30 (m)*, Sarah A. E. 49
DANIEL, Louisa 60*
WARREN, Wm. H. 7*
NUNNELY, D. 36 (m), Juetty 17, James B. 11
ROBERTS, B. F. 29 (m), S. J. 25 (f), Ruth 3, Wesley 1
ELBERT, Theodore 39, Margaret A. 28, Sarah R. 7, Lucy E. 5, Cathrine J. 3
BOYD, Saml. M. 35, S. A. F. 24 (f)
ROBB, Joseph 28, B. J. 24 (f), Mary E. 1
NUTTER?, James 51, Mary 49, Wm. 24, John 20, Robert 18, Mary E. 8
GRIMES, John 41*, Edward 11, Virginia 10, John 9, Cathrine 7
SUTTON, Wm. 22*, Mary A. 17
HANEY, Patrick 25*, Mary 22, John 2, Cathrine 1, Charles 21, Daniel 14
CARNEY, John 19*, Daniel 35
CRAWLEY, Dennis 28*, Michael 28
BRADLEY, Barney 28*
MALORY, Arther 36*
NUTTER, Ann 56, Martha L. 17
KEISER, C. M. 42 (m), Nancy A. 39, John W. 17, Wm. J. 14, David C. 13, James A. 6

Schedule Page 176

MCKENNA, Stafford 30*
LOGUE, John 23*
MCLANE, James 20*
FRANEY, Moses 30*
COLLINS, James 32*
CAMPBELL, John 30*
FRAIL, James 26*
HIGGINS, Patrick 23*
COLEMAN, Eliza B. 47, Elizabeth 30, Saml. M. 28, W. P. 24 (m), Sallie H. 18, Frances 16
FLOURNOY, Victor F. 40*, Betsey 38
MEDLICATT, John 70*
WALLACE, Nancy 66*, Louisa 29
COILE, Nancy 38*
SMITH, J. B. 44 (m)*, Henrietta M. 42
WHITT, Ann E. 21*, Rosabell 17
MARTIN, Wm. 40, Sarah 40, Mary 21, Elizabeth 18, Gabriel 16, Sarah 9, Margaret 6, M. A. 4 (f), W. H. 2 (m)
APPLETON, Joseph 51, Charles 10, Joseph C. 8, David F. 6
SAMPSON, James 36
GRAVES, Geo. W. C. 41, Sidney J. 36 (f), John R. 18, F. Q.? 16 (m), Francis H. 14, Henry C. 12, M. J. 10 (f), James B. 1, Georgetta E. 6, Irene H. 3
WALLACE, Geo. H. 54, Amanda 29, Julia F. 3, James R. 2, Jane E. 2/12

1850 Census Fayette County Kentucky

HANES, Simeon 69*, Jane 55, Mary 35, Sarah 33
HANEY, Elizabeth 31*, Catherine 21, Saml. 19, Charity 16
ARMSTRONG, Sarah 91*
RANDOLPH, John H. 34*, Mary 31, Wm. H. 6, Harriett F. 4, John W. 7/12
FORD, Hannah 62*, Wm. 34
GAUGH, Percival 42, Julia O. 35, James P. 13, Sarah L. 11, Chas. E. 7, Wm. W. 4, Richard P. 2
WRIGHT, Morgan 40, Ann E. 28, Mary E. 11, Thos. 9, Robt. M. 7, Sarah E. 5, Jane H. 3, Susan S. 1

Schedule Page 177

PRICE, Elenor 37 (m), Mary J. 34, Charles B. 12, Mary E. 10-, Isaiah W. 8, Margaret A. 4, E. M. 6/12 (m)
BRECKENRIDGE, Thos. 55, Jane 47, James 21, Sarah 18, Greenup 14, Nancy 12
MURFREE, John 28*, Catherine 22
ESTILL, Thos. 3*
GORHAM, John G. 40*, Mary J. 29, Geo. L. 5, John A. 2/12
ESTILL, Mary 47, Wallace 23, John 16, Mary E. 14, Eliza 12, Elenora 9, Thos. 6, James 25
LAUDAMAN, Wm. 40, Cyntha Ann 34, John J. 13, Mary E. 11, Joseph 7, Sarah C. 5, Wm. 1
ADAMS, Wm. 32*, Mary T. 25, John 7, James 6, Geo. 4, Mary E. 7/12
MERRELL, David 40*
BRYAN, John O. 46, Ellen O. 31
WILSON, James 65*, Nathan H. 25
ROBERTS, Agness A. 30*, E. J. 8 (f)
LEEDS, M. A. 14 (f)*, Luther R. 12, Jessa? J. 7 (f), Fanny M. 4
DOWNING, Margaret 60*, B. F. 39 (m), Frances 10, Leticia 6
LEWIS, David J. 23*, Margaret 14
MARTIN, Barnett 45, Sarah 44, Margaret 23, Hannah 18, Gabriel 16, Barnett 10, Joseph W. 4
EARDMAN, John A. 34*
POWELL, John 24*
LUCAS, John 26, Irene 19, Albert 3, Barbary A. 8/12
LAWSON, David 68, Catherine 60
ANDERSON, O. H. 44 (m)*, Catherine 45
PARMER, Nancy 50*, Mary E. 14
CRAIN, J. P. 25 (m), Margaret 17
SPATIS, Levi 45, Ammy 49

Schedule Page 178

SPATIS, Noah 42, Ann 35, W. W. 14 (m), Mary 11, Virginia 9, John 8, Leticia 6, Amanda 3, Isabella 6/12
JOHNSON, M. B. 42 (f), Caroline L. 36, Christopher 55(B)
MOORE, Margaret 67*, B. F. 20 (m), R. H. 34 (m)
MANSON, Albert 21*
DEVERS, H. B. 35 (m), Jane 34, Geo. W. 9, F. M. 7 (m), John G. 6, Susan 5, Mary 1
RICE, John 39, Caroline 37, S. E. 14 (f), John W. 13, Sarah F. 11, W. C. 9 (m), James H. 8, Mary 6, Joseph 5, H. E. 3 (f), Edward P. 1
KENIDAY, Geo. 27*, Sarah C. 17

1850 Census Fayette County Kentucky

SCOTT, Telitha 44*, Robt. C. 11, Talbott 9, Benj. 5
JOHNSON, J. B. 47 (m)*, Elizabeth M. 43, Robt. F. 12
TILLON, Sarah F. 15*
SPEAKE, W. F. 26 (m)*
SHIRLEY, Magdaloney 51, David 26, Mary E. 23, John D. 21, Susana 18, James W. 15, W. F. 11 (m)
VANCE, John 28?, Lidia 54, David 21
SALYERS, Robt. C. 36, Elizabeth 25, Saml. J. 9, Sharlotte A. 7, Rebecca P. 5, John A. 2
RANDOLPH, Moses 74*, Sarah 70, Moses 30, Rachael 17
MAGUIRE, David 22*, Eliza D. 19
CROMWELL, Eliza D. 19*, Rachael 50
HARRISON, Humphrey 24*
ATCHISON, Sarah 39*
WEST, James W. 26*, Isabella 21, Mary E. 3, Hamilton A. 1
MOORE, Wm. G. 31, Sarah B. 29, John W. 9, Mary E. 7, Hannah 3
ENNIS, Robt. 75*, Catherine A. 29, Lucy C. 3, Margaret E. 1

Schedule Page 179

THOMPSON, James C. 1*
SIMPSON, Thos. 31*
INNIS, E. E. 66 (f)*
COX, Frances 40, James 17, John 14, Geo. 12, L. A. 10 (f), Hopson 8, Daniel 7, Franklin 5, Emarillis 1 (f)
DOWNING, Salem 46*, Margaret 46, Susan E. 14, Julia 11, Josephine 5
MCINTIRE, Benj. 21*
PERKINS, James 23*
HUGHES, Thos. 45*, W. T. 18 (m), R. H. 12 (m), Ann W. 8, Sarah C. 6
CARTER, Geo. G. 31*, Mary 31
MASON, Wm. 46, Jane 44, John K. 22, E. A. 20 (f), Carr 17, Killis 14, Charles R. 12, Tabitha 9, Mary J. 6
DOMIGAN, James 48, Nancy 34, Hector 24, Thos. 22, Nancy 15, Sarah 13, Cabble 10 (m), John 8
LEWIS, Granvill? 50 (B), Emily 34
BRENHAM, Danl. 40* (B), Mary 34, Albert 16, Mary E. 14, Danl. 9, Emily 7, Rosey 6, Betty 4, Sarah F. 2, Ellen 1
DOOLEY, Doxey 80* (B)
GIBBONS, Thos. 70, Matilda 51, Joseph B. 14, Richard J. 10, Samuel S. 7
TAYLOR, Bird 39*, Paulina 32, W. R. 12 (m), Mary A. 8, Joseph H. 6, John 4, Chas. E. 6/12
HECKELL?, John 40*
DOOLIN, Robt. 29* (B), Mary A. 25, John L. 3/12
JOHNSON, Christopher 44* (B)
WENDOVER, R. H. 30 (m)*, Susan M. 27, A. C. 5 (m), M. C. 3 (f), W. A. 1 (m)
DUNLAP, Harriett 30*
ELLEDGE, Sharlott 17*
LAUSLEY, Lucinda 36, Geo. H. 13, James 8
GARRARD, Jas. D. 27*

1850 Census Fayette County Kentucky

Schedule Page 180

LEWIS, Hector P. 72*, Rebecca T. 20
VANMETER, Isaac 30*, Frances H. 28, Charles 7, Sarah E. 5, Edwin 3, Wm. S. 1
HULL, J. C. 35 (f)*, Ann A. 12
GIBBS, John 76, Elizabeth 66
LEWIS, Isaac 38, Maria 36, Louisa 19, Saml. 18, Mary J. 17, Sarah 16, Wm. 14, Lidia A. 10, Albert 8, Caroline 7, James 3, Bawler P. 2, Robt. 8/12
HARPER, Saml. 54, Mary 51, Elizabeth 21, Martha 17, Nancy 15, Lemira 13, Sarah 12, Samuel 3
PEEL, Priscilla 39, James 19, Margaret 18, Mary 16, Maria A. 15, Wm. 12, Richard 10, Eliza J. 7
HAYSE, Sarah 60*, Wm. 45, Martha 29
WILSON, Mary E. 12*, Lucy J. 8
RAGAN, Mary 51, Ann 19
PARKER, Jacob 37, Nancy 32, Jmaes 10, Mary 8, Emily J. 6, Jiram 5, Martha 1, Ellen 1
HUTCHISON, John 37, Alley 39, Wm. 20, Livina 18, Chas. 16, James 12, Nancy J. 10, Geo. 9, Lucian 8, Alsy 5, Mary 2
MCCARTY, Danl. 49, Pheeby 45, Cintha 20, Wm. 19, Susan 17, Jane 15, Jerry 12 (m), Pheeby 9, Danl. 6, Casius 3
DIXSON, Benj. 39*, Julia 41, Sarah M. 17, Harrison 13, Benj. 12, Saml. 8, Richard 2
HOGAN, Shelton 11*, Catherine 12

Schedule Page 181

CONQUEST, Lunsford 35*, Nancy 25, James 7, John 5, Thos. 3, Linsey 2
CUNNINGHAM, Rosey 45*, Mary 15
GRIGGS, Lucian 22*, Polly A. 23
JAMES, Tabatha 18*, Wm. R. 16, Geo. 11
EADES, Sallie 48, Margaret 24, Sarah 19, A. J. 17 (m), Polly 14, Thos. 12, James 10, John 8, Lewis 6, Nancy 3
MCKINNEY, Susana 30, Robt. 12, A. J. 8 (m), W. J. 6 (m), Angeline 10, Joseph 4, Sallie A. 2, Henry 1
MOORE, Francis 29, Susan 25, John 4, Wellington 1
JACKSON, Thos. 44*, Sarah 44, Andrew W. 15, Elizabeth 65
RIDDELL, Nancy 70*
LAUDEMAN, John 45*, Geo. A. 24
HELLENMEYER, Francis 35*, Caroline 37, Jane 9, Caroline 7, Catherine 5, Alfred 3, Hector 1
LATSCH, Teresse 41*
ONEAL, Patrick 33*, Margaret 28, Mary 12, Chas. 10, Michael 7, John 2
DOHAD, Thos. 21*
CROMWELL, Oliver 50*, Elizabeth 48, Edward 15, Robt. 12, Eliza 10, Thos. 9, Susan 6
LAUDEMON, David 20*
KAY, Robt. 72, America 20
BUCKNER, Geo. 55 (B)
DOWNING, Saml. 34, Amanda 28, Samuel 8, Sabret 5 (m), May E. 3, Alfred 1
MCMURTRY, Levi 29*, E. H. 27 (f), David 6, James 2
TURNER, David 67*
TARLTON, Cabb 46, Mary A. 39, Chas. 20, Wm. H.? 24, Caleb 14, Margaret 12, Nancy 10, Joel 6, Mary E. 4, Ellen 2, Martha 6/12

1850 Census Fayette County Kentucky

Schedule Page 182

TARLTON, Wm. B. 36
TAYLOR, Harrison 30
CASTLEMAN, David 64, Virginia H. 44, Virginia H. 22, Robt. H. 19, David 16, Mary A. 14, Frances E. 7, Umphreys 7, Sarah B. 4, Geo. A. 2
FRAZIER, James O. 30, Elizabeth M. 27, Anna 6, Lettitia 4
DALHAM, Letitia 60*, Littitia 30
RITTER, Valentine 29*
MEREDITH, Jane 60*
SIMRALL, John G. 40, Sarah B. 35, James 14, Walter 12, John G. 10, Wm. T. 8, Joseph B. 6, Martha B. 2, Saml. B. 5/12
READ, R. W. 46 (f), Saml. 17, Wm. 15, Oliver 12, Richard 9, Thos. S. 14, John W. 11
GRISSIM, John D. 32, H. M. 25 (f), Mary A. 4, Eliza C. 2
MOORE, Chas. C. 60, M. A. H. 45 (f), Wm. H. 18, Chas. C. 12, Mary Ann 10, Amanda J. 4, Alice W. 1
WALLACE, Wm. 23, Letitia 22, John W. 6/12
NUTTER, Robt. 49, Sallie 44, Mary E. 16, Geo. W. 11, Robt. H. 9, Sarah J. 7, Amelia 5, A. R. 4 (f), John T.? 1
NUTTER, David 24, Sarah F. 22
HURST, James 43*, Rebecca 43, Wm. H. 16, Amelia 13, John F. 11
NUTTER, Matilda 14*
LOGAN, David 49, Joseph J. 14, Esther M. 12, Sophia S. 10
WOOD, Jas. B. 45, Celina 34, Ferdinand 14, Mary J. 12, Sarah A. 9, John 7, Wm. 5, Margaret 2

Schedule Page 183

COYLE?, Wm. 39, Elizabeth 31, James M. 12, May E. 10, John L. 7, Ann R. 6, Barton S. 5 (f), Susan F. 2, Wm. 1/12
HAMILTON, Thos. J. 65*, Martha 65
DUVALL, Ann 53*, Payton 13
SPEAKE, Thos. C. 61, Margaret 45, James 14, Robt. 8, Isaac 6, Mary E. 2
MOORE, Henry C. 37, Elizabeth A. 27, Laura J. 4, Sarah A. 2/12
ROSS, Wm. 74*, Wm. 18
CHILDERS, Margaret 22*, John 26, Mary E. 2/12
INNES, John P. 38*, Margaret 10, James 8, Susan 6, Elizabeth 3, John 4/12
SPEAKE, John O. 24*
RICE, Abraham 53*, Margaret 40, Martin 28, Ann E. 20, Martha M. 18, Wm. A. 11
SIMMS, Margaret 3*
RICE, Martin 28, Eliza J. 21, Mary F. 4, Ann M. 8/12
SHOVER, James 37*, Mary Ann 23, Mary F. 2, Sarah E. 1
WOOD, Alexander 20*, A. R. 14 (f)
NUTTER, Wm. 57, Temperance 54, John R. 23, Clement C. 21, Mary A. 17, Sarah H. 14
WOOD, B. B. 32 (m)
READ, Ellen 68*
BOSWELL, W. D. 20 (m)*
BEVANS, Mary 24*
HICKS, John 29, Elizabeth 22, David 3, Frances 1, Abraham 64, Martha 60, Harvey 22

1850 Census Fayette County Kentucky

VANCE, Harvey 24, Geo. A. 24, Susan E. 5, Lidia A. 2, Levi 21
HUFFMAN, Michael 40*, Eliza 22, Saml. 12, Mary J. 9, John 4, Lidia C. 3/12

Schedule Page 184

CROFFORD, H. 75 (m)*
SAYRE, David A. 57, Abby V. 51, Ephraim D. 30, Mary E. 23, C. P. 63 (f)
VERTNER, David 78*, Elizabeth 63, Margaret 16
JOHNSON, C. M. 30 (m)*, Rosa 24, Vertner 2
HERREN, Virginia 16*
CHISM?, Wm. 30* (B)
GOUGH, Perry W. 33*, Mary J. 23, Michael 7
WEBB, John 23*
MORGAN, Creth? 22 (m)*
CLARK, Joseph 20*
BROWN, John P. 20*
HALEY, Randolph 30*
MCCARTER, Geo. M. 33*, Ann 25
MCMAINS, Mary 23*
ROBERDS?, L. C. 32 (m)*
MAROMAN, G. W. 25 (m)*
MYERS, John 25*
LOGAN, James 68, John 30, Lavina 70 (B)
PAYNE, H. B. 55 (m)*, Amanda 47, Sarah A. 21, Margaret G. 18, J. H. D. 12 (f)
PERRIN, Felix 45*, Hippolyte 21
POLK, Jmaes 23*
MURAIN, D. H. 22 (m)*
BASSETT, B. F. 20 (m)*
ATKINS, Dudley 40, Sarah 27, Thos. 7, Mary 5, Dudley 3
EDINDGTON, Benj. T. 30*, Mary J. 26
WOODHOUSE, Margaret 44*
MILLER, John J. 27*, Elizabeth H. 23, W. F. 3 (f), B. C. 1 (m)
SETTELS, Josephene 12*
HUKLE, John 30, Mary 65, Martha 38, Eliza 35
HARRISON, Carter H. 25*
HULETT, Jas. 19*
HEDGES, Alexander 78*
BOWMAN, Abram 65
BOWMAN, Nancy 60*, Thos. 24
GILBERT, John 50, Elizabeth 46, Chas. J. 19, John 18, Letitia 15, James 13, Thos. 11, Wm. 9
CROMWELL, John W. 20, Susan 19
FRAZER, Wm. 51*, Ann O. 45, Wm. 22, Mary 20, Martha 18, James O. 17, Robt. 14, Rebecca 9
HULETT, Elizabeth 19*

1850 Census Fayette County Kentucky

Schedule Page 185

GARNETT, Virginia 3*
NUTTER, Jas. R. 22*
HINAS, Thos. 50* (B)
JOHNSON, Isaiah 40* (B), Adam 70
OUTEN, Mathias 54*, Margaret H. 54, Wm. L. 27, Celia 26, Elizabeth 24, Thos. 22, Margaret 20, America 18, Mary 16, Sarah R. 14
ANDERSON, John 40* (B)
HILL, Thos. 82*
LYLE, John J. 46*, Jane J. 34, Paulina P. 11, Robt. J. 5
PLEASANTS, Susan R. 62*
LYONS, Chas. O. 25*
SHUCK, Valentine 45*
HULITT, Granvill 33, Sarah 35, Mary A. 16, Isaac? 3
MICHAEL, Elizabeth 48, Geo. 16
YOWELL, Conner 41, Susan 44, Emasetta 19, Geo. W. 18, Minerva 15, Almanth? 13, Benj. 11
JEWETT, Jane 56*, Catherine 50, Mary 27, Chas. 19, Ellen 13
HOFFMAN, John B. 4*
WILLIAMS, E. 38 (m), Ann 27, Mary E. 8, Lucy J. 6, Robt. W. 2, John 1
SMITH, E. R. 33 (m)*, M. C. 24 (f), J. D. 6 (m), Susan H. 4, Joseph W. 3, Minerva E. 1, David M. 18
RANSDALE, Margaret 19*
SMITH, Lucy 70*
SIDNER, Andrew 33, Jas. A. 8, Jacob W. 7
OTWELL, John F. 29, Mary 29, Mooris 4
OFFUTT, Mary A. 37, Mary E. 16, Marian 10 (m), Jasper 8
COOK, Elizabeth 52*, Dudley 23, Susan H. 23, E. F. 20 (f)
DINGLE, Mary 38*, M. A. 16 (f)
WILSON, Samuel 69, Rebecca 50, Mary E. 24, Catherine 20, Saml. R. 18, Rebecca 16
GAINES, Jonas N. 32*, Nancy B. 28, Sarah F. 6, Saml. S. 1

Schedule Page 186

THOMPSON, Wm. O. 26 (m)*
GAINES, Franes 70*, Polly S. 58, Permelia 27, Wm. J. 10, john S. 6
MCCOY, Joseph 80* (B)
CALWELL, Jane 50*
WINCHESTER, Ann E. 27*, John 19
WOOD, Wm. 27*
BRYAN, Saml. 60*, Elizabeth 47, Chas. C. 21, Virginia A. 18, Edwin 16, Ann R. 13, Sarah H. 11, Saml. 9, John G. 5, Alace 1
BYRNES, Ann E. 8*, Mary C. 6, Whitney 4
BYRNES, Aaron 36
CARROLL, James 27*, Jane 26, Martha A. 6, Thos. H. 4, Wm. 2/12
WYNNE, Lewis 28*
HURBERSON, Setphen 50* (B)
GANETT, Walker 60*, Alsey 55, Elizabeth 50, Mary J. 16
SHINGLETON, Thos. 90*

1850 Census Fayette County Kentucky

CHILDERS, Linsey 58*, Catherine 52, A. L. 31 (m), S. A. 21 (b), Mary C. 18
SMITH, Sarah C. 4*, Lindsey C. 2
DICKERSON, Benj. 10*
BUGGINGTON, Taylor 37*, Ann 36, Julian 3 (m), Cirene B. 1/12
ADAMS, James 23*
SIDNER, Daniel 51
LYDICK, Jacob 44, Mary S. 43, Ann R. 15, AndrewW. 14, Elizabeth R. 11, Louisa F. 10, Stephen T. 8, Laura B. 6
PHILLIPS, Wm. 34, Elizabeth 32, Mary A. 14
BENNETT, John 31, Sarah A. 25, James W. 10, Rebecca E. 8, M. E. 6 (f), Eliza G. 4, John T. 2, Rice 1
CAVENDER, Reuben 39*, Elizabeth 25, Eliza A. 9, Nancy A. 7, Sarah F. 5, Wm. T. 3, Arrebella 1/12
SHINGLETON, David 19*
CAVENDER, Daniel 35, Sallie 25, George 10, Thomas 8, Sophrena 6, Barthenia 4, A. 1 (f)

Schedule Page 187

HUFFMAN, Henry 80*, Joanna 50, Lindsey R. 24
SIDNER, Jacob 62, Polly 61, John A. 29, Jacob 26, Jsoeph 20, Mary A. 3, Martin 32
HALL, Elizabeth F. 11*
SIDNER?, Sarah 32*
RUFFMAN, Benj. 22*
SMITH, Benj. 36, Frances 29, J. S. 9 (f), Laura H. 7, A. F. 4 (m)
WOOD, B. B. 59 (m), Mary 49, Sarah 18, Susan A. 16, Ann R. 14, John 12, Elizabeth A. 10, Alexander 20
FISHER, Elizabeth 54*, James 24
VAUGHN, Masterson 27*
MOORE, Margaret 63, Robt. 30, Franklin 19
HANNAH, Saml. 35, Margaret 25, Wm. J. 6, John E. 5, Saml. A. 3
JONES, Saml. 34, Hannah 26, Sallie A. 6, Abraham 4, Wm. 1
PILCHER, Chas. 53, Cahrine 35, Lucy A. 19
MOORE, Benj. 30, Susan 20, Wm. G. 7
MCLANE, Wm. 24, Nancy C. 23, Henrietta 2, Chas. 17
HARP, Cabble 36, Elizabeth 29, Mary J. 12, W. H. 10 (m), Eliza 8, John W. 5, Stephen 3, Cabble 1
SIDNER, Wm. 49, Matilda 40, Geo. W. 21, Thos. J. 17, W. H. H. 15 (m), Paulina D. 13, Abram H. 11, John G. 8, Benj. F. 6, Irena S. 4, Zachariah T. 2
HARP, Baston 38, Bethiah 35, John H. 16, Abram 14, Malvina 12, Loyd 10
SIMPSON, Saml. 35, Elizabeth 26, Ann E. 6, Nancy 4, Sallie 4, Emily 1

Schedule Page 188

SCOTT, Francis 43, Matilda 39, Susan J. 14, Wm. N. 10, Ann E. 7
WALLACE, Richard 46, Sallie A. 27, Margaret A. 9, James C. 7
CROMWELL, Vincent 53, Nancy 49, W. V. 24 (m)
ETHINGTON, Sarah 57, Hiram E. 36, Mitchel 24, Hartwell 18, Elizabeth 20, Mary R. E. 2, Robt. M. 2/12
DERAN, James 50, E. L. 47 (f), Saml. 21

1850 Census Fayette County Kentucky

HARP, Geo. 39*, Julia 38, Mary 15, Elizabeth 14, Theodocia 12, John W. 9, Lidia A. 10, Emely 7, Geo. W. 4, Thos.J. 4
LAWRENCE, James 64*
HARP, Lea 60, Jefferson 22
HARP, John 34, Matilda 31, Isabell 12, John F. 10, Margaret 8, Geo. W. 6, Tabitha 5, Henry 4, Lyman 2, Geo. 1/12
HURST, David 31, Sarah 28, Ann E. 8, Margaret F. 5, Nancy J. 2
CURTIS, Lyman 38*, Tennell 28, Caroline M. 1
HUTCHINGS, Newton R. 17*
HARP, David 30*, Mary E. 28, Louisa 8, Mary A. 6, Dursilla 4, Lea M. 3, Wm. 1
RANEY, John 16*
SMITH, Chas. M. 37, Nancy 34, James 12, Geo. 10, Mary 8, John 5, Chas. 2
MYALL, Johnathan 27, Sarah 20, Ann J. 2, Mary 1/12
ZIMMERMAN, David 40*, Nancy 35, Mary T. 13, D. L. 7 (m), Thos. J. 2, Sarah E. 2
MCROBERTS, Elizabeth 19*, Agness 14
APPLETON, John 26*, Chas. 12
BUTLER, Jas. C. 38*, Lucy A. 25, Geo. 6, Alex. 18

Schedule Page 189

LONG, O. D. 18 (m)*
PARRISH, W. D. 22 (m)*
COOPER, John H. 40*, Elizabeth 64, Sallie C. 16, Mary E. 13, Susan F. 11
CARROLL, Dempsey 35*
DESHA, John R. 6*, Mary C. 31, Ben. 9, Eliza 7, Adalade 4, Mary 2/12, Frances E. 16
PICKETT, John J. 26*
INNIS, Chas. W. 28*, Mary N. 18, Nancy 48
WEBB, Mary T. 79*
NUTTER, John 22*
MORGAN, C. C. 51 (m), Henrietta 40, Kitty 16, Henrietta 11, Richd. C. 14, Charlton 12, Thos. 5, Frank 3
MCMURTRY, John 38, Elizabeth 25, Sarah 12, Geo. C. 6, Elizabeth C. 4, John W. 2, James 1
WOOLLEY, Sallie 43, Robt. W. 21, Margaret 20, Chas. W. 19, Eller 12, Howard 10, Vertne 8, Frank 6, Adrian 3
LOYD, Thos. W. 34, Elizabeth 25, W. 3 (m), no name 1 (m)
WOOD, Benj. C. 48, Susan A. 42, Elizabeth 19, Robt. 16, N. F. 13 (m), Ann M. 9, Ambrose C. 6, Susan A. 4, Benj. C. 1
BRECKENRIDGE, John C. 29, Mary C. 24, J. C. 5 (m), C. R. 3 (m), Frances 2
ROGERS, C. C. 31 (m), L. R. 26 (f)
PAYNE, O. F. 42 (m), Geo. A. 40 (f), Mary S. 16, Darwin J. 14, John B. 12, O. F. 10 (m), Geo. Ann 7, James S. 4, Humphries 2
CROMWELL, John E. 42, Harriett 39, JaneE. 16, Benj. F. 14, L. G. 12 (f), John E. 10, Mary E. 7, Eliza H. 5
190 RICE, Soloman 43, John M. 22, Sarah 20, Catherine E. 18, Allen 16, Maria 13, Joann 11, Levi 8, Mary J. 5

1850 Census Fayette County Kentucky

Schedule Page 190

STIPES, Harvey 28, Mary A. 23, John 6, Sarah C. 3, Mary 13
WEBB, Garland 40*, Lucy J. 15, Marcus 13, Garland 11, John 9, Willis 7
PATTENT, John C. 21*
APPLEGATE, Joseph 20*
LEARY, Wm. A. 53*, Mary A. 45, Catherine 19, Wm. 17, Mary 13, Saml. 8, Sarah 73
TROTTER, Cordelia 40*, Georgetta 30
CURD, Wm. P. 36, Mary A. 36, Nanney E. 17, John 14, Richard A. 12
MCKEE, Jane W. 38, Martha 13, Geo. W. 8, Wm. R. 6
JACKSON, Saml. G. 49*, Ann S. 50, James F. 21, Ann 16, Saml. 14, Israel 12, Caroline 11, Lewis 9, Mary 3
JONES, ---- 22 (m)*
SUTTON, Geo. W. 45*, Laura C. 44, Louisa 14
CONKLIN, --- 50 (m)*
ONEAL, Daniel 35, (f) 30, no name or sex 2
MARFIELD, Loyd 51*, Mary J. 16, Loyd 11, Edward 7, Henry 5
BURBANK, Elmira 25*
MCCOY, Alexander 31, Mary 22, Jane 20, Ann 18, James 25
SNOWDEN, John D. 32*, Susan 29, Mary F. 7, John J. 5, Margaret A. 3
SHEVATTER, Jackson 26*
WEBB, Joshua 60, Jane 60
MCCAN, Peter 42, Beddy 40, Mary 19, Cathrine 15, Christopher 12, Ann 11, James 9, Jane 5, Peter 3

Schedule Page 191

TURNER, Mathew 37, Luoisa 25
WALLS, Richard 36*, Mary 38, Ann 33, Margaret 19
OMARA, Michael 36*
GREEN, Ann 7*
ATER, W. W. 65 (m)*, Elizabeth 50, Frances 18, W. W. 17 (m)
DUDLEY, Mary 63*, Elizabeth 7, Ethelbert 5, Wm. 3
WHEELER, Geo. W. 31, Sarah 36, John 4, Mary C. 1
HARP, Clemency 31*, Mary E. 10, Maria W. 8, James A. 6, Wm. 4
ALLEN, Elizabeth 25*
LONG, Adam 56
FURGOSON, John M. 38*, Ann R. 12, Sallie 6
JUTPHIN?, John B. 26*
CALVIN, George 19*
SANDERS, Cobb J. 57, Nancy 53
BUNIER, Wm. 32, Rebecca 34
FIELD, Sabina 51*, Amelia 26
BEATY, Margaret 85*
JEFFIE?, Sarah 48*
BASCOM, Henry B. 54*, Eliza 39, Laura 9, Henry R. 7
BRYANT, Zerilda 19*
BOULT, Henry B. 40*, Emaline 39, Jesse 3, Edward B. 6/12, Hellen 7
BENJAMIN, Theadore 16*

1850 Census Fayette County Kentucky

PASTLETHWAITE, G. L. 44 (m), Sarah 38, Ann M. 19, Lewis 12, Wm. M. 11, Sarah E. 10, Gabriella W. 4
MARSHALL, Thos. A. 56*, Eliza 55, Eliza A. 13
PRICE, Susan 73*
CROGHAN, Francis 64*, Francis 9
SMITH, James M. 44, Junius 12, Saml. 11, Orlando 9, Alice 7, Margaret 5
WORLAND, Thos. L. 44*, Mary A. 40, Sarah C. 14, Ann E. 12, Susan E. 10, James B. 9, Mary F. 7, Margaret A. 5, Lidia F. 3, Thos. C. 6/12
FRELEY, Thos. 19*

Schedule Page 192

FERGUSON, Ann 27 (B), Edward 29, Betsey 4, Campbell 2, Spencer1/12
ROBINSON, Cordilia 22* (B)
STEEL, Mary 13* (B)
SIMPSON, Anna 29* (B), George 4
FICKLIN, Mary 60* (B)
KAY, Glovina 29 (B)
FOSTER, Mary 22 (B), Ellen 5, Richard 3, Richard 5-
JENKINS, Cara 39 (B), Flordia 22, Ann E. 2, Zilpha 19, Josiphene 5, Lafayette 11, Pheoby 7, amanda 5, Henry 2, Chas. 20, Edward 18, Zilpha 55
MARTIN, David 24, Nancy 19
BELL, David 40*, Charlotte C. 32, Mary R. 16, Ellen B. 13, Jane M. 11, Nannie H. 9, George R. 6, Charlotte R. 3, Bettie H. 1
TODD, Jane 76*
SHAW, Alex 55*
CRANLEY, Edward 28*
ELLEN, Prudence 66
DUDLEY, B. W. 64 (m), W. A. 26 (m), M. J. 25 (f), Winslow 3, Chas. 9/12
DOWNING, Marcus 37, Ann 35, Lidia 12, Mary 10, Bettie 8, Caroline 6, Hellen 4, John A. 1
BOSWORTH, D. H. 54 (m)*, Minerva 44, D. B. 21 (m), Geo. A. 18, H. W. 16 (m), E. A. 14 (f), F. L. 12 (m), W. E. 10 (m), Thos. M. 8, F. B. 6, Robt. T. 4
COX, Martha 21*
RUSSEL, S. L. 40 (f), A. M. 20 (f), M. E. 16 f), M. J. 14 (f), L. V. 9 (f), Thos. A. 6
MCCOY, Thos. A. F. 35, Nancy 21, Lucy A. 1
KENNEY, R. P. 64 (m)*, Sallie 57, Robt. 26, Mathew 23, Wm. 20
BRYAN, Elizabeth 22*, Robert 23
COLLINS, Sallie 60 (B)

Schedule Page 193

INNES, Robt. 22*, Sophia 20, Mary 4/12
FLOURNOY, Mary 46*
FINK?, John 20*
MCINTIRE, Elizabeth 52, John A. 26, James 28, Alla 17
SHELBY, Isaac 55, M. B. 53 (f), Maria L. 21, Isaac 18, John 15, Henry C. 10
MCGOFFIN, Saml. 49, Susan H. 23, James W. 1, Joseph 17

1850 Census Fayette County Kentucky

BRECKENRIDGE, Mary H. 81*
LEWIS, Elizabeth 74*
FRAZER, Oliver 40, Martha B. 33, Betty 7, Fanny 5, Catherine 3, Nannie 2
_____, Judith 50 (B)
SIMPSON, Gilbert 56, Elizabeth 47
GILBERT, Henry 27*, Juliett 21, John H. 7/12
OFFUTT, Maria 85*
HALL, Malinda B. 45*
CALCLAZURE, Geo. W. 30, Elizabeth 26, R. 2 (m)
COOPER, Reuben H. 36*, Elizabeth J. 35, John M. 13, Daniel 12, Wm. B. 10, Sarah A. E. 5, Stephen 2
MCALISTER, Edward 45*, Eliza 38
JENKINS, Zilphy 60* (B), Casah 40, Henry 44, Chas. 18, Edward 16, L. 12 (m), Florida, Zelphy 15
BOON, Gabriel 52* (B), Henry 50
BALL, Hambal 40* (B), Spencer 42
CAMPBELL, Bryant 38* (B)
BROWN, Jacob 37* (B)
ROBINSON, F. 28 (m)* (B), Nelson 26
FERGUSON, E. 32 (m)* (B)
WELLINGTON, Wm. 16* (B)
FICKLEN, L. B. 8 (m)* (B)
COMBS, Leslie 56*, Mary E. 27, Howard 15, Magleslie 13 (f), E. B. 2/12 (f)
BROWNWELL, Silvester 22*
MAN, Mary E. 4*
DOWNING, J. L. 60 (m), Mary A. 54, Richd. 22, Mary A. 18, Caroline 15
RYMAN, Robt. 51, Hester 42, Lucy 15, Jacob 13, Rachael 79

Schedule Page 194

GRATZ, Benj. 57, A. M. 42 (f), Herman C. 24, Cary 20 (m), Miriam 6, Anna M. 2
MCCANN, F. M. 28 (m)*, Joanna P. 24, Joseph 5, Smith 2
DEAN, John A. 24*
MARSH, Richd. 31, Isabella 27, Julia B. 5, R. B. 4, Laura 1
ALLEN, John R. 36*, Elizabeth 30, James J. 1
PATTERSON, Louisa 24*
CUNNINGHAM, J. W. 23 (m)*
HOLLADY, James 33*
WITHROW, Jane 40*
BURCH, Mary 30*
PROFUT, Nancy 26*
PERRY, Ellen 25*, Mary 23
HENY, Margaret 32*, Elizabeth 20
QUINN, Ann 25*
FITZPATRICK, Garret 25*, Phillip 30
THORNTON, Geo. 45*
MCKEE, Phillip 30*
SAUNDERS, Alex 21*
COOK, John 32*
SMITH, John 30*

1850 Census Fayette County Kentucky

BRIDWELL, Ann 27*
DUVALL, John 25*
YATES, A. 23*, Lucy 17
MARTIN, John B. 21*
SATTERFIELD, Wm. 30*
USSERY, James 28*
RIKER, Ann 40*
RONALDS, Margaret 55*
WHITE, T. C. S. 45 (m)*
HUGHART, John 24*
SRASLER, Mary 25*
BOYD, John D. 48*
WADE, Marston W. 29*
PARKS, John 46*
HEBSON, Wm. 33*
BURROWS, Uphemia 24*
CROW, John 22*
FENNEL, Elijah 60*
CARR, Reuben 26*
MILLER, R. 60 (m)*
EVANS, Wesley 48*
THOMPSON, Almira 30*
HAY, James C. 36*
CLARK, A. B. 28 (m)*
MINOR, Tabitse 26*
BOBBITT, Rebecca 45*
DUNBAR, James 34*
ELLIOT, Boone 44*
MCGEE, David 28*
LAND, W. L. 23 (m)*
LEWIS, John 30*
JENKINS, _____ 25 (m)*
MCCANN, Mike 23*
WHITING, Chas. 60*
DOGGET, John 25*
TAYLOR, Thos. 34*
GILBERT, Mrs. _____ 20*
FERREL, Jane 42*
WHEATLY, Ignatius 33*
BEAVER, Mary 35*
GOODMAN, Nancy 45*
SCOFIELD, Coleman 35*
CAIR?, Lamb 30 (m)*
BENNET, James 28*
JOHNSON, J. G. 29 (m)*
BOWER, May 26*

Schedule Page 195

PHELPS, John B. 31*
DONEGAN, Wm. 32*
MCCALISTER, John 37*
HAMILTON, Alex 37*
GRAY, Mary C. 30*
HOGAN, Dan. P. 33*
HERM, Fility 48*
MARTIN, Robt. 48*
NORTON, Sarah E. 32*
KING, Richd. 39*
COLEMAN, Henry 58*
GREEN, Nancy 52*
OATY, Augustus 36*
ERNEST, Theoe. 43*
CARLAN, Melvina 33*
MOORE, John 35*
FERRIS, Jas. 41*
TALIEFARO, Geo. 32*
MCWILLIAMS, Ellen 31*
LINDSEY, Jas. 33*
BASCOMB, Mary B. 36*
BURROWS, Thos. 45*
VILLIER, Peter 40*
SHUVLY, Fred. 31*
PULLY, Jesse 30*
BEARD, David C. 31*
HEAD, Jas. 39*
WELLER, Ann 36*
HELWICH, Augustus 40*
HARRISON, Abner 55*
APPLEGATE, Judith 45*
BURGER, Fanny 35*
DRAKE, Sarah 57*
BEARD, John 27*
COOPER, Lucy 28*
COLEMAN, P. L. 34 (m)*
WALKER, Maria 39*
THOMPSON, Josephene 25*
CANNON, John 59*
MOORE, Duke 28*
HICKLIN, Jas. 28*
MORRIS, Eliza 43*
HILL, Mary 59*
WEBBER, Ann W. 33*
GRAVES, Thos. 29*

MOORE, Jas. G. 39*
DAVIS, Henrietta 43*
ANDERSON, Jas. 48*
BLACK, Peter 35*
SPEARS, Elizabeth 41*
SMITHERS, Rebecca 27*
VALENTINE, Rebecca 29*
BRISLEY, Elizabeth 52*
BYRIE, Wm. 35*
MILLER, Wm. 65*
CAVISTON, John 42*
RUCKER, Ben 47*
SESSIONS, Susannah 37*
MCDANIEL, Washington 37*
WEDDLE, Geo. 42*
ROBERTS, Thos. 27*
FOSTER, Patsy 20*
FREDRIC, Theresa 22*
THOMPSON, John D. 17*
COBURN, Jane 62*
HANY, John 34*
ENNIS, Jas. 29*
WINSTERNLY, Mrs. 37*
CRUSH, John 41*
YATES, C. 21 (f)*
JOHNSON, Ann 55*
MATHEWS, Sarah J. 10*
BRIDWELL, Malinda 28*
CARPENTER, Isaac 24*
BURKHEAD, Nelson 23*
SHELBY, Jas. 40*
CUNNINGHAM, Jas. 40*
HARDY, Wm. 30*
JOHNSON, Jas. 50*
TAYLOR, A. 31 (m)*
RUST, Lewis P. 35*
DURHAM, Jas. 34*
RUCKER, Willis A. 50*
BARNETT, Fanny 40*

Schedule Page 196

KENNEY, Mary 43*
HEFBORN, Mary 27*
GLOVER, Matse 59 (f)*
NELSON, Sam 58*

1850 Census Fayette County Kentucky

POTTER, Nancy 53*
SMEDLY, Biddy 43*
DALLY, Alex W. 65*
ROGERS, Jas. 33*
CLAY, Theoc. W. 40*
MARTIN, Sarah H. 44*
LACKET, Caroline 58*
PECK, Caroline 37*
THRASHER, Sarah 38*
BARNETT, Nick 28*
HERNDON, Polly 57*
DENT, Mildred 44*
BAKER, Job 58*
RAMSDEN, Jas. 30*
DAILY, Lucy A. 22*
SCOTT, Nancy 49*
HOKE, Rudy 43*
JONES, Henrietta 28*
BURNS, Matilda 49*
WARD, Sarah 46*
EVANS, Rebecca 57*
DEWIT, John 40*
BOHANNON, Ann 65*
STEWART, Olive 45*
BACON, E. L. 45 (m)*
STANFORD, E. D. 54 (m)*
KENNARD, Andrew 60*
BARNES, Mary 38*
ROGERS, Jacob 46*
ISLER, Geo. F. 40*
CANNON, Greenup 42*
COVINGTON, Benj. 38*
PULLEN, Agnes 58*
CLAYFOOL, Rebecca 63*
SMITH, Mary A. 46*
ROGERS, John D. 37*
MURPHY, Ad. 41 (m)*
METCALF, Eliza 54*
COKE, Abram 41*
ARNOLD, Thos. 36*
MCMEEKIN, Jas. 49*
REED, Mary 51*
HUNTER, Margaret 43*
LIGHTER, David 46*
WILLIAMS, Susan 65*
LYONS, Mary 65*
SPARKS, Humphry 48*

RILEY, Lidia 46*
DAVIDSON, Jas. 62*
WALKER, Chas. W. 42*
TINDER?, Anthony 41*
MCBRIDE, Danl. 45*
MAHONE, John 35*
TODD, Madisonia 48*
DEAL, Mike 31*
WINTER, Walter 46*
WHITAKER, Betsy 31*
BRAVARD, Saml. 50*
CLARK, Alex 57*
POMPHRY, A. B. 36 (m)*
ROGERS, Chas. 55*
SANE, George 33*
MORRIS, Jas. 43*
MCKEE, Wm. 36*
AVERY, Phil B. 43*
SCHENK, John C. 39*
STONE, Mary 39*
WERNE?, John 39*
MCABRAM, Rosella 40*
DUVAL, Eliza 46*
JACKSON, Allis 32*
STRADER, Christ 32*
MILLER, Nancy H. 32*
DENTON, Nancy 46*
CLELLAND, John 34*
BURT, Betty 25*
TROTTER, Geo. T. 42*
STOLL, Christiann 67*
CAMPBELL, Robt. 20?*
WORD, Fredric 32*

1850 Census Fayette County Kentucky

Schedule Page 197

MARSHALL, Sarah R. 23*
BENNINGFIELD, Henry 28*
RUNALDS, Vincent 41*
QUERTEMOUSE, Sarah 20*
BROWN, Josiah 24*
THERMAN?, C. 18 (f)*
RICE, Lewis C. 30*
GRAY, Mary 27*
ROGERS, _____ 52 (m)*
PIGG, Henry 45*
ANDERSON, John H. 35*
HENCHIN, Marshall 17*
GORDON, _____ 40 (m)*
OVERTON, Jane 37*
SELLER, Mary 37*
OVERTON, Frances 72
GOMER, E. C. 33 (m)*
EAGLE, E. E. 32 (m)*
FISHBACK, James 36, Mary 26, Mary L. 5, Will E. 4, Laura 5/12
RAYMON, Mrs. 78*
FISHBACK, John 21*
GEORGE?, Lucy 22*
TALBOTT, Charles 36*
DALLIS?, Michael 28*

Schedule Page 198

MCGOWAN, Tho. B. 53*, Nancy 45, James P. 30, Jo. R. 28, Eliz. 26, Martha J. 22, Tho. J. 19, Hany B. 6, Charles C. 1, Jos. 3, Ruth 70 (B), Ellen H. 8/12
HASTINGS, Ellen 22*
MCCRACKEN, W. 30 (m)*
_____, Henry 25 (B), Allen 22, Caroline 30, Jerry 1, Eliza Jane 18, Mary 15, Celey 30
KINKEAD, George B. 38, Eliza? 26, Ro? J. 4 (m), John 2
HARRISON, James O. 46, Margeretta P. 40, Richard P. 17, Geo. B. 15, Mary E. 12, James O. 10, Margeretta 8, Ellen 6, Albert 3
TAYLOR, Charlotte 34* (B), John H. 30, James 25, George 21, William 19, Robert 17, Mary Ann 33, Catharine 15, Ann 16, Charles? 13, John 54
JACKSON, Malvina 19* (B), Virginia? 10/12
MAXWELL, Viley? 70 (f)* (B)
PICKETT, Courtney 53, Sarah J. 26, Ann B. 22, George B. 24, Ulen? D.? 22
ELLIOTT, Alex J. 44, Caroline 30, William 15, Mary 6, Alfred J. 4
SAYRE, Andrew J. 30, Mary 40, Sarah 65, Mary Jane 20
CRAIG, Parker 45*, Susan M. 33, Mary Ellen 16, William 11, Joseph 9
MOFFETT, Mary 56*, Ann 27
KENNEDY, C. W. 35 (m), Sarah 25, Cliffton 2, Mary 4/12
WOODS, Mary 50, Harriett 24, Thomas J. 18

1850 Census Fayette County Kentucky

OWENS, Peter 30*, Mary 26
MARTIN, Catharine 2*
TAYLOR, John 27 (B), Emily 26, George 4, Mary 2, Charlotte 4/12

Schedule Page 199

MURPHEY, Susanah 71*, Jerry 40, James 23, Margaret 27, Susannah 24
GRAVES, Edward O. 2*
BEARD, Joseph 72 (B)
FELIN, Jno. 41
PRONELL?, J. W. 30 (m)
BARLOW, Milton 33*, Addotacia 24, Margaret 3, Virginia 11/12, Tho. H. 59, Keziah 51, Eliz. H. 21, Elizabeth 11, William 9, Milton 7, Mary 4
WHEELER, Susan 18* (B)
LEWIS, Artomecia 23*
FREED, Mary 15*
TAYLOR, Mary Ann 21*
WEIL, Patrick 30*, Joseph 27, Sydney 17
MCENESLEY?, John 30*
CAIRL, Daniel 35*
GRAF, Lewis 21*
KINNARD, James W. 24*
WATSON, John 22*
KANE, John 22*
BOYD, Jos. B. 21*
KROUSS, Jacob 23*
STEELE, Mary 34*, Martha 8, Charles? 7, Drusilla 6
BEECH, Virginia 16*
MCCARTY, John 32, Juana? 31, Daniel 4, John 1
LACKENS, Margaret 28*, John 31, Mary C. 6, Geo. E. 4, Sarah J. 2, John W. 3/12
SIMPSON, George 69*, Catharine 46
CUNNINGHAM, Kate 31?*
WEST, Harriet E. 20*
BRECKENRIDGE, Mary 17*
SHEENY, Eliz. 17*
WRIGHT, Elias 18*
STOHLS, George 31*, Mary Jane 26, George jr 8
PEIS?, Blackburn 21*
ARMAN?, Andrew 19*
SHINDLEBOROUN, Tho. 17*
STOLL, Chas. 23*
ADAMS, Israel 17*
LYTTLE, Ulm 17*
CRISTOPHER, Horrens 17*
KING, David A. 20*
HUNT, P. K. 33 (m), Julia G. 31, Maria B. 6
TROTTER, G. R. 34 (m)*, Amanda 30, James G. 9, Eliz. 8
WEBB, Eliz. 8*, Lucy 24, Louisa 40, Richd. A. 38

1850 Census Fayette County Kentucky

WILSON, John J. 38, Lydia 27, Laura 9, Anna L. 1
EVENS, Geo. W. 36*, Julia 35, Theodore 9, Blanch 6, Wilson P. 9/12

Schedule Page 200

WILSON, Mary E. 21*
INGLES, Davis 52* (B), Eliza A. 35
DUSEY, Nancy A. 5* (B)
WHEELEN, Mary 16* (B)
MORTON, Eliz. 55* (B)
LEWIS, Matilda 29 (B)
PUNCEON?, Mathew 34
MALON, William 25*, Mary 22
STALL, Henry 21*
ARMSTED, Henry 35*
MCCURDY, Alex 55*, Catharine 51, Jno. 15, George 13, Alax 8
WALLINGFORD, Cath 25*, Florence 3
ROBBINS, W. H. 40 (m), Mary A. 26, W. H. H. 11 (m), Mary A. 9, Alred 6
PEMBLETON, Bowlen 58, Lydia 57
HENRY, Danl. 40*, Mary 40, Catharine 15, Patrick 13, Mary 11
MCCLEAVER, Michl. 16*
MCCRASTLE, Chas. 35*
CENOY, Margaret 25*, John 1
MULLIN, Rosa 18*
DALLAS, Eliz. 27*
DANLY, Hugh 22*
MUTTEN, Clarissa 28 (B), John H. 7
BEARD, William 47, Martha J. 16, Ann 15, Eliza 14, Catharine 12, Clara 10
CROPPER, Nathaniel 35*, Eugene 17
PRIEST, Mary 20*, P. H. 26 (m)
GEORGE, Joseph 45*, Mary A. 38, Sarah 17, John W. 16, Joseph F. 12, Mary E. 6, Martha J. 5, Lucy 74
WILSON, Eliz. 16*
ELLIS, Jesse 46*, Mary 46, Ambrose 14
HAUN, John H. 30*, Mary H. .19
GEROGE, Rebecca L. 30*, Caroline 12, William 10, Joseph 6, John 8/12
TUCKER, Margaret 16*
PROBEIT, Tho. 25*, Mary E. 24, Atlanta 2, Mary 42, William 15
BRIDGES, John 55*
HIGGINBOTOM, Ben 25*
HEADINGTON, Jaban 77*, Moses 55
BOWMAN, John 45*, Pamela 41

Schedule Page 201

DAWSON, James W. 36*, Maria 31, Joseph 4
FROST, Joshua 45*
GISH, Catharine 41 (B), Eliz. 21, Catharine 10, Sarah 14, Nathaniel 12, Amlet 8

1850 Census Fayette County Kentucky

HARRIS, Philus 55* (B)
GIVENS, Harriett 9* (B)
BROWN, Diana 56 (B), John 60
ANDERSON, Mildred 43*, Richd. T. 11, John E. 5
MCCLELLAND, Sarah E. 17*, Noah H. 17
BAKER, Jesse H. 32*
MCCAW, John 59, Cecily 44, Sarah 23, Frances 21, Mary 17, Thomas 12, Emma 10, Lucy 6, Wm. R. 4, Nina 1
WOODRUFF, Jesse 32*, Ann 30, Nancy 55
KILROY, Tho. C. 10*
LONG, Samuel 169*, Margaret 59, John 27, Edward 24, Margaret 20, Letitia 9
TUTT?, Margaret 7*, William F. 5
SCOTT, Isaac W. 35, Susan B. 34, Mathew I? 10, Mary M. 7, Joseph 5, Susan 1
HENRY, John 64*, Sarah 61
DOZIER, Geo. W. 42*, Mary W. 37, Mary Jane 13, George H. 9, Oliver P. 5, John C. 1
HENRY, John P. 31*
MARSH, Richard 35, Isabella 26, Julia 5, Richard 4, Laura 6
GROSS, Joseph R. 25, Julia 19
PATTERSON, John W. 38*, Margaret 22, Archey 8, Julia 4, Kate 1
SHIVETT, Maria 18*, Kate 16
ALLENDER, Edwd. 20*
BROWNING, Tho. 18*
GARRARD, James 19*
DOWNING, Lilburn 26, Carolilne 26, Albert B. 3, Marcellus 1
DAY, William 39, Eliza J. 29, Ann V. 3
CARTER, Landon 50, Nancy 52, Rebecca H. 14

Schedule Page 202

HOLMES, John 60 (B), John 14
EDMONDSON, Kesiah 55 (B)
TUCKER, Mathew 65 (B), Nathan 19
PEEL, Taylor 31*, Mary A. 30, William T. 1
SMITH, Charles R. 16*
WEBSTER, Lawson 22*
WREN, Jane 73
THOMAS, Elizabeth 47*, Eliz. 27, Ellen 22, Moses 20, John W. L. C. 18, Robert 11, George H. 8, Sarah C. 5
SPUR, Mary Jane 10*
WHITE, Mary E. 8*
WINGATE, Debra 43*, Joseph 45
WATNER, William 8*
BELART, Thomas 30, Rebecca 19, Alice M. 2/12
ATKINSON, John 28, Mary 19
MARSH, Nancy 55*
MOREY, Mary 29*, Augustus J. 23
WHITE, James 35, Mary 33, Andrew J. 3
LEWIS, John A. 23*, Martha J. 20, John B. 3

1850 Census Fayette County Kentucky

BELL, Sarah 56*
KIDD, James 32, Margaret J. 21, James L. 2
LUXON, William 44, Eliz. 43, Eliz. 18, William E. 16, Thomas C. 6, Laura B. 3
MCDANIEL, Alex 55*, Catharine 54
BRIDGFORD, Geo. 27, Mary 55, Harriet 22, R. 15 (m), Thos. 11, James 30
MARSHALL, Margaret 58* (B)
BRECKENRIDGE, Wm. 13* (B)
BUTLER, Andrew 37, Julia 6/12, Nancy 35, William 10, Andrew 10, Andrew 7, Mary J. 5, Jane 2
BERRY, James 75 (B), Eve 55
HUNTER, Harriet 35 (B), Andrew 8, Jane 6, Westly? 4, John 1
WINFREED, Samuel 50 (B), Harriett 45, Emily 20, Nate 8, Mary 6, Ann 10/12
CRAVENS, Elisha B. 44, Elmeda 35, John 10, Elisha 9, Mary 5

Schedule Page 203

CHILDS, Luther 32, Sarah 24, Sarah C. 3
HOSTETLER, Francis 40*, Rebecca 36, James 29
HAMMOND, Jalvey? 10 (m)*, Mary 8
SHAY, Henry 25*
ROBINSON, William 22*
WILSON, James 50, Geo. Ann 33, Henry M. 14, Luther 13, Mary E. 11, Geo. W. 7
BRUCE, Wm. W. 29*, Eliz. J. 28, Margaret 9, Nancy M. 7, James S.? 5, Wm. W. Jr. 3, Betty 8
NAVEN, Patrick 21*
BRYANT, Clifton 50*
RUCKER, Nancy 68*, Rebecca 21
ROBERTSON, Jno. E. 47*
RICHARDSON, L.? M. 38 (f), William 20, George 19, Louis 16, Emily 13, Edwd? 8, Bonner 6, Albert 4, Reynolds 2
BRAND, Geo. W. 37*, Eliz. 10, Jno. H. 7, Nannie 6, Harriett 5
ANDERSON, Eliz. 65*
ROBBINS, John 30 (B), Winney 51
BRENT, Mary 55*
JOHNSON, Massey 86 (f)*
BOSWORTH, Jos. 37*
GULPIL?, Wm. 31*
MORGAN, Griffeth S. 37*
HUTCHESON, And. 27*
CULLEN, Charles 23*
PAWL, John P. 24*
HITCHCOCK, Lester 22*
CLARKE, Enoch 28, Judith 54, Augustus 24, Sarah E. 12
TAYLOR, B. B. 38 (m)
MORRISON, M. B. 48 (m)*, Catharine A.? 40, Richd J. 24, Edwin A. 19, Mary A. 17, Moses B. 15, Kate P. 13, Lilla A. 9, Hellen M. 7, Ida 5
TAYLOR, M. A. 84 (f)*
BROWN, Hadric? R. 28*
PRICE, Samuel W. 31*
FRAZER, Robert Sr. 51*, Catharine 34, John C. 16, James K. 12, Wm. C. 8, Francis 6, Mary E. 2

1850 Census Fayette County Kentucky

HERBERT, Catharine 13*
FRAZER, R. 80 (m)
ATWOOD, Wm. 24
CARR, Charles D. 25

Schedule Page 204

LOGAN, L. M. 29 (m), S. E. 24 (f), William 1
EMMAL?, Wm. B. 32, Catharine S. 24, Sarah H. 5, Margaret 3, Will S. 3/12
YATES, James M. 18*
SUTTON, Thomas 22*
MCELLEHANY, R. 35 (m)*
MILLTON?, Allison 20
BRYANT, Benjamin 19
MYERS, Frank 23
BROCK, Ro S. 25 (m)
FOX, W. H. 28 (m), Sarah 21, William F. 1
CLARK, John P. 31 (B), Catharine 24, Samuel 17
EDGE, John T. 28
WILLIAMS, Z. B. 29 (m)*
HARSNER?, A. G. 25 (m)*
CARPENTER, Geo. W. 20*
GRAMMAN?, Isadore 35*, Ernstien? 32 (f), Sarah 10, Henry 9, Dawte? 7 (f), Edward 6, Eliza 5
SAYRE, David T. 18*
GILLROY, Pat 21*
GREEN, Thomas 21*
OWENS, Grandison? 29
WARREN, O. S. 26 (m)
BURBANK, David 29
HICKEY, David R. 30
BAIN, Hutbert H. 16
ROGERS, J. 21 (m)*
DRAKE, D. S. 18 (m)*
LOCKWOOD, John 70*, Eliz. H. 65
MCKINNEY, Charlot 45*, Eliz. J. 14, John L. 11, Charlot W.? 10, Jaliner? S. 7 (f)
BURDEN, Jane 54 (B)
MCCRACKEN, Henry 27*
MOONEY, Francis 17*
STRAUS, G. 21 (m), S. 41 (m)
HARRIS, Kitty 70 (B)
MOSEBY, Augustus 24, Ferdinand 16
FAY, William M. 25*
MCCURDY, John 15*
SYMONDS, A. J. 19 (m), P. 25 (m)
MORTON?, W. B. 24 (m)*
HOLLOWAY, E. H. 23 (m)*
WICKLIFFE, R. N. 40 (m)*
CALDWELL, A. B. 30 (m)*

1850 Census Fayette County Kentucky

MYERS, C. F. 40 (m)*
RATSEL, W. 32 (m)*
MATHENEY, W. 27 (m)*
FARREN?, Charles 15*
MCKEE, John 15*
POPPAL, Lewis 38*, Dorothy 25
DARLINGTON, R. D. 25 (m)*, Henrietta 23
EVANS, John 32*
GURMLY, James 28, Biddy 20
LOUGHRIN?, Patrick 31*, Rose 30, Ellen 12, Mary W. 3, Catharine 1
CAMPBELL, Mary 40*, Biddy 33

Schedule Page 205

CONNELL, Patrick 65, Margaret 63
DOUGHERTY, Hugh 29, Laura 28, Mary J. 4/12
FINLEY, Thomas 40
HENRY, Biddy 28, Arthur P. 6, Mary A. 4, Joseph 3, Margaret 8/12
RURDEN?, Patrick 26*
RYAN, Jeremiah 22*
MCKINNEY, Henry 29*, Eliz. 26, Daniel 1
MCCALISTER, M. 19 (m)*
ARMSTRONG, Samuel 30, Jane 22, Sarah J. 1
DOUGLASS, William 30, Margaret 26, Susan 1
MCCALISTER, James 35, Sarah 35, Ann 13, John 8, Pat 2 (m), James 1/12
BEACH, Samuel 55, Mary W.? 34, Margaret J. 10
WOOD, Thomas 52, Rebecca 48, Mary J. 17, Thomas 15, Edward 11, William 10, Ellen R. 8
GILLMAN, M. 29 (m)
SHORT, Wm. 31
WESSELS, H. A. 25 (m)
HOMEN?, Patrick 35
DAVER?, Feliso 32
MANLIGAM, Dennis 32*, Ellen 28, James 5
DOUGHERTY, Danl. 29*
MURKEY, Patrick 27*
RICE, Emeline 38*
TIMBERLAKE, Geo. W. 18*, F. M. 16 (m), W. J. 8 (m)
FINLAY?, Jos. 22*
HYDE, Humphrey 24*
REYNOLDS, Russell 30*
MARRS, Richard 52, Winaford 40, Ann E. 13, W. R. 9 (m), Catharine 6, Joel B. 3, Samuel 1
GRAVES, Richmond 34 (B)
MAYDWELL, Alex 42, Martha 35, Alex 12, Wm. 10, Catharine 8, Sarah 3
METCALF, William 41*, Eliz. 39, James 13, John T. 11, Chas. 19, James W. 15, Richard 12, Milton O. 7
WELDEN, Margaret 37*
BRIGGS, Sarah A. 27*
MCKEE, Thomas 24*

1850 Census Fayette County Kentucky

BROWN, James 32*
LAMBDEN, Geo. J. 25*
ANTHONY, Ben 34*

Schedule Page 206

BRIGGS, Chas. A. 3*
SEALS, Dennis 66 (B), Letty 59, Enoch 19
PERRY, George 35 (B), Mary Ann 38, Lucinda 11, Charles H. 9, Darcus 57
HARRISON, Jane 47*, Joseph H. 19, James W. 17, Margaret J. 9, Eliz. 8, Lucinda 17
REILEY, Chas. M. 25*, Mary Jane 20, Mary E. 3, John W. 2
SPRING, Amos 34, Martha A. 29
LAWRENCE, Hiram 27, Jane 22, Samuel 5, Mary J. 3
TANDY, George 35 (B), Hannah 30
GRAYSON, Mary E. 25 (B), Mary F. 7, Henrietta 4, Emily 2, W. E. 1 (m)
SPANNER?, Nancy 75* (B)
STRAUSS, Reubene 30 (f)* (B)
BRADFORD, Daniel 73, Eliza P. 62, Matilda 27, Isabella 24, James 15, Caroline 12
MOODY, James 67, Margaret 63?, Eliza 19, Julia Ann 17, W. G. 25 (m), James 12, Virginia M. 2
HIGGINS, Richard 38, Jane N. 30, Sally A. 4, Frank C. 2
WATERS, Tho. H. 58, Caroline 49, Anne E. 18, Sally A. 16, Frank W. 13, Mary W. 9
BOYER, Geo. A. 35*, Mary A. 30, Geo. W. 2, Clarence S. 1
CHRISTOPHER, Columbus 14*
THOMAS, Andrew 14*
HARWOOD, A. 34 (m)*, Mary D. 28, Mary 8, Lucretia 6, Emma L. 3
RUGG, Orwell 24*
SCROGGINS, Seana 25* (B), Diana 60, Sarah J. 26
MITCHELL, Henry 9* (B), Jos. 6
HANSON, Clark 60* (B)
BUCKLEY, Charles 50 (B), Sarah 45, Julai 24, Ulin 16
ROSETY, Jane 85*
HOGAN, Elihu 52*, Isabella 50, Jas. C. 20, John J. 18, William P. 16, Jos. L. 13, Mary Z. 5

Schedule Page 207

HILTON, J. S. 39 (m), Isabella 26, Isabella 6
CROOK, Walter 43, Sarah 39, Richd. C. 17
OLDHAM, Saml. A. 56* (B), Daphney 49, Saml. C. 22
TAYLOR, Henry 19* (B)
MORRISON, Mary E. 15* (B), Hezekiah 9
MALLERY, Peter 16* (B)
SULIVANS?, P. E. 38 (m)
MEGOWAN, Geo. J. 30, Mary J. 19, Lilla 1
KING, William 40*, Eliz. 40, Eliz. 6, Henry W. 3, Hellen W. 6/12
KINNARD, Mary 66*
ALLEN, Alfred 19*
GIBBON, James W. 22*

1850 Census Fayette County Kentucky

SHEPHERD, Juretta 50*, Mary E. 12, Alphius 6
WALLACE, G? W. 35 (m)*, mary 39
DOWNY, Nancy 40*, Andrew 6
BUTLER, Easter 40* (B), Bob 54
BARKER, Moses 51, Lucinda 39, Wm. H. H. 11
WILLIAMS, Marshall 40, Rachel 40, Cerilda 19
SMITH, Harvey 36, Elizabeth 24, John 15, Cornelius 9
DONEGAN, Hector 24*, Amanda 20, John 2/12
PEERS, Eliza 26*
COOK, James W. 21*, Eliza 24, William 3, Geo. W. 2/12
MCPETERS, Margart 75*
WILSON, R. Spaulding 336*, Sarah 34, Robert 15, Marian 13
HUNTER, Jane 61*
HUNTER, John 26*, Augusta 22, Shelton 2, Rosa 4
MCCONNELL, Cely 50* (B)
SHEPPARD, Genevieve 9*
TRELAURNCEY, Henry 28, Elizbth. 21
MITCHELL, Milton 35, Martha 35, John M. 12, Sarah W. 8
KENSEL, Christian 40*, Mary A. 40, Isabella 16, Geo. 13, Frederick 10, Mary 8, Cinteynetta 6
LORD, Isabella 39*
TAYLOR, Ellen 13*
MCDANIEL, J. C. 30 (m), Mary 22, Margaret A. 5, Seles? 3 (f), Charles 1

Schedule Page 208

YOUNG, Alfred 23, Eliz. 19, William 3/12
DOUGLASS, Alfred 42, Sarah 40, Rosannahh 15, Wiliam 11, James 11, John 8, Gran 5, Alfred R. 2
MERRELL, David 31, Mary 28
SPARKS, Thomas 25, Charles Ann 23, Sarah J. 3
MCULANE, Nancy 55
ROSS, Liberty 30* (B), Mary Ann 30, Mary F. 4, William J. 2, C. B. 2/12 (f)
FRENCH, Virginia 9* (B)
INGLES, John S. 60*, Mary 64, William 26, John 25, Jennett 27
HOLLIDAY, James 27*, Isabella 28, John 3, Mary 1
MORGAN, Lucy 52, Jane 30, William 28, James 24, Nancy E. 18, Lucy W. 16, Josaphine 14
BEARD, Joseph 38, Julia 27, Mary E. 1
WILLIAMS, Edward 38 (B), Nancy 1
VANPELT, William 35*, Margaret E. 43, Margaret S. 13, Martha C. 12
LITTLE, William 24*
KAPPS, Henry J. 25*
SISSEN, Lucy 73 (B)
POINDEXTER, W. 58 (m), Sallie 53, Charles 33
MUNCEY, John 24, Ann 24, James 3, John 1
BAKER, Nancy 23*
PENDAGESS, Adaline 20*
JONES, Virginia 24*
HOSDETTER?, Frances M. 5/12*
GEORGE, Lucy 212*

1850 Census Fayette County Kentucky

BAKER, Christine 23*
TURNER, William 62, Eliz. 49, William H. 13, Sarah M. 5
LAN, Richard 48*
LOND, Julia A. 35*, Franklin J. 22, Richd. 19, Dane 16, Mary E. 14, Geo. 11, John 9, Hiram 7, Louisa 5, Jerome 2
COOPER, Joseph B. 48*, Susan 37, Eliz. 15, John 19, William 9, Sarah J. 1

Schedule Page 209

BOSWELL, Hartwell 17*
MCCONTY, Jackson 16*
DUDLEY, Jeptha 47, Lucy 39, Jeptha 12, John 10, Howard 6, Taylor 2
VANPELT, William 65, Ann M. 61, James 24, J. B. 42 (m), James C. 15, Saml. D. 12, Ann E. 11, Mary 9
KISSINGER, John 31, Louisa 22, Julia 2
COFER, Elizab. 30, Joseph 13, William 3, Emma D. 9/12
ROSS, Lucy 52
BUTLER, Sarah 50
KING, Sarah 40*
OVERSTREET, Margaret 20*
SMITH, Margaret 26*
ELLIOTT, Sarah 25*
TREADWAY, Jane 24*
BURNES, Nancy 25*
WAGGEN, Ann 40
ROBINSON, Martha 57*
VAUGH, Charity 105*
HAWKINS, A. T. 52 (m)*, Ellen A. 48, John L. 18, S. J. 11 (m)
PECK, Julia Ann 5*, Eliza B. 68
HEUBOT, Wesley 24* (B)
DRAKE, Abram 26, Catharine 21, Hanna 1, Hanna 62
MONTMOLLEN, F. 52 (m)*, Sallie 46, F. 23 (m), Sallie P. 18, Adda 16, James 12, Ulen 11, Cardine 8, Lizzie 6
ELLIS, Moses P. 51*
BEARD, Oliver 28, Rebecca 18, Perry 1/12
BYRNS, Robert 38*, Mary 27, Ulm 15, Patrick 8, Clarke 5, Ann E. 3, Mary E. 9/12
GIVIN, Jane 28*
CARTY, Mary 76, W. F. 50 (m), Rebecca 30
CARTY, John 43*, Mary E. 28, M. S. 6 (f), Helen 4, Maria 2
PARISH, Dabney W. 47*
JOUETT, Margaret 57*, George P. 32, Martha H. 22, John 26
MENIFEE, Sarah B. 31*, Richd. J. 14

Schedule Page 210

MERCHANT, William 27, Amanda 22
COCHRAN, J. W. 36 (m), J. S. 26 (f), John 11, Mathew P. 7, Mary C. 4

1850 Census Fayette County Kentucky

ROBERTSON, Geo. 59*, Ellener 56, Alex 30, James 18?, Geo. 12
WOODS, David 24*
TROUTMAN, Mercellus 20*
SMITH, John R. 40, Sarah J. 32, Sallie W. 12, Amee E. 11, Ruth A.? 9, Benj. W. 7, John R. 3
WINFIELD, Elisha N.? 27, Eliz. H. 23, Harriet H. 3
MCCHESNEY, Wm. 50, Polly A. 38, CAtharine 18, Juliet 15, Jno. W. 16, Cave J. 13
ROYSTON, John W. 30, Anna A. 25, Mary F. 1, Celest 2/12
MORTON, Jno. 66*, Sarah 59
SCROGGIN, Geo. 30* (B)
SCOTT, J. P. 32 (m), Jemima 28
MORTON, Geo. W. 39, Eliz. 32, Eliz. 12, Mary 9, Alice 5, Virginia 3, James 6/12, George 72
WOOD, W. F. 56 (m)*, Rebecca 54
JOHNSON, Amanda 33*, Frances W. 8
COCKLEISURE, Maria 34, Geo. A. 8, Ro W. 3/12 (m)
BLINCOE, Ben C. 41, Lydia B. 37, Tho H. 16, James D. 14, Benj. 12, Martha F. 10, Sarah E. 8
HUNT, Michael 24, Mary 23, Mary 1
SUTTEN, Jos. T. 40*, Celest B. 25, James W. 5, Charles M. 3, Elizabeth 80, Tabitha 44, Sarah 30
BARBEE, Susan 20*
COCKLEISURE, Julia A. 12*
HAMPTON, Thos. 35*, Selina 27
ANDERSON, Andrew 16*
SHICK, Peter 6*
ASHTON, Jacob 29, Sarah C. 45, Rebecca 21, Charlton H. 12, Horace 9
BAILEY, Benj. 48*, Susan A. 43, Ro H. 16 (m), James T. 13, Jos. C. 10, Sallie 7, Lucy D. 4

Schedule Page 211

DUFREE?, Lucy 62*
BECK, James B. 27, Jane W. A. 24, Margaret 1
MORGAN, George 38*, Rebecca 26, Lucy A. 12, Mary J. 11, James B. 7, Caroline 5, John A. 3
SECHREST?, John 14*
YOUNG, Richd. B. 44*, Jane E. J. 33, Ambrose 8, William 6, Richard 3
RIGGOLD, Maria 37* (B)
SPIRES, Jeremiah 51, Mandy 54, Jmaes M. 14
SPENKS, James 32, Mary 25, Mary A. 4, Eliz. C. 2
WARNER, Derrick 50, Martha B. 33, Debora 17, Kate 9, Henry C. 7, Nathan T. 3, Selia J. 1
MILLER, Martin W. 36*, Catharine 29, William S. 11, Thos. R. 9, Chances 1, Kate 7, Maud 5
ROGERS, Thomas H. 62*
DEMOSS, Sarah 28*
SPIRES, Mary Ann 19*
TAYLOR, Matilda 41*, Henrietta 6, Mancey? 3, Martha J. 1
JANUARY, James 11*
EDGAR, Rebecca 55*, Sally A. 35, A. B. 24 (m), Jerome 22, Alex 8
ASBERRY, Rebecca 17*
FRAZER, Jerry T.? 43*, Ellen A. 35, William 16, Thomas 15, Tilghman 13, Christopher 10, Jerome 7
JONES, Woodson 16*
SAYRE, John 13*
GAUGH, Jerry 28*, Ann E. 24, Sarah J. 5, Mary E. 1, Jerry 3/12, Michael 72, Sarah 62, Augusta 18

1850 Census Fayette County Kentucky

SOUTEN?, Mary 12*
GAUTER, Daniel 30*
SMITH, Richd. 21*
SPRAKE, John O. 54*, Ann 44, Sarah 21, James 18, Mary 14, Ann E. 12, John 10, Lydia A. 8, Isaac 4, Bettie 2, Lydia 57

Schedule Page 212

KENNEY?, William 33*
LOEKLIN?, Arthur 35*
STONE, M. P. 34 (m)
ATHLEY, Robert A. 24
WALLACE, M. A. 52 (f)*, Sarah C. 22, Caroline 19, W. C. 18 (m), Mary P. 16, Eliz. 14, Caleb 12
BEASLEY, John 20*
FLOURNOY, J. F. 19 (m)*
MORGAN, Alex 18*
BROWN, Saint 35*, Anna 25
LILLY, James 55 (B), Lucy 30, Joseph 21, Mary 14, John 13
MASON, Anna 25 (B), Fanny 4, Sylva 5/12, Patrick 4
DAGANS?, Betsey 58 (B)
FOREMAN, Cloa 46, Julia 23, Joana 17, Mary 15, Thomas 11
CRAIG, E. W. 70 (m), Mary 23, Lucy 16, Horace 15, Almyra 12, Albert 9, Fanny 6
HUKILL, E. W. 33 (m)*, Mary E. 29, W. B. 17
BRYANT, Martha 11*
OREAR, Susetta 40, Julia E. 17, John W. 13, George W. 9, Mary E. 6
UTTINGER, Fred 50, Saint L. 3
IRVINE, James 52, Margaret A. 29, Henry C. 23, Lucretia 19, Eugene 17, Edward 15, Elizabeth 6, Emily 5, Victoria F. 4, James 2, Johnson 2/12
DRAKE, S. N. 30 (m)*, Josephene P. 22, Laura 2
GAINES, Alonzo 22*
FAHEY, Daniel 33*
JOHNSON, Henry 55*, Betsey J. 50, Robert A. 33, Henry 23, Charles F. 21, Ben F. 18, Mathew F. 11, Mary B. 9, Eliz. J. 25
TILFORD, Emily 25*, Eliza J. 8, Henry T. 5, John 2, Franklin 1, Frank 30

Schedule Page 213

ELLY, William R. 33*, Louisa E. 24, Mary 3/12
LONG, Ann 57, William 71
MCCAULEY, John 43, Mary M. 30, William H. 2
TATES, Loudon 72 (B), Jemima 40
LYTTLE, Eliz 53, Mary J. 21, John 20, Frances C. 13
LOVE, John 62
SCOTT, Lucy C. 49*, Joseph 20, Mathew T. 17, Winney 14, David 11, Isaac W. 24
HOLLOWAY, Lucy 12*, Elizabeth 10
STEWART, Michael 21*
BOYD, Almeda 27*, Francis M. 9, Robert 6, John 5

1850 Census Fayette County Kentucky

WEBSTER, Mary 55*
MCFADDEN, James 34, Martha A. 30, Rebecca C. 7, James F. 5, Mary E. 3, Margaret A. 1
KEMP, J. L. 40 (m)*, Mary A. 26, William V. A. 4, Charles E. 2, Josiah L. 10
MARCH, Sallie B. 2*, James W. 8
CUNNINGHAM, Arthur B. 50, Eliza 48, Adeline 18, James 15, Clarinda 12, A. B. 8 (m)
GOLDEN, Margaret 40 (B)
COOK, Samuel 40, Cerilda 27, James 6, John 3, Eliz. 6/12
BARKER, John 47*, Mary 31, Mary A. 12, Thomas W. 2/12
HARDIN, Mary 17*
BALDWIN, Ulen? 57*, Eliza 50, Anna 15, Mary A.? 13, Samuel 11, Alfred 7
PENDLETON, Edwd. 23*
WOODHOUSE, Frances 9* (B)
BEACH, James 56*, Maria 52, Jane 29, Catharine 7
NORTON, W. H. 40 (m), Ann 30, Emma 14, George 8, Wash 6, John 2, William 1/12
HOWARD, Chas. 25*, Catharine 32, M. C. 5 (f), Marie E. 2

Schedule Page 214

DART, Mary 25*
CRIDLAND, S. W. 28 (m)*, Marion 15, Martha 11, Amelia 9, Lavinia 6, Laura 3
BROOKS, Solomon S. 33, Mary A. 33, Amelia 8
LYKES, Marshall 41 (B), John 12
ANDERSON, O. 56 (m), Louisa 53, Jane L. 16, Robert 15, John 13, Kate 11, Lelia 7
GOODLOE, David S. 38, Sally A. 30, Speed S. 13, W. Cassius 8, David L. 6, Green Clay 4, A. W. 13 (m)
BEACH, Elisha 27*, Elizabeth A. 24, Henry 3, Thomas 20
BERTON, Jane 19*
CRAIG, Sarah 18*
LOVE, Elizabeth 16*
COOK, Susan N. 54*
RATTELL, Mary 58*
STRIBLING, R. A. 40 (f)*, Margaret 15, Portia 12
BARRY, Cathe. A. 53*
MATTHEWS, Mary 29*, James Y. 34, Ellen 11, Julia 9, Laura 7, Vertna 4 (m), Rosa 2, James 1
HALSEY, ____ 35 (m)*, Elizabeth 22, Edward 1/12
COOPER, A. 35 (m)*
BARRON?, Jack 25*
BIGGS, Joseph 50*, Hanna 40, Rebecca 16, Edward 12, Laura 6
HERNDON, Judith 83*, Mary Ann 17
REED, Lucy 46, Charles 46, Thomas 22, Mary Ann 20, Marshall C. 11, Joseph N. 8, Eliza J. 3/12
REESE, Lavinia 33, Lloyd B. 8, Mary E. 6
ANDERSON, Priscilla S. 75* (B)
COLEMAN, Becky 75* (B)
YOUNG, Charity 36 (B), Benjamin 19, Sanford 12, Nancy J. 10, Catherine 9, Huldy Ann 6
DRAKE, James F. 32*, Mary 26, Hanna 10, Benj. 8, Edwin 6, Cornelia 4, Rebecca 2

1850 Census Fayette County Kentucky

Schedule Page 215

HOAGLAND, Edmund 33*, Julian 24 (m)
NUTTER, Lizzie 14* (B)
CRAIG, Dudley M. 48*, Henrietta 36, Dudley 10, Elizabeth 12, Mary Ann 7, Richard 5, Elijah 2
DOWNING, Elizabeth 58*
BELL, H. C. 55 (f)*, W. E. 35 (m), Mary H. 21, Walter C. 17
GIST, Jude 33 (m)*, Eliza M. 30
WIRT, J. C. 26 (m)*, Jane 20
TANDY, Elizabeth 12*
RANDALL, Thomas G. 36*, Susan P. 77, A. P. 21 (m)
CHEATHAM, Matilda G. 50*
RANDALL, S. C. 48 (m), Martha 35, Brice 20, Achilles 12, Mildred A. 10, Martha J. 6, Laura 5, Nancy N. 3, L. C. 4/12 (m)
LAWRENCE, James M. 28*, Margaret 27, Oliver P. 1
MERRILL, John 22*
COLEMAN, John 26*
CHRISTIE, Margaret L. 43, Josephine 18, Laura 16, Henrietta 14, Catherine 12, John 10
LEWIS, John 49, Verenett 43, Thomas 22, Ann M. 20, James B. 18, Mary P. 14, Artemisia 12, Verenett 10, Hiram 8, Juniette 6
WARFIELD, Benj. 60, Nancy 60, Benj. 19
MONTGOMERY, William 38*
PAYNE, Martha A. 50*, John B. 47, Elizabeth T. 34, Elizabeth T. 13, Victoria A. 12, John B. 1
HIGGINS, Joel 47, Ann L. 45, Randall G. 20, John H. 18, Joel 16, William 14
SAYRE, E. K. 40 (m), Elizabeth S. 27, Charlotte J. 5, Elizabeth 1
LETCHER, S. M. 45 (m), Ellen M. 37, George R. 15, William B. 13, Margaret 11, Saml. M. 9, Ellen 4, Tony 1
WARFIELD, William 23, Mary C. 22, Sophonisba P. 6/12

Schedule Page 216

WALKER, Elizabeth 40*, Charles E. 21
MANN, Mary Ann 35*, James 38, Shelby 5, Romily 4
HILL, Charlotte 30*
GRIMES, Jane 28*, Geo. W. 11
WARNER, O. S. 27 (m), Mary E. 23
HUNT, John 25, Minerva P. 23
VERDEN, Artemisia 26, Mary 11, Daniel 9, Morner 9 (m)
LAYTON, Amanda 42, David 22, Thomas 16, Amanda 13, William 11
FLEMING, Susan 65*
ROBINSON, Priscilla 42*
SMITH, John 41*, Sarah 41, Ellen 14
OWENS, Elkanah 21*, Mary 19, Elnar 1, Sarah 2/12, William J. 23, Mary J. 20, Eliza B. 5/12
JINGLE, Jesse 50, Sarah 48, John 19, Edward 9, Riland 5
CURRY, Francis M. 36*, Margaret 25, John 6, Alice 8/12
RYNER, Jane 45*
GANEY, Michael 42, Bridget 40, Kate 7
TOMPKINS, Whitfield 36, Elizabeth 33, Emily 9, John W. 7, Betty 4, Virginia 2

1850 Census Fayette County Kentucky

DONELLY, Charles 35*, Julia 28, Ellen 3, Rosanna 1
MULAY, Lucy 30*
THORNTON, Ann 16*
MCKEE, Owen 19*
METEER, Elizabeth 36, Thomas 12, Mary J. 11, John 9, Ann E. 7, James 5, Charles 4
ANDERSON, Charles 27*, Ann J. 28, Mary F. 4/12
BAXTER, Jane 50*
NOBLE, Frances 22*
BELART, B. F. 44 (m)*, Charlotte 42
NEAL, Anne 44*
UTLEY, John 53, Nancy 46
BROWN, Charles 36, Hannah 36, Robert 14, Charles 12, Catherine 7, Mary 2

Schedule Page 217

NEWBERRY, William H. 39, Amanda 31, George 16, Amanda 1
TURNER, Robert 40, Eliza E. 28, John L. 12, Henrietta 10, Oteria 8, Thaddeus C. 6, Robert W. 3
WHITE, Jacob 44, Hannah 41, Mary E. 9, Emily 7, Kate 1
DAVIDSON, James T. 25*, Catherine M. 23, Mary E. 6, Kate A. 4, Sarah J. 1
HULL, Sarah J. 17*
HULITT, Richard 45, Mary L. 46, Walker 20, Sand. R. 18, Amanda D. 5
HOPPER, Mary 32, William 4
BESORE, John 36*, Lucinda 24, Julia 6, Mary C. 4
HANIWAY, Chas. 18*
MCCAUL, James 19*
HIBITT, Frederick 22*
BUSH, Frederic 43*, Maria 45, William 15, Sarah A. 13, James E. 11, Mary E. 9
WININS, Alexr. 23*, Joanna 18
SULLIVAN, Enoch G. 21*, Catherine 23
PEEL, James 29, Caroline 24, Sarah E. 4, Nancy E. 2, Hugh T. 1/12
HULITT, David 30, Sarah 30, Ellen 11, David E. 2
RALSTON, Thos. N. 44, Josephine 41, Elizabeth 5
HAMILTON, Emily C. 55*, James C. 23, Mary W. 18, W. G. 15 (m)
MILLER, Elizabeth 49*
FORD, John 28*, Joseph H. 2, Mary J. 26
WINN, Sarah 64*, Julia 35, Anne E. 6
DOOLY, Ethelinda J. 7*, Robert B. 5
LOGWOOD, Thos. S. 39, Susan P. 34, Thos. S. 11, Edmund C. 7
GARDINER, Joseph T. 40, Susan A. 35, Ann C. 13, Theodore T. 3
JONES, James 28*, Ann R. 24, John 22
READ, James 8*

Schedule Page 218

MCMAHON, A. 55 (m)*
BRAND, P. W. 40 (f)*, Mary 19, John 16
HIGGINS, Elizabeth 21*, Richard Jr. 23, Ann G. 2/12

1850 Census Fayette County Kentucky

HALL, B. H. 42 (m)*, L. B. 28 (f)
SULLIVAN, John 13*
WEIR, James 45*, Frances 37, Elizabeth 18, Frances 16, Lavinia 14, Henry 11, Lucy 9, Mary 7, James 5, Camilla 3
BOWERS, E. J. 22 (m)*
IRION, M. F. 17 (m)*
MILLER, Joel 16*
HALL, G. B. 38 (m), Emily 32, Amelia 11, Wm. W. 5, Anna B. 3, Garland B. 6/12
GORDON, John 73*, Jemmima 52, Joseph 19, Mary M. 7, Elisha S. 5, John R. 3, Georgiette 1
SMOOT, William 29*
HUNT, Rebecca 42, Elisha W. 24, Kate J. 18, R. Charlton 15
DUNLAP, Elizabeth 66, James 39, Cecilia 25
SCROGGINS, Louisa 35 (B), Charles 12, Thomas 7, Tucker 2, Horace 1
WEBSTER, Ruth 34, Jacob 17, Sarah F. 10, Marcus 8
SCROGGIN, Jas. 34, Panthea 32, Mary E. 10, Alice 5, Ethelbert D. 1
MCCAFFRAY, James 35*, Ellen 30, James M. 10, Sarah F. 8, Virginia 6, Emma J. 5/12
GIBBONS, Isabella 19*
WEAVER, Francis 55*, Tercia 19, Adelaide 16
BAILY, Augustus 31*, Frances 27, Sarah C. 20
WEAVER, Thomas 56, Ann 50
MILLIGAN, Joseph B. 50, Sarah 32, John A. 6, Sarah J. 3, Joseph B. 1
SMITH, Eleazer 39, John 6, W. 5 (m)
ELEY, Benj. 39, Martha 29, W. R. 12 (m), Charles M. 9, Joseph E. 7, Alexr. 5, Jos. S. 4

Schedule Page 219

WELCH, Elizabeth 35, Mary A. 19, Edward 13, Louisa 10, John 8
ONEALY, Jas. 37*
DIGGINGS, Patrick 37*
YOUNG, Charles 41, Jane 41, Emily 16, Jane 14, Washington 6, Cassius 4, Ellen 2
THOMPSON, John 36, Augusta 33
HARING, Peter 33*, Susanna 29, Fred M. 4, James S. 1
THOMPSON, John 8*
HARLOW, George 57*, Rhoda 65
PICKETT, Mary 72*
KALE, George W. 40, Jane 35
KASTLE, John 45, Sophy 54, John 18, Caroline 22, Charles 12, Daniel 14, Rebecca 16
TAYLOR, Elizabeth 60*, George 38, James 26
NELSON, Elizabeth 25*, Elizabeth 16
COOK, Isaac 44, Alvira 40, Mary 12, Eda 4, Emeline 1
IRVINE, Thos. H. 33*
WEAVER, Francis T. 24*
HIGBY, Hestra 76, Cassandra 56 (B)
HALL, Augustus 48, Sarah M. 41, James 16, Isabella 8, William 6, Samuel 3, Sarah 1
RICHARDSON, George P. 52, Sarah A. 47, David D. 18, Henry C. 11, George Ann 9, Mary F. 7
ROBB, Ellen 74, Ellen 31
WICKLIFFE, Charles H. 48, Louisa 32, Susanna 16, Mary 14, Virginia 12, James 10, Charles 8, Drusilla 4, Edwin 2

1850 Census Fayette County Kentucky

SULLIVAN, Maria 42, John W. 14
HAPPY, Josephus 39*, Louisa 32, William 16, Mary Ann 14, Emma 12, Charles 10, James 8, Rebecca 5, John 3, Josephus 1

Schedule Page 220

DONN, John C. 26*
KIDD, William C. 45, Elizabeth H. 38, Robert 19, James 17, Philip 15, Mary T. 12, Ann E. 7
FORD, Edwin 35, Eliza J. 25, Lou Ann 4, Thomas 2, Ada 2/12, Eliza J. 31
JACKSON, James 35, Rebecca 34, Andrew 14, William 9, James 5, Joseph 2
MULLIN, Peter 35, Alice 32, Frank 14, Margaret 12, William 8, Mary 7, John 5, Henry 3, Peter 1
GOODWIN, Joseph 29, Rosanna 23
SCRUGHAM, Joseph 73, Mary 63, James 24
SMITH, Louisa 49*
ROSS, John W. 17*, Louisa S. 14
LILLY, Caleb 28*, Henrietta 21, Minerva A. 22
DOWNING, Elizabeth 18*, Catherine 16
SMITH, Beverly 27 (m) (B), Lucinda 25, Charlton 9, Malcom 7, Mary B. 6, Nora 5, Martha 2
HOLMES, Harriett 38 (B)
FLEMING, Nancy 59, Elizabeth 38, Matilda 24, Sarah 18
FARRAR, Betsy 50* (B)
LANOM, Philicianne 91* (B)
THOMPSON, Aggy 50 (B)
TAYLOR, Henry 73* (B), Martha 60, Harriet 30, Susan 28, Newman 25, Amanda 23
HUMMINGS, W. H. 7 (m)* (B), Eleazer 6, John H. 3
SLAUGHTER, William 40 (B), Susan 22, Henry 1/12
WEBSTER, Amanda 25, thos. 9, Francis M. 7, Kentucky 4 (m), Anna Bell 1
HARRISON, W. E. 26 (m), E. 51 (f), Mary A. E. 22, Sand. B. 28 (m)
DUNCANSON, E. D.? 46 (m), Catherine 32, Edward 15, Mary 12, Alice 10, Kate 7

Schedule Page 221

GOSS, Chas. 34, Margaret E. 27, Charles 7, John W. 2
NORTON, Charles 28, Virginia 25, Stephen 2, Charles 3
CHEVIS, David 35, Melissa 37, Harriet 22
HAMPTON, John A. 36, Susan 36
CHISM, John 41*, Julia A. 41, James W. 9, John H. 8, Imogine 5, Benj. L. 2, Robt. 8/12
STUBBS, Elizabeth 15*
HENDRICKS, Cornelius 47, Rebecca 45, Elizabeth 23, Ellen 14, Cornelius 13, Hetty A. 11, Mary 10, Eliza 8, Nancy 5
MCCHESNEY, John 46, Jane 45, Sam 22, Margaret 17, Wallace 12, John 9
EDEN, Asa 29*, Catherine 22, Henrietta 2, Mary 6/12, Elizabeth 6/12, Anderson 26
JONES, Thomas 18*
NICHOLS, E. 58 (m), Sidney 55 (f), William 27, Sally Ann 21, Rebecca 14, Emily 13, James A. 12
CHEVIS, Sam 26*, George Ann 16
GIBBONS, Zac 21*
MCMAHON, James 20*

1850 Census Fayette County Kentucky

WALKER, Calvin 33*
HARLAN, Margaret 25*
SKILLMAN, Elizabeth 64*, Henry 25
HOWARD, Thomas S. 7*
WELCH, Elizabeth 64*
JOHNS, Thos. H. 34*, Ann 36, W. E. 8 (m), Virginia 5, Chas. A. 3, Thos. H. 5/12
GRIMES, James 18*
GRACE, Daniel 19*
BADDEN, Henry 60*, Minerva 43
LAWLESS, Margaret 19*, Martha 13
WICKLIFFE, D. C. 40 (m)*, Virginia 26
MERCHANT, Caleb 17*
HERBERT, James 16*
PRATHER, Lloyd 34, Mary 31, Lewis K. 8, James H. 3, Mary E. 8/12

Schedule Page 222

COOPER, Mary H. 55, Henry 20, Robert W. 18, Helen Julia 14, Anna 12
FERRELL, London 59 (B), Eleazer 18, Elizabeth 13
ANDERSON, Wilkins 50 (B), Julyy 27, Wm. 4, Emly 2, Mary J. 2
BERRY, Sam 35, Susan A. 30, Susan 8, Sarah V. 2
HENRY, William 26, Mary Ann 57, Eliza 16
KRUISER, James 49, Susan 44, Mary M. 13, Susan H. 8, Henry Theo. 3
ALLEN, John G. 34, Ellen 30, John G. jr 7, Henry W. 5, Charly Ker 3, Ellen Rebecca, 6/12
REDD, Saml. 71*, Sarah C. 60, Saml. J. 27
MCDONELL, Saml. 11*
TILMAN, John 65*
ASA, Marianne 35*
RODES, Mary W. 38*
MEGOWAN, David 64, Nancy 62, James 26, Nancy 21, Caroline 16, Robert 21, Lucinda 22
BELL, Henry 40*, Clara 36, William 19, Noah 16, Henry 10, Clarence 9, D. Heron 10/12
CONWAY, Sally Ann 38*, Saml. 17
MEGOWAN, Stewart 69, Catherine 70
MCCALLISTER, Edward 47, Elizabeth 38
BROWN, Joseph C. 35
JOHNSON, E. P. 52 (m), Betsy 47, James W. 26, E. P. jr 17 (m), Margaret 18, Nanny 11
RICHARDSON, John C. 66, Mary Ann 38, Margaret 1
BRUCE, Sanders D. 25*, Labella S. 21, Leslie C. 1
GILLIS, Thos. H. 31*
DEWEES, Farmer 58, Mary Ann 50
MURPHY, William 35
BERRYMAN, Jack 50 (B)
SPARKS, Wm. 56, Catherine 590, Sam 24, Mary A. 17
WHEATLY, Chas. 32, Nancy 28, Lucian 7, R. Ridgly 3, Nancy 59, Walter S. 17

1850 Census Fayette County Kentucky

Schedule Page 223

MCCRACKEN, John 71*, Emily 54
MYERS, Frederic 35*
MCFARLAND, C. 44 (m)*
MOORE, T. J. 29 (m)*
MOSEBACK, Augustus 24*
KANZ, Charles 25*
HANNA, James 40*
CLAY, Henry 73*, Lucretia 69, John M. 29
HALL, Sarah 80*
MENTILLE, Victoria C. 80*, Louisa 45, Rose 40
WINTER, Jane 10*, Hannah 6, Emma 5
LEWINSKY, Mary 9*
LUSBY, John H. 62*, Elizabeth 60, John 23
BENNETT, Eliza A. 24*, Mary E. 4, Thomas Ann 2
GOVERIN, Thomas 26, Catherine 25, Mary Ann 3/12
CLAY, Thomas H. 46*, Mary R. 43, Lucretia 11, Henry B. 9, Thomas H. jr 7, Rose V. 5, Mary R. 2
WATKINS, Edward 13*
PETTIT, Rebecca 50*, Martha 17, Benj. 12
DENISON, Catherine 80*
TRUE, John P. 33, Mary Ann 32, Willis J. 11, Sarah C. 8, John A. 5, Thomas 3, Adeline H. 1
MORTON, William 59, Mary 47
BERRY, William 34*
MCCONATHY, George 24*
DRURY, Isabella 40*
CROWE, Theodora 24*
OMEALLY, Generose 32*
DUNLAP, Felicity 33*
GIBBONS, Antonia 32*
MCGINNIS, Genevieve 30*
GALIO, Eulalia 28*
RANKIN, Maria 15*
BURR, Margaret 13*
MCCANN, Mary 30*
ALTON, Frances 12*
ANGLIN, Margaret 17*
SMITH, Maslam 53, Mary A. R. 45, Mary E. 16, S. M. 14
CASSELL, Mary 57*
LAWES, Lucullus 25*, Mary L. 24
HULLS, Mary 4*
WISEMAN, William 68
SHY, Saml. 38, Mary 31, James A. 12, Mary M. 10, Laura L. 8, Ann M. 6, John 4, Jane L. 60, John 21
KENNY, John S. 40*, Jospeh S. 27

1850 Census Fayette County Kentucky

Schedule Page 224

DUDLEY, Nelson 51*
WILSON, Abner 30
CHRISTIAN, John 52, Simeon 17, John 2
HAWKINS, Wa;ler 64*, E;ozabetj 62, Amm 30, Bemkm/ 28
ROUTE, Walker 7*
PETTIT, James O. 27, Mary F. 22, Sarah R. 4, Mary J. 2, Nathaniel H. 2/12
STONE, David 40, Harriet 30, Mary 18, Martha 17, Puss 10
BRINK, Daniel 46, Mary A. 31, George D. 15
ATCHISON, William 69, Catherine 63, Alexander 33, Rebecca 28
HEADLEY, James 57, George W. 22, James A. 19, William 14
GOODWIN, Lloyd 58, Mary J. 54, James L. 18, Lloyd B. 14, Lucinda V. 12
GOODWIN, Joseph P. G. 22, Eliza 18
SHIVERY, G. W. 57 (m), Mary 59
GOODLOE, Thos. W. 36*, Mary W. 35
HART, Susan G. 10*
WARE, Joseph S. 17*
THORNS, John 39*, Theodocia 34, Margaret E. 17, Ann J. 8, john F. 6, Joseph T. 3
CHAPLIN, Jacob 52*, Sally 45, John 14
JONES, Wm. R. 38, Drusilla 35, Susan A. 12, Lydia M. 10, George 8, William 6, James 4, Walter 3
VEAL, Dudley 37, Julia A. 33, John 14, Catherine 12, Mary E. 10, James 8, Milton 6, Thomas 4, Susan F. 1
LEWIS, S. H. 40 (m), William 15, Margaret 13, Saml. 11, Catherine 7, Leanna 5, Theodore 2, Leo. 37
EASTIN, A. F. 58 (m)*, Nnacy 34, William H. 24, James M. 22, Jno. Augustine 15, George D. 9, Preston H. 6, Stephen 3

Schedule Page 225

BOLT, Saml. R. 35*
PREWITT, Levi 30, Mary Ellen 22, Margaret W. 3, Elizabeth 1
GRAVES, R. B. 37 (m), Jane 27, Jacob 4, Elizabeth 2
BULLOCK, Joseph J. 37*, Caroline L. 35, Waller 16, Mary S. 12, Caball B. 10, Joseph J. 7, Letitia B. 4, Jno. M. 2
SATTERWHITE, Mary S. 17*
COLEMAN, Florence 17*, Eugenia 12
ELSTON, Penelope 17*
DESHA, Frances 17*
TODD, Jane 17*
MCKNIGHT, Mary J. 16*
BERRY, Lucy 17*
WACIR?, Frances 17*
ARNOUR, Alice 17*
MARTIN, Mary 16*
HOWELL, Elizabeth 16*
EVERETT, Mary 16*
BRECKENRIDGE, Maria 14*, Sally 17, Mary 65
RICE, Sarah 17*

1850 Census Fayette County Kentucky

TAYLOR, Mary W. 14*
THOMPSON, Harriet 13*
SMITH, Mary 15*
JAMES, Eliza 14*
MCCAW, Emma 12*
BOORAM, Paulina 16*
SPURR, Estelle 16*
HARRISON, Georgeanne 17*
DONLEY, Melinda 16*
TODD, Virginia 15*
KERR, Jane 17*
SIMMS, Sarah 14*
WARFIELD, Ruth 17*
PRINCE, Mary 15*
PARKHILL, Letitia 25*
JOHNSON, Eliza 16*
CHILES, Susan 13*
SIMPSON, Mary 16*
MOORE, Patty 16*
FAULKNER, Margaret 16*
HIGGINS, Eliza 15*
WIER, Lavinia 15*
SMITH, Granville 43*, Sarah 29, Sarah 4, Julia E. 3, Wm. B. 1
WHITAMORE, Wm. 20*
SHY, James 58, Lucinda 44
SHELBY, Thomas 70 (B)
MCCONNELL, James 72, Sarah 67, Frank 36, Wm. 5, Benj. F. 4, Jane 3
MCMAHON, Daniel 30*, Rose 30, James 3, Ater 1
MAINEY, John 21*
DOYLE, Luke 24*
CORNER, Maurice 45*
ATKINS, Saml. 41*
RADKIN, Patrick 40*

Schedule Page 226

MCMAINS, Jno. 70, Polly 61
CLUGSTON, John 57, George 22, George 63, Jane 54, Mary 20
CHRISTIAN, Thomas 59*, Harriet 51, Dodridge G. 23, Lethe A. 17 (f), Sarah A. 16, James 13, W. H. H. 10 (m)
WARNOCK, John 35*, Henrietta 21, Ristis 2 (m)
KENT, Wm. 40*
DOWNING, Richard 51, Mary 48, William 28, Samuel 21, Hugh T. 18, John 16, Richard 13, George 8, Joseph 10, James 5, Margaret 2
JONES, R. B. 23 (m), Elizabeth 24, James 50, John 16
DOWNING, William 25*, Sarah A. 20, Aristeus 1/12
KEISER, Hester 50*
HICKS, Alexander C. 25*

1850 Census Fayette County Kentucky

ELLIS, William A. 29*, Ellen C. 23, Wm. A. 6, Edward 4, Martha 2
HICKS, Beverly A. 35 (m)*, Mary 54, Mary 30, Lucy 16, Charles 16, Eveline 10
ELLIS, Mary 9*
AINSWORTH, John 17*
MARTIN, Greene 12*
MCCANN, Joseph 38, Maria 22
OVERTON, Mary S. 42, John 23, James 20, Mary 18, Richard 16, Lucy 13, Susan 11, William 8
DUDLEY, John W. 24, Harriet A. 28, Alice E. 6, Thomas P. 3
ELLIS, Hezekiah 81*, Mary 37, Lucy Jane 24
MCCANN, Lucy Ann 18*, Mildred 15
BRYAN, Mary Ann 8*
SMITH, Mary Elizabeth 20*
KENNARD, Joseph 57, James G. 22
GOODWIN, J. J. 35 (m)*, Joseph 8, Thomas 6, Elizabeth 4, Polly 1
GRAVES, Polly W. 60*
CHILES, Richard 65, Lucy 43, George L. 41

Schedule Page 227

ESTELL, W. R. 36 (m)*, Amanda 29, Clifton F. 8, William 2, Mary E. 4/12
FERGUSON, Amanda 44*
DIDLAKE, Mary B. 16*
DAMABY, James A. 34
GRAVES, Coleman 43, Elizabeth F. 35, Tarlton 18, Wm. H. 16, Robert 14, Samuel 12, Lethe Ann 10, Clementina 8, Henry 6, Walker 4
HUNT, Jno. M. 48, Martha J. 18, Richard J. 15, Gavin D. 14, Mary C. 12
DAMALEY, John H. 42, Edward L. 35
LOW, Noah 45, Eda 30, Mary 7, Buford A. 6, John 4, Lucy 1
CRIM, Fielding 63*, Winny 63, Benj. M. 30, Martha 20, Susan 18
ROSSELL, Fielding 14*
UTTINGER, Samuel 3*
CARTER, James 56*, Mary 59, Edward 18
DOWNING, Lucy 30*, Mary 8, Elizabeth 6
COOK, Thomas 31*, Susan 18
SINGLETON, James 19*
DUDLEY, Thomas P. 58, Caroline E. 53
DUDLEY, James 73, Morning S. 51, Sarah E. 12
DUDLEY, A. F. 44 (m), Ann M. 39, James 16, Ann M. 14, Mary E. 13, Wm. R. 12, Thos. P. 10, John 8, Virginia 6, Felix R. 4, Maurice 2, Carter H. 9/12
ELLIS, William 55, Susanna 53, Elvira J. 20, Perpetua 12, Robert 9
ELLIS, Charles C. 24, Elizabeth 18
DAMABY, Wm. 64*, Malinda 59, Francis S. 36, Joel S. 30, James E. 23, Simeon A. 21, Lydia Sarah 19
STEVENSON, Thomas 12*, Wm. 10, Margaret 7
DAMBY, Edward 57*, Catherine 54, Elizabeth 24, William H. 22, Malinda C. 20, Sidney S. 18, Fabricius E. 13

1850 Census Fayette County Kentucky

Schedule Page 228

DILLARD, R. T. 53 (m), Pemelia A. 48, Wm. D. 26, John 20, Almira 16, James M. 14, Ann Rebecca 9, Maria L. 5
DUDLEY, William 74, Polly 74
BRYANT, Wm. 66, Susan 66, Barnard 40, David M. 22
DAMABY, Wm. 55*, Joseph W. 4, Richard 1
CHILDERS, Jacob G. 33*, Mildred 21, Mary Agnes 1
CARTER, Joseph J. 49*, Elizabeth G. 52
MCCAMMOCK, Mary F. 17*
EWING, James 62, Louisa Ann 38, Martha A. 19, Mary J. 19
WHITE, Albert 23*, Minerva J. 25, Joseph 25, Thomas J. 21
PORTER, Henrietta 22* (B), John 4
BRYANT, Enoch 77*, Jane 70
WHITE, Eliza 40*, Joseph W. 7, Mary C. 4
BRYANT, James A. 29, Judith A. 28, Edward F. 8, Wm. A. 6, John S. 4, James T. 2, Augustus 1/12
RICHARDSON, John H. 40, Sarah 36, Alice M. 15, James M. 14, Mary E. 12, George D. 10, Wm. C. 8, Emily 7, John 5, Sarah E. 4, Isaac 2, Abagil A. 1/12
DUNLAP, William T. 46, Pemelia H. 40, William 19, James 16, Enoch 14, John 12, Thomas 9, George 7, Mary Louisa 6, Joseph 4, Harriet A. 3
BARR, Edmund 50*, Eliza 55
MCCREARY, Mary 60*
RICHARDSON, Thomas 24, Catherine 23
DOWNING, Sarah 50, Joseph 16, Stark 14, Samuel 10, Jeremiah 8
BARKER, Charles 34, Ellen 34, Catherine 50

Schedule Page 229

DAWSON, James 67, Lucinda 46, Mary E. 17, Sarah E. 14, Alvina 13, Mariam 9
MCCANN, William E. 44
CAVINS, John 62*, Mary H. 57, Thomas 35, Robert 32, Jane 30, Josephine 22
TAYLOR, Anarchy 80 (f)* (B)
BALLARD, Henry 56, Lucy 52, William 34, Benj. F. 22, Elizabeth 18, James H. 15
GOODNIGHT, Michael 54, Lucinda 39, John C. 16, Thomas J. 14, George S. 9, Noah H. 4
ALEXANDER, Moses 60* (B), Micky 59 (f), Emeline 19, Amelia E. 2
WEST, Charlotte 7* (B)
ALEXANDER, Davy 30 (B), Della M. 35, Henry 6, Emily 3, Jane M. 6/12
BERRY, J. C. 30 (m), Mildred W. 27, Mary J. 7, Augustine 5, Lucy Ann 3, Nancy E. 1
KEISER, William 30, Amanda 18, Mary H. 1/12, Nancy Jane 25, John 81
EASTIN, Thomas E. 25, Ann L. 26, William 3, Mary 1
DODD, Jane 36, Nancy 35, Sally 33, Daniel 24, Charles 22
GRAVES, Spencer C. 45, Nicy 67
ALEXANDER, John 49* (B), Melinda 40
NUTTER, Lucy 14* (B)
HAYES, Samuel F. 33, Armacinda 27, Polly 11, Georgiette 9, Armacinda 1
ALLEN, John R. 32*, Sarah A. 21, Barbara J. 9, Ann 55, Simeon B. 18
VAUGH, James H. 37*
ALLEN, Buford E. 50, Eleonora 45, Benj. R. 23, Buford 18, George 14, Sarah 12, Adeline 10, Eleonora 8, Thomas 6, Simeon 4

1850 Census Fayette County Kentucky

Schedule Page 230

MUIR, Ann 70, Ann 7
KENT, A. D. 25 (m)*, Ann E. 18, Elizabeth C. 1
KIBLER, David 33*, Salrah 62, James 5
KENT, Lewis 26, Emily J. 21, Thomas D. 1
HAYES, Thomas T. 44, Nancy 39, Lucy 19, John 17, Margaret 15, Sarah 13, Thomas 11, Robert 5
MCCANN, Neal 51*, Elizabeth 33, Thomas 14, Howard 10, Susan 8, Sarah 5
PULLUM, W. A. 40 (m)*, Armstead B. 11, William M. 3
WOODS, Schuyler 35*
HALL, George W. 28*
PIPER, William C. 28*
OWENS, Elizabeth 24*
CLAUSON, Richard 31, Julia A. 28, Austin 10, Mary E. 8, Richard A. 4, William J. 1
COLEMAN, Samuel 45, Elizabeth C. 43, Woodson 17, Lucy Hawes 9, Elizabeth A. 7, Ann E. 5, Benjn. L. 2
PREWITT, William C. 62*, Catherine 50, Elizabeth 22, Richard H. 17, David 10, Robert 25
WOOD, Greene C. 25*
HICKMAN, Lucy 75* (B)
ALBERTI, Jno. Chs. 60, Nancy M. 50, John L. B. 26
COLEMAN, Marquis 21*, Cicero 16, Ann B. 50
THOMPSON, Q. A. 21 (m)*
MCCANN, Mary 50, Rufus 24, Sidney 23, James 18, Hezekiah 14
MCGRADDY, Hugh 24, Alicia 27, Mary F. 1, Margaret A. 1/12
COONS, William C. 30*, Ann 30, Morrison 10
FEANISTER, Susan Ann 23*
GOODWIN, Joseph G. 62, Rachel 48, Benjn. G. 30, Martha Ann M. 12, Josephine R. 10
WHITESIDE, Pembroke 30*, Marinda 27, Thomas 2
ELLIS, Polly 75*
TRULL, Sarah Ann 11*
CRIM, Lewis 48, Susan R. 43, James L. 21, Clifton F. 19, Claibourn E. 18, Woodson B. 16, Frances M. 15, Thomas J. 14, Ann Eliza 12, David F. 10, Samuel H. 8

Schedule Page 231

ROBINSON, Roger 60, Lucy Ann 48, Radford M. 25, Mary E. B. 23, John M. 22, Lucy Ellen 16, Amanda M. 15, William 10, Joseph K. 6, Lucy 87
TRUE, Ellen 50*, Emay E. 22, Elizabeth 21, Phebe 19
HURT, Laura 6*
SHIPP, Dudley 62, Eliza T. 50, Thomas J. 22
SHEFFER, J. Howard 42*, Julia M. 30, Jacob H. 8, Ruth W. 6, Elizabeth H. 4, Laura J. 2
MURRAY, Thomas A. 23*
HUGHES, Jacob 59*, Sarah A. 45, Harriet 23
SKINNER, Thomas 18*
ROBERTSON, Solomon 33, Eliza 33, Henry 12, Margaret 9, Mary E. 7, Daniel 5, Belle 3

1850 Census Fayette County Kentucky

TAYLOR, Hubbard D. 38*, Alice T. 33, Mary T. 7, Newton F. 5, George F. 2
LANE, Mildred 67*
MITCHELL, George 62*, Frances 50, Alison 31, Claibourn 26, Joseph 21, George 18, Sarah 15, Lucy 12, Benjamin 13, Julia Ann 10, Mildred 8
LYON, Thomas 39*, Mildred F. 15, William T. 14, George A. 12
CARTER, George 33*, Robert 28, Lunsford 24
ELLIS, Claibourn 38*
WHITE, Austin 55, Jacob 43
LEWIS, Enoch 35, Mary A. 27, Ann E. 10, James 8, Mary 5, Charlton 1
WEATHERS, Polly 50, Caswell 25, Ambrose 40, Grenville 22, Amanda 21

Schedule Page 232

WEATHERS, Albert 27*, Sarah 24, Howard 1
SCOTT, Margaret 40*, Andrew J. 42
HALEY, Mary 57*
PARISH, John 24*, Mary 24
WEATHERS, Lucinda 28*, William 3, Thomas J. 5, Mary E. 10
DAMABY, George M. 28*, Agnes E. 26, James M. 6, Lucy E. 3
MITCHELL, Wandy 58*
LOW, Solomon 47, Rebecca 46, Charlton 20, John M. 17, Mary C. 15, Dillard 12, Helena 8, George Ann 6, Zachary T. 3, Eliza Jane 4/12
HALEY, William 35, Susan 28, Ambrose 5, Mary A. 2
WILSON, Thos. 38*, Nancy 34, Abner 9, Sarah E. 3, Davidella 2, Martin 1/12
STEVENS, Mary C. 15*, Margaret J. 12
WILSON, Nancy 58, Lydia Ann 40, Elizabeth 34, Matilda J. 23
WILSON, Moses 62, Lydia 28, Abner 16, Amelia 14, Pemelia 8, Matilda 4
WINN, Jesse D. 39*, Mary E. 19, Catherine E. 17, Benjamin S. 16, William H. 14, George G. 12, Lucy 11, Mary 77
ROGERS, David E. 1*
WARE, James T. 34, Abraham 29, George C. 27, John W. 22
SHRYOCK, John F. 87, Fanny 85, Samuel 40, Ellen 30
FERGUSON, Abraham L. 46, Mary K. 40, William 19, Noah S. 17, Lewis 12, Robert 9, Mary E. 6
WOODGATE, Jackson B. 35, Louisa 29, James 6, Margaret 5, Oscar 2
WHITE, Richard 40, Robinson 26
DAMABY, George W. 55*, Elizabeth 51, Catherine M. 24, Thomas E. 21, James L. 18, Sarah A. 17, Lucy 10

Schedule Page 233

TINGLE, David 25*
MITCHELL, Frank 55* (B), Emily 35, Sally 15, Dick 9, Esther 8, Betsy 5, Moses 2
ROBINSON, Milly 65* (B)
DAMABY, John 59, Melinda 49, Ann E. 31, Luther W. 30, Emerine 27, Lucinda 25, John E. 23, George E. 18, James M. 14, Mary E. 12, Judith C. 9, Louisa 7
COONS, George W. 47, Eveline 43, John J. 18, James J. 14, Charles E. 11, George R. 9, David E. 7, Zachary Taylor 5, Llewellyn 3

1850 Census Fayette County Kentucky

COONS, Edward H. 36*, George A. 30, Mary E. 1
NORTON, Jerry 50* (B)
DAMABY, Benjn. M. 22, Elizabeth A. 20, George B. 2
COONS, Joshua 66, Judy 65, Thomas 29, Elizabeth 24, Joshua A. 21
MATTHEWS, Saml. 59, Polly 58, Benjn. J. 17
HUNT, Drummond C. 55*, Letitia 45, George 16, Mary D. 15, Philemon B. 12, Albert G. 10, Gavin Drummond 8
PARISH, Howard E. 18*
COONS, William B. 32, Lucy M. 30, Mildred 8, Judith Ann 6, Clifton 1
OWEN, Thos. 43*, Susanna 26, Robert 6, Mary E. 4, Nancy A. 1
HEARNE, Robert C. 19*, Wm. T. 15, James W. 11
BARNETT, Ambrose H. 35*, Emily 32, Charles W. 11, John H. 9, Richard P. 5
THOMASSON, Wm. P. 22*
COLEMAN, Fauntleroy 21*
KERTLEY, AManda M. 48*
BERKLEY, William S. 34*, Henrietta 24
ROGERS, Clifton R. 33*

Schedule Page 234

CHRYSTAL, James E. 37*, Sarah A. 37, James H. 11, Richard S.? 9, George W. 5, Charles E. 3, Benjn. F. 6/12
BIVEN, John W. 17*
MERRIWETHER, Eliza J. 19*
TAYLOR, Harry 36* (B)
KALMES, W. T. 40 (m)*, Lucinda 34, Samuel 16, Benjamin 12, W. T. 8 (m), Marcus 4, James 2
BRECKENRIDGE, Roddy 40*
DUDLEY, Albert G. 40*
SMITH, Polly 52*
DAMABY, Susan 67*
KEYESE?, John L. 35*, Mary 2, Nelson 1, Mary Ann 35
ROGERS, Joseph 10*, Susan 9, Charlton V. 8
ROBERTS, Frank 80* (B)
BRUNNETT, William 28*, Sarah 40
BRECKENRIDGE, Susan 7*
CLARK, William 59*, Betsy 51, George 18, Elizabeth 15
HEDGER, Jonathan 31*
ROGERS, C. F. 36 (m), Margaret F. 26, Rebecca 5, Charles F. 3, James 1
BARNETT, Charles 50, Ann 50, James A. 10
ATCHISON, James 50, Amelia 50, James 23, Lethe J. 19 (f), John 18, Stephen 11, Clifton 9, Elizabeth 7, Aurilla 6
HULITT, Joseph 27, Elizabeth 29, Mary E. 1/12
WARFIELD, Elisha 70, Maria 64, Ann E. 32
SKINKER, Marshall 45 (B), Susan 84, July A. 35, Louisa 4
WEBSTER, America 33, George S. 16, Florida A. 14, Margaret A. 13, Daniel 10, John B. 8, Edward 6, Isabella 4
PARKER, Howard S. 23, Montgomery H. 28, Maria W. 20, Wilson H. 1
THOMPSON, James K. 34*, James C. 1

1850 Census Fayette County Kentucky

STONE, William C. 39*, Paulina N. 36, Margaretta 12, Alice S. 7, Betty Keith 4
HAMMOND, A. D. 30 (m)*, Eliza Jane 35, Lucy 1, George 28
MORRISON, Asa 49*

Schedule Page 235

KELLER, David 31, Hannah G. 31, John Eastin 8, Lucy B. 3, Kate Hobson 2, Eliza Spears 1/12
HAMILTON, Jesse T. 39, Nancy 46, John A. 14, Robert A. 12, James W. 10
BRADLEY, James S. 50, Mary 47, W. J. 26 (m), Margaret 22
YEARING, Dennis 40*, Ellen 32, Mary 1
ROACH, David 27*
FORAN, John 22*
BAKER, John H. 28, Amanda 21, James B. 3, John W. 1
MUIR, Harriet 47*, Samuel 21, Thomas F. 19, William 16, Malvina 14, Henrietta 9, Sarah F. 7, Harriet 5
WEBSTER, Laura 5*
CHILES, John 37, Nanny 26, Sally 3
LEWIS, Thomas 23*
MCDANIEL, Jno. 22*
ARMSTRONG, John 59*, Mary 42, Sarah Ann 18
AGIN, Philip 26*
BARRY, John 52*
PATTERSON, Joseph 38*, Mary 35
CLINCH, William 35*
KERR, John 59, Rachel 42, Mary P. 21, James H. 20, Jane 17, Sarah 14, Nancy R. 12, Kate 9, Ella 7, John 3
PERKINS, William 62, Rebecca 50, James 23, Edward 22, Catherine 8, Mary C. 12
PERKINS, James 23*, John 21
KEMPER, Tilman 22*
HENDERSON, James 31, Susan 27
HARDISTON, George C. 37, Lucinda 30, Nancy Jane 8, William T. 6, John H. 4, George R. 2, Cornelia 1
JOHNSON, John 66*, Elizabeth 64, Ozreel 38, Richard 34, John 32, James 28

Schedule Page 236

YATES, George 49*
HARDESTER, Henry 85, Sarah 64, Judy 25, Frances 20
YATES, Abner 57, Lucy 48, William 21, Dorcas 20
HARDESTER, Benjn. 74, Nancy 23, Susan 19, Moses 13
HUTSELL, Jesse 28, Ann 26, Sarah F. 1
HULITT, Perry 30, Eliza 24, Zachary T. 3, Catherine 1
SCOTT, Andrew 72*, Elizabeth 69, Nancy 44, Thomas M. 42, Ruth 40, Eliza Ann 31, Jane 23, Agnes 34
MCCOWAN, Nancy 80*
DAUSON, Levi 24, Absolom 25, Sarah 54, Eliza 22, Cynthiana 21, Melinda 18, Elizabeth 16
SCOTT, Andrew T. 45, Elizabeth 37, Nancy 17, William 15, Polly 13, Sally 11, Julius 9, Catherine 7, Eliza 2/12

1850 Census Fayette County Kentucky

WHITE, John P. 39, Sidonia 35, Dabney 13, John D. 11, William 6, Polly B. 4, Obebria 2
DEJARNATT, Greenup 45, Mary Ann 35, Robert L. 17, John T. 16, Amelia 12, William 10, George 7, James 4, Susan 1
MARTIN, David 50, Sophia 50, Isabella 20, Mary Ann 14, Sarah J. 12, Elizabeth 6
COONS, James M. 40*, Sarah D. 35
YATES, William 30*
HULITT, Joseph 60, Elizabeth 45, Ann 18, Jackson 16, Henry 13, William 10, Catherine 7, Amanda 4, Bicky 2 (f)
WHITE, Caswell 26*, Elizabeth 25
MARTIN, James H. 23*, Nancy 22, James 2, Margaret 1

Schedule Page 237

WARFIELD, Nicholas 65*, Susan 54, Mary E. 25, Ruth 16, Caroline 14
THORNTON, Rebecca 22*
ORR, William 46*
BAKER, Catherine 53, Charles 33, Ellen 28
PULLUM, Major 70 (B), Judy 67
VAUGHN, William 49*, Julia Ann 41, William 14, Thomas M. 11, George 4
HAMPTON, Sarah 21*, Jerry 27, Julia 1
GEORGE, Lucy 18*
EWING, Samuel 46, Sally 40, Saml. M. 18, Sophia 16, Ryland 14, James 90, Susan 6, John 2
SLAUGHTER, Charles 55 (B)
DOWNING, George 45*, Kitty J. 35, Richard 19, Thomas 16, George 12, Frances 11, Catherine 9, Becky 6, Ann M. 4, William 3, John 1
DOWNTON, Elizabeth 65*
SLAUGHTER, Thomas 26* (B)
ALLEN, Joseph G. 26, Barbara J. 17, Mary B. 11/12
BARR, Thomas J. 39, Lenora 30, Thomas J. Jr. 12, Isaac 11, Robert 9, Lenora 7, Archibald 3, Mary C. 4, Harriet A. 6/12, Martha A. 65
BACON, Enoch 41*, Mary 39, Mary E. 8, Richard W. 6
GILL, Martha 15*
STONE, Cordelia 32*
MCCLANAHAN, Elijah 37*, Harriet 36, Louisa 17, Thomas 15, Mary 13, William 11
DUNLAP, Andrew J. 28*
FOSTER, Henry 53*, Mildred 49
SUTTON, Matilda 48*
KENT, Washington 27*
HUNTER, Thomas 50*, Mary 55
BALTIMORE, Lucky 70 (f)* (B)
PRATHER, John 65, Telitha 18
STIP, George 66*, Emily 30, Isaac 13, John 29
EPPERSON, John 15*

1850 Census Fayette County Kentucky

Schedule Page 238

ROBINSON, John 71, Mildred 30, Kitty 21, Joseph 39, Elijah H. 31
PATTESON, A. A. 32 (m), Jane W. 28, Augusta 8, Jean F. 6, Alexander L. 4, Susan Archy 1
RODES, William 58, Margaret B. 51, Waller J. 33, Levi T. 19, Sarah E. 23
ANDERSON, Reuben 65 (B), Hannah 50, John 35, Timothy 30, Reuben 27, Ann Maria 25, Mary 20
MARSHALL, Robert 50, Elizabeth 43, George 25, Richard 22, Robert 19, Joseph 18, Mary Ann 15, Silas 14, Ann E. 12, Jane 10, Margaret 8, William 5
DOWNING, James 42, Elizabeth 35, James Jr. 15, Francis 6, Margaret A. 3
MCMAHAN, John 42, Mary 62, Lucinda 39, Sally 32, Nancy 30, Martha 25, Eliza 23, Samuel 21, Benjn. 28
HUNT, P. G. 46 (m), Isabella A. 30, Waller B. 17, Maria B. 15, Joseph G. 12, Josiah B. 4, Sally K. 1
DUNLAP, John R. 57, Emily 45, George R. 14
TWAY, Patrick 30, Cate 28, Patrick 4, Kitty 2
GARRARD, Eliza T. 49*
KEY, Albert 30*, Robert 25
VEALE, Dudley 50, Elizabeth 39, George O. 17, Nathaniel W. 15, Sarah J. 14, Elizabeth 12, James 9, Dory 7 (m), Newton 6, Theodocia 5, Warren 3
BERKLEY, Burgess 56, Maria 30, Susan 25, Amanda 24, John Q. A. 22, Julia Ann 18, Benjn. F. 16, Elizabeth 15, Burgess 10

Schedule Page 239

WILSON, Abner 31*, Lucy 25, Alnette 7, Laura 4, Ruffle 2
ESTES, Clement 29*
SPURR, Richard 41*, Martha A. 36, Richard A. 13, Levi 10, Marcus 6, H. Clay 4, Robinson Crusoe 2
SPURR, B. A. 50 (m)*, Eliza J. 43, George Ann 8
HAVELY, John 24*
PREWITT, Alexander 34, Martha E. 27, Laura 7, Margaret M. 5, William A. 2
SHARP, Allenton B. 31*, Polly Ann 28, Stephen G. 7, Milton D. 4
BENTHEL, Richard 45*
HUDSON, John 68, John Jr. 32, Elizabeth 23, Susan 5/12
VALLANDINGHAM, James 47*
SHARP, James 35*, Nancy 30, Polly 28, Marshall 10, Martha A. 8, Llewellyn 7, Morton 4, Louisa 1
GRIMES, Jane 75, C. W. 33 (m), Mary A. 30, Erasmus B. 10, Joe E. 7, Chas. W. 5, Martha 6, Edwin 4, Eusebius 2, William W. 3/12
GESS, Mary 54, Sarah J. 27, Martha Ann 25, George 23, John 19
DAVIDSON, James 21*, Sally A. 18, Jonathan 1
LANGBY, Catherine 44*, William 4
GRIMES, Sidney S. 44, Judy Ann 44
JOHNS, Joseph 35*, Cynthia 25
FISHER, Ratcliff 31*
PARKER, John 54, Rebecca 37, Alexander T. 18, Mary 16, Lucy 14, Stafford 11, Martha 9, John 7, Sarah 5, Watts 2
HARRISON, George B. 41, Catherine 27, Ann E. 11, Charles 9, George 7, James 3
GRAVES, Joseph 42*, Margaret A. 36, William 18, Lucy 15, George 13, Mary 12, Ann 10, Ellen 5, Joseph 3

1850 Census Fayette County Kentucky

Schedule Page 240

HAYES, Lucy 77*
CHRISTIAN, Wm. 25, Martha 23, Sidney 14
AUBREY, R. J. 33 (m)*, ANn 28, Mary E. 10, Harriet A. 9, Sarah 7, Martha J. 3, Martin L. 25
MCCAN, John T. 10*, Ann E. 12
FAULKNER, Harriet 55*, Mary 17
GEORGE, Moses 44, Maria 44, Lucy Ann 19, Jane 14, Lenora 12, Susan 10, William 8, Benjn. F. 7, Owen 5, Z. Taylor 2
HUNDLEY, Allen 25, Mary 25, Richard 7, Samuel 5, Joseph 2
KENT, David 75*, Elizabeth 64, Melinda 42
HALSEY, Jane 26*, Thomas 23, Cassius 4/12
CRISTOPHER, Catherine 28*, Columbus 13, George 8, Minerva J. 5
KENT, David Jr. 23*
SMALLWOOD, Abraham 32, Frances C. 33, Frances A. 12, William T. 6, John 4, George 2
RATCLIFFE, Francis 57*, Mary 46
SEARCY, Nancy E. 10*
STIVERS, E. Y. 31 (m), Lucy 24, Mary A. 2, James W. 3/12
MAGEE, Sidney S. 30, Miranda 20
WHITE, Thomas 29, Virginia 29, John Thomas 2, Joseph 31, Elizabeth 23, John T. 4, Chas. 2
NICHOLS, Polly 47, Wm. 22, Harvey 21, Mary 16
HALL, William 48, Docia 29, Ann E. 5, James P. 8, Henrietta 4, Netta 3, Cassius 4/12
JONES, James 40, Sarah 50, George Ann 5

Schedule Page 241

AUBREY, Rebecca 38*, Charity 85, French 46, Francis M. 17, Henry C. 7, Margaret 9, Henry C. 15
VAUGHN, John B. 45*
BENTLEY, Washington 53*
MCPHADDEN, J. D. 32 (m)*
ERSKINE, Wesley J. 35*, Sarah 30
EVE, George 69*, Jane 60, Fanny 20
WATTS, Oscar 7*
NELSON, Harvey 36*
PREWITT, B. A. 28 (m)*
BERRY, Thos. H. 32*
MORRIS, Wm. B. 51*
HUNDLEY, Chas. 27, Zach H. 55, Prudence 58
BERRY, B. L. 36 (m), Sarah J. 30, Josephine E. 9, Julia 7, Edwin M. 4, John M. 30
MAYHUGH, N. B. 28 (m)*, Ann 21, Robinson 2
ROBINSON, Eliza 22?*
DONELLY, John 46*, Mary A. 48, George W. 18, Melinda A. 16, John 12
LAYNG, Violetta B. 6*, Francis L. 4
HOWES, Orion 26, Mary 21, Lydia F. 2
WATSON, Drury 43*, Polly A. 34
BOONE, Eleanor 17*, Jesse 19
SPURR, William 32, Mary A. 31
MUNDAY, Edmund P. 35*, Mary Ann 28, Lucy Ann 9, Nancy 7, Mary 3, Amanda 1

1850 Census Fayette County Kentucky

TALBOT, Daniel 20*
RATLIFFE, Wm. D. 24*
CARTER, Allen 32*, George Ann 31, Mary J. 11, John W. 8, James L. 6, George A. 4, Thomas 2, Susan 60, Logan 30, Alexander 23
HAROLD, Nancy 17*
HALSEY, Benjamin 58*, Mary 40, Elijah 17, Mary F. 16, Lucy Ann 15, Milton 5
SUTTON, Jane 22*, Lewis 22
HARRISON, Isaac W. 35*, Elizabeth 34, Mary 7, George G. 5, Sarah B. 3, Elizabeth 2

Schedule Page 242

ALEXANDER, John 22*
MCMAHAN, Geo. W. 36*
ROGERS, Frances H. 65*, Judith C. 27
DOUGLAS, Pleasant 43, Nancy 31, Margaret A. 16, Tarlton 14, Pleasant Jr. 12, Sarah E. 10, Adeline 8, Julia Ann 6, Z. Taylor 3, Nancy 1/12
STONE, David 41, Harriet 31, Maria L. .8
GRIMES, Rachel 54*
LINDSEY, Wm. 28*, Mary 25, John 5, William 4, Mary 2, Philip 1
BARKER, Joseph 64, Nancy 63, Thomas 23, Robert 20, Jane 18
EDDLEMAN, Robert 60, Alice 34
HATTAN, James 62, Polly 66, Joanna 23
BANFORD, James C. 45, Frances 41, Mary 20, Lucy 18, William 16, Elizabeth 14, Susan 12, Sarah 9
EDDLEMAN, Peter 88, Mary 57, Elizabeth 54
EDDLEMAN, Jones 38, Harriet 31, John R. 13, Susan F. 11, William C. 6, James T. 3
CHRISTIAN, Ann 35, Annice 4, William 28, July 70 (B)
WATTS, Frances C. 39*, Benjn. 24
MORETON, Susan F. 16*
SHAW, Nancy 18*
VALLANDINGHAM, Judy 38, Elizabeth 21, Jane 18, John 17, Julia Ann 3, Mary 25, Mary F. 8, Henrietta 3, George 1
DUNCAN, Levicy 53, Thomas 29, Sarah A. 21, William 15
CHRISTIAN, Tumer? 53, Mary 50, Martha 23, Margaret A. 22, Marion D. 21, Thomas 19, James 17, Theodore 15, Mary F. 13
GRIMES, William 67, Sarah 60, Mary 37, James W. 35, Martha A. 19

Schedule Page 243

WALLACE, Thomas M. 52, Susan T. 24, Maria L. 9, James W. 7, Susan ANn 6, Thomas W. 4, Oliver 2, Elizabeth 6/12, Mary 22
EMBERSON, Harry 54*, Elizabeth 25
TINELL, William 26*
WATTS, David T. 18, Telitha A. 24
WATTS, Larrett? 43*, Lucinda 45, Garrett J. 4, David 50
FERGUSON, Martha A. 10*
TWYMAN, George 9*

1850 Census Fayette County Kentucky

HAYES, William 44, Mary 36, Mary J. 18, Lucy 16, Robert 14, Margaret 12, William 10, Alexander 8, Sarah A. 6, Joseph 4, James 5/12
HUDSON, James 31, Margaret 26, Milton 27
RICHARDSON, Sam Q. 34, Elizabeth Ann 22, Andrew W. 8, James T. 5, Mary E. 3
WINN, Owen D. 44*, Amanda 19, Phebe 10, Susan 62
GRIMES, John 23*
EMBRY, Jacob 52*, Nancy C. 44, James W. 21, Sarah F. 17, Ann E. 13, Virginia 11, Sidney 8, Cary 2 (f)
FOWLER, Franklin 22*
JOHNS, Susan 56, Susan Jr. 33
SPURR, James 50, Frances 56
WINN, Jerry 70 (B), Violet 75
NELSON, John 75*, Dicy 75
BOGARD, William 23*, Lauretta 20, Mary 1
SEARCY, P. M. 45 (f), Mary A. 18, George W. 16, Martin D. 14, Susan 12, Henry D. 8, Frances 5, W. W. 1 (m)
CLARKE, George W. 52
ADAMS, Richard 39, Nancy 27, Sarah J. 11
DEVORE, Harrison 35*, Love Allen 28, Ellen 25, Amanda A. 5, John W. 2, Lucinda L. 1

Schedule Page 244

FULLERLOVE, Dulcinea 16*
WILLIAMS, O. H. 28 (m)*
STIVERS, Sidney 41, Mary J. 31, Jacob 9, William 8, Elizabeth 6, Edward 5, James T. 2/12
FRANKLIN, Judith W. 48, Betty 20, Bernard A. 17
THURMAN, William 30, Cynthia Ann 24, Richard 4
MCDANIEL, Lampton 43, Susan 35, Nancy Thos. 15, Wm. T. 12, Elias W. 10, Susan F. 9, Nathanikel 4, Rebecca 2
TILLET, William 20, Mary 18
HART, Minor 60*, Milly 63, John 39, Anna 27
STIVER, George M. 8*, Susan 5
STONE, Calvin 35*
HART, Levi 31, Lydia 27, Josephia 4, Napoleon 3, China 4/12 (f)
DEVORE, David 73*, David Jr. 26, Martha 24
HARDIN, Calvin 13*
GESS, Mary Ann 34, Newton 9, James Wm. 6, John W. 6, Isaac 3, Ann 1, Ann 68
CURLE, Sophia 39, Mary 16, Fanny 13, Ellen 10, James 8, Jane 19
HART, Lou Ann 34, John H. 38, Mary C. 13, Lucy D. 11
SHELBY, Evan 26*, Amanda 25, Mary P. 5
BROWN, Stephen 70* (B)
SHELBY, Isaac 35*
WHEELER, John 30*
DOWNING, Josiah 45*
CRAWFORD, Mary 60
CARR, Charles 74, Elizabeth T. 68
CARR, Thomas 48, Nancy 46, Thomas D. 23, Lucretia 16, Ann M. 6
MCCANN, Ben 45*, Emily 31, Martha B. 18, Robert 15, George 7, "Sis" 6, Betty 4

1850 Census Fayette County Kentucky

TAYLOR, Joseph 33*
SHELBY, Isaac P. 28
SHELBY, Thomas 63*, Mary C. 24, Thomas H. Jr. 21, Fanny T. 18, Edmund P. 17

Schedule Page 245

WEBB, William 30*
LITRELL, Robt. 28, Maria 21, Chas. W. 1, Margaret F. 4/12, Alexander 23, Amanda 19, Phoebe Ann 1/12
STEP, George Jr. 24*, Sarah 24, Laura 2, Mary 4/12
FAULKNER, William 22*
EVANS, Silas 30, Pemelia 31, Elizabeth 12, Sarah 10, Nancy J. 8, Richard F. 5, Telitha 3, Louisa 1, Sarah 66
EVANS, Peter 45*, Rebecca 39, Sarah J. 17, Richard 13, Elizabeth Ann 7, thomas 6, Peter 3
FERGUSON, Martha 68*
HUMPHRY, Catherine 76*
CUNNINGHAM, Geo. W. 35, Martha Ann 33, Saml. W. 11, Martha 6, Judith 2, Geo. R. 1/12, Sarah E. 1/12
MCNEAL, James 50, Sarah 50, Sarah 92
MCCROSBY, Rebecca 55, Mary 35, Thomas 31, Ann 27, Minerva 21, Alexander 18, Almarine 17
SMITH, Green Berry 88, Rebecca 73, Becky 45, Kate 42, John 39, Aquilla 38, Elijah 36, Mary 32
BAXTER, German 52, Elizabeth 42, Elizabeth P. 25, Polly Ann 22, James 20, Sally Ann 16, Reuben 15, William H. H. 12, Lucinda Ann 9, Mary 76
BAXTER, America 48, George 21, Abernathy 83
BAXTER, Andrew J. 30, Amanda 23, Ella E. 3, Kate 1
CRAWLEY, Asa 46*, Elizabeth 67, Cynthia Ann 27, Elizabeth 22, Isabella 22, Washington 40, Sanford 38, Harrison 36, Tilford 27, Milton 24, Harbard 22
BEASLEY, Sally 48*

Schedule Page 246

LYLE, John R. 50*, Sarah M. 41, William J. 9, Robert B. 7, Edwin R. 4, Joseph L. 1
ST. CLAIR, W. P. 23 (m)*
BRISTER, Judith 73*
BRINK, Archd. 48, Judy 18, Demarus 16 (f), Archer 6, Cynthia 1
BROADDUS, E. Samuel 28*, Elizabeth 23, John F. 9, Frank Webb 2, Mary E. 1, Wm. A. 1/12
BOWLING, WM. 21*
STIVERS, John 19*
PRATHER, Thos. Sr. 73, Mary 62, James 24, Sarah 16
PRATHER, Walter 23, Mary 22
SCHROCK, Mary D. 50*, Edward 14
PRATHER, Wm. J. 18*, Sarah 15, Robert J. 26
PRATHER, Reuben 56*, Rachel 60
GRIFFY, George 22*, Sarah 22
BRINK, Hibard 39*, Louisa 32, Emma J. 4, Mary E. 2, George W. 5/12
LIPSICOMB, William S. 45, Patsy 46, Humphrey J. 20, Nathan M. 18, Patsy Ann 17, James J. 14, Mary W. 9

1850 Census Fayette County Kentucky

BAILEY, John R. 56, Rosalina 44, Elijah 25, Sarah J. 18, Amanda 16, David 8, James F. 4
BAILEY, Samuel 31, Mary 27, Martin L. 5, Mary 6/12
BRINK, Martha 70*, James 28, Joseph C. 24, William S. 23, Becky Jane 6, Philip 47, Isaac 17
GRIFFY, Elizabeth 10*, Thos. 14
COSBY, Winfield M. 45, Amanda 41, James W. 16, Ausey D. 15, Edward 12, Lucy C. 14, John W. 9, Oliver 8, Charles D. 6, Z. Taylor 4, Ann Amanda 1

Schedule Page 247

BAILEY, Wm. G. 60, Pemelia 55, John H. 23, George G. 21, Mary Ann 16, Sarah 13
STIVERS, Elizabeth 56*, James 35, Benjn. 27, Elijah 25, George 23, Joseph 16, Cristopher 14, Elizabeth 11
GRIFFY, Melissa Ann 17*
PIKE, Samuel 68*
GRIFFY, Sally Ann 27*, Peggy 20, Jesse 4, Peter M. 2
BRINK, Ephraim 36*, Mary Ann 25, James W. A. 2
PIKE, Elizabeth 18*
GESS, George Wash 31, Phoebe Ann 21, Wilson F. 10, Rebecca F. 8, William Jane 6, Mary C. 4, George 1/12
GRIFFY, William 50, Ruth 45, Sally 18, Daniel 15, William 13, Becky 11, Polly 8, Martha 5, Demains 2 (f)
GRIMES, James 45, Sally Ann 40, John W. 13, Elizabeth 10, Matilda 8, Ruth 6, Eliza 5, Jackson 4, Martha 2
ROBINSON, Thos. 35, Ruth 27, John S. 8, Joseph 7, Sarah 5, Eliza Ann 3, William P. 2
BAILEY, David 35, James 28, Frances 37
CHRISMAN, Jefferson 45, Jenette 43, Henry H. 10, Benjn. D. 3
MARTIN, James H. 70, Polly 60, Matilda 22
BAXTER, Priscilla 59*, Samuel 30, John 21
BRYANT, Emeline 25*, Demarias 13 (f), Henry 9
TAPPS, P. W. 36 (m), Emily J. 28, Lewis W. 10, John 8, Mildred 6, L. Montague 4, Ben Johnson 2, Susan F. M. 1
SPURRS (SPEARS), Lee W. 46, Frances G. 33, Sarah J. 15, Charles L. 13, Mary L. 11, Riley F. 9, Chrisman 7, Geo. Wash. 5, Luther W. 3, Mildred F. 3/12

Schedule Page 248

SPEARS, John 80, Margaret 73
BAXTER, German 63, Martha 50, Napoleon 25, Jerome 24, Descartes 20, Martha 17
TAUL, Benjn. M. 48, Sally Ann 42, Saml. 23, Joseph C. 22, Mary J. 21, Jesse 18, John 16, W. H. H. 14 (m), Susan 13, Sarah F. 11, Nancy E. 8
WILSON, Jonas 26, Mary J. 21, Benjn. H. 1
CHRISMAN, Joseph 50, Eleanor 47, Joseph 16, John 25, Jane 23, Laura 1
SOPER, John H. 59*, Mary D. 45, H. Clay 18
JOHNSON, Mahaly 35*, Henry T. 13, Frank 11
MITCHEN, Mary 4*
MARTIN, Richard 57, Sarah 43, James H. 23
WEBB, Allen 30, Emily J. 24, Othriah 6 (m), Mary J. 3, Elizabeth A. 7/12

- 175 -

1850 Census Fayette County Kentucky

COTTON, Nancy 56 (B), Joe 12
LAFFOON, James M. 37, Elvira 33, James A. 13, Frances 12, Emily J. 7, Elijah 6
BAKER, Allen 62, Ann 93
LITTELL, Henry 48 (B), Rose 31, John H. 17, Charles 15, Letcher 9, Robert 7, Henry 5, Mary 3, Virginia 6/12
COLE, Benjamin 55 (B), Milly 50, Rosanna 27, Mary J. 25, David 24, Ben 13, Melinda 10, Junius 5, Almeda 4, Henry 5, Sidney 3, John 3, Hannah 4, Hannah 92
SIMPSON, Robert 46, Sidonia 39, Minor 14, John 10, Mary 11, Matthew 8, Robert 5

Schedule Page 249

DUMAS?, Spotwood 27, Sally 65
MARTIN, Lewis 43, Ann 40, William 14, Ann E. 12, La Belle 10, Mary 8, Cornelia 6, Shreve 4 (m), Lou Ann 2
WALKER, Margaret 52, Lucinda 26, Rankin 24, John 22, Martha 20
MARTIN, John W. 34, Elizabeth 20, Anna 3, Catherine 1
CAVE, Patsy 65*
BELL, John H. 44*, Mary A. 33, Maria 14, William 10, Ann Eliza 6, Fanny 2
SAFFRON, A. B. 40 (m)*, Maria 41, Dudley 15, John W. 10, Anderson 7, George 4, Riland D. 1/12, Eliza J. 5
BOTTS, Moses 45*
RETHERFORD, Jesse 77*
MCCUDDY, Timothy 37*
DOWNING, John 36*
WATSON, Betsy 77*
VARBLE, Nancy 45, John 20, Mary E. 18, Isaac 13, Thos. W. 12
STEWART, Lyttleton 27, Sarah 48, Mary 30, Joseph 18, Moses 16
YOUNG, Roland 40*, Eliza 78, Eliza 52
STEWART, Moses 80*
YOUNG, Moses 42*, Martha 38, Elizabeth 9, John 5, Catherine 3, Emily 1
STEWART, Wesley 54*
MCISAAC, Isaac 42, Jane 43
MCISAAC, James 72*, Elizabeth 32, Zilla 30
STIVERS, Robert 14*
BELL, John W. 24*
VARBLE, Jacob 16*
ARMSTRONG, James 24, Eliza C. 18
ARGOBRIGHT, John 41, Elizabeth 33, Mary E. 15, Ann E. 13, Victoria 11, Jas. W. 10, John H. 8, R. Menifee 6, Lucy 2

Schedule Page 250

CLARK, James 46*, Jane 82, Lydia 15
MCCOY, Jane 30*
LYLE, Elizabeth Ann 34*, Joseph G. 7, Eliza V. 6
IRVINE, Robert A. 15*, Judith E. 14
ARMSTRONG, Andrew 59, Jane 58, Lafayette 26, Charlotte A. 22, Clinton 16

1850 Census Fayette County Kentucky

GOSS, Henry 37*, Susan 18, James 16, Mildred 70, Jane 68
JOHNSON, Amos 58*, Ann 30
HART, Edwin 49, Betsy 41, John 19, Margaret 15, Edwin 13, Bryan 6, Thomas 7/12
MITCHELL, Boswell 66, Lucy 21
BERRY, James W. 35, Susan 28, May 5, Willilam L. 2
SUTHERLAND, James 28*, Dulcenia 21, Louis F. 2
JONES, William 35*
THOMPSON, A. H. 24 (m), Mildred 21
BULLOOCK, Waller 76, Maria L. 60, Martha P. 44, Robert S. 22
BULLOOCK, E. O. 22 (f)*, Waller C. 7, Dabney O. 5, Sam R. 1
WHITNEY, Sarah Ann 52*, William 15
HULET, Boswell 25*
GARAY, John 21*
BARRY, Martha B. 30*, Lucy C. 15
OVERTON, John W. 59*, Dabney C. 49, Eliza D.? 40, Catherine S. 12, Waller 11, Frederick 9, Sallie Ann 6, Archibald 5, Eliza 3, Julia Ann 2
SPRAUL, Julia 28*
PICKETT, Robert 53* (B)
CALDWELL, Robert 16* (B), Benjamin 15, William 13, Elizabeth 12, Nancy 9, Mary 5, Betsy 37
GIBSON, C. C. 36 (m), John 25
GAUNT, Lettitia 45, Anthony 20, John 17, Joseph 14, George 12, Thomas 10, Francis 9

Schedule Page 251

HART, Mary 65, Nathaniel 24, Mary Ann 3/12
HART, C. C. 45 (m), Nancy P. 38, David 17, Isaac 15, Sarah 14, Mary 12, Isabella 10, William 8, Nannie 6, Thomas 4
SMITH, Fleetwood 48*, Harriet 46, Nancy 20, Ellen 18, Warren 15, Harriet 13, William 13, Benj. Arnett 6/12
ARNETT, Amanda 23*
HEADLEY, A. 37 (m), Eliza 30, John 12, James 11, Victoria 9, Mary C. 7, Jane 5, Margaret 3
MOORE, John 42, Alex 33, Mary 20, Kate 5/12
WILSON, Samuel S. 30, Nancy 27, Mary Ellen 4
CAMPBELL, Sarah Ann 68*
MORRISON, Martha 63*, Robert S. 17
WILKERSON, John W. 41, Mary 45, William W. 12, Martha J. 9
EVES, Lewis 35*, Mary J. 25, Martha 12, Huldy 11, Alfred 9, Lewis 5, Agness 2
JENKINS, Jane 69*
TODDHUNTER, John 28, Mary C. 27, John 7, Thomas 4, Catherine 2, Robert 6/12
SPARKS, W. C. 33 (m), Mariam W. S. 31, Ann E. 8, Mary C. 7, James W. 3, Cora E. 1, Charlton 20
EDWARDS, G. W. 44 (m), Amanda 29, John 7, Geo. Wash 5, Thos. J. 4, Lucinda 2, James H. 3/12
CARR, David 46, Ann 41, Richard 22, Sarah 20, Lucy Ann 18, Jane 14, Dabney 12, Lunsford 7, Mary E. 4
DROSDALE?, Eliza 43, James 17, Sarah J. 15

1850 Census Fayette County Kentucky

Schedule Page 252

MOORE, Joseph A. 36, Elizabeth 25, Jane 7, Elizabeth 5, John W. 2
WILSON, John H. 56, Catherine 54, John H. Jr. 27, W. M. 24 (m)
WEBB, John 28, Sarah 26, Joicy 20
BOGGS, Robert C. B. 56*, Nancy 67
CRIM, Joseph 25*
HARRISON, Elizabeth 70, Winny 27, George Ann 17
SAYRE, C. C. 19 (m), Margaret 20
WILSON, B. R. 37 (m), Agnes 30, Sarah 15, Mary 14, Lucinda 13, Judith Ann 12, Abner 10, William 9, Lucretia 8, H. Clay 7, Lydia 6, Sarah 82
FISHBACK, William 32*, M. L. 25 (f)
THOMPSON, J. J. 25 (m)*
STEVENS, Sarah P. 27*, Sally 5, Catherine 2
SCOTT, Thos. J. 49*, Jane 49, Ann J. 18, James A. 16
HARDISTER, Benjamin 25*
MARTIN, James H. 30, Mary Ann 23, James H. Jr. 2, Elizabeth M. 1
BUSH, Roland 62*, Susan 60, Alexander 22
HUSTON, Mary 24*, William 2
CLARKE, John 54, Maria L. 44, Mary H. 16, Henrietta M. 15, Kitty 13, Elizabeth N. 11, Margaret 9, John W. 7, Ann M. 4
TRUE, thomas 37*, Fanny 40, Mary J. 12, Frances 11, William H. 6
ADAMS, Mary 50*
TRUE, Willis 28, Elizabeth 27, Letitia C. 5, John 3, Peter C. 2, Robert 62, Catherine 55, Downing 10
MCCLELLAND, John T. 29, Margaret B. 25, William T. 1, Nancy 52
HEADLEY, John 47, Lucinda 43, James 20, John 18, Charlton 4

Schedule Page 253

GIBSON, James 68, Elizabeth 64, Mary A. 28, Thomas F. 23
MCCLANAHAN, Robert 33, Nancy E. 25, Laura T. 5
MCCLELLAND, Thos. 23, Virginia 16
BERRY, Nathaniel P. 41, Lucy 33, Nat F. 10
MERRILL, Jonathan 29*, Ruth 39, Elizabeth 14, Lucy Ann 9, Mary Magdaline 3
GEARS, Robert 27*
CALDWELL, John 45*, Sarah T. 30, Margaret 11
MCCLANAHAN, Mary 18*, Elizabeth 14
CLEMENS, Robert 32*, Paulina 21, Maria E. 6, Margaret E. 4, Mary E. 5/12
SUTTON, George 19*
MARS, William 33, Rebecca J. 27, Mary 1
BUGESS, Henry W. 60, Rebecca 47, John T. 24, Quincy 19, Nancy 17, Mary 6, Edgar 4
HALLIGAN, William 27, Elizabeth 26, Nat 2, John 24, Robert 23, Elizabeth 13
BERRY, John 31, Catherine 22
SECRIST, Martha 68
DARNABY, George W. 28, Mary 18
ARNETT, Ellison 40, Emily 35, George W. 12, Ben M. 2
FEATHERSTON, Robert 47, Elizabeth 43, William 19, Charels 15, Franklin 14, Elizabeth 12, John 9, Milo 7, Susan 5, Warren 3, Oscar 6/12

1850 Census Fayette County Kentucky

FEATHERSTON, Jeremiah 74, Elizabeth 80
PETTIT, Harry 53, Julia G. 49, Nancy 18, William 16, Nat 13, Rebecca 10
AXLINE, Jacob 36*, Mary C. 30, John T. 4, George M. 1
KENNEDY, Henry J. 26*
SALLE, James E. 20*
SHANKLIN, John 25*
CASSEL, Saml. F. 33*, Sarah 30, Eudora 11, Margaret 9, Willialm 7, Maltha 5, Eugene 3

Schedule Page 254

BRADLEY, Leland 24*
MOORE, John 55, Cynthia 45, Sarah 16, Catherine 14, George 13
MOORE, Nathaniel sr 71*, Sallie E. 69
SELF, Patsey 30*, Bright 30, Sarah 7, Nathanael 5, Jenivra 3, William 1
MOORE, Nathaniel 34, Paulina 25, Nancy 5, Sarah C. 3/12
MCCONATHY, Asa 50, Rebecca 46, Jacob 23, Newton 20, Elizabeth 16, Asa 14, Eliza 12, James 10, Mary 8, Martha 5, Isabella 3
MCCLELLAND, James M. 27, Lucy A. 25, George W. 3, James C. 1, Gov. M. 22
MONTAGUE, Thos. 62*, Elizabeth 54, Joseph 30, Elizabeth 18, Thomas jr 17, Emeline 14
WALLS, James 17*
MOORE, Moses 28*, Matilda 28, James K. 6
WILSON, Sarah 20*
HICKEY, William 68, Elizabeth 69, William J. 34, Nancy 34, James T. 10, Mary E. 8, William S. 6, Margaret J. 4, David 1
KIRKPATRICK, William 38*, Sarah Ann 38, Sarah 11, Nathiel 9, William 4
SMITH, Jasper 70*, Sarah 56
MERRELL, James J. 22*
MCMILLAN, Andrew F. 60, Lucretia 42, Bettie 12, Drucilla 7, Andrew 6, John 4
BAKER, Dudley 34, Martha 24, Edwin R. 3, John C. 9
THEOBALD, G. P. 58*
TODD, St. Blair 25*
BARBEE, Junius W. 30*
CARTER, Susan 37
DUNCAN, Henry T. 50, Eliza 43, Henry T. jr 14, Mary 10, Ellen 8, Elzia 3

Schedule Page 255

BERRY, Geroge 71, Nancy 68, James 30
BRAND, Harriet W. 41, Wm. H. 24, Mary A. 21, Horace H. 18, Harriet H. 14, Emily A. 11, John W. 9, Catherine M. 8, George C. 6
KIRTLEY, R. B. 35 (m), Sallie Ann 39
TILFORD, John 66*
EVANS, William 48*
SWIFT, Stephen 54, Lucia 44, Charles H. 19, Ellen E. 17, Sarah F. 14, Lucia J. 12, Aaleline C. 10, Stephen T. 7, Wm. E. 4, Elizabeth B. 3
CHILES, John C. 56*, Elizabeth 44, Hamlet W. 25, Othello 22, Marcellus 20, Narcessus 17, Desdemonia 15, Almanza 12, Las Cassus 10, Aline 8

1850 Census Fayette County Kentucky

SMITH, Ophelia 24*, Mary C. 3
MORGAN, Sallie 28*
CHILES, Eddy 22 (f)*, Bettie 2, George Ann 2
WEBSTER, Lauson 38*
MYRES, Fred 24*
DARBY, William 29*
COGLE, Cornelies 30*
MYERS, John 26*
WILLIAMS, Tom 40*
MORRIS, Richd. 27*
WILLIAMS, Philip 30* (B)
BLANTON, Elizabeth 60, Florida 33, Christopher 31, Levi 28, Daniel 23
BONNAN, Abram 65, Nancy B. 60, Thomas 24
BRYAN, Woodson 46, Martha A. 20, William 17?

1850 Census Garrard County Kentucky

Schedule Page 205

ROBINSON, Michael 44, Margaret 37, Mary Ann 19, Silas C. 17, James B. 15, Sarah Jane 13, John 11, Gabrila 9, Margaret 7, George N. 5, Serany B. 3 (f), Michael jr. 5/12
DUNN, James G. 26, Emely 19
FLOYD, George W. 24, Sarah 17
YANTIS, Robert P. 29, Elzabeth J. 27, Catharine L. 2
MERRELL, Azariah M. 31, Susan An 30, Frances 12, John Ann 10 (f), James W. 8, Berry 7, Azariah jr. 6, Sarah Jane 4, Susan M. 1
MERRELL, William 26, John W. 5, Sarah 3, Caroline 1, Martha 23
KEYS, Jesse 46, Debosa 44, Elizabeth 19, Eliza Jane 17, James 15, Isabella 13, MArtha 11, George 9, Richard 7, Wm. 5
ANDERSON, Peyton 50, Ruth 30, Emily M. 22, Clayton 19, Elner An 16 (f), Moses 14, John 5, Joann 3, Sarah A. 7/12
MERRELL, William 65
BROWN, John 72, Fanny 68
FORD, John P. 28, Polley 27, John W. 7, Asa S. 5, Sarah F. 2
BROWN, Asa 33, Jane 32, Mar F. 9, Thomas W. 7, Sarah E. 5, Martha J. 3, Leroy F. 1
BIRCHELL, John 48, Jane 35, Rachel 23, Owen 22, Henry 20, Louisa 18, John 16, Sally 14, Elizabeth 6, Polly Ann 4, Wm. 10/12
MCKINNEY, William 54, Mahala 60
CLEAVELAND, Elizabeth 65*, Wm. 30, Sarah 44, Philip G. 68

Schedule Page 206

HARDWICK, George 28*
DUNN, Philip G. jr. 35, Nancy Ann 31, Charles 11, Erasmus Ann 9, Walter S. 3, James W. 1
SCHOOLER, James 45, Martha 48, Joseph 13, Eliza Jane 10, Martha 6
WAGEMON, David 36, Mary 38, Hastings M. 11, Barbary A. 9, John G. 7, James C. 4, Will P. 4, David G. 2
KEMPER, John 56, Frances 37
KEMPER, William 85
NEWTON, Samuel 56, Ketturah 47, John 23, Wm. 21, Frances 18, James 16, David 12, Sarah 10
SMILEY, Marce 50, Jonothan 18
BERCHEL, Isaac 71, Sarah 73, Neoma 23
DUNCAN, Isaac 28, Harriett 2, Elizabeth 7, Almyra 5, Jane 3, Eliza Ann 2, Sarah A. 4/12
SCOTT, David 43, Lucy B. 33, Morton 9, Mary An 7, Cate 5 (f), David T. 2, Margaret 3/12
BROWN, Willia 33, Eliza Jane 18, James R. 7/12
BACK, Jeremiah 44, Salley 22, Polly 9, Sarah E. 7, Joseph 4, Isaiah 2, Lydia Ann 1/12
CLEAVELAND, George 28, Susan 23, Wm. B. 4, Mary E. 1
ISON, Charles 47, Nancy 38
BEVERLY, Benj. 46*, Mary 39, Mary jr. 12, Elza 10, Henry 8, John 6, Elenor 4
DISMUKES, Elizabeth 59*
PULLIAM, Busrod 43*, Hariett 32, Sarah 19, Nancy 18, George 14, Marion 13, Albert 11, Frances 8, Mary 4, Bushrod 6/12

1850 Census Garrard County Kentucky

Schedule Page 207

CAYES, Parey 29 (m)*
HARLAN, Jeremiah 23*, Isabella 33, Wm. 9/12
CULBERSON, James H. 9*
HOCKER, Clayton 35, Martha Ann 37, Sarelda Jane 9?
CHRISTOPHER, Andrew 44, Sarah 39, Thomas 96, Isabella 13, Telitha 12, Will 8, David N. 3
PITTS, John L. 31, Lucy Ann 20, Richard G. 2
LANE, Thomas P. 27, Maria C. 22, Sarah E. 3, Benjamin G. 1
CONAGAM, James 72, Elzabeth 50, Mary 22, Thomas 15
PERKINS, Joseph D. 42, Mary 35, Edmund 18, John 16, Hardin 14, Sarah 12, Wm. 4
SMITH, Brady 40, Martha 26, Derastus 6, John 4, Sarah 2, Henry 6/12
DUNCAN, Lewis 30, Elza 30, Isaac 8, John 5
LAM, Johnson sr. 56*, Sally 58, Almyra 27, Montro 23, Elzabet 22, Garrett 20, America 16, Clarinda 13
BACK, Winney 84*
ISON, William 47, Jane 42, James N. 23, Willia 19, Mary E. 16, George B. 13, Hester Ann 12, Emily J. 10, Ann D. 8, Henry V. 6
DUNCAN, Joseph 57, Elzabet 49, Will 25, John 20, Owen 15, David 12, Joseph jr. 10, Nancy 7
HARRIS, Thomas 24, Sally 18, Henry T. 5/12
GREEN, Zachariah 65, Elnor 55, Ali 20 (m), Lydia 16, Alfred 15
MCDANIEL, George 35, Prunette 27, Sarah E. 10, Clara 8, Joseph 6, Robert 3, George 1

Schedule Page 208

BROWN, Green 37, Mary 26, Mary Jane 6, Susan E. 4, Eliza T. 2
URTON, Henry 53*, Susan 43, Wiatte 18, Erasmus10, John 9, Janah 7, Benj. 5, Elizabeth 3
BURROWS, Elizabeth 16*
MERRITT, Peter 60*, Nancy 63, Nancy sr. 86, Isaiah 17
SAMS, Jesse 21*
ROBINSON, Benj. F. 24, Mary 22, Margaret 4, Mary S. 2, Martha 4/12
PUMPHREY, Harrison 36, Harriet 33, Lucy Ann 14, Benj. F. 12, James W. 10, Thomas E. 8, elijah 6, Henry 4, Lemuel 2
CECIL, James 40, Mary 35
SCOTT, Benjamin 22
MURPHY, Aaron 30, Mary 28, George 11, Kitty A. 9, Clarey 7, Charles 4
DAVIS, John H. 36*, Almyra 38, James F. 12, Mary Ann 3, George M. 6/12
FORBUSH, Betsy J. 12*
EDGERTON, William 82, Hannah 38, Josiah 15
SCOTT, William 28*, Ann 8, Samuel 6, Mary J. 2
MERRITT, Uriah 25*
SCOTT, Joseph 52, Sally 53, Robert 24, George 22
ROBINSON, Richard M. 33, Margaret 25, Mary E. 9
JONES, Benah 45 (m), Martha 43
DUNN, Benjamin 85, Margaret 74, Isaiah 39
MILLER, Robert B. 42, Lucy 31, Will B. 13, Jane E. 9, Marthe e. 6, Richard R. 3, Robert E. 2/12
HOSKINS, John S. 32*, Mariah 27, William F. 11, Mary A. 9, Sarah B. 7, Robert C. 4, John 2

1850 Census Garrard County Kentucky

Schedule Page 209

ASQUEN, Bell 17*
HOSKINS, William 66*, Elizabeth 57, Eliza 27, James T. 17, Wm. A. 23, Fanny 21, Mary E. 3, Lucy 1
HILL, John 28*
KIMBLE, David 35*
HUFFMAN, William 65, Nancy 60, Cornelia 14
SWOPE, John 37
HACKLEY, George E. 41, Judith 34, Richard 13, Thornton 9, Martha J. 5, Margaret A. 2
PRICE, Reben 45, America 42, James 20, Keziah 20, Mary Ann 21, Sarah E. 15
BURDETT, Daniel O. 45, Elizabeth 33, Lysander 14, Isham 12, Daniel 8, Frederick 6, America 8/12
WEST, Richard S. 41, Illena 41, Joseph 20, Ongisby 18, Catharine 15, Jemima 13, Nancy 11, Thomas E. 9, James 7, Eliza 2
WORNER, John 43, Margaret 43, George W. 21, Bejamin 18, Sarah J. 17, Susan Ann 15, James 13, Mary 11, Martha 9, Burdett K. 7, Victory 5
CORNELIOUS, Lorenzo 38, Permelia 25, George 8, Warren 5, Richard 2, Sena 2/12
SMITH, Elizabeth 69, Henry D. 36
JOHNSON, Samuel 34, Margaret 29, Simeon 10
SMITH, John L. 29, Elizabeth 25, Catharine 7, M. A. 4 (f), James 1, Jesse 22
WEST, Sarah 36, John H. 16, Margaret E. 12
BOWEN, Nancy 55
KINCAID, John 46, Clinton 33 (f?), Mary Ann 11, Eveline 9, Andrew 7, Jeremiah 5, James 3, Frederick 1/12
DUNN, Silas B. 26*
OATMAN, Peter 56*

Schedule Page 210

SMITH, Peyton W. 24*, Frances 23, John T. 7/12
BURROUGHS, John 8*
SMITH, John 73, Frances 59, Mary 43, Nancy 0
SMITH, Hiram 36, Jane 36, Frances 8, James 3
BLAND, Alamander 33 (m), Margaret 32, Alex M. 5, Charles 8, John 6
RAY, Hezekiah 48, John 20, James 20, Zachariah 18, Ann 14, Richard 12, Patsey 10, Charlotte 8, Enoch 6, Mary 4, Winfield 2
BYERS, Edmund 69*, Nancy W. 65
FISHER, Mary Jane 18*
BIRCH, James 71*
TATUM, Margaret 49*, John 26, Wm. 17, Benjamin 20, George 14, Mary E. 12
BOURNE, Francis 65*, Sally 63
HERRING, Sarah 20*
WHITE, George 28, Sally 33, Elizabeth 21, Will 19
DUNN, Erasmus 56, Eliza 44, James 25, Wm. 22, John 21, Ruth A. 14, Erasmus 10
BOYD, Malinda 50, Moses 28, Samuel 26, James 16
MERSHORN, Furnace 54 (m)*, Robert 57
LOVE, Marshall 18*
MERSHORN, Burkett 53, Calley 47, Andrew 21, Clementina 18, Furnace 17 (m)

- 183 -

1850 Census Garrard County Kentucky

MERSHORN, Ben F. 43*, Emily 35, Wm. 18, Francis M. 16, Montreville 14, Furnace 12, Clementina 10, Carrol K. 8, Calley A. 6, Ben F. 4, O. P. 1 (m)
JENNINGS, Emily 14*
HOUSE, Rury 8 (f)*
SUTTON, Sarah 51*, Mortimore 28
ANDERSON, Jane 46*, James B. 19, Margaret 16
HUMPHREY, S. E. 10/12 (f)*

Schedule Page 211

WILFON, Horatio 46, Thursa 46, John 17, Elizabeth 13, Eberle 11 (m), Emley J. 9, Martha C. 7, Horatio 5
WILFON, Will 20, Catharine 20
WILMOT, James 26*, Elizabeth 20, Matilda C. 3
GARDNER, Azariah 25*
JENNINGS, James 8*
CRAIG, David 28*, Susan 28, Wm. 4, Sarah 3, Margaret 1
BLACKABEE, Elizabeth 67*
HOUSE, Aaron 18*
HUTCHERSON, John 30, Mary Ann 20, Sarah E. 7/12
BLACKABEE, George 41, Martha 40, Franklin 21, John 19, NAncy 17, Jane 16, Thomas 14, Samuel 10, George 7, Wm. 4, Sarah 3/12
HERRING, Nancy 22, James 24, Parey 23 (m), Henry C. 18, Thomas 15, Margaret 13
MILLER, Harrison 37, Mary A. 26, J. Thos. 4, Robt. H. 3
ELLIOTT, George 37, Mary 36, Thomas 14, Irvine 12, Luther 11, George Ann 9, Mary F. 7, Betsy 6, Alexander M. 1
IRVINE, George 8, Amanda 23, Charity 6, Wm. 5, Mary E. 3, Susan C. 1
AUSTIN, Prudence 52, George 22
ONSTOTT, William 48, Austin 36 (f), Nic. S. 19 (m), Len A. 17 (m), Mary A. 16, Henry C. 14, Sarah 12, George W. 10, Will H. 9, Robert M. 7, Jeremiah 5, Eliza. J. 3, Ephm. S. 2(m), Martha Ann 1
ONSTOTT, Mary 86
WATERS, John sr. 52, John jr. 22, Margaret 51, Lucinda 19, Nancy J. 17, Eliza 15

Schedule Page 212

GRIMES, W. H. 39 (m), Eliz. J. 34, Charles 13, Wm. 10, James 8, Sarah 5, Benjamin 2
JENNINGS, John B. sr. 66, Eliza F. 66, Henry Clay 23, Sarah E. 28
BENNETT, William 32, Mary 24, Artameta 5, John Wm. 3, Caroline 1
BENNETT, Roda 70, Samuel D. 34, James H. 17, Amanda 25
PULLIAM, William sr. 27, Delila 23, Wm. 3, Nancy A. 1
CLEAVELAND, John 35*, Mary Jane 22, Eliza B. 1
RYAN, Isabella 18*
REYNOLDS, Barney 51, Elizabeth 50, Will M. 19, Eliza O. 17, Morimore 14, Price 12, Elliott 9, Georgge 7, Frances 4
FIGG, Silas 37*, Margaret 26, Eliza 4
BURNSIDES, Margaret 67*
DAVIDSON, Mary J. 7*

1850 Census Garrard County Kentucky

GALLIMORE, John 42, Sarah 38, Will S. 15, Martha E. 13, James M. 11, Thomas J. 10, Sarah E. 8, Jonathan R. 7, Mary M. 3, Prudence R. 7/12
GREEN, Joab 58, Martha 57, James 24, Martha 26, Lorenzo 22, Susan 16, John 8
HOLTZCLAW, Jesse 68, Edward 30, Frederick 28, Sarah 20
LANE, William 36, Margaret J. 28, Mary R. 6, Barnet E. 5, Calberd W. 2 (m)
FRAZER, Austin 36, Dorcas 8, Mary D. 6, Robert L. 4, Benjamin H. 3
VANCE, Jacob 70, George W. 33, Casander 24, Mary 5, Emily J. 2, James W. 1
BEAUMONT, Nancy B. 41*, Mary L. 15, Willis 21
DUGGINS, Hamilton 25*, Susan A. 19

Schedule Page 213

MARKSBURY, Will 24, Almyra 26, Margaret 6, Allen 1
BONER, John C. 24, Mary J. 21, Will 3
EVANS, Hickman 47, Mary B. 27, Susan E. A. 6, Samuel S. 4, Henry H. 2, Joseph D. 9/12
DUNN, James 48, Sally A. 39, John 19, Shebel 14 (f), Augustine 12, Richard 10, Joshua 8, Mary 5, Sally Ann 1
BROWN, Nelson 37*, Naoma 34, Elza A. 11, Will H. 9, Mary J. 7, Margaret 5, Edna 3, Martha B. 11/12, Ann 63
HUFFMAN, Eliza 60*
BROGAL, Martin 45*, Saly 40, Martha Ann 15, Clara 12, John 10, Joseph R. 5, Mariah 4, Martin 2, Eliza F. 2
DAVIDSON, Abner 5*
PULLIAM, John B. 30, Judy 29, Enoch 6, J. Brady 4, John 3, Isaac 7/12
ADAMS, Fothergail 47, Clara 36, Sally A. 17, John W. 12, James 7
ALLEN, Lucy 62, Clara 28, Estham 25 (m), Wm. 18, Susan 16
TOTTEN, Polly 26*, Almyra 4
BUTLER, Will 2*
SADLER, asa 53*, Rebecca 49, Joseph 22, Wm. 21, Salem 18, Henry 15, Asa M. 14, Rebecca J. 13, Almyra 11
LAIR, James N. 5*
WALL, William 60, Lima? 43 (f), Mary A. 19, Edwin 16, Sally 15, James 13, Robert 11, Wm. 6, Nancy 1
GORDON, Samuel 21, Sall 21, Madoree D. 3 (f), James R. 6/12

Schedule Page 214

CHRISMAN, William 38*, Nancy F. 29, Elizabeth E. 11, James T. 9, Salina 7, Amanda L. 3, Mary Ann 9/12
COOKE, John 21*
MURPHY, Hardin 30, Nancy 27, Wm. 10, Susan 8, James 7
BAKER, Allen 36, Elizabeth 41, Mary 22, Josephine 21, Elizabeth 15, Malinda 13, John 11, Allen jr. 9, Freeman 7, George 5
BAKER, Abraham 63, Susan 58, Malinda 25, Patsey 23
HILL, Elizabeth 1, James 1
RAY, Michael 58*, Martha 60, George 5
TEETER, Rebecca E. 12*

1850 Census Garrard County Kentucky

BOGA, Patsey J. 12*
DAVIDSON, Jesse 41 (m), Rosana 41, Louisa 18, Louisiana 17, Leander 15, Almyra 13, Eliza 11, Sarilda 10
GULLEY, Drury 76, Hannah 3
GULLEY, Griffin 41, Ellenor 36, Hannah jr. 7, Griffen jr. 5
WORD, Thomas 50, Mary 48, Malinda 22, Drury 21, Amanda 18, Elenor 14
CLOUSE, William 20, Mar 19, Moses 1/12
REYNOLDS, Moses 66*
BAKER, Moses 21*
BEAUMONT, Thomas 18*
MASTERS, William G. 28, Eliza 28, Sally F. 4, Harrison 2
ROSS, James 24, Eliza 24
SADLER, Edmund 26, Rebecca T. 22, Edward L. 4, Quincy T. 2, Elizabeth E. 5/12
WEAVER, William 42, Amanda 35, Wm. jr. 6, Abram 3, Sarah 1, Barbara 60
HUMPHREY, Solomon 36, Fanny 36, Mary Jane 10, Peter 8, Russell 7, Sally A. 4, Beryamin 2

Schedule Page 215

TURNER, Samuel 43, Sarah 43, James 19, Wm. 16, Almyra 14, Claibourn C. 12, Sarah E. 10, Joseph P. 8, Isabella 5, Ellen 3
CONE, Solomon 27, Letty J. 21
TEETER, Paris 70*, Rebecca 62, Robert 27
WEAVER, Thomas 14*
SANDERS, Giles 40*, Sally 40, Martha A. 14, James 12, Semira 4, Nancy 84, Isaac 45
CHANDLER, Alexander 20*
DAVIS, Henry B. 51*, Sally 45, Louisa 20, Wm. C. 18, Rodolphus 16, Totten 14 (m), Angeline 12, Cyrus 10, Sally A. 8, Ambrose 4, Ann 2
MONTGOMERY, Sarah F. 7*
WORD, James 27*, Nancy J. 24, Jordan 10, Alexander 4, Eliza S. 1
GIBBS, Alexr. 4/12 (f?)*
TEETER, Russel H. 36, Susan 37, Samuel 15, James 13, Wm. 11, Moses 9, Patsy Jane 7, Robert 5, John 3, Sarah 2, Josephine 1
MCCULLON, Elizabeth 85, Eliza Jane 15
TAYLOR, Jonathan 40*, Mary 9, Charles T. 10, Sarah J. 5, Reuben S. 2
SHORT, Susan 70*
LEWIS, Hannah 29, Wm. 10, Mary E. 2, Thomas H. 1
LEWIS, Elizabeth 50, Howard 18
ROSSER, William 40, Lena 28, James 10, Sarah 8, Charles 6, John 3
PRUETT, Solomon 65*, Elizabeth 47
WARREN, William 16*
WALKER, James 33, Eliza 33, Caledonia 4, Charles E.F. 2/12
SMITH, Will L. 38, Elizabeth 20, Thomas P. 6, Sarah F. 8/12

Schedule Page 216

SIMPSON, George 38, Martha 40, James W. 10, John Willis 8, Mary Ann 6, Lucinda E. 2
PRATHER, James jr. 20, Louisa 8, Lucinda 3, Sarah A. 9/12

1850 Census Garrard County Kentucky

HARDIN, John 58, Caroline 32, James 29, Uriah 27, Merrell 22, Hervey 16, Albert 9
PRATHER, Hannah 77, Sarah 38
FLETCHER, William 39, Patsey 37, John F. 18, Sarah 15, Hannah 13, Ellen 11, Thomas 9, James P. 7, Martha 1
ARNOLD, Henry B. 32*, Ann H. 27, Mary E. 6, James A. 4, Jeremiah S. 1
BEAZLEY, Royal H. 23*, James S. 18, John A. 16
GIBBS, Hillary 43 (m), Martha 33, Permelia 10, Eliza 8, Clara 5, James 2
ALVERSON, John B. 55*, Sophia 40, Henry B. 30, George W. 19, Lucy 17, James 14, John 12, Thomasw 8, Alexander 5
BLAND, John 20*
BAKER, John 74
KENNEDY, James M. 32, Mary Ann 25, Samuel T. 5, Jesse B. 3, Clayton C. 1
AUSTIN, Walter 40, Martha Jane 29, Arthusa 11, Thomas T. 9, Mary 6, Martha J. 4, Samuel 1
DOTY, Benj. F. 32*, Eliza J. 9, A. 7 (m), Tabitha 5, Amanda 3, Brunette 10/12
ARNOLD, Tabitha 50*, Clara 25, Horatio C. 27
POINTER, Walker S. 29, Arsonel 25 (f), Wm. T. 5, Lila A. 3, Vincent 1
POINTER, William 44*, Nancy 49, John H. 11
HALL, Vincent W. 22*, Elizabeth 16

Schedule Page 217

POINTER, Squire 40, Rachel 35, James V. 15, John 13, Wm. 11, Mason 9, Mary Susan 5, Cassey 2
HAMMOCKS, George 36, Elizabeth 42, Ephraim 15, Rebecca J. 12, Sarah E. 10, Andrew J. 8, James M. 5
JOSLIN, James 28, Hannah 20, John H. 1, Rebecca 83
BAKER, henry 46, Nancy 46, Eliza A. 23, Mary J. 22, Lucinda 18, Wm. 22, Nancy 16, Rachel 14
POINTER, William H. 20, Permelia 19, John M. 10/12
MERIDETH, Joseph 53, Mary 47, Daniel 17, Elizabeth 14, David 12, Isabel 6
WHITICO, Charles 33, Mary A. 26, Mary E. 8, Louisa Ann 5, James W. 3, Margaret F. 2
FAULKNER, Thomas 45, Jemima 49
LUNSFORD, Benjamon 53, Nancy 27, Jane 46, Mary F. 17, Daniel 15, Judith 10, Elizabeth 7, Harrison 3, William 6, Joel 3
KENNEDY, David 59*
DOLLINS, James 44*, Eliza 37, Nancy 16, Wm. 14, John 14
MIDDLETON, Yantis 34, Elizabeth 34, Mary J. 12, Louisiana 11, Christopher 9, Isaac 1
LEWIS, Jesse C. 31, Mariam 23
POINTER, John 48, Ann 47, Jane 21, Meredith 20, Ellen 17, Mary 16, Wm. 14, John 11, Margaret 7, Susan 2
MAYFIELD, James 64*, Martha 63
HUTCHERSON, Margaret 17*
JONES, Daniel 22, Lucinda 22, Margaret 1

Schedule Page 218

HAMMOND, Lucy 43, John R. 21, Wiatt 19, Will H. 17
JOHNSON, John sr. 79, Elizabeth 66
MAYFIELD, Milton 22, Mary Ann 25, James M. 5, Bonaparte 3, George T. 2, Mariam 10/12

1850 Census Garrard County Kentucky

GREEN, Jackson 34, Lucy 34, Martha 13, Lucinda 10, James K. P. 4, Sarah 19
HUDSON, Morgan 39, Elizabeth 27, Lucy A. 5, Mar S. 3, Benjamin F. 2
DUGGINS, Thomas 50, Permelia 45, Synthia A. 20, Alsina 16, Eliza 13, James 11, Louisa 10, Alexander 6, Susan A. 3, Henry 24
HUTCHERSON, Silas 34, Nancy 1
DUGGINS, Daniel 48, Sarah 52, Elijah 22, Mary 19, Elizabeth 14, Daniel 11, Jennings 8
DUGGINS, Elizabeth 74, Mahala 36, Wilfon 22 (m), Elizabeth 13
DUGGINS, John 56, Martha 45, Wm. 15, Telitha 12, Sarina 10, Martha E. 8, John R. 3
BURNSIDES, Richard 60 (B), Lucy 50
SPRATT, Charles 29, Nancy 27, Elizabeth 8, John T. 6
ALFORD, Morgan 66*, Mary 52, Warren R. 32, George sr. 23
HALEY, James 15*
ALFORD, Elizabeth 40, Smith 26, Oliver P. 23, Richard 20, America 13, John 10, Mary C. 7, Peachy 1
ALFORD, Carey 25, Margaret 18
BURDETT, Nelson 56, America 50, Robert L. 19
BURDETT, Stephen L. 24, Sarah B. 17, Peachy M. 15, B. F. 12 (m), George 17

Schedule Page 219

DUNN, Isaac 48, Malinda 47, David 19, Martha 9
BAUGHMAN, Thomas 25, Sally 17
ROBERTS, Jefferson 43*, Eliza J. 29, Louisa F. 10, Lewis 8, Robert 6, Jefferson jr. 1
VANDIVER, Martha 26*
MOORE, George 39, Mary J. 26, Richard 12, Elizabeth 9, Thomas 7, Jane 4, Caroline 3, Charles 2, Edna 8/12
BROWN, Joseph 30, Lucy 25, Mary 4, David 1
MOORE, Margaret 60*
BOONE, Charles 27*, Margaret 16
HUNTER, John 44, Mary J. 32, Laura D. 10, Alexander D. 8, William B. 5, Mary P. 2
COLLEY, Nancy 80, Ellen 35
COLLEY, Pleasant 38, Jane 35, George W. 12, Elizabeth A. 10, America 8
COLLEY, Samuel 27, Mary 24, Reuben T. 7, Sarah B. 2, Mary 4/12
SWANSON, C. J. 35 (m), Sarah J. 32, Martha J. 9, Wm. R. 6, John 3, Lucinda 2
COOVERT, David sr. 65, Mary 65, David jr. 27, Isaac 22
COOVERT, Garrard 35, Elizabeth 35
COOVERT, Sarah 24, James D. 2, Eliza 3/12
FARLY, Cassander 69, George 39
FARLY, William B. 41, Sarah 30
SCOTT, Rachel 48, John 23, Martha A. 18, Martha J. 16
SMITH, Harold F. 46, Catherine 32, John C. 12, Virginia 10, Peachy 6, David 4, Albert G. 10/12, Henry G. 8
WILDS, Benjamin F. 35, Eliza G. 27, Harrison G. W. 3, Elizabeth J. 2
SAMME?, Lewis 33

1850 Census Garrard County Kentucky

Schedule Page 220

POOR, Robert C. 41, Mahala 41, Sarah 15, James 13, Mary 11, Malinda 9, Elizabeth 5, Martha 2
WEST, Westly 40, Lucy 45, Susan J. 15, Mary A. S. 12, Martha M. J. 8, Mahala 6, Kitty E. 3
SMITH, Merrill 40, Hannah 39, Edmund 18, Mary J. 15, Sarah E. 6, Jeremiah 4, Henry G. 2
SCOTT, John 52, Louisa 38, John F. 16, Martha A. 13, Robert L. 11, Joshua 7, Winfield T. 2
WILMORE, Jacob W. 30, Mary J. 23, Elizabeth J. 8, James 6, David C. 4, Sarah C. 1
POOR, John W. 28, Martha A. 20, Hannah E. 2, Mary B. 5/12
PINDEGRAS, Abijah 57*, Charlotte 54
GREEN, Joseph 16*
OVERSTREET, William F. 30, Almyra E. 27, Peachy J. 6, Sarah B. 2
CROW, James E. 36, Elenro 36, James T. 15, Delitha T. 14, Samuel 11, Jalila 9, Sarah A. 7, Susan 5, Mary D. 3, Zachary Taylor 2, Rebecca S. 1
BROWN, Buford 40*, Caroline 36, Robert N. 12, Isaiah 9, Juliann 2
PORTER, Clarinda 16*
HAMILTON, Isham 48, Sarah 38, Henry C. 16, Sarah A. 14, Emily J. 11, Hester A. 8, Permelia 6, Nancy 4, Isham 1
POOR, Thomas 35, Martha A. 23, Robert 6, Stephen W. 5, John 1
FORD, Edward 24, Josephine 21, Jas. Clayton 9/12
FORD, Will W. sr. 54, Will W. 21, Mary 19

Schedule Page 221

KERSEY, William 42, Ann 42
FORD, James M. 24, Martha 19, Mary B. 2
DUNN, Joshua 52, Sarah 45, William 23, Charles 19, Joshua 17, Elizabeth 14, Sarah 11, Wilson 9, Eliza 5
DUNN, Benjamin 23*, Jesse 21
TATUM, Jackson 23*
BYERS, James 29, Mary J. 27, Sarah E. 7, Hariett 5, John 1
HARDIN, George 49, Mary 54, Louisa 21, Kitty Ann 19, Mary J. 14, Josephine 12, Robert N. 8
TURNER, George 45, Milley 47, Jane 15, Susan A. 15, Wm. 14, Elzina 12, Tima 10 (f), John 8
SWOPE, Dorcas 54, Benedict 22, Margaret 30
BURNAUGH, Will F. 27, Sarah 16
PHILIPS, Lewis 43, Indiana 39, Martha A. 21, James M. 19, Nancy 17, Margaret 14, John 12, Isaac 9, Lucy J. 7, Lewis T. 4
BARKER, Jane 41, Thomas 7, Benjamin 4
MONTGOMERY, Dorinda 43*
LAMB, Darias 17 (m)*, Warren 15
BURROUGHS, Michael B. 49*, Juriah 42, Michael B. 14, Westly 12
BROWN, Thomas 48*, Elizabeth 47, John T. 16, Martha J. 18, Wm. 11, Elizabeth 7
GRIMES, Nancy 60, Sally 33, John 31
GRIMES, Luke 33, Teresa 23, Henry P. 5, Nancy J. 4
DENIS, Henry 39*, Mary 37, Selina 11, Lucinda 7, Mary E. 5, Martha E. 3, Malinda 1
HILL, Eliza A. 6*, Malinda C. 4

1850 Census Garrard County Kentucky

Schedule Page 222

MARKSBERRY, Daniel 30, Maria 36, Sally 12, Horatio 3
COLLIER, Mary 67*, Citty A. 27, William 7, James S. 4, Perry 2
SHERROW?, NAncy A. 24*, Mary 1
COLLIER, Moses 81*, Mary 76
TAYLOR, Mary 17*
ISOM, Samuel 12*
TAYLOR, Jesse 40*, Elizabeth 40, Mary A. 3, Henry Clay 1
ISON, Moses 10*
TAYLOR, Winston 53, Nancy 53, Lud An 23, Elizabeth 21, Sally T. 19, Henry 17, Volentine 15, Eliza 13
PRESTON, William jr. 22, Alvira 21, James 2
ANDERSON, Cornelious 44, M. 41 (f), William 17, John E. 11, George 5, Martha 5
ANDERSON, William 50, Citty A. 51 (f), George W. 27, Cornelious 24
BURNSIDES, James 71*, Martha 74
DUNN, Gatewood 22*
BURNSIDES, Allen 33, Susan 28, Margaret P. 7, Lucy J. 5
HOGAN, Mary 55, Ellen 16, Wm. M. 18
HOGAN, John M. 20, Elizabeth 21
GRAHAM, William 32, Elizabeth 22, John W. 7, Elisha H. 4, Martha 5, Garland 3 (m), Nicholas 1
DUNN, Richard B. 24, Mary J. 24, James B. 26
TURPIN, James sr. 72, Fanny 38, Juliann 36, Elinor 33, Nancy 27, Artisia 24, James 21, Sally N. 19
DUNN, Benjamin 63, Rosa 53, Hannah 15, Cooper 13, Wm. G. 11, Sarah M. 9
HILL, John 59, Wm. 34, Ann Eliza 27, Nancy J. 12, Perry jr. 10, James T. 8

Schedule Page 223

RAY, Robert C. 37, Malinda 39, James 15, Michael 8, Wm. H. 5
ALVERSON, James 43
WARREN, John 37, Margaret 34, Louisa 15, Ashley 13 (m), Mary A. 11, Catharine 9, George M. 7, Enoch 5, Griffin 3, John A. 1
WARREN, Thomas 58, Rebecca 40, Selitha 22, Elizabeth 20
WARREN, John jr. 29, Mary 25, Thomas 5, Lucy 3, William P. 4/12
RUNYON, Asa G. 46, Mary 38, John M. 18, James L. 17, Richard A. 14, Sarah J. 12, Margaret R. 8, Silas R. 6, Asa G. jr. 4, Belinda B. 2
WORD, William 52*, Elizabeth 45, John W. 18, Lucinda 14, Wm. jr. 11, Thomas 3
SIMPSON, Martha 3/12*
TURNER, David E. 44, Elizabeth 39, Eliza J. 22, Elizabeth R. 18, Matthew W. A. 16, Ambrose A. 10, James H. 8, Elenor M. 5, Paulina 3, Alphonsa C. 1 (m)
WEST, William 38, Sarah 34, Samuel L. 16, James 12, Thomas N. 7, Richard 5, Perry 2, America 9
HUMES, Absalom W. 35, Hetty 35, Mary 13, Martha 10, Manerva 7, Sarah A. 5, Susan 3
WORD, James 32, Sally 25
BAKER, Lewis 34, Joanna G. 37, John 12, Mary E. 10, Margaret 9, Abram 7
EAST, James 30, Elizabeth 26, John 2, Alexander 10/12
SIMPSON, George jr. 28, Malinda 26, Michael 5, Rebecca J. 3, Mary 2

1850 Census Garrard County Kentucky

Schedule Page 224

PHERIGO, Benjamin F. 33, Elizabeth J. 28, Mary E. 6, James R. 3
LONG, Perry C. 30, Elizabeth A. 24, Allen B. 3, Jesse W. 1
SANDERS, James 64, Mary 52, Emily 23, Mary 16, Lucy 14, Nancy 12, Wm. 9
DAVIS, Levi 36, Minerva 33, Elizabeth 13, Paris 12, Sarah 10, Samuel 8, Levi jr. 6, Tima 5 (f), Wm. 4, Minerva 2, Nancy 1/12
TATUM, Nicholas S. 67, Hetty 65, Thomas 22
MAY, Jackson 32, Matilda 30, James R. 9, Robert 8, John W. 5, Susan A. 2, Malcolm 3/12
CHARLOTTE, John W. 52, Elizabeth 23
MCMILLAN, William 44, Clara 44, John 21, Jerome __
LAND, Thomas 47, Sally 45, Martha 22, Overton L. 18, Shelton 15, Wm. H. 14, Lucy 11, Thomas F. 8, Robert B. 5, James S. 2
REYNOLDS, Henry 31, Lydia 34, America E. 12, Wm. 10, Susan 7, James 5
MURPHY, William 36, Fanny 36, James 17, george 16, John 14, Jane 12, Elizabeth 10, Wm. 8, Daniel 6, Joseph 4
HIATT, Oliver 35, Eliza 32, Wm. T. 8, alzina 6, Fany Y. 3, Martha J. 11/12
WARREN, Drury 51, Hetty A. 41, Wm. 19, Sarah J. 17, Mary E. 14, Robert 12, John jr. 10, Catharine 7, George 4, Burdett K. 2

Schedule Page 225

BURTON, Alfred 39*, Elizabeth 23, Emily 16, Clayton 14, Irvine 12, Sarilda 10, Martha J. 2
TEETER, Alfred 7*, Yima 5 (f), Buanna 3
WEST, Tyre 29 (m), Elizabeth 22, Tecora 7/12 (f)
DAVIS, Nancy 50, Thomas 57, John 30, Wm. 25, Moses 23, Avory 21
DAVIS, James 28, Lucinda 23, Mary J. 5, Eliza 4, Almyra 1
ADAMS, Walter 41, Barthena 21, Nancy J. 14, Mary L. 1/12, Judah 67
STORMS, E. L. 32 (m)*, Zerelda T. 36, John M. 6
BURTON, Jesse 18*, Frances A. 11
STINNETT, John 30*, Rebecca 30, James 9, Elza 8, Mary J. 6, Jesse 4, Sally A. 11/12
DENTON, Elizabeth 15*
ARNOLD, Humphrey 61, Ann 56, Humphrey F. 22, Camilla 15
ROW, William 74
PHILIPS, Isaac 76, Lucy 74, Larinda 47
HARRIS, Russel 40, Rachel 68, Overton 26
COLLIER, William 50, Martha 49, George 22, Zachariah 21, Alexander 18, Rebecca 16, Hezekiah 13, Isaiah 11, Sarah 9
REYNOLDS, Levi 31, Rachel 33, Mary E. 6, Rutha E. 3
ARNOLD, David 30, Mar 31, Reuben 8, Margaret A. 6, Judith E. 4, Zerilda J. 3, Wm. A. 23
ARNOLD, George B. 26, Mary 21, Maria J. 4, Margaret A. 2, Isaac 8/12
HOUSE, James 24, Mary A. 21, Samuel 18, Nancy 12

Schedule Page 226

LAMASTER, James R. 36, Mary A. 16, Leslie C. 2
HOLTZCLAW, Abner 71, Harrison 40

1850 Census Garrard County Kentucky

HOLTZCLAW, Willia 24, Zerilda 18
COLLIER, Alexander 55, Jane 50, Robert 30, Wm. 16, Mary J. 15, James 12, Daniel 9
ADAMS, Abra 52, Lucy J. 51
NAYLOR, Edward 24, Clara A. 22, Margaret E. 3
ARNOLD, Elijah 53, Sandrel 41 (f), John 24, Elzabeth 16, Elenor 14, Ann M. 12, Hervey 10, Mary T. 8, Nancy S. 6, Margaret 4, Eliza M. 1
PERREL, William S. 47*, Elzabeth 43, Lucy A. 16, Eliza E. 8
WOOLEY, Mary C. 13*, James 11, John 9, Elizabeth 7, Serena D. 5
BAKER, Thomas 27*
PRATER, Willis 41, Martha 37, Eveline 12, Wm. F. 10, James P. 8, John 6, Philip 4, Squire 3, Jefferson 2, Nancy E. 6/12
PRATER, Philip 46, Sarah A. 17, Wm. 13, Sophia J. 12
POSEY, Thomas 30, Sally A. 32, William D. 5, Mary E. 3, Daniel 26
ODER, Albert 35, Missania 37, Martha E. 9, Margaret J. 6, Dudley H. 5, Alexander L. 2
SOPER, Dennis 35, Emily 31, Charles T. 9, James W. 8, Wade 5, Robert 4, Car 6/12
ALDRIDGE, Samuel G. 51, Catharine 46, Joshua 22, Ruth Ann 16, Catharine J. 14, James 11, Elizabeth 7, George 5
MCMANNIS, Nelson B. 36, Samuel 20

Schedule Page 227

DAVIDSON, Ahab 30
NAYLOR, Absolem 32, Martha 28, Josephine 6, Jennings 4, Julia Ann 3
PHILIPS, Sidney S. 42 (m), Martha B. 27, Lorinda D. 4
ANDERSON, James 50, Sarah 48, William 22, Thomas 21, James 18, Elizabeth 16, John 12, Samuel 6
SCHOOLER, William 30, Martha 26, Nancy 4, Margaret 3, Eliza 1
HUTCHERSON, Willis 28, Docia 25, Druzera 3, John T. 1
HUTCHERSON, Ruth 64
PRYOR, John 26, Polly 24
PRYOR, Angelina 38*, Liberty H. 4 (m)
CARPENTER, Sally 88*
MADDIX, Mary 29, Margaret A. 13, Elizabeth 10, Mary 8, Richard P. 5, Madosa 2
COMLEY, James H. 25, Emily 28, Sarah J. 2, William 6/12
EASON, Rebecca 50, Jerusha 30, Walton 20, Minerva 18, Nancy J. 16, John P. 14, Joseph M. 12
RAY, Daniel 60, Martha 31, Abner G. 12, Elzina 10, Zachariah 7, Alexander 5, Wm. T. 3, Chestina 6/12
JENNINGS, Samuel B. 50, Rosanna 49, Zachariah M. 20, Emarine 17, Wm. 23, George 21, Nancy E. 15, Mason 10, Fanny 10
MCQUERRY, William 51, Ann 52, Malinda 28, Emily 23, Elizabeth 16, Alexander 15, Daniel W. 8
BAKER, William 42, argaret 34, Martin 21, Wm. 14, Lewis 9, Joseph 6, Isham 3
BAKER, Robert 23*, Nancy J. 17
LEWIS, Edna J. 11*
DUFF, Elizabeth 43*

Schedule Page 228

KIDD, Anderson 28, Elizabeth 65, Polly 22
BAKER, Jesse 25*, Caroline 35

1850 Census Garrard County Kentucky

ANDERSON, William 5*
OVERSTREET, Sally 48*
BYNUM, William 48, An 45, Sally A. 21, Rebecca 20, Nancy 18, David 16, Harriett 14, Harrison 12, Isabinda 10, John R. 8
CARVER, Lucinda 60, Elizabeth 23
POSEY, Harrison 56, Sarah 53, Josiah 20, Margaret 18, Sarah A. 16, Elizabeth 12
WARMOUTH, Philip 23, Mary 25, Lucinda 2, Susan F. 6/12
WILLIAMS, Shipton 23, Mary 21, Squire 1
BROOKS, William 40, Mary E. 34, John T. 12, Robert A. 10, Thursa J. 8, Charles G. 6, George C. 3, James L. 1
WIATT, Green B. 22, Mary N. 24
LOGAN, Elijah 33, Charlotte 30, Mary J. 11, John R. 10, Lucy 8, Arthursa A. 2
JONES, David 25, Emily 28, Mary E. 1
SADLER, Reuben 31, Nancy 24, James A. 2, John A. 4/12
CARVER, Will 31, Lucinda 25, Elizabeth J. 6, Alexander 4, Lafayette 1
LOGAN, John 64, Mary 63, Mason 23, Joseph R. 20
LOGAN, Morgan 40, Mary 37, America 19, Sarah 17, Mary 1
LAIR, Claibourn 44, Susan 45
ODER, George C. 36*, Sarah 32, Timothy 10, Hugh 8, Clara E. 7, James N. 6, Wm. S. 4, Thomas J. 1
PHILIPS, Madison 15*
ARBUCKLE, John W. 26*, Lucy T. 18
GILLASPIE, Mary 53*, Wm. J. 25

Schedule Page 229

BRIGHT, Thomas sr. 62, James H. 32, Thomas jr. 28, John R. 25, Martha 19, George 18
LOGAN, Timothy 30, Sarah 26
ODER, Elizabeth 43, Sarah J. 20, John 18, Emily 14, Eliza 12, Harvey 10, Thomas C. 8, William 5
LOGAN, Sarah 65
MILLER, Aminadab 35 (m), Anne 33, George 4, Timothy S. 3, Sarah 1/12
LOGAN, William 35, Sophia 31, Lee 9 (m), Josephus 7, James H. 1
LAIR, James 56, Margaret 52, Margaret jr. 18, Samuel 15
BURTON, Jesse 38, Lucy 28, George 10, Robert 8, Susan An 6, James A. 1
LAIN, Will 62, Lucy 30, Peter 26, Alexander 21, Rebecca 17
PEEL, Samuel 39, Mary 35, Ephraim 14, Mary E. 12, James 9, Wm. 7, Charles 5, Richard 2
DICKINSON, Morgan 38, Sally A. 36, John H. 12, Moses M. 10, Sarah E. 9, Hiram 7, Joseph L. 5, Morgan jr. 3, Zachariah T. 1
WOODS, Urban 53, Jane 54, Mary 22, Malinda 20, Eliza J. 18, Urbin 16, Will 13
POOR, Elizabeth 52, Elizabeth Jane 22, James G. 19
BROWN, Will 41, Nancy A. 44, John S. 18, Nancy G. 13, Isabella 10, Mary E. 7
NEWTON, Joseph 53, Lydia 48, Nancy A. 22, Cassander 17, Joseph A. 15, Samuel G. 13, Elijah 8
HARRISS, Richmond 56, Henry 27

Schedule Page 230

SCOTT, Samuel 44, Mahala 44, James 19, Emily J. 18, Samuel 14, Thomas 10
CECIL, Richard 43, Lavina 35, Wm. 16, Isabella 14, Henry 12, Margaret 10, Martha 8, Thomas 6, Isaiah 4, Warren 7/12

1850 Census Garrard County Kentucky

BROWN, Caroline 38, John R. 14, David 9, James W. 7, Martha J. 4, Isabella 2
JONES, Judith 67*
TAYLOR, Fielding 38*
BURDETT, Enoch 50, Francis 20, Joseph S. 15, Mary 12, Will Almira 9
BUSSING, John 58*, Mary 35, Harve 13, Mary 9
JOHNSTON, Will H. 20*
BROWN, Samuel 65, Martha 60
WILDS, John R. 50, Hoba B. 50 (f), Elizabeth 20, Sarah Ann 16, Nancy T. 12, Benjamin R. 8
TRACEY, James 28, Lucy 60
BURDETT, Simeon 40, Manerva 30
ISO, Jonathan 30, Elizabeth 21, Martha J. 1
PERKINS, Hardin G. 36, Harriett 29, Benjamin 11, George B. 3
FORD, Reuben 5, Citty 53, Mariah 16, Citty 14, Caroline 12, Joseph 10, Martha 8
ISON, Hardin 24, Frances 21, Logan 3/12
HUFFMAN, William 37*, Clarinda 40
REESE, Granville 22*
TRACEY, James B. 45, Angelina 33
TRACEY, James T. 20, Nancey 17, Frances 17, Sarah Anne 15, Franklin 13, Charles W. 11, Nathaniel R. 9, Caroline 7, John 3
SHROPSHIRE, Asa 46, Rebecca 42
MCMURTRY, Alex 76, Mary 75, Alex 22
BURNSIDES, Nancy 56, Edmond 33

Schedule Page 231

BERNAUGH, Robert 30, Mary 29, Elizabeth C. 5, Nancy J. 2
WOOD, James 26, Martha 24, Mary E. 1
BURDETT, George F. 40*, Sarah Ann 31
MOORE, Thomas S. 8*
BEASLEY, Nancy 44
FLOYD, Merrill H. 21, Amanda 18, Sarah 63, T. Smith 19
FARMER, William 46, Harriet 39, Martha A. 16, Mary 14
WEST, Peyton 53, Rebecca 52, Hunly 28, John 22
SUTTON, Henry O. 33, Lucy J. 23
HUGHES, Tharp 38, Tabitha 35, Virginia 12, Wm. H. 10, America 8, Abner D. 5
OBANON, Mary 58, Daniel 23, Virginia 14
POLLARD, Elizabeth 56, James 37, Thornton 35, Will 33, Franklin 22, Granville 16
POLLARD, Thompson 25, Mary A. 18
POLLARD, Mason 39, Tiliphus T. 11, Lucinda 9
BAKER, John 31, Elizabeth F. 20
SMITH, George R. 31, Elizabeth 24, Margaret A. 9, Mary F. 7, Sarah E. 4, Lardy B. 2 (f)
ROUT, Robert L. 30, Sarilda 30, Henry 11, Lucy J. 9, John 7, Nancy 4, Lewis 2
BURNAM, John F. 33, Martha 20, Allen 5
BOWEN, John 40, Emily 30, Terrill 8 (m), Mary A. 6, Paulina 4, Sally A. 2
IRVINE, Annanias 64, Charity 50
SUTTON, Benjamin 46, Harriett E. 34, Will 20, Elcinda 15, John 13, Eliza J. 11, Mary A. 8, America B. 5, Samantha 2
JOHNSTON, John jr. 45, Mahala 40, Chestina 14, J. Saml. 11

1850 Census Garrard County Kentucky

Schedule Page 232

ENNIS, John 52, Elizabeth 46, Lewis 21, George 14, Sarah 12, Elizabeth 5
BOYLE, Rufus 45*, Theresa 40, Will 15, Mary E. 12, Wallace 9, Nancy J. 7, Manerva 5, Edria 3 (f), Elizabeth 1
BARKER, Charlotte 65*, Ann 42, Samantha 7
CROCKETT, Elizabeth 80*
BONER, William 57*, Eliza 55, Henry 22, Dulcina 18, Alford 16, William 14
MOORE, Jane 7 (m?)*
PULLIAM, Stephen 25
BLAND, John 43, Citty A. 35, JEremiah 4, James H. 2, Martha E. 8/12
BLAND, Elija 45, Joseph 38, Hiram 36, Elizabeth jr. 17, Henry 8
BERRY, Moab 29, Almira 23
MAY, Jesse 23, Nancy 21, John W. 4/12
TARRANT, Charity 85, Achilles 48, Richard 10, Achilles 8
TUGGLE, Rebecca 52, Clanci 18 (f), Mahala 16, Reuben 15, James 13, Peter M. 10
WILLIS, William 39, Elizabeth 40, Ellen 16, Catharine 15, Sterling 13, Emaline 12, Eliza 10, George Ann 8, Josaphine 6, Napoleon 3
ADAMS, James 29*, Cynthia A. 29, Mary A. 7, John H. 5, James B. 3, Caroline E. 1
SUSBURY, Sarah 16*
HOPSON, Willard 17*
ROBINSON, William 32, Sarah 23, John S. 1
GREEN, Alexander 27, Mary 21, James 2, John 1
WILEY, Benjamin 57, Magaret 60, Mary 28
WILEY, William 26*, Tima 20, Margaret 1
RICHARDSON, Luraney 4 (f)*

Schedule Page 233

BURROUS, Laban 44
MIDDLETON, Buford 44, Mary 34, Nancy 12, Elizabeth 10, Jordon 2
COLLIER, Benjamin 28, Eliza A. 22, Jacob 5
NAYLOR, Reuben 26, Margaret A. 18, Isabella 3/12
BEASLEY, George 0, Elizabeth 18, Robert 18
CECIL, James sr. 49, Nancy 32, Elizabeth 16, Sarah 11, James H. 10, Mary C. 8, America 6, Silas 4, Martha 2
STINNETT, James 26, Desa 22
ANDERSON, John 48, Matilda 42, Sophia 21, Nancy E. 19, Mary J. 16, Louisa 13, Lavinia 3
GRAHAM, James 37, Milly 24, Mahala 12, Moses 11, Pleasant 1
SPURR, Ruth 65*
MILLER, Jacob 18*
RICHARDSON, Joseph 31, Lucy 31
COLLIER, Hyram 47, Margaret 28, Benjamin 7, Robert 2
HUDSON, James H. 41, Elizabeth 36, Margaret 14, Robert 12, Nancy 10, Sally 7, James 4, George 2
BORALLY, Peter D. 58
ROBINSON, George 56
ANDERSON, James 34, Lurinda 25, Emily 8, Elenor 6, John T. 2
TAYLOR, James 79, Sarah 80

1850 Census Garrard County Kentucky

RANEY, John 45, Sarah 33, Mary J. 16, George 15, Ruth A. 13, Henry H. 9, Silas 7, Sarah F. 5, John 4, Mary D. 2
WOODS, John 76, Martha 40
BROWN, Ephenetus 32, Elizabeth 27, John W. 9, Nancy A. 7, Elenor 5, James A. 10/12
LANE, Johnson 27, Mary J. 24, Margaret 8?/12

Schedule Page 234

SALTER, Susan 35, Robert 16, Elizabeth E. 14
CLARKE, William 39, Nancy 26, Elizabeth 8, Simon 7, Wm. 5, Sarah A. 3, James 1
ROYSTON, Willia 27, Martha 8, Eliza 9, John 7, Thomas, Sally A. 1
CHILDERS, Baley 35, Solomon 16, Wm. 9, Lucy 6, Elizabeth 2
PARKS, Harvey 45, Nancy 32, Mary J. 14, Allen 12, Frances 10, Martha A. 8, Newstina 6, James 3, Will L. 1
BROOKSHIER, Charles H. 21, Martha 22, Mary E. 2
KINDER, Will 54, Mary 51, Nancy 15, Isaiah 12
RAY, Alexander 35, Elizabeth 30, Martha 7, Abraham 4, Allen 2
HARDEN, William 45, Elizabeth 36, John W. 12, Decy 10 (f), Will G. 8, Arthusa J. 5, Elizabeth E. 4, Mary C. 1
ANDERSON, Hall 52*, Emily 36, James 15, Clayton 13, Clifton 11, simeon 9, Hall 7, Wm. 5, Reece 3
JENNINGS, Alexander 27*
TEETER, William 50, Elizabeth 41, Nancy J. 16, Will T. 13, Sarah A. 8, Mary S. 6, John C. 4, Robert 2
TAYLOR, John J. 54, Elenor 48
SIMPSON, Charles 48, Elizabeth 44, Will 22, Melissa 20, James 18, Charles 16, George 14, Elijah 12, Zachariah 10, Margaret 7, Sally 4
GRAHAM, Nicholas 23, Hester 20, Wm. H. 1

Schedule Page 235

SHORT, Joel 45, Susan 19, Elija J. 17, Mary 15, Sally 13, Letty 11, Cynthia E. 8, Sina 6
HUMES, James 76, Margaret 40, Will 23, Jane 20, Charles 18
SIMPSON, Willis 26, Carey 28 (f), George A. 4, Elizabeth 1
RAY, George 30, Emily 25, Mary J. 7, Martha E. 6, Will H. 4, Michael 2
HARRIS, Brinkley 38, Nancy 40, Armeda J. 14, Elizabeth 11, Kizziah 7, America 4
ROLAND, P. B. 26 (m), Nancy J. 20, Hulda 2, Amanda J. 6/12
SIMPSON, Elijah 40, Mary 39, Mary 14, Margaret 10, Emily 7, Sarah 5
BURTON, William H. 26, Sarah 22, Martha E. 2
BOLTON, John 64, Sally 57, Sidney 22 (m), Walter 18, Pamelia 11
FRY, John 22, Sally 22, Thomas 1/12
BOLTON, Melissa 38, elizabeth 30, Talitha 10, Napoleon 8, Eliza 6, William 4, John 4/12
BOLTON, Elbert 34, Nancy 32, Sarah 12, James 10, Josiah 8, Clinton 6, Randolph 4, Elbert 1
BOLTON, Ballard 30, Nancy 26, Elizabeth 8, David 5, John 1
BAKER, Mary 42, David 22, Patsey J. 20, Nancy 18, Sally 14, Elizabeth 10, Susan 8
BURTON, Allen 64, Elzabeth 49, John 19, Lucy 16, Sally A. 13, Allen jr. 10

1850 Census Garrard County Kentucky

Schedule Page 236

LONG, Uriah 40, Rebecca 21, Squire T. 11, Nancy E. 8, Stephen T. 5, Thomas N. O. B. 2, Mary E. 2/12
WOOD, Ameter 29 (m), Nancy 29, Nancy A. 3, Elizabeth 9/12
BAKER, Samuel 54, Nancy 47, Sally 20, Jane 18, Joseph 14, Allen 11, Martha 6
HUMES, James 27, Mary 23, Absolem W. 6
WARREN, James 33, Martha 35, Bransen 4, John M. 3, Wm. J. 9?/12
WARREN, Athur 22, Mary 19, Elizabeth 2, Zarilda 4/12
SIMPSON, Josph 26, Artimeca 24, Mary F. 5, Wm. 2, George W. 1/12
GULLY, Squire 24, Eliza 21, Mary E. 3, Moses 4/12
WEST, Walker 68, Martha 66, Furlingo 4 (m)
LAIN, Sherrod 46 (m), Virginia A. 39, Lawrince? 20, Lansdown 18, Isaiah 16, Lucotha 14 (f), Minor 12, Freeman 10, Malachi 5, David 4, Nancy Jane 3, Thomas 1
HAM, Thomas 35, Mary 25, Will O. B. 5, Thomas S. 2, Susan J. 6/12
HUDSON, Thomas 26, Margaret 21, John 2, Mary 1
PETTY, Garrett S. 40, Elizabeth 35, John 15, Joseph M. 13, Albert G. 11, Barbara E. 8, Hannah T. 4, Benjamin 1
HATTEN, Benjamin sr. 83, Hannah 69, Mary 26, Permelia 24, Benjamin jr. 22, Joseph 21
SCOTT, David 43, Mary 43, George H. 19, John W. 16, Susan M. 13, Gabrella 9, Thomas M. 8

Schedule Page 237

SHIPMAN, John 37, Julia Ann 33, Maria 15, Anne E. 12, Frances 10, Margaret L. 5
SALTER, Thomas R. 36, Martha 28, John S. 5, Jane 3, Elizabeth 1
RASEY, Joel 31, Nancy 31, Margaret 7, George 5, Mary 2
BOWEN, Daniel 40, Susan A. 28, John 13, Wm. 10, James 7, Martha A. 4
RANEY, George 36, Maria 30, Alexander 10, Anne 7, Elenor 5, Albert 3, Almira 7/12
BARLON, Henry 48, Mary T. 25
CLARKE, Thomas 35, Polly 60
NAYLOR, James 29, Elzabeth 23, James S. 3
MURPHY, Will L. 73, Levicay 40 (f), John 15, Elizabeth 10, Malinda 8, Nancy A. 2
BURNSIDES, Josiah 43, Almira 32, Elijah 13, James 12, Josiah 11, Martha 9, Susan 8, Wm. 6, Richard 4, Tabitha 1
VAUGHN, Joseph 61, Elenor 57, James 19, Louisa 15, Burdett K. 13 (m), Hiram T. 10
VAUGHN, George W. 26, Martha 25, Joseph 5, Wm. M. 3, Mary E. 1, George 1/12
ROBINSON, Will B. 35, Clara 22, Mary E. 1
GRAHAM, Robert 36, Catharine 37, Martin 9, Wm. 7, Mary 2, John C. 6/12
DUNN, Jefferson 45*, Nancy 30, Henry 14, John H. 11, Thomas 9, Isaac 7, Mary 2, Alice 4/12
HILL, John A. 28*
MIDDLETON, Charity 50, Catharine 86

Schedule Page 238

WELLS, Amie 34, Wm. S. 13, Mary S. 9, George W. 7, Emily J. 5, Delila 3, Catharine 4/12
WILSON, William 46*, Nancy 45, Will jr. 23, Elizabeth 20, Mary A. 18, Samel 15, Sophia 13, Tima 11 (f), Horatio 9, Fountain 7, Isaiah 4, Amanda 2
JENNINGS, Eliza E. 5*

1850 Census Garrard County Kentucky

MARKSBURY, Daniel 6, Louisa 6, Joshua C. 3, James F. 1, Tabitha 20, John 18, Fanny 14
DENNIS, John 25
HUFFMAN, Fountain 35, Susan 22, Will H. 2, Mary Ann 3/12
MONTGOMERY, Nancy 64, Mary 27, Jane 24, Rhoda 18
PHILIPS, William 50, John 25
PHILIPS, Erasmus 23, Josaphine 22
TRACEY, Thomas 66*
PORTER, Clarinda 17*
COMELY, John 60*, Martha 55, Emily 18, Susan 15, Ann Eliza 13, Wm. 20
SPRATT, William 26*, Almira 20
NAYLOR, Will 23*, Cynthia 23
COMELY, Perry 27, Elzabeth 24, Emily A. 5, Mary E. 3
NAYLOR, Will 54, Ann 50
NAYLOR, John 24, Sally N. 20
ADAMS, Wesley 38, Elizabeth 33, Nancy J. 8, Martha A. 6, James C. 4, Mary S. 2
NAYLOR, George 34, Sarah 35, Margaret A. 9, John P. 8, Martha 6, George W. 4, Luann 3, James D. 1
NAYLOR, Luama? 54 (f), Leann jr. 20, Horatio 18
MALAIR, John 39*, Nancy 37, James 19, Dica 17, Sally 86
MCMAMIS, Dica 39*
PORTER, Mary 12*

Schedule Page 239

SELLERS, Nancy 50, John 32, Samuel 28, Wm. 12, Sarah A. 10, Herrod 5, James 2
BEAUMONT, William 72, Susan 71, Wm. jr. 36, Herrod 28
MARKSBURY, Samuel 50
LEAVELL, Squire T. 41, Catarine 35, Rachael 14, James 12, John 10, Squire jr. 8, Mary Jane 5, Sarilda 1
HIX, William 34, Fanny 30, Joseph 11, Elizabeth 9, William 7, Catharine 5, Mary A. 1
LEAVELL, John T. 30, Mary A. 28, Thomas 7, James 5, Mildred 3, Isaac 1
TOMLINSON, Joseph 36, Eliza A. 28, Mary E. 10, Henry J. 8, Robert 5, Judith Ann 3
BURCHIL, Owen 23*, Mary 20
PORTER, Pa__y 10 (m)*
RENFRO, James 35, Mary 23, Edmond 7, Sarah E. 5, Mark 3, John 2, Arthur 4/12
KING, Mary 45, Wm. 21, Samuel M. 15, James A. 13, Marion W. 11, Franklin P. 8, Mary E. 6
MERRITT, Zachariah 34, Margaret 30, John R. 9, Peter 7, Adaline 5, Zachariah T. 1
SUTHERLAND, William 26, Frances 23, Milly A. 5, Sarah J. 3, James H. 1
SPILMAN, Pamelia 50, Charles 20
TERRILL, E. J. 35 (m), Susan B. 31, Wm. A. 6, Elizabeth S. 5, Robert J. 3, John A., Patrick H. 4/12
ISON, Lunnda? 57 (f)*, James Hartford 34, Stephen 24, Simon P. 20, Zacharia T. 18, Emily 15, John N. 12
PORTER, Thornton 20*

Schedule Page 240

PRESTON, George W. 38, Emily 40, George 10, Granville 8
BROWN, Buford 40*, Caroline 36, Robert N. 12, Isaiah 9, Julia A. 3

1850 Census Garrard County Kentucky

PORTER, Clarinda 17*
CROUCH, Absolem 51, Louisana 42, Wm. 21, Cordelia 17, Sophia 15, Mary G. 14, David 12, Oliver 10, Robert 8, Ophelia 4
DOWNING, William 60, James 26, Elizabeth 15
DICKERSON, Hiram 40, Susan 36, John 17, Mary E. 15, Sally Ann 13, Thomas W. 12, Josaphine 10, Martha M. 8, Susan 6, Margaret 4, Henry A. 2
ISON, James H. sr. 77, Mary 56
COMPTON, Burrus 64*, Ann 65, James 30, Mary 26, Emily 21, Vardimon 23, George 19, George M. 10
WINTERS, George 10*, Amanda 7, Hester A. 2
PEACH, Thomas W. 4*
ASKINS, John 60*, Ann 56, Louiza 24, Susan Mary 15, William 12
WESTERFIELD, Lucasley 23 (f)*
BURKS, Direnda 64*
KEMPER, James H. 46, Burilla 42 (f), George 20, America 18, John H. 7
STONE, Smith 62, Mary 60, George W. 22, Robert S. 21, Smith T. 18, Isaac A. 16
OBANON, Algernon S. 40, Artimeca 34, L. B. T. 3 (f), S. S. 1 (m)
WEST, Simeon 53, Louisa 50, John 18, Simeon 16
TARRANT, Eastham 50, Cynthia 26, Eliza 8
BIXLER, Susan 54
BIXLER, David M. 31, Nancy 26, Harriett 10, Susan 7, John 5, Margaret 3, Sarah 3/12

Schedule Page 241

TEMPLE, William 34, Talitha 33, George Ann 6, Lervy? B. 4 (f), James W. 2
COOKE, Elijah 40*, Zerilda 38, James W. 9, John W. 7
ADAMS, Will 33*
KEMPER, Thornton 70, Eliza 67, A. J. 32 (m)
BURDETT, Wilhelmina 67
BURDETT, Isham 46, Catharine 33, Lysander 38
BURDETT, Hyram 52*, America 20, John 30
WEST, Lysander 30*
AUSTIN, James 30, Elenor 24
HUTCHESON, Jemima 46, Eliza 21, Will 19
SUTTON, John 68, Mary 59, Alexander 32
SUTTON, Walter 34, Eliza 28, Ben Duncan 7, John 5, Seneca 3 (m)
HERRING, Augustus 52*
DALE, Nancy 55*
POLLARD, Elizabeth 35*, Ruth 12, Robert 10, Thornton 8, Wm. 5, Margaret 3, Timolean 1 (m)
BOURNE, James 28, Susan Ann 21, Wm. 4, John 2
JENNINGS, William 30, Zorelda 24, Wm. P. 13, John 10, Robert M. 8, Margaret E. 6, Almira 4
CHEATHAM, Joseph 30, Jane 30, Elizabeth 6, Fany 4, Wm. 1
RAMSEY, Thomas 75, Nancy 40
RENFRO, John 27, Elizabeth 21, George Ann 4, Mary F. 2, Martha 10/12
THURMON, John D. 50, Martha 22
GEORGE, Flemming 28

1850 Census Garrard County Kentucky

EDS, William 31, Lucy A. 30, Sarah A. 12, Martha J. 10, Lucy A. 8, Eliza C. 5, Wm. M. 3, Mary F. 3, Margaret E. 1
EVANS, Jefferson 35, Ann 35, Martha J. 12, John Patterson 6, Josaphine 3, Almira T. 6/12

Schedule Page 242

HARMON, Mary 51, Sally 66
HARMON, Reece 60, Nancy 60, Eliza 28, Jane 26, Almira 23, Nelson 20
BRADY, Harrison 36, Mary A. 30
BEELER, Jo 27 (m), Frances 25, John H. 7
BEELER, George 59*, Louisa 59
LAWSON, Salina 20* (B), Joseph 1
HALL, Matthew 26, Eliza 24, Fielding 4, Eliza A. 6/12
RAMSEY, Burdett 23 (m)
EDMONSON, Thomas 42, Eliza 37, Jane 17, Wm. 15, Telitha 12, James T. 10, John W. 8, David 6, Lewis 4
BERRY, John 33, Amanda 26, Enoch 3, Milton 2, Harris 6/12
HOLTSCLAW, John W. 37*, Frances 30, Wm. 12, Alexander 8, Mary A. 6
LUSK, Will 20*
LUSK, Samuel jr. 24, Martha A. 24
HAWKINS, Jason 20
WILCOX, Rodolphus 35, Margaret 33, Mary B. 4
JENKINS, Letty 55, Eliza 26
LOWE, Manerva 49, Leannah 16, Jared 14, Angelina H. 12, Moses 9
LOWE, William 27, Mahala 24, James R. 5, Mary C. 3, Margaret 2
MARKSBURY, Randolph 40, Nancy 32, Henry 11, Mary E. 9, Susan A. 5, Benoni 3
BARKER, Joseph 50, Eliza 35, Smith 13, Richard 12, America 11, James W. 9, Mary 7, Robert 6, Willis 4, John T. 1
GROOMS, Nancy 51, James 22, Maria E. 16
GROE, Peter 29, Sarah 22, Wm. N. 1
BROWN, John 31, Mary 25

Schedule Page 243

THORNTON, John 57, Eliza 53, Jepthey 26 (m), Wm. 16, Franklin 14
HUDSON, Commodore P. 22, Eliza 18, James A. 3/12
EVANS, Lemuel 26, Mary 21, Elizabeth 5
BEAUMOUNT, Wesley 45, Paulina 44, Susan 19, James 17, John 15, Mary 13, Nancy 11
GORDON, David 54, Mary 54, Hetty 22
RANEY, William 44, Mary 40, Elizabeth 19, James H. 17, Nancy J. 15, George M. 13, Wm. 11, Sally A. 9, Robert M. 7
RANEY, Salley 66, Susan 40, Sally 11
LITTREL, Richard 28*, Malvina 37, Elizabeth 17
WILLIAMS, Milly 16*, Elizabeth 13, Delila 39
TURNER, Susan 62*
RUNNELS, George 15*
HARRIS, John 55, Anne 50, Elijah 18, samuel F. 16, Mary 13, Martha 8, almira 7

1850 Census Garrard County Kentucky

HARRIS, Robert 50*
PEARL, Robert 16*, Martha 14
LAIR, Will 60, Elizabeth 45, Jude 21 (f), Susan A. 18, Wm. D. 6, Ben D. 4
BROADUS, Mitchel 32, Lucy 30, Thomas 10, Elizabeth 8, Elijah 6, Margaret 3, Mary F. 1
MCMILLIN, Samuel 61, Ann 62
ODER, Gabrael 33, Ellen 28, Maria E. 10, John M. 4, James C. 3, Oliver T. 1
LAMASTER, Alexander 38, Nancy 30, Mary E. 9, Sarah A. 7, James W. 5, Sarilda J. 3, Jude E. 11/12 (f)
ANDERSON, John M. 38, Samantha 15, John M. 13, Jason 11, Sandford 10, Victoria 7, Mary 5

Schedule Page 244

PRATHER, James B. 38, Lucinda 40, Ellen 17, John 14, George 12, Susan 12, Rebecca 8, Freeman 7
HOLHIMER, Eldridge 34, Mary 35, George D. 11, Salina J. 10, Will R. 8, Mary E. 6, Lucy A. 4, Sandford C. 3, Oliver P. 1
HARRIS, Jefferson 45, Penelope 34, Will 12, Ann Eliza 10, Robert 8, Josaphine 5, Overton 4, Francis M. 3, Nancy E. 1
BYNUM, Kinhan? 40 (m), Lucinda 40, James T. 19, Stephen 16, Artemecia 14, Rolinda 11, Eliza 8, Isabella 5
TATUM, Samuel A. 45, Lucinda 40, Mary J. 19, James W. 16, Hetty A. 15, William 12, John S. 8, Samuel 6, Moses H. 4, Thomas A. 2
GARRISON, Willis 25, Delila 27, Owen 6/12
ODER, Joseph jr. 23, Elizabeth 21
PATTERSON, James 40, Elzabeth 27, Isabelle 7, Margaret 2
WILLIAMS, David 51, Elizabeth 50, Jude W. 16 (f), Amanda 31
RINDER, Reuben 32*, Thursa 35, Elizabeth 10
SIMPSON, Mary 32*
TURNER, Will 38, Rolinda 37, James H. 16, Joseph J. 14, John W. 12, Malinda 10, Eliza J. 8, Wm. 2
KELLY, John 43, Eliza 38, Margaret 19, Elijah 12, John R. 11, Sarah E. 8, Anne 40, Susan 80, Ben L. 6, Mitchel 4
HARDWICK, Ben F. 33, Mary A. 31

Schedule Page 245

LAYTON, Henry 27, Martha J. 22, Eliza 3, Wm. 2, Mary A. 11/12
COLLIER, Moses 26*, Mary 24, James B. S. 3
BEASLEY, George W. 14*, Robert 12
LAYTON, Davis 56, Clara 53, Will N. 18
LAIR, William G. 43, Talitha 28, Almanda 16, Lucinda 16, Elizabeth 2
BURDETT, Andrew 34, Eliza 27, Wm. 8, Martha A. 6, Margaret J. 2, George 1
LEWIS, William 37, Rebecca 26, Greenberry 17, Clara 12, Michael 11, Wm. 9, Bright 7 (m), Nancy J. 5, Robert 3, Howard 1
LEAR, Elijah 30*, James 5
ANDERSON, Thornton 18*
WALKER, Ed H. 26*, Martha J. 20, Alexander 1, John M. 4/12
LAWLES, James 10*
JENNINGS, Alexander A. 70, Nancy 70, Alexander H. 30

1850 Census Garrard County Kentucky

JENNINGS, Benjamin F. 24*, Angelina 17, Wm. A. 5/12, Eliza 24
BURTON, George W. 12*, John 8
HERRING, John A. 33, Eliza 32, Daniel 5, Hiram 3
HOLTSCLAW, Charles 33, Mary 22, Abraham S. 2
KING, Davis C. 33, Katharine 25, Sarah A. 1
KING, Robert E. 31, Mary 33, John J. 9, James A. 4, Edge E. 3 (f)
GREEN, Henson G. 53*, Delila 50, Elizabeth 22, Mary 20
HARDWICK, Christopher 41*, Pleasant 24
KING, John R. 35, Mary A. 33, Elza A. 8, Zerilda 6, Peachy 4, John R. 2
BAST, Sarah 52
AUSTIN, William 27, Joan 20, John 25

Schedule Page 246

EVERLY, Will 55, Eliza 56, Mary E. 38, Sarah E. 23, Pamelia E. 19, Wm. H. H. 16
DAVIS, Sarah B. 54*, Asel B. 26 (m), James H. 24, Robert 17, George 15, Milton 13, Wm. F. 10
TUCKER, Susan 51*
ALLEN, Eliza B. 1*
ADAMS, Jones L. 40*, Catharine 28, Crawford 19, Wm. 18, James G. 15, Caroline 14, Jones 10, America 6, Rebecca 4, Nelson 1
COX, Rebecca 67*, W. 24 (m)
RICE, Jacob 60, Sarah 45, Robert 23, Mary 21, Andrew 18
BAKER, Lucretius 40 (m)*, Lydia 30, Mary 12, Amelia 2, Wm. 1
JOHNSON, William 25*
REMBLE, David 34*
BEAUMONT, John 36, Sarah 27, Lindsey 8 (m), Jerome 5, Margaret E. 3, Lydia 3/12
HART, John P. 28, Maria F. 23, Ed E. 5, Zachariah T. 3, Cumberland S. 1
LYNAM, Charles 64*, Winney 56
BAKER, Eliza 16*
GREEN, Mary A. 94*
HERNDON, Albert G. 43*, Nancy B. 51, Lucinda F. 17, Eliza C. 15
NUTTALL, Mary C. 24*
ANDERSON, John 49, Susan 47, James H. 21, Wm. 18, Eliza 15, Eliza Ann 13, David 10
LETCHER, John 25, Rebecca 21, Sarah 18, Joshua 16, Martha 13
LAWLESS, Peter C. 53, Margaret J. 46, George 18, Martha J. 14, Margaret A. 11, Emily F. 6, Sarah J. 4, Alexander B. 1
WILLIAMSON, John 39, Emily C. 23, John D. 13, James F. 10, Nancy J. 7, William J. 5, Eliza 5, Samantha J. 3

Schedule Page 247

MIDDLETON, Walter B. 47, Sally 45, Chloe 20, Mary A. 17, Sam 16, Wm. 8, Walter B. 5, Henley F. 2, James 9/12
MCMILLIN, George W. 29
SEBASTIAN, Wylie sr. 58, Margaret 60
HARRIS, James 60, Sarah 54, James 21, Margaret 16, Martha 14
EVANS, Samuel g. 27, Mary 24, Nancy E. 1/12

1850 Census Garrard County Kentucky

MYERS, William E. 45, Minerva 43, George 20, David 18, Lucy an 15, Wiley S. 10, Felix H. 8, Susan 4, Bud 2
ROBINSON, Jacob 52, Maria 46, James F. 25, John W. 24, Angelina 17, Alexander 16, Will 14, Joseph 13, Jacob C. 10, Thomas 7
ARNOLD, James B. 25, Nancey E. 20, Eliza E. 1
HARRIS, William G. 61*, Elizabeth 59, Tyre S. 24 (m), Margaret 29, Nancy 23
HILL, Margaret 66*
COMELY, Sabril 68 (m), Eliza 67, Theresa 30
HARDIN, Robert 63*, Eliza 63, Robert M. 24
WARREN, Nancy 21*, Greenberry 21
DOTY, Jesse 67, Sally 66
DOTY, Cyrus 38, Sarah 31, Anne L. 3, Julia P. 1
NEVIEUS, Cornelius 39, Sally 25, John 6, Mary 3, Judith 9?/12
BLACKABY, Benjamin 27, Catharine 22, Martha J. 2, Zachariah T. 7/12
TERRILL, Overton 42, Sarah 42, Allison 18 (m), Eliza 16, Henry T. 13, Eliza E. 5
ARNOLD, John B. 35, Sarah J. 26, Mary jane 7, Zerilda 5, Elizabeth 4, James H. 1

Schedule Page 248

LUSK, William 57, Eliza 56, John 23, Jenings 15
LUSK, Baylor 28, Elizabeth 25, John 4, Thomas 2
HAWKINS, William W. 39, Ellen t. 39, Sallie C. 15, Wm. W. 13, Xenophan 9 (m), Ellen T. 7
ALSPAUGH, Henry 29, Eliza 22, Cynthia T. 6, Simeon 3, Eliza H. 6/12
BURTON, Robert D. 52, Eada 45, Will 23, Richard 18, Robert 16, John 14, Sarah 12, Margaret 10, Squire T. 8, Blythe 6
BURNSIDES, Robert 24
BEASLEY, James A. 34, Elizabeth 21, Allen 30
HEATH, Polly 60, ann 42, Eliza 26, Rachael 19, John 8, Sally 7, Wm. 4
BRYANT, Mary 41, Eliza 24, Amanda 22, Nancy 20, Paulina 18, Greenberry 15, John 12, Mary G. 5, Sarah F. 3
BRYANT, Susan 41*, Sally 17, Eliza 15, John 13, James 11, Anne 9
GROOMER, Elizabeth 61*
WARE, Squire 30, Julia A. 25, Nathan H. 3, Jackson 2
WARE, William 25*
JACKSON, Thursa 35*, Elizabeth 13, Wm. W. 9
WALDRIDGE, Peter jr. 40, Matilda 41, Mary F. 9, Ellis 7, Peter 5, Elizabeth 1
MATTHEWS, Thomas 56*
BROWN, Jack 34*, Emily 34, James W. 15, Joan 12, Samuel M. 9, Louis C. 6
ROMANS, William sr. 65*, Sally 58, George 21
JAMESON, Eliza 13* (B)

Schedule Page 249

NAYLOR, Sally 54*
BURDETT, Amelia 30*, Sally Ann 11
MARKSBURY, Margaret 59, Sally 39, Louisiana 23, Meriam 21, Overton 17, Sally 12
PHILIPS, James 27*, Sally 36, Isabella 3, Nancy 4/12

1850 Census Garrard County Kentucky

POLLARD, Mary A. 17*, Edmond 14, Absolem 12, Martin 10, Cynthia A. 7, George 6
WALKER, Kemp jr. 28*, Nancy 30
WALKER, Elijah M. 6*, George W. 4, James H. 2, Wm. W. 1
POLLARD, John 62, ann 54, John T. 11, Thomas J. 9, James 25, Elizabeth 25, Margaret Ann 5, Mary C. 2
BALL, Thomas 49, Lucinda 59, Susan W. 24, Almada 20, Ann Eliza 16
BURNSIDES, Williamson 47, Elizabeth 34, Joseph 21, Bill 19, Martha 10, Sarah 8, James 6, Opha 4, Mary 1
ANDERSON, Jo 41 (m), Alvire 34 (f), Catharine 21, Andrew 19, James R. 17, Richard T. 15, John W. 13, Frederick 11, Benjamin 9, Sally A. 7, Joseph 5
JAMESON, David 66, Eliza 52, David jr. 20, Cassy A. 18, Eliza 17, Ashford 15, Merideth K. 13, George 11
PRESTON, William 55, Eliza 52, George 15, Joseph J. 13, David 10
PRESTON, Enoch 70, Nancy 28, Susan 18, Nancy 3
PRESTON, Elice 25 (m)*, Margaret 25, Martha J. 24, Mary J. 3, Wm. 2
SHEARER, Martha 65*
HADE, Joseph 24, Sally 20, Jane 2

Schedule Page 250

FLOYD, Davis 62, Frances 58, Ezra 31, Talitha 25, Frances A. 5, Sarah A. 2
MIDDLETON, Henry 40, Sally 43, Wm. 16, Mary 14, Matilda 11, Henry 9, Margaret 7, Emily 5
BRYANT, Martha 28, Kitty Ann 3, James W. 8, John Tolton 44, Margaret 45, Mary J. 23, Garret 22, Eliza 19, Washington 17, Emily 15, John 13, Nancy E. 11, Logan 13
HILL, Russel 36, Delila 27, Frederick 8, Will P. 6, Sally Ann 4, Elizabeth E. 2, James 12
MCMAMIS, William 70*
SCOTT, Jenny 50*
MILLS, Maglin 50 (f)*
ENGLISH, Rachael 10*
MCCORMACK, Will 40*
BRADY, John 66*
HILL, Frederick 38, Jane 36, John 16, James 14, Russel 12, Mary 10, Jesse 8, Lucy 6, Jane 4, George 3, Eliza 2
HAYS, John 37, Mary 30, James 8, Catharine 6, Alexander 4, Elzina 2, Will 5/12
GILL, Samuel 38, Cely 28, Malinda 12, John 9, Alexander 7, Catharine 5, Samuel 2
STORMS, Catharine A. 40, James R. 16, Robert H. 14, Sally O. 12, Coonrod 10, George H. 7, Jonathan W. 4
MURPHY, James 50, Paulina 39, Wm. 24, John 22, James 17, Daniel 15, Sarah Jane 13, Francis M. 8, Elzina 4, Vicilla 2

Schedule Page 251

WALDRIDGE, Peter sr. 70*, Fany 66, Sarah 40, Agnes 36, Mary 30, Benjamin 23, Milly 21, Martha 18
MATTHEWS, Nancy 32*, Eliza 8, Ellis 6
HOLLAND, Tracey 44*, Wm. 23
BAKER, James 30*, Sally 30, susan J. 10, Eliza 8, John 7, Abram 5, Martha 4/12
BEASLEY, John 32, Sarah A. 26, Amanda 9, Elijah 7, Will 5, John 2

1850 Census Garrard County Kentucky

BETTIS, Fanny 40*, Wm. 19, Anne 11
RODINE, Mary 70*
TOMPKINS, Susan 59*
STEPHENS, Frances J. 19*
STEPHENS, Sarilda J. 21*, Marietta 3, Martha A. 2
JENNINGS, George 21*
JENNINGS, Thomas B. 42*, Anne 44, Sarah C. 11, Anne R. 7, T. Benj. 4
GREEN, William 11*
JENNINGS, Baylor 55*, Lavinia 51, Sarah E. 24, Baylor 20, Thomas 19, Russell 14, John A. 11, James H. 7, Gabrael B. 3
BROWN, Eliza 94*
STORMS, Nathaniel 53*, Nancy 53, Cornelius 30, Nancy 20, Mar 16, Martha 16, Paulina 12
WEAVER, Andrew J. 12*
BROWN, George 23, Sarah A. 18, Wm. 5/12
ARNOLD, Thompson 46, Sarah J. 35, John L. 17, Mary E. 15, Joseph H. 13, Thompson M. 11, Paulina J. 9, Frances S. 7, Andrew R. 5, Alex. T. 3, Zachariah T. 6/12
COMELY, James 67, Mary A. 24, George 21
COMELY, John 26*, Salley 29, Eliza 8, Wm. 5, James 4, Nancy J. 2
SANDERS, Sarah E. 2*

Schedule Page 252

JENINGS, Abraham 28, Nancy G. 23, Carrol B. 8 (m), Cicero P. 6, Elija 4, Overton 2
BROWN, Joseph S. 55, Margaret 22, Martha A. 20, Wm. 18
BROWN, Smith 30, Tabitha 21, Robert 3, Clara 1
CLARKE, Comely 34 (m), Frances 23, Eliza 11, Amanda 9, Emily J. 8, Nancy T. 6, Marinda 4
HILL, Isaiah 43, John 22, Wm. 21, James 17, Jesse 15, Mary 13, Parrey 11, Isaiah 10, Matilda 8, Randolph 6, Elizabeth 6, Josaphine 4, Col. Russell 2, Lucy 6/12
PEARCE, Rachael 41, Will H. 24, Almira J. 22, Amanda G. 16
SANDERS, James M. 25, Almira 20, John A. 7/12
ALFORD, Jesse 57, Lucinda 54, Rosa E. 17, Clay 15
ALFORD, John Q. 26, Nancy 24, Mary E. 6, Sarah m. 4, Jesse 3/12
ASKINS, Charles G. 42, Nancy 39, Wm. A. 17, Margaret 15, Emily 8, Eliza 6, John 4
REED, Barbara 70, Will P. 34, Mary A. P. 24, James C. 10, Marietta 2
TEETER, Nelson H. 30*, Pamelia 38, Solon R. 19, James H. 17, Will C. 16, Paulina T. 13, John N. 11, Martha J. 9, Paris M. 7, Allen 5, Zachariah T. 3, Elizabeth 2
DUNN, Theodrick 24*, Mary E. 22, Ed A. 11/12
BOWMAN, George 68, Sarah 54
HARRISON, Sally 20*, Sally H. 3, David Ella 8/12
WHITE, Will 24*

Schedule Page 253

ODER, Joseph 59*, Clara 61, James 29
SSBURY, Miriam 15*
GOFF, C. P. 28 (m), Lucy 24, Elzabeth 5, John H. 2, Annabiller 8/12

1850 Census Garrard County Kentucky

YEATER, Matilda 45, Jacob 17, Nancy 15, Mary A. 14, Matilda 10, Wm. 8, Margaret 5
WARMOUTH, Thomas S. 29, Miriam 24, Henry Clay 5, Oliver H. 3, James 1, Jesse Y. 1/12
BROADUS, John E. 30, Ann M. 22, Wm. T. 7, Sarah J. 5, Mary M. 3
WELEFORD, Charles 35*, Elizabeth 21, Sarah 2, Mary E. 1
MERRITT, John sr. 64*, John jr. 29, Josephus 26, Addison 24, Wade H. 22, Mitchell 21, Lurana 20, Margaret 19, Stephen 36
YEATER, Henry 20*
SMITH, James 13*
GAY, John 29, Catharine 29, James 8, Benjamin 5, Lucinda 4
BOLTON, Burt 20, Paulina 18
PULLIAMS, Alvah 31 (m), Matilda 36, Samtha 34, Amelia 24, Amanda 22, Nanc 20, Samuel 18, Charles W. 11
OBERLY, Allen B. 23, Elizabeth 23, Laura 1
MERRITT, George S. 38, Eliza 30, John 8, Ann 6, Smith 4, Mary 2
SHUMATE, Mitchell sr. 58, Catharine 51, Eveline 18, Mary 13, Francis 9
SHUMATE, Daniel 80
SHUMATE, Mitchell jr. 23, Martha 19, Martha 1/12
BROWN, richard 44, Nancy 46, Charles J. 23, Granville 21, Lafayette 17, Amelia 13, Elizabeth 10, Nancy C. 2

Schedule Page 254

FERELL, Micajah 48, Margaret 43, John R. 17, Margaret 13, Mary E. 6
ROTHWELL, Fountain 51, Jane 48, James m. 24, Wm. 18, Sally Ann 15, Gideon 13, John 11, Samuel 9, Alexander M. 7
BROWN, Stewart 40*, Jane 41
FERRELL, Stewart 20*
DOTY, A. 69 (m), Elizabeth 54, John 21, Wm. 15
BLACK, James 40, Emily 25
RAY, John 68, Jane 62, Eli 27, Jane jr. 20
YEATER, Thomas sr. 43, Eliza 40, John 12, Nancy 10, Henry 8, Jane 6, Alexander 3
HURT, John W. 34, Cassander 26, Wm. 9, Sally 6, Jane 3, Citty Ann 1
NICHOLSON, Jeremiah J. 36, Lucinda 30, John R. 8, Mary F. 6, James M. 4, Arthusa M. 1
LEISURE, William 66*, Mary 52, Elizabeth 24, Joseph 23, Alexander 19, Selema 17, George 16, Wm. 14, Marion 12, Nathaniel 10
HUBBARD, John H. 7*, Wm. 5
HENDERSON, Elizabeth Y. 50, Margaret A. 25, Alexander 23, Crutchfield 20, James 18, Eliza 15, Samuel 15, Martha 13, John 9
LACKEY, Gabriel 66, Hannah 54
BASHFORD, Eli D. 34*
MCKOY, John 40*, Elizabeth 38
ENKINS, Marcy 71*
LOGAN, David 33, Nancy 33, Martha T. 11, Hugh 10, Oliver 8, John 6, timothy 4, Mary E. 2, James M. 3/12

1850 Census Garrard County Kentucky

Schedule Page 255

MYERS, Isaac M. 63, Caroline 49, Martha A. 21, Emily 18, Josaphine 16, Clay 14, Thompson 11, Isaac 9, Marcy 6
LAIN, James 52, Milly 50, William J. 27, James 18, Marcy J. 16, Elizabeth 13
CLOUSE, James W. 22, Sarah A. 22, Will E. 1
WHICK, Elizabeth 41, Mary J. 15
DENTON, Eliza 50, Milley 20, Salley 22, Eliza 16, Margaret J. 13, Catharine 6
TOTTEN, Joseph 59, Nancy E. 59, Will M. 24, Mary F. 14
TOTTEN, Juan L. 30 (f), Lucinda E. 8, John 7, David R. 6
CLOUSE, James 34, Catharine 25, Isham 1
NAVE, John 48, Serefina W. 36, Joseph P. 16, James D. 15, Malinda F. 13, Alexander 11, Mary E. 8
PRYOR, Jourdon 50, Nancy 53, Chastina? 15, Eveline 12, Mary A. 9
PRYOR, Will 22, Elza 22, Isaiah 15
RAY, Harrison 38, Sarah 30, Wm. 13, Martha J. 11, Malinda 9, Susan 8, Michel 6 (m), Lindsey 5 (m), Harrison B. 4, James T. 2
LETCHER, James H. 40
HURT, Eleven 34 (m), Eliza J. 28, Sireney 11 (m?), Sarah 9, Robert 5, Nathaniel 2
BURTON, Robert A. 52, Sarah 53, Woodson 22, Amanda 16, Sarah 8
JONES, John 40, Elza 44, Nancy 21, Mary A. 15, Simpson 14 (f?), Sarah J. 11, Eliza 5, David N. 3, Emily 1

Schedule Page 256

JONES, Will 44, Matica 41 (f), Catharine 18, John 16, Virginia 14, Elza 12, Gerorge 10, Will 8
WARREN, John 65, Sarah 65
PRATHER, Freeman 52, Nancy 44
WARREN, Danica 44 (f), William 18, Howard 16, Martha 15
CLARK, David 20, Eliza 16, Susan M. 1
CASEY, Lucy 35, Mary A. 17, John W. 14, Rolinda 12, Reuben 10, Analiza 5
GOINS, Samuel H. 31, Elza 28, Will C. 8, Minerva J. 6, Mary A. 4, Hester F. 2, Lucinda E. 2/12
CLARKE, martin 40, Mary 30, Sidney 17 (m)
WOODFORK, Thomas 36, Margaret 36, Mary A. 6, Nancy J. 4, Josaphine 3
TATUM, William M. 25, Eliza 16
NOEL, Robert C. 46, Nancy 37, Will S. 17, Thomas A. 16, Lewis L. 14, Robert A. 9, Mary A. 4, Nancy J. 3
TUDER, William 29, Mary 18, Lucinda 7, Kinchen 4 (m), Pamelia 6/12
MCCOLLON, Ezekiel 35, Theresa 35, Mary A. 12, Squire 9, Taylor 7, Parey 5, Lowrey 2
SEBASTIAN, Wiley 23, Emeline 21, Margaret E. 4, James M. 2
JONES, David 50, America 46, Joseph 25, Daniel 23, Thomas 20, Jane 17, John 15, Will 13, Andrew 11, Caroline 9, James 7, Anderson 5
TOMPKINS, John M. 27, Martha A. 24, Will M. 2, John T. 10/12
MCMILLIN, Travis 46, Eliza 45, Ann 20, James A. 11

- 207 -

1850 Census Garrard County Kentucky

Schedule Page 257

SANDERS, Elijah 32, Jane 25, Clifton 8, Margaret A. 5
SANDERS, Siras 28 (m), Malinda 26, James R. 7, Susan A. 5, Sarah F. 3, Richard 6/12
BOWAN, John 22*, Martha 17
BROADUS, Overton 20*
WARREN, Harvey 22*
BROOKS, John 70*
SMITH, Susan 50*
WHEELER, Nathaniel 25, Frances 57
LEWIS, Mitchel 32, Clarey 32
WHEELER, James 46, Sarah 41, Benjamin 22, Henderson 20, Eliza 18, Susan 16, Sally A. 14, James 10, Clary 8, Squire 6, Angelina 4
EMBRY, Burrill 30, Lucinda 24
RISPOON, Robert 32, Martha 21, James D. 2, Lucy J. 6/12
SEBASTIAN, Alexander 30, Lucinda 30, Talitha J. 8, Isabel 7, Eliza 5, Harris 4, Maranda 3, James 1
SEBASTIAN, Howard 28, Maranda 24, Serepta 8, Alexander 5
SEBASTIAN, Washington 32, Mary 28, Sarah 11, Will 10, James 8, America 7, Thomas 6, John 5, George 3, Marilda 4/12
SEBASTIAN, William 40, Zorada 36, George 18, Harvey 16, Charlotte 14, Margaret 12, Mary A. 9, James A. 11, Thompson 7, Amanda Y. 4
EMBRY, Talton 53, Matilda 50
WHEELER, Abel 34, America 26, Will A. 7, Horace B. 4, America S. 1
SINGER, Ephraim 45, Lucy 40, Will 12, Azariah 10 (m)

Schedule Page 258

LAYTON, Thomas 30, Josaphine 27, Andrew J. 5, Napoleon T. 3, Lycurgus 2
LOGAN, Hugh 60*, Nancy 45, Mary A. 16, Judith E. 1
BEASLEY, Walter A. 7*, Clary E. 5
LOGAN, James 25, Elza 20, David 2
STAGNER, Barnett 36, Miriam J. 32, Martha A. 11, John M. 8, Salam W. 7 (m), Margaret J. 4, Ward H. 1
ROBERTS, James 25, Emily 22, Margaret 2
ROYSTON, Ann 40, Sally A. 17, Jesse 10, Anne R. 8, James A. 4
DENNY, Margaret 66*
ALLEN, Margaret 28*
DENNY, George 25, Eliza 17
HENRY, Brank 28 (m), Eliza 30, James R. 10, Mar A. 8, Burnett G. 6 (m), Elza 4, Harvey 1
HENRY, Robert B. 59, Eliza J. 32
SPILMAN, James H. 42*, Ann 30
BURROUS, Charles M. 27*, Mary 40
LSEARS, Moss 40*, Lavica 24
ALSPAUGH, Nelson 43*, Elza 28, Lucy J. 9, Nancy 7, John H. 5, Sally A. 2
MOGEE, George 37*
SPILMAN, Charles T. 30, Nancy E. 27
SHARP, Temperance 64, Will 24, Temperance 21
BATES, James W. 33, Gabrella 30, Matcour? 5 (m), Ann Mariah 2

1850 Census Garrard County Kentucky

WILLIAMSON, John 40*, John 5, Wm. 2
WARREN, Thomas C. 26*
BUCHANAN, Alex 40, Nancy 35, George 17, Mary 14, Benjamin 12, Joseph 10, Lysander 6, Rufus 4
SLAVINE, John 94
SLAVINE, James G. 49, Nancy 42, Will 22, Isabella 20, Sally A. 18, John 16, Benjamin 14, James W. 12, Mary C. 9, Edward 7, George 4, Cynthia 1

Schedule Page 259

OGLESBY, Jacob 52, Harriett 33, Sally A. 11, Hannah A. 1
LEAVELL, Edm. 37 (m), Rebecca 30
ANDERSON, Irvin 28, Sarah M. 28, Salom 6 (m), Robert 4, Eliza 2
NICHOLSON, Archibald 54, Mary 37, Thaddeus W. 14, James M. 11, Emily J. 8, Thomas S. 6, Will N. 4, Gabrael 4/12
WARMOTH, Madison 27, Margaret J. 24, John H. 8, Henry Clay 6
GIBBS, Alexander 35, Mary J. 20, Anne P. 2, Zachary T. 1
LAYTON, William 58*, Susan 32, Elza 31, John 28, Henry 26, James 24, Mary 22, Martha 20, Abraham 18
BYARS, John 66*, John 16, Jeremiah 12
ANDERSON, Alexander 46, Susan 28, Will 11, Robert 9, Mary 7, Allen T. 5, Martha 3, Sally 1
SALTER, Gabrael Y. 41, Barbara 37, Richard 20, Mary j. 18, Sally A. 16, Osa 13, Michael 11, Amanda 9, California 6/12
SALTER, Elijah Hiatte 79*, Martha 62, Allen 22
ALLEN, John 65*
TERRILL, Martha 49*
BANTON, James 20*
LAYTON, James 24, Mary J. 19
HUGHES, Will 36*, Martha J. 27, George W. 8, James m. 6, Oliver T. 4, John H. 1
BANTON, Eliza 19*
ALCORN, Will 29, Juda? 29, Will P. 10, Eliza J. 8, John H. 6, Matilda A. 5, James 3, Lafayette 1

Schedule Page 260

CLARKE, John 86*, Deca 74, Mary 54, Sally 45
FORD, Mariah 18*
MYERS, John 51*, Eliza 47, Mary F. 8
DOTY, Rebecca 14*, Eliza A. 12
SCARBRO, Jacob 24*
TRAYLOR, Jane 86*
HURT, Will 32*, Ann 36, Mary 10, Sarah M. 8, Susan A. 6, Joshua 4, John 2, Will 1, Joshua 30
HUGHES, Eliza 30*, Sarah 18, James 76
HARRIS, A. J. 34 (m), Elenor T. 35, Alex 12, Tyre 10 (m), Overton 6, Mary E. 6/12
FINDLEY, Houston 45, Malinda 41, Milton 16, Martha 14, Clayton 12, Mary 10, Chloe 8
FERRILL, Isaac 75 (B)
YATES, Thomas jr. 23, Clarissa 18, Marcy 1
COMELY, David 49, Pamelia 26, David jr. 21, Martha 19, Reuben 17, Susan 15, Daniel 2, Eliza 6/12
MCDANIEL, Daniel 45, Eliza 39, Nancy 17, Jane 16, Elzina 14, Mary 11, James 8

1850 Census Garrard County Kentucky

HARRIS, Elemuel 39, Eliza 35, Will O. 15, Samuel 12, Elijah 8, James B. 3
ARNOLD, Jane 45, Daniel 18, Patience 16, Isaac 14, Alex C. 12, Sarah E. 10, Margaret 23, Wm. 21
ROMANS, Will jr. 36, Judith 28, Margaret J. 12, Adaline 10, Eliza 8, John 6, Elizabeth 4
BURDETT, James T. 45, Eliza 25, Samuel 4/12
BURDETT, Francis 28*, Nancy 30, John P. 7, Will H. 2, Penelope 1

Schedule Page 261

ALDRIDGE, Joseph 20*
KEMPER, Burdett 62 (m), Jemima 52, Frederick 27, James T. H.? 20, Henry C. 18, Joshua 13
BALLARD, William 40, Mary A. 30, James H. 5, Lucy E. 3, Mary A. 9/12
REYNOLDS, O. P. 34 (m), Mary A. 25, Lee 2 (m)
TILLETT, E. G. 52 (m), Martha 36, Oscar 20, Analiza 14, Margaret 11, Amanda 9, Walton 8, Martha 6, Malcom 4, Joshua 2
DISMUKES, James m. 40, Louisa 37, Elizabeth J. 13, Joseph 9, Peter F. 7, John W. F. 5, Clarissa F. 3, James J. 1
GRAHAM, Samuel 30, Clintena 22, Margaret J. 4, Jack 1
COSBY, James D. 66*, James 24, Nicholas 23, Benjamin W. 18
DAVIS, Elizabeth 26*, George Ann 2
MIZNER, Samuel S. 34, Rosa 20, John 4, Caroline 2
STEPHENS, Harrison 37, Mary 36, Susan F. 13, Victoria 10, Mary Moore 6, Emily B. 4, Amelia 2
HALEY, Sidney 36 (m)*, Almira 24, Edmond 6, Caleb 4, John 2, Mary E. 9/12
MCMURTRY, Ed 57* (B)
WELCH, Sally A. 38*, Benjamin W. 11, Charles S. 9, Josephine 7, Mary J. 47, Sally A. 1
SMITH, Nancy A. 17*
NORRIS, James 46*, Elza 41
PARKS, Sally A. 21*, Eliza 16, Will 23, Eliza 20
LYONS, Moses 34, Susan 34, Samuel 3, Isaac 1
SWOPE, John sr. 59*, Fanny 54, Joseph 17, Jesse 15, Zerilda 13, John 9

Schedule Page 262

FLOYD, Mary J. 21*
HUFFMAN, Will L. 47, Sarah 45, Granville 25, Israiel 22, Eliza 19, John 17, Jane 12, Willey 10 (f), William 7, Albert 5, Gabrael 3
KURTZ, Henry A. 32*, Josaphine 31, George W. 8, Hester A. 7, Isaac C. 5, Mary J. 3, Henry 1
DEARING, William R. 23*
FARLEE, Peter 26*
BROWN, Hamlett 23*
ALSPAUGH, D. C. 32 (m), Elenor A. 35, Mary J. 6, Texas 4 (f), Ruth 1
DAVIS, Jesse 60, Mary 67
HARDWICK, James 39, George 33
MEEKER, A. R. 50 (m), Lucinda 40, Will J. 17, Mary A. 10, Westley 7
TRACEY, Emaliah 50 (f), Smith 30, Sally A. 24, Benjamin 10, Elizabeth 8, Thomas F. 28, Wm. 20
HUFFMAN, Jack 48*, Jane 41
FARLEE, Martha A. 20*, John 2

1850 Census Garrard County Kentucky

CAMPBELL, Whitico H. 65 (m), Pernell H. 39 (f), Opah P. 13 (f), Alias H. 10 (m), John L. 8, James W. 6, Benj. 4, Hiram B. 1
JENNINGS, Richard B. 41, Martha A. 36, John W. 17, Sarah A. 14, Thomas S. 10, Eliza 7, Richard B. 3
COLLIER, Aron 63, Miriam 67, Louisa 38
SMITH, Edmond 71, Jane A. 66
SMITH, David F. 28, Martha A. 22
COLLIER, Sarah 52, John 21, Martha J. 18, Sarah 16
JOHNSON, Merryman 27, Susan 23, Sarah E. 3, Nancy J. 10/12
DUNN, Walter 72
DUNN, Will 38, Mary 27, James 9, John 2, Elizabeth 4/12

Schedule Page 263

LANDRAM, Lewis 50, Eliza Ann 30, Paulina D. 12, Joseph J. 10, John 7, Susan A. 6, James R. 3, George R. 1
ARNOLD, John Bruce 32*, Rosanna 32, Speed Smith 8, Horatio C. 3, Bennett 1
BRUCE, Brunette 54*
KENNEDY, Elbert D. 35, Elizabeth 38, Mary 15, Eliza 13, Mildred 9
HENDERSON, John 28, Mary E. 19
DUNN, Uriah 53, Virginia 48, Harrison 27, Will 18, Sarah 15, Rhoda a. 14, Uriah 13, Benjamin 10
DUNCAN, Benjamin F. 42*, Jane 32, Martha 8, John 6, Margaret 4, Charlotte 2, Wm. 1
MCKEE, George R. 40*, Samuel 15
STEWART, Rice L. 60*
MORGAN, M. M. 26 (m)*
JACKMAN, Houston 33*
EVANS, Hezekiah 48, Nancy 46, Elijah 22, Samuel 19, Thomas 17, James 15, Shropshire 13, Nancy J. 10, Sarah 8, Lysander J. 6, Emily 3
CARP, Henry 46, Nancy 44, George 21, Elizabeth 19, Jane 16, Jesse 14 (m), John 12, Nancy 10
GILL, John 64, Martha 47, Malcom 18
GILL, John S. 23
ANDERSON, Clayton 41, Elzina 23, Margaret M. 3, Elza 1
ANDERSON, Margaret 68
MURPHY, Willis G. 29*, Mary A. 28, Mary C. 4
MCKEE, James 17*
EVANS, Isaac 35, Caroline 34, Mary A. 13, Eliza C. 11, Joseph A. 9, Angeline 7, Susan A. 5, Isaac N. 2, Houston 7/12

Schedule Page 264

HILL, O. P. 36 (m), Eliza 31
PRICE, Jennings 43, Susan 35, Will C. 15, Martha 7, Jane 1
HUDSON, L. B. 34 (m)*, Eliza 32, Jennings P. 12, Lytle R. 11, Benjn. 10, Eliza 8, Will O. 6, Lynn 4 (m), John B. Conn 23
DODD, Travis 46*, Nanc 30, Ephraim S. 11
BROWN, Thomas 73*
SALTER, Osa 68*
COMELY, Jennings 26*

1850 Census Garrard County Kentucky

DUGGINS, Daniel 24*
HILL, James 17*
BEDSTER, Nelson 16*
GABBORD, John 19*
GORDON, Hetty 21*
GREEHAM, Benjamin 63*, Mary W. 28, Benjamin 13
EVANS, Morgan 20*
MCMURTRY, James 47, Martha 36, Nancy 11, James L. 9, Robert 6, Mary 4, Alexander 2
MCQUERY, Louisiana 40*, James T. 16, martha A. 14
KERSEY, James 16*
PIERCE, Jeremiah 47, Eveline 33, John 16, James 14, Braxton 12, Wm. 7, Alice 2
BROWN, A. J. 64(m), Nancy 59, Harvey 25, Breathitt 18
HUTCHESON, Arthusa 36, fredreick 15, Zerilda 13, Barthena 9, Silas 7
ARNOLD, Alexander 24, Margaret 22, Breathitt 6/12
BROWN, George A. 44*, Mary 36, A. J. jr. 21 (m), George 18, Creath 16 (m), Ricks 9, Margaret 7, Martha 5
WHITE, Martha 16*
CARTER, Collin C. 37, Catharine A. 34, James H. 12, Eliza A. 10, Pamelia B. 8, Oliver 6, Virginia B. 3, Thomas L. 1
GREENLEAF, Will 36*, Lucinda B. 35, Lee 14 (m), Gabreal 6
HUFFMAN, Davidson 20*

Schedule Page 265

SMITH, George W. 38, Eliza 26, James 12, George 9, Martha 7, Robert 5, Sarah 3, Mary 2, Miriam 6/12
LETCHER, James H. 49*, Nancy T. 36, Thomas K. 20, Benjamin 18, Margaret 14, Elizabeth 12, Mary 9, Ann 7, James 4, Robert 6/12
OFFICER, Mary 18*
GARFIELD, Lucy C. 26*, Jane E. 24
KENNEDY, Aggy 68 (f)* (B)
DISMUKES, James W. 32, Malinda 27
DISMUKES, Mary 30*, Will F. 13, Eliza J. 12, John E. 7, Malinda A. 4, George F. 1
MCKINNEY, Huldah 58*
DENTON, Dudley H. 36*, Nancy 26, Catharine 7, Alex 3, Henry 1
SCOTT, Timothy 15* (B)
RENFRO, Wilson 12* (B)
SERGACY, Henry 34, Matilda 34, Sarah J. 12, Malinda 10, Daniel 5, Jesse 3 (m), Henry 9/12
HINDS, Henry? 26, Sally A. 25, Mary B. 3, John T. 7
GRESHAM, Will R. 34, Margaret 21, Nancy 4, Louisa 1
LOGAN, Hugh 71, Catharine 60, Catharine 20, Hannah J. 17
MASON, James B. 29, Elizabeth 22
RYANT, Will 22*, Frances 20
SMITH, Lorenzo? 36*
HIX, Henry 44, Bethiah 44 (f), Perry 22, Clarinda 21, Mary J. 20, Embry 19, Andrew J. 17, Paulina 16, Rebecca 14, Will H. 12, Eliza F. 12, Zachariah T. 4, Josiah Leak 1
SANDIFER, Nicholas 33, Mary J. 23, Henry G. 4, Joseph P. 1
HILL, John M. 32*, Mary E. 7

1850 Census Garrard County Kentucky

SANDIFER, James 23*
ONEAL, John 22*

Schedule Page 266

CROW, Joseph R. 40*, Emaline 28, Mary E. 8, Susan 6
GREEN, Eliza 19*
WILMOT, Benjamin 32*, Mary A. 25, Ephraim 6, Martha A. 4, James 1
JOHNSTON, Thomas 22*
MERSHON, Henry 21*
HARLAN, Joseph 18*
HASELDON, John H. 39*, Mary E. 34, John S. 8, Mary 6, Rodger S. 4, Joseph C. 2
DUNN, Alexander 21*
HART, John 36, Elizabeth 30, Charles 4, James 2
SARTAIN, George F. 24*, Ann 20, Mary 1
TAYLOR, Mariah 26* (B)
COOKE, Sarah 57*, Ed 21
HOPPER, William H. 26*
BURTON, A. A. 28 (m)*
LUSK, Samuel 51, Elza A. 36, Alexander 20, Wm. 14, Mary 11, Ann 10, John 6, Eliza 4
YOUNG, Frances 59, Elizabeth 16
AKIN, Josaphine 28, Elizabeth 13, Joseph P. 12, Mildred 9, Dudley 6
DUNLAP, George W. 36*, Nancy 25, Ugenia 10, Mary 7, John 4, George 1
JENNINGS, James 20*, John 18
BAILEY, Walter C. 42, Desdemonia 38, Adelia 17, Isabella 14, John S. 8, Will T. 6, Elizabeth 2
LOGAN, John F. 35, Sarah E. 28, Walter E. 3
STEPHENSON, Jane 36, Mary L. 8, Albert W. 7, Martha 3
YANTIS, James H. 42, Margaret A. 33, Will C. 16, Mary D. 14, Robert H. 12, Arthusa 11, Ann B. 8, Thomas L. 4, Jane 2
MCKEE, Alexander R. 35, Martinette H. 26, Lucy 3, Elizabeth 1

Schedule Page 267

BROWN, Ephariam 33, George Ann 25, George P. 10
BRUCE, William 49, Ann 49, Mary 17, James H. 15
YANTIS, John Q. 32, Eliza 25, Clarey 4 (f), Salley 1
YANTIS, Jesse 53 (m), Martha R. 50, R. F. 22 (m), Sarah F. 17, Martha E. 14, Jacob W. 12, Jane R. 10, Ann M. 7
EVANS, Jesse 38 (m), Roanah 39, Mary A. 21, Lucinda 15, Rebeca 14, John 12, Marcus W. 10, Enoch 8, Margaret 6, Elijah 3

Schedule Page 268

PRICE, N. B. 36 (m), Hariott A. 23, Wm. A. 4, Charles 2
GARDNER, James 57, Ann 47, John 21
HILL, John 28, Martha 28

1850 Census Garrard County Kentucky

THORNTON, John 24, Margaret A. 21, Noel F. 4/12
QUINN, John B. 34, Martha J. 28, James A. 5, Robert H. 2, Mary J. 8/12
MILLER, Thomas 54, Catharine 49, Jacob 24, Luei 22 (m), Polley A. 18, L. Taylor 17, Thomas 14, Nancy J. 12, Fealding 9, Joseph 5
JOHNSTON, John W. 55, Edna 35, John T. W. 5, Hiriam S. 2
LOVE, Thomas P. 25, Frances 21, Mary E. 4
HIATTE, Samuel 30, Mary 80, Franklin 21
CAROLILE, Solomon 30, Mary J. 19, Elizabeth J. 7/12
DENNIS, Elisha 24, Martha 25, Mary A. 2
STUGER, James 50, Rebecca 50, Margaret 17, Elizabeth 15, Francis M. 13, Susan 10, James C. 8, John 6
WHITE, Will 40, Salley 39, Amelia 19, George 16, James 14, Elzabeth 9, Polley A. 7, Salley A. 5
RAMSEY, Alexander 65, Polley 55, James 27, Elizabeth 28, Polley 24, Alexander 23
HIATTE, Harrison 36, Zarilda 30, Mary A. 8, James 7, Will 5, John 4, George 3, Elizabeth 1
EDMINSON, Thomas 41
RICHARDSON, Will jr. 38, Jane 36, Martha A. 15, Elizabeth J. 10
DUMEY, Elijah 33
RICHARDSON, Will sr. 62, Elizabeth 64
RIGSBY, Lucy 43, Elizabeth S. 8, Wm. 7, Mary J. 5, James H. 2

Schedule Page 269

RIGSBY, will 69*, Lucy 71, Susan 40
ADAMS, Martha 44*, Will 16 (f?)
NAYLOR, George T. 41, Jane 41, Alexander 16, Will E. 14, Daniel 11, John 10, Margaret 8, Mary E. 6, George W. 4, Elizabeth S. 4
NAYLOR, Edward B. 72, Jane 71
GEORGE, James 60, Nancy 56, Charlott 32, Nancy 26, Elizabeth 24, Martha A. 18, Ansel 17, Sarah 14, Mary 8
FOLEY, Elijah 50, Elizabeth 34, John M. 19, Nancy A. 16, Absaim? 14 (m), Elmanda 12, Gabriel A. 11, Rachal 10, Sarah E. 7, Margaret F. 6, Thomas 3, George M. 9/12
PERKINS, John 54, Tabitha 55, Lucinda 34, Silas 21, Thomas 17
RAMSEY, Thomas 30, Martha J. 23
DOOLIN, Jonson 46, Mary 34, Will 14, Thomas 11, Margaret E. 9
PERKINS, Stacy 45, Thomas 12, Cook 6
AUSTIN, Polley 23, Arteminda 20, Samuel 17
PERKINS, Isadinda 30, Nancy J. 12, Richard 11, James 9, Wm. 7
PERKINS, James 64, Nancy 56
LAWSON, James M. 35, Catharine 35, Wm. 15, John 13, Louisa 12, Benjamin F. 10, Moses 8, Nancy 6, James 3
PERKINS, Newel 28, Salley 27, James 7, George 5, Neneon? 4 (m), Wm. 3, Emanuel 1
BELL, Elizabeth 41, Willis 17, Nancy 15, Louisa 13

Schedule Page 270

BELL, James 28*, Elizabeth 28, Mary F. 1
BRADY, Crofford 10*

1850 Census Garrard County Kentucky

ANDERSON, Levi 44, Nanc 43, Samuel D. 20, Sarah J. 18, Will 16, Eli 13, George 11, Eliza A. 7, Nancy E. 7, Jemima 5, Mary S. B. 3
PHERIGO, James 23, Catharine 20, Will 11/12
PAIN, robert 49, Sarah 45, Kitty J. 20, Robert 18, Julian 18, Nancy 16, Martha S. 3
ANDERSON, David 46, Eliza 44, Will H. 21, Daniel M. 17, John 11, James M. 9
SHROPSHIER, N. J. 31 (m), Sarah J. 25, Will 8, Susan J. 6, Mary B. 4, John O. 2, Sophia A. 10/12
GRAVES, Will 82*
PROCTOR, John 21*
EVERT, Will 37, Susan 20, Darius 4, Mary T. 2
EDMUNSON, robert 61, Nancy 50, Ann 56
ADAMS, John 31, Margaret 30, Achilas 10, Nancy E. 7, George W. 3, John T. 1
RIGSBY, Will 27, Margaret 23, Mary E. 2, Eliza J. 1
RIGSBY, David 26*, Mary 30
DOOLIN, Margaret 12*
KENNEDY, Margaret 56, David 20, Falkner 16, Joseph 12, Barbary J. 8
CHASTEEN, Jesse 55, Learea 55, Roda 18, Jesse 17, Nicholas 14, Orson 12, Margaret 10
MEQUARY, Thompson 38, Salley 24, Mary S. 7, James D. 2, Eliza F. 3/12
ODUNCAN, John 44, Salley 28, Mary S. 7
KENNEDY, Will 29, Amelia 23, Agnas 3, Edna 6

Schedule Page 271

AUSTIN, Samuel 50, Sylva 37, Louisa 11, Thomas 9, Aaron C. 8, Miriam 3, James W. 11/12
AUSTIN, Jane 75, Almira 16, Elizabeth J. 5
ROTHWELL, Will 42, Nancy 31, Mary J. 5, Samuel 2
ROSS, Thomas K. 50, Mildred 38, James W. 17, Samuel 11, Mary A. 8
SPOONEMORE, Henry 34, Lurana 30, Will H. 11, Greenberry 8, Nancy E. 5, Uriah 2
COOKE, Grove 78, Polley 80
HENRY, James H. 51*, Martha 42, Solon B. 7, Eliza F. 3, Rachel 1
DOOLIN, Polley 76*
KENNEDY, Samuel 43, Martha 29, Sarah 18, James 15, Samuel F. 14
MULLINS, Will 54*, Mariah H. 40, John G. 15, Will J. 12, Benj. 6, Mary 3
PROCTOR, George Ann 16*
PETTUS, Will H. 22, Elizabeth 23, John F. 18, Margaret A. 14
MILLER, Will 43, Polley 33, Eliza J. 18, Willis G. 16, Will H. 15, Margaret A. 14, Lucy R. 12, Henry C. 10, Malinda S. 8, Zerilda 7, Daniel 6, Elizabeth 3, Mary S. 2
FRAZER, Will 30, Delila 23, Hugh H. 8, Will J. 3
MILLER, John 80, Margaret 72, Susan J. 8
MILLER, Cornelious 38
NICHOLSON, Will 43, Margaret 33, Mary 13, Amos 9, Harriott 6, Martha 5
LAWSON, Will 62, Nancy 50, John 25, Roy 22, Thomas 18, Elizabeth 14, George 12

Schedule Page 272

JOHNSTON, Thomas 45, Malinda 32, Jane 76, Phiba 38
STANTON, Merela 45, Roy 16, Lewis 12, Mary E. 10, James 5, Mildred J. 8
LAWSON, William jr. 30, Martha 26, John 4, Nancy J. 2

1850 Census Garrard County Kentucky

WORLD, Elijah 35
PRICE?, Fedrick 25, Mary A. 26, Robert 3, Sarah E. 1
NICHOLSON, John 56, Juliann 34, Mary J. 20, Will H. 14, Martha E. 12, Jeremiah P. 10, Rachel 9, Sarah m. 6, James 4, Charles 2
NICHOLSON, James 49, Elizabeth 46, James P. 22, William 20, Mary A. 18, Edna 15, Sarah J. 12, Elenor C. 5
ADAMS, W. B. 35 (m)*, Amelia J. 29, James 8, Robert 4, Wm. 2
NICHOLSON, James sr. 80*
WRIGHT, Elisha 33, Lucinda 34, Salley J. 15, Margaret 13, Will 10, Patsey A. 7, Mary A. 5, Nancy 2
AUSTIN, Elizabeth 52
MCCORMIC, Robert 30, Sarah 26, Rachel A. 7, Sarah J. 6, Elizabeth D. 4, John W. 2/12
MCCURDA, Hugh 50*, Jain 54, John 52, Sarah 12
MCDONALD, Mary 50*
HALL, Nancy 60, Cyntha 20, Jane 16, Salley E. 2
MEQUAREY, Will 40, Edna 27, Mary A. 15, Sarah J. 13, Abner E. 11, Zarilda 9, Thompson 5, Martha A. 3, Polley 8/12
MCQUARY, Joseph 30, Mary F. 18
AUSTIN, Ann 33*, Mitchel 10, Mary J. 8, Sylva 7
ALLEN, Polly 82*
WOODALL, John 83, Mary 34

Schedule Page 273

SIMS, Elvira 70, Elizabeth 27, George W. 3
CONNER, John M. 75*, Manerva 36
CHASTEEN, Mary 25*
CONNER, Paris 36, Barthena 31, Sarah E. 11, John M. 5, James T. 3, Will C. 1, Elizabeth 40, Frances M. 15
WILMUT, Nathaniel 23, Mary A. 28, James T. 1
SCOTT, Joseph 50, Elizabeth 50, Fanney 26, Isabella 24, Dica 23, Stephen 20, Salley 19, Ann 18, Charles 15
NEELEY, James F. 35
MCAFEE, John 75*, Dica 50
BENNETT?, Emeley 22*
SIMS, James 41, Mary 41, Mildred 18, Martha A. 16, Robert 13, Nancy J. 12
CONN, Elizabeth 60, Sarah E. 20
STANTON, Fleming 60, Mary 58
KENNEDY, James 25, Edna 25, Amelia G. 3, Mary B. 1
STUGALL, James 40, Almira 39, Mary 20, Almira 16, Elvina 14, Elvira 12, George Anna 10, John 8, Misurea 6, James J. 3
DAVIS, James M. 25*, Nancy J. 22
THORNTON, Louisa 16*, David 45, Nancy 46
REYNOLDS, Oliver 42, Elizabeth 33, Serena 13, Elenor 11, John 10, Ruth J. 7, Jesse 5, Eli 2, Ruth 68
BAKER, John 35, Salley 40, Polley 17, Jesse 15, Martha 13, James 10, Elizabeth 8, Ann 5
BAKER, Henry 47, Nancy 47, Patsey A. 24, Mary J. 22, Will P. 20, Lucinda 17, Nancy 15, Rachael 14

1850 Census Garrard County Kentucky

Schedule Page 274

POINTER, Vincent 29, Nancy 32, Isaac 6, Mary A. 5, Nancy J. 3, Martha J. 2/12
STANTON, Cyntha A. 44, Almira 16, James H. 15, John C. 13, Wm. 11, Mary 10, Sarah E. 7, Cyntha 4, Nancy A. 1
BURNETT, Reuben 26, Mary A. 25, John H. 4, Sarah T. 2, George S. 1
ABBOT, Abner 35
SIMS, Levina 35, James 23
FALKNER, Peter 67*
KING, Luvena? 22*
CARPENTER, Silas 42, Polly 37, Jeremiah 19, Elizabeth 17, Reuben 16, Solomon 14, Almeda 13, John 10, Mary A. 8, Mildred 6, Eliza 2
CARPENTER, C. B. 38 (m), Elizabeth 37, Almeda 15, Bufus? 12 (m), Mary E. 10, Rebeca 8, Barton W. 6, Robert 4, Sarah J. 2
CARTER, Will? W. 25, Sarah 24, Hiriam 5, Joseph 3
AUSTIN, Will 21
MORAN, Franklin 45, Amanda 40, John S. 13, Adison 10, Robert 8, Florance 3 (m)
HENRY, Will F. 28, Sarah A. 22, James R. 1
CRUTCHER, Will 31, Mar 35, George W. 12, Owen E. 12, Green E. 7, Judiania 4, Nancy J. 3, John W. 2
PALMER, Will 47, Esther 70, Elizabeth 30, Sarah 28, Jane 28
DAVIS, Joseph C. 56, Caroline 52, Mary 23, Elizabeth 18, Joseph 16, Lafayett 14, Will J. 12, Charles W. 11
BURA, Will 44, Mar 40, Archibald L. 18, John F. 16, James L. 14, Joseph S. 9, Henry F. 7, Will A. 11, Martha R. 4, Eliza J. 2

Schedule Page 275

POINTER, James 36, Margaret 34, Mary C. 12
COLLIER, Moses 74*, May 77
BRUCE, Will 16*, Mary 13, Jane 9, Eliza 7, Elizabeth 3
PALMER, Nenion? 44 (m)*, Eliza 37, John M. 21
YEATES, Mary A. 5*
CLINTON, George 60, Salley 26, Monroe 32
DOTSON, George 23
COLLIER, Mary 60, Lafayett 23, Luvina 25, Will L. 21
READY, Theresa 35, Mary A. 6, Elon? T. 4 (f)
CROOKE, Jabez 62*, Ann 58, George 29
ANDERSON, Jane 20*
ENNIS, John 23, Elizabeth 19, Nancy J. 8
BRADY, Elizabeth 26, Nancy J. 2
DANCER, Will 27, Stacy 23, Jane 6, Mary 4, Henry 1
BOULTON, Maliki 36, Elizabeth 32, Tabitha J. 11, Napoleon 9, Ann E. 6, Will 4, John 3/12
HAMMOND, Silas 59, Elizabeth 50, James 25, Will 21, Campbell 18, John 16, Leonidus 13
LEVELL, John Y. 33, Jane S. 24, Benja. F. 5, Elizabeth G. 4, Ezariah D. 1
HERT, John H. 28, Jane 28, Mary C. 9, Amanda 7, Susan 5, Henry 3, Joshua 1
HERT, James jr. 21, Elizabeth 25, Will 3
HERT, Henry jr. 20, Martha J. 18, Henry 2

1850 Census Garrard County Kentucky

SIMPSON, Will 31, Martha 28, Mary E. 7, Clary 4, Jane 6/12
WILEY, D. J. 27 (m), Elizabeth 25, Mary J. 4, Sarah m. 2, Angelina 1

Schedule Page 276

BRUCE, Horatio 56
DOTY, Sabert 44, Susan A. 13, Will 12, Alexander 10, Sarah 8, Mary F. 7, Elizabeth 5, Jesse 1
ROSS, David 41
CARPENTER, Samuel D. 36, Eliza 31, Lucinda 12, Will D. 9, John M. 7, Josephean 5 (f), James 3, Eliza 6/12
GATES, George B. 44, Carey 13 (m), Margaret P. 12, George R. 8, James H. 5, Mary E. 3
MCCARLEY, Moses 58, Elizabeth 45, Will 26, Salley A. 21, James 19
ROSE, George W. 32, Will B. 5, George W. 2
SAMUEL, Henry D. 53, Henry W. 19, Reuben 18, Mariah 16, Gabriel 14, James 12, Patsey 8
SAMUEL, Reuben sr. 85
ADAMS, W. S. 37 (m), Elizabeth A. 29, Elizabeth C. 5, Will G. 3, Martha A. 1, Mary A. 16, Hariott 14
WILEY, Harvey 41, Ruth A. 38, Eliza J. 14, Salam W. 13 (m), Margaret E. 11, Martha A. 10, Mary C. 8, Susan T. 6, Will F. 4, John L. 2
FOLEY, John 40, Mary 38, Uphama 19, James M. 17, Whitley C. 15, Will L. 13, Solomon R. 11, Mary A. 8
BURNTSIDES, John 36, Elizabeth J. 24, Martha B. 1
POLLARD, Absolum 50, Elizabeth 42, Will G. 24
WELSOA?, Charles S. 28, Mary A. 24, David F. 3, Sarah E. 2, James T. 6/12
SCHOOLER, Benjamin 63, Margaret 54, Lytle 23, Margaret 16, Lucrecia 13

Schedule Page 277

HOOD, Will 24, Elizabeth 21, Edward 2/12
SMITH, Auston 72*
BROWN, Matilda 44*, Armsted 15
POPE, Thomas 39, Elizabeth 33, Will 13, Margaret 11, Robert A. 9, Elizabeth 7, Abner 6, Samuel 3, Wordon 10/12
ELKIN, Will 31, Margaret A. 31, Mary E. 9, Robert 6, Thomas S. 4, William 2
SIMPSON, Aly 57 (f)
THORNTON, James B. 27
DODD, Jane 50, Croford 28, Will 24
DODD, Samuel 30, Margaret 28, James S. 6, John 4, Will 2
BALDOCK, Will 30, Elizabeth 22, John 6, James 4
JENNINGS, John B. 30, Sarah J. 26, Samuel H. 6, Elizabeth E. 5, Salley A. 3
COMLEY, Will 26, Elizabeth 22
HET, Henry sr. 58, Susan 32, Andrew 13, Mary 10, Salley J. 8, Lucinda 6, Martha T. 3
HENDERSON, Suan 60
HERT, Able 30, Sarah 41, John H. 13, Joshua 11, Will A. 9, Eli 6, James 4, David 8/12
RAY, Oliver J. 30, Eliza J. 26, Will 5, Elie A. 4 (m), Lucy J. 2, Mary S. 2/12
PERKINS, Emanuel 22
WHITICO, James 42, Julian A. 18 (f), David 22, Martha J. 14, John W. 12
SADLER, Mary 60*, James 25

- 218 -

1850 Census Garrard County Kentucky

YEATES, Elizabeth A. 11*, Wm. 10
SPAYINGHOWER, Henry 41, Eliza 36, Will H. 9, Hariott 8, Catharine E. 7, Peter . 5, Nicholas P. 3, Salley A. 1
RAY, Hampton 38, Mahaley 36, Elizabeth 15, John L. 13, Artusa J. 11, James A. 8, Henry H. 6, Eli S. 3, Mary J. 1

Schedule Page 278

HENDERSON, Robert A. 29, Nancy 63
MORIMOR, Jacob 42, Eveline 42, James B. 21, Henrietta 15, Samuel 13, Lucy A. 11, Will T. 9, Isham 7, Emina J. 6, Elizabeth R. 3
WILEY, Carey A. 45 (m), Elizabeth L. 36, Mary E. 11, John L. 8, Sarah M. 6, Will A. 4, Nancy E. 1, Salley 73
MONTGOMERY, Will 40, Pulina 23, Jane F. 12, Isabella 8, Thomas 3
COOKE, Reuben 48, Mary 42, Caroline 2, Grove 20, John 17, Mary A. 17
BROCK, Peyton S. 38, Casander 40, Elizabeth 15, Eliza 14, Susan 12, Albert c. 11, Mary? E. 9, George W. 7, Peyton S. 5, Casander B. 3, Salley 2
COCHRAN, Samuel 35, Isabella 37
BOATMAN, Nelson 40, Elizabeth 25, James C. 8, Nancy J. 6, Martha 4, Joel W. 2, Richard J. 1
DENNEY, Alexander F. 43, Massey B. 29 (f), Salley 14, Jane 12, Isabella 5, George 2
ROYSTON, Lytle 55, Frances 37, Margaret 9, Jemima 7, Alexander 5, Will 3, Emely 1
DOTY, Josephean 23*
LETCHER, James 50* (B), Bob 13 (W?)
SAMMONS, John 56, Mary A. 52, Mary J. 16, John R. 15, Levena 14
ADAMS, P. C. 29 (m)
ELLIOTT, Thomas 44, Zerilda 29, Wm. 10, Salley A. 8, Thomas 6, Zerilda 5, Mary A. 3, America C. 2, Masula J. 16 (f)

Schedule Page 279

SKINNER, Clark 56, Lucinda 38, Peyton S. 19, Will 17, Elizabeth J. 15, Mary P. 13, Sarah 11, James H. 9, John R. 8, David J. 3, Malvina F. 9/12
SCARBO, Harvey 42, Salley 35, Jacob 9, ary A. 6, David 5, Catharine 2
COOLEY, Hannah 64, Eliza 35, Arthusa 10, John 14, James M. 8, Thomas 5, Angelina 3
DURHAM, Jesse 39, Lucy A. 24, Jane G. 6, Will P. 5, Thomas C. 3, Rolla 9/12 (m)
WINKLER, Jacob 24, Sarah 26, John 5, Angelina 3, Frances A. 2, Emley M. 1/12
ALDRIDGE, Mary 55, Thomas F. 16
HUBBORD, Robert 35, Ann 23, Mary J. 10, John H. 7, Wm. 5
COOLEY, Polley 37, Wm. 18, Amelda 13, Martha A. 11, Salley 8, Elizabeth 4, Alcena 3
CARPENTER, Jeremiah 62, Jane 62, Solomon 23, Jeremiah jr. 21, Jane jr. 7
MASON, W. B. 33 (m), Rachel J. 26, Joseph 6, Talitha E. 4, Rachel 1
DAVIS, Alford 27, Elizabeth A. 24, Sophrona 5, Elizabeth 3
HOLMS, Catharine 25
FALKNER, Peter 25, Sarah 18
JOSLIN, John 37, Arthusa 35, James W. 16, Mary A. 14, Elizabeth 12, Sarah E. 5
STORMS, Stephen 35, Lucinda 35, Elizabeth 14, Mary A. 11
RENFROE, Isaac 35, Sally 39, Mary 6, Emily 2, Arthusa 1/12

1850 Census Garrard County Kentucky

Schedule Page 280

RAMSEY, Jonson 37, Lockey 38, Thomas 12, Hanah E. 10, James 8, Martha A. 6, Samuel 3, Will 1
DUNHAM, Asa 30
REED, Anda 41 (m), Luvisa 40, Rachel A. 12, Hanah F. 10, Mary 7, Will B. 5
CARPENTER, Robert 24
MCCARDY, James 25
FLINT, John 31, Rosanah 31, John 14, Will 9, James T. 2
FORD, Henry 22*
AUSTIN, Thomas 21*
CARTER, John 24, T. Jane 19
AUSTIN, Mitchel 38, Elizabeth 5
KIRKINDOL, Richmond 80*, Elizabeth 54
HALL, Joseph 14*
HALL, Salley 45, Almira 18, Mary J. 16, Josiah 14, George W. 7, Lafayette F. 4
LEWIS, Will 31, Jaire? 21 (f), Jane 7/12
HIGGINBOTHAM, Almira 9
SIMS, Edna 28, Mary J. 9, David 7, Salley A. 6, Angelina 2, Levisa F. 7/12
HALL, Abner 30, Nancy 49, Polley 16, Binda 15, Nancy A. 12, Hiriam 11, Jane 10, Samuel 7
KENNEDY, Eliza 32, Andrew 12, Jane 11, Wm. 9, Mary A. 8, Sarah 5, Elbert 3, Elizabeth 1
KENNEDY, David 80*, Jane 76
FORSYTHE, Elizabeth 13*, Cyntha 11
BANTON, Oliver 26*, Susan 31, Haston 1
CONN, Alexander 13*, Camp W. 9
HALL, Sidney 23 (m), Nancy 18
GAFNEY, Moton 39, Betsey 39, Elza 17, Matha J. 16, Mary A. 14, Polley Ann 12, James 10, Will 8,
    John 6, Sherod 1/12 (f)

Schedule Page 281

GAFNEY, Susan 30, Julia A. 12, Nancy 8
HARRIS, Willis 40, Julia 34, Lucinda 10, Sophia 4
KENNEDY, Rebecca 53, Arthusa 30, Mary E. 22, Rebeca 20, Will H. 19, Samuel 14
RENFROE, Lydia 45, James 26, Mary 22, John H. 21, Will 20, Elizabeth 17, Thomas B. 16, Elbert 13,
    Alvis 10 (m), Rodusea 7, Martha 4, John B. 3, Nancy 2
BROCK, David 49, Mary 44, John 23, Will J. 21, Levina 14, Nancy 10
MOBERLY, Mahala 50, Lucinda 20, Mary J. 13, Martha 10, Alexander 7, Eliza 5, Easther 4 (f),
    Edna 8/12
GIBSON, Pleasant 44, An 40, Will 15
JOHNSTON, Will 47, Jane 46
THOMPSON, George 27, Martha 26, John M. 6, Columbus M. 4, George 2
HOLCOM, Stephen C. 32, Elizabeth 25
SINGLETON, James 34, Martha 23, Samantha 6
RODGERS, Joseph 25, Ellen 20, Martha A. 1, Elizabeth 5/12
MCCOY, Hector 47, America 27, Will 15, Sarah C. 5, Alava J. 4, Taylor 1
HUGHS, Person 30, Margaret 24, Joshua J. 6, Meredith A. 5, Elizabeth H. 3, Will E. 2, Ann E. 6/12
GOOLSBURY, Julian 35 (f), Will 7
HOPKINS, H. J. 30 (m), Ann 0, Angeline 2

1850 Census Garrard County Kentucky

HOPKINS, Jesse 27 (m)
HIGGINBOTHAM, Will 40*, Ellon 34, Elizabeth 10, John M. 9, Joseph 7, James M. 6, Will 5, Eliza 3, Ellon M. 2

Schedule Page 282

HENRY, Mary A. 16*
BAUGH, Samuel 17*
YEAKEY, John 26, Jane 58, Sarah 25, Mary 24, Fedrick 23
COMO, J. T. 28 (m), Elizabeth 30, Elizabeth J. 5
WOODS, Rice G. 36*, Rachel 9, Elizabeth 5, Sarah 3, Martha H. 1, Elizabeth 64, Arthusa 38
BRANK, Sophia 54*
CARPENTER, Robert 67, Mary 62, Nancy 30, Erasmus 27, Laura 21, Will 19
SHUMATE, Champ 25*, Martha 33, Jason 9/12
OLIVER, Jasper 10*
ROTHWELL, Thomas 36, Matilda 31, Albert 8, John M. 7, James F. 5, Hiriam 4, Elizabeth 3, Will 2, Mary 1
BUNDA, Joseph 42, Lusanna 30, George W. 7, Jane E. 5, Susan C. 4, Louisa 2
HALL, Josiah 76, Fanney 69
WOODS, Will 65, Mary 56, Caleb D. 12
WOODS, James R. 35, Susan 27, Horace 6/12
MONTGOMREY, W. C. 29 (m), Mary E. 25
HOOZER, Lorenzo 46, Ame 40 (f), Lucy J. 19
RENFROE, Thomas 35, Mary 30, Elizabeth 7, John 5, Wm. 4, Martha A. 9/12
NORMAN, Will 38, Mary 39, Humphrey 15, Clarissa 13, Mary F. 11, Susanah 8, Edward 4, Will 1
PATERSON, John 69, Rhoda 58, Allen 33, John 28, Asa 23, Rhoda 21, Nancy J. 18, Margaret 16

Schedule Page 283

WILEY, Salley 37, Rhoda 15, John 8, Martha 5
COLLIER, Mason 32
PHILPOT, Rebecca 39
SCOTT, Salley 39, John 13
BAUGH, Jesse 54, Elizabeth 37, Edna 24, Martha 19, Elizabeth 15, Mary G. 13, James W. 11, Nancy 7, Isamanda 5, Robert 3, Arabella 1
SCOTT, Will 26, Susa 31, Julia A. 8, Nancy M. 6, Rebeca 4, Stephen T. 1
FOSTER, Daniel 75, Mary 76, Elizabeth 36, Daniel F. 10
ROBERTS, Nathaniel 50, Catharine 30, Rebeca J. 21, Namoa? 16 (m), Phillip 13, Easther A. 12 (f), Mary F. 11
LANSFORD, Alexander 20, Jane 34, Wilmuth 12 (m), George A. 1
BAKER, Elias 50, Martha 47, Amanda 16, Elizabeth 14, James 13, Josephian 7 (f), Charles 4
BAKER, James M. 20, Nancy J. 19, Mary E. 2, Martha J. 1
HIGGINBOTHAM, Emanuel 79*, Isaminda 21
MCCLUNG, Andrew 50*
MAUPIN, Jefferson 28, Jane 23, Adam W. 3, Dorcas 2, Margaret 10/12
HENRY, J. Harvey 34, Emeline F. 29
ROLLINS, Will W. 28*

- 221 -

1850 Census Garrard County Kentucky

CALLISON, Nancy 31*, Samartha 5, Jane 4, Margaret 1
HENDERSON, Margaret 56, Keron W. 26 (m), Elizabeth 22, Saphrona 20
CAVENAUGH, Archibald 36, Dorcas 28, Will 9, Martha J. 7, Joseph 5, Martha L. 8/12
TAYLOR, David W. 37, Eliza 36, Louisa 11, Harrison 9, Charles W. 7, Stephen 6, Elbert5, Elizabeth 3, Mary 1

Schedule Page 284

REED, Elizabeth 55, George 32, James 22, Bell 15 (f)
KENNEDY, Andrew A. 57, Mary 58, Robert 33
REED, James M. 37, Mary J. 26, Foreftus 7 (m)
MCCORMICK, John C. 32*, Ange 22 (f)
LACKEY, Polina 52*, Gabriel 20, Elizabeth 22, Samuel 18, Polina 15
NAHAM?, John 30, Louisana 27, Will 8, Mary E. 7, John R. 5, James S. 3, Frances J. 7/12
DUMEY, James G. 52, Amelia 45, Will 21, Alexander 19, Elizabeth 14, Martha J. 12, James 10, Margaret 4
CROOKE, James 34, Isabella 25, Jabes 7 (m), Elizabeth 3, Mary C. 7/12
DOTSON, Jeremiah 49, Catharine 46, Eliza 24
PERKINS, Wiatte 32, Margaret 33, James 7, John 4, Nancy 2, Fanney 12 (B)
PERKINS, Ama 45 (B)
ADAMS, John Q. 37*, Angelina 30, Rodna D. 7 (m), Mary E. P. 5, John W. 4, Charles 2
WALDEN, Elizabeth 68*
BERRE, Susan 56, Will 16, Susan 15, Martha 14, Milton 12, Frances 10
JONSON, Robert A. 35, Peachy 34, Mary 2
TERRELL, H. T. 47 (m), Fanney 42, Cleland 16, Eliza 14, John H. 11, Mary F. 5, Oliver T. 5/12
MERSHOW, Robert 31, Susan 30, James A. 6, Wm. 5, Luther 3, Susan F. 1
COMO, Flavous J. 43*, Celia 38, Allen 16, Juliann 13, Frances 11, Elizabeth 7

Schedule Page 285

DOTSON, Nancy 18*, Wm. 16, Catarine 11, Margaret 10, John 8, Francis 6, Jeremiah 3
COMO, Robert R. 4*, J. Waller 1
NEELY, Nathaniel J. 27, Eliza 27, Cornelious H. 5, Mary S. 4, Charles 5/12
BURNARD?, Henry 27, Mary 21, James 21
HARRIS, Anderson 37, Ann 27, Edna 12, Misouria 10, George M. 8, Sarah E. 2
WILEY, David 46, Jemima 42, Sarah J. 22, James H. 19, Elizabeth 15, John 13, Artusa 11, Almira 9, Permilia 6, David B. 4, Simpson 1
WILEY, Jesse 21, Mary A. 19
BIRD, Nathaniel H. 31, Wm. T. 21, Nancy A. 27, John C. 19, Permelia 57
OGELSBY, David 52, Owen W. 20, Will 18, Mary J. 16, John 12, Sarah M. 11
MITCHELL, Will D. 49, Elizabeth H. 40, Isabella 14, Mary S. 12, Samuel D. 6, Harriott 3, Benjamin F. 3/12
OGELSBY, John 36, Sarah 26, James M. 8, Jacob H. 6, Mary E. 5, Samuel K. 4, Will P. 2
CHAMP, Franklin W. 34, Mary A. 32, Will H. 5, Susan H. 4, Robert F. 1
HIGGINBOTHAM, Samuel 47*, Jerome 14, Samuel 12, Sarah 10, Almira 9, Louisa 7, Virginia 5, Emanuel 3
CLARK, Salley 45*

1850 Census Garrard County Kentucky

COCHRAN, Walker 32, Salley A. 25, John W. 4, Wm. 2
EADS, Will 41, Martha 28, Sarah 15, Jerdon 13, Mary 10, Nancy 9, Elizabeth 3, Tyrie 1 (m)

Schedule Page 286

BEST, Will H. 38, Manervey 23, Cyntha A. 5, Mary J. 4, Dulcena 3, George 2
SCOTT, James 39, Mary 37, Rebeca J. 14, Hester 11, Mathew 8, Betsey 7, James 5, John 1
FOSTER, John sr. 45, John jr. 39, Mary J. 13, Salley A. 11, Martha 9, Emeley 7, Manerva 5, Wm. 3
BEST, Tyrie 43 (m), Martha 32, Mary A. 8, Elizabeth E. 6, Frances 1, Martha J. 2/12
ADAMS, John L. 39, Keziah 37, Mary J. 17, Amanda E. 12, Amelia 9, James 7, John 5, George 2
LEVELL, Benjamin sr. 77, Cyntha 26, Benjamin jr. 24, Lewis Y. 22
EADS, John 28, Cyntha 24, James 6, Mary 5, Sarah 3
HARN, Pheoba 50, Wm. 23, Ephariam 76
WHITICO, James jr. 20, Rhoda 19
NICHOLSON, Robert 36, Elizabeth 35, Samuel 10, James 8, Mary S. 6, Eliza J. 4, Elizabeth W. 3, Salley E. 1
HOLMS, Samuel 33, Elza 35, Ephariam 9, Dudley 7, John 4, Samuel M. 2/12
STEWART, Lewis 56
STEWART, Roy 58, Susan 30, Mildred A. 13, Elizabeth F. 10
WAIN, Henry 68*, Jane 65
MCMANNIS, T. 16 (m)*, James 14
ENNIS, Archabald 48, Nancy 46, Mellty? 18 (f), George 12, Mary E. 10, Lewis 8, Catharine 6
HENDERSON, John 28, Mary E. 19

Schedule Page 287

CONN, Will 38, Margaret 39, Mary E. 18, Samuel 17, Margaret 11, Wm. 10, Susan 8, Andrew 7, James 6, Ann E. 5, Salley E. 3
RUSSELL, Ephariam 23
GRAY, Will 54, Mary A. 50, Joanah 20, James 16
MILLER, Will S. 56, Mary J. 17, Sarah F. 6, Elizabeth A. 4, Will S. 2
COMSKI?, Samuel E. 42, Amanda 27, Hanah A. 6, Sarah M. 3
CASEY, Samuel E. 26
LANDRAM, W. J. 22 (m)*, Sarah A. 20
WALKER, Catharine 21*
WALL, Michiel 35
BISHOP, Thomas 40*, Mariam 36, Sarah 17, Mary 15, Betsey B. 13, Alexander 11, Darius 9, Pernell 7, James 5, Nancy 4, Samuel 2
DALY, Charles M. 26*
DABNEY, Spencer G. 26, Dorcas? 26, Logan 5, David B. 13
MILLER, John S. 22, Samuel 21
WALKER, John 48*, Jane M. 41, Mary 13, John 12, Stephen 9, Edwin 7, Wade 3, Jane 1
FALKNER, Margaret 15*
HOPPER, John 45*
BUFORD, Thomas 74*, Mary 44
LOVE, Margaret 14*, Thomas 12, Alexander 10
BRYANT, Will O. 39, Archabald 23

1850 Census Garrard County Kentucky

PEACOCK, Thomas 32, Mary 30, George F. 6, Cora 5, Salley 3, Albert H. 1
KINNAIRD, Will H. 28*, Martha 23, Bob 3, Gillen 1 (f)
MCKEE, Elizabeth 60*
WHIRETT, Will H. 21*
BRYANT, Will S. 25, Frances 20

Schedule Page 288

PETTY, John A. 43, Miriam 33, James 15, Martha S. 13, Hugh 8, Simon 6, Charles 4, Kindor 18 (B)
GREEN, Hiriam 41, Ann M. 30, Willard 12, William 10, George W. 8, Josephean 6 (f), Hiriam 4, James 2
ELGIN, Susan 68 (B), Chany 40 (f), Mandana 12 (f)
HIX, Colmon 37, Martha 33, George W. 5, Charles H. 3, Oliver 5/12
CRUTCHFIELD, Henderson 28, Sarah 30, Calvin J. 4, Montroe 3, Tina 2/12
BAKER, Abner 75, Sarah L. 68, Almira 30, Patsey 23
GRAHAM, Nancy 35, Emely 13, Lucy 12, Wm. 7
HIX, Lindsey 40 (m), Susan 35, Alexr. 17, Sarah A. 13, Squire 11, Parey 9 (m), Salina 2, Margaret 2/12
BURDETT, Joshua 26, Edna 21, Wm. 4
PALDING, Jane 60 (B)
MCKEE, Talitha 35* (B), Mariah 32, Mary E. 17, Ann 11, Eliza 4, Margaret 4
HUFFMAN, Plesant 44, Elsy 44, Susan A. 17, John W. 14, Sarah F. 12
SIMPSON, Delila 49 (B), Montroe 10, Isiah 8, Margaret 2, Edmon 68
FOX, Susan 50, Mary 25, Elizabeth 16, Charles 24
BAKER, Patsey 35 (B)
JONES, Robert 65 (B)
SMITH, Mary 65
DISMUKES, Mary 32, Will 14, Eliza J. 12, John 6, Malinda 4, George 1
SMITH, James J. 30*, Mary 27, Joetha 6, Silas 1
TOMPKINS, Asa 19*

Schedule Page 289

MILLER, William 18*
TILLETT, John G. 22*, Abby W. 20
WARREN, Catharine 26*, Mary B. 2
DUNN, Alexander 18*
BOURNE, F. M. 26 (m)
CHETHAM, Nancy 42, Joseph 15, Elizabeth M. 13, Rachel 12, Jane D. 10, Mariah B. 6, Nancy W. 2?, Henrietta 1/12
FREDERICI, Elizabeth 46, Benja. F. 23, Elizabeth 16
TAYLOR, Thompson 24*, Jane E. 22, Will W. 3
ANDERSON, Noah 12*, George P. 9
YANTIS, John 32, Lucy M. 24, Ben m. 4, Sarah B. 2, Mary 3/12
LUSK, Robert D. 48*, Susan A. 36
HARRISON, W. B. 29 (m)*
CONN, Thomas K. 24
EAGON, Charles B. 45*, Nancy M. 29, Joseph 9, Will C. 4, Alice 1

1850 Census Garrard County Kentucky

WALDRIDGE, Robert 19*, Almira 17, Elizabeth 13, John 8
BARNES, James C. 62, Mariah 67
POOR, John S. 30, Amelia 23
PHILLIPS, James M. 34, Mary A. 32, Mary E. 13, Isaac 11, Joseph 8, Susan 6, Arabella 4, Marget C. 4/12
NIVENS, Will 35, Elizabeth 29, Malcom 7, Sarah 5, George Ann 3, Elizabeth 1
EVANS, Nancy 65, Mary 27, George 24
PERKINS, Jordon 40, Martha 28, Napolion B. 7, Obanion 5, James 3, Emanuel 2, Lucus 1
CURAN, Marietta 34, America 11, Marietta 7, James 5, Robt. Soper 56
HOPPER, Simon 43*, Ann 24, Will 9, Margaret 7, Jane 5, Mariah 3
CROULEY, Catharine 22*
PENELSTON, Will 18*
BRUCE, Will 49, Ann 49

1850 Census Jessamine County Kentucky

Schedule Page 1

LOWEN, Lewis 45*, Jane 30, Martha 9, Lucy L. 7, Morten L. 3, Elizabeth C. 11?
NELSON, Elizabeth 18*
MCCRISTLE, Arthur 30, Mary 30, Mary 10, Michael 8, Bridget 6, John 2, Catharine 6/12
KERSEY, Absalum 43, Rebecca 42, Margaret 21, John 18, George 15, Mary 13, Emily 10, Josephine 7, Thomas 1
PEYTON, Zachariah 38*, Susanah 37, Manerva 12, Ann Eliza 8, Arabella 6, Benjamin 1, Joseph 30
HARBAUGH, Phebe 40*
DAVIS, James E. 38, Elizabeth 28, William C. 10, John P. 8, Jane 6, James G. 55
DAVIS, William 78, Hannah 60, George W. 25, Oliver 22, Russel 18, Jane 25, Nancy Bell 2, Margaret 1/12, Henry 26
SOCHRIST, Joshua 26*, Paulina 28, George W. 3, Jemima J. 2
BOONE, John 38*
KINES, Lorenzo D. 35, Eliza 33, William 12, George 10, Casander 8, James H. 4, Otho R. 2, Oldrige 37
RUTHERFORD, James 57, Precilla 45, Harriet H. 13, Lauri Ann 11, William 9, Martha E. 5, Benjamin F. 3
RUTHERFORD, Joseph 28, Susan 30, Paulina 5, Sarah B. 2, Elizabeth 1
RUTHERFORD, Clayborn 37, Eliza J. 35, Sarah J. 11, James E. 9, Julia E. 5, Mary E. 3, Charles C. 1, James 25
BEASLEY, Sarah 87*, William 60, Gustavus 57
HARRISON, Rose Jane 18*

Schedule Page 2

MARSHAL, Henry 51, Sally 51, Henry 21, Ellen 19, Sarah 18, Martha 15
HOCKERSMITH, Wilkinson 30, Mary E. 29, Lucy 29, Martha J. 7, David 4
CARLISLE, Robert 62, Robert G. 28
MUIR?, Thomas 46, Elizabeth E. 33, Ann 14, Thomas 12, John B. 10, George S. 8, Joseph B. 6, Rebecka 3, Elizabeth 1/12
RICHERSON, James 28*, Ann 20, Samuel M. 2
MIDDLETON, Samuel 16*
CRUTCHER, Jefferson 16*, Lewis 13, Samuel 12
BRYANT, John H. 12*
COBB, Ambrose 19*
COMSTOCK, Alexander 24*
ROBINSON, James S.? 40*, Melvina 35, Frances 17, Margaret 13, John W. 10, Eliza 8, Mildred 6
PARISH, James R. 18*
BIBB, Benjamin 21.*
ROBINSON, John 70*, Fanna 64, Thomas 42
MITCHEL, Susan 43*, Mary F. 19, Mildred 13, Ann E. 10
CARNAHAN, Catharine 28*
ROBINSON, Allen 30, Cathy 25, Laura B. 5, Buenavista 2
PATTEN, John E. 32, Margaret 30
PERRY, John 67, Sally 64, Jane A. 27, Morten 23, Ellen 18
ROBINSON, Jeremiah T. 26*, James T. 21
VAUGHAN, Isabella 1*
MITCHEL, William J. 25*, Tabitha S. 23, Benjamine 1/12, Elizabeth 21

1850 Census Jessamine County Kentucky

PHELPS, George 30*
BOURNE, James 51, Catharine 31, Elijah 17, Sarah 15, John 12, James 10, Robert 7, Charles 1
HAPPY, James 46*, Catharine 42, Elijah 17, Cornelius 10
BRUEN, Daniel 30*, Nancy 21, Catharine 5, Frances 3, John 1

Schedule Page 3

HAPPY, Harvey 19, Sarah 18
BEASLEY, Frances 47*, Elizabeth 23, Harrison 21, Mary 19, James M. 17, William 15, Ann 13, Sarah J. 11, John L. 7
DAVIS, Mary 2*, John 1/12
CRAWL, Elizabeth 37*, John B. 15, Mary C. 13, Nancy J. 12, Thomas J. 10, Sarah E. 7, Joseph W. 5
WISE, John 80*, Nancy 65
WHITTEN, Hester 5*
BRYANT, Joseph C. 28*, Mary 34, Ann 10
MASONER, Ann R. 6*
VINCE, Abraham 66, William 38, John 30, Elizabeth 25, Matilda 7, John 5, James 2, William 10/12
ADAMS, George W. 42, Elizabeth 41, Nancy A. 14, Mary E. _, Martha J. 10, Thomas 8, Ellen 4
ELMORE, William 62, Lucretia 62, Richard T. 30, John 25, Lucretia E. 22, John F. 6, William W. 2, Martha J. 1
MASONER, James 50*, Martha 40, Sarah 10, Armilda 8, Jane 6, John 2, Joseph 2/12
HAGER, William 65*
FITZJERE?, George 35, Rebecca 50, William 13, Solomon 11, Caroline 11, Casander 10, Sarah 6
MASONER, Marillis 84 (f), Catharine 52
PRICE, JAmes C. 22, Frances A. 18
HORINE, John 51, Margaret 42, Henry 19, Harrison 16, Amanda 14, Elizabeth 8, Huldah 6, Anderson 10
ROBINSON, William G. 28*
PARISH, Paulina 47*, Eliza 23?, Thomas J. 13

Schedule Page 4

HAGER, Elijah 21*
ALLEN, James 15*
UTINGER, George 70, Barbary 74, Joseph 46, Jane 41, George W. 18, James W. 14, Elizabeth 12
PARISH, John W. 26*, Mildred 22, A. L. 10/12 (m)
ALLEN, Jefferson 20*
ROBINSON, Benjamine 34, Virginia 27, Martha 7, James B. 5
DICKERSON, John 43, Paulina 38, Mary E. 14, Virginia W. 12, Sarah J. 11, Andrew W. 9, Louisa 7, John F. 5, Ann P. 3
WALLACE, John 57, Lucy 52
YOUNG, Mary 75*
SMITH, Martha 48*
NEATT?, Isaac S. 27*
HAYDEN, Thomas 26*, Lucy 22, William S. 5, Harrison 4/12
WYATT, Thomas J. 40*, Susan A. 21, Elizabeth J. 13
WADE, Charles S. 46*, James S. 45

1850 Census Jessamine County Kentucky

YOUNG, Walter C. 42, Henrietta 38, Laura J. 18, Adelade L. 16 (f), Semones? 13 (f), Eliza P. 11, Isadore 9 (f), Maria L. 7, Walter C. 3
STEWART, Robert 57, John 59, Charles 50, Mary 53
ARNETT, Burrus 66, Margaret 56, Samuel 32, William 23
YOUNG, A. M. 33 (m), Frances 77, Paulina 20
HIGGINS, Nancy 70
NEAT, George W. 39, Nancy 37, Jane 15, John W. 13, Melvina 10
CASSELL, Sarah 66*
STEPHENS, Huldah 25*, Alvin 6, Sarah 4, Mary S. 2, Margaret 4/12
CASSELL, Leonard 40*, George W. 17, Susan 11, William H. 9, Mary E. 7, Margaret L. 4
SPEAK?, George 24*
STEWART, Joseph 17*

Schedule Page 5

SMITH, Hannah 33, Jasper 35, Robert 23, Benjamin 21, Abraham 17, William 11, Hannah 9, Martha 14
FARROW, George 56, Delila 35, William 14, Samuel 10, George 6, Emaly 3
SMITH, Andrew 33, Margaret 21, Emina 6/12
MCFARLAND, Sandusky? 33, Mary 30, W. H. 11 (m), J. E. 8 (m), J. R. 6 (m), H. D. 5 (m), Warren 2
HARBAUGH, Casper 39*, Catharine 35, Martha E. 4, William 1, Catharine 75, Lewis 55, Elisbeth 56
MARSHAL, John A. 23*
JACOBS, Sally A. 18*, Flavina 1
MCCAMPBELL, James 45, Andrew 12, James 10, Susan 8, Jane 6, Mary E. 4, Eliza 1
SAFFOON, Richard 45, Lucretia 43, William 21, J. E. 17 (m), Sarah 15, Elira 10, Delila 8, Manerva 5
CROW, Eliza 46*, Mragaret 22, Elizabeth 19, John 17
MCCUNE?, George 25*, Zerelda 23, Joseph 22
DAVIS, C. C. 26 (m)*, Mary 24
TRUS, Phebe 20*
MARES, James 35, Lucinda 34, Martha 7, William 9, George 2
ALLISON, George W. 36*, Jane R. 38, Eleanor 6, Susan 4, James 2
RICE, Charles 18*
WILSON, Bazel D. 35, Rachael 70, Mary 36, Mary J. 9
TODHUNTER, Parker E. 52*, Catharine 52, Jacob F. 30, Robert P. 23, Edwin 18, Ryland 11
VARBLE, Mary 23*
RYLAND, Edwin 12*
CILE, John J. 28*

Schedule Page 6

BARNET, Elizabeth 50, Edwin 23, Martha 17, Victoria 10, Laura 8
YOUNG, William D. 53*, Elizabeth 75
JETER, Elizabeth 34*, John 6, Leonard 6
TAYLOR, Parker 54, Sarah 49, Rebecca 15, George B. 14, Layfayett 11, Elijah 6
TAYLOR, Timier? 26 (m), Jane 21, Margaret 2, William 3/12
SHERLEY, Elijah 39, Elira J. 30, Sarah E. 6, Alvisa 3, Margaret 2
HINES, Jonathan 50*, Ann 45, Margaret 17, Amanda 14, John 1
MESSICK, Manuel 16*

1850 Census Jessamine County Kentucky

ZIMERMAN, Martin 23, Mildred 49, Mary 22, E. A. 19 (m), William 16, Julia 14, Daniel 12, Luann 10, Lucy 7, M. P. 4 (m)
LOWEN, John 76*, Sarah 66
BOURNE, Sarah 7*
MESSICK, Jacob 52, Ann 44, Mary A. 24, Elizabeth 22, William 20, Thomas 17, Emanuel 14, Mathew 13, J. P. 10 (m), Sarah 8, Ann 2
DENIS, David 24, Martha A. 26, Elira H. 1, Mary A. 14
SMITH, Robert 47, Mary 32, John 8, Mary E. 4, James L. 9/12
MITCHELL, George S. 37, Mary E. 32, Mary E. 6, Susan A. 4, Mildred 2, John B. 1
WEST, Wilson H. 38, Elizabeth 35, C. R. 13 (m), Fletcher 10, James 8, Henry 7, Thomas E. 2, Minia? 55 (B), Fanny 20 (B), Martha 7 (B), Hetty 24 (B), Thomas 6 (B)

Schedule Page 7

DUNCAN, William 62*, Nancy 39, Robert 23, Benjamin 21, Charles 29, Sarah 25, Mary A. 14
BLACKFORD, Thomas 13*
BURCH, Ezekiel 40, Roda 34, Mary A. 10, Richard M. 6, Elizabeth 4, William 42
SPRAGGINS, Margaret 31, Stephen 10, William 8, Jesse 6, Joseph 3
CLEMENTS, William 32, Melvina D. 21, Elizabeth 2/12
SALLEE, Henry M. 25, Susan J. 19, Squire J. 6/12
MARTIN, Rebecca 53, Eliza 20, John W. 3
LUSK, Ellen 57*
WELCH, Matilda 22*, Sally 2
DILLON, Elizabeth 65*
BALL, Margaret 58, Charles P. 22, Mary Ann 21, Sally J. 6/12
KERBY, Atlantic O 64 (f)
MCMURTRY, John 23*, Martha 25
SPARKS, Moroe 10 (m)*, Eudora 8, Louisa 5
BURCH, Nancy 64, Cortney L. 21 (m)
BODINE, Matilda 53?, John 23, William 23, James 21, Jorden 20, Jane 17, Martha A. 9
MUIR, Samuel 49, Susanah 40, Elijah 16, Lavina 10
MURPHY, William 27, Athaline 29, Jordon 3, Sarah E. 1, Lindsey 1
HAMBRICK, Green 28, Martha 27, Nancy J. 6, Ann M. 1
HAMBRICK, Thomas 31*, Frances 26, H. H. 11 (m), Mary A. 8, John T. 6, James A. 5, Jane E. 3, Frances W. 2
JACOBS, Mathew 63*
SPARKS, Isaac 44, Mary A. 41, Joseph 19, J. C. 17 (m), J. N. 14 (m), E. R. 11 (m), J. S. 6 (m), John W. 3 (m), T. T. 1 (m)

Schedule Page 8

NEWLAND, Richard T. 26, Philadelphia 21, Roland 3, Thomas 1
BOURNE, Elijah 80
HUNTER, J. H. 27 (m), Er_lla 23 (f), George W. 5, Eudora 1
BOURNE, Davis 36, Mary Ann 33, Huldah 13, Francis 10, Nancy 7, Mary 5, M. 2 (f)
WATERS, Harry 43, Paulina 43, Madison 16, George 12, Neplian 10, Harvey 5, William 1, Prusilla 17, Mary 14, Ann 8, Sarah 6

1850 Census Jessamine County Kentucky

ALLEN, George W. 44, Eliza S. 42, Mary E. 14, Sarah Ann 12, John H. 10, Richard M. 9, Hugh G. 6, Samuel P. 4, George W. 3?, Susan E. 38
HAWKINS, Benjamin 38, Catharine 35, James 2, John 3/12
CAMPBELL, Lucy M. 50*
YOUNG, Sally A. 13*, Lucy M. 11, Parthina 46
GREAG, James M. 28, Samuel M. 5, Martha 24, James M. 1
BAXTER, John J. 39*, Susan 23, James 3, Emely 2, James M. 26
CRAVEN, Elizabeth 62*
SIMPSON, Samuel 60, James 50, Robert 21
BIBB, Agnes 60, William M. 31
PERRY, John jr. 32, Elizabeth 30, William 1
BRYANT, Ruben 31, Elizabeth 26, Ann 6, John H. 1
BOURNE, David A. 35, Casander 34, John M. 10, C. P. 8 (m), S. M. 4 (m)
DAVIS, A. F. 27 (m)*, Mary 27, Henrietta 8, Garret 5, Laura 2
BURCH, Catharine 65*, Henry 30
ASHFORD, Joseph 18*
CONNER, Malinda 54, Mary C. 20, Margaret 16

Schedule Page 9

HAWKINS, James 44, Mary 38, Josey 18 (f), Mary A. 16, Thomas E. 13, Strother 10
DOWNING, Fanny 46, Susanah 68, James 18, Sarah E. 15
MCCONNELL, Mary 2_, Jemima 26
MEREDITH, William 38*, Mary E. 40, Mary V. 10, Phebe A. 8, N. B. 6 (m), William P. 1/12
BRAY, Robert J. 20*, Richard L. 18
BURCH, Robert 32, Mary J. 29, James S. 12, Frances A. 7
NETHERLANG, Theadocia 80
SANDERS, S. B. 38 (m)*, Phebe 36, C. B. 10 (m), Mary S. 9, Henry C. 7, Lochy V. 4, Arrena 2, George S. 2/12
BROWN, Martin 21*
MESSICK, John 38, Richard M. 15, John 10, Tilford 8, Hetty J. 6, James 3, Thomas F. 10/12
WALLER, Stephen 38, Malinda B. 34, Benjamin F. 12, Eliza F. 10, Edmund 25
GRIMES, B. R. 37 (m), Hannah M. 31, James S. 9, John W. 7, Charles M. 5, Thomas E. 3, George A. 1
PRICE, Klebar F. 43 (m), Elizabeth M. 41, Ezra R. 18, William H. 11, Lewis S. 8
YOUNG, Lidia 76*, Minor 43
EVANS, James 4*
GIBNEY, Hinton 26, Armasinda 18, Thomas C. 1
PHELPS, Athony 58*, Elizabeth 56, William C. 30, Samuel 28, Richard S. 21, N. B. 25 (m), Anthony 16, Edwin 13, Sarah E. 18, Rebecca 9
BROSIN, Rebecca P. 54*
JOHNSON, Benjamin 67, Phebe 38, Martha 22, Benjamin D. 19
DOUGLASS, William 85, Elizabeth 80, Keelin 47 (m), Adaline 36

Schedule Page 10

MARTIN, Wilson 36*, Mary A. 30, James T. 10, John M. 7, George F. 5, Benjamine L. 2, Lucy 11, Frances E. 8

1850 Census Jessamine County Kentucky

PEAK, James F. 18*
BIBB, James 51, Elizabeth 48, Robert 18, Richard 13, Rowland 9
DOUGLASS, John 49, Mary A. 21, Margaret 20, Adeline 17, Judith A. 6, Alfred R. 16, Elias 14, George W. 13, John M. 10
NEWMAN, George 20, Sarah A. 18
WILSON, Roda 44, Elizabeth A. 22, Mary Ann 18
FRANKUM, _____ 45 (m)*, Frances A. 34
HARVEY, Sarah A. 16*, John A. 14, Robert 7
GRAY, William 41*, Elizabeth 45, George P. 10, Benjamin F. 7
NEWMAN, Robert 29*
STAFFORD, William 33*, Matilda 33
COOK, R. P. 1 (m)*
NEWMAN, Edmund 27, Euphea 27, George T. 5, James W. 4, Z. T. 2 (m)
JACKSON, Isham 60*, Elira __, Ashford 30, Lavina 2
NEWMAN, Sarah T. 13*, Mary E. 1/12
SMITH, Elira A. 24*, Olonzo 6, Quintila A. 5, Charles E. 3, Sarah E. 10/12
STAFFORD, Isabella 78, Jerman 28, Elizabeth 32
CARROL, Richard H. 39, Rebecca 26, James W. 4, Samuel E. 43, Lucinda G. 24, Joseph B. 1, John H. 2/12
MILLER, Allen A. 51, Susan 49, Daries 28 (m), Spicea 19 (f), Ann 11, James A. 13, Sarah 8, Mary 4, Allen 2, Mary E. 1
EASLEY, Obediah 55, Mary 49, Emeline 27, Eliza J. 24, Mary A. 16, Elizabeth 27

Schedule Page 11

DAVIS, William 49*, Martha 46, Thomas A. 18, Elizabeth M. 17, William 15, Robert 13, John P. 12, Ambros L. 9
RICKITS, Martha 90*
SCRUGHAM, Clabourn 47, Sarah 40, Mary 20, Virgsilla 18, Joseph 16, Sanford 14, George 13, Dicy C. 10, Elizabeth 8, Jackson 4
DOOMES, James F. 43, Elizabeth 24, Almeda 9, Jerman 6, Polly A. 3, Sarah M. 1
DAVIS, A. P. 38 (m), Martha 34, Mary E. 12, O. M. 9 (m), July A. 6, James E. 4, Thomas H. 2, Sarah H. 1
HARRIS, Bright B. 27, Ruben B. 24, J. W. 20? (m), H. R. 20 (m)
FOSTER, Robert P. 22*, Mary 18
SINCLAIR, Amanda 12*
BOURNE, Roger P. 22*
STAFFORD, John W. 18*
ARNOLD, Samuel 53*, Elizabeth 25, Sophia 16, John 14, George 13, Mary 11, Almira 8
SPEARS, George C. 52*, Ann 49
MASTERS, Henry W. 26, Sarah E. 22, Mildred D. 5, Ruben 1, John H. 3, Thomas E. 3/12
BOURNE, Isaac 34*, Jane 20
BALLARD, Paulina 40*, John W. 17, David T. 15, Paulina 12, Isaac H. 6
MCCABE, Hugh T. 39*, Martha 45, James A. 14
RICHERSON, James 26*
WILSON, Thomas 23*
MOORE, Morang? 45 (m)*, Dianah 33, Margaret 16, Mary J. 14, Martha M. 12, Nancy E. 9, Elizabeth J. 7

1850 Census Jessamine County Kentucky

WATSON, William 20*
BROWN, George 31*, Ann 23, Morer? 5 (m), Andrew H. 3, George J. 1
GLEAN, Samuel 23*

Schedule Page 12

GREEN, Alexander 36, Nanc 26, Harrison Ann 12, John 8, Emine? J. 6, Moses 4, Alexander 3, Catharine 1
BROWN, George J. 65, Catharine W. 46, Mary H. 15, William 12, Sally 9
NAVE, Jonathan 51*, Maranda 46, John L. 20, Jacob 18, Huldah J. 15, Amanda 14, James M. 13, Michael H. 11, Virginia 9
SPRINGER, Rice 34*
HOOVER, George D. 25*, Amadna B. 22, Catharine B. 2
LAND, William S. 25*
HOOVER, Catharine 47, David E. 22, Samuel T. 20, Woodson D. 16, William R. 11, Jacob F. 9, Catharine E. 6
WILEY, Mathew 71, Mary 64, W. F. 25 (m), Matilda 26
HULET, Allen 43, Emily 39, Edmon 22
HOCKERSMITH, David 64, Susan 45, E. C. 16 (m), Sarah 15
BALLARD, James L. 24, Catharine 19, Dove H. 1/12 (f)
ARNOLD, Reuben 40, Luiza J. 30, Jane E. 10, John W. 8, David 7, Susan 5, Lucy 3, Hudson 1
HORINE, Henry 75, Esther 77, Christopher 31, Francis 18
MILLER, William 47*, Mahala 36, Mason 7?, Jesse 14, Robert 10, W. B. 7 (m), J. W. 1 (m)
LAWS, Welcome 35 (m)*, Eveline 22
FORD, Daniel 34, Sarah 30, Edward H. 8, Cordelia L. 6, Josephene 5
MCCLURE, R. S. 59 (f)*, Sarah B. 22
STURGUS, John J. 26*
BURNAUGH, Sarah 56
TAPP, Mildred 70*, William 41
GRAY, Emily 28*, Lewis M. 6
COLEMAN?, Charles 34*

Schedule Page 13

SOPER, James __, Elizabeth 41, Nancy 18, James R. 14, William 17, Benjamin 12, David 10, John E. 8, Oromandle? 5 (m), Amos B. 1
JOHNSON, Jeptha 46, America 44, Martha 21, William S. 19, Margaret 17
SIMMONS, Benjamin 50
HUNTER, Joseph 73, James 52, Squire 47, David 38, Robert 35, Sydna 30 (m), Amadna 24, Sarah E. 3
ARNOLD, David 62*, Mary 43, Catharine B. 18, Mildred 16
LOGAN, James B. 28*, Lucy R. 20, Ann M. 3/12
ARNOLD, Joshua 26, Margaret 18
HUNTER, Mesy? 40 (m)*, Lucy 38, Sary A. 18 (f), Lucy Jane 14, Catharine E. 12, James A. 10, Robert 8, Serena 6, Riland D. 4, Nancy A. 2, Mary E. 3/12
WOOD, Sarah 38*
HUNTER, Samuel 35, Julia 25, Mary E. 10
HUNTER, Ellen 80*, Mary 56, Hannah 45

1850 Census Jessamine County Kentucky

GIBNEY, An 48*
FAIN, John 24*, Mary E. 22
ENGLISH, William 46*, Sarah 34, Lafayett 15, Columbus 12, Martha 11, Elizabeth 9, Mathew 7, W. T. 5 (m), Cintha A. 3, Leroy M. 1
SPARKS, Mary 20*
DAVIS, Joshua 38, Nancy 32, William 12, Margaret 9, Greenbery 7, Zach T. 1
HAMBRICK, John 23, Amanda 25, James L. 2, W. W. 6/12 (m)
FAIN, Mastin 25, Mary 19, Seminda 5, William 3
WILLIS, Green B. 39, Catharine A. 37, Nancy 16, Letty 14, Mary J. 12, Juda A. 10, Mastin F. 8, Angeline 6, Malinda 4, Thomas H. 1

Schedule Page 14

HOLLYDAY, Samuel 36*, Elizabeth 36, Catharine 9, Greenup H. 7, John J. 6
BURNS, Elizabeth 76*
HAGER, Polly 41, James T. 17, Matha 13, John F. 8, E. H. 6 (f), Ann E. 4
LAND, Fountain 35*, Martha 30, Mary A. 2
WILLIS, Elizabeth 16*, Henry 58
HAGER, Daniel 20*
HILL, John 35, Saly 34, James J. 15, Nancy J. 13, Eda 10, Elizabeth 8, Henry 6, John T. 3, Gerard 10/12, Roda J. 12
SANDERS, David 46, Rebecca 33, Oliver J. 13, James W. 11, Amanda E. 9, Peter F. 7, Judithann 5, David C. 3, Rebecca D. 1
MASTERS, Nancy 56*, John J. 20, Ellis Ann 16, William C. 14
DANIEL, Harrison 52*, Lucy A. 46, William H. 23, Richard P. C. 13, Fanny L. 19, Lucy C. 12, Eleanor E. 11, Sarah H. 10, Cath. P. 6
WILMORE, James 66, Susan 48, George 17, Mary R. 20
TAUL, John M. 34, Tabitha 28, Margaret 7, B. F. 4 (m), Nancy J. 2
SPIRES, G. P. 45 (m)*, M. 15 (f), F. 11 (f), Green 9, Ann T. 15, Walter 6, Cashus M. C. 2, Zephaniah 56
GLAZE, Bazel 32*, Joseph 9, Elizabeth 27
BROWN, Moroe? 35 (m), Sarah E. 22, F. C. 8 (f), Elizabeth M. 3
SHREVE, John M. 39, Susanah 27, Juliet A. 6, Tolbert T. 2
BLUNT, Charles W. 17

Schedule Page 15

MAYES, Samuel 58*, Ann 50, George Ann B. 18
REYNOLDS, Elizabeth 50*, Samuel R. 11
SCOTT, Richard 25*
DUNCAN, Alexander 61*, Hannah 30
SANDERS, Charles 22*, Z. C. 17 (f)
DEBOE, Martin 52, Lidia 44, Maltha E. 13
WILMORE, John W. 39*, Maranda S. 30
BALLARD, John P. 13*
WILMORE, Thomas D. 37, Permelia 34
FAIN, R. C. 30 (m)*, Mary 22
WILLMORE, O. A. 32 (m)*, Isabella 28

1850 Census Jessamine County Kentucky

WELCH, John C. 27*, Susan W. 22, W. M. 7/12 (m)
MCBRYOR, Polly 47*, F. S. 25 (m)
ALLCORN, James 18*
DANIEL, Ellen 10*
COSBY, Edward 42, Mary J. 22, Eliza 4, Margaret 5/12?, Sally 5/12
PORTWOOD, Ambrose 19, Louisa 19, Armstead 8/12
HOVINE, Isaac? 53*, Catharine 23, Eliza 21, Andrew 18, Margaret 11
BOURNE, Catharine 9*
WELCH, Samuel R. 31*, Catharine C. 24, James A. 2, Elizabeth 30, Sarah F. 15, Alexandra 72
SHELY, Nancy 40*
WILMORE, Elizabeth 7*
BURCH, James J. 45, Nancy B. 38, Ann E. 15, Martha 2
WILMORE, James C. 40*, Mary A. 39, James A. 18, Nancy B. 16, Henry F. 14, Robert S. 12, Ann J. 10, Mary D. 8, James W. 6
OLDS, Tucker W. 25*
GREEN, Thomas 52*, Frances 61
SCANLAND, Matilda 22*, Charles 16
WELCH, George W. 30
WELCH, Nathaniel 68, Nathaniel jr. 29, Mary C. 25, Sarah 4, Thomas 2, Isabella 3/12
HUNTER, John 48
NORTON, R. H. 28 (m), Ann M. 26, Margaret 4, J. R. 6/12 (m)
JACOBS, Mary 66, Oliver 19

Schedule Page 16

JACOBS, Lewis 35, Mary 38, America 14, Elizabeth 10, Charles A. 8, Amanda 6, Nancy 2
REYNOLDS, John M. 43, F. E. 22 (f), T. E. 2 (f), M. D. 1 (m)
SALE, John 36*, Lucy A. 27, Mary E. 2
MCCABE, William 22*
DICKERSON, Newton 38*, Elizabeth 35, Mary E. 12, Malinda 10, Matilda 6, Woodson 2, Woodson 29, William 21
FUNK, James M. 23*
CARROL, Thomas 37, Mary 25, James C. 8, Eliza A. 7, Nancy J. 4
JACOBS, Andrew 34, Lucy J. 34, Anderson 5, Maryann 3, John 1
RAGSDALE, Clifton 24, Caroline 18, Edger L. 1/12
CREATH, Jacob 73, Mildora? 70, Shaline 9 (f), Alberty 7 (f)
MCAFEE, Allen L. 25, Elizabeth R. 22, Archibald 1/12
HOVINE, Jacob 34, Malinda 34, Sarah V. 7, Catharine 5, Henrietta 4, Mary L. 1, Joseph L. 3/12
ARNSPIGER, Samuel 39, Sally 37, George H. 13, Mitten M. 9, Margaret 5, Jacob 3, Emely C. 1
HOVINE, Joshua 40*, Margaret 32, Mary A. 5, Thomas J. 3, Milton 2
ROBERTS, James 23*, Nancy 18
PATTERSON, William 52*, Martha 52, Sarah 1_, Virginia 14
RICHERSON, Moses 20*, Susan 17
WALKER, Thomas L. 25*
FAIN, Thomas 17*
SWITZER, Moses 27, Margaret 19, William 1/12
MASTERS, John 37, Elizabeth 31, William 9, Joseph 7, James 5, Gabriel 2

1850 Census Jessamine County Kentucky

Schedule Page 17

MASTERS, Moses 39*, Frances 37, John S. 15, William 12, Nancy J. 9, Moses 3, Mary F. 1
STANLY, Nancy 56*
HACKET, Allen 46, Matilda 41, Humfrey 20, John 18, Malinda 16, Charles 12, Mary A. 10, Allen 8, S. M. 6 (f), Matilda 3/12
PARMER, Lavina 83, Agnes 31
HUNTER, William 66, Elizabeth 60, James 23, Charles 13
HAMBRICK, John 60, Elizabeth 58, Malinda 14
HUNTER, John P. 38, Eda 27, Allen 12, Jane 10, Catharine 8, Margaret 7?, James 5, John 2
LAND, Thomas 66, Jane 55
BOURNE, Francis 42*, Elizabeth 38, Jane 13, John B. 8/12
SINCLAIR, Eliza 7*
OWENS, David 38, Sarah 22, Fleming S. 17, Elizabeth 15, John M. 13, James H. 12, Dana L. 9 (m), Milton 7
FISK, Wiley B. 31, July F. 31, Mary E. 15, John R. 10, Wily B. 8, Jams F. 5, July F. 2, Martha C. 3/12
FOSTER, Pleasant 50*, Martha 47, Harriet 13, Franklin 7
MCDAVIS, William 49*
DAVIS, Russel 39*, Jane 24, Charles 5, George 4, Squire 2
CLARK, Thomas 24*, Robert 15
PAGGET, Charlotte 25, Sarah J. 7, Mary F. 1/12
DUNCAN, Charles 36, Lucy J. 23, Joseph 7, Mary 5, Robert 3, Ann 1
WOODARD, Heelery 50 (m), Nancy 42, Frances 15, Jordan 13, Robert 11

Schedule Page 18

WOODARD, Lavina 72, James 30, John 15
SCOTT, Jorden 48*, Margaret 30, George C. 7
WAKE, Celia 51*
HUGGINS, Sarah 26*, Thomas 3, Margaret 2/12
FAIN, Leta 52, Scarlet 26 (m), Lela 22, Thomas 17
NAVE, Elizabeth 72*
BOURNE, Paulina 41*, Harrison 22
SCOTT, Harvey 46, Elizabeth 35, Mary 13, Catharine 11, Arabella 8, John 6, Ann 1
MILLER, Meriman? 45*, Celia 44, Susan 18, Sally 16, William 13, John 11, Catharine 9, Meriman 7, Celia 1
TREADAWAY, Micaga 23*
GRIFFIN, Jasper 66, Catharine 65
GOSS, Robert 36*, Elizabeth 24, Catharine E. 8, Thomas H. 1
BARNETT, Mary E. 2*, John 1/12
VANTRICE, Daniel 45, Mary Ann 42, John 22, C. 19, E. 17 (f), Laura 13, W. H. 10 (m), James M. 6, Emanuel 3, Rosanna 3/12
KNOX, Samuel __*, Elizabeth 54, Thomas 29
POOR, Mary W. 20*, Allice 1
ALCORN, John 49*, Betsy 30, James 16, Willis 14, Sarah 13, John 9, Henley 7, Mary A. 2, Emely 3/12
BARNETT, John 7*, William 4

1850 Census Jessamine County Kentucky

CARTER, Lewis 46?, Emely 35, William 12, Elizabeth 10, Lewis 9, Charles 7, Anderson 5, John 3, Allen 1
BARNETT, Dudley 35, Frances 27, Daniel 19, James 9, A. J. 7 (f), Jesse 5, Robert 4

Schedule Page 19

BOURNE, George 34*, Sally A. 22, Stephen 4, Mary F. 2, Joseph 2/12
GRANT, Ellen 16*
WATTS, William 29*, Elizabeth 23, Charles 9, John B. 7, Susan 2
WEAVER, Betcy J. 23*
GOFOURTH, Thomas 23, Berzilla 23, Amanda 6/12
GOFOURTH, Sarah 53, Milton 17, David 15
BROWN, Mary J. 39*, Henrietta 13, Magy V. 12 (f), Victora 10, Margaret 6, Thomas J. 3
HARRIS, Nathaniel 45*, Margaret A. 33, Mary P. 1
CLARK, William 45*, Margaret 40
TUCKER, Charles 28*
MARSHALL, A. K. 40 (m)*, Lucy 35
MCDOWEL, Elizabeth __*, Lucian 24
PAYNE, Charles F. 28*, Elizabeth 20
MAYES, Samuel 25*
FRITSLAN, Joseph 21*
HOWARD, Robert S. 23, Lavina 18, Eliza 50
MACKE, John B. 40, Agnes 28, Joseph 9, Elizabeth 7, Francis H. 5, William 11/12
GLASS, Casper 43*, Elizabeth 44, John 11, William 9, Margaret 7, Mary 4, Ann E. 1
ECHHELA?, Barnet*
WILLIAMSON, Thomas B. 30, Mary J. 29, Josephine 10, Sarah 7, Mary 3
HARRIS, John 58, Dica 60, William 28, Emely 20, Susan A. 17, Henry J. 25
LAND, John 29*, Sally 28, Mathew 7, Chary 1 (f)
WOODARD, David 19*
ARNSPIGER, Delila 35*
HOOVER?, Sarah 13*
DAVIS, Michael 32, Hetty 32, Hetty J. 13, John W. 11, Sarah E. 8, James O. 6, Michael 4, Joseph 2, Thomas 1/12

Schedule Page 20

SMITH, Mark A. 38, Sarah 33, William 12, Ann 10, Thomas 5, Henry 1/12
STIPE, Margaret 37*, Mary 12, Margaret 9, John 8, Samuel 1, Frances 2/12
LIVINGSTON, Betcy 80*
RUTLEY, Phillip 77*, Mary 38
THOMAS, Josephine 7*
LINDSEY, Harvey 50, Mary A. 34, Sarah J. 16, Amanda R. 14, Joseph M. 11, William 3, America 1/12
DELPH, James 30, Delphia 26, Martha 6, William 3
SHORROW, William 24, Amanda 22
BLAKEMAN, James 25, Almeda 19
FAIN, Larkin 41*, Zerada 35, Mitchel 13, Frances 10, Georg 7, Wilson 4, Tilford 3, William 1
BURTON, Pharis 34*, Lydia 18

1850 Census Jessamine County Kentucky

HAMILTON, William 25, Margaret 21, Albert 1
EASLEY, Josiah 30, Martha J. 27, Sarah A. 8/12
MAYES, William 53, Elizabeth 36, Nelson 8, Frances 7, Martha 6, Arkansas 2 (f)
KNIGHT, Francis 35, Elizabeth 41, Nancy 14, Robert 12, Elizabeth 10, Margaret 9
BACK, Enoch 37, Mahala 21, Mary 1, Jeremiah 3/12
WALLACE, William 34*, Martha J. 37, Elizabeth 2, Mary C. 1
UNDERWOOD, John 18*
FERREL, Washington 35, Leanner 37, John C. 5
GROW, Daniel 25, Armela 16
MCCONNEL, Andrew 54*, Nancy 43, James 24, George 19, Andrew 17
OWEN, Amanda J. 18*, Ann 70
POTTS, Ann 69, Nepoleon 18

Schedule Page 21

SHERROW, Isaac 53*, Polly 53, Martha 18, Isaac 15, Michael 13, James 10
SEWEL, Sally Ann 30*, Beraman 9, Josiah 7, James W. 5, George W. 3
SHERROW, Jefferson 23, Sarah 19
DEAN, Harrison 38, Nancy Ann 30, Merel J. 12, James H. 10, William H. 9, John A. 6, Mary E. 4, A. M. 1
PRESTON, Richard 34, Susan A. 25, Samuel T. 8, Pinkney 7 (m), Mary D. 5, Lewis M. 2, William W. 4/12
DICKENSON, Jeremiah 74
SWITZER, Samuel 60, Polly 57, Lidia 14, Samuel 10
SHARP, Alexander 22, Mary J. 22, Mary 5/12, Lewisa 18
WALTERS, William 62*, Ruth 64, Rachael 39, Daniel 32
HUNTER, Ellen 35*
GAYHART, Daniel 49*, Relinda 29, Lucinda 12, William 9, Elizabeth 5, Relinda 3, Daniel 7/12
SWITZER, Alexander 20*
PRESTON, Jilson 28*, Amanda 24, Grattan 4 (m), Granville 1, William 3/12
WALTERS, Ann 28*
SWITZER, David 22, Catharine 27, Nancy 5, Mary E. 4, William R. 2, Franklin 1, William 28, Cintha A. 28, Sarah 6
COLEMAN, William 37, Mary 37, Martha 16, George A. 10, JEremiah 7
WEAVER, Catharine 55?
SAGACY, Jefferson 37*, Nancy 36, James F. 15, William 14, Charles W. 7, Harrison 5, Margaret 4, Sarah 3
WALLACE, Rebeca 30*
CAMERON, Ruth 70, William 24, Ruth 22

Schedule Page 22

SAGACY, Federick 74*
WATTS, George 23*
SAGACY, Jacob 50, Sarah 40, George 20, John 15, Eliza 16, Daniel 13, Federic 9, Henry 7, Sarah 5, Margaret 2, Jacob 1/12
LAND, Jackson 32, Elizabeth 34, Ruth 13, William 9, Mary E. 7, James W. 5, Henry M. 1

1850 Census Jessamine County Kentucky

CAMERON, America 17
SAGACY, Henry 46, Nancy 44, Federic 21, George 17, David 14, James 12, G. B. 10 (m), Henry 8, Sarah E. 6, J. 4 (m), Robert 1
PORTWOOD, John 63, Rebecca 52, Dudley 26, Louisa 23, Mary 17, SArah 12, John 10
PORTWOOD, Siquir? 31 (m), Eliza 20
ROBERTS, Thomas 23, Polly 23, Ann M. 1
HUNTER, Henry 48, Malinda 20, Fanna J. 17, Margaret 15, Paulina 13, Ann M. 11, Henry 9, Levina 6
HUNTER, Nathan 50, Atha 45, Mildred 12, Armidia 14, Emely 16
GIBNEY, William 27, Frances 24, Mary E. 5, William O. B. 2
HUNTER, Martin 20, Mary 18, Martha 1/12
UNDERWOOD, Gerret 26*, Bashaly 28 (f), Harrison 10, Charles 7, Gustavus 1, George W. 1
MASTERS, Sally 46*, Joseph 14, John 13, Lewis 11, Garret 22, Sally 22, Seminda 7/12
TAYLOR, Franklin 37, Sophina 28, Leroy 11, John M. 7, William 4, Elizabeth 1

Schedule Page 23

MASSEY, Jefferson 39, Nancy 41, Ruben F. 16, Asa 14, Lucinda 9, Benjamin 7, Sally Ann 1
LAND, Ellen 62*, Leroy 30, John T. 22
ROBERTS, Charles T. 26*
FARRER, Joseph 29, Hester 19, Elizabeth 5/12
HUNTER, Richmond 44, Roda 44, Joseph 20, James C. 15, Roda 14, Richmond 12, Samuel 10, Mary J. 8, William 23, Matilda 20
HUNTER, Thomas 50, Mary 51, James G. 26, Richard 25, Thomas 22, Mary 19, John 17, Jacob 14, William 11, Martin 8
MURPHY, Susanah 46, James 16, Polly 13, Hardin 10, William 8, Sally 6, Betcy 4, Fanny 3
STINNETT, King A. 40*, Huldah 46, John W. 20, Elizabeth 17, Harrison 15, Adison 13, Charles 10, Ruben 7, Michael 4
MURPHY, John 2*
MURPHY, Lindsey 23, Susanah 27, John 1
STINNETT, Lindsey 56 (m), Susanah 59, James 25, Lucinda 23
STINNETT, Charles 29, Lucinda 70, Martha A. 29, Mary E. 5, Louisa 4, Jackson 2, Mahala 9/12, Anthony 20
FAIN, Thomas 40, Lucinda 25, Sally 8, John 6, William 2, James 2/12
FAIN, Lindsey 21 (m), Lucinda 18
WALKER, John 50, Matilda 38, William 17, Elizabeth 15, Samuel 13, Martha 14, Pollyann 8, July A. 4, Susan 3, Easter 1

Schedule Page 24

HAGER, Moses 46*, Elizabeth 50, Tempa 21, David 18, Sherod 17, Elizabeth 14, Lidia J. 13, Letty M. 8, Parris 6
REYNOLDS, Catharine 69*
REYNOLDS, John 43, Thomas 16, James 12, Nancy 40, John 14, Fanny 10, Prosaphine 8, William 4, Moses 5, Dudley 1
REYNOLDS, William 48, Mary 50, Paulina 18, Jefferson 21, Willis 16, Lindsey 14 (m), Joseph 12, Levy 11, Nancy 8
ROBERTS, John 49, Lucinda 38, William 20, John 17, Fountain 15, Ellen 11, Mesa 8 (m)

1850 Census Jessamine County Kentucky

STINNETT, Lindsey 25 (m), Emily J. 28, Leanah 3, Martha J. 1
FAIN, John 35, Susan 28, Frances 8, Catharine 6, John B. 4, Mastin 1
FAIN, Price 43, Keziah 40, Larkin 15, Scarlet 13 (m), Magaret 10, Ellen 6, William 3
TAYLOR, John 49, Mary Ann 22, Marion 8, Mary E. 2
STINNETT, Jackson 35, Mahala 35, Emily 16, James 14, Lusetta 12, Mary 10, Mourel? 7 (m), Elizabeth 6, Jackson 3, Sally A. 6/12
REYNOLDS, Thomas 41*, Nancy 32, Araminta 16, Elizabeth 11, F. M. 6 (f), Henry J. 1
MASSEY, Richard 45*, Matilda 45, Caroline 9
FISHER, Isaah 30*, Lydia 36
STINNETT, Mary T. 4*
BAKER, Benedic? 22, Nancy 18

Schedule Page 25

REYNOLDS, Henry 76, Elizabeth 76, Polly 53, Levy 17, Morten 12
WILEY, Henry 25, Lucinda 21
REYNOLDS, Moses 41, Araminta 40, William 12, Elizabeth 10, Oskar 8, Nancy 6, Thomas 4, Mary L. 2, Sarah G. 1
REYNOLDS, Henry 50, Patcey 46, Eliza B. 16, Susan 14, Sulada 12, John 15, William 6, Louisa 4
HAGER, Thomas 21, Mary Ann 22
WILLIS, Hezekiah 32, Martha 24, Margaret 9, William 7
BRUMFIEL, Joel 50, Roda 50, Jane 20, Luisa 11
HILL, Green B. 26*, Mary 19, Nancy E. 1
PRUETT, Tamor? 69 (f)*
ALLISON, George 23*, Mahala 27
FAIN, Bailey 16*
STINNETT, Rubin 31, Juliann 34, Morton 9, John 7, Mary 5, William 4, Luticia 2, Susan 4/12
TREADAWAY, Silas 21, Lavina 18
REYNOLDS, William 37, Polly 34, Absalum 11, Harrison 9, Lindsey 7 (m), Hugh 4, A. R. M. 1 (m)
STINNETT, Reuben 37, Nancy 27, Henry 14, Catharine 13, Isaah 10, Charles B. 8, George 2
LOWIN, James 54, Elizbeth 39, Mary 15, Sarah 14, Chilton 12, Ambrose 10, Margaret 8, Johnson 6, Catharine 4, James 1
DAVIS, Absalum 40, Jane 37, Matilda 15, William 13, Frances 9, Mary J. 7, Sarah E. 4, Gabriel M. 1

Schedule Page 26

CHRISMAN, Henry 50, Margaret 43, Conrad 20, Ann 13, Clarissa 10, Joseph 7, Zachry 3
FALKNER, George 54, Margaret 50, George 23, Bethy 19, John 17, Mildred 15, Martha 13, Joseph 11
HOLLIDAY, Harrison 40*, Matilday 40
WATERS, Hetta 20*, Matilda 16, Sarah J. 13
PRICE, Daniel B. 61*, Mary J. 46, Samuel 22, Daniel 12, Eliza V. 10, Robert 7, Margaret 3, Matthew B. 28
ROBERTSON, George 21*
COONS, John F. 35*
WHEELER, Thomas 32, Mary 20, Sodinky? 2 (f), Susanah 9/12
ALEXANDER, Thomas 70*, Frances 56, Susan 22
WEBSTER, Thomas J. 9*, Francis J. 7, Kentucky 5

1850 Census Jessamine County Kentucky

BAKER, Jonathan 57, Margaret 53, Benjamin 25, John A. 20, William 18, Jonathan 15, George W. 12, Margaret E. 13
NORTHERN, James H. 25, Nightingale 24, Robert B. 1?
WHEELER, James 29, Manerva 28, Mary 8, Thomas 6, John 3, Amanda 8/12
LAND, Joseph 33, Mary 30, Almarinda 10, Sarah A. 9, Willis 7, John J. 2, James H. 18
BRUNER, Levi 37, Nancy 24, Mary 6, Levina 4, America 1
SANDERS, Mary 34, William 16, Sarah 14, Susan 10, Francis 7, Mary 5
HUNTER, William 27, Nancy 18
PEEL, William 28, Betcy Ann 23, James T. 5, Margaret 3, Frances 2

Schedule Page 27

HOOVER, Peter 61*, Eve 60, William 25, Sophina 17, Malinda 15, Mary 32, Josephine 13, Louisa 9, John L. 6
STIPE, James T. 28*
SHARP, Thomas 48*, Mary 34, Frances 12, Willie? 9 (f), Harvey 6, Mary E. 3
BARNETT, Elizabeth 58*
BLAKEMAN, James 48, Frances 44, James 16, William 12, Martha 10, Emely 8, George C. 6
WATERS, Buford 23, Polly 23, Perry 3, Levisa 1, William 20
GRANT, Abraham 29*, Levisa 28, Mary P. 6, James 4, Stephen 1
RHIRNENS?, Gilla 16*
NEWLAND, William 38, Arthusa 32, Mary F. 7, Elizbeth 5, Squire R. 2
BAYLEY, Daniel 31, Delila 24, William 4, Mahala 2, John L. 5/12
TATIM, George 28, America 27, Lucinda 20
RUE, William 40, Lucinda 38, Nancy J. 10, Athalona 7, Mary T. 6, Josiah 3
COLEMAN, Francis 19, Sarah 19
WILLIS, Benjamin 50*, Lucinda 42?, Andrew 21
WATERS, Thomas 26*
REYNOLDS, Joseph 32, Sarah 29, Mary 11, Henry T. 9, William 7, Mahala 5, Frances 1
HOUSE, James 46, Polly 45, Daniel 13, John 11, Samuel 9, Benjamin 7, Hesekiah 2
RUE, Joseph 36, Milly 35, Lewis 13, Joseph 10, Francis 8, William 6, Perpetua 4, Richard 5/12

Schedule Page 28

BURTON, Singleton 36*, Roda 30, Russel 5
UNDERWOOD, Thomas 35*
HILL, Sally 88*
MASTIN, Jackson 26*, Casander 21, John W. 10/12
LEAR, Massa 48 (f)*
LEAR, Henry 57, Mary 19, Caroline 18, Nancy 15, David 14, John 8, William 10, Hebron 6, Lucy E. 3
HOCKER, Jeremiah 29, Elizabeth 30, Mary J. 12, Ann E. 10, Zerada 5, George W. 2, Frances 2, Annetta 1/12
FAIN, Pillard 25, Mary Ann 29, Millerd 4, Frances 1
WALTERS, William 32*, Eliza 31, Alfred 10, Margaret 8, Jackson 7, Nancy E. 5
BRUMFIEL, Elizabeth 35*
MASTERS, George W. 34, Elizabeth 31, Fanny 7, James 4, John T. 2

1850 Census Jessamine County Kentucky

REYNOLDS, John W. 37, Caroline 30, Sarah E. 10, James P. 8, Moses 6, William 3, Lucinda 3, Thersey 1
PEEL, Thomas 60, Margaret 48, James 25, Hugh 22, John 20, Thomas 15, Catharine 14, Margaret 10, George 7
FAIN, Matton 76, Francis 69
FAIN, Hardin 26, Emeline 23, Richard 1
TAYLOR, James 46, Esther 34, Frances 6, Joseph 2
TREADWAY, Hiram 45*, Betcy 44, Daniel 22, Leaty 17 (f), William 12, Barbary 9, Betcy 8, Thomas 3
WILLIS, Leaty 82 (f)*
TAYLOR, Elizabeth 67, Anica 21
MASTERS, James 20, Martha 22, Nancy 65, Patsey 24, Isabinda 9/12

Schedule Page 29

BURCHEL, Daniel 42, Elizabeth 37, Aron 18, Mary 17, Isaac 14, Sarah E. 12, William 9, Eliza 6, Mary J. 4, Sarah J. 3, Josephine 12, Josephine 10/12
MASTERS, Irvin 33?, Rebecca 32
TREADWAY, Francis 35*, Eda 36
HILL, John 12*
TAILOR, John 40, Susan 26, Jane 18, Mary 8, Phebe 5, Rebecca 3, Josephine 3/12
SHORT, James 22, Elizabeth 17, John 7/12
COBBS, Charles 34, Lucinda 31, John P. 9, James M. 7, Panthy 5 (f), Catharine 3, Ambrose 8/12
UNDERWOOD, John 58*, Sally 41, Jorden 22, Wesley 20, Charles 18, Leroy 9
REYNOLDS, Nancy 59*
UNDERWOOD, Emeline 29, Green B. 10, America 7, Sally 5, Samantha 1, Martha 3
FAIN, Mary __, Nancy 25
UNDERWOOD, Russel 27, Mary 20, Celia 6/12
BRUMFIEL, Sarah 65, Vincent 20, Mary 22
WALTERS, Jordon 26, Catharine 23, James 4, Martha E. 6/12, Martha 65
BRUMFIEL, Nelson 31, Martha 30, Zantipa 15, Rebecca 13, Jordon 11, Martha 7, Sarah C. 7, Daniel 5, Levina 2
JACKSON, David 30, America 23, William 1
OVERSTREET, Samuel 23, Martha 21, John 1
POTTS, William 32, Elizabeth 30, Albert 9, Beaty C. 6, Almira 4, Benjamine 1

Schedule Page 30

BLAKEMAN, John 42, Polly 41, Susan 20, America 18, Jincy 16 (f), Aron H. 9, Elizabeth 5, Frances 3
MYERS, William 34*, Jane 30, Ann E. 10, William E. 9, Charles J. 6, Jacob D. 4, David H. 1
HUDSON, Ellen M. 21*, David 22
ROBERTS, Samuel 18*
DUNBAR, George 18*
RICHERSON, Moses 17*
ENGLAND, James 31*
PERRY, Oliver 34, Frances 32, Robert 2, John 1
HAMILTON, Andrew 54*, Mary 46, Martha 15, Allice 13
FOSTER, Leanah 68*

1850 Census Jessamine County Kentucky

HOGAN, William 36, Eleanor 39, Mary J. 16, Elizabeth 15, Sarah E. 13, Rebecca 10, Nancy 8, James 5, Mary 3, Adam 1, Nancy 62
WELCH, Thomas 32*, Elizabeth 26, James 8, George 5, John A. 2
RUCKER, Gideon 24*
DEBOE, Joseph 56, Milly 50, Mary 23, Martha 23, Margaret 23, Jane 19, Fanny 18, Thomas 19, Lauretta 15, Sarah 14, Time? 12 (f), Joseph 10
WALKER, Matthew 73, Mary 53, Henry B. 23, William B. 20, Allexander 17, George B. 15, Elizabeth 13
HAMILTON, Duke _2*, Sarah 41, Margaret 16, James 13, Mary 12, Elizabeth 10, George 8, Richard 5, Sarah 2
KNIGHT, Hardin 32*
HAMILTON, Robert 87, Elizabeth 77
CLARK, Wesley 22, Eliza 22, George 2, Wilson 10/12

Schedule Page 31

PRESTON, Milton 33, lucy 30, Caroline 7, M. M. 5 (m), Francis 5, Eliza 3, Gabriel 2, Sarah 1/12
PRESTON, Lewis 62, Eliza 62
PRESTON, Berryman 30, Matilda 25, Green B. 7, Sarah 5, Eliza 3, Mary L. 1
FERREL, Daniel 74, Elizabeth 70
FERREL, Andrew 25, Susanah 30, James W. 7, Ephram 5, Harvey 2
SACREY, John? 49, Margaret 47, Thomas 21
WALTERS, Thomas 36, Sally A. 28, Serenuda 5
STANLEY, Luke 56*, Tabitha 50, Ellen J. 17, Richard P. 13
GROOMS, John T. 31*, Martha 22
BURCHEL, Aron 19*
GULLY, Mason 30*, Eliza 22, Mary 6, William 4, James 1
PRESTON, Asbury 18*
HILL, George 42, Catharine 41, Malsena 16, Rebecca 13, Sarah 11, Hannah 9, Elizbeth 6, Thomas 4, John P. 9/12
EASLEY, Andrew 29, Malinda 24, George 8/12
MCMANIS, A. W. 52 (m), Agnes 52, James 21, William 17
EASLEY, Andrew 48*, Rachael 45, Elizabeth 22, Eleanor 18, Washington 17, Alford 15, Amos 12, Mary 5
HOOVER, Henry 24*, Katharine 21, Betcy 4/12
QUIMBEY, George 61, Rachael 34, Elizabeth 32, Mary 34, Sarah 24, Frances 22, Ephraim 20
CARTER, Charles 79, Susan 68, Polly 22
MCDONAH, Daniel 66, Sarah 65, Jane 19, Frances 1

Schedule Page 32

BRYANT, John 33*, Martha 34, Thomas 11, George S. 9, John 7, William 5, Oliver 2, William 19
VAUGHN, Arthesa 36*, Elizabeth 1
DUNCAN, Harker 24*, Mary J. 20
BROWN, Samuel 16*
EASLEY, Christopher 54*, Nancy 50, Margaret 20, John 20, Maliza 17, George T. 15, Nancy 12, James 11, Dudley 9, Green B. 5

1850 Census Jessamine County Kentucky

KNIGHT, William 24*, Catharine 25
ROBERTS, Rankin 52, Nancy 42, Susan 17, Mary J. 16, Emely 14, Arabella 12, Florida 10, James 8, William 6, Rankin 4, Nancy 2
BLAKEMAN, Aron 35*, Eliza 32
WHITE, Jane 39*
MCMILLEN, James 14*
WHITE, James 45*
DAVIS, John H. 36*, David N. 25
BOURNE, James D. 12*
WATERS, Thomas 75, Margaret 57
WATERS, Andrew 22, Sally A. 20, Lucinda 1
COLEMAN, J. C. 26 (m)*, Mary 21, Lucretia 2
HILL, Nancy J. 15*
SHARP, Ezekiel 30*, Nancy 27, William 11, Rebecca 9, James 7
WATERS, Thomas 29*
SCOTT, Elizabeth 21*
CARTER, Paschal 37*, Fanny 38, Charles 11, John 9, James 7, Mary 2
TREADWAY, Franky 14 (f)*
CATLET, John 75, Fanny 68, Eliza 38, Betcy 26, Washington 21
WATERS, Thomas 30, Matilda 25, George 7, Campbell 4, Rilly C. 1 (m)
CATLET, Charles 25*, Mary 28, Julia 4, James 1
EDGERTON, Susan 50*
PRESTON, Tabien? 5 (m)*

Schedule Page 33

CARTER, James 29, Jane 31, Martha 3, Zerada 8/12
WOODARD, William 39, Keziah 40, Gabriel 18, Lavina 16, Peter 14, William 12, Alfred 10, Margaret 8, Elizabeth 6, Benjamine 4
SHORT, James M. 22, Elizabeth 17, John 6/12
MURPHY, Stephen 48, Pency 45 (f), Woodson 23, Linda 24, Thomas 16, Sidney 14 (m), Polly 12, Betcy 10, Simeon 8, Siminda 6, Meriman 4, Margaret 2
BRUNER, Frances 71*
SMITH, Moses 35*, Elizabeth 25
WOODARD, William 7*
PRICE, Littleton T. 37, Margaret 37, James C. 13, Mary E. 12, Josiah 10, Thomas J. 7, Rebecca 5, Buenavista 2
PRICE, William 73, Elizabeth 75
TETER, P. M. C. 30 (m)*, July Ann 27, R. L. 5 (m), M. G. 4 (m), S. E. 3 (f), Rebecca 1
SCOTT, Elijah 19*
MASTERS, Wesley 40, Maltha 37, Sophina 16, William 14, Permelia 11, Levi 10, Eli 8, John 5, Irvine 4, Lafayett 2, Nancy 4/12
JENNINGS, William E. 31*, Elizabeth 40
OVERSTREET, John P. 15*
BRUMFIEL, David 28*, Nancy 27, Mary 4, Newton 2, Moses 1/12
RUE, Juliann 25*
WADE, William 63, William H. 24, Louisa 23, Mary 1
BLAKEMAN, Adam 27*, Matilda 25, John 2

1850 Census Jessamine County Kentucky

COLLINS, Betcy A. 23 (m)*
BLAKMAN, George 60*, Frances 57, Aron 21, William 19
IRVINE, James 95*

Schedule Page 34

TREADAWAY, John 45, Jane 44, Martha 19, James 15, Nancy 12, Matilda 10
DAVIS, J. 22 (m)*, Mary 23, William 3, Joseph J. 1, Sarah 56
WADE, Mary 64*
HOOD, John 23, Polly 21, Susan E. 1
COBB, John 33, Sarah 27, James 8, Nathan 6, Henry 4, Sophrona 1, Susan 59, Ambrose 19
WILLIS, Henry 23, Margaret 22
HUNTER, William 28, Dianah 26, Sarah E. 7, Ann E. 5, Howard R. 3, Susanah 9/12
MASTIN, Henry 30*, William 10, Franklin 8, Singleton 5
EMERSON, Elizabeth 60*
BURTON, Lucy 39, William 23, Sarah 18, Sadiney 16 (f), Mead 14 (m), Mary 21
HEMPHILL, Andrew 49*, Mildred 44, Mary 20, James 18, Charles 17, Lewis T. 15, Catharine 11, Arkansas 9 (f), Hugh C. 7, Laura 5
PRIESTLEY, Michael 45*
TURPIN, Thomas 35, Harriet 32, William 11, David 9, Lucy 7, George 3, Nancy A. 2/12
BRUNER, Green 36, Caroline 34, Edward 11, Calvin 10, Tilford 9, Moses? 7, Augustus 2
HUDSON, Eliza 50
HUDSON, Jesse 26, William 20, Elizabeth 15, Polly 14, Juliann 23
FERREL, William 29, Mahala 27
CARTER, Montacue 42, Mary 33, Ann 9, Jane 7, William 6, John 5
CARTER, James 19*, Jane 30
MCMILLEN, James 36*

Schedule Page 35

BALL, Benjamin 4_, Delitha 41, Susan 16, Nancy 11, Sarah E. 9, Mary 7, Brunetta 6, Margaret 3, James 18, George 16, Burdit 14 (m), Daniel 10, William 1
BRUNER, Enoch 50, Frances 49, William 18, John 16, Franklin 12, Elizabeth 14, Mary A. 10, Green B. 18, Lucy A. 6
GULLEY, William 82*, Sarah 56, William 30
SADORE, Elizabeth 36*, William 18, Manervy 16, Elizabeth 14
MCQUERRY, Charles 47*, Mary A. 43, William 17, George 15, James 12, Alford 9, Ghage? 6 (m), George 38
BRIM, Abner 24*
SLAUGHTER, John 21, Elvina 26, Edwin 8, James 6
GREEN, William 29*, Martha J. 27, Thomas H. 8, John C. 5, Mary E. 3, Nancy 8/12
HILL, Sarah J. 12*
CANTER, John 30*, Lucy 27, John 9, William 7, Jane 5, Lucy 1
SLAUGHTER, Edward 50*, Roda 10, Amanda 12
RICHERSON, Bailey 68, Elizabeth 71
RICHERSON, James 32, Almira 30, Amos 2, Amanda 10
SCOTT, George 46, Artemacy 41 (f), George 18, Woodson 16, Joeann 6

1850 Census Jessamine County Kentucky

SAGACY, Daniel 60, Bethiah 61 (f), Sally 24, Susan 16, John 12
CANTER, Thomas 23, Martha 22
SAGACY, James 25, Patsey 20, Perry 9/12
QUIMBEY, Daniel 28, Margaret 20, George 4, Josephine 2, Allice 1/12

Schedule Page 36

BAKER, Henry 55*, Emeline 35
PRESTON, Rosanna 15*, Emily 13, Lrinda 11, Henry 8, Oliver 6, Sarah 3
FAIN, Scarlet 55 (m)*, Matilda 42
WOODS, Margaret 15*, Joshua 13, Elira 11?, George 9
SEWEL, Sarah 50, Mary 19, John W. 13, Louisa 10, George 8, Benjamin 6
SEWEL, Sarah A. 30, Josiah 10, James W. 6, George W. 4
SHERROW, Henry 26, Elira 23, John W. 2, Christopher 1/12
WOODS, C. C. 38 (m)*, Eveline 34
SHERROW, James 38*, George W. 13
CLARK, George 60, Nancy 60, Benjamin 14
CLARK, Polly 20, Joseph 4, William 1/12
PRESTON, Toliver 71, Sally 63, Martha 19, Sarah 16
CRUTCHFIEL, Mordica 62 (m), Nancy 57, Moses 22
CRUTCHFIEL, Mordica 25 (m), Frances 25, Mary 3, Louisa 1
ALLEN, Achilles 30*, Mary 24
VANDERPOOL, William 9*
PRESTON, Elias 31, Malinda 23, James 5, Lidia 4, William 2
JOHNSON, James __ *, Richard 4/12
PRESTON, Emily 25*, James 2
ROBB, Joseph 44, Nancy 34, John 14, James 13, Emeline 11, Jonas 10, Elira J. 6, Mary E. 5, Sarah B. 2, Joseph C. 4/12
CHRISMAN, Lewis H. 36, Hester 35, Lucy J. 8, Adison 6, America 4, Mary B. 2, Elizabeth 1
BONNER, Silas 41, Jane 30, Estella 12, Charles 9, Perry 6, Florida 2

Schedule Page 37

BERRY, Newton 43, Catharine 36, Mary E. 8, Nancy P. 6, Catharine 4, Lucy 2
DAVIS, Joseph 26*, Henrietta 21, Margaret 4, Juliann 2, Charles 1
JAMERSON, Casan 23 (f)*
LYLE, Alexander 33*, Isabella 46, Mary 44
JEFFRES, Thomas 32*
KARSNER, Jonathan 56*, Jennetta 50
WENDIVER, Susan M. 26*, Albert C. 5, Mildred C. 3, William A. 1
PAGGET, Mary J. 18*
MASTERS, Gabriel 40*, Malinda 38, Margaret 16, Wilson 12, Martin 10, Elizabeth 8, H. H. 6 (m), Maranda 4, William 1
DURHAM, George W. 30, Nancy 25, Mary 7, Sarah 5, James 3, Octava 1
WILLIAMS, Samuel 23

WILLIAMS, Sam 73* (B)
LEWIS, Lety 75* (B)
REYNOLDS, Tom 70* (B)
SUFFIT, Elen 23* (B), John 11, Ellen 8, Dan 4
PAGGET, Harvey 26 (B), Emerine 8
WOODFORK, Julias 77* (B)
WATTS, Vicky 75 (f)* (B)
HARRIS, Orange 85 (B), Peachy 80
CLARK, Denis 43 (B), Malinda 26, Milton 10, Christina 8, Cotton 1
MCPHETERS, Relin 55 (m)* (B)
DENIS, Milly 51* (B), Charles 12, Bellyann 2, Alexander 9
ROBERTS, Sarah 80* (B)
MASON, Dave? 12* (B), Isaac 11, Evan 4
SUTTON, Manuel 70 (B), Matilda 60, Squire 21
WALKER, Cupid 75 (B)
PERRY, Fanny 50 (B), Elira 6

Schedule Page 39

ROWLAND, Jeremiah 48*, Celia R. 42, Nathaniel 22, Celia E. 20, Tabitha A. 14, William H. 10, Sarah T. 7, Malinda C. 2
WALTERS, Rebecca 17*, Stephen 26
KEENE, Robert W. 12*
TANKSLEY, Margaret 20*
SIMMONS, J. T. 50 (m), Mary A. 24, Nancy J. 23, Joseph A. 19, Josephine 16, Elizabeth 15, B. D. 12 (m), Sarah E. 7
ADAMS, John H. 36, Nancy 38, M. A. 12 (f), James 9, Ben 6, Charles 3
QUEST, George 63, Malinda 45, Jessa 20, Alvina 22, S. J. 12 (f), G. A. 10 (m), S. H. 5 (m)
SMITH, Clem 24, A. 27 (f)
FORD, William M. 26, M. A. 25 (f), W. T. 2 (m)
CHANCELER, Rebecca 53
FORD, E. D. 23 (m)*
CROSBY?, William 24*
STINNETT, _____*, L. 28 (f), M. J. 6 (f), E. _ (f), L. L. 2 (m)
TURPIN, M. 74 (f)*, N. 40 (f)
SMITH, R. 31 (m), S. M. 21 (f), H. 3 (m), P. 1 (f)
COMBS, W. 26 (m), S. 22 (f), M. L. 3 (m), Thomas W. 6/12
BOWMAN, John 42, C. 35 (f), J. 16 (m), Joseph 14, John 11, L. 8 (f), C. 6 (m), E. 3 (m)
CORMAN?, George 24, M. 17 (f), L. Isaac N. 8/12
TRISLER, Nancy 33
KETRON, Joseph 24, A. 28 (f)
WALLACE, Joseph 71, Sarah 70
WALLACE, James 38, Mary N. 24
THOMAS, Reuben 40, A. M. 40 (f), J. 16 (m), James H. 14, J. L. 9 (m), Ed 8, J. A. 6 (f), E. J. 4 (f), L. 2 (m)
HAZLEWOOD, Rebecca 59, Mary F. 22

1850 Census Jessamine County Kentucky

Schedule Page 40

COLEY, William 64, Sarah 60
WATSON, Joseph 21
COMBS, Jeremiah 29, M. A. 28 (f), William E. 7, M. J. 5 (f), H. A. 3 (f), E. J. 1 (f)
ZIKE, Joseph 50*, Sarah 53, Lydia 18, Jordan 16, Susan 14, Joseph 12, George H. 9
GOFORTH, John 49*
JACOBS, Kitty A. 26, Joseph 8, Melvin L. 6, Mary 4, George Ann 1
HILL, William N. 31*, Katharine 26, M. K. 2 (f)
SMITH, B. Franklin 22*
RUFFNER, Samuel 54, Martha 23, George 19, Sanford 16, John 12, E. 9 (f), D. 5 (m)
SPARKS, J. B. 42 (m), S. D. 43 (f), J. E. 19 (f), J. B. 17 (m), M. P. 15 (f), E. E.? 13 (f), W. H. 11 (m), Jerome 9, S. C. 7 (f), E. 4 (f), M. B. 2 (f), N. 5/12 (f)
SPARKS, Paulina 43, R. J. 18 (m), James 15, H. B. 11 (m), George W. 7, M. E. 20 (f)
EVANS, Mary 35
CAMPBELL, Mathew 62*, Elizabeth 59, Robert 21, Martha 18, Mathew Jr. 16, Peter 13
JOHNSON, James 22* (B), Frank 21, Peter 18
CAMPBELL, Robert 90*, Katharine 86
JOHNSON, Harriett 16*
CAMPBELL, James 34*, William 8, Mary 7, Eliza 4, John 6, K. 3 (f), A. 2 (f)
WALTERS, Sarah 32*, L. 10 (f), Ben 8
JOHNSON, Courtney 26 (m), Elizabeth 19, John 2
STULL, John 57, Paulina 38, P. A. 20 (f), E. 18 (f), J. 15 (f), J. T. 11 (m)

Schedule Page 41

HAWKINS, William W. 37*, M. A. 28 (f), Thomas 24
WILMORE, James 6*
STEELE, Gavin 49, S. A. 35 (f), M. M. 18 (f), D. W. 16 (m), G. A. 10 (m)
CHRISMAN, Hugh jr. 22*
ADAMS, James 60*, J. 45 (f)
RICHARDSON, Moses 50, Nancy 42, James 16, P. 19 (f), N. J. 14 (f), D. C. 11 (m), C. H. 9 (m), Moses 21
EVANS, James 36, S. 28 (f), J. B. 8 (m), J. W. 6 (m), W. R. 5 (m), D. 2 (m)
COGAR, M. H. 27 (m), M. A. 27 (f)
EVANS, R. T. 38 (m)*, M. N. 42 (f), J. T. 26 (m)
ENGLAND, Caroline 28*, E. 32 (f)
FORD, S. 18 (f)*
TRISLER, James 17*
WILSON, Thomas 26*
HANCOCK, _____ 53 (m)
_____, Hannah 56 (B)
BATES, John 26*, Ann 24, William T. 4, M. J. 3 (f), J. T. 9/12 (m), William 24, Thomas 22, John 51, H. 40 (f), E. J. 20 (f), L. 18 (f)
FIGG, James 27*
BRADSHAW, John 51*, Nancy 45, Joseph 24, H. C. 11 (m), William 6
JOHNSON, Sarah A. 26*, A. 6 (m), Joseph 4, Thomas 3/12
ST CLAIR, Nancy 26*

1850 Census Jessamine County Kentucky

CRUTCHER, Sarah 58, Thomas 20, Susanna 15
CURD, R. S. 29 (m), M. E. 21 (f), G. S. 2 (m)
CURD, Joseph 53*, Frances 49, M. F. 19 (f), S. H. 13 (f)
REED, James R. 3*
REED, John 26, P. 23 (f), M. E. 2 (f)
SMITH, D. 45 (m), F. D. 45 (f), Sarah 22, M. E. 20 (f), E. T. 18 (f), E. A. 15 (f), B. T. 13 (m), D. 12 (m), M. 10 (m), J. H. 7 (m), M. F. 4 (f), H. J. 3 (f)

Schedule Page 42

JOHNSON, Willis 30 (B), Patsy 26, George 21, James 5, W. H. 1 (m)
JOHNSON, Sally 35 (B), C. A. 20 (f), L. 17 (f), M. 6 (f), M. 3 (m)
WALTERS, David 48, Sarah 46, John? C. 24, Sarah 16, H. 14 (f), S. W. 8 (m)
JOHNSON, Cesar jr. 25 (B), E. 28 (f), E. 7 (f), R. 1 (m)
JOHNSON, Cesar sr. 60 (B), Malinda 17, E. 10 (f), M. A. 6 (f)
JOHNSON, Julia 50 (B), Nancy 20, W. 3 (m), R. 3 (f)
CROW, Milton 33, E. 29 (f), H. 32 (f)
BEYMER, Samuel 36, Mary 34, William H. 7, E. A. 5 (f), K. I. 4 (f), R. 3 (m), G. E. 3/12 (m)
EVANS, P. E. 35 (m)*, E. 25 (f), L. 5 (f), R. 4 (m), M. 1 (f)
MORGAN, S. 25 (f)*
CRUTCHER, Peter 34, E. 28 (f), M. 4 (f), J. P. 2 (m), N. 7/12 (m)
SUTTON, D. P. 42 (m), Isabella 33, James W. 13, M. J. 10 (f), Mary N. 8, Martha 8 (twins), Richard 5, George 3, D. 8/12 (m), Jane 72
MINTER, James C. 30, J. 35 (f), M. A. 2 (f), Jane 4/12
WILSON, William T. 68, Mary 70, Joseph H. 36, C. A. 31 (f), M. E. 15 (f), Joseph M. 10, S. M. 5 (f), M. J. 2 (f), William T. 8/12
SHEPHERD, ____ 60 (m) (B)
CRUTCHER, James 26, M. E. 20 (f), Thomas E. 3, S. W. 8/12 (m)
HOOVER, John sr. 44, Mary N. 28, S. E. 14 (f), J. W. 12 (m), H. C. 8 (m), T. B. 7 (m), C. M. 6 (m), K. H. 3 (m), D. B. 1 (m)

Schedule Page 43

HOOVER, Moses 50, Sarah 40, Phebe 76, Richard 21, Andrew 17, P. A. 14 (f), E. B. 7 (f), Margaret 4
ROWLAND, Thomas 45*, E. J. 37 (f), E. A. 14 (f)
HALL, William 12*
ROWLAND, John 42, M. J. 33 (f), A. E. 10 (f), G. T. 8 (m), Mary P. M. 6 (f), L. 4 (f), N. 3 (f), E. 1 (f), J. W. 11 (m)
COGAR, Cap? Tho. T. 52*, Ruth 49, Tho. jr. 25, A. 23, John 19, Mary 17, Jesse 14, Elizabeth 11
VANARSDALE, Abm. 35 (m)*, Con. 23 (m)
FOWLER, E. 16 (f)*, Mary 13, Margaret 7, Martha 3
SPAULDING, Harrison 34, Nancy 24, James W. 5, N. J. 2 (f)
ROWLAND, Jemima 65, William 25
ROHRER, Jacob 54, Mary 49, Sarah 29, John 25, N.? C. 23 (m), Daniel 20, T. J. 18 (m), Samuel 15, M. H. 6 (m)
BAUGHN?, Joseph 54*, Patsy 53, Jackson 21, James H. 16, K. J. 13 (f), Thomas M. 9
WOODWARD, Allen 23*, Eliza 23, Joseph 2

1850 Census Jessamine County Kentucky

OGLE, John 64*, Jane 63
OVERSTREET, Frank 15*, William W. 18
HARRIS, Rice jr. 33, Mary 30, James W. 14, D. 7 (f), M. 4 (f), E. 1 (f)
OVERSTREET, James sr. 54, Thomas J. 20, M. A. 15 (f), M. P. 13 (f), M. F. 10 (f), J. H. 8 (m), G. C. 6 (m), C. E. 3 (f)
POTTS, C. A. 32 (f), Alexander 13

Schedule Page 44

REDMAN, Lloyd 24*, Harriett 26
RICHARDSON, John 21*, Margaret 15
BROWNFIELD?, Mary 80, Westley 49, Samuel 46, Anna 35, Malvina 30
GILBERT, Andrew 56* (B)
HUMPHREYS, Betsy 24* (B), H. 9 (m), Sharlott 3
OVERSTREET, William 33, F. E. 23 (f)
OVERSTREET, Nancy 58, Monroe 27, Samuel 22, Mary A. 20
HARRIS, Rice sr. 56*, Sarah 49, James 21, Jane 19, Sarah 10
WALKER, Mary A. 23*
KETRON, Peter 60, E. 61 (f), Samuel 27, Saly 31, William 5, Frances 3
WEST, Woodford 26, Katharine E. 17
BRYANT, G. B. 31 (m), E. P. 25 (f), M. E. 7 (f), G. H. 5 (m)
DORMAN, James 25, Ann E. 22
LEE, Strother 38*, Elizabeth 40, Emily 13, Melvin L. 10, E. S. 3 (f)
DORMAN, William 19*, John 21, N. J. 17 (f)
WALTER, Richard 68*, James C. 25, Peter P. 22, Levi H. 19
MINTER, Benjamin F. 30*
LYNN, Grand 45*
JEWELL, John 38, Mary A. 31, James H. 8
BROWN, Jacob 48, Jane 45, Cate 20 (f), George W. 18
HOOVER, Joseph 35, Juliann 30, Marshall 12, Areis? 10 (f), Merit 8, L. 6 (f), F. 4 (f), Tenn. 2 (f), ____ 11/12 (f)
WEST, Charles jr. 45*, Elvin 48 (f)
MYERS, James M. 22*
REYNOLDS, Susan 40, Sarah T. 19, George W. 11
HARRIS, James sr. 60*, Jeriah 57 (f), Lewis 29, Lucy A. 15
THOMPSON, Eliza Ann 20*
HICKS, John 35, M. Jane 28 (f), Louisa 10, James 8, Sarah 5, Thomas 1

Schedule Page 45

PHILLIPS, Elizabeth 66*, H. H. 38 (m), Matilda 37, Martha 15, S. E. 14 (f), William 12, Theodore 6, D. 3 (m), Katharine 8/12
HIGHTOWER, George W. 21*
EASLEY, Joseph H. 46, R. A. 43 (f), Thomas M. 22, Archibald 15, M. 13 (f), Edward 9, S. F. 6 (f), Emma 3
HANLY, John H. (Maj.) 70*, Margaret 60, S. Gratten 25, Ann S. 18, M. L. 15 (f)
MCKENZIE, J. H. 10 (m)*

1850 Census Jessamine County Kentucky

BONNER, J. H. 7 (m)*
FOLEY, David 64*
RUBLES, Henry 28, Martha 26, F. 5 (m), Charles 3
BARNETT, Archibald E. 29*, Sally A. 23, Thomas D. 8, James A. 5, A. E. 3 (f), John 3/12
SHARP, Louisa 14*
MOSS, Ray sr. 70, Jane 71, America 45, Joseph 33
MOSS, Ray jr. 31 (f)
MOSS, John M. 27, Elenor 18
FRY, Fry 51 (B)
HICKS, John sr. 58, Elizabeth 59, Sarah 23, Joseph 21
HICKS, William 34, Elizabeth 37, Almira 13, Mary J. 10, Clarinda 6, William 2, Mary A. 17
FITCH, P. S. 40 (m)*, M. H. 30 (f), Joseph C. 9
FRY, Thomas 13* (B)
PRESTON, Samuel 27*, Emmasetta 31
SPRUCE, John M. 9*
PRESTON, Benjamin F. 1*
GUTHRIE, Mary 45*
SCOTT, Mary 64*, Thomas B. jr. 35
THOMAS, Daniel 13*
MCKENZIE, A. P. 56 (m)*, Nancy 37, James 12, Edmond 9, Mary 7, E. A. 5 (f), M. H. 3 (f), William 1
WELCH, S. D. 25 (m)*
WHITE, Lewis 40*
PADGETT, Martha 40*
HANLY, James 32, Mary J. 19, J. Hilery 8 (m), Thomas B. 6

Schedule Page 46

CORMAN, John jr. 31, Elizabeth 28, M. E. 7 (f)
SCOTT, R. S. 33 (m)*, E. C. 23 (f), Nancy 29
PRICE, Cassa 42*, Samuel D. 11, Mary 8
ROBERTS, Mary 36*
DOWNS, R. J. 37 (m), Nancy 43, S. A. 15 (f), Maria 13, S. 12 (f), James 10, Martha 8, M. 6 (f), R. 2 (f), ____ 2/12 (f), E. A. 4 (f)
MASTERS, Madison 34, M. A. 27 (f), M. J. 11 (f), M. 9 (m), Nancy 5, A. 4 (f), Margaret 2
ROHRER, Samuel 51, James 21, Levi 19, H. 17 (m), Hulda 15, Jeff 12
BUTLER, John 37, Mary A. 34, Thomas 14, E. 12 (f), Mary 10, M. 7 (f), Lucy 4, Catharine 1, Catharine 25
CORMAN, A. H. 35 (m), Sarah 30, Margaret 12, G. W. 10 (m), G. 8 (m), G. A. 6 (f), M. E. 4 (f), Jer.? 2 (f), M. 4/12 (f)
MITCHELL, George W. (Dr) 39, Caroline W. 25, Sarah E. 17, James T. 15, E. W. 12 (f), Caroline B. 7, G. W. 2 (m)
THOMAS, Ann 23, A. E. 5 (f), J. W. 3 (m)
THOMAS, Simeon 50*, E. 23 (f), S. E. 3 (f), G. A. 2 (f)
TRISLER, Elizabeth 63*
GOFORTH, Mary 46, William 16, M. J. 13 (f)
JEFFRIES, Leanna 80*, William 30
CROW, A. 22 (f)*
CORMAN, Coon. 33 (m), Margaret 22, M. 9 (f), E. J. 7 (f)

1850 Census Jessamine County Kentucky

COMBS, Sophia 62, C. A. 28 (f)
CORMAN, John 52, Susanna 47, Joseph 23, Caroline 20, Mary A. 18, H. 15 (m), Harriett 15, John L. 14, Susanna 10, D. 8 (f), S. J. 5 (f)

Schedule Page 47

CORMAN, Jonas T. 27, Margaret 23, A. 5 (f), A. J. 3 (m), Elizabeth 1
BARKLEY, James T. 36, E. M. 35 (f), C. J. 14 (f), S. J. 9 (m), George M. 2
SCOTT, Newton 40
FUNK, Peter 49, Susan 40, Richard 20, Caroline 18, John 16, M. 12 (m), Henry E. 8, Mary 6, E. 4 (f)
HUFNER, Margaret 42, William A. 15, B. F. 7 (m)
CARROL, James 62*, A. 62 (f)
GOFORTH, Zepp 35*, N. J. 32 (f), Gen 13 (m), James W. 11, E. J. 5 (f), D. B. 2 (m)
COOLEY, Reuben 57, Lucy 50, Elizabeth 20, Mat 18 (f), G. D. 16 (m), William D. 14, Margaret 11, Katharine 8
BUSTER, West 56 (B)
REYNOLDS, Margaret 86*
ROWELL, S. B. 39 (m)*, Nancy 40, Love A. 3
FUNK, Amanda 42*
ROBERTS, Lucy 49*, Margaret A. 21
WILLIS, John A. 27*, Robert 12
BOWMAN, Isaac 38, Mary A. 32, J. E. 13 (f), Robert 10, N. 8 (f), S. 6 (f), Richard 5, D. 2 (m)
BOWMAN, Elizabeth 57, Elizabeth 24
ROBINSON, Isom? 47*, T. W. 20 (m), G. H. 16 (m), J. M. 14 (m), M. E. 11 (f)
EWAN, John B. 28*, Elizabeth 21, M. 2 (f)
BOSWELL, George 17* (B)
BALLARD, Wm. J. (Dr.) 47*, Elizabeth 47, Lucy J. 20, William A. 18, E. F. 16 (f), M. E. 14 (f), L. E. 9 (f), Joseph E. 7

Schedule Page 48

MCAFEE, Martha E. 18*
ROWLAND, Henry 46*, Amanda 38
WALLACE, Charles 38, Katharine 34, Amanda 14, Elizabeth 13, James 9, Margaret 6, Henry 2
KETRON, William 34, Mahala 33, Margaret 9, M. H.? 7 (f), James 5, Elizabeth 3
JACOBS, William 32, Mahala 32, John T. 8, H. 5 (f), M. 3 (f), M. J. 2 (f)
WILMORE, John sr. 63, Hannah 53, Jacob C. 31, William A. 26, John M. 23, Jane A. 21, H. J. 19 (f), Mary E. 16, Sarah M. 13, M. E. 9 (f), Florida M. 3
SPROWL, William 39, Mary 36, Richard 9, Frances 8, Sarah J. 6, A. T. 3 (m), N. A. 10/12 (f), Lettitia 74
MASTERS, James 46*, Mary 46, John S. 20, William J. 18, Sarah J. 15, S. W. 13 (f), M. F. 11 (f), H. G. 9 (m), M. C. 7 (f), M. L. 4 (m), Joseph H. 3/12
HOLMES, Frances 60*
CAWBY, Martin 32, Elizabeth 22
TURPIN, Daniel 52, Sarah 37, Mary J. 15, Matilda 14, William M. 12, James 10, Thomas J. 9
RICHARDSON, William 26, Martha 27, A. F. 4 (m), R. 2 (m)
UTLEY, Alley 75 (f)*

1850 Census Jessamine County Kentucky

TRILER, Lucy A. 32*
HOOVER, William T. 14*, Alvina 12
HOWSER, Peter 50*, Sarah 42, Margaret 22, Harrison 20, Malinda 15, Peter jr. 12
SMITH, Richard 24*, Mary J. 21, Melvin L. 7/12
CORMAN, George 58, Abigal 53, James M. 19, Henry 15, Harrison 12, Isaac 9

Schedule Page 49

MATHEWS, William H. 43, Sarah A. 24
GILMAN, Harvey 50, Mary 40, Sarah 17, James jr. 15, Henry 14, Lucy 12, Alphia 11, Benjamin 9, Mary 7, Harvey 6, Susan 4, Nancy 2, James sr. 56
SMITH, David 49*, Susan 47, John 25, George 19, Mary A. 20
BRUNER, Benjamin 26*
TRISLER, Mary 76*, John 50, Woodson 9
TURPIN, Enoch 29, Sarah J. 27, John 9, N. A. 6 (f), William 3, Levi 18, James 17
SMITH, Andrew 53*, Sophia 50, Willis B. 25, Thomas 22, Milton 20, George 16, Mary C. 14, Lucy A. 10
CAWBY, John M. 9*
STINNETT, William 33*, Polly 37, Absalom 5, Ann E. 4, P. J. 2 (f)
DEAN, John 17*, James 16
STINNETT, Nancy 56, Elizabeth 34, Katharine 32, S. L. 22 (m), Elijah 20
STONESTREET, David 40 (B), Mary 24, William 13, Margaret 11, Mary 9, Benjamin 7, Nancy 5, Martha 2
CORMAN, William 28, Susan 25, Amanda 5, G. M. 3 (f), Mariah 1
JOHNSON, Stephen 48*, Jemima 40, Mary A. 2, Peter 2 (twins)
HUNT, Harrison 58*, Nancy 54, William A. 8, James T. 6
WEAVER, Polly 16*
HILL, Greene 55, Frances 50, Greene B. 17, Arabel 15
FRAZER, Martin 63, Mary 65, M. B. 23 (m), Mary 16
SMITH, Charles F. 37

Schedule Page 50

SMITH, Quintrella 22*, Edward 2, M. E. 4/12 (f), Alonzo 6
ASON, Susan 20* (B)
FORD, Benjamin B. 39, Martha A. 34, Margaret E. 15, Juliet 9, Mary 7, Sarah 5, Victoria 2
MITCHELL, James A. 35, E. W. 28 (f), P. A. 10 (f), C. W. 9 (m), Elizabeth 5
NEAL, David 42*, R. A. 41 (f), Mary E. 19, James L. 17, Lewis? C. 14, S. M. 10 (f)
ELMORE, James 86*
EASLEY, James H. 25, Mary 23, Christopher 3, Martha A. 2
BARKLEY, William L. 39, Adaline 26, Martha 6, Margaret 3, M. A. 4/12 (f), Martha 60
BARKLEY, Isaac 40, Ann E. 32, John C. 17, Elizabeth 12, M. J. 9 (f), Ann E. 7, Samuel C. 3, Joseph H. 1
HAWKINS, Thomas (Esq.) 55*, Mary 52, Thomas W. 25, Elizabeth 16, Mary 16, William 14, Katharine 10, George J. 6
WRIGHT, Elizabeth 11*
BARKLEY, Jane 63, Samuel 29, George M. 26

1850 Census Jessamine County Kentucky

GREGG, Samuel H. 26, E. J. 27 (f), C. R. 3 (f), A. T. 1 (m)
CRUTCHER, Mary 70, Spencer 50
DEAN, John W. 49, Mary 46, Katharine 20, Sarah 16, Sophia 14, Hulda 12
GROW, Peter 45*, Sarah 44, Stephen 23, Marcus 17, Milton 15, Elizabeth 12, Sarah 6, David 10, Martha 4
CROW, Nancy 20*, Eli jr. 20
SHIELDS, James 69, Sarah 54, Jane G. 22, Isabel J. 20, E. M. 18 (f), Sarah M. 16
NAVE, George T. 27, Elizabeth 25, John R. 5, Thomas M. 3, Joseph A. 6/12

Schedule Page 51

STIPE, David 54*, Martha 54, David jr. 18, Mary 22, Susanna 20, Martha A. 16
SALE, Ann 40*
WATTS, Susanna 49*, Frederick 21, John 17, Andrew 15, Mary A. 13, Monroe 12, J. W. 10 (m)
ENGLAND, Clia A. 22*, Ed 3, Susan 1
EASLEY, George 40, Elizabeth 23, M. E. 3 (f)
WAMSLEY, Thomas E. 42, Elizabeth 38, J. S. 18 (m), Charles H. 16, F. M. 13 (m), Margaret K. 11, William T. 9, M. W. 7 (m), M. B. 5 (f), Mary S. 4, James L. 2
KETRON, John 37, Louisa 37, William M. 6, James W. 4, John H. 3, G. Ann 1, Mary 40
BOOTHE, Mary 34, Mariena? 11, Elizabeth 9, Leanna 3, James? 2
GLOSSOM, Ellen 25
BOWMAN, David 62, Elizabeth 40
YOST, George J. 44*, Elizabeth 38, Margaret 14, Alvina 12, William 11, Katharine 9, Elizabeth 7, Sophia 5, James 3, George 2, Katharine 78
RITTER, John 34*
BOWMAN, Sarah 63*
BROWN, Polly 37*, Sanford 19, Thomas 15, Robert 13
MICHAEL, Robert 20, Eliz. A. 26, Mary K. 7
HOOVER, Alfred 30, Elizabeth J. 24, Ann E. 6, John W. 2, Jacob F. 7/12
RICE, Daniel 48*, Lear 45 (f), Jasper 19, William B. 15, Caroline 14, Newton 11, Henry H. 8, M. B. 4 (f), Alice A. 6/12

Schedule Page 52

WALTERS, Morton 19*
LOWEN, William 49*, Eliza K. 21, Lucy M. 1
STIPE, Robert S. 25*, Ann L. 23, Mary O. 1
NETHERLAND, Benjamin 54*, Joseph H. 22, James T. 15, Ann O. 13, Mary L. 10, Ellen L. 8, Benjamin P. 5
FLOURNOY, A. Eliz. 17*
SHEELY, Katharine H. 41*, Dewit C. 18, James W. 17, Katharine A. 14
WILLIS, Alex W. 6*
HORINE, John (Genl.) 45, Lucy B. 35, Susan O. 13, Ann M. 12, E. T. 10 (f), Alex P. 9, James M. 6, Sarah 4, Elizabeth 2, John H. 8/12
HORINE, Katharine 63*, Elizabeth 43, Susan 41
HICKS, Samuel 36*, Matilda 21, Katharine A. 8, James W. 6, Lucy 2
ELMORE, Thomas B. 43*, Juliann 34, Samuel D. 17, James E. 15

1850 Census Jessamine County Kentucky

RAYMOND, J. K. 22 (m)*
TODHUNTER, John 73*, Mary 64
WILLIAMS, Eliz. A. 49*
MCDOWELL, Samuel 63*, Mary 52, William 22, Mary R. 8
SPEARS, John 14*, Sidney 12 (m)
CALDWELL, George Mc. 14*
ANDERSON, Mort. C. 38, Jane 32, Georgeann 13, Mary E. 10, Samuel Mc. 8, Sarah E. 5, James W. 2
TRAINER, James 45, Eliz. 33, Mary 12, John 10, James 6, Henry 1
DUNCAN, Louisa 33, Eliza J. 10, Nancy 9, Susan M. 6, John W. 3, James 27
NEAL, Moses H. 40, Matilda E. 35, Sarah D. 16, James W. T. 12, John A. 9, Mary E. 7, William M. 6, Joseph R. 4, M. J. 1 (f)
BRYANT, Joel 55, Martha 41, Jesse 15, Julia A. 13, James 12, America 7, Martha 5, Rufus 4

Schedule Page 53

JENISTON, Rebecca 68, Susan 33, Price N. 30, William 28
WALLS, Susanna 65, Eliza 36, N. C. 26 (m), Henry C. 24 (m), W. T. B. 24 (m)
FANA, Aaron 58*, Sarah 57, Bnenjamin F. 31, Charles A. 18
NEET, Lucy 82*
ROBB, John 56, Katharine 53
LOWRY, Nathaniel 37, Harriett 33, Margaret 10, Mary L. 8, George N. 5, Ann T. 3, John G. 2
LOWRY, Prudence 62*
THOMPSON, John F. 39*, Latitia 39
LOWRY, William J. 37, Julia A. 30, G. F. 9 (m)
BERRY, Richard 43, Mary 37, Z. 16 (m), Mary J. 9, John 7, F. M. 2 (m), James R. 1
HAYDON, Benjamin 25, Mary E. 18, James L. 1
RUCKER, Minty 61*, John J. 35, Katharine 39, Elizabeth 24, William 22, Sarah A. 18
RAMSEY, James 18*, Martha 16, Isaac 13, John 11
OWINGS, Samuel J. 34, Mary A. 28, Jesse P. 10, Thomas M. 9, James M. 7, William H. 5, E. A. 3 (f), Owen W. 1
ASHUNT, Craig 45*, Sally 40, Robert 17
CLEMMONS, Elizabeth 66*, John 49, Rankin 26
CLEMMONS, James 45, Elizabeth 41, Mary J. 21, Malinda 19, James 17, Stephen 16, Henry 14, Emily 12, John 10, Jesse 8, Elizabeth 6, Sarah 4, ____ 3/12 (f)
BRYANT, Daniel 25, Sarah 22, Joseph 6/12

Schedule Page 54

FARRA, Oliver 49, Nancy 45, James A. 21, Aaron 17, Margaret 13, William 12
WALLS, Joseph L. 16, Thomas N. 28, M. J. 32 (m)
MYERS, Albert H. 49*, Elizabeth 38, George W. 18, Francis M. 16, Susan M. 13, Margaret H. 11, Elizabeth A. 9, Alex C. 5, Ann E. 2
CAWBY, Susan 62*
LACKEY, Nathan 45, Polly 46, Martha 20, John 19, Peter 16, Thomas 12, Mary A. 10, Jane 8, Emiline 6
NAVE, Jefferson 42*, Mahila 40, Paulina E. 16, William T. 15, Waller 14, E. A. 11 (f), Mason 8, Chats.? D. 6 (m), Robert C. 4, Tennessee 9/12
DEAN, James D. 19*

1850 Census Jessamine County Kentucky

NAVE, Peter sr. 80*, Mary 75, David G. 27, Malinda 27, Alexander J. 4, Robert 3, John 2, George Ann 1/12, Tilford 14
GOSSOM, Lucy A. 18*
NAVE, Jacob 34, Myrom 32 (f), William J. 2, Adaline 1
WOOLFOLK, Absalom 40* (B), Frances 37, George 14
STONESTREET, Jane 18* (B)
LYNUM?, Katharine 60 (B), Thomas 24
CARSON, Joseph 48*, Elizabeth 35, Eliza J. 16, Bell 14, William 11, Harriett 8, Andrew F. 5
HOLLIS, Mary K. 17*
OVERSTREET, Samuel 38* (B), Gracy A. 26, Mary J. 6/12
JOHNSON, Lucy A. 9* (B)
OVERSTREET, William 40 (B), Edy 57
BOATRIGHT, James 85, Mildred 63
ROWLAND, Robert G. 39*, Martha A. 38, Mary E. 13, Mariah L. 12, Martha J. 9, George W. 7
PATTERSON, John 63*, Nancy 59, John C. 26, James M. 23, Samuel 16

Schedule Page 55

ATKINS, Brockman 63, Mary 58
MCMURTRY, Mary 45, Nancy H. 21, James T. 20, John W. 18, David S. 15, Mary J. 12, Gavin 10, Lewis B. 8
CHAMBERLAIN, J. S. 71 (m)*, Mary A. 34, Sophrona E. 6, Namoi? 4, Semantha J. 2
BUTLER, Mary (Mrs.) 53*, Eliz. Jane 18, Sally W. 15, Susan J. 13
DRYSDALE, B. A. 26 (m)*
LIVINGSTON, Nannie J. 20*
KERBY, Richard 50* (B)
RICHARDSON, Thomas 52*, Cyntha 52
HENRY, Cynthia 16*, Thomas 18
HOOVER, John Q. A. 22, Sarah E. 15, Juliann 16
STEVENSON, William 35, Jamima R. 38, Benjamin 12, Mary J. 8, James M. 6, Priscilla M.? 4, Margaret 74, J. A. 2 (f)
HORD, F. J.? 22 (m)*, Mildred C. 22
BURTON, John 25*
BURCH, William H. 40*, Nancy 37, Lavinia 6, Parallee 8/12
CORMAN, Elizabeth 54*
NOVE?, Nimrod 40, Lucy P. 35, Andora 12, James D. 11, Thomas J. 9, Mary A. 8, E. R. 6 (f), Sarah M. 3, Zack T. 1
CORNETT, A. J. 33 (m)*, Mary 27, F. Josephus 11, A. A. 8 (m), E. J. 6 (f), William L. 4, Alexander L. 1, Eliza D. 31
GRACE, David L. 25*, Elizabeth 29, Loretta J. 2
CHAMPION, Sarah 35, Mary J. 18, Sarah T. 5
REED, John W. 27, Sarah C. 19, Sarah E. 3, Mary M. 2, L. Jane 1
WATSON, D. P. (Capt.) 45, Nannie 19, James 8, Katharine 6, Ann 4, Hetty 1
JOHNSON, Amanda 12
MCTYRE, Alfred 34*, Mary 29, Joseph 5, William 4, James 1

1850 Census Jessamine County Kentucky

Schedule Page 56

YATES, James W. 40*, Frances 4/12
MCLAUGHLIN, Bernard 35*
DRYSDALE, Samuel J. 28, Malinda P. 25, James E. 3, Mary A. 2, Ann E. 7/12
CAMPBELL, Peter 50, Paulina 36, Richard 15, Stephen 12, Marth A. 6
THOMPSON, John H. 52, Mary 44, John A. 22, J. B. 21 (m), James W. 14, Armilda 9, Arabel 5
GILLESPIE, Nancy B. 48*, Caroline A. 17, James M. 14, Nancy G. 11, Margaret C. 9, Thomas M. 7
KERBY, C. T. 35 (m)*, Martha H. 30, Mary E. 13, James W. 9
OAKS, Katharine 70, Monroe 25
DENNIS, David 79, Margaret 77, D. Westley 25, Jane 40, Amanda 17
CORMAN, Jonas 47, Roseann 42, David H. 20, Amanda 18, Archibald Y. 16, William J. 13, Rose Ann 11
SHIELDS, Thomas 37*, Margaret 28, William S. 8, James B. 6, Frances M. 3, John O. 1
HENAN, Mathew 27*
TURPIN, Isaac 64*, Anney 50
DEARINGER, Eliza 21*
HOLLOWAY, Samuel 54*, Jane P. 45, James 16, Thomas 14, William 13, Samuel jr. 10, Charles 7, George 5
JONES, William 35*
CHOWNING, Mary 48*, Martha 18, Robert 9
COOK, Philip 33*, Susan 21
BRYANT, Patsy 45*
COOK, Thomas 49, Paulina 23, Philip 13, Sarah J. 11, Mariam 1, Nancy A. 5
MCKEE, Archd. 53, Eliz. 57, Nancy 26, Mary J. 21, William S. 20

Schedule Page 57

GARRISON, John 64*, Isabel 41
MCNULT, Samuel 67*
CAMPBELL, John M. 14*
HOGAN, Joseph 25, Mary 25, Mary J. 3, Love 2
FOSTER, Thomas 60*, Lucy 60, Mary 26, James W. 24, Nancy 19
PRYOR, George R. 10*
ROBARDS, Otho 66*, Cassa 47, John M. 21, Eliz. D. 18, Y. Petts? 17 (m), Gabrella K. 13, James H. R. 10, Linis? L. 5 (m), Susanna 61
BLACK, Sam 60* (B), Lewis 40
ROBARDS, James 58 (B), Lewis 9
HORN, James 53*, Mary 38, Mary A. 29, Susan J. 18, John E. 17, William C. 15, James M. 12, George W. 10, Henry C. 10, A. S. 7 (m), Bettie B. 3
CROCK, Joseph 38*
NEET, Jacob 55, Sarah 47, Susan 22, George 18, Frederick 16, Eliz. 13, John 11, William 9, Hetty 6, Mary B. 3
KEENE, William R. 34*, Eliz. 28, William P. 10, George S. 7, E. W. 5 (m), Worth 2
SUTLEY, Frederick 18*
HUMPHREYS, James 23* (B)
SHANKLIN, Sarah 60*
HILL, James D. 48, Margaret 51, Margaret J. 17, Sarah B. 13, Mary 75

1850 Census Jessamine County Kentucky

WOODSON, Tucker 45*, Evelyn 40, William C. 16, Ann M. 13, Jessamine? 10, Ann R. 69
RANDOLPH, Evelyn B. 19*, Jane 13, John H. 53
ROHRER, Jonas 43*, Elizabeth 33
CAWBY, Sarah 16*
BENNETT, Robert 24, Martha 20, Sarah F. 2
HAVEY, James O. R. 26, Elizabeth 20, M. Agness 1
CARTER, Edward 54*, Eliza 40, Frances 17, William S. 16, James L. 14, Joseph 10, Eliz. 8, Lucy 7, Alfred 5, Anny? 4
WOODSON, Sarah T. 22*

Schedule Page 58

MARRS, Mary 75, Margaret 46, Nancy 42, Eliza 36, John 28, Martha 21, Mary S. 1
BRYAN, William T. 62, Margaret 54, Lewis 28, Daniel 26, Alexander 16, Andrew 14, Christopher 12, Marianella 10
CRAVENS, Thomas 54, Jane 49, Hugh K. 19, John 18, Jenetta? F. 16, Sarah D. 12, Rebecca J. 8, William 6
TALBOTT, Mary A. 72, L. B. 31 (m), Ann P. 27, William C. 4
FOLEY, Richard 52*, Mary 50, John 20, Henry 16, Sanford 13, George 12, Peter 9, Rachael 73
RICE, Michael 28*, Margaret 22, Mary E. 1
HUFNER, John 20*
RICE, Isaac 50, Malinda 46, Salina 28, William S. 24, Martha 22, John B. 20, Amanda 18
RICE, Elizabeth 76*
BENNETT, Mary A. 9*
GATEWOOD, Richard 66, William 36, Sarah 32, Susan 23
HENDLEY, Marshall 41, Margaret 28, Charles W. 10, James 18
ADAMS, Dudley 31, Nancy 39, Betsy A. 11, NAncy J. 9, Mary K. 8, Charles W. 6, John Q. 4, E. B. 2 (f)
ROSE, Thomas 52, Margaret 47, Lewis Jr. 26, William T. 23, Isaac J. 21, George W. 20, Charity E. 19, Allen C. 15, Mary A. 14, Joshua 10, Katharine R. 8, Margaret J. 12, Lucy A. 6

Schedule Page 59

HAWKINS, Giles 39, Martha 29, Martha A. 9, Mary E. 7, James W. 5, Lucretia J. 3, Malinda F. 2/12, Jacob W. 20, Polly A. 22
NEAL, Elijah 62, Polly 58
FUNK, John 54, Nancy D. 50, Andrew 23, Morton 21, Mary 18, Jacob 16, Lucy A. 13, Henry 12
DAVIS, Henry 74, Sarah 64, Greene 22
HIGBEE, Peter 53*, Elizabeth 48, Ellison 27, Emma E. 22, Eliz. 4, Emily J. 2, Susan M. 10/12, asa 13, Nancy 17, Sarah E. 15
DEARINGER, Levi 25*
NEAL, James K. 26*, Susan W. 21
MONROE, Elizabeth 15*, Marquis 11
NEAL, George 57*, Francissina? 26, Mason S. 23, Elijah B. 10, Jesse C. 3, Elizabeth 83
DOUGHERTY, Patrick 26*
MONOHON, William 32*
EAVES, Willis 42*, Nancy 35, Eliz. 17, William 15, James 5
STEPHENS, Mary A. 18*

1850 Census Jessamine County Kentucky

GEORGE, William 30, Eliza 30
HEADLEY, Hamilton 23*, Sally A. 22, George A. 6/12
ATCHISON, Hamilton 14*
DUNN, Nathaniel F. 47*, Hulda J. 32, Helen W. 6, James W. 13
CASSELL, Barbary 45*
RIAL, John 27*, Amanda J. 24, James W. 6, Cassa J. 5, Isaac K. 2, Merit 7/12
BEASLEY, James 52*
WATSON, William H. 18*
GENNIS, Samuel 40*, _____ 34 (f)
MEGLONE, Edward 14*
YOUNG, Ephraim 31*, Mary A. 19, David M. 7, Mary A. 1
DUNN, Amanda M. 15*
YOUNG, George P. 29*, Nancy 35, Mary E. S. 9, William H. 7, D. K. 4 (m), John L. 1

Schedule Page 60

HIGBEE, John 18*
MAHAN, James 20*
HUNT, John W. 20*
WALKER, Samuel 19*
MARKWELL, William A.? 35, Katharine 33, William A. J. 12
COFFMAN, David 71, Katharine 58, Martha (Miss) 22, John J. 21, Emily 18, Susan 14
CARTMILL, Robert 75 (B)
ARNSPIGER?, Gabriel 38, Malinda 43, Thomas J. 8, Mary E. 5, James S. 3, George W. 1
ALLEN, Richard 42*, Rosa A. 42, Martha 20 (twin), Ann 20 (twin), Mary 13, George 10, William 6,
    Frank 3, Eliza L. 63
MCCLARY, Robbin 60 (m)* (B)
ELGIN, James H. 29, John S. 20
JENKINS, Elisha 42*, Elsy 38, William 20, Nathaniel 17, Nancy J. 13, Wilson 10, John 7, Newton 5,
    Betsy? 2 (m?), Keziah 95
DAVIS, Betsy? 23*
KENNY, S. B. 38 (m)*, Margaret H. 34, Eliza J. 12, William H. 2
ALLEN, Polly 45*
SMITH, Alice 6*, Margaret 4
YOUNG, Andrew M. 28*, Mary A. 23, Dillard 1
BAXTER, William 19*
GEORGE, William 60, Juliann 44, Mildred E. 14, William Jr. 8, Henrietta C. 5, Mary A. 1
TANNER, William 54, Nancy 54, Margaret 22, Marquis L. 20
ALLEN, Edward 33, Mary E. 27, William 8, Margaret B. 6, Rich W. 3, John P. 1
DEDMAN, Robert 30, Martha 27, Sims? 7, Elizabeth 5, William 3, Patsy 1
LAFON, Anna 76*, William 52
BRODUS, Margaret 22*, Edward 2
BLACKFORD, Nathaniel 50, Rebecca 38, Epsin? 18 (m), John H. 9, Ann 6, Jessamine 4, Nathaniel Jr. 2

1850 Census Jessamine County Kentucky

Schedule Page 61

RICE, Jasper D. 64, Polly 51, Anapias? 30 (m), Robert 26, Mary E. 22, Jerome 19, Julia A. 14, Jane W. 5
SETTLE, Thomas J. 27, Alice A. 25
EVANS, James 48, Jane 41, William W. 17, Ann E. 13, Harriett 11, Martha J. 9, John W. 6, Mary H. 4, James H. 2, Mary 55
PEYTON, Elizabeth 52*, Susan 46, Ann 43
MOSELEY, James L. M. 32*, Eliz. 31, David S. 11, Ann E. 9, Margaret F. 7, Benjamin F. 2, James T. 1
RICE, Elizabeth 64*
LONG, John W. 4*
THORNTON, James 27, Margaret 23
SODOWSKY, Jonathan 31, Lewis E. 9, John D. 7, William 16
SODOWSKY, Ephraim Sr. 69, Hester 35, H. Clay 16, Ephraim jr. 2
SODOWSKY, John E. 32*, Hannah 26, Jacob 6, Chilton A. 4, John W. 2
NEAL, Charles W. 16*
MCGEE, Dean 53*, Ann L. 45, Dean M. 20, Ann E. 16, Sarah C. 14, Marietta? 12
CRAVENS, Martha J. 17*
CAVENOR, Patrick 24*
MCGEE, Seth 59*, Susan 50, James R. 15, Rebecca F. 13
POWELL, John 25*, Margaret J. 18
SODOWSKY, Ann E. 27, Ephraim jr. 8, S. G. 7 (m), Julia A. G. 3, James M. 1
GRAVES, Richard C. 46*, James M. 24, Laura 18, Florida 15
CAVE, Alice 3*
MITCHUM, Mary 60*
CRAIG, Samuel H. 77*
DOWDEN, Martin 36*
MURRAY, John 30*
HAWKINS, Thomas 35*, Emeline 33, Thomas 7, James 5, Ellen F. 4

Schedule Page 62

ELLIOTT, Augustus N. 26*, Nancy 18, James A. 2
WEAVER, Matilda 35 (B), Andrew 12, Charles 10, Harvey 8, ____ 7 (f), Frances 6, ____ 4 (m), ____ 1 (f)
COLLINS, Lewis 70*, Ambrose 27, Frances A. 20, George L. 18
SODOWSKY, Malina 13*
ELLIOTT, Andrew 58*, Lucinda 54, J. H. 30 (m), William A. 23, Thomas D. 16
HAMILTON, Frances E. 32*
HUGHES, John M. 26, Lucy J. 22, James T. 6, Sarah E. 4, Mary L. 2
SMITH, G. P. 50 (m), Mary 40, John W. 23, Florida A. 21, Lucy A. 12, James F. 9, William A. 7
MOSELEY, Frances 60*, William B. 45, Martha E. 20, George W. 15
HENSPERGER?, H. C. 27 (m)*, J. Ann 22, John M. 1
SALLEE, Jacob B. 52, Sydney 43 (f), Susan E. 18, William E. 16, Eliz. 13, James 11, Katharine F. 9
LANCASTER, John 76, Hannah 72, John N. 30, Eliz. 25, Samuel C. 4, Susan M. 3
HUDSON, L. M. 46 (m), Sophia 47, Samuel 17, Manerva 14, William J. 11, Jesse 9, John 8, Mary J. 5
CRAIG, Lewis S. 25, Martha A. 22, Alice 4, William 1
SIMS, John G. 39, Marilda F. 35, Eliz. A. 17, Mary L. 14, Lucy A. 12, Margaret 9, Malinda F. 4

1850 Census Jessamine County Kentucky

NAVE, Peter D. 62*, Eliz. 59, Joseph 22
HOOVER, Mary 21*
IRVIN, J. P. 14 (m)*
KNIGHT, Grant 40, Nancy G. 36, Melvin L. 18, John P. 16, Thomas B. 14, James W. 12, Marquis D. F. 10, Alex H.? 6, Sarah A. 4, Mary A. J. 2, Elizabeth 90

Schedule Page 63

LEWALLEN, James 35, Mary J. 26, James F. 3, Sarah M. 1
GROW, Samuel 52, Nancy 46, Andrew 26, Isaac 17, Morton 13, James A. 12, William G. 10, Martha 18, Margaret 15, Mary E. 8, Cassa Ann 6, Malinda 4
GROW, Sarah 49, John 26 (twin), Joel 26 (twin), Martha 23, Frances A. 23, Henry 22, Amanda 20, Francis 14, Almeda 2, Isabel 1, Frances 1, Henrietta 6/12
WELCH, Thomas 37, Margaret 37, George 15, Eliz. 11, Caroline 10, Josephine 8, John 6, James 4, Mary J. 1
LASENER, Jasper C. 34*, Catharine 40, Susan 15, James 13, Mary 11, John 9 (twin), Sidney 9 (f), Betty 1
SHASTEEN, Eliz. 93*
SALLEE, William A. 40*, Martha A. 40, George 12, Mary E. 10, William 8, Philip 6, John T. 3, James K. Polk 1
MOTHERSHEAD, Mary A. 39*, Louisa M. 4
MATHEWS, Thomas 33*, Margaret 26, Jesse D. 7, Hester A. 5, Susan 2, James D. 9/12
DIXON, Elizabeth 24*, George 23, Thomas 17
HAYDON, Sarah 86*, Thomas 45, Isaah B. 22
KING, Patsy 60*
ROBERTS, Mary A. 4* (B)
EAVES, Henry 27, Malinda 21, Jane 7, Henry 4, Thomas 2, James 6/12
FOLEY, Andrew 26, Martha A. 21, Mary S. 3, David 1

Schedule Page 64

HAYDON, Jane 53, Lucy C. C. 15, Ezekiel W. 12
BARKLEY, James L. 48*, George W. 23, Merit S. 18, James 16
LONG, William T. 29*, Lucy J. 21
KNIGHT, John 65* (B)
DEADEMA, _____ 30 (f) (B)
HAYDON, Whitfield 46, Sarah E. 24, Sanford T. 3, William 1
BROCK, Winfield 55, Sarah 55, Sarah M. 20, Eliz. 17, Rebecca 14
HAMPTON, Andrew 53*, Hester 33, Samuel T. 23, William R. 16, Amanda W. 14, Eliza A. 12, Simon R. 7, H. A. 5 (f), Jesse C. 1
ROBINSON, DeWit C. 11*
BUNIER?, Jacob 42*, Eliza 30, John S. 6, Samuel 45
MCCROSKY, Martha 35*
PROCTOR, L. H. 39 (m), Adelia F. 34, Sarah M. 15, Mary A. 13, William H. 10, Hamilton 8, A. T. 6 (f), Lucy J. 4, R. A. 2 (f)
HERRING, A. M. 27 (m), M. T. 19 (f), M. E. 2 (f), A. A. 1/12 (f)
BRYANT, O.? D. 41 (m)*, Martha M. 36, Benjamin 9, Martha 7, Dudley 5, Alexander 3

1850 Census Jessamine County Kentucky

SINGLETON, S. E. 15 (f)*, Joel 12
COLLINS, Whitfield 31, Mary A. 27, John W. 4, M. A. 2 (f)
ADAMS, James 36, Mary 34, Benjamin 13, Margaret 10, Cynthia A. 8, Eliz. 6, Thomas 4, Susan 2, Thomas 30, Susan 23, Nancy 70
HACKNEY, Samuel 41, Mary 38, Sarah M. 17, Ruth A. 16, Mary C. 14, S. E. 12 (f), William 11, Sidney A. 9 (f), Samuel H. 7, Nancy E. 2
MCTYRE, Larkin C. 50*, Margaret 57

Schedule Page 65

BENNETT, John 59*
COROTHERS, Mary B. 48*, James 19, Samuel 16, Mary 50
HACKNEY, William C. 28*, Mary 21, Lucy C. 6/12
LANCASTER, Mason? T. 40, Polly 34, John S. 14, Sarah M. 12, Jane E. 10, Ambrose D. 1, Lewis M. 4
WOODS, Richard 63, Esther 59, Andrew 34, John 25, Rice 19
WOODS, Morton 29*, Ann M. 24, William R. 2, Hester A. 2/12
BLAIR, Ann 60*
WOODS, Merit 31, Eliz. 24, William 3, Lewis R. 1
CLEVELAND, George sr. 88*
COLLINS, George P. 25*, Nancy 22, John 2
LANCASTER, Merit P. 35, Ann E. 28, Abm. 9, Mary 3, Johnson 22
JONES, Thomas B. 41, Jane 40, Joanah 14, Mary 2
WALLER, William E. 47*, Eliz. 45, Eliza 21, Ann E. 17, Margaret 14, Joseph 11, O Liva? 7 (f)
FIELDS, William 19*
MCCABE, Johns 51*, Mariah 45, James T. 25, Joseph 20, Thomas 16, Frances 14, David 7, George 4
MOSELEY, George S. 28*, Martha 24, Mary 5, H. C. 3 (m), William 1
BROUGHTON, Thomas S. 30*, Henrietta E. 26, Marshall 7, _____ 10/12 (m)
TUTT, Adeline 41*
SALLEE, Eliz. 74, Frances 47, Eliza 43, Thomas 36, Mary A. 30, John M. 28
ELKIN, John B. 28, Nancy J. 19, Sidney 4 (m), Benja. 5/12
GRANISON, John A. 23*, Sarah K. 26, Mary A. E. 9/12
STEELE, Samel Mc. 8*, William L. 6, John 4

Schedule Page 66

SHANKLIN, Ephraim 26*
DUERSON, John B. 33*, Eusebia 32, Margaret A. 10, Lucy K. 4, Susan E. 2, Mary T. 6/12
FROST, Samuel 28*, Nancy A. 29
KIDD, Walter 40*
MANING, Thomas 19*
BROOKS, Parker 18* (B)
WHITE, John 41*, Martha J. 36, E. C. 13 (f), William W. 11, John H. 6, E. K. 2 (m)
HEAD, E. J. 16 (f)*, John K. 21
COX, William D. 40, Mary 43, David B. 16, Columbus 15, Matilda J. 14, Martha 11, Rachael 8
MAHAN, William 37, Nancy 33, Sarah 14, Arch Ann 13, Mary 12, Eliza 9, Charles 7, John 6, Malvina 4, Walter 1
ROSE, A. J. 28 (m), Eliz. 19, Sarah E. 2, Simeon 1

1850 Census Jessamine County Kentucky

LUNDY, Thomas 43, Mary A. 40, George 17, Mary A. 16, St. Clair 12 (m), Ann E. 10, Martha 8, Laura 5, James T. 2
BARBEE, Jos. R. 32*, Margaret 32, Mary 14, Josephene 13, John L. 10, Joseph 6, James W. 4, Charles S. 1
____, Kitty 30* (B)
FOSTER, Thomas U.? J. 26*, Lucy J. 24
NEET, Charles M. 21*
LONG, J. C. 73 (m)*, Nancy 66, James J. 37, A. Dudley 27, Mildred 24, Thomas P. D. 25, James R. 14, Susan A. 10
HOLLOWAY, John 27*
COONS, T. M. 33 (m)*, Susan F. 26, Sarah J. 8, Eliz. K. 4, Clay M. 1
COLLINS, William P. 22*
SINGLETON, Elijah 54*, Mariah 45, Atwell 18, Armilda 15, Joseph T. 12, Katharine 9, Thomsonann? 6

Schedule Page 67

WALLER, Napoleon B. 24*
BAUGHN, David 27*, Eliz. S. 22, Ruth R. 3, Alice S. 1
WEBSTER, William 26*
JOHNSON, John J. 17*
PERKINS, Mary J. 29, Benja. H. 13, Robert 8, William 6, David 4, Rebecca 2
BRYANT, Benja. 67, Darcus 65, Woodson 24, Parker 22
BRYANT, Harrison E. 38, Nancy D. 35, Mary B. 13, Thomas 11, Simon P. 10, William 7, Parker 5, Eliza 9, Benja. 2
OAKS, Thomas 32*, Priscilla 35, T. Milton 7, American 5, Wm. O. Butler 2, Polzey K. 1 (f)
KITLEY, Sarah 52*
BRYANT, James 17*
VEATCH, John W. 57, Elenor 56, Christopher 24, Mary 27, Hannah 18, Nancy 26, Priscilla 78
SHIELDS, Hugh 35, Mira? 25, James W. 4, George T. 2, Samuel G. W. 1
KIRTLEY, Francis 36, Mary J. 24, Thompson G. 7, Mary L. 5, Margaret 4, Sarah J. 2
LOWRY, Robert 78, Samuel C. 44, Eliza 40, John C. 18, Sarah J. 16, James C. 14, Samuel C. 11, David J. 10
WHITE, John 77, Nancy 71
WRIGHT, Gabriel J. 37, Sarah 36, Martha 18
WRIGHT, Robert G. 35, Elizabeth 34, James L. 9, Margaret 7, Charles 3, Lucy 1
LYONS, Jospeh 24, Mary C. 28, Paralee 1
BARKLEY, Mason S. 32, Narcissa 28, Cassa J. 7, James F. 5, Susan A. 6/12
CLEVELAND, George jr. 44*, Parthena 29, Martha E. 13, Horace W. 6, Amanda H. 3, James L. 1

Schedule Page 68

MORAN, Jigg? 45 (m)*
SISSON, Charles 35, Elizabeth 29, John 14, Thomas J. 8, Charles Henry 6, James S. 3, Marquis 1
MOSELEY, Thomas J. 43, Martha 29, Mary E. 13, Nancy 11, Thomas 8, H. Clay 6, Eliz. 2, John 1
HUGHES, John B. 24*, Mary J. 22, Juliett D. 3, Mary A. 1
JOHNSON, D. Francis 28*

1850 Census Jessamine County Kentucky

SINGLETON, Mason 44*, Nancy 43, Richard M. 18, Walter 16, Joseph B. 15, Nathaniel L. 13, James B. 11, William H. H. 9, Frances A. 7, Katharine M. 5, Jackson L. 1
POSTLETHWAIT, Lewis 42*, Sarah 38, Lewis jr. 12, William 11, Sarah A. 9, G. 4 (f)
FLETCHER, Horace 31*, Margaret M. 30, Cordelia S. 2
LUFON, Edward 51*
TAYLOR, Robert 23* (B)
BRADLEY, Patrick 30*
WHITESELL, Lewis 30*
SANFORD, Mary 46, David C. 23, Margaret E. 16
MOSELEY, Samuel H. 27*, Mary A. 22, Anna B. 4, Charles H. 1, H. Clay 25, Theressa 24
COLLINS, John C. 20*
SEA, L. M. 28 (m)*, Mary M. 23
MCMILLEN, Mary 15*, Martha 10
ROBERTS, Margaret 10* (B)
LANCASTER, Sarah J. 28, Lucy A. 8, William D. 6, Levi B. 3
HENDRIX, Samuel J. 34*, Elizabeth 24, John C. 4, James M. 2, Charles F. 1, Sarah 58
CHOWNING, Thomas 24*, Mary 16
WHORTON, Susan M. 51, Mary 17, Lovy 23, Lucy A. 11
CAMPBELL, William M. 40, Nancy H. 34, Joseph R. 7, Mary A. 5, John G. 1
BRIZENDINE, William L. 29*, Katharine M. 38, Joseph R. 7

Schedule Page 69

EVANS, William W. 18*, Katharine M. 15
SEA, Joseph M. 16*
CAMPBELL, Samuel A. 35*, Sophrona 18, Mary S. 1
FORGUSON, Richard S. 38*, Eliz. H. 26, Eliz. G. 8, Nancy 81
LEWIS, Joseph G. 6*
LYNE, Daniel 34*, Sarah E. 22, James 21
LONG, R. D. 21 (m)*
LANCASTER, James H. 22*
DEAN, William R. 24, Martha E. 19, Thomas 5, Mary 3?
ROBBINS, John L. 34, Lavisa B. 30, Emily A. 8, William J. 3
HOLLOWAY, Spencer 57*, Katharine 53, Samuel S. 15, Walter 14, Sarah E. 12, Robert H. 10
PRUITT, Sarah 56*
POAGE, Samuel 51, Emily 44, William H. 18, J. H. 16, Mary A. 12, Ellen 10, George 8, Lucy 6, A. Frances 4, Jonathan 2
TRABUE, C. C. 45 (m)*, Malinda 46, Martha J. 19, Samuel 17, Susan 15, Eliza 12, Sarah 7
MCPHETERS, William 28*, Malvina 26, Harriett 3/12
GORDON, N. M. 36 (m), Katharine M. 23, Eliza C. 3/12, Ro. J. 20 (m)
DAVIS, William 22, Margaret 22
EASLEY, Pleasant 60*, Patience 60, Thomas 18
COOK, Mary E. 16*
COOK, Reubin 49*, Eliz. 27, Reubin jr. 1
EASLEY, ____ 20 (f)*
MOSELEY, Robert 51, Mary 49, Thos. 25, Julia A. 22, Ephm. 18, Betsy A. 21, Edward 15, Mary H. Clay 6

1850 Census Jessamine County Kentucky

SMITH, James sr. 64, Peter 57, George H. 26, James jr. 29, America 24, Mary A. 22, Thos. L. 20, Louisa 17, John W. 16

Schedule Page 70

GAYLOR, George 37*, Margaret A. 28, A. H. 8 (f), Mary J. 6, Stateria? A. 2, Cosby A. 9/12
CORNETT, Eliza D. 22*
LEVISY, James 23*, Eliz. 22, Sarah J. 9/12
REDMAN, Sarah 11*
FROST, John 58, Margaret 57, Cyrus W. 24, Eliz. J. 23, John N. 20, William J. 18, Stephen 68
STEPHENS, Garner 40, Eliz. 50, James 23, Mathew 20, David 19, William 17, Katharine 16, Garner 14, Anna 12, Mary 11, Paulina 9, Florida 7, John 4
WATKINS, Phil J.? 84* (B)
WALTERS, Zelpha 35* (B), E. J. 18 (f), Rebecca 16, Jennings 14, Eliz. 13, Moses 7, Frances 4
WEST, Milton 29, Naomi 25, Eliz. J. 4, William 3/12
WEST, Charles sr. 56, Martha A. 34, Emma 14, Susan 12
DAVENPORT, R. W. (Dr.) 38, G. H. (Dr.) 45, Charles M. 17, Margaret 16, Sarah 14
MAJOR, James P. 42*, Margaret 28, Thos. 5, Joanna 3, Leslie C. 1/12(m)
GOSSOM, Ellen 24*
COOK, John B. 41*, Eliz. 36, James L. 14, Thos. B. 8, John W. 6, Robert 4, Mary J. 2
DUNBAR, Dulcena 17*
WHITE, William W. 41*, Jane 38, Rebecca 16, Morton 14, Mary J. 10, Samuel 8, Alex C. 6, Katharine M. 3, W. H. 2 (m)
DOUGLASS, James 19*
MCCABE, Robert 27*
HALL, S. B. 37 (m), Mary A. 33, Charles F. 13, O.? S. 12 (f), O. R. A. 10 (f), Mary A. 8, Elisha H. 6, Julia A. 4, Mariah M. 2, S. B. jr. 4/12

Schedule Page 71

SMITHEY, Austin 36*, Lucy A. 36, Jos. C. 10, Sally A. 8, Mary V. 7
MASONER, Lucy 48*
MAJOR, C. M. 31 (m), Emily 29, Geo. Ann 11, Julia 9, Sarah V. 7, James D. 5, William A. 3, Jos. C. 3/12, Sarah 55
COOPER, L. W. 37 (m)*, Hester A. 35, Sarah E. 11, Amanda M. 7, Nancy J. 5, Rice H. 2
DANDRIDGE, Angeline 27* (B), America 12, Sarah J. 8, Luther 6, Eliz. 3
BRUMFIELD, James 43, Eliz. 39, Thos. D. 15, Lucy W. 13, Jas. jr. 9, Samuel 7, Mary 5, Margaret 3
TURPIN, Perry 35, Susan 33, Martha J. 16, Margaret 14, Mary 12, Harrison 9, Hugh H. 7, Amanda E. 5, Maranda E. 2, Emily F. 2 (twns)
MITCHELL, George 25*, Jane 25, James 3
HOOVER, Martha 2*
WORLEY, C. T. 32 (m), Mary 29, Frank H. 4
CHAPIZE, Henry 3, Lucy B. 31, Benja. F. 10, Mary L. 4, F. P. K. 16 (m)
RILEY, William J. 36, Nancy 36, Samuel J. 14, W. J. jr. 10, John 6, Francis 1
DENNIS, John B. 46, Sarah J. 34, John W. 15, Jos. T. 14, Charles A. 10, Mary F. 5
WILSON, James 42, Charlott 30, Tho. J. 9, James A. 7, Sarah E. 5, Mary H. 3, Nancy R. 1
WEBSTER, Hannah 96, Jonathan 50, Elender 47, Eliza 21, Sarah 14, Harvey 11, Geo. W. 7

1850 Census Jessamine County Kentucky

Schedule Page 72

WOODS, Archibald 64, Mary 61, Jane 29, Eliz. 27, William 24, Thos. 21
MCCANLEY, James 58, Mary 44, Tho. J. 27, John 20, Nancy 8, Hugh 10, William P. 7, Dulcina 5
MAHAN, William 47, Sally T. 41, Wm. T. 17, Jane E. 14, Georgeann 13, Thomas W. 10, Urial D. 7
RILEY, Elizabeth 57*, Jno. F. 28, Samuel E. 20, Archd. A. 18
COLE, Katharine 45*
LYONS, James 30, Patsy 24
GWYNN, Andrew 32*, Isabel 22, Sarah J. 4, James B. 3
WALKER, Robert S. 28*
YOUNG, Archibald 58, Eliza 40, Saml. D. 19, Thomas 17, Mathew 13, Martha 12
HUGHES, Henry 28, Mary A. 22, D. D. 18 (m)
RUSSELL, Hezekiah 60*, Elizabeth 66, Nathaniel H. 31
OCCONNELL, Hugh 15*
ENGLAND, John 25, Amanda 22, S. 17 (m)
WOODS, William 50, Eliza 37, Martha A. 19, Nancy 17, Luther 15, Benja. B. 11, Margt. J. 8, William H. 6, Eliz. 3, Mary D. 1
BOURNE, John 70, Betsy 66, John M. 27, Sarah A. 24
YOUNG, Brown 27*, Emeline J. 23, Adelia 5
DRAKE, Adelia H. 18*
RIDDLE, Isaac 62 (B), Lizzy 60
CROW, Eli 54, Martha 45, Eliz. 18, Nancy L. 11, William H. 9, Eli C. 7
THOMPSON, Sarah 64, John P. 38, Rachael 26, Alexr. 25, Washington 23, Joseph 30, Martha H. 21, Frances N. 18

Schedule Page 73

MAUPIN, John H. 39*, Margt. 33, Sarah F. 12, Susan M. 11, Robert J. 9, John R. 7, Thompson T. 5, Margt. W. 3, Ann E. 1
MOSELEY, John R. 30*
QUEST, Charles 17*
HOOVER, David S. 52, Eliz. 34, Thos. A. 21, Dent 17 (m), Sarah? E. 15, David jr. 12, James R. 9, Henrietta 5, Mary B. 2, Jonas 43
STORMS, Asa 48*, Eliz. 50, William L. 24, James T. 23, Rosanna 21, George T. 20, Jno. A. 18, Nancy M. 17, Willis 15, Eliza A. 12, Emily 11, Asa jr. 8
LAND, William 25*, Jane 25
REYNOLDS, Mary W. 48*, Geo. Ann 18, Wm. F. 16, Mary 12, Jas. S. 31
WILSON, Sophia 60*, Martha A. 24
ANDERSON, Sarah W. 25*
DISHMAN, John 28*, Jane T. 21, Mary L. 1, Eliza E. 1/12
BRONAUGH, John S. 29*, Louisa V. 23
SMITH, James H. 44, Hetty 46
HUGGINS, Harvey C. 42, America 41, Oliver B. 19, Mary E. 15
PEYTON, Thomas 44*, Rebecca 44, Mary E. N. 20, Joseph P. 18, Sarah 14, Wm. T. 6, Edward P. 3, Nannie 3/12
DUDLEY, William S. 25*
CHAMBERS, James P. 33*
HAMILTON, Alex 38*, John 33, Martha B. 26, Edwin 7

1850 Census Jessamine County Kentucky

HOOVER, Andrew 26*
JACKSON, Milton 21*
KING, Henry 20*
FRAZER, George 38, Sarah W. 36, Susan M. 13, Emily 12, Joann 7, Martin 5, Wm. C. Lowry 3, _____ 6/12 (m)
MARRIOTT, William H. 34*, Emily G. 33
HEIFNER?, Henry 17*

Schedule Page 74

BROWN, Talmadge 18 (m)*
HARRIS, Thomas 36*, Mary A. 31, Eliza O. 16, Perpetus? 14 (f), Marquart? 10 (m), Margt. 8, Maranda J. 4
CORN, Ellis 53*, Emily 37, Josephene 16, Ann Mary 14, Samuel T. 9, Kathn. 6, Eliz. 4, Henry E. 1
LEMONS, John 32 (B), Fame A. 24 (f), Alexr. 6, Sarah E. 4, Martha 2
DAY, Margaret 43 (B)
BRUCE, James G. 40, Nancy 34, Eliz. 14
METCALF, Henry 49*, Eliz. D. 44, John 22, Jas. F. 18, Sarah J. 16, Mary B. 14, Geo. W. 12, Chas. W. 9, Alice J. 6, Bettie 1
WOODSON, R. e. 33 (m)*
LUCE?, Myron 32*, Sarah E. 23
WILDER, R. E. 40 (m)*, Ann 23, Henry Q. 1, John 21
OVERSTREET, James 24*
KAPPES, J. H. 26 (m)*
INNES?, Amanda 27*
GIBNEY, R. A. 33 (m)*, Amanda 26, Virgil 2
MATTINGLY, Albert E. 20*
LOWRY, Charles F. 31*, Miranda H. 20, Eliz Jane 7, Susan H. 2, Mary F. 1
NEAL, George M. 18*
MASTERS, Meredith 17*
BLACKFORD, Robert P. 33, Susan V. 20
SCOTT, William S. 42*, Lucy A. 30, Frances A. 18, Richard R. 16, Robert 11, Edwin R. 7
OVERSTREET, Milton 25*
MARTIN, James C. 38*, Eliza B. 36, Martha D. 14, Mary E. 12, Elenor J. 10, James H. 8, Charles E. 3
HAMPTON, Margaret A. 27*, Geo. W. 11, Kathn W. 7
TRUE, Eliza B. 16*, Verginia 1
DAVIDSON, Thomas 25*
MENTZEL, Louis 28*
HORD, Mary 56
SCROGIN, John A. 30*, Mary W. 22, Mary Virginia 5, Martha S. 3, Eliz. 2/12

Schedule Page 75

MCCLONE, Louis 18*
TEVIS, N. B. 16 (m)*
CROW, Holeman 33*, Eliz. A. 28, Mary J. 5, Sarah B. 1, Geo. 17
SMITH, Aaron 22*

1850 Census Jessamine County Kentucky

TRISLER, William 18*
COOK, Pleasant 17*
WILSON, Neal 22*
BRUCE, Judith 58, Mariah 50 (B), David 11 (B), Milly 17 (B), Malinda 6/12
CAMPBELL, Emily 35, Geo. 15, Femonds? 10
WELCH, James M. 39, Eliz. 27, Virginia 14, Jas. W. 2
MASON, Roseanna 26* (B), Squire 9, Thos. 6, Patsy A. 4
VANOY, Squire 65* (B)
WATKINS, Sharlotte 58 (B)
MASON, Fanny 50* (B), Celia 14, Otho 21, Hudson 24
LEWIS, Melson sr. 70* (B)
DAVIS, Sarilda 24 (B), Eliza 7, Eliz. 5, Smiley 2
BURKETT, Eliz. R. 58, Mary H. 45, Bettie A. 19, Jno. W. 17
SINGLETON, Agatha 63 (B)
HIGHTOWER, Elizabeth 37*, Martha 14, Nancy 11, John 8, Mary 5, Kathn. 2
CHRISTOPHER, Sarah 62* (B)
DRAIN, Thomas J. 36, Margaret A. 31, Mary J. 10, Sarah J. 7, Margaret A. 3
LETCHER, Joseph P. 42*, Wm. C. 19, Benja. 13, Ann M. 10, Ellen C. 5
ROBARDS, William O. 20*
KITCHEN, Greene C. 26*, Levina 24
DOZIER, Eliza 17*
YOUNG, Robert 46, Josephene 38, Daniel P. 17, Robt. P. 12, Eliz. 9, Bennett H. 7, Susan D. 4, Melanethon 1 (m)
WALLER, Joseph H. 34, Sirena 29, Ed. M. 6, Mary4, Geo. 1, Henry 18
RIDGELY, Jane B. 55, Richd. R. 33, Martha F. 29, Jane E. 10, Johnanna C. 8, Daniel B. 4, Mary L. 2

Schedule Page 76

SHANKLIN, William 66*
MCCAMPBELL, John G. 48*
MONTAGUE, John 35*, Mary A. 25, Ophelia 4, Julia 2
SANDERS, Charles 22*, Zelpha 18, Sarah 49
WILSON, Valentine H. 27, Eliz. 21, Amanda J. 1
SIMPSON, William 53, Lutitia 44, Henrietta 17, Martha 16, Wm. 14, James 12, John 5
WEST, Thomas E. 62, Eliz. 45
CROZER, David 54*, Margt. 42, Matilda H. 21, Ann H. 19, James M. 16, Hugh C. 15, Martha J. 12, Wm. 11, Eliz. C. 9, Cathn. B. 6, Margt. 4, David jr. 4, Mary T. 1
MINTER, Edwin F. 20*
PRUITT, Mariam 50 (f), Courtney H. 27(f), Berry 26, Frank 22, Mariam V. 18, Angeline 16, Sarah L. 14, Fleet H. 6 (m)
HAWKINS, Anna 64*, Jane 34, Jno. W. 28, Kathn. 26
JOHNSON, Joseph 19* (B)
BOURNE, Andrew 48, Isabel 13, Morton 11, Margt. 71
DRAKE, Ephraim 42*, Zerelda 32, Wm. 14, James 7, Eliz. 4, Jno. C. 3, Nancy 2, Jane 1
LEE, Ephraim 44*
MCCLARY, Alexander 38* (B)
WALTER, Stephen 85*, Sarah 55, Richard G. 20
STULL, Mary 21*

1850 Census Jessamine County Kentucky

LEWIS, Peggy 100* (B)
CORMAN, Abraham 49, Eliz. 41, Sarah 21, Emily 19, Hardin W. 18, Sedonia 16, Eliza 14, Martha 12, Amanda 11, Archd. L. 9, Eliz. 6, Lewis Cass 4, Thos. Barton? 1
SHANKLIN, George S. 39, Martha 28

Schedule Page 77

DAY, Collins 55* (B), Malinda 46
THOMAS, Phebe 70* (B)
CASSELL, Thomas J. 46, Susan M. 36, Wm. H. 17, John L. 15, Benja. F. 13, Susan M. 6, Abert G. 4, Thos. J. jr. 1
MURRAM?, William 54, Lydia 58, Martha J. 18, Geo. Ann 16
CRAVENS, Elisha 23, A. 25 (f), E. 1 (f)
MAYS, John D. 22, Elenor J. 20, Geo. B. 1/12, Carey 30 (m)
GWYNN, Samuel R. 46, Martha K. 17, Robt. J. 15, Jno. W. 12, Ed. N. 9
GWYNN, Jane E. 17, Jas. W. 15, Robt. N. 11, Sarah H. 8, Mary B. 5, Saml. R. 2
HILL, James 56*, Thos. 20, Jane 17, Andrew J. 16
EARTHENHOUSE, Polly 39*
LOWRY, William C. 28, Nancy E. 23
CAMERON, James 35*, Prosepine? 33 (f), Artemecia 10, Jno. S. 4, Jas. P. 1
WEBSTER, Margaret 13*
SIMPSON, Benjamin 26*, Eliz. 26, Phebe 3, Naomi 1
HOOVER, Margaret 20*
REYNOLDS, Joseph 27, Lucy 25, Amanda 8, John 6, Wm. 4, _____ 3/12 (m)
LIVINGSTON, John 52, Arabel 37, Jas.? H. 16, Bettie A. 12, Kathn. 10, Jno. W. 6, Jasper G. 2, Sarah J. 7/12
COGAR, William G. 38*, Sarah E. 14, Andw. J. 13, Nancy L. 12, Wm. C. 8, Mary A. 4, Jaes 3, Eliz. 75
DAVENPORT, Nancy 64*
MINTER, John C. 26*
CAMPBELL, John jr. 26*
HARRIS, Willis 45* (B)
CAMPBELL, John 36*, Eliz. 21, Kathn. 4, Sarah 3, Mathew 1
MOORE, David 25*, John 21

Schedule Page 78

DEAN, Francis 24*, M. 22 (f), Molly 1
WHITE, Joel 46*, Manerva J. 32, Kitty A. 1
TILLETT, Sarah W. 14*, Mary F. 16
GWYNN, Joel 14*
FISHER, Wm. 41*, Sarha 34, Mary A. 14, Tavner? 18 (m), John 12, Tinner? 10 (m), Joseph 7, Caroline 3
HAGAN, Mathew 33*
JONES, Darnel S. 44*, Jane 40, Jesse H. 8, Margt. D. 1
LIVINGSTON, Mary 42*
BENTHREL, Sarah 16*
NEAL, Julia 13*

- 269 -

1850 Census Jessamine County Kentucky

WILMORE, Jacob 57, Mary 42, Hannah 60, Jane 55, Mary J. 19, H. Ann 17, Sally W. 15, Margt. J. 12, Nancy D. 12, John R. 10, Kate C. 8, Susan E. 3
TRISLER, Elizabeth 30*, Levina 10, Jackson 8, Mary E. 4, Philip 1
MOORE, Nancy 65*, Matilda 14
BRONAUGH, William 53*, Mary 42
DISHMAN, Syrena 52*, Eliza 17
HOGAN, Elizabeth 23*, Milton 20
DUNN, N. F. jr. 24 (m)*, Ann 18, Sophrona 16, Josephus 21
FORD, Timothy 30*, Sarah 26, Benja. F. 7
SHANKLIN, Jesse 28*, _____ 23 (f), _____ 3 (m)
WOODWARD, Oliver 19*
COLEY, Charles 23*
MCFARLAND, William 22*
OVERSTREET, John 16*
LEMON, John 25*
BATES, Alvin 25*
RICHARDSON, Edward 25*
HOLLIS, James 21*
HART, John 28*, Harriett 23, _____ 5/12 (f)
COLE, Edward 28*
MCDAVID, Charles 25*
STACK, Robert 30*
PATRICK, _____ 30 (m)*
DAVIS, Joseph 35*
BRONAUGH, William jr. 18*, Kitty 8 (B), Sam 6 (B), John 3 (B)
ROWLAND, Christopher 45, Eliz. 36, Mildred A. 18, John H. 15, George W. 12, Edwin 5

Schedule Page 79

LOWRY, James H. 47, Nancy D. 47, James K. 20, Margaret B. 13, Melvin T. 26

1850 Census Madison County Kentucky

Schedule Page 200

SMITH, John Lynn? 57, Eliza 52, James? C. 27, M. Abay? 23 (m), James B. 17, Mary S. 15, J. Spur? 5
CARPENTER, Fielding 52*, Nancy 43, Wm. 16
TODD, Isaac 27*, Nancy J. 21, Nancy T. 7
BRADLE, William 33, Mary E. 33, Sally T. 11, Ann E. 9, Paulina P. 7, Umphrey 5, Susan B. 3, Mary E. 1
LAKES, Robert 29, Sally 31, Mary E. 8, Lucy J. 5
LAKE, Timothy 26*, Elzabet 36, Henry 13, Jerry 11 (m), Array 5 (m)
CARTER, Timothy 1*
LAKES, John 31, Ruthy J. 25, Wm. 7, Sally E. 5, Nancy J. 3, Susan 3/12
HILL, Harrison 37, Martha 42, Murphey? 16, Susan 15, Elizabeth 13, Wm. 11, James 9, Elemiel? 6 (m)
GENTRY, Bayley 43, Lucinda 33, James W. 14, Iam B. 12, Miranda 10, Plesant 8, Richard 6, Mary F. 3
ADAMS, Andrew T. 27, Dility A. 25, Susan 6, John S. 5, Louisa E. 3
MOBERLY, Emily 42 (m?), Paulina 40, Napoleon 18, Mary C. 16, W. E. 14, John F. 11, Susan A. 9, Martha 5, Eliza L. 3, ___ 7/12 (f)
HILL, Silas 31, Mary 26, Wm. 7, Dorothy 6, Charles 3, Thomas 1
REEVES, Willia S. 44, Lavina 43, Jerry 21 (m), Richard 17, Wm. 17, Stepen 13, Licena 11, Woodson 10, Mary 8, Joseph 6, Thomas F. 3

Schedule Page 201

COX, David D. 47, Paulina 41, Margaret 21, Mary E. 19, Sally An 16, John 15, Robert 13, Paulina 11, Stephen 8, delila 6, Joseph A. 4, Martha 3, Rosa Bell 1/12
HALEY, Hamilton 40, Rhoda 28, Shelby 18 (), Wm. H. 15, David 13, Gravil 11, Dorinda 8, Eliza A. 4, Sarah M. 1
LAVINE, Watson 34, Martha 28, Mary J. 9, Wm. 6, Thomas 4, Warfield, John 23
BALLARD, John 44, Wm. 14, Edward D. 8, John 6, Permelia 4
MILLION, Elam jr. 36, Paulina 37, Ira 14, Joel 12, Mary A. 10, Nancy 8, Lucy A. 6, Lurana 4, Frances 8/12
BARNES, James 29
WHITAKER, John 35, Sally 35, Mary 6, Jane 7, Wm. 5
GIMBELL, Elizabeth 70*, James 29
TURNER, Mary 18*, Wm. 17, Samuel 16, George 14
MILLION, Squire 34, Martha 22
RICE, James 62, Eliza 52, Elizabeth 22, Mary 20, Wm. 18, Samuel 17, Thomas 15, Robert 13, Charles 11, Judith 10, Nancy 7, James 25, Meredith 24
WRIGHT, James B. 35, Sarah M. 25, James 8/12
WILLIS, Moses 51*, Mary 34, Cyrus 15, Barbry 12 (f), Nancy 10, John W. 8, Layfaette 6, Richard 4, Elkany 2 (m)
GULLIN, Orlena 21*

Schedule Page 202

MOREMAN, William 22*
HOWARD, Benjamin 54*, Sarah 44, Zedilan 24 (m)

- 271 -

1850 Census Madison County Kentucky

WATTS, David P. 18*
PERKINS, Gerge T. 33, Mary 27, Permelia 5, Samuel 3, Larah? 1 (f)
PERKINS, Susan 78*
TATUM, Mary Ann 16*
UMBRY, William 33, Georgeanna 25, Joshua 3, Sally 7, Talton 2, Nannie 5/12
MILLION, Travis 23, ary A. 15
SIMMONS, Josiah P. 42*, Patsy 45, Leanna 20, Mary e. 19, Wm. 13, George E. 11, Sarah? E. 10, Tabitha 8, Josiah 6
COWS?, Samuel E. 23*
MOORE, Joseph W. 23, Margaret 24, Reubin 1
PERKINS, John F. 32, Tilothy 27 (f), Archy S. 11, Wm. S. 9, Nancy A. 6, Elzy 4 (m), John W. 1
MOBERLY, Thomas 49, Clarkey 46 (f), Louisa 18, Lucinda 18, Squire D. 14, Wm. C. 13, Margaret 10, Lorah Jane 9, James T. 5
BLACK, samuel 45, Eliza J. 35, Alexander 16, Thomas 14, John D. 12, Mary A. 10, Lucy J. 3
JENNINGS, Jesse 40, Robert 42, Cynthiann 38, Margaret 4, Wm. 2, Robert 3/12
MILLION, Green 53, Elizabeth 46, John Fox 10, Travis 45
DEJARNULT?, James 73, Elizabeth 68, George 35, Sarah 24, Samuel 4/12
JENNINGS, Isiah 70, Margaret 60, Rebecca 36, Catharine 25, Squire 24, Matilda 23
GUESS?, John 54, Ana 46, J. _ Smith 14
MOBERLY, Jacob 45, Catharine 38, Squire 20, Amanda 18, Stephen 16, Phoeba 12, Wm. 8

Schedule Page 203

WHITE, Adderson 26, Sarah 26, Elijah 4, Alice 2, Susan 1/12
WHITE, Durrett 20*
WILLIAMS, Samuel 26*
BURNETT, Samuel 43, Elizabeth 33, Wm. 14, John 12, James 11, Susan A. 6, David 8, Walter 2
WATTS, Charles S. 48*, Elzabeth 45, Wm. 15, Jane 13, George 11, Charles 9, Joseph 6, James 6/12
WALKER, Jane 70*
MILLER, Rebecca 57*
BUSBY, Elizabeth 26*, Rebecca 8/12
WILLIAMS, James 28*, Ann 23
DOOLIN, Hiram 45, Milaud? 34 (f), Martha 15, Eliza 14, Elizabeth 11, Nancy 6
SMITH, Solomon 40, Maria 38, Wm. 18, Thomas 15, George 12, Bethi 8 (f)
WHITE, Claiborn 54, Susan 45, Richard 28, Patsy 25, Susan 2, Ann 2/12
RUSSEL, richard 45, Sally 36, David 15, Mary 12, Ann 10, Claibourn 7, Susan 6, Ellen 4, Hugh 1
JARMAN, E. B. 40 (m)*, Juliett 32, Mary E. 12, Ann E. 8, John 6, Sally 3
FRANCIS, John B. 30*, Eliza C. 19, Martha 4
BOULERAN, John 22*
HARRIS, John D. 35*
CASTLE, William 23*
LITTLE, Samuel 34*
MCCRACKEN, Anoy? 28 (m)*
GROOMLY?, Hugh 21*
CROOK, John 23*
BROUSTON, Thomas 32*, Charles 2
BOULDON?, James 27*

1850 Census Madison County Kentucky

ROBERSON, Robert 30*
GODDIN, S. J. 55 (f), Jane P. 33, Thomas J. 27, Mary 18

Schedule Page 204

WHIRETT, Samuel 51, Mary J. 39, Robert 15, Samuel 13, Thomas 11, Clark 17, Clarinda 8, Elizabeth 6, Sally 1
BALL, C. C. 37 (m), Emily 33, Ellen 8, Louis 6, Frances 4, Christopher 3, Caroline 9/12
FARLEY, John 39, Caroline 25, Margaret 7, James 5, Ann 3
TAYLOR, John G. 39*, Elizabeth 33, Mary E. 17, Henry H. 12, Virginia 7, Charles 6, James 5, Wm. 3, Colley 1 (m)
GRANT, Anthony 38*, Emily 22, Eliza 1
BROWN, Mary 18*, Benj. H. 9
SHACKELFORD, William 40 (B), Caroline 35, Mary J. 11, Euginia 5, Willis 5, Elizabeth 2, Lavina 1
GRANHALGH?, Izrial 43, John R. 9
BROWN, George 69, Elizabeth 69, John 35, Sally Ann 17
WORE, Samuel C. 39, Sarah A. 31, Wm. 9, Martha 7, Iranda? 4, Amanda 2
WALTERS, Owen? 45, Carlile 38 (f), Sarah 14, Catharine 9, Owen? 7, Cabet 5 (m), James 3, Junius? S. 1
WALKER, Joel 50*
MOCKERY, Albert 35* (B)
TURNER, Lidany G. 31 (m), Rebeca 27, George E. 3
WIMSCOTT, M. D. 33 (m)*, Angeline 21, Nannie 4, Martha 2, Wm. 18
JOHNSON, James 25*
SHUTER, James 26*
NIBBINS, Henry 26*
BURRISS?, Charles 23*
KANISEY, Thomas 18*
SMITH, Peter M. 44, Martha 37, Laura 16, Amelia 14, Mary 12, James 9, Jasper 7, Matha 5, Wm. 3, Sally T. 9/12

Schedule Page 205

MILLER, John 52, Bethy 42, Susa 18, Sarah 16, Margaret 14, Bethi 10 (f), Mary 8, John 6, Lucy 4
BLACK, James 50, Sarah 11, Almira 8, John 6
BUCK, Daniel sr. 61, Jane T. 56, Edward 19, H. E. 16 (f), C. H. 14 (m)
BUCK, Daniel jr. 28, Elizabeth 27
PATTERSON, Perry 32, Elizabet 30, Archy 8, Wm. 6, Rebecca 4, Mary A. 2, Elizabeth 8/12
PALMER, Thomas 60*, Nancy 55
EMBRY, Jesse 33*, Milaud? 30 (f), Henry 11, Nancy 9, Thomas 6, Mary 3, Joel 1
TODD, Colemon 28*
JAMESON, William 30, Sarah 28, Sarah 8, John 2?, Norris? 3, Milaud 6/12 (f)
BARNES, Thomas H. 27, Ann H. 24, John W. 9/12
SMITH, John B. 33, Susanna 34, Isaac 12, Anna 9, Thomas 6
MOORE, William 34, Mary A. 21, Isabell 6, Rebecca 5, Rachael 3, Sally Ann 1
SHUTER, John 26, Mary 30, Thomas 3/12
SHEOPORD?, William 37, Mary A. 34, John 11, Jason 7, Irvin 4, George 1

1850 Census Madison County Kentucky

WHITE, James 56*, Frances 46, David G. 13, George 12, McCand 10 (m), Rachael 8, Henry A. 4
BENNET, James 16*
SCOTT, John 40, Mary J. 35, Thomas 9, Lamuel 7, Elvira 5, Frances 3, Marian? 1 (f)

Schedule Page 206

IRVINE, David 53*, David 18
BURT, Samuel 25*
CAMBELL, John S. 30*, Harriett B. 24, Mary R. 1
LYLE, Bethi V. 20 (f)*
JONES, Murphey 80, Mary 52
KINNARD, George W. 36, Biddy 31, James 11, Ann 8, Eliza 5, Wm. 3, Fayett 8/12
SHELBY, Edward 77 (B), Sally 40
BAKER, James E. 24, Lucy 27
CALDWELL, James C. 40, Amanda 37, Robert 14, Jacob W. 12, James 10, Fany 7, John C. 5, Patty W. 1
HAWKINS, Cary 43 (m), Celia 41, Jasin 20, Lucy 15, Nicholas 11, Malissa 8
CRUTCHER, James U. 38, Mary A. 27, Wm. 11, Samuel 11, Tabitha 7
GREEN, Irvine T. 35*, Nancy 35, Francis 8, John 1
MILLER, Martha 55*
KING, Jackson 35*, Margaret 23, Mary L. 1
POWELL, William 22*
FRANCIS, Louis 59, Edi 58 (f), Joseph S. 30, John W. _7, Martha A. 5
BROADDUS, D. R. 23 (m), Lucy A. 20
FOX, Isham 67*, Nancy 41, John 34, Richard 26, Ophelia 18
CRUSE, Isham 16*
DUDLEY?, James W. 43, Sarah V. 36, William 14, Eliza R. 12, Ambrose 10, Robert H. 7, Clifton 5, Catharine 2
IRVINE, Shelby 22 (m)*
ROBERTS, Talton 28*
JARMAN, Lidury? 26 (m), Mar 19
WAGLE, Thomas 56, Mary 40, Susan 11
BIGGERSTAFF, Isaac W. 48, Mary 45, Minerva 20, Penelton 18, Orville 16, Elizabeth 11, Isaac 8, David 13, Wm. 5, Winihfield 2 (m)

Schedule Page 207

FOWLER, James 45, Eliza T. 35, Wm. B. 13, John Smith 10, James C. 9, no name 5/12 (m)
CLOY, Cassius M. 39, Mary J. 35, Warfield 15, Green 12, Mary B. 10, Sallie 8, Cassius 6, Brutus 3, Laura 1
RILSY?, Jackson 29, Talithy 23, Sidney 5 (m), Mary J. 3, Elizabeth 2, Wm. 2/12
BARNES, Clifton K. 20, Margaret 19
MANION, James P. 30, Mary A. 23, Lyonial 1 (m)
MANION, John O. 57, Mary 57, Zarsco Z. 30 (m)
WILLIAMS, Lemuel 39, Louisa 35, William 16, James 14, Elizabeth 12, Mary 10, Louisa 8, Lemuel 5, Harrison 3
WILKERSON, William 69*, Bashey 65 (f), Lucy 17

1850 Census Madison County Kentucky

BARNES, Betsey 45*, Elizabeth 6
SHACKELFORD, Zachery 58*, Frances 69, Tabitha 22, Andrew J. 17
ELLIS, Richard 10*
LANKFORD, Stephen 37, Rebecca 47
JOHNSON, Robert 35, Cyntha 38, Susan F. 12, James F. 11, Plesant W. 5, Thomas J. 4
PERKINS, William H. 45, Eliza 45, Lucinda 20, Elizabeth 18, Caroline 16, Patsy 13, Mary S. 12, Merida 10 (m), Mildred 8, Nancy A. 6
THOMASSON, Daniel 50, Mahaly 29, Lenate 1 (m), Richard 5, Nancy A. 2
THURNAM?, John 25, Rosanna 21, William 3, Louellen 2 (m), Henderson 2/12
IRVINE, Nathaniel 42*, Malina 32, Thomas 12, Sally Ann 7, Mary E. 4
WOODARD, Lucy 70* (B)

Schedule Page 208

HARRIS, Solm? 38 (m)*, Sally A. 33, Robert 11, Carlile 9 (f), Edney 7 (f)
MILLER, Sarah E. 17*
ERWIN, John 71, Sally 65, John C. 26, Nancy 23, Martha 21
VARBEL, Samuel 26, Mary 31, Martha 6
ROSSEL, Anthony 45, Nancy 41, Elizabeth 18, Alexanan 14 (m), Martha 12, Nancy 10, John 8, Margaret 8, Owen 3
PARRISH, Samuel 55*, Susan 54, Ann E. 18, Samuel 15
SHEARER, Michael 42*, Castrisa 23
GRYARD, Josephus 23*
GRIFFIN, John 19*
RAIBOURN, John 30, Harriett 23, Benj. H. 3, Frances H. 1
FOWLER, Thomas 57, Elizabeth 20, Margaret 8, Mary 7, Thomas 6, Judiann 5
FOWLER, Joseph 59, Mary 33, Nancy E. 11, William H. 9
FOWLER, William 56, James 21, Benj. 18, Sidney 15 (m), Elizabeth 13, Mary 19
FLANIGA, Carigan 57, Frances 43, Martha 0, Parthena 18
ROWLAND, James 52, Caroline 47, Mary F. 18, Caroline 17, Amelia 15, Robert 15, Ann 12
QUINN, Susan 58*, Robert 29
WATTS, Frances 39*
NUBY, Woodson 40*, Ophelia 41, Frances 16, John 14, George 13, Wilson 12, Fulton S. 11, Robert 8, Nancy J. 8, Catharine 6, Thomas 4, _____ 2/12 (m)
MOORE, Willis G. 24*
ROSSEL, James 26, Mary 25
GIBONY, Daniel 25, Susan 24, Marion 4 (m), Nancy 1

Schedule Page 209

SHANKS, Charles 50, Sally 48, Simon 20, Hiram 18, John 16, Lucy 14, James 12, John 10, Sally 8, Sidney 6 (m), Mary 3
TAYLOR, Samuel 31, Frances 30, John 7, Jesse 5, Mary J. 5, Patsy A. 3
NUBY, John 31, Lucinda 25, Nancy J. 6, Mary C. 4, Towrison 1 (m)
SAMUELS, James M. 37*, Martha 30, George M. 12, Malissa 10, Robert 7, Thomas 5, Clifton 3, James 1
LANOM, Benj. 45*

- 275 -

1850 Census Madison County Kentucky

JENNINGS, Kasiah 64*, Sarah J. 17
CHRISTOPHER, Daid 32 (m)*
MILLION, Ir G. 46 (m), Frances 46, Franklin 14
PERKINS, Sally 61, Thomas 22, Major 15
NUBY, William 30, Winny 27, William 4, Ann E. 4, James T. 9/12
NUBY, John 41, Susanna 36, Rebecca 7, Mary A. 4, John J. 2, no name 8/12 (m)
MASTIN, Edward 35, Ritta 30, Woodson 10, Susan 8, John A. 6, Elly 4, Edward 2
LOWERY, Green 24, Rusilla 23
MATTICKS, Hesiah 34 (m), Amanda 37, John 15, George T. 13, Argela 11, Isabella 9, Elby 6 (m), Wm. 6/12
ROBERTS, Nathan 38, Eva 38, Sallie 5, George 3, John D. 1
PERKINS, Jesse 30, Emeline 25, Frances 8, Mary 6, Thomas 4, Jesse 9/12 (m)
KNUTZER, George 42, Juda 45
BAKER, Jacob 35, Nancy 27, Malvina 9, Ellen 7, Elizabeth 5, James 1

Schedule Page 210

KIDWELL, Johnty 53 (m)*, Susan 50, Betsy 16, Thomas 19, Samuel 14
COLE, Mary 33*, Susan 14
KIDWELL, Vinson 22, Sally A. 18
LAY, Talton 28, Lydia 25, Francis 10, Wm. 8, Lucy A. 6, Nancy 4, Ellen 2
PARRISH, Sequel 66 (m), Betsey 2, Isham 17, Volney 14 (m), Henry 10, Mary 3
KNUK?, George 40, Lynda 33, Martha 5, no name 11/12 (m)
JENKINS, George W. 22, Rebecca 20, Catharine 1
MORE, William 38, Emma 24, Nancy 9, Mary 7, Wm. 11, Lumptha 3
BAKER, Josiah 38, Sarah 25, Ann E. 5, Mary R. 3, Thomas M. 1
HURST, Smith W. 37*, Rebecca 29
ALEXANDER, Jacob 5*
SHINGLES, Jacob 60*
DAVENPORT, Powoton 52 (m)*
MILLION, Townson 43, Susan 30
HARTHEMAN, John 44, Mariann 30, Elzy 20 (m), Elzabeth 16
PARRIS, Ezekiel 65, Elizabeth 22, Isham 16, Volney 14 (m), Henry 9
MILLION, James S. 40, Sally 38, Francis __ 4, Nancy 3
MONDAY, Andrew 30, Louisa 26, Reubin 10, Mary A. 5, John C. 1
BALLARD, nancy 45, James W. 21, Sally Ann 11
BURRISS, Nelson D. 23, Martha 18
COSBY, Wingfield 59, Emisy? 19 (m), Ann 13, Malinda 13, Catharine 10
CROW, John 46*, Larah 40, Zebedan? 10 (m), John W. 9/12
BROWN, Marion 12 (m)*, Charles 14

Schedule Page 211

LAIRD, Polly 42*, Edward 13, Milam 7, Barterton 5, Mary J. 4
HOLIDAY, Mary 29*
TAYLOR, William 52, Mary 48, Wm. 22, Owen 12, Martha 8
TAYLOR, Barterton 31*, Eliza J. 25, Cyrus T. 4, Jay Z. 1

1850 Census Madison County Kentucky

MONTGOMERY, William 14*
TAYLOR, Talton 67, Elizabeth 67, Rebecca 10, Marion 7
AGEE, James 32, Agnes 31, Eliza 10, Woodson 8, Frances 6, Nancy 4, John 8/12
HADIN, John W. 50, Hannah 48, James 20, Mary A. 17, Henly W. 15, Elizabeth 13, Levi 9, Leroy 9
TAYLOR, Jesse 47*, Elizabeth 45, Permelia 16, Nancy 14, Jesse 2
MONTGOMERY, Columbus 8*
HADIN, Thomas H. 24, Frances Ann 23, Robert W. 4, John T. 5/12
WRIGHT, Jackson 29, Emily 26, John W. 4
RENFROE, Joseph 70, Joseph W. 24, Nancy 21, James P. 20
RENFROE, James W. 27, Mary 24, Mary 1/12, Peter 60, Nancy 16
NUBY, Andrew J. 33, Elizabeth 24
NUBY, Jesse 27, Arsminda 21, Tabitha 8, James 6, Jesse 4 (m), Mary A. 10/12
NUBY, Winaford 60 (m), James 35
PERKINS, Richard 23, Winney 25, Wm. 3
PERKINS, Richard 55, Mary 55, Joseph 35, Kasiah 21
ROACH, Squire 26, Eliza 27, Frances 5, Ophelia 3
MILLION, Burrel 58, Harriett 42, Robert 32, Nancy 14, Chris 9 (m)
MAGEE, Ralph 54, Elnaw 56 (f), Wm. 18, Benj. W. 16

Schedule Page 212

KENITZER, Jacob B. 44, Rhoda 41, Mary 17, James 16, Richard 15, Sidney 14 (m), Fanny 10, John 10, Lethadin 8 (f), Elizabeth 6, Jesse T. 2, Nancy 8/12
FOSTER, Paten 48, Henr E. 44, John 18, Elizabeth 17, Wm. 15, James 14, Caroline 12, Mariann 11, Robert 8, Cloyretta 5
TUDER, Allen 44, Nancy 20, John T. 8/12, Christopher 13, Elizabeth 11, Sally 63
HATHMAN, Joseph 35, Mary 27, Nancy 7
NUBY, Bryant 65, Lucy 63, Talton 26, Susan 24, Nancy 22, Monen? 21 (f), Jesse 20 (m), Harriett 19
MILLION, Bowland 33, Elizabeth 30, Telithy 8, George 6, Frances 4
GREEN, William R. 41, Jane 40, James 23, Margaret 18, Daniel 11, Moses 9, Jane 7, Mary 2
PARKS, Johnathan 35, Barthana 32, Minerva 13, Sidney 12 (m), Almilda 9, Wm. 7, Hiram 3, Rhoda 1
BRANSTON, Thomas 58, Emily 19, Harriett 14, Jacob 12
ANDERSON, Allen 54, Margaret 54, James R. 20, Ann W. 18, Wm. 16, Samuel 14, Sarah A. 12
TUDER, Daniel 56, Rhoda 51, Daniel W. 22, Sally Ann 20, Martha 18, Christo. 9
CAMBELL, James 50, Mary A. 40, Thomas 22, James 20, William 18, Samuel 16, John 14, Susan 11, Alexander 9, Reubin 62

Schedule Page 213

CORNELISON, Albert 33, Martha 30, Wm. 11, Ann E. 9, Martha 7, Mary 4, John 2, Joanna 54
HILL, Isaac 52, Maria 53, Mary 22, Martin 21, Isaac 20, John 18, Elizabeth 14, Ann M. 12, Laura 6
LAIRD, Howard 26, Sarah 25, Harriett 1, Squire 30, Elza 30, Louisa 16, Betsy 10, Mary 8
IRVINE, Albert G. 47, Christopher 10, Adam C. 8, Latvy A. 7 (f), Arneta 5, Elizabeth 4, Margaret 1
BATES, Thomas E. 47, Cyntha 44
HARLOW, David M. 29, Jerome 30, Isabelle 5, Carlile 4 (f), Alice 2, Sarah 3/12
BOGGS, Benj. 42

1850 Census Madison County Kentucky

GROCH, C. J. 41 (m), Eliza 31, Cornelius 17, Arzelia 15, Thomas 14, Nancy 12, Burrus 10, Mary 8, Henry 6, Joean 4, Lashiel 2 (m)
FARRIS, Johnithan 34, Bethenia 27, Wm. 9, Michael 4, Nancy 2
MILLER, John H. 40, Patsy 35, Elizabeth 14, Martha 13, James 10, E. H. F. 8 (m), Amelia 6, Julia 4, Mary B. 6/12
KNIGHT, Curtis 34, Emily 29, Mary 6, James 4, Sarah 3
HIATT, William 47*, Martha 30, Margaret 1, Jerushia 1/12
WHITE, Richard 55*
MARCH, Anderson 33*, Lorinda 19, John 1

Schedule Page 214

HOOVER, Nancy 61*, Woris? 16 (m)
MCCLANIHAN, William 61*, Irvine 23, Jane 22, Ezekiel 18
STNE, Willia 20*, Thomas 15
TRIBBLE, Alexander 40, Nancy 30, Mary 7
MAUPIN, William 32*, Margaret 26, Mary E. 7, Robert 4, Partheny 2
LYMAN, A. B. 26 (m)*
CHAISE, William 26*
MCWILLIAMS, John Q. 22*
BRAWNER, Samuel 17*
GILLISPIE, Louis H. 70, Mary 98
HALEY, William 34, Nancy 30, Archy 11, James 9, Elzabeth 7, Dicy E. 5, Jane 3
OWENS, E. J. 25 (m), Mary 19, Ellena 1, Sarah 4/12
MCWILLIAMS, A. C. 55 (m), Jane 50, Almira 17, Harriett 15, Ophelia 13, Cornelia 11, Virginia 9, Julia 7
ARMSTRONG, Wesley 29, Amelia 19, George 1
BIN, Joel 64, Jane 56, Eliza 14, Warren 10, Paten 8
FICHURMER?, Samuel 35*, Caroline 28, Mary 4, Delia 2
BENNETT, Samuel 17*, Mary 15
GAY, John 54, Lucinda 35, Rebecca 12, Matilda 10, Thamy 9 (f), George 7
ELMORE, James 53, Sarah 45, John 24, Robert 16, Sarah 14, Jane 12, Ann 10, James 7, Jefferson 5
LYLE, Thomas 45, Mary 23, James 18, Urskin 8, Thomas 6
BUTNER, James 24, Angelia 20, Robert 1
BROWN, William 41, Mary A. 33, Mary E. 8, Thomas 6, Wm. 5, George 1

Schedule Page 215

MCCORD, William D. 46, Theodocia 45, Benj. F. 18, Emily 15, Charles 13, Mary 10, Martha 8, Sarah 4
ROGERS, Samuel 31, Talitha 29, Wm. 8, Elizabeth 7
BOULDAN?, William 34*, Arthusa 28, Lusan A. 10 (f), Malissa 8, James K. 6, Salem W. 4 (m), Elizabeth 1
BOWEN, James 14*
BRYANT, Elizabeth 36*
WILLIAMS, Jefferson 48*, Cyntha 45
SNODDY, Jane 75*, John 35
BUTNER, John 18*

1850 Census Madison County Kentucky

ROBERSON, Mary J. 12*
MILLER, John 28, Sally 26, Owen 2
BUCKHANEN, Caleb 49*, Sally 40, John 13, Anderson 8, Mary 4
WOODS, Wiley 79*, Talitha 32
WHITE, William 24*
HUNT, Richard 26*
THOMPSON, Joseph 21*, James 19
SNOOKS, R. P. 19 (m)*
BING, David 23*
FARREL, Patrick 30*, Mike 24
MAUPIN, Thomas 85, Margaret 50, Jesse 19
DAVIS, Samuel 28, Mary 25, Easter 3, Edwin? 1
DOSHNIR?, John 34*, Nancy 33, Margaret 12, Mary 10, Nancy J. 7, Malissa 5, Susan 3, George Ann 1
ODER, Thomas 27*
MCWILLIAMS, Sidney 21 (m)*
CHITEY, Matthew 49, Pricilla 53, Sarah 4
HARDEN, Sally 42, Josiah 17, John T. 5, Oliver 3, James K. 1
MCWILLIAMS, Elihu 50
SIMS, William 50, Elizabeth 48, John 21, Theadore 20, Susan 17, Melvin 15, Cabin? 12 (m), Eliza 7, George 5
TODD, John 45, Nancy 35, James 17, John 16, Levi 14, Elizabeth 12, Edward 10, Ledonia 8, Lesilia 4, William 4/12

Schedule Page 216

ELDER, Andrew 62, Lucinda 58, Anderson 26, Lucinda 24, Nancy 23, Andrew 20, Mary F. 18, Elvira 17, Charles 10
WALKER, Lucy 60, Eliza 25, Leann 23
CORNELISON, Alitha 37, Martha 12, Sarah 10
SOAPER, James 47, Susan 37, James 18, Elizabeth 16, Thomas 14, Denis 12, Sarah 10, John 8, Tobias 6, Aoline 4 (f), Mary A. 2, Edward 6/12
CAMBELL, David 27, Emily 24, Frances 7, Edley 4 (m), Mary J. 3, David J. 1/12
WATSON, Sally 60, Paulina 25, Joel 2
CAMBELL, Edley 82 (m), Hannah 64, Nancy 28
CAMBELL, Archibal 30, Margaret 27, Wm. 6, Archibal 2
MCWILLIAMS, William G. 51*, Frances 45, Sally Ann 14
SPILLMAN, Hardin 20*
BOULNAN?, Hardin 31, Ruthe 31, Mary 10, Brutus . 8, Jefferson 6, Taylor 3, Josephine 1
ROBERTS, James 33, Nancy 28, Thomas 7, Elzabeth 5, Margaret 4, Howard 3, Cyntha 1
MCWILLIAMS, Mary 70, Harrison 38, James 28, Paulina 17
MCHENRY, David 30, Lucy 23, Andrew 4, Martha 5/12
MCHENRY, John E. 49*, Rebecca 45, James 19, Mary A. 16, Nancy 13, Wm. 7
GOLDEN, Dudley 28*
MOODY, Andrew J. 33, Luvina 43

1850 Census Madison County Kentucky

Schedule Page 217

BURNETT, William C. 32*, Louisa 40, Wm. 8, Edley 5 (m)
HOOTEN, Jesse 9 (m)*
WITT, William 63, Jae 48, David 20, George 16, Sally Ann 14, Elisha 12, Thomas 10, Elizabeth 8, Malissa 5
MOORE, Franklin 29, Sally Ann 28, Frances Cloy 4, Charles E. 5/12
CAMBELL, William 34, Selina 31, Mary J. 13, Nancy 11, George W. 9, Wm. 7, James A. 5, Sarah 1
WILSON, William 44, Patsy 43, Thomas 19, Nancy J. 16, Sarah 15, ames 11, Agathy 9, Wm. 8, Elizabeth 6, Martha 1
KINCAID, Thomas 60*, Sarah 37
BUSH, William 17*
BALLARD, James B. 73, Frances 70
HARDIN, Jemima 91, Mary A. 49
HUBBARD, Granville 36, Mary 33, John W. 10, Michael 8, Margaret 7, James F. 6/12
CORNELISON, M. G. 37 (m), Sarah 39, Margaret 16, Richard 14, John P. 10, Duranda 8, Dosha 6
KIDD, W. B. 26 (m)*, Virginia 23, Isabelle 2
ERMAN, Elizabeth 55*, Eliza 20, George 16
MCWILLIAMS, Andrew 46, Hannah 45
MAIDEN, Samuel 50*, Hannah 45, Daniel 30, Sarah 27, Elizabeth 22, Eliza 19, Hannah 5, Patsy 3
BOWMAN, Green? 5*
DIGGS, Morgan 25*
GABBARD, John 63*, Elizabeth 50, Margaret 23, Eliza 22, Mary 20, Susan 18, John 16, Elizabeth 13
MONROE, James 1*

Schedule Page 218

HILL, Murphy 65*, Mary 62, Martha 10, John 10, Mary 9
MCWILLIAMS, Mary 25*, John 4
GOLDEN, Fielding 22, Mary 19
GOLDEN, Harrison 21
HULLET?, Joseph M. 25*, Nancy 25
GABBARD, Eli B. 25*
HART, James 28, Suasn 31, Nancy A. 7, Mary J. 5, George W. 4, Martha 2
DAVIS, Ennis 35, Hannah 29, Ennis 1
DOUDEN, James 28, Elizabeth 26, Malissa 2
DOUDEN, Michael 59, Nancy 50, John 21, Minerva? 18
GABBARD, Hiram 27*, Nancy 35, Elizabeth 8, Sarah 6, Frances 4, Nancy 8/12
CIMBRELL, Sally 40*, John 17
BLAKE, Samuel 45, Nancy 45, Reubin 10, Thomas 7, James G. 10
KINNARD, John 28*
DOUDEN, Margaret 6*
CLIFT, Thomas 40, Anna 35, Thomas 12, Mary 10, Emaline 7, Louisa 4
JERMAN, William 35, Amanda 30, Mary A. 12, James 10, Srah 7, Wm. 4, Jane 2
PARKES, William 30, Martha 30, James 10, Sarah 8, Richard 6, Wm. 5, Martha 4, Mary C. 4, Eliza 1
HARLOW, Bartlett 35, Margaret 30, Thomas 18, Daniel 15, John 7, Jacob 5, Louisa 4, Anna 2, Eliza 1
JOHNSON, Alfred 30, Elizabeth 25
JOHNSON, William 37*, Anna 30, Mary 14, Wm. 11, Plesant 8, Martha 1, Emaline 4

1850 Census Madison County Kentucky

Schedule Page 219

HOOTEN, John 65*
DENNISEN?, Jesse 49, Eliza 38, John 17, Martha 12, Elza 8, Elizabeth 6, Minerva 4
DENNISEN?, Bowen 26, Jane 17, Whitfield 6/12
JOHNSON, Easter 50*, Major 28, Franklin 19, Isham 17, John 15, Hannah 13
CLIFT, Archibol*
DAVIS, Samuel 28, Mary 26, Easter 3, Eanos 1
MOODY, James 27, Patsy 27, Mary A. 6, David A. 2
HOSKINS, Jack 52, Lucy 50, Colman 26, Nancy 16, Lucinda 14
HOSKINS, William 25, Elizabeth 23
PARKS, John W. 47*, Elizabeth 35, Samuel 20, Margaret 18, Elizabeth 16, Jefferson 13, Frances 8, John B. 6, James 3, Mary W. 1
SMITH, William 45*
NEWLAND, Silas 47*, Emily 40, Isaac 23, Sally Ann 18, Broaddus 15, Elizabeth 13, China 11 (f), Mary 9, Patsy 7, Thany 5 (f), Allis 3 (f), Cloyretta 1/12
KATES, Isai 47 (m)*
VANWINKLE, James 55, Fanny 50, Martha 18, Vianna 14, Robert 13, Julia 11, James 9
POWELL, Abram 28, Leander 24, Emily 2
LAMB, Madisn 39, Jenny? Ann 33, Mary 15, Mahala 12, Wm. 11, John 8, Isaac 5, Elizabeth 3, Lucinda 8/12
LAMB, Oliver 19, May 25, Susan 1/12
WILLIAMS, Abraham 50, Patsy 45, John 25, Silas 20, Volentine 16, Lelia 21

Schedule Page 220

POWELL, Michael 48, Nacy 42 (f), Richard 21, Martha 19, Michael 17, Robert 15, Hiram 12, Sally Ann 8, Mary J. 6, Susan 5, Margaret 3, Samuel 1/12
THOMAS, Jesse 39, Sally A. 26, James M. 8, Willia 6, Levi 5, Sally A. 4, David 6/12
CLIFT, George 30, Elizabeth 30, Wm. 2
BENNETT?, William 45, Mary 45, Frances 23, Paulina 21, Sally 15, Jane 12, James 10, Wm. 8, John 2, _____ 8/12 (m)
PARKER, Susan 48, James 30, Elizabeth 27, Sally Ann 22, John 21, Nancy 17, Frances 15, Robert 13, Michael 11, Margaret 7, Elzira 8
COLE, William 50, Harriet 35, Maria 20, Marion 8, James 6, Mary 3
WILLIAMS, Joseph 33, Patsy 28, Howard? 8 (f), Sally A. 6, Abraham 4
BLAND, Franklin 40, Mary A. 40, Thomas J. 19, Catharine 17, Nancy J. 14, Julia 12, Clifton 8, Mary 3, Sarah 9/12
CORNELISON, Richard 59, Frances 25, Elzira 16
CARR, William 62, Patsy 47, Elender 14, Eve 12, Gentry 10, Jane 9
HARPER, Jefferson 32, Sophia 39, Patsy 15, Talitha 11, Thomas 10, Maranda 8
WEST, Robert 32, Manerva? 30, Elizabeth 6, Manerva? 3, Margaret 3/12

Schedule Page 221

JOHNSON, William 38, Frances 35, Mary F. 13, Wm. 9, Plesant 6, Martha 8/12
RHODES, James W. 30, Margaret 25, Elizabeth 5, Samuel 3, Agee 9/12

1850 Census Madison County Kentucky

JOHNSON, Schuyler 31*, Laura 24, Alexander 7, Mary M. 4, Squire F. 7/12
TODD, Mary 50*, Mary A. 20
HART, Caleb 25*, Jane 26, Jasper 12, Amanda 9, Mary 7, Wm. 3, John 6/12
KERBEY?, Elisha P. 21*
JOHNSON, Major 65, Elizabeth 63, Daniel 23, Reuben 21
ROBERTS, Jackson 35*, Elizabeth 31, Jesse 11, Mary 7, Nancy J. 4, Wm. 2
SIMMS, Nathaniel 74*
TERREL, William T. 44, Perthena 37, John 17, Wm. 15, Daniel 13, Robert 11
TERREL, Beverly 39 (m), Mary F. 16, James H. 14, Napoleon 11, Lurenda 7
EASTEN, Reuben J. 53, Nancy 51, Samuel 17, John 15, Loftis 13, George 7
WEST, James B. 65, Sarah 60, Wm. 30, Kasiah 23, Permelia 21
MCWILLIAMS, James 30, Paulina 18, Renner? 2/12 (m), Mary 60, Harrison 40, John 5
STOPP, William 54, Sharlett 48, David 15, Lucy 11
CARR, James 73, Thomas 34, Dicy 32, Patsy 30, Owen 27
PARRISH, John H. 28, Susan 24, Julia A. 4, James 3, Mary 1
MILLER, Alfred 23*, Minerva 23, J. T. S. 3 (m)
MATHEWS, Mosilda 18*, Jane 8

Schedule Page 222

DAVIS, Joab 25, Permelia 33, Wm. 7, Robert 5, Levi? 3
CORHOM, Robert 64, Martha 58, Ann 47, James 24, Edward 18
MOSS, William 55, Jane 54
MOORE, James 81*, Mary 72
ELAN, John 35*, Emily 31, James 10, Mary 7, Elizabeth 5, Thomas 3, Lucinda 1
CAMBELL, Samuel 56, Nancy 46, Mary 21, Wm. 19, Samuel 16, Margaret 14, Minerva 11, John 9, Josephine 6, George 4, Martha 4
HESTER, Jerry M. 60 (m), Mary 56, Edward? 21, Eliza 19
FARRIS, Michael 60*, Michael 20, Lucy A. 15
GENTRIAGE?, Ann 30*
HOCERDAY, Richard 38*, Elizabeth 28, Amanda J. 9, James 7, George 4, Lucy 2
CORHOM, Maria 17*
ROSS, George M. 40*, Eliza 39, Eugine 9/12
PINMOODY, Ann M. 11*
MOBERLY, Elias 50, Isalinda 40, Elizabeth 17, Charles 15, Mary 1
BARNETT, Willia 79*, Mary A. 27
ATKERSON, Mary E. 33*
DAVIS, Jackson 34, Mary J. 24, Joseph 8, Barnett 6, Margaret 4, Nancy 2, Schuyler 35
MOBERLY, Susan 40, Margaret 22, Mary A. 21, Clifton 15
MORAN, Robert 56, Elizabeth 50, James 25, Rebecca 19, Ann M. 15, Robert 1
MANZEY, Mary 65*, Margaret 35, Harrison 30, Lucinda 26
ROLSTIN, John 19*, Mary 15, William 15
ROSS, Susan 66, Madilla 44, James 43, Margaret 33, Fountain 28

1850 Census Madison County Kentucky

Schedule Page 223

SCOTT, Susan 55, Thomas 30, Susan 25, Nancy 24, Reubin 21, Joeann 18, Jane 17, James 15, John 13
FITZPATRICK, Frances 64*, Alexander 42
TURNER, Elizabeth 56*, Eliza 38, Merian? 26 (f), Cyrus 24
DUFF, William 34, Minerva 25, Mary A. 7, Wm. 6, Irvine 3, no name 3/12 (m)
BASSETT, Nancy 80*
DUFF, Lotsy 44*
OGLEBEE, Jesse 86*, Celia 71
WALLACE, Susan 33*
MITCHEL, Fielding 53, Margaret 59
WILLY, Mary 47, John 25, Nancy 21, Elizabeth 18, Sally Ann 16, Permelia 13, Letturia 11, John 4
PATTERSON, Samuel 68, Margaret 42, Joel 38, Wm. 34
LUNSFORD, Enoch 26, Lucinda 24, Thomas 4, Mary 2
HULETT, Catharine 46, Granvil J. 26, Nancy J. 21, Ephram 19, Catharine 18, Jasper 16, Rosa 14, Amanda 12, Elias B. 9
WALLACE, James 66*, Margaret 62, Margaret 22, Sarah 30, Rebecca 25, Elias 21, Rachael 18
BAKER, Elizabeth 83*
STINSON, Mary 55, Patsy 32, Sarah 20, Richard 23, Nancy 22, Grissom 15, David J. 12
STINSON, Edward 38, Mary A. 28, John H. 10, James M. 9, Rosa 7, Wm. 5, Mary J. 3, Elizabeth 1
KINNARD, Davi? 30, Amelia 28, John 3, Mary E. 1

Schedule Page 224

MOORE, Walter 48*, Sarah 37, Ann E. 9, Jane A. 7, Elizabeth 5, Thadius 4, _____ 8/12 (f), John 56
ROLLINS, Moses 23*
STEPHENSON, Mary A. 23*
BLACKBURN, James 57, Nancy 48, Disey 21 (f), Susan 19, James 21, Oliann 15, Jesse 12, Nancy 8, Martha 5
SMITH, Benagy 35 (m), Elizabeth 31, Alvarin? 7 (m), John M. 6, Mary J. 5, Wm. 4, Susan 2
ELDER, Judith 58, Margaret 34, Alsy 32 (f), Josephine 12, Wm. 3
HULETT, Thomas 26, Susan 28, Wm. 3/12, Granvil 28, Ephram 19
ELDER, Robert 31, Lucinda 21, Amanda 8, John J. 6, Ann Rachael 5, Anderson 1
KERBEY, elisha 68, Rebecca 67, Reuben 16, Mary A. 19
LEE, John 33, Ann 26, Martha 2, Mary 1/12
CARR, Harrison 36, Mary 8, Wm. 3
WRIGHT, Sally 42, Martha 22, Arthusa 20, Julia A. 18, Jesse 15, Mary J. 14, Dianna 12, Palestine 10 (m)
ANDERSON, Charles 23, Amanda 20, George E. 1
BOATRIGHT, James 49*, Rebecca 30, Hemetra 10, Samuel 8, Wm. 6, Lucinda 3
WILISFORD, Samuel 66*
BESS, Samuel 25*, Nancy 30, Ann E. 2, Mary 1, John 17
SIMS, James 23*
BALLARD, William 30, Nancy 25, Margaret 8/12
BALLARD, George C. 52, Larissa 50, James 28, Edward 26, Elizabeth A. 23, John 22, Thomas 16, Catharine 14, Richard 13, Caroline 10

1850 Census Madison County Kentucky

Schedule Page 225

NOWLAND, William 41, Elizabeth 29, Wm. 17, Elizabeth 15, Edward 12, Martha 10, Frances 1
FRANKLIN, Jesse 55*, Mary 47, Benj. L. 21
MANIS, Susan 80*
GATES, James 35, Agnes 30, John 6, Martha 4, Margaret 2, Patience 80
FOLEY, william 47, Mary A. 35, Betsey 20, Nancy 18, Susan 13, Alexander 15, Almira 12, Eliza 6, Thomas 4, Margaret 3, Mary 2, Robert 11/12
JOHNSON, David 45, Elizabeth 43, Margaret 21, John H. 19, Lucinda 17, Amanda 15, Malissa 13, Lidonia 10, Eliza W. 6
BOATRIGHT, Elizabeth 71*, Alexander42, Sally A. 24?, Martha 19, Ellna? 15, Eliza 11
KELLRY, Martha G. 51*
LOCKEY, Samuel 70, Jane 55, Andrew 25, Delany 21 (m), Robert 15, Malcom 13
BARNETT, Robinson 38, Minerva 38, John 13, Eugine 10, Boyd 5
BARNETT, William 77, Mary 32
CRAGLER, John 38, Galville 25 (f), Lucy A. 9, Sally A. 7, Phoeba 6, George 4, John C. 1
MITCHELL, Leroy 45, Margaret 88
KINCAID, Samuel 50, Margaret 31
THOMPSON, James H. 24, Rebecca 26, Sarah 3, Mary J. 1
WALKUP, Samuel 57, Mary54, Lucinda 20, Harvie 18, Kasiah 15, Robert 26, Finley 28 (m)

Schedule Page 226

GUTRIDGE, John G. 74, Mary 60, Patsy 35, Nancy 23, James 22, Lucy 20, Sally 19, Wm. 15, Elizabeth 7, James 12
TATUM, Thomas 58, Mary 52, John 28, Jemima 30, Mary A. 10
TODD, Baxter 36, Eliza 37, Jenny 16, Nancy 14, Elizabeth 13, John W. 10, Wm. 8, James 6, Samuel 3, Christopher 2
VAUGHN, Ann 52*, America 24, Fayette 23, Elizabeth 21, Martha 19, Nancy 12, Alexander 10, Benj. F. 8
MOBERLY, Camron? 40*
WALKUP, William 30, Sophia 26, Martha 9, Mary A. 7, Richard 5, Elizabeth 3, Thomas 2/12
DAVIS, Josephus G. 32, Virginia 28, Constantine 8 (m), Cephus 5, Robert 3, Wm. 1
TODD, Madison 42*, Sarah 37, John M. 14, Mary E. 11, George 9, James M. 7, Nancy 5, Waller 2, Wm. 1/12
FLETCHER, James 24*
FLETCHER, Mary 55, Elizabeth 18, Lucy 16, Patterson 15
TODD, Joel 50, Nancy 53, Irvine 22, Newton 20, Amanda 16, Lucy 14, Mary 13, Joel 10
TODD, John 25, Martha 23, Lucinda 2, _____ 1/12 (m)
ELDER, James 27, Martha 26, Nancy 3, Mary 1, Joel 2/12
COURR?, Jesse 57, Elizabeth 47, Stephen 11, Sally 50

Schedule Page 227

WEST, George 46, Elender 35, Susan 16, Elizabeth 14, Eliza 2
RENFROE, Thomas J. 40, Frances 35, Caroline 19, Elizabeth 15, Green 13
HINTON, William 21*

1850 Census Madison County Kentucky

DOOLY, Nancy 65*
HOPER?, Eliza 60, Tamer 66 (m), Matilda 20
BURRUS?, Nancy E. 30*, James M. 6, Eliza M. 5, Luvina 2, _____ 1/12 (f)
BIGGS, John 26*
COCHRAN, John 58*, Wm. 23, Walker 18
HARDEN, James 37*
FREEMAN, James H. 46*, Mary 44
WALKUP, William 20*, Nancy 17, James 12, Jerry Miah 10 (m)
WALKUP, Samuel 93*
HARDEN, Elizabeth 25*
MASON, Joseph 43, Nancy 20, Lucy 2, Rachael 60, Zerilda 17
GALOWAY, John 63*, Elizabeth 50, Franklin 26, Johnathan 22, Granvil S. 20, Tyrey B. 11 (m)
BLAND?, John 40*
MASON, John 66, John W. 36, Margaret 33, Samuel 31, Mary A. 22
HOCKERDAY, James S. 32, Luisa 28, Nancy 8, Wm. 7, Elizabeth 5, Laura 1
HOCKERDAY, Samuel 58
MILLER, Malcom 38, Mary J. 27, Wm. 10, Virginia 7, Lessly 5 (m), no name 10/12 (m), Wm. 14
DUNCAN, Lucy 64*, John A. 36
GOODLOW, Levia 32*, Emily 11, Duncan 10, Wm. 7
HARRIS, William 45, Malinda 42, John D. 20, Nancy J. 18
BLACK, Sarah 80, Elizabeth 49, Patsy? 47
OGG, Johnithan 50*, Martha 40, Mary 16, Martha 15, Elizabeth 13, Miranda 12, Howard 10, Tabitha 8, no name 8/12 (f)

Schedule Page 228

KERBEY, Marion 18 (m)*, Arminta 16, Sally A. 14, Rebecca 12, Lucinda 10, Wm. 8
GARVIN, Martin 32*, Jane 6, Mary 7, Malinda 6, Paulina 4, Margaret 3/12
HARRIS, Joseph 30*
CLUB, Joshua 26*
MCWILLIAMS, John C. 63, Nancy 54, James 32, Richard 38, Schuyler 25, John 21, Samuel 19, Sidney 17 (m), Elizabeth 14, Dudley 12, Nancy 10
OGG, William 50, Elizabeth 48, Martha 21, Wm. 18, Elizabeth 17, Mary A. 15, Nancy 13, Thomas 12, Napoleon 9, Susan 6
THOMAS, Churchill 61, Barbry 47, Nataniel 21
THOMAS, William 23, Sally 20, Susan G. 1
TAYLOR, William C. 29, Elizabeth 22, Martha 7, Jacob 4, James 2
RHODUS, William 39, Jane 33, Talita 11, James 8, Amanda 6, Elizabeth 3, Richmond 1
YATES, Anderson 41, Malinda 28
CROUCHER, Edward 46, Naomy 49, Thomas 15, Martha 13, Rebecca 9, Nancy 6, Susan 3, John W. 6/12
WALKER, Stephen 30, Paulina 27, Lucy A. 7, Sally 5, John 3, D. W. 1 (m)
MAUPIN, Washington 43, Susan 30, James 20, Caldwell 14, Archibal 12, Seth W. 11, George W. 9, Joel 6, Anna 4, Martha 2
MAUPIN, King 39, Nancy 35, John W. 18, Socrates 14, Wm. 12, Sarah 10, Sidney 8 (m), Julia 6, Harriett 4, Nancy 3, Henry 2, Franklin 1/12

1850 Census Madison County Kentucky

Schedule Page 229

YATES, James 42, Sally 64, Brewster? 40 (m), Milton 3
BALLEW, George 48, Frances 42, Sally A. 22, Elizabeth 19, Nancy 17, Owen 15, Mary E. 13, Talitha 11, Martha 8, James 7, Robert 6, Margaret 4, George 2
KEELY, Arminta 46, Howard 21, Green 18, Mary 15, Barnett 13, Brook 10, Elizabeth 5
CARDWELL, George 40, Jemaima 37, Louisa 16, Levi 16, Martha 8, Thomas 7, Huston 6, Edmund 4, Andrew 1
YATES, John 80, Anna 65
CRAIG, William 26*, Elizabeth 27, Sarah 5, Malissa 3, James 1
SHOEMAKER, Marion 17 (m)*
RAIBOURN, Milton 39*, Paulina 34, Wm. 16, James 14, Sarah 12, Milton 5, Mary 3
LAY, Henry 50*
CARTER, William 45*
ESTILL, Wallace 76, Elizabet 62, Clifton 27
JACKSON, James 23, Jane 16
MASON, James R. 29, Margaret 22, Wm. 4, Sarah 3, Mary 2
CORNELISON, Edward 27, Ann 20, Patsy 5/12
CHRISTOPHER, George 34, Laura 28, James 9, Reubin 5, John 3, Elizabeth 4/12
CORNELISON, Garland 40 (m), Ely 30, Alexander 28, Miland 25 (m), Patsy 63
RYAN, T. P. 32 (m), Martha 29, John 6, Wm. 5, Bertie 4 (f), Patsy 2, Miland 9/12 (f)

Schedule Page 230

STONE, Samuel 60, Nancy 54, James G. 27, Matilda 24, Samuel 8/12
CHINAULT, William 44*
DRENNAN?, Amanda 24*
MILLER, James 32*
COSHOUR?, Robert 25*
KINNARD, Fields 23*
THARP, George 23, Elizabeth 20, Emma 5/12
LAMB, Lucy 70, Eliza 24, Jefferson 21, Johnithan 21, Arzela 11, Thomas 2
LAINE, Alvy 39 (f), Wm. 19, Lucinda 17, Milly 16, Amanda 13, John 12, Martha 10, James 2
LAMB, Richard 35*, Elizabeth 30, Warren? 14
WALTON, Elizabeth 63*
BALLARD, Nicholas 55*
HUDSON, Edward 29*
CARPENTER, William 29*, Eliza 24, Louis 1
BALLARD, T. B. 30 (m), Miranda 27, Leonard 9, Palestine 7 (m), Thomas 5, Ellen 3, Christy 1 (m)
SMITH, Thomas 33, Marola 32 (f), Elizabeth 11, John 9, Miland 7 (f), Ellen 6, Robert 3, Wm. 2, Cyrus 5/12
PINKSTONE, Eli 77, Elenda 63
JARMAN, John J. 34, Agnes 35, Thomas 11, Viney 10 (f), Nancy 9, Plesant 7, Miland 6 (f), Ersana 4, George 9/12
BROWNING, John W. 38, Mary 30, Ellen 14, Louisa 13
QUINN, Elizabeth 54, Benj. 28
BARNY?, Jerry 58, David 25, Minerva 28, Wm. 23, Iranda 22, Lucinda 18, Elizabeth 15

1850 Census Madison County Kentucky

WITT, Littleberry 38, Mary 37, Margaret 16, John 14, Thomas 12, Paulina 8, Lotty A. 6, Allen B. 4, Last 6/12 (f)

Schedule Page 231

QUINN, James W. 23, Elizabeth 16
QUINN, Leanny N. 33 (m), Sally A. 26, Narcissa 4, Mary 3, Elizabeth 11/12
BARTLETT, Peter 54, Elizabeth 48, Florinda 16, Nancy 10, Fayett 5
BARTLETT, Amos 31, Minerva? 23, James 8/12
BARTLETT, William 23, Mary 19, Jesse 8/12
BARTLETT, Spud 25, Hannah 20, James 3, Sarah 1
HILL, William 40, Margaret 26, Frances 12, Jane 8, Richard 10, Robert 6
WARFORD, Camron? 66, Mary 62
QUINN, Hiram 25, Eliza 18, James 1
HUNTER, Ruth 85
KINDRED, William 56, Mary 53, Elzira 20, Joshua 18, Julina 16, Caleb 14, Daniel 11
KINDRED, Nathaniel 27, Elizabeth 32, Andrew 5, Robert 3, James 2, Lucinda 3/12
HUNTER, John 57, Elizabeth 56, Wm. 26, Thomas 21, Arthusa 18, Jane 15, Minerva 13, Susan 7
ABRAMS, Joseph 38, Lucinda 41, John B. 19, Bossel 17 (m), Leluster 15 (f), Nancy 11, McKursy 8 (m), Williamson 7, Thomas 5, Maria 3
ROBERTS, James M. 34, Permelia 34, Lawford 11, Owen 7, Mary 4, Margaret 2
HENDRIX, David 36, Susan 32, George 16, James 13, Dudley 10, John 9, Joshua 6, Judy A. 5, Amanda 2, Silars 4/12 (m)

Schedule Page 232

KELLY, William 25, Larilda 25, Mary 3, Rachael 2
BUFORD, James 46, John 87
GENTRY, James H. 27, Amanda 27, Mary 7, Nancy 5, Minerva 3
BICKEREL, Thomas 29, Mary A. 25, Wm. 5
GENTRY, Plesant 22, Maria 21, Curtis 2/12
KINDRED, John 30, Minerva 27, Reubin 8, Minna? 6, Cynthiann 4, Amanda 2
MARSH, John 33*, Mary 35
PRESLY, Enoch 15*, James 12, Lydia 10, John W. 7, Thomas 5, Robert 3, Elizabeth 2
LEWIS, Woodson 44, Ellmair? 50 (f), James 23, Asa 19, John 17, Mary 14, Elizabeth 12, Josiah 11, George 8
EASTER, William 42, 43, Patsy 20, James 19, Susan 15, Milly A. 13, Mary 10, Catharine 9, Nancy 5, Ducilla 73
WEBBER, Elizabeth 44, Minion? 21 (m), John 20, George 18, Cassius 15, Ann F. 12
BURGESS, Charles W. 31, Mahala 35, Eliza A. 8, Thomas 6, John W. 1
HARRIS, Overton 30, Maoma 26 (f), Ellen A. 7, Minerva? 5, Milly J. 4, Josephine 1
SMITH, Asa 46, Catharine 46, John 7
DIXON, Bastin 29, Jane 29, Wm. 9, Franklin 4, Sarah 2
GRIGGS, James 24, Lucy 23, Sarah 1
HISEL, John W. 41*, Catharine 40, Mary J. 17, Willis 14, Leroy 1, Algin 10 (m), John 8, Augustin 6, James 4, Walker 2

1850 Census Madison County Kentucky

Schedule Page 233

WILSON, James 28*
FRITZ, Jacob 47, Jane 36, Amanda 16, Michael 14, Phillip 9, Martha 5, Dillard 1/12
HALL, Allen 50, Amanda 44, Richard 21, Elihu 17, Mary 13, Elizabeth 11
EDWARDS, Jesse 40, Susan 22, Minerva 12, Joseph 10, Belinda 8, Daniel 5, Cynthian 3 (f), John 1
ADAMS, Thomas 50, Thomas 23, Paten 18, Elisha 17, Mary 12, Wm. 10, Alexandrew? 8, Strowder 6 (m)
SHIFFLET, Fountain 50, Rebecca 48, Clifton 25, Jacintha 23, Rebecca 21, Margaret 20, Christopher 18, Joel 15, Irvine 14, Biddy 11, Martha 9, Hardin 6
ROBERTS, Coler 42 (m), Mahaly 41, Lawrence 18, David 17, Margaret 15, Susan 12, Mary 9, Martha 9, Enoch 8, Andrew 5, Rebecca 4, John M. 3, George 1
PARKES, Levi 26, Margaret 28, Wm. 4, Litha J. 3, Elizabeth 1
BAKER, Litha 53, Wanley 17, Sharlott 13
VANWINKLE, John 29, Martha 33, James 14, Racheal 12, Amanda 11, Easter 9, Sarah 6, Mary 2, Cassius C. 9/12
SHIFFLET, Thomas 41, Anna 41, James O. 15, Cyrena 12, Thomas 10, Hannah 8, Miland 3 (m)

Schedule Page 234

MCQUINN, Nancy 38, Cary 19 (m), Thomas 19, Polly 17, Martha 14, Richard 8, Sally 8, John 4, Samuel 11
BURK, John 58*
COVINGTON, Ama 64*
COX, Robert 54, Jane 30, Absolum 10, Robert 9, John 6, Jefferson 4, David W. 1
HUDSON, John 51, Frances 50, John 19, Wm. 18, Lucinda 16, Emily 14, Louisa 13, Jessia? 11 (m), Cyrena 9, Mary 3
DAVIS, Louis 48, Margaret 31, Elizabeth 12, Minerva 11, Isaac 7, Lydia 5, Alexander 2
BAKER, Washington 29, Elizabeth 28, John W. 9, Basil 7, Susan 5, Reubin 3, Wm. 1
HUDSON, Eliza 28 (m?), Frances 20, John 1
BAKER, Birgus 54 (m), Mary 54, James 18, Mary 14, John 15
GILES, Mary 35, Nancy 90
VANWINKLE, Benjamin F. 87, Hester 67
ABRAMS, James 48, Sally 40, James 15, Sally 13
BAKER, Edwin G. 26, Frances E. 19, Mary A. 9/12
COYLE, William 26, Lydia 21, Thomas 21, Thomas 8/12
LAMBERT, John 25, Elizabeth 23, Eliza A. 5, Mary F. 4, Jefferson 1
KERBEY, Layton R. 37, Elzabeth 29, Shelton 10, Sarah 8, John 6, Richard 5, Wm. 8/12
LEWIS, Rowlin 35, Elizabeth 35, Louisa 15, Wm. D. 13, Nancy 11, James W. 9, Laura 5, Elizabeth 4, Josephine 7/12

Schedule Page 235

ASBEL, Joseph 32, Emaline 26, Palestine 6, James O. 5, Wilson K. 3
HUNT, William 48, Mary 43, Esekiah 13, Josiah 11, David 9, Louisa 7, Margaret 5, Elizabeth 3, Nancy 1
STEPHENS, David 63, Nancy 52, Andrew 22, Eliza 17, Elihu 15, David 13, James 12, Alexander 9

1850 Census Madison County Kentucky

BROCKMAN, Ambros 29, Caroline 25, Elizabeth 4, Shelton 3, Godfrey 1, Ellender 8/12
BROCKMAN, Shelton 61*, Ellender 57
BAKER, Margaret 23*, Frances 2
BROCKMAN, John 24, Nancy 22
ISAACS, George W. 26, Mary 27, Sally 7, Ellender 5, Samuel 2
POWEL, Manuel 24, Susan 22, Abram 7, Mary 5, Manuel 3, Wm. 1
CRAWFORD, George W. 27, Martha 25, Thomas 2, Eli 9/12
HARRISON, John B. 43, Sally 33, Shelton 17, Elisha 15, Elizabeth 13, Layfaett 12, Ellender 10, Nancy 8, Hannah 4, Margaret 2
ISAACS, Samuel 24, Jane 21, Elizabeth 8/12
BICKEREL, Thomas 88*, Nancy 63, Silvester 21
ASBEL, Overton 15*
WILLIAMS, William 36, Elizabeth 33, James U. 9
SKINNER, Midad? 45 (m), Nancy 35, Jackson 18, Emily 15, Wm. 12, Reubin 8, Lucinda 5, Perry 3, Daniel 1

Schedule Page 236

POWEL, Lorily? 59 (m), Sally 56, Washington 17, Calvin 15, Hudson 13
POWEL, Larkin 21, Rhoda 23, Nancy 5, Malinda 4, Elizabeth 2, Sally 6/12
BROCKMAN, Birgus 33, Nancy 27, Mary A. 8, John D. 6, Ellender 4, Joranda 1
ABNER, William 59*, Delila 56, Frances 18, Delila 14, Sally 12, samuel 10, Wm. 7, John 4
RICHARDSON, Thomas 25*, Levina 25, Julia A. 4, Dulley 1 (m)
BAKER, Green 60, Nancy 52, Dudley 17, Adron 15, Sherna? 13 (m), Wanley 11 (m), Frances 7, Wm. 4
KINDRED, Harvin 24 (m), Ellender 23, John 4, Mary 1
POWEL, Cleveland 37, Malinda 35, amos 16, Richard 13, Aba Jane 7, Monday 5 (m)
POWEL, John 32, Eliza 27, Almira 8, Lucinda 7, Mary 4, John 2, Emiria? 3/12
LAWS, James 30, Margaret 25, John 14, Milton 12, Leann 10, Garland 8 (m), Wm. 5, Elizabeth 2, Elzira 8/12
COX, Thomas 36, Rhoda 31, Mary 8, Joel 6, Martha 4, Columbus 2, Plesant 6/12
GENTRY, Brightberry 65, Cynthia 55, Wm. 17, Nancy J. 13, Martha 11
GENTRY, Owney 55 (f), Jane 40, Winny 36
TODD, Isham F. 31, Nancy 31, Spud W. 8, Joseph A. 7, Isaac F. 5, Elizabeth C. 3, George B. 1

Schedule Page 237

THOMPSON, Tramon? 45 (m), Mary 43, Diana 21, Arthusa 19, Wm. 17, Stanton 15, Leann 13, Amanda 11, Frances 8
BOWMAN, John 62*, Nancy 43, Malony? 18 (f), Wm. 15, Mary 11, John 6
TUCKER, Paulina 22*
WOOL____, George G. 68, Susan A. 68, Ellen 35, John 33
JONES, M. J. 54 (m), Trucilla? 45, Catharine 20, James 19, Elizabeth 16, Zantith 14 (m), Joseph 10, Moritt 7 (m), Caroline 5, Mar 3
EDWARDS, Peter 61
JONES, John 65, Mary 75, Mary 11
CLIFT, Thomas 39, Anna 39, Mary E. 11, Wm. 9, Eliza A. 6, Joseph 1
BING, Rice 39, Sally A. 33, Cyntha 17, Susan A. 15, James 13, John 10, Patsy 6, Wm. 4

1850 Census Madison County Kentucky

HESTER, Hamilton 30, Aminda 26, George A. 4 (f), Louisa 3, Zacery 1
NICHOLS, Eli 42, Betsy 33
MORAN, Cyrus 26*
HOLLAND, William 30*
ROBERSON, John 21*
STROP, Robert 18*
BICKEREL, William J. 24, Elizabeth 21, Nancy J. 11/12
HALEY, Willis G. 25, Elizabeth 21, Nancy 3, Mary 2/12
MOODY, Whitfield 40, Lucinda 27, Elizabeth 18, Margaret 13, Wm. D. 8, Thomas J. 7, James K. 5, Cassius C. 2
BAKER, William 25, Nancy 18
JACKSON, James H. 21, Martha 16
BAKER, James R. 31, Margaret 22, Ann E. 2
JACKSON, Isaac 21, Sally W. 18

Schedule Page 238

BING, Thomas 46, Nancy 50, Isaac F. 14, Samuel 12
JACKSON, Thomas 32, Malinda 32, Wm. 11, Elihu N. 9, Julia A. 7, James K. 5
HARRISON, George 41, Rachael 37, Isaac 18, Nancy 13, John B. 11, Iphy 7 (m), Elisha 5, Minerva 1
HALL, John F. 36, Rachael 38
SMITH, D. K. 23 (m), Susan 20
PERVIS, Alfred 54, Hannah 35, Lucinda 12, Henry J. 9, Alfred 7, Nancy 5, Zacery T. 2
CRUSE, Jackson 33, Cirena? 27, Miam 12 (m), Ham 9 (m), Armilda 8, Leann 6, Andrew 4, Amanda 2, John D. 1
VANWINKLE, Sidney 27 (m), Julia A. 28, Wm. 7, Nancy 5, Bassel 3 (m), James 1, Hester A. 1
FRANCIS, Thomas 26, Elzabeth 27, James 7, Mary S. 6, Permelia 4
FRANCIS, Thomas 61, Mary 54, Wm. 22, Daniel 20, Margaret 16, Edy 15 (f), Julia 13
COYLE, Isaac 60, Massy 48, Isaac 13, Paulina 11, Joseph 9
VANWINKLE, Joseph 25, Juranda 21, Missouri 4, Frances 3, Sally A. 3/12
HUNT, Dudley 24, Elizabeth 24
JOHNSON, Thomas 43, Rhoda 36, George W. 17, Louis C. 15, Samuel M. 13, Elizabeth 10, Mary A. 8, Leanna 6, Nancy V. 4, Noah F. 2
ISAACS, James 45, Elizabeth 35, Lucinda 22, Louisa 21, Lonatta 19, Esekiah 15, James K. 13, George W. 12, Elizabeth 10, Euriah 8 (m), Silas 6, Isaac 4, Rhany? 4 (f), Jenny 3, Cyrus 1

Schedule Page 239

ISAACS, John 38, Isabell 32, Grafny 8 (m), John 5, Derbey 4 (m), Rachael 1
BAKER, Thomas R. 26, Ann 26, Mary J. 4, Elina 3, Nancy 1
MAYSE, Peter 28, Rebecca 28, John 7, Alfred 4
JACKSON, A. P. 24 (m), Jane 30, James 6, Susan 4, Wm. 2
ABRAMS, Gabriel 45, Susan 40, Nancy 13, Solomon 12, Friendly? 10 (m), Elijah 8, Elizabeth 6, Sally 4, Murphey 3, Henry 1
LYNX, Riley 29, Frances 25, Margaret 7, Anderson 6, Leann 5, Louisa 3, Ellender 6/12
BAKER, Benj. F. 35, Easter 22, James E. 3, Nancy 1
BAKER, Bassel 56, Rachael 50

1850 Census Madison County Kentucky

COOPER, Samuel 34, Nancy 36, Squire 15, Mary 13, John 11, Bathulia 10, Edward 8, Thomas 6, F. 3 (f), Samuel 1
FOWLER, James 40, Alitha 38, Murphey 15, Patsy 10, Celia 7
WILLIAMS, Abner 34, Anna 13, Margaret 11, Jane 9, Patsy 7, Susan 5, Rhoda 3, Joseph 1
BAKER, William 46, Susan 24, Sally A. 3, Solomon 1
LEABORN, Jacob 21, Cyntha 19
GABBERT, Jacob 25, Mahaly 26, Mary 3, Nancy 2, Edward 1

Schedule Page 240

FORBUSH, Franklin 20, Laviney 22 (f), Daniel 9/12
ROBERTS, Wiley? 20, Mary 21
HARRISON, Nathaniel 25, Sally A. 25, Nancy 4, Elizabeth 2
GABBRT, Edward 51, Sally 50, Margaret 16, Jane 12
GABBERT, John W. 30, Alethy 30, Green 12, Mary A. 10, Jacob 8, Wm. 7, Nancy 6, Sally 5, Susan 4, Edward 3, Cyntha 2, Jacob 80
TILERY, Isaac 81*, Elizabeth 40
JOHNSON, Anna 21*, Elijah 20, Herod 14, John 4, Nancy 4
MARCUM, John 25, Mary 19
ISAACS, Godfrey 75, Betsey 60, Wm. 38, Rebecca 20, Anna 18, Henry 16, Elizabeth 29
COLLINS, John 30, Nancy 30, James 7, Susan 5, Nancy 3, John 2, Emily 1
ISAACS, Godfrey 23, Emily 20, James 3, Mary 3/12
CABER, John 40, Mary 35, Reuben 6, John 4, Mary J. 2, Juransy 1 (f)
ROSE, William 23, Elizabeth 30, samuel 11, Elmanda 8 (m), Sarah 6, Ayhinda 3 (f)
ASBEL, William 60, Mary 37, Alithy 16, George 10, Talithy 13, Elisha 7, Lydia 5
JOHNSON, Thomas 60
JONES, Robb 40, Mary 37, John 13, Susan 11, Wm. 10, Murphey? 8, Elihu 7, Mary A. 6, Robert 3, Elizabeth 2, Catharine 1

Schedule Page 241

CLEMMS, John 34, Catharine 30, Mary J. 10, John F. 7, Gravil 5, Emily 1
LAKERS, Thomas 23, Susan 21, Jacob 1
LAKERS, John 60, Susan 30, Isabinda 9, Miranda 7, Mary 6, Joel 3, Betsey 10/12
LAKERS, John 27, Nancy 27, John jr. 2, Margaret 5/12
ROSE, John 27, Martha 24, Leseann 8 (f), Paulina 6, Martha 4, John 2, Lucinda 10/12
ROSE, Samuel 59*, Sally 58, Sally 35, Nancy 26, Tillet 26 (m), Betsey 24, Berry? 22, Mary 18, John M. 13, Martha 11, Eliza 8, Betsey 1
RUNYON, Mary 21*, Sally 2
JOHNSON, James 62, Aley 60 (f), James 17, Madison 12, Wm. 10, Lucinda 8, Maria 6
JOHNSON, William 28, Lucinda 38, Anna 16, Arlithy 13 (f), Nancy 7, Daniel 5, Susan 3, Louis 1
ROSE, Isreal 50, Betsey 50, Levina 18, Edward 16, Martha 14, Nancy 12, Mary 10, Jefferson 9, James 8, Sally 8
LACKERY, Gabriel 35, Rhody 28, Jane 10, Samuel 8, Mary 6, Eliza 4
HARRIS, William 33, Elizabeth 26, Milley 6, Rufus 3, Sarah 9/12
WHITE, John B. 40, Mary 32, Martitia 14, Ephram 13, John M. 11, James A. 10, Nicholas 7, Martha 3, David 1

1850 Census Madison County Kentucky

Schedule Page 242

MOORE, Levi 56, Mary 56, Christopher 23, George W. 18
TURNER, William 40, Nancy 38, James 15, Susan 13, Wm. 11, Sarah 9, John 5, Amanda 3, Mary 1
BOGGS, Robert 50
JARMAN, John 15, Beverly 38 (f), Zelinda 32, John F. 4, James E. 4, Wm. 1
LOGAN, Isaac 42, Margaret 46, Hazle 18 (m)
DILLINGHAM, Henry B. 27, Margaret 22, Mary B. 2
GIBBS, Alexander 73, Permelia 63, Thomas 22, Joel 20, John 17
HUME, Margaret 31, Wm. 11, Sally A. 9, Robert 7, Frances 5
MOBERLY, Nancy A. 37, Granvil 16, Stephen 14, Susan 12
GIBBS, James 25
OLDHAM, Richard 35, Mary 32, Wade 15, Eli 13, Wm. 11, Napoleon 9, Samuel 7, James B. 4, Richard 8/12
GRIDER?, Volentine 18*, Susan 15, Leroy? 60, Sally 55
JELNER?, Huldey 6*
BAXTER, Milo? 37, Patty 13, Jerusha 12, Edmund 16, Silas 8, George 6, Jacob 4, Mary 2, Zerilda 6/12
FARIMAN, E. 35 (m), Ellen 51, Mary 1
OGG, William 60, Elizabeth 59, Steiner? 45, Elizabeth 35
RICHARDSON, James 27*, Sarah 26, Thomas 9?, Sarah 6, Mary 4, Rosabella 1

Schedule Page 243 (no 244, 245)

MURREL, Nicholas 19*
WHITE, Stephen 16*
WHITE?, Sally 50, Martha 30, Leth 22 (f), Sally 20, James 5, Martha 3, John 1, Sally 6/12
JENNET?, Mary 80, James 39, Ally Jane 37, Frances 10, James 8, Emelin 6, Wm. 5, Jasper 4, Susan 2, Lavina 1
ALEXANDER, Betsy 42*, Jasper 20, Sally 13
CROUCHER, Malinda 25*, Humphry 4
LAMB, Johnithan 20*, Palmira 16
MOORE, Sally 45*, Emily 7
FREEMAN, Hannah 45*, Sarah 4
JONES, William 33, Lucinda 38, Euna? 18 (m), J. 16 (f), Mitchel 12, John 10, Margaret 9, Patty 6
TODD, Silas 31, Hanah 23, Mary 4, Calet 2 (m)
TODD, William 28, Malinda 20, Mary 4, Wm. 2
ROBERSON, Elizabeth 50, Elizabeth 23, John 19, Wm. 17
WOOLWINE?, John 32, Margaret 22, George 3, Amanda 1
MONDAY, Reubin 42, Nancy 46, Mary 17, Bettie 17 (f)
BORMAN, Harrison 30, Nancy 28, Mary 10, John 6, Nicy 3
LAMBERT, Mary 50, John 18, Mary 16, Wm. 14
YATES, Elijah 54*, Margaret 53
OLDHAM, Arthusa 33*, Josph 13, Richard 11, Oscar 9
ELLERSON, Amos 45, Sally 35, Harvey 14, Elizabeth 13, James 11, Lydia 9, George 7, Thomas 6, Phoeba 2

1850 Census Madison County Kentucky

Schedule Page 246

JOHNSON, George 61, Anna 48, Francis B. 23, George M. 16, May 11, Elizabeth 10, James M. 8, Rhoda 7, Wm. 5, Amanda 4
DILLION, Boston 32, Elizabeth 32, F. W. 9 (m), Wm. 7, James K. 5, A. W. 2 (m)
SHIFFLETT, Sidny 26 (m), Martha 24, S. A. 1 (f)
LAYNE, William 43, Elizabeth 47, Margaret 16, Susan 13, Mary 10, Lucy 9, Minerva 7, Sally A. 3
MOBERLY, Peter 79, Frances 60
CARR, William 49*, Hetty 33, Simpson 20, Louisa 17, John U. 16, Frances 11/12
TAYLOR, Sally A. 10*
HUNTER, William 43, Jenny 50, Irvine 23, Alvin 20, Wm. 17, John U. 14, Allen A. 11, Talitha 6
KINDRED, Garland 29 (m), Nancy 24, Mary F. 7, Patsy 5, Susan 4, Humphrey 1, Eliza 1/12
LAINE, Willis 21, Susan J. 22, Wm. 1/12
WOOLNY, James 49, Margaret 55, Josiah 22, Emaline 17, Argustus 13, Mary E. 12, Sally A. 20
LAINE, James 59*, James 61, Frances 22, Mary 17, Mary J. 13, Adam K. 13
SPAULDING, Sally A. 25*, Eliza J. 8
KINDRED, Overton 27, Eliza J. 26, Mary 6, Nathaniel 4, James W. 3, Sally A. 1/12
MOBERLY, Simon 46, Arthusa 44, Wm. 20, Henry 16, Leanna 13, Margaret 12, Manerva 10, Zerilda 8, Benjamin 9, Layfaett 2, Talitha 18

Schedule Page 247

PINKSTON, Allen 39, Elizabeth 37, Green Berry 16, Eliza J. 11, Lucinda 9, Sally A. F. 7, Mary W. 4, Elizabeth 1
MOBERLY, John N. 28*, Martha 54
COX, John N. 30*
SEARCEY, Joseph 52, Nancy 52, Rufus P. 23, Sally A. 20, Mary F. 18
LAUB?, Thomas G. 50
HEATHERLY, Thomas S. 25, Susan A. 16
MOBERLY, Benjamin 52*, Benjamin 20, James S. 18, Cimion 16 (m), John U. 13
BAKER, Bassel 22 (m)*, Mary 21
STEWART, Benjamin 26, Racheal 22, James 6, Catharine 4, Sally F. 2
TODD, Thomas C. 51, Susan A. 45, Robert 15, George 11, Susan A. 11
BAKER, Hiram 51, Jane 47, Thomas 25, Barthena 21, Serilda 17, Anna 15, Levi 14, Susan 12, Jane 11, David B. 8, Wm. W. 6, Hiram 3
WHITE, Elias 22, Eliza 18, James W. 2
VAUGHN, John 47, Nancy 40, Elizabeth 20, Rebecca 16, Wm. 12, James 12, George W. 5
LAMB, John 78, Sarah 30, Thomas 25
BLEVINS, Daniel 34, Sally 26, Alfred 7, James 5, Christopher 3, Wm. 6/12
BURTON, James 59*, Anna 54, Daniel 23, Jesse 16, Wm. 12, John 10, Susan 20, Margaret 15, Elizabeth 14
LACKEY, Andrew 26*, Nathan 21
CAGER, Thomas 29*, Daris 50 (m), Joel 65, Horain 18 (m)

1850 Census Madison County Kentucky

Schedule Page 248

CLEET?, Margaret 65*
ELLIS, James H. 36, Mary A. 27, Peter 11, Elizabeth 5, Virginia 4
CROCHER, William 47*, Nanc 35, Mary 3
LAINE, Francis 14*, John 93
THOMAS, Arthurius 63, Sarah 58, Wm. 23, Tyry 19 (m), Mary E. 17, Winnaford 13 (m), Nathan 11
TODD, Isaac 67, Catherine 56, Daniel 56
FREY, David B. 28*, Mary J. 21, Mary E. 1
MAUPIN, Robert 17*
EVANS, Henry 42*, Sarah 51
REID, Susan G. 15*
KIDWELL, James 60, Nancy 54, James 22, Minerva 16, Mary 22, Sally 25
PRUNTY, Thomas 40, Elizabeth 40, Delina 13, John W. 11, Robert 10, Susan 7
WEST, Richard 46, Licena 40, John 20, Joseph 18, Michael 14, Paulina 10, Ephram 7, Jerina? 2 (m)
THARP, Alexander 55, Frances 54, Leander 24, Elizabeth 22, Thomas 19, Wm. 16, Catharine 13, George 12, Sarah 10
COVINGTON, William 66, Edith 63
COVINGTON, William 29, Elizabeth 22, Robert 3
COVINGTON, Jeptha 35, Mary 37, Sally 5, Leanna 4, Lucy 2
HOLLINSWORTH, Jeremiah 27*, Mary 19, James R. 5, John U. 2, B. J. 9/12 (m)
MCQUINN, Mary 19*
TODD, Alvin W. 24, Arthusa 24, Wm. 3, Frances 1
BAKER, Bassil 44 (m), Elizabeth 43, Melvin 17, Suasn 12, Sellrend? 11 (m), Sanford 10, Raibourn 7, Murrel 6, Armilda 5

Schedule Page 249

PRUETT, Joseph 24, Rebecca 61, Rebecca 21, Catharine 18, Julia 16, Robert 12, Thomas 7
DUNBAR, Abijah 47 (m), Joicy 48, Mary 19, Nancy 12, Sally 7, Joicy 3, Susan 6/12
KINDRED, James W. 36, Susan 32, Adderson 5, Nancy 11, E. J. 9 (f), Prisilla 7, Reubin 5, Zachery 2, John 9/12
OGG, John 51
MARTIN, Jerrymiah 41, Susan 21
MOBERLY, Alfred 44*, Lucinda 38, Rufus 20, Thomas 15, Susan 14, Mary 11, M. E. 9 (f), James V. 3
POST, John 25*, Lucinda 20, Alfred 1
KIDWELL, Jonathan 26*, Mary 21, James 3, Louis 1/12
FORT, Hasting 15*, Alfred 13, Elizabeth 12, Josephine 10, John S. 8
HYSE, Thomas 29, Catherine 38, Thomas 3, Mary 2
BAKER, Reason 22, Elizabeth 21, Nancy 11/12
ARSEL, Joseph 66, Juda 49, George 6, Rodes 21, Maria 20, Mary 18, Minerva 15, John 12, Julia 10, Samuel 8, James 6
TRIBBLE, John 59, A. J. 14 (m), Mary 12, John C. 10, D. M. 8 (m)
EMBRY, Thomas E. 41*, Amanda 47, M. F. 14 (), L. F. 12 (m), Mary 10, Joel 8, Ellen 6, Wm. 2
JONES, John 23*
CAVENAUGH, Ruth 51
WHITAKER, John 35, Sally 28, _____ 6/12 (f)

1850 Census Madison County Kentucky

Schedule Page 250

DOYLE, Patrick 38, Mary 24
GODDIN, Thomas J. 46*, Alzira 34
ROBERTS, Jane 12*
KELLY, Robert E. 54, Rosa F. 51, Benjamin 16, Ann E. 15, James S. 9, Richard K. 7
SHACKELFORD, Edmund 48, Margaret 44, Susan F. 16, Edmund 8, Margaret 6
LITTLE, Thomas G. 62*, Nancy 46, Lucinda 18, Samuel 23, James 20, Mary 13, Bettie 9
KENERDAY, Rosa 26*
BRAUNER, Wiley 13*
TURNER, Joseph 56, Jane 53, Edward 20, Sallie 18
HOLLOWAY, William 40, Elizabeth 38, Amelia 18, Ezekial 16, Patsy 11, James B. 9, Clarence 8, Mary 6, Wm. 5, Ann F. 3
BOYD, William 26*, Sophia 20, Elizabeth 40
BOYLE, Sally Ann 27*, Elizabeth 21, Matilda 13, Amanda 11
NEWMAN, T. T. 34 (m), Mary E. 34, Mary J. 9, John R. 7, Harrison 4, Elizabeth 1
BOYD, Thomas W. 46, Elizabeth 46, Wm. 18, Thomas 16, Mary 13, Henry 11, John 9
LONG, William 31, Nancy 27, Allis 5 (f)
LETCHER, William R. 56, William R. 5
MILLER, Fayett 26, Catharine 23, Bettie 2
ROWLAND, David J. 47*, Mahaly 47, Sidney 19 (m), Dan P. 17, James 17, Henry 12
RIX, George J. 61*
OCONNER, James 30*
FREEMAN, Samuel 37, Sophia 37, Ann A. 13, Robert 11, Fanny L. 9, David R. 6, Jackson 3
WHITE, Milton 47, Julia 18

Schedule Page 251

ROBERTS, Elisha 39*, Mary 20, Patsy 7/12
BARNES, Richard 20*
NEWMAN, William 22*
WEBSTER, Dudley 63*, Mary 50, Louisa 21, Rosa F. 19, John B. 9
PICKLES, George M. 35*, Arsiminta 32, Thomas 3, Mary 9/12
SHACKELFORD, James 38*, Malissa 33, George T. 13, Edmund 9
GILBERT, John W. 27*, Isabelle 19, James 1
HALEY, Henry 35*, Martha 20, Henry 2
HETCH?, Samuel 21*
SMITH, Isaac D. 30*
EMBRY, James H. 22*
HATCHER, Isaac 24*
KINETT?, Elias 42*
ALLERSON, Henry T. 32*
RUST, Jacob 20*
WALKER, William J. 35*, Sarah A. 30, Charles 14, Mary J. 10, James 8, Ann E. 6, Wm. 4, Sarah 2, Joel 1
GIBSON, Edmund 20*
FIELDS, Ezekiel 68, David J. 29, Edmund 26, Mary 20, Isabell 17, Ezekiel 14, Patsey 2
WEBSTER, Benjamin 27, Rhoda A. 23, Sally B. 3, Mary 1

1850 Census Madison County Kentucky

WHITE, William 26*, Elizabeth 21, Daniel 5, Charles 3
HARRIS, Robert 29*
LAPELLMAN, Louis 23*
BRONSTON, Thomas 29*
BARNETT, William 30*
FRANCIS, Louis 23*
HATCH, Willia 19*
TELLYIA, Alfred 25*
EMBRY, William 22*
FERREL, Micheal 27*, Patrick 25
CONROY, Patrick 27*
SULIVAN, Patrick 25*
WOODS, James 30*
WILSON, Edmund 28*
RUNYON, Richard 31*
BOWEN, John W. 40*, Sarah A. 26
GIBBERT, Susan F. 19*
SHAPARD, John 30*, Lucy 24, Eugine 3
WILKERSON, Agnus 38*
BURNARD?, Curtis F. 30, Sarah H. 24, A. R. 4 (m), Sallie 2, Thompson 20
RICE, Thomas 30*, Margaret 34, Josephine 3, Louisa 2

Schedule Page 252

HAGER, David 20*
OWENS, Samuel 26*
TURNER, Squire 57, Elizabeth 50, Thomas 29, Mary A. 21, Catharine 18, Charles 8
MCKEE, Alexander 34, Mary 27, Samuel 7, Ashby 5, Logan 2
CAPERTON, William 53, Eliza 50, Woods 28, James 24
WALKER, Charles 50, NAnc 40, James W. 17, Fulton E. 15, Mary E. 12, C. B. 10 (m), William 8, Florence 5, Charles J. 4, N.? J. 2 (m)
FORD, John J. 34, Louisa 28, Wm. 10, Sally A. 5, Malissa 3/12
FIELDS, Curtis 27, Martha 23, Sarah 4, Rosana 2
WILKERSON, Patsy H. 1/12*, Wyatt 41, jAcob W. 1
HOWELL, Emaline 20*
WHITE, Jacob S. 50*, Martha 56, Sarah 35, John A. 25, Mary L. 22, Amera? V. 21 (m), JAcob D. 17, James W. 13, Martha 11, Jacob 6, Oscar 4
CALE, John Y. 26*, E. H. 26 (f)
WHITE, R. P. 28 (m), Anna 21
HUFFMAN, P. A. 28 (m)*, Caroline 26, Walter 4, John 1
VAUGHENSTOCK, V. 23 (m)*
LENYN?, Augustus 22*
WILL, E. W. 15 (m)*
JEFFREYS, Richard 44, Mary 45, Minerva 20, Thomas 17, Edney 13 (f), Rebecca 11, Laura 7, Nancy F. 5, Thomas 2
TAYLOR, Paten W. 23, Anna 21, Sarilda 4/12
BENTLY, James 27, Susan 6/12
BENTLY, William 54, Mahala 52

GUESS, William 28*, Nancy 23
CUNNINGHAM, John 23*
BARNES, John M. 18*
WILKERSON, Foster 1*

Schedule Page 253

MANLY, John 43, Elizabeth 42, Wm. 14, Walter 13, Mary 11, David 9, Daniel 7, Nancy 6, Emmet 4
MANION, John C. 28, Zerilda 22, M. E. 3 (f), E. B. 2 (m)
PURSELL, Daniel 70*, Thallata 72
ABRAMS, Mary 43*
PURSELL, Cyrus 38, Kasiah 38, Sally A. 13, Daniel 11, Mary G. 7, Senate 4 (m), Nancy 2
BURGEN, Temple 44, Sophia 34, Narcissus 10 (f), Lucy 11, Hannah 8
BURGEN, Akillis 52 (m), Amelia 37, Thomas 18, Wm. 17, Argella 15 (m), Patsy 14, Eisom 11 (m), Akilles 9, Elias 7, Elizabeth 4, Jasper 2
RICHARDSON, Thomas 59, Mary 57, Mary 20, Sanford 16, Benjamin 14, Sally 18
HALLEY, Samuel 52, Minerva 46, Elizabeth 22, Fannie 15, Edwin 12, Henry 10, Virginia 8
CHINAULT, Walter 46, Talitha 32, Elzabeth 14, Wm. 12, Joseph 10, Susan 8, Carlile 6 (f), Christopher 4, Waller 2, Nancy 1/12, David 25
CHINAULT, Josiah P. 39, Narcena 36, Ulysses 16, Wm. 14, Abner 12, Josiah 10, Susan 9, Lanina 7, Waller 6, Edwin 5, Ann 3, Reubin 2, Hellen 4/12
CHINAULT, David 22, Pattie 18
CHINAULT, Ann 40, Wm. 18, Matilda 15, Henry 12, Henry 10

Schedule Page 254

CHINAULT, Nancy 59*
HARRIS, Christopher 29*
ALEXANDER, Amanda 11*
TEVIS?, James 14*
HARRIS, Sidney W. 35 (m)*, Nancy 30, Wm. 14, Christopher 10, Solen 4 (m), Sidney 2 (m), James 6/12
MILLER, Caledonia 12*
SMITH, John 38*, Nancy 47, Sally 21
ALEXANDER, Ruth 12*
RICHARDSON, Elliot 30, Susan 28, Bugby 53 (m)
FOWLER, Malinda 40, Robt.? 19, Clifton 17, Sally 15, Wm. 13, Rebecca 10, Margaret 8
BENTLY, John E. 75, Sally E. 73
BATHSTON, Henry 35, Susan 19, Presly 2
BURGIN, Allen 56, Emily 45, Clayton 19, Arilda 13, Lelia 15, Samuel 14
WOODS, George 45, Disy 33
SMITH, James 46, Nancy 39, Presly 22, Wm. 17, Jerome? 15, James 13, Solm 8 (m), Benjamin 6, Eugine 4, Catherine 2
COCKRELL, Henry C. 31, Catharine 37, Martha 8, Sarah 4, Cyrus 2, Wm. 1
BUSH, Tilman 62, Sally 56
BUSH, Z. E. 30 (m), Arcella Nerah? 6, T. C. 4 (f), Wm. 2, Sarah 6/12
LILE, Henry 52, Susan 50, Richard 19, Virginia 17, Isabelle 15, Chilton 14, Arabella 12, Arzelia 11, Thomas 10

1850 Census Madison County Kentucky

GENTRY, Plesent 36, Mary 30, Amanda 9, Lucy 8, Andrew 6, Benjamin 4, Paulina 2
LITTLE, John 48, Nancy 28, Wm. 13, Sarah 11
SEARCEY, Bryant 40, Frances 35, Elias 11, Mary 9, Elizabeth 7, Charles 5, Nathan 4, Alonzo 3, George 2

Schedule Page 255

KERBEY, Elisa P. 32*, A. E. 30 (f), John N. 8, Catherine 10, David 6, Joseph 4, Clifton 2
BAKER, Lucinda 50*
QUISHENBERY, Joseph 37, Sally 34, James 15, Louis 13, Talitha 12, Cassius 9 (f), Chloe 7, Elizabeth 5, Sophia 3, Lettie 2
RAIBOURN, James 50, Nancy 43, Maria 17, Catharine 9, Hester 7, Joseph 5
HUGENLY?, John M. 30, Nancy 23, John 6, Cabel 3 (m), Emily 3/12
HUGENLY?, R. 71 (f)
MARTIN, David 47, Lamira 43, James 22, Elizabeth 12, David 7, Margaret 15
BOGGS, Edward C. 36, E. J. 3 (f), James 14, Phoeba 12, E. J. 10 (f), Rebecca 40
IRVINE, William 25, Elizabet 20, Susan 2, Adam 1/12
MILLER, Robert 65*, Sally 69, Robert 30, Laben? 40, Sally 18
TERIS?, Robert M. 20*
RICE, Fountain 34, Malinda 27, James 9, Fountain 8, Taylor 5, Theadore 3, Richard 6
GENTRY, Stanton 30, Patsy 22, David 7/12
TRIBBLE, Dudley 53, Matilda 45, U. 24 (m), Peter 20, Nancy 18, Patsy 15, Alexander 13, Janus 11 (f), Robert 9, Lucy 7, Dudley 5, Andrew 2
ESTILL, Jonathan 28, Louisa 23, Laura 1/12

Schedule Page 256

WHITE, Richard J. 22*, Lucy A. 21, Volintine 3, Wm. 2
TAYLOR, Elizabeth 37*
WALKER, William E. 48, Sallie 23, Emaline 15, John 12, Harvie 8, James 6
RAMSEY, William U. 36*, Martha 33, James W. 10, Frances 8, Martha 6, Lucy 3
FOOT, Thomas M. 22*
DALTON, Edley A. 29 (m), Racheal 33, Jasper 10, nEwton 10, Mary C. 4, Daniel 1
BLACKBURN, Sally 54, Amanda 32, Louisa 21, John M. 16, P. Q. 15 (m), Henry 11, Roda 7
MOORE, Willia 34, Mar E. 27, Isabella 7, Rebecca 6, Racheal 3, Sally 1
MAUPIN, John D. 21, Mary 17, Elizabeth 53
SHIFFLETT, Allen 35, Nancy 28, Joshua 7, Sarah 5, John 4, Mary 2
TODD, Thomas 27
CORNELIS, Nancy 45, Mary 17, Allen 21, John 15, Emily 14, Millie 12, Susan 10, Wm. 9, Henry 6, Eli 4
MCCOY, Mary 40, Martha 15, Nancy 12
BOULVORE?, Greenberry 25, Eliza A. 18
HARRIS, Robert 63, Jael 54 (f), Paulina 22, Nancy 17, Susan 15, Sarah 13, Wm. 11
YATES, Robert 30, Marian 25 (f), Leanna 5, Margaret 1
THORP, Dodson 31, Cristine 33, Wm. 10, Lydia 7, Elzabeth 3, T. C. 8/12 (f), James 23
TODD, William 60*, Elizabeth 60, Sidney 22 (m), James 18

1850 Census Madison County Kentucky

Schedule Page 257

THARP, Frances 26*, Green B. 10, James 7, Wm. 4
WATSON, Zerilda 14*
CHAMBERS, Victoria 42, Mary E. 16, Joseph 6
THOMAS, William T. 23, Sarah 24, Susan 1
HISLE, Sampson 55, Sallie 60, Sampson 22, Ann 19, Susan 17, Milley 62
GRIFFITH, Patsy 50, Mary 13, James 11
BROADUS, China 40 (f), Marcellus 20, Temple 16, Benjamin 14, Laura 12, Lycurgus 9
STEPHENS, Taltn 30*, Susan 27, Frances 4, Drucilla 3
TODD, Thomas J. 21*
TODD, Thomas 58, Charity 47, Mary 21, Sally A. 20, James 16, Nancy 16, Wm. 12, Arshura 8
GILBERT, Jareptha? 34 (m)*, Julia A. 25, James 3, Jail 1 (f), R. E. B. 1/12 (m)
WHITE, William 18*
BOGGS, James 56*
CORNELISON, Robert 28*, Mary 35, Elizabeth 2, Adalaide 3/12
COLLINS, Ann 39*, Milton P. 30
WATTS, William 23*, Sally G. 22
RHODUS, Douglas 24*, Martha 25, Margaret 2
LAMB, Thomas 29*
PARKS, Joshua? D. 39, Mary 30, Diana 14, Cyrus 11, Walter 8, Baubus 3 (f), James 2/12
HARRIS, John A. 46, Isabella 26, Mary 5
ARMSTRONG, Mason 60, Mary 50, Lucinda 21, Mason 22, Mary 18, Lamira 16, Ely 12, Malvina 11
WATSON, John 50, Mary 46, Richard 20, Nancy 17, John C. 13, Joseph 13, Salli 10, James 9, Elizabeth 7

Schedule Page 258

HISEL, Ira 34, Margaret 25, Wm. 5, Alexander 4, John R. 1
TODD, Ninevah 30 (m), Sirena 25, Sarah 5, Mary 4, Isaac 3, Nancy 5/12
BROADDUS, W. C. M. 35 (m), Nancy 35, Susa 9, James 6, Mary 16
MAUPIN, Thomas 26, Elizabeth 21, Thomas 5, Clay Smith 3, Margaret 65
MAUPIN, S. O. 40 (m)*, Martha 23, John D. 15, Brutus 9, Waller 6, Sulana 5 (m)
FRY, William 23*
WEST, John 43, Margaret 42, Richard 20, Bright Berry 18, Martha 16, Mary 14, Elza 11, Amanda 9, Elizabeth 3
BROADDUS, George 44, Eliza 41, Nicholas 20, Henry C. 18, Mary A. 14, Newland 11 (f), Martha 9, James 5, Wm. 4, Thomas 2
WARD, Mary 44, Elizabeth 24, Mary 21, James 18, W. P. 23 (m), Margaret 16, Benjamin 14, Thomas 13, Walker 11, John 10, Lear 8 (m), Stanton 5, Mary E. 3/12
REEVES, Stephen 40, Louisa 28, Thomas 4, Mary 2
ELLIS, Thomas C. 30, Julia 27, Susan 5
SEARCEY, Charles 36, Lucinda 34, Louisa 10, Hana? 7 (f), Mary 4, Charles 2, Susan 3/12
HUMES, Nancy 53*, Thomas 25, William 23, John 20
EMBRY, John 22*, Susan 22

1850 Census Madison County Kentucky

Schedule Page 259

EMBRY, Joseph 55, Nancy 47, Canais 17 (f), Nancy 16, Joel 12, William 10, James 6
WEBB, George M. 25, Elizabeth 19
THARP, Thomas 50*, Anna 47, Martha 23, Harris 21, Stanton 18, Thomas 15, M. F. 12 (f), Louisa 9, Susan 6
CULLIN, Bryan 21*
RILEY, George S. 43, Elizabeth 44, Julia 18, Samuel 17, Martha 16, Serilda 15, Thomas 11, George 8, Wm. 8, James 1
WILLIAMS, John 62*, Sally 65, John 19
SAMS, Sally A. 31*
AMERINE, John T. 22*, Mary 17, George 28
HOPPER, George 13*
PORTWOOD, Silas 48, Caroline 37, John M. 22, Thomas 17, Silas 7, Joseph 6, Rufus 4, Samuel 2, Daniel 6/12
COX, William 21, Sally A. 20
HOPPER, William 22, Elizabeth 23, Sally 1/12
PORTWOOD, Joseph 45, Lucy 40, Benajah 20 (m), Minerva 17, Susan 15
ELLINGTON, Thomas P. 31, Cynthiann 35, Hiram 7, Thomas 6, Sarah 5, James 2, John 9/12
HARRIS, William 23, Jamima 60, Nancy 12
RHODUS, Joseph 69, Elizabeth 70
RHODUS, Abner 23, Leana 18, Josephine 6/12
HALL, Jesse 56, Permelia 30, Martin 14, Martha 10, Bryant 7, Mary 4, S. 3 (m), James 7/12
DASHIER, Levi 49, Sarah A. 20, Dulana 16, Martha 13, Rebecca 7

Schedule Page 260

ABRAHAM, Hezekiah 63, Mary 53, William 28, Margaret 18, Charles 16, Abner 13, Mary E. 9
OLDHAM, Thomas 26*, Nancy 21, Eliza 2, Murphey 7/12
STONE, Louis 19*
TAYLOR, Hiram 45, Susan 35, Wm. 16, Parker 14, John 10, Mary 8, America 6, Amanda 4
CAMBELL, Andrew 40, Mary 30, Marinni? 14 (m), Reubin 10, Elza 8, Sidney 5 (m), Nancy 3/12
RHODUS, Burrel 35, Phoeba 33, John 14, James 12, Sally 10, Mary 6, Thomas 4, Josiah 2, Elizabeth 1
MORRIS, Ennis 35, Susan 30, Franklin 15, Sally A. 11, Elizabeth 5, Joseph 3
HART, Joseph 30, Elizabeth 17, John 4/12
PORTWOOD, John P. 22*, Martha 22, Thomas 2, Elizabeth 8/12
BEALEY, Elizabet 19*
TAYLOR, James C. 72, Nancy 60, Francis 17
COX, Jesse 72, Mary 70
SHIFFLETT, Hillery 26 (m), Jemaima 24, Mary E. 4, Christopher 2
COX, John 45, Mary 42, Rebecca 21, Wm. 18, Louis 16, John 10
COFFEY, Richard . 55*, Catherine 50, Wm. 28, E. McDowell 21, Mary 12, Martha 9
WILLIAMS, Lutticia 27*, Mary 4, Euginia 6/12
MOORE, Jarret 29, Susan 20, Sarah 9, Solen 8 (m), Obediah 5, Wm. 3, J. 1 (m)

1850 Census Madison County Kentucky

Schedule Page 261

PARKS, George W. 21, Patsy 18
KURRS, Jeremiah 68*, Darona 64 (f), Jeremiah 22, Wm. 10
FINNEY, Elizabeth 16*
MAUPIN, William 43, Susan 39, Mary E. 14, Callum 12 (m), Susan 9, Christopher 6, Cassius Clay 4
DILLINGHAM, John P. 37, Amanda 25, Elihu 20
FNNEY, Cyntha 36, Nancy 14, Amelia 11
COVINGTON, Wilton 38, Paulina 35, Mary 16, Wm. 15, Milly 13, Martha 11, Amanda 8, Robert 4, John 1
KIDWELL, Harrison 36, Eliza 28, Thomas 7, Eliza 6, Paulina 4, Margaret 2, Nancy 6/12
PARKS, Eli 63, Winnaford 55 (f), Elizabeth 12
WOOLERY, Isaac 54*, Franky 56 (f)
MOBERLY, John F. 19*, Sally A. 17, Malvina 13
REEVES, Jefferson 37, Elizabeth 32, Henry 8, E. W. 7 (m), Harvy 6, Jeremiah 2
SHIFFLETT, Margaret 53*, John 33, Susan 27
BAILEY, Mary E. 7/12*
HARRIS, Christopher 62, Elizabeth 50, John M. 29, Mary 26, Margaret 83
DILLION, Rowlin 54, Elizabeth 67, Mary 24, Edney 21 (f)
HARRIS, Robert 63, Mary 52, Fannie 20, James 22, Mary 11, Thomas 6
WHITE, Bassel 52 (m), Mary 45, Edward 18, Mary 11, George 8, Wm. 6
EDGE, William 34, Catharine 34, Larkin 13, Eliza 12, Allen 7, James 5, Sally 4, Samuel 2, Milton 1

Schedule Page 262

GARRISON, Thomas 58, Ana 46, Mary A. 24, Nancy 22, Laticia 20, Minerva 18, Martha 16, James 13, Eliza 11, Paulina 9, Frances 6
COMBS, William 33, Frances 27, James 2, Julia 6/12
SIMPSON, Benjamin 39, Milly 32, Sarah 13, Julia 9, Ann 7, Paulina 5, Mary 3, Wm. 1, James 7/12
ROBARDSON, William 23, Nancy 16, Malvina 1
WILKERSON, Mary 56, John C. 23, Frances 21, Susan 15
HISLE, Richard 24, Amanda 23, Sarah 4, Frances 2
TODD, Elizabeth 45, Joseph 18, James 15, Mary 12, Henry 10, Robert 4
OGG, Henderson 55, Margaret 52, Robert 18, Tabitha 16, Coleman 11, Millie? 9
FINNEY, Joshua 75, Nancy 72
ESTUS, John H. 65, Susan 60
LEE, Samuel 45, Mary 35, Joshua 14, Elihu 11, Alfred 7, Horinda 6, Josephine 5, Lucinda 3, Susanna 2
QUINN, William R. 30, Sally 31, Ann 5, Maria 3
MOBERLY, John 59*, Patsy 57, Susan 28, Nancy 25, Louis 24, Mary 22, Icabud 20, Elizabeth 14, Arzelia 12
QUINN, Susan 5*
SIMPSON, Richard B. 66*, susan 60, Alfred 33, James 26
ESTER, Elijah 17*
BURKS, Laura 8*
HOOKER, Nicholas 68, Miland 45 (f)
WATSON, William 47, Sally 53, Joab 10

1850 Census Madison County Kentucky

Schedule Page 263

TADER, Hardin 49, Elizabeth 47, Lycurgus 23, Lurinda 15
CROOK, Kiah 50 (m), Sally 48, Bejamin 21, Brutus 19, Cassius 16, Wm. 13, Elizabeth 11, Sally 9, Tobey 6
POWLL, Jeremiah 66, Nancy 49, Wm. 29, Josia 22, Mary 18, Susan 12, George 11
RUNYON, Abslum 67, Mary 66, James 43, Nancy 41, Charity 30
GENTRY, Josiah 82, Mary 50, Martin 44, Josiah 18
GENTRY, Elizabeth 49, Ann 18, Currard 15 (m), Thomas 13
DUNN, James 53, Elizabeth 42, Paulina 19, Archie 17, Ann 15, Margaret 12, James 8, Butler 6
JAMES, Henry 56*, Sarah 70
MOBERLY, Rosanna 7*
COLLINS, Jerrymiah 36, Mary 24, Edwin 10, John 7, James 1
REED, John 65*, Eliza 50
WOODRUFF, Benjamin 75*
GREEN, Mastin 45*, Mary 38, Catharine 18, Congrove 15 (m), John 14, Mastin 12, Wm. 10, Sarah 7, Racheal 5, Stephen 4, Jacob 3, Willis 1
STAGNER, Nancy 21*
REED, John 33*, Minerva 24, Sharlotte 7, Celia 5, Martha 2
GRIFFEY, Jane 18*
FRENCH, Robert 33*, Lucy 28, Ann 2
HAWKINS, Rhoda 34*, Phoeba 70
REED, Margaret 54 (B), Hannah 60
TRIBBLE, Jerusha 66, Zerilda 39, Columbus 38, Andrew 24, Elizabeth 22

Schedule Page 264

BAXTER, Edmund 78*
TURNER, Martha 16*
BERRY, John W. 31, Zerilda 28, James 6, Ellen 4, David 1
CANIDA, Anderson 29, Patsy 24, Celia 3
THOMAS, James 47, Julia 47, Sally 20, Mancy 18 (f), Robert 16, James 14, John 10, George 8, Elizabeth 7, Daniel 4, Ibson 2 (m)
BURRISS, James 27, Julia 18
LANDER, John 42, America 12, Lear 7 (m), William 6
HAWKINS, Squire 42, Rebecca 35, Rhoda 10, Sarah 9, Harvey 6, Benjamin 2
COLLINS, Josiah 71*, Millie 68
HALE, Ann 30*
GRIFFIN, Caroline 23
ROYSTN, Thomas 60*, Sally 64, John 35
WOOMER, Daniel 20*
KINEE, John J. 38, Anna 3, Wm. 16, Archibald 14, Malinda 12, Elzabeth 10, Sally 7, Patsy 3
GRIFFEY, Jesse 54, Fannie 56
TURPIN, Solomon 29, Elza 32
CORNELISON, Susan 44*
SIMMONS, Susan 25*, Wm. 6, Susan 4, Amanda 2
CHURCH, James 32*, Nancy 32, James 5/12
EWIN, Aray? 23 (f)*, Elizabeth 2

1850 Census Madison County Kentucky

GRIFFEY, James 26*
WARNER, William 33, Mary 27, Martha 8, Mary 7, Elizabeth 6, Zacheria 4 (m), Wm. 2
DURRIVEY?, Samuel 50*, Kasiah 40, Eliza 16
MOBERLY, John 2*
SIMMONS, John 57, Jane 52, David 14, Benjamin 12, Adalaide 8
TODD, Newton 29, Margaret 16
TODD, Peter 75, Amanda 17, Peter 1

Schedule Page 265

GRUBS, Wiliam 41, Owen? 40, James 9
TILLETT, John 23, Arzela 16, Elizabeth 7/12
GREEN, Haram 41, Adalaide 41, Theodore 11, Fidelia 9, Ann 7, Edmund? 5, Isabella 3, Horner 2, Adaline 3/12, Elizabeth 15
BLEVINS, Charles E. 30*, Malinda 20, Mary 3, Nancy 11/12
JARMA, M. H. 18 (m)*
MILLER, Thomas 38*, Mary J. 25, Susan 8
BARNES, Richard 20*
HUDSON, Thomas 30, Nancy 22, Abner 1, Milton 4
COVINGTON, Robert 46, Anna 37, Robert 15, John H. 12, Mary 10
MILLER, C. J. 37 (m)*, Tabitha 36, Sarah 13, Robert 11, James 9, John F. 7, C. J. 3 (m), Susan 1/12
HARRIS, Shelton 29*
HERNUS?, Stanton 58, Susan 46, Mary L. 12
DUNCAN, William 50, Elizabeth 55, George 23, Wm. 19, Archibald 16, Susan 13
PARKES, John M. 43, Martha 38, Jefferson 15, Milly 11, Mary 9, Talitha 4, Sarah 8/12
WAGES, Ambrose 51*, Jamima 47
WHITE, Lucinda 26*
LOGSTONE, Abner 14*
CONNER, Ambrose 8*
ELLIS, Peter H. 32*, Sarah 50
CARTER, Milam 8 (f)*, Elizabeth 24, Wm. 5
CHASE, Charles 30*
SHIP, Mary E. 10*
BUTLER, Walker T. 52?*, Catharine 73?
POTTS, Nancy 50*
MINTER, William 18*
BUTLER, Brook 60*
CHILLIS, John 50, Amanda 35, Nancy 11, Wm. 9, John 7, Edwin 5, Thomas 3, Leonidas 1

Schedule Page 266

CAR, Louis P. 28*, Elizabeth 24
PORTWOOD, Elizabeth 6*
ELLINGTON, William 64, Frances 64
EMBRY, Wyatt B. 44, Celia 25
JOLLY, Spear 45 (m), Susan 34, William 18, Joseph 12, Thomas 10, Daniel 8, James 6, Henry 4, Marshall 1

1850 Census Madison County Kentucky

OLA, Andrew 44, Gilly 34, Andrew 15, Amanda 12, Wm. 8, James K. 6, Wilson 5, Susan 3, Armilda 4/12
JONES, George W. 40, Cynthia 33, James 12, Wm. 10, Martha 8, John 6, George 4, Othreul? 7/12 (m)
CAMPBELL, William 27*, Mahala 22, Millie 7, Mary 5, Julia 1
SHIVERS, Reubin 65*
STEPHENS, William P. 45, Francis 21, Leroy 18, Thomas 16, Caleb 14, Amanda 12, Nancy 10, John B. 8, Richard C. 7, Sarah E. 11/12, Mary E. 34
ELLINGTON, William 25, Jane 12, James 11, John 7, Sarah 3, Wm. 2, Richard 1, Mary 36
GIBBERT, Jacob 31, Jane 9, Wm. 7, James 5, John D. 3, Ann E. 8/12, George 28
WILKERSN, Bartlett 18, Martha 30
HOLMAN, Elisha 27, Mary 9, James 7, Wm. 6, Lucy 5, George 3, Martin 1, Charles 32
HAMILTON, Simon 32*, Minerva 15, Squire 12, Angelina 7, James 15, Andrew 4, Arthusa 2, Hannah 7/12

Schedule Page 267

ALEXANDER, Nancy 50*
COX, Green 43, Permelia 40, Frances 14, Elizabeth 11, Mary 9, Permelia 7, John 5, Jane 3
HISEL, Benjamin 70, Mary 60, Franklin 27, Henry 25, Abner 23, Jamima 22, Christopher 20, John 18
GARRISON, Samuel 46*, Lucy 17, Margaret 14, Mary 12, Mathew 9, Elizabeth 50
LAMB, Alonzo 33*
WHITE, John 22, Lucinda 22
RINGO, Elizabeth 86, Grayham 40, Spicy Ann 37, Sallie W. 13
SAUTER, Alexander 50*, Sarah 45, Harvey? 24, Sallie 20, Wm. 18, John 14, Elizabeth 12
WEBB, Milly 104*, Fontain 54, Sallie Ann 23
JORDAN, Robert 6*
COVINGTON, Coleman 49*, Matilda 46
HORNSBY, Lucy 26*, Robert 18
BURNET, Maria 4*
OLDHAM, Caleb 63, Abby 50, Shelton 26, Elizabeth 21, Paulina 19, Dianna 17, Preston 15, Mary 13
STEWART, John 22*, Mary 16
TODD, Henry 18*
ELKINS, Joel 42, Celia 29, ancy 12, Martha 11, Sally 8, Wm. 3
OLDHAM, Susan 61, Amanda 17
SHIFFLETT, Dudley 35, Icy Binda 34, William 15, Thomas 12, Almilda 9, Stephen 7, Mahala 5, Elizabeth 1
GENTRY, John P. 67*, Mary 54
FREEMAN, Morton 5*
LONG, James 49*, Eliza 40, Martha 16, John 14, James 12, Nancy 10, Eliza 6

Schedule Page 268

CARNEY, Martha 30*
DOTSEY, Volney 80 (m), Hannah 30, Charles 27, Bayle 8 (m), James 6, Azariah 4
BROADDUS, Jerremiah 2*
BROADDUS, Julia 26*, Andrew 19
PADEN, Joseph 2*, Rachael 25, Sarah 24

1850 Census Madison County Kentucky

PADMAN, Sarah 11/12*
WILLS, Henry 45, Jane 35, Thomas 44, Wm. 11, Sally 9, Milo 7, George 6, Cyrus 4
JETT, Isaac J. 1*
SOUTHERLY, Augustus 55*
OLDHAM, Thompson 21, Nancy 31, Camilia 27, Wm. 6, Margaret 5, Louis 3
BENTLY, William 3/12*
BENTLY, Temperance 43*, Elizabeth 40
HARDIN, John 23*
BENTLEY, Daniel 40, Matilda 40, Maross 42 (m), Wm. 18, Virginia 16, Daniel 6, Cassius 3
BENTON, Milton 30, Martha 28, Ruthy 4, Elizabeth 1
TODD, Benjamin 69, Alsey 65, Mary 21, Minerva 20, Jamima 10, Eliza 6, David 2?, John 2?, Alfred 1?
GRINSTEAD?, John B. 39, Mary 35?, Smith 16, Margaret 13?, Julia 12?, Catharine 8, Joel 10, George 7, Elizabeth 5, Mary 3
STEPHENS, Richard 29, Sarah 26, Elizabeth 8/12
LYKINS, Isaac L. 32, Elvira 28, Wm. 5, James 3, Martha 2, Mary 1/12
MARTIN, Liberty 40*, Elizabeth 36, Austin 9, Josiah 7, Lucy 3, Eliza 1
MORRIS, Henry 43*
STEPHENS, Thornton 50, Nancy 50, Juliana 18, Nancy 15, Martha 14, Charles 5

Schedule Page 269

STEPHENS, William 23, Eliza 23, Mary 2/12
AMORINE, John 66, Catharine 56, Mary 19, James 18, Charlotte 13, Jane 26, Kesiah 19, James Cassius 1
NIBLICK, John C. 38*, Maria 30, Amelia 15, Elizabeth 13, Wm. 10, Thomas 8, Amanda 6, Mary E. 7/12
CREED, John 80*, Mary 70
BAXTER, Thomas 45, Eliza 33, Sarah 14, Moab 13, Nancy 11, Elizabeth 10, John 7, Binona 4 (m), Thomas 3
SMITH, Elisha 25, Margaret 21
SMITH, Jessee R. 57, Juria 51, Sally A. 24, Ellender 15, King Solomon 13, Emily 9, Juria 6
MILLER, James P. 34, Rachael 34, Fayette 9, John Spud? 6, Nancy 5, Zackaria 2
ABRAMS, James 18, Nancy 27
SMITH, James 19, Matilda 17, Henry 20
ROGERS, Adam 64, Frances 40, Cynthia 10, James 8, Joel 7, Bejamin 4, Elizabeth 2
BROADDUS, Andrew 54, Gracy 53, Sydney 17 (m), Jackson 15, Martha 12, Elizabeth 10
MOORE, Samuel 44*, Agness 47, David 24
HARAM, James 23*
OLDHAM, Nathaniel 66, Lacada 50 (f), Amarine 25, Dominica 17, Elizabeth 16, Mary 15
ESTILL, Johnathan 39*, Judith 28, Peter W. 28, Richard 6
ROGERS, Joseph 25*
OLDHAM, Edith 8*, Edith 70
OLDHAM, David D. 38, Susan 33, Elizabeth 13, Abner 8

Schedule Page 270

MOBERLY, Thomas 46*, Nanc 29, Alla 4, Patsey 1
DUDLY, Elizabeth 62*, Jamima 16, Richard 11

1850 Census Madison County Kentucky

KING, Jackson 37, Margaret 22, Mary 2
BAKER, David E. 54*, Jamima 39
DASHIN, John 25*
STAGNER, Thomas 19*
KAVANAUGH, Charles 63, Margaret 63, Humphrey 26, Archibald 21
CHILLIS, Milly 89*, Ann 45, Nancy 43
COULTER, Paulina 17*, James 13
TODD, Peter 56, Nancy 45, Montraville 22, Franklin 18, Nancy 16, Louisa 29, Peter 13, Henry 11, Elizabeth 9
FIELDER, William 30, Elizabeth 28, Ambrose 10, Mary 7, Wm. 5, Dillard 3, Milly 2, Jane 6/12
HILL, Henry S. 30, Martha 9, Alexander 7, Louis 6
FIELDER, Curtis 34, Louisa 28, Frances 14, Ellender 8, Sarah 6, Wm. 73, Milam 68, Minty 28
WATERS, Thomas 27, Malinda 24, Emily 2, Eliza 1
EVANS, Stephen 55, Elizabeth 53, Angeline 15, Mary 18, Stephen 13, Joseph 10, Arthuisa 60
HILL, Eliza 2*
VAUGHN, Julia 53*
DOUTHETT, Hiram 53, Francis 28, Benjamine 22, Armilda 1, Margaret 35
JOHNSON, George 30, Lucy 10, Laura 8, Wm. 6, Jefferson 4, John 1, Barthena 23
NORRIS, Napoleon 17, Minerva 25
JENKINS, P. A. 23 (f)*, Jacob 4, Lucy 13, Henry 1/12

Schedule Page 271

VAUGHN, William 34*
MOORE, Smuel 40, Margaret 49, John W. 12, Mary E. 10, James 7, Laura 6/12
LOWREY, Thomas 35, Willy 28, Mary 7, Nancy 4, John 1
LOWEL, Turner 36, Hannah 24, Better 13, James 12, Patsey 6, George 4, Arthusine 3, Eliza 1
WATSON, William 43, Amelia 42, John W. 9, Sarah E. 8
COBB, James 43, Leander 45, Thomas 18, Robert 16
CLARKE, James W. 34, Martha 31, Wm. 10, Leander 8, James 6, Tarlton 4, Henry 2, Ann 1
MANSFIELD, William 58, Nancy 53, Green 36, Calista 25, Ibsan 20
MOORE, William R. 47*, Amanda 40, Wm. 7, James 5
STAGNER, David 17*
REYNOLDS, James W. 29, Hester 24, Virginia 6, Monroe 1/12
MOORE, William J. 28*, Eliza J. 23, Augusta 7, John 5, Rosa 3, Elizabeth 1
WITT, Robert 25*
GIMSTEAD?, M. D. 36 (m), Eliza 35, Elizabeth 10, wesley 9, George 7, John 5, Mary 3, Edward 2, Charlotte 1/12
MCKINNY, D. C. 33 (m), Mary Ann 23, Wm. 6, James 5, Mary S. 3, Francis M. 1
JACKSON, J. G. 44 (m), Betsey 39, Emeline 17, Josiah 14, Nancy 11, Wm. 8, Frances 6, Nancy? 3
JOHNSON, George 38, Lucy 37, Louisa 12, William 8, George 5, John 2, Parthina 7/12

Schedule Page 272

WATERS, Larkin B. 29, Edwin 25, Samuel 8, John 6, Nathan 4, Wm. 1
SHEARRER, Thomas 44, Nancy 39, Tilman 20, Armilla 15, Astilda 13, Nancy 8, Sarah 5, Thomas 2
HOWARD, Obediah 29, Elizabeth 28, John 10, James 8, Wm. 6, Lackey 3 (m), Laura 1

1850 Census Madison County Kentucky

GREEN, James 60, Henry 11, Anna 17, Betsey 21
NORRIS, Hamilton 40*, Eliza 33, Laura 14, Simpson 13, James 10, Sarah 6, Wm. 4, Mary 2
MCDIAL, William 40*, Younger? 20 (m), Walter 18, Lucy 44, Dudley 10
TILEY, Joel 8*, Mary 5
TILEY, Edward 21, Eliza 24
TUCKER, Willis 32, Clarissa 30, Malinda 11, Eliza 3, Permelia 4/12
CHENAULT, David 79, Nancy 72, Anderson 38
NOLAND, John 63*, Julia 12
WATSON, Elender 30*
NOLAND, Martha 30, Nathan 33, Margaret 19, Elbridge 2, John A. 6/12
WOOD, Simpson 25, Mahala 22, James 4, Robert 8/12
OLIVER, Isaac 59, Elizabeth 45, Josaphine 12, Tabitha 9, Elizabeth 4
PARKER, Courtney 35 (f), Francis 19, Cassinda 15, Christopher 14, Samuel 10, James 8, Ann 1
DENNY, John 33, Minerva 34, Francis 11, Margaret 10, Zeria 8, Rachael 3

Schedule Page 273

FRELAN, John 30, Cyntha 25, Elizabeth 6, Talton 1
WILCOX, Squire 35, Agnus 35, Amanda 15, William 12, Sarah 8, Jesse 3, _____ 9/12 (f)
CHAMBERS, John 37, Temperance 21, John 6, Ann 4, Harvey 3, _____ 1 (m)
JONES, Thomas 35, Sally 25, Hardin 7, Patsey 4, _____ 1 (f)
MASTIN, John 23*
FLUTY, William 23*
WEBB, Joseph 37, Joicy 37, Henry 16, Elisha 15, Elizabeth 14, Lucy 8, Columbus 13, James 7, Liby 6, Mancy 3 (f), _____ 4/12 (m)
NOLAND, William 74, Liby 28, Jackson 34, Lucy 28, Levi 12, Patsy 8, Cynthia 5, William 4
WIDDLE, George 56, Squire 54, Cassius 18
KINDRED, J. J. 28 (m), Nancy 28, Mary 13, Elizabeth 11, Frances 10, Nancy 9, J. J. 6/12 (m)
CANE, John 65, Susan 60
HISLE, Jeferson 27, Amanda 21, James 1, Zacheria 1/12
MOORE, Jeremiah 25, Arminta 23, Lucy 9/12
MCKINNEY, James 56, Ellender 53, John 26, Wm. 23, Colley 21 (m), Murrel 20, Mary 17, David 10
BROCK, Martin 35, Charlotte 29, Frances 12, Mary 11, Wm. 8, John 6
WHITE, Benjamin 26, Sarah 22, Henry 3, Margaret 2, Maria 1/12
MOORE, Thomas 26, Thursey 26, Robert 2, James 1

Schedule Page 274

GOLANE, Sally 30, Catharine 17, Emily 14, Wm. 10, Frank 5
NOLAND, James 35, Ann 30, Mary 13, Ann 11, Hesekiah 9, John 7, Orthunial 5 (m), Nathan 4, Margaret 1
BARNES, William 40, Margaret 40, Henry 21, Ana 17, Titury? 16 (f), Joel? 15, John 12, Wm. 11, Ellen 4
CANADA, Mary 59*
WEST, William 16*
ANDERSON, George 30*, Arzelia 29, Amos 9, Mary 5, Elizabeth 4, John 1
CANADA, James 65*

1850 Census Madison County Kentucky

WEST, John M. 32, Mary 23, James 10, Wm. 7, Mary 5, George 2
BERRY, Celure? 38 (m), Harriett 31, Martin 17, Grant 15, John 10, Silars 6 (m), James 1
JONES, John 60, Mary 54, Sally 27, Martha 18, Murrel 16, Marcellus 13, Jasper 9
LAUTER?, Newton? 23*, Martha 19
CHRISTOPHER, Thomas 23*, Amanda 20, John D. 2/12
FREEMAN, John 25, Elizabeth 18
FREEMAN, Claibourne 27, Nancy 23, Margaret 2, Mary 1
PORTWOOD, Rice 27*, Mary 33, George 6, Eliza 4, James 10/12
WILSON, Elizabeth 18*, John 20, Perry 15, Alfred 14
TODD, Haram 33, Lucy 33, Emily 12, Ailsey 10, John 8, Paulina 6, Elizabeth 9/12
FORD, Anna 62, Caroline 30, Benjamin 24, Emily 11, Thomas 5, Marcus 3

Schedule Page 275

PORTWOOD, Thomas 57, Nancy 56, Wesley 18, Wm. 11, Susan 21
JONES, Bright 45, Easter 42, Susan 14, U. B. 12 (m)
CRUSE, William 38, Nancy 39, Martha 16, Mary 14, Margaret 12, Amanda 10, Rebecca 8, Elizabeth 5, John 3, Nancy 2, Robert 9/12
WELLS, Richard 43, Joel 36, Henry 16, Margaret 13, Elizabeth 8, Anna 6, Wm. 5, Richard 4, John E. 2, ____ 2/12 (m)
LIPSCOMB, Josiah 32, Eliza 22, Oscar 5, Amanda 3, Wm. 1
OLDHAM, Orthenal 33 (m), Lydonia 27, John 11, Hesekiah 9, James 7, Mary 4, Susan 1
TURPIN, John 22, Elizabeth 24, Eliza 2, Mary 5/12, Hannah 55
TURPIN, Mary 81, Mourning 43, Nancy 20, Lucinda 18, Richard 16
TURPIN, Solomon 48, John 30, Smith 22, Nancy 17
LIPSCOMB, Nancy 66*
TURPIN, Henry 31*
WALDEN, Elisha 41*, Martha 40, Elizabeth 16, Wm. 14, Josiah 13, John 12, Robert 11, Harvie 9, Leanna 6, Jackson 5, Elijah 4
BROTHERTON, Robert 21*, Arsela 20
TURPIN, Andrew 17*
TURNER, Harriett 50, Lena 15, Armilda 12, Cassius 9, Wm. 17, Martha 16
BRUCE, Tina 31 (m)*, Nancy 26, Alminda 5, James 2
WALDEN, Thomas 13*

Schedule Page 276

KINN?, Samuel 31, Louisa 35, Nancy 7, John 5, Leanna 3, Wm. 1
KINN?, William 28, Mary 22, John 6, Mary 5, Elizabeth 3, Samuel 1
KINN?, Thompson 28, Louisa 23, Isabella 2
TURPIN, John 60, Elizabeth 57, John 22, Leanna 18, Ann 15, Allen 12, Henry 28
OWENS, James W. 48, Mary 42, John 17, Mary 16, Emily 14, Wm. 12, Amanda 8, Martha 6, Frances 4
PARCAN, Ephram 22, Louisa 22, W. 11/12
POWELL, Joel 35, Jane 23, Benjamin 3, Jonathan 1
PINKSTON, John W. 33, Anna 26, Sarah 9, Mary 6, Martha 4, Adalaide 2, Sally 60
HAMILTON, Bluford 40*, Permelia 32, James 16, John 14, Wm. 4, Rosaline 2
BROWNING, Jesse 70*

HOLINS, Thomas 69*
COLTER, James 69*
HIATT, Fanny 68*
JOHNSON, John 68*
FRENCH, William 28*, Sophia 22, Mary 4, Susan 2
FORD, Silas 38*
WATTS, Robert 27, Millie 21, Wm. 5, Green 3, Ann 1
ROBES, William 56*, Paulina 48, Isabella 18, Paulina 12
STONE, Robert H. 29*, Eliza 27, Sally 5, Wm. 3, James 1
BECK, Robert S. 24*, Martha 23, Paulina 2, Wm. 1/12
YOUNG, John C. 50, Margaret 50, Sally 20, Matilda 18, Thomas 16, Mary 14, John 12

Schedule Page 277

BOGGS, James S. 31, Mary 31
JONES, Newland 25*, Mary 20, Margaret 2/12
FOX, William 42
WRIGHT, Flensy? W. 26 (m), Ellender 23, Margaret 5, Rosa 3, _____ 1 (f)
PORTWOOD, Hardin 27, Maria 22, Margaret 4, Harrison 2
CHINAULT, Cavel? 55 (m), Emily 45, Robert 24, Elverell 16 (f), David 12, Cavel 10, Anderson 7, Jeptha 5, Harvey 2
LAY, Talton 31, Lydia 25, Francis M. 9, Nancy 7, Wm. 6, Lucy 4, Elizabeth 2
KRINE?, James 55, Frances 45, Susan 21, Franklin 18, Matilda 17, Elizabeth 16, John 14, Robert 12, Zuna? 9 (m), Mary 5
CHANY, William 28, Nancy 25, Wilson 4, Amanda 11/12
DUNN, Edmund 43, Mary 40, Wm. 22, Jasper 20, Scuyler 18, James 12, Elizabeth 9
IRVINE, Samuel 66*, Racheal 50, Samuel 23 (B), Susan 17 (B), William 20 (B), Isaac 18 (B), Christopher 12(B), Georgeanna 5 (B)
SMITH, Mary 50, Elizabeth 26, _____ 1 (m)
COBB, Zine 52 (m)*, Provicence 48, Silas 18
SMITH, John 6*
WALTON, W. R. 25 (f)*, Susan 27
CHRISTOPHER, Howell 18*, Ann 12
TROWER, James A. 35, Permelia 30, Nancy 9, Thomas 7, James 6, Susan 3
WADKINS, Thomas 48, Mary 40, Emily 15, Thomas 9, John W. 7, James 5, Mary 3

Schedule Page 278

PULLEY, Robert J. 31, Nancy 31, Jackson 4
WOODS, Louisa 36, Elizabeth 18, Nancy 16, Leanna 15, Joel C. 13, Elliot 9, Alexander 10, Wm. 5, Louisa 2
SIMMONS, William 33*, Mourning 32, Willis 14, Jemaima 12, Elizabeth 10, Nancy 8, Louisa 4, John 2, _____ 9/12 (f)
WALDEN, Jemaima 57*
FORD, Schuyler 41, Sarah 43, Schuyler 13, Louisa 12, Charlotte 11, Silas 9, Sarah 8, John 6, Mary 5, Leslie 4, Alice 2

1850 Census Madison County Kentucky

PINKSTON, Ann 67 (B), Robert 45, Squire 40, Hester 30, Racheal 18, Squire 15, John 9, Susan A. 6, Martha 4, James 3, Louisa 1, George 7/12
MILLER, William 60 (B), Nancy 55
MILLER, Peggy 58 (B), Elizabeth 40
STAGNER, Thomas 57, James 31, Harvy 17, Richard 14, Thomas 12
STAGNER, John S. 21*, Julia 20, Jesse 66
MONROE, Turner? 25*, Wm. 23
DENNY, Samuel 50, Cira? 40 (f), Elzira 16
CURCH, Mathew B. 30*, Elizabeth 18, James 4
LAMB, Lucinda 28*
COBB, Henry 25, Sarilda 17
MCELROY, E. R. 46 (m), Lavina 40, Martha 16, James 12
PORTWOOD, Leonard 20*, Martha 19
FARAR, Rebecca 30*, Ann 10, Samuel 8, James 5
PORTWOOD, Zacaria 22*, Squire 17, Mary 12

Schedule Page 279

FIFE, Daniel 11*, Samuel 9, Alexander 8, Mary 4
SMITH, Jacob 58, Eliza 56, Ellen 24, Caroline 20, Ann 17
STONE, Caleb 65, Mary 37, Caroline 19, James 13, Thomas 11, Mary 6, Wm. 5, Caleb 3, Cyrus 3/12
JOHNSON, Tennie? 38, Fountain 36, Mary 70
ANDERSON, Matilda 45, Amanda 20, Paulina 18, Nancy 16
HAYNES, Nathan 40, Catharine 42, Margaret 37
TERRY, Joseph 46, Manerva 39, Edna 13, Mary 10, Lavinda 8, Joseph 1
COX, Manerva 70
HOLMEN, James 32, Frances 34, John 10, Bryant 8, Andrew 6, Sydney 4 (m), James 2
LAY, Jessee 55, Susan 50, Edward 30, Manerva 20, Wm. 16, Jessee 12
MORAN, William 55, Daniel 21, Solon 19, James 16, Elizabeth 14, Nancy 12
SMITH, John R. 30*, Charlotte 22, Mary 5
CRUSE, Samuel 18*
MORAN, Nathan 48, Nancy 30, Adalaide 19, David 13, Hugh 1
BENSUTT, Samuel 40*, Nancy 41, Moses 19, Humphrey 17, Susan 14, Mary 12
WILLIAMS, Robert 24*
KELLOGG, Chester 47*, Susan 37
PEYTON, Griffin 51, Elizabeth 51, Amanda 20, Nancy 19, George 17, Margaret 15, Emily 10
PEYTON, James T. 25, Maria 26
BALLARD, James A. 48*, Elzabeth 18
SMITH, Nancy 1*
BALLARD, Permelia 4*

Schedule Page 280

DAVIS, Lucy 54, Paulina 25, Wm. 22, Tanner 19, James 17
WILLIS, Thomas 50*, Nancy 53
BINTER, Mary 82*
LAND, G. W. 27 (m), Sarah 24, Mary 6, John 23
GILLEN, William 27, Ann 22, Nancy 1

1850 Census Madison County Kentucky

LONG, Henry 32, Martha 29, E. J. 10 (f), Nancy 8, Sarah 6, Mary 4, Rhoda 1
CHRISTOPHER, Frances 27
GULLIE, John 60, Lucinda 45, Jackson 28, Wm. 20, Willis 17
DOLLIN, John P. 46, Patsy 44, Mary 20, Eliza 19, Martha 12, Phoeba 10, Sarah 8, Caroline 6, Nancy Clay 3
JOHNSON, Mary 54, Mary 28, James 26, Perry 20, Jasper 3, Elizabeth 20
ROBERSON, Butler 43*, Allen 28 (f?), Mary 6, Nancy 4, Sarah 2, Absolum 3/12
BALLEW, Richard 22*
WORLAND, James 42, Lucinda 36, Mary 12, Dianna 10, Wm. 8, Susan 6, James 4, Harriett 2
STAGNER, Joseph 60, Mary 56
RAIBOURNE, Harrison 35, Minerva 35, Matilda 4
WILKERSN, Plesant 36, Sophia 34, Rebecca 8, Sarah 7
BETTERWORTH, John 54, Barbery 45, Walter 2
ANDERSON, John 54*, Mary 53
MARSH, William 62*
DAVIS, Joshua 23, Agnus 22, Crelia? 4/12
FOSTER, William 21, Margaret 21
WOOD, John G. 32, Susan 33, Wesley 10, Araminta 8, Mary 2

Schedule Page 281

SHIPTON, Jesse 75*, Mary 65, Nancy 44
GILLISPIE, Susan 68*
SHIPTON, Green 40, Louisa 19, Robert 12, Mary 9, Margaret 5, Lucy 5, _____ 2/12 (f)
BLACKWELL, John R. 26*, Frances 68
ATKINS, Frances 15*
TIVIS, Silas 39, Martha 39, E. J. 15 (f), Thomas 14
BATTERTON, A. G. 32 (m), betha25, Christopher 2, Emily 8/12
BENTLY, China 35 (f), Tilman 8, Louisa 7, Jaran 5 (m), Susan 3
BATTERTON, Abraham 70, Susan 60, Mahala 37
MORAN, Barrutt 60, Sophia 56, Isaac 17, Malinda 11
CANIDA, Malinda 30*, Elizabeth 12, Malissa 10, Joan 7, Lucy 5, Michael 1
ASCUR, James 24*
REED, John J. 33, Margaret 32, Wm. 13, N. G. 10 (f), Margaret 9, Mary 7, John 1
WALLACE, Ann J. 61*
HARRIS, Jane 50*
HUGHES, William 31, Jane 25, Wm. 6, Thomas 3, John 7/12
MORAN, John G. 30, Elizabeth 25, Victoria 7, Margaret 5, Lee 3 (m), Sallie 1
BOULWAN, Madison 36, Wilmoth 32, Wm. 11, John 9, Perthana 7, James 5, Lucy 3, Mary 1
SINGLETON, Merret 34, Talitha 23, Margaret 3, Wm. 1, Lyne 3/12 (m), Mary 30, Daniel 23
HAGUE, James 52, Cyntha 48, Wm. 23, John 21, James 18, Robert 5
DAVIS, John 40*, Jane 30

Schedule Page 282

JUDTSELL?, Josiah 27*
GENTRY, Benaja 72, Paulina 66, Benjamin 30, Aulsan 26 (m)

1850 Census Madison County Kentucky

FORTUNE, Emily 45, Jesse 18 (m), Wm. 15, Jerone 10 (m), Mary 9, Minerva 4
OLDHAM, Frances 70, Nathaniel 34, Jackson 32, Hesekiah 25, Mildred 12
JIMMERSON, Nancy 60*
SEARCY, Samuel 55*
WOODS, Frances 50, Patsy 45
OLDHAM, Nathan 46*, Rebecca 46
RAIBOURNE, Miranda 28*
ALEXANDER, Samuel 7*
PARKES, Joseph 46*, Sophia 46, Samuel 17, Margaret 16, Robert 10, Wm. 6
TILLETT, Jane 20*
CARR, Adam 32*, Elizabeth 31, Elizabeth 9, John B. 4, Ann 2, _____ 2/12 (m)
OLDHAM, Ibsan 40 (m)*
ANDERSON, Green 31, Hettie 25, Wm. 3, Patsy 2
GENTRY, James 47, Nancy 42, Susan 19, Robert 17, James 15, Josiah 14, Rebecca 11, Wm. 10,
    Thomas 9, Richard 3, Martin 7/12, Lucy 50, Elizabeth 45
DOY, Malinda 18 (B), Edy 2/12 (f)
HARPER, Henry 40, Susan 38, Elizabeth 13, James 6, Nancy 5, Thomas 4, Wm. 4/12
COX, Daniel 45, Milinda 38, Nancy 6, Dillard 5
PORTWOOD, Clifton 30, Mary 36, Alexander 3, Robert 2
HACKETT, Owen 27, Bassel 24 (m), Sarah 60
TEVIS, Mar A. 39, Wm. 20, Noah 18, Nancy 16, Joel 15, Mary 12, John 10, Robertson 8, Nathaniel 3

Schedule Page 283

BARNETT, John 40*, Mary 35, Rebecca 6, Jasper 5
WOODSON, Francis 17*
HUNTER, Jesse 50*, Mary 48, Elizabeth 16, ann 14, Mary 13, George 8, Samuel 7, Jacob 12
RICE, Thomas 30*
OWENS, Samuel 23*
RICE, Margaret 24*, Josephine 3, Louisa 2
HAYNE, Davis 20*
DUNHAM, James 25*, Mary 17, Murrel 11/12
MCQUINN, Thomas 19*
PARKES, Louisa 41*, Wm. 18, James 12, Letha 7, Thomas 5, Elizabeth 3
STAMPER, William 50, Elizabeth 30, John 10
MILLION, william 29, Mary 23, Milton 5, Sarilda 3, Jeremiah 1
DOZIER, Richard 57, Margaret 55, Mary A. 28, Rebecca 24, Bradford 23, James 22, Fostimetus? 19(f),
    Alford 16, Thomas 11
STAGNER, Abner 26*, Zerilda 22, Sarah 2, John 1/12
MOBERLY, Thomas 10*
BENTLEY, Sarah 43
COBB, Samuel 37, Permelia 31, Robert 11, Owen 10, Joel 4, Rufus 3, Nancy 6/12, Nancy 77
PARKS, Hesekiah 37*, Elizabeth 29, Agnus 10, Jeptha 8, Margaret 6, Martha 4, Stephen 2, Wm. 7/12
PORTWOOD, Milton 22*
OWENS, Bartheny 67 (f)*
BERRY, Thomas 16*
OLDHAM, Hiram 26, Emily 21, Rosa 1
EBOND, Samuel 30*, Susan 25, Elizabeth 6, Thomas 4, Debby 2

1850 Census Madison County Kentucky

PORTWOOD, Conwell 27*
PARRISH, Wesley 55, Harriett 51, Harvey 23, Socrates 21

Schedule Page 284

PARRISH, Owen 32, Mary 25, Wm. 9, June 8, Elizabeth 6, Ann 4, John 3, Martha 2, Joel 1/12
PARRISH, Albertis 27, Margaret 23, Harriett 1
JONES, Stephen 45, Agnus 42, Emeline 19, Wm. 13, Jason 8
MOORE___, Charles C. 55, Ellener 50, Martha 22, Elizabeth 18, James 16, Mary 13, Ellender 11, Charles 8
GOODLOE, William 81, Suasn 72, Amia 19, Mary 15
FRANCIS, Thomas R. 33, Mary 29, Edney 11, Susan 4, Edy 3, Eliza 3/12
GOODLOE, William C. 45, Almira 42, Susan 20, Amanda 18, Sallie 15, Wm. 13, Caroline 11, Archibald 8, Lucey 5, Mary B. 8/12
BALLARD, John R. 25, Emeline 25, Mary S. 3, Nancy 1
BALLARD, Elizabeth 65, Mary 32, John 16, Nancy 14, Harrison 10
STONE, John 75, Sally 70, Samuel 33, Alfred 29, Mary A. 19, John 4/12
PHELPS, George 45, Nancy 35, Thomas 15, James 10
EVANS, George 44, Mary 35, Louisa 14
EVANS, Mary 73
HARLOW, Thomas 21, Milam 17 (f)
WILLIS, John 53, Susan 47, Amos 25, Nancy 19, David 18, Elizabeth 15, Samuel 12, John 11, Robert 4, Josiah 2
FIFE, Alexander 50*, Mary 46, James 15, Wm. 13

Schedule Page 285

PARRISH, Paulina 18*, Martha 14, Jacob 11, Squire 9, Celia 5
PARRISH, William 58, Celia 35, Martha 20
SCIDDER?, William 55*, Lucy 48, Nancy 20, Wm. 19, James 17, Louisa 16, Charity 13, Richard 9, Lucey 5
FOWLER, Richard 64*
PARKS, Rebecca 24*, Rufus 3
EMBRY, Joseph 50, Racheal 46, Mary 23, Josephus 21, Catherine 19, Henry C. 16, Martha 13, Paulina 10, Wm. 5
ADAMS, John T. 22, Millie 19, Sarah 4/12
WILLIAMS, Nathan 52, Celia 52, Neoma 23, Amanda 21, Celia 19, Nathan 17, Daniel 16
WILLIAMS, William 29, Emily 26, Julia 6, Taylor 4, Mary 2
BENTLY, Nancy 10*
DANIEL, Mary 32*
MARCH, Joshua 42*, Mary 41
BENTLY, Susan 13*, Creed N.C.S. 10, Mary T.W.B.C.H. 3, Thomas C.J.T.F. 2
OWENS, John 56, Matilda 47
LANHAM, John 40, Mary 39, Josephus 25, America 13, Lear 10 (m), Wm. 5
HUGUELY, Jacob 43*, Florence 38, Susan 16, Racheal 12, James 10, Squire 8, Martha 6, Jacob 4, Harriett 2
RUNYON, Matilda 47*

1850 Census Madison County Kentucky

WOODRUFF, Harvey 30, Mary 25, Hiram 2, John 5/12
OLDHAM, David 41, Martha 38, Nancy 16, Nathaniel 12, Wm. 11, Jesse 8/12
OLDHAM, Abner 67*, Hannah 63, Hellen 29, Miranda 27

Schedule Page 286

DAVIS, Isabella 15*, Margaret 12, Abraham 10, Sarah 7, Thomas 5, Sophia 5, Harriett 6/12
FOX, Samuel M. 44, Martha 41, John 13, Josephina 10, Laura 7, Patsy 4, Samuel 2
JENNINGS, William 65, Malinda 60, Paulina 30, Laura 26, Vinia 24, Wm. 25, Leaney 22 (f), Elizabeth 20, Amanda 18
CORNELISON, Franklin 37*, Angeline 33, Susan 5, John 3, Wm. 5/12
ROWLAND, Thomas 13*
LAND, James W. 30, Pricilla 31, Mary 7, Ann 5, James 2
WHITAKER, James 37, Sally 37, James 15, Archibald 13, Nancy 11, Sarah 9, Johnson 7, Catharine 5, William 3, John 2
SCOTT, John 55, Eliza 50
ESTILL, Samuel 63, Rebecca 63, James 30, Erasmus 28, Elvira 25
BOGER?, John B. 25*, Elizabeth 21, Benjamin 3, John 1
BALL, Edney 22 (f)*
MASTIN, Alexander 40, Mary 35, Wm. 15, Dianna 14, Marion 12 (f), John 8, Horian? 7 (m), _____ 4 (f), George 7/12
CALICO, Mary 40, James 17, John 16, Margaret 15
ELKINS, Jacob 35, Racheal 30, Mary 13
WHITATON, Marcus 37*, Morning 37, Patsey 16, Sidney 14 (m), Irvine 12, Wm. 13, Thomas 11, John 10, Johnson 8, Eliza 4, Fannie 3, Margaret 1

Schedule Page 287

TAYLOR, Ann 62*
CURRINS, Jacob 85*
HOWARD, Elijah 29*, Nancy 24, Angeline 3, Napoleon 1, _____ 1/12 (m)
LAND, Hiram 27, Sally 25, Cassius C. 1, _____ 1/12 (m)
HAM, Joseph 48, Marina 43, Massey 21 (f), Elizabeth 19, Clara 17, Sidney 16 (m), Margaret 13, William 11, John 8, James 5, Woodson 2
HAM, John 72, Mary 60
KENATZER, Christopher 30, Amanda 27, Columbus 9, Eliza 7, Wm. 3, Mary 2/12
YANCY, Thomas G. 37, Cynthianna 34, Arminta 12, John 9, Wm. 4
POND, Joseph R. 70, Nellie 70, Malissa 30, Cyrena 27, Mary 24, Margaret 23, Amanda 20
SALLE, Stephen 86, Sarah 83, Mary 53, Malinda 46, Cyntha 40
SMITH, James 59, Mary 61
SALLE, Stephen 39*, Martha 40, Mary 10, Sarah 7, John 5, Wm. 3, _____ 8/12 (f)
HAGEN, Jane 44*
ISBELL, William 58, Abner 32, Wm. 20, Siminda? 25, John 5, Henry H. 4
SALLE, John F. 24, Elizabeth 28, Sarah 4, Dudley 3, _____ 8/12 (f)
ALVERSON, Jesse 49*, Nancy 50, Milton 23, Cincinattus 21, Charlton 17, Maryetta 14, Amada 11
CARVER, Sarah 54*

- 314 -

1850 Census Madison County Kentucky

ELKINS, Henry 53, Mary 55, John 25, James 23, Rosa 20
SMITH, william 49, Sallie 55, Thomas 25

Schedule Page 288

GILLESPIE, Jeremiah 28, Harriett 25
GOGGIN, William 50, Sabill 45 (f), Mirrena 18
FERREL, Archer 56*, Mahala 34, Martha 17
MILLION, Benson 75*
JEFFRIES, Absolm 32, Mary 19, Mary 1
HARVIE?, Green B. 36, Winney 22, Norris 4, John 1
STRATTS, William 40, Chana 32, Sophina 15, Andy W. 14 (f), Louisa 7, Wm. 5, Mahala M.C.M.M. 3, Cyrus J.J.C. 8/12
HENDROW, Oliver 42*, Elizabeth 27, Margaret 1
HAND?, John W. 15*
PATTERSON, Clark 37*, Milard 4 (f), George 2
WHITAKER, Zacheria 25*, Susan 17, George 5/12
TURNER, Amanda 15*, Nancy 13
SALLE, Alvin? A. 49, Phoeba 44, Sarah 12
CARPENTER, Job 50, Susan 63
GILL, Margaret 50, Alminda 17, Shelby 14 (m)
TUDER, Stephen 36, Jane 30, Wm. 6, Margaret 4, James 1
TUDER, Daniel 56, Rhoda 51, Sallie 20, Martha 17, Christopher 10
LONG, James 47, Martha 23, Mary 18, John 17, Malinda 14, Miland 12 (f), Morris 10, Sidney 9 (m), Albert 8
TUDER, John 27, Permelia 27, James 7, Nelson 6, George 3, Paulina 1
TUDER, Woodson 30, Sallie 27, George 8, Wm. 6, Isabelle 5, Levi 2, _____ 3/12 (m)
LOGSTON, James 27, Susan 22
LONG, James J. 25*, Amanda 18, James 1

Schedule Page 289

TUDER, John M. 14*
LONG, Daniel 40*, Elizabeth 30, Wm. 15, Haden 14, Marion 13, Sidney 12 (m), Martha 11, Howard 10, Mary 8, _____ 6/12 (f)
MOBERLY, Ann 83*
HAVERY, Johnathan 25, Isabelle 16, Henry 3/12, Charles 22
BAGER, Daniel 40, Isabele 12, George 10, Marcus 9, David 5, Amanda 2
SHEARER, Lammion? 29 (m), Amanda 23, Baretha 2
SHEARER, William 26, James 26
VAUGHEN, Catharine 40, Elizabet 17, Henry 15, Wm. 14, Jacob 13, Robert 10, Eliza 11, Debranna 6, Sarah 2
JONE?, Elizabeth 68
AGEE, Ann 40, Irvine 18, Amanda 17, Nancy 16, Susan 14, Elizabeth 10, Squire 6, Howard 5
SHEARER, Nicholas 60, Rebecca 51
ROSS, Gabriel 65, Mary 62, George 27, Nancy 23, Richard 21, Lydia 83
COLTON, James 35, Nancy 32, Mary 12, Richard 9, Joseph 7

1850 Census Madison County Kentucky

ROSS, Stephen 33*, Elizabeth 25, Malinda 7, Andrew 5, Minerva 3, Lycurgus 6/12
WHITE, Jeremaih 25*
WHITLOCK, Albert 25, Adaline 20, John 5/12
WHITLOCK, Richard 21, Elizabeth 16
ROSS, Morris 35*, Anna 25
STEPHENSON, Mary J. 7*
ROGURS, Ellen 24, John 15, Robert 12, Elizabeth 10, Silas 7
LONG, John S. 38, Emily 25, ____ 1/12 (f), May 49
GOINS, Lucy 42*, Alexander 14, William 12, Beverly 11 (m), John 8, Mary 6, Cyrus 4, Robert 2

Schedule Page 290

WHITLOCK, James 24*, Mary 20
BOGER, Thomas 46, Frances 30, Mary J. 14, Thomas 12, Sallie 9, Joseph 6, Margaret 4
HAWKINS, William 61
MILLER, James B. 42, Juliet 27, Leslie 4 (m), Mary 1
ROBINSON, Sarah 50*, Jefferson 37
HUNDREN?, Lucinda 15*
KIRKENDALL, Samuel 46, Louisa 45, John 18
SULIVAN, Mary 64, Lucy 37, Mary 28
GARRET, Samuel 30*, Elizabeth 30, Charles 5, Mary 2
BURRISS, Green 17*
RAGSDALE, Thomas 48, Mary 47, Amanda 17, Wm. 15, Thomas 12, Mary 11, Margaret 9
CROOK, John P. 35, Catharine 34
SMITH, William S. 41, Elizabeth 18, Thomas 7, Sarah 2
TIVIS, Elizabeth 37, Robert 19, Sallie 17, Franklin 11, Wm. 9
ELKINS, Henderson 26, Elizabeth 25, Matilda 4, Mary 4/12
HASE, Thomas 42, Jane 36, Samuel 16, Mary E. 15, Nancy 14, Cyrus 11, James 9
MILLER, Alexander 65*, Sarah 36
BACON, John M. 7*
FOX, Charles 56, Nancy 50, Joel 33, Samuel 23
EADES, Nelson 36, Lucretia 32, Thomas 10, John C. 6
HORN, John 55, Louisa 50
BROWN, Lucey 35, James 9, Susan 8, ____ 5 (m)
FULLERLOOR?, Nancy 40, Wm. 48, Malinda 14, Andrew 12, Spicy 10 (f), Thomas 8

Schedule Page 291

FULLERLOOR?, Nancy 45, Milton 18, Sallie 15, Florinda 12
GARNET, Thomas H. 70, Elizabeth 60
MOODY, Samuel 60, Sophia 55, Amelia 30, Joseph 21, Robert 12, Benjamin 6
HARRIS, James K. 49, Nancy 43, Elizabeth 18, George 20, James 14, Lucy 8
IGO, Murberry? 35 (m)*, Mary 19
JOHNSON, Robert 36*, Susan 30, Mary 9, Margaret 8, Maria 7, Lucy 5, Susan 1
GROIN, Thomas 34, Matilda 32, nancy 13, James 10, Sarah 7, Elizabeth 5, Thomas 1
HOCKER, William 30*, Virginia 27, Sarah 3, Nicholas 5/12
BROWN, Catharine 18*
COLIBAN, Rebecca 20*

1850 Census Madison County Kentucky

Schedule Page 292

WILSON, robert 49*, Nancy 40, James 22, Wm. 21, Josiah 18, Levi 16, Mary 14, Robert 13, John 11, Sarah 9, Margaret 7, Vaby? 15 (m)
MAGEE, Nancy 25*, Cassius C. 2
HELPHINSTINE, T. H. 36 (m), Margaret 30, Wm. 8, Nancy 7, Elizabeth 5, John 2, Benjamin 1/12
HISLE, Louis 31, Clarissa 28, Martha 6, elizabeth 5, Sarah 3, John 1/12
WILLUBY, Silvester 25, Margaret 21, Elizabeth 1/12
HISLE, Irvine 28, Elizabeth 27, James 9, Lucy 4, Jackson 3, Napoleon 2
TILY, Lucy 44, Edward 21, Dudly 7, Joel 5, Mary 3
TIPTON, William 36, Catharine 31, Hammon 8, Wm. 5?, Absolum 3, Mary 1/12
WHITE, Austin 28*, Catharine 28, Benjamin 8, Henry C. 6, James 4, Levi 2
GROIN?, Sarah 45*, Nancy 22, John 10
LANDRON, Abram 72, Mary 59, Nancy 40, Henry 34, Elzabeth 29, Sarah 28, John 23, Susan 19
ELLIOT, Dorson 68, Permelia 65, LEvi 34, Permelia 20, Wm. 17, Edmund 14, Frances 10
JACKSON, James F. 39, Sarah 34, John 15, Sarah 13, Joshua 11, Elizabeth 9, Zerilda 7, Martha 4, Mary 2
BALDWIN, W. W. 22 (m), Mary 20, Louisa 1

Schedule Page 293

HISLE, Jackson 32, Sarah 30, Elizabeth 13, Laben 12, Thomas 10, Mary 7, Amanda 5, Wm. 2
THOMAS, James 57, Hannah 56, Jane 30, Elizabeth 34, Nancy 31, Kasiah 29, Araminta 27, Zaceriah 18, Josiah 14, Catarine 15, John 6
REEVES, John 50, Nancy 52, Jerry 25, Margaret 24, Sarah 21, Elzabeth 18, John 15, Owen 14
BURRS, William 32, James 10, John 7
KINDRED, J. J. 30 (m), Nancy 26, Lucinda 8, Mary 6, Martha 4, Cornelia 2, Peter 11/12
BAXTER, Edmund 38, Fancy 39, Louisa 16, Sarah 14, Elzabeth 12, Amelia 10, Eliza 8, Arathusa 6, Margaret 4, Celia 3, Benjamin 1
HOOLER, Robert 29, Evelina 30, John 7, James 5, America 3, Anna 2, Madison 6/12
CHRISTOPHER, Ambrose 30, Mary 40, John 7, Wm. 4, Wiley 2, Catharine 1/12
BLACKWELL, Joseph 45, Jamima 30, Wm. 18, Schuyler 15, Harrison 12, Armilda 10, Ely 8 (m), Nancy 6, Benjamin 5, Joseph 6/12, Delila 2
BROOKS, John 22, Mary 18, Archibald 7/12
CAIN, Hugh 38, Zerilda 22, Levi 7, Daniel 6, Permelia 4, Dorson 2 (m)
IRVINE, David L. 60, Sarah 60, Elizabeth 26, Miranda 23, Wm. 7, David 8, Thomas 6, James 5

Schedule Page 294

BABER, James 27, Catharine 27, Arminta 3, Celey 2
BABER, John M. 25, Asenith 50, Elizabeth 22, America 20, John 18, Wm. 16, Claraminta 14, Asenith 12, Davis 10, Mary 8
EADES, Louisa 61, Samuel 24, Jackson 16
JARMAN?, Elford 24, Susan 22, Darcus 3, Wm. 2, Cyntha 1
EADES, Plesant 29, Debby 24, Elizabeth 7, Stephen 5, Lucy 3, Marshon? 1 (m)
EADES, Thomas 37, Amanda 25, Wm. 6, Louisa 3, Samuel 1
KINDRED, Martin 67, Elizabeth 64

- 317 -

1850 Census Madison County Kentucky

KINDRED, Lorenzo D. 42, Mary 42, James 13, Wm. 12, Elizabeth 9, Paulina 8, Lucinda 6, John 5, Mary 3, Lorenzo 1/12
HATTEN, Martha 42, Robert 26
SHEARER, Perten 42 (m), Louisa 41, James 17, Mary 15, Nancy 14, Robert 12, Frances 9
DUNBAR, Daniel 56, Anna 57, Simpson 22, Arzila 17
DUNBAR, John 51, Sarah 30, Dudly 25
OLD, John 50, Mary 30, Milly 19, Eliza 15, Ely 15 (m), Doshia 11 (f)
WATTS, Barnett 35, Cyntha 30, Oscar 22, Jordan 21, Mary 15, Elvira 13, Sarah 12, Elizabeth 10
WOOLSY, James 31, Catharine 30
ADAMS, John G. 27, Sophia 27, Enoch 7, James 5, Pascal 3, John 1

Schedule Page 295

FIELDS, Timothy 95 (B), Judith 70
LANTER, Jefferson 28, Margaret 21, Sarah 1
FREEMAN, Sarah 50, Wm. 22, James 20, Reubin 5
POWELL, Thomas S. 32, Mary 28, John 8, Ibsan 5, Sarah 1, Mary 1
POWELL, Obediah 56, Rebecca 58, Sarah 20, Rodolphus 17
BLACKWELL, William 45, Ellener? 70
MOORE, Pheby 50, Lucy 28, Louis 22, Madison 17, Susan 13
LANTER, Alexander 55, Sarah 50, Harvie 26, Sarah 20, Wm. 18, John 15, Elizabeth 14
CHRISTOPHER, John 72, Catharine 72
ANDERSON, James 30, Margaret 25, James 8, Mary 6, John 4, Sarah 1
SHEARER, Benjamin 37, Julia 26, James 3, Hannah 2
SHEARER, Martha 82, Hannah 72, Absolum 26, Susan 19
DAVIS, Richard 35, Arothusa 16, Albert 13, Clifton 11, James 9
MCCORD, David 44, Ebina 37, Wm. 19, Andrew 17, John 15, Rufus 13, Emily 10, Dorcus 9, Evan 6
TIPTON, Davis B. 35, Mary 26, George 9, Francis 2
DAVIS, Josiah 25, Sophia 20
OWENS, John 51, Matilda 46
SHEARER, Samuel 50, Mary 46, Hiram 19, Thompson 16, Samuel 12, Gavin 10, John 7, James 4

Schedule Page 296

BUSH, Joseph 50, Elizabeth 51?, Wm. 20, Dillian 18 (m), Willis 15, Elcany 12 (m), Clifton 9, Jerry 6, Lucy 14
WHITE, Francis 36, Lelia 27, Mary 6, Angeline 5, James 3
ISOM, James 65, Mary 50
ISOM, George 24, Amanda 22
WELCH, Henry 53, Cyntha 34, Thomas 18, Wm. 15, Sarah 10, Martha 8, Frances 6, Jane 4, Benjamin 1
POWELL, Stephen 31, Martha 30, Wm. 10, Susan 12, Jasper 8, Hesekiah 7, Perry 6, Elizabeth 4, John 2
POWELL, Elizabeth 56*, Casander 19
REED, John 54*, Eliza 48
DUNN, William 23, Mary 19
COLLINS, Jerry V. 34, Mary 27, Edwin 10, John 8, Wm. 1
PARRISH, John G. 62, Leah 50
WEST, Martha 57*, Harriett 15, Nancy 13

1850 Census Madison County Kentucky

KENADY, Anderson 30*, Patience 23, Betty 4
REEVES, James 35, Julia 17
SHEVAT?, John 40, Lucretia 38, Hiram 19, Samuel 17, Arzelia 15, Absolum 13, Robert 11, Harrison 7, Zerilda 5, John 4, Amanda 1
POWELL, Little B. 67, Sarah 15, James 14, Ann 71
POWELL, Joel B. 33, Sarah 22, Benjamin 3, Johnithan 1
POWELL, Benjamin 31, Julia 17
POWELL, Samuel S. 38, Agnus 33, Elizabeth 13, Harriett 11, Mary 10, Agnus 9, Delila 9, Huston 6, Wm. 3, Berry 3/12

Schedule Page 297

SMITH, Eleander 46 (f)*, Elizabeth 19, Rosanna 16
WALDREN, Silamin 21 (m)*
MILLION, Rodney 80, Lucy 46
MOORE, Leach 22 (m), Rebecca 20
JOHNSON, Thomas 52, Rebecca 48, Elizabeth 21, Margaret 19, Amanda 17, Sarah 15, Robert 14, Rebecca 13, Mary 11, James 8, Louisa 6, Thomas 1
TURPIN, Talton 42*, Mary 30, Mary Webb 3
DIX, Stephen 22*
BOWERS?, Sarah 44, Amelia 21, Margaret 20, Elizabeth 18, Sarah 17
DENNY, Croas? 45 (m), Elizabeth 31, Arminda 7, Susan 6, Mary 4, James 1
RIVERS?, Jeremiah 50, Sarah 44, Wm. 21, Lucy 16, Rebecca 13, Mary 11, Hiram 7, Sarah 4/12
THOMAS, robert 40, Elzabeth 36, Mary 3
DUNCAN, John 79, Janie 69
KENNEDY, Nancy 50, Martha 15, Susan 13
CAINE, Gidron? 35 (m), Milly 32, Susan 15, George 13, Martha 10, John 9, Elizabeth 7, James 5, Lydia 3
FRAZIER, Jeremiah 28
DUNBAR, Susan 31, Malvina 14, Florinda 12
WILSON, Robert 48, Nancy 38, James 23, Wm. 21, Joseph 19, Levi 17, Mary 15, Robert 13, John 11, Sarah 9, Margaret 5, Colby 1 (m)
WILSON, William 90, Delpha 38
LANTER, David 60, Sarah 50, Joicy 10

Schedule Page 298

POWELL, Joel H. 36, Hester 21, Elizabeth 4, Wm. 2
POWELL, Elizabeth 55, Debby 25, Pattie 22
PARRISH, John G. 29, Ellen 25, James 11/12
PETTIFORD, Fanny 65 (B), James 13
PETTIFORD, George 27 (B), Amanda 23, Wm. 7, Georgeanna 4, Emily 3, Kesiah 6/12
HAWKINS, Louisa 50 (B), Alexander 10, Mary 10, Pattie 8
BAXTER, Charles 60 (B), Murphry 40, Nathaniel 19, Henry 15, Wm. 23, Paulina 25, Hulda 13
PETTIFORD, Alfred 38 (B), Ailcy 43, Milton 22, Narcissus 18 (f), Edmund 12
WRIGHT, Katurah 49, Samuel 15, Price 10
WRIGHT, William B. 23, Laura 20, John 3/12

1850 Census Madison County Kentucky

TIPTON, Shanon 50 (m), Jane 41, Abner 18, Leannah 16, John 9
BAXTER, Bejamin 85
BROUGHTON, Pattie 43, Martha 10, Celia 7
LANRUM?, Mary 64*, Sarah 33
TEVIS, William 20*
WRIGHT, John 45, Ruth 41, Mary 20, Elizabeth 18, Nancy 16, Sarah 12, Florina 7, Amanda 1
ROBERTS, Shadrich 53, Nancy 46, Wm. 21, Hannah 18, Lucy 16, James 12, Joseph 9
MOORE, Nancy 35, Wm. 17, Susan 14, ____ 9 (m), ____ 5 (f)
WEBB, Susan 30
SEARCY, Francis 23?, Malinda 33, John 8, Wm. 1
BAYLY, Mary 47, Rebecca 20, Easter 18, Lucilla 13, Cyntha 11

Schedule Page 299

SMITH, John 77, Sarah 34, Thomas 14
LANTER, Mary 50, Julia 24, Wm. 19, James 5, Jasper 2
CHANCY, James 30, Nancy 25, Jamaima 9, Mary 5, John 3, Milton 2/12
STIVERS, Absolem 49, Mary 40, Elzabeth 12, Eliza 10, Walter 7, Milton 5, Mary 2
BRUCE, James 67, Margaret 61, Elizabeth 37, Racheal 25, Wm. 19
DUNN, Absolem 22, Mary 17?, Nancy 8/12
GOLDEN, Richard 50, Abajail 49 (f), Dudle 27, Mar 18, Martha 16, Elizabeth 14, James 12, Richard 10, Emily 8
GOLDEN, James 46, Elizabeth 40, Amanda 21, Napoleon 19, Catharine 76, Minerva 24, Dicy 48
CHINAULT, Cabel 56 (m), Emily 44, Haney 24, Elvina 17, David 13, Cabel 10, Anderson 8, Joeptha 5 (m), Harvie 2
PHOENISTER, E. J. 40 (m), May 25, Joseph 5, Margaret 4, Wm. 2
DOZIER, Sidney 26 (m), Louisa 22, Ibsan 5 (m)
PHELPS, Samuel 62, Tabitha 49, Samuel 22, Ann 16, Marcus 14, Thomas 12, Josiah 11
CROSSWHILE, Reubin 79*
PHELPS, Tabitha 81*
BRASSHORE, Lucy 90*
DUNHAM, William F. 30, Elizabeth 28, Nancy 2
PARKS, Cortes 35 (m), Amanda 29, George 10, Morvel? 7 (m), Eliza 5, Harris 3, Pracia 1 (f)

Schedule Page 300

LOGSTON, William 28, Eliza 23, George 3, John 6/12
LOGSTON, Edward 26, Margaret 28, George 6, Sarah 5, Wm. 4, Malinda 3, Aaron 2
PHELPS, Peter T. 26, Angeline 21, Alvira 1
NOBLES, David 55, Rebecca 50, Samuel 23, George 22, Paul 20, Jefferson 16, David 14, Sidney 12 (m), Saleas 10 (m)
PORTWOOD, Fanny 28*, Rebecca 8
DOZIER, Yotman 49*
DAVIS, John 24, Elizabeth 18, Mary 6/12
EPPERD, Samuel 50, Susan 22, Elizabeth 6, Thomas 3, Dudley 1
CARR, Joel 44, Elizabeth 35, Hesekiah 10, Sarah 7, Robert 5, Mary 3, Wm. 2
TATE, Casuel 30, Amanda 22, Plesant 3, Mary 1

1850 Census Madison County Kentucky

BURGIN, John 56, Mary 49, Clifton 28, Easom 25, Calvin 23, Louisa 22, Tastur? 20 (m), Overton 16
CARR, Thomas 38, Lucy 35, Paulina 13, Sarah 10, Wm. 8, Perry 5, Eursua? 3 (f)
GENTRY, Claibourne 32, Nancy 28, Benjamin 7, Lucy 5
HARBER, Thomas 63*, Sarah 51, Marion 17, Wm. 10, Sarah 6
WHANKS, Mary 80*
ANDERSON, Elizabeth 40*, Mary 18, Solon 15, John 14, Sarah 13, _____ 1 (f)
STAYLY, Rebecca 55, William 23, Lydia 21, Luvicy 20, Abraham 18, Rebecca 15, Zerelda 13
SHANKS, James 34, Talitha 30, Thomas 13, Sidney 11 (m), Wm. 10, Milo 8, Schuyler 8, Taltn 5, Mary 2

Schedule Page 301

DOZIER, Peter 50, Elizabeth 47, James 20, Francis 16, Elizabeth 11, Peter 6, Sarah 2
DOZIER, William 24, Amelia 19, Waller 3, Ann 9/12
PARKS, James 59, Ellener 45, Catharine 16
BURGIN, Elias 39, Mary 28, Elizabeth 7, Lucy 4, Leann 2, Mary 10/12
DOZIER, James 44, Jane 33, Wm. 16, Louisa 14, Sophia 12, Robert 10, Elizabeth 8, Martha 3, Frances 3/12
HICKS, Archibald 34, Mary 23, Susan 12, Samuel 10, Nancy 8, Cassius 3, Major 4/12
TAYLOR, Jesse 48*, Elizabeth 48, Perelia 17, Nancy 14, Jesse 2
MONTGOMERY, Barterson 8*
DAVIS, Lawrence 35, Hester 34
KNUTZER, Sarah 0, Margaret 50, Christopher 20
HADEN, William 22, Miranda 18, Joel 5/12
HARVIE, Martha 30, Wm. 4
STOCKER, Sidney 19 (m), Delphy 25
STOCKER, William 21, Mary 30
BROWNFIELD, Moses 50, Amy 35
PERKINS, Jefferson 30, Nancy 27, Elizabeth 8, Columbus 6, Harrison 5, Susan 10/12
PERKINS, Mitchel 34, Marina 30, Ann 8, Eldridge 7
TAYLOR, Andrew 28, Lucinda 26, Andrew 6, Mary 5, David 3, James 1, Frances 6, Paulina 2

Schedule Page 302

CHINAULT, Anderson 62, Samuel 32, Waller 26, Robert 20
TEVIS, Elizabeth 40
TIPTON, Ann 50, Joel 60, Elizabeth 82
BOULIN, Benjamin 35, Susan 24
BOULIN, Elizabeth 85, Margaret 45, Ely 15 (m), Nancy 6
POWELL, Andrew J. 22, Elizabeth 20
MILLION, Hannah 72, Doritha 38, Thana 22
WRIGHT, Henry 34, Mary 24, George 5, James 4, Samuel 1
LOGSTON, George 56, Sarah 52, George 19, James 12, John 8
DUNBAR, Martin 24, Malinda 22, Sarah 2, Daniel 10/12
RILEY, William 40, Nancy 42, Ambros 15, Frances 13, Mary 12, John 10, Elza 8, Wm. 5, Noah 4
RILEY, William 64, Margaret 62, Mary 33, Julia 28, Martha 9
CLAY, Isreal 41 (B), Emeline 31

1850 Census Madison County Kentucky

DETHERIDGE, Birgus 68*, Sarah 56, Akillis 31, Franklin 22, Birgus 17, John 15
NEWLAN, Margaret 12*, David 10
PHELPS, Janett 74 (m)*, Miland 70 (f)
STONE, William 35*, Miland 32 (f), Charles 12, Sarah 9, Nancy 7, Wm. 2
WALKER, James 53, Amanda 47, Laura 16
PARIS, William 25, emily 20, Nancy 2, Wm. 1
FIELD, Curtis 69, Rosanna 60, Thompson 22, Lucinda 16
JONES, Joseph 30, Nancy 23, George 3, Nancy 2, Tabitha 2, Sarah 2
PARKS, Shipton 66, Margaret 55, Harris 25, Shipton 21, Caleb 18, Hester 13

Schedule Page 303

DETHERIDGE, William 30, Mary 17, Allen 27, George 34
LAUTER, Richard 26, Minerva 25, Wm. 2
FULLERTON, Brutus 22, Julia 26
WRIGHT, William 80, Nancy 66, Samuel 26, Emily 25, James 2, Laura 10/12
NEWLAND, Anderson 29, Mary 18, Isaac 3, John 1
KNUTZER, Richmond 38
HENDRON, Dover 39, Lucy 38, James 13, Squire 11, Elizabeth 9, Irvine 6, Merret 5/12
BARKER, William 30*, Frances 23, Emily 11/12
MOMAN, Matilda 47
HENDRON, Enos 77, Margaret 69
HENDRON, Irvine 26, Malinda 24, Martha 2, Richmond 1/12
WILLIAMS, Samuel 58*, Virlinder 54 (m), Martha 26
CHINAULT, Anderson 21*, Ann 17
MILLION, Green 50, Elizabeth 44, John 10
BARRUS?, Joel 35, Elizabeth 36, Leathy 19 (f), Sarah 11, Frances 9, Wm. 7, Emily 5
COATS, Rice 38, Mary 37, Rebecca 16, Isham 15, Margaret 15, Robert 11, Rice 10, Amos 7, Joseph 4, Curnan? 8/12 (m)
TURNER, Alfred C. 44, Martha 27, Talton 5, Ann 3, Brutus 6/12
KNUTZER, James 50, Mary 46, Elizabet 17, James 15, Mary 12, Harmon 11, Minerva 9, John F. 7
KNUTZER, Jacob K. 21, Amanda 18
MARSH, Thomas 47*, Elizabeth 46
STEWART, Miller 23?*, Nancy 26, James 6, Wm. 5, Robert 8/12

Schedule Page 304

ROBERTS, Francis 47, Patty 35, Lucinda 22, Squire 20, Clfton 18, Daniel 17, Elizabeth 15, Cassius 13, Prudy 10, Amanda 8, Leathy 7
FOSTER, John 50, Sarah 42, James 18, Mary 17, Emaline 13, Ellen 9, Nancy 6, Thomas 5, Andrew 4
TURNER, Barnett 29, Mary 29, Thomas 8, Blady 6 (f), Catharine 4
RUTNER, William 50, Catharine 22, Kasiah 3 (m), Adam 1
ROBERTS, Mar 58, Malinda 19, Nathan 17, Ferryman? 14 (m)
JOHNSON, Henry F. 48, Nancy 43, Samuel 16, Sarah 5
NEWBY, Nelson 42, Susan 29, Permelia 10, Asher 7 (m), Woodson 1/12
DENBAR?, William 43, Margaret 40, Ellen 13, Angeline 8, Nancy 6, Rebecca 2, Highly 6/12 (f)
DEJAMETT, James 37, Nancy 37, Elizabeth 12, James 10, Jefferson 7

1850 Census Madison County Kentucky

HATHMAN, Johnithan 70, Sarah 70, John 25, Wm. 22
HATHMAN, Joseph 74, Elzabeth 60, Woodson 27, Jane 24, Thomas 22, Mary 20
LEAR, David 22, Jane 24, Mary 1
MILLION, Elzy 65 (m), Martha 61
KENATZER, William 79, Elizabeth 50, Jane 24, Elizabeth 17
NUBY, Allen 55, Sarah 55, Elizabeth 23, Squire 21, Nancy 17, Andrew 15, Green 13

Schedule Page 305

KENATZER, William B. 25, Elizabeth 20
MOORE, William 37, Emma 24, Serrepetha 13 (f), Wm. 12, Nancy 10, Mary 8
MAGER, Ralph 55, Ellener 50, Wm. 19, Benjamin 17
MILLION, Mary 50, Joel 25, Mary 23, Woodson 15
TAYLOR, J. V. 41 (m), Mourning 30, John 12, Nancy 11, Wm. 10, Mary 9, Lucinda 7, Allen 2, Frances 7/12
NUBY, John 37, Sharlott 34, Mar 10, Talton 8, Wm. 6, Owen 4, Alvira 2, Susan 6/12
WILLIS, John 38, Eliza 30, Letty 13, Wm. 11, Reubin 9, Elizabeth 7, Irvin 5, Miland 3 (f), Mary 4/12
ROACH, James 35, Nancy 60, Martha 30, Nancy 21, Louisa 18, Bailey 17
KENATZER, William 46, Dianna 33, Andrew 14, Martha 12, John 6, Elizabeth 4, Mary 1
FOSTER, James 24, Emily 20
PERKINS, Madison 40, Mary 35, Lucy 11, Elizabeth 10, Winyfield 7 (m), Nancy 2
NUBY, Andrew 28, Elizabeth 24
SINNIS, William 54, Martha 52, Sarah A. 26, Talitha 21, Nancy 19, Cassander 17 (f), George 15, Wm. 12
JACKSON, Robert 74, Ann 39, Mary 21
FOSTER, George 26, Mary 23, Elizabeth 6, Joel 4, Nancy 1
ROBERTS, Merrel 28, Emily 30, Martha 2, Andrew J. 1

Schedule Page 306

FOSTER, Elisha 28, Talitha 22, Nancy 7, Wm. 5, George 2, Frances 1
PERKINS, Plesant 62, Susan 56, Susan 20, Juranda 18
PERKINS, Terry 35, Paulina 22, Bolin 11 (m), Louisa 10, Talton 9, Elizabeth 8, Strauder 7 (m), George 2, James 8/12
PERKINS, Richard 23, Winny 26, William 3
TAYLOR, Grooms 40, Mary 27, Cassanda 17 (f), Lucy 15, Elby 14 (m), Schuyler 12, Elizabeth 11, Calaway 7, Elvira 8, Allen? 5, Mahala 3, Thomas 1
TAYLOR, Andrew J. 28, Lucinda 26, Andrew 6, Mary 5, Cassius 3, Major P. 4/12
TAYLOR, Jesse 48*, Elizabeth 48, Permelia 17, Nancy 14, Jesse 2
MONTGOMERY, Barterson 8*
DAVIS, Lawrence 35, Hester 34
KNUTZER, Sarah 70, Margaret 50, Christopher 20
HADER, William 22, Mirander 18 (f), Joel 5/12
HARVIE, Martha 30, Wm. 4
STOCKER, Sidney 19 (m), Delphy 25
WOODS, Dudley 50, Phanna 40 (f), Mary 17, Drucilla 16, James 14, Jane 13, Richard 11, Thomas 10, Elizabeth 7, Jesse 5, Nancy 2, Susan 3/12, John 19

1850 Census Madison County Kentucky

LAY, Green 41, Mary 34, Wm. 14, Elizabeth 13, Prudy 11 (f), Joel 4
KNUTZER, Nancy 45, Sarah 21, Elizabeth 19, Mary 17, Henry 16, John 14

Schedule Page 307

HOWARD, James 60, Sarah 48, Hannah 24, Wm. 22, Squire 20, John 16, Mahala 15
ROBERTS, Daniel 30, Prudy 30, James 10, Merrel 8, Mary 6, Prudey 1 (f)
STAPP, Thomas 48, Lucy 37, Elizabeth 17, Reubin 16, Charles 14, Mary 12, Caroline 10, Catharine 7
FOSTER, Paten 49, Henryetta 44, John 19, Elizabeth 17, Wm. 15, James 14, Caroline 12, Marianne? 10, Robert 7, _____ 5 (f)
PERKINS, John H. 38, Jane 32
KNUTZER, Jacob 40, Rhody 38, Mary 20, James 17, Richmond 15, Sidney 13 m), Fanny 10, John 11, Leathy Ann 9, Elizabeth 7, Jesse 5, Nancy 1
WILLIAMS, William 28
MILLION, Green B. 27*, Isabella 27, Mariah 4, Charles 2, Thomas 7/12
GREEN, Samuel*
GREEN, Frances 88, Sarah 45
TURNER, Samuel 75, Judith 40, Thomas 23, Stephen 21, Elizabeth 18, John 16, Sarah 12, Lucy 10, Ann 75
TURNER, James B. 31, Mary 26, Ann 8, Matilda 6, Thomas 2, Dudley 4/12, Elizabeth 50
HILL, Isaac 50, Maria 45, Mary 24, Martin 23, Isaac 21, John 18, Elizabeth 15, Ann 12, Laura 7
EMBRY, Wiley 46, Sarah 43, Joel 16
BARNES, Turner? 50, Frances 41, Richard 21, Samuel 14, Margaret 12, Thomas 10, Jesse 8, Mary 6, Licker 3 (m), Sophia 2/12

Schedule Page 308

HARVIE, William 42, Martha 41, James 19, Nancy 17, Cyntha 16, Rebecca 15, Susan 13, Wm. 11, Martha 9, Mary 7, George 5, Bernetta 3, Boalitta 3, Sarah 1
HARBOUR, David M. 33, Jerome 33 (f?), Mary 6, Carlile 4 (f), Sarah 2, Frances 5/12
GULLY, Squire 46, Elzabeth 49, Orleny? 25 (f), Emily 23, Mary 16, Malinda 13, John 9, Moses 4
BARNS, Hardin 39, Elzabeth 28, Mary 9, Cyntha 7, Nancy 5, Sarah 2
CLARK, David 67, Elizabeth 76, Susan 44, Robert 49
CLARK, James 33, Talitha 36, Mary 14, Elizabeth 13, James 11, Sarah 8, David 6, Wm. 4, Thomas 2
CLARK, John 37*, Malijnda 42, Nancy 13, Richard 12, Martha 10, Wm. 6, John 2, Charles 5/12
WOODS, Susan 55*
MASTIN, Jacob 85*, Catharine 60, Margaret 19
BROADDUS, Mary 7*
MARTIN, James 35*, Catharine 33, Mary 12
VARNING?, William O. 66*, Mary 60
LEAR, William 22*
STEWART, Thomas 70*
OGER, David 28*, Margaret 21, Matha 5, Elizabeth 3
TUDER, William 15*
DICKERSON, James 37, Lucy 33, Harrison 12, John 8, Caroline 6, Margaret 3, Mary 10/12

1850 Census Madison County Kentucky

Schedule Page 309

COLLINS, William 40, Mary 33, Joseph 10, Thomas 8, Lucy 4, _____ 2 (m)
LAND, Squire 32*, Eliza 30
BRONSTON, Charles 2*
LAND, Thomas 29*, Sarah 23, Harriett 1
MCMANIS, Lavicy 18 (f)*
REAGAN, Elizabeth 49*, Mary 8
LONG, Howard 25*
AGEE, Sarah 53*, Elzabeth 21, William 20, Sarah 20, Green 17
BROADDUS, Frances 28*, Wm. 9, James 6
LEWIS, Adam 50*
AGEE, Robert 26, Nancy 28, Martha 3, James 2
MASTIN, George 21, Nancy 22
ELKINS, Robert 32, Mary 32, Minerva 14, Malvina 10, Sarah 3, Mary 2
ROBERTS, William 50, Lettie 46, Talton 30, Haley 19 (f), Charity 16 (f), Quiller 18 (m), Miland 14 (f), Wm. 12, Catharine 10, Elizabeth 6, Jacob 3, Andrew 2
ROBERTS, Elihu 40, Paulina 37, Irvine 15, Phillip 12, Cassinda 11, Robert 8, Susan 5
TAYLOR, Thomas 45*, Sophia 42, Sidney 20 (m), Rowlin 16, Elizabeth 15, Jason 12, Nancy 9, Harriett 6, Talton 3, Frances 1
MILLION, Allen 21*, Lucy 19
MILLION, John 50, Clarke 47 (f), Fryman 25 (m), Harriett 20
LOWERY, James 58, Prudy 53, Squire 25, Nathan 20, Reubin 19, Green 24, Mary 16
BURNS, Green 28, Sarah 2, Leathy 9/12

Schedule Page 310

BURRIS, Nathaniel 28, Artecia 28, John 22
JONES, Thomas 19, Emily 18
HANN?, William 47, Resina 30, Emily 20, Watson 17, Clarinda 14, Eliza 12, Elizabeth 9, Sarah 7, Levicy 5, Bowman 4, Mary 5/12
STAPP, J. Speed 29 (m), Mary 20, George 3, Joseph 21, Margaret 17, Wm. 9/12
BOGER, Andrew 49, Almira 32, Ellener 25, Martha 12, Malinda 7, Susan 5, Robert 4, James 2, Mary 4/12
BOYER, Andrew 41, Susan 30, Sarah 13, James 11, Diana 10, Frances 9, Mary 7, Perry 5, Emaline 3
DUNBAR, Sarah 35, Ann E. 10, Martha 8, Mary 7, Lucinda 5, Lucretia 1, Ann 36, Samuel 19, James 18
BARNS, Nancy 45, James 25, Sidney 18 (m), Temple 17 (f), Paulina 14
AGEE, Sarah 58, Nancy 21, Lucinda 19
COX, William 52, Sarah 45, Samuel 25, Hanson 22, John 21, Miranda 17, Richard 15, Bolen 13, Elvira 10, Amanda 8, Susan 5
LOWERY, Irvin 28, Emily 27, Elizabeth 3
STEPP, Robert 52, Mildred 47, Irvine 23, John 20
STEPP, Jesse 22, Elizabeth 17
MARTIN, Meret 41 (m), Nancy 32, Wm. 15, Elizabeth 14, Lucy 11, Casander 8, Isabella 6

1850 Census Madison County Kentucky

Schedule Page 311

PERKINS, Harrison 39*, Sarah 43, Green 17, Christopher 15, Eve 13, Lucy 10, John 7, Sarah 5
BARNES, Susan 32*
ROBERTS, James 35, Lucinda 37, Shadrich 15, Isham 12, Ealine 9 (f), Silas 6, Wm. 4, Casanda 1
STEPP, John 49, Margaret 46, Jackson 23, Mary 22, Paulina 20, Milton 19, Cassius C. 17, Oliver 13, Ellender 6
BARNS, Nathan 48, Mary 45, Thomas 23
CUSIE, Martha 30, Robert 6, Jacob 4, James 10/12
MASTERS, Joseph 47, Minerva 41, Mary 16, Wm. 12, Henry 9, Henry 7, Joseph 7, Minerva 5, John 2
DAVIS, Phillip 42, Mary 43, Mary 10, Martha 6, Susan 4, Lucy 1
BARNES, Lucy 40, Wm. 17, Sophia 5
MARTIN, Andrew J. 26, Cemurius? 18 (f), James 6/12
ROBERTS, Joel 36, Louisa 21, Elvira 8, Mary 6, John 1
STEPP, Maglin? 74 (f), Irvin 34
SANDERS, Osbern 40, Miland 26 (f), Cyrus 4, James 2, Carlile 1 (m)
BIRD, Camillus 24 (m), Lamira 26
HARVIE, Levi 35, Amy 30, James 9, Elbridge 7 (f), Nancy 5, Sylvin 3 (m), Levi 3/12
CODDLE, John 45, Nancy 34, Thomas 12, Wm. 10, Winny 8, Nanc 6, Susan 3
NUBY, Winny 46

Schedule Page 312

NUBY, Jesse 29, Arminda 23, James K. 9, Tabitha 8, Jesse 6, Mary 8/12
NUBY, James 31, Mahala 26
RENFROE, Peter 62, Nancy 16
RENFROE, John 48, Mary 37, Arzelia 18, Thomas 17, John 13, Alminda? 11, Wm. 9, Mary 6, Peter 4, Sarah 1
HOLIDAY, John 63, Jane 55, Nanc 30, Mary 26, Jane 24, Emily 23, Amony 20 (m), Martha 19, Elizabeth 17
FOWLER, Zepheniah 62, Margaret 55, Thomas 33, Cyntha 30, Wesley 26, Linsey 24 (f), Sarah 22, Mary 21
GOIN, Francis 68, Nancy 65, Thomas 29, Mary 31, Lorinda 5, Jane 1
DUNCAN, Valentine 39*, Ann 30, Oliver 10, Nancy? 8, Peter 6, Lucy 4, John 2, Wingfield 6/12(m)
HILL, Nancy 20*
BOWMAN, Nancy 11*
BURRIS, James 55*, Maria 38, Wm. 15, Alminia? 12, Sophia 11, Nancy 9, Jerry 7, Newton 3, Jospeh 6/12
COOPER, Sophia 42*
COOPER, John 40, Elizabeth 34, James 7, Harriett 2
BOATMAN, James 33, Elizabeth 36, Sarah 7, Wm. 6, James 3, Charles 2/12
WRIGHT, William B. 25, Martha 25, Andrew J. 5, George W. 3, Burdit 84
BROADDUS, Thomas 49*, Elizabeth 25?, Andrew 4, John 2, Rubin 1
MONDAY, Nancy 57*

1850 Census Madison County Kentucky

Schedule Page 313

MCMILLAN, John V. 24, Mary 23
FATHERGILL, David 56, Sophia 56, Curtis 27, Minerva 26, Nancy 20, Washington 16
STEPP, Washington 25, Rebecca 18
BURRIS, Elizabeth 58*, Price 32, James 28
COOPER, Mary 35*
LAND, Berry 27, Louisa 24, Margaret 2, John 10/12
COSBY, Linsey 19 (m), Lotty 16
BALLARD, Nancy 40, Woodson 26, Sarah 12
CHRISTOPHER, George 35, Loving? 25 (f), James 10, Reubin 6, John 3
PERKINS, Stephen 62, Nancy 52, James 26, Stephen 20, Granderson 17, Hendly 15, Talbot 13, Linsey 5
COSBY, Meredith 55, Elizabeth 81
HARVIE, Nancy 67, Charles 23, Norris 16
MARSH, Abraham 61, Susan 50, Absolum 32, Mary 25, John 21, Edith 18
BARNS, Elias 62, Catharine 59, James 35, Sarah 25, Wm. 19, Milton 17, Cyrus 15, Elias 13
BERRY, James 47, Emily 40, Mary 21, James 20, Susan 14, Wm. 12, Samuel 10, Nancy 8, Lucinda 3, Sarah 89
REILBERT, James? 36, Lucinda 38, Susan 12, Pattie 10, Lucinda 7, Samuel 5, Sarirs? 1 (m), Susan 72
BERNARD?, Thompson 61, Lucinda 57, Burnet? 23, Thompson 20, Edmund 18, Euginia 13
CHAMP, William 80, Hannah 70, John 40
FOSTER, William 31, Anna 31, Lucy 5, Levi 3, Susan 1

Schedule Page 314

ROGERS, Nathaniel 30, susan 27, Margaret 3, Samuel W. 2/12
WALLACE, John 55, Eliza 38, Wm. 14, Elizabeth 12, Ann 10, Mary 8, Oliver 5, Margaret 1, Lolue? 1/12 (m)
BOULTON, Beverly 27 (m), Mary 25, Ann E. 5, Catharine 3, Armilda 1
DOZIER, Ephram 55, Elizabeth 20, Thomas 18
NINNARD, James 4, Mary 23, Zachary 8?
GENTRY, Peter 30, Martha 23, Benjamin 5, Joseph 3, James 2, Peter 1
MOBERLY, John J. 36, Elza 22, Isy B. 3 (f), Lens? 10/12 (m)
ASKY, Nancy 50, Sarah 13, Eliza 10
FENNELL, Azariah 38, Jane 32, Jasser? 12 (m), Mary 10, Abner 8, Samantha 6, Elizabeth 3, Wm. 7/12
ROSS, Alexander 56*, Susan 40, Malinda 18, Jason 15, Solun 12(m), Alexander 10, Argen 6 (m)
BROADDUS, Beverly 26 (m)*, Nancy 4, Layfayette 8/12
ROSS, David R. 40*
PHILLIPS, Catharine 48*, Louisa 20, John 16, Sarah 13, Mary 10
VANORSDAL, David 40, Ann 24, Monroe 3
ROSS, Nicholas 28, Elizabeth 23, Mar 3, Martha 2
PULLINS, William 28, Minerva 23, Nancy 1
ELMORE, William 34, Elizabeth 19, Thomas 2
ROSS, Riceton 31, Fanny 30, Mary 10, Nancy 7
GREEN, Irvine 26, Emily 25, Mary 7, James 4, James 80

1850 Census Madison County Kentucky

Schedule Page 315

KING, Edmund 48, Martha 43, Orthunile? 20 (m), Elizabeth 18, Susan 16, Nancy 14, Joann 12, John 7, Margaret 4, Ibsan 4 (m), Edline 1 (f)
KING, John 27, Caroline 26, Nancy 60, Sidney 6 (m)
CURTIS, Job 60, Nelly 50, Mordica 23 (f), Mary 15
MURPHY, Joseph 25*, Sarah 19
GAIL, Eliza 25*, John 15
HILL, James 28, Margaret 22, Catharine 8, Eliza 3, Amanda 1
TURNER, Charles 35, Mary 37, Plesent 47, Isa 21, Miland 1 (f), John 15, Nancy 13, Napoleon 10
TURNER, Reubin 50, Martha 45, Plesant 24, Reubin 22, Mary 20, Martha 18, Louisa 17, Elzira 15, Minnie? 13, Elizabeth 11, James 9, Sarah 7, Wm. 5, Eliza 2
TURNER, Squire 27, Martha 23, Mary 11/12
PREWIT, Johnithan 22, Patience 20
EVANS, Olnster 28(m), Sarah 23, Nancy 6, Lucy 4, Edaline 1
WILLIS, Mary 47, Emily 16, Mary 15, Robert 13, Christopher 12, Nancy 10, Wm. 9
COY, Tandy 42, Mary 39, Tandy 12, Napoleon 4
CURTIS, Washington 22, Minerva 19, David 2/12
WARMOTH, Sidney 21 (m), Elizabeth 22, Sarah 6, James 2, Mary 3/12
ROSS, Filmore 42, Martha 39, Lucy 13, Isabel 11, Gabriel 9, Mary 6, Jasper 2

Schedule Page 316

WILLIAMS, William 27, Fanny 20
WARRING, John 21, Nancy 17, Bell 1
ANDERSON, Woodson 32, Talitha 26, John 4, Wm. 2
PRUETT, James 36, Marilda 26, Wm. 9, Frances 8, David 5
BROADDUS, Martin 24, Mary 20
LAYRE, Andrew 60*, Nancy 53
STEPHENSON, Sarah 8*
PREWETT, William 30, Mildred? 28, Margaret 8, Wiley 6, Mary 4, America 2
WALKER, Samuel 57, Milly 40, Fraicy 19 (f)
PREWETT, James 26, Edney 22
PREWETT, David 38, Lucy 38, James 10, Margaret 9, Mary 6, Martan 4, Eliza 17
WILLIAMS, William 25, Fanny 19
TAYLOR, Nathaniel 35, Susan 25, James 10, Elizabeth 8, Nancy 4, Thomas 3, John 7/12
WARREN, Jacob 50, Sarah 55, Nancy 18, Dicy 17, Thomas 15, Margaret 12
WARMOTH, Green B. 32, Sarah 30, James 9, Thomas 7, Nathaniel 4, Nelson 2
WARREN, John 22, Nancy 16, Sarah 1
WARMOTH, Thomas 50, Mary 45, Sarah 25, Thomas 18, John 16, Able 13, Paton 10, Nancy 6
WARMOTH, Bright B. 30, Hanah 35, John 10, Wm. 6, George 3
BROADDUS, William 35, Lucy 37, Mary 14, Albert 9, Wm. 6, America 4

Schedule Page 317

MCMILLION, William 25, Isylinda 24, Asbell 7 (f), James 4, Harriett 3, Cassius 1
COTTEN, Paulina 35, Wm. 18, Lucinda 13, James 11, Mary 8, Martha 4, Sarah 2

1850 Census Madison County Kentucky

COTTEN, William 45, Elizabeth 40, Thomas 18, Milton? 16, Rolinda 13, Risa 11, Wm. 9, Jane 7, Isabell 5, Matilda 2
PREWETT, Wiley 43, Nancy 40, Alexander 17, Jane 12, John 10, Nancy 7, Susan 4, Rebecca 2
LAND, Owen D. 22, Elizabeth 18
WEST, Perry 24, Susan 21, Wm. 1
PREWETT, Elizabeth 55*, Selia 30, Daniel 35
TAYLOR, Malvina 10*
PREWETT, Henry 32, Sarah 22, Wm. 10, James 8, Robert 4, _____ 1 (f)
CLARK, Benjamin 44, Terretta? 45 (f), John 19, Bryant 15, Nancy 9
EAST, Conrad 32, Susan 32, John 9, Wm. 7, James 4
GULLY, John 71, Rosana 69
GULLY, William 29, Margaret 26, Berry 9, Mary 7, John 4, Sarah 1
GULLY, John 20?, Sarah 24
LOCKER, John 35, Belinda 32, Elizabeth 14, Mary 12, Amanda 10, Margaret 8, Eliza 6, Wm. 5, John 3, Allen 4/12
BURTIN, Abraham 84, Lucy 67
HURDUN?, Harrison 43, Cyntha 43, Susan 15, Wm. 11, James 10, Lucy 8, Lorenzo 2

Schedule Page 318

LAND, John F. 52, Rebecca 36, Levi 20, Fleming 15, America 12, Wm. 4
LOLLY, William 62, Hanah 47, Malinda 24, Stephen 22, Cyntha 21, Martha 19, Minerva 17, Sarah 15, John 13, Mary 11, Wm. 8, Hannah 6
GOIN, Franklin 23, Hannah 21
DENTON, William 25, Lucy 23, Benjamin 3
LOWERY, William 50, Elizabeth 33, Nancy 13, Martha 11, Susan 10, Wm. 8, Martha 7, John 6, Sarah 4, Woodson 2
THOMAS, John 29, Cyntha 24, Elizabeth 7, James 5, Nancy 6/12
BUTNER?, Jesse 60, Rebecca 50, Charles 25, Isaac 23, Elizabeth 20, Andrew 18, Sarah 17, Rebecca 14, Nancy 8, Jesse 6
BOGEN, James 33, Barbery 30, Wm. 7, Levi 6, George 3, Eliza 1
JOHNSON, William 43, Ellender 44, Mary 12, Margaret 9, Amanda 3
PILANT, James 56*, Sarah 54, Wm. 32, Lucinda 23
HONERS?, Elizabeth 18*
TEATER, Fletcher 36, Emaline 32, Rebecca 13, Michal 11, Wm. 5, Martha 3, George 2
RUNNELS?, Thomas 83*, Elizabeth 67
PREWETT, William 25*
GOGGIN, William 47, Sabiny? 39 (f), Minerva 18
CHISER, John 45*, Sarah 34
FOSTER, Lucretia 16*
REYNOLDS, George T. 33, Harriett 25, Mary 1

Schedule Page 319

WHEELER, William 26, Timanty 24 (f), Henderson 6, Green 4, Lucinda 2
WHEELER, Mary 60, Elzy 30
REYNOLDS, Levi 53, Henryetta 53, Mary 17, Elizabeth 15

1850 Census Madison County Kentucky

TURPIN, Nancy 42, Ellender 16, Mary 14, Emily 10, Amanda 6/12
MASTIN, William 67, Nancy 62, Henry 23
HARRIS, Richmond 88, Mary 54
GAINES, John 38, Rhody 36, Theopulus 17, Nancy 14, Frances 13, Wm. 12, Talot 9, Mary 7, Martha 5
REYNOLDS, Thomas 38*, Elizabeth 18, Wm. 8
WILLIS, Lettie 55 (f)*
TURPIN, Sarah 26*
COLLINS, Ephram 45, Elizabeth 24, Wm. 22, Stephen 21, Nancy 20, Margaret 16
COLLINS, John 57, Elizabeth 47, Sophia 17, Lephranna 14, Cary 10 (m), John 5, Louisa 3
COLLINS, William 30
WEST, Turpin 34, Eliza 34, John 10, Martha 8, Sarah 7, Wm. 3
WARRING, William 30, Sarah 32
RAY, Susan 40*
TAYLOR, James 30*, Susan 16, Talitha 1
LAND, John 45, Rebecca 38, Busby 16 (m), America 15, Wm. 4
TAYLOR, Robert 52, Actoria 28, Even 16 (m), George 13, Martha 10, Elizabeth 6, Ezekiel 7, Susan 3
HILL, Harrison 26, Martha 22, Josephine 5
MOODY, Willia 35, Lucinda 34, Elizabeth 10, John 8, Sophia 6, Newton 4, Barnett 1

Schedule Page 320

GAINES, Pollard 55, Elizabeth 20, Judith 18, John 17, Wm. 16, Mary 11, Thomas 9
TISDEL, Thomas 48, Sarah 48, Eliza 22, James 21, Thomas 19, George 19
STONE, Robert R. 33, Elizabeth 25, Ann 5
BALLEW, Frances 69, Thomas 31, Jane 20, Elizabeth 2
BATES, John 50*, Sarah 27
COCHRAN, Sarah 25*
OWENS, Mastin 42, Susan 50, Meldira? 18 (f), George 15
TODD, Caleb 56, Susan 55
HARRIS, Dianna 50, Wm. 16, Mary 15, Susan 12, Elizabeth 11
TOMLIN, Sarah 60
MOYR, Easter 82 (f), Nelly 89, Mary 57, Delory 52 (m), Lucy 50
BOULNARD?, Calvin 25, Mary 23, Sampson 4, McCandis 2 (f), Nancy 4/12
GOLDEN, William 27*, Martha 28, Doctor 9, Jefferson 7, Mary 5, Ann 2
ARNOLD, William 27*
TILLET, John 24, Arzelia 18, Elizabeth 11/12
STAGNER, Mary 75, Lucinda 40, Sarah 37, James 36, Elizabeth 30
BLYTHE, James 56*, Jane 44, Mary 15, Lucy 12, _____ 5 (f)
REESE, Mary 34*
MAHONY, James 30*
BROOKS, John 30, Elizabeth 25, Arasmus 7, Newton 4, Pochuntas 1 (f)
SMITH, Benjamin 59, Judith 51, Francis 21, Elizabeth 18
WATERS, Singleton 34, Minerva 25, Harriett 4, Henry 5/12
JONES, Humphrey 28, Elizabeth 21, Olivia 6
BROWER, Thomas 32?*, Amelia 25, Nancy 7

1850 Census Madison County Kentucky

Schedule Page 321

MCMILLON, John 20*
WOOD, Anderson 39, Lucy 34
SMITH, Robert 25, Paulina 19
COSBY, Austin 50*, Mary 25, Charles 18, James 16, Wm. 14, John 12, Fletcher 9
ALEXANDER, Eliza 17*
THORP, George 24, Elizabeth 20, Emina 8/12
SUMATE, Willis 28, Almeda 34, Racheal 9, Almilda 7, Mary 4
CUZICK, William 38, Catharine 28, Elizabeth 15, Nancy 12
BRYBURN?, James 70*, Ann 52, William 24
SHREWSBERRY, Penelope 21*, Eliza 18, Sarah 15, Ann 14, Robert 13, Drewery 11
DANSON, Paulina 39*, Layfaett 17, John 14, Mary 12, Ann 10, Willis 8, Baldridge 7, Nancy 4, Lucy 2, _____ 7/12 (f)
DURTON, Nancy 57*
AGEE, Racheal 46, Clarky 16, Albert 13, Mary 11, Elizabeth 9, Sidney 7 (m), Emily 4
PREWITT, Solomon 45, Mary 42, James 14, Nelson 2
HURBURD, William 31, Eliza 27, Levi 9, Laura 6, George 4, Mary 9/12
AGEE, John 30, Clarissa 27, Amos 9, Mary 7, Patsy 4, Harriett 3, Ambrus 1
TUDER, Daniel 65, Nancy 52, John 33, Martin 29, Winnaford 38 (f)
TUDER, Blumer 24 (m), Sarah 8, Wm. 5, America 2, Josephine 34
SMITH, William 28, Jane 12, Elizabeth 10, Benjamin 10, Josephine 8, Maria 7, Matilda 6, Susan 4

Schedule Page 322

WHITAKER, Irvine 28, Tabitha 23, Thomas 7, James 5, Charles 2, Martha 1
WILLIAMS, Moses 47, Nancy 40, Sarah 22
TUDER, Mark 20, Phatima 38 9f), Albert 40?, Stephen 25, Allen 18, Martha 16, John 19, Morris 15, Mary 9?, Jason 8, Levica 7, Louisa 5, Susan 4, Thompson 10/12
TUDER, Phoeby 55, Irvine 27, George 19, Sidney 15 (m), Absolum 13
LONG, Samuel 29, Sarah 24, Nancy 4
LONG, Perry 33, Susan 32, John 13, Wm. 11, Morris 9, Leanda 7 (f), Robert 5, George 3, _____ 10/12 (m)
WILLIAMS, William 29, Eliza 25, Nathan 6, James 3, John 2
WILLIAMS, Nathan 52*, Elizabeth 49, James 20, Thomas 16, Elizabeth 14, Lydia 12, Catharine 10
LONG, Thomas 12*
TAYLOR, Elizabeth 3*
ELKIN, John 85*, Sarah 74
LONG, William 58, Nancy 59, Drewry 14, Levi 22, Sarah 22, Wm. 1
TURNER, Boswell 41, Mary 36, Thomas 19, Archabol 16, Malinda 14, Squire 13, Woodson 10, Andrew 6, Wm. 3
BOGER, James 42, Sarah 42, Thomas 19, Emily 18, David 16, Wm. 14, Howard 12, Sarah 10, Taylor 8, Andrew 5, Robert 4

- 331 -

1850 Census Madison County Kentucky

Schedule Page 323

ROBERTS, Absolum 28, Mary 23, George 3, Angeline 4/12
FERREL, William 41, Martha 39, woodson 20, Minerva 17, Wm. 16, Thomas 14
WHITE, John 41, Matha 33, Marticia 14, Ephram 13, John 11, Alexander 10, Nicholas 7, Martha 3, David 1
BURTIN, Abraham 34, Martha 29, Nancy 7, Mary 3, Pattie 1, Martha 55
JENNINGS, John 36, Nancy 35, Elizabeth 18, Allen 15
VINSON, David 58, Mahala 49, Joel 26, Hanah 24, Sarah 21, Ezekiel 20, Wm. 18, Caperton 16, Oliver 13, Peter 10, Allen 9, James 7
GOGGIN, Stephen 61, Mary 60
TUDER, Nancy 50, Walker 22, Martha 20, Raichad 19 (m), Wm. 14
FARRIS, Evan 24, Lucinda 20, Sarah 2
HARRIS, James m. 36, Caroline 31, George 6, Wm. 5, Smiley 1
MORAN, Joshua 63, Elizabeth 63, Sophia 21, Mary 17
MORAN, Stephen 31, Martha 21
MILLER, John 45, Pattie 42, Elizabeth 19, Martha 18, Wm. 14, Harrison 12, Stephen 9, George 7, Sarah 4, Margaret 2
COOLY, Levi 36, Elizabeth 24, Lucinda 12, Eliza 10, Susan 9, Sarah 5, Jacob 4, Letty 6/12 (f), Patience 73

Schedule Page 324

MURPHEY, Charles 32, Elizabeth 25, James 6, Almeda 1, Sarah 75
PHILLIPS, James 60, Morriney? 50 (f), Delore 17 (f), Simeon 15, Isalinda 12, James 10, Reeves? 8
MURPHEY, Elitia 47 (m), James 17, Catherine 15, Elizabeth 13, Sarah 11, Hettie 7
CARRIER, Harvie 32, Eliza 32, Mary 7, Sarah 6, Harvie 4, Almira 2, Easter 4/12
GOODMAN, Jesse 66, Mary 60
WILEY, Alexander 76, Hannah 76, Thomas 50
WILEY, William 44*, Elizabeth 28, Susan 3, Hannah 1
HILL, Leminda 26*
WILEY, John 53*, Hannah 50, Lucinda 16, Leminda 13, William 10, Hannah 7
STOCKER, Hester 22*
DAVIS, John 24, Elizabeth 22, Armetia 2, James 4/12
MASTERS, Joseph 44, Elizabeth 47, Minerva 19, Hanah 17, Catharine 16, Louisa 14, Wm. 13, Micheal 11
WARREN, Henry 44, Fanney 37, James 14, Louisa 11, Sarah 9, Alexander 7, Charles 4
COOLY, Jesse 37, Sarah 24, Mary 8, James 7, Garret 4, Wm. 2
WARREN, Alexander 43, Sarah 46, Simpson 23, Wm. 22, Alexander 20, Elitia 17, Amanda 13, Catharine 9
COOLY, William 46, Catharine 44, Silas 18, Amanda 16, Wm. 8, Mariann 12, Thomas 5, Nancy 4, Mary 1

Schedule Page 325

SALLE, John 56, Mary 49
ADAMS, Giles 35, Martha 26, Margaret 12, Sarah 10, Wm. 8, James 5, Mary 2, Lucretia 1

1850 Census Madison County Kentucky

HILL, Jarret 54, Fanny 53, Eliza 22, George 20, Martha 17, John 16, Jarret 14
SMITH, Shelton 53, Mary 52, Thomas 28, Elizabeth 21, James 18
FERREL, James 46*, Jane 38, Wm. 18, Archibald 16, Mahaly 14, Parker 12, Harrison 10, Lurinda 8,
  Henry 5
HOOVER, Catharine 47*
ROACH, William 37, Mary 37, Squire 17, Nancy 15, Lucinda 14, Mary 11, Talton 8, Susan 5, Fanney 5
MILLION, Sarah 28, George 8, James 4, Sarah 1

1850 Census Montgomery County Kentucky

Schedule Page 1

YOUNG, Acquilla 57*, Elizabeth 49, Mary J. D. 21, Henry 17, Adaline 19, James 14, M. L. 12 (f)
BUFORD, L. M. 35 (m)*
DANIELS, C. B. 26 (m)*
APPERSON, J. E. 28 (m)*
ADAIR, R. M. 25 (m)*
HAMILTON, A. W. 30 (m)*, Henrietta 28
FOGG, Rufus 30, Mary E. 25, Cyrus 7, Thomas 5, William 3, Margaret 1
BARNES, A. M. 38 (m)*, Elizabeth H. 33, Clarince _. 4
THOMAS, Emily A. 13*
JONES, G. D. 25 (m)*
TIPTON, Samuel E. 34*, L. S. 26 (f), Marcia 5, Frances W. 3
NEWMAN, Leroy 27*
BINGHAM, Thomas _. 26*
CHAPMAN, Zimra 20 (m)*
NELSON, Mary 18*
HOFFMAN, Mary 20*, Elizabeth 18
STEVENS, A. J. 35 (m)*, S. F. 25 (f), William A. 7, M. E. 4 (f), B. A. 3 (m), George S. 2/12
WILLIAMS, Louisa 14* (B)
BARNES, Thomas C. 52*, Amelia A. 39, Louisa C. 14, F. C. 12 (m), Juliet F. 9, Howard 7, Alvin 5, William L. 4, Thomas C. 2
LEE, W. M. M. 22 (m)*
BUSBY, Samuel 39*, Catharine 32, J. E. 10 (m), Mary 6
FITZGERRALD, Thomas 35*, W. 26 (f)
CHILES, Walter 38, Caroline 28, Mary A. 7, Landon F. 5
STOCKTON, George F. 342*, Gusta Ann 31, William E. 10, Robert H. 8, Mary F. 6
SOMMERSALE, F. M. 49 (f)*
BROWN, A. F. 24 (m)*, Lucinda 22
HOWARD, George 75*, Catharine 60, Henry C. 24
LITTLE, William 23*
THOMAS, George H. 18*
BARNES, Robert M. 26, Paulina 20, Thomas R. 4, Robert M. 9/12
HAZELRIGG, Thomas F. 47*, Nancy H. 35, Edward 3, Ralston 1
DEAN, J. N. 37 (m)*

Schedule Page 2

WHEATLEY, Albert 34*, Mary A. E. 26
COSS, Martha 15*
WRIGHT, Edwin 10*
JANNAH?, John A. 40*, Polly 30
HARRISON, Polly 65*
JONES, Henry 39*, Frances 27, Henry 4
PAGE, George 51*
MORRISON, Nathan 37*, Elizabeth C. 30
COX, Mary B. 50*
GROOMS, Moses 63*, Nancy 55, B. R. 18 (m)

1850 Census Montgomery County Kentucky

SMITH, R. F. 20 (m)*
NICHOLSON, Thomas 33, Lucy 24, James 5
HANSLEY, John 35*, Margaret A. 30, Mary 13, William F. 11, Margaret G. 9, James G. 3, John 1
LEWIS, James G. 21*
JONES, A. F. 18 (m)*
FERGUSON, L. C. 16 (m)*
CARTER, George 40*, Mary 35, James R. 8, Mary A. 4
LACY, Edgar 23*
VORIS, John 40*, Nancy 35, Armilda 13, Alexander 10, William 8, Mary 5, Mary Jane 30
GAINES, John P. 24, Mildred 31, Henrietta 14, Olando 6
WALLACE, Joseph W. 28, A. E. 22 (f), William H. 1, John 66, Martha Jane 30
COOK, Stephen M. 28*, Catharine E. 21, Elizabeth J. 3
RODGERS, Eliza 12*
LINDSEY, James 54, Susan Ann 48, Sarah 16, Mildred 12, George 8
JACKSON, Samuel 27*, Cynthia A. 21
CROSSWAIT, Perry 23*
WILSON, John 28*, Sarah 25
BURDEN, John L. 32, Mary Jane 18, Mary E. 2, L. T. 4/12 (m), Mary Ann 50
PALMER, Asa W. 45*, Sarah 45, Angeline 22, Perry P. 14, Dallas 4
ALLISON, James 23*
BAKER, William 32, Ella B. 23
RUNYON, John 26, Lydia 33, Mary E. 7, Martha W. 4, M. E. 2 (f), Leroy 18

Schedule Page 3

FIZER, Samuel 55, Sarah 50, George 28, Matilda 23, Mary A. 22, Samuel 20
MITCHELL, Boone 37, Urana 29, William B. 4
MULDROW, Merrit 33 (B), Addison 30
CHAMLON, William B. 28*, Sarah 34, Jefferson J. 8, A. L. 5 (m), Martha 1
SMITH, William B. 23*, Virginia 20
CLEVELAND, Amaha 48 (f)*
DICKEY, Paulina 30*
DEADMAN, Clary 60 (B)
TIPTON, Charles 45 (B), Sylvia 39, Charles 5
HART, Peter 30 (B), Eliza 22
ARMSTRONG, Mary Ann 53, Susan 33, George M. 28
TUCKER, Peter G. 43, John P. 6, America A. 4
BUTLER, Franky 55* (B), Maria 29, Henrietta 26, William 5, Moses 4, Martha A. 5/12, Angeline 4/12, John Henry 6, Frances Ann 3
BOTTS, Margaret 90* (B)
FIZER, Charles B. 31, Sarah 29
KENNARD, James E. 57, Frances 45, Mary F. 20, Joseph 19, Eliza 16, William H. 13, Reuben C. 10, Emily 6
BOTTS, Polly 33 (B), Louisa 10, America 8, Walter 5, Sarah E. 1
BRUNER, Henry 24*, Sarah E. 19, John W. 1/12
GARRETT, Henry 18*
BLYTHE, Robert 19*
MULLEN, James 30*

1850 Census Montgomery County Kentucky

HAZELRIGG, Dorothy 41*, Margaret 10, Adaline 8, James G. 5, Mary O. 2
BOURN, Berya F. 31 (m)*, Elizabeth 19
REED, Sophia 28 (B), Catharine 27, Benjamin 4, James S. 1
DEBARD, Lewis 36*, Elizabeth 27
RUSSELL, James 18*
PERRY, H. J. 43 (m), Melvina 26, Ann E. 14, Esther Jane 12, Laura W. 5, Virginia M. 2/12

Schedule Page 4

LINDSEY, John 44, Osea 35, Joseph 5, eliza 4, Charles 2, John 7/12
MOORE, James W. 30*, Mary V. F. 27, Helan 12
BOURN, William 27*
WILLIAMS, Maria 45, Frances 19, Caroline 73
SMITH, Charles H. 39, Susan 14, Mary 12, George 10, Elen 9, John 5
COOPER, Milton 30*, Mary Ann 25, William A. 6, John M. 4, Elizabeth 2, George W. 5/12
PARKER, Pleasant 25*, Elizabeth 23, James 4/12
SCOTT, Frances 16*
KELLEY, James 18*
COOPER, John H. 18*
PATTERSON, Edward 18*
MCDONALD, John W. 29, Gillian 16 (f)
THOMPSON, William 72, Mary 66
MITCHELL, William 31*, Malinda 25, Lucretia C. 5
EMBRY, Ann E. 12*, Virginia E. 10
HOPWOOD, Sarah 34 (B)
MANIER, Nancy 39*, John A. 17, Charles A. 14, Mary E. 10
THOMAS, Bary 17*
RIGGING, Mary 29, Louisa 8, John W. 6, Sarah 4
SMITHERS, Alexander 30*, Cordelia 31, Marium 5, Henry T. 3, Florence N. 1
WHITTMANN, Sarah Ann 14*, William 13, Edward 8
MORRIS, McLane 18*
LINDSEY, Alexander 41*, Rachel M. 36, Edward _. 16, Mary M. 14, Martha R. 12, Sarah _. 10, Robert S. 8, Emma 6, Laura 6, Virginia C. 2, Rachel P. 4/12, Rebecca 80?
STOCKTON, Matilda 60?*
KIRTLEY, Fleming A. 24*
SMITH, William 15*
LINDSEY, Robert R. 36*, Harriet C. 32, Robert 13, Samuel D. 11, Louisa 9, Samantha 7, Edward W. 5, Henry H. 3, Cassandra H. 1

Schedule Page 5

ALLIN, Lewis A. 20*
HOWELL, Lewis M. 20*
PEARCE, E. B. 18 (m)*
OREAR, Patsey 35* (B)
THOMPSON, Charles 35*, Rebecca 62, Mary 8, William 7, James 5, Caroline 1
JUSTICE, W. W. 23 (m)*

1850 Census Montgomery County Kentucky

OWENS, Richard 37*, Eliza 33, Eliza Ann 11, Mary Jane 10, Catharine B. 7, Richard H. 5, James W. 2
MANFELL, William 37*
SMITH, John 65, Nancy 57, Emily F. 21, Mary 19
CROMWELL, William 43*, Catharine 38, William 16, James C. 12, Margaret 9, John 7, Mary 5, Clayetta? A. 1
LANGLEY, William S. 27*, Eliza J. 20
WORD, Eliza 18*
FADELY, Elizabeth 48*
TROWBRIDGE, James 32*
JOHNSON, James 17*
DOTTS, George W. 22, Juliet C. 19
TURPIN, Wilkinson 45*, Jane 50
ISOM, Joseph B. 40*
FOSTER, Ephraim 28*
CLAIBOURN, Solomon 48 (B), Ann 46, Phebe 12
DORSEY, O. B. 31 (m)*, Virginia M. 25, J. S. 17 (m)
PARK, Cora Bell 6*
STOCKTON, Maria T. 48*
STEVENS, James 18*
HARRISON?, Ephraim 20*
WALKER, Charlott 50*, Marium 16 (m), Sobina 13
WILLIAMS, Eveline 27* (B), John 8
RANEY, Ruhama 48, Ann L. 25, Susan 23, Rebecca 17, Henry C. 15, Maria 13
JOHNSON, Moore 55*, Eliza 55, Eliza Jane 21, Mary 19, Marcus 17, Walter S. 13
MARSHALL, Lemon T. 27*
CHAMBERS, John R. 37*, Susan B. 36, Elizabeth A. 14, Minirva 11, Samuel H. 9, Harriet 7, Thomas J. 5, Charles C. 1

Schedule Page 6

STAPLES, Joshua 17*
CLEMM, Mary 25*
THOMAS, Edward A. 28*
MAYO, Margaret 9* (B), David 8
WALLACE, Joseph S. 49*, William 22, Mary E. 16, Joseph S. 12, Edward S. 5, Charles S. 2
TENNEY, O. S. 26 (m)*, Junia 22
EVERIT, Samuel D. 59*, Henrietta 47, Marcus R. 22, John 21, Mary 17, Emily 15, Samuel D. 12, Peter M. 11, George C. 9, William S. 7
BLACKBURN, Henrietta 24*, William 3, Levenia 1
TODD, Hugh? B. 37*, Eliza 36, Mary W. 14, Laura 10, Rufus 8, Francis 7, Marcus 14
SARY, William B. 11*, Eliza 9, Sarah 7
BARKESON, John 16*
PRICE, Dillard 18*, John 15
DAVIS, William 16*
BUSH, William 14*
STEWART, Patterson 17*
HARPER, William 20*
WELLS, N. B. 23 (m)*

1850 Census Montgomery County Kentucky

RUNYON, Benja. 28*
WARFORD, James 21*
ADAIR, Robert 14*
HAYS, Margaret 16*
YOUNG, Georgean 15 (f)*
BEAN, Mary 16*
OWINGS, Ann 15*
HANELINE, Julia 16*
YATES, Frances 15*, Amanda 16, Susan 13
GRAVES, Mary F. 16*
THOMAS, M. C. 14 (f)*
TREADAWAY, Ann 13*
JAMISON, Molly 15*
ABBOT, Louisa 15*
HOWELL, Susan 12*
STONES, Frances 13*
BEAN, Martha 11*
CARRINGTON, Frances 14*
WATRONS, Warren P. 28?*, Unice 28, James L. 5, Josephine 2
LEWIS, Rosetta 30*
ELLIS, H. C. 53 (m)*, Elizabeth 31, Mary F.? 15
WELLS, Joseph 35*, Lucretia 34, Mary W. 5
WILLIAMS, Mary 16* (B)
WILKINSON, Aberam 58*, Maria 52, Jackson 22, Preston 18, Zelinda A. 13, William 8

Schedule Page 7

HOWARD, James 35*
CLAKE, Rog. S. 24*
GATEWOOD, Asa B. 20*
TURNER, H. H. 26 (m)*
DANIEL, Vivian 33 (m)*
MUNSON, O. 55 (m)*
BARNES, Alvin 52*
EVERITT, Peter 50*
BUTLER, George 23*
NEWMAN, Peyton 24*
BROWN, John 26*
RAMEY, Bartlett 30* (B)
BUSBY, Harvey 43*
HADEN, Matt J. 22*
JOHNSON, Isaac E. 25*
GIST, George W. 28*
HERNDON, Samuel G. 55*, Henry 24, Betty 22, Margaret 21, Samuel 15
DANIEL, John 45*
DANIEL, Henry 57
DUNBAR?, William W. 31, Elizabeth 20, James 8/12
HOFFMAN, William 32, Julia A. 30, Thomas 5, Albert 3, Mary 1

1850 Census Montgomery County Kentucky

BOTTS, Thomas 58, Virginia 45, John 24, Louisa 17, Marium 13 (m), America 10, Issabel 6
WILLIAMS, Charles S. 50*, Louisa B. 36, Arrabella A. 17
MORROW, Robert 77*
PREWITT, Willis 53*, Theodocia 49, Nelson 25, Jeremiah 23, Robert H. 13
NELSON, William A. 46*, Charlott 47, Jesse D. 21, Eliza J. 19, James 18, Frances 16, Harvey G. 9
GRIGSBY, James B. 56, Ann 49, Lewis B. 23, Ann M. 14, Charlott 12, James B. 12
OLDHAM, Richard jr. 36, Sebra E. 34, Benja. F. 12, A. M. 10 (m), Sarah Ann 3
HAGGARD, Noe 36 (m)*, Elizabeth 31, Roseline 13, Saberary 10 (f), William H. 6, Zachariah 2
RUPERD, Louisa 15*, Mary 17
MCCLURE, John 49, Mahala 36, Catharine 15, Milton 13, Margaret 12, Susan 10, Elizabeth 8, John 7, Richard 5, Andrew 4, S. E. 2 (f)

Schedule Page 8

WALDEN, Tilson 30, Susan 26, Ma__ S. 6 (f), Thomas 1, Tilman J. 20
RAYBOURN, Thomas 56, Christina 51, Samuel 25, Franklin 22, Sarah 18, Elizabeth 16, Thomas 14
RAYBOURN, William 28, Mary 23, Julius F. 3, Thomas H. 10/12
SHOUSE, William 43, Susanna 37, Lucinda 18, James M. 16, Henry W. 13, Elizabeth 15, R. G. 10 (m), William A. 9, S. J. 7 (m), Ann M. 4, Bluford A. 3, Mary 1
BARROW, William 59, Goodwin 32? (f), N. B. 27 (m), S. B. 20 (f), Mary 18, David 16, Elizabeth 10, Thomas 6
WHITSETT, Jilson S. 32 (m), Mary 27, Sarah E. 5, James A. 3
WHITSETT, Elizabeth 65, Preston S. 20
WILLOUGHBY, James 31, Amanda Jane 22, Nancy Jane 5, James S. 3, J. D. 3 (m), William F. 10/12, William 24
MORRIS, Daniel W. 35, Elizabeth 26, Martha Ann 9, Amanda 7, Justina 5, James E. 4, Martin A. 2
BLACK, Miller 40*, Margaret B. 37, Amanda 15, Mary E. 13, Eliza Jane 11, Margaret M. 8, George 6, Sarah A. 4
YOUNG, George 20*
FRAME, William G. 23*
DANIEL, Charles W. 45*, Matilda A. 40, Jesse M. 8
RISK, Margaret 40*
REED, Joseph 71, Sibba 64, Barbara 28, Turner 26, Joseph 23, Mary 14

Schedule Page 9

PREWITT, Nelson 43, Mary Ann 41, Martha C. 19, Lucy C. 17, John W. 14, Ann 11, William H. 8, Henrietta C. 6, Charles C. 4
COFFEE, Rawley 43, Ale Ann 28, Jesse A. 16, Samuel C. 12, Elizabeth B. 9, Nancy C. 7, Ann H. A. 6, A. L. 4 (f), Nicholas H. 3, Nelson J. 6/12
PREWITT, James 49, Henrietta 38, Henry C. 20, Josiah 16, Thomas 14, Emily 12, James 10, Caswell 8, Robert 18, Allin 6, Clifton 3
FLETCHER, William 58*, Nancy 60, William 28, Francis M. 24
ROBINSON, Laura 11*
WHITE, Jeremiah 43, Nancy 42, Preston D. 15, Elizabeth 12, Alvin B. 10, George W. 8, Susan F. 5, William S. 3

1850 Census Montgomery County Kentucky

HADDEN, Nicholas 51, Nancy 44, Samuel S. 26, Jesse A. 24, Perry M. 22, Marion B. 19 (m), Dillard T. 17, Sally B. 15, Columbus 13, Nicholas 11, Mary N. 7, Rufus 4
KITCHENS, James 76*, Martha 72, Ann 46
MCCLURE, Martha 44*
MCKEE, James 53*, Sally 45, John 21, Elizabeth 18, Samuel 16, Melvin 14, Mary 11, Moses 9, Asena 6, James 4, Sally 2
GARRETT, Joseph 43* (B)
GARRETT, Findley 60, Polly 46, Lucy 22, Adalida F. 18, James 15, Mary M. 13
FLETCHER, John 74, John 35, Elizabeth 31, Waller 16
RAGAN, William 50, Louisa 17, Mary C. 15, Elizabeth 13, Willie 12 (f), Sarah 10, Frances 8, Laura 7, Eliza Ann 3

Schedule Page 10

JONES, George W. 35*, Elizabeth J. 32, Charles F. 11, Mary F. 9, Clementine A. 5, Caroline 1
MARSH, Polly 60*
SUMMERS, William 59, Sarah 57, Frances 17, Harvey 15, John 11
RAGAN, Alfred 42, Lucinda 43, Mary C. 11, William S. 9, Charles G. 8, Andrew J. 6, George W. 4, Alfred M. 1, Charles 58, James 17 (B)
YOUNG, Amon 29, Susan A. 18, Mary E. 2, Emma B. 3/12
HADEN, John J. 28*, Anna M. 25, Mary T. 4, James C. 11/12
FLINT, J. A. 12 (f)*
WOODFORD, Sarah A. 32*, Mary E. 13, William H. 6
SEWELL, George A. 38, Elizabeth 36, John H. 7, Barton G. 5, Mary E. 3, George T. 3/12
JONES, Elizabeth 81, Lucy 50
FRENCH, Richard 58, Mary T. 44, James H. 26, Charles S. 21, Mary E. 16, Ann C. 11, Richard jr. 8
GRIFFIN, Terry 84 (m), Prince 86 (f)
TREADAWAY, Stephen 44*, Martha A. 39, Elizabeth 19, Mary 16, Nancy 15, Martin M. 12, Kaziah 10, Samuel P. 7, Susan 5, James S. 3
DRUMMOND, Betsey 40*
CONGLETON, John M. 40*, Malvina 39
METCALF, Thomas 12*
MCINTIRE, Washington J. 19*
REED, Paul W. 32*, Frances A. 24, Elizabeth 4, Newton 3, Harvey W. 8/12
SMITH, William P. 43*, Lerra 41 (f), Robert H. 18, Elizabeth 15, Catharine 12, John R. 9

Schedule Page 11

CLUKE, James 22*
MCCULLOUGH, Samuel 56*, Elanor 49, Nancy 23, Owens 20, Emily 21, Sarah 18, Verlinda 16, John 15, Albert 10, Samuel 8, James 5
WALLER, John 68*
TADE, Lucy 11*, Mary 7
ROSS, George 7*
BAKER, Andrew 49, Martha 37, Jesse 20, Sarah 18, Rebecca 16, Rachel 14, Lucy Ann 11, David 9, Paulina 7, Eliza Jane 5, Martha 3, Edward S. 10/12

1850 Census Montgomery County Kentucky

BARROW, Augustus 51, Elizabeth 38, Mary 35, Cordelia 20, Eliza Ann 16, Amanda 13, Margaret 11
WHITE, John 38*, Jane 26, Elizabeth L. 4, Thomas E. 2, Elza W. 11/12
HULTZ, Garret 17*
BARROW, David G. 53, Lucy 48, Christopher C. 24, Robert E. 23, Sarah E. 15
HULTZ, William 41*, Mary 37, Amanda 18, Nancy A. 13, Mary 11, Margaret 8, Henrietta C. 5, Edward Ann 2
BAKER, Sarah 80*
MAYO, Nelson 7* (B)
DONAHOO, John J. 42, Elizabeth 29, Joseph D. 16, Sarah Ann 10, Mary W. 8, Thomas B. 6, Nancy C. 6/12
PATTERSON, Jacob S. 47, Nancy 42, Sarah A. 17, Emily D. 15, Tamer L. 14 (f), Mary F. 10, George H. 8, Martha G. 5, Nancy 11/12
OREAR, Tamer 75 (f)*, Sophia 45, Sarah 37, John 33, Joseph 31
BLACK, Charlott 45* (B), Jane 18, Usual 9 (m)

Schedule Page 12

OREAR, Daniel 54, J. Henry 27, Erasmus 22, Robert M. 17, Addison 15, Elizabeth 13, Charles D. 10
ANDERSON, John F. 46, Dorcas 40, William 21, John W. 17, Dorcas 11, James 8, Strother 4
RAGAN, Thomas 47, Lucy 44, Lucy A. 22, Milly 20, Alfred 18, Charles 17, John 13, Mary C. 7
BOTTS, Benja. F. 40, Mary C. 34, Elizabeth F. 10, Robert H. 6, Mary E. 6/12
SPURGIN, Samuel S. 27, Ann R. 25, Agnes H. 5
ALLISON, James jr. 48, Rachel 32, Sarah 12, James 10, Jane 8, Cynthea G. 6, Milton 4, William C. 2
GRUBBS, Jesse 56*, Nancy 52, Thomas 14, Sarah 12
FESTER, Andrew 33*, John G. 6, Joel 4
BUTLER, Levi H. 32, Julia 30
ROBERTS, Willis 41, Lucetta 22, Louisa 12
JOHNSON, Thomas 38*
DONSON, John 25*
SMITH, Daniel 35*
MIFFETT, Melson 40*
WILSON, Harvey 55, Amelia 39, E. Smith 29, William 13, Thomas 8, Theodore 6, Mary 4, E. L. 2 (f)
EVANS, Robert 57, Susan 45, Margaret 16, Eleanor 14, Joseph 12, Susan 10
TERRY, James 45, Winafred 40, Sarah T. 9
BEAN, James 50, Ann E. 22, Martha 10, Robert 7, John 6, James 2
METIER, Sarah 58, William 29, James 27, Sarah 22, Elizabeth 17

Schedule Page 13

BAKER, Nathan 31*, Julia 20, Martha Jane 3, Mary M. 2, William H. 10/12
PITTITT, Mary 16*
OREAR, Robert 69*, George 30, Edward 23, Jesse 21
GEORGE, James J. 39*, Mary C. 30, Robert 7, Joel 4, Mary E. 2, Melinda 9/12
MARSHALL, Elizabeth 27*, James R. 9, Peter C. 5
HODGES, Jonas 63*, Maria 53
HOOD, John W. 52*, Docia 47, William 16, Keziah 10
STAPLES, Andrew J. 20*

1850 Census Montgomery County Kentucky

BENNETT, Daniel 60* (B)
FRENCH, Enoch 55* (B)
FLEETY, Ezekiel 51*, Lucy 48, Elizabeth 28, John M. 19, Amanda Jane 21, Thomas M. 18, Joseph 15, Frances A. 12, Milton 6
YOCUM, Nancy E. 4*
JONES, Closs T. 58, Permelia R. 39, Benja. S. 21, Spencer F. 19, Emily J. 15, Hiram F. 11, Mary W. 9, Lydia M. 7
BARNES, Otho 50, Margaret 45, Mary 25, Thomas 22, Strother 15
STONE, James M. 33, Nancy R. 23, Sarah M. 6, Charles W. 4, Nancy B. B. 5/12
MCCARTY, T. M. 30 (m), Judith 27, James H. 6, Robert C. 3
HART, Benjamin 64*, Jane 55, Benjamin 20, John F. 15, Lucretia 13
ROBERTSON, Emma 3*
PETERS, Belvard J. 43*, Elizabeth A. 33
FARROW, Kencey 55 (m)*, Susan 53, Edward R. 23, Elizabeth B. 18, Stephen F. 20
TIPTON, Burwell 26, Sarah 64
SMITH, Harriet 53, William H. 31, Ann E. 21, Ellen 24, John L. 22, Robert T. 16

Schedule Page 14

SMITH, Enoch 54, Sally 48, Enoch L. 16, Susan 14, Martha 12, Loretta 10, Virginia C. 6
GRUBBS, Thomas 76*, Caty 66
WILLIS, Alfred 30*
WILLIAMS, John 62*, Caroline 44, John L. 17, Cordelia R. 14, Robert T. 12, Louisa C. 10, Samuel L. 8, Garret D. 2
COLVER, Charles P. 27*
JUDY, William 30*, Delean? 29 (f), Samuel 8, Andrew 6, Elizabeth Jane 4, Margaret C. 2
MASON, John W. 28*
OLSON, Abram 21*
HART, Peter 26* (B)
NELSON, Joseph 55, Thomas 21
DEVINE, Nathan 64*, Andrew J. 28, Ann 14, Caroline 13, Julia 8
BULLOCK, James 27*, Susan 20, Sarah 2
SMITH, John M. 42*, Patsey JAne 28
MCQUIN, Charles 28*
LUMBERT, Machael 45*
FITZGERRALD, Thomas 28*
SIDENER, J. H. 33 (m), George W. 18
ANDERSON, Robert S. P. 36, Amanda 36, Mary E. 12, Julia F. 10, Ann A. 8, Joetta 3
FERGUSON, William 63*, Susan 61, Franklin 23, George 20, Christopher C. 17, Ellen 15
STITH, Harriet E. 7*
GRUBBS, Joel H. 25, Mary G. 20, William J. 1
ROBERTS, James Y. 32*, Susan 25, Mary E. 2
GEORGE, Preston 17*
FLETCHER, Walter 27, Louisa 26, John W. 4, Merillus 1 (f)
WILKINSON, Nimrod A. 48, Maria 42, James M. 23, Annis 20, Thomas J. 21, William A. 14, Elizabeth 16, Joseph A. 10, John A. 8, Mary F. 6, Ann M. 3, Minera K. 10/12
CALK, Thomas 66*, Elizabeth 56, Thomas 29, Isaac F. 23

1850 Census Montgomery County Kentucky

Schedule Page 15

STOCKTON, Emily 27*, Ashton Y. 3, Larmatine 1 (m)
HODGE, William 53, Nancy N. 42, Elizabeth 27, Mary 21, Robert 17, Louisa 15, John 14, Samuel 12, Eli 10, Walter 6
WILLIAMS, William 54, Sally 50, Elizabeth 28, Sarah 14, Lucy Ann 12, Stephen 11, Lee M. 8, Marth Jane 5, Susan C. 5
BRUTON, James 50, Susan G. 45, Francis J. 20, Enoch 18, Jonah 16, William 14, Martha S. 9, Rebecca 7, James G. 5
HAYS, Benjamin F. 40, Mary 3, James M. 11, S. C. 9 (f), John 7, Ann B. 1
SAUL, Micha 44 (m)*, Mary 41, Sarah 23, Elizabeth 21, Susan 19, Jonathan 16, Mary 8
WRIGHT, William H. 4*, Jonathan W. 2, Charles B. 2/12
SAUL, Susan 64
WARNER, Willis 35, Catharine 32, William 16, Isabella 14, Samuel 12, Julian 10 (f), Mary 7, Evaline 5, Elizabeth 2, M. L. 2/12 (f)
KINGS, Joseph 87, William H. 36, Harriet _. 33, Mary L. 10, Joseph W. 8
FIZER, David B. 32, Judith L. 34, America C. 8, Malinda B. 5, Adam S. 4, William H. 1
FIZER, Bright 45, Martha 44, Mary 21, Margaret 19, Elizabeth 17, Samuel 14, Charles 12, Metilda 10, James 7, Martha 3

Schedule Page 16

BONJURANT, Joseph 57*, Elizabeth L. 54
GLOVER, Joseph B. 28*, Mary 26, Martha 4, Peter 2, Joseph 7/12, Ann 24
OWINGS, Joshua 50
RAMSEY, David 43, Rachel 39
HOWELL, David 51*, Ann R. 32, David G. 11, Rezin 9 (m), Henry C. 7, Howard C. 4, Clayton 2
STAPLES, John 15*
ALLISON, Milton 38*, Sarah J. 17, James W. 15, Eliza Ann 13, John C. 11, Benjamin F. 9, Joseph A. 7, Leliza 5, R. B. C. 4 (f)
FRAKES, Joseph jr. 21*
ALEXANDER, John 58*, Polly 50
GLOVER, Austin 18*
ALLISON, William 47, Nancy V. 6, Elizabeth 5, Letza 3, James 10/12
BUTTS, James 47, Sarah 53, James 22, Nancy J. 21, Susan J. 21, Milton W. 20, Benjamin C. 18, Mary E. 15, Eliza A. 15, Sarah F. 13
WREN, James W. 69*, Anna 59, Elza 36, Frances 34, Emily 32, Mary J. 15
RANKINS, James 13*, Lousa 15
JOHNSON, Anna 62, James 28, Ignatius 16
JONES, William 30, Margaret 25, Horatio T. 1, Benjamin 25
WEBSTER, Thomas 49*, Caroline 15, Mary 13, Ann D. 5, Charles W. 6
KINCADE, Allen 32*
THOMAS, Frances 62*
JAMESON, Milton 43*, Sarah 37, David B. 14, Sarah 10, Caroline 7, Permelia 4, Lucy 2
WALDEN, James 6*
MCDONALD, John 23*
WILLIAM, Henry 14* (B)
GUNSAULEY, A. 24 (m)*, Mary Ann 23, Levia 24

1850 Census Montgomery County Kentucky

Schedule Page 17

STEVENS, William 73*
BRADSHAW, William A. 50*, Acenia 28, Drucilla 24, Polly 19, David 16, Peter T. 12, Louisa 6, Joseph 9
MCGUIRE, Nancy 68*
DARNALL, William T. 49, Phebe A. 57, James T. 19, John W. 10, Lee M. 8, Alvin 5, Daniel 78
SCOTT, Green 26, Andrew 23, Mary 37
JUDY, Alexander 47*, Susan 42, John 18
BOWLES, Frances 20*, Permelia 3, Susan 1, Docian 17 (f), Mary Anna 15, Daniel S. 13, Garret D. 11, Alexander 7, James H. 4, Elza 1
DENTON, J. W. 31 (m), Elizabeth 27, Frances 6, James 4, William 2, George 1, John W. jr. 2/12
DUCKWORTH, George 47, Agnes 37, Mary 16, Jane 15, John W. 12, Delila 10, Melinda 7
ARNOLD, Perry 32*, Evelene 27, Sarah F. 7, Lucy Ann 5, Elijah 3, Mary E. 2, William A. 1
ALLIN, Francis W. 20*
NORTHCUT, William 64*, Mary 51, William 18, Ann W. 15
CRIM?, Frances 74*
EDMUNDSON, William 54, Amelia 27, Sandford W. 9, Sarah E. 6, William M. 5, Eliza Jane 2, Louisa E. 6/12
GARDNER, Elias H. 34*, Sarah 30, Richard D. 2, Sarah F. 1, Elias jr. 10/12
SAUL, Thomas 30*, Mary A. 29, Henry C. 2, A. S. 22 (m)
CRAWFORD, Alexander B. 26*
MOORE, James 30, Martha A. 31, Metilda F. 6, George A. 5, Samuel E. 4, Mary E. 2, James M. 1

Schedule Page 18

PRIEST, Daniel 55, Mildred 45, Sarah A. 20, Fielding 18, Simeon S. 13, Thomas W. 9
GRINSTEAD, Lewis 50, Jane 33, John W. 15, James L. 13, Elizabeth N. 7, Mary C. 5, John G. 95, Reuben 65
SMAWLEY?, Josh__d 39 (m)*, Susanne 42, Francis M. 16, Andrew J. 14, James M. 12, Nancy J. 10, Lewis A. 7
DAVIS, Acquilla 58* (B)
KENEPER, Edward 36, Volentine R. 38, Lucy Ann 34, Zerilda 25
BERKLEY, Benjo. 41*, Isabel 32
NELSON, George 25* (B)
BARNEBY, Landie 36 (m), Maria 24, Lydia Ann 7, John W. 5, James C. 3, Landie J. jr.7/12, Milly 65 (B)
DOUTHETT, Lewis 57*, Eliza 50
HAVELINE, James L. 11*
SHOUSE, Jacob 77, Esther 55, Julia 20, Betsey Ann 11, Henry C. 5, Darius 17
DANIEL, Carter 64, Elizabeth 54, Micelberry 24, Elizabeth 17
BARTLET, James 48*
HOFFMAN, John 28*, Sarah 24, Richard 2
ELLIOTT, William A. 33, Paulina 28, John N. M. 10, Joel S. 8, Benjamin F. 6, Lucy C. 4, Margaret E. 1
HOWARD, Micelberry 33, Eliza 34, William 11, Gipson 9, Sidney J. 5 (f)
TREADAWAY, Edward E. 24, Lucinda 18, Christo. C. 11/12
SMITH, Elijah H. 31*, Caroline 25, Metilda 4, William Taylor 3, Elizabeth M 11/12

1850 Census Montgomery County Kentucky

CLARK, Catharine 17*
HAGGARD, John F. 46*, Elizabeth M. 45
GARNER, Allen 29* (B), Eleanor 23, Nancy Jane 5, Amand M. 3, Mary E. 1

Schedule Page 19

TAYLOR, James 37* (B)
WILLS, Andrew 55*, Eleanor 44, Armistead L. 20, Harriet 19, James 16, Thomas 14, Mary E. 9
SMITH, Mary E. 10*
SMITH, John A. 54, Elizabeth 54, George C. 22, Larana 19, William 19
SHOUSE, Andrew 47, Elizabeth 52, James 16, Temperance 23, Catharine 15
HANELINE, Jesse 61, Charlotte 55, Daniel W. 21, Alfred B. 19, John A. 17, Ennis C. 12
ROSE, Ezekiel 50*, Ally 45, Henry B. 19, Sarah Ann 17, Mary E. 15, Louisa H.? 9, Alley L. 7 (f)
SHOUSE, Caroline 8*
GIPSON, Levi J. 35, Matha Ann 22, Mary D. 11/12
BALDWIN, Samuel 28, Nancy F. 21
ANDERSON, James 50*, Sarah M. 37, David L. 21, MArgaret A. 17, George W. 12, Mary J. 10, Julia F. 5, Thomas T. 1
HOFFMAN, James A. 1*
HANKS, Stephen E. 37*, Eliza 38, Gillian 15 (f), Amanda M. 12, George W. 10, Oliver 8, John W. 6, Fielding V. 4, Lucretia C. 2
ANDERSON, James v. 22*, Emily J. 17
PENCE, Henry R. 37, Matilda 36, William 12, JAmes 10, Eliza Ann 8, John 4, Mark 6, Melinda 2
SPRY, James 38, Elizabeth 41, Martha Jane 14, John W. 12, James H. 10, George A. 8, Melinda 6, Pleasant B. 4, E. L. 1 (m)
CHOAT, John W. 44*, Mary 45, Margaret 20, Thomas A. 18, Milly R. 16, Isaac 14, Mary R. 10, Griella 8, Andrew J. 6, Elizabeth 3

Schedule Page 20

RAMEY, Elizabeth 18* (B), Ann 65
ALLIN, William 62*, Catharine 62
WHITE, Lucinda 25*
GROVES, James 43*, Emily E. 32, Julia C. 12, John W. 10, James 7
JARVIS?, James H. 35*
REYNOLDS, William 48, Rebecca L. 40, Edward S. 17, Sarah E. 15
GATEWOOD, Robert H. 44, Mary A. 31, Sarah F. 11, James W. 9, Emily J. 6, Robert C. 3, William H. 14, Mary E. 9
FITZPATRICK, Peter 50, Drussilla 21, William T. 5, John C. 3
BROTHERS, John 72, Sally 44, Thomas P. 14, Margaret A. 10
REBELIN, William 59, Martin L. 30, Mary Ann 26, Martha 24, George W. 15, Benjamin _. 12
MOORE, Reuben 48, Eliza Ann 35, John C. 11, Martha C. 8, Dulcenia 7, Mary P. 5, William 3, Emeline 1
TURLEY, Willis 29, Sarah Ann 27, Mary E. 3, Joseph C. 1, Jesse Y. 2/12, Mary 66
THOMPSON, Green 38, Lucy 37, John A. 12, William H. 10, Joseph B. 8, Mary E. 6
TURLEY, John 31*, Elizabeth S. 30, Willis Steele 21
GLOVER, Chesley J. 20*

1850 Census Montgomery County Kentucky

JACKSON, Chloe Ann 93, John 58, Nancy 68
MONTGOY, Travis 38*, Nancy 28, Garret W. S. 9, John W. 7, Mary E. 4, Hannah 6/12
CASE, Joseph 40*
CONNER, Daniel 36, Luranda 34, Joseph D. 10, Martha L. 8
GLOVER, Lyndoff A. 28 (m), Elizabeth 25

Schedule Page 21

MONTGOY, Garret 66, Hannah 63, Amanda 20, Elizabeth 18, Garret 26
SKILLMAN, Thomas _. 29
GRAVES, Benjamin H. 48, Julia 42, Thomas C. 20, Eliza F. 13
WARDER, Horace 32, Elizabeth 34, Quinnella 23
SPILLER, Mildred 56*
ANDERSON, Milton 32*
WOOD, George 33*
JACKSON, Jane 31*, Georgian 10 (f), Mary 8, Thomas 5, Elizabeth 2
STEVENSON, Isaac 48*, Lucinda 46, Mary F. 19, James 17, Crocean 13 (f), William 11
LEE, Elizabeth 36*
RAMSEY, Sarah 13*
BRUTON, David 45*, Rebecca 36, Samuel 15, Israel G. 14, James 12, Sarah 10, Absalom R. 6, Amand S. 4, David 9/12
FISK, Thomas 66* (B), Aggy 50
OREAR, Newton 39*, James H. 15, John S. 13, Robert F. 11, Joseph H. 9, Wallace H. 7, Ann E. 7, Sarah Jane 3
EVANS, Jane 85*, Polly 45
GATEWOOD, Lucy 65, James S. 32, Molly E. 21
GATEWOOD, William F. 37, Olivia 23, Frances 6, James 4, Susan F. 2, Emely G. 18, Plenney F. 16 (m)
WARNER, Henry H. 35, Ellen Jane 37, George W. 2, Clay 11/12, Jane 73
RUSSELL, Joseph 60, Elizabeth 57, Catherine 20, Emily 18, Harvey 15, Elizabeth 12
ROBINSON, Benjamin 45*, Emily 42, Henrietta C. 14, Sarah 13, Joseph 11, Ann C. 6, Marcus 2
RICHARDSON, Marcus 82*, Mary R. 5, Marcus 2
FORTUNE, Archibald 28*

Schedule Page 22

HOWARD, John B. 74, Preston A. 38, Louisa 27, James 31, John B. 8, Elizabeth 7, Rebecca 5, James 4, Thomas 1
FORTUNE, Benjamin 44*, Thomas 17, Leonard 16, Elizabeth 14, Benjamin 12, Polly Ann 11, Sally Ann 10, Lewis 9
NICHOLS?, Elizabeth 78*, Jacob 54
PRITCHETT, Milly 56, Kitty 28, James R. 10, Alfred 3
DOOLEY, Benjamin T. 32, Sarah Ann 31, william O. 6, Elizabeth Ann 4, Albert W. 1, Elizabeth 51
REDMAN, Squire P. 34*, Elizabeth 27, John W. 10, Mary Margaret 8, Wallace 6, Frances 5, Nancy 3
BATY, Frederick 20* (B)
MANIER, Nancy 14*
GILLMORE, John 42, Nancy 41, Emily 16, Sarah 11, Patsey 9, James H. 7, Leah 3, Elizabeth 1, Sarah 72

1850 Census Montgomery County Kentucky

PHELPS, John 44, Amanda 41, Mary E. 19, Margaret A. 17, Joseph 16, Sarah Jane 14, William W. 12, James H. 10, John H. 5
MCGINNES, James P. 44*, Mary 38
JENKINS, Jane 16*
WHITE, William F. 49, Ann 28, Charles W. 13, John W. 11, George A. 9, L. J. 7 (f), Martha 90, Edmund P. 23
WILLIAMS, Uriah 32, Catharine 26, Louisa 5, Harriet 3
JACKSON, William 33, Amanda 25, Samuel 5, Louisa 3, Elzira 6/12
EVANS, Jesse 85*, Eleanor 70, Rawley 38
CRAWFORD, Rose 65* (B)
MASTERSON, Peter 38, Sarah 30, William 8, Thomas 5, John 2, Peter 5/12

Schedule Page 23

STULL, Lotty 45, George 22
STRINGER, Amy 51, William 25, Mary 20
CONLEY, James 33, Ann 32, William 14, Elizabeth 13, Catharine 11, George 8, Moranda 5, Mary 1/12
MORLOY, Josiah 36, Melinda 35, Mildred 7, George H. 6, Margaret C. 4, Mary W. 1, Mildred 68
PLEAK, James O. 34, Phebe Ann 25, Mary E. 7, M. Frances 5, Margaret J. 2, Eliza Ann 6/12
JONES, John T. 38*, Mary 38
ROBERTS, Edward 32*, Margaret 26
GRAHAM, Ellen 12*
SMITH, John 48, Nancy 44, William M. 18, Arastus 17, Mary 14, Joseph 12, Samuel B. 10, Wallace C. 8
YATES, Jesse 55, Mary 49, Oliver B. 13, Robert M 9, Mary 5, Emily 3
WHITE, William 47, Angelina 37, Elizabeth C. 12, Emily 4, Edward 40
THOMPSON, Edgar 26, Lucinda J. 18, Charles Care? 14
THOMPSON, Horatio 67*, Sally 58
JONES, Emily 30*, William E. 3, Emily W. 4/12, Henry Care 12
KELLY, William 70, Nancy 43, Emanuel 22
KELLY, Elizabeth 50, Lemebridge 25, Ann Mary 22, Virginia 20, Joseph 18, Susan 15, Melinda 13
PAYNE, Thomas 40*, Margaret 41, John W. 13, Louisa 11, Samuel W. 9, Maria G. 7, Mary W. 6, Thomas C. 3, Sarah F. 6/12

Schedule Page 24

POWERS, Martin 55*
KEATH, Uriah 40, Sarah Ann 31, Judith 17, John 15, Mary 13, Elizabeth A. 11, Amanda 8, Sarah F. 5, Eliza Ella 3, Judith 63
CHEATHAM, James 63, Mary 20
RYAN, Philip A. 76, Lloy H. 37, Louisa 33, Juliet H. 5, Margaret A. 3, Julian J. 1 (f)
TURLEY, James 43, Mahala 40, Martha Ann 20, James 16, George 14, William 12, John 10, Elizabeth 8, Milton 6, David Q. 4
ALEXANDER?, Harrison 37, Winifred 32, William 14, Sarah Ann 9, John 6, Thomas J. 3, M. L. 6/12 (f)
WOOLS, John 31, Mary 28, Ellen 3, Mary 2, John 1
BARNES, Edmund 38, Amanda 35, Frances A. 9, John _. 7, Nancy J. 5, Anna E. 3
DARNAL, Milton 40, Mary 33, John W. 16, Richard _. 13, David O. T. 9, James M. 7, Susan Ann 1

1850 Census Montgomery County Kentucky

MITCHELL, John 59, Margaret 56, John W. 21, Benja. F. 19, Thomas J. 17, Catharine 15
WILSON, Samuel 56, NAncy 50, Samuel J. 22, James _. 19, William M. 16, David _. 14, Benja. T. 10
FINCH, John H. 35, NAncy 36, Sarah E. 14, Lucy M. 12, John T. 9, Cynthia E. 4, Samuel D. 2
HANOLEY?, John A. 39, Susan 36, M. C. 8 (f), William S. 6, Josephene 4, John S. 2, Isaac N. 11
TERRY, Enoch 52*, Mary 50, Emily R. 20, Tobitha 16, Maria L. 13, Thomas L. 11

Schedule Page 25

FERMAN, Richard S. 26*
SCOBY, William 47, Nelly Jane 48, Alexander 22, James W. 19, Elizabeth 13, Nelly Jane 8
SCOTT, William 50, Eliza L. 39, Mariam 17, Winfield 14, Fanny 12, Margaret G. 11, Benjamin F. 10, William M. 8, Elsira 7, Caroline 5, Elizabeth L. 2, Candance G. 1
TOMLINSON, Lewis C. 45, Elizabeth 37, Harriet 18, William 16, Lydia 14, Mary 12, James A. 11, Susan 6, George W. 4, Sarah E. 2, John H. 10/12
ALLISON, James jr. 80*, Lucretia 79
HANNAH, Amanda 35*, Sarah Ann 7, Elizabeth C. 6
FURGUSON, Joseph 14*, Albert 10
FERGUSON, Josiah 66*, Mary Ann 36, Elizabeth 31, Masha Jane 23, Mary S. 21, John 7, Molly 3, Eliza Ann 26
RAGLAND, Drusilla 26*, Frances 7, Mary Jane 1
HARRIS, Charles 45, Nancy 43, Molly Ann 21, Amanda 16, Nancy 14, Margaret 12, Electious 9, Joseph B. 6, Charles 1
MORROW, A. S. 28 (m), Mary 26, Francis M. 2, William B. 5/12
JONES, David L. 40*, Julian 27 (f), John M. 16, Henry L. 14, James H. 14
WALDEN, Benjamin 5*
NELSON, William 52, Ann 50, Nancy 20, James F. 19, John B. 17, Susan Jane 15, Seby F. 13 (f), Emili T. 11, Cerilda H. 9, Theodocia H. 7, Margaret C. 5, Tobitha C. 3, Fanny 26 (B)

Schedule Page 26

CRAVENS, William 63, Polly 55
HARDMAN, John 45, Nancy 35, James C. 16, George F. 13, John H. 11, Ann Eliza 9, Mary C. 7, Charles W. 4
SMITH, Henry 41*, Elizabeth 37, William J. 14, Eliza Jane 12, James H. 8, Margaret Ann 5, John H. 3, Elizabeth 1
SADE, James 23*
WARNER, Joseph 44*, Julian 38 (f)
ENSOM, Angeline 18*, Lafayette 10/12
CARRINGTON, Samuel 45, Margaret 35, Mary 17, George 16, John 14, Frances 13, Martha 11, Emily 9, Samuel 7, William S. 5, Levi B. 3
WALKER, Daniel 60*, Sarah C. 61, Daniel P. 27, Joanna 30, William C. 22
YOUNG, Nancy 62*
GLOVER, Mary 15*
FIZER, Adam 56, Melinda 55
MOBERLY, Thomas J. 61, Sarah 55, Caleb O. 28, America 23, Julia B. 21, James G. 18
TRIMBLE, William 32, Susan V. 33, William W. 7, Samuel 5, Albert E. 4, Sarah Jane 3, Mary 1, Jane 60, Margaret Jane 25

1850 Census Montgomery County Kentucky

MOORE, Lewis 93*, Riley 49
CONLEY, Sylvia 60* (B)
COLIVER, Samuel 32, Susan 30, Nancy F. 3, Richard T. 2, Thomas 36
CLARK, James 54, Elza 54, Michael B. 23, James 17
GARRATT, Nimrod 80*, Elizabeth 70, benja. 19
GILLMORE, Sally 20*, Patsey 16
DAVIS, Patsey 48*, James B. 22, Robert 20, William 18, Samuel 16, Josiah 13, Frances 6, Dianna 19

Schedule Page 27

LLOYD, Elijah 28*, Elizabeth 28, William 3
REED, Henry P. 40, Mary 25, Richard 11, Josiah D. 10, Flora D. 7, William 5, Patsey D. 3, Mary V. 1
MORTER, Armstead 63, Patsey 64
RAGLAND, Isaac N. 43*, Minerva 20
THOMPSON, Hannah 70* (B)
RIGGS, Greenberry 52, Mary 32
RIGGS, John D. 46*, Hannah 43, Mary E. 12, Henry H. 9, Ann E. 7, James G. 4
NELSON, Milton 31* (B)
WILSON, William W. 25, Lucinda 24, Mildred A. 6, John W. 4, James 2, Richard 4/12
SAUL, Willey J. 30*
MCCRERY, Decius 6*
CALLAGHAN, Aaron 32*, Harriet 21, Sarah E. 4/12
OWDEN?, Crepan 23 (m)*
HARROW, Polly 45*
WREN, Hugh B. 50*, Malindrea 52
GIST, Rachel 50*
WILSON, Henrietta C. 22*, Hiran C. 2
DAVIS, Polly 43, Ann E. 17, John S. 14, William H. 12, Sarah L. 10, Benjamin S. 7
PIERCE, Thomas W. 45*, Nancy 33, Daniel H. 14, George W. 12, Ellinder 10, Rachel Ann 8, Louisa 6, William 3, Joseph 6/12
REYNOLDS, Nancy 30*
MITCHELL, William 69, Elizabeth 39, James 32, Warren 30, William 16, Benjamin 14
BONDURANT, Edward 47
THOMAS, George W. 43
THOMPSON, Van 35, Mary 28, MArgaret 10, George C. 9, Mary 7, Sarah W. 4, Caroline 3, Wilmot 58 (f)
DAVIS, James H. 29*
MCCORMICK, James P. 22*
WREN, Nelly 80* (B)

Schedule Page 28

SCOBY, Robert 24, Caroline 22, Emma 10/12
BRAKE, William 39, Lucy Ann 35, Sarah Ann 12, Mary Ann 10, Edmond 6, James W. 4
STITH, Preston 38*, Lydia B. 31, George 7, James 5, Lucy 3, Leonard 2, Warren 8/12, Joseph 68, Hannah 65
GELVIN, James 22*

1850 Census Montgomery County Kentucky

ALLIN, James 56*, Sarah 54, Harrison 24, Paulina 17, James 17, William 15, George 11
TURNER, Marth 12*, Margaret 10
FRAKES, Joseph 61*, Nancy 50, Henry D. 6
ARMSTRONG, Juliet 27*, John S. 18, Robert N. 15
STEELE, Jacob 42, Rachel 38, Andrew J. 30, George W. 18, Acquilla Y. 16, Lucinda 14, Alfred R. 12, Catlett R. 10, Moses S. 8, Louisa 6, Emily 4
DONOHOO, Nancy 29, Willis 12, Daniel B. 9 (m), Elizabeth 7, William O. 5
STEVENSON, Samuel M. 24, Edith 19
BOURN, Walker 60*, Willie B. 34 (f), James M. 12, Sarah Ann 9, Prmelia L. 7, Butler 5, Edgar 4, Nannie 3, Mary B. 4/12, Henry G. 4
LANE, Sarah 64*
RAMEY, Harry 55* (B)
MOORE, James B. 42*, Parthenia 34, Eliza Jane 11, Martha Ann 10, Thomas J. 7, Laura 5, Juliet T. 2
TAYLOR, James L. 18*
FOSTER, Thomas 44*, Rebecca 49, Mary Jane 18, Marth Ann 14, Elzira 12, Amon F. 10, Rebecca 6
YOUNG, Ephraim 83*
WILSON, James R. 44, Hannah 30, Nancy 2

Schedule Page 29

MOBERLY, John 30, Nancy 26, William T. 3, Edmund B. 1
DALE, William 52, Rebecca 50, Mary E. 23, Patterson 18, Dorothy Jane 14, James T. 12, John W. 11
LANDER, William 53, Laura A. 35, William H. 6, Levi Green 23
ODEN, James W. 26, Ellen 23
WILLIAMS, Oliver B. 44, Maria 36, John W. 14, Joseph G. 12, George N. 10, Sarah A. 7, Daniel B. 5, Margaret C. 2
MOORE, William 40, Angeline 38, John 15, James F. 14, George S. 12, Susan 10, William 7, Margaret 5, Thomas K. 1
JONES, Thomas 60*, Frances 58, David 25, James 21
HARRIS, Martha A. 4*
ARNOLD, William M. 28, Nanny J. 17, Mary L. 4
THOMPSON, John 51, Ellen 50, Polly 21, William 19, Margaret 17, Martha 15
MAGOWAN, James G. 46, Rebecca 44
BRIDGES, Hiram 62, Elizabeth 58, Willis D. M. 18, Nancy J. 16, Levia B. 12
RODGERS, Horace 61, Elizabeth 55
MITCHELL, James H. 28, Rebecca 22
PHELPS, James 55, Dorothy 78
PASSMORE, Joseph 59*, Ellen 55, George 18, Elizabeth 25, Martha 15
BRANDENBURGH, Ann 30*
GILLESPIE, Nelson 40*, Mary 35, Volney 18, John 16, Isaac 13, William 13, Milton 11, Henry C. 8, Julian 4 (f)
OWINGS, Hannah 63* (B)
MASON, John 74*, Elizabeth 33, Ann A. 13, Emily 11, Elizabeth 8, John H. 6, Andrew J. 5, William J. 7/12

1850 Census Montgomery County Kentucky

Schedule Page 30

NELSON, Robert 60*
FREELIN, William G. 30, Jane 27, Ann Eliza 6/12
BOURN, Jack 55
ALEXANDER, John W. 29, Mildred 30, Nancy 5, Felix G. 11
DENSMORE, John 30, Martha Ann 24, George W. 5, Henry T. 3, David C. 1
HODGES, John T. 32*
WHITE, William 25*, Emily 19
DABNEY, Elizabeth 55, Ann 28, John A. 29
CLARK, John 58*, Aceneth 51
LANE, Frances 16*
JOHNSON, Joseph 24*, Amanda 23, Margaret B. 11/12
DUCKWORTH, James 35, Jane 36, Mary E. 12, William H. 10
GILLISPIE, Garrett 38, Mary J. 32, James H. 16, William F. 14, Nancy A. 13, John S. 10, Miles C. 8, Amy E. 5, Mary J. 3, Christopher C. 1
NORTHCUT, Jeremiah 40, Nancy 30, James F. 5, Thomas J. 3, Margaret A. 1
GELVIN, Hugh 65, Sarah 63, Nancy 37, Jeremiah 20
LEGATE, David 54, Mary 38, Hugh T. 13, William R. 11, Moses Y. 9, David C. 7, John 4, Sarah Jane 2
JOHNSON, John T. 50, Margaret 50, Conawawy 14
JOHNSON, Jacob 44, Hannah 44, Cythia 25, Elizabeth 23, Margaret 21, Nancy 19, Armilda S. 17, Matilda 14, Squire 12, Silas 13, Daniel 8, Sarah 6, Jacob 1
BIRCH, John J. S. 24, Sally 24
LEGATE, William 34, Amanda 29, Hugh 5, Mary Ann 4, Susan E. 3, John T. 10/12

Schedule Page 31

LEGATE, Hugh 49, Hannah 45, Susan 36, Jeremiah 8
RODGERS, James T. 42*, Polly 37, Lucy Ann 4
HAWKMAN, Joseph 50*
DUNKIN, James A. 31, Mary Ann 30, Joseph W. 7, William D. 5, David T. 2, Edward J. 7/12
JOHNSON, Moses W. 28, Margaret 28, Sarah E. 7, Mary Jane 4, William H. 1
COLIVER, Thomas 25, Sarah 60, Henrietta 33, Francis M. 4, Sarah Ann 2, Abner 31
CAYWOOD, John T. 51, Ann 44, Isaac 20, Margaret 18, Rachel 16, James 14, William 12, Nery? 9 (f), Kitty Ann 7, John 3, Samuel 1
CAYWOOD, Dudley 27, Lydia 32, James 6, Harrison 4, John 4/12
JOHNSON, Jahoda 59, Harrison 36
JOHNSON, Richard T. 34, Caroline D. 31, David S. 11, Nancy C. 10, Julia 6, Sarah 3, Jahoda Jane 10/12
JOHNSON, Thomas 41, Deborah 36, Nancy 13, David 11, Michael 10, Mary Jane 8, Margaret Ann 6, Thomas 3
FRAZIER, Alexander 76, Mary 71, Margaret 40, Polly 30, Frances 32, Jane 25, Alexander M. 24, Margaret 14, Harriet 12
RODGERS, Granville S. 28, Mary Jane 16
COMBS, Jackson 37, Sarah A. 32, Horace 12, Martha Ann 9, John 7, Elizabeth 5, Lydia 3, William O.B. 6/12
DUNCAN, Lucy 53, William D. 32, Edward 28, Andrew J. 22, Emily Jane 18, Coleman R. 14, Minerva 30, Louisa 7

1850 Census Montgomery County Kentucky

Schedule Page 32

DALE, Mary 47*, Susan 19, David 15, James 13, John W. 9, George W. 6
HOOVERMAIL, Nancy J. 28*, Mary F. 4
DALE, Thomas 23, Elizabeth 18
DALE, Thomas 23, Elizabeth 18
JOHNSON, Thomas 24, Elizabeth 21
WILSON, David 55, Elizabeth 56, Joseph 34, Julian 27 (f), Hoda 24 (f), Nancy J. 22, Keziah 19, Susan 17, Margaret 15
WILSON, Johnson 32, Sarah 25, Mary E. 5, Keziah Ann 4, William R. 1
COLIVER, Rachel 51, Elijah 17, Elizabeth 14
ROBINSON, Jefferson S. 43, Jemima 34, Nancy 16, Margaret 14, Sarah 13, Emily 11, Richard 8, Elizabeth 6, Mary 3, John M. 11/12
CLARK, James P. 24*, Sarah 22, John T. 4
DUCKWORTH, Nancy 20*
DUCKWORTH, John 34*, Melinda 24, Elizabeth 65
REYNOLDS, James 19*
DERICKSON, William P. 23, Nancy B. 28, Margaret E. 9, Charles S. 7, Mary A. 5
GELVIN, Joseph 38, Nancy 43, Hannah F. 15, Minerva J. 13, Samuel M. 12, James A. 8, Mary Ann 6, Preston 4, Andrew J. 2, John W. 1
BARKER, John 65*, NAncy 50
HODGE, Joseph 7*
REED, Newton 50, Evaline 42, Enoch S. 16, James N. 14, William H. 12, Washington 8, Sarah E. 5, Edwin R. 3, Maria Lane 34 (B)
CAYWOOD, Morrison 36, Ann 36

Schedule Page 33

TARPIN, Abraham 58, Nancy 54, Mary J. 24, Lucy Ann 21
MITCHELL, James M. 23*, Mary E. 19
BURTON, Christopher 20*
SIDENER, John A. 35, Mary T. 27, Mary E. 7, William E. 5, Sarah E. 3, John A. 8/12
TREADAWAY, John D. 50, Polly M. 41, Nancy A. 12, Mary F. 10
REED, Arustus 35, Mary 31, William T. 14, James M. 11, Ann E. 8, Sandford 7
THORNTON, Charles 38, Catharine M. 25, William T. 8, Charles T. jr. 6, Philip H. 4, John A. 2
HENRY, George 27, Sarah 21, Mary L. 2, Elizabeth A. 9/12
DALE, Mary 60, Issabella 58
ANDERSON, Peter H. 30, Emily 28, Mary E. 9, Joseph M. 7, William 5, James 3, Leah 1
GREEN, John 45, Lucy 41, Addison 23, William 22, Richard 20, Thomas 17, Samuel 15, Elizabeth 13, Jefferson 11, John jr. 9, Susan 8, Lucy Ann 6, James 4
DOBBYNS, Thomas T. 54, Sarah G. 43, John B. 27, Thomas P. 22, Samuel T. 16, Sally B. 11, Mary A. 6, Julia F. 1, Julia F. 18
JEFFRIES, Enoch 59
WEBSTER, Volentine 36, Louisa 31, Daniel 14, Mary E. 12, Hester M. 10, Susanna 6, Emma L. 5, Paul 3, Peter 2
STEWART, A. C. 22 (m), Evaline 30, Caroline 3, Henrietta 6/12
CLARK, Martin 50*, Sarah 40, Martin jr. 12
BRUTON, Elizabeth 18*, Sarah 1

1850 Census Montgomery County Kentucky

Schedule Page 34

WREN, George S. 30, Caroline 28, Eliza Ann 7, Sarah F. 5, William Z. T. 4, Mary Ellen 11/12
WREN, Eleanor Ann 60
DONAHOO, John 50, Celia 50, James W. 24, Mary 22, Martha 21, Margaret 20, John 19, Alfred 17, Rachel 16, Andrew J. 14, Amanda 12, Austin 10
TRIPLETT, John 45, Sarah Ann 37, Sarah E. 15, Harriet S. 13, Mary Ann 11, William H. 9, John R. 3, Thomas F. 9/12, Elizabeth 46
THOMPSON, Lloyd 60, Elizabeth 54, Margaret 30, Mildred 16
RODGERS, John 67, Matilda 48, Emarine 21, Lucy A. 19, Eliza 10, George W. 9, Susan 7
BEAN, William 54, John B. 27, George A. 22, James 19, William 11, Elizabeth E. 24
STONER, Michael L. 33*, Carlile 24 (f), Nancy H. 4, George O. 2, Tolitha 1, Andrew 50
SHELTON, Frances 80*
MASTERSON, Aaron 65*, Clemens 30, Aaron 20, William W. 17, Moses 15
HAWKINS, James 25*, Frances 21, Eugene 3, Elizabeth H. 1
CARRINGTON, John 50, Permelia 45, William T. 23, Margaret 21, James 19, John H. 17, Strother 15, Samuel 13, Elizabeth 11, Permetia A. 9, Eliza 7, Taylor 4, Benja. F. 1
HAMMONS, Priscilla 61*
TAYLOR, James 32*, America 29, Samuel W. 10, Mary P. 8, Richard S. 5
WEBSTER, John 27, Roda Ann 24, Sally E. 3, David 9/12

Schedule Page 35

CRAVENS, William 30, Mary Jane 22, Margaret 1
CRAVENS, Elijah 24, Emily Jane 16
CRAVENS, David W. 26, Cerena 23, Mary 4, Nancy 3, Julia M. 1
JOHNSON, Jackson 49*, Elizabeth 34, Mary Jane 12, Sarah E. 14, Jackson V. 10, Margaret E. 8, Charlott N. 6, Elenor C. 3
NICHOLSON, Judy 45*, Mary 9, Margaret 7, Michael 24, John 21, William 15, Thomas 13
RILEY, John 49*, Mary 28, Mary E. 7, John 4, Issabella 2
DEVAN, Patrick 24*, Mary 20, John J. 6/12
POWELL, Providence 52*
MURRY, Philip 27*
CONNALL, Martin 28*
CURRY, Thomas 23*
BRENNAN, John 20*
SULLIVAN, Thomas 27*
KELLY, John 26*
QEESTER?, Michael 30*
BOLERTINE, Thomas 23*, James 25
FLOOD, Patrick 25*, Edward 30, Luke 28
FARRELL, James 28*
MCDONNOUGH, William 27*
SKERRY, John 26*, Patrick 19
MOONEY, Thomas 21*
HEHOON?, Patrick 24*
MALONEY, John A. 25*
KING, Thomas 27*

1850 Census Montgomery County Kentucky

KENNEDY, Francis 38*
DOWNES, John 38*
FORD, Thomas 27*
DOOLEY, Patrick 21*
SAMMON, James 26*
WINN, Larrey 18*
RYNE, Michael 23*, Patrick 32, Thomas 28
HOWARD, Thomas 30*, Michael 25
FITZGERRALD, Edward 30*, John 22
MELOY, Thedy 23 (m)*
POWER, Lenn 32*
MALEY, James 29*
WOOD, Joseph 40*
HATHAWAY, David 49, Peggy 35, Mary B. 18, Thomas L. 16, Elizabeth A. 12, Philip 8, David 6, Sarah 4, Emily Clay 3, Catharine F. 1, Nancy 66

Schedule Page 36

CONNER, Coleman 73, Nancy 56, James 25, Mary 20, Lydian 15 (f)
WILSON, John 77, Lucy 77, Jery W. 32 (m), Louisa L. 28, William 5
DOOLEY, Jabez 42*, Rebecca 37, Ann E. 18, Obediah 16, Robert S. 14, Samuel 12, Mary C. 10, James 8, Sarah J. 4, Issabella 1
FOSSETT, Samuel 27*
HART, Thomas M. 50*, Mary W. 43, James E. 21, Lucy C. 16, Susan M. 14, Eligene C. 12 (f), Eveline _. 10, Augustine C. 7, William P. 24, Catharine 18
THOMPSON, Abert 17*
STEVENSON, William 17*
LOWREY, John R. 14*
TULLEY, David O. 43, Catharine P. 40, Margaret E. A. 13, David T. 11, Mary Lucy 9, Anthony 6, Charlotte B. 2, Fanny W. 4
PAYNE, Edward 27*, Mary E. 21
COOK, Edwin A. 19*
MAN, Richard W. 9*
MARK, John H. 32*, Nancy 27, Robert W. 10, James 8, Sarah E. 6, Jason 5, Susan 3, John T. 1
COMBS, Lydia 50*
NORTHCUT, Thornton M. 35, Rachel 32, Elizabeth 8, Margaret 6, Arrabel P. 3
HIGHLAND, Denman 46, Susanna 42, Martha F. 18, Maria 17, John 15, Lurana 12, James T. 10, David D. 3
BENTON, Horace 50*, Louisa 42, John H. 19, Emily C. 17, Charles H. 14
AMBROSE, Clements 19*
FRAZIER, George 44, Phebe 43, William A. 17, Martha A. 15, Sarah F. 11

Schedule Page 37

COMBS, John 68, Walker 20
GATESKILL, Henry 34, Catharine T. 24, Silas W. 3, John C. 2
BUTLER, Gabriel 68 (B), Squire 7

1850 Census Montgomery County Kentucky

HAZELWRIG, David 44, Catharine 41, Julia F. 16, Mary D. 15, Thomas F. 19, JAmes N. 13, Marion E. 11 (m), Mildred A. 10, Amanda 8, Ellen B. 6, William G. 2, Lucy B. 10/12
BIRCH, John S. 24, Sarah 28
BRADLEY, William 46, Mary Jane 13
BROCK, Calvin 26, Nancy 25, Mary E. 3
HAMPTON, James 79*, Delpha 80, Nancy 40, Polly 35, William C. 27
CLARK, Henry M. 7*
BASSELL, John 56, Rebecca 30, Nancey 11, Jackson 6, Sarah Ann 5, Betsey 4
MOORE, John 64, Rebecca 60, Walker 25, Kely 23
MARK, William P. 26*, Lucy Ann 23, John L. 2, Louisa D. 11/12
PARTON, Asher 18* (B)
LAMB, Edwin 38 (B), Levenia 37, Sally 16, George 26, Theressa 7, Mary E. 5, Benja. E. 3, Susan A. 1
BULLOCK, James 32, Mary E. 25, Mary E. 9, Margaret J. 6, James 3
BEDFORD, Daniel C. 30*, Mary A. 30, Asa K. 11, Susan H. 9, Ashby M. H. 7, Charles T. 5, Mary L. 3, Elizabeth E 10/12
HARRIS, Susan 70*
DOOLEY, George J. 22*, Mary 24
MOORE, Elisha 66*, William 16
GOODWIN, John 31 (B), Nancy 26, Bristo 85
BIBB, James M. 27, Sarah 28
JEFFRIES, Harvey 42, Margaret 79, Mary 46

Schedule Page 38

GREEN, Frances 80, Samuel T. 39, Elizabeth 26, Sarah Ann 11, Lucian B. 3
GREEN, Richard D. 60, Elizabeth J. 43, Lafyette 20, Edward D. 12, Emma 10, Bell 8, Florence E. 1
GREEN, Thadeus 51*, Mariel? 50, James 25
HALZELWRIGG, James H. 1*
WILLIAMS, Samuel L. 68, Fanny 53, Thomas J. 22, Caroline F. 17, H. Amanda 16, Benja. W. 13
YATES, William 85, Lucy 65, Jenney 65 (B)
HICKMAN, William 75, Sarah 71
LANE, Hiram 51*, Ann C. 43, MArgaret D. 12, John B. 10, Archibald S. 8, Edwin 6, Emma 6, Ann 2
SUMMERS, Archibald 72*
HAYS, Ann 45* (B)
WILLIAMS, Mary 5* (B)
HOLLAND, Nancy 44, Elizabeth 23, William 24, Isabella 20, Newton 18, Thomas 14, Andrew J. 12, George 10, Mary F. 6
BURROGH?, George H. 40, Dulcenia 34, Mary Jane 13, Martha Ann 11, James W. 9, Priscilla 7, Eliza Ann 5, Moranda J. 10/12
ROBERTS, John 38, Chloe Ann 38, Alfred J. 20, Willis 18, John W. 16, Edward 14, Mary C. 12, Horace C. 10, James H. 8, George W. 5, Eliza Ann 11/12
ROBERTS, Woodford 38*
FEMAS?, Nancy 30*, William 9, James 8, Melinda 6, Joseph W. 4, Henry B. 3, Frances E. 1
KING, James 42, Martha 32, Sarah 6, Melvina 4, George R. 1, Levinia 60
THOMPSON, William 50, Sydney 35 (f)

1850 Census Montgomery County Kentucky

Schedule Page 39

THOMPSON, Lucinda 50*, James H. 24, Joseph 22, William 20, Enoch 18
TURLEY, Louisa 27*
MOORE, Reuben 50, Emily 48, Sarah F. 12
CRAIG, Robert 50, Catharine 60, Mary B. 22, James B. 20
QUISENBERRY, James T. 30, Anzy M. 25 (f), Emily Jane 7, Robert S. 6, James R. 4, Margaret 2, Sarah A. 9/12
NELSON, William M. 27, Mary E. 24, Mary M. 3, Joseph R. 11/12
WREN, Thomas 40, Nancy J. 40, MAry E. 19, JAmes W. 17, Lucinda B. 15, Sarah A. 13, John H. 11, Thomas S. 9, Ubert C. 7, Nancy J. 5, Harriet E. 3
BRADSHAW, William 59, Nancy 33, John 15, Lafyette 13, Alexander 10, Isabella 1
HAMILTON, James C. 33*, Margaret 26
JOHNSON, Joseph 22*
HATCHER, George 33* (B)
CHAPEL, William 25*, Lucy 22
FRISLY, JAmes 27*
WHITE, James A. 47, Frances 37, Mary 14, John 12, William 10, Sarah 9, James K. 4, Emma E. 2
GLOVER, Lydoff D. F. 44, Eliza 38, Daniel B. 15, Charles A. 10, Sarah C. 8, Joseph S. 6, William P. 4, Lydoff A. 1
MOORE, John B. 22, Surlina 23, Mary E. 2, Georgian 5/12 (f)
GLOVER, Samuel 67, Sally 52, Chesley 16
GOODPASTURE, Anderson 30, Henrietta P. 24, Sarah Ann 9, Patience 7, Mary J. 5, George H. 3, Patsey E. 1, Lucinda 6/12
BLACKBOURN, William F. 24, Susan 21, Sarah A. 6, Louisa F. 4, Charles B. H. 1, Almaranda 16

Schedule Page 40

WHITE, Thomas 53, Polly 48, James 24, Joseph 22, Mary Jane 16, Susan E. 11
MCKINNEY, Thomas H. 38, Elizabeth A. 26
BIRD, Nimrod 22, Ellen 22
LANE, Frazier 42 (B), Allen 40, Jerry 56
OWINGS, Samuel 46*, Lucy 40, George 21, Julia V. 14, Elizabeth B. 12, Ormazinda H. 8, Thomas J. 4
JOHNSON, Richard M. 27*, Mary 19, Alberta R. 6/12
COLEMAN, George M. 26*
HARROW, Mary 42*, Mary 18, JAmes W. 12, Joseph D. 7
OWINGS, William 65* (B), Hannah 55
CRANE, Samuel B. F. 32*, Maranda R. 31, Elizabeth E. 2, Louisa Jane 1
GROVES, Elizabeth 72*
WREN, Enoch S. 42*, Harriet W. 41, Andrew J. 16, Elizabeth E. 2, Louisa D. 6/12
TRIPLETT, Presley 30*, Julian 28 (f)
JOSIETT?, Jack 56, E. B. 45 (f), Elizabeth R. 29, Cha. E. 24 (m), Louisa 20, M. H. 17 (m)
COX, Benigroves 65* (B)
REED, Caroline 5* (B)
CRAWFORD, John A. 85*, James M. 20
MILLSPAUGH, Levi Y. 58*
MOOROW, Nancy T. 48*, Mary C. 24
CLUKE, Mary W. 16*

1850 Census Montgomery County Kentucky

DALE, George W. 21, Elizabeth 7, Mary Jane 9/12
CRAVENS, Jeremiah 54, Nancy 51, Elizabeth 19, John 17, James 15, Archibald 14, Samuel 12
BROCKWAY, Samuel A. 30, Eliza Jane 27, Augustus 8, Lucy 6, Horace B. 4, Metilda 2, Henrietta 9/12
GILKEE, Elizabeth 37, Ann 10, Charles 9, Mary 7, Louisa 5

Schedule Page 41

ALLIN, Archibald 23, Metilda 21, James 1, Mary 6/12
GOODWIN, Simeon 37 (B), Mary 30
HOWARD, James O. 32*, Frances 35, James H. 3, Joseph H. 8
MEREDITH, Melinda 60*
CALDWELL, Mary 35*, Sarah E. 7, Robert 5, Mary 1, Mary 18
COMBS, Caroline 22*, James 17

Schedule Page 42

SWOPE, Andrew 49*, Catharine 38, M. D. 17 (m), R. J. 14 (m)
HALLY, Milly 14* (B)
FORTNER, F. 78 (f)*
GARRETT, J. H. 18 (m)*
MURRELL, Andrew D. 32, L. D. 23 (f), Sarah Jane 2, William L. 8/12
BLYTHE, James 37, Amy 28, S. E. 11 (f), N. J. 9 (f), Hiram 8, Polly A. 6, R. J. 2 (f), E. C. 1 (f)
ROBERTS, William 28, Catharine 25, A. P. 2 (m)
BOWLIN, Hiram 34, Emily 30, Green 12, John Q. 9, Thomas 7, Mary Jane 5, Elizabeth 2
WHITE, Thomas 66*, Mary 67
MILLER, Sarah 29*
HOLLEY, James 18* (B)
ADAMS, A. M. 25 (m), Margaret L. 17, Mary E. 2/12
JUDY, F. C. sr. 55 (m)*, Elizabeth 51, Mary Ann 27, Martha 25, George H. 24, Thomas C. jr. 22
WHITE, L. 39 (f)*
HOLLY, Judy Ann 12* (B)
ADAMS, James S. 26, P. 22 (f), Mary A. 8, Lucretia 4, John M. 3, Greer 4/12
BELFORD, R. W. 45 (m), Mary A. 34, A. W. 10 (m), Ellen N. 8, Mary E. 2/12
BLYTHE, Robert 70, Elizabeth 68, Greenberry 27, William 7
JOHNSON, Isaac 45, C. 46 (f), Kindred 23, Jane 21, Elizabeth 18, John 17, William 14, Emily 12, Hugh 11, Mary C. 8, Margaret 5, Nancy 3
FRENCH, John sr. 45*, Ann 42, John 12, William 8, Ellen O. 5, Susan 2, A. Smoothers 14, Andrew 15
DAVIS, Margaret 20*, Z. T. 2 (m), A. 1 (f)

Schedule Page 43

BOTTS, Joseph 35, Julia A. 30, Mary T. 14, Susan L. 11, Amy G. 9, Elizabeth C. 6/12
FRANKLIN, James W. 22, Mary E. 21, John H. 9/12
TRACY, Augustin 61, Sarah 47, Rebecca 16, S. 15 (m), Elias 14, P. A. 12 (f), Catharine 10, Obediah 8, Ellen 6, Sarah 4
BENNINGFRED, Henry S. 28, Levina 25, Caroline 5, Nancy J. 3, John H. 1

1850 Census Montgomery County Kentucky

HOLLY, Emanuel 55 (B), Nancy 38, Daniel 10, MArgaret 7, John 3, Joseph 2
WELCH, William 54, Cynthea 44, Zena 21 (m), Amanda 18, Nancy 16, Arthur 15, James 13, Lucy 10, Irene 6, Richard 8, Thomas Johnson 2, Robert C. 1
HOLMES, Benjamin 43, Mary 27, Orlando 14, Narzembra 12 (m), Celia A. 11, L. C. 9 (m), Velanda 3, Ardena 5
CONLEY, Henderson 31, Maria 24, E. A. 6 (f), Louisa 2, Henderson 13
HOLDER, Gary 66, Maria 25, John 5, Weeden 2
HATTON, Ephraim 66, Susan 65
HATTON, Hiram 33, Susan 26, Fantleroy? 5, A. M. 1 (f)
HATTON, William 44, Patsey 33, J. M. 14 (m), F. M. 13 (f), A. E. S. 11 (f), A. J. 7 (f), Henry 5, M. A. 3 (f), Mary 2
HATTON, John sr. 47, Metilda 30, George T. 10, Gary 8, Susan 5, Ephriam 4, Mary A. 3, John H. 2

Schedule Page 44

HATTON, George W. G. 41, Julian 38 (f), Martha J. 12, Susan 9, Mary E. 6, Richard A. 4, Emily J. 4/12
BRADSHAW, James 48, Elizabeth 48, David 13, Louisa 11
GARRETT, Westley 49, Louian 34 (f), Sarah E. 10, Susan C. 8
RANDALL, William 27, Elizabeth 38, Lourinda 2, Susan 4/12
THOMAS, Greenberry 41, Mary J. 34, Gipson 13, Clifton 12, Louisa 10, Rianzo 8 (m), Catharine 5, W. J.? W. 3 (m)
EWING, John 50, Margaret 48, Sarah 23, Hugh 22, John R. 19, Arraminta 15
CURRY, William 53
HATTON, Thomas W. 35, Evaline 35, Susanna 14, George W.G.B. 11, W. H. 6 (m), C. A. 5 (f), Melvina 2
CLARK, Mary 77, Christo. T. 27, Elizabeth T. 28, S. B. 6 (m), D. H. 4 (m)
GARRETT, Jesse 48*, Elizabeth 45, Westley 22, Richard 21, Henry T. 19, Caroline 16, Eveline 15, Greenberry 13
MONSEY, Franklin 22*
MAUP9IN, Nancy 76, Mary 19
HATTON, Adam 38, Mary A. 42, Monterville 21, Eliza Ann 18, H. B. 15 (m), William H. 13, W. G. M. 11 (m), Ellen 9, S. A. R. 8 (f), Lucinda 5, Catharine 1
PATTON, Thomas 54, Mary 43, F. M. 12 (m), Sarah Ann 10, Morgan 3
PATTON, John 21, Eliza 19, Thomas 14, Margaret 1
DANIEL, Almanza 27 (m), Elizabeth 25, Anna 4, James 24
WRIGHT, Solomon 65*, Patterson 18, Nelly 12, Ryina 10, Levin 9

Schedule Page 45

MILTON, Elizabeth 22*, Kindred 6/12
RANDALLY, Samuel 26, Susan 23, Laurinda 3, Elizabeth A. 1
RANDALL, Samuel jr. 61, Mary 50, Catharine 13, Joseph 11, James H. 9, Richard A. 6, Armina 4, Aramenta 4
CRAW, Daniel sr. 52, Rachel 52, Evaline 28, Elizabeth 25, Rebecca 21, Daniel jr. 19, James S. 14, David 12, Nancy A. 10, Paulina 7
PATTON, George W. 22, Mary A. 22
FLINN, Harvey 54, Ruth 42, Preston 11, James 7, John 5, Nancy 2

1850 Census Montgomery County Kentucky

ANDERSON, Richard 60 (B), Susan 60
FRAZIER, James 53*, Catharine 45, William 22, Aaron 20, James 18, F. M. 15 (m), John 13, MArgaret 9, Rebecca 8, Catharine 7, Lovinia 7, Lydia 3
JOHNSON, Robert 40*
HOWELL, George W. 39, Hannah 36, mahulda 16, Paul 13, Thomas 10, S. A. 7 (f), Berry 4, Hannah 2, David 1/12
HALL, Thomas 43, Melinda 34, Simpson 14, Allen 10, Lucy 8, M. A. 7 (f), Patsey 6, Caroline 4, A. J. 2 (f), Perry 9/12
REYNOLDS, Henry 31, Emily 29, Martha 3, Benja. F. 1
LAMBERTON, Jeremiah 51, Mary 42, MArgaret 25, Joshua 23, John 18, Richard 16, Mary 14, Elizabeth 12, Jeremiah 10, Andrew 6, Sarah C. 3, Ellen 4/12

Schedule Page 46

RODGERS, George M. 31, Cythia 32, James W. 11, Margaret E. 9, ludd S. 7, Elihu J. 5, Levina 1
POWELL, Thomas 70, Hannah 67
LARRINSON, Jacob 36, Fanny 34, Elizabeth A. 13, Nancy 10, William 8, Edy 6 (f), L. A. 3 (m), Mary Jane 6/12
REED, Daniel 60, Sarah 45
MEDOWS, Catharine 28, William S. 10, Mary A. 9, James F. 8, John W. 6, Jacob 4, Harrison 1
POWELL, Marcus 44, Sarah A. 42, Marth Jane 18, Elizabeth 16, Hannah 14, John W. 12, Hyberd 10, Anna 8, Hulda 4, Benja. F. 1/12
CENTERS, Solomon 60, Nancy 56, William 20, Mary 18, Fanny Jane 16, Jackson 14, William 12
CENTERS, James 27, Nancy 27, Matthew? 6, Stephen 5, William T. 3, Farlena 6/12
REYNOLDS, H. H. 54 (m)*, Martha 50, John H. 25
LEWIS, Thomas 16*
CENTERS, Solomon jr. 28, Mary 25, Paulina 4, F. Jane 2
CENTERS, Powell 20
HALE, John M. 24, Ellen 24, Richard 5, Alonzo 3, Caleb 1
HALL, Caleb 45, Susan 43, James M. 17, Zerilda 19, Beverly 15 (m), Bazil 13, Henry H. 11, Armstead 9, Ginsey 7
CROW, Richard sr. 49, Mary 53, Catharine 28, Sarah 25, Richard jr. 22, Nancy 20, Mary 18

Schedule Page 47

JOHNSON, Kindred 32, Martha 42, Mary Jane 15, Cynthea A. 10, John 9, Margaret 7, William 5, Harrison 4, George 21
HALL, Sarah 55, Philip 23, Mary 21, Nancy 19, Lucy 17, Maland 16 (m)
MARTIN, Benjamin 37, Priscilla 37, John F. 17, M. E. 15 (f), Barbery E. 13, Endicy 11 (f), Martha 9, Almanzo 7 (m), James 5, Ruth J. 3
DANIEL, Hiram B. 37, Sarah Jane 31, Mary A. 8, Susan F. 5, Sarah J. 4
JOHNSON, William 48, Ruth Jane 45, Laurinda 21, Alfred 20, Franklin 18, Gilley Ann 15
JOHNSON, Socretion 23, Elizabeth 25, Marium 6/12 (m)
FLETCHER, Garret 40, Caroline 36, Sarah E. 16, Mary W. 8, Thomas J. 5, Elizabeth A. 3
SMITH, Joseph 74*
WHITE, Margaret 41*, Menefee 12, James B. 8

1850 Census Montgomery County Kentucky

MAXFIELD, Hugh 73, Mary 48, Alexander 24, Zindarella 22, Margaret 18, Sarah 16, Hugh 15, Elizabeth 13, Robert 11, John 9
FOREMAN, Samuel S. 30, Elizabeth A. 29, John W. 10, William H. H. 8, Bazil 7, Henry H. 6, Sarah jane 4, Mayland 1/2 (m)
WILLS, Martin 32, Mary 33, James 11, Sarah A. 10, John 8, Lucinda 6, William 5, Elizabeth 3
KIRKPATRICK, Ira 41, Susan 41, James 18, Priscilla 16, Mary Jane 14, William P. 12, Amy 10, John 8, Marvilla 8, Arraminta 6, Isaac 4, Licordus 2 (m)

Schedule Page 48

DANIEL, James M. 62*, Mary 25, William H. H. 7, Sarah A. 3, Beverley 89 (m)
STARNS, James O. 15*
STARNES, James 34, Lorusa H. 24, Mary 6, Josephene 1
STEWART, Madison 40*, Celia 34, Patterson 16, Jinsey 13 (f), Louisa 11, Ann 9, Sarah F. 6, Mary J. 3
HOLLEY, Robert 12* (B)
MUNSEY, Reuben 56, Delila 40, Enoch 14, Nancy 12, Elizabeth 11, Samuel 7, James W. 5, Mary A. 3, Ruth Jane 6/12
WILLIAMS, Louisa 44, Henrietta 18, John W. 13, James 10, Boone H. 7, George H. 5
HARDWICK, Mitchell P. 76, Lucy 54, Sarah 23, America 22, Ann 18, James W. 16
HATTON, Benjamin 62, William J. 12, McDonald 11, Alwilda 7, Nancy 4, Demarion 2
BENINGFIELD, John 55, Nancy 39, Martha F. 17, Adaline 15, Nancy J. 13, Mary E. 9
BIRCH, Daniel 50*, Nancy 51, Jane 21, Nancy 19, Elizabeth 17, Jane _/12
COMBS, William M. 21*
WELCH, Tilford 27, Arraminta 23, James M. 1, Louisa E. 22, Sarah 20, Sophia 18, John W. 14
HARDWICK, John N. 29, Mimerva 24, James R. 5, Lucy E. 3, Sarah F. 1
RAVER, Hezekiah 41, Mary 40, Margeret 21, Amanda 17, Newton 13, Sarah E. 11, William 8, Morton 5, John 3, Armstead 1

Schedule Page 49

HANKS, Vancover 35*, Harriet 26, Armilda 8, Nancy 5, Mary 3, Ruth 2, Randall 1/12, John 45
STARNES, Lucinda 40*
MARTIN, Littleton 39, Lucinda 39, Mary C. 15, William 12, George W. 11, John 8, Leonard 6, James 3, Andrew 1
LOCKRIDGE, James 75
EVERMAN, Elisha 44, Mary 43, Jinsey 12 (f)
CORELEY, Charlotte 33, Henry C. 4, John W. 2
THARP, Jesse 52*, Sarah 50
WALLER, Lucy A. 5*
HANELINE, James H. 28, Frances 27, William F. 7, Martha E. 3, Weden C. 1
MARTIN, William 45, Elizabeth 42, Luke 20, Susan 18, Sylvester 16, Mary 14, Thomas 11, Ellin 7, Lucy 4, Margaret 1
BOWEN, William 45, Mary 22, Jinsey 4 (f), Celia 2, Armasetta 8/12
BOWEN, Armstead 28*, Joseph 20
ANDERSON, Cythia 32*, Morton 2
MORTON, Hezekiah 50, I. Margaret 45, Jehu 75, Hezekiah 19

1850 Census Montgomery County Kentucky

MORTON, Richard 56, Elizabeth 40, Joab 17, Margaret 15, Moses 12, Richard 10, William 9, James O. 4, Maria 23 (m)
SEA, Nimrod 42*, Docia 24, William 20, Sarah 19, George 18, John 16, Berry 14, Benja. 19, Anna 8, Cynthia Jane 6, Jasper? 3, James 2

Schedule Page 50

GREEN, Laura 1*
CENTERS, Tandy 22 (m), Elizabeth 19
OLIVER, Julia 29, Jane 16, Elizabeth 10, Louisa 7, Mary L. 3
KNOX, Thomas 47*, Nancy 34, John 17, George 11, Mary A. 9, Sally 7, Henry 6, Caroline 3, Benjamin F. 3/12
CENTERS, Caroline 15*
CENTERS, Stephen 66, Brittain 13 (m)
CENTERS, Joshua 70*, Cynthia 53
STAMPER, John C. 12*
SEA, Almanza 22*, Elizabeth 21, Mary A. 1
TACKETT, Philip 43, Nancy 30, Margaret 12, William R. W. 7, William 7, Cynthia 5, Nancy 4, Elizabeth 1
NOLAND, Sarah 41, Norvell 17, Martha Ann 16
HALL, Arthur 50, Sally 44, James 20, Westley 18, Salley 14, Benja. 12, Eliza Jane 9
HALL, Sarah 36, Eveline 15, Amoris 13 (m), Mildred 63
KNOX, George 50*, Rebecca 40, Mary 19, James H. 18, Elizabeth Jane 15, William 13, John 11, Adaline 10, Benjamin 8, Amanda 5, Sidney 2 (m)
MORTON, Solomon 50* (B), Rachel 70
WRIGHT, Joshua 45, Sarah 33
HALL, Green 68, Mary 69, Millison 20
BLACKBOURN, James K. 49, Nancy 40, Jacob S. 16, Elizabeth Jane 14, Eliza A. 12, Joseph T. 8, James K. H. C. 2
HALL, Thomas B. 38, Patsy 38, James H. 14, Mayland 9 (m), Henry C. 6, Albert 3
HANKS, William 47, Eliza 43, Fielding 19, Mary A. 17, Lydia A. 16, James H. 14, Elizabeth 13, William J. 11, Henry 7, Millison 4, Eveline 2

Schedule Page 51

SHAWLEY, David 53*, Elizabeth 53, James 20, Martha 18, Eliza 12, Elizabeth 10, Morton 7, William H. 37
GRAY, Emily 16*, Joseph 22
SHAWLEY, John B. 26, Catharine 24, Lucy 3, Elizabeth 1, Henrietta 4/12
TOWNSEND, Elizabeth 57, Elkana 22, Hiram 18
TOWNSEND, William 24, Margaret 18, James 1
GRAY, William 63, Lucy 53, Susan 16, Louisa 15
ESTIS, Obadiah 23, Sarah 19, Mary Jane 2
ROSE, Josiah C. 35*, Mary D. 25, Robert 6, Asa 4, Mary F. 3, William 1
PLEAKS, Amanda 30*
ROSE, Powell 48, Nancy 40, John A. 22, David 20, James B. 17, R. D. 15 (m), Mary A. 13, William L. 11, Rebecca 10, Rachel 8, Israel 5, Esther 3

1850 Census Montgomery County Kentucky

MCDANIEL, Samuel M. 24*, Lucinda 39, Daniel 5, James 3, John M. 8/12
LEWIS, Armina 12*
JONES, Wiley 27*, Elizabeth 26, Mary A. 13, Cythia Jane 11, Rebecca 9, Ally 7 (f), Susan 5, Greenberry 3
WALLER, John 30*, Hucaba 35, Turner 13, Peter 10, George W. 9, Lucy 4, Mary 1
HATTON, George W. 40*, Amanda 20, Lucinda 15, John P. 13, William D. 1
FORTNER, Jonas 44, Nancy 43, Orlando 22, Orbra 18 (m), Ornaldus 16, Isra 14 (f), Normanda 12 (m), Cynthea 10, Squire 5, Alagin 3 (m)

Schedule Page 52

WILLIS, John 56, Anna 42, Malinda Jane 13, William S. 12, James H. 10, Mary Ann 8, Peter 6, Emily 5, Amanda 2
MILLER, John 45, Jonas 20, John 19, William P. 16, Marshell 13, Anabal 10 (m), Osbourn 8, Nancy Jane 6, Arraminta 4, Armina 2
HALL, James H. 35*, Mary 33, Nancy Jane 10, Henry F. 9, Green H. 7, Marcus L. 5, Zach T. 3, Josiah _. 2, John W. 4/12
COX, E. K. W. 23 (m)*
FORTNER, Henry 57, Sarah 36, Eleanor 14, Morton 10, Armstead 8, Cythia 5, Jesse 4, Nancy 1
WELCH, A. W. 45 (m), Elizabeth 40, Green A. 20, Franklin T. 18, James H. 17, McDonald 15, Hugh L. 13, A. C. 11 (m), John L. 9, Mary 7, Amanda 5, Nancy Jane 4, Lou A. W. 2 (f)
HORN, Isaac 40, Ermina D. M. 37, Verdonia 20, Samuel 17, Joseph 15, Achland 13 (m), Isaac 10, Nancy E. 8, Thomas L. 4
FORTNER, Jesse 31, Elizabeth 21, Margaret E. 1, Richard H. 1/12
WILLS, James S. 23, Istra 19, Leander G. 1
GRAY, Robert D. 51*, Mary Jane 40, Weden D. 16, Elizabeth C. 14
SMITH, Sarah F. 36*
MORTON, Richard 23*
EVANS, Robert J. 24*

Schedule Page 53

HANKS, Hanibal 31, Armilda 26, Mary 11, M. V. 8 (m), William 5, Issabella 4, Romulous 2, Urmina 6/12
HOHN, William 53, Sarah 54, Joseph 19, William 19, Richard 16, Mary Jane 15, Archibald 13, Gillean 9 (f), Joseph 75, Eleanor 60
HOLMES, John 38, Susan 40, Almanza 17 (m), James 14, John 12, Emeline 10, Catharine 8, Jinsey 5 (f)
FROST, William 26, Fanny Jane 23, Simeon 2, Nancy A. 1
FOREMAN, Hamilton 67, Priscilla 64
MARTIN, John L. 51, Ruth 43, Massagill 20, Priscilla 22, Van C. 18, Mary E. 16, James 14, Luther 13, Roan 9 (f), Melvina 8, John L. 6, Robert 3
HOLMES, William 30, Elizabeth 64, Elizabeth 25, Lenora 22
ANDERSON, Harrison J. 31*, Sarah 28, Martha A. 8, John H. 5, Wingate 4, Josiah 2
STARNES, Joseph 76*
MANSFIELD, James M. 24, Mary 21, William P. 8/12
EWING, William 27*, Jane P. 24, Mary E. 6, Weden 4, John H. 2/12
HOLDER, Gary 17*

1850 Census Montgomery County Kentucky

KIRKPATRICK, John 46, Cavilla 43, Martilla 20, Elizabeth 14, Hannibal D. 10, John 7, James 5, Alfred 3
HALL, Henry W. 32, Lucinda 31, Elizabeth 8, Sarah 6, Bazel 3, Lucy E. 1/12
CONLEY, James 69, Priscilla 69, William 26, Henderson 13, P. Jane 11

Schedule Page 54

CONLEY, Henry 38, Elizabeth 34, William 15, Sarah A. 13, Hamilton 11, Mary C. 8, John W. 5, M. S. 2 (m)
ARTHUR, John 48, Luvisa 18, Susan 16, Arraminta 10, A. P. 8 (m)
FICKLIN, William 28, Mary 27, Elizabeth 3, Mary E. 1
HUDSON, James 35, Elizabeth 25, Angeline 5, Westley 3
STEPHENS, James Q. 19, Mildred J. 20
SHUBART, Lewis 57, Emily C. 60, Elihu 21
COUCHMAN, Peter 58, Frances 56, George A. 12
STEWART, William H. 28*, Julia A. 27, S. A. 3, Mary C. 8/12
FROST, Nancy 18*, Cynthea A. 20
WILLOUGHBY, William 45, Mildred 45, Phebe A. 18, Emily J. 16, John 14, William jr. 13, Henry 12, Robert 11, Elizabeth J. 10, R. 8 (m), Madison 2
GORDON, Randall 63, Rachel 65, Nancy G. 34, R. R. 28 (m)
GORDON, William B. 38, Lydia 28, John B. 7, William R. 5, R. R. 2 (m), Thomas 3/12
GEORGE, Joel S. 36, Nancy 36, David C. 4/12
TIMBLE, David F. 25, N. J. 22 (f), E. J. 3 (f), John H. 9/12
FICKLIN, John 64, Judith 47, Margaret 21, Fanny 16, Charlott 14, John 13, George 11, Clifton 9, Benja. 5
MYRES, Francis 52, Agnes W. 52, Amanda J. 16, Mary E. 14, William W. 12, Dulenia 9, H. D. 22 (m)
ESTEP, Elijah 37, Sarah 22, Elizabeth 10, Emily J. 3, Elider 1 (f)

Schedule Page 55

INGRAHAM, Job 33, Emily 33, Mary J. 11, Matha A. 10, Puras 5 (f), Rachel 4, William J. 2
HALSEY, Moses 39*, Anna 46, Margaret 14
TIPTON, Christanna 18*
SIMPKINS, Robert 66, Margaret 55, Emily J. 9, R. A. 6 (m), Lucy A. 4, Mary A. 2
INGRAHAM, William 27, Elizabeth 23, Thomas 5, H. T. 3 (m), William J. 1
LAWSON, James 23, Elizabeth 22, Benja. F. 1
IGO, Thomas 25, Martha A. 23, Lucretia 3, James F. 1
GLOVER, Creed T. 56*, Nancy 47
HINDER, Sarah A. 21*, A. J. 17 (f)
LAWSON, James jr. 62, Mary 46, F. S. 15 (m), Cythea 13, Nancy 10, Henry 8, John 8, Jerry 6, George W. 4
WILLOUGHBY, Mayland 30 (m), Mary J. 25, P. A. 4 (f), Mary A. 3, William 8/12, Phebe 40
WILLIAMS, Nathan 26*
DAVIS, Rebecca 52*
STEWART, C. M. 26 (m)*, Catharine 22, Mary T. 3, James S. 2
STEPHENS, Catharine 53*, Aurelia 10
HEDGER, John 45*, Eliza 26, Jane 6, John 1

1850 Census Montgomery County Kentucky

BALLARD, Malinda 22*, Phebe 50
PEYTON, Philip 63*, Elizabeth 56, Barbary 21
YOCUM, Sylvester 9*
GREEN, William F. 21, Minerva 21, Levi H. 4/12, Ellen 40
FRAME, John 62, Elizabeth 56, Nancy 26, Joseph A. 21
WARMSLEY, John 63, Sarah 73, A. D. 31 (m), Sarah 25, John M. W. 3, James M. 2, Nancy A. 8/12

Schedule Page 56

CRAIG, Fleming 46, Elizabeth 49, John G. 17, Nancy S. 15, Verlinda T. 13, Mary D. 11, John 81
DANIEL, Harvey 37, Mary F. 33, William J. 9, James E. 7, P. J. 5 (m), Armina J. 2
SHUBART, William C. 32, Elizabeth 26, James L. 5, Leah 3, E. C. 1 (f)
STEVANS, J. Y. 62 (m), Cynthea 52?, Alfred 23, Dolly 22, Berry 14, Martha 12
YOCUM, Jesse 35, Susan 32, Mericem? 13 (f), Martha A. 7, William 6, Elizabeth 5, Cistira 1
WILLOUGHBY, Wade 33, Judy 35, James 16, Reuben 14, P. W. 13 (m), Mayland 6 (m), Benja. 4, John 8/12, Eliza J. 8, E. A. 3 (f)
FROST, Joshua 50, Elizabeth 40, Angeline 14, John 13, Fanny 10, Voluntine A. 8, Mary A. 6, James K. P. 5, Eliza J. 3, Elizabeth 2
DANIEL, Eastridge 68, Mary 67, James Q. 27, Marium 21 (f), John 3/12, Elizabeth 7
HENSLEY, John 38, Martha 27, Joseph 8, Sarah C. 5, Laura J. 4, C. B. 2 (m), Elihu 70, C. A. Fox 17 (f)
MEANS, William C. 40, Frances S. 30, W. A. 15 (m), George H. 13, P. A. 11 (f), C. B. 8 (m)
WALKER, M. C. 46 (m), Melinda 43, John 15, William 14, George 7
HINDER, James 42, J. A. 22 (f), John 17, James 11, Lucinda 8, George W. 4

Schedule Page 57

CLEMM, Patterson 34*, Mary 1
WRIGHT, Mary 34?*
RYMERS, John 46, Elizabeth 34, Joseph W. 16, Asa H. 14, John E. 10, Mary J. 7, Martha A. 5, Henrietta 2
ALLIN, R. G. 30 (m), Theressa 37, E. Jane 13, Margaret A. 9, George 5, William J. 3, Terrace 1/12 (f)
KERTLEY, Mary 45, John F. 26, Louisa 22, Mary 20, William 18, James 15
TOMLINSON, H. 46 (m)*, Margaret 40, Marsha E. 6, Nancy F. 4, Georgian 2 (f), James J. 9/12
BANEFIELD?, William W. 10*
STEWART, David 48, Rose 50, Sarah 22, Elizabeth 20, John 18, Mary 16, Armilda 14, Robert 12, Martha 10, Margaretta 8
HAZELWRIGG, Dillard 50, Delila 36, George 29, John 22, James 16, Martha 10, Charles 2, Sarah 3/12
APPERSON, Richard 51, Harriet S. 35, Coleman R. 4, Lewis 2, Caroline 3/12
POINTER, Matthew 42, Rebecca 45, Thomas F. 19, William M. 16, Sarah H. 14, James P. 12, George W. 5
MCCORMICK, John 54*, Ruth 53, A. B. 24 (m), Newton 18, Thomas 14, George 8
WYMER, Peter 30*
ENRIGHT, John L.? 28
KIRK, James A. 43, MArtha 43, Angeline 20, Haden 17, James W. 14, Leroy 9, Mary E. 5, Shelly 1
WILSON, William S. 51*, Matilda 53, J. D. 24 (m), Susan 22, Rebecca 20, Lucretia 16

- 365 -

1850 Census Montgomery County Kentucky

Schedule Page 58

DAVISS, Clerrissa 37*
HOLLEY, Uriah 40*, Sarah 28, Mary J. 3, Ann E. 1
HELMS, Nancy 14*, Andrew 12
WILLIAMS, Zedekiah 29*, Mary Emily 28, Mary 2, James C. 9/12
HOLLEY, Nancy 60*
FICKLIN, Alexand W. 35, Eliza 30, John 7, Sarah 6, Andrew 5, Thomas 4, Walker 2
MYRES, Walter S. 40, Margaret 42, William 15, T. J. 10 (m), Mary 7, John 5, Margaret 4, Elizabeth 2
JEFFRIES, John 35*, Issabel J. 30, Mary 8, Nancy N. 6, William F. 4, James 2
BLEVINS, John 18*
MYRES, John S. 71, John H. 25
KIRKPATRICK, James 50*, Margaret 40, Armilda 24, Sarah L. 23, Margaret 19, Jane Hinder 22, Mary H. 19
PATTERSON, Thomas 24*
PRATHER, Walter 25, Jane 23, Mary 6, George H. 4
WELCH, Robert Y. 44, Caroline 36, Elizabeth 16, Nancy J. 14, John H. 12, Robert D. 10, Mary 5, Emily 4, Caroline 1
RECMAN, Thomas W. 36, Mary A. 32, Squire F. 13, William H. 7, Sarah H. 6, John S. 4
KINCADE, George W. 37*, Frances M. 32, Richard F. 6, Armstead S. 1
COLLINS, Sarah 70*
HALL, Mary M. 43, William C. 18, Edwin R. 15, S. G. 12 (f), James S. 9, John B. 7
STEVENSON, James M. C. 49*, JEstina 23, Andrew S. 5, J. H. 4 (m), Drusilla 9/12, George 26

Schedule Page 59

GENTRY, John B. 35*
EVANS, William B. H. 30, Joanna 27, Mary C. 4, Elizabeth M. 3
SMITH, Obediah 47*, Levisa 37, Mary A. 10, George 8, Drusilla 1, Sarah F. 1, Julia F. 13
SHOUSE, Obediah 19*
MERSHON, A. J. 26 (m)*
SPRATT, Mary 73*
ANDERSON, Jesse 24, Sarah E. 18, James T. 11/12
HOWARD, John 55, Sydney 42 (f), Amanda 16, Henry 14, C. Lou 13 (f), Emily 9, Frederick 6
SHOUTS, William 33, Mary 37, Carter 8, Mahala 6, Jackson 5, William E. 8/12
PIERCE, N. H. 23 (m), Martha 22, Mary E. 2
NOELL, Robert 30, Nancy E. 30
WARE, Robert E. 65, Frances 50, Samuel 35, William 13, James 11, Martha 9, Andrew 4, Lucy 22
WARE, John 60, Silas 20, Nancy 16, William 14, Margaret 12
BARNETT, Claibourn 48, Delila 44, Milly 19, James A. 16, Mary 14, Lewis 12, William W. 10, Bergaham E. 8 (m), J. C. 6 (m), Nelson 4
CLARK, McKinney 41, Milly 37, Mary F. 14, Nancy J. 12, Joseph 10, John 9, Richard 7, Elizabeth 5, Emily A. 2
WELLS, Nancy 63, Rose 45, Fielding 18, Silas 12, Eleanor 10, William T. 4
YOUNG, Martha P. 35*, Martha Jane 20, Amanda Jane 19, Wingate A. 16, F. Jane 14, William H. F. 9, Sarah A. J. 7, Nancy E. J. 4

1850 Census Montgomery County Kentucky

Schedule Page 60

ANDERSON, Letty J. 87*
RANDOLPH, Robert 30, Hannah 30, Elizabeth A. 13, Mary 12, Margaret 8, Paulina 7, Catharine 4
HATTON, Cassandra 40*
WILCOX, Catharine 60*
LAWRENCE, H. H. 36 (m)*, Elizabeth 35, John C. 13, Ennis B. 11, Louisa 9, William G. 7
GARNER, Elizabeth 16 (B)*, Rachel 63
LAWRENCE, William 27*, Martha 23, Virginia 6/12
RICHARDS, Sarah 56*
CRAIG, William F. 58, Elizabeth 58, Elizabeth 14, William F. jr. 26, Uphrana 27, William 6/12
PHILIPS, Mary A. 53*, John 27, Mary 18
BLACK, George F. 26*
MORRIS, William 36, Nancy A. 31, MArtha J. 14, M. C. 12 (f), E. C. 10 (f), Lucinda A. 8, Charles W. 6, T. Harriet 3, Nancy M. 8/12
DUNCAN, Joshua 47*, Harriet 35, Mitchell 13, Catharine 10, Robert 8, Levina 6, Ann 4, Silas 4, Rebecca 2
ROSS, Jane 15*, Benja. 11, Allen 10
HOLDER, Margaret 20*, Mary E. 1
ANDERSON, H. G. 48 (m), Sarah 41, Elizabeth 17, C. Kitturra 14(f), Bingham 10, Permelia 8, William H. 7, Peter J. 6, H. J. 4 (m), Henry W. 2
MORRIS, Joseph 50*, Lucinda 51, Jacob W. 20, John W. 17, Armilda J. 13, Joseph 10
ANDERSON, Mary 27*, Susan C. 20
WILSON, David A. 62, Mary 58, Elizabeth 28, Sarah 24, James 22, David 19, Mary 18, John 15

Schedule Page 61

WILSON, Jesse M. 30*, Nancy 39
BARKER, James H. 13*
LOCKNANE, Miles B. 21, Cordelia 20
BRANHAM, Thomas 32, Lydia P. 28, John W. 7, Susan C. 4, Nancy A. H. 8/12
WESTBROOK, James 28, Susan 23
HULTZ, David 45, Sarah 46
WYCKOFF, J. 52 (m), Levisa 38, Nancy A. 18, Catharine 16, Benja. F. 6, Julia 3, Esther 2
SUMMERS, William 22, Mary F. 20, Sarah M. 6/12
SUMMERS, Doel 60 (m)*, Sarah 56, Richard 9, Mary L. 6, John H. 4
LAWNES, A. 27 (m)*
HANELINE, Volentine C. 27, Julia A. 23, Mary C. 3
SMITH, James 37, Sarah 34, William M. 14, Hester E. 13, Sarah E. 10, Mary F. 4
WHITE, Ann 60, Eveva A. 20
STONE, Richard 36, M. Jane 31, J. W. 7 (m), Hannah E. 4, George W. 1
HANELINE, Thomas M. 25, Paulina 22, Thomas M. 1
SPRATT, Alexis _. 27, Nancy 23, John B. 1
SPRATT, Solomon 45*, Martha A. 27, John B. 22, Louisa 10, Andrew G. 6, S. T. 2 (m)
HOLLAND, Tobitha 22*
GARRETT, Owen C. 31, Catharine E. 21, John M. 6, Mary J. 5, James S. 3, Owen T. 11/12
GARRETT, James jr. 36*, Nancy J. 32, John H. 5, James 90, Susan 80, Maria J. 28
BARTETT, William 23*

1850 Census Montgomery County Kentucky

PHELPS, Charles G. 35, Mary J. 27, Elizabeth A. 10, Amanda F. 8, John W. 6, Mary H. 4, Ann 2, James W. 4/12
GARRETT, John 50*
CRAIG, James 24*

Schedule Page 62

ADAMS, John 49, Mary 52, William 22, Luth B. 20 (f), Sarah C. 17, Lou Ann E. 16, John A. 14, Mary C. 12
PHILIPS, Harvey 32, Amanda 26, Mary E. 9, Margaret 8, Nancy J. 4, Patsey 6/12
FLETCHER, Ezekiel 44*, Susan 50, C. Jane 11
DOUGLASS, James 23*
BRANHAM, William 47, Joanna 30, NAncy 10, William 8, Mary S. 6, Sarah 4, Lydia Jane 1
HEDGER, Benjamin 40*, Matilda 39, Angeline 20, S. W. 17 (m), John 15, Samuel 13, Sally A. 7, F. Jane 6, William 5
BALLAD, Frances 60*
PHILIPS, Garrett 30*, Margaret 26, James W. 3, John W. 1
ROSS, Joseph 8*
GARRET, Alexander 48, Lodusca 39, Gipson 17, R. N. 14 (m), H. T. 8 (m), John S. 6, William J. 4, Q. Taylor 1
TATE, David 45*, Jeftina? 38, Cindarilla 15, Moses R. 13, David jr. 11, Tilman 9, William H. 7, Andrew L. 5, Elizabeth 3, Francis 1
TREADAWAY, M. H. 24 (m)*
VAUGHN, Josiah J. 24, Mary P. 18, James 9
CONNER, William 26, Amanda 24, John 6, Ezekiel 5, Martha A. 3, William H. 1/12
HASKIN, William 35, Martha 34, Nancy 11, Arraminta J. 8, John 5, Jesteen 3 (f), Martha E. 6/12
ADAMS, Robert 60, Rose 50, Anderson 21, Lucretia 16, Sarah 13
PIGG, Woodford 30, Elizabeth 24, Adaline 7, William L. 5, Mary L. 3, Thomas M. 1, Anderson 78

Schedule Page 63

MARTIN, Elsberry 27*, Nancy 23, James A. 7, Lucy E. 5, Hugh 2
JEWELL, Lesly 30 (m)*
HUDSON, James 40*, Nelly 40, Susan 17, Abram 16, Randall 10
RICHARDSON, Jesse 14*
KONKRIGHT, Abram 77*
HUOFON?, Benjamin 13*
STRANGE, John 34*, Ellen 37, George W. 12, Mary A. 9, Lucretia 7, John W. 5, Martha E. 3, James W. 5
KONKRIGHT, R. Jane 18*, Eliza Jane 15, Benjamin 14
DONAHOO, Jacob 34*, Jane 34, Sarah 17, John H. 10, Alexander 7, Amy 4, E. J. 3 (m)
WALLER, Rachel M. 23*
KENNEDY, John 39
MCLAUGHLIN, David 50, Elizabeth 45, John 22, Clerrissa Jane 21, Thomas G. 20, Sarah A. 18, Elizabeth 16, Susan 15, Andrew P. 9, Hugh 7, Christopher 5, James H. 28
POWELL, Samuel M. 25*, Mary 16
WHITE, Vina J. 13*

- 368 -

1850 Census Montgomery County Kentucky

MCLAUGHLIN, Sarah 51*
LILLY, Elizabeth A. 6*
KONKRIGHT, Elizabeth 30*
WOODARD, Joseph 45, Richard 11
FRENCH, William 43*, Ann 42, John 20, Elizabeth 17, Nicholas 15, Mary Jane 13, William 10, Josephene 6, Irene 3
KNOX, Robert 20*
HALL, Fanny 21*
JOHNSON, Hugh 44, Sarah 45, T. J. 23 (m), Elizabeth 20, Mary 18, William 15, James M. 10
GROOMS, Madison 45*, Barzilla 28, Elizabeth 3, William H. 2
STARNES, James 12*

Schedule Page 64

MAGOWAN, John 8*, Thomas C. 5
OTTER, Stephen 92*
BRADSHAW, John H. 24, Mary 20, Caroline 3, Mary Jane 1
HOHN, Malinda 44, Lycordas 21, Almanza 19, Eastlard 18, Mary E. 16, John 14, Amand Jane 11, C. Ann 9, Elizabeth 7, Armanda 4, Isaac 2
YOCUM, William 50, Ella 37, Anderville 2, Alonzo 3/12
PRATHER, Nathaniel 51, Mary Jane 45
WILLOUGHBY, Ben J. 39, Amanda 35, Sarah E. 15, William 13, Mary 11, Margaret A. 9, James 7, Castrina? 5, Moses 3, Isaac 3, Melinda 1
ROBBINS, Haman 49, Mary 41, James F. 18, William A. 17, Lucinda 16, Mary A. 14, Melind Jane 12, John M. 10, George W. 8, Elizabeth 5, Luther G. 2
HOHN, Moses J. 29, A. B. 26 (f), A. V. 3 (m), Olevia W. 1
YOCUM, John M. 26, Mary Jane 25, Elizabeth E. 3, Mary A. 2, William A. 20, James H. 19, Mary A. 13, Eliza Jane 9, Harriet 7, George 5
FRAME, Samuel 65*, Margaret 40
KENNEY, Jane 15*, Nancy 13
HUDSON, Thomas 30, Louisa 30, James 4, Nancy E. 3, Samuel 6/12
TRIMBLE, David 33, Sophia 39, Elizabeth 15, William T. 11, Mary 8, JAmes G. 7, Caroline 5, Almanza 6/12 (m)
BRISTOE, Morris 35* (B), Eliza 27, Jane 14
RAMEY, David 17*
YOCUM, Abel 42, George 87

Schedule Page 65

PRINCE, Arthur 42, Nancy 40, George W. 18, John W. 16, James M. 14, Rose A. 12, Sarah A. 4
MEANES, James 35, Elizabeth 23, Nimrod 6, William 4, Sarah 2
FOX, Washington 42, Mary 35, Emily Jane 17, Sarah A. 15, Solomon 13, Alfred 13, George 10, Catharine 5, Joseph 3, Benjamin 2
ANDERSON, Ann 62, Asena 25, Mary 6, Frances 2
HENSLEY, Evan S. 41, Annie 40, Emily Jane 15, John W. 13, Julia A. 12, Joseph A. 10, William F. 8, James A. 5, Isabella 4, Charlotte 8/12
FOX, Harrison 34, Barbara 33, Anna 12, John 8, Elizabeth 6, Joseph 5, Cenia 3, James F. 8/12

1850 Census Montgomery County Kentucky

FOX, John 25, Mary 24, Joseph 8, Elizabeth 6, William T. 3, Sarah A. 8/12
COX, William 33, Mary 30, James F. 13, Elizabeth 10, William H. 6, Angeline 5, John 2, Solomon 1
WILLS, Andrew H. 21, Mahala 31, John C. 1, John jr. 22
MAGOWAN, John B. 43*, Mary A. 39
MILLER, James L. 20*
BARFIELD, Aprida? 13 (f)*
KIRK, Matthew 71, Hannah 73
REFFETT, Levi 27, Julia 27, Mary A. 7, Cordelia 4, Letty 1
WHITE, Allen 44, Eliza Jane 38, George N. 19, Frances M. 17, William Sea 14, James A. 10, A. M. 7 (m), Phebe Jane 6, Sarah A. 8/12

Schedule Page 66

EDWARDS, William 89*, Mary 88
NICKS, Nancy 46*
BALLARD, James 39, Fanny 53, Garret 18
HENSLEY, William 35, Margaret 39, Fielding 47, James 15, Lucinda 13, John S. 11, Mary A. 10, E. Jane 8, William M. 7, Annice 4, Sarah M. 2
WHITE, John 24, Lucinda 18, Mary Jane 1
COOK, John 24*, Mary Jane 22
COOLE, Jacob 75*
ROWLAND, Melissa 40*, Maria 11
COX, David 25, Margaret M. 20, Louisa Jane 4, Winfield S. 1
CARTER, William 59*, Nancy 59
TRIMBLE, Sarah 22*
KING, Elizabeth 14*, William 13
FRAZIER, Vina 11*
DANIEL, Isham 33, Mary Jane 31, Narcissa 9, James H. 8, John C. 6, Joseph 5, Leroy 3, Mary L. 1
HENSLEY, Almanza 28 (m), Elizabeth 26, Nancy Jane 8, Martha 6, William J. 4, Samuel O. 3, Mary E. 8/12
KERSLEY, Travis 48, Mary 46, William 19, Mary Jane 21, Frank 17, Eveline 16, Julia A. 13, Thomas 11, Nancy 6
KERSLEY, Rebecca 26, James M. 6, Abby Jane 5, David F. 4, Lucinda 2, Mary 40
WYMER, Lucinda 50*, Margaret E. 14, Martha H. 12
KINNEY, John 22*, Caroline 17, Mary E. 11/12, Frank 8
YOCUM, Franklin 31*, Queene Ann 31, Eliza Jane 7, Barbary E. 5, James 2, Franklin 76, Anna 76, Catherine 42, Maria 40
BRUSH, James O. 19*

Schedule Page 67

YOCUM, Jesse 36*, Elizabeth 21, Aaron 3/12
KENNEY, Mary 14*, Aaron 19
BLEVINS, John 18*
WYMER, David 27*, C. A. 26 (f), Philander 5, James 4, Lucy E. 2, John 1
OTTER, Nancy 14*

1850 Census Montgomery County Kentucky

SMITH, Henry 46, Louisa 41, Harriet 13, Sarah A. 11, B. P. 10 (m), Tolitha 8, Elizabeth 6, Maria 5, Lucinda 3, Mary C. 3/12
WILLOUGHBY, James W. 52*, Mary 40, John 17, Marian 12 (m)
KINNEY, Lucinda 17*
MARTIN, Elijah 55, Phebe 50, Susan 22, James 20, Salley 17, Clinton 13, Benjamin 11, Rily 9
MARTIN, William S. 26, Martha 22, Greenberry 2, Benjamin L. 8/12
KONKWRIGHT, Benjamin L. 33, Lucinda 33, Elijah 14, Nancy Jane 12, William 10, Elsberry 9, Isaac 7, F. M. 5 (m), Mary A. 3, Susan 1
YOCUM, Jinsey 40 (f), Stephen 13, Melvina 11, Louisa A. 7, George 5, Sarah M. 3
HANDLEY, William 55*
LOCKRIDGE, Mary A. 65*
WYMER, Peter 27, Nancy 28, James A. 5, Barbary A. 2, John 6/12, John sr. 22
MAXWELL, James 27*, Elizabeth 26, Roan 6/12 (f)
COOPER, Margaret 45*, Mary 8
BELLOWS, James 30*
CRAIG, Daniel 60, Jane 64, Louisa T. 23, William D. 28, Susan Jane 27, Louisa 3, John H. 5/12
LANCE, Eleanor 53, Amanda 26, Sarah Jane 24, M. Ellen 22

Schedule Page 68

FICKLIN, Frances 60, Archibald 25, Richard 22, Charles 16
THOMAS, Eleanor 30, William 10, Garret 8, Mary E. 6
TURNER, George 59, Priscilla 59, William 19, James 23, Susan 21
WOOD, William 25*, Lucretia 25, Amelia 6, George 4, William 2, John 1
DICKSON, Sarah A. 21*
GILKEY, William 67, Barbary 56
GILKEY, Charles 48, Clementine 20, Benjamon T. 14, Maria L. 11
BALDWIN, Thomas 58, Jesse 26, Sarah A. 22, Thomas E. 1
BALDWIN, William 68*
COLLINS, Samuel R. 27*, Sarah 21, William 8/12
FOSTER, John H. 54*
WILLS, Andrew 20*
DAULTON, Adaline 21*
HANELINE, Ann 47, John R. 26, Samuel M. 25, Catharine 19, Franklin F. 17, Elizabeth A. 16, George W. 14
DICKEY, Daniel 47, Martha 39, George W. 15, Mahala 12, Margaret 11, Martha 10, Mary F. 2
DICKEY, William 41, Levina 38, Elizabeth 18, Mary Jane 15, Robert 13, Lou Ann 11, Jennet 8 (f), Newton 6, Etera 4, P. V. 2 (f), Adam 86, Elizabeth 50
MASON, Benson 68, Margaret 64, Charles B. 20
DICKEY, Maria 49, Vashatie 25 (f), William 23
BLACK, George 75
GREGSBY, R. T. A. 28 (m), A. M. 28 (f), A. E. 8 (f), John F. 5, James B. 2
COCKERELL, William 48, Sarah 45, Jeremiah 21, William 17, Benjamin 15, George 13, Peter 11

1850 Census Montgomery County Kentucky

Schedule Page 69

BLACK, Andrew 42, Margaret 39, Louisa 18, Mary A. 16, Elizabeth 14, Margaret 12, Permelia 10, Sarah 8, George W. 6, R. M. 4 (m), Jane 2, Virginia 6/12
HAZELWRIGG, Charles 64, Nancy 63
STOFER, John 54, Mary 50, Albert 21, William 19, Elizabeth 16, Richard 12, Silas 9
SAPPINGTON, John 59*, Sarah 51
KENNEDY, Leah 34*, James 28
WARD, Thomas 14*
COCKRELL, Jane 37, Thomas 15, Richard 13
TIPTON, N. P. 41 (m), Elizabeth 42, Waller 16, Samuel 13, Lether 11 (m), James 6, Mary 43
OLDHAM, Richard 63*, Sarah 44, Marian 19 (m), Catharine 14, Sarah 11, John 9, Junietta 7, William 5
HURT, James 22*
PARRISH, Grandison 38*, Sarah 35, John C. 15, Thomas J. 13, William T. 11, James 10, Sarah 8, Martha 6, Mary 3, E. Taylor 1
SPRATT, Mary E. 18*
WILSON, L. D. 34 (m)*, Eliza M. 28, Nancy E. 10, Luther M. 8
JEFFRIES, Luther C. 30*, Ann 28
ANDERSON, Josiah 28, Martha C. 26, Luckett 6 (f), Albert 4, Ann B. 2, Mary 3/12
OREAR, Welsley 40, Emily 40, Mary 19, Louisa 17, Elizabeth 14, Nancy 12, Georgean 10 (f), Albert 8, Joseph 6, Lucy 6/12
SONS, Matthew 40, Hannah 42, William 18, Melinda 16, Mary 14, Sarah 13, Elizabeth 11, George W. 10, John M. 9, James K. P. 6, Matthew 3/12

Schedule Page 70

BARNES, John 30, Nancy Jane 21, William M. 6, Mary F. 1
CLEMIN, A. G. 32 (m)*, Elizabeth 29, William T. 11, James F. 9, L. Jane 7, F. M. 5 (m), Leroy E. 4, D. P. 2 (m), A. S. 6/12 (m)
SMITH, James 21*
DUNCAN, Nancy An 20*, Z. Taylor 1
GREENWADE, Henry 20, Emily 19, James S. 8/12
BARNETT, Elizabeth 75, Mary 60, Nancy 55, Susan 53, William 50, Virginia 48, Joseph 45, George 40, Lucinda 37, JAmes 35, Mahala 23, Elizabeth 14
GREENEWADE, Samuel 58*, Leanna 50, Mary 13
HALL, Jesse 18* (B)
KING, William 40, Nancy 25, John 14, Henry 10, Moses 6
KING, Stephen 37, Elizabeth 23, Richard 17, Elizabeth 14, William 13, Nancy 10, Henry 7, John 5, Stephen 1, Mary 3/12
BIGGERS, Harrison 41, Eliza A. 38, Matilda 13, Elizabeth 10, Landy 8 (m), Harrison 7, William 1
RICHARDSON, John 42*, Elizabeth 38, John L. 11, Mary 9, James W. 8, Robert 5, Elizabeth 4
PATTON, Margaret 10*, Louisa 8
RINGO, Solomon 32, Julia 28, James F. 10, Jackson 7, William W. 5, Thomas J. 3, John H. 4/12, Christenia 34, Elizabeth 60

1850 Census Montgomery County Kentucky

Schedule Page 71

MCMAHILL, Ambrose 42*, Elizabeth 43
PITT, Cornelia 21*
MANYON, Thomas 68, Parthenia 59
PETITT, Asa T. 40*, Sarah A. 39, Nancy 16, Martha 14, George 12, William 10, Mary 8, James 6, Sarah 4
MYRES, C. R. 30 (m)*
RAMY, Benjamin 40* (B)
HOLLEY, John 30*, Armanda 28, Angeline 5, Cassandra 3, Boone C. 2/12
JONES, Martha 56*, Issabella 45, Uriah Helms 12
CRAWFORD, Lorinda 15* (B)
JONES, James F. 30*, Nancy 32, John D. 10, William T. 1
HELM, Thomas 17*
RICHARDSON, Eliza 14*
HINDES, Benja. F. 30, Mary 30, Elizabeth E. 3
HINDES, Edwin 32, Mary 28, Martha 6, Catharine Jane 4, Sarah Jane 6/12
GIPSON, William 44, Roan 34 (f), Mary 14, Nancy J. 13, George 11, Martha 9, Barbary 7, Milton 5, Samuel 2
GIPSON, Samuel 77, Jane 77, John N. 13
JOHNS, Anderson 61*, Nancy 61, Julia 24, James R. 20
KEY, Sarah 88*
RYMUS?, Sarah 50* (B)
SCOTT, Eliza 15* (B)
JOHNS, Joseph 28, Eliza Jane 30, John A. G. 6, Mary J. 5, S. G. 3 (f), Martha H. 1
CHEATHAM, David 47, Mary 38, Marian 19 (m), Evaline 13, Truman? 12, Harriet 9, Maria 7, David jr. 3
MEANS, John 46, Mary 30, Caroline C. 19, Elizabeth 17, Julia A. 16, John W. 14, George C. 12, James R. 6
GIPSON, James 40, Gillean 36 (f), Salina 14, Elizabeth 12, Nancy 10, Sarah Jane 7, Amanda 4, Campbell 3, Ann 1

Schedule Page 72

JAMUSON, Benjamin F. 27*, Margaret 24, William 4, Sarah A. 2
CRITZER, Leander 27*
COOPER, George 79*, Mary 80
CLARK, James 46*, Elizabeth 34, Harriet 7, George W. 5, Mary E. 3, James C. 6/12
OREAR, Edwin G. 30*, Amanda B. 28, Lucy Jane 4, Mary E. 2
MITCHELL, Greenberry 25*
CRAIG, John M. 22*
GILKEY, B. F. 45 (m)*, James F. 14, William T. 11, Mary E. 7, William O. 39
SPURGIN, Samuel 22*
MEANS, J. F. 21 (m)*, Nancy 32, Sarah E. 4, G. F. 2 (f), H. A. 1 (m)
CLURE, Sarah 14*
DESHONG, A.? 35 (m), Mary J. 26, John 4, James 2
DEAN, Jeremiah 37, Zerilda 36, Mary E. 3, Nancy Jane 1

1850 Census Montgomery County Kentucky

YOCUM, Levi 42, Lucy 36, Rachel 14, Sarah A. 12, Randall 10, Jesse 8, Lucy Jane 6, Mary E. 4, William 1
TRIMBLE, John 51, Nancy 53, William 24, Sarah 22, John W. 18, Angeline 16, Lucinda 14, Richard 12
TRIMBLE, Isaac 55, Mary 56, Lucy A. 30, Cythea A. 15, Martha 12
HAWKINS, Henry B. 32, Drussilla 28, John 12, Elizabeth 8, William 6
WALKER, William 23*, Nancy 22
NORTON, William W. 52*
WALKER, Mary 38, Cassandra A. 83
ANDERSON, Nimrod 29, L. M. 26 (f), George W. 7, James K. P. 5, Barbary A. 4, John W. 1

Schedule Page 73

STEPHENS, Jesse 46, Elizabeth 31, S. E. D. 17 (m), James W. 15, E. M. 12 (m)
PORTER, R. C. 33 (m)*, Mary 25, James m. 7, Mary 5, Ann E. 3/12
STEPHENS, Narcissa 15*
PORTER, Lyman 31*, Caroline A. 25, Ransom 5, George 3, Clara A. 2, William 6/12
HOPWOOD, Permelia 44*, Louisa 19, William 17, Sarah B. 9, Jesse 7, John 4
OREAR, Jeremiah jr. 49, Levenia 39, Josephine 15, Marshall 13, Asberry 11, Columbus 9, Luther 7, Peter 4, Julia 2
SHUBART, John N. 28, Mary 19, Lucy D. 1
BRUER, Thomas 27, Rebecca 19
TRIMBLE, James H. 28, Harret 25, F. M. 7 (m), Mary E. 5, James F. 4, Licortus? 2 (m)
FOX, Thomas 34, Martha 31, James W. 10, William H. 8, George 6, Mary Jane 4, L. M. 1 (m), John sr. 70, Elizabeth 68
STEWART, Eli 44*, Sidney 43 (f), Sophia 17, Marchesa 14, Elisha 12, L. M. 10 (f), William J. 6, Amanda B. 4, Eli A. 1
JONES, Rebecca 23*, John M. 5
STEPHENS, John 37*, Mary A. 26, James W. 9, John C. 5, Joseph A. 3, Sarah C. 1
CAYWOOD, Mary E. 10*
CROSSIT, Mary 60*
BEESON, Phebe 27*, John O.? 7, F. Jane 3
MCDONALD, George 44*
ALEXANDER, Patsey 55*, Nathan 26, Joseph W. 22
GREEN, Agnus 19*
ROBERTSON, John 15*, Sarah 14, Joseph 9

Schedule Page 74

REFFIT, Derret 34 (m), Catharine 28, JAmes A. 10, George W. 6, W. H. 3 (m)
STONE, Martin 23, Julia A. 28, A. M. 7 (m), Marsh A. 4 (f), Joseph W. 2
TADE, John 26*, Vina 26, Nancy Jane 5, Emily 2, Louisa 2
BARFIELD, Robert F. 11?*, Susan 43, Matilda 6, Franklin 4, Mary 2
WILLIAMS, Minerva 20*, John 5, Jesse 3
WILLS, James 48, Aletha 46, Aletha 16, John H. 14, Docia 12, Caroline 9, Sarah B. 6, James T. 4, Amanda Jane 2, Nancy 25, Nimrod 4, Mary 1
COMBS, William 45, Wilmoth 45, Clinton 21, Catharine 17, Amanda 14, Achillis 12
COMBS, Washington 35, Nancy 22, America 8, Farellinder 4 (f)

- 374 -

1850 Census Montgomery County Kentucky

LAWSON, Henry 40*, Nancy 28, Alexander L. 17, Travis 15, William 13, JAmes 6
ALEXANDER, Jackson 4*, Mary 2
LAWSON, Daniel 23, Fanny 21, Angeline 1
LAWSON, Travis 27, Margaret 23, Sarah E. 4, Simeon 2, Mary 7/12
LAWSON, Joseph 35, Susan 34, Lucinda 14, Fanny 12, Mary 9, Julian 7 (f), Louisa 5, William F. 3, Susan 1
RATCLIFF, William 26, Mary A. 21, J. W. 1 (m), Jane 7/12
RATCLIFF, James 50*, Elizabeth 60, Jeremiah 29, Henry 23, Robert 21, Elizabeth 15

Schedule Page 75

OWEN, Robert 76*
COMBS, Laban 29, Margaret 25, Luther 9, Margaret 7, Lucinda 5, Eans 21 (m), Emily Jane 15
LAWSON, William 46, Mary 44, Jeremiah 21, John 18, MArtha 16, Joseph 14, William B. 12, E. G. 10 (m), Mary A. 9, Fletcher 6, Davis 4, Benja. F. 1, Travis 84
DAVIS, David 36, Mary A. 30, Jackson 14, John 12, Eveline 8, William F. 4, Jefferson 2, Newton 3/12
GORE, Henry 44, Elizabeth 42, Mary A. 19, James P. 16, R. Jane 14, John M. 13, Lucinda 10, Lewis G. 8, Gillian 6 (f), George F. 5
CORNWELL, James 35, Elizabeth 28, James R. 8, Mary Jane 6, Rebecca A. 2
BARNS, Uriah 84, Mary 63
ALEXANDER, James 29*, Emily 23
ROBERTSON, James 11*
BECRAFT, Thomas 40, Jemima 30, Rebecca 13, Solomon 11, William 9, John 4, Elizabeth 1
CORNWELL, Rebecca 50*, William 24
RINGO, Zerilda 14*, Nancy 10
CORNWELL, Jesse 35, Fanny 30, William 12, Rebecca 10, Jackson 8, Nancy Jane 2
HALL, Levi 34, Allegan 6 (m), Elizabeth 6, Mary J. 2, Mildred 63
REFFITT, James jr. 25, Elizabeth 34, Nancy A. 12, William H. 7/12, Henry 21
TOLAND, James 73, Washington 15, John 13
BARNS, Dempsey 53 (f), James 24, Emily Jane 17, Patience? 37, Elizabeth 24, Thomas 21, Mary A. 14, Z. T. 10 (m), Sarah A. 7, Minerva Jane 2

Schedule Page 76

PITTS, Washington 35, Sarah A. 24, Mary A. 9, George W. 7, Henry 5, Thomas J. 3, Emily Jane 7/12
HODGE, Robert 37, Lucinda 30, Elizabeth 15, James 10, Ally A. 8 (f), Jonathan 6, Levi 2
BOOHER, John H. 33*, Tamer R. 26 (f), William 4, May 1
YOCUM, Melvina 11*
MORRISON, Sophia 44*, Martha Jane 21, Clementine 18
MORRISON, Daniel 15*, James F. 5
REFFITT, James 66, Nancy 55, Amos 27, William 23, Thomas 17, John 14, Lucinda 11
WILLS, Nimrod A. 30*, Letty M. 30, Peter 7, Martha 5, James C. 4, Catharine 2, John H. 1
FROST, Anpaline 14 (f)*
DONAHOO, John 47, Elizabeth 34, Ara 17, Elizabeth 15, John H. 12, Alligan G. 10, George W. 8, Lean C. 6 (f), J. F. 3 (m), Julia 2
HEDGER, Robert 48, Mary 39, William 24, John 20, Abigail 18, David 13, George 11, Emily 4
CARTER, William 41*, Elizabeth 38, Cynthea A. 15, Washington 7, John W. 4

1850 Census Montgomery County Kentucky

DONAHOO, Joseph 43*
DOWNES, Elizabeth 45, Levinda 18, George W. 15, William M. 13, Elizabeth 10, John 8
BALLARD, Garret 43, Rachel 36, Thomas B. 20, Mary J. 17, Arrabella 15, John 12, Melvina 10, Eliza 7, John W. 5, Elizabeth 3, Cestra 7/12

Schedule Page 77

GREEN, William F. 21, Manerva 21, Levi H. 7/12, Nelley 40
GREENE, Elizabeth 32, Levi 26, James E. 17, Letty 43
SMITH, Joseph 30*, Mary 34, Elizabeth 10, James 9, Samuel 5, Joseph jr. 3, Josephene 1/12
HAWKINS, Thomas 36*
HENSLEY, Harvey 30, Cenia 26, Joseph 10, James H. 8, William C. 6, John T.? 4, Evan S. 2, Henry C. 11/12
HUBBARD, Peter 25, Rachel 25
ANDERSON, Thomas T. 57, Margaret 54, A. P. 20 (m), B. B. 19 (m), Mary 16, Margaret 13
HUBBARD, Archibald 25, Nancy 30, Nathan 75, Winney 69, Eliza Jane 3
RAMSEY, Hannah 58 (B), Henry 24, M. H. 22 (m), Ellen 19, Alfred 16, Henry 15, Levi 10
STEPHENS, Mary A. 24, Luther F. 3, Armilda Jane 1
HUBBARD, Hannah 30, James C. 11, Matilda Jane 9, Julia A. 6, Andrew F. 3, Sarah B. 1
DANIEL, Shelby 42 (m)*, Cythea A. 35, William E. 16, James H. 14, Armilda Jane 12, Randall R. 10, Mary L. 3
WYMER, Lucinda 33*
STEVENS, Matthias 56, Rebecca 48, Sarah A. 18, Amanda R. 15, John F. 12, George W. 9, Albert 7, Margaret 5
ANDERSON, James 24, Elizabeth 26, Henry 9, Newton 7, Mary 5, Margaret Jane 3
MYRES, George 28, Sarah 28, Elizabeth 6, Henrietta 4, Mary E. 3, James L. 2

Schedule Page 78

ALEXANDER, Joseph 30, Louisa Jane 30, Thomas A. 7, Mary F. 5, Louisa Jane 2
PENDLETON, John 25, Sarah 24, Thomas H. 3, Jesse 1
MAGOWAN, James S. 76
FORTUNE, Lewis 49*, Hannah 49, James F. 22, Lydia A. 19, Andrew 15, Archibald 31
CLEMM, Theressa 26*
CLEMM, John 69, Mary 63, Patsey 42
HICKS, Thomas 61*, Martha 33
ALEXANDER, Marth 9*
MYRES, Hiram 26*, Mary 26, Lydia A. 2
CLARK, Margaret A. 12*
MILLER, William J. 38, Elizabeth 38, F. A. 13 (f), R. H. 13 (m), William H. H. 10, Ann E. 7, Nancy Jane 4, John 44
STEWART, Henrietta 54, Jane 32, Emily 22, James 21, John 19, Louisa 18, Franklin 16, Elizabeth 14, John W. 12
STEPHENS, Mary 60, W. P. 29 (m)
STEPHENS, Milton P. 30, Catharine 22, Stateira 3 (f), William P. 2
GOODLOW, Henry 66, Rachel 30
FICKLIN, Garret P. 33, Maria 22, William 7/12

1850 Census Montgomery County Kentucky

STEPHENS, John M. 32*, Elizabeth 26, John F. 4, Mary Jane 3, William 2, David 1/12
PIERCALL, Jane 16*
SHUBERT, R. J. 23, Mary 24, Lucy Jane 2, Amos 7/12
WARMSLEY, M. 33 (m), Caroline 27, Susan M. 7, Nancy Jane 5, George M. 2
MOSS, Nathaniel O. 53*, Jane 50, Edwin 19, Sarah 15, Thomas D. 10, Laura A. 7
REDMAN, Garret 21*, Rebecca 21

Schedule Page 79

HALL, James 37, Sarah A. 30, James M. 10, Louisa 7, Z. Taylor 2
KELLEY, Richard P. 59, Sarah C. 59, Henry 20, John J. 32, Mary 32
COMBS, R. W. 43 (m)*, Cyrena 32, Joseph A. 16, John B. 9, Eliza B. 7, James C. 5, Susan C. 4, Sarah B. 2, Eunice? 7/12
BEATY, Sarah 80*, Robert 53
POWELL, E. S. 26 (m), Martha Jane 21, Fanny B. 2, John A. 2/12
MCCLURE, Margaret 62, Joel 37, Mitton 35, Margaret 24, Andrew 22, Mary 20, Emily 16, Elizabeth 12, James M. 22
WILSON, Samuel 54*, Elizabeth 50, James M. 17
BONDURANT, Mary 11* (B)
WYATT, Haden 47, Mary 47, John 24, Luther H. 20, Julia A. 18, James F. 16, Lemuel 13, Benjamin F. 10, Joseph D. 7
CRAY, Lorenzo D. 45, Ruth 48, Thomas 19, Emily 17, Joseph 13, Lear Jane 13
ALLEN, Isaac N. 29, Margaret 25, Lucy Jane 4, Fanny 1
STEPHENS, John L. 38, Mary 38, John D. 7/12
CHENAULT, Tandy 43 (m), Virginia 41, Joel 19, David W. 17, Benjamin F. 14, Nancy 11, Westley 9, Ann 6, William F. 3
COONS, John 76*, Elizabeth 72, Benja. F. 28
URIETH?, George K. 58* (B)
BEATY, Thomas 19* (B)
FLETCHER, Johnson 53, Permelia 48, Jesse 21, Martha A. 18, Melvina 16, Elizabeth 13, William H. 10, R. L. 6 (m)

Schedule Page 80

BEATY, George 45*, Susan J. 32, Sarah A. 9, Mary E. 8, Laura J. 5, Susan P. 3, Nancy A. 2
TADE, Sarah 19*
PHIPPS, Abram 40*, Nancy 42, Emily F. 4, John J. 2, Susan A. 1
RAMSEY, Jacob 75*
GRUBBS, John 29*, Minerva 24
PROCTOR, Washington 40*, Nancy M. 25
BERRY, John sr. 57, John jr. 17
FOSTER, James M. 26*
BRADSHAW, Nancy 40*, Narcissa 18, Margaret 16
SHOUSE, M. M. 29 (m), Gillean 25 (f), Mary Jane 6, Cynthea 5, W. O. 1 (m)
TIPTON, John 66, Mary 50, Benjamin 20, Oliver 15, Jemima A. 13
TIPTON, William 56, Sarah 48, Milton W. 20, John C. 15, James E. 10, Melissa Jane 7
WOODARD, Judith 50, Eliza 25, Susan 23, Hannah 21, Lance 19, John 17, William 12

1850 Census Montgomery County Kentucky

BOTTS, Robert 70, Elizabeth 60, Catharine 26, Elizabeth 24, George 22
HOWARD, Samuel 25, Nancy 20
OREAR, Harrison 39, Amy 32, John 6/12, Joseph 37, William 32
GILKIE, Thompson 36, Mary 7, James T. 3
MYRES, Harvey 37*, Eliza 30, William H. 8, Thomas B. 2
JORIETT?, Frank 72* (B)
SHROCK, John G. 28, Elizabeth 25, Allen 8, William D. 6, Sarah E. 4
STEPHENS, Joel 35, Mary A. 26, Mary C. 2
ALEXANDER, John 25, Araminta Jane 27
WILLIAMS, Amos 60, Rebecca 53, Elihu 34, Emily 31, Elizabeth 29, William 26, Frederick 20, John S. 14, Felix A. 3

Schedule Page 81

WRIGHT, Meredith 45, Harriet 43, Meredith jr. 18, Jane 12, James 9, Robert 7, Sarah K. 6
HENSLEY, Jackson 33, Ruth S. 26, Hezekiah 4, Ann 1
BURHOPP, George P. 44*, Dorothy 43, Jesse 14, John M. 7, Sarah E. 6, Caroline J. 4, Georgean 1 (f)
STEPHENS, Jehu 91*
OREAR, Jeremiah C. 68*, Lucy 62
GEORGE, Violet 86* (B)
MANIER, John 45, Ann 41, W. H. 20 (m), Mary J. 18, John jr. 16, Martha 13, Robert 11, Joseph 9, Thomas 2
RAMEY, Robert 36, Caroline 25, W. F. 2 (m), Mary 69, Henrietta 24
MAGOWAN, James P. 48, Eliza Jane 44, William C. 22, James A. 19, John J. 16, Ann E. 14
DENT, Johnston 35* (B), Eliza 40, William S. 3/12
JORIETT?, Margaret 12* (B), Thomas J. 9, Lyndia 7
BLACK, Guardian Ann 45 (B), Nancy 20, Alfred 13, Christopher C. 8, Henrietta 6, Patsey A. 4
OREAR, John D. 68, Mary 42, Benja. F. 21, John D. jr. 16, Sarah A. 14, James M. 12, Davis O. 10, Louisa 7, Emily 4, Rebecca 3
HENSLEY, William 78, Lucy 74, Lucinda 44, Milton 26, Lucy Ann 13
BOTTS, Seth 55, Adaline 16, Seth jr. 14, Emily 12, John 7, Susan 48 (B), Seoney 10 (B,f), Nancy 6 (B), Robert 5 (B)

Schedule Page 82

MCCULLOUGH, Daniel 42, John W. 17, Susan 15, Eleanor E. 12, Emily 10, William 5, John 44, Hannah 32
MCDANIEL, Alexander 23*, Sarah Jane 22, Mary _. 60
TAPP, Mary 84*
RICKETTS, H.? 50 (m)*, Mary 46, James 24, Louis 16
HELMS, Peter J. 3*
WILSON, Joshua 65 (B), Patsey 65
LUDLOW, William 30*, Elizabeth 24, Martha 5, Samuel 3, Catharine 1
ARTHUR, Elizabeth 17*
WELCH, Francis 31, Hannah 26, Daniel 4, Nancy Jane 2
THOMAS, Robert 68, Mary 64, Eermy? C. 21 (m), W. A. 19 (m), Robert A. 17, Sarah A. 14, Edith 12, James 9, Thomas H. 6, Mary H. 5

1850 Census Montgomery County Kentucky

TURLEY, James 38*, Julia 28, Mary 8, Amos 6, Henretta 4, Samuel 28
TAYLOR, Zachariah 3*
RAMEY, Randall 40* (B)
RUSSELL, Chilton 47*, Caroline 30, George 12, Sarah 10
PARISH, Frances 17*
MITCHELL, Strother D. 25, Ann E. 21, Mary E. 2, Richard A. 3/12, James W. 9, A. T. 7 (m)
BERKLEY, John 65*, Ann 47, Sarah 40, Elizabeth 26, Samuel 33, George W. 25
STEPHENS, William 42*, Mary 36, Henrietta 6/12
HADEN, Polley 65* (B)
RAMEY, Thomas 22* (B)
JAMESON, William O. jr. 69, Amanda 64, Elizabeth 24, W. J. jr. 22 (m), Eliza 19
JAMESON, John H. 34, Catharine 28, Elizabeth 11, Charlott 9, Louisa 7, Will A. 4, Ellen 3, Marium 5/12 (f)

Schedule Page 83

JONES, John H. 35*, Verraby 25 (f), Eleanor Jane 12, William M. 8, James J. 5
HANKS, Armilda 1*
MCCULLOUGH, Margaret 22*
BONDURANT, Eliza 15* (B)
WILSON, Simeon 27, Sarah Jane 24, Mary J. 11/12, Joseph 29
SMITH, Joseph 55, Mary 58, James M. 24, Mary 18
MCCORMICK, Adam F. 29*, Susan 29, Mary 2
BLEVINS, Mary A. 14*
HANKS, Jackson 33, Catharine 32, William F. 8, Mary E. 6, Joseph M. 2, Olevia 6/12
WADE, Carter P. 27*, Cordelia C. 23, Nancy 2, Permelia 5/12
STARK, Benja. F. 25*, Thomas 22, Issabella 90 (B)
MAUPIN, Wilson R. 46, Mary 45, Daniel 22, John 18, Spencer 8
CHEATHAM, Jerry 24, Celinda 23, John D. 1
SADDLER, John R. 29, Nancy Jane 23, Amanda 4, Lucinda 1
KEMBER, Jepthah 50, Nancy 48, Thomas 23, Martha 21, Susan 17, Reuben 14, Samuel W. 11, John 7
LOCKRIDGE, Lucy A. 42, Charles 19, James 17, Mary Jane 14, Andrew 9
KEMPER, J. V. 39 (m), Mary 38, Mildred 14, Emily 12, Sandford 11, Mary 10, Jacob 9, Washington 8
MYRES, Aaron 44, Martha 21, T. M. 18 (m), R. W. 14 (m)
CHEATHAM, Firman 28, Louisa 25, Mary 8, Mildred 5, John 2
REDMAN, William F. 51, Phebie Jane 60, George W. 18
COONS, Permelia 30*, Elizabeth 12, John F. 4

Schedule Page 84

WADE, Nancy 56*
WADE, Robert 37*, Frances 32, Ida 11, John B. 9, Thomas 4, Robert jr. 2
RICHARDSON, James 30*
BARKER, Hezekiah 25*
KIRK, Susan 53, Martin 30, Mary A. 25, John W. 24, James A. 19, Sarah A. 13
ADAMS, Martin 60, John 28, James 26, George Q. 14, Mildred 12, Nancy 60

1850 Census Montgomery County Kentucky

ROSE, John 45*, Eliza A. 36, Ally Jane 17, Serena A. 14, James F. 15, Sarah E. 9, Robert 7, John W. 7, Chilton R. 1
PLEAK, Jane 54*
CHANDLER, Federick 80 (B), Macalinda 50
NORTHCUT, Benjamin 63*, Elizabeth 63, Benja. jr. 24
JOHNSON, Julia A. 29*, Benjamin 11, Harrison C. 10, Thornton M. 8
INGRAHAM, Abram 68*, Elizabeth 62, Melinda 27, Eliza Jane 25, Patsey A. 23, Thomas_. 25, William C. S. 22, John C. J. 21, Matilda 19, Mary E. 5
CONNER, William H. 87*, William 53
EANS, John C. 60, Ann 50, Nancy 30, Maria 27, Elizabeth 25, Elkana? 21, John 18, Russell 14, Rebecca 11
EVANS, L. D. 24 (m), Margaret 24, Sarah Jane 1
FOSTER, Jeremiah 56, Nancy 53, Thomas 31, Georgian 23 (f), George W. 18, Amanda 12, William M. 20
STOKELY, William 25*, Lucindia 28, Achilles 6, John S. 11/12
BROCK, Rebecca 15*
KONKRIGHT, Cevilla 11*
DAWSON, John A. 29, Caroline 20, John W. 1
GARRETT, Sandford 55, Nancy 50, Mary 22, JAmes 16, Sarah 14, Sandford jr. 11, Joseph 9

Schedule Page 85

STEVENS, Walker 40

1850 Census Owsley County Kentucky

Schedule Page 277

WILLIAMS, William 53*, Sophia 41, John L. 24, Catharine 21
LEES, Joseph 19*
WALKER, Joseph J. 38, Jane 19
JUDD, Rowlin 66, Frances 64, Leander 25, Frances 26, Allace 23, Maria 18, Elvira 17
DICKERSON, A. R. 33 (m), Emely 24, William 4, Letitia 3/12
HAMBLIN, Francis 45*, Martha 40, Daniel 19, Statira 11, Benjamin 8, Henry 6, James 4, Allice 3
MITCHEL, E. C. 28 (m)*
CHASTAIN, S. A. 25 (m)*
BRANDENBURGH, Lewis 19*
MOORE, A. J. 32 (m), Sarah 28, A. H. 10 (m), Virginia A. 9, John H. 4, Andrew 1
THOMAS, James 22, Jalina 17
HUNDLEY, Samuel 36, Elizabeth 34, James 14, Clarinda 12, Theophilus 7, John 5
TRUIT?, William 34, Elizabeth 30, Elias 8, Wilie 7, Jackson 5, Sarah 1
REYNOLDS, Richard 30, Isey 23 (f), Rebeca 1, William 3/12
HAMELTON, C. W. 26 (m), Silvester 28 (f?), Nancy 6, Mary 3, Martha 10/12
LUTES, Henry 28*, Eveline 21, Francis 3, Mary 1, Mary 80
SMITH, Richard 8*, Huston 6
WARD, Jelson 77*, Rutha 66, Lawrance 25, Rebecca 22, G. W. 12 (m)
PRITCHET, Elizabeth 27*, Bonepart 5
BRANDENBURGH, Samuel 23, Sally 20, William 6, Debby 4, Susan 2, Martain 1/12
MOORE, James R. 28, Jane 29, Ann 1
ROSE, James B. 32, Henrietta 32, B. F. 9 (m), Robert G. 7, John A. 5, William H. 4, Allison 2 (m), Martha 2/12

Schedule Page 278

REESE, David*, Susan 27, Sarah 5, Jane 2
STEWART, Daniel 26*, Matilda 18
JOHNSON, Jessee 41, Elendor 38, Elizabeth 16, Rachal 13, Robert 10, Shedrick 7, Jessee 4, Elendor 6/12
GABBARD, Jacob jr. 36, Elizabeth 28, Henry 5, William 3, Margaret 1, Henry sr. 82
MORRIS, William jr. 32*, Mary 28, Izabell 7, John 5, George 3, Thomas 1
BEATY, Robert 40*, Elizabeth 38, William 18
REYNOLDS, Richard sr. 48, Mima 43, John 19, LEvi 15, Eli 14, Elihue 10, Jeremiah 6
BOWMAN, Elizabeth 62
HACKER, Julious 46, Elizabeth 36, Theophilus 12, Sophia 10, William 7, Mary 5, Plesant 3, Joseph 1
HACKER, John 25, James 27
WILSON, Polley 27, Elizabeth 6, Phillip 2
SANDLIN, Ezekiel 34*, Sarah 27, Elizabeth 9, Lewis 7, William 4, Martha 1
HUNTER, Nathan 22*
HAMMONS, James 26, Lucindia 22, Jane 1
PHILLIPS, Mason 50, Mary 40, Margaret 19
PONDER, Joseph 45, Nancy 46, Catharine 16, Josephus 15
HAULKMAN, Nathan 26, Sally 20, Mason 1/12
PITMAN, Starling 35*, Nancy 34, Elizabeth 14, Darias 12, Sarah 10, Penell 8 (m), Easter 6, John M. 4
STEWART, Henry 19*

1850 Census Owsley County Kentucky

Schedule Page 279

RATLIFF, Reubin 28, Sarah 24, Mary 5, Lucinda 4, Silas 9/12
HACKER, Isaac 24*, Ester 24, America 1
MOELIR, William J. 21*
PONDER, Zadoc 29, Sally 21, Nancy 3, John 1
DAUGHERTY, Evin 34*, Caroline 33, Nancy 12, Levi 10, Josiah 8, JAckson 5, Jane 3, John 3/12
STEWART, John 23*
BUCKNER, William 20*
HUNT, Johnathan 81*, Patsey 82
WILLIAMS, Louisa 18*
GILBERT, Patsey 50, Abner 20, Elizabeth 14
MCCOLLUM, Daniel 43, Lydia 43, David 21, Henderson 20, Elizabeth 17, Perry 15, Luther 13, Rachal 11, Daniel 9
MCCOLLUM, George 38, Sally 34, Easter 15, David 11, Robert 9, William 7, Nancy 5, Jane 2
SPIVEY, James 41, Mary 38, Sarah 21, Patsey 19, Charles 16, Nancy 14, Julious 12, Susan 10, Russell 7, Theophilus 5, Margaret 3, Isaac 1
BOWLING, Graham 23, Nancy 19
BREWER, Ambrose 35, Susan 33, Lucindia 13, John 11, James 9, William 7, Elizabeth 5, George 2
VON, John 29, MArtha 23, Hamilton 8, Elizabeth 6, Martha 4, Jane 1
CENTERS, George 23
GILBERT, A. B. 35 (m), Martha 32, John 9, James 6
BOWMAN, WilliM 35, Nancy 32, Ibby 11 (f), Elizabeth 8, Susan 6, Henry 4, Cornelious 2

Schedule Page 280

COMBS, Harvey 34, Elizabeth 36, Susan 18, Elizabeth 11, James H. 8
JOHNSTON, Samuel jr. 40, Rachal 32, George 17, Anderson 18, Henderson 16, Levi 12, Hijah 8 (m), Elizabeth 5, Nancy 1, Jane 17, Samuel sr. 69
SMITH, Alexaner 39, Mary 40
GABBARD, Isaac H. 45, Jane 39, Elizabeth 20, G. W. 19 (m), James B. 18, JAcob 16, Michial 14, Polley 12, Able 10, Abijah 8, Rachal 6, Margaret 4
STAPLETON, Plesant 28*, Ann 29, JAmima 7, Harrison 6, Lewis 5, Russell 4, Letcher 7/12 (m)
JOHNSTON, Andy 21*
STAPLETON, Mason 22, Fanney 24
STAPLETON, Edward sr. 65*, Sally 87
WOODS, Rebecca 53*
STAPLETON, William 42, Eliza 40, Nancy 13, Granvill 11, William 9, Elizabeth 7, Martha 5, Edward 3, Emiley 1
BOWLING, William 23, Edy 22 (f), James 3, Elizabeth 7/12, Polley 18
GABBARD, Henry jr. 43*, Polley 36, Noah 12, Beckey 10, Elizabeth 7, Nancy 4, John 2/12
WOODS, Ibby 18 (f)*
WOODS, John 34, Viney 17
MOORE, Elias sr. 60, Cealia 54, Easter 20, Lydia 17, Richard 15, William 12, Plesant 9
YORK, William 38, Elizabeth 76, Fanney 41, John 22, Lear 11 (f)
TRUIT, Reddin 31*, Elizabeth 34, Sarah 3, William 1

1850 Census Owsley County Kentucky

Schedule Page 281

YORK, Elenor 10*, Jeremiah 8, John 7, Alford 5
GABBARD, Peter 50, Susan 39, Elish 15, Henry 13, Margaret 12, John 10, Mathias 8, Lewis 6, Thomas 5, William R. 4, Sophia 1
COMBS, Harden 55*, Nancy 55, Caroline 24, Pop 18 (f), Perlinia 16, Sally 3
MARSHAL, Joseph 22*
SIZEMORE, Smith 36, Matilda 31, Abijah 11, William 9, Elizabeth 6, Armicia 5, Silvania 1
THOMAS, Jesse 34, Martha 29, Sylvania 6, Elizabeth 4, Margaret 8/12
ISAACS, Godfrey 25, Lydia 28, Emlia 3, Kisia 1, Frances M. 3/12
AMBROSE, M. M. 45 (m)*, Ann 43, William 20, Jane 17, John 15, Henry 13, Marion 6 (m), Mary 9, Barton 4, Martha 2
MCDOWEL, Nathan 53*, Easter 52
MORRIS, Henry jr. 22, Elizabeth 22
STAPLETON, William 63*
HART, Jane 47*, John 8, Henton 5
ABNER, William 43, Jane 42, Susan 17, David 16, Mary 14, Easter 12, Nancy 10, Lewis 8, Elizabeth 6, William O. 4, Sophia 1
STRONG, Daniel 36, Rebecca 34, John 14, Phillip 12, Alexander 10, Maria 8, Susan 6, Sally 4, William 2, Plesant 2/12
COMBS, John 58, Elizabeth 47, Samuel 18, John 16
PETERS, John 36, Margaret 29, Lilbourn 12, Susan 10, Anderson 8, Sarah 6, William B. 4, John P. 1

Schedule Page 282

ABNER, Elisha 67*, Nancy 61, Elizabeth 41, Willis 26, Enoch 20
BAKER, Matilda 23*
ABNER, Lacy 39 (m), Cintha 31, Maria 12, Polley 10, Nancy 10, John 8, Manerva 6, Catharine 3, Elizabeth 2/12
BUENES?, William 50, Rachal 41, Perry 21, Andy 20, William 18, Lydia 16, John 15, Wilie 14, Zilphy 10 (f), Nancy 9, Sally 7, Joicey 5, Franklin 2
CARMACK, John 30, Ibby 24, Polley 6, William 4
BAKER, Andy sr. 38, Polley 34, John 15, Nancy 13, Robert 11, Louisia 8, Jackson 6, Martha 3, Lydia 1
BAKER, Robert jr. 50, Hettia 32, Robert 19, Nathan 17, George 13, Lucinda 11
COUCH, William 35, Dougherty 30 (f), Sampson 14, Elijah 12, John 10, David 8, Polley 6, Henry 4
SANDLIN, Lewis 25, Nancy 28, Willis 4, Mary 3, Zilphey 6/12
SANDLIN, James 52, Zilphey 44, Joicey 29, Andy 18, Robert 16, James 14, Catharine 12, Niram? 10 (m), Hugh 7, William 4, Jackson 8, Rachel 3
BAKER, John H. 55, Lucindia 44, Susan 20, Chiney 21 (f), Wilie 18, Robert 16, Catharine 14, Ester 13, James 12, Granvill 10, Isaac 7, Jane 4, Massey 1 (f), Jacient? 1 (m), Mary Ann 6

Schedule Page 283

BAKER, Robert sr. 76, Catey 73 (f), Andy 23, Polley 24, William 1, Margaret 21
GABBARD, Wilson 30, Susan 29, Jackson 10, Willis 7, Polley 5, Elisha 2
GABBARD, John 37, Margaret 26, Peter 13, Rebecca 10, Julious 7, Benjamin 5, Isaac 2
FOX, John 60, Hannah 22, Fountain 6, Marinda 4, Malinda 2, George 22

1850 Census Owsley County Kentucky

FOX, Isaac 26, Almarinda 16, Mary 1
ABNER, John sr. 56, Lewis 18, William 16, Elisha 13, John 7
WILLIAMS, James 32*, Lucindia 32, Matilda 6, Polley 5, Eliza 4, Nancy 1
CLARK, Anderson 16*
STAPLETON, Edward 42, Nancy 38, Sarah 7, Edward 5, William 4, Elizabeth 1
REYNOLDS, Plesant 59*, Rebecca 55, Plesant 27, Thomas 19, Elias 21, Henry 16
WILLIAMS, Nancy 27*
FROST, Elizabeth 20*
WILSON, Lemuel 53, Elendor 42 (f), Polley 24, Sally 22, Johnathan 20, John 17, Marinda 15, Elizabeth 9, Mahaly 7, America 3
WILSON, Phillip 40, Polley 38, William 13, Robert 10, America 8, Phillip 6, Debby 4, Jackson 3, Plesant 1, Samuel 8/12

Schedule Page 284

REYNOLDS, Moses 36, Nancy 32, Mary 13, Henderson 11, Lewis 9, Malan 7 (m), Martha 5, Elias 3, Plesant 7/12
COMBS, William 32, Elizabeth 35, William 13, Malan 10 (m), Mahaley 8, Moses 6, Sebo__ 3 (m), Edward 1
REYNOLDS, Wesley 34, Nancy 37, Perlinia 13, Meridia 12 (m), Elizabeth 10, Martha 9, Emeline 7, Gilbert 3, Mary Jane 1
PERKEY, William 21, Martha 25, Lavenia 5, John 11/12
SMITH, Elias 21, Elizabeth 22
PENNINGTON, Levi 28*, Rachal 25, Elihue 6, Jane 5, Preston 4, Elendor 2, Martha 6/12
CORNWALL?, Elijah 17*
TURNER, John C. 30, Mary 27, Minetree? 9 (m), Rachal 8, Nancy 6, William 4, Able 2
TURNER, Tempey 54, Pleasant 20, Cealia 18, Rachal 14, Nancy 12, Salley 75
PENNINGTON, Able 53*, Elizabeth 56
MCGEE, Nancy 20*, Lucretia 3, Robert 1
SMITH, Joseph 23*
ERLEY, William 41, Lucey 33, Preston 7, Debby 6, Hiram 3, Louisia 1
CUNNIGIM, Wilie 38, Rachal 30, Sevralus 9 (m), Lewis 7, Jane 6, Clark 5, Elizabeth 3, Nancy 1
REESE, John 28, Debby 30, Joseph 1
THOMAS, Elisha 34, Rachal 22, Simeon 5, Byned 3 (m), Susan 1
THOMAS, Betsey 45, JAckson 23, Vincient 21, Arnold 18

Schedule Page 285

2PENNINGTON, John 23, Sarah 25, Mary 4, Able 3, Elias 1
2FROST, Simeon 48, Jane 32, Elias 17
2ANGELL, Ephram 45*, Susan 32, Viney 12, Andy 9, Elizabeth 5, William 3, Emley 1, Hamelton 17
2RICHARDSON, James 13*, Reney 11 (f), Sally 9
2COOPER, William 42, Nancy 35, John 8, William 7, Rachal 6, Thomas 4, Martha 2, MArgaret 1, Lucretia 2/12
2BOWMAN, John 33, Susan 25, Edard 12, Ann 10, Henry 8, William 6
2BOWMAN, Thomas 29, Marium 26 (f), Minty 8 (f), Polley 6, Daniel 4, Jackson 2
2MOORE, John jr. 25, Polley 23, America 1

1850 Census Owsley County Kentucky

2BOWMAN, Henry 38, Elizabeth 36, Perlinia 9, Sturgis 6, Tipton 4, Elizabeth 5/12
2EVANS, Edward 46, Sarah 44, Martha 20, John 11, Henry 9, Delila 7, Elizabeth 2
2GIBSON, James E. 36, Bethany 32, William 10, Manervia 8, Chiney 6 (f), Letitia 4, Zacrey 1
2ANGELL, James 43, Elizabeth 43, Wilie 18, Lucindia 20, Squire 15, America 12, Lizabonner? 10(f), Josephine 7, Littleton 6, Wade 4, James 2
2HAMELTON, Harvey 40*, Mary 41, Amanda 16, Paulinia 13, Sidney 10 (m), Mary 7, James 4
2AGEE, Elenor 22*
2WILSON, Gaberrel 23*

Schedule Page 286

COMBS, Clabourne 46, Sally 46, Mecey 19 (f), Kenneth 17, Tinsley 13, James 3
PETERS, James 25, Eliza 22, Elizabeth 4, Ann 7/12
MOORE, James 45, Jane 43, Madison 13, Nancy 12, Joseph 11, Hardin 10, Henry 7, Martha 5
MOORE, James jr. 20, Emley 20, America 3/12
BRANDENBURGH, Joseph 46, Rody 39, James 21, Samuel 18, Henry 17, Joseph 16, Simpson 15, Jaley 13 (f), Hardin 12, Joel 10, Jeptha 9, Jackson 7, Thomas 6, Sophia 5, Felix 2, Patrick 5/12
MOORE, John 28, Lucretia 26, Debby 6, Edmond 4, Elizabeth 2, Morton 5/12
SMITH, Robert 49, Polly 39, Henry 18, William 16, Mary 14, Beckey 10, Nancy 7, Stacey 2 (f)
STEWART, Isaac 33*, Catharine 24, Eliza 7, William 5, Sarah 2, James 4/12
CORUM, William 22*
WILSON, John jr. 26, Vicey 30 (f), Alford 3, Edmond 1
WILSON, Alford 21, Debby 23, Mary Ann 1
WILSON, Davis 49, Beckey 48, William 19, Plesant 16, Sarah 13, Mary Ann 9, Davis 4
LUNSFORD, Hiram 45, Lydia 44, Maria 21, Cealia 18, Elisha 17, Hiram 14, James 12, Sally 9, George 4, Permelia 2
SEAL, Joseph W. 32, Martha 24

Schedule Page 287

MARION, Anderson 22, Sarah 22, Henry P. 1
FRYER, Timothy 28, Mary Ann 23, William 4/12
ROBERTS, James 49*, Ann 53, Madison 19
SMITH, Polley 13*
BRANDENBURGH, George H. 48*, John 18, Samuel 16, Angelina 14, Nancy 13, Abreham 12, Henry 10, Delinia 9, David 7, Taylor 5
WILLIAMS, Jacob 21*
CONGLETON, Isaac 45*, Delinia 35, John 14, James 12, Joseph 11, Margaret 9, Martha 7, Thomas 6, Isaac 5, Samuel 2
MAHAFFY, William C. 24*
PORTER, Eli 43*, Hiram 8, Ann 6, William 4, Lewis 2
COLE, Margaret 28*
CHAMBERS, Gideon 35, Mary 24, Rachal 4, Elijah 6/12
THOMAS, Isaac 43*, Elizabeth 28, William 9, John 7, Nicholas 5, Nancy Ann 1
PHARRIS, Mary 15*
SMITH, Asa 30, MArgaret 25, Polley 13, Algin 6, Henry 25
THOMAS, James 40, Polley 28, Ann 6, Presley 5, Amanda 4, America 6/12

1850 Census Owsley County Kentucky

SMALLWOOD, James 41, Caroline 32, Emeline 14, William 12, James 10, Mary 8, Edmond 6, Randolph 4, John 1
DUNEWAY, Benjamin 53, Elizabeth 46, David 26, William 23, Derney 19 (f), Thomas 17
JOHNSTON, William 58, Catharine 32, Russell 32, Sally 19, William 15, Julia Ann 5, Narcissa 1
STEEL, Andrew 49, Nancy 46, William 24, Andrew J. 22, Jane 19, Sally 18, Daniel 17, Henry 14, John 15, Lucindia 12, Rebecca 10, Martha 6, Mary Ann 4

Schedule Page 288

HALL, Aaron 32, Margaret 25, William 6, Harvey 3, John 1
KINDRICK, John F. 33, Lucey 25, William 2, Thomas 4/12
HALL, Harvey 36*, Mary 25, Sarah 6, Aaron 4, Joseph 2
WHITE, Shelton 16*
THOMAS, Joseph 27, Elizabeth 23, Lucy 74
MCGUIRE, James 77*, Dianah 76, Felix 49, Prisciller 43
MANN, America 19*
DUNEWAY, William 22*
VANDERPOOLE, Abraham 27, Amandia 25, Isaac 7, Jane 4, William 3, Margaret 1
MCGUIRE, James jr. 45*, Eveline 36, Greenville 12, Felix 10, Susan 6, Caroline 5, Fletcher 3, Bascom 1
GOOSEY, Reney 19 (f)* (B)
THOMAS, Anthony 36, Perlia 30, David 13, Jessee 11, Henry 8, James 7, Anthoney 4, Felix 3, Sebastian 1
SNOWDIN, James 29, Lucy 19
SHOEMAKER, Jacob 34, Catharine 32, Daniel 8, Woodford 7, Jane 5, Andrew 4, William 1
NOLAND, Henry 37, Nancy 36, Thursey 18, William 16, Sally Jane 14, Didenia 11, David 9, Nicholas 5, Margaret 3
BUSH, Harvey 44, Margaret 25, James 15, Enoch 14, Nancy Jane 12, Robert 10, Margaret T. 6, An 4 (f), Perlinia 1

Schedule Page 289

SNOWDIN, Greenbury 25, Amelia 20, Marion 1 (m)
ADAMS, Squire 23, Nancy 22, Daniel 5, Mary 1
CUNDIFF, William 40, Virginia 27, Theophilus 15, Elizabeth 14, Lucy 11, Margaret 1
LUTES, John 54*, Prisciller 50, Buford 21, Christopher 16, James 14, Joseph 11, William 7
ROBERTS, Lucindia 16*
TREDWAY, Thomas 29, Demanda 26, Caroline 2, Prisciller 1
SPENCER, Gulman 26, Pheby 25, Jacob 6, Jane 4, Matilda 2, Elizabeth 3/12
JONES, Mathew 30*, Jane 26, Andrew 9, John 5, Robert 3, Elizabeth 1
EASTIS, Sarah 5*
LUTES, Charles 24, Lucindia 24, Nancy 2, John 1
GRAY, Thomas 47*, Lucey 45, Thomas 17, Sarah 5
TUT, Michial 20*
WERTMAN, John 21*
HEYRONIMUS, Samuel 62*, Sally 43, Frank 28, Demirious 18 (f), Geoge 16, Thomas 12, Emelia 9
DAVIS, Charles 26*, Nancy 20, James 4, Charles 2
WHITE, Whitfield 66*, Judith 63, Zerildia 30, Reubin 28, Robert 22

1850 Census Owsley County Kentucky

COCKRELL, Jaulia 38*, Zerildia 3
CHANDLER, Samuel 40*, Nancy 42
CALLEMEASE, George 9*
CAMMEL, Stephen 40*, Elizabeth 34, Debby 14, Darcus 12, Elizabeth 5, Lucindia 2
CABLE, Casper 24*
EVERSOLE, John 65, Betsey 63
EVERSOLE, Hiram 22, Polley 22, John 4, Armenia 2, Susan 3/12

Schedule Page 290

GIMMERSON, John 55, Elizabeth 44, Ann 17, Martha 15, Jane 13, P. Elizabeth 11, Patience 9, John D. 7, Marion 5 (m)
SPENCER, William T. 36*, Mima 29, James 10, Ann 7, Malachia 5 (m), Mark 2
COUCH, Catey 19 (f)*
STAMPER, John A. 42, Lucindia 35, James A. 17, Armitia 13, Preston 11, Pheby 7, Levi 4, John 1
STAMPER, Larkin 37, Edy 31 (f), Ann 13, James 10, William 8, Mary 7, Joseph 6, Nancy 5, Sandford 4, Elisha 3, Rebecca 2, John 3/12
CHILDERS, Joseph 28*, Leviner 22 (f), John 2, JAne 4/12
STAMPER, William 15*
CHILDERS, William 62, Winney 56, Cealia 20
CHILDERS, John 38, Polley 34, Richard 16
OLIVER, James 38, Nancy 24, James M. 15, Samuel 4, Walker 2, George 6/12
STAMPER, James 29, Maria 31, Emlia 9, William 7, Marcus 6, Sally 5, Lucindia 3, Susan 2, James 1
WIENICK?, Michal 39*, Elizabeth 39, Jane 17, William 15, Eliza 13, Catharine 11, James 9, Sarah 7, Leander 4, Samuel 1
STURGEN, Eli 18*
STAMPER, Joel 64, Polley 65
LACEY, Perry 28, Beckey 23, Sally 4, Ellen 2, John 1, Milton 23
SALBEY, James 55, Elizabeth 58, Elizabeth 24, James 22, Judy 17

Schedule Page 291

SOULSON, Stephen? 33, Peggy 29, Jane 11, Isaac 8, William 5, Nancy 1
SALBEY, Archibald 25, Elizabeth 19, Nancy 2, William 7/12
SALBEY, William 32, Cealia 24, Caroline 6, Elizabeth 5, William 3, Isaac 2
COCKRUM, James 28, Emlia 24, John 7, James 4, William 2, William 23, Martain 21
COCKRUM, William 56, Elizabeth 54, Miles 17, Elijah 15, Daniel 12
BAKER, Benjamine 44, Polley 44, Alexaner 20, Elizabeth 18, Sarah 16, Beckey 8, Amanda 7, Virginia 10/12
HOBBS, Absalom 25, Lila 20, Mary 3, Jobe 3/12
HOLLAND, Jackson 26, Sally 26, Jane 10, Elisha 8, Larkin 7, Martain 6, Elizabeth 5, John 4, Ellcaney 2
WRIGHT, Elish 50*, Ann 48, Marion 16 (m), Lucindia 12, Lewis 10, Hamelton 7
KING, Nancy 18*
WIERMAN, John 32, Elizabeth 21, Silvester 3
JOHNSON, James A. 25, Martha 20, Hamelton 5, Marion 2, Jerome 4/12
SPENCER, Joseph sr. 48*, Delilia 47
CALVIN, John 11*

1850 Census Owsley County Kentucky

DEATON, Joseph 16*, Daniel 14, Izabeler 81 (f)
ALLEN, Thomas 22*
SPENCER, John 35, Arminda 37, Henry 13, Hiram 12, Fereby 9, Allen 8, Benjamine 5, Elijah 3, Alexander 1
SHEFFIELD, George 40, Tamer 36 (f), Sarah 13, Susan 10, James 6, George 4, Margaret 1

Schedule Page 292

CARTER, Asa 36, Mahaley 27, LEwis 14, Emlia 12, Ann 7, James 4, Joseph 3, Asa 8/12
KILBERN, George 29*, Rachal 25, Martain 7, Polley 3
SPENCER, John 16*
NOBLE, John 43, Sally 39, Cealia 16, Peggy 14, Polly 12, Elizabeth 10, Ira 8, Isom 5, George 1
KING, Isam 24*, Polley 16
MCDANIEL, Anney 37*, John 4
HALL, Lenard 36, Angeliner 36 (f), William 12, Green 10, John 8, Thomas 5, Nancy 4, Elizabeth 1
RAULEY, James 58, Anny 58, Nancy 18, John 13
CARROL, Noland 35, Druister 25 (f), William 9, Daniel 7, John 5
SPARKS, Harvey 26, Nancy 23, Polley 5, Jane 3, Sarah 5/12
HARRIS, Mathew 35, Cealia 33, Samuel 14, Susan 12, John 7, Lizaney 5, Luzaney 3, Benjamine 1
WHITE, Marue? 26 (m)*
DUFF, Alexander 21*
CABLE, Joseph 26*
SPENCER, John D. 42*, Phebey 42, Nancy 18, Joseph 16, Charlotey 13, John 12, David 9, Isaac 7, George W. 4
SPARKS, Tobias 20*, Peggy 18
SPARKS, Ephraim sr. 68, Charlot 72
SPARKS, Ephraim jr. 30, Sarah 26, Ann 11, Nancy 8
BOOTH, William 63, Sarah 36, John 18, Mithias? 16 (m), Clarinda 12, Jamima 9, Marlain 11 (m), Lucindia 8, Rachal 4, Isaac 2

Schedule Page 293

BOOTH, William jr. 22, Elizabeth 17
WIATE, John 70, Jane 50, Catharine 20, William 14, Calvin 12, Alson 12, Noah 10, Jane 6
SPENCER, William 37, Nancy 37, Amelia 18, Elizabeth 15, James 12, Presley 9, John 11, Jamima 8, Hannah 6, Lawson 4, William 2
SPENCER, Hiram 26, Jane 23, Sarah 3, Ann 1
SPENCER, Allen 26, Arminda 23, Hezekiah 3, Kenis? 1 (m)
SPENCER, Elijah 30, Delilia 30, Elizabeth 12, Fereby 10, Jamima 8, James 6, Catharine 5, Ellen 1
WISMAN, Michial 34, Izabella 32, John 15, Moses 13, Mary Ann 11, James 9, Hiram 8, Elizabeth 6, Lavinia 4, David 1
SHOEMAKER, James 40, Pheraby 40, Delia 15, Tempey 13, William 11, Viney 9, Louisia 6, Lydia 4, Sarah 8/12, Phebey 19
SPENCER, Joseph 38, Isabeller 30, John 12, Nicholas 11, Simeon 9, Henry 7, Brantley 3, Lucindia 8/12
FULKS, Thomson 27, Elizabeth 23, Henry 2, Isaac 6/12
COX, Jacient 40 (m), Lydia 41, Joel 15, Sampson 11, William 8, Branton 6, Lydia 4, Polley 12, Ambrose 2

- 388 -

1850 Census Owsley County Kentucky

Schedule Page 294

COX, Branton 69*, Nancy 72
PROFFIT, Stephen 26*, Nancy 16
STAMPER, Joel 23, Polley 23, John 3, William 2
SPENCER, Alexander 25, Emelia 23, Gulman 3, Allen 1
MASTERSON, Patrick 90*, Mary 47, Phebey 14, Lucey 12
SPARKS, John 21*
SPENCER, Moses jr. 28*, Lucindia 24, Wesley 9, Elizabeth 7
HOBBS, Isaac 22*, Hezekiah 21
SPENCER, Moses sr. 64*, Elizabeth 57, Brantley 21, James 18, Jamima 16
ROBERTS, Joseph 22*
SPENCER, Strong 24, Nancey 20, Luraney 3, Lucindia 2
HENTON, Thomas 28, Silvania 27, Mary 7, John 1
PROFFIT, Eli 24, Sarah 50, Jeremiah 20, Pheby 18
SNOWDIN, David 63, Margaret 53, Marion 23 (m)
CONGLETON, William 49, Nancy 39, Eustrius 14 (m), Lavinia 12, Archillus 11, Derias 8, William 6, Robiney 3 (f)
MANN, John 52*, Pattey 48, Martain 29, Samuel 24, Jackson 20, Joseph 19, Thelix 16, Prisey 16 (f), William 14, James 12
GILBERT, Catharine 20*
VANDERPOOLE, Joseph 26, Lavinia 26, John 6, Mary 4, Patsey 1
RATLIFF, Peter 20, Telithey 18, Berry 1
MCGUIRE, John 39, Elizabeth 36, Jane 9, William 7, John 4, Ann 2
CRAWFORD, Simson 25, Elizabeth 17
ANDERSON, Frank 23, Jane 20, America 5/12

Schedule Page 295

EVANS, Silvester 19, Lucindia 21
CARREL, Thomas 49, Sarah 55, Elizabeth 20
SEAL, John K. 41*, Therese 30, Mary Ann 10, James F. 8, William 6, Margaret 4, Martha 2/12
REYNOLDS, William 24*
JUDD, Frankey 28*
ISAACS, Elijah 42, Sally 30, Silvester 18, Preston 16, Henderson 9, Stephen 7, William 5, Isaac 4, Jacob 2/12
MOORE, William sr. 64*, Debery 60 (f), Izabeller 24, William 20, Henry 15
COLE, John 6*
PETERS, Elisha 50*, Ann 50
REESE, William 24*, Elizabeth 18
PRICE, Adam 52*, Polley 47, Almanda 17, Caroline 13, Jane 11, Silvania 6, Henry 5, Nelson 3
PRADINGTON, Mary 4*, Ellen 2
BURNES, John 52, Louisia 37, John 14, Abijah 12, Meredith 7, Ann 10, Brice 5, Mary 2
BOWMAN, R. S. 30 (m), Polley 25, Elizabeth 5, Silvaney 3, Cornelious 1
BOWMAN, Levi 24, Elizabeth 23, Elizabeth 4, Cornelious 3, John 1
CUNNIGIM, Samuel 30, Sally 25, Ellen 5, Margaret 4, Jane 3, John 1
PRICE, Elias 31, Cealia 26, Elizabeth 6, PErlinia 4, Jane 3, Stephen 6/12
MOORE, Lewis 22, Margaret 23

1850 Census Owsley County Kentucky

SLAUGHTER, James L. 27*, Lucindia 20
HAM, Ellen 28*
SMITH, Thomas 30*
MOORE, John sr. 70*, Judy 70
BALES, John 31, Nancy 20, Susan 4, James 3, Daniel 1

Schedule Page 296

ANGLIN, John 36*, Cleracy 31, Huldy 14, James 12, Catharine 9, Elizabeth 6, Mason 7, Nancy 3
PHILLIPS, Persar? 29 (m)*, Jamima 75
MORRIS, George 58, Elizabeth 48, Emley 19, Silvaney 17, John 13, Elizabeth 11, George 9
REYNOLDS, Joseph 24*, Easter 22, James 3, Henry 1
BLAIR, Samuel 26*
SCHOOLCRAFT, Michial 59*, Patsey 54, Overton 32, Polley 27, Madison 17, James 15, Nathan 11
HOBBS, Elizabeth 8*
BOWMAN, Jacob 22, Elizabeth 21, Margaret 4, Emeline 3, Nelley 60
MCKINNEY, James 30, Easter 34, Izabeller 10, James 5, Jane 1/12
ROBERTS, William 36, Cealia 25, Perlinia 7, William 6, Cealia 2, Edy 1/12 (f)
BULLOCK, John C. 37, Isabeller 34, Jane 12, Irminey 10 (f), Amanda 8, Thomas 6, David 4, Mary 4, William 2
BOND, William 72, Sarah 57, Fletcher 19, Oliver 17, HArriet 16
MCQUINN, Hamelton 25, Nancy 24, Stephen 1, John 22
GABBARD, Cornelious 28, Mary 27, Hiram 8, Elizabeth 6, Susan 4, Meridey 1 (m)
WILSON, Sally 72, Beckey 38, Lear 17
WILSON, Robert 33*, Sally 32, John 12, Jane 9, Robert 7, Daniel 4
FLANERY, William 25*
WYNE, Elkaney 32 (m)*
SMITH, James 17*

Schedule Page 297

WILSON, Jessee 32*, Betsey 30, Polley 9, John 7, Delaney 5 (m), Robert 3, Ibby 1
BOWLES, James 17*
BRUMMIT, Benjamin 44*, Elizabeth 44, Walter 18, William 16, John 12, Josiah 10, Polley 8, Jane 5, Louisia 3
RADER, Jane 78*
MARCUM, James 40, Betsey 36, Alferd 16, Polley 14, Richard 12, Hiram 4, Phillip 1
DURHAM, Isaac 49, Elizabeth 41, David 19, John 18, Joseph 21, Martha 22
HUGHES, M. C. 44 (m)*, Elizabeth 40, Newton 18, Margaret 16, Franklin 12, M. C. 2 (m)
HELLEN, Sarah 9*, Clara 9, Mary Jane 6
FOSTER, James 26*, Frances 17, Mary 1
RECTOR, Thomas 23*, Mary 19
WOODS, Samuel 25, Sally 21, Joseph 2
ANGLIN, Martain 23, Debora 22, Isaac 1
WEST, Buford 32, Jane 34, Louisia 9, Lenard? 7, Polley 6, Isaac 5, Thomas 3, John 1
WILLIAMS, Moses 50, Nancy 48, Nathan 21, James 18, Lydia 15, George 10, Nancy 8, Absalum 5
AMBROSE, Moses 68, Mary 50

1850 Census Owsley County Kentucky

RECTOR, Eli 31, Sarah 26, Vianey 8 (f), Franklin 3, Lydia 1
HEARD, Rober 20, Emley 23
REESE, Joseph 23, Judy 22, Elijah 8/12
WOODS, John 65, Tobithey 66, Thersey 16
MARCUM, Thomas 75*, Polley 70, Phillip 26, Nancy 8

Schedule Page 298

HACKER, Betsey 18*
RECTOR, Phillip 26, Tildey 18 (f), Frankey 5/12 (f)
WILDER, William 40, Sally 38, Larkin 26, Henry 15, Woodson 12, Malinda 8, Silas 6, Jane 5
SPIVEY, Charles 39, Elizabeth 35, Moses 14, Sarah 12, Julious 9, Mary 6, Ann 4, David 1
ANGLIN, Isaac 26, Martha 27, Jane 2
MCHONE, John 34, Margaret 34, Nancy 10, Martha 8, Chaney 5 (f), John 4, Robert 2
BROWNING, John 29, Alsey 27, Joseph 2, George 9/12
HALKMAN, Absalum 40, Jois 40 (f), Allen 18, Polley 21, Henry 16, Levi 13, Sarah 12, Darcas 10, John 7, Jane 5, James 2
WORD, John 41, Milley 41, Daniel 18, Abbert 16, Susan 11, Joseph 8, John 6, Mars 4 (m)
AMBROSE, Joseph 27*, Rachal 27, Alsey 4, Nancy 3, John 9/12
BISHOP, Nancy 30*
HEDRICK, William 44, Tempey 37, Anney 15, John 11, Samuel 5, Elizabeth 2
MAHAFFEY, Ela 43 (f), Hiram 21, Malinda 25, Jessee 18, Ann 17, Elizabeth 15, John 13, Martain 11, James 9
CRAWFORD, John 35, Maria 21, Adaline 8/12
STRONG, Isaac 40, Judy 42, John 18, Margaret 12, Jane 1

Schedule Page 299

GABBARD, Jacob sr. 51, Susan 49, Hiram 25, Abreham 22, Margaret 19, William 13
PHILLIPS, Thomas 48, Edy 50 (f), Polley 25, Ansel 21 (m), Debby 16, Theophilus 13, Mary 11, Elizabeth 9
BAKER, Joannah 28, Jane 10, George 8, James 6, Sarah 3, John 3/12
ALFORD, Charles 49, Margaret 30?, Charles 15, William 12, George 7, Elizabeth 3
ALFORD, James 26, Emiley 24, Jane 1
COLE, Jahue 38, Elendor 35, Jahue B. 7, James R. 5
GOOSEY, David 27, Susan 20, Ellen 2
MOORE, James 30, Matilda 25, Nancy 14, Rodey 12, Daugherty 10, Elizabeth 9, Mary 8, Simeon 6, Cornelious 3, Martha 5, Lucey 1
MOORE, Cornelious 37*, Jestine 34, MArtha 11, William 9, Debby 7, James 5, Harvey 3, Eli 5/12
TURNER, Zeperiah 28 (m)*
EVANS, Huram 24*, Nancy 20, Hiram 2, Margaret 6/12
STAMPER, John 12*
NEWMAN, William 26, Jane 22, Frances 4, Leanner 2 (f)
TINCHER, Rebecca 51, Eli 30, William 21, Elias 17, Hose 16, Henry 12, Price 6
NEWMAN, Harrison 33, Susan 24, William 10, Elias 8, Henry 6, Balinda 2
NEWMAN, John 23, Susan 23, Daniel 3, Mary 1
HAMELTON, Owen 22, Anney 25

1850 Census Owsley County Kentucky

Schedule Page 300

MAYS, William 56*, Polley 50, William 15, Peggy 13, Rudey 4 (f)
EASTERS, Jessee 14*
MAYS, Andrew 25, Rachal 23, Giles 5/12
CARTER, Sollimon 29, Lucy 26, Susan 5, Elizabeth 2
GORDIN, Kennedy 56, Polley 36, Elizabeth 14, Susan 11, Mary 6, Lucy 2
GROSS, John 40, Polley 40, Polley 17, Margaret 14, Emeline 12, Susan 7, Sarah 5, Elizabeth 1
NEWMAN, John 60, Lear 55 (f), Morris 23
EVANS, Edy 45 (f), John 21, Jessee 16, Henderson 15, Henry 12
BOWMAN, Absalum 28*, Maria 26, America 5, Frances 4, Squire 2
GROSS, America 10*
EVANS, Hiram 27*, Polley 28, Edy 5 (f)
STAMPER, William 19*
MOORE, Elias jr. 36, Sally 34, William 10, George 9, Nelley 8, Margaret 6, James 4, Alexander 2
BREWER, Howel jr. 29, Mary 29, Moses 6, Susan 4, Salley 46, Nancy 20
THOMAS, Cornelious 50*, Margaret 44
KELLEY, Simson 7*
ROSS, George 30* (B)
KENDRICK, Jane 22*
ROSE, Robert sr. 70*, Easter 59, Hezekiah 13
CHAMBERS, William 23*, Rebecca 22, Ester 4, Rachal 2
ROSE, John 22
MOORE, Edard 40*, Manervia 39, Rachal 16, Judy 14, Elizabeth 12, Jackson 10, Ann 8, Javirs? 6 (m), Margaret 2
CARPENTER, Preston 9?*
POLE?, William __*, Matilda __, Martha 7, Alexander 5, Lucy 4, Nancy 2, Aaron 2/12

Schedule Page 301

COLE, Mathew 76, Catharine 68, Susan 26, Mary 2?
YIREY, John 50, Julia 27, Thomas 21, John 15, Oliver 14, Amos 13, Marcallis 12, Elizabeth 11, Calvin 4, Mary 2
WILSON, Edwin 25, Easter 19, Robert 6/12
POLE, John 50, Margaret 44, Jarome 18, William 14, Elizabeth 11, Charles 8, John 5, Mary 2
MCGUIRE, James 45, Elizabeth 31, Anderson 20, Hiram 18, Lewis 17, Henry 15, John 10, Margaret 9, Archibald 7, Christena 4, Tabitha 2, Everly 6/12 (f)
ABNER, John 37*, Chesner 25, Mary 10, Elisha 8, William? 6
MCJUNCHIN, W. 60 (m)*, Mary 60
CLARK, Wm. 34, Tabitha 36, Sarah 17, Anderson 15, Edward 13, Rachael 12, Henry 10, Martha 8, Lucinda 6
BOWLING, Sanford 45, Catharine 44, Martin 18, John 17, Ira 15, Alfred 14, Abraham 5, William 3, Patterson 3/12
BRANDENBURG, Samuel 50*, Sally 28, Jonathan 10, Joseph 7, Nancy 5, Henry 3, Samuel 3/12
ISAACS, Elisha 25*
ROSS, Levi 34 (B)*, Sally 28, Mary 7, William 5, Hiram 2
BURNS, John 14*

1850 Census Owsley County Kentucky

WHITE, Aqquilla 58?, Sally 48, Elizabeth 23, Thomas 22, Polly 18, Shelton 16, Francis 14, Sally 12, Cultis 7 (m)

Schedule Page 302

MORRIS, Henry 40*, Caroline 36, Louisa 13, William 11, Levi 8, Jacient 4 (m), John 2
ALLISON, John 22*
CLARK, Elhannon 37, Rachael 40, Henry 14, William 13, Tabitha 9, Hiram 8, Edwin 5, Emily 4, Annity 12 (B)
MORRIS, Jancent? 34 (m), Jane 30, John 14, Sally 12, Job 10, William 8, Hannah 5, Thomas 3, Lear 1 (f), John N. 21
MORRIS, Robert 53*, Susan 53, Minta 14
ROBERTSON, John 24*
FRANCIS, Lemuel 65*
STRONG, Alexander 62, Ann 38, Ibly 16 (f), Marinda 14, Rachael 12, Sally 10, Thomas 8, Ellander 6 (f), Cordelia 4, John 2
KELLY, William 32*, Nancy 22
BADFORD, Israel 26*
NOE, Martin 18*
PETERS, William 22*, Emily 17, Harden 10/12
WHICKER?, Zachariah 21*, Martha 22, Elizabeth 1/12
MCGEE, Robert 38*, Easter 34, Polly 18, Lucretia 15, William 12, Hannah 11, George 8, Andy 5, Nancy 3
WILLIAMS, Nathan 20*
ROSE, Robert jr. 26*, Fanny 21, _ee 1 (m)
WILSON, John 19*
HAMILTON, Speed 26 (m), Lucinda 26, Margaret 3, Easter 2, George 1/12
PHILLIPS, Asa 24, Margaret 23, James 4, Jamima 2
STRONG, Henry 36, Polly 28, Amanda 17, Isaac 15, William 13, Samuel 10, Jane 11, James 8, Alexander 7, Rachael 5, Catharine 4, Taylor 2, Patsa? 75 (f)

Schedule Page 303

SMITH, John 38*, Lucy 30, Mary 11, William 9, Sarah 7, Milton 5, Harrison 2, George 2/12, Margaret 16
KELLY, Speed 21*
ALLENBAUGH, William 38, Delilah 34, Sally 11, Andrew 9, Dolly 7, James 5, Peter 5, Nancy 4, Lucy 1
BRANDENBURGH, James 42*, Nancy 34, Castio? 12 (f), Lucy Ann 10, Nancy 8, William B. 6, James B. 4
ROSS, Sanford 15* (B)
FIREY?, Caroline 28*
WALTERS, Baily 46*, Elendar 45, Henry 17, Baly 13, Elizabeth 12, Alexander 8, Andrew 6
HATTING, Thomas 47*
ANGELS, James jr. 22, John 21, Leanney 14 (f)
HILTON, Stokely 24, Aurraney 21, Ellandor 2, Serrilda 5/12

1850 Census Owsley County Kentucky

BOWMAN, Elisha 39, Mahulda 35, Jane 17, Cornelius 15, Elizabeth 13, Simpson 11, Ann 9, William 7, Mary 1
REESE, Marion 24 (m), Nancy 27
SMITH, Frank 34, Lucretia 35, Samuel 14, John 12, Sarah 9, Meshick 6 (m), Evelina 4, Alexander 2
MORRIS, William 55*, Margaret 50, Rachael 18, James 15, Thophelus 13, Nancy 10, Henry 7
JASPER, William 23*
SIZEMORE, Anderson 24, Minerva Q. 25, Ann 3, John 4?/12

Schedule Page 304

REARD, William 55, Rebecca 47, John Q. 28, William N. 15, Sebina 11, George 9, Tunsel 7, Joseph 4
BOWLES, William A. 63, Lucy 45, Thomas 23, Hughs 21, James 19, William 14, Sarah 8, Margaret 5
MORE, Elizabeth 50, Bresley 19, Sutton 17, Nicholas 14, Hiram 10
MORRIS, Hardin 24, Sarah 22, Elizabeth 1, Nancy 1/12
WILLIAMS, James 56, Susan 56, Elijah 21, Lucy 17, Juda 12 (f), William 7, Susan 3
WILLIAMS, William 29, Patsy 23, Becky 1, Isaac 3
BAILY, Hiram 22, Catharine 50, Sarah 16, Sally 19, Robert 25, George 19
MCGUIRE, Ansen? 24 (m), Easter 23, Marticia 66
COLE, John 23, Jessee 21
COLE, Barton 24*, Emily 21, Polly 3, William 1
EVANS, Palina 22*
CRAWFORD, A. G. 24 (m)
COLE, Ose 45 (m), Palina 34, William 17, John 14, Speed 12, Marticia 10, Thomas 6, Orson 9/12
COCKRAM, John 44?
STONE, William 23, Susan 22, Nancy 3, John 1
ADDISON, Isaac 29, Mary 26, Polly 4, Adam 1
BRICE, Price 34*
SHORT, John 24*
SEAWART, Robert 28*
JONES, John 28
TURLEY, Mitchell 28, Rebecca 23
HELTON, James 21, Matilda 30, Margaret 10, John 8, William 6, Dema 5, Elizabeth 3, James 2

Schedule Page 305

HOWERTON, Jacob 40*, Rebecca 41, Sereena 20, Mary 18, William C. 16, Nancy 15, Horry 12 (m), Alfred 10, Duke 7, John 3
BAKER, William 23*
KASERD, David 25*
TREADWAY, E. B. 26 (m)*
BLUNT, Charles 58, Jane 53, James 27, Charles 26, George 22, Mariah 20, Lafayette 18, Louisa 14, William 14, Gustavus 8
DANIEL, John M. 38*, Mary 30, George 19?, Caroline 18, Thomas 14, Sarah 12, Lucinda 10, Henry 8, Laura 4, Scott 2/12
ROSS, Emily 18* (B)
HURLEY, James 41, Jane 38, Lewis 12, Davis 10, Hannah 16, Hester 16, John 8, Elizabeth 5, Lavina 2
MIZE, N. J. 45 (m), Rebecca 44, William 18, John 16, Milton 12, Martha 9, Butler 5, Harrison 3

1850 Census Owsley County Kentucky

MCGUIRE, Hiram 47*, Frances 48, Archibald 25, Berry 23, James 21
WILER, Samuel 30*
WALKER, William 31, Jane 25, Julea 7, Milton 5, William 1
SMALLWOOD, William 34, Margaret 26, James P. 7, William 4, John 8/12
TREADWAY, William 50*, Margaret 43, Mary 13, Simpson 12, Susan 10, Hellen 8, Laura 4, William 3
ALFORD, John 23*, Welton 15
HURLEY, Spencer 20*
SYLABAR, Thomas 25*
SHARER, Albert 25, Narcissa? 23 (f)
ORCHARD, David 65* (B), Jane 45, Jane 6, Cornelius 4, Sarah 2

Schedule Page 306

JENKINS, Clemins 25* (B)
CORNETT, Lewis 35, Elizabeth 27, John 9, Maticia 7, Sueney 5 (f), Dick 1
FULKERSON, William M. 28, Peter 62, M. E. Sine 45
SPARKS, William 34, Jane 25, Benjamin 6, Jane 2
CORNETT, John 62, Hetty 59, Sarah 20, James 16, David 14
MARSH, Eastis 48*, Mary 37, Laura 17
LEWIS, James 45*
FOCKNER, John 25*
SMITH, William 24*
PEBWORTH?, Stephen 33, Matilda 30, Squire 21
HAMMOND, James 26, Martha 17, Nancy H. 9
MIZE, William 36*, Caroline 26, William H. 4
SMITH, Josa? 12 (m)*, Sylvania 8
GRAY, James 32*, Sally 38, Angeline 14, Hiram 12
HATTEN, Thomas 35*, Irvin 8, John 6
GUN, John 23, Ellen 17
WILLIAMS, George S. 33*, Ermine 27, John 1
RILLY, Rachael 20*
DAVIS, Joseph 51, Harry 55
WHITE, John 33, Polly 27, Aquilla 10, Rachael 8, Martha 4, Jane 3, Elizabeth 1
NORMAN, James 57*, Perrina 35 (m), Owin 12
MASCAL, Stephen 7*
PITMANN, Micager 38 (m), Norma 36, Susan 19, Sally 15, Nancy 13, Jessy 7, William 11
KELLY, John 24, Herodia 55 (f)
FULKES?, Leapold 35, Lucinda 26, Henry 6, Ann 3, Joseph 9/12
FRILEY, Benjamin 36, Elizabeth 32, Catharine 12, Mary 11, Caroline 8, Butler 6, Stephen 4, Rachael 1

Schedule Page 307

HOWARD, George 31*, Martha 26, Thomas 6, Ann 3, Susan _/12
SMITH, Pleasant 18*
HOWARD, Clement 23*, Nancy 26, Mary 10/12
EDENS, Jeptha 15*
ASHCRAFT, James 23, Nancy 21, Nancy 1

1850 Census Owsley County Kentucky

BATLY, Samuel 56*, Patience 38, James M. 14, Jane Collar 12, Ann 10, William 7, Elizabeth 4, John 1
REYNOLDS, John 25*
PENNINGTON, Peter 28, Patsy 28
DAY, Newberry 25, Dianna 20, Robbert 2/12
REDVINE?, William 22
PETTICORD, John 25
EVANS, Warren 22, Robert 24
PORTWOOD, Ennis 25, Elvina 24, Joseph 5, Samuel 3
JONES, A. C. 30 (m), Elizabeth 18, Roena 3, Mary 1
MCGUIRE, Archibald 71*, Catharine 36, Elizabeth 13, Joseph 12, Thomas 11, Jonathan 9, Christopher 8, Francis 5, Franky 4 (f)
WARD, Rebecca 50*
PORTER, Thomas 39, Polly 35, Eli 15, Manerva 14, Sally 12, Benjamin 11, Lucinda 9, Martha 6, Rachael 2, William 1, Thomas 87
JACKSON, B. F. 29 (m), Estels? 25 (f), Mary 8, Elisha 6, Julia 3, Zacharia 2
MAYS, Andy 47, Margaret 40, Elizabeth 16, Rebecca 13, Sarah 10, William 8, Patric 5, Anir? __ (f), Isa? 19 (f), Margaret 10
MORE, James W. 42*, lucinda 41, Zacharia 21, Margaret 19, Just___ 18 (f), Susan 14, Lucinda 12, Sarah 10, Mary 7, Tabitha 4, Jane 1

Schedule Page 309

WILLIAMS, Alfred 30*
PONDER, Joseph 18*
ROSS, Herod 43 (B), Manerva 35, Polly 12, Elizabeth 11, Castira 9, Henry 8, Nancy 7, Rachael 3, Eliza 8
ROACH, Sally 45, Anderson 23, Kitty 17, Armina 12
PATRICK, James 24, Polly Ann 19, Margaret 1, Joanna 65
TINCHER, William? 42, Margaret 38, Mary 22, James 20, John 18, Emerine 16, William 14, Eliza 12, Polly Ann 10, George 8, Randolph 6, Milly Ann 2
ASBELL, H. H. 39 (m)*, E. Jane 31, Sally 11, John 8, Henry 6, Catharine 5, Susan 3
JOHNSON, Timothey 20*
SMALLWOOD, Randolph 70, Rachal 65
WILLIAMS, Mason 30, Prisciler 30, Sandford 10, Sarah 7, Mary 5, Wilie 2
HAMILTON, Henry 35*, Dicey 35, John 12, Elizabeth 10, Preston 8, Mary 5, Jefferson 3, Anderson 2
KERLY, Kiz 23 (f)*
PHILLIPS, B. F. 44 (m), Susan 41, John 21, Nancy 19, Zackeriah 17, Silas 15, James 13, Eliza 11, Benjamine 9, Susan 7, Rody 5, Thomas 3, Henry 2
FRILEY, Martin 34, America 26, John 11, Thomas 9, Caney 8 (f), Mary 7, Sally 5, Henry 3, Benjamine 1/12
EATIS, Ansel 23, Cealia 23, Lavina 1, Sarah 1/12

Schedule Page 310

BEATY, Decator 29*, Emley 23
GIMERSON, Robert 23*
ROBERSON, Jane 11*

1850 Census Owsley County Kentucky

GUM, William 31*, Lucinda 26, Mily 11 (f), Michial 9, John 7, William 4, Lucinda 1, Susan 16, Berry 21
JONES, Samuel 25*
PETTICORD, John C. 22*
ETENS, Wesley 25*
MALONEY, William 49*, Pernelia 36, John 17, Greenbury 13, Jeremiah 11, Daniel 8, Susan 6, Luraney 4, George 3, Nancy 8/12
BARRART, John 62*
ASHCRAFT, John 18*, Nancy 16
BOND, Henderson 30, Sally 25, Jane 6/12
FRANCIS, Morgan 26*, Sarah 40, James 18, Manerva 20
BALLARD, Malinda 24*, James 2, Peter 4/12
LANE, Melvin 2*, Clarinda 4/12, Fidella 4/12
ASHCRAFT, James 47, Elizabeth 48, Nancy 20, John 18, Sally 10, Harriett 13, William 7
HEFFLEBEAN, Susan 51, Alesey 24 (f), Perlina 18, Creca 15, Thomas 3
BUSH, William 31, Sarah 20, Coleby 7, Lucy 5, Charles 4, Joseph 1
ELLIOTT, Martin 53*, Elizabeth 50, Mary 24, Joicy F. Ann? 19
SHOEMAKER, William 38, Nancy 39, Louisa 9, Mary 6, Phillip 4, Nancy 2
SHOEMAKER, Pheba? 60, Andy 24, Elisha 17, Elijah 19, Elizabeth 15
EASTIS, William 50, Jane 50, Pracilla 23, William 20, Margaret 16, Frances 14, Almyra 12, Boderick 10, Sally 9, Mary 7

Schedule Page 311

SANDLES, Hiram 50, Susan 40, Elizabeth 14, Joseph 12, Lucinda 10, Cynthia 7, Susan 5, Hiram 3
CHRISTIAN, William? 25*
SHOEMAKER, Andy 24*
KINGKADE, Socretas? 24 (m), Elizabeth 28, Ciladeth? 2/12(f)
KINGKADE, Edward 52*, Mariam 47, Miles 18, Samuel 17, Anna 15, Margaret 13, Malisaa 10, Edward 8, Scott 2
PLUMES, Samuel 96*
DUCKHAM, Thomas 64*
KINGKADE, Lycurgus 20, Malinda 20
PROFFIT, Jerry 59, Phoeba 53, Phoeba 22, William 21, Samuel 18, Ira 10, Polly 3, Rosy 1
PROFFIT, John 25, Sally 21, James 2, William 1
PROFFIT, Stephen 43, Rebecca 35, John 8, Nancy 5, Jeremiah 3, Elizabeth 2
BURTON, John 26*, Nancy 28, David 1, Mason 6/12
MORRIS, James 8*
SHAWLEY, William 23, Sophia 24, Dolly 3, Elizabeth 1
ROWARK, Carter 26, Polly 22, John 2, Dicy 1
GILLEN, Levi 35, Malinda 33, Sarah 14, Phoeba 13, Hiram 11, James 9, John 5, Polly 2
WRIGHT, Hiram 34, Susan 32, Polly 14, Celia 12, Jane 10, Phoeba 5, Susan 2
SHAWLEY, Allen 30*, Matilda 28, Milla 4, Elias 3, Henry 3/12
DUNE, Rachael 10*, Washington 10
SEBASTIAN, Nelly 31, James 11, Matilda 8, John 6, Jacob 3

1850 Census Owsley County Kentucky

Schedule Page 312

MCGUIRE, William 37, Polly 32, John 19, Archibald 16, Dillard 9, Henry 7, Thomas 5, Pracilla 4, Margaret 1
BUSH, Luallen? 47 (m), Martha 29, Elis 13, John 7, William 6, Mary 4, Elizabeth 3, James 1
MCGUIRE, John P. 34*, Jane 35, Gilleann 9, Houston 7, Dedema 4, Crittendon 2
COLE, William 27*
VANDERPOOL, Jacob 25*
HOWARD, Phillip 38, Finno__ 32 (f), Lancy 12 (f), Susan 10, Mary 8, Lucy 6, Jordan 4, Ellen 1
PERRY, William 30, Elizabeth 25, Henry 8, Nancy 7, Washington 2
HALL, John 45, Polly 35, Micager 21, Mary 20, Rachael 17, Elizabeth 14, John 13, Milly 10, Rebecca 6, Arminta 2
ACRES, William 50, Delia 45, Clifton 24, Ann 23, William 21, John 20, Martha 18, Catharine 16, Milton 14, Smith 12, Stephen 7
SPARKS, Isaac 50*, Jane 55, Sylvester 25
DUNAWAY, John 27*, Perlina 24, Elizabeth 4
ROBERTS, Allen 34, Peggy 30, Hrom? 13 (m), John 10, Isaac 5, Margaret 3
CATCHUM, John 25, Hally 50 (f), Marietta 20, Jane 14
BACON, A. J. 34 (m)*
KING, William H. 37*
HAMILTON, John 43*
HAMONDS, John 92?*
ACRES, Nancy 2*

Schedule Page 313

CAMBELL, Hugh 35*
HAMMONDS, Thomas 50, Allis 49
YORK, Alferd 35, Sally 33, Martica 6, William 10, Luticia 3
ROBINSON, Catharine 26*, Malowur? 4 (f), Mahala 2, Hugh 1, Maria 18
CARTER, Caroline 27*
JOHNSON, Rody 56, Betsey 39, Ellen 2
BUTCHER, Isaac 40 (B), Phereby 40, Christeny 16, Jane 12, Mary 8, Fanney 4, Isaac 2, Frank 2, Hannah 1
AKERS, Patsey 53, William 33, Hardin 29, John 21, Patsey 18, James 16, Henderson 13, Eveline 10
BAKER, Henry 39, Henerietta 32, John 19, James 5, Elizabeth 1
HOWEL, Gains 33, Mary 29, Elias 10, Samuel 9, Mary 6, Rebecca 2, Henriettia 2
ROACH, Thomas 25*, Mary 25, William 3, Stephen 2
ESTIS, Vicey 18*
DURBIN, John jr. 25, Sarah 21, Joseph 5, James 4, Mary 1
DUKE, John 18, Margaret 17
DURBIN, Edward 32, Patience 26, Margaret 9, Elizabeth 8, Nancy 7, Malinda 5, Perdellia 3, Joseph 1
ARMSONG, John 19*
SIMONS, Mary 28*
LYNCH, Elizabeth 12*, Sidney 10 (m), Edward 8
DURBIN, Joseph 51, Margaret 51, Joseph 18, James 21, Ambrose 13, Ann 11
DURBIN, John 41?, Ann 30, Serilda 18, Ambrose 16, John 15, Caroline 10, _____ 8 (m), Susan 6, Abraham 5, Elizabeth 3, Julia 1

- 398 -

1850 Census Owsley County Kentucky

Schedule Page 314

PATRICK, William 40, Nancy 30, Harrison 6, Hu__ 4 (m), Dolly 3, James 1
BRANDENBURG, Joseph 81, Delilah 79, Elizabeth 34, Bethy 31
BRANDENBURG, John H. 48*, Debby 36, Hardin 15, Elijah 12, Ansel 9, Samuel 7, John 5, Delinas 2
LACKEY, James 21*
SMITH, Richard 32, Margaret 22, Henry 7, Hiram 5, John 3, Lucy 1, Lutitia 10
HAMILTON, Patrick 65*, Sally 55, William 24, Wesley 21, Elisha 18, Randolph 15
STRONG, Sally 45*
HAMILTON, Thomas 27, Polly 25, Sarah 5, John 4, Rhoda 3, Margaret 1
MAYS, Giles 34*, Polly 30, Jane 7, William 6, Samuel 4, Rachael 1
ISAACS, Alkney? 70 (f)*
GRAY, John 40*, Dolly 37, Lavinia 15, Armana 12, Ann 8, John 5, Artimecey 3
FRUSSELL?, French 38*
HATTENS, Polly 80*
NEWTON, Allen 38*, Rachael 35, _alton 12 (m), Nancy 10, Illy 8 (f), Godfrey 7, Deanna 6, William 5, John 4, Sally Ann 2
FOLLDS?, Harvy 35*
SHARP, Martha 25, Jackson 4, Elijah 1
ESTIS, Feldin 25, Emily 20, Mary 3, Sally 10/12
GRAY, Charles 36, Minerva 30, Polly 14, Betsy 12, Nancy 10, William 6, Eliza 1

Schedule Page 315

PORTWOOD, Solomon 60, Betsy 55, Eliza 30, John 8, Betsy 6, William 4, Sarah 1
CROWFORD, Joseph 42*, Nancy 38, Elihu 16, Levi 14, Josiah 12, Polly 9, Nancy 7, Marcus 6, Marshall 4, John P. 2
CRATER, Lavinia 16*
ISAACS, Samuel 27, Eliza 18, Nancy 2, Mary 9/12
BRANDENBURG, Nancy 45*, David 15, Catharine 12, Louisa 10, Jackson 8, Joanna 3
FARMER, James 25*, Matilda 17, John 5/12
CREECH, Elijah 38*, Nancy 26, Sally 8, John 6, Martha 4, Mary 6/12
HARRIS, George 19*
CREECH, Gilbert 30, Rebecca 30, Betsy 6?, Sally 4
RADER, George 45, Polly 48, Sally 26, Jane 24, Henry 23, Elizabeth 19, Polly 21, Roderick 13
YOUNG, John 48, Sarah 37, Hiram 18, Julius 16, Pleasant 13, David 10, James 8, Lucinda 5, Elizabeth 2, Nancy 5/12
ROBINSON, David 50, Nancy 45, William 22, Susan 22, James 18, Polly 12, Minerva 10, Elizabeth 8, Henry 6, Drusilla 1
RAMSEY, Garret 41*, Delight 35 (f), Mary 16, John 15, Zaddock 13, Job 11, Robert 9, Henry 7, Mary 5, William 2, Sarah 7/12
HALCOM, Mary 81*
BOWLES, Anderson 27, Emily 22, Mary 5, Lucy 4

1850 Census Owsley County Kentucky

Schedule Page 316

GILBERT, Ezakies? 31 (m), ane 23, James 4/12
PHILLIPS, Abram 24, Betsy 30, Joel 13, Polly 12, William 10, John 8, Charles 5, James 3, Harvy 2
PHILLIPS, Hardy 45, Elizabeth 40, Mima 20, Austin 19, William 15, Charles 13, John 11, Mary 9, Martha 7, Nancy 4, Clara 1
SMITH?, James 35, Jane 36, Sarah 12, Martha 10, Polly 8, Eda 7, Nimrod 6, James 4, Simpson 3, Elizabeth 1/12
MORE, Jessee 30, Elizabeth 35, William 8, Emily 5, Lewis 4, Cornelius 2
BAYLS, James 30, Sally 25, Nancy 6, Malinda 4, John 3, David 1
CULTON, William J. 33*, Martha 32, Charles 9, James 7, Mary 5, Permelia 4, William 1, John 31, Nancy 19
ALLSUP, Martha 21*
HELLARD, John 25*
HORN, Isaac 31, Mary 30, Elizabeth 11, Frances 7, John 4, Martha 8/12
HAMMONDS, Mary 56, Franky 23 (f), Arther 17, Cerlestia 14, Jefferson 13
ANDERSON, Jessee 41, Betsy 41
ANDERSON, Jacob 34, Margaret 28, Henry 6, Laura 4
ANDERSON, William 49, Nancy 47, William 20, James 17, Mary 15
HUNT, James 22*, Nancy 22, Malinda 3, Mary Jane 8/12

Schedule Page 317

ANDERSON, Abijah 12*, Isaac 9, Francis 6, Mack 4
ANDERSON, Jessee K. 24, Martha 17, Nancy 6/12
MORGAN, Mark 38, Mary 28, Jane 9, Adam 6, William 4, Alfred 1
LEE, Andrew 40, Sarah 40, Polly 10, Mahala 14, David 9, Catharine 8, Nancy 5, William 7/12
FERRINGTON, William 34*, Peggy 22, Sally 4, Sally 50, Gilbert 21, Polly 16, Sarah 14, John 12
SUKER, Lewis 19*, Calvina 16
SUKER, James 26, Betsy 23, Catharine 5, Sarah 2, Jacob 80
WOODS, William 35, Nancy 25, Henry 10, Joseph 8, Elizabeth 6, John 4, George 2
CHANDLER, Larkin 27, Peggy 24, John 5, William 4, Noah 1
CALLAHAN, Mack 23, Lucy 22, James 1
CALLAHAN, Ezekiel 39, Polly 22, Becky 5, Robert 3, Martha 1
HERD, Elijah 28, Nancy 19, James 4
DAVIDSON, Robert 28, Nancy 26, Samuel 6, Rachael 4, Chaney 2 (m), Reniz? 62 (m)
DAVIDSON, Hansford 24, Becky 22, Katty 3 (f), Ellen 2, James 6/12
RADFORD, Richard 58, Polly 58, Polly 18, Stephen 20, Tilda 15, Celia 14, Pollyann 14, Nancy 14, Stephen 5, Julius 5
RADFORD, Nancy 29, Betsy 21, Malissa 5, Stephen _

Schedule Page 318

RADFORD, Sally 30, Sylvania 9, Vica 22
RADFORD, Nathaniel 37, Richard 14, Fanney 13, Elizabeth 11, Jessee 8, Mahala 4, Phoeba 3, Nancy 1
RADER, Henry 41*, Susan 38, William 16, John 11, Martha 6, Mary 5, Sarah 4/12
PONDER, Betsy 26*

1850 Census Owsley County Kentucky

RADER, John 37, Jane 37, Adam 9, Henry 8, Ellen 7, George 6, John 5, Betsy 4, William 2, Mary 1
WOODS, Joseph 34, Patsy 26, Cynthia 4, Catharine 2, William 1
SPARKS, Robert 28, Mary 24, Isaac 4, Theresa 3, Daniel 1
ANGLIN, James 67, Jane 64, Henry 19
SIMPSON, John 36, Jane 30, John 8, Patsy 6, Polly 5, Bosly 2, Dilly 6 (f)
SMITH, Charles 28, Margaret 25, James 7, Isom 5, Jane 3, Susan 2, Nancy 7/12
ROBINSON, S. J. 42 (m), Suky? 32 (f), George 5
PENNINGTON, James 51, Catharine 41, Calaway 20, Mahala 18, Mary 16, Sarah 11, Edward 9, John 5, Nancy 4
MARCUM, Sewel 34, June 26, John 6, Peter 4, Thomas 3, America 2
WICKER, Z. J. 21 (m), Martha 22, Nancy 4/12
EVANS, William 26, Elizabeth 25, James E. 3, George 2, William 1
CAPS, Daniel 32, Nancy 28, Louisia 6, William 4, Mary 2, Nancy 4/12

Schedule Page 319

WILSON, Rachal 55, Theophilus 18, Emeline 16, Anderson 14
WILSON, Alford 25, Ann 22, Sally 5, William 4, Lucey 3, Anderson 1
WILSON, Phillip 30, Jane 44, Harden 8, Cordelia 6, Thornton 4, Thomas 2
BALES, Hawkins 26, Elizabeth 22, Martha 1
AMBROSE, James 28, Malinda 28, Julius 6, Joseph 4, Sereney 3, Charles 1
BREWER, Howel 55, Polley 50, Nickolas 12, John 10, Vallentine 8, Morris 6, Emley 2
WILSON, John 37, Amey 36, William 12, Mary 8, Jackson 6, Nancy 2
GUM, Stephen 50, Eilzabeth 45, Lucinda 13, Margaret 12, Sally 10, Milley 8, Stephen 6, William 3
BOLES, William sr. 55, Elizabeth 50, Edy 22 (f), Garrardo 20
BOLES, Elbert 37, Nancy 35, James 16, Jeddy 14 (m), Eliza 12, John 8, Stephen 5, Thomas 5, Daniel 3
BOLES, William 21, Susan 17, Edy 1 (f)
MCQUEEN, Beaty 23, Edy 16 (f)
GUM, Abraham 24, Matilda 16, Stephen 8/12
PRICE, Charles 23, Louisia 22, Hully 3 (f), William 1
TURNER, Jessee 61, Cytha 56, Polley 38, Matilda 33, James 21, Nancy 16, Julia 15, Rachal 14, Abijah 12

Schedule Page 320

BOWMAN, Enoch 27, Alvirey 22 (f), Mary 3/12
RADNER, Clabourn 26, Jenina 24, Stephen 28, Elhannon 21, Noah 2/12
BOWMAN, Thomas 68*, Polley 60, Squire 24, Rodey 26, Martha 2, Maria 6/12
CAMPBELL, John 23*, Emiley 21
CALLIHAN, Wilson 37, Sally 36, Jeremiah 17, Mahala 15, Ridy 13 (f), John 11, Susan 9, Maria 4, William 2, Luther 5/12
RILEY, James 30, Ann 28, Rachal 6, John 4, Samuel 6/12
PETERS, Elijah 29, Margaret 29, Samuel 11, Elizabeth 10, Rebecca 7, John 5, Martha 3, Sarah 1
BOWMAN, Elizabeth 40, Cornelious 21, Elenor 19, Rachal 15, Robert 13, Nancy 9, David 5
SPEAR, A. J. 30 (m), Elizabeth 24, Jane 8, William 6, Walter 3, Martha 1
DOOLY, James 46, Mary 36, John 18, Mary 16, Jacob 13, George 11, Johnson 9, Elizabeth 8, Dolly? 8, James 7, William 5, Susan 1

- 401 -

1850 Census Owsley County Kentucky

BRAWNER, Luther? 39, Marid 35, Amelia 15, Lucinda 13, Mary Ann 11, Nathan 10, Elizabeth 7, Lutitia 5, Catharine 3, Daniel 3/12
MCDOWELL, William F. 30, Cyntha 23, Serenia? 5, James 3, Sophia 1
MCDOWELL, Irwin 25
GLOVER, Harrison 37, Mary 25, Henry 11, Frances 9, Sarah 3, Theodore 1

Schedule Page 321

THOMAS, Joseph 50, Anna 45, William 22, Jane 20, Polly 18, Mima 16, Elizabeth 14, Elisha 12, Eli 10, Levi 10, Elijah 8, Catharine 7, Rebecca 6
MCGUIRE, Benjamine 45, Dema 40, John 22, Margaret 20, Elisabeth 18, Gideon 16, Archibald 14, Schelton 12, Dema? 10 (f), Benjamin 8, Ibyan 7 (m)

INDEX

Index

ABBOT
  Abner 35 (GD-274)
  Louisa 15* (MT-6)
ABBOTT
  Aaron 44 (B) (CL-66)
  Eliza 26* (F-130)
  Eveline 42 (CL-66)
  Isabella 70 (B) (CL-69)
ABERNATHY
  George W. 40* (F-136)
ABNER
  Arzela 13* (ES-99)
  Elisha 67* (OS-282)
  John 37* (OS-301)
  John sr. 56 (OS-283)
  Lacy 39 (m) (OS-282)
  William 43 (OS-281)
  William 59* (MA-236)
ABNEY
  Allen 36 (ES-49)
  Clem 31 (m) (ES-49)
  Coleby 23 (ES-68)
  Daniel 28 (ES-48)
  Elijah 41 (ES-47)
  Liley 9* (ES-90)
  Littlebury 62 (ES-73)
  Madison 24 (ES-73)
  Paulina 16* (ES-81)
  Tucker 50 (ES-49)
  William 22 (ES-86)
  William 22 (ES-91)
ABRAHAM
  Hezekiah 63 (MA-260)
ABRAMS
  Gabriel 45 (MA-239)
  James 18 (MA-269)
  James 48 (MA-234)
  Joseph 38 (MA-231)
  Mary 43* (MA-253)
ACKMAN
  John 38 (F-116)
ACRES
  Nancy 2* (OS-312)
  William 50 (OS-312)
ACTON
  Francis 40 (CL-17)
ADAIR
  R. M. 25 (m)* (MT-1)

Robert 14* (MT-6)
ADAMS
  A. M. 25 (m) (MT-42)
  Abra 52 (GD-226)
  Andrew t. 27 (MA-200)
  Berryman 56 (ES-55)
  David 38* (ES-54)
  David C. 32 (ES-56)
  Dudley 31 (JE-58)
  Elizabeth 52* (F-121)
  Fielding 24 (CL-62)
  Fothergail 47 (GD-213)
  Frances 37* (F-153)
  Frankey 26 (f)* (CL-58)
  George W. 42 (JE-3)
  Giles 35 (MA-325)
  Israel 17* (F-199)
  Jackson 29 (ES-79)
  James 23* (F-186)
  James 29* (GD-232)
  James 36 (JE-64)
  James 60* (JE-41)
  James S. 26 (MT-42)
  Jesse 37* (ES-80)
  Jesse 68 (ES-53)
  John 31 (GD-270)
  John 49 (MT-62)
  John 60 (CL-62)
  John G. 27 (MA-294)
  John H. 36 (JE-39)
  John L. 39 (GD-286)
  John Q. 26 (CL-45)
  John Q. 37* (GD-284)
  John T. 22 (MA-285)
  John T. 34 (ES-73)
  Jones L. 40* (GD-246)
  Lewis 29 (CL-16)
  Martha 44* (GD-269)
  Martin 60 (MT-84)
  Mary 27* (F-116)
  Mary 50* (F-252)
  Mary 61* (F-122)
  Nathan 33* (ES-104)
  P. C. 29 (m) (GD-278)
  Peyton 52* (CL-73)
  Richard 33 (ES-104)
  Richard 39 (F-243)
  Robert 27 (ES-66)

Robert 60 (ES-63)
Robert 60 (MT-62)
Sarah J. 17* (F-171)
Sarah L. 11* (F-150)
Squire 23 (OS-289)
Stephen 33* (CL-27)
Tandy 23 (CL-30)
Thomas 37 (CL-62)
Thomas 38* (CL-44)
Thomas 44 (F-129)
Thomas 50 (MA-233)
W. B. 35 (m)* (GD-272)
W. S. 37 (m) (GD-276)
Walter 41 (GD-225)
Wesley 38 (GD-238)
Will 33* (GD-241)
William 29* (ES-68)
William 61* (CL-31)
William 64* (CL-44)
William 79 (ES-95)
William H. 20* (CL-28)
William R. 19* (CL-49)
Wm. 14* (F-165)
Wm. 32* (F-177)
ADDISON
  Isaac 29 (OS-304)
AGEE
  Ann 40 (MA-289)
  Elenor 22* (OS-285)
  James 32 (MA-211)
  John 30 (MA-321)
  Racheal 46 (MA-321)
  Robert 26 (MA-309)
  Sarah 53* (MA-309)
  Sarah 58 (MA-310)
AGIN
  Philip 26* (F-235)
AINSWORTH
  John 17* (F-226)
AKEBY
  Lott 38* (CL-64)
AKEN
  Gryza 74* (F-120)
AKERS
  Patsey 53 (OS-313)
AKIN
  Elizabeth 59* (F-128)
  Josaphine 28 (GD-266)

Index

AKIN
  Richard 17* (F-136)
  Saml. 27* (F-166)
  W. A. 37 (m)* (F-166)
ALBERTI
  Jno. Chs. 60 (F-230)
ALBY
  Fanny 9* (CL-33)
ALCORN
  John 49* (JE-18)
  Will 29 (GD-259)
ALDRIDGE
  Fanny 45* (CL-29)
  Honor 66 (f)* (CL-30)
  James 18* (CL-36)
  James 41 (CL-27)
  Joseph 20* (GD-261)
  Mary 55 (GD-279)
  Richard 48 (CL-24)
  Samuel G. 51 (GD-226)
  Squire 45 (CL-29)
ALDRIGE
  Noah 34 (CL-29)
ALEXANDER
  Amanda 11* (MA-254)
  Betsy 42* (MA-243)
  David 46* (F-120)
  Davy 30 (B) (F-229)
  Edmund 45* (B) (F-147)
  Eliza 17* (MA-321)
  Hiram 48 (CL-65)
  Isabella 68 (F-160)
  Jackson 4* (MT-74)
  Jacob 5* (MA-210)
  James 29* (MT-75)
  James 38 (ES-80)
  James 69* (ES-102)
  John 22* (F-242)
  John 25 (MT-80)
  John 29 (ES-98)
  John 49* (B) (F-229)
  John 58* (MT-16)
  John 70* (CL-65)
  John W. 29 (MT-30)
  Joseph 30 (MT-78)
  Joseph 34 (ES-64)
  Joshua 28* (ES-66)
  Marth 9* (MT-78)

Moses 60* (B) (F-229)
Nancy 50* (MA-267)
Patsey 55* (MT-73)
Ruth 12* (MA-254)
Samuel 7* (MA-282)
Thomas 70* (JE-26)
ALEXANDER?
  Harrison 37 (MT-24)
ALEXANDERS
  James 45 (CL-65)
ALFORD
  Carey 25 (GD-218)
  Charles 49 (OS-299)
  Elizabeth 40 (GD-218)
  James 26 (OS-299)
  Jesse 57 (GD-252)
  John 23* (OS-305)
  John 34 (F-163)
  John Q. 26 (GD-252)
  Morgan 66* (GD-218)
ALGAIER
  Charles A. 28* (CL-44)
ALLCORN
  James 18* (JE-15)
  James 39 (ES-59)
  John 35 (ES-96)
ALLEN
  A. M. 21 (m)* (F-150)
  A. S. 26 (m)* (CL-46)
  Achilles 30* (JE-36)
  Albert 26 (F-170)
  Alfred 19* (F-207)
  Buford E. 50 (F-229)
  Celia 28* (B) (F-119)
  Celia 39 (ES-64)
  Charles 50* (CL-40)
  Chilton 64* (CL-41)
  Edward 33 (JE-60)
  Eliza B. 1* (GD-246)
  Elizabeth 25* (F-191)
  Elizabeth 50* (F-160)
  Francis S. 29* (CL-34)
  George W. 44 (JE-8)
  Isaac N. 29 (MT-79)
  James 15* (JE-4)
  James 41* (CL-47)
  Jas. H. 45* (F-167)
  Jefferson 20* (JE-4)

Jerry 73 (B) (F-158)
John 29* (F-170)
John 45 (CL-57)
John 65* (GD-259)
John E. 45 (CL-57)
John G. 34 (F-222)
John R. 32* (F-229)
John R. 36* (F-194)
John S. 63 (CL-3)
John Will 24 (CL-70)
Joseph G. 26 (F-237)
Lucy 62 (GD-213)
Margaret 28* (GD-258)
Patsey 80 (CL-34)
Polly 45* (JE-60)
Polly 82* (GD-272)
Richard 32* (CL-57)
Richard 42* (JE-60)
Richd. 39 (F-148)
Sarah 15* (F-114)
Stephen 28* (ES-58)
Thomas 22* (OS-291)
Thomas 52* (CL-57)
Thomas 74 (CL-92)
Thomas B. 37* (CL-47)
W. W. 24 (m)* (F-168)
William 43 (CL-57)
William P. 40 (CL-84)
ALLEN?
  Simeon 18* (F-123)
ALLENBAUGH
  William 38 (OS-303)
ALLENDER
  Edwd. 20* (F-201)
ALLENDER?
  Thomas 25 (F-143)
ALLERSON
  Henry T. 32* (MA-251)
ALLEY
  William 58 (ES-68)
ALLIN
  Archibald 23 (MT-41)
  Francis W. 20* (MT-17)
  James 56* (MT-28)
  Lewis A. 20* (MT-5)
  R. G. 30 (m) (MT-57)
  William 62* (MT-20)

- 404 -

Index

ALLISON
  George 23* (JE-25)
  George S. 20* (F-150)
  George W. 36* (JE-5)
  James 23* (MT-2)
  James jr. 48 (MT-12)
  James jr. 80* (MT-25)
  John 22* (OS-302)
  Milton 38* (MT-16)
  William 47 (MT-16)
ALLSUP
  Martha 21* (OS-316)
ALSPAUGH
  D. C. 32 (m) (GD-262)
  Henry 29 (GD-248)
  Nelson 43* (GD-258)
ALTON
  Frances 12* (F-223)
  Mildred 15* (F-142)
ALVERSON
  James 43 (GD-223)
  Jesse 49* (MA-287)
  John B. 55* (GD-216)
AMBROSE
  Clements 19* (MT-36)
  James 28 (OS-319)
  Joseph 27* (OS-298)
  Joseph 52* (ES-83)
  M. M. 45 (m)* (OS-281)
  Moses 68 (OS-297)
AMERINE
  John T. 22* (MA-259)
AMES
  S. F. 39 (m)* (ES-87)
AMORINE
  John 66 (MA-269)
ANDERSON
  A. T. 17 (m)* (F-141)
  Abijah 12* (OS-317)
  Alexander 27 (CL-72)
  Alexander 46 (GD-259)
  Alexaner 46 (CL-18)
  Allen 54 (MA-212)
  Andrew 16* (F-210)
  Ann 62 (MT-65)
  Archibald 48 (CL-66)
  Charles 23 (MA-224)
  Charles 27* (F-216)

Charlott 30* (B) (F-137)
Clayton 41 (GD-263)
Cornelious 44 (GD-222)
Cythia 32* (MT-49)
David 46 (GD-270)
Eliz. 65* (F-203)
Elizabeth 40* (MA-300)
Frank 23 (OS-294)
George 25* (B) (F-128)
George 27* (B) (F-148)
George 30* (MA-274)
George 58 (CL-89)
Green 31 (MA-282)
H. G. 48 (m) (MT-60)
Hall 52* (GD-234)
Harrison J. 31* (MT-53)
Irvin 28 (GD-259)
Jacob 34 (OS-316)
James 24 (MT-77)
James 30 (MA-295)
James 34 (GD-233)
James 35 (CL-67)
James 50 (GD-227)
James 50* (MT-19)
James v. 22* (MT-19)
Jane 20* (GD-275)
Jane 46* (GD-210)
Jas. 48* (F-195)
Jesse 24 (MT-59)
Jesse 37 (CL-84)
Jessee 41 (OS-316)
Jessee K. 24 (OS-317)
Jo 41 (m) (GD-249)
John 12* (CL-5)
John 24 (CL-66)
John 26* (CL-94)
John 40* (B) (F-185)
John 48 (GD-233)
John 49 (GD-246)
John 54* (MA-280)
John F. 46 (MT-12)
John H. 35* (F-197)
John M. 38 (GD-243)
Josiah 28 (MT-69)
Letty J. 87* (MT-60)
Levi 44 (GD-270)
Margaret 68 (GD-263)
Maria 45 (B) (CL-47)

Mary 27* (MT-60)
Matilda 45 (MA-279)
Mildred 43* (F-201)
Milton 32* (MT-21)
Mort. C. 38 (JE-52)
Nancy 47* (F-167)
Nimrod 29 (MT-72)
Noah 12* (GD-289)
O. 56 (m) (F-214)
O. H. 44 (m)* (F-177)
Peter H. 30 (MT-33)
Peyton 50 (GD-205)
Preston M. 27 (CL-75)
Priscilla S. 75* (B) (F-214)
R. 33 (m)* (F-131)
Reuben 65 (B) (F-238)
Richard 60 (B) (MT-45)
Robert S. P. 36 (MT-14)
Sarah W. 25* (JE-73)
Thomas T. 57 (MT-77)
Thornton 18* (GD-245)
Wilkins 50 (B) (F-222)
William 18* (CL-47)
William 40* (CL-85)
William 41 (CL-42)
William 49 (OS-316)
William 5* (GD-228)
William 50 (GD-222)
William H. 14* (CL-74)
William M. 29 (CL-63)
Wingate 50 (CL-67)
Woodson 32 (MA-316)
ANDREWS
  A. M. 57 (m) (F-167)
ANEME?
  Thomas G. 35 (ES-112)
ANGELL
  Ephram 45* (OS-285)
  James 43 (OS-285)
ANGELS
  James jr. 22 (OS-303)
ANGLIN
  Isaac 26 (OS-298)
  James 67 (OS-318)
  John 36* (OS-296)
  Margaret 17* (F-223)
  Martain 23 (OS-297)

Index

ANNAN
  Saml. 50 (F-167)
ANTHONY
  Ben 34* (F-205)
APPERSON
  J. E. 28 (m)* (MT-1)
  Richard 51 (MT-57)
APPLEGATE
  Joseph 20* (F-190)
  Judith 45* (F-195)
APPLETON
  John 26* (F-188)
  Joseph 51 (F-176)
  Joseph 7* (F-155)
  Philadelphia 21* (F-142)
ARAINE
  Joseph 28 (ES-61)
ARBUCKLE
  John W. 26* (GD-228)
ARGOBRIGHT
  John 41 (F-249)
ARMAN?
  Andrew 19* (F-199)
ARMSONG
  John 19* (OS-313)
ARMSTED
  Henry 35* (F-200)
ARMSTRONG
  Allen 30* (CL-18)
  Andrew 59 (F-250)
  James 24 (F-249)
  John 59* (F-235)
  Juliet 27* (MT-28)
  Mary Ann 53 (MT-3)
  Mason 60 (MA-257)
  Samuel 30 (F-205)
  Sarah 91* (F-176)
  Thos. 21* (F-151)
  Wesley 29 (MA-214)
ARNETT
  Amanda 23* (F-251)
  Burrus 66 (JE-4)
  Ellison 40 (F-253)
ARNOLD
  Adaline A. 23* (CL-10)
  Alexander 24 (GD-264)
  David 30 (GD-225)
  David 62* (JE-13)

Elijah 53 (GD-226)
Frances 40* (CL-16)
George B. 26 (GD-225)
Henry 59* (CL-10)
Henry B. 32* (GD-216)
Humphrey 61 (GD-225)
James 29* (CL-15)
James B. 25 (GD-247)
Jane 45 (GD-260)
John B. 35 (GD-247)
John Bruce 32* (GD-263)
Joshua 26 (JE-13)
Perry 32* (MT-17)
Reuben 40 (JE-12)
Richard 40* (CL-9)
Samuel 53* (JE-11)
Tabitha 50* (GD-216)
Thompson 46 (GD-251)
Thos. 36* (F-196)
William 27* (MA-320)
William M. 28 (MT-29)
ARNOUR
  Alice 17* (F-225)
ARNSPIGER
  Delila 35* (JE-19)
  Samuel 39 (JE-16)
ARNSPIGER?
  Gabriel 38 (JE-60)
ARSEL
  Joseph 66 (MA-249)
ARTHUR
  Elizabeth 17* (MT-82)
  John 48 (MT-54)
ARTIS
  Robert 52 (CL-71)
ARVINE
  James 31 (ES-86)
  John 45 (ES-98)
  Nancy 69* (ES-106)
  Nathaniel 43* (ES-107)
  Sally 35 (ES-99)
  William 35* (ES-97)
ASA
  Marianne 35* (F-222)
ASBEL
  Joseph 32 (MA-235)
  Overton 15* (MA-235)
  William 60 (MA-240)

ASBELL
  H. H. 39 (m)* (OS-309)
  James 28 (ES-96)
  John 31 (ES-86)
  Joseph 30 (ES-82)
  Joseph 60 (ES-73)
  Levi 23 (ES-73)
ASBERRY
  Rebecca 17* (F-211)
ASCUR
  James 24* (MA-281)
ASHBURN
  Ambrose 15* (CL-46)
ASHCRAFT
  James 23 (OS-307)
  James 47 (OS-310)
  John 18* (OS-310)
ASHCROFT
  Amos 50 (ES-72)
  Gideon 49 (ES-106)
ASHFORD
  Joseph 18* (JE-8)
ASHLEY
  Josiah J. 31* (CL-77)
ASHTON
  Jacob 29 (F-210)
ASHUNT
  Craig 45* (JE-53)
ASKINS
  Charles G. 42 (GD-252)
  John 60* (GD-240)
ASKY
  Nancy 50 (MA-314)
ASON
  Susan 20* (B) (JE-50)
ASQUEN
  Bell 17* (GD-209)
ATCHISON
  Hamilton 14* (JE-59)
  James 50 (F-234)
  Sarah 39* (F-178)
  William 69 (F-224)
ATER
  W. W. 65 (m)* (F-191)
ATHLEY
  Robert A. 24 (F-212)
ATKERSON
  Mary E. 33* (MA-222)

Index

ATKINS
  Brockman 63 (JE-55)
  Dudley 40 (F-184)
  Frances 15* (MA-281)
  Margaret 57 (F-121)
  R. J. 48 (m) (F-117)
  Saml. 41* (F-225)
  W. 30 (m)* (F-153)
ATKINSON
  John 28 (F-202)
  Joseph 25 (CL-23)
  Washington 20 (CL-22)
  William 32 (CL-24)
ATWOOD
  Wm. 24 (F-203)
AUBREY
  R. J. 33 (m)* (F-240)
  Rebecca 38* (F-241)
AUDDRETH?
  Thomas 44 (CL-77)
AUSBURN
  William T. 35 (CL-35)
AUSTIN
  Ann 33* (GD-272)
  Elizabeth 52 (GD-272)
  H.?P. 25 (F-115)
  James 30 (GD-241)
  Jane 75 (GD-271)
  Mitchel 38 (GD-280)
  Polley 23 (GD-269)
  Prudence 52 (GD-211)
  Robert 51 (B) (F-137)
  Samuel 50 (GD-271)
  Thomas 21* (GD-280)
  Walter 40 (GD-216)
  Will 21 (GD-274)
  William 27 (GD-245)
  William 32 (F-115)
AVERY
  Phil B. 43* (F-196)
AXLINE
  Jacob 36* (F-253)
AYERS
  Martin 35* (CL-52)
BABB
  J. M. 18 (f)* (F-146)
BABCOCK
  George W. 28 (F-115)

BABCOCKE
  John 23* (F-131)
BABER
  James 27 (MA-294)
  James 34 (CL-20)
  John M. 25 (MA-294)
  Jonathan 55 (CL-27)
  Thomas W. 26 (CL-26)
BACCUS?
  L. A. 12 (m)* (F-142)
BACK
  Enoch 37 (JE-20)
  Jeremiah 44 (GD-206)
  Winney 84* (GD-207)
BACON
  A. J. 34 (m)* (OS-312)
  E. L. 45 (m)* (F-196)
  Enoch 41* (F-237)
  John M. 7* (MA-290)
BADDEN
  Henry 60* (F-221)
BADFORD
  Israel 26* (OS-302)
BAGER
  Daniel 40 (MA-289)
BAILEY
  A. M. 29 (m)* (ES-81)
  Benj. 48* (F-210)
  David 35 (F-247)
  Elizabeth J. 28* (CL-91)
  John 42 (CL-82)
  John R. 56 (F-246)
  Mary E. 7/12* (MA-261)
  Samuel 31 (F-246)
  Walter C. 42 (GD-266)
  Wm. G. 60 (F-247)
BAILY
  Augustus 31* (F-218)
  Eliza 39 (CL-51)
  Hiram 22 (OS-304)
BAIN
  Hutbert H. 16 (F-204)
  M. L. 57 (f)* (F-148)
BAKER
  Abner 75 (GD-288)
  Abraham 63 (GD-214)
  Allen 36 (GD-214)
  Allen 62 (F-248)

  Andrew 49 (MT-11)
  Andy sr. 38 (OS-282)
  Bassel 22 (m)* (MA-247)
  Bassel 56 (MA-239)
  Bassil 44 (m) (MA-248)
  Benedic? 22 (JE-24)
  Benj. F. 35 (MA-239)
  Benjamine 44 (OS-291)
  Birgus 54 (m) (MA-234)
  Catherine 53 (F-237)
  Christine 23* (F-208)
  David E. 54* (MA-270)
  Dudley 34 (F-254)
  Edwin G. 26 (MA-234)
  Elias 50 (GD-283)
  Eliza 16* (GD-246)
  Elizabeth 83* (MA-223)
  Green 60 (MA-236)
  Henry 39 (OS-313)
  Henry 47 (GD-273)
  Henry 55* (JE-36)
  Hiram 51 (MA-247)
  Jacob 35 (MA-209)
  James 30* (GD-251)
  James 35 (CL-81)
  James E. 24 (MA-206)
  James M. 20 (GD-283)
  James R. 31 (MA-237)
  Jerry 60* (CL-51)
  Jesse 25* (GD-228)
  Jesse H. 32* (F-201)
  Joannah 28 (OS-299)
  Job 58* (F-196)
  John 31 (GD-231)
  John 35 (GD-273)
  John 54 (F-136)
  John 74 (GD-216)
  John H. 28 (F-235)
  John H. 55 (OS-282)
  John William 23* (ES-56)
  Jonathan 57 (JE-26)
  Josiah 38 (MA-210)
  Lewis 34 (GD-223)
  Litha 53 (MA-233)
  Lucinda 50* (MA-255)
  Lucretius 40 (m)* (GD-246)
  Margaret 23* (MA-235)
  Mary 42 (GD-235)

Index

BAKER
Matilda 23* (OS-282)
Moses 21* (GD-214)
Moses 49 (ES-56)
Nancy 23* (F-208)
Nathan 31* (MT-13)
Patsey 35 (B) (GD-288)
R. 53 (f)* (F-131)
Reason 22 (MA-249)
Robert 23* (GD-227)
Robert jr. 50 (OS-282)
Robert sr. 76 (OS-283)
Samuel 54 (GD-236)
Sarah 80* (MT-11)
Thomas 27* (GD-226)
Thomas R. 26 (MA-239)
Washington 29 (MA-234)
William 23* (OS-305)
William 25 (MA-237)
William 32 (MT-2)
William 34 (ES-79)
William 42 (GD-227)
William 46 (MA-239)
William H. 34 (CL-83)
henry 46 (GD-217)
BAKERS
Susan 50* (CL-58)
BALDOCK
Will 30 (GD-277)
BALDWIN
John W. 19* (CL-24)
Samuel 28 (MT-19)
Thomas 58 (MT-68)
Ulen? 57* (F-213)
W. W. 22 (m) (MA-292)
William 68* (MT-68)
BALES
Hawkins 26 (OS-319)
John 31 (OS-295)
BALL
Benjamin 4_ (JE-35)
C. C. 37 (m) (MA-204)
Charles 30* (F-151)
Edney 22 (f)* (MA-286)
Hambal 40* (B) (F-193)
John 57* (CL-45)
Margaret 58 (JE-7)
Thomas 49 (GD-249)

BALLAD
Frances 60* (MT-62)
BALLANCE
William 47 (CL-72)
BALLARD
Byrom 25* (ES-57)
Eliza 60 (CL-65)
Elizabeth 65 (MA-284)
Garret 43 (MT-76)
George C. 52 (MA-224)
Henry 56 (F-229)
James 38 (CL-45)
James 39 (MT-66)
James A. 48* (MA-279)
James B. 73 (MA-217)
James L. 24 (JE-12)
Jane 60* (CL-28)
John 23 (CL-27)
John 44 (MA-201)
John 57 (ES-79)
John 65 (CL-21)
John P. 13* (JE-15)
John R. 25 (MA-284)
Malinda 22* (MT-55)
Malinda 24* (OS-310)
Mordica 21 (m) (ES-57)
Nancy 40 (MA-313)
Nicholas 55* (MA-230)
Paulina 40* (JE-11)
Permelia 4* (MA-279)
T. B. 30 (m) (MA-230)
Wiley 29 (CL-65)
William 30 (MA-224)
William 40 (GD-261)
Wm. J. (Dr.) 47* (JE-47)
nancy 45 (MA-210)
BALLARD?
Byrd W. 28* (CL-5)
BALLEW
Frances 69 (MA-320)
George 48 (MA-229)
Richard 22* (MA-280)
BALTIMORE
Lucky 70 (f)* (B) (F-237)
BANEFIELD?
William W. 10* (MT-57)
BANFORD
James C. 45 (F-242)

BANTON
Eliza 19* (GD-259)
James 20* (GD-259)
Oliver 26* (GD-280)
BARBEE
George 27 (CL-6)
Jos. R. 32* (JE-66)
Junius W. 30* (F-254)
Susan 20* (F-210)
BARFIELD
Aprida? 13 (f)* (MT-65)
Robert F. 11?* (MT-74)
BARKELY
James 58 (F-151)
BARKER
Ann 37* (F-117)
Charles 34 (F-228)
Charlotte 65* (GD-232)
Hezekiah 25* (MT-84)
James H. 13* (MT-61)
Jane 41 (GD-221)
Jincey 29 (f) (ES-106)
John 47* (F-213)
John 65* (MT-32)
Joseph 50 (GD-242)
Joseph 64 (F-242)
Lewellin 3* (F-117)
Moses 51 (F-207)
Polly 34* (ES-102)
William 30* (MA-303)
William 42 (ES-95)
BARKESON
John 16* (MT-6)
BARKLEY
C. H. 29 (m) (F-133)
Hiram 25 (CL-92)
Isaac 40 (JE-50)
James L. 48* (JE-64)
James T. 36 (JE-47)
Jane 63 (JE-50)
Mason S. 32 (JE-67)
Silas 33 (CL-94)
William L. 39 (JE-50)
BARLON
Henry 48 (GD-237)
BARLOW
Milton 33* (F-199)

Index

BARNEBY
Landie 36 (m) (MT-18)
BARNES
A. M. 38 (m)* (MT-1)
Alvin 52* (MT-7)
Betsey 45* (MA-207)
Catharine 16* (ES-65)
Catty 48 (f)* (ES-79)
Clifton K. 20 (MA-207)
Edmund 38 (MT-24)
Hannah 68 (ES-68)
Israel 36 (CL-50)
James 23 (ES-50)
James 29 (MA-201)
James C. 62 (GD-289)
John 23* (ES-104)
John 30 (MT-70)
John 49 (ES-66)
John 54 (ES-58)
John M. 18* (MA-252)
Lucy 40 (MA-311)
Mary 38* (F-196)
Otho 50 (MT-13)
Richard 20* (MA-251)
Richard 20* (MA-265)
Richard 36 (ES-49)
Robert M. 26 (MT-1)
Sidney M. 29 (ES-87)
Susan 32* (MA-311)
Thomas C. 52* (MT-1)
Thomas H. 27 (MA-205)
Turner? 50 (MA-307)
William 37 (ES-49)
William 40 (MA-274)
BARNET
Elizabeth 50 (JE-6)
BARNETT
Ambrose H. 35* (F-233)
Archibald E. 29* (JE-45)
Berry 38 (ES-73)
Celia A. 35* (ES-76)
Charles 50 (F-234)
Claibourn 48 (MT-59)
Dudley 35 (JE-18)
Eliza 63* (F-114)
Elizabeth 58* (JE-27)
Elizabeth 75 (MT-70)
Fanny 40* (F-195)

Franklin 21 (ES-76)
James 27* (ES-49)
James 34 (ES-47)
John 40* (MA-283)
John 7* (JE-18)
John W. 35 (ES-75)
Mary E. 2* (JE-18)
Mathew 30 (ES-98)
Nick 28* (F-196)
Robert 31* (ES-104)
Robinson 38 (MA-225)
Stanten 24 (ES-103)
Willia 79* (MA-222)
William 30* (MA-251)
William 50 (ES-49)
William 77 (MA-225)
BARNS
Dempsey 53 (f) (MT-75)
Elias 62 (MA-313)
Hardin 39 (MA-308)
Nancy 45 (MA-310)
Nathan 48 (MA-311)
Uriah 84 (MT-75)
BARNS?
William 15* (F-146)
BARNY?
Jerry 58 (MA-230)
BARR
Edmund 50* (F-228)
Thomas J. 39 (F-237)
BARRART
John 62* (OS-310)
BARRON?
Jack 25* (F-214)
BARROW
Asa 33 (CL-83)
Augustus 51 (MT-11)
David G. 53 (MT-11)
Hencher G. 59 (CL-95)
William 59 (MT-8)
BARRUS?
Joel 35 (MA-303)
BARRY
Cathe. A. 53* (F-214)
John 52* (F-235)
Martha B. 30* (F-250)
BARTETT
William 23* (MT-61)

BARTLET
James 48* (MT-18)
BARTLETT
Amos 31 (MA-231)
J. C. 34 (m)* (F-143)
Peter 54 (MA-231)
Spud 25 (MA-231)
William 23 (MA-231)
BARY
Mercer 29 (CL-15)
BASCOM
Henry B. 54* (F-191)
BASCOMB
Mary B. 36* (F-195)
BASHFORD
Eli D. 34* (GD-254)
BASSELL
John 56 (MT-37)
BASSETT
B. F. 20 (m)* (F-184)
Nancy 80* (MA-223)
BASSITT
Squire 27* (F-151)
BAST
Sarah 52 (GD-245)
BASTON
Polly 100* (F-156)
BATEMAN
William 31 (B) (F-127)
BATES
Alvin 25* (JE-78)
James W. 33 (GD-258)
John 26* (JE-41)
John 50* (MA-320)
Thomas E. 47 (MA-213)
BATHSTON
Henry 35 (MA-254)
BATLY
Samuel 56* (OS-307)
BATTAILE
James E. 28* (CL-3)
BATTENSHELL?
William 38 (CL-82)
BATTERTON
A. G. 32 (m) (MA-281)
Abraham 70 (MA-281)
Henry T. 20* (ES-68)

Index

BATY
  Frederick 20* (B) (MT-22)
BAUCHAMP
  H. 27 (m)* (F-169)
  Jesse 47* (F-169)
BAUGH
  Jesse 54 (GD-283)
  Samuel 17* (GD-282)
BAUGHMAN
  Thomas 25 (GD-219)
BAUGHN
  David 27* (JE-67)
BAUGHN?
  Joseph 54* (JE-43)
BAWZER?
  Robert 35* (F-114)
BAXTER
  Abner 40* (CL-82)
  America 48 (F-245)
  Andrew J. 30 (F-245)
  B. 24 (m)* (F-140)
  Bejamin 85 (MA-298)
  Charles 60 (B) (MA-298)
  Edmund 38 (MA-293)
  Edmund 78* (MA-264)
  Geo. 30 (F-171)
  Geo. 32 (F-174)
  German 52 (F-245)
  German 63 (F-248)
  Green 43* (CL-54)
  Jane 50* (F-216)
  John 65* (CL-32)
  John J. 39* (JE-8)
  Mary 59* (ES-68)
  Mary 75 (ES-111)
  Milo? 37 (MA-242)
  Priscilla 59* (F-247)
  Reuben 27* (F-171)
  Richard 38* (CL-50)
  Simeon? 26* (F-136)
  Thomas 45 (MA-269)
  Thomas B. 50 (F-125)
  William 19* (JE-60)
BAYES
  Elizabeth 31* (CL-91)
BAYLE
  Henry 66 (ES-47)

BAYLESS
  S. M. 40 (m)* (F-160)
BAYLEY
  Daniel 31 (JE-27)
BAYLISS
  Jesse 47? (F-114)
BAYLS
  James 30 (OS-316)
BAYLY
  Mary 47 (MA-298)
BEACH
  Elisha 27* (F-214)
  James 56* (F-213)
  Samuel 55 (F-205)
BEAL
  Burgess 27 (m)* (CL-28)
BEALEY
  Elizabet 19* (MA-260)
BEALL
  Durrett 27 (CL-40)
  Leonard 53 (CL-94)
BEAN
  Eli 55 (CL-88)
  Eve 74 (CL-91)
  James 50 (MT-12)
  Martha 11* (MT-6)
  Mary 16* (MT-6)
  Peter 47 (CL-88)
  William 54 (MT-34)
BEARD
  David C. 31* (F-195)
  John 27* (F-195)
  Joseph 38 (F-208)
  Joseph 72 (B) (F-199)
  Martha 30* (F-134)
  Oliver 28 (F-209)
  William 47 (F-200)
BEARDEN
  Cyrus 32* (F-134)
BEASLEY
  America 29* (CL-8)
  Frances 47* (JE-3)
  George 0 (GD-233)
  George W. 14* (GD-245)
  James 52* (JE-59)
  James A. 34 (GD-248)
  John 20* (F-212)
  John 32 (GD-251)

  Nancy 44 (GD-231)
  Sally 48* (F-245)
  Sarah 87* (JE-1)
  Walter A. 7* (GD-258)
BEATY
  Decator 29* (OS-310)
  George 45* (MT-80)
  Margaret 85* (F-191)
  Robert 40* (OS-278)
  Sarah 80* (MT-79)
  Thomas 19* (B) (MT-79)
BEAUMONT
  John 36 (GD-246)
  Nancy B. 41* (GD-212)
  Thomas 18* (GD-214)
  William 72 (GD-239)
BEAUMOUNT
  Wesley 45 (GD-243)
BEAVER
  Mary 35* (F-194)
BEAZLEY
  Royal H. 23* (GD-216)
BECK
  James B. 27 (F-211)
  Robert S. 24* (MA-276)
BECKNELL
  Perry 34* (ES-72)
BECKWELL
  Hiram 28 (ES-72)
  Linfield 65 (m) (ES-72)
BECRAFT
  Thomas 40 (MT-75)
BEDFORD
  Daniel C. 30* (MT-37)
BEDSTER
  Nelson 16* (GD-264)
BEECH
  Virginia 16* (F-199)
BEELER
  George 59* (GD-242)
  Jo 27 (m) (GD-242)
BEESON
  Phebe 27* (MT-73)
BELART
  B. F. 44 (m)* (F-216)
  Thomas 30 (F-202)
BELERT?
  George 44* (F-116)

Index

BELFORD
R. W. 45 (m) (MT-42)
BELL
Betty 60* (B) (F-159)
Billy 80* (B) (F-161)
Chas. S. 28 (F-132)
David 40* (F-192)
E. 50 (f)* (B) (F-125)
Edward 24* (CL-74)
Elizabeth 41 (GD-269)
H. C. 55 (f)* (F-215)
Henry 40* (F-222)
James 28* (GD-270)
James H. 24* (ES-59)
John H. 24* (CL-43)
John H. 44* (F-249)
John W. 24* (F-249)
Otha 46 (m) (CL-82)
Sarah 56* (F-202)
BELLIS
Hiram 27 (ES-61)
Thomas 54 (ES-79)
BELLOWS
James 30* (MT-67)
BENINGFIELD
John 55 (MT-48)
BENJAMIN
Theadore 16* (F-191)
BENNET
James 16* (MA-205)
James 28* (F-194)
BENNETT
Daniel 60* (B) (MT-13)
Eliza A. 24* (F-223)
Elizabeth 20* (CL-53)
John 31 (F-186)
John 59* (JE-65)
Joseph 45* (F-128)
Lucy 16* (F-145)
M. B. 50 (f)* (F-141)
Malinda 41 (ES-77)
Mary A. 9* (JE-58)
Robert 24 (JE-57)
Roda 70 (GD-212)
Samuel 17* (MA-214)
Thomas 47* (ES-54)
William 32 (GD-212)

BENNETT?
Emeley 22* (GD-273)
William 45 (MA-220)
BENNING
James 22* (B) (CL-2)
James 50 (B) (CL-82)
Sarah 79 (CL-50)
BENNINGFIELD
Henry 28* (F-197)
BENNINGFRED
Henry S. 28 (MT-43)
BENSUTT
Samuel 40* (MA-279)
BENTHALL
Seth 54 (CL-44)
BENTHEL
Richard 45* (F-239)
BENTHREL
Sarah 16* (JE-78)
BENTLEY
Daniel 40 (MA-268)
John 16* (CL-46)
Sarah 43 (MA-283)
Washington 53* (F-241)
BENTLY
China 35 (f) (MA-281)
James 27 (MA-252)
John E. 75 (MA-254)
Nancy 10* (MA-285)
Susan 13* (MA-285)
Temperance 43* (MA-268)
William 3/12* (MA-268)
William 54 (MA-252)
BENTON
B. G. 15 (m)* (ES-85)
Cyrus 27 (ES-96)
Eli 39* (ES-111)
Hiram 16* (ES-90)
Horace 50* (MT-36)
Jesse 62 (ES-105)
Joseph 28 (ES-97)
Judy 18* (ES-113)
Merrill P. 22 (ES-81)
Milton 30 (MA-268)
Milton 35 (ES-108)
Norval 47 (CL-86)
Richard T. 40 (ES-109)
William 38 (ES-61)

BERCHEL
Isaac 71 (GD-206)
BERK
Laura 6* (F-124)
BERKEY
John W. 39 (CL-17)
BERKLER
Reuben 57 (CL-6)
BERKLEY
Benjo. 41* (MT-18)
Burgess 56 (F-238)
Daniel 65 (CL-12)
Daniel 89 (CL-7)
E. F. 36 (m) (F-147)
John 65* (MT-82)
Leven 35 (CL-7)
Ludwell 53* (CL-12)
Samuel 34 (CL-6)
William S. 34* (F-233)
BERNARD?
Thompson 61 (MA-313)
BERNARKE?
John 27* (F-138)
BERNAUGH
Robert 30 (GD-231)
BERRE
Susan 56 (GD-284)
BERRY
B. L. 36 (m) (F-241)
Benj. 36 (F-161)
Celure? 38 (m) (MA-274)
David 45 (CL-46)
Eliza 13 (F-161)
Geroge 71 (F-255)
Grant 45 (CL-46)
H. K. 42 (m) (F-161)
Isaac N. 30 (CL-68)
J. C. 30 (m) (F-229)
James 47 (MA-313)
James 75 (B) (F-202)
James W. 35 (F-250)
John 31 (F-253)
John 33 (GD-242)
John 8* (CL-47)
John W. 31 (MA-264)
John sr. 57 (MT-80)
Levi 41 (ES-64)
Lucy 17* (F-225)

Index

BERRY
  Moab 29 (GD-232)
  Nathaniel P. 41 (F-253)
  Newton 43 (JE-37)
  Richard 43 (JE-53)
  Robert 23* (CL-7)
  Sam 35 (F-222)
  Thomas 16* (MA-283)
  Thomas 55* (CL-68)
  Thomas J. 26 (ES-82)
  Thomas J. 33* (CL-43)
  Thos. H. 32* (F-241)
  Washington 35* (CL-68)
  William 34* (F-223)
  Williar C. 59* (CL-14)
BERRYMAN
  Alexander 28 (CL-38)
  J. S. 61 (m) (F-160)
  Jack 50 (B) (F-222)
  James 49 (ES-80)
  John 60 (ES-68)
  Richard 5* (ES-84)
  Samuel 38 (ES-69)
BERTON
  Jane 19* (F-214)
  John 20* (F-160)
BESORE
  John 36* (F-217)
BESS
  Samuel 25* (MA-224)
BEST
  Jackson 33 (ES-62)
  John 15* (ES-69)
  Tyrie 43 (m) (GD-286)
  Will H. 38 (GD-286)
BETTERWORTH
  John 54 (MA-280)
BETTIS
  Fanny 40* (GD-251)
BEVANS
  Mary 24* (F-183)
BEVERLY
  Benj. 46* (GD-206)
BEYMER
  Samuel 36 (JE-42)
BIBB
  Agnes 60 (JE-8)
  Benjamin 21* (JE-2)

  James 51 (JE-10)
  James M. 27 (MT-37)
BICKEREL
  Thomas 29 (MA-232)
  Thomas 88* (MA-235)
  William J. 24 (MA-237)
BIGGERS
  Harrison 41 (MT-70)
  Kitty 46 (CL-94)
  Landie 63 (m)* (CL-90)
  Mary 10* (CL-94)
  Mary 30 (B) (CL-90)
  Nancy 60 (CL-90)
BIGGERSTAFF
  Isaac W. 48 (MA-206)
BIGGS
  John 26* (MA-227)
  Joseph 50* (F-214)
BIN
  Joel 64 (MA-214)
BING
  David 23* (MA-215)
  Rice 39 (MA-237)
  Thomas 46 (MA-238)
BINGHAM
  Thomas _. 26* (MT-1)
BINTER
  Mary 82* (MA-280)
BIRCH
  Abel 36 (ES-104)
  Daniel 50* (MT-48)
  George 38* (CL-50)
  James 71* (GD-210)
  John J. S. 24 (MT-30)
  John S. 24 (MT-37)
BIRCHELL
  John 48 (GD-205)
BIRD
  Camillus 24 (m) (MA-311)
  Nathaniel H. 31 (GD-285)
  Nimrod 22 (MT-40)
BISHOP
  Nancy 30* (OS-298)
  P. 54 (m)* (F-146)
  Thomas 40* (GD-287)
  William 50 (CL-61)
BIVEN
  John W. 17* (F-234)

BIXLER
  David M. 31 (GD-240)
  Susan 54 (GD-240)
BLACK
  Andrew 42 (MT-69)
  Charlott 45* (B) (MT-11)
  George 75 (MT-68)
  George F. 26* (MT-60)
  Guardian Ann 45 (B) (MT-81)
  James 40 (GD-254)
  James 50 (MA-205)
  James W. 45 (CL-30)
  Miller 40* (MT-8)
  Peter 35* (F-195)
  Sam 60* (B) (JE-57)
  Sarah 80 (MA-227)
  samuel 45 (MA-202)
BLACKABEE
  Elizabeth 67* (GD-211)
  George 41 (GD-211)
BLACKABY
  Benjamin 27 (GD-247)
BLACKBOURN
  James K. 49 (MT-50)
  William F. 24 (MT-39)
BLACKBURN
  Henrietta 24* (MT-6)
  James 57 (MA-224)
  Sally 54 (MA-256)
BLACKFORD
  Benj. 9* (F-162)
  Nathaniel 50 (JE-60)
  Robert P. 33 (JE-74)
  Thomas 13* (JE-7)
BLACKWELL
  Armstead 45* (CL-21)
  John R. 26* (MA-281)
  Joseph 45 (MA-293)
  Nancy 51* (ES-112)
  William 45 (MA-295)
BLAIN
  David 38 (F-128)
BLAIR
  Ann 60* (JE-65)
  Caroline 40 (B) (F-120)
  Malinda 16* (B) (F-117)
  Samuel 26* (OS-296)

Index

BLAKE
  Samuel 45 (MA-218)
BLAKEMAN
  Adam 27* (JE-33)
  Aron 35* (JE-32)
  James 25 (JE-20)
  James 48 (JE-27)
  John 42 (JE-30)
BLAKEMORE
  Eliza 34* (F-158)
  Ellen 44 (CL-35)
  James S. 25 (CL-40)
BLAKMAN
  George 60* (JE-33)
BLANCHARD
  Hester 60 (F-170)
BLAND
  Alamander 33 (m) (GD-210)
  Elija 45 (GD-232)
  Franklin 40 (MA-220)
  John 20* (GD-216)
  John 43 (GD-232)
BLAND?
  John 40* (MA-227)
BLANTON
  Elizabeth 60 (F-255)
  G. D. 36 (m)* (ES-68)
  William 42 (ES-72)
BLAYDES
  Hugh T. 27* (CL-9)
BLEDSOE
  Thomas C. 48* (F-152)
  William 60* (CL-30)
BLEVINS
  Charles E. 30* (MA-265)
  Daniel 34 (MA-247)
  John 18* (MT-58)
  John 18* (MT-67)
  Joseph 45 (ES-84)
  Mary A. 14* (MT-83)
BLINCOE
  Ben C. 41 (F-210)
BLUNT
  Ann 7* (F-144)
  Charles 58 (OS-305)
  Charles W. 17 (JE-14)
  Margarett 34 (CL-44)

BLYTHE
  James 37 (MT-42)
  James 56* (MA-320)
  Robert 19* (MT-3)
  Robert 70 (MT-42)
  Samuel 4* (ES-104)
BOATMAN
  James 33 (MA-312)
  Nelson 40 (GD-278)
BOATRIGHT
  Elizabeth 71* (MA-225)
  James 49* (MA-224)
  James 85 (JE-54)
BOBBITT
  Rebecca 45* (F-194)
BODINE
  Matilda 53? (JE-7)
BODLEY
  C. S. 27 (m) (F-127)
BOGA
  Patsey J. 12* (GD-214)
BOGARD
  William 23* (F-243)
BOGEN
  James 33 (MA-318)
BOGER
  Andrew 49 (MA-310)
  James 42 (MA-322)
  Thomas 46 (MA-290)
BOGER?
  John B. 25* (MA-286)
BOGGENS?
  Cyntha 45 (CL-92)
BOGGS
  Benj. 42 (MA-213)
  Edward C. 36 (MA-255)
  James 56* (MA-257)
  James S. 31 (MA-277)
  Robert 50 (MA-242)
  Robert C. B. 56* (F-252)
  mary 26* (F-140)
BOHANNON
  Ann 65* (F-196)
BOLERTINE
  Thomas 23* (MT-35)
BOLES
  Elbert 37 (OS-319)
  William 21 (OS-319)

  William sr. 55 (OS-319)
BOLT
  Saml. R. 35* (F-225)
BOLTON
  Ballard 30 (GD-235)
  Burt 20 (GD-253)
  Elbert 34 (GD-235)
  John 64 (GD-235)
  Melissa 38 (GD-235)
BOND
  Henderson 30 (OS-310)
  Preston 26* (ES-81)
  William 72 (OS-296)
BONDURANT
  Edward 47 (MT-27)
  Eliza 15* (B) (MT-83)
  Mary 11* (B) (MT-79)
BONER
  John C. 24 (GD-213)
  William 57* (GD-232)
BONEY
  Edward 30* (F-124)
BONFILES
  Cunard? 17* (F-145)
  Luvenia 51* (F-145)
BONJURANT
  Joseph 57* (MT-16)
BONNAN
  Abram 65 (F-255)
BONNER
  J. H. 7 (m)* (JE-45)
  Silas 41 (JE-36)
BONNEY
  Mary Ann 55 (ES-70)
BONNY
  Nathaniel 26 (CL-62)
BONTA?
  Abraham 48* (ES-60)
BOOHER
  John H. 33* (MT-76)
BOON
  Gabriel 52* (B) (F-193)
BOONE
  Charles 27* (GD-219)
  Eleanor 17* (F-241)
  George 44 (CL-81)
  George 68 (CL-7)
  Jeptha 28 (CL-76)

Index

BOONE
John 38* (JE-1)
M. R. D. 28 (m)* (ES-103)
Nancy 30 (CL-67)
Samuel 33 (CL-81)
Squire 45 (CL-80)
Thomas 64 (CL-56)
Thomas N. 23 (CL-75)
BOORAM
Paulina 16* (F-225)
BOOTH
William 63 (OS-292)
William jr. 22 (OS-293)
BOOTHE
Mary 34 (JE-51)
BORALLY
Peter D. 58 (GD-233)
BORHITE
John A. 28 (F-120)
BORMAN
Harrison 30 (MA-243)
BOSTICK
L. B. D. 57 (m)* (ES-86)
BOSWELL
George 17* (B) (JE-47)
Hartwell 17* (F-209)
James M. 35 (CL-5)
Thos. E. 55 (F-166)
W. D. 20 (m)* (F-183)
BOSWORTH
Ann W. 51 (F-171)
Benj. 28 (F-168)
D. H. 54 (m)* (F-192)
Eliza 50* (F-140)
Geo. 19* (F-168)
Jos. 37* (F-203)
BOTTS
Benja. F. 40 (MT-12)
Joseph 35 (MT-43)
Margaret 90* (B) (MT-3)
Moses 45* (F-249)
Polly 33 (B) (MT-3)
Robert 70 (MT-80)
Seth 55 (MT-81)
Thomas 58 (MT-7)
BOULDAN?
William 34* (MA-215)

BOULDON?
James 27* (MA-203)
BOULERAN
John 22* (MA-203)
BOULIN
Benjamin 35 (MA-302)
Elizabeth 85 (MA-302)
BOULNAN?
Hardin 31 (MA-216)
BOULNARD?
Calvin 25 (MA-320)
BOULT
Henry B. 40* (F-191)
BOULTON
Beverly 27 (m) (MA-314)
Maliki 36 (GD-275)
BOULVORE?
Greenberry 25 (MA-256)
BOULWAN
Madison 36 (MA-281)
BOUREN
Alfred F. 31* (CL-41)
BOURN
Berya F. 31 (m)* (MT-3)
Jack 55 (MT-30)
Walker 60* (MT-28)
William 27* (MT-4)
BOURNE
Andrew 48 (JE-76)
Catharine 9* (JE-15)
David A. 35 (JE-8)
Davis 36 (JE-8)
Elijah 80 (JE-8)
F. M. 26 (m) (GD-289)
Francis 42* (JE-17)
Francis 65* (GD-210)
George 34* (JE-19)
Isaac 34* (JE-11)
James 28 (GD-241)
James 51 (JE-2)
James D. 12* (JE-32)
John 70 (JE-72)
Paulina 41* (JE-18)
Roger P. 22* (JE-11)
Sarah 7* (JE-6)
BOWAN
John 22* (GD-257)

BOWEN
Armstead 28* (MT-49)
Daniel 40 (GD-237)
James 14* (MA-215)
John 40 (GD-231)
John W. 40* (MA-251)
Nancy 55 (GD-209)
William 44* (ES-110)
William 45 (MT-49)
BOWER
May 26* (F-194)
BOWERS
E. J. 22 (m)* (F-218)
BOWERS?
Sarah 44 (MA-297)
BOWLES
Anderson 27 (OS-315)
Frances 20* (MT-17)
James 17* (OS-297)
William A. 63 (OS-304)
BOWLIN
Hiram 34 (MT-42)
BOWLING
Graham 23 (OS-279)
Sanford 45 (OS-301)
WM. 21* (F-246)
William 23 (OS-280)
BOWMAN
Abram 65 (F-184)
Absalum 28* (OS-300)
Andrew 42 (ES-90)
David 62 (JE-51)
Elisha 39 (OS-303)
Elizabeth 40 (OS-320)
Elizabeth 57 (JE-47)
Elizabeth 62 (OS-278)
Enoch 27 (OS-320)
Geo. H. 57* (F-164)
George 68 (GD-252)
Green? 5* (MA-217)
H. C. 24 (m) (F-163)
Henry 38 (OS-285)
Hezekiah 37* (ES-91)
Isaac 38 (JE-47)
Jacob 22 (OS-296)
John 33 (OS-285)
John 42 (JE-39)
John 45* (F-200)

Index

BOWMAN
  John 62* (MA-237)
  Joseph 56 (F-162)
  Levi 24 (OS-295)
  M. M. 33 (m) (ES-103)
  Nancy 11* (MA-312)
  Nancy 60* (F-184)
  Polly 80* (CL-50)
  R. P. 37 (m) (F-142)
  R. S. 30 (m) (OS-295)
  Sarah 54* (ES-105)
  Sarah 63* (JE-51)
  Thomas 28 (ES-103)
  Thomas 29 (OS-285)
  Thomas 68* (OS-320)
  WilliM 35 (OS-279)
  Wm. 60* (F-161)
BOWREN
  Cornelius 65* (CL-1)
  Elizabeth 38 (CL-43)
BOWYER?
  Ezra 36* (F-115)
BOYD
  Almeda 27* (F-213)
  John D. 48* (F-194)
  Jos. B. 21* (F-199)
  Malinda 50 (GD-210)
  Robt. 38 (F-153)
  Saml. M. 35 (F-175)
  Thomas W. 46 (MA-250)
  William 26* (MA-250)
BOYER
  Andrew 41 (MA-310)
  Geo. A. 35* (F-206)
BOYLE
  Rufus 45* (GD-232)
  Sally Ann 27* (MA-250)
BRADEY
  George 49 (ES-84)
BRADFORD
  Daniel 73 (F-206)
  Thomas T.? 52 (F-128)
BRADLE
  William 33 (MA-200)
BRADLEY
  Barney 28* (F-175)
  Dennis 92* (CL-53)
  James S. 50 (F-235)

  Leland 24* (F-254)
  Patrick 30* (JE-68)
  Richard N. 35* (ES-103)
  Samuel 40* (CL-31)
  Sarah 58 (CL-31)
  Thomas 29* (F-145)
  William 46 (MT-37)
  William N. 6* (CL-31)
BRADLY
  William 8* (CL-49)
BRADSHAW
  James 48 (MT-44)
  John 51* (JE-41)
  John H. 24 (MT-64)
  Nancy 40* (MT-80)
  William 59 (MT-39)
  William A. 50* (MT-17)
BRADY
  Crofford 10* (GD-270)
  Elizabeth 26 (GD-275)
  Harrison 36 (GD-242)
  John 66* (GD-250)
BRAGG
  Grace 38 (F-171)
BRAKE
  William 39 (MT-28)
BRAND
  Geo. W. 37* (F-203)
  Harriet W. 41 (F-255)
  P. W. 40 (f)* (F-218)
BRANDENBERG
  Ruth 60* (CL-8)
BRANDENBURG
  John 20 (ES-83)
  John H. 48* (OS-314)
  Joseph 35 (ES-82)
  Joseph 81 (OS-314)
  Nancy 45* (OS-315)
  Peter 54 (B) (CL-67)
  Samuel 24* (CL-73)
  Samuel 50* (OS-301)
  Sarah B. 10* (ES-57)
BRANDENBURGH
  Ann 30* (MT-29)
  George H. 48* (OS-287)
  James 42* (OS-303)
  Joseph 46 (OS-286)
  Lewis 19* (OS-277)

  Samuel 23 (OS-277)
BRANEGAR
  Sally 35* (CL-95)
BRANHAM
  Thomas 32 (MT-61)
  William 47 (MT-62)
BRANK
  Sophia 54* (GD-282)
BRANSTON
  Thomas 58 (MA-212)
BRASFIELD
  Eliza 55* (CL-45)
BRASSHORE
  Lucy 90* (MA-299)
BRATTON
  David 40 (CL-90)
BRAUNER
  Wiley 13* (MA-250)
BRAVARD
  Saml. 50* (F-196)
BRAWNER
  Luther? 39 (OS-320)
  Samuel 17* (MA-214)
BRAY
  Robert J. 20* (JE-9)
BRECKENRIDGE
  A. 70 (m)* (F-156)
  John C. 29 (F-189)
  Maria 14* (F-225)
  Mary 17* (F-199)
  Mary E. 32 (B) (F-116)
  Mary H. 81* (F-193)
  R. J. 50 (m) (F-167)
  Robt. H. 52* (F-133)
  Roddy 40* (F-234)
  Susan 7* (F-234)
  Thos. 55 (F-177)
  Wilcher 64 (B) (F-152)
  Wm. 13* (B) (F-202)
BRENHAM
  Danl. 40* (B) (F-179)
BRENNAN
  John 20* (MT-35)
  John 62* (F-143)
BRENT
  Mary 55* (F-203)
BREWER
  Ambrose 35 (OS-279)

Index

BREWER
　Howel 55 (OS-319)
　Howel jr. 29 (OS-300)
　John 38* (F-173)
　Thomas 17* (ES-78)
BRICE
　Henry 40 (B) (F-119)
　Price 34* (OS-304)
BRIDGES
　E. A. 8 (f)* (F-123)
　Hiram 62 (MT-29)
　Isaac 15* (F-129)
　John 55* (F-200)
BRIDGFORD
　Geo. 27 (F-202)
BRIDWELL
　Ann 27* (F-194)
　Malinda 28* (F-195)
BRIENT
　S. O. 9 (m)* (B) (F-144)
BRIGGS
　Chas. A. 3* (F-206)
　Sarah A. 27* (F-205)
BRIGHT
　Thomas sr. 62 (GD-229)
BRIGHTON
　William 43 (CL-89)
BRIM
　Abner 24* (JE-35)
BRINEGAR
　David S. 32 (ES-80)
　Israel 58 (ES-79)
　Jacob 56* (ES-58)
　John S. 26 (ES-47)
BRINIGAR
　Sam 75 (B) (CL-32)
BRINK
　Archd. 48 (F-246)
　Daniel 46 (F-224)
　Ephraim 36* (F-247)
　Hibard 39* (F-246)
　John A. 25 (CL-11)
　Martha 70* (F-246)
BRISBY
　David 43 (F-143)
BRISCO
　Catharine 52 (F-132)

BRISH
　Pleasant 58* (CL-32)
BRISLEY
　Elizabeth 52* (F-195)
BRISTER
　Judith 73* (F-246)
BRISTOE
　Morris 35* (B) (MT-64)
BRITTEN
　Thos. 74 (B) (F-152)
BRIZENDINE
　William L. 29* (JE-68)
BROADDUS
　Andrew 54 (MA-269)
　Beverly 26 (m)* (MA-314)
　D. R. 23 (m) (MA-206)
　E. Samuel 28* (F-246)
　Frances 28* (MA-309)
　George 44 (MA-258)
　Jerremiah 2* (MA-268)
　Julia 26* (MA-268)
　Martin 24 (MA-316)
　Mary 7* (MA-308)
　Thomas 49* (MA-312)
　W. C. M. 35 (m) (MA-258)
　William 35 (MA-316)
BROADDUS?
　Edward J. 36 (ES-108)
BROADUS
　China 40 (f) (MA-257)
　John E. 30 (GD-253)
　Mitchel 32 (GD-243)
　Overton 20* (GD-257)
BROCK
　Amanda 16* (B) (CL-35)
　Calvin 26 (MT-37)
　David 49 (GD-281)
　Isaac 17* (F-115)
　James 22* (B) (CL-38)
　James S. M. 23 (CL-35)
　John jr. 45 (CL-34)
　John sr. 74 (CL-36)
　Joshua 50 (ES-77)
　Martin 35 (MA-273)
　Peyton S. 38 (GD-278)
　Rebecca 15* (MT-84)
　Ro S. 25 (m) (F-204)
　Simpson W. 22* (CL-36)

　Winfield 55 (JE-64)
BROCKMAN
　Ambros 29 (MA-235)
　Birgus 33 (MA-236)
　Jacob B. 23* (CL-14)
　James T. 29* (CL-14)
　John 24 (MA-235)
　Roger P. 6* (CL-12)
　Shelton 61* (MA-235)
　Wm. 37* (F-169)
BROCKWAY
　Abby S. 34* (F-152)
　Mary E. 34* (F-152)
　Samuel A. 30 (MT-40)
BRODUS
　Margaret 22* (JE-60)
BROGAL
　Martin 45* (GD-213)
BROMBOYER
　John 65* (F-169)
BRONAUGH
　James H. 32* (CL-40)
　John S. 29* (JE-73)
　William 53* (JE-78)
　William jr. 18* (JE-78)
BRONSTON
　Charles 2* (MA-309)
　Thomas 29* (MA-251)
BROOKING
　Caroline 37* (B) (CL-5)
　Robert E. 69* (CL-3)
BROOKS
　John 22 (MA-293)
　John 30 (MA-320)
　John 70* (GD-257)
　Parker 18* (B) (JE-66)
　Solomon S. 33 (F-214)
　William 40 (GD-228)
BROOKSHIER
　Charles H. 21 (GD-234)
BROOKSHIRE
　Ann 55* (CL-32)
　Elizabeth 60* (CL-20)
　Feriby 21* (CL-26)
　Hampton 30 (CL-24)
　Johnson 26 (CL-29)
　Judieth 35 (CL-25)
　Martin 42 (CL-32)

Index

BROOKSHIRE
  Wiley 33 (CL-31)
BROSIN
  Rebecca P. 54* (JE-9)
BROTHERS
  John 72 (MT-20)
BROTHERTON
  Robert 21* (MA-275)
BROUGHTON
  James G. 37 (CL-63)
  Pattie 43 (MA-298)
  Ruth 62* (CL-42)
  Thomas S. 30* (JE-65)
BROUSTON
  Thomas 32* (MA-203)
BROWER
  Thomas 327* (MA-320)
BROWN
  A. 41 (f) (B) (F-123)
  A. F. 24 (m)* (MT-1)
  A. J. 64(m) (GD-264)
  Anderson 28 (CL-18)
  Asa 33 (GD-205)
  Buford 40* (GD-220)
  Buford 40* (GD-240)
  Caleb 46 (F-127)
  Caroline 38 (GD-230)
  Catharine 18* (MA-291)
  Charles 36 (F-216)
  David 39 (CL-23)
  Diana 56 (B) (F-201)
  Edgar A. 37* (F-150)
  Eliza 94* (GD-251)
  Elizabeth 58* (ES-89)
  Ephariam 33 (GD-267)
  Ephenetus 32 (GD-233)
  Francis G. 45 (CL-8)
  Geo. 33* (F-173)
  George 23 (GD-251)
  George 31* (JE-11)
  George 69 (MA-204)
  George A. 44* (GD-264)
  George J. 65 (JE-12)
  Green 37 (GD-208)
  Hadric? R. 28* (F-203)
  Hamlett 23* (GD-262)
  Henry 32 (CL-19)
  Jack 34* (GD-248)
  Jacob 37* (B) (F-193)
  Jacob 48 (JE-44)
  James 32* (F-205)
  James 65* (ES-104)
  John H. 44* (F-148)
  John 26* (MT-7)
  John 31 (GD-242)
  John 52* (F-134)
  John 72 (GD-205)
  John P. 20* (F-184)
  Joseph 13* (CL-26)
  Joseph 30 (GD-219)
  Joseph C. 35 (F-222)
  Joseph S. 55 (GD-252)
  Josiah 24* (F-197)
  Katy 50* (B) (F-173)
  Lucey 35 (MA-290)
  Marion 12 (m)* (MA-210)
  Martin 21* (JE-9)
  Mary 18* (MA-204)
  Mary J. 39* (JE-19)
  Matilda 44* (GD-277)
  Moroe? 35 (m) (JE-14)
  Nelson 37* (GD-213)
  Perry 27 (CL-54)
  Polly 37* (JE-51)
  Saint 35* (F-212)
  Samuel 16* (JE-32)
  Samuel 65 (GD-230)
  Smith 30 (GD-252)
  Stephen 70* (B) (F-244)
  Stewart 40* (GD-254)
  Talmadge 18 (m)* (JE-74)
  Thomas 48* (GD-221)
  Thomas 73* (GD-264)
  Will 41 (GD-229)
  Willia 33 (GD-206)
  William 41 (MA-214)
  richard 44 (GD-253)
BROWNFIELD
  Moses 50 (MA-301)
BROWNFIELD?
  Mary 80 (JE-44)
BROWNING
  E. C. 31 (m) (CL-6)
  Jesse 70* (MA-276)
  John 29 (OS-298)
  John W. 38 (MA-230)
  M. C. 40 (m) (F-141)
  M. E. 42 (m) (F-141)
  Mary 39 (F-146)
  Sally 69* (F-167)
  Tho. 18* (F-201)
  W. P. 36 (m)* (F-151)
BROWNSTON
  Susan A. 34* (F-121)
BROWNWELL
  Silvester 22* (F-193)
BRUCE
  Benjamin G. 23* (ES-103)
  Brunette 54* (GD-263)
  Eli 27 (CL-57)
  Eli 55 (CL-28)
  Horatio 56 (GD-276)
  James 67 (MA-299)
  James G. 40 (JE-74)
  James M. 27 (F-140)
  Judith 58 (JE-75)
  Margaret 60* (F-146)
  Sanders D. 25* (F-222)
  Tina 31 (m)* (MA-275)
  Will 16* (GD-275)
  Will 49 (GD-289)
  William 49 (GD-267)
  Wm. W. 29* (F-203)
BRUEN
  Daniel 30* (JE-2)
  Wm. 24 (F-158)
BRUER
  Thomas 27 (MT-73)
BRUIN
  James 25 (F-119)
  M. 50 (f) (F-120)
BRUMFIEL
  David 28* (JE-33)
  Elizabeth 35* (JE-28)
  Joel 50 (JE-25)
  Nelson 31 (JE-29)
  Sarah 65 (JE-29)
BRUMFIELD
  James 43 (JE-71)
BRUMMIT
  Benjamin 44* (OS-297)
BRUNER
  Benjamin 26* (JE-49)
  Enoch 50 (JE-35)

Index

BRUNER
  Frances 71* (JE-33)
  Green 36 (JE-34)
  Henry 24* (MT-3)
  Jackson 26* (CL-45)
  John W. 34 (CL-41)
  Joseph 27 (CL-70)
  Levi 37 (JE-26)
BRUNNETT
  William 28* (F-234)
BRUSH
  James O. 19* (MT-66)
  William 50 (CL-73)
BRUTON
  David 45* (MT-21)
  Elizabeth 18* (MT-33)
  James 50 (MT-15)
BRYAN
  Elijah 26 (F-163)
  Elizabeth 22* (F-192)
  John O. 46 (F-177)
  Joseph 53 (F-166)
  Mary Ann 8* (F-226)
  Saml. 60* (F-186)
  Thomas 50 (F-133)
  William T. 62 (JE-58)
  Wm. 43 (F-163)
  Woodson 46 (F-255)
BRYANT
  Benja. 67 (JE-67)
  Benjamin 19 (F-204)
  Benjamin 20* (F-132)
  Clifton 50* (F-203)
  Daniel 25 (JE-53)
  Elizabeth 36* (MA-215)
  Emeline 25* (F-247)
  Enoch 77* (F-228)
  G. B. 31 (m) (JE-44)
  Harrison E. 38 (JE-67)
  Harvey 38 (CL-78)
  James 17* (JE-67)
  James 30 (ES-54)
  James A. 29 (F-228)
  James H. 40 (CL-20)
  Joel 55 (JE-52)
  John 33* (JE-32)
  John H. 12* (JE-2)
  Joseph C. 28* (JE-3)

  Keziah 63* (CL-79)
  Martha 11* (F-212)
  Martha 28 (GD-250)
  Mary 41 (GD-248)
  O.? D. 41 (m)* (JE-64)
  Patsy 45* (JE-56)
  Ruben 31 (JE-8)
  Susan 41* (GD-248)
  Will O. 39 (GD-287)
  Will S. 25 (GD-287)
  Wm. 66 (F-228)
  Zerilda 19* (F-191)
BRYBURN?
  James 70* (MA-321)
BUCHANAN
  Alex 40 (GD-258)
BUCK
  Daniel jr. 28 (MA-205)
  Daniel sr. 61 (MA-205)
BUCKHANEN
  Caleb 49* (MA-215)
BUCKLEY
  Charles 50 (B) (F-206)
BUCKNER
  A. H. 40 (m)* (CL-41)
  Charlotte 34* (CL-47)
  Geo. 55 (B) (F-181)
  William 20* (OS-279)
BUCKNERS
  william S. 40 (CL-79)
BUENES?
  William 50 (OS-282)
BUFORD
  James 46 (MA-232)
  Jeremiah 47 (B) (F-118)
  L. M. 35 (m)* (MT-1)
  Thomas 74* (GD-287)
BUGESS
  Henry W. 60 (F-253)
BUGGINGTON
  Taylor 37* (F-186)
BULEY
  Samuel M. 36 (ES-47)
BULLARD
  Heny 35 (m) (CL-59)
BULLOOCK
  E. O. 22 (f)* (F-250)
  Waller 76 (F-250)

BULLOCK
  Elizabeth 8* (F-161)
  James 27* (MT-14)
  James 32 (MT-37)
  John C. 37 (OS-296)
  Joseph J. 37* (F-225)
BUNCH
  Benjamin W. 40 (CL-80)
  Elijah 45 (CL-80)
BUNDA
  Joseph 42 (GD-282)
BUNERD?
  K. A.. 22 (m)* (F-131)
BUNIER
  Wm. 32 (F-191)
BUNIER?
  Jacob 42* (JE-64)
BUNNELL
  Jessee 44 (F-122)
  Martha 18* (F-143)
BURA
  Will 44 (GD-274)
BURBANK
  David 29 (F-204)
  Elmira 25* (F-190)
BURBERRY
  David 28* (CL-44)
BURBRIDGE
  Thomas 53 (CL-5)
BURCH
  Catharine 65* (JE-8)
  Ezekiel 40 (JE-7)
  James J. 45 (JE-15)
  Mary 30* (F-194)
  Nancy 64 (JE-7)
  Robert 32 (JE-9)
  William H. 40* (JE-55)
BURCHEL
  Aron 19* (JE-31)
  Daniel 42 (JE-29)
BURCHIL
  Owen 23* (GD-239)
BURDEN
  Jane 54 (B) (F-204)
  John L. 32 (MT-2)
  William 31 (F-131)
BURDETT
  Amelia 30* (GD-249)

Index

BURDETT
Andrew 34 (GD-245)
Daniel O. 45 (GD-209)
Enoch 50 (GD-230)
Francis 28* (GD-260)
George F. 40* (GD-231)
Hyram 52* (GD-241)
Isham 46 (GD-241)
James T. 45 (GD-260)
Joshua 26 (GD-288)
Nelson 56 (GD-218)
Simeon 40 (GD-230)
Stephen L. 24 (GD-218)
Wilhelmina 67 (GD-241)
BURGEN
Akillis 52 (m) (MA-253)
Temple 44 (MA-253)
BURGER
Fanny 35* (F-195)
BURGESS
Charles W. 31 (MA-232)
John 42 (CL-24)
BURGHER
John 24 (ES-77)
Manson 59 (ES-77)
Nicholas 33 (ES-77)
BURGIN
Allen 56 (MA-254)
Elias 39 (MA-301)
John 56 (MA-300)
BURHOPP
George P. 44* (MT-81)
BURINGER
Henry 24 (F-139)
BURK
James H. 31 (CL-49)
John 58* (MA-234)
BURKETT
Eliz. R. 58 (JE-75)
BURKHEAD
Nelson 23* (F-195)
BURKS
Direnda 64* (GD-240)
Laura 8* (MA-262)
BURNAM
John F. 33 (GD-231)
BURNARD?
Curtis F. 30 (MA-251)

Henry 27 (GD-285)
BURNAUGH
Sarah 56 (JE-12)
Will F. 27 (GD-221)
BURNELL?
Anthony 55 (B) (F-114)
BURNES
Catharine J. 10* (CL-43)
John 52 (OS-295)
Nancy 25* (F-209)
BURNET
Maria 4* (MA-267)
BURNETT
Reuben 26 (GD-274)
Samuel 43 (MA-203)
William C. 32* (MA-217)
BURNS
Elizabeth 76* (JE-14)
Green 28 (MA-309)
John 14* (OS-301)
Matilda 49* (F-196)
BURNSIDES
Allen 33 (GD-222)
James 71* (GD-222)
Josiah 43 (GD-237)
Margaret 67* (GD-212)
Nancy 56 (GD-230)
Richard 60 (B) (GD-218)
Robert 24 (GD-248)
Williamson 47 (GD-249)
BURNTSIDES
John 36 (GD-276)
BURR
Margaret 13* (F-223)
BURRIS
Elizabeth 58* (MA-313)
James 55* (MA-312)
Nathaniel 28 (MA-310)
BURRISS
Green 17* (MA-290)
James 27 (MA-264)
Nelson D. 23 (MA-210)
Thomas 50 (CL-65)
BURRISS?
Charles 23* (MA-204)
BURROGH?
George H. 40 (MT-38)

BURROUGHS
John 8* (GD-210)
Michael B. 49* (GD-221)
BURROUS
Charles M. 27* (GD-258)
Laban 44 (GD-233)
BURROWS
Elizabeth 16* (GD-208)
Thos. 45* (F-195)
Uphemia 24* (F-194)
William P. 23* (CL-14)
BURRS
William 32 (MA-293)
BURRUS?
Nancy E. 30* (MA-227)
BURT
Betty 25* (F-196)
Samuel 25* (MA-206)
BURTIN
Abraham 34 (MA-323)
Abraham 84 (MA-317)
BURTON
A. A. 28 (m)* (GD-266)
Agnes 68* (ES-89)
Alfred 39* (GD-225)
Allen 47 (ES-98)
Allen 64 (GD-235)
Christopher 20* (MT-33)
George W. 12* (GD-245)
Isom 32 (ES-71)
Jackson 35* (ES-92)
James 59* (MA-247)
Jesse 18* (GD-225)
Jesse 38 (GD-229)
John 25* (JE-55)
John 26* (OS-311)
John 44* (ES-108)
Lucy 39 (JE-34)
Pharis 34* (JE-20)
Robert A. 52 (GD-255)
Robert D. 52 (GD-248)
Samuel 42* (ES-74)
Singleton 36* (JE-28)
William 29* (ES-76)
William H. 26 (GD-235)
BUSBY
Elizabeth 26* (MA-203)
Harvey 43* (MT-7)

Index

BUSBY
  Samuel 39* (MT-1)
  William 56 (F-134)
BUSH
  Allen N. 30* (CL-55)
  Ambrose 72* (CL-7)
  Ambrose E. 24* (CL-88)
  Anbose G. 27 (m) (CL-14)
  Anderson 44 (ES-58)
  Barbara 59* (CL-9)
  Barbara S. 13* (CL-14)
  Christopher C. 26 (CL-20)
  Colby 38 (CL-10)
  Dillard 19* (CL-22)
  Fielding 35 (CL-21)
  Frederic 43* (F-217)
  George W. 51 (CL-39)
  Harvey 44 (OS-288)
  Heyman G. 29* (CL-32)
  Howard 36 (CL-17)
  J. M. 40 (m)* (F-144)
  James 51* (CL-94)
  Jeremial 42* (CL-14)
  John 26* (CL-76)
  Jonathan 70 (CL-11)
  Joseph 50 (MA-296)
  Joseph 78 (CL-15)
  Landen 56* (CL-14)
  Luallen? 47 (m) (OS-312)
  Mahal 25* (ES-56)
  Moses 54 (CL-16)
  Nacy J. 6* (CL-39)
  Nancy 78* (ES-110)
  Nancy G. 65* (CL-11)
  Nancy H. 55 (CL-13)
  Nancy J. 13* (CL-13)
  Nelson 60 (CL-59)
  Oliver E. 25* (CL-13)
  Philip W. 38 (CL-9)
  Pleasant 25 (CL-7)
  Pleasant 27* (CL-34)
  Richard G. 37 (CL-10)
  Roland 62* (F-252)
  Sally T. 6* (CL-13)
  Sarah 69* (CL-1)
  Susan 18* (CL-13)
  Thomas G. 35 (CL-8)
  Thomas J. 31* (CL-35)
  Tilman 62 (MA-254)
  William 14* (MT-6)
  William 17* (MA-217)
  William 31 (OS-310)
  William 40* (CL-3)
  William S. 2* (CL-20)
  William T. 31 (CL-23)
  Z. E. 30 (m) (MA-254)
BUSLEY
  N. B. 35 (m)* (ES-80)
BUSSARD
  Nancy 74?* (F-119)
BUSSING
  John 58* (GD-230)
BUSTER
  West 56 (B) (JE-47)
BUTCHER
  Isaac 40 (B) (OS-313)
BUTLER
  Andrew 37 (F-202)
  Brook 60* (MA-265)
  David 25* (CL-83)
  Easter 40* (B) (F-207)
  Franky 55* (B) (MT-3)
  Gabriel 68 (B) (MT-37)
  George 23* (MT-7)
  James D. 24* (F-149)
  Jas. C. 38* (F-188)
  John 37 (JE-46)
  Levi H. 32 (MT-12)
  Lucy 30* (CL-58)
  Mary (Mrs.) 53* (JE-55)
  Mary 2* (F-129)
  Sarah 50 (F-209)
  Thompson 23* (F-163)
  Thomson 21* (F-163)
  Walker T. 52?* (MA-265)
  Will 2* (GD-213)
BUTNER
  James 24 (MA-214)
  John 18* (MA-215)
BUTNER?
  Jesse 60 (MA-318)
BUTTS
  James 47 (MT-16)
BYARS
  John 66* (GD-259)
BYBEE
  Araminta 32* (CL-23)
  Fielding L. 25 (CL-59)
  James 49 (CL-22)
BYERS
  Edmund 69* (GD-210)
  James 29 (GD-221)
BYNUM
  Kinhan? 40 (m) (GD-244)
  William 48 (GD-228)
BYRD
  John S. 37 (ES-63)
  Mitchel 74* (CL-85)
BYRIE
  Wm. 35* (F-195)
BYRNES
  Aaron 36 (F-186)
  Ann E. 8* (F-186)
  Felix 47* (F-150)
  John 23* (F-124)
  Morgan 48 (F-150)
BYRNS
  Robert 38* (F-209)
  Wm. 66* (F-172)
CABER
  John 40 (MA-240)
CABLE
  Casper 24* (OS-289)
  Joseph 26* (OS-292)
CADWALADER
  Andrew 6* (ES-86)
CAGER
  Thomas 29* (MA-247)
CAHILL
  Margarett 31* (CL-44)
CAIN
  Hugh 38 (MA-293)
  James 45 (ES-101)
CAINE
  Gidron? 35 (m) (MA-297)
CAIR?
  Lamb 30 (m)* (F-194)
CAIRL
  Daniel 35* (F-199)
CALCLAZURE
  Geo. W. 30 (F-193)
CALCLOYER?
  Livina 27 (F-168)

Index

CALDWELL
 A. B. 30 (m)* (F-204)
 Andrew 52 (F-125)
 George Mc. 14* (JE-52)
 James C. 40 (MA-206)
 John 45* (F-253)
 Mary 35* (MT-41)
 Robert 16* (B) (F-250)
CALE
 John Y. 26* (MA-252)
CALELAZER?
 Sarah 28* (F-114)
CALICO
 Mary 40 (MA-286)
CALIHAN
 Mary 59 (ES-111)
CALINES?
 Henry B. 46* (CL-8)
CALINNIS?
 Eveline 16* (ES-51)
CALK
 Thomas 66* (MT-14)
CALLAGHAN
 Aaron 32* (MT-27)
CALLAHAN
 Ezekiel 39 (OS-317)
 Mack 23 (OS-317)
CALLEMEASE
 George 9* (OS-289)
CALLIHAN
 Wilson 37 (OS-320)
CALLIN
 Ellen 28* (F-132)
CALLISON
 Nancy 31* (GD-283)
CALLOWAY
 William 33* (F-116)
CALMES
 John W. 28 (CL-67)
 William 66 (CL-71)
CALVIN
 A. H. 37 (m)* (F-133)
 George 19* (F-191)
 John 11* (OS-291)
CALWELL
 Jane 50* (F-186)
CAMBELL
 Andrew 40 (MA-260)

Archibal 30 (MA-216)
David 27 (MA-216)
Edley 82 (m) (MA-216)
Hugh 35* (OS-313)
James 50 (MA-212)
John S. 30* (MA-206)
Samuel 56 (MA-222)
William 34 (MA-217)
CAMERON
 America 17 (JE-21)
 James 35* (JE-77)
 Ruth 70 (JE-21)
CAMMEL
 Stephen 40* (OS-289)
CAMPBELL
 A. D. 51 (m)* (ES-67)
 A. L. 11 (m)* (F-148)
 Andly 41 (m) (ES-61)
 Betty 8* (F-154)
 Bryant 38* (B) (F-193)
 Catharine 3* (F-124)
 Chilton 27* (CL-57)
 Emily 35 (JE-75)
 Enos 32* (F-114)
 James 34* (JE-40)
 John 15* (ES-66)
 John 23* (OS-320)
 John 30* (F-176)
 John 36* (JE-77)
 John B. 37* (F-166)
 John M. 14* (JE-57)
 John jr. 26* (JE-77)
 Julia A. 22* (F-169)
 Lucy M. 50* (JE-8)
 Mary 40* (F-204)
 Mathew 62* (JE-40)
 Peter 50 (JE-56)
 Robert 57 (F-140)
 Robert 90* (JE-40)
 Robt. 20?* (F-196)
 Sally A. 14* (ES-62)
 Samuel A. 35* (JE-69)
 Sarah 50* (CL-63)
 Sarah Ann 68* (F-251)
 Stephen 17* (F-131)
 Sudieth? 82 (f)* (CL-2)
 Whitico H. 65 (m) (GD-262)
 William 20* (F-120)

William 27* (MA-266)
William M. 40 (JE-68)
CANADA
 James 65* (MA-274)
 Mary 59* (MA-274)
CANE
 John 65 (MA-273)
CANIDA
 Anderson 29 (MA-264)
 Malinda 30* (MA-281)
CANLIN
 James 28 (F-125)
 James 5* (F-132)
CANNON
 Greenup 42* (F-196)
 James 40* (F-173)
 John 59* (F-195)
 Whitney 32?* (F-126)
CANOVER
 Chas. 40* (F-128)
CANTER
 John 30* (JE-35)
 Thomas 23 (JE-35)
CAPERTON
 William 53 (MA-252)
CAPPS
 Caleb 72 (CL-2)
CAPS
 Daniel 32 (OS-318)
CAR
 Louis P. 28* (MA-266)
CARBIN
 John 43 (F-155)
CARDWELL
 George 40 (MA-229)
CAREY
 Harry 30* (B) (CL-45)
CARLAN
 Melvina 33* (F-195)
CARLISLE
 Robert 62 (JE-2)
CARMACK
 John 30 (OS-282)
CARMICLE
 George 45 (ES-57)
CARNAHAN
 Catharine 28* (JE-2)

Index

CARNER
  Sally 50* (CL-22)
CARNEY
  John 19* (F-175)
  Martha 30* (MA-268)
CAROLILE
  Solomon 30 (GD-268)
CARP
  Henry 46 (GD-263)
CARPENTER
  C. B. 38 (m) (GD-274)
  Fielding 52* (MA-200)
  Geo. W. 20* (F-204)
  Isaac 24* (F-195)
  Jeremiah 62 (GD-279)
  Job 50 (MA-288)
  Preston 9?* (OS-300)
  Robert 24 (GD-280)
  Robert 67 (GD-282)
  Sally 88* (GD-227)
  Samuel D. 36 (GD-276)
  Silas 42 (GD-274)
  William 29* (MA-230)
CARR
  Adam 32* (MA-282)
  Charles 74 (F-244)
  Charles D. 25 (F-203)
  David 13* (ES-89)
  David 46 (F-251)
  Edmund 34 (CL-61)
  Eliza 44 (F-153)
  Harrison 36 (MA-224)
  James 73 (MA-221)
  Joel 44 (MA-300)
  Reuben 26* (F-194)
  Simeon 43 (CL-61)
  Thomas 38 (MA-300)
  Thomas 48 (F-244)
  William 49* (MA-246)
  William 62 (MA-220)
CARREL
  Thomas 49 (OS-295)
CARRICK
  Robt. 55* (F-166)
CARRIER
  Harvie 32 (MA-324)
CARRINGTON
  Frances 14* (MT-6)

  John 50 (MT-34)
  Samuel 45 (MT-26)
CARROL
  James 62* (JE-47)
  Noland 35 (OS-292)
  Richard H. 39 (JE-10)
  Thomas 37 (JE-16)
CARROLL
  Dempsey 35* (F-189)
  James 27* (F-186)
CARSON
  Joseph 48* (JE-54)
  Thomas H. 42 (ES-85)
CART
  O. R. 27 (m)* (CL-41)
CARTER
  Allen 32* (F-241)
  Asa 36 (OS-292)
  Caroline 27* (OS-313)
  Charles 79 (JE-31)
  Collin C. 37 (GD-264)
  Edward 54* (JE-57)
  Geo. G. 31* (F-179)
  George 33* (F-231)
  George 40* (MT-2)
  James 19* (JE-34)
  James 29 (JE-33)
  James 45* (CL-40)
  James 56* (F-227)
  Jane 70* (B) (F-125)
  John 24 (GD-280)
  Joseph J. 49* (F-228)
  Landon 50 (F-201)
  Lewis 46? (JE-18)
  Milam 8 (f)* (MA-265)
  Montacue 42 (JE-34)
  Paschal 37* (JE-32)
  Saml. 60 (B) (F-116)
  Sollimon 29 (OS-300)
  Susan 37 (F-254)
  Timothy 1* (MA-200)
  Will? W. 25 (GD-274)
  William 41* (MT-76)
  William 45* (MA-229)
  William 59* (MT-66)
CARTMILL
  Robert 75 (B) (JE-60)

CARTWRIGHT
  James L. 25 (CL-9)
CARTY
  John 43* (F-209)
  Mary 76 (F-209)
CARVER
  Lucinda 60 (GD-228)
  Sarah 54* (MA-287)
  Will 31 (GD-228)
CASE
  Joseph 40* (MT-20)
CASEY
  Lucy 35 (GD-256)
  Samuel E. 26 (GD-287)
CASKY
  Frederick 24* (CL-40)
CASS
  Abba 40* (B) (F-120)
CASSEL
  Saml. F. 33* (F-253)
CASSELL
  Barbary 45* (JE-59)
  Leonard 40* (JE-4)
  Mary 57* (F-223)
  Sarah 66* (JE-4)
  Thomas J. 46 (JE-77)
CAST
  Dudley S. 28 (CL-27)
CASTLE
  William 23* (MA-203)
CASTLEMAN
  Charles W. 39* (F-161)
  David 64 (F-182)
  M. P. 66 (f)* (F-160)
CATCHUM
  John 25 (OS-312)
CATES
  Alexander 42 (ES-92)
CATHERWOOD
  John 44 (CL-41)
CATLET
  Charles 25* (JE-32)
  John 75 (JE-32)
CAUSEY
  Robert 43* (F-150)
CAVE
  Alice 3* (JE-61)
  Patsy 65* (F-249)

Index

CAVENAUGH
  Archibald 36 (GD-283)
  Ruth 51 (MA-249)
CAVENDER
  Daniel 35 (F-186)
  Reuben 39* (F-186)
CAVENOR
  Patrick 24* (JE-61)
CAVINS
  John 62* (F-229)
CAVISTON
  John 42* (F-195)
CAWBY
  David 35 (F-170)
  John M. 9* (JE-49)
  Martin 32 (JE-48)
  Sarah 16* (JE-57)
  Susan 62* (JE-54)
CAWGILL
  James 27* (F-158)
CAYES
  Parey 29 (m)* (GD-207)
CAYWOOD
  Dudley 27 (MT-31)
  John T. 51 (MT-31)
  Mary E. 10* (MT-73)
  Morrison 36 (MT-32)
  William D. 37* (CL-76)
CECIL
  James 40 (GD-208)
  James sr. 49 (GD-233)
  Richard 43 (GD-230)
CENICK
  Wm. 33* (F-152)
CENOY
  Margaret 25* (F-200)
CENTERS
  Caroline 15* (MT-50)
  George 23 (OS-279)
  James 27 (MT-46)
  Joshua 25 (ES-53)
  Joshua 70* (MT-50)
  Powell 20 (MT-46)
  Solomon 60 (MT-46)
  Solomon jr. 28 (MT-46)
  Stephen 66 (MT-50)
  Tandy 22 (m) (MT-50)
  William 29 (ES-53)

CHADWICK
  S. S. 30 (f)* (F-130)
CHAISE
  William 26* (MA-214)
CHAMBERLAIN
  J. S. 71 (m)* (JE-55)
CHAMBERLIN
  William 36 (ES-112)
CHAMBERS
  Evaline 7* (ES-108)
  Fayett 32* (F-124)
  George 35* (F-135)
  Gideon 35 (OS-287)
  James 14* (ES-60)
  James P. 33* (JE-73)
  Jane 45* (F-147)
  John 37 (MA-273)
  John R. 37* (MT-5)
  Sarah 10* (ES-61)
  Victoria 42 (MA-257)
  William 23* (OS-300)
CHAMBLIN
  Isabella 17* (F-131)
CHAMLON
  William B. 28* (MT-3)
CHAMP
  Franklin W. 34 (GD-285)
  William 80 (MA-313)
CHAMPION
  Sarah 35 (JE-55)
CHANCELER
  Rebecca 53 (JE-39)
CHANCELLOR
  Julius 51* (F-124)
CHANCY
  James 30 (MA-299)
CHANDLER
  Alexander 20* (GD-215)
  Federick 80 (B) (MT-84)
  Larkin 27 (OS-317)
  Samuel 40* (OS-289)
CHANEY
  Hiram 23 (ES-111)
  John 65 (ES-111)
  Joseph 37 (ES-58)
  Thomas 20 (ES-88)
CHANY
  William 28 (MA-277)

CHAPEL
  William 25* (MT-39)
CHAPIZE
  Henry 3 (JE-71)
CHAPLIN
  Jacob 52* (F-224)
CHAPMAN
  Zimra 20 (m)* (MT-1)
CHARLES
  Joseph 40 (ES-47)
CHARLOTTE
  John W. 52 (GD-224)
CHASE
  Charles 30* (MA-265)
CHASTAIN
  S. A. 25 (m)* (OS-277)
CHASTEEN
  Jesse 55 (GD-270)
  Mary 25* (GD-273)
CHEATHAM
  David 47 (MT-71)
  Firman 28 (MT-83)
  James 63 (MT-24)
  Jerry 24 (MT-83)
  Joseph 30 (GD-241)
  Matilda O. 50* (F-215)
CHENAULT
  David 79 (MA-272)
  Tandy 43 (m) (MT-79)
CHETHAM
  Nancy 42 (MT-289)
CHEVIS
  David 35 (F-221)
  John G. 50 (CL-92)
  Sam 26* (F-221)
CHEW
  S. H. 30 (m)* (F-155)
CHILDERS
  Baley 35 (GD-234)
  Jacob G. 33* (F-228)
  John 38 (OS-290)
  Joseph 28* (OS-290)
  Linsey 58* (F-186)
  Margaret 22* (F-183)
  William 62 (OS-290)
CHILDS
  Luther 32 (F-203)

Index

CHILES
  Ambrose 70 (B) (CL-76)
  Eddy 22 (f)* (F-255)
  John 37 (F-235)
  John C. 56* (F-255)
  Laura 12* (CL-3)
  Richard 65 (F-226)
  Samuel W. 47* (CL-9)
  Susan 13* (F-225)
  Thomas D. 36* (ES-60)
  Walter 38 (MT-1)
  William 72* (ES-103)
  William P. 28* (ES-109)
CHILLIS
  John 50 (MA-265)
  Milly 89* (MA-270)
CHINAULT
  Anderson 21* (MA-303)
  Anderson 62 (MA-302)
  Ann 40 (MA-253)
  Cabel 56 (m) (MA-299)
  Cavel? 55 (m) (MA-277)
  David 22 (MA-253)
  Josiah P. 39 (MA-253)
  Nancy 59* (MA-254)
  Walter 46 (MA-253)
  William 44* (MA-230)
CHINN
  Rachael 60 (B) (F-114)
  William 30* (B) (F-145)
CHIPLEY
  W. S. 39 (m)* (F-137)
CHISER
  John 45* (MA-318)
CHISM
  Calvin 27* (CL-39)
  James 62 (CL-23)
  John 41* (F-221)
  Nathaniel 62 (CL-61)
  Thomas 82* (CL-51)
  William 27 (CL-27)
CHISM?
  Wm. 30* (B) (F-184)
CHITEY
  Matthew 49 (MA-215)
CHOAT
  John W. 44* (MT-19)

CHORN
  Samuel 63 (CL-77)
  Samuel S. 25 (CL-84)
CHOWNING
  Mary 48* (JE-56)
  Thomas 24* (JE-68)
CHRISLY
  John 45 (F-147)
CHRISMAN
  Henry 50 (JE-26)
  Hugh jr. 22* (JE-41)
  Isaac 52 (ES-55)
  Jefferson 45 (F-247)
  John 24* (F-164)
  Joseph 50 (F-248)
  Joseph H. 50* (F-163)
  Lewis H. 36 (JE-36)
  William 38* (GD-214)
CHRISTIAN
  Ann 35 (F-242)
  James 32* (F-121)
  John 52 (F-224)
  Lucinda 25 (CL-6)
  Thomas 59* (F-226)
  Turner? 53 (F-242)
  William? 25* (OS-311)
  Wm. 25 (F-240)
CHRISTIE
  Margaret L. 43 (F-215)
CHRISTOPHER
  Ambrose 30 (MA-293)
  Andrew 44 (GD-207)
  Columbus 14* (F-206)
  Daid 32 (m)* (MA-209)
  Frances 27 (MA-280)
  George 34 (MA-229)
  George 35 (MA-313)
  Howell 18* (MA-277)
  John 72 (MA-295)
  Sarah 62* (B) (JE-75)
  Thomas 23* (MA-274)
  Wily M. 44 (ES-66)
CHRISTY
  Hannah 73* (CL-52)
  Julius 43 (CL-57)
CHRYSTAL
  James E. 37* (F-234)

CHURCH
  James 32* (MA-264)
CILE
  John J. 28* (JE-5)
CIMBRELL
  Sally 40* (MA-218)
CLABOURN
  John 35 (B) (F-117)
CLAIBOURN
  Solomon 48 (B) (MT-5)
CLAKE
  Rog. S. 24* (MT-7)
CLAMPET
  Henry 90* (CL-50)
CLANAHAN
  Sarah 30* (CL-39)
CLANCY
  Lewis 56 (CL-37)
CLARK
  A. B. 28 (m)* (F-194)
  A. H. 40 (m)* (F-148)
  Alex 57* (F-196)
  Anderson 16* (OS-283)
  Benjamin 44 (MA-317)
  Catharine 17* (MT-18)
  Charity 70* (B) (CL-3)
  David 20 (GD-256)
  David 67 (MA-308)
  Denis 43 (B) (JE-38)
  Elhannon 37 (OS-302)
  Gemima 75* (B) (CL-42)
  Georg e60 (JE-36)
  Harriett 41* (CL-2)
  Henry M. 7* (MT-37)
  James 33 (MA-308)
  James 46* (F-250)
  James 46* (MT-72)
  James 54 (MT-26)
  James P. 24* (MT-32)
  John 28* (CL-89)
  John 37* (MA-308)
  John 58* (MT-30)
  John 63 (F-144)
  John P. 31 (B) (F-204)
  John W. 39* (F-136)
  Joseph 20* (F-184)
  M. B. 23 (f)* (B) (F-151)
  Manuel 57 (B) (F-131)

Index

CLARK
  Margaret A. 12* (MT-78)
  Martin 50* (MT-33)
  Mary 77 (MT-44)
  McKinney 41 (MT-59)
  Polly 20 (JE-36)
  Richard 75 (B) (F-159)
  Robert 57* (ES-88)
  Robt. 40* (B) (F-160)
  Rody 70 (B) (F-159)
  Salley 45* (GD-285)
  Thomas 11* (ES-105)
  Thomas 12* (ES-55)
  Thomas 24* (JE-17)
  Wesley 22 (JE-30)
  William 45* (JE-19)
  William 59* (F-234)
  William J. 37* (ES-59)
  Wm. 34 (OS-301)
  Zachariah 23* (F-162)
CLARKE
  Comely 34 (m) (GD-252)
  Enoch 28 (F-203)
  George W. 52 (F-243)
  James A. 5* (CL-82)
  James W. 34 (MA-271)
  John 52 (CL-84)
  John 54 (F-252)
  John 86* (GD-260)
  Mary 53* (CL-84)
  Mary E. 2* (CL-83)
  Thomas 35 (GD-237)
  William 39 (GD-234)
  martin 40 (GD-256)
CLARKSON
  Jas. M. 37 (CL-93)
CLARY
  John 40 (F-128)
CLAUSON
  Richard 31 (F-230)
CLAWSON
  Jesse 32 (CL-56)
  Pleasant 35* (CL-81)
CLAY
  Henry 73* (F-223)
  Isreal 41 (B) (MA-302)
  John W. 28* (CL-41)
  Sarah 20* (CL-77)

  Theoe. W. 40* (F-196)
  Thomas H. 46* (F-223)
CLAYFOOL
  Rebecca 63* (F-196)
CLEAVELAND
  Elizabeth 65* (GD-205)
  George 28 (GD-206)
  John 35* (GD-212)
  Mary 60* (F-122)
CLEET?
  Margaret 65* (MA-248)
CLELLAND
  John 34* (F-196)
CLEM
  James 40 (CL-51)
  John W. 31 (CL-17)
  Joseph 22 (CL-63)
  Joseph 50* (CL-57)
  Josiah 34 (CL-68)
  Leroy 30 (CL-39)
CLEMENS
  Robert 32* (F-253)
CLEMENTS
  Jonathan 42 (ES-96)
  William 32 (JE-7)
CLEMIN
  A. G. 32 (m)* (MT-70)
CLEMM
  John 69 (MT-78)
  Mary 25* (MT-6)
  Patterson 34* (MT-57)
  Theressa 26* (MT-78)
CLEMM?
  George 70* (ES-69)
CLEMMONS
  Elizabeth 66* (JE-53)
  James 45 (JE-53)
  Madison 22* (F-163)
  Thos. C. 28 (F-165)
CLEMMS
  John 34 (MA-241)
CLESER
  Elizabeth 13* (F-172)
CLEVELAND
  Amaha 48 (f)* (MT-3)
  George jr. 44* (JE-67)
  George sr. 88* (JE-65)
  John H. 30 (CL-72)

CLIFT
  Archibol* (MA-219)
  George 30 (MA-220)
  Thomas 39 (MA-237)
  Thomas 40 (MA-218)
CLIMES
  M. Q.? 32 (m) (F-153)
CLINCH
  William 35* (F-235)
CLINKENBEARD
  Harriet 30 (B) (CL-90)
  Lewis 17* (CL-44)
CLINKENBUND?
  John 57 (CL-77)
CLINTON
  George 60 (GD-275)
CLOUD
  Harriet 35* (F-146)
  R. T. S. 34 (m)* (F-159)
CLOUSE
  James 34 (GD-255)
  James W. 22 (GD-255)
  William 20 (GD-214)
CLOWERS
  James M. 32 (ES-85)
CLOY
  Cassius M. 39 (MA-207)
CLUB
  Joshua 26* (MA-228)
CLUGSTON
  John 57 (F-226)
CLUKE
  James 22* (MT-11)
  Mary W. 16* (MT-40)
CLURE
  Sarah 14* (MT-72)
COATNEY
  William 16* (ES-88)
COATS
  Rice 38 (MA-303)
COBB
  Ambrose 19* (JE-2)
  Henry 25 (MA-278)
  Henry 48 (ES-62)
  James 43 (MA-271)
  Jesse 34 (ES-63)
  John 33 (JE-34)
  Richard 32 (ES-63)

Index

COBB
  Samuel 37 (MA-283)
  Zine 52 (m)* (MA-277)
COBBS
  Charles 34 (JE-29)
COBURN
  Jane 62* (F-195)
COCHRAN
  J. W. 36 (m) (F-210)
  John 58* (MA-227)
  M. 40 (m)* (F-129)
  R. E. 4 (f)* (F-167)
  Samuel 35 (GD-278)
  Sarah 25* (MA-320)
  Walker 32 (GD-285)
COCKERELL
  William 48 (MT-68)
COCKLEISURE
  Julia A. 12* (F-210)
  Maria 34 (F-210)
COCKRAM
  John 44? (OS-304)
COCKRELL
  Henry C. 31 (MA-254)
  Jane 37 (MT-69)
  Jaulia 38* (OS-289)
COCKRILL
  E. L. 28 (m)* (ES-105)
COCKRUM
  James 28 (OS-291)
  William 56 (OS-291)
CODDLE
  John 45 (MA-311)
COFER
  David T. 23* (CL-87)
  Elizab. 30 (F-209)
COFFEE
  Coleby 50 (ES-95)
  Rawley 43 (MT-9)
COFFEY
  Richard . 55* (MA-260)
COFFIELD
  B. G. 22 (m)* (F-129)
  Margaret 33* (F-128)
COFFMAN
  David 71 (JE-60)
  Saml. 30* (F-150)

COGAR
  Cap? Tho. T. 52* (JE-43)
  M. H. 27 (m) (JE-41)
  William G. 38* (JE-77)
COGGSHELL
  John B. 29 (F-115)
COGLE
  Cornelies 30* (F-255)
COGWELL
  George 47* (F-133)
COILE
  Nancy 38* (F-176)
COKE
  Abram 41* (F-196)
COLBERT
  Thomas 17 (F-141)
COLCLOZURE?
  John 44 (F-156)
COLE
  Barton 24* (OS-304)
  Benjamin 55 (B) (F-248)
  Edward 28* (JE-78)
  Jahue 38 (OS-299)
  James 40 (ES-111)
  James W. 44 (CL-45)
  Jerry 27* (B) (CL-43)
  John 23 (OS-304)
  John 6* (OS-295)
  Katharine 45* (JE-72)
  L. W. B. 30 (m) (F-175)
  Margaret 28* (OS-287)
  Mary 33* (MA-210)
  Mathew 76 (OS-301)
  Ose 45 (m) (OS-304)
  William 27* (OS-312)
  William 50 (MA-220)
COLELAZER
  James 40* (F-115)
COLEMAN
  Becky 75* (B) (F-214)
  David S. 26* (F-166)
  Eliza 70* (F-168)
  Eliza B. 47 (F-176)
  Fauntleroy 21* (F-233)
  Florence 17* (F-225)
  Francis 19 (JE-27)
  George M. 26* (MT-40)
  Henry 58* (F-195)

  J. C. 26 (m)* (JE-32)
  John 26* (F-215)
  Marquis 21* (F-230)
  P. L. 34 (m)* (F-195)
  Paul 35* (B) (F-118)
  Rosetta 5* (B) (CL-4)
  Samuel 45 (F-230)
  William 37 (JE-21)
COLEMAN?
  Charles 34* (JE-12)
COLEY
  Charles 23* (JE-78)
  William 64 (JE-40)
COLIBAN
  Rebecca 20* (MA-291)
COLIVER
  Rachel 51 (MT-32)
  Samuel 32 (MT-26)
  Thomas 25 (MT-31)
COLLEY
  Nancy 80 (GD-219)
  Pleasant 38 (GD-219)
  Samuel 27 (GD-219)
COLLIER
  Alexander 55 (GD-226)
  Aron 63 (GD-262)
  Benjamin 28 (GD-233)
  Hyram 47 (GD-233)
  Mary 60 (GD-275)
  Mary 67* (GD-222)
  Mason 32 (GD-283)
  Moses 26* (GD-245)
  Moses 74* (GD-275)
  Moses 81* (GD-222)
  Sarah 52 (GD-262)
  William 50 (GD-225)
COLLIN
  Randolph 29* (F-146)
COLLINS
  Ann 39* (MA-257)
  Asa 45 (F-125)
  Betcy A. 23 (m)* (JE-33)
  Eli C. 49* (ES-84)
  Ephram 45 (MA-319)
  George P. 25* (JE-65)
  James 32* (F-176)
  James 40* (CL-43)
  James 67* (ES-102)

Index

COLLINS
Jerry V. 34 (MA-296)
Jerrymiah 36 (MA-263)
John 27* (F-128)
John 30 (MA-240)
John 57 (MA-319)
John C. 20* (JE-68)
Joseph 39 (ES-92)
Josiah 71* (MA-264)
Levi 36 (ES-101)
Lewis 24* (F-136)
Lewis 70* (JE-62)
Sallie 60 (B) (F-192)
Samuel R. 27* (MT-68)
Sarah 70* (MT-58)
Whitfield 31 (JE-64)
William 27 (ES-102)
William 30 (MA-319)
William 40 (MA-309)
William P. 22* (JE-66)
COLTER
James 69* (MA-276)
COLTON
James 35 (MA-289)
COLVER
Charles P. 27* (MT-14)
COMBS
Allen 40* (B) (CL-9)
Caroline 22* (MT-41)
Clabourne 46 (OS-286)
Cuthbert 49 (ES-79)
Cuthbert 67 (CL-60)
Edward 22 (CL-10)
Edward M. 32 (CL-75)
Glenmore 36* (CL-75)
Harden 55* (OS-281)
Harvey 34 (OS-280)
Jackson 37 (MT-31)
James P. 40 (CL-69)
Jeremiah 29 (JE-40)
John 58 (OS-281)
John 68 (MT-37)
Laban 29 (MT-75)
Leslie 56* (F-193)
Lydia 50* (MT-36)
Marem 44 (CL-66)
Paul __ * (CL-67)
R. K. 39 (m) (ES-84)

R. W. 43 (m)* (MT-79)
Sophia 62 (JE-46)
Stephen D. 25 (CL-10)
W. 26 (m) (JE-39)
Wallace 26* (CL-10)
Washington 35 (MT-74)
William 32 (OS-284)
William 33 (MA-262)
William 45 (MT-74)
William M. 21* (MT-48)
COMELY
David 49 (GD-260)
James 67 (GD-251)
Jennings 26* (GD-264)
John 26* (GD-251)
John 60* (GD-238)
Perry 27 (GD-238)
Sabril 68 (m) (GD-247)
COMLEY
James H. 25 (GD-227)
Will 26 (GD-277)
COMO
Flavous J. 43* (GD-284)
J. T. 28 (m) (GD-282)
Robert R. 4* (GD-285)
COMPTON
Burrus 64* (GD-240)
COMSKI?
Samuel E. 42 (GD-287)
COMSTOCK
Alexander 24* (JE-2)
CONAGAM
James 72 (GD-207)
CONALL
M. A. 11 (f)* (F-122)
CONDA
Thomas J. 14 (F-147)
CONE
Solomon 27 (GD-215)
CONGLETON
Isaac 45* (OS-287)
John M. 40* (MT-10)
William 49 (OS-294)
CONKLIN
— 50 (m)* (F-190)
CONKRIGHT
John 42* (CL-36)
John M. 13* (CL-32)

Ketura 68 (f) (CL-32)
Pleasant P. 11* (CL-32)
CONLEY
Henderson 31 (MT-43)
Henry 38 (MT-54)
James 33 (MT-23)
James 69 (MT-53)
Louisa 36 (F-119)
Sylvia 60* (B) (MT-26)
CONN
Alexander 13* (GD-280)
Elizabeth 60 (GD-273)
Thomas K. 24 (GD-289)
Will 38 (GD-287)
CONNAH?
Margaret 58* (F-142)
CONNALL
Martin 28* (MT-35)
CONNELL
Catharine 70 (F-135)
James 31 (CL-11)
Patrick 65 (F-205)
CONNER
Ambrose 8* (MA-265)
Coleman 73 (MT-36)
Daniel 36 (MT-20)
Ezekial 35 (ES-48)
George 24 (ES-58)
James 50* (ES-65)
John M. 75* (GD-273)
M. A. 29 (f)* (F-122)
Malinda 54 (JE-8)
Moses 25 (CL-36)
Nancy 19* (ES-50)
Paris 36 (GD-273)
Patrick 30* (CL-94)
William 26 (MT-62)
William H. 87* (MT-84)
CONQUEST
Lunsford 35* (F-181)
CONROY
Patrick 27* (MA-251)
CONWAY
Sally Ann 38* (F-222)
COOK
Edwin A. 19* (MT-36)
Elizabeth 52* (F-185)
Isaac 44 (F-219)

Index

COOK
  James W. 21* (F-207)
  Jas. D. 43 (F-159)
  John 24* (MT-66)
  John 32* (F-194)
  John 56 (F-154)
  John B. 41* (JE-70)
  Mary E. 16* (JE-69)
  Nancy 63* (B) (F-145)
  Philip 33* (JE-56)
  Pleasant 17* (JE-75)
  Prissilla G. 43 (F-173)
  R. P. 1 (m)* (JE-10)
  Reubin 49* (JE-69)
  Samuel 40 (F-213)
  Stephen M. 28* (MT-2)
  Susan N. 54* (F-214)
  Thomas 31* (F-227)
  Thomas 49 (JE-56)
  Thomas B. 50 (F-122)
  William 47 (F-123)
COOKE
  Elijah 40* (GD-241)
  Grove 78 (GD-271)
  John 21* (GD-214)
  Reuben 48 (GD-278)
  Sarah 57* (GD-266)
COOLE
  Jacob 75* (MT-66)
COOLEY
  Hannah 64 (GD-279)
  Polley 37 (GD-279)
  Reuben 57 (JE-47)
COOLIDGE
  Loonrisla? 11* (F-130)
COOLY
  Jesse 37 (MA-324)
  Levi 36 (MA-323)
  William 46 (MA-324)
COONEY
  Thomas V. 36* (F-126)
COONS
  Edward H. 36* (F-233)
  George W. 47 (F-233)
  James M. 40* (F-236)
  John 37* (F-133)
  John 76* (MT-79)
  John F. 35* (JE-26)
  Joshua 66 (F-233)
  Permelia 30* (MT-83)
  T. M. 33 (m)* (JE-66)
  William B. 32 (F-233)
  William C. 30* (F-230)
COONS?
  Nancy 27* (CL-3)
COONY
  James 28 (F-120)
COOPER
  A. 35 (m)* (F-214)
  Eleanor 40 (CL-30)
  George 46 (ES-75)
  George 79* (MT-72)
  James M. 43 (CL-31)
  John 40 (MA-312)
  John H. 18* (MT-4)
  John H. 40* (F-189)
  Joseph B. 48* (F-208)
  L. W. 37 (m)* (JE-71)
  Lucy 28* (F-195)
  Margaret 45* (MT-67)
  Mary 35* (MA-313)
  Mary 74 (CL-53)
  Mary H. 55 (F-222)
  Milly 13* (CL-30)
  Milton 30* (MT-4)
  Reuben H. 36* (F-193)
  Samuel 34 (MA-239)
  Sophia 42* (MA-312)
  William 38* (F-134)
  William 42 (OS-285)
  William C. 45 (CL-57)
COOVERT
  David sr. 65 (GD-219)
  Garrard 35 (GD-219)
  Sarah 24 (GD-219)
CORDREY
  John L. 29* (F-123)
CORDWELL
  E. C. 36 (m) (F-129)
  James 37* (F-129)
CORELEY
  Charlotte 33 (MT-49)
CORHOM
  Maria 17* (MA-222)
  Robert 64 (MA-222)
CORMAN
  A. H. 35 (m) (JE-46)
  Abraham 49 (JE-76)
  Coon. 33 (m) (JE-46)
  Elizabeth 54* (JE-55)
  George 58 (JE-48)
  John 52 (JE-46)
  John jr. 31 (JE-46)
  Jonas 47 (JE-56)
  Jonas T. 27 (JE-47)
  William 28 (JE-49)
CORMAN?
  George 24 (JE-39)
CORN
  Ellis 53* (JE-74)
CORNELIOUS
  Lorenzo 38 (GD-209)
CORNELIS
  Nancy 45 (MA-256)
CORNELISON
  Albert 33 (MA-213)
  Alitha 37 (MA-216)
  Edward 27 (MA-229)
  Franklin 37* (MA-286)
  Garland 40 (m) (MA-229)
  M. G. 37 (m) (MA-217)
  Richard 59 (MA-220)
  Robert 28* (MA-257)
  Susan 44* (MA-264)
CORNER
  Maurice 45* (F-225)
CORNETT
  A. J. 33 (m)* (JE-55)
  Eliza D. 22* (JE-70)
  John 62 (OS-306)
  Lewis 35 (OS-306)
CORNWALL?
  Elijah 17* (OS-284)
CORNWELL
  James 35 (MT-75)
  Jesse 35 (MT-75)
  Rebecca 50* (MT-75)
COROTHERS
  Mary B. 48* (JE-65)
CORUM
  William 22* (OS-286)
COSBY
  Austin 50* (MA-321)

Index

COSBY
 Edward 42 (JE-15)
 James D. 66* (GD-261)
 Linsey 19 (m) (MA-313)
 Meredith 55 (MA-313)
 Winfield M. 45 (F-246)
 Wingfield 59 (MA-210)
COSHOUR?
 Robert 25* (MA-230)
COSS
 Martha 15* (MT-2)
COTMAN
 Benjamin 45 (CL-79)
 Tubman 50 (CL-62)
COTTEN
 Paulina 35 (MA-317)
 William 45 (MA-317)
COTTON
 John 45* (B) (F-119)
 Nancy 56 (B) (F-248)
COUCH
 Catey 19 (f)* (OS-290)
 William 35 (OS-282)
COUCHMAN
 John 61* (CL-11)
 Nathaniel 32* (CL-46)
 Peter 58 (MT-54)
 William 43* (CL-3)
COUCHMEN
 Frederick 49 (CL-8)
COULTER
 Paulina 17* (MA-270)
COURR?
 Jesse 57 (MA-226)
COVINGTON
 Ama 64* (MA-234)
 Benj. 38* (F-196)
 Charles 20 (ES-85)
 Coleman 49* (MA-267)
 Jeptha 35 (MA-248)
 Rachael 55 (ES-91)
 Robert 46 (MA-265)
 William 29 (MA-248)
 William 66 (MA-248)
 Wilton 38 (MA-261)
COWELL
 C. 24 (f)* (F-133)
 Julian 31 (f)* (F-134)

COWS?
 Samuel E. 23* (MA-202)
COX
 Benigroves 65* (B) (MT-40)
 Benjamin 30 (ES-102)
 Benjamin 56 (ES-102)
 Branton 69* (OS-294)
 Charles 69* (ES-86)
 Daniel 45 (MA-282)
 David 25 (MT-66)
 David D. 47 (MA-201)
 David H. 28* (CL-41)
 E. K. W. 23 (m)* (MT-52)
 Frances 40 (F-179)
 Green 43 (MA-267)
 Jacient 40 (m) (OS-293)
 James 33 (ES-102)
 Jesse 72 (MA-260)
 John 37 (ES-100)
 John 45 (MA-260)
 John N. 30* (MA-247)
 Joshua 25* (F-168)
 Lewis 38 (ES-48)
 Manerva 70 (MA-279)
 Martha 21* (F-192)
 Mary B. 50* (MT-2)
 Perry 25 (ES-95)
 Rebecca 67* (GD-246)
 Robert 54 (MA-234)
 Sarah 50 (CL-70)
 T. M. 25 (m)* (F-141)
 Thomas 36 (MA-236)
 William 21 (MA-259)
 William 25 (ES-112)
 William 33 (MT-65)
 William 52 (MA-310)
 William D. 40 (JE-66)
COY
 Tandy 42 (MA-315)
COYLE
 Alfred 51 (ES-92)
 Francis M. 26 (ES-96)
 Isaac 60 (MA-238)
 Jesse 69* (ES-96)
 Tilford 33 (ES-72)
 William 26 (MA-234)
COYLE?
 Wm. 39 (F-183)

CRABTREE
 Jacob 52 (ES-52)
 John T. 26 (ES-51)
CRAFFORD
 Harvey 43 (ES-105)
CRAGLER
 John 38 (MA-225)
CRAIG
 Daniel 60 (MT-67)
 David 28* (GD-211)
 Dudley M. 48* (F-215)
 E. W. 70 (m) (F-212)
 Fleming 46 (MT-56)
 Herman T. 21* (ES-80)
 Jacob 42 (ES-76)
 James 24* (MT-61)
 John M. 22* (MT-72)
 Lewis S. 25 (JE-62)
 Mary 70* (F-158)
 Parker 45* (F-198)
 Robert 50 (MT-39)
 Samuel H. 77* (JE-61)
 Sarah 18* (F-214)
 Sarah M. 32 (ES-80)
 Sharlott 15* (F-154)
 William 26* (MA-229)
 William F. 58 (MT-60)
CRAIN
 J. P. 25 (m) (F-177)
CRANDELL
 J. B. 22 (m) (F-171)
CRANE
 Samuel B. F. 32* (MT-40)
CRANLEY
 Edward 28* (F-192)
CRATER
 Lavinia 16* (OS-315)
CRAVEN
 Elizabeth 62* (JE-8)
CRAVENS
 David W. 26 (MT-35)
 Elijah 24 (MT-35)
 Elisha 23 (JE-77)
 Elisha B. 44 (F-202)
 Geo. 58 (F-162)
 James C. 21* (F-162)
 Jeremiah 54 (MT-40)
 Martha J. 17* (JE-61)

Index

CRAVENS
  Milton 31 (F-165)
  Thomas 54 (JE-58)
  William 30 (MT-35)
  William 63 (MT-26)
CRAW
  Daniel sr. 52 (MT-45)
CRAWFORD
  A. G. 24 (m) (OS-304)
  Alexander B. 26* (MT-17)
  George W. 27 (MA-235)
  John 35 (OS-298)
  John A. 85* (MT-40)
  Lorinda 15* (B) (MT-71)
  Mary 25* (B) (ES-98)
  Mary 60 (F-244)
  Oliver 45* (ES-51)
  R. Lee 45 (ES-51)
  Rose 65* (B) (MT-22)
  Simson 25 (OS-294)
  Volentine 73 (m) (ES-51)
CRAWL
  Elizabeth 37* (JE-3)
CRAWLEY
  Asa 46* (F-245)
  Dennis 28* (F-175)
CRAY
  Lorenzo D. 45 (MT-79)
CREATH
  Jacob 73 (JE-16)
CREECH
  Elijah 38* (OS-315)
  Gilbert 30 (OS-315)
CREED
  John 80* (MA-269)
  Julian 22* (CL-20)
  Robert B. 51 (ES-69)
CRIDLAND
  S. W. 28 (m)* (F-214)
CRIM
  Albien 23* (CL-3)
  Benjamin Y. 45* (CL-3)
  Elizabeth 65* (CL-28)
  Fielding 63* (F-227)
  George W. 34* (CL-28)
  James 34 (CL-17)
  John 20* (CL-22)
  John W. 20* (CL-13)
  Joseph 25* (F-252)
  Lewis 48 (F-230)
  Peter 39 (CL-15)
  Sally 13* (CL-47)
CRIM?
  Frances 74* (MT-17)
  John 40* (CL-23)
CRISSEL
  Margaret 37 (F-118)
CRISTOPHER
  Catherine 28* (F-240)
  Horrens 17* (F-199)
CRISTY
  W. 45 (m)* (F-141)
CRITENDEN
  Mary W.? 57* (F-144)
  Nancy 35?* (F-142)
CRITZER
  Leander 27* (MT-72)
CROCHER
  William 47* (MA-248)
CROCK
  Joseph 38* (JE-57)
CROCKETT
  Elizabeth 80* (GD-232)
CROFFORD
  H. 75 (m)* (F-184)
CROGHAN
  Francis 64* (F-191)
CROMWELL
  Aben W. 36 (F-168)
  Benj. 67 (F-168)
  Benj. 6y7 (F-155)
  Eliza D. 19* (F-178)
  John E. 42 (F-189)
  John W. 20 (F-184)
  Mary 1* (F-165)
  Oliver 50* (F-181)
  Vincent 24 (F-128)
  Vincent 53 (F-188)
  W. B. 33 (m)* (F-124)
  William 43* (MT-5)
CROOK
  John 23* (MA-203)
  John P. 35 (MA-290)
  Kiah 50 (m) (MA-263)
  Walter 43 (F-207)
CROOKE
  Jabez 62* (GD-275)
  James 34 (GD-284)
CROPPER
  Nathaniel 35* (F-200)
CROSBY?
  William 24* (JE-39)
CROSS
  A. A. 44 (f)* (F-123)
CROSSIT
  Mary 60* (MT-73)
CROSSWAIT
  Perry 23* (MT-2)
CROSSWHILE
  Reubin 79* (MA-299)
CROTH
  S. 49 (f)* (B) (F-127)
CROUCH
  Absolem 51 (GD-240)
  James 53 (ES-79)
  Mary 5* (ES-99)
  Mima 30* (ES-79)
  N. 24 (m)* (F-130)
CROUCH?
  Thomas 46* (ES-112)
CROUCHER
  Edward 46 (MA-228)
  Malinda 25* (MA-243)
CROULEY
  Catharine 22* (GD-289)
CROW
  A. 22 (f)* (JE-46)
  David 26 (CL-70)
  Eli 54 (JE-72)
  Eliza 46* (JE-5)
  Holeman 33* (JE-75)
  James 47 (ES-84)
  James E. 36 (GD-220)
  Job B. 45 (ES-71)
  John 22* (F-194)
  John 28* (CL-94)
  John 46* (MA-210)
  John 52 (CL-68)
  John 76 (CL-38)
  Joseph R. 40* (GD-266)
  Milton 33 (JE-42)
  Nancy 20* (JE-50)
  Nathanel 21* (CL-5)

Index

CROW
  Nicholas 36 (CL-56)
  Polly 55* (B) (CL-31)
  Randall 37 (ES-80)
  Rhoda 57 (CL-71)
  Richard sr. 49 (MT-46)
  Robert 43 (ES-84)
  Samuel 28 (ES-74)
  Thomas 13* (ES-71)
  William 22 (CL-63)
  Zachariah 25 (CL-71)
CROWE
  Theodora 24* (F-223)
CROWFORD
  Joseph 42* (OS-315)
CROWLEY
  David 47* (F-132)
CROZER
  David 54* (JE-76)
CRUMBAUGH
  Ezra 53 (F-160)
  John 41 (F-161)
CRUSE
  Isham 16* (MA-206)
  Jackson 33 (MA-238)
  Samuel 18* (MA-279)
  William 38 (MA-275)
CRUSH
  John 41* (F-195)
CRUTCHER
  James 26 (JE-42)
  James U. 38 (MA-206)
  Jefferson 16* (JE-2)
  Mary 70 (JE-50)
  Peter 34 (JE-42)
  Sarah 58 (JE-41)
  Will 31 (GD-274)
CRUTCHFIEL
  Mordica 25 (m) (JE-36)
  Mordica 62 (m) (JE-36)
CRUTCHFIELD
  Henderson 28 (GD-288)
  John 28* (CL-27)
  John 48 (CL-33)
  Martin 53 (CL-25)
  Sutton 45 (CL-34)
CUDLESS
  George 24* (F-146)

CUFF
  John 30* (CL-47)
CULBERSON
  James H. 9* (GD-207)
CULBERTSON
  David 60* (CL-27)
CULLEN
  Charles 23* (F-203)
CULLIM
  Jack 70* (B) (CL-18)
CULLIN
  Bryan 21* (MA-259)
CULLUM
  Charles 60* (B) (CL-27)
CULTON
  William J. 33* (OS-316)
CUMER?
  John 27* (F-128)
CUMMINGS
  William H. 35 (CL-33)
CUMMINS
  Harriett 2* (CL-26)
  Hester 81* (CL-55)
  John S. 12* (CL-21)
  Saml. 21* (CL-54)
CUNDIFF
  William 40 (OS-289)
CUNN
  Batris 51 (f)* (F-159)
CUNNIGIM
  Samuel 30 (OS-295)
  Wilie 38 (OS-284)
CUNNINGHAM
  Abner 48* (CL-91)
  Arthur B. 50 (F-213)
  David 19* (ES-86)
  Geo. W. 35 (F-245)
  Isaac 45 (CL-94)
  J. W. 23 (m)* (F-194)
  Jas. 40* (F-195)
  Jesse 53 (CL-91)
  John 23* (MA-252)
  Kate 31?* (F-199)
  Nancy 39* (F-162)
  Polly 75* (CL-91)
  Rosey 45* (F-181)
  T. 21 (m)* (F-144)
  William 42 (ES-59)

CURAN
  Marietta 34 (GD-289)
CURCH
  Mathew B. 30* (MA-278)
CURD
  Eleanor 46 (F-144)
  John 51 (F-164)
  Joseph 53* (JE-41)
  Nancy J. 21* (ES-103)
  R. S. 29 (m) (JE-41)
  Wm. P. 36 (F-190)
CURLE
  Sophia 39 (F-244)
CURRINS
  Jacob 85* (MA-287)
CURRY
  Abed 39 (m) (CL-58)
  Andy 4* (ES-57)
  Charles 50 (CL-95)
  Elias 47 (CL-58)
  Francis M. 36* (F-216)
  Joseph 26 (CL-64)
  Thomas 23* (MT-35)
  William 33 (ES-52)
  William 53 (MT-44)
  William E. 30 (CL-79)
CURSEY
  M. 17 (m)* (F-146)
CURTIS
  A. A. 32 (m)* (ES-60)
  Addison 44 (ES-76)
  Benjamin 20 (CL-34)
  Dudley 12* (ES-76)
  George 26 (ES-78)
  Harrison 28 (CL-70)
  Jacob 42 (B?) (CL-70)
  James J. 32 (CL-32)
  Jeremiah J. 35 (ES-77)
  Jesse 49 (ES-78)
  Job 60 (MA-315)
  John 58 (ES-77)
  John J. 32 (CL-32)
  Kitty 24* (CL-35)
  Levi 50 (CL-36)
  Lyman 38* (F-188)
  Mary A. 20* (CL-66)
  Ranson O. 38 (CL-18)
  Sally 22* (CL-32)

Index

CURTIS
  Thomas 53 (CL-64)
  Washington 22 (MA-315)
  William 20 (CL-34)
  William 62 (ES-77)
  William 64 (ES-77)
  William F. 37 (ES-77)
CUSIE
  Martha 30 (MA-311)
CUZICK
  William 38 (MA-321)
DABNEY
  Elizabeth 55 (MT-30)
  Spencer G. 26 (GD-287)
DAGANS?
  Betsey 58 (B) (F-212)
DAILY
  Lucy A. 22* (F-196)
DALE
  George W. 21 (MT-40)
  Mary 47* (MT-32)
  Mary 60 (MT-33)
  Nancy 55* (GD-241)
  Thomas 23 (MT-32)
  Thomas 23 (MT-32)
  William 52 (MT-29)
DALEY
  Benjamin 44 (F-115)
  Lawrence 57 (F-166)
DALHAM
  Letitia 60* (F-182)
DALLAS
  Eliz. 27* (F-200)
DALLINGHOUSE
  G. H. 35 (m)* (F-140)
DALLIS?
  Michael 28* (F-197)
DALLY
  Alex W. 65* (F-196)
DALTON
  Edley A. 29 (m) (MA-256)
  Thomas 36 (ES-72)
  Timothy 39 (ES-73)
DALY
  Charles M. 26* (GD-287)
  John G. 28* (F-129)
DAMABY
  Benjn. M. 22 (F-233)

  George M. 28* (F-232)
  George W. 55* (F-232)
  James A. 34 (F-227)
  John 59 (F-233)
  Susan 67* (F-234)
  Wm. 55* (F-228)
  Wm. 64* (F-227)
DAMALEY
  John H. 42 (F-227)
DAMBY
  Edward 57* (F-227)
DANCER
  Will 27 (GD-275)
DANDRIDGE
  Angeline 27* (B) (JE-71)
DANDY
  William C. 29* (CL-40)
DANIEL
  A. C. 28 (m)* (ES-61)
  Almanza 27 (m) (MT-44)
  Ansil 49 (ES-87)
  Carter 64 (MT-18)
  Charles W. 45* (MT-8)
  Eastridge 68 (MT-56)
  Ellen 10* (JE-15)
  Esther 65 (CL-89)
  Harrison 52* (JE-14)
  Harvey 37 (MT-56)
  Henry 57 (MT-7)
  Hiram B. 37 (MT-47)
  Isham 33 (MT-66)
  Jackson M. 38* (CL-46)
  James M. 62* (MT-48)
  John 45* (MT-7)
  John M. 38* (OS-305)
  Louisa 60* (F-175)
  Mary 32* (MA-285)
  Pleasant 54 (ES-87)
  Robert 51 (CL-72)
  Shelby 42 (m)* (MT-77)
  Venon 32 (m)* (CL-74)
  Vivian 33 (m)* (MT-7)
  Willis 36 (CL-93)
DANIELS
  C. B. 26 (m)* (MT-1)
DANLY
  Hugh 22* (F-200)

DANSON
  Paulina 39* (MA-321)
DARBY
  J. C. 38 (m)* (F-138)
  M. R. 3 (m)* (F-139)
  William 29* (F-255)
DARLINGTON
  C. 22 (m)* (F-128)
  R. D. 25 (m)* (F-204)
DARNABY
  George E. 18* (CL-12)
  George W. 28 (F-253)
  Sydnia S. 17 (m)* (CL-27)
DARNAL
  Milton 40 (MT-24)
DARNALL
  William T. 49 (MT-17)
DARR
  Sarah M. 15* (F-114)
DART
  Mary 25* (F-214)
DASHIER
  Levi 49 (MA-259)
DASHIN
  John 25* (MA-270)
DAUGHERTY
  Evin 34* (OS-279)
DAUGHETEE
  William 52 (ES-76)
DAUGHETER
  Andrew J. 27* (ES-74)
DAULTON
  Adaline 21* (MT-68)
DAUSON
  Levi 24 (F-236)
DAVENPORT
  Louiser 7* (F-174)
  Nancy 64* (JE-77)
  Powoton 52 (m)* (MA-210)
  R. W. (Dr.) 38 (JE-70)
DAVER?
  Feliso 32 (F-205)
DAVIDSON
  A. 23 (m) (F-151)
  Abner 5* (GD-213)
  Ahab 70 (GD-227)
  Hansford 24 (OS-317)
  James 21* (F-239)

Index

DAVIDSON
James T. 25* (F-217)
Jas. 62* (F-196)
Jesse 41 (m) (GD-214)
Mary J. 7* (GD-212)
Polly A. 19* (CL-17)
Robert 28 (OS-317)
Thomas 25* (JE-74)
DAVIS
A. F. 27 (m)* (JE-8)
A. P. 38 (m) (JE-11)
Absalum 40 (JE-25)
Acquilla 58* (B) (MT-18)
Alford 27 (GD-279)
Betsy? 23* (JE-60)
C. C. 26 (m)* (JE-5)
Catharine 11* (F-124)
Charles 26* (OS-289)
David 36 (MT-75)
E. 35 (f)* (F-127)
Elizabeth 26* (GD-261)
Elizabeth 42* (F-123)
Ennis 35 (MA-218)
Geo. 35 (F-162)
George 11* (B) (F-116)
George S. 30* (CL-21)
Henrietta 43* (F-195)
Henry 74 (JE-59)
Henry B. 51* (GD-215)
Isabella 15* (MA-286)
J. 22 (m)* (JE-34)
Jackson 34 (MA-222)
James 28 (GD-225)
James E. 38 (JE-1)
James H. 29* (MT-27)
James M. 25* (GD-273)
Jesse 43* (F-162)
Jesse 60 (GD-262)
Joab 25 (MA-222)
John 24 (MA-300)
John 24 (MA-324)
John 40* (MA-281)
John 57 (CL-12)
John H. 36* (GD-208)
John H. 36* (JE-32)
Joseph 26* (JE-37)
Joseph 35* (JE-78)
Joseph 51 (OS-306)

Joseph C. 56 (GD-274)
Josephus G. 32 (MA-226)
Joshua 23 (MA-280)
Joshua 38 (JE-13)
Josiah 25 (MA-295)
Lawrence 35 (MA-301)
Lawrence 35 (MA-306)
Levi 36 (GD-224)
Louis 48 (MA-234)
Lucy 54 (MA-280)
Margaret 20* (MT-42)
Mary 2* (JE-3)
Mary 31* (F-127)
Michael 32 (JE-19)
Nancy 50 (GD-225)
Patrick 25* (CL-42)
Patsey 48* (MT-26)
Phillip 42 (MA-311)
Polly 43 (MT-27)
Rebecca 52* (MT-55)
Richard 35 (MA-295)
Richard 54 (CL-43)
Russel 39* (JE-17)
Samuel 28 (MA-215)
Samuel 28 (MA-219)
Sarah B. 54* (GD-246)
Sarilda 24 (B) (JE-75)
W. P. 32 (m) (F-154)
W. R. 31 (m) (F-166)
William 16* (MT-6)
William 22 (JE-69)
William 49* (JE-11)
William 78 (JE-1)
William C. 25 (CL-13)
DAVISS
Clerrissa 37* (MT-58)
D. M. 32 (m) (CL-94)
DAWES
James 20* (F-160)
John 21* (F-160)
DAWS
Joseph 30* (ES-81)
DAWSON
James 67 (F-229)
James W. 36* (F-201)
John A. 29 (MT-84)
Jonathan 40 (CL-66)
Lydia 84* (CL-58)

Patsey 30* (CL-78)
DAY
Collins 55* (B) (JE-77)
John 35* (CL-7)
Margaret 43 (B) (JE-74)
Newberry 25 (OS-307)
Sarah 61* (F-142)
William 39 (F-201)
DEACON
John 33 (CL-10)
Joseph 37 (CL-11)
DEADEMA
_____ 30 (f) (B) (JE-64)
DEADMAN
Clary 60 (B) (MT-3)
DEAL
Mike 31* (F-196)
DEAN
Ellis 62 (CL-78)
Francis 24* (JE-78)
Harrison 38 (JE-21)
J. N. 37 (m)* (MT-1)
James D. 19* (JE-54)
Jeremiah 37 (MT-72)
John 17* (JE-49)
John A. 24* (F-194)
John W. 49 (JE-50)
Simpson M. 35 (CL-78)
William H. 23 (CL-45)
William R. 24 (JE-69)
DEARBON
John 24* (CL-40)
DEARING
William R. 23* (GD-262)
DEARINGER
Eliza 21* (JE-56)
Levi 25* (JE-59)
DEARMOND
Hester A. 40* (F-121)
DEATON
Joseph 16* (OS-291)
DEBARA
Treobe 48 (m) (CL-37)
DEBARD
Joseph 21* (CL-54)
Lewis 36* (MT-3)
Marcus 45 (CL-61)

Index

DEBOE
  Joseph 56 (JE-30)
  Martin 52 (JE-15)
DEDMAN
  Richmond 27 (F-161)
  Robert 30 (JE-60)
DEGARRIS
  Isaac 32* (F-138)
DEGARRIS?
  John 36 (F-135)
DEJAMETT
  James 37 (MA-304)
DEJARNATT
  Greenup 45 (F-236)
DEJARNULT?
  James 73 (MA-202)
DELHOUSE
  John 45* (B) (F-148)
DELONY
  Andrew 30* (F-173)
DELPH
  J. 48 (m)* (F-166)
  James 30 (JE-20)
DEMOSS
  Sarah 28* (F-211)
DENBAR?
  William 43 (MA-304)
DENIS
  David 24 (JE-6)
  Henry 39* (GD-221)
  Milly 51* (B) (JE-38)
DENISON
  Catherine 80* (F-223)
DENNEY
  Alexander F. 43 (GD-278)
DENNIS
  David 79 (JE-56)
  Elisha 24 (GD-268)
  John 25 (GD-238)
  John B. 46 (JE-71)
DENNISEN?
  Bowen 26 (MA-219)
  Jesse 49 (MA-219)
DENNY
  Croas? 45 (m) (MA-297)
  George 25 (GD-258)
  John 33 (MA-272)
  Margaret 66* (GD-258)

  Samuel 50 (MA-278)
DENSMORE
  John 30 (MT-30)
DENT
  Johnston 35* (B) (MT-81)
  Mildred 44* (F-196)
DENTON
  Dudley H. 36* (GD-265)
  Eliza 50 (GD-255)
  Elizabeth 15* (GD-225)
  J. W. 31 (m) (MT-17)
  Nancy 46* (F-196)
  William 25 (MA-318)
DEORE
  Joseph 66 (CL-57)
DERAN
  James 50 (F-188)
DERICKSON
  Jesse 29 (ES-87)
  William P. 23 (MT-32)
DESHA
  Frances 17* (F-225)
  John R. 6* (F-189)
DESHONG
  A.? 35 (m) (MT-72)
DESMOND?
  George 21* (F-138)
DETHERIDGE
  Birgus 68* (MA-302)
  William 30 (MA-303)
DEVAN
  Patrick 24* (MT-35)
DEVERS
  H. B. 35 (m) (F-178)
DEVINE
  David 20* (F-129)
  David 22* (F-135)
  Nathan 64* (MT-14)
DEVLIN
  Frances 25* (F-128)
DEVORE
  David 73* (F-244)
  Harrison 35* (F-243)
  R. H. 27 (m) (F-156)
DEWEES
  Farmer 58 (F-222)
DEWIT
  John 40* (F-196)

DEWITT
  Smalwood 18* (CL-23)
DIAMOND
  Jas. 20* (F-166)
DICKEN
  Sarah 59* (ES-88)
DICKENSON
  Jeremiah 74 (JE-21)
DICKERSON
  A. R. 33 (m) (OS-277)
  Benj. 10* (F-186)
  Hiram 40 (GD-240)
  James 37 (MA-308)
  John 43 (JE-4)
  Newton 38* (JE-16)
  Susan 62 (ES-67)
  William 27 (ES-76)
DICKEY
  Daniel 47 (MT-68)
  Maria 49 (MT-68)
  Paulina 30* (MT-3)
  William 41 (MT-68)
DICKINSON
  Morgan 38 (GD-229)
DICKSON
  E. 28 (m)* (B) (F-124)
  Sarah A. 21* (MT-68)
DIDLAKE
  Edmond H. 52 (CL-2)
  Mary B. 16* (F-227)
  Robert Q. 39* (CL-45)
DIGGINGS
  Patrick 37* (F-219)
DIGGS
  Morgan 25* (MA-217)
DILLARD
  R. T. 53 (m) (F-228)
DILLEN
  Michael 25* (F-117)
DILLINGHAM
  Henry B. 27 (MA-242)
  Henry H. 59 (ES-110)
  John P. 37 (MA-261)
DILLION
  Boston 32 (MA-246)
  Rowlin 54 (MA-261)
DILLON
  Elizabeth 65* (JE-7)

Index

DILLS
  Proctor 30* (CL-46)
DIMMETT
  John B. 43 (ES-84)
DINGLE
  Mary 38* (F-185)
DISHMAN
  John 28* (JE-73)
  Syrena 52* (JE-78)
DISMUKES
  Elizabeth 59* (GD-206)
  James W. 32 (GD-265)
  James m. 40 (GD-261)
  Mary 30* (GD-265)
  Mary 32 (GD-288)
DIX
  Stephen 22* (MA-297)
DIXON
  Bastin 29 (MA-232)
  Elizabeth 24* (JE-63)
  Isabella 60* (B) (F-119)
  John 38 (CL-88)
DIXSON
  Benj. 39* (F-180)
DOBBYNS
  Thomas T. 54 (MT-33)
DODD
  James B. 43* (F-144)
  Jane 36 (F-229)
  Jane 50 (GD-277)
  Richard 17* (F-128)
  Samuel 30 (GD-277)
  Travis 46* (GD-264)
DOGGET
  John 25* (F-194)
DOHAD
  Thos. 21* (F-181)
DOLAN
  Patrick 27 (F-174)
DOLEN
  Wm. 70 (F-172)
DOLLIN
  John P. 46 (MA-280)
DOLLINS
  James 44* (GD-217)
DOMIGAN
  James 48 (F-179)

DONAH
  M. 23 (m)* (F-129)
DONAHOO
  Jacob 34* (MT-63)
  John 47 (MT-76)
  John 50 (MT-34)
  John J. 42 (MT-11)
  Joseph 43* (MT-76)
DONALDSON
  Patrick H. 50 (CL-91)
  Thomas F. 45 (CL-43)
DONAVAN
  Sallie A. 26* (F-171)
DONEGAN
  Hector 24* (F-207)
  Wm. 32* (F-195)
DONELLE
  Robert 25* (CL-42)
DONELLY
  Charles 35* (F-216)
  John 46* (F-241)
DONIVAN
  Archy 36* (CL-89)
DONLEY
  Benj. D. 16* (CL-1)
  Melinda 16* (F-225)
DONN
  John C. 26* (F-220)
DONOHOO
  Nancy 29 (MT-28)
DONSON
  John 25* (MT-12)
DONYHESS?
  Thomus 26* (CL-42)
DOOLEY
  Ann __ (CL-90)
  Benjamin T. 32 (MT-22)
  Doxey 80* (B) (F-179)
  George J. 22* (MT-37)
  Jabez 42* (MT-36)
  Obediah 34 (CL-90)
  Patrick 21* (MT-35)
DOOLIN
  Hiram 45 (MA-203)
  Jonson 46 (GD-269)
  Margaret 12* (GD-270)
  Polley 76* (GD-271)
  Robt. 29* (B) (F-179)

Thomas 40* (CL-89)
DOOLY
  Ethelinda J. 7* (F-217)
  Henry 21* (CL-90)
  James 46 (OS-320)
  Nancy 65* (MA-227)
  William 46 (CL-90)
DOOMES
  James F. 43 (JE-11)
DORMAN
  James 25 (JE-44)
  William 19* (JE-44)
DORNIGAN?
  Thomas 45 (CL-91)
DORSEY
  O. B. 31 (m)* (MT-5)
DOSHNIR?
  John 34* (MA-215)
DOSIER
  Joseph 27 (ES-56)
DOTSEY
  Volney 80 (m) (MA-268)
DOTSON
  George 23 (GD-275)
  Jeremiah 49 (GD-284)
  Nancy 18* (GD-285)
DOTTS
  George W. 22 (MT-5)
DOTY
  A. 69 (m) (GD-254)
  Benj. F. 32* (GD-216)
  Cyrus 38 (GD-247)
  Jesse 67 (GD-247)
  Josephean 23* (GD-278)
  Rebecca 14* (GD-260)
  Sabert 44 (GD-276)
DOUDEN
  James 28 (MA-218)
  Margaret 6* (MA-218)
  Michael 59 (MA-218)
DOUGHERTY
  Danl. 29* (F-205)
  George 23* (CL-36)
  Hugh 29 (F-205)
  Patrick 26* (JE-59)
  William 60 (CL-38)
DOUGLAS
  Pleasant 43 (F-242)

Index

DOUGLAS
  Robert 19?* (F-131)
DOUGLASS
  Alfred 42 (F-208)
  James 19* (JE-70)
  James 23* (MT-62)
  John 49 (JE-10)
  William 30 (F-205)
  William 45 (ES-78)
  William 85 (JE-9)
DOURGHTY?
  Danl. 50* (F-129)
DOUTHETT
  Hiram 53 (MA-270)
  Lewis 57* (MT-18)
DOWDEN
  E. W. 41 (m)* (F-126)
  Martin 36* (JE-61)
DOWEN
  John S. 46 (CL-68)
DOWNER
  Peggy 58 (B) (CL-47)
DOWNES
  Elizabeth 45 (MT-76)
  John 38* (MT-35)
  Wm. H. 35* (F-169)
DOWNEY
  William S. 27* (CL-41)
DOWNING
  Benj. 17* (F-145)
  Elizabeth 18* (F-220)
  Elizabeth 58* (F-215)
  Fanny 46. (JE-9)
  George 45* (F-237)
  J. L. 60 (m) (F-193)
  James 42 (F-238)
  John 36* (F-249)
  Josiah 45* (F-244)
  Lilburn 26 (F-201)
  Lucy 30* (F-227)
  Marcus 37 (F-192)
  Margaret 60* (F-177)
  Richard 51 (F-226)
  Richard 60 (F-168)
  Salem 46* (F-179)
  Saml. 22* (F-161)
  Saml. 29* (F-165)
  Saml. 34 (F-181)

  Sarah 50 (F-228)
  William 25* (F-226)
  William 60 (GD-240)
  Wm. 55 (F-165)
DOWNS
  Benj. 62 (F-156)
  Jackson P. 33 (F-174)
  R. J. 37 (m) (JE-46)
DOWNTON
  Elizabeth 65* (F-237)
DOWNY
  Nancy 40* (F-207)
DOY
  Malinda 18 (B) (MA-282)
DOYLE
  Dennis 47 (CL-18)
  James 21 (CL-89)
  James 39 (F-154)
  John 45 (F-120)
  Luke 24* (F-225)
  Patrick 38 (MA-250)
DOZIER
  Eliza 17* (JE-75)
  Ephram 55 (MA-314)
  Geo. W. 42* (F-201)
  James 44 (MA-301)
  Peter 50 (MA-301)
  Richard 57 (MA-283)
  Sidney 26 (m) (MA-299)
  William 24 (MA-301)
  Yotman 49* (MA-300)
DRAIN
  Thomas J. 36 (JE-75)
DRAKE
  Abram 26 (F-209)
  Adelia H. 18* (JE-72)
  B. P. 41 (m) (F-142)
  Catharine 30 (B) (F-119)
  D. S. 18 (m)* (F-204)
  Ephraim 42* (JE-76)
  James 27* (F-129)
  James F. 32* (F-214)
  S. N. 30 (m)* (F-212)
  Sarah 57* (F-195)
  William M. 35 (F-118)
DRENNAN?
  Amanda 24* (MA-230)

DRIVER
  A. 53 (m) (B) (F-124)
DROSDALE?
  Eliza 43 (F-251)
DRUMMOND
  Betsey 40* (MT-10)
DRURY
  Hensfro? 37 (CL-54)
  Isabella 40* (F-223)
DRYSDALE
  B. A. 26 (m)* (JE-55)
  Samuel J. 28 (JE-56)
DUCKE?
  Susan 29* (F-125)
DUCKHAM
  Thomas 64* (OS-311)
DUCKIMER?
  Catharine 66* (F-121)
DUCKSON
  Richard 59 (CL-76)
DUCKWORTH
  George 47 (MT-17)
  James 35 (MT-30)
  John 34* (MT-32)
  Nancy 20* (MT-32)
  Thomas 47* (CL-53)
DUDLEY
  A. F. 44 (m) (F-227)
  Albert G. 40* (F-234)
  B. W. 64 (m) (F-192)
  C. W. 28 (m)* (F-167)
  E. A. 43 (m) (F-145)
  E. L. 32 (m)* (F-144)
  James 73 (F-227)
  Jeptha 47 (F-209)
  John J. 33 (F-145)
  John W. 24 (F-226)
  Mary 63* (F-191)
  Nelson 51* (F-224)
  Thomas P. 58 (F-227)
  William 74 (F-228)
  William S. 25* (JE-73)
DUDLEY?
  James W. 43 (MA-206)
DUDLY
  Elizabeth 62* (MA-270)
DUERSON
  John B. 33* (JE-66)

Index

DUFF
  Alexander 21* (OS-292)
  Elizabeth 43* (GD-227)
  Lotsy 44* (MA-223)
  William 34 (MA-223)
DUFFEE
  Thomas 46* (CL-87)
DUFFY
  Barny 32* (CL-89)
DUFREE?
  Lucy 62* (F-211)
DUGAN
  Hugh 12* (CL-52)
  John W. 24 (ES-51)
DUGGINS
  Daniel 24* (GD-264)
  Daniel 48 (GD-218)
  Elizabeth 74 (GD-218)
  Hamilton 25* (GD-212)
  John 56 (GD-218)
  Thomas 50 (GD-218)
DUGLASS
  Hesekiah 24 (F-160)
DUKE
  John 18 (OS-313)
DULAND
  Terry 39 (m) (F-123)
DULSEM?
  W. Van __ (m)* (F-138)
DUMAS?
  Spotwood 27 (F-249)
DUMEY
  Elijah 33 (GD-268)
  James G. 52 (GD-284)
DUMFORD
  Solomon 60 (CL-37)
DUNAWAY
  Easter 54* (ES-55)
  James 22* (ES-104)
  John 27* (OS-312)
  Joseph 22* (ES-88)
  William G. 30* (ES-50)
DUNBAR
  Abijah 47 (m) (MA-249)
  Daniel 56 (MA-294)
  Dulcena 17* (JE-70)
  George 18* (JE-30)
  James 34* (F-194)
  John 51 (MA-294)
  John P. 22* (ES-83)
  Martin 24 (MA-302)
  Peter 25* (CL-13)
  Sarah 35 (MA-310)
  Susan 31 (MA-297)
DUNBAR?
  William W. 31 (MT-7)
DUNCAN
  Alexander 61* (JE-15)
  Benjamin F. 42* (GD-263)
  Charles 27* (CL-56)
  Charles 36 (JE-17)
  Harker 24* (JE-32)
  Henry T. 50 (F-254)
  Isaac 28 (GD-206)
  Jesse 49 (B) (CL-42)
  Jesse 85 (B) (CL-72)
  John 79 (MA-297)
  Joseph 53* (CL-44)
  Joseph 57 (GD-207)
  Joshua 47* (MT-60)
  Levicy 53 (F-242)
  Lewis 30 (GD-207)
  Louisa 33 (JE-52)
  Lucy 53 (MT-31)
  Lucy 64* (MA-227)
  Margaret 72 (CL-91)
  Michael 32* (F-132)
  Nancy An 20* (MT-70)
  Valentine 39* (MA-312)
  William 50 (MA-265)
  William 55 (CL-33)
  William 62* (JE-7)
  William R. 32 (CL-91)
DUNCAN?
  James 30* (F-164)
DUNCANSON
  E. D.? 46 (m) (F-220)
DUNE
  Rachael 10* (OS-311)
DUNEWAY
  Benjamin 53 (OS-287)
  William 22* (OS-288)
DUNHAM
  Asa 30 (GD-280)
  James 25* (MA-283)
  Susan 76* (F-123)
  William F. 30 (MA-299)
DUNIEN
  Bryant 25* (CL-42)
DUNKIN
  James A. 31 (MT-31)
DUNLAP
  Andrew J. 28* (F-237)
  Elizabeth 66 (F-218)
  Felicity 33* (F-223)
  George W. 36* (GD-266)
  Harriett 30* (F-179)
  John R. 57 (F-238)
  William T. 46 (F-228)
DUNN
  Absolem 22 (MA-299)
  Alexander 18* (GD-289)
  Alexander 21* (GD-266)
  Amanda M. 15* (JE-59)
  Benjamin 23* (GD-221)
  Benjamin 63 (GD-222)
  Benjamin 85 (GD-208)
  Edmund 43 (MA-277)
  Erasmus 56 (GD-210)
  Gatewood 22* (GD-222)
  Isaac 48 (GD-219)
  James 48 (GD-213)
  James 53 (MA-263)
  James G. 26 (GD-205)
  Jefferson 45* (GD-237)
  Joshua 52 (GD-221)
  N. F. jr. 24 (m)* (JE-78)
  Nancy 58* (F-154)
  Nathaniel F. 47* (JE-59)
  Philip G. jr. 35 (GD-206)
  Pleasant 46* (CL-53)
  Richard B. 24 (GD-222)
  Silas B. 26* (GD-209)
  Stephen 57 (CL-51)
  Theodrick 24* (GD-252)
  Uriah 53 (GD-263)
  Walter 72 (GD-262)
  Will 38 (GD-262)
  William 23 (MA-296)
DURBIN
  Edward 32 (ES-107)
  Edward 32 (OS-313)
  Francis 30 (ES-107)
  James 25 (ES-97)

Index

DURBIN
John 41? (OS-313)
John jr. 25 (OS-313)
Joseph 28 (ES-73)
Joseph 51 (OS-313)
Pias 30 (m) (ES-67)
William H. 21 (ES-107)
DURHAM
George W. 30 (JE-37)
Isaac 49 (OS-297)
Jas. 34* (F-195)
Jesse 39 (GD-279)
DURRIVEY?
Samuel 50* (MA-264)
DURTON
Nancy 57* (MA-321)
DUSEY
Nancy A. 5* (B) (F-200)
DUVAL
Eliza 46* (F-196)
DUVALL
Ann 53* (F-183)
Daniel 34* (CL-3)
Geo. H. 75 (F-171)
John 25* (F-194)
Perry 64 (B) (CL-3)
Thomas D. 7* (CL-36)
DYCKE
Henry 33* (CL-16)
DYCKES
James 59* (CL-15)
DYKES
Benjamin 60* (CL-10)
EADES
Louisa 61 (MA-294)
Nelson 36 (MA-290)
Plesant 29 (MA-294)
Sallie 48 (F-181)
Thomas 37 (MA-294)
EADS
Isaac 21* (F-157)
John 28 (GD-286)
Jourdan 44 (CL-62)
Thos. 46 (F-168)
Will 41 (GD-285)
EAGLE
E. E. 32 (m)* (F-197)

EAGON
Charles B. 45* (GD-289)
EANS
John C. 60 (MT-84)
EARDMAN
John A. 34* (F-177)
EARP
Joshua 55 (F-127)
EARTHENHOUSE
Polly 39* (JE-77)
EASLEY
Andrew 29 (JE-31)
Andrew 48* (JE-31)
Christopher 54* (JE-32)
George 40 (JE-51)
James H. 25 (JE-50)
Joseph H. 46 (JE-45)
Josiah 30 (JE-20)
Obediah 55 (JE-10)
Pleasant 60* (JE-69)
Sallie 60* (F-162)
_____ 20 (f)* (JE-69)
EASON
Rebecca 50 (GD-227)
EAST
Conrad 32 (MA-317)
James 30 (GD-223)
EASTEN
Reuben J. 53 (MA-221)
EASTER
James D. 28 (ES-105)
William 42 (MA-232)
EASTERS
Jessee 14* (OS-300)
EASTIN
A. F. 58 (m)* (F-224)
Thomas 60 (CL-73)
Thomas E. 25 (F-229)
EASTIS
Berry 15* (ES-87)
Charles 56 (ES-106)
David 46 (ES-61)
Elisha 49 (ES-106)
Elisha 52* (ES-102)
Henry 21* (ES-51)
Jackson 32 (ES-49)
James 23 (ES-51)
John 33 (ES-51)

Lott 44 (ES-61)
Milton 27 (ES-51)
Sarah 22* (ES-65)
Sarah 5* (OS-289)
William 50 (OS-310)
EASTON
Elizabeth 22* (F-163)
EATIS
Ansel 23 (OS-309)
EATON
John 60 (CL-64)
Jonta 62 (m)* (CL-14)
Mary 5* (F-132)
Sarah S. 10* (CL-23)
Thomas 24* (CL-53)
Wm. J. 29 (CL-21)
Zachariah 65 (CL-23)
EAVES
Henry 27 (JE-63)
Willis 42* (JE-59)
EBOND
Samuel 30* (MA-283)
ECHHELA?
Barnet* (JE-19)
ECTON
Burgess 44 (CL-77)
Horatio 56* (CL-50)
James S. 22 (CL-50)
James S. 27 (CL-52)
John 31* (CL-52)
Nancy 76 (CL-79)
Smalwood 63 (CL-58)
Theodore 59 (CL-50)
Theodore jr. 35 (CL-52)
EDDLEMAN
Jones 38 (F-242)
Peter 88 (F-242)
Robert 60 (F-242)
EDDY
Clara J. 27* (F-146)
EDEN
Asa 29* (F-221)
EDENS
Jeptha 15* (OS-307)
EDGAR
Rebecca 55* (F-211)
EDGE
B. F. 31 (m)* (F-146)

Index

EDGE
  John T. 28 (F-204)
  Mary 70 (F-150)
  Saran A. 27* (F-146)
  William 34 (MA-261)
EDGERTON
  Judith 64* (CL-53)
  Susan 50* (JE-32)
  William 82 (GD-208)
EDINDGTON
  Benj. T. 30* (F-184)
EDMINSON
  Thomas 41 (GD-268)
EDMONDSON
  Kesiah 55 (B) (F-202)
EDMONDSON?
  J. E. 51 (f)* (F-145)
EDMONSON
  Archy 24* (CL-87)
  James 27 (CL-81)
  James 65 (CL-81)
  Nathan 29 (CL-81)
  Thomas 42 (GD-242)
EDMUNDSON
  William 54 (MT-17)
EDMUNSON
  robert 61 (GD-270)
EDS
  William 31 (GD-241)
EDWARDS
  Cynthia A. 2* (CL-31)
  G. W. 44 (m) (F-251)
  James 26 (CL-65)
  Jesse 40 (MA-233)
  Martha 60* (F-169)
  Peter 61 (MA-237)
  William 89* (MT-66)
EGENTON
  Charles 35 (CL-41)
ELAN
  John 35* (MA-222)
ELBERT
  J. L. 42 (m) (F-150)
  Pollard 37 (F-150)
  Theodore 39 (F-175)
ELDER
  Andrew 62 (MA-216)
  David L. 36* (F-122)

James 27 (MA-226)
Judith 58 (MA-224)
Robert 31 (MA-224)
ELEY
  Benj. 39 (F-218)
ELGIN
  Dick 60* (B) (CL-31)
  H. S. 60 (m)* (F-163)
  James H. 29 (JE-60)
  Susan 68 (B) (GD-288)
ELIATH
  Nancy 63 (F-137)
ELKIN
  Enoch 41 (CL-14)
  Ezekiel 33 (CL-35)
  Ezekiel P. M. 26* (CL-11)
  Frances 16* (CL-35)
  James 50 (CL-62)
  James M. 24 (CL-69)
  John 85* (MA-322)
  John B. 28 (JE-65)
  Lewellen 40 (CL-16)
  Mildred 32 (CL-13)
  Reuben H. 35* (CL-13)
  Robert M. 24 (CL-14)
  Smalwood A. 44* (CL-11)
  Will 31 (GD-277)
  William 26* (CL-62)
  Willis 39* (CL-13)
  Zach 21 (CL-2)
ELKINS
  Anna 43 (ES-98)
  Elizabeth 18* (CL-23)
  Henderson 26 (MA-290)
  Henry 53 (MA-287)
  Jacob 35 (MA-286)
  Joel 42 (MA-267)
  Robert 32 (MA-309)
ELLAGE
  John 49* (CL-53)
ELLEDGE
  Sharlott 17* (F-179)
ELLEN
  Prudence 66 (F-192)
ELLERSON
  Amos 45 (MA-243)
ELLEY
  Thos. 23* (F-152)

ELLIDGE
  Sarah 69* (ES-88)
ELLINGTON
  Thomas P. 31 (MA-259)
  William 25 (MA-266)
  William 64 (MA-266)
ELLIOT
  Boone 44* (F-194)
  Dorson 68 (MA-292)
ELLIOTT
  Alex J. 44 (F-198)
  Andrew 58* (JE-62)
  Augustus N. 26* (JE-62)
  George 37 (GD-211)
  J. W. J. 14 (m)* (F-172)
  James L. 35* (F-144)
  Joel 60 (CL-74)
  Joel T. 30 (CL-74)
  Martin 53* (OS-310)
  Priscilla F. 23* (CL-6)
  Sandford 28 (ES-56)
  Sarah 25* (F-209)
  Sarah 35* (ES-50)
  Thomas 36 (ES-105)
  Thomas 44 (GD-278)
  Uriah 28* (F-154)
  William A. 33 (MT-18)
ELLIS
  Charles C. 24 (F-227)
  Claibourn 38* (F-231)
  Dick 67 (B) (CL-4)
  H. C. 35 (m) (F-126)
  H. C. 53 (m)* (MT-6)
  Hegekeah 30* (F-152)
  Hezekiah 81* (F-226)
  Ira 35* (B) (F-153)
  James H. 36 (MA-248)
  Jesse 46* (F-200)
  M. S. 15 (f)* (F-154)
  Mary 9* (F-226)
  Moses P. 51* (F-209)
  Peter H. 32* (MA-265)
  Polly 75* (F-230)
  Richard 10* (MA-207)
  Saml. 14* (F-148)
  Sarah 24* (B) (F-152)
  Thomas C. 30 (MA-258)
  William 55 (F-227)

Index

ELLIS
  William A. 29* (F-226)
ELLISON
  Mary A. 40 (ES-56)
  Travis 21 (ES-90)
  Travis 48 (ES-60)
  William 45 (ES-97)
ELLY
  John W. 45* (F-165)
  William R. 33* (F-213)
ELMORE
  James 53 (MA-214)
  James 86* (JE-50)
  Thomas B. 43* (JE-52)
  William 34 (MA-314)
  William 62 (JE-3)
ELSBERRY
  Benjn. 72 (CL-88)
  Jackson 18* (CL-87)
  John R. 47 (CL-49)
  Mary 15* (CL-50)
ELSTON
  Penelope 17* (F-225)
EMBERSON
  Harry 54* (F-243)
EMBRE
  Tarlton 42 (CL-19)
EMBREE
  Sophia 40 (CL-54)
  William 44 (CL-72)
EMBRY
  Ann E. 12* (MT-4)
  Burrill 30 (GD-257)
  Jacob 52* (F-243)
  James H. 22* (MA-251)
  Jesse 33* (MA-205)
  John 22* (MA-258)
  Joseph 50 (MA-285)
  Joseph 55 (MA-259)
  Talton 53 (GD-257)
  Thomas E. 41* (MA-249)
  Wiley 46 (MA-307)
  William 22* (MA-251)
  Wyatt B. 44 (MA-266)
EMERSON
  Elizabeth 60* (JE-34)
  Francis 58* (CL-23)
  Francis M. 30* (CL-22)

Henry H. 38 (CL-17)
EMMAL?
  Wm. B. 32 (F-204)
EMMERSON
  Tilly 33* (CL-32)
EMMS
  Moses 50 (ES-68)
ENGLAND
  Caroline 28* (JE-41)
  Clia A. 22* (JE-51)
  James 31* (JE-30)
  John 25 (JE-72)
ENGLISH
  Rachael 10* (GD-250)
  William 46* (JE-13)
ENKINS
  Marcy 71* (GD-254)
ENNIS
  Archabald 48 (GD-286)
  Elijah 39* (F-117)
  Jas. 29* (F-195)
  John 23 (GD-275)
  John 52 (GD-232)
  Josiah 42* (F-130)
  Robt. 75* (F-178)
ENRIGHT
  John L.? 28 (MT-57)
ENSOM
  Angeline 18* (MT-26)
EPPERD
  Samuel 50 (MA-300)
EPPERSON
  Ambrose 12* (CL-30)
  Francis 30 (CL-16)
  James 39 (CL-40)
  Jane 36* (F-152)
  John 15* (F-237)
  Nancy 38 (CL-32)
ERD
  Francis 25* (F-131)
ERLEY
  William 41 (OS-284)
ERMAN
  Elizabeth 55* (MA-217)
ERNEST
  Theoe. 43* (F-195)
ERSKINE
  Wesley J. 35* (F-241)

ERWIN
  John 71 (MA-208)
  John M. C. 64 (F-174)
  Mary 67* (F-119)
ESTELL
  W. R. 36 (m)* (F-227)
ESTEP
  Elijah 37 (MT-54)
ESTER
  Elijah 17* (MA-262)
ESTES
  Bulah 70 (CL-92)
  Clement 29* (F-239)
ESTHAM
  Malinda 30 (F-136)
ESTICE
  John 37* (F-136)
ESTILL
  Johnathan 39* (MA-269)
  Jonathan 28 (MA-255)
  Mary 47 (F-177)
  Samuel 63 (MA-286)
  Thos. 3* (F-177)
  Wallace 76 (MA-229)
ESTIS
  Feldin 25 (OS-314)
  J. D. 13 (m)* (F-137)
  Obadiah 23 (MT-51)
  Vicey 18* (OS-313)
ESTUS
  John H. 65 (MA-262)
ETENS
  Wesley 25* (OS-310)
ETHINGTON
  Sarah 57 (F-188)
EUBANK
  Achilles W. 26 (CL-16)
  Philip C. 41* (CL-21)
  Stephen 60* (CL-12)
  Stephen B. 37* (CL-16)
EUBANKS
  Achilles 26* (CL-60)
  Price 50 (CL-69)
EVANS
  Edward 46 (OS-285)
  Edy 45 (f) (OS-300)
  George 44 (MA-284)
  Henry 42* (MA-248)

Index

EVANS
 Hezekiah 48* (GD-263)
 Hickman 47 (GD-213)
 Hiram 27* (OS-300)
 Huram 24* (OS-299)
 Isaac 35 (GD-263)
 Isabella 17* (F-172)
 James 36 (JE-41)
 James 4* (JE-9)
 James 45* (CL-21)
 James 48 (JE-61)
 James 57 (ES-53)
 Jane 85* (MT-21)
 Jefferson 35 (GD-241)
 Jesse 38 (m) (GD-267)
 Jesse 85* (MT-22)
 John 32* (F-204)
 John 33* (ES-90)
 John 39* (F-147)
 John 56 (CL-90)
 John 60* (CL-23)
 John S. 44* (CL-50)
 Joseph 40* (F-147)
 L. D. 24 (m) (MT-84)
 Lemuel 26 (GD-243)
 Marcus C. 43* (CL-50)
 Mary 35 (JE-40)
 Mary 73 (MA-284)
 Morgan 20* (GD-264)
 Nancy 65 (GD-289)
 Oliver P. 29 (CL-50)
 Olnster 28(m) (MA-315)
 P. E. 35 (m)* (JE-42)
 Palina 22* (OS-304)
 Paul J. 57* (CL-67)
 Peter 42 (CL-12)
 Peter 45* (F-245)
 R. T. 38 (m)* (JE-41)
 Rainey 51 (f)* (ES-75)
 Rebecca 57* (F-196)
 Robert 57 (MT-12)
 Robert J. 24* (MT-52)
 Sally 65* (ES-75)
 Samuel g. 27 (GD-247)
 Silas 30 (F-245)
 Silas 38 (CL-52)
 Silvester 19 (OS-295)
 Stephen 55 (MA-270)
 Warren 22 (OS-307)
 Wesley 48* (F-194)
 William 26 (OS-318)
 William 48* (F-255)
 William 7* (B) (F-135)
 William B. H. 30 (MT-59)
 William W. 18* (JE-69)
EVE
 George 69* (F-241)
EVENS
 Geo. W. 36* (F-199)
EVERETT
 Mary 16* (F-225)
EVERIT
 Samuel D. 59* (MT-6)
EVERITT
 Peter 50* (MT-7)
EVERLY
 Will 55 (GD-246)
EVERMAN
 Arthur 36* (CL-66)
 Elijah 48 (CL-70)
 Elisha 44 (MT-49)
 James 56 (CL-70)
 Presly 30 (CL-65)
 Samuel 63 (CL-66)
EVERSOLE
 Hiram 22 (OS-289)
 John 65 (OS-289)
EVERT
 Will 37 (GD-270)
EVES
 Lewis 35* (F-251)
EWAN
 John B. 28* (JE-47)
EWELL
 John W. 33 (CL-63)
 William 64 (CL-63)
EWIN
 Aray? 23 (f)* (MA-264)
EWING
 James 62 (F-228)
 John 50 (MT-44)
 Samuel 46 (F-237)
 William 27* (MT-53)
EXEM
 Benjamin 42 (CL-10)
FADELY
 Elizabeth 48* (MT-5)
FAHEY
 Daniel 33* (F-212)
FAIN
 Bailey 16* (JE-25)
 Hardin 26 (JE-28)
 John 24* (JE-13)
 John 35 (JE-24)
 Larkin 41* (JE-20)
 Leta 52 (JE-18)
 Lindsey 21 (m) (JE-23)
 Mary __ (JE-29)
 Mastin 25 (JE-13)
 Matton 76 (JE-28)
 Pillard 25 (JE-28)
 Price 43 (JE-24)
 R. C. 30 (m)* (JE-15)
 Scarlet 55 (m)* (JE-36)
 Thomas 17* (JE-16)
 Thomas 40 (JE-23)
FAIRHEAD
 Robert 25 (F-136)
FALKNER
 George 54 (JE-26)
 Margaret 15* (GD-287)
 Peter 25 (GD-279)
 Peter 67* (GD-274)
FANA
 Aaron 58* (JE-53)
FANK?
 Frances 2* (CL-53)
FARAR
 Rebecca30* (MA-278)
FARDING
 Jeremiah 33 (ES-110)
FARIMAN
 E. 35 (m) (MA-242)
FARIS
 Granville 27 (CL-52)
 Harvey 40* (CL-54)
 John 84 (CL-54)
FARLEE
 Martha A. 20* (GD-262)
 Peter 26* (GD-262)
FARLEY
 John 39 (MA-204)
 Richard 16* (CL-73)

Index

FARLY
  Cassander 69 (GD-219)
  William B. 41 (GD-219)
FARMER
  Irvine 39 (CL-20)
  James 25* (OS-315)
  Milton 12* (CL-31)
  Sarah 29* (CL-19)
  William 46 (GD-231)
FARNEY
  Benjamin F. 28 (CL-38)
  Green E. 35* (CL-39)
  Hudson 64 (CL-38)
  Polly A. 9/12* (CL-38)
  Robert 33 (CL-61)
FARNSWORTH
  B. F. 53 (m)* (F-173)
FARRA
  Oliver 49 (JE-54)
FARRAR
  Betsy 50* (B) (F-220)
FARREL
  Patrick 30* (MA-215)
FARRELL
  James 28* (MT-35)
FARREN?
  Charles 15* (F-204)
FARRER
  John M. 50* (F-168)
  Joseph 29 (JE-23)
FARRIS
  Evan 24 (MA-323)
  Johnithan 34 (MA-213)
  Michael 60* (MA-222)
FARROW
  George 56 (JE-5)
  Kencey 55 (m)* (MT-13)
FATHERGILL
  David 56 (MA-313)
FAULCONER
  Joseph 49 (F-163)
  Lewis 74* (F-165)
FAULKNER
  Harriet 55* (F-240)
  Margaret 16* (F-225)
  Margarett 22* (CL-10)
  Thomas 45 (GD-217)
  Thomas 50* (B) (CL-45)

  William 22* (F-245)
FAY
  William M. 25* (F-204)
FEANISTER
  Susan Ann 23* (F-230)
FEATHERSTON
  Jeremiah 74 (F-253)
  Robert 47 (F-253)
FEEMSTER?
  Sarah 40* (CL-44)
FEENEY
  Peter 20* (F-137)
FELIN
  Jno. 41 (F-199)
FEMAS?
  Nancy 30* (MT-38)
FENNEL
  Elijah 60* (F-194)
FENNELL
  Azariah 38 (MA-314)
FERELL
  Micajah 48 (GD-254)
FERGUSON
  Abraham L. 46 (F-232)
  Amanda 44* (F-227)
  Ann 27 (B) (F-192)
  E. 32 (m)* (B) (F-193)
  Josiah 66* (MT-25)
  L. C. 16 (m)* (MT-2)
  Lucy 49* (CL-1)
  Martha 68* (F-245)
  Martha A. 10* (F-243)
  William 63* (MT-14)
FERMAN
  Richard S. 26* (MT-25)
FERREL
  Andrew 25 (JE-31)
  Archer 56* (MA-288)
  Daniel 74 (JE-31)
  James 46* (MA-325)
  Jane 42* (F-194)
  Micheal 27* (MA-251)
  Washington 35 (JE-20)
  William 29 (JE-34)
  William 41 (MA-323)
FERRELL
  London 59 (B) (F-222)
  Stewart 20* (GD-254)

FERRILL
  Isaac 75 (B) (GD-260)
FERRINGTON
  William 34* (OS-317)
FERRIS
  Jas. 41* (F-195)
FESTER
  Andrew 33* (MT-12)
FICHURMER?
  Samuel 35* (MA-214)
FICKLEN
  Joseph 75* (F-151)
  L. B. 8 (m)* (B) (F-193)
FICKLIN
  Alexand W. 35 (MT-58)
  Frances 60 (MT-68)
  Garret P. 33 (MT-78)
  John 64 (MT-54)
  Mary 60* (B) (F-192)
  William 28 (MT-54)
FIELD
  Curtis 69 (MA-302)
  Sabina 51* (F-191)
FIELDER
  Curtis 34 (MA-270)
  Harvey 42* (CL-17)
  Tarleton 50 (ES-65)
  William 27 (ES-65)
  William 30 (MA-270)
FIELDS
  Curtis 27 (MA-252)
  Ezekiel 68 (MA-251)
  Timothy 95 (B) (MA-295)
  William 19* (JE-65)
FIFE
  Alexander 50* (MA-284)
  Daniel 11* (MA-279)
FIGG
  James 27* (JE-41)
  Silas 37* (GD-212)
FILLAYSON?
  James 28* (F-119)
FINCH
  John 25* (F-129)
  John H. 35 (MT-24)
FINDLEY
  Houston 45 (GD-260)

Index

FINK?
  John 20* (F-193)
FINLAY
  John 38 (F-125)
FINLAY?
  Jos. 22* (F-205)
FINLEY
  Martha 72* (F-159)
  Thomas 40 (F-205)
FINNELL
  Fountain 47 (ES-70)
  John 20 (ES-69)
  John 50* (ES-64)
  Jones 26 (CL-37)
  Mary 16* (F-130)
  Mary 30* (F-124)
  Nelly A. N. 40* (ES-70)
  Simpson 22 (ES-70)
FINNEY
  Amos 42 (ES-111)
  Bailey 33* (ES-51)
  Elizabeth 16* (MA-261)
  John 50 (ES-61)
  Joshua 75 (MA-262)
  Peter 34* (F-124)
  Squire 51 (ES-111)
FIREY?
  Caroline 28* (OS-303)
FISHBACK
  George T. 37 (CL-4)
  James 36 (F-197)
  John 21* (F-197)
  Samuel _. 30 (CL-4)
  Susan 58* (F-152)
  William 32* (F-252)
FISHER
  Elizabeth 54* (F-187)
  Elizabeth 60 (CL-65)
  Isaah 30* (JE-24)
  John 50* (F-148)
  John 53 (CL-61)
  Mary Jane 18* (GD-210)
  Matthias 33 (CL-61)
  Ratcliff 31* (F-239)
  Rebecca 65* (CL-12)
  Thomas 30 (CL-65)
  William 35 (CL-64)
  Wm. 41* (JE-78)

william 39 (CL-73)
FISK
  Thomas 66* (B) (MT-21)
  Wiley B. 31 (JE-17)
FITCH
  P. S. 40 (m)* (JE-45)
FITZGERALD
  S. F. 42 (m) (F-172)
FITZGERRALD
  Edward 30* (MT-35)
  Thomas 28* (MT-14)
  Thomas 35* (MT-1)
FITZJERE?
  George 35 (JE-3)
FITZPATRICK
  C. 19 (m)* (F-166)
  Emily 52 (F-158)
  Frances 64* (MA-223)
  Garret 25* (F-194)
  James 24* (CL-27)
  Peter 50 (MT-20)
FIZER
  Adam 56 (MT-26)
  Bright 45 (MT-15)
  Charles B. 31 (MT-3)
  David B. 32 (MT-15)
  Samuel 55 (MT-3)
FLANAGAN
  William 45 (CL-46)
FLANERY
  William 25* (OS-296)
FLANIGA
  Carigan 57 (MA-208)
FLEETY
  Ezekiel 51* (MT-13)
FLEMING
  Mary Susan 38* (F-120)
  Nancy 59 (F-220)
  Susan 65* (F-216)
FLETCHER
  Ezekiel 44* (MT-62)
  Garret 40 (MT-47)
  Horace 31* (JE-68)
  James 24* (MA-226)
  John 74 (MT-9)
  Johnson 53 (MT-79)
  Mary 55 (MA-226)
  Rufus 16* (CL-8)

Walter 27 (MT-14)
William 22* (CL-12)
William 39 (GD-216)
William 58* (MT-9)
FLINN
  Harvey 54 (MT-45)
  Levi 47 (ES-100)
  William 23 (ES-101)
FLINT
  J. A. 12 (f)* (MT-10)
  John 31 (GD-280)
FLIRTY
  Ezekial 31 (ES-112)
  John 27 (ES-64)
  John 58 (ES-64)
FLOOD
  Patrick 25* (MT-35)
FLOURNOY
  A. Eliz. 17* (JE-52)
  J. F. 19 (m)* (F-212)
  Mary 46* (F-193)
  S. C. 50 (m)* (F-123)
  Victor F. 40* (F-176)
FLOYD
  Davis 62 (GD-250)
  George W. 24 (GD-205)
  Mary 32* (ES-89)
  Mary J. 21* (GD-262)
  Merrill H. 21 (GD-231)
FLUTY
  William 23* (MA-273)
FLYNN
  Dudly 27* (CL-84)
  John 30 (CL-84)
  Mary 58* (CL-74)
  Mason 25* (CL-82)
  Michael 50 (CL-58)
  Sarah 65* (CL-88)
FLYNT
  Margarett 36 (CL-4)
FNNEY
  Cyntha 36 (MA-261)
FOCKNER
  John 25* (OS-306)
FOGG
  Rufus 30 (MT-1)
FOGLE
  W. E. 39 (F-143)

Index

FOLEY
  Almira 46 (F-161)
  Andrew 26 (JE-63)
  David 64* (JE-45)
  Elijah 19* (F-170)
  Elijah 50 (GD-269)
  Elizabeth 67 (F-165)
  James 37* (F-158)
  Jane 74* (F-152)
  John 40 (GD-276)
  Margaret 24* (F-165)
  Rebecca 50 (CL-43)
  Richard 52* (JE-58)
  Thos. 28* (F-163)
  William 24* (ES-86)
  william 47 (MA-225)
FOLLDS?
  Harvy 35* (OS-314)
FONNARD?
  J. E. 42 (m) (F-145)
FONNER
  Warren 5* (F-120)
FOOT
  Thomas M. 22* (MA-256)
FORAN
  John 22* (CL-42)
  John 22* (F-235)
FORBUSH
  Betsy J. 12* (GD-208)
  Franklin 20 (MA-240)
FORD
  Amanda 25* (CL-28)
  Anna 62 (MA-274)
  Benjamin B. 39 (JE-50)
  C. W. 33 (m) (F-139)
  Daniel 34 (JE-12)
  E. D. 23 (m)* (JE-39)
  Edward 24 (GD-220)
  Edwin 35 (F-220)
  Hannah 62* (F-176)
  Henry 22* (GD-280)
  James M. 24 (GD-221)
  John 28* (F-217)
  John J. 34 (MA-252)
  John P. 28 (GD-205)
  Margaret 57* (F-139)
  Mariah 18* (GD-260)
  Reuben 5 (GD-230)
  S. 18 (f)* (JE-41)
  Schuyler 41 (MA-278)
  Silas 38* (MA-276)
  Thomas 27* (MT-35)
  Timothy 30* (JE-78)
  W. H. 41 (m)* (F-166)
  Will W. sr. 54 (GD-220)
  William M. 26 (JE-39)
FORDING
  Dudley 59 (ES-83)
  Hezekiah 35 (ES-83)
  Zachariah 29* (ES-83)
FORDS
  Malinda 40 (CL-87)
FOREMAN
  Cloa 46 (F-212)
  Hamilton 67 (MT-53)
  John 28 (F-168)
  Samuel S. 30 (MT-47)
FORGUSON
  Richard S. 38* (JE-69)
FORMAN
  Dana W. 36 (m) (CL-85)
  Saml. 29* (F-120)
FORSYTH
  Ann 65* (CL-47)
  J. M. 30 (m)* (F-114)
FORSYTHE
  Elizabeth 13* (GD-280)
FORT
  Hasting 15* (MA-249)
FORTNER
  F. 78 (f)* (MT-42)
  Henry 57 (MT-52)
  Jesse 31 (MT-52)
  Jonas 44 (MT-51)
FORTUNE
  Archibald 28* (MT-21)
  Benjamin 44* (MT-22)
  Emily 45 (MA-282)
  Lewis 49* (MT-78)
FOSSETT
  Samuel 27* (MT-36)
FOSTER
  Daniel 75 (GD-283)
  Elisha 28 (MA-306)
  Ephraim 28* (MT-5)
  George 26 (MA-305)
  Henry 53* (F-237)
  James 24 (MA-305)
  James 26* (OS-297)
  James M. 26* (MT-80)
  Jane 38* (CL-89)
  Jeremiah 56 (MT-84)
  John 50 (MA-304)
  John 66 (CL-49)
  John H. 54* (MT-68)
  John sr. 45 (GD-286)
  Leanah 68* (JE-30)
  Lucretia 16* (MA-318)
  Mary 22 (B) (F-192)
  Mary 13* (CL-46)
  Nancy 35 (B) (CL-43)
  Paten 48 (MA-212)
  Paten 49 (MA-307)
  Patsy 20* (F-195)
  Pleasant 50* (JE-17)
  Robert P. 22* (JE-11)
  S. E. 19 (f)* (F-152)
  Thomas 44* (MT-28)
  Thomas 60* (JE-57)
  Thomas U.? J. 26* (JE-66)
  William 21 (MA-280)
  William 31 (MA-313)
FOURSLER
  M. C. 22 (m)* (F-128)
FOWLER
  E. 16 (f)* (JE-43)
  Franklin 22* (F-243)
  Isaac 23 (ES-100)
  James 40 (MA-239)
  James 45 (MA-207)
  Jeremiah 48 (ES-48)
  Joseph 59 (MA-208)
  Malinda 40 (MA-254)
  Martha 26* (CL-47)
  Perdilla 35 (ES-102)
  Richard 64* (MA-285)
  Sally A. 14* (CL-45)
  Thomas 57 (MA-208)
  William 56 (MA-208)
  Zepheniah 62 (MA-312)
FOX
  Alfred 40* (CL-78)
  Beaufred 38 (CL-54)
  Benjamin 70 (CL-55)

Index

FOX
  Boaz 41 (CL-79)
  Catharine 60 (ES-100)
  Charles 56 (MA-290)
  Elizabeth 21* (ES-86)
  George 44 (CL-53)
  H. P. 24 (m)* (F-145)
  Harrison 34 (MT-65)
  Isaac 26 (OS-283)
  Isham 67* (MA-206)
  John 25 (MT-65)
  John 6* (ES-99)
  John 60 (OS-283)
  Samuel 29 (ES-59)
  Samuel M. 44 (MA-286)
  Susan 50 (GD-288)
  Thomas 34 (MT-73)
  W. H. 28 (m) (F-204)
  Washington 42 (MT-65)
  William 42 (MA-277)
  William 75* (CL-55)
FRAIL
  James 26* (F-176)
FRAKES
  Joseph 61* (MT-28)
  Joseph jr. 21* (MT-16)
FRAME
  John 62 (MT-55)
  Samuel 65* (MT-64)
  William G. 23* (MT-8)
FRANCIS
  Danl. 91* (B) (F-143)
  John B. 30* (MA-203)
  Lemuel 65* (OS-302)
  Louis 23* (MA-251)
  Louis 59 (MA-206)
  Morgan 26* (OS-310)
  Thomas 26 (MA-238)
  Thomas 61 (MA-238)
  Thomas R. 33 (MA-284)
FRANEY
  Moses 30* (F-176)
FRANKLIN
  Elizabeth 25* (CL-49)
  H. B. 36 (m)* (F-166)
  Harrison 39 (CL-55)
  James W. 22 (MT-43)
  Jesse 55* (MA-225)
  John L. 25* (ES-107)
  John W. 59* (CL-52)
  Josephine 11* (ES-54)
  Judith W. 48 (F-244)
  Lucy 56 (F-122)
  Lydia J. 14 (CL-49)
  Reuben S. 55* (CL-53)
  Sarah M. 17* (CL-31)
FRANKUM
  _____ 45 (m)* (JE-10)
FRAZER
  Austin 36 (GD-212)
  George 38 (JE-73)
  Jerry T.? 43* (F-211)
  Martha 35 (F-125)
  Martin 63 (JE-49)
  Mary 72* (F-150)
  Oliver 40 (F-193)
  R. 80 (m) (F-203)
  Robert Sr. 51* (F-203)
  Will 30 (GD-271)
  Wm. 51* (F-184)
FRAZIER
  Alexander 76 (MT-31)
  George 28* (F-134)
  George 44 (MT-36)
  James 53* (MT-45)
  James O. 30 (F-182)
  Jeremiah 28 (MA-297)
  John M. 36 (ES-47)
  Vina 11* (MT-66)
  Warren 45* (CL-45)
  William 5* (ES-57)
FREDERICI
  Elizabeth 46 (GD-289)
FREDRIC
  Theresa 22* (F-195)
FREDRICK
  L. 33 (m) (F-148)
FREED
  Mary 15* (F-199)
FREELIN
  William G. 30 (MT-30)
FREEMAN
  Claiborne 27 (MA-274)
  Delila 14* (ES-92)
  Edna J. 4* (ES-85)
  Hannah 45* (MA-243)
  James H. 46* (MA-227)
  John 25 (MA-274)
  Moab 56 (ES-100)
  Morton 5* (MA-267)
  Samuel 37 (MA-250)
  Sarah 50 (MA-295)
  Thomas 50 (CL-64)
  William 27* (CL-3)
  William 28 (ES-93)
FRELAN
  John 30 (MA-273)
FRELEY
  Thos. 19* (F-191)
  Thos. 20* (F-154)
FRENCH
  Enoch 55* (B) (MT-13)
  James 34* (ES-84)
  John sr. 45* (MT-42)
  Richard 58 (MT-10)
  Robert 33* (MA-263)
  Virginia 9* (B) (F-208)
  William 28* (MA-276)
  William 43* (MT-63)
FREY
  David B. 28* (MA-248)
FRIEND
  George 55* (ES-91)
  Samuel K. 28* (ES-91)
FRILEY
  Benjamin 36 (OS-306)
  Martin 34 (OS-309)
FRISLY
  JAmes 27* (MT-39)
FRITSLAN
  Joseph 21* (JE-19)
FRITTS
  Elizabeth 37* (CL-38)
  Isaac 36 (CL-38)
FRITZ
  Jacob 47 (MA-233)
FROMAN?
  Daniel C. 36* (ES-88)
FROST
  Anpaline 14 (f)* (MT-76)
  Elizabeth 20* (OS-283)
  John 58 (JE-70)
  John M. 48* (F-142)
  Joshua 45* (F-201)

Index

FROST
  Joshua 50 (MT-56)
  Nancy 18* (MT-54)
  Samuel 28* (JE-66)
  Simeon 48 (OS-285)
  William 26 (MT-53)
FRUSSELL?
  French 38* (OS-314)
FRY
  Benj. 50 (F-175)
  Catharine 61 (ES-97)
  Chrystopher 25* (F-121)
  Fry 51 (B) (JE-45)
  Green B. 45* (CL-82)
  John 22* (CL-84)
  John 22 (GD-235)
  Julia 80* (CL-83)
  Thomas 13* (B) (JE-45)
  Thomas J. 28 (F-143)
  Thos. C. 54* (F-171)
  William 23* (MA-258)
FRYER
  Timothy 28 (OS-287)
FUDGER
  E. 50 (f)* (F-130)
FULKERSON
  William M. 28 (OS-306)
FULKES?
  Leapold 35 (OS-306)
FULKS
  Thomson 27 (OS-293)
FULLERLOOR?
  Nancy 40 (MA-290)
  Nancy 45 (MA-291)
FULLERLOVE
  Dulcinea 16* (F-244)
FULLERTON
  Brutus 22 (MA-303)
FUMY
  Henry 35* (CL-41)
FUNK
  Amanda 42* (JE-47)
  James M. 23* (JE-16)
  John 54 (JE-59)
  Peter 49 (JE-47)
FURGOSON
  John M. 38* (F-191)

FURGUSON
  Joseph 14* (MT-25)
GABBARD
  Cornelious 28 (OS-296)
  Eli B. 25* (MA-218)
  Henry jr. 43* (OS-280)
  Hiram 27* (MA-218)
  Isaac H. 45 (OS-280)
  Jacob jr. 36 (OS-278)
  Jacob sr. 51 (OS-299)
  John 37 (OS-283)
  John 63* (MA-217)
  Peter 50 (OS-281)
  Phillip 50 (ES-101)
  Wilson 30 (OS-283)
GABBERT
  Jacob 25 (MA-239)
  John W. 30 (MA-240)
GABBORD
  John 19* (GD-264)
GABBRT
  Edward 51 (MA-240)
GAFNEY
  Moton 39 (GD-280)
  Susan 30 (GD-281)
GAIL
  Eliza 25* (MA-315)
GAINES
  Alonzo 22* (F-212)
  Franes 70* (F-186)
  John 38 (MA-319)
  John P. 24 (MT-2)
  Jonas N. 32* (F-185)
  Martha P. 6* (CL-18)
  Pollard 55 (MA-320)
  Thomas 40 (CL-54)
GAITSKILL
  John 33 (CL-86)
  Jon. 50 (m)* (CL-86)
  William 60 (CL-77)
GALAGER
  M. T. 5 (m)* (F-142)
GALIO
  Eulalia 28* (F-223)
GALLAGHER
  John 30* (CL-89)
GALLIMORE
  John 42 (GD-212)

GALOWAY
  John 63* (MA-227)
GAMBOE
  Eda 49 (CL-30)
  Greenberry 24* (CL-31)
GAMLEY
  Patrick 50 (F-164)
GAMUNDY?
  Thomas 20* (CL-89)
GANETT
  Walker 60* (F-186)
GANEY
  Michael 42 (F-216)
GARAY
  John 21* (F-250)
GARBER
  Frederick 41 (F-121)
GARDINER
  Joseph T. 40 (F-217)
GARDNER
  Azariah 25* (GD-211)
  Elias H. 34* (MT-17)
  James 57 (GD-268)
  John 80 (CL-87)
  Mary 13* (CL-88)
  Thomas 38 (CL-83)
GARFIELD
  Lucy C. 26* (GD-265)
GARLAND
  Peter 20* (CL-47)
GARLEND
  Patrick 20* (CL-42)
GARNER
  Allen 29* (B) (MT-18)
  Elizabeth 16 (B)* (MT-60)
  John C. 39* (CL-2)
  Landford 32 (CL-19)
  William 39 (CL-42)
GARNERS
  Laura 80* (CL-79)
GARNET
  Thomas H. 70 (MA-291)
GARNETT
  Virginia 3* (F-185)
GARRARD
  Eliza T. 49* (F-238)
  James 19* (F-201)
  Jas. D. 27* (F-179)

Index

GARRATT
  Nimrod 80* (MT-26)
GARRET
  Alexander 48 (MT-62)
  Samuel 30* (MA-290)
GARRETT
  Andrew 32 (ES-109)
  Ezekiel E. 30* (CL-53)
  Findley 60 (MT-9)
  Henry 18* (MT-3)
  J. H. 18 (m)* (MT-42)
  James jr. 36* (MT-61)
  Jesse 48* (MT-44)
  John 50* (MT-61)
  John 52 (CL-57)
  Joseph 43* (B) (MT-9)
  Owen C. 31 (MT-61)
  Sandford 55 (MT-84)
  Westley 49 (MT-44)
  William 23* (F-129)
GARRISON
  John 64* (JE-57)
  Morgan 30* (ES-110)
  Samuel 46* (MA-267)
  Thomas 58 (MA-262)
  Willis 25 (GD-244)
GARTON
  Henry 35* (B) (CL-5)
GARTSKELL
  Albert G. 28 (CL-90)
  William 25 (CL-90)
GARVIN
  Martin 32* (MA-228)
GARY
  James 57* (CL-87)
  John Dunlap 46 (CL-87)
  Robert 23 (CL-87)
GARY?
  David 22* (CL-87)
GASPER
  Lucy A. 1* (CL-33)
  Peter 63* (CL-40)
  Thomas 36* (CL-30)
GATES
  George B. 44 (GD-276)
  James 35 (MA-225)
GATESKILL
  Henry 34 (MT-37)

GATEWOOD
  Asa B. 20* (MT-7)
  Lucy 65 (MT-21)
  Richard 66 (JE-58)
  Robert H. 44 (MT-20)
  William F. 37 (MT-21)
GATSON
  William 17* (CL-90)
GAUGH
  Jerry 28* (F-211)
  Percival 42 (F-176)
GAUNT
  Lettitia 45 (F-250)
GAUTER
  Daniel 30* (F-211)
GAY
  Benjamin P. 60 (CL-89)
  Jacob W. 49 (CL-88)
  John 29 (GD-253)
  John 54 (MA-214)
GAYHART
  Daniel 49* (JE-21)
GAYLOR
  George 37* (JE-70)
GEARS
  Robert 27* (F-253)
GELVIN
  Hugh 65 (MT-30)
  James 22* (MT-28)
  Joseph 38 (MT-32)
GENKINS
  Esther 50 (B) (F-124)
GENKINS?
  Margaret 14* (F-136)
GENNIS
  Samuel 40* (JE-59)
GENTRIAGE?
  Ann 30* (MA-222)
GENTRY
  Bayley 43 (MA-200)
  Benaja 72 (MA-282)
  Brightberry 65 (MA-236)
  Claibourne 32 (MA-300)
  Elizabeth 49 (MA-263)
  Jaila 51 (f) (ES-95)
  James 47 (MA-282)
  James H. 27 (MA-232)
  John B. 35* (MT-59)

  John P. 67* (MA-267)
  Josiah 82 (MA-263)
  Owney 55 (f) (MA-236)
  Peter 30 (MA-314)
  Plesant 22 (MA-232)
  Plesent 36 (MA-254)
  Stanton 30 (MA-255)
GEORGE
  Flemming 28 (GD-241)
  Harrison 26* (F-116)
  James 60 (GD-269)
  James J. 39* (MT-13)
  Joel S. 36 (MT-54)
  John 43 (CL-14)
  Joseph 45* (F-200)
  Lucy 18* (F-237)
  Lucy 212* (F-208)
  Lucy 80* (CL-15)
  Melurath 30 (F-114)
  Moses 44 (F-240)
  Preston 17* (MT-14)
  Reuben 23* (F-118)
  Violet 86* (B) (MT-81)
  William 30 (JE-59)
  William 60 (JE-60)
GEORGE?
  Lucy 22* (F-197)
GEROGE
  Rebecca L. 30* (F-200)
GESS
  George Wash 31 (F-247)
  Mary 54 (F-239)
  Mary Ann 34 (F-244)
GIBBERT
  Jacob 31 (MA-266)
  Susan F. 19* (MA-251)
GIBBON
  James W. 22* (F-207)
  Nancy A. 60* (F-121)
GIBBONS
  Antonia 32* (F-223)
  Isabella 19* (F-218)
  Thos. 70 (F-179)
  Zac 21* (F-221)
GIBBS
  Alexander 35 (GD-259)
  Alexander 73 (MA-242)
  Alexr. 4/12 (f?)* (GD-215)

Index

GIBBS
  Hillary 43 (m) (GD-216)
  James 25 (MA-242)
  John 76 (F-180)
GIBNEY
  An 48* (JE-13)
  Hinton 26 (JE-9)
  R. A. 33 (m)* (JE-74)
  William 27 (JE-21)
GIBONY
  Daniel 25 (MA-208)
GIBSON
  Anna 68* (CL-6)
  C. C. 36 (m) (F-250)
  Chas. 39* (F-151)
  Edmund 20* (MA-251)
  F. B. 37 (m) (CL-72)
  Henry 37* (CL-6)
  James 68 (F-253)
  James E. 36 (OS-285)
  John 72 (F-175)
  M. J. 37 (f)* (F-151)
  Pleasant 44 (GD-281)
GILBERT
  A. B. 35 (m) (OS-279)
  Andrew 56* (B) (JE-44)
  Catharine 20* (OS-294)
  Ezakies? 31 (m) (OS-316)
  Henry 27* (F-193)
  Jareptha? 34 (m)* (MA-257)
  John 50 (F-184)
  John W. 27* (MA-251)
  Mrs. ____ 20* (F-194)
  Patsey 50 (OS-279)
GILES
  Mary 35 (MA-234)
GILKEE
  Elizabeth 37 (MT-40)
GILKEY
  B. F. 45 (m)* (MT-72)
  Charles 48 (MT-68)
  William 67 (MT-68)
GILKIE
  Thompson 36 (MT-80)
GILL
  John 64 (GD-263)
  John S. 23 (GD-263)
  Margaret 50 (MA-288)

Martha 15* (F-237)
Samuel 38 (GD-250)
Therissa 17* (F-168)
GILLASPIE
  Mary 53* (GD-228)
  Thomas J. 33 (ES-105)
GILLEN
  Levi 35 (OS-311)
  William 27 (MA-280)
GILLESPIE
  Jeremiah 28 (MA-288)
  Nancy B. 48* (JE-56)
  Nelson 40* (MT-29)
GILLETT
  L. 19 (m) (B) (F-141)
GILLIS
  Thos. H. 31* (F-222)
GILLISPIE
  Garrett 38 (MT-30)
  Louis H. 70 (MA-214)
  Susan 68* (MA-281)
GILLMAN
  M. 29 (m) (F-205)
  Martin 28* (F-129)
GILLMORE
  John 42 (MT-22)
  Sally 20* (MT-26)
GILLROY
  Pat 21* (F-204)
GILMAN
  Harvey 50 (JE-49)
GILMORE
  Andrew? 38 (F-136)
GILTNER
  David 15* (F-154)
GIMBELL
  Elizabeth 70* (MA-201)
GIMERSON
  Robert 23* (OS-310)
GIMMERSON
  John 55 (OS-290)
GIMSTEAD?
  M. D. 36 (m) (MA-271)
GIPSON
  James 40 (MT-71)
  Levi J. 35 (MT-19)
  Samuel 77 (MT-71)
  William 44 (MT-71)

GISH
  Catharine 41 (B) (F-201)
GIST
  George W. 28* (MT-7)
  John 58* (F-165)
  Jude 33 (m)* (F-215)
  Rachel 50* (MT-27)
GITON
  W. H. 12 (m)* (F-164)
GIVENS
  Harriett 9* (B) (F-201)
GIVIN
  Jane 28* (F-209)
GLASS
  Casper 43* (JE-19)
  David 68 (F-172)
GLAZE
  Bazel 32* (JE-14)
GLEAN
  Samuel 23* (JE-11)
GLEASON
  Joset 33 (m)* (CL-47)
GLOSSOM
  Ellen 25 (JE-51)
GLOVER
  Austin 18* (MT-16)
  Chesley J. 20* (MT-20)
  Creed T. 56* (MT-55)
  Daniel 70* (B) (CL-40)
  Harrison 37 (OS-320)
  James 32* (CL-33)
  Joseph B. 28* (MT-16)
  Lydoff D. F. 44 (MT-39)
  Lyndoff A. 28 (m) (MT-20)
  Mary 15* (MT-26)
  Matse 59 (f)* (F-196)
  Owen 45 (CL-37)
  Samuel 67 (MT-39)
GODDIN
  S. J. 55 (f) (MA-203)
  Thomas J. 46* (MA-250)
GOFF
  C. P. 28 (m) (GD-253)
  David 75 (B) (CL-72)
  John 29* (CL-73)
  Nancy 51* (CL-73)
  Strawder 48 (CL-92)

Index

GOFFNEY
  Thomas 41* (F-117)
GOFORTH
  John 49* (JE-40)
  Mary 46 (JE-46)
  Zepp 35* (JE-47)
GOFOURTH
  Sarah 53 (JE-19)
  Thomas 23 (JE-19)
GOGGIN
  Stephen 61 (MA-323)
  William 47 (MA-318)
  William 50 (MA-288)
GOHAGAN
  E. 55 (f)* (F-128)
GOHAM
  Nancy 60* (F-155)
GOIN
  Francis 68 (MA-312)
  Franklin 23 (MA-318)
GOINES
  Americus 43* (F-171)
GOINS
  Lucy 42* (MA-289)
  Samuel H. 31 (GD-256)
GOLANE
  Sally 30 (MA-274)
GOLDEN
  Dudley 28* (MA-216)
  Fielding 22 (MA-218)
  Harrison 21 (MA-218)
  James 46 (MA-299)
  Margaret 40 (B) (F-213)
  Richard 50 (MA-299)
  William 27* (MA-320)
GOLIN
  Michael 30* (CL-94)
GOMER
  E. C. 33 (m)* (F-197)
GOODE
  Walter R. 47 (CL-61)
GOODLOE
  David S. 38 (F-214)
  Thos. W. 36* (F-224)
  William 81 (MA-284)
  William C. 45 (MA-284)
GOODLOW
  Henry 66 (MT-78)

  Levia 32* (MA-227)
GOODMAN
  Jesse 66 (MA-324)
  Nancy 45* (F-194)
GOODNIGHT
  Michael 54 (F-229)
GOODPASTURE
  Anderson 30 (MT-39)
GOODRICH
  Elizabeth 82* (CL-71)
GOODWIN
  J. J. 35 (m)* (F-226)
  John 31 (B) (MT-37)
  Joseph 29 (F-220)
  Joseph G. 62 (F-230)
  Joseph P. G. 22 (F-224)
  Lloyd 58 (F-224)
  Simeon 37 (B) (MT-41)
GOOLMAN
  Martin 40 (CL-70)
  Mary 60* (CL-59)
GOOLSBURY
  Julian 35 (f) (GD-281)
GOOSEY
  David 27 (OS-299)
  Nancy 15* (CL-65)
  Reney 19 (f)* (B) (OS-288)
  William C. 54* (CL-58)
GORDIN
  Kennedy 56 (OS-300)
GORDON
  David 54 (GD-243)
  David M. 48 (CL-19)
  Hetty 21* (GD-264)
  Jackson 36 (CL-30)
  John 73* (F-218)
  N. M. 36 (m) (JE-69)
  Randall 63 (MT-54)
  Richardson 46* (CL-53)
  Samuel 21 (GD-213)
  Sarah 75* (CL-30)
  William B. 38 (MT-54)
  _____ 40 (m)* (F-197)
GORE
  Henry 44 (MT-75)
  Lewis 5* (F-124)
  Sophia 24 (F-153)

GORGAN
  Patrick 30* (F-129)
GORHAM
  John G. 40* (F-177)
GORTNEY
  J. F. 30 (m) (F-156)
GOSS
  Chas. 34 (F-221)
  Henry 37* (F-250)
  Robert 36* (JE-18)
GOSSOM
  Ellen 24* (JE-70)
  Lucy A. 18* (JE-54)
GOUGH
  Perry W. 33* (F-184)
GOVERIN
  Thomas 26 (F-223)
GRACE
  Daniel 19* (F-221)
  David L. 25* (JE-55)
GRADY
  John 26* (F-165)
  Wm. 80* (F-170)
GRAF
  Lewis 21* (F-199)
GRAHAM
  Ellen 12* (MT-23)
  James 37 (GD-233)
  Nancy 35 (GD-288)
  Nicholas 23 (GD-234)
  Robert 36 (GD-237)
  Samuel 30 (GD-261)
  William 32 (GD-222)
GRAMMAN?
  Isadore 35* (F-204)
GRANHALGH?
  Izrial 43 (MA-204)
GRANISON
  John A. 23* (JE-65)
GRANT
  Abraham 29* (JE-27)
  Anthony 38* (MA-204)
  Ellen 16* (JE-19)
  G. W. 28 (m) (F-140)
  Hannah 70* (CL-53)
  Thomas 64* (F-140)
GRATZ
  Benj. 57 (F-194)

Index

GRAVES
  B. F. 45 (m)* (F-124)
  Benjamin H. 48 (MT-21)
  Coleman 43 (F-227)
  Edward O. 2* (F-199)
  Geo. W. C. 41 (F-176)
  John 48* (F-115)
  Joseph 42* (F-239)
  Lidia 52* (F-173)
  Mary F. 16* (MT-6)
  Polly W. 60* (F-226)
  R. B. 37 (m) (F-225)
  Richard 40* (B) (F-145)
  Richard C. 46* (JE-61)
  Richmond 34 (B) (F-205)
  Spencer C. 45 (F-229)
  Thomas P. 51 (F-141)
  Thos. 29* (F-195)
  W. W. 62 (m)* (F-160)
  Will 82* (GD-270)
GRAVETT
  Elizabeth 60 (CL-25)
  Ellis 60* (CL-26)
  Ellis jr. 27 (CL-4)
  George S. 34 (CL-26)
  John 34 (CL-25)
  Nancy 27 (CL-36)
  Nicholas 33* (CL-36)
GRAVITT
  George 62 (ES-74)
  John S. 22 (CL-36)
  Thomas 37 (ES-73)
GRAW
  Levi 22* (F-163)
GRAY
  Charles 36 (OS-314)
  Emily 16* (MT-51)
  Emily 28* (JE-12)
  Henry 33* (F-118)
  James 32* (OS-306)
  John 40* (OS-314)
  Marcus 68 (ES-99)
  Mary 27* (F-197)
  Mary C. 30* (F-195)
  Matthew 60 (CL-70)
  Robert D. 51* (MT-52)
  Thomas 47* (OS-289)
  Will 54 (GD-287)
  William 41* (JE-10)
  William 63 (MT-51)
GRAYSON
  Mary E. 25 (B) (F-206)
GRAZER
  Davel 23 (F-139)
GREAG
  James M. 28 (JE-8)
GREAT HOUSE
  Fanny 30* (B) (F-137)
GREEHAM
  Benjamin 63* (GD-264)
GREEN
  Agnus 19* (MT-73)
  Alexander 27 (GD-232)
  Alexander 36 (JE-12)
  Ann 7* (F-191)
  Bayless M. 50 (ES-88)
  D. 54 (m) (F-156)
  Daniel 29 (CL-82)
  Edmond 60* (CL-9)
  Edward 60 (CL-84)
  Eli 25 (ES-70)
  Elias 57 (ES-101)
  Eliza 19* (GD-266)
  Frances 80 (MT-38)
  Frances 88 (MA-307)
  Frances __ * (B) (F-117)
  Haram 41 (MA-265)
  Henson G. 53* (GD-245)
  Hiriam 41 (GD-288)
  Irvine 26 (MA-314)
  Irvine T. 35* (MA-206)
  Jackson 34 (GD-218)
  James 60 (MA-272)
  Jesse P. 61 (CL-8)
  Joab 58 (GD-212)
  John 42 (CL-52)
  John 45 (MT-33)
  John H. 30 (CL-8)
  Joseph 16* (GD-220)
  Laura 1* (MT-50)
  M. 40 (m)* (F-128)
  Mary A. 94* (GD-246)
  Mastin 45* (MA-263)
  Nancy 52* (F-195)
  Rebecca 77* (F-135)
  Richard D. 60 (MT-38)
  Samuel* (MA-307)
  Thadeus 51* (MT-38)
  Thomas 21* (F-204)
  Thomas 22* (CL-82)
  Thomas 34* (B) (CL-4)
  Thomas 52* (JE-15)
  Thomas C. 65* (CL-8)
  Thomas P. 27 (CL-8)
  William 11* (GD-251)
  William 29* (JE-35)
  William F. 21 (MT-55)
  William F. 21 (MT-77)
  William R. 41 (MA-212)
  Zachariah 65 (GD-207)
  Zachary 31* (ES-74)
GREENE
  Elizabeth 32 (MT-77)
GREENEWADE
  Samuel 58* (MT-70)
GREENHOW
  Sarah 35* (F-123)
GREENING
  Henry 50* (CL-28)
GREENLEAF
  Will 36* (GD-264)
GREENWADE
  Henry 20 (MT-70)
GREGG
  R. 20 (m)* (F-156)
  Samuel H. 26 (JE-50)
GREGSBY
  R. T. A. 28 (m) (MT-68)
GRESHAM
  Will R. 34 (GD-265)
GREY
  John 35 (CL-58)
GRIDER?
  Volentine 18* (MA-242)
GRIFFEY
  James 26* (MA-264)
  Jane 18* (MA-263)
  Jesse 54 (MA-264)
GRIFFIN
  Caroline 23 (MA-264)
  Jasper 66 (JE-18)
  John 19* (MA-208)
  Terry 84 (m) (MT-10)

Index

GRIFFITH
  Benjamin F. 33 (ES-107)
  Mary 18* (ES-86)
  Patsy 50 (MA-257)
  William 50 (CL-64)
GRIFFY
  Elizabeth 10* (F-246)
  George 22* (F-246)
  Melissa Ann 17* (F-247)
  Sally Ann 27* (F-247)
  William 50 (F-247)
GRIGGS
  Allen 21* (CL-33)
  David 52 (ES-47)
  Fielden 55 (ES-113)
  Hannah 44 (F-157)
  James 24 (MA-232)
  John 71 (CL-34)
  Lucian 22* (F-181)
  Martin 19* (CL-30)
  Minor 31* (CL-36)
  Nancy 41 (CL-32)
  Noah 21* (F-136)
  Rice 22 (F-157)
  Roland 27* (ES-77)
  Samuel 1* (ES-74)
  Susan R. 16* (CL-30)
  Vergis 47 (F-157)
  Wade H. 21* (ES-76)
GRIGSBY
  Charlott 75* (CL-1)
  James B. 56 (MT-7)
  John 51* (CL-2)
  John V. 24* (CL-1)
GRIMES
  B. R. 37 (m) (JE-9)
  Carla 40 (m) (CL-7)
  James 18* (F-221)
  James 45 (F-247)
  Jane 28* (F-216)
  Jane 75 (F-239)
  John 23* (F-243)
  John 41* (F-175)
  Luke 33 (GD-221)
  Mary 1* (B) (F-117)
  Nancy 60 (GD-221)
  Rachel 54* (F-242)
  Sally 32* (CL-6)

  Sidney S. 44 (F-239)
  W. H. 39 (m) (GD-212)
  William 67 (F-242)
GRINSTEAD
  Jas. A. 36* (F-167)
  Lewis 50 (MT-18)
  Robt. 26 (F-172)
GRINSTEAD?
  John B. 39 (MA-268)
GRISSIM
  John D. 32 (F-182)
GROCH
  C. J. 41 (m) (MA-213)
GROE
  Peter 29 (GD-242)
GROEN
  Sarah 19* (CL-50)
GROIN
  Thomas 34 (MA-291)
GROIN?
  Sarah 45* (MA-292)
GROOMER
  Elizabeth 61* (GD-248)
GROOMLY?
  Hugh 21* (MA-203)
GROOMS
  Benja. 26* (CL-93)
  Dorothea 18* (CL-25)
  James 35* (CL-55)
  James 38* (F-152)
  Jane 65* (F-124)
  Jesse 37 (CL-80)
  John T. 31* (JE-31)
  Madison 45* (MT-63)
  Moses 63* (MT-2)
  Nancy 51 (GD-242)
  Sarah 60* (F-127)
GROSS
  America 10* (OS-300)
  John 40 (OS-300)
  Joseph R. 25 (F-201)
GROVER
  Elizabeth 15* (CL-40)
GROVES
  Elizabeth 72* (MT-40)
  James 43* (MT-20)
  Nelson 35 (CL-70)
  Sally 74* (CL-31)

  Travis 60 (CL-70)
GROW
  Daniel 25 (JE-20)
  Peter 45* (JE-50)
  Samuel 52 (JE-63)
  Sarah 49 (JE-63)
GRUBBS
  Jesse 56* (MT-12)
  Joel H. 25 (MT-14)
  John 29* (MT-80)
  John O. 26* (ES-55)
  Thomas 76* (MT-14)
GRUBS
  Wiliam 41 (MA-265)
GRUCON?
  William 35* (F-125)
GRUK?
  Ann 9* (F-141)
GRUNDELL?
  John 33* (F-117)
GRUNDID?
  Louisa 25* (F-128)
GRUNT
  Jesse 40 (ES-88)
GRUNT?
  A. 30 (f)* (D) (F-130)
GRYARD
  Josephus 23* (MA-208)
GUESS
  William 28* (MA-252)
GUESS?
  John 54 (MA-202)
GUINN
  James 27 (CL-27)
GULLEY
  Drury 76 (GD-214)
  Griffin 41 (GD-214)
  William 82* (JE-35)
GULLIE
  John 60 (MA-280)
GULLIN
  Orlena 21* (MA-201)
GULLY
  John 20? (MA-317)
  John 71 (MA-317)
  Mason 30* (JE-31)
  Squire 24 (GD-236)
  Squire 46 (MA-308)

Index

GULLY
  William 29 (MA-317)
GULPIL?
  Wm. 31* (F-203)
GUM
  Abraham 24 (OS-319)
  Stephen 50 (OS-319)
  Stephen B. 30 (ES-91)
  William 31* (OS-310)
GUM?
  John P. 27 (ES-71)
GUN
  John 23 (OS-306)
GUNKLE
  John 32* (F-142)
GUNSAULEY
  A. 24 (m)* (MT-16)
GURMLY
  James 28 (F-204)
GURS
  James 66 (F-124)
  Thomas 17* (F-125)
  William 40 (F-125)
GURS?
  James 26* (F-123)
GUSS?
  Jane S. 10* (F-115)
GUTHRIE
  Mary 45* (JE-45)
GUTRIDGE
  John G. 74 (MA-226)
GWYNN
  Addison 31 (CL-51)
  Andrew 32* (JE-72)
  Jane E. 17 (JE-77)
  Joel 14* (JE-78)
  Samuel R. 46 (JE-77)
HACKER
  Betsey 18* (OS-298)
  Isaac 24* (OS-279)
  John 25 (OS-278)
  Julious 46 (OS-278)
HACKET
  Allen 46 (JE-17)
HACKETT
  Granville 28 (ES-113)
  Owen 17 (MA-282)

HACKLEY
  George E. 41 (GD-209)
HACKNEY
  Samuel 41 (JE-64)
  William C. 28* (JE-65)
HADDEN
  Nicholas 51 (MT-9)
HADE
  Joseph 24 (GD-249)
HADEN
  John J. 28* (MT-10)
  Matt J. 22* (MT-7)
  Polley 65* (B) (MT-82)
  William 22 (MA-301)
HADER
  William 22 (MA-306)
HADIN
  John W. 50 (MA-211)
  Thomas H. 24 (MA-211)
HAGAN
  David 78* (CL-22)
  John 40 (CL-22)
  Mathew 33* (JE-78)
HAGARD
  Augustin L. 30* (CL-27)
HAGEN
  Jane 44* (MA-287)
HAGER
  Daniel 20* (JE-14)
  David 20* (MA-252)
  Elijah 21* (JE-4)
  Moses 46* (JE-24)
  Polly 41 (JE-14)
  Sarah 48 (F-170)
  Thomas 21 (JE-25)
  William 65* (JE-3)
HAGGARD
  Bartlett 22* (CL-14)
  David D. 38 (CL-28)
  David D. 43 (CL-25)
  David S. 22 (CL-27)
  David T. 54* (CL-40)
  Dewitt? 38 (CL-31)
  Fraces 44 (CL-14)
  James 18* (CL-9)
  James H. 27* (CL-26)
  John 55 (CL-26)
  John F. 46* (MT-18)

  Lewis 33* (CL-27)
  Martin 24 (CL-32)
  Martin 60* (CL-26)
  Mary 32* (CL-51)
  Nathaniel 70 (CL-49)
  Nathaniel 74 (CL-15)
  Noe 36 (m)* (MT-7)
  Pleasant 72 (CL-25)
  William 43 (CL-28)
  Zachy 48 (m) (CL-80)
HAGGART
  John S. 38 (CL-26)
HAGGIN
  Samuel 67 (F-155)
HAGGINS
  Patrick 26* (F-128)
HAGUE
  James 52 (MA-281)
HALCOM
  Mary 81* (OS-315)
HALDEN
  Josephine 12* (F-114)
HALE
  Ann 30* (MA-264)
  John M. 24 (MT-46)
HALEY
  Hamilton 40 (MA-201)
  Henry 35* (MA-251)
  James 15* (GD-218)
  Johnson 54 (F-133)
  Mary 57* (F-232)
  Randolph 30* (F-184)
  Randolph 47 (F-134)
  Sidney 36 (m)* (GD-261)
  William 34 (MA-214)
  William 35 (F-232)
  Willis G. 25 (MA-237)
HALKMAN
  Absalum 40 (OS-298)
HALL
  Aaron 32 (OS-288)
  Abner 30 (GD-280)
  Achilles 37 (CL-26)
  Allen 50 (MA-233)
  Ambros 33 (CL-22)
  Arthur 50 (MT-50)
  Augustus 48 (F-219)
  B. H. 42 (m)* (F-218)

Index

HALL
Bryant 48 (ES-63)
Caleb 45 (MT-46)
David E. 33 (ES-73)
Elizabeth 54* (F-116)
Elizabeth F. 11* (F-187)
Evan 21 (ES-74)
Fanny 21* (MT-63)
G. B. 38 (m) (F-218)
George W. 28* (F-230)
Green 24 (ES-53)
Green 68 (MT-50)
Harvey 36* (OS-288)
Henry W. 32 (MT-53)
James 27* (CL-19)
James 37 (MT-79)
James 46 (ES-63)
James 60 (CL-85)
James H. 35* (MT-52)
Jefferson 40 (ES-94)
Jesse 18* (B) (MT-70)
Jesse 56 (MA-259)
Jessee A. 23 (F-126)
John 38 (F-123)
John 45 (OS-312)
John F. 36 (MA-238)
John W. 27* (CL-87)
Joseph 14* (GD-280)
Josiah 76 (GD-282)
Lenard 36 (OS-292)
Levi 34 (MT-75)
Malinda B. 45* (F-193)
Mary M. 43 (MT-58)
Matthew 26 (GD-242)
Mayse 22 (m)* (ES-74)
Morton 51 (ES-63)
Nancy 58 (CL-26)
Nancy 60 (GD-272)
Rebecca 60* (ES-57)
S. B. 37 (m) (JE-70)
Salley 45 (GD-280)
Samuel 59 (ES-74)
Sarah 36 (MT-50)
Sarah 55 (MT-47)
Sarah 80* (F-223)
Sidney 23 (m) (GD-280)
Thomas 43 (MT-45)
Thomas 64 (ES-52)
Thomas B. 38 (MT-50)
Vincent W. 22* (GD-216)
William 12* (JE-43)
William 48 (F-240)
HALLER
Benjamin 70* (F-139)
HALLEY
Samuel 52 (MA-253)
HALLIGAN
William 27 (F-253)
HALLY
James H. 41* (CL-53)
Milly 14* (B) (MT-42)
HALMON
Cornelius 62 (F-174)
HALSEY
Benjamin 58* (F-241)
Jane 26* (F-240)
Moses 39* (MT-55)
____ 35 (m)* (F-214)
HALSTEAD
Sarah 16* (F-168)
HALTON
Tho. 60 (m) (CL-6)
HALZELWRIGG
James H. 1* (MT-38)
HAM
Ellen 28* (OS-295)
John 72 (MA-287)
Joseph 48 (MA-287)
Thomas 35 (GD-236)
HAMBLETON
Hezekiah 39 (CL-69)
HAMBLIN
Francis 45* (OS-277)
HAMBRICK
Green 28 (JE-7)
John 23 (JE-13)
John 60 (JE-17)
Thomas 31* (JE-7)
HAMBROUGH
F. C. 50 (f)* (F-123)
HAMELTON
C. W. 26 (m) (OS-277)
Harvey 40* (OS-285)
Owen 22 (OS-299)
HAMILTON
A. W. 30 (m)* (MT-1)
Alex 37* (F-195)
Alex 38* (JE-73)
Alexander D. 38 (ES-108)
Anderson 39 (ES-106)
Andrew 24* (ES-94)
Andrew 54* (JE-30)
Andrew 75 (ES-76)
Bluford 40* (MA-276)
Duke _2* (JE-30)
E. W. 11 (m)* (F-147)
Elizabeth 60 (ES-108)
Emily C. 55* (F-217)
Frances E. 32* (JE-62)
Henry 35* (OS-309)
Huldah 50* (CL-49)
Isham 48 (GD-220)
James 53 (F-147)
James C. 33* (MT-39)
Jesse T. 39 (F-235)
John 43* (OS-312)
Lewis D. 45 (ES-106)
Mary 31 (F-121)
Patrick 65* (OS-314)
R. B. (m)* (F-147)
Robert 87 (JE-30)
Simon 32* (MA-266)
Speed 26 (m) (OS-302)
Thomas 27 (OS-314)
Thos. J. 65* (F-183)
William 25 (JE-20)
William 26 (CL-24)
HAMMOCKS
George 36 (GD-217)
HAMMOND
A. D. 30 (m)* (F-234)
Jalvey? 10 (m)* (F-203)
James 26 (OS-306)
Lucy 43 (GD-218)
Silas 59 (GD-275)
HAMMONDS
Mary 56 (OS-316)
Thomas 50 (OS-313)
HAMMONS
James 26 (OS-278)
Priscilla 61* (MT-34)
HAMONDS
John 92?* (OS-312)

Index

HAMPTON
 A. H. 42 (m) (CL-18)
 Andrew 53* (JE-64)
 Andrew H. 11/12* (CL-13)
 Catharine 2* (CL-47)
 Esther 4* (CL-34)
 George 73 (CL-17)
 James 79* (MT-37)
 James 9* (ES-56)
 Jesse 65 (CL-22)
 Jesse 77 (CL-26)
 John 38 (CL-8)
 John A. 36 (F-221)
 Jonathan 82* (CL-17)
 Leonard 36 (CL-52)
 Lewis 36* (CL-41)
 Margaret A. 27* (JE-74)
 Nancy P. 14* (CL-20)
 Parnetha 33* (CL-34)
 Sally 52* (CL-26)
 Sarah 21* (F-237)
 Sarah 60 (CL-52)
 Thos. 35* (F-210)
 Wade 45* (CL-50)
 Willis 40* (ES-63)
HANCOCK
 ____ 53 (m) (JE-41)
HAND?
 John W. 15* (MA-288)
HANDLEY
 William 55* (MT-67)
HANDY
 Orla 47 (m) (CL-74)
HANELINE
 Ann 47 (MT-68)
 James H. 28 (MT-49)
 Jesse 61 (MT-19)
 Julia 16* (MT-6)
 Thomas M. 25 (MT-61)
 Volentine C. 27 (MT-61)
HANES
 Jefferson 30 (B) (F-121)
 Lucinda 52* (F-160)
 Simeon 69* (F-176)
HANEY
 Elizabeth 31* (F-176)
 Patrick 25* (F-175)
 Robt. 23* (F-160)

HANIKER
 M. 38 (m) (F-153)
HANIM?
 David D. 20* (F-116)
HANIWAY
 Chas. 18* (F-217)
HANKER
 Elizabeth 90* (F-117)
HANKS
 Armilda 1* (MT-83)
 Hanibal 31 (MT-53)
 Jackson 33 (MT-83)
 Stephen E. 37* (MT-19)
 Vancover 35* (MT-49)
 William 47 (MT-50)
HANLEY
 W. J. 20 (m)* (F-129)
HANLY
 James 32 (JE-45)
 John H. (Maj.) 70* (JE-45)
HANN?
 William 47 (MA-310)
HANNA
 James 40* (F-223)
HANNAH
 Amanda 35* (MT-25)
 Saml. 35 (F-187)
HANOLEY?
 John A. 39 (MT-24)
HANSEN
 Samuel 64* (CL-42)
HANSLEY
 John 35* (MT-2)
HANSON
 Clark 60* (B) (F-206)
HANY
 John 34* (F-195)
HAPPS
 George 30* (F-137)
HAPPY
 Harvey 19 (JE-3)
 James 46* (JE-2)
 Josephus 39* (F-219)
HAPTON
 Polly 75* (CL-18)
HARAM
 James 23* (MA-269)

HARBAUGH
 Casper 39* (JE-5)
 Phebe 40* (JE-1)
HARBER
 Thomas 63* (MA-300)
HARBERT
 Mary 45 (B) (F-119)
HARBOUR
 David M. 33 (MA-308)
HARDEN
 Elizabeth 25* (MA-227)
 James 37* (MA-227)
 Sally 42 (MA-215)
 William 45 (GD-234)
HARDESTER
 Benjn. 74 (F-236)
 Henry 85 (F-236)
HARDESTUN
 H. E. 30 (f) (F-148)
HARDESTY
 Sarah 33 (F-124)
HARDIN
 Calvin 13* (F-244)
 George 49 (GD-221)
 Jemima 91 (MA-217)
 John 23* (MA-268)
 John 58 (GD-216)
 Mary 17* (F-213)
 Robert 63* (GD-247)
HARDING
 Blaney? 20* (F-140)
 James W. 26* (CL-42)
 P. 21 (m)* (F-129)
 Wm. 30* (F-158)
HARDISTER
 Benjamin 25* (F-252)
HARDISTON
 George C. 37 (F-235)
HARDMAN
 George 39 (CL-86)
 John 45 (MT-26)
HARDWICK
 Ben F. 33 (GD-244)
 Christopher 41* (GD-245)
 George 28* (GD-206)
 James 39 (GD-262)
 John N. 29 (MT-48)
 Mitchell P. 76 (MT-48)

Index

HARDY
  Wm. 30* (F-195)
HARING
  Peter 33* (F-219)
HARLAN
  Jeremiah 23* (GD-207)
  Joseph 18* (GD-266)
  Margaret 25* (F-221)
HARLIN
  Mary 17* (B) (F-137)
HARLOW
  Bartlett 35 (MA-218)
  David M. 29 (MA-213)
  George 57* (F-219)
  Mary A. 32* (CL-27)
  Thomas 21 (MA-284)
HARMON
  John S. 3 (CL-75)
  Mary 51 (GD-242)
  Reece 60 (GD-242)
HARN
  Pheoba 50 (GD-286)
HARNEY
  Charels 16* (F-146)
HAROLD
  Nancy 17* (F-241)
HARP
  Baston 38 (F-187)
  Cabble 36 (F-187)
  Clemency 31* (F-191)
  David 30* (F-188)
  David 34 (F-174)
  Geo. 30 (F-155)
  Geo. 39* (F-188)
  Henry 32 (F-167)
  John 34 (F-188)
  Lea 60 (F-188)
HARPER
  Henry 40 (MA-282)
  J. 31 (m)* (F-141)
  Jefferson 32 (MA-220)
  Matheas 25* (CL-32)
  Saml. 54 (F-180)
  William 20* (MT-6)
HARRIS
  A. J. 34 (m) (GD-260)
  Anderson 36 (ES-105)
  Anderson 37 (GD-285)

Archibald 21 (ES-75)
Bowles 41* (ES-88)
Bright B. 27 (JE-11)
Brinkley 38 (GD-235)
Charles 45 (MT-25)
Christopher 29* (MA-254)
Christopher 62 (MA-261)
Dianna 50 (MA-320)
Ed. 52* (F-139)
Edward 43 (F-136)
Elemuel 39 (GD-260)
Elijah 68 (CL-43)
Eliza 30* (B) (F-138)
Eliza 9* (CL-18)
Elizabeth 71* (ES-91)
George 19* (OS-315)
H. 15 (f)* (F-152)
Henry 26 (ES-65)
James 60 (GD-247)
James 63 (B) (F-158)
James K. 49 (MA-291)
James m. 36 (MA-323)
James sr. 60* (JE-44)
Jane 50* (MA-281)
Jane 60* (ES-77)
Jefferson 45 (GD-244)
Jeremiah V. 39 (ES-96)
John 55 (GD-243)
John 58 (JE-19)
John A. 46 (MA-257)
John D. 35* (MA-203)
John P. 29* (ES-50)
John V. 36 (ES-74)
Joseph 30* (MA-228)
Joseph 37* (F-148)
Josiah 34 (ES-55)
Josiah 42 (ES-76)
Kitty 70 (B) (F-204)
Leland 29 (ES-65)
Lindsey 22 (m)* (CL-75)
Martha A. 4* (MT-29)
Mathew 35 (OS-292)
Milton V. 30 (ES-108)
Nathaniel 45* (JE-19)
Orange 85 (B) (JE-38)
Overton 30 (MA-232)
Philus 55* (B) (F-201)
Rice jr. 33 (JE-43)

Rice sr. 56* (JE-44)
Richard F. 35* (CL-20)
Richmond 88 (MA-319)
Robert 29* (MA-251)
Robert 50* (GD-243)
Robert 63 (MA-256)
Robert 63 (MA-261)
Russel 40 (GD-225)
Sarah 58 (ES-65)
Shelton 29* (MA-265)
Sidney W. 35 (m)* (MA-254)
Solm? 38 (m)* (MA-208)
Susan 70* (MT-37)
Thomas 24 (GD-207)
Thomas 27 (ES-65)
Thomas 36* (JE-74)
Thomas 45 (F-149)
Webber 70 (ES-51)
William 23 (MA-259)
William 33 (MA-241)
William 45 (MA-227)
William G. 61* (GD-247)
Willis 40 (GD-281)
Willis 45* (B) (JE-77)
HARRIS?
  Madison 27 (B) (F-131)
HARRISON
  Abner 55* (F-195)
  Carter H. 25* (F-184)
  Elisha 28 (ES-93)
  Elizabeth 70 (F-252)
  George 41 (MA-238)
  George B. 41 (F-239)
  Georgeanne 17* (F-225)
  Humphrey 24* (F-178)
  Isaac W. 35* (F-241)
  Iva 60 (ES-102)
  James O. 46 (F-198)
  Jane 47* (F-206)
  John B. 43 (MA-235)
  John C. 49 (CL-64)
  Nathaniel 25 (MA-240)
  Polly 46* (CL-95)
  Polly 65* (MT-2)
  Rose Jane 18* (JE-1)
  Sally 20* (GD-252)
  Saml. 29* (F-114)
  Thomas 35 (ES-94)

Index

HARRISON
 Thomas J. 39 (F-119)
 W. B. 29 (m)* (GD-289)
 W. E. 26 (m) (F-220)
 William 23 (ES-102)
 William 7* (ES-57)
HARRISON?
 Ephraim 20* (MT-5)
HARRISS
 Richmond 56 (GD-229)
HARROW
 Joseph 30* (CL-75)
 Mary 42* (MT-40)
 Polly 45* (MT-27)
 Thomas A. 29* (CL-45)
HARSNER?
 A. G. 25 (m)* (F-204)
HART
 A. M. 35 (f)* (F-141)
 Benjamin 64* (MT-13)
 C. C. 45 (m) (F-251)
 Caleb 25* (MA-221)
 Camillus J. 25* (CL-91)
 Edwin 49 (F-250)
 James 28 (MA-218)
 Jane 47* (OS-281)
 Jesse G. 33* (CL-21)
 John 28* (JE-78)
 John 36 (GD-266)
 John P. 28 (GD-246)
 Joseph 30 (MA-260)
 Levi 31 (F-244)
 Lou Ann 34 (F-244)
 Mary 65 (F-251)
 Minor 60* (F-244)
 Peter 26* (B) (MT-14)
 Peter 30 (B) (MT-3)
 Susan G. 10* (F-224)
 Thomas 54 (CL-93)
 Thomas M. 50* (MT-36)
HARTHEMAN
 John 44 (MA-210)
HARTHEY
 Thomas 28* (F-137)
HARVEY
 Joseph 27* (F-151)
 Sarah A. 16* (JE-10)

HARVIE
 Levi 35 (MA-311)
 Martha 30 (MA-301)
 Martha 30 (MA-306)
 Nancy 67 (MA-313)
 William 42 (MA-308)
HARVIE?
 Green B. 36 (MA-288)
HARWOOD
 A. 34 (m)* (F-206)
 A. 53 (f)* (F-135)
HASE
 Thomas 42 (MA-290)
HASELDON
 John H. 39* (GD-266)
HASKIN
 William 35 (MT-62)
HASTINGS
 Ellen 22* (F-198)
HATCH
 Willia 19* (MA-251)
HATCHER
 George 33* (B) (MT-39)
 Isaac 24* (MA-251)
HATHAWAY
 David 49 (MT-35)
HATHMAN
 Johnithan 70 (MA-304)
 Joseph 74 (MA-304)
 Joseph 35 (MA-212)
HATON
 John 23 (CL-16)
HATTAN
 James 62 (F-242)
HATTEN
 Benjamin sr. 83 (GD-236)
 Martha 42 (MA-294)
 Thomas 35* (OS-306)
HATTENS
 Polly 80* (OS-314)
HATTER
 James 72 (CL-63)
HATTING
 Thomas 47* (OS-303)
HATTON
 Adam 38 (MT-44)
 Benjamin 62 (MT-48)
 Cassandra 40* (MT-60)

Ephraim 66 (MT-43)
George W. 40* (MT-51)
George W. G. 41 (MT-44)
Hiram 33 (MT-43)
John sr. 47 (MT-43)
Lucinda 14* (ES-57)
Mary 20* (ES-74)
Thomas W. 35 (MT-44)
William 44 (MT-43)
William H. 38 (ES-90)
HAULKMAN
 Nathan 26 (OS-278)
HAUN
 John H. 30* (F-200)
HAVELINE
 James L. 11* (MT-18)
HAVELY
 John 24* (F-239)
HAVERY
 Johnathan 25 (MA-289)
HAVEY
 James O. R. 26 (JE-57)
HAW?
 Alexander 60 (F-121)
HAWES
 Mildred 13* (CL-42)
HAWKINS
 A. T. 52 (m)* (F-209)
 Anna 64* (JE-76)
 Benjamin 38 (JE-8)
 Cary 43 (m) (MA-206)
 Elizabeth 66* (F-123)
 Giles 39 (JE-59)
 Henry B. 32 (MT-72)
 James 25* (MT-34)
 James 44 (JE-9)
 Jason 20 (GD-242)
 Lawson 60 (B) (F-135)
 Louisa 50 (B) (MA-298)
 Moses 25 (ES-69)
 Rhoda 34* (MA-263)
 Squire 42 (MA-264)
 Thomas (Esq.) 55* (JE-50)
 Thomas 35* (JE-61)
 Thomas 36* (MT-77)
 Thomas 62 (ES-105)
 Wa;ler 64* (F-224)
 William 61 (MA-290)

Index

HAWKINS
William 70 (ES-68)
William W. 37* (JE-41)
William W. 39 (GD-248)
HAWKMAN
Joseph 50* (MT-31)
HAY
James C. 36* (F-194)
HAYDEN
Andrew 34 (CL-51)
George 40 (CL-85)
Thomas 26* (JE-4)
HAYDON
Benjamin 25 (JE-53)
Jane 53 (JE-64)
Sarah 86* (JE-63)
Whitfield 46 (JE-64)
HAYES
Lucy 77* (F-240)
Samuel F. 33 (F-229)
Thomas T. 44 (F-230)
William 44 (F-243)
HAYNE
Davis20* (MA-283)
HAYNE?
John 25* (F-137)
HAYNES
Nathan 40 (MA-279)
HAYS
Ann 45* (B) (MT-38)
Benjamin F. 40 (MT-15)
David B. 53 (CL-8)
Henetta 33* (F-123)
John 37 (GD-250)
Margaret 16* (MT-6)
Thomas 20* (F-137)
HAYSE
R. A. 37 (m) (F-164)
Sarah 60* (F-180)
HAZELRIGG
Dorothy 41* (MT-3)
Thomas F. 47* (MT-1)
HAZELWRIG
David 44 (MT-37)
HAZELWRIGG
Charles 64 (MT-69)
Dillard 50 (MT-57)

HAZLEWOOD
Rebecca 59 (JE-39)
HEAD
E. J. 16 (f)* (JE-66)
Jas. 39* (F-195)
HEADINGTON
Jaban 77* (F-200)
W. 58 (m)* (F-140)
HEADLEY
A. 37 (m) (F-251)
Hamilton 23* (JE-59)
James 57 (F-224)
John 47 (F-252)
Saml. 52* (F-171)
HEARD
Rober 20 (OS-297)
HEARNE
Robert C. 19* (F-233)
HEATH
Polly 60 (GD-248)
HEATHER
Mary Ann 17* (ES-88)
HEATHERLY
Thomas S. 25 (MA-247)
HEATHMAN
Elias 44 (F-133)
HEBSON
Wm. 33* (F-194)
HECKELL?
John 40* (F-179)
HEDGER
Benjamin 40* (MT-62)
John 45* (MT-55)
Jonathan 31* (F-234)
Robert 48 (MT-76)
HEDGES
Alexander 78* (F-184)
Preston 42 (CL-83)
HEDRICK
William 44 (OS-298)
HEFBORN
Mary 27* (F-196)
HEFFLEBEAN
Susan 51 (OS-310)
HEFNER
Peter 22* (F-163)
HEHOON?
Patrick 24* (MT-35)

HEIFNER?
Henry 17* (JE-73)
HEISLE
Christipher 22* (CL-24)
HELLARD
John 25* (OS-316)
HELLEN
Sarah 9* (OS-297)
HELLENMEYER
Francis 35* (F-181)
HELM
Thomas 17* (MT-71)
HELMS
Nancy 14* (MT-58)
Peter J. 3* (MT-82)
HELMSTINE?
John P. 38 (ES-66)
HELPHINSTINE
T. H. 36 (m) (MA-292)
HELTON
James 21 (OS-304)
HELWICH
Augustus 40* (F-195)
HEMMINGWAY
Thomas 49 (F-135)
HEMPHILL
Andrew 49* (JE-34)
HENAN
Mathew 27* (JE-56)
HENCHIN
Marshall 17* (F-197)
HENDERSON
Carcus 40 (ES-69)
Elenor 37 (ES-95)
Elizabeth Y. 50 (GD-254)
Ellenor 59 (ES-69)
J. C. 34 (m) (F-158)
James 31 (F-235)
James 35 (F-149)
James W. 70 (F-172)
John 28 (GD-263)
John 28 (GD-286)
John 80* (ES-90)
M. E. 2 (m)* (B) (F-127)
Margaret 56 (GD-283)
Robert 29 (ES-69)
Robert A. 29 (GD-278)
S. G. 36 (m) (F-167)

Index

HENDERSON
  Samuel 27* (CL-9)
  Suan 60 (GD-277)
  William 28 (ES-69)
HENDLEY
  Marshall 41 (JE-58)
HENDRICKS
  Cislia 36 (f) (ES-90)
  Cornelius 47 (F-221)
  Julia 79* (ES-90)
  Milly E. 16* (ES-97)
  William 59 (ES-94)
HENDRIX
  David 36 (MA-231)
  Samuel J. 34* (JE-68)
HENDRON
  Dover 39 (MA-303)
  Enos 77 (MA-303)
  Irvine 26 (MA-303)
HENDROW
  Oliver 42* (MA-288)
HENIP
  Joshua 20* (CL-46)
HENKILL
  Eda 27* (CL-20)
HENNASSY
  J. R. 29 (m)* (F-122)
HENNESSY
  Richard 26* (CL-42)
HENRY
  Absolom 56 (ES-50)
  Angeline 24* (ES-58)
  Ann 75* (F-131)
  Biddy 28 (F-205)
  Brank 28 (m) (GD-258)
  Charles 10* (B) (F-162)
  Charles 35* (F-173)
  Cynthia 16* (JE-55)
  Danl. 40* (F-200)
  Elizabeth 43* (ES-50)
  Evan 39 (CL-32)
  George 27 (MT-33)
  J. Harvey 34 (GD-283)
  James H. 51* (GD-271)
  John 64* (F-201)
  John P. 31* (F-201)
  Mary A. 16* (GD-282)
  Peggy 48 (ES-112)

  Polly A. 15* (CL-24)
  Robert B. 59 (GD-258)
  Sarah 56* (F-161)
  Will F. 28 (GD-274)
  William 26 (F-222)
HENSHALL
  Jenney 15* (F-150)
HENSLEY
  Almanza 28 (m) (MT-66)
  Evan S. 41 (MT-65)
  George W. 32* (CL-1)
  Harvey 30 (MT-77)
  Jackson 33 (MT-81)
  John 38 (MT-56)
  William 35 (MT-66)
  William 78 (MT-81)
HENSLY
  John W. 41 (CL-74)
HENSPERGER?
  H. C. 27 (m)* (JE-62)
HENTON
  Thomas 28 (OS-294)
HENY
  Margaret 32* (F-194)
HERBERT
  Catharine 13* (F-203)
  James 16* (F-221)
HERD
  Elijah 28 (OS-317)
HERKEL?
  Thos. 54* (F-172)
HERKILL
  David 40 (CL-29)
HERM
  Fility 48* (F-195)
HERNDON
  Albert G. 43* (GD-246)
  Elijah 39 (ES-60)
  Judith 83* (F-214)
  P. J. 48 (f)* (CL-47)
  Polly 57* (F-196)
  Samuel G. 55* (MT-7)
  William 80* (CL-44)
HERNUS?
  Stanton 58 (MA-265)
HERREN
  Virginia 16* (F-184)

HERRING
  A. M. 27 (m) (JE-64)
  Augustus 52* (GD-241)
  John A. 33 (GD-245)
  Nancy 22 (GD-211)
  Sarah 20* (GD-210)
HERT
  Able 30 (GD-277)
  Henry jr. 20 (GD-275)
  James jr. 21 (GD-275)
  John H. 28 (GD-275)
  Julia F. 22* (F-167)
HESTER
  Hamilton 30 (MA-237)
  Jerry M. 60 (m) (MA-222)
HET
  Henry sr. 58 (GD-277)
HETCH?
  Samuel 21* (MA-251)
HEUBOT
  Wesley 24* (B) (F-209)
HEWETT
  John M. __* (F-138)
HEYRONIMUS
  Samuel 62* (OS-289)
HIATT
  Fanny 68* (MA-276)
  Oliver 35 (GD-224)
  William 47* (MA-213)
HIATTE
  Harrison 36 (GD-268)
  Samuel 30 (GD-268)
HIBITT
  Frederick 22* (F-217)
HICKENBOTTOM
  Mary 26* (F-142)
HICKEY
  David R. 30 (F-204)
  James 27* (CL-47)
  William 68 (F-254)
  Willis 43 (F-126)
HICKLIN
  Jas. 28* (F-195)
HICKMAN
  Joel 88* (CL-6)
  Lucy 75* (B) (F-230)
  William 61* (CL-40)
  William 75 (MT-38)

Index

HICKS
  Alexander C. 25* (F-226)
  Archibald 34 (MA-301)
  Beverly A. 35 (m)* (F-226)
  Hager 14* (F-170)
  Hendley 49 (CL-22)
  John 29 (F-183)
  John 35 (JE-44)
  John D. 31 (F-170)
  John sr. 58 (JE-45)
  M. A. 26 (f)* (F-124)
  Samuel 36* (JE-52)
  Thomas 61* (MT-78)
  William 24* (CL-10)
  William 34 (JE-45)
HIERONYMUS
  Benjamin 77 (CL-10)
HIGBEE
  Alex 21* (F-163)
  John 18* (JE-60)
  Peter 53* (JE-59)
  S. E. 37 (f)* (F-130)
HIGBY
  Hestra 76 (F-219)
HIGGENBOTTOM
  A. 70 (m)* (F-127)
HIGGINBOTHAM
  Almira 9 (GD-280)
  Emanuel 79* (GD-283)
  Samuel 47* (GD-285)
  Will 40* (GD-281)
HIGGINBOTOM
  Ben 25* (F-200)
HIGGINS
  Charles 11* (F-172)
  Eliza 15* (F-225)
  Eliza 60* (F-173)
  Elizabeth 21* (F-218)
  Joel 47 (F-215)
  L. A. 7 (f)* (F-129)
  Nancy 70 (JE-4)
  Patrick 23* (F-176)
  Richard 38 (F-206)
  W. K. 35 (m)* (F-141)
HIGHLAND
  Denman 46 (MT-36)
HIGHLY
  John M. 31 (ES-76)

William 22* (ES-76)
HIGHTOWER
  Elizabeth 37* (JE-75)
  George W. 21* (JE-45)
HILL
  Charlotte 30* (F-216)
  Eliza 2* (MA-270)
  Eliza A. 6* (GD-221)
  Elizabeth 1 (GD-214)
  Frederick 38 (GD-250)
  Geo. W. 31 (F-158)
  George 42 (JE-31)
  George W. 29* (CL-8)
  Green B. 26* (JE-25)
  Greene 55 (JE-49)
  Harrison 26 (MA-319)
  Harrison 37 (MA-200)
  Henry S. 30 (MA-270)
  Herndon 54* (CL-77)
  Isaac 50 (MA-307)
  Isaac 52 (MA-213)
  Isaiah 43 (GD-252)
  James 17* (GD-264)
  James 27* (F-125)
  James 28 (MA-315)
  James 32 (CL-1)
  James 56* (JE-77)
  James 58 (ES-100)
  James D. 48 (JE-57)
  Jarret 54 (MA-325)
  Jefferson A. 27 (ES-48)
  John 12* (JE-29)
  John 28* (GD-209)
  John 28 (GD-268)
  John 35 (JE-14)
  John 59 (GD-222)
  John A. 28* (GD-237)
  John M. 32* (GD-265)
  Leminda 26* (MA-324)
  Leonard 33* (CL-14)
  Lorenzo 20* (F-134)
  Margaret 66* (GD-247)
  Mary 59* (F-195)
  Moses 36* (CL-7)
  Murphy 65* (MA-218)
  Nancy 20* (MA-312)
  Nancy J. 15* (JE-32)
  O. P. 36 (m) (GD-264)

Russel 36 (GD-250)
Sally 88* (JE-28)
Sarah J. 12* (JE-35)
Silas 31 (MA-200)
Thomas 25 (B?) (CL-10)
Thos. 82* (F-185)
William 40 (MA-231)
William N. 31* (JE-40)
HILLICKS
  Wm. 19* (F-174)
HILTON
  J. S. 39 (m) (F-207)
  Stokely 24 (OS-303)
HINAS
  Thos. 50* (B) (F-185)
HINDE
  Anna 24* (CL-45)
  James O. 40 (CL-75)
HINDER
  James 42 (MT-56)
  Sarah A. 21* (MT-55)
HINDES
  Benja. F. 30 (MT-71)
  Edwin 32 (MT-71)
HINDS
  Henry? 26 (GD-265)
  James B. 31* (ES-59)
  Samuel 29 (ES-108)
HINES
  Jonathan 50* (JE-6)
HINSHALL
  Mary 55* (F-152)
HINTON
  William 21* (MA-227)
HINTON?
  Mary R. 6/12* (F-114)
HIRONEMUS
  W. T. 44 (f)* (F-170)
HIRST
  Doctor 25* (CL-89)
HISEL
  Benjamin 70 (MA-267)
  Ira 34 (MA-258)
  John W. 41* (MA-232)
HISLE
  Daniel 28 (ES-97)
  Irvine 28 (MA-292)
  Jackson 32 (MA-293)

Index

HISLE
  Jeferson 27 (MA-273)
  Louis 31 (MA-292)
  Margaret 56 (CL-73)
  Richard 24 (MA-262)
  Sampson 55 (MA-257)
  Willis 39 (ES-66)
  Younger 51* (CL-79)
HITCHCOCK
  Lester 22* (F-203)
HITER
  C. M. Y. 33 (m)* (F-163)
HIX
  Colmon 37 (GD-288)
  Henry 44 (GD-265)
  Lindsey 40 (m) (GD-288)
  William 34 (GD-239)
HOAGLAND
  Edmund 33* (F-215)
  L. 83 (f)* (F-153)
  Thos. 64 (F-153)
HOBBS
  Absalom 25 (OS-291)
  Elizabeth 8* (OS-296)
  Isaac 22* (OS-294)
  Susan 22* (CL-40)
HOCERDAY
  Richard 38* (MA-222)
HOCKADAY
  Ametia 22* (CL-42)
  Edmond W. 46 (CL-9)
  Elizabeth 18* (CL-41)
HOCKER ·
  Clayton 35 (GD-207)
  Jeremiah 29 (JE-28)
  William 30* (MA-291)
HOCKERDAY
  James S. 32 (MA-227)
  Samuel 58 (MA-227)
HOCKERSMITH
  David 64 (JE-12)
  Wilkinson 30 (JE-2)
HODGE
  Cretea T. 45 (f)* (CL-87)
  Joseph 7* (MT-32)
  Robert 37 (MT-76)
  William 53 (MT-15)

HODGES
  John T. 32* (MT-30)
  Jonas 63* (MT-13)
HODGKIN
  Philip B. 40* (CL-20)
HODGKINS
  James 29 (CL-20)
  Samuel 64 (CL-17)
HOFFMAN
  James A. 1* (MT-19)
  John 28* (MT-18)
  John B. 4* (F-185)
  Mary 20* (MT-1)
  William 32 (MT-7)
HOFFUTT
  Richard 20* (F-150)
HOGAN
  D. F. 33 (m) (F-130)
  Dan. P. 33* (F-195)
  Elihu 52* (F-206)
  Elizabeth 23* (JE-78)
  James 29* (CL-78)
  John 60 (F-161)
  John M. 20 (GD-222)
  Joseph 25 (JE-57)
  Martha 59* (F-116)
  Mary 55 (GD-222)
  Shelton 11* (F-180)
  William 33 (CL-29)
  William 36 (JE-30)
HOHN
  Malinda 44 (MT-64)
  Moses J. 29 (MT-64)
  William 53 (MT-53)
HOKE
  Rudy 43* (F-196)
HOLBROOK
  John 26 (CL-59)
HOLCOM
  Stephen C. 32 (GD-281)
HOLDER
  Francis M. 10* (CL-66)
  Gary 17* (MT-53)
  Gary 66 (MT-43)
  Margaret 20* (MT-60)
HOLEMAN
  George W. 35* (ES-81)
  Margarett 30* (ES-63)

HOLHASS
  Henry jr. 30 (CL-45)
HOLHIMER
  Eldridge 34 (GD-244)
HOLIDAY
  John 63 (MA-312)
  Mary 29* (MA-211)
HOLINS
  Thomas 69* (MA-276)
HOLLADAY
  Benj? 19* (F-151)
  Joseph 59* (CL-6)
  Waller 53* (CL-5)
HOLLADY
  James 33* (F-194)
HOLLAND
  Eliza 7* (F-150)
  Jackson 26 (OS-291)
  John 49* (F-128)
  M. A. 18 (f)* (F-145)
  Nancy 44 (MT-38)
  Tobitha 22* (MT-61)
  Tracey 44* (GD-251)
  William 30* (MA-237)
HOLLENKEMP
  H. 30 (m)* (F-140)
HOLLEY
  James 18* (B) (MT-42)
  John 30* (MT-71)
  Nancy 60* (MT-58)
  Robert 12* (B) (MT-48)
  Uriah 40* (MT-58)
HOLLIDAY
  Harrison 40* (JE-26)
  James 27* (F-208)
HOLLINSWORTH
  Jeremiah 27* (MA-248)
HOLLIS
  James 21* (JE-78)
  Mary K. 17* (JE-54)
HOLLOWAY
  E. H. 23 (m)* (F-204)
  John 27* (JE-66)
  Lucy 12* (F-213)
  Samuel 54* (JE-56)
  Spencer 57* (JE-69)
  William 40 (MA-250)

Index

HOLLY
  Emanuel 55 (B) (MT-43)
  James 65 (CL-80)
  Jefferson 23* (CL-80)
  Judy Ann 12* (B) (MT-42)
  Patrick 33* (CL-47)
HOLLYDAY
  Samuel 36* (JE-14)
HOLMAN
  Edward 30* (F-174)
  Elisha 27 (MA-266)
HOLMEN
  James 32 (MA-279)
HOLMES
  Benjamin 43 (MT-43)
  Frances 60* (JE-48)
  Harriett 38 (B) (F-220)
  James 33* (F-120)
  John 38 (MT-53)
  John 41* (F-138)
  John 60 (B) (F-202)
  William 30 (MT-53)
HOLMS
  Catharine 25 (GD-279)
  Samuel 33 (GD-286)
HOLTSCLAW
  Charles 33 (GD-245)
  John W. 37* (GD-242)
HOLTZCLAW
  Abner 71 (GD-226)
  Jesse 68 (GD-212)
  Willja 24 (GD-226)
HOMEN?
  Patrick 35 (F-205)
HONERS?
  Elizabeth 18* (MA-318)
HOOD
  Andrew 54 (CL-46)
  James M. 30* (CL-47)
  John 23 (JE-34)
  John W. 52* (MT-13)
  Will 24 (GD-277)
HOOKER
  Nancy 65* (F-149)
  Nicholas 68 (MA-262)
HOOLER
  Robert 29 (MA-293)

HOOTEN
  Jesse 9 (m)* (MA-217)
  John 65* (MA-219)
HOOTON
  Nicholas 50 (CL-16)
  William 74 (CL-10)
HOOTREL?
  Matthias 45 (CL-73)
HOOVER
  Alfred 30 (JE-51)
  Andrew 26* (JE-73)
  Catharine 47 (JE-12)
  Catharine 47* (MA-325)
  Daniel 44 (ES-100)
  David S. 52 (JE-73)
  George D. 25* (JE-12)
  Henry 24* (JE-31)
  John Q. A. 22 (JE-55)
  John sr. 44 (JE-42)
  Joseph 35 (JE-44)
  Margaret 20* (JE-77)
  Martha 2* (JE-71)
  Mary 21* (JE-62)
  Moses 50 (JE-43)
  Nancy 61* (MA-214)
  Pelina 15* (F-121)
  Peter 61* (JE-27)
  William T. 14* (JE-48)
HOOVER?
  Sarah 13* (JE-19)
HOOVERMAIL
  Nancy J. 28* (MT-32)
HOOZER
  Lorenzo 46 (GD-282)
HOPER?
  Eliza 60 (MA-227)
HOPKINS
  H. J. 30 (m) (GD-281)
  Jesse 27 (m) (GD-281)
  P. T. 42 (m)* (CL-9)
  William 30* (F-128)
HOPPER
  George 13* (MA-259)
  Hiram 22* (ES-68)
  John 25 (ES-67)
  John 45* (GD-287)
  Mary 32 (F-217)
  Simon 43* (GD-289)

  William 22 (MA-259)
  William H. 26* (GD-266)
HOPSON
  Willard 17* (GD-232)
HOPWOOD
  Permelia 44* (MT-73)
  Sarah 34 (B) (MT-4)
  Smith 15* (CL-55)
HORD
  F. J.? 22 (m)* (JE-55)
  Mary 56 (JE-74)
HORINE
  Henry 75 (JE-12)
  John (Genl.) 45 (JE-52)
  John 51 (JE-3)
  Katharine 63* (JE-52)
HORN
  Aaron 51 (ES-107)
  Elizabeth 44 (ES-106)
  Isaac 31 (OS-316)
  Isaac 40 (MT-52)
  Jackson 30 (ES-107)
  James 53* (JE-57)
  John 55 (MA-290)
  Simpson 22 (ES-106)
  Susan 76 (ES-107)
  Warren 36 (ES-107)
HORNBACK
  Anthony 64 (CL-79)
  Harry 25 (m)* (CL-88)
HORNSBY
  Lucy 26* (MA-267)
HOSDETTER?
  Frances M. 5/12* (F-208)
HOSKINS
  Jack 52 (MA-219)
  John 43 (ES-57)
  John S. 32* (GD-208)
  Nancy 64* (ES-57)
  William 25 (MA-219)
  William 66* (GD-209)
HOSTETLER
  Francis 40* (F-203)
HOSTETTER
  Jacob 33* (F-155)
HOUGHTON
  F. R. 33 (m) (F-135)
  Reuben 59 (F-135)

Index

HOUGHTON
  W. F. 31 (m)* (F-129)
HOUS
  James C. 23 (CL-49)
HOUSE
  Aaron 18* (GD-211)
  George W. 34* (CL-31)
  James 24 (GD-225)
  James 46 (JE-27)
  Rury 8 (f)* (GD-210)
  Samuel 40 (CL-80)
  Squire B. 32 (CL-30)
  Thomas B. 47* (CL-28)
HOUSTON
  John B. 37* (CL-41)
HOVINE
  Isaac? 53* (JE-15)
  Jacob 34 (JE-16)
  Joshua 40* (JE-16)
HOW
  Mary 34* (F-139)
HOWARD
  Benjamin 54* (MA-202)
  Chas. 25* (F-213)
  Clement 23* (OS-307)
  E. 74 (f)* (F-143)
  Elijah 29* (MA-287)
  George 31* (OS-307)
  George 75* (MT-1)
  Henry H. 53 (ES-87)
  Isabella 100* (CL-65)
  J. L. 45 (m) (F-162)
  James 35* (MT-7)
  James 60 (MA-307)
  James O. 32* (MT-41)
  John 55 (MT-59)
  John B. 74 (MT-22)
  Lucy Jane 7* (F-134)
  Mary A. 19* (F-122)
  Micelberry 33 (MT-18)
  Nancy 13* (ES-74)
  Nancy 14* (ES-77)
  Obediah 29 (MA-272)
  Phillip 38 (OS-312)
  Robert S. 23 (JE-19)
  Samuel 25 (MT-80)
  Thomas 30* (MT-35)
  Thomas S. 7* (F-221)

  William 31 (ES-49)
  William D. 27* (ES-71)
HOWEL
  Gains 33 (OS-313)
HOWELL
  A. J. 32 (m) (ES-81)
  David 51* (MT-16)
  Elizabeth 16* (F-225)
  Emaline 20* (MA-252)
  George W. 39 (MT-45)
  H. R. 30 (m)* (F-115)
  Lewis M. 20* (MT-5)
  Lucy 66 (ES-104)
  Susan 12* (MT-6)
HOWERTON
  Jacob 40* (OS-305)
HOWES
  Orion 26 (F-241)
HOWSER
  Peter 50* (JE-48)
HUBBARD
  Archibald 25 (MT-77)
  Granville 36 (MA-217)
  Hannah 30 (MT-77)
  John H. 7* (GD-254)
  Peter 25 (MT-77)
HUBBORD
  Robert 35 (GD-279)
HUBER
  Joseph 40* (F-117)
HUDGENS
  Thomas 44 (ES-86)
HUDSON
  Commodore P. 22 (GD-243)
  Edward 29* (MA-230)
  Eliza 28 (m?) (MA-234)
  Eliza 50 (JE-34)
  Ellen M. 21* (JE-30)
  Isabella 9* (F-123)
  James 31 (F-243)
  James 35 (MT-54)
  James 40* (MT-63)
  James H. 41 (GD-233)
  Jesse 26 (JE-34)
  John 51 (MA-234)
  John 68 (F-239)
  L. B. 34 (m)* (GD-264)
  L. M. 46 (m) (JE-62)

  Morgan 39 (GD-218)
  Thomas 26 (GD-236)
  Thomas 30 (MA-265)
  Thomas 30 (MT-64)
  Thomas 40 (ES-70)
HUDY
  Hester J. 24* (F-114)
HUFFMAN
  Davidson 20* (GD-264)
  Eliza 60* (GD-213)
  Fountain 35 (GD-238)
  Henry 80* (F-187)
  Jack 48* (GD-262)
  Michael 40* (F-183)
  P. A. 28 (m)* (MA-252)
  Plesant 44 (GD-288)
  Will L. 47 (GD-262)
  William 37* (GD-230)
  William 65 (GD-209)
HUFNER
  John 20* (JE-58)
  Margaret 42 (JE-47)
HUGENLY?
  John M. 30 (MA-255)
  R. 71 (f) (MA-255)
HUGGINS
  Harvey C. 42 (JE-73)
  Sarah 26* (JE-18)
  Thomas 50* (F-129)
  Thos. 17* (F-152)
HUGHART
  John 24* (F-194)
HUGHES
  Betsey 45* (B) (F-130)
  Eliza 30* (GD-260)
  Ferdinand 35* (F-122)
  George W. 32 (CL-39)
  Henry 28 (JE-72)
  Jacob 59* (F-231)
  John 41* (CL-39)
  John B. 24* (JE-68)
  John M. 26 (JE-62)
  M. C. 44 (m)* (OS-297)
  Margaret 69 (ES-101)
  Mary 22* (F-122)
  Matthew 43 (CL-39)
  Tharp 38 (GD-231)
  Thos. 45* (F-179)

Index

HUGHES
  Turner 40 (ES-67)
  Will 36* (GD-259)
  William 31 (MA-281)
HUGHS
  Daniel 40 (CL-64)
  Loucinda 44 (ES-93)
  Person 30 (GD-281)
  Thomas 36* (CL-38)
HUGUELY
  Jacob 43* (MA-285)
HUKEL
  Leslie 7* (F-172)
HUKELL?
  John 22* (F-172)
HUKILL
  E. W. 33 (m)* (F-212)
  Robbert 30* (F-122)
  Robt. 51 (F-139)
HUKLE
  John 30 (F-184)
HULET
  Allen 43 (JE-12)
  Boswell 25* (F-250)
HULETT
  Catharine 46 (MA-223)
  Elizabeth 19* (F-184)
  Jas. 19* (F-184)
  Jesse 33 (CL-73)
  Jesse 53 (CL-92)
  Robert 56 (CL-92)
  Silas 26* (CL-73)
  Thomas 26 (MA-224)
  Wyatt 66 (CL-74)
HULITT
  David 30 (F-217)
  Granvill 33 (F-185)
  Joseph 27 (F-234)
  Joseph 60 (F-236)
  Perry 30 (F-236)
  Richard 45 (F-217)
HULL
  Henry 16* (F-161)
  J. C. 35 (f)* (F-180)
  John C. 30* (F-154)
  Rebecca 34* (F-172)
  Sarah J. 17* (F-217)

HULLET?
  Joseph M. 25* (MA-218)
HULLS
  Mary 4* (F-223)
HULSE
  Elizabeth 61 (CL-80)
  James 21* (CL-68)
  John 71 (CL-76)
  Joshua 39 (CL-58)
  Paul 48 (CL-77)
  Richard 23 (CL-67)
  William 29 (CL-19)
HULSE?
  Stephen 40 (CL-95)
HULTZ
  David 45 (MT-61)
  Garret 17* (MT-11)
  William 41* (MT-11)
HUME
  Esther 81 (CL-92)
  Margaret 31 (MA-242)
  Matthew D. 46* (CL-88)
  Robert 40 (CL-92)
HUMES
  Absalom W. 35 (GD-223)
  James 27 (GD-236)
  James 76 (GD-235)
  Nancy 53* (MA-258)
HUMMINGS
  W. H. 7 (m)* (B) (F-220)
HUMPHREY
  Mahala 22* (B) (F-127)
  S. E. 10/12 (f)* (GD-210)
  Solomon 36 (GD-214)
HUMPHREYS
  Betsy 24* (B) (JE-44)
  James 23* (B) (JE-57)
HUMPHRY
  Catherine 76* (F-245)
HUMPSTON
  William 36 (CL-72)
HUNDLEY
  Allen 25 (F-240)
  Chas. 27 (F-241)
  Samuel 36 (OS-277)
HUNDREN?
  Lucinda 15* (MA-290)

HUNT
  Agness 8* (B) (F-158)
  Armina 18* (ES-105)
  Arthusan 40 (f)* (ES-96)
  Drummond C. 55* (F-233)
  Dudley 24 (MA-238)
  Harrison 58* (JE-49)
  James 22* (OS-316)
  James 47 (CL-51)
  Jeptha 45* (CL-51)
  Jno. M. 48 (F-227)
  John 114? (44?) (B) (F-141)
  John 25 (F-216)
  John W. 20* (JE-60)
  Johnathan 81* (OS-279)
  Jon_ 75 (m)* (CL-51)
  Michael 24 (F-210)
  P. G. 46 (m) (F-238)
  P. K. 33 (m) (F-199)
  Rebecca 42 (F-218)
  Reuben 43 (CL-92)
  Richard 26* (MA-215)
  Sarah 48* (F-165)
  Thompson 43 (F-135)
  Washington 17?* (F-128)
  William 48 (MA-235)
  Wilson S. 40 (F-154)
HUNTER
  Ellen 35* (JE-21)
  Ellen 80* (JE-13)
  Harriet 35 (B) (F-202)
  Henry 48 (JE-21)
  J. H. 27 (m) (JE-8)
  J. J. 38 (m) (F-146)
  Jane 61* (F-207)
  Jesse 50* (MA-283)
  John 26* (F-207)
  John 44 (GD-219)
  John 48 (JE-15)
  John 57 (MA-231)
  John P. 38 (JE-17)
  Joseph 73 (JE-13)
  Margaret 43* (F-196)
  Martin 20 (JE-21)
  Mesy? 40 (m)* (JE-13)
  Nathan 22* (OS-278)
  Nathan 50 (JE-21)
  Peter 33* (CL-92)

Index

HUNTER
  Richmond 44 (JE-23)
  Ruth 85 (MA-231)
  Samuel 35 (JE-13)
  Thomas 50* (F-237)
  Thomas 50 (JE-23)
  Thomas C. 35* (ES-104)
  William 27 (JE-26)
  William 28 (JE-34)
  William 43 (MA-246)
  William 66 (JE-17)
HUNTON
  John C. 40 (CL-69)
HUOFON?
  Benjamin 13* (MT-63)
HURBERSON
  Setphen 50* (B) (F-186)
HURBURD
  William 31 (MA-321)
HURDUN?
  Harrison 43 (MA-317)
HURLEY
  James 41 (OS-305)
  Spencer 20* (OS-305)
HURONYMUS
  Franklin 25* (CL-40)
HURST
  David 31 (F-188)
  James 43* (F-182)
  Smith W. 37* (MA-210)
HURT
  Eleven 34 (m) (GD-255)
  James 22* (MT-69)
  John W. 34 (GD-254)
  Laura 6* (F-231)
  Will 32* (GD-260)
HUSTON
  Mary 24* (F-252)
HUTCHERSON
  John 30 (GD-211)
  Margaret 17* (GD-217)
  Ruth 64 (GD-227)
  Silas 34 (GD-218)
  Willis 28 (GD-227)
HUTCHESON
  And. 27* (F-203)
  Arthusa 36 (GD-264)
  Jemima 46 (GD-241)

HUTCHINGS
  Africa 51 (m) (B) (CL-42)
  Newton R. 17* (F-188)
HUTCHINS
  E. 18 (f)* (F-132)
HUTCHINSON
  Betty 13* (F-142)
  Margaret 68* (F-120)
  Sarah 49* (F-135)
HUTCHISON
  D. 70 (f) (F-156)
  John 37 (F-180)
HUTSELL
  Jesse 28 (F-236)
HYDE
  Humphrey 24* (F-205)
HYMER
  Andrew P. 42* (CL-90)
  William 25 (ES-86)
HYSE
  Thomas 29 (MA-249)
IGO
  Murberry? 35 (m)* (MA-291)
  Thomas 25 (MT-55)
IMFREL?
  Darly 60 (f)* (CL-50)
INGELS
  Andrew 32 (F-167)
  H. B. 35 (m)* (F-164)
INGLEHEART
  Joseph 22* (F-153)
INGLES
  Davis 52* (B) (F-200)
  John S. 60* (F-208)
  William 30* (F-120)
INGRAHAM
  Abram 68* (MT-84)
  Job 33 (MT-55)
  William 27 (MT-55)
INGRAM
  Hardin 29 (ES-107)
  William 26 (ES-67)
INNES
  John P. 38* (F-183)
  Robt. 22* (F-193)
INNES?
  Amanda 27* (JE-74)

INNIS
  Chas. W. 28* (F-189)
  E. E. 66 (f)* (F-179)
INSKEP?
  A. 78 (m)* (F-172)
IRION
  M. F. 17 (m)* (F-218)
IRVIN
  J. P. 14 (m)* (JE-62)
IRVINE
  Albert G. 47 (MA-213)
  Annanias 64 (GD-231)
  David 53* (MA-206)
  David L. 60 (MA-293)
  George 8 (GD-211)
  James 52 (F-212)
  James 95* (JE-33)
  Nathaniel 42* (MA-207)
  Robert A. 15* (F-250)
  Samuel 66* (MA-277)
  Shelby 22 (m)* (MA-206)
  Thos. H. 33* (F-219)
  William 25 (MA-255)
  William 47 (CL-57)
IRWIN
  M. E. 20 (f)* (F-168)
ISAACS
  Alkney? 70 (f)* (OS-314)
  Elijah 42 (OS-295)
  Elisha 25* (OS-301)
  Fielden 34 (ES-101)
  George W. 26 (MA-235)
  Godfrey 23 (MA-240)
  Godfrey 25 (OS-281)
  Godfrey 75 (MA-240)
  James 45 (MA-238)
  John 38 (MA-239)
  Samuel 24 (MA-235)
  Samuel 27 (OS-315)
ISBELL
  William 58 (MA-287)
ISLER
  Geo. F. 40* (F-196)
ISO
  Jonathan 30 (GD-230)
ISOM
  George 24 (MA-296)
  James 65 (MA-296)

Index

ISOM
  Joseph B. 40* (MT-5)
  Samuel 12* (GD-222)
ISON
  Charles 47 (GD-206)
  Hardin 24 (GD-230)
  James H. sr. 77 (GD-240)
  Lunnda? 57 (f)* (GD-239)
  Moses 10* (GD-222)
  William 47 (GD-207)
ITCHER?
  Wrily 62? (f)* (B) (F-117)
JACKMAN
  Houston 33* (GD-263)
JACKSON
  A. P. 24 (m) (MA-239)
  Allis 32* (F-196)
  B. F. 29 (m) (OS-307)
  Chloe Ann 93 (MT-20)
  David 30 (JE-29)
  Francis F. 73* (CL-24)
  Isaac 21 (MA-237)
  Isham 60* (JE-10)
  J. G. 44 (m) (MA-271)
  James 23 (MA-229)
  James 35 (F-220)
  James F. 39 (MA-292)
  James H. 21 (MA-237)
  Jane 31* (MT-21)
  John H. 21* (F-160)
  Josiah A. 42* (ES-104)
  M. 41 (m)* (B) (F-151)
  Malvina 19* (B) (F-198)
  Milton 21* (JE-73)
  Peter 64 (B) (F-116)
  Robert 74 (MA-305)
  Sally 78* (CL-50)
  Saml. G. 49* (F-190)
  Samuel 27* (ES-54)
  Samuel 27* (MT-2)
  Thomas 32 (MA-238)
  Thos. 44* (F-181)
  Thursa 35* (GD-248)
  W. 65 (m)* (F-146)
  W. G. 29 (m)* (ES-86)
  W. T. 17 (m) (F-129)
  William 33 (MT-22)
  Wm. 19* (B) (F-152)

JACOBS
  Andrew 34 (JE-16)
  David 65 (B) (CL-94)
  Isaac 37 (CL-93)
  Kitty A. 26 (JE-40)
  Lewis 35 (JE-16)
  Mary 66 (JE-15)
  Mathew 63* (JE-7)
  Nathan 52* (ES-88)
  Sally A. 18* (JE-5)
  William 32 (JE-48)
JACOBY
  Andrew 42* (F-157)
JAMERSON
  Casan 23 (f)* (JE-37)
JAMES
  Eliza 14* (F-225)
  Henry 56* (MA-263)
  Hezekiah J. 22* (CL-44)
  John G. 50* (F-162)
  John M. 41 (CL-82)
  M. R. 58 (m) (F-172)
  Tabatha 18* (F-181)
JAMESON
  David 66 (GD-249)
  Eliza 13* (B) (GD-248)
  John H. 34 (MT-82)
  Milton 43* (MT-16)
  William 30 (MA-205)
  William O. jr. 69 (MT-82)
JAMISON
  Irvine 20* (ES-97)
  Molly 15* (MT-6)
JAMUSON
  Benjamin F. 27* (MT-72)
JANNAH?
  John A. 40* (MT-2)
JANUARY
  James 11* (F-211)
JARMA
  M. H. 18 (m)* (MA-265)
JARMAN
  E. B. 40 (m)* (MA-203)
  John 15 (MA-242)
  John J. 34 (MA-230)
  Lidury? 26 (m) (MA-206)
JARMAN?
  Elford 24 (MA-294)

JARVIS?
  James H. 35* (MT-20)
JASPER
  William 23* (OS-303)
JEFFERS
  Affd? 29 (f)* (F-154)
JEFFIE?
  Sarah 48* (F-191)
JEFFRES
  Thomas 32* (JE-37)
JEFFREYS
  Richard 44 (MA-252)
JEFFRIES
  Absolm 32 (MA-288)
  Enoch 59 (MT-33)
  Harvey 42 (MT-37)
  John 35* (MT-58)
  Learna 80* (JE-46)
  Luther C. 30* (MT-69)
  Smith 50 (CL-45)
JELNER?
  Huldey 6* (MA-242)
JENINGS
  Abraham 28 (GD-252)
JENISTON
  Rebecca 68 (JE-53)
JENKINS
  Ann M. 13* (CL-1)
  Benjamin 18* (CL-94)
  Cara 39 (B) (F-192)
  Charles 28* (F-151)
  Charles 32* (F-116)
  Clemins 25* (B) (OS-306)
  Daniel 36 (ES-75)
  Elisha 42* (JE-60)
  George W. 22 (MA-210)
  James 22* (F-149)
  James 25* (F-163)
  James 27* (F-124)
  Jane 16* (MT-22)
  Jane 69* (F-251)
  Josephine 56* (F-139)
  Letty 55 (GD-242)
  Lewis 60 (F-135)
  P. A. 23 (f)* (MA-270)
  Thomas 45 (CL-21)
  Willis 45 (F-165)
  Zilphy 60* (B) (F-193)

- 465 -

Index

JENKINS
    ____ 25 (m)* (F-194)
JENNET?
    Mary 80 (MA-243)
JENNINGS
    Alexander 27* (GD-234)
    Alexander A. 70 (GD-245)
    Baylor 55* (GD-251)
    Benjamin F. 24* (GD-245)
    Eliza E. 5* (GD-238)
    Emily 14* (GD-210)
    George 21* (GD-251)
    Isiah 70 (MA-202)
    James 20* (GD-266)
    James 8* (GD-211)
    Jesse 40 (MA-202)
    John 36 (MA-323)
    John B. 30 (GD-277)
    John B. sr. 66 (GD-212)
    Kasiah 64* (MA-209)
    M. 28 (f)* (F-127)
    Pascal 39 (F-120)
    Richard B. 41 (GD-262)
    Samuel B. 50 (GD-227)
    Thomas B. 42* (GD-251)
    William 30 (GD-241)
    William 65 (MA-286)
    William E. 31* (JE-33)
JERMAN
    William 35 (MA-218)
JESSEE
    Thomas J. 24 (ES-111)
JETER
    Benjamin 32? (F-132)
    Elizabeth 34* (JE-6)
    Hugh 45* (F-127)
JETT
    Isaac J. 1* (MA-268)
JEWELL
    Ewell 60 (CL-56)
    John 38 (JE-44)
    Lesly 30 (m)* (MT-63)
    Thomas S. 34* (CL-29)
JEWETT
    Jane 56* (F-185)
JIMMERSON
    Nancy 60* (MA-282)

JINGLE
    Jesse 50 (F-216)
JOHNS
    Anderson 61* (MT-71)
    Joseph 28 (MT-71)
    Joseph 35* (F-239)
    Susan 56 (F-243)
    Thos. H. 34* (F-221)
JOHNSON
    Alexander 29 (ES-106)
    Alfred 30 (MA-218)
    Amanda 12 (JE-55)
    Amanda 33* (F-210)
    Amos 58* (F-250)
    Ann 55* (F-195)
    Anna 21* (MA-240)
    Anna 62 (MT-16)
    Armstead 30* (CL-35)
    Benjamin 67 (JE-9)
    C. M. 30 (m)* (F-184)
    Cesar jr. 25 (B) (JE-42)
    Cesar sr. 60 (B) (JE-42)
    Charles 4/12* (B) (CL-43)
    Christopher 44* (B) (F-179)
    Courtney 26 (m) (JE-40)
    D. Francis 28* (JE-68)
    David 45 (MA-225)
    David 60 (F-172)
    E. P. 52 (m) (F-222)
    Easter 50* (MA-219)
    Edward 30* (ES-78)
    Elijah 54 (CL-34)
    Eliza 16* (F-225)
    George 30 (MA-270)
    George 38 (MA-271)
    George 61 (MA-246)
    Hamson 22* (F-156)
    Hannah 13* (ES-88)
    Harriett 16* (JE-40)
    Henry 55* (F-212)
    Henry F. 48 (MA-304)
    Hugh 44 (MT-63)
    Isaac 32 (ES-48)
    Isaac 45 (MT-42)
    Isaac E. 25* (MT-7)
    Isaah 27* (B) (F-137)
    Isaiah 40* (B) (F-185)
    J. B. 47 (m)* (F-178)

    J. G. 29 (m)* (F-194)
    Jackson 49* (MT-35)
    Jacob 28* (F-173)
    Jacob 44 (MT-30)
    Jahoda 59 (MT-31)
    James 17* (MT-5)
    James 22* (B) (JE-40)
    James 25* (MA-204)
    James 30 (ES-49)
    James 62 (MA-241)
    James A. 25 (OS-291)
    James __ * (JE-36)
    Jas. 50* (F-195)
    Jeptha 46 (JE-13)
    Jessee 41 (OS-278)
    John 66* (F-235)
    John 68* (MA-276)
    John J. 17* (JE-67)
    John T. 50 (MT-30)
    John sr. 79 (GD-218)
    Joseph 19* (B) (JE-76)
    Joseph 22* (MT-39)
    Joseph 24* (MT-30)
    Joseph 27 (ES-110)
    Julia 50 (B) (JE-42)
    Julia A. 29* (MT-84)
    Kindred 32 (MT-47)
    Louvisa 22 (ES-101)
    Lucy A. 9* (B) (JE-54)
    M. B. 42 (f) (F-178)
    M. C. 41 (m) (F-145)
    Mahala 39 (CL-71)
    Mahalia 3* (ES-70)
    Mahaly 35* (F-248)
    Major 65 (MA-221)
    Manerva 12* (ES-83)
    Martin 39 (ES-71)
    Martin 47 (CL-16)
    Mary 18* (CL-16)
    Mary 54 (MA-280)
    Massey 86 (f)* (F-203)
    Merryman 27 (GD-262)
    Moore 55* (MT-5)
    Mordica 50 (m) (ES-83)
    Moses 60 (ES-58)
    Moses W. 28 (MT-31)
    N. B. 30 (CL-10)
    Nancy 22* (ES-106)

Index

JOHNSON
Peter 34* (F-118)
Ramsey 70* (F-138)
Richard M. 27* (MT-40)
Richard T. 34 (MT-31)
Robert 35 (MA-207)
Robert 36* (MA-291)
Robert 40 (ES-52)
Robert 40* (MT-45)
Rody 56 (OS-313)
Sally 35 (B) (JE-42)
Samuel 34 (GD-209)
Sarah 40 (B) (F-114)
Sarah A. 26* (JE-41)
Schuyler 31* (MA-221)
Socretion 23 (MT-47)
Stephen 27* (CL-1)
Stephen 48* (JE-49)
Tennie? 38 (MA-279)
Thomas 24 (MT-32)
Thomas 38* (MT-12)
Thomas 41 (MT-31)
Thomas 43 (MA-238)
Thomas 52 (MA-297)
Thomas 60 (MA-240)
Timothey 20* (OS-309)
Verbeda 50 (F-148)
William 25* (GD-246)
William 28 (MA-241)
William 37* (MA-218)
William 38 (MA-221)
William 40 (CL-17)
William 43 (MA-318)
William 48 (MT-47)
William 69 (CL-16)
Willis 30 (B) (JE-42)
Wm. 22* (F-175)
JOHNSTON
Alexander M. 60 (CL-70)
Andy 21* (OS-280)
H. 23 (m) (F-140)
Henry 25* (F-130)
James 30* (F-121)
John W. 55 (GD-268)
John jr. 45 (GD-231)
Polly 18* (CL-64)
Samuel jr. 40 (OS-280)
Tamie 70* (B) (F-152)

Thomas 22* (GD-266)
Thomas 45 (GD-272)
Will 47 (GD-281)
Will H. 20* (GD-230)
William 30 (CL-60)
William 58 (OS-287)
JOLLY
Spear 45 (m) (MA-266)
JONE?
Elizabeth 68 (MA-289)
JONES
— 22 (m)* (F-190)
A. C. 30 (m) (OS-307)
A. F. 18 (m)* (MT-2)
Abslom 42 (CL-26)
Alfred F. 38* (F-140)
Ansil D. 24 (ES-91)
Benah 45 (m) (GD-208)
Bright 45 (MA-275)
Cadwallader 30* (CL-41)
Cleopatra 10* (CL-74)
Closs T. 58 (MT-13)
Danford D. 69* (ES-104)
Daniel 22 (GD-217)
Darnel S. 44* (JE-78)
David 25 (GD-228)
David 50 (GD-256)
David L. 40* (MT-25)
Ducon 62 (CL-50)
Edmond 63* (CL-18)
Elizabeth 60* (CL-10)
Elizabeth 81 (MT-10)
Emily 30* (MT-23)
Fauntleroy 33* (CL-6)
G. D. 25 (m)* (MT-1)
George W. 35* (MT-10)
George W. 40 (MA-266)
Henrietta 28* (F-196)
Henry 39* (MT-2)
Hiram 30 (CL-81)
Hiram 45* (CL-51)
Humphrey 28 (MA-320)
James 28* (F-217)
James 40 (F-240)
James F. 30* (MT-71)
John 23* (MA-249)
John 27 (CL-27)
John 28 (OS-304)

John 29 (CL-24)
John 40 (GD-255)
John 60 (MA-274)
John 65 (MA-237)
John 70 (CL-33)
John H. 35* (MT-83)
John H. 37 (F-117)
John T. 11* (CL-28)
John T. 38* (MT-23)
Joseph 30 (MA-302)
Joseph 44 (F-159)
Judith 67* (GD-230)
L. B. W. 51 (m) (ES-56)
L. D. 46 (m)* (F-142)
Linney 90 (f)* (CL-50)
Lucy 17* (B) (ES-80)
M. A. 27 (f)* (F-142)
M. J. 54 (m) (MA-237)
Martha 56* (MT-71)
Mary 7* (F-158)
Mathew 30* (OS-289)
Murphey 80 (MA-206)
Newland 25* (MA-277)
R. B. 23 (m) (F-226)
Rebecca 23* (MT-73)
Richard 25* (F-166)
Robb 40 (MA-240)
Robert 65 (B) (GD-288)
Roger 31 (CL-5)
Saml. 34 (F-187)
Samuel 25* (OS-310)
Stephen 45 (MA-284)
Tarleton 31 (ES-110)
Thomas 18* (F-221)
Thomas 19 (MA-310)
Thomas 34 (ES-103)
Thomas 35 (MA-273)
Thomas 54 (CL-29)
Thomas 60* (MT-29)
Thomas B. 41 (JE-65)
Virginia 24* (F-208)
W. C. 12 (m)* (F-159)
Wiley 27* (MT-51)
Will 44 (GD-256)
William 26 (CL-68)
William 27* (CL-52)
William 30 (MT-16)
William 32* (CL-57)

Index

JONES
  William 33 (MA-243)
  William 35* (F-250)
  William 35* (JE-56)
  William C. 23* (CL-31)
  Wm. 40* (F-140)
  Wm. R. 38 (F-224)
  Woodson 16* (F-211)
JONES?
  Lucy 56* (B) (F-144)
JONETT
  Lou 50 (f)* (CL-68)
  Lynch 44 (CL-75)
JONSON
  Joseph 50 (F-164)
  Joseph M. 50 (F-171)
  Robert A. 35 (GD-284)
JORDAN
  Betsey 60* (CL-21)
  Robert 6* (MA-267)
  Sarah 25 (CL-11)
  Shurshall? 49 (m) (CL-74)
  Thomas 35* (CL-24)
JORIETT?
  Edward S. 20* (CL-41)
  Frank 72* (B) (MT-80)
  Margaret 12* (B) (MT-81)
JOSIETT?
  Jack 56 (MT-40)
JOSLIN
  James 28 (GD-217)
  John 37 (GD-279)
JOUETT
  Margaret 57* (F-209)
JOURDON
  James R. 44 (ES-90)
JUCHO?
  William 46 (F-144)
JUDD
  Frankey 28* (OS-295)
  Rowlin 66 (OS-277)
  Sarah 84* (F-117)
JUDTSELL?
  Josiah 27* (MA-282)
JUDY
  Alexander 47* (MT-17)
  David B. 34 (CL-77)
  F. C. sr. 55 (m)* (MT-42)

Henry M. 31* (ES-105)
Henry M. 34* (ES-55)
Hetty 65 (CL-87)
John 63 (CL-86)
John A. 30 (CL-86)
Martin 40 (CL-85)
William 30* (MT-14)
JUSTICE
  W. W. 23 (m)* (MT-5)
JUTPHIN?
  John B. 26* (F-191)
KALE
  George W. 40 (F-219)
KALMES
  W. T. 40 (m)* (F-234)
KANE
  John 22* (F-199)
KANISEY
  Thomas 18* (MA-204)
KANNON
  Robert C. 24* (ES-58)
KANZ
  Charles 25* (F-223)
KAPPES
  J. H. 26 (m)* (JE-74)
KAPPS
  Henry J. 25* (F-208)
KARRICK
  James V. 45* (CL-67)
  Samuel 26* (CL-42)
KARSNER
  Jonathan 56* (JE-37)
KASE
  A. 35 (f)* (F-152)
KASERD
  David 25* (OS-305)
KASTLE
  John 45 (F-219)
KATES
  Isai 47 (m)* (MA-219)
KAVANAUGH
  Charles 63 (MA-270)
KAY
  Glovina 29 (B) (F-192)
  Mary B. 44 (F-164)
  Robt. 72 (F-181)
KEARSEY
  Silas 59 (ES-85)

KEAS
  Aurelius 31 (CL-38)
  James 74* (CL-65)
  William B. 48* (CL-39)
KEATH
  Uriah 40 (MT-24)
KEELER
  Lucy 65* (B) (F-145)
KEELY
  Arminta 46 (MA-229)
KEEN
  E. L. 10 (f)* (F-144)
  Geo. F. 42 (F-159)
  Oliver 30 (F-158)
KEENE
  Mary 66* (F-159)
  Robert W. 12* (JE-39)
  William R. 34* (JE-57)
KEISER
  Benj. 56* (F-128)
  C. M. 42 (m) (F-175)
  Hester 50* (F-226)
  William 30 (F-229)
KEISER?
  John __ * (F-138)
KEITH
  Andrew M. 49 (CL-47)
  James W. 61 (CL-47)
  M. L. 24 (m)* (F-145)
KELLER
  David 31 (F-235)
KELLEY
  Alexander C. 10* (ES-60)
  Emanuel 43 (ES-92)
  Green B. 39 (ES-82)
  Harrison 36 (ES-95)
  James 18* (MT-4)
  James 37 (ES-83)
  John 36 (F-153)
  Patrick 30* (F-166)
  Rachael 43 (ES-96)
  Richard P. 59 (MT-79)
  Simson 7* (OS-300)
KELLOGG
  Chester 47* (MA-279)
KELLRY
  Martha G. 51* (MA-225)

Index

KELLY
  Charles S. 12* (CL-42)
  Dolly 66 (ES-106)
  Elizabeth 50 (MT-23)
  Griffin 80 (CL-92)
  John 24 (OS-306)
  John 26* (MT-35)
  John 43 (GD-244)
  John 46 (ES-71)
  Robert 36* (F-120)
  Robert E. 54 (MA-250)
  Speed 21* (OS-303)
  William 25 (MA-232)
  William 32* (OS-302)
  William 70 (MT-23)
KEMBER
  Jepthah 50 (MT-83)
KEMP
  Henry 35* (CL-47)
  J. L. 40 (m)* (F-213)
KEMPER
  Burdett 62 (m) (GD-261)
  J. V. 39 (m) (MT-83)
  James H. 46 (GD-240)
  John 56 (GD-206)
  Thornton 70 (GD-241)
  Tilman 22* (F-235)
  William 85 (GD-206)
KENADEY
  Dolly 56* (CL-87)
KENADY
  Anderson 30* (MA-296)
KENATZER
  Christopher 30 (MA-287)
  William 46 (MA-305)
  William 79 (MA-304)
  William B. 25 (MA-305)
KENDALL
  Bailey 40 (CL-3)
KENDRICK
  Jane 22* (OS-300)
KENEPER
  Edward 36 (MT-18)
KENERDAY
  Rosa 26* (MA-250)
KENIDAY
  Geo. 27* (F-178)

KENITZER
  Jacob B. 44 (MA-212)
KENNARD
  Andrew 60* (F-196)
  James E. 57 (MT-3)
  Joseph 57 (F-226)
KENNEDARY
  James 47 (CL-16)
KENNEDAY
  Robert sr. 65* (CL-44)
KENNEDY
  Aggy 68 (f)* (B) (GD-265)
  Andrew A. 57 (GD-284)
  C. W. 35 (m) (F-198)
  David 59* (GD-217)
  David 80* (GD-280)
  Elbert D. 35 (GD-263)
  Eliza 32 (GD-280)
  Francis 38* (MT-35)
  Henry J. 26* (F-253)
  James 25 (GD-273)
  James M. 32 (GD-216)
  John 39 (MT-63)
  Leah 34* (MT-69)
  Margaret 56 (GD-270)
  Nancy 50 (MA-297)
  Rebecca 53 (GD-281)
  Samuel 43 (GD-271)
  Will 29 (GD-270)
KENNER
  Jane L. 80* (CL-93)
  Willis 7* (CL-55)
KENNEY
  Jane 15* (MT-64)
  Mary 14* (MT-67)
  Mary 43* (F-196)
  R. P. 64 (m)* (F-192)
KENNEY?
  William 33* (F-212)
KENNON
  Robert 55 (CL-49)
KENNY
  John S. 40* (F-223)
  S. B. 38 (m)* (JE-60)
KENSEL
  Christian 40* (F-207)
KENT
  A. D. 25 (m)* (F-230)

  David 75* (F-240)
  David Jr. 23* (F-240)
  Jane 36* (CL-76)
  John W. 14* (CL-36)
  Lewis 26 (F-230)
  Washington 27* (F-237)
  Wm. 40* (F-226)
KERBEY
  Elisa P. 32* (MA-255)
  Layton R. 37 (MA-234)
  Marion 18 (m)* (MA-228)
  elisha 68 (MA-224)
KERBEY?
  Elisha P. 21* (MA-221)
KERBY
  Atlantic O 64 (f) (JE-7)
  C. T. 35 (m)* (JE-56)
  Rebecca 21* (ES-94)
  Richard 50* (B) (JE-55)
KERFOOT
  Elizabeth 40* (ES-82)
KERLEY
  George S. 34 (ES-61)
KERLY
  Kiz 23 (f)* (OS-309)
KERNS
  Patrick 38* (CL-94)
KERR
  Jane 17* (F-225)
  John 59 (F-235)
  Parthenia 11* (CL-46)
KERSEY
  Absalum 43 (JE-1)
  James 16* (GD-264)
  K. A. 28 (m)* (F-138)
  William 42 (GD-221)
KERSLEY
  Rebecca 26 (MT-66)
  Travis 48 (MT-66)
KERTLEY
  AManda M. 48* (F-233)
  Mary 45 (MT-57)
KETRON
  John 37 (JE-51)
  Joseph 24 (JE-39)
  Peter 60 (JE-44)
  William 34 (JE-48)

Index

KETTLE
  Henry 23* (CL-4)
KEY
  Albert 30* (F-238)
  Sarah 88* (MT-71)
KEYESE?
  John L. 35* (F-234)
KEYS
  Jesse 46 (GD-205)
  John L. 34* (F-133)
KIBLER
  David 33* (F-230)
  Susan 7* (F-115)
KIDD
  Anderson 28 (GD-228)
  Frances 30* (F-164)
  George W. 40* (F-138)
  James 32 (F-202)
  P.? H. 37 (m)* (F-132)
  Robert 42 (CL-73)
  S. A. 32 (m)* (F-154)
  W. B. 26 (m)* (MA-217)
  Walter 40* (JE-66)
  William C. 45 (F-220)
  Zadick 46 (CL-72)
KIDWELL
  Harrison 36 (MA-261)
  James 60 (MA-248)
  Johnty 53 (m)* (MA-210)
  Jonathan 26* (MA-249)
  Mary 37* (F-164)
  Vinson 22 (MA-210)
KILBERN
  George 29* (OS-292)
KILROY
  Tho. C. 10* (F-201)
KIMBLE
  David 35* (GD-209)
KIMBRELL
  Elizabeth 78* (ES-75)
  James 45 (CL-65)
  John 48 (ES-80)
  Wiley 41 (CL-66)
KIMES
  William 40 (CL-92)
KINCADE
  Allen 32* (MT-16)
  George W. 37* (MT-58)

KINCAID
  John 45 (ES-106)
  John 46 (GD-209)
  Samuel 50 (MA-225)
  Thomas 60* (MA-217)
KINDER
  Will 54 (GD-234)
KINDRED
  Anderson 29 (ES-92)
  Garland 29 (m) (MA-246)
  Harvin 24 (m) (MA-236)
  J. J. 28 (m) (MA-273)
  J. J. 30 (m) (MA-293)
  James W. 36 (MA-249)
  John 30 (MA-232)
  Lorenzo D. 42 (MA-294)
  Martin 67 (MA-294)
  Nathaniel 27 (MA-231)
  Overton 27 (MA-246)
  William 56 (MA-231)
KINDRICK
  John F. 33 (OS-288)
KINEE
  John J. 38 (MA-264)
KINES
  Lorenzo D. 35 (JE-1)
KINETT?
  Elias 42* (MA-251)
KING
  Benjamin 38 (ES-75)
  Celia 82 (ES-62)
  Daniel 24 (ES-85)
  David A. 20* (F-199)
  David A. 32 (CL-13)
  Davis C. 33 (GD-245)
  Edmund 48 (MA-315)
  Elizabeth 14* (MT-66)
  Francis 25 (CL-63)
  Garland 34 (ES-62)
  Henry 20* (JE-73)
  Isaah 36 (F-120)
  Isam 24* (OS-292)
  Jackson 35* (MA-206)
  Jackson 37 (MA-270)
  James 42 (MT-38)
  John 15* (F-140)
  John 27 (MA-315)
  John 33 (CL-86)

  John R. 35 (GD-245)
  Joshua D. 38 (ES-94)
  Luvena? 22* (GD-274)
  Margaret 71* (ES-99)
  Mary 45 (GD-239)
  Merida 27 (ES-89)
  Nancy 18* (OS-291)
  Nancy 69* (F-159)
  Patsy 60* (JE-63)
  Presley 22 (ES-47)
  Richd. 39* (F-195)
  Robert D. 25 (CL-15)
  Robert E. 31 (GD-245)
  Robert S. 63 (CL-22)
  Samuel 19 (ES-89)
  Samuel 42 (ES-78)
  Samuel 52 (ES-70)
  Sarah 40* (F-209)
  Scuyler 50 (m) (ES-81)
  Simon P. 29 (ES-112)
  Stephen 37 (MT-70)
  Thomas 27* (MT-35)
  William 40* (F-207)
  William 40 (MT-70)
  William 48 (ES-68)
  William 50 (ES-68)
  William H. 37* (OS-312)
  Zackary 76* (ES-62)
KINGKADE
  Edward 52* (OS-311)
  Lycurgus 20 (OS-311)
  Socretas? 24 (m) (OS-311)
KINGS
  Joseph 87 (MT-15)
KINKEAD
  Chunn 38 (F-162)
  E. 35 (m)* (F-150)
  George B. 38 (F-198)
  H.? 46 (m) (F-120)
  John 21 (F-130)
KINN?
  Samuel 31 (MA-276)
  Thompson 28 (MA-276)
  William 28 (MA-276)
KINNAIRD
  Will H. 28* (GD-287)
KINNARD
  Davi? 30 (MA-223)

Index

KINNARD
 Fields 23* (MA-230)
 George W. 36 (MA-206)
 James W. 24* (F-199)
 John 28* (MA-218)
 John 40 (F-140)
 Mary 66* (F-207)
KINNEY
 Ellen 51 (F-128)
 John 22* (MT-66)
 Lucinda 17* (MT-67)
KINNY
 W. 28 (m)* (F-146)
KINSEY
 James 38 (F-145)
KIRBEY
 Elisha 56 (ES-109)
KIRBY
 Elisha 22 (ES-109)
 Elizabeth 30* (ES-88)
KIRK
 James A. 43 (MT-57)
 Matthew 71 (MT-65)
 Susan 53 (MT-84)
 William G. 24 (ES-79)
KIRKENDALL
 Samuel 46 (MA-290)
KIRKINDOL
 Richmond 80* (GD-280)
KIRKPATRICK
 David 25 (F-172)
 Ira 41 (MT-47)
 James 50* (MT-58)
 John 46 (MT-53)
 Mary 18* (F-174)
 R. 50 (m)* (F-124)
 W. 22 (m) (F-172)
 William 38* (F-254)
KIRTLEY
 Fleming A. 24* (MT-4)
 Francis 36 (JE-67)
 R. B. 35 (m) (F-255)
KISE
 Harriet 49* (F-173)
KISEN
 Thomas 28* (CL-32)
KISSINGER
 John 31 (F-209)

KITCHEN
 Greene C. 26* (JE-75)
KITCHENS
 James 76* (MT-9)
KITLEY
 Sarah 52* (JE-67)
KITTMAN?
 Ann 71* (F-115)
KITTS
 Polly 54* (F-131)
KLINGER
 Danl. 24* (F-142)
KNIGHT
 Curtis 34 (MA-213)
 Francis 35 (JE-20)
 Grant 40 (JE-62)
 Hardin 32* (JE-30)
 John 65* (B) (JE-64)
 Sarah F. 3* (CL-23)
 William 24* (JE-32)
KNOBLE
 David 34 (F-114)
KNOX
 George 50* (MT-50)
 Robert 20* (MT-63)
 Samuel __* (JE-18)
 Thomas 47* (MT-50)
KNUK?
 George 40 (MA-210)
KNUTZER
 George 42 (MA-209)
 Jacob 40 (MA-307)
 Jacob K. 21 (MA-303)
 James 50 (MA-303)
 Nancy 45 (MA-306)
 Richmond 38 (MA-303)
 Sarah 0 (MA-301)
 Sarah 70 (MA-306)
KOHLHASS
 Theodore 37 (CL-47)
KONKRIGHT
 Abram 77* (MT-63)
 Cevilla 11* (MT-84)
 Elizabeth 30* (MT-63)
 R. Jane 18* (MT-63)
KONKWRIGHT
 Benjamin L. 33 (MT-67)

KOPPUKUS
 A. 38 (m)* (F-138)
KRAUSE
 Martha 27* (F-135)
KRINE?
 James 55 (MA-277)
KROUSS
 Jacob 23* (F-199)
KRUISER
 James 49 (F-222)
KUGER?
 James 22* (F-127)
KUHLMAN
 B. 24 (m)* (F-140)
KUNTY
 Chas. 26* (F-140)
KURRS
 Jeremiah 68* (MA-261)
KURTZ
 Henry A. 32* (GD-262)
KYLE
 John 39* (F-121)
LACEY
 Perry 28 (OS-290)
LACKENS
 Margaret 28* (F-199)
LACKERY
 Gabriel 35 (MA-241)
LACKET
 Caroline 58* (F-196)
LACKEY
 Andrew 26* (MA-247)
 Gabriel 66 (GD-254)
 James 21* (OS-314)
 Mildred 38 (CL-93)
 Nathan 45 (JE-54)
 Polina 52* (GD-284)
 Thomas 61 (CL-93)
LACY
 Edgar 23* (MT-2)
 Thos. 39* (F-151)
LAFAYETT
 James 21* (CL-5)
LAFFOON
 James M. 37 (F-248)
LAFOE
 M. 19 (f)* (F-153)

Index

LAFON
  Anna 76* (JE-60)
LAID
  Saml. 69 (F-133)
LAIN
  James 52 (GD-255)
  Sherrod 46 (m) (GD-236)
  Will 62 (GD-229)
LAINE
  Alvy 39 (f) (MA-230)
  Francis 14* (MA-248)
  James 59* (MA-246)
  James 62* (CL-24)
  William H. 9* (CL-22)
  Willis 21 (MA-246)
LAIR
  Claibourn 44 (GD-228)
  James 56 (GD-229)
  James N. 5* (GD-213)
  Will 60 (GD-243)
  William G. 43 (GD-245)
LAIRD
  Howard 26 (MA-213)
  Polly 42* (MA-211)
LAKE
  Timothy 26* (MA-200)
LAKERS
  John 27 (MA-241)
  John 60 (MA-241)
  Thomas 23 (MA-241)
LAKES
  John 31 (MA-200)
  Rebecca 48* (ES-102)
  Robert 29 (MA-200)
LALEY
  Dennis 48* (F-117)
LAM
  Johnson sr. 56* (GD-207)
LAMASTER
  Alexander 38 (GD-243)
  James R. 36 (GD-226)
LAMB
  Alonzo 33* (MA-267)
  Darias 17 (m)* (GD-221)
  Edwin 38 (B) (MT-37)
  Harry 45* (F-145)
  John 78 (MA-247)
  Johnithan 20* (MA-243)

  Lucinda 28* (MA-278)
  Lucy 70 (MA-230)
  Madisn 39 (MA-219)
  Oliver 19 (MA-219)
  Richard 35* (MA-230)
  Thomas 29* (MA-257)
LAMBDEN
  Geo. J. 25* (F-205)
LAMBERT
  Barnes? 33* (F-131)
  John 25 (MA-234)
  Mary 50 (MA-243)
LAMBERTON
  Jeremiah 51 (MT-45)
LAMKIN
  V. 16 (f)* (F-136)
LAMME?
  Jane 33* (F-171)
LAN
  Richard 48* (F-208)
LANCART
  William 29 (F-137)
LANCART?
  Lewis 20* (F-145)
LANCASTER
  Henry 40* (F-123)
  James H. 22* (JE-69)
  John 76 (JE-62)
  Mason? T. 40 (JE-65)
  Merit P. 35 (JE-65)
  Sarah J. 28 (JE-68)
LANCE
  Eleanor 53 (MT-67)
LAND
  B. Jackson 32 (ES-94)
  Berry 27 (MA-313)
  Ellen 62* (JE-23)
  Fountain 35* (JE-14)
  G. W. 27 (m) (MA-280)
  Hiram 27 (MA-287)
  Jackson 32 (JE-21)
  James 21* (ES-51)
  James W. 30 (MA-286)
  John 29* (JE-19)
  John 45 (MA-319)
  John F. 52 (MA-318)
  Joseph 33 (JE-26)
  Owen D. 22 (MA-317)

  Sarah M. 7* (ES-50)
  Squire 32* (MA-309)
  Sylvester 11* (ES-55)
  Thomas 29* (MA-309)
  Thomas 47 (GD-224)
  Thomas 66 (JE-17)
  W. L. 23 (m)* (F-194)
  William 25* (JE-73)
  William S. 25* (JE-12)
LANDER
  John 42 (MA-264)
  William 53 (MT-29)
LANDRAM
  Lewis 50 (GD-263)
  W. J. 22 (m)* (GD-287)
LANDRETH
  A. E. 50 (f)* (F-170)
LANDRON
  Abram 72 (MA-292)
LANDRUM
  Stephen H. 28* (CL-78)
LANE
  Frances 16* (MT-30)
  Frazier 42 (B) (MT-40)
  Hiram 51* (MT-38)
  James B. 21 (ES-110)
  John C. 29* (ES-61)
  Johnson 27 (GD-233)
  Jon. N. 15 (m)* (CL-76)
  Melvin 2* (OS-310)
  Mildred 67* (F-231)
  Sarah 64* (MT-28)
  Thomas P. 27 (GD-207)
  William 28* (ES-110)
  William 36 (GD-212)
  William N. 30* (ES-90)
LANGBY
  Catherine 44* (F-239)
LANGDON
  Ann 73 (F-116)
  Harriet C. 45 (F-145)
LANGHORN
  Levi 36 (F-114)
LANGLEY
  Eliza 20* (CL-36)
  James W. 38* (CL-39)
  Robert W. 30* (CL-36)
  William S. 27* (MT-5)

Index

LANGSTON
  Joab 26* (CL-69)
LANHAM
  John 40 (MA-285)
LANKFORD
  Stephen 37 (MA-207)
LANKHART
  Edward 38 (F-173)
LANOM
  Benj. 45* (MA-209)
  Philicianne 91* (B) (F-220)
LANRUM?
  Mary 64* (MA-298)
LANSFORD
  Alexander 20 (GD-283)
LANTER
  Alexander 55 (MA-295)
  David 60 (MA-297)
  Jefferson 28 (MA-295)
  Mary 50 (MA-299)
LAPELLMAN
  Louis 23* (MA-251)
LARRINSON
  Jacob 36 (MT-46)
LARRISON
  David 45 (ES-50)
  George 24 (ES-68)
LASENER
  Jasper C. 34* (JE-63)
LASWELL
  James 43* (F-137)
LATHAM
  Robt. T. 42* (F-164)
LATSCH
  Teresse 41* (F-181)
LAUB?
  Thomas G. 50 (MA-247)
LAUCENT?
  Joseph 59* (F-135)
LAUDAMAN
  Wm. 40 (F-177)
LAUDEMAN
  David 38 (F-131)
  John 45* (F-181)
LAUDEMAN?
  Margaret 16* (F-120)
LAUDEMON
  David 20* (F-181)
LAUDERMAN
  J. H. 26 (m)* (F-164)
LAUDMAN
  Malinda 47* (F-173)
LAUGHLIN
  Benjamin 56 (CL-64)
  John W. 23* (CL-5)
  John W. 28 (CL-64)
  Lucy W. 65* (CL-47)
  Simeon 73* (CL-25)
LAURENCE
  Robert 48 (CL-33)
LAUSLEY
  Lucinda 36 (F-179)
LAUTER
  Richard 26 (MA-303)
LAUTER?
  Newton? 23* (MA-274)
LAVINE
  Watson 34 (MA-201)
LAW
  Jackson 22 (ES-48)
LAWES
  Lucullus 25* (F-223)
LAWLES
  James 10* (GD-245)
LAWLESS
  Margaret 19* (F-221)
  Peter C. 53 (GD-246)
  Richard 50* (F-128)
LAWNES
  A. 27 (m)* (MT-61)
LAWRENCE
  Andrew J. 23 (CL-38)
  Ann 55 (F-117)
  Frances 60* (CL-29)
  Frances M. 26* (CL-28)
  H. H. 36 (m)* (MT-60)
  Hiram 27 (F-206)
  J. M. 30 (m)* (CL-80)
  James 64* (F-188)
  James M. 28* (F-215)
  James M. 35* (CL-35)
  John B. 65 (CL-72)
  Merideth 64 (CL-19)
  Nancy J. 12* (CL-54)
  Will H. 33 (CL-54)
  William 27* (MT-60)
  William 45 (CL-54)
  William H. 29 (CL-37)
LAWS
  James 30 (MA-236)
  Welcome 35 (m)* (JE-12)
LAWSON
  Daniel 23 (MT-74)
  David 68 (F-177)
  Henry 40* (MT-74)
  James 23 (MT-55)
  James M. 35 (GD-269)
  James jr. 62 (MT-55)
  John 25 (ES-91)
  Joseph 35 (MT-74)
  Patsy 32* (ES-110)
  Salina 20* (B) (GD-242)
  Theresa 38 (ES-110)
  Travis 27 (MT-74)
  Will 62 (GD-271)
  William 46 (MT-75)
  William jr. 30 (GD-272)
LAY
  Carter 58 (ES-83)
  Green 29 (ES-102)
  Green 41 (MA-306)
  Henry 50* (MA-229)
  Jessee 55 (MA-279)
  Talton 28 (MA-210)
  Talton 31 (MA-277)
  Willis 31 (ES-99)
LAYNE
  James 66 (F-149)
  William 43 (MA-246)
LAYNG
  Violetta B. 6* (F-241)
LAYRE
  Andrew 60* (MA-316)
LAYTON
  Amanda 42 (F-216)
  Davis 56 (GD-245)
  Henry 27 (GD-245)
  James 24 (GD-259)
  Thomas 30 (GD-258)
  William 58* (GD-259)
LEABORN
  Jacob 21 (MA-239)
LEACH
  Jas. B. 71* (F-167)

Index

LEAKER?
  Jestes 56* (F-168)
LEAR
  David 22 (MA-304)
  Elijah 30* (GD-245)
  Henry 57 (JE-28)
  Massa 48 (f)* (JE-28)
  William 22* (MA-308)
LEARY
  Wm. A. 53* (F-190)
LEAVELL
  Edm. 37 (m) (GD-259)
  John T. 30 (GD-239)
  Squire T.! 41 (GD-239)
LEE
  Andrew 40 (OS-317)
  Benjamin 38 (ES-53)
  Eliza 37* (B) (F-153)
  Elizabeth 36* (MT-21)
  Elizabeth 60* (ES-53)
  Ephraim 44* (JE-76)
  John 33 (MA-224)
  Mary F. 23* (F-132)
  Samuel 45 (MA-262)
  Strother 38* (JE-44)
  Turner 37 (ES-58)
  W. M. M. 22 (m)* (MT-1)
LEEDS
  M. A. 14 (f)* (F-177)
LEES
  Joseph 19* (OS-277)
LEGATE
  David 54 ·(MT-30)
  Hugh 49 (MT-31)
  William 34 (MT-30)
LEGRAND?
  Abner 75* (F-144)
LEISURE
  William 66* (GD-254)
LEMON
  Beverly 60 (m) (B) (F-142)
  John 25* (JE-78)
LEMONS
  John 32 (B) (JE-74)
LENNESSEE?
  James 21* (F-149)
LENVILLE
  Goon 53* (CL-79)

LENYN?
  Augustus 22* (MA-252)
LETCHER
  James 50* (B) (GD-278)
  James H. 40 (GD-255)
  James H. 49* (GD-265)
  John 25 (GD-246)
  Joseph P. 42* (JE-75)
  S. M. 45 (m) (F-215)
  William 70* (F-117)
  William R. 56 (MA-250)
LEVELL
  Benjamin sr. 77 (GD-286)
  John Y. 33 (GD-275)
LEVINGSTON
  R. W. 33 (m)* (CL-28)
LEVISY
  James 23* (JE-70)
LEWALLEN
  James 35 (JE-63)
LEWINSKY
  Mary 9* (F-223)
LEWIS
  A. E. 7 (f)* (F-147)
  Adam 50* (MA-309)
  Alpheus 51 (CL-78)
  Armina 12* (MT-51)
  Artomecia 23* (F-199)
  Asa K. 4* (CL-3)
  Asa K. 69 (CL-89)
  Danl. 30 (f)* (B) (F-125)
  David J. 23* (F-177)
  Edna J. 11* (GD-227)
  Elizabeth 50 (GD-215)
  Elizabeth 74* (F-193)
  Enoch 35 (F-231)
  Evaline 45 (B) (CL-4)
  George W. 34* (CL-27)
  Granvill? 50 (B) (F-179)
  Hannah 29 (GD-215)
  Hector P. 72* (F-180)
  Isaac 38 (F-180)
  Isaac 43 (F-157)
  James 45* (OS-306)
  James G. 21* (MT-2)
  Jesse C. 31 (GD-217)
  John 24* (F-122)
  John 30* (F-194)

  John 49 (F-215)
  John A. 23* (F-202)
  Joseph G. 6* (JE-69)
  Lety 75* (B) (JE-38)
  M. 16 (f)* (F-131)
  Malinda 44* (F-156)
  Matilda 29 (B) (F-200)
  Melson sr. 70* (B) (JE-75)
  Mitchel 32 (GD-257)
  Peggy 100* (B) (JE-76)
  R. A. 13 (f)* (B) (F-143)
  Rosetta 30* (MT-6)
  Rowlin 35 (MA-234)
  S. H. 40 (m) (F-224)
  S. B. 49 (m) (F-119)
  Saml. 44 (F-127)
  Stephen D. 58 (CL-91)
  Thomas 16* (MT-46)
  Thomas 23* (F-235)
  Thornton 56 (CL-76)
  Thos. M. A. 23 (F-169)
  Will 31 (GD-280)
  William 32 (CL-87)
  William 37 (GD-245)
  William 75 (ES-66)
  Woodson 44 (MA-232)
LIGHTER
  David 46* (F-196)
LIGHTFOOT?
  John 24* (F-130)
LILE
  Henry 52 (MA-254)
LILLY
  Caleb 28* (F-220)
  Elizabeth A. 6* (MT-63)
  Ervin 34* (F-147)
  James 22 (ES-75)
  James 51* (ES-75)
  James 55 (B) (F-212)
LILLY?
  Louisa 8* (F-148)
LIMFORST?
  Francis 75* (F-168)
LINCH
  Mary 13* (F-173)
LINCOLN
  John K. 28* (F-133)

Index

LINDSEY
  Alexander 41* (MT-4)
  Charles 53 (CL-78)
  Harvey 50 (JE-20)
  James 54 (MT-2)
  Jas. 33* (F-195)
  John 44 (MT-4)
  Robert R. 36* (MT-4)
  Thomas 60 (CL-78)
  Wm. 28* (F-242)
LINGENFELTER
  John 40* (F-150)
  John jr 85* (F-150)
LINGINFELTER
  Philip 18* (CL-1)
LINN
  Mary 50* (F-158)
LIPSCOMB
  Josiah 32 (MA-275)
  Nancy 66* (MA-275)
  Nathan 33 (CL-27)
LIPSICOMB
  William S. 45 (F-246)
LISLE
  Claiborn 30* (CL-21)
  James 64* (CL-15)
  Manson 26 (CL-22)
  Rufus 32* (CL-41)
LITRALL
  John 59* (CL-14)
  Richard 25 (CL-16)
LITRELL
  Robt. 28 (F-245)
LITTELL
  Henry 48 (B) (F-248)
LITTLE
  John 48 (MA-254)
  Samuel 34* (MA-203)
  Thomas G. 62* (MA-250)
  William 23* (MT-1)
  William 24* (F-208)
LITTREL
  Richard 28* (GD-243)
LIVINGSTON
  Betcy 80* (JE-20)
  John 52 (JE-77)
  Mary 42* (JE-78)
  Nannie J. 20* (JE-55)

LLOYD
  Elijah 28* (MT-27)
  W. H. 28 (m) (F-153)
LOCKER
  John 35 (MA-317)
LOCKEY
  Elias 60 (ES-89)
  James 19* (ES-91)
  Mary 62* (ES-90)
  Samuel 70 (MA-225)
LOCKHART
  Henry 47* (F-131)
LOCKNANE
  Charles S. 37 (CL-30)
  James T. 39 (CL-40)
  Jane 30 (CL-49)
  John M. 49 (CL-31)
  Miles B. 21 (MT-61)
LOCKRIDGE
  James 75 (MT-49)
  Lucy A. 42 (MT-83)
  Mary A. 65* (MT-67)
LOCKWOOD
  John 70* (F-204)
LOEKLIN?
  Arthur 35* (F-212)
LOGAN
  David 33 (GD-254)
  David 49 (F-182)
  Elijah 33 (GD-228)
  Hugh 60* (GD-258)
  Hugh 71 (GD-265)
  Isaac 42 (MA-242)
  James 25 (GD-258)
  James 68 (F-184)
  James B. 28* (JE-13)
  Jas. H. 50 (F-167)
  John 64 (GD-228)
  John F. 35 (GD-266)
  L. M. 29 (m) (F-204)
  Morgan 40 (GD-228)
  Robt. B. 31* (F-150)
  Sarah 65 (GD-229)
  Timothy 30 (GD-229)
  William 35 (GD-229)
  William 45* (F-134)
  William S. 34 (ES-100)
  Wm. 60* (F-174)

LOGSDEN
  John B. 47 (ES-92)
LOGSTON
  Edward 26 (MA-300)
  George 56 (MA-302)
  James 27 (MA-288)
  William 28 (MA-300)
LOGSTONE
  Abner 14* (MA-265)
LOGUE
  John 23* (F-176)
LOGWOOD
  Thos. S. 39 (F-217)
LOLLY
  William 62 (MA-318)
LOMAS
  Elizabeth 48 (CL-63)
LOND
  Julia A. 35* (F-208)
LONEGAN
  James 1/12* (F-132)
LONEY
  Hugh 56* (F-124)
  Peter 23* (F-124)
LONG
  Adam 56 (F-191)
  Ann 57 (F-213)
  Daniel 40* (MA-289)
  George 50 (CL-3)
  Hannah 39 (F-147)
  Henry 32 (MA-280)
  Howard 25* (MA-309)
  J. C. 73 (m)* (JE-66)
  James 47 (MA-288)
  James 49* (MA-267)
  James J. 25* (MA-288)
  John S. 38 (MA-289)
  John W. 4* (JE-61)
  O. D. 18 (m)* (F-189)
  Perry 33 (MA-322)
  Perry C. 30 (GD-224)
  R. D. 21 (m)* (JE-69)
  Robert 40* (F-144)
  Samuel 29 (MA-322)
  Samuel 169* (F-201)
  Thomas 12* (MA-322)
  Thomas? 35* (CL-89)
  Uriah 40 (GD-236)

Index

LONG
  William 31 (MA-250)
  William 58 (MA-322)
  William T. 29* (JE-64)
LORD
  Isabella 39* (F-207)
LOTT
  Elizabeth 55 (CL-15)
LOUDENSUN
  R. H. 10 (m)* (F-149)
LOUGHRIN?
  Patrick 31* (F-204)
LOVE
  Elizabeth 16* (F-214)
  John 62 (F-213)
  Margaret 14* (GD-287)
  Marshall 18* (GD-210)
  Thomas P. 25 (GD-268)
LOVELY
  John V. 36 (CL-86)
LOW
  Isom 27* (ES-58)
  Noah 45 (F-227)
  Solomon 47 (F-232)
LOWE
  Frederick 32* (CL-56)
  James R. 28* (CL-9)
  Manerva 49 (GD-242)
  William 27 (GD-242)
  William 34* (CL-1)
  William 50 (CL-33)
LOWEL
  Turner 36 (MA-271)
LOWELL
  Andrew 49* (ES-86)
LOWEN
  John 76* (JE-6)
  Lewis 45* (JE-1)
  William 49* (JE-52)
LOWERY
  Green 24 (MA-209)
  Irvin 28 (MA-310)
  James 28 (ES-54)
  James 58 (MA-309)
  W. G. 35 (m)* (F-154)
  William 50 (MA-318)
LOWIN
  James 54 (JE-25)

LOWREY
  John R. 14* (MT-36)
  Thomas 35 (MA-271)
LOWRY
  Charles F. 31* (JE-74)
  Flora 24* (F-135)
  Garnett 45 (CL-62)
  James 57 (CL-49)
  James H. 47 (JE-79)
  Ludwell 53 (ES-54)
  Nathaniel 37 (JE-53)
  Nathaniel 39 (F-135)
  Prudence 62 (F-135)
  Prudence 62* (JE-53)
  Robert 78 (JE-67)
  W. R.? 38 (m) (F-135)
  William 27 (CL-61)
  William C. 28 (JE-77)
  William J. 37 (JE-53)
LOYD
  Stephen 25* (F-153)
  Thos. W. 34 (F-189)
LSEARS
  Moss 40* (GD-258)
LUBA
  Henry 43* (CL-45)
LUCAS
  John 26 (F-177)
LUCE?
  Myron 32* (JE-74)
LUDLOW
  William 30* (MT-82)
LUFON
  Edward 51* (JE-68)
LUMBERT
  Machael 45* (MT-14)
LUNDY
  Thomas 43 (JE-66)
LUNSFORD
  Benjamon 53 (GD-217)
  Enoch 26 (MA-223)
  Hiram 45 (OS-286)
LUSBY
  John H. 62* (F-223)
  W. H. 33 (m) (F-131)
LUSK
  Baylor 28 (GD-248)
  Ellen 57* (JE-7)

  Robert D. 48* (GD-289)
  Samuel 51 (GD-266)
  Samuel jr. 24 (GD-242)
  Will 20* (GD-242)
  William 57 (GD-248)
LUTES
  Charles 24 (OS-289)
  Henry 28* (OS-277)
  John 54* (OS-289)
LUTZ
  John 48* (F-152)
LUXON
  William 44 (F-202)
LYDICK
  Jacob 44 (F-186)
LYKES
  Marshall 41 (B) (F-214)
LYKINS
  Isaac L. 32 (MA-268)
LYLE
  Alexander 33* (JE-37)
  Bethi V. 20 (f)* (MA-206)
  Elizabeth Ann 34* (F-250)
  George 20* (CL-64)
  John 25 (ES-105)
  John J. 46* (F-185)
  John R. 50* (F-246)
  Thomas 45 (MA-214)
  William H. 24 (ES-47)
LYMAN
  A. B. 26 (m)* (MA-214)
LYNAM
  Charles 64* (GD-246)
LYNCH
  Calvin 29 (ES-102)
  Elizabeth 12* (OS-313)
  John D. 21 (ES-67)
  Sidney 27 (m) (ES-95)
LYNE
  Daniel 34* (JE-69)
LYNG
  Dennis 26* (CL-88)
LYNN
  Grand 45* (JE-44)
LYNUM?
  Katharine 60 (B) (JE-54)
LYNX
  Riley 29 (MA-239)

Index

LYON
 Eligah 55 (CL-92)
 Hezekiah 67* (CL-95)
 Thomas 39* (F-231)
LYONS
 Chas. O. 25* (F-185)
 James 30 (JE-72)
 Jospeh 24 (JE-67)
 Mary 65* (F-196)
 Moses 34 (GD-261)
LYSLE
 John E. 54 (CL-12)
LYTTLE
 Eliz 53 (F-213)
 Ulm 17* (F-199)
MABERRY
 Elizabeth 20* (CL-39)
MABERY
 Sally 23* (CL-39)
MACHEAD
 John 44 (CL-68)
MACKE
 John B. 40 (JE-19)
MADDIX
 Mary 29 (GD-227)
MADOX
 Samuel 32 (F-150)
MAGEE
 Mary 14* (B) (F-121)
 Nancy 25* (MA-292)
 Ralph 54 (MA-211)
 Sidney S. 30 (F-240)
MAGER
 Ralph 55 (MA-305)
MAGOWAN
 James G. 46 (MT-29)
 James P. 48 (MT-81)
 James S. 76 (MT-78)
 John 8* (MT-64)
 John B. 43* (MT-65)
 Sarah 21* (CL-81)
MAGUIRE
 David 22* (F-178)
MAHAFFEY
 Ela 43 (f) (OS-298)
MAHAFFY
 William C. 24* (OS-287)

MAHAN
 James 20* (JE-60)
 William 37 (JE-66)
 William 47 (JE-72)
MAHONE
 John 35* (F-196)
MAHONY
 James 30* (MA-320)
MAIDEN
 Samuel 50* (MA-217)
MAIDLOW
 James 74* (F-159)
MAINEY
 John 21* (F-225)
MAJOR
 C. M. 31 (m) (JE-71)
 James P. 42* (JE-70)
MALAIR
 John 39* (GD-238)
MALAND
 Patrick 40* (F-129)
MALEY
 James 29* (MT-35)
MALLERY
 Peter 16* (B) (F-207)
MALON
 William 25* (F-200)
MALONEY
 John A. 25* (MT-35)
 William 49* (OS-310)
MALORY
 Arther 36* (F-175)
MAN
 Mary E. 4* (F-193)
 Richard W. 9* (MT-36)
MANFELL
 William 37* (MT-5)
MANIER
 John 45 (MT-81)
 Nancy 14* (MT-22)
 Nancy 39* (MT-4)
MANIFREED
 Sally 26* (CL-62)
MANING
 Thomas 19* (JE-66)
MANION
 James P. 30 (MA-207)
 John C. 28 (MA-253)

 John O. 57 (MA-207)
MANIS
 Susan 80* (MA-225)
MANLEY
 Allen 34 (F-140)
MANLIGAM
 Dennis 32* (F-205)
MANLY
 John 43 (MA-253)
MANN
 America 19* (OS-288)
 John 52* (OS-294)
 Mary Ann 35* (F-216)
MANOR
 Marcus 25 (CL-27)
MANSFIELD
 James M. 24 (MT-53)
 William 58 (MA-271)
MANSHIP
 Jane 20* (F-127)
MANSON
 Albert 21* (F-178)
MANYON
 Thomas 68 (MT-71)
MANZEY
 Mary 65* (MA-222)
MAPEL?
 George W. 28* (ES-87)
MAPLES
 Shadrack 60* (CL-1)
MAPPIN
 Elizabeth 23 (CL-22)
MARCH
 Anderson 33* (MA-213)
 James 45* (B) (F-152)
 Joshua 42* (MA-285)
 Sallie B. 2* (F-213)
MARCUM
 James 40 (OS-297)
 John 25 (MA-240)
 Sewel 34 (OS-318)
 Thomas 75* (OS-297)
MARDAC?
 Anna 16* (F-119)
MARDEN
 John 19* (CL-44)
MARES
 James 35 (JE-5)

Index

MARFIELD
  Loyd 51* (F-190)
MARION
  Anderson 22 (OS-287)
MARITT
  Joseph 32 (F-123)
MARK
  John H. 32* (MT-36)
  William P. 26* (MT-37)
MARKER
  Malinda 60* (B) (F-124)
MARKSBERRY
  Daniel 30 (GD-222)
MARKSBURY
  Daniel 6 (GD-238)
  Margaret 59 (GD-249)
  Randolph 40 (GD-242)
  Samuel 50 (GD-239)
  Will 24 (GD-213)
MARKWELL
  William A.? 35 (JE-60)
MAROMAN
  G. W. 25 (m)* (F-184)
MARRIOTT
  William H. 34* (JE-73)
MARRS
  Mary 75 (JE-58)
  Richard 52 (F-205)
MARS
  William 33 (F-253)
MARSH
  Abraham 61 (MA-313)
  Catharine 63* (F-130)
  David 32 (F-128)
  Eastis 48* (OS-306)
  John 33* (MA-232)
  Nancy 55* (F-202)
  Polly 60* (MT-10)
  Richard 35 (F-201)
  Richd. 31 (F-194)
  Thomas 47* (MA-303)
  William 62* (MA-280)
MARSHAL
  Henry 51 (JE-2)
  John A. 23* (JE-5)
  Joseph 22* (OS-281)
MARSHALL
  A. K. 40 (m)* (JE-19)

Elizabeth 27* (MT-13)
Glass 40* (F-174)
Lemon T. 27* (MT-5)
Margaret 58* (B) (F-202)
Robert 50 (F-238)
Sarah R. 23* (F-197)
Thos. A. 56* (F-191)
William N. 43* (CL-8)
MARTIN
  Andrew J. 26 (MA-311)
  Barnett 45 (F-177)
  Benjamin 37 (MT-47)
  C. 60 (f)* (B) (F-126)
  Catharine 2* (F-198)
  David 22* (F-172)
  David 24 (F-192)
  David 47 (MA-255)
  David 50 (F-236)
  Elijah 55 (MT-67)
  Elsberry 27* (MT-63)
  Fanny 17* (CL-9)
  Greene 12* (F-226)
  Hezekiah 37* (F-157)
  Hudson 45 (CL-39)
  Hudson 52 (CL-10)
  Jack H. 39 (ES-87)
  James 35* (MA-308)
  James C. 38* (JE-74)
  James H. 23* (F-236)
  James H. 30 (F-252)
  James H. 70 (F-247)
  Jane 23 (CL-65)
  Jerrymiah 41 (MA-249)
  Job 73* (CL-84)
  Joel 48 (ES-65)
  John 52 (CL-78)
  John B. 21* (F-194)
  John L. 51 (MT-53)
  John W. 26 (CL-35)
  John W. 34 (F-249)
  Lewis 43 (F-249)
  Liberty 40* (MA-268)
  Lilburn B. 28 (ES-83)
  Littleton 39 (MT-49)
  M. T. 23 (m)* (F-155)
  Manlius 21* (F-170)
  Mary 16* (F-225)
  Meret 41 (m) (MA-310)

Milton 27* (ES-82)
Peggy 55* (CL-9)
Pleasant 35 (CL-88)
Rebecca 53 (JE-7)
Richard 57 (F-248)
Robert 28* (CL-10)
Robert E. 55* (CL-3)
Robt. 48* (F-195)
Samuel D. 59 (CL-4)
Sarah H. 44* (F-196)
Thomas 65 (ES-83)
Thos. B. 55 (F-167)
Thos. B. 55 (F-169)
Valentine 76* (CL-11)
William 38 (ES-60)
William 45 (MT-49)
William S. 26 (MT-67)
Willis 25* (B) (CL-4)
Wilson 36* (JE-10)
Wm. 40 (F-176)
MASCAL
  Stephen 7* (OS-306)
MASON
  Anna 25 (B) (F-212)
  Benson 68 (MT-68)
  Dave? 12* (B) (JE-38)
  Fanny 50* (B) (JE-75)
  Frances 46* (F-135)
  James 80* (CL-40)
  James B. 29 (GD-265)
  James R. 29 (MA-229)
  John 66 (MA-227)
  John 74* (MT-29)
  John W. 28* (MT-14)
  Joseph 43 (MA-227)
  Rodd 30 (f)* (B) (F-125)
  Roseanna 26* (B) (JE-75)
  Saml. 28* (B) (F-130)
  W. B. 33 (m) (GD-279)
  William 26* (F-137)
  Wm. 46 (F-179)
MASONER
  Ann R. 6* (JE-3)
  James 21 (F-153)
  James 50* (JE-3)
  Lucy 48* (JE-71)
  Marillis 84 (f) (JE-3)

Index

MASSEY
  Jefferson 39 (JE-23)
  Richard 45* (JE-24)
MASSIE
  A. W. 41 (m)* (CL-43)
  William R. 65* (CL-28)
MASTERS
  Gabriel 40* (JE-37)
  George W. 34 (JE-28)
  Henry W. 26 (JE-11)
  Irvin 33? (JE-29)
  James 20 (JE-28)
  James 46* (JE-48)
  John 37 (JE-16)
  Joseph 44 (MA-324)
  Joseph 47 (MA-311)
  Madison 34 (JE-46)
  Meredith 17* (JE-74)
  Moses 39* (JE-17)
  Nancy 56* (JE-14)
  Sally 46* (JE-21)
  Wesley 40 (JE-33)
  William G. 28 (GD-214)
MASTERSON
  Aaron 65* (MT-34)
  Mary 40* (F-153)
  Patrick 90* (OS-294)
  Peter 38 (MT-22)
MASTIN
  Alexander 40 (MA-286)
  Curtis 26 (ES-78)
  Edward 35 (MA-209)
  George 21 (MA-309)
  Henry 30* (JE-34)
  Jackson 26* (JE-28)
  Jacob 85* (MA-308)
  John 23* (MA-273)
  William 67 (MA-319)
MATHENEY
  W. 27 (m)* (F-204)
MATHERLY
  James C. 36 (ES-80)
MATHEWS
  Mosilda 18* (MA-221)
  Sarah J. 10* (F-195)
  Thomas 33* (JE-63)
  William H. 43 (JE-49)

MATTHEWS
  Mary 29* (F-214)
  Nancy 32* (GD-251)
  Pleasant 36 (CL-13)
  Saml. 59 (F-233)
  Thomas 56* (GD-248)
  Thomas 84* (CL-44)
MATTICKS
  Hesiah 34 (m) (MA-209)
MATTINGLY
  Albert E. 20* (JE-74)
MAUP9IN
  Nancy 76 (MT-44)
MAUPIN
  Jefferson 28 (GD-283)
  John D. 21 (MA-256)
  John H. 39* (JE-73)
  King 39 (MA-228)
  Robert 17* (MA-248)
  S. O. 40 (m)* (MA-258)
  Thomas 26 (MA-258)
  Thomas 85 (MA-215)
  Washington 43 (MA-228)
  William 32* (MA-214)
  William 43 (MA-261)
  Wilson R. 46 (MT-83)
MAUVER?
  Albert 19* (F-131)
MAXFIELD
  Hugh 73 (MT-47)
MAXLEY
  John M. 50* (F-140)
MAXWELL
  James 27* (MT-67)
  Viley? 70 (f)* (B) (F-198)
MAY
  Jackson 32 (GD-224)
  Jesse 23 (GD-232)
MAYBERRY
  John 55 (ES-78)
  Mary 19* (ES-78)
MAYDWELL
  Alex 42 (F-205)
MAYES
  Samuel 25* (JE-19)
  Samuel 58* (JE-15)
  William 53 (JE-20)
MAYFIELD

  James 64* (GD-217)
  Milton 22 (GD-218)
MAYHUGH
  N. B. 28 (m)* (F-241)
MAYLONE
  Maria 30 (F-126)
MAYO
  Margaret 9* (B) (MT-6)
  Nelson 7* (B) (MT-11)
MAYS
  Andrew 25 (OS-300)
  Andy 47 (OS-307)
  Giles 34* (OS-314)
  John D. 22 (JE-77)
  William 56* (OS-300)
MAYSE
  Peter 28 (MA-239)
MCABRAM
  Rosella 40* (F-196)
MCAFEE
  Allen L. 25 (JE-16)
  James 47* (F-149)
  John 75* (GD-273)
  Martha E. 18* (JE-48)
  Wm. 47* (F-170)
MCALISTER
  Edward 45* (F-193)
MCBRIDE
  Danl. 45* (F-196)
  M. 22 (m)* (F-129)
MCBRYOR
  Polly 47* (JE-15)
MCCABE
  Hugh T. 39* (JE-11)
  Johns 51* (JE-65)
  Robert 27* (JE-70)
  William 22* (JE-16)
MCCAFFRAY
  James 35* (F-218)
MCCAFFRY
  Margaret 93* (CL-55)
MCCALISTER
  James 35 (F-205)
  John 37* (F-195)
  M. 19 (m)* (F-205)
MCCALLA
  James D. 25* (CL-6)
  John 15* (CL-44)

Index

MCCALLISTER
  Edward 47 (F-222)
  Patrick 35* (CL-42)
MCCAMMOCK
  Mary F. 17* (F-228)
MCCAMPBELL
  James 45 (JE-5)
  John G. 48* (JE-76)
MCCAN
  John T. 10* (F-240)
  Peter 42 (F-190)
MCCANLEY
  James 58 (JE-72)
MCCANN
  Ben 45* (F-244)
  F. M. 28 (m)* (F-194)
  John 27 (F-164)
  John 34 (CL-92)
  Joseph 38 (F-226)
  Lucy Ann 18* (F-226)
  Mary 30* (F-223)
  Mary 50 (F-230)
  Mike 23* (F-194)
  Neal 51* (F-230)
  Virginia 10/12* (F-150)
  William E. 44 (F-229)
MCCANTRY
  F. T. 41 (m)* (F-158)
MCCARDY
  James 25 (GD-280)
MCCARLEY
  Moses 58 (GD-276)
MCCARTER
  Geo. M. 33* (F-184)
MCCARTY
  Danl. 49 (F-180)
  Jerimiah 48* (F-116)
  John 32 (F-199)
  T. M. 30 (m) (MT-13)
  Tandy 30 (CL-30)
  Zerelda 19* (F-130)
  ____ 23 (m)* (F-133)
MCCAUL
  James 19* (F-217)
MCCAULEY
  John 43 (F-213)
MCCAW
  Emma 12* (F-225)

John 59 (F-201)
MCCAY
  Mary 23* (F-156)
  Mary 24* (ES-86)
  William 50 (ES-67)
MCCHESNEY
  John 46 (F-221)
  Wm. 50 (F-210)
MCCHRISTY
  Jesse 45 (CL-34)
MCCLANAHAN
  Elijah 37* (F-237)
  Mary 18* (F-253)
  Robert 33 (F-253)
MCCLANIHAN
  William 61* (MA-214)
MCCLARY
  Alexander 38* (B) (JE-76)
  Robbin 60 (m)* (B) (JE-60)
MCCLEAVER
  Michl. 16* (F-200)
MCCLELLAND
  James M. 27 (F-254)
  John T. 29 (F-252)
  Sarah E. 17* (F-201)
  Thos. 23 (F-253)
MCCLONE
  Louis 18* (JE-75)
MCCLUNG
  Andrew 50* (GD-283)
MCCLURE
  John 49 (MT-7)
  Margaret 62 (MT-79)
  Martha 44* (MT-9)
  Mary 62* (CL-40)
  R. S. 59 (f)* (JE-12)
  Thomas 29* (F-117)
  W. 18 (m)* (F-138)
MCCOLLON
  Ezekiel 35 (GD-256)
MCCOLLUM
  Daniel 43 (OS-279)
  George 38 (OS-279)
MCCONATHY
  Asa 50 (F-254)
  George 24* (F-223)
MCCONETHY
  H. 40 (m) (F-152)

MCCONNAT
  V? 30 (m)* (F-148)
MCCONNEL
  Andrew 54* (JE-20)
MCCONNELL
  A. W. 46 (f)* (F-145)
  Cely 50* (B) (F-207)
  Elizabeth 45 (CL-88)
  Herbert 22* (F-115)
  J. E. 36 (m) (F-126)
  James 72 (F-225)
  Lucinda 33* (CL-92)
  Mary 2_ (JE-9)
MCCONTY
  Jackson 16* (F-209)
MCCORD
  David 44 (MA-295)
  Samuel 6* (CL-5)
  William D. 46 (MA-215)
MCCORMACK
  Will 40* (GD-250)
MCCORMIC
  Robert 30 (GD-272)
MCCORMICK
  Adam F. 29* (MT-83)
  James P. 22* (MT-27)
  John 54* (MT-57)
  John C. 32* (GD-284)
MCCOWAN
  Nancy 80* (F-236)
MCCOY
  Alexander 31 (F-190)
  Hector 47 (GD-281)
  Jane 30* (F-250)
  Jas. 57* (F-156)
  Joseph 80* (B) (F-186)
  Mary 40 (MA-256)
  Thos. A. F. 35 (F-192)
MCCRACKEN
  Anoy? 28 (m)* (MA-203)
  Henry 27* (F-204)
  John 71* (F-223)
  W. 30 (m)* (F-198)
MCCRACKIN
  H. 28 (m)* (F-151)
MCCRASTLE
  Chas. 35* (F-200)

Index

MCCREARY
  Jincy 43 (f)* (ES-54)
  Mary 60* (F-228)
MCCRERY
  Decius 6* (MT-27)
MCCRISTLE
  Arthur 30 (JE-1)
MCCROSBY
  Rebecca 55 (F-245)
MCCROSKY
  Martha 35* (JE-64)
  W. Jim? 11 (f)* (CL-8)
MCCRUM
  Junius 45* (CL-89)
MCCRUNE
  James 38* (CL-47)
MCCUDDY
  Timothy 37* (F-249)
MCCULLON
  Elizabeth 85 (GD-215)
MCCULLOUGH
  Daniel 42 (MT-82)
  Margaret 22* (MT-83)
  S. D. 47 (m)* (F-125)
  Samuel 56* (MT-11)
MCCUNE?
  George 25* (JE-5)
MCCURDA
  Hugh 50* (GD-272)
MCCURDY
  Alex 55* (F-200)
  John 15* (F-204)
MCDANIEL
  Albert 30 (CL-90)
  Alex 55* (F-202)
  Alexander 23* (MT-82)
  Anney 37* (OS-292)
  Daniel 45 (GD-260)
  Francis 60 (CL-93)
  George 35 (GD-207)
  Hugh 35 (CL-92)
  J. C. 30 (m) (F-207)
  Jno. 22* (F-235)
  John 78 (CL-85)
  Lampton 43 (F-244)
  Nathan 38 (CL-92)
  Samuel M. 24* (MT-51)
  Washington 37* (F-195)

MCDAVID
  Charles 25* (JE-78)
MCDAVIS
  William 49* (JE-17)
MCDIAL
  William 40* (MA-272)
MCDONAH
  Daniel 66 (JE-31)
MCDONALD
  Chas. 30* (F-150)
  George 44* (MT-73)
  John 23* (MT-16)
  John W. 29 (MT-4)
  Lucy 13* (CL-42)
  Mary 37* (CL-1)
  Mary 50* (GD-272)
MCDONELL
  Saml. 11* (F-222)
MCDONNOUGH
  William 27* (MT-35)
MCDOWEL
  Elizabeth __ * (JE-19)
  Nathan 53* (OS-281)
MCDOWELL
  Elizabeth 40 (ES-56)
  Irwin 25 (OS-320)
  S. P. 61 (m)* (F-149)
  Samuel 63* (JE-52)
  Thomas 57 (ES-103)
  William F. 30 (OS-320)
MCELLEHANY
  R. 35 (m)* (F-204)
MCELROY
  E. R. 46 (m) (MA-278)
MCENESLEY?
  John 30* (F-199)
MCFADDEN
  A. 44 (m) (F-142)
  James 34 (F-213)
MCFARLAND
  C. 44 (m)* (F-223)
  Sandusky? 33 (JE-5)
  William 22* (JE-78)
MCFARRIN
  William 46* (CL-39)
MCGARVEY
  John 6* (F-129)
  Peter 30 (F-173)

MCGEE
  David 28* (F-194)
  Dean 53* (JE-61)
  Nancy 20* (OS-284)
  Robert 38* (OS-302)
  Seth 59* (JE-61)
  Thomas J. 50 (B)(F-117)
MCGINNES
  James P. 44* (MT-22)
MCGINNIS
  Genevieve 30* (F-223)
MCGOFFIN
  Saml. 49 (F-193)
MCGOWAN
  Tho. B. 53* (F-198)
MCGRADDY
  Hugh 24 (F-230)
MCGUIRE
  Ansen? 24 (m) (OS-304)
  Archibald 71* (OS-307)
  Benjamine 45 (OS-321)
  Hiram 47* (OS-305)
  James 45 (OS-301)
  James 77* (OS-288)
  James jr. 45* (OS-288)
  John 39 (OS-294)
  John P. 34* (OS-312)
  Nancy 68* (MT-17)
  William 37 (OS-312)
MCHENRY
  David 30 (MA-216)
  John E. 49* (MA-216)
MCHONE
  John 34 (OS-298)
MCILROY
  Thos. 58 (F-151)
MCINTIRE
  Benj. 21* (F-179)
  Berry 47* (F-151)
  Elizabeth 52 (F-193)
  Mary 75* (F-166)
  Washington J. 19* (MT-10)
MCINTOSH
  Bayless 27 (ES-54)
  Francis 32 (ES-54)
  Frederick 58 (CL-26)
  Jesse 57 (ES-93)
  John 56 (ES-62)

Index

MCINTOSH
  Nancy 30* (ES-66)
  Peter 48 (ES-62)
MCISAAC
  Isaac 42 (F-249)
  James 72* (F-249)
MCJUNCHIN
  W. 60 (m)* (OS-301)
MCKEE
  Alexander 34 (MA-252)
  Alexander R. 35 (GD-266)
  Archd. 53 (JE-56)
  Elizabeth 60* (GD-287)
  George R. 40* (GD-263)
  James 17* (GD-263)
  James 53* (MT-9)
  Jane W. 38 (F-190)
  John 15* (F-204)
  Owen 19* (F-216)
  Phillip 30* (F-194)
  Talitha 35* (B) (GD-288)
  Thomas 24* (F-205)
  Wm. 36* (F-196)
MCKELLIPS
  Daniel 30* (CL-64)
MCKENNA
  Stafford 30* (F-176)
MCKENNON
  John 30* (F-117)
MCKENZIE
  A. P. 56 (m)* (JE-45)
  J. H. 10 (m)* (JE-45)
MCKINNEY
  Charlot 45* (F-204)
  Curtis 23 (ES-67)
  David R. 46 (ES-79)
  Henry 29* (F-205)
  Huldah 58* (GD-265)
  James 30 (OS-296)
  James 56 (MA-273)
  James B. 26 (ES-56)
  James F. 31* (ES-88)
  Joseph 29 (ES-76)
  Mathew 37 (ES-78)
  Pleasant 30 (ES-80)
  Richard 65 (ES-56)
  Susana 30 (F-181)
  Thomas H. 38 (MT-40)

  Thomas S. 29 (ES-55)
  Wilda 19 (m) (ES-77)
  Wilda 67 (m)* (ES-76)
  Wilda E. 24 (m)* (ES-47)
  William 26* (CL-1)
  William 40* (ES-81)
  William 54 (GD-205)
  William A. 22* (ES-79)
MCKINNY
  D. C. 33 (m) (MA-271)
MCKNIGHT
  Mary J. 16* (F-225)
MCKOY
  John 40* (GD-254)
MCLANE
  James 20* (F-176)
  Thos. 17* (F-149)
  W. 24 (m)* (F-149)
  Wm. 24 (F-187)
MCLAUGHLIN
  Bernard 35* (JE-56)
  David 50 (MT-63)
  J. H. 38 (m)* (F-129)
  Sarah 51* (MT-63)
MCLEAN
  Isabella 55* (F-165)
MCLEAR?
  Francis 61 (F-144)
MCMAHAN
  Geo. W. 36* (F-242)
  James 30* (CL-94)
  John 42 (F-238)
  Julia 30* (CL-43)
MCMAHILL
  Ambrose 42* (MT-71)
MCMAHON
  A. 55 (m)* (F-218)
  Daniel 30* (F-225)
  James 20* (F-221)
MCMAHUN
  William 40 (ES-84)
MCMAINS
  Jno. 70 (F-226)
  Mary 23* (F-184)
  robert 32 (F-119)
MCMAMIS
  Dica 39* (GD-238)
  William 70* (GD-250)

MCMANIS
  A. W. 52 (m) (JE-31)
  James 23 (F-123)
  Lavicy 18 (f)* (MA-309)
MCMANNIS
  Nelson B. 36 (GD-226)
  T. 16 (m)* (GD-286)
MCMEEKIN
  A. 53 (m) (F-149)
  A. F. 29 (m)* (F-156)
  Jas. 49* (F-196)
  Jeremiah 31 (F-156)
  William 47* (F-136)
  William 55 (F-123)
MCMEEKINS
  L. 14 (f)* (F-135)
MCMILLAN
  Andrew F. 60 (F-254)
  James 42* (CL-3)
  James 56 (CL-22)
  James W. 18* (CL-8)
  John V. 24 (MA-313)
  William 44 (GD-224)
MCMILLEN
  James 14* (JE-32)
  James 36* (JE-34)
  Mary 15* (JE-68)
MCMILLIN
  George W. 29 (GD-247)
  Samuel 61 (GD-243)
  Travis 46 (GD-256)
MCMILLION
  William 25 (MA-317)
MCMILLON
  F. 23 (m) (B) (F-146)
  John 20* (MA-321)
MCMINNEY
  W. 61 (m)* (F-156)
MCMONIGAL
  Aaron 18* (ES-105)
MCMULLEN
  Ann 26* (B) (F-152)
MCMURRAY
  Edwin 39* (F-129)
  James 68 (F-148)
MCMURTRY
  Alex 76 (GD-230)
  Ed 57* (B) (GD-261)

Index

MCMURTRY
  James 47 (GD-264)
  John 23* (JE-7)
  John 38 (F-189)
  Levi 29* (F-181)
  Mary 45 (JE-55)
  Mary J. 27* (F-148)
MCNEAL
  James 50 (F-245)
MCNULT
  Samuel 67* (JE-57)
MCPETERS
  Margart 75* (F-207)
MCPHADDEN
  J. D. 32 (m)* (F-241)
MCPHERSON
  Rachael 65* (ES-82)
MCPHETERS
  Andrew 51 (F-158)
  Relin 55 (m)* (B) (JE-38)
  William 28* (JE-69)
MCQUARY
  Joseph 30 (GD-272)
MCQUEEN
  Beaty 23 (OS-319)
  John 47 (ES-101)
MCQUERRY
  Charles 47* (JE-35)
  William 51 (GD-227)
MCQUERY
  Louisiana 40* (GD-264)
MCQUIN
  Charles 28* (MT-14)
MCQUINN
  Hamelton 25 (OS-296)
  Mary 19* (MA-248)
  Nancy 38 (MA-234)
  Thomas 19* (MA-283)
MCROBERTS
  Elizabeth 19* (F-188)
MCSWINE
  William 49 (ES-72)
MCTYRE
  Alfred 34* (JE-55)
  Larkin C. 50* (JE-64)
MCULANE
  Nancy 55 (F-208)

MCWILLIAMS
  A. C. 55 (m) (MA-214)
  Andrew 46 (MA-217)
  Elihu 50 (MA-215)
  Ellen 31* (F-195)
  James 30 (MA-221)
  John C. 63 (MA-228)
  John Q. 22* (MA-214)
  Mary 25* (MA-218)
  Mary 70 (MA-216)
  Patrick 26* (CL-42)
  Sidney 21 (m)* (MA-215)
  William G. 51* (MA-216)
MEADOWS
  Green 43 (ES-53)
MEANES
  James 35 (MT-65)
MEANS
  J. F. 21 (m)* (MT-72)
  John 46 (MT-71)
  William C. 40 (MT-56)
MEARICK
  William 28* (ES-80)
MEBREARY?
  James 41 (ES-67)
MEDER?
  Saml. 33* (F-130)
MEDERS?
  John 60* (F-122)
MEDIGATE
  C. 39 (f) (F-126)
MEDLICATT
  John 70* (F-176)
MEDOWS
  Catharine 28 (MT-46)
MEEKER
  A. R. 50 (m) (GD-262)
MEFFORD
  Leonard 23* (CL-41)
MEGLONE
  Edward 14* (JE-59)
MEGOTHLIN
  Wylie 14* (ES-92)
MEGOWAN
  David 64 (F-222)
  Geo. J. 30 (F-207)
  Stewart 69 (F-222)

MELOY
  Thedy 23 (m)* (MT-35)
MENELL
  Polly 65 (CL-61)
MENIFEE
  Sarah B. 31* (F-209)
MENIR
  Robert 22* (CL-15)
MENTILLE
  Victoria C. 80* (F-223)
MENTZEL
  Louis 28* (JE-74)
MEQUAREY
  Will 40 (GD-272)
MEQUARY
  Thompson 38 (GD-270)
MERCHANT
  Caleb 17* (F-221)
  John 40* (F-116)
  William 27 (F-210)
MEREDITH
  Jane 60* (F-182)
  Melinda 60* (MT-41)
  William 38* (JE-9)
MERIDETH
  Jane 60* (F-123)
  Joseph 53 (GD-217)
MERIDITH
  David 19* (CL-38)
MERRECK
  Wright 50 (F-146)
MERRELL
  Azariah M. 31 (GD-205)
  David 31 (F-208)
  David 40* (F-177)
  James J. 22* (F-254)
  William 26 (GD-205)
  William 65 (GD-205)
MERRILL
  Chilton A. 28* (CL-28)
  Isabella 65* (F-120)
  John 22* (F-215)
  Jonathan 29* (F-253)
MERRITT
  Abram 38* (CL-38)
  George S. 38 (GD-253)
  John sr. 64* (GD-253)
  Peter 60* (GD-208)

Index

MERRITT
  Uriah 25* (GD-208)
  Zachariah 34 (GD-239)
MERRIWETHER
  Eliza J. 19* (F-234)
MERRYMAN
  Betsey 50* (F-153)
MERSHON
  A. J. 26 (m)* (MT-59)
  Henry 21* (GD-266)
MERSHORN
  Ben F. 43* (GD-210)
  Burkett 53 (GD-210)
  Furnace 54 (m)* (GD-210)
MERSHOW
  Robert 31 (GD-284)
MESIR?
  John 59 (CL-23)
MESSICK
  C. T. 34 (m)* (F-126)
  Jacob 52 (JE-6)
  John 38 (JE-9)
  Manuel 16* (JE-6)
METCALF
  Eliza 54* (F-196)
  George 35* (F-118)
  Henry 49* (JE-74)
  Thomas 12* (MT-10)
  William 41* (F-205)
METCALFE
  Thomas 48* (CL-53)
METEER
  Elizabeth 36 (F-216)
METIER
  Sarah 58 (MT-12)
MEYRES
  W. C. 25 (m)* (F-154)
MICHAEL
  Elizabeth 48 (F-185)
  Robert 20 (JE-51)
MIDDLETON
  Buford 44 (GD-233)
  Charity 50 (GD-237)
  Henry 40 (GD-250)
  Samuel 16* (JE-2)
  Walter B. 47 (GD-247)
  Yantis 34 (GD-217)

MIFFETT
  Melson 40* (MT-12)
MILBOURN
  John D. 36* (F-128)
MILES?
  Charles 41 (B) (F-147)
MILIGON
  W. 47 (m)* (F-143)
MILLER
  A. F. 21 (m)* (F-136)
  Alexander 65* (MA-290)
  Alfred 23* (MA-221)
  Allen A. 51 (JE-10)
  Aminadab 35 (m) (GD-229)
  Andrew 32* (F-143)
  C. J. 37 (m)* (MA-265)
  Caledonia 12* (MA-254)
  Cornelious 38 (GD-271)
  David 66 (CL-12)
  Elijah 28 (CL-57)
  Elizabeth 49* (F-217)
  Fayett 26 (MA-250)
  Green K. 30 (CL-68)
  Harrison 37 (GD-211)
  Isaac 27 (CL-21)
  J. F. 48 (m)* (F-146)
  Jacob 18* (GD-233)
  James 32* (MA-230)
  James B. 42 (MA-290)
  James L. 20* (MT-65)
  James P. 34 (MA-269)
  Joel 16* (F-218)
  John 28 (MA-215)
  John 45* (F-138)
  John 45 (MA-323)
  John 45 (MT-52)
  John 52 (MA-205)
  John 80 (GD-271)
  John H. 40 (MA-213)
  John J. 27* (F-184)
  John S. 22 (GD-287)
  Lucinda 13* (CL-75)
  M. 66 (m)* (F-127)
  Malcom 38 (MA-227)
  Martha 55* (MA-206)
  Martin W. 36* (F-211)
  Meriman? 45* (JE-18)
  Nancy H. 32* (F-196)

  Noah 54 (CL-85)
  Peggy 58 (B) (MA-278)
  R. 60 (m)* (F-194)
  Rebecca 57* (MA-203)
  Rebecca 76 (CL-87)
  Robert 65* (MA-255)
  Robert B. 42 (GD-208)
  Sarah 29* (MT-42)
  Sarah E. 17* (MA-208)
  Sophia 45* (F-122)
  Thomas 38* (MA-265)
  Thomas 54 (GD-268)
  Thomas 62 (ES-93)
  Tunstall Q. 32 (ES-79)
  Washington 52* (CL-28)
  Will 43 (GD-271)
  Will S. 56 (GD-287)
  William 18* (GD-289)
  William 47* (JE-12)
  William 60 (B) (MA-278)
  William J. 38 (MT-78)
  Wm. 65* (F-195)
MILLERS
  Alice 30* (CL-84)
  Eilzabeth 15* (CL-84)
MILLIGAN
  Joseph B. 50 (F-218)
MILLION
  Allen 21* (MA-309)
  Benson 75* (MA-288)
  Bowland 33 (MA-212)
  Burrel 58 (MA-211)
  Elam jr. 36 (MA-201)
  Elzy 65 (m) (MA-304)
  Green 50 (MA-303)
  Green 53 (MA-202)
  Green B. 27* (MA-307)
  Hannah 72 (MA-302)
  Ir G. 46 (m) (MA-209)
  James S. 40 (MA-210)
  John 50 (MA-309)
  Mary 50 (MA-305)
  Richard 34 (ES-71)
  Rodney 80 (MA-297)
  Sarah 28 (MA-325)
  Squire 34 (MA-201)
  Townson 43 (MA-210)
  Travis 23 (MA-202)

Index

MILLION
 William 29 (MA-283)
MILLS
 John 69* (CL-41)
 Maglin 50 (f)* (GD-250)
MILLSPAUGH
 Levi Y. 58* (MT-40)
MILLTON?
 Allison 20 (F-204)
MILTON
 A. 17 (m)* (F-132)
 B. F. 42 (m) (F-141)
 Eben 54* (F-160)
 Elizabeth 22* (MT-45)
MILTON?
 Wm. E. 39* (F-114)
MILWARD
 Henry F. 23 (F-130)
 Joseph 47* (F-130)
MIMMS
 M. A. 18 (f)* (F-163)
MINOR
 Tabitse 26* (F-194)
MINTER
 Benjamin F. 30* (JE-44)
 Edwin F. 20* (JE-76)
 James C. 30 (JE-42)
 John C. 26* (JE-77)
 William 18* (MA-265)
MIRGUN?
 Thomas 28* (CL-85)
MISSMER?
 M. A. 16 (f)* (F-119)
MITCHEL
 E. C. 28 (m)* (OS-277)
 Fielding 53 (MA-223)
 Susan 43* (JE-2)
 William J. 25* (JE-2)
MITCHELL
 Boone 37 (MT-3)
 Boswell 66 (F-250)
 D. W. 18 (m)* (F-151)
 F. T. 28 (m)* (CL-42)
 Frank 55* (B) (F-233)
 George 25* (JE-71)
 George 62* (F-231)
 George S. 37 (JE-6)
 George W. (Dr) 39 (JE-46)

Greenberry 25* (MT-72)
Henry 9* (B) (F-206)
James A. 35 (JE-50)
James H. 28 (MT-29)
James M. 23* (MT-33)
John 59 (MT-24)
Kitty 39 (F-142)
Leroy 45 (MA-225)
Mary 25* (F-137)
Maryman 24* (F-170)
Milton 35 (F-207)
Sallie 60* (F-170)
Strother D. 25 (MT-82)
Wandy 58* (F-232)
Will D. 49 (GD-285)
William 31* (MT-4)
William 69 (MT-27)
MITCHEN
 Mary 12* (CL-41)
 Mary 4* (F-248)
MITCHUM
 Mary 60* (JE-61)
MITTON
 William 25* (CL-23)
MIZE
 Isaac 56* (ES-108)
 Joshua 68* (ES-81)
 Martin W. 27* (CL-74)
 N. J. 45 (m) (OS-305)
 R. S. 24 (m)* (ES-87)
 William 36* (OS-306)
MIZNER
 Samuel S. 34 (GD-261)
MOBERLY
 Alfred 44* (MA-249)
 Ann 83* (MA-289)
 Benjamin 52* (MA-247)
 Camron? 40* (MA-226)
 Elias 50 (MA-222)
 Emily 42 (m?) (MA-200)
 Jacob 45 (MA-202)
 John 2* (MA-264)
 John 30 (MT-29)
 John 59* (MA-262)
 John F. 19* (MA-261)
 John J. 36 (MA-314)
 John N. 28* (MA-247)
 Lucinda 40 (CL-29)

Mahala 50 (GD-281)
Nancy A. 37 (MA-242)
Peter 79 (MA-246)
Rosanna 7* (MA-263)
Simon 46 (MA-246)
Susan 40 (MA-222)
Thomas 10* (MA-283)
Thomas 46* (MA-270)
Thomas 49 (MA-202)
Thomas J. 61 (MT-26)
MOBLEY
 Tandy 18* (CL-21)
MOCKERY
 Albert 35* (B) (MA-204)
MOELIR
 William J. 21* (OS-279)
MOFFETT
 Mary 56* (F-198)
MOFFUTT
 M. M. 18 (f)* (F-119)
MOGEE
 George 37* (GD-258)
MOMAN
 Matilda 47 (MA-303)
MONDAY
 Andrew 30 (MA-210)
 Nancy 57* (MA-312)
 Reubin 42 (MA-243)
MONKS
 Thomas 56* (F-148)
MONKS?
 Ellen 12* (F-145)
MONOHON
 William 32* (JE-59)
MONROE
 Elizabeth 15* (JE-59)
 James 1* (MA-217)
 Martha 23* (ES-70)
 Matilda 42 (ES-70)
 Turner? 25* (MA-278)
 William 27 (CL-37)
MONSEY
 Franklin 22* (MT-44)
MONTAGUE
 Elijah 32 (F-121)
 Jas. C. 30 (F-155)
 John 35* (JE-76)
 Thos. 62* (F-254)

- 485 -

Index

MONTAGUE
  Wm. 24* (F-164)
MONTGOMERY
  Barterson 8* (MA-301)
  Barterson 8* (MA-306)
  Columbus 8* (MA-211)
  Dorinda 43* (GD-221)
  Nancy 64 (GD-238)
  Sarah 27* (F-132)
  Sarah 65 (CL-58)
  Sarah F. 7* (GD-215)
  Will 40 (GD-278)
  William 14* (MA-211)
  William 38* (F-215)
MONTGOMREY
  W. C. 29 (m) (GD-282)
MONTGOY
  Garret 66 (MT-21)
  Travis 38* (MT-20)
MONTMOLLEN
  F. 52 (m)* (F-209)
MONZ
  Maria 45* (F-149)
MOODY
  Andrew J. 33 (MA-216)
  James 27 (MA-219)
  James 67 (F-206)
  Samuel 60 (MA-291)
  Whitfield 40 (MA-237)
  Willia 35 (MA-319)
MOON
  Smalwood 47 (CL-30)
MOONEY
  Francis 17* (F-204)
  Thomas 21* (MT-35)
MOONY
  F. 20 (m)* (F-129)
MOORE
  A. J. 32 (m) (OS-277)
  Alexander 45* (F-167)
  Benj. 30 (F-187)
  Butler 77 (F-158)
  Catahrine 9* (F-121)
  Chas. C. 60 (F-182)
  Cornelious 37* (OS-299)
  David 25* (JE-77)
  Duke 28* (F-195)
  Edard 40* (OS-300)

  Eli 54 (ES-82)
  Elias jr. 36 (OS-300)
  Elias sr. 60 (OS-280)
  Elisha 66* (MT-37)
  Evan 42 (ES-61)
  Eveline 51 (CL-93)
  Francis 29 (F-181)
  Franklin 29 (MA-217)
  George 39 (GD-219)
  Harrison 35* (ES-50)
  Harvey 47 (F-121)
  Henry 33* (F-124)
  Henry C. 37 (F-183)
  James 30 (MT-17)
  James 30 (OS-299)
  James 45 (OS-286)
  James 64 (ES-105)
  James 81* (MA-222)
  James B. 42* (MT-28)
  James R. 28 (OS-277)
  James W. 30* (MT-4)
  James jr. 20 (OS-286)
  Jane 7 (m?)* (GD-232)
  Jarret 29 (MA-260)
  Jas. G. 39* (F-195)
  Jeremiah 25 (MA-273)
  John 28 (OS-286)
  John 35* (F-195)
  John 42 (F-251)
  John 55 (F-254)
  John 64 (MT-37)
  John B. 22 (MT-39)
  John M. 50 (CL-60)
  John jr. 25 (OS-285)
  John sr. 70* (OS-295)
  Joseph A. 36 (F-252)
  Joseph W. 23 (MA-202)
  Joshua 52* (ES-85)
  Leach 22 (m) (MA-297)
  Leander 20 (CL-25)
  Levi 56 (MA-242)
  Lewis 22 (OS-295)
  Lewis 68 (ES-89)
  Lewis 93* (MT-26)
  M. 45 (m)* (F-125)
  Marcus 23 (F-134)
  Margaret 60* (GD-219)
  Margaret 63 (F-187)

  Margaret 67* (F-178)
  Mary 32* (CL-9)
  Mashall? 41 (CL-19)
  Morang? 45 (m)* (JE-11)
  Morton P. 32* (ES-94)
  Moses 28* (F-254)
  Moses 31* (ES-71)
  Nancy 35 (MA-298)
  Nancy 60 (F-165)
  Nancy 65* (JE-78)
  Nathan 37 (ES-85)
  Nathaniel 34 (F-254)
  Nathaniel sr 71* (F-254)
  Patty 16* (F-225)
  Pheby 50 (MA-295)
  Reuben 48 (MT-20)
  Reuben 50 (MT-39)
  Richard 58 (F-121)
  Robt. 49 (F-168)
  Sally 45* (MA-243)
  Samuel 25 (ES-105)
  Samuel 44* (MA-269)
  Sarah 18* (ES-108)
  Sidney 26 (m) (ES-83)
  Smuel 40 (MA-271)
  T. J. 29 (m)* (F-223)
  Thomas 26 (MA-273)
  Thomas 46 (ES-56)
  Thomas 46 (ES-89)
  Thomas H. 29* (CL-92)
  Thomas S. 8* (GD-231)
  Walter 48* (MA-224)
  Willia 34 (MA-256)
  William 22 (ES-101)
  William 34 (MA-205)
  William 37 (MA-305)
  William 40 (MT-29)
  William 41* (ES-106)
  William 47* (F-146)
  William J. 28* (MA-271)
  William J. 38* (ES-94)
  William R. 47* (MA-271)
  William sr. 64* (OS-295)
  Willis G. 24* (MA-208)
  Wm. G. 31 (F-178)
  Yelley 74 (F-158)
MOORE___
  Charles C. 55 (MA-284)

Index

MOOROW
 Nancy T. 48* (MT-40)
MOPPIN
 Jane 28 (CL-37)
MORAN
 Barrutt 60 (MA-281)
 Cyrus 26* (MA-237)
 Franklin 45 (GD-274)
 Jigg? 45 (m)* (JE-68)
 John G. 30 (MA-281)
 Joshua 63 (MA-323)
 Nathan 48 (MA-279)
 Robert 56 (MA-222)
 Stephen 31 (MA-323)
 William 55 (MA-279)
MORE
 Elizabeth 50 (OS-304)
 James W. 42* (OS-307)
 Jessee 30 (OS-316)
 William 38 (MA-210)
MOREHEAD
 William 30* (CL-74)
MORELAND
 Elijah 40 (CL-37)
 Enoch 35 (ES-71)
MOREMAN
 William 22* (MA-202)
MORETON
 Susan F. 16* (F-242)
MOREY
 Mary 29* (F-202)
MORGAN
 Alex 18* (F-212)
 C. C. 51 (m) (F-189)
 Creth? 22 (m)* (F-184)
 George 38* (F-211)
 Griffeth S. 37* (F-203)
 Jno. H. 25* (F-146)
 Lucy 52 (F-208)
 M. M. 26 (m)* (GD-263)
 Mark 38 (OS-317)
 Nicholas 32* (F-139)
 Raleigh 25 (CL-5)
 S. 25 (f)* (JE-42)
 Sallie 28* (F-255)
 Van 59* (CL-3)
MORGERSON
 Elijah 52 (CL-34)

MORIMOR
 Jacob 42 (GD-278)
MORLIN
 Isaac 36* (F-151)
 James 1* (F-151)
MORLOY
 Josiah 36 (MT-23)
MORRIS
 Daniel W. 35 (MT-8)
 Eliza 43* (F-195)
 Ennis 35 (MA-260)
 George 58 (OS-296)
 Hannah 69 (F-173)
 Hardin 24 (OS-304)
 Henry 40* (OS-302)
 Henry 43* (MA-268)
 Henry jr. 22 (OS-281)
 Jacob E. 33 (ES-108)
 James 8* (OS-311)
 Jancent? 34 (m) (OS-302)
 Jas. 43* (F-196)
 Joseph 30* (MT-60)
 Mason 45 (CL-79)
 McLane 18* (MT-4)
 Prucilla 46 (CL-79)
 Richd. 27* (F-255)
 Robert 53* (OS-302)
 Saml. 40 (F-125)
 Samuel 85 (CL-90)
 W. P. 35 (m)* (F-172)
 Washington 46 (CL-90)
 William 36 (MT-60)
 William 55* (OS-303)
 William jr. 32* (OS-278)
 Wm. B. 51* (F-241)
MORRISON
 Asa 49* (F-234)
 Daniel 15* (MT-76)
 Dick 40* (B) (F-153)
 Harriet 50* (CL-5)
 M. B. 48 (m)* (F-203)
 Martha 63* (F-251)
 Mary E. 15* (B) (F-207)
 Nathan 37* (MT-2)
 Sophia 44* (MT-76)
MORROW
 A. S. 28 (m) (MT-25)
 James 60 (F-157)

Robert 77* (MT-7)
MORTER
 Armstead 63 (MT-27)
MORTON
 Asa W. 32 (ES-103)
 Clowry 70 (f)* (B) (F-145)
 Eliz. 55* (B) (F-200)
 Gabriella 32* (F-143)
 Geo. W. 39 (F-210)
 George G. 32 (CL-7)
 Hezekiah 50 (MT-49)
 Jno. 66* (F-210)
 John 50* (CL-2)
 Jonathan 70* (CL-6)
 Richard 23* (MT-52)
 Richard 56 (MT-49)
 Solomon 50* (B) (MT-50)
 William 59 (F-223)
MORTON?
 W. B. 24 (m)* (F-204)
MOSBAK
 Furnudad 26* (F-140)
MOSEBACK
 Augustus 24* (F-223)
MOSEBY
 Augustus 24 (F-204)
MOSELEY
 Frances 60* (JE-62)
 George S. 28* (JE-65)
 James L. M. 32* (JE-61)
 John R. 30* (JE-73)
 Robert 51 (JE-69)
 Samuel H. 27* (JE-68)
 Thomas J. 43 (JE-68)
MOSELY
 Martin B. 35* (ES-59)
MOSS
 Francis B. 46* (CL-44)
 John M. 27 (JE-45)
 Nathaniel O. 53* (MT-78)
 Ray jr. 31 (f) (JE-45)
 Ray sr. 70 (JE-45)
 William 55 (MA-222)
MOTHERSHEAD
 Mary A. 39* (JE-63)
MOTZBAUGH
 David 42* (CL-67)

Index

MOUNTS
 Adam 44 (ES-57)
 George 42 (ES-57)
MOYR
 Easter 82 (f) (MA-320)
MUCK
 Joseph 34 (ES-101)
 Joseph 60 (ES-101)
MUDAY
 David 27 (CL-35)
MUIR
 Ann 70 (F-230)
 Harriet 47* (F-235)
 Samuel 49 (JE-7)
MUIR?
 Thomas 46 (JE-2)
MULAY
 Lucy 30* (F-216)
MULDER
 S. J. 23 (f)* (F-158)
MULDROW
 Merrit 33 (B) (MT-3)
MULLEN
 James 30* (MT-3)
MULLIN
 Peter 35 (F-220)
 Rosa 18* (F-200)
MULLINS
 Gordon C. 31 (CL-24)
 James 49 (CL-18)
 Mary A. 16* (CL-27)
 Will 54* (GD-271)
MULOCK
 M. 30 (m) (F-127)
MUNCEY
 James 44 (ES-78)
 John 24 (F-208)
MUNDAY
 Edmund P. 35* (F-241)
 James 63* (CL-25)
MUNEY
 Dudley 53* (F-160)
MUNEY?
 Isaac S. 29* (ES-48)
MUNSEY
 Reuben 56 (MT-48)
MUNSON
 O. 55 (m)* (MT-7)

MURAIN
 D. H. 22 (m)* (F-184)
MURE
 E. 57 (m) (F-150)
MURFREE
 John 28* (F-177)
MURKEY
 Patrick 27* (F-205)
MURPHEY
 Charles 32 (MA-324)
 Elitia 47 (m) (MA-324)
 Susanah 71* (F-199)
 William 38 (ES-93)
MURPHREE
 John 42 (F-174)
MURPHY
 Aaron 30 (GD-208)
 Ad. 41 (m)* (F-196)
 Hardin 30 (GD-214)
 Jack 28 (B) (F-119)
 James 50 (GD-250)
 John 2* (JE-23)
 John 41 (ES-102)
 John 84 (ES-102)
 Joseph 25* (MA-315)
 Lindsey 23 (JE-23)
 M. A. 50 (f) (F-125)
 Stephen 48 (JE-33)
 Susana 29* (F-154)
 Susanah 46 (JE-23)
 Will L. 73 (GD-237)
 William 27 (JE-7)
 William 35 (F-222)
 William 36 (GD-224)
 Willis G. 29* (GD-263)
MURRAM?
 William 54 (JE-77)
MURRAY
 David 43 (F-118)
 John 30* (JE-61)
 Joseph 53 (B) (CL-12)
 Thomas A. 23* (F-231)
MURREL
 Nicholas 19* (MA-243)
MURRELL
 Andrew D. 32 (MT-42)
MURRY
 Philip 27* (MT-35)

MUTTEN
 Clarissa 28 (B) (F-200)
MYALL
 Johnathan 27 (F-188)
MYERS
 Albert H. 49* (JE-54)
 C. F. 40 (m)* (F-204)
 Frank 23 (F-204)
 Frederic 35* (F-223)
 Isaac M. 63 (GD-255)
 James M. 22* (JE-44)
 John 25* (F-184)
 John 26* (F-255)
 John 51* (GD-260)
 William 34* (JE-30)
 William E. 45 (GD-247)
MYRES
 Aaron 44 (MT-83)
 C. R. 30 (m)* (MT-71)
 Francis 52 (MT-54)
 Fred 24* (F-255)
 George 28 (MT-77)
 Harvey 37* (MT-80)
 Hiram 26* (MT-78)
 John 40 (F-115)
 John S. 71 (MT-58)
 Walter S. 40 (MT-58)
 N. 29 (M)
  (F-139)
NAGHEL
 E. J. 23 (m) (F-133)
NAHAM?
 John 30 (GD-284)
NAHM
 Leopold 31* (CL-41)
NAPPER
 Sallie 27* (F-147)
NAVE
 Elizabeth 72* (JE-18)
 George T. 27 (JE-50)
 Jacob 34 (JE-54)
 Jefferson 42* (JE-54)
 John 36* (F-169)
 John 48 (GD-255)
 Jonathan 51* (JE-12)
 Peter D. 62* (JE-62)
 Peter sr. 80* (JE-54)
 Robt. 35* (F-169)

Index

NAVEN
  Patrick 21* (F-203)
NAYLOR
  Absolem 32 (GD-227)
  Edward 24 (GD-226)
  Edward B. 72 (GD-269)
  George 34 (GD-238)
  George T. 41 (GD-269)
  James 29 (GD-237)
  John 24 (GD-238)
  Luama? 54 (f) (GD-238)
  Reuben 26 (GD-233)
  Sally 54* (GD-249)
  Will 23* (GD-238)
  Will 54 (GD-238)
NEAL
  Anne 44* (F-216)
  Charles W. 16* (JE-61)
  Chas. 55 (F-149)
  Creath 36 (m) (ES-111)
  David 42* (JE-50)
  Edgar 39 (CL-55)
  Elijah 62 (JE-59)
  George 57* (JE-59)
  George M. 18* (JE-74)
  James K. 26* (JE-59)
  Jourdan 23 (ES-55)
  Julia 13* (JE-78)
  M. O. 44 (f)* (F-152)
  Moses H. 40 (JE-52)
  Richard 26 (ES-49)
  Samuel 33 (ES-49)
  William 35 (ES-96)
NEAT
  George W. 39 (JE-4)
NEATT?
  Isaac S. 27* (JE-4)
NEBLACK
  William 71* (CL-63)
NEEL
  M. H. 16 (f)* (F-142)
NEELEY
  James F. 35 (GD-273)
NEELLY
  Ann B. 65* (CL-40)
NEELY
  Nathaniel J. 27 (GD-285)

NEET
  Charles M. 21* (JE-66)
  Jacob 55 (JE-57)
  Lucy 82* (JE-53)
NELSON
  Elizabeth 18* (JE-1)
  Elizabeth 25* (F-219)
  George 25* (B) (MT-18)
  Harvey 36* (F-241)
  James? 50* (CL-5)
  John 75* (F-243)
  Joseph 55 (MT-14)
  Mary 18* (MT-1)
  Milton 31* (B) (MT-27)
  Robert 60* (MT-30)
  Sam 58* (F-196)
  Warner 45 (B) (CL-43)
  William 52 (MT-25)
  William A. 46* (MT-7)
  William M. 27 (MT-39)
NESBIT
  Mary 68* (CL-90)
NETHERLAND
  Benjamin 54* (JE-52)
NETHERLANG
  Theadocia 80 (JE-9)
NEVIEUS
  Cornelius 39 (GD-247)
NEWBERRY
  William H. 39 (F-217)
NEWBY
  Nelson 42 (MA-304)
NEWCANT
  James 12* (F-154)
NEWKIRK
  Sytha 23* (CL-58)
NEWLAN
  Margaret 12* (MA-302)
NEWLAND
  Anderson 29 (MA-303)
  Richard T. 26 (JE-8)
  Silas 47* (MA-219)
  William 38 (JE-27)
NEWMAN
  David J. B. 24 (ES-85)
  Edmund 27 (JE-10)
  George 20 (JE-10)
  Harrison 33 (OS-299)

  John 23 (OS-299)
  John 60 (OS-300)
  Leroy 27* (MT-1)
  Peyton 24* (MT-7)
  Robert 29* (JE-10)
  Samuel W. 50 (ES-91)
  Sarah T. 13* (JE-10)
  T. T. 34 (m) (MA-250)
  William 22* (MA-251)
  William 26 (OS-299)
NEWTON
  Allen 38* (OS-314)
  Joseph 53 (GD-229)
  Samuel 56 (GD-206)
NIBBINS
  Henry 26* (MA-204)
NIBLACK
  Luallen 51 (CL-71)
NIBLICK
  John C. 38* (MA-269)
NICHOLAS
  George A. 38* (CL-88)
  Judy 10* (F-137)
  Laura 42 (B) (F-119)
  Primus 55 (B) (CL-4)
  Robert C. 35* (CL-47)
  S. A. 14 (f)* (F-139)
  William 13* (CL-28)
  William C. 43* (CL-25)
NICHOLS
  E. 58 (m) (F-221)
  Eli 42 (MA-237)
  Frederick B. 63 (CL-92)
  Geo. 28* (F-129)
  Polly 47 (F-240)
NICHOLS?
  Elizabeth 78* (MT-22)
NICHOLSON
  Archibald 54 (GD-259)
  James 49 (GD-272)
  James sr. 80* (GD-272)
  Jeremiah J. 36 (GD-254)
  John 56 (GD-272)
  Judy 45* (MT-35)
  Robert 36 (GD-286)
  Thomas 33 (MT-2)
  Will 43 (GD-271)

Index

NICKERSON
  William 45 (ES-96)
NICKS
  Nancy 46* (MT-66)
NICKSON
  James 15* (F-115)
NILES
  Isaac 34* (F-142)
NINNARD
  James 4 (MA-314)
NIVENS
  Will 35 (GD-289)
NOBLE
  D. E. 39 (m) (F-153)
  Frances 22* (F-216)
  John 43 (OS-292)
NOBLES
  David 55 (MA-300)
NOE
  Harvey 40 (CL-56)
  Landon 71 (CL-57)
  Martin 18* (OS-302)
  Nimrod 19* (CL-3)
  William F. 46* (CL-53)
NOEL
  Richard 22 (CL-33)
  Robert 35 (CL-73)
  Robert C. 46 (GD-256)
NOELL
  Robert 30 (MT-59)
NOLAN
  Thomas 38* (CL-89)
  Wm. 53 (F-157)
NOLAND
  Abraham 38 (ES-66)
  Hayard P. 27 (ES-98)
  Henry 37 (OS-288)
  James 35 (MA-274)
  John 31 (F-172)
  John 42 (ES-66)
  John 63* (MA-272)
  Joseph P. 48 (ES-82)
  Joshua 38 (ES-58)
  Martha 30 (MA-272)
  Obed 46* (ES-85)
  Sarah 41 (MT-50)
  Stephen 32 (ES-87)
  William 74 (MA-273)

  William P. 45* (ES-88)
NONLEY
  A. 45 (m) (F-159)
NORDMAN
  Fredrick 1* (F-131)
NORMAN
  James 57* (OS-306)
  Will 38 (GD-282)
NORRIS
  Hamilton 40* (MA-272)
  James 46* (GD-261)
  Napoleon 17 (MA-270)
  Thomas 42* (F-136)
NORTHCUT
  Benjamin 63* (MT-84)
  Jeremiah 40 (MT-30)
  Thornton M. 35 (MT-36)
  William 64* (MT-17)
NORTHERN
  James H. 25 (JE-26)
NORTON
  Amos 42 (ES-48)
  Benjamin 46 (ES-87)
  Charles 28 (F-221)
  James H. 38 (ES-59)
  Jerry 50* (B) (F-233)
  Malinda 27* (F-132)
  R. H. 28 (m) (JE-15)
  Sarah E. 32* (F-195)
  W. H. 40 (m) (F-213)
  William W. 52* (MT-72)
NOVE
  Daniel 47 (F-159)
NOVE?
  Nimrod 40 (JE-55)
NOWLAND
  William 41 (MA-225)
NUBY
  Allen 55 (MA-304)
  Andrew 28 (MA-305)
  Andrew J. 33 (MA-211)
  Bryant 65 (MA-212)
  James 31 (MA-312)
  Jesse 27 (MA-211)
  Jesse 29 (MA-312)
  John 31 (MA-209)
  John 37 (MA-305)
  John 41 (MA-209)

  William 30 (MA-209)
  Winaford 60 (m) (MA-211)
  Winny 46 (MA-311)
  Woodson 40* (MA-208)
NUNLY
  Sarah 63* (F-166)
NUNNELY
  D. 36 (m) (F-175)
NUTLER?
  Henry 30* (F-136)
NUTTALL
  Mary C. 24* (GD-246)
NUTTER
  Ann 56 (F-175)
  David 24 (F-182)
  Jas. R. 22* (F-185)
  John 22* (F-189)
  Lizzie 14* (B) (F-215)
  Lucy 14* (B) (F-229)
  Matilda 14* (F-182)
  Robt. 49 (F-182)
  Wm. 57 (F-183)
NUTTER?
  James 51 (F-175)
OAKS
  Katharine 70 (JE-56)
  Thomas 32* (JE-67)
OATMAN
  Peter 56* (GD-209)
OATS
  Sampson 50 (F-137)
OATY
  Augustus 36* (F-195)
OBANNON
  E. 45 (m)* (F-167)
OBANON
  Algernon S. 40 (GD-240)
  Mary 58 (GD-231)
OBERLY
  Allen B. 23 (GD-253)
OBRADY
  Dennis 30* (CL-89)
OCCONNELL
  Hugh 15* (JE-72)
OCONNER
  James 30* (MA-250)
ODEN
  James W. 26 (MT-29)

Index

ODEN
  John 51 (CL-86)
ODER
  Albert 35 (GD-226)
  Elizabeth 43 (GD-229)
  Gabrael 33 (GD-243)
  George C. 36* (GD-228)
  Joseph 59* (GD-253)
  Joseph jr. 23 (GD-244)
  Thomas 27* (MA-215)
ODONALD
  John 24 (F-126)
ODUNCAN
  John 44 (GD-270)
OFFICER
  Mary 18* (GD-265)
OFFUT
  Mary A. 37 (F-139)
OFFUTT
  Maria 85* (F-193)
  Mary A. 37 (F-185)
  Sandford 35 (F-169)
OGDEN
  John 48 (CL-60)
  Smalwood 39 (CL-49)
  Thomas 31* (CL-15)
OGDON
  Aquilla 32 (CL-28)
OGELSBY
  David 52 (GD-285)
  John 36 (GD-285)
OGER
  David 28* (MA-308)
OGG
  Henderson 55 (MA-262)
  John 51 (MA-249)
  Johnithan 50* (MA-227)
  William 50 (MA-228)
  William 60 (MA-242)
OGLE
  John 64* (JE-43)
OGLEBEE
  Jesse 86* (MA-223)
OGLESBY
  Jacob 52 (GD-259)
OHERRIN
  Dennis 37* (F-173)

OLA
  Andrew 44 (MA-266)
OLD
  John 50 (MA-294)
OLDHAM
  Abner 11* (CL-32)
  Abner 67* (MA-285)
  Arthusa 33* (MA-243)
  Caleb 63 (MA-267)
  David 41 (MA-285)
  David D. 38 (MA-269)
  Ed 57* (F-155)
  Edith 8* (MA-269)
  Frances 70 (MA-282)
  Hiram 26 (MA-283)
  Ibsan 40 (m)* (MA-282)
  John C. 30 (ES-90)
  Mary 56* (ES-63)
  Nathan 46* (MA-282)
  Nathaniel 66 (MA-269)
  Orthenal 33 (m) (MA-275)
  Richard 35 (MA-242)
  Richard 63* (MT-69)
  Richard jr. 36 (MT-7)
  Saml. A. 56* (B) (F-207)
  Susan 61 (MA-267)
  Thomas 26* (MA-260)
  Thompson 21 (MA-268)
OLDS
  Benjamin 20* (CL-13)
  John T. 15* (CL-12)
  Micajah 51 (CL-10)
  Tucker W. 25* (JE-15)
OLIVER
  Catharine 19* (CL-26)
  Elizabeth 48 (CL-54)
  Funky? 50 (f)* (B) (F-124)
  Isaac 59 (MA-272)
  James 38 (OS-290)
  Jasper 10* (GD-282)
  Joel 50 (CL-35)
  Joel S. 21* (CL-35)
  Julia 29 (MT-50)
  Raney 69 (f)* (CL-12)
  Robert 27 (CL-44)
OLSON
  Abram 21* (MT-14)

OMARA
  Michael 36* (F-191)
OMEALLY
  Generose 32* (F-223)
ONEAL
  Daniel 35 (F-190)
  John 22* (GD-265)
  Patrick 33* (F-181)
ONEALY
  Jas. 37* (F-219)
ONIEL
  Parlor 29* (CL-89)
ONSTOTT
  Mary 86 (GD-211)
  William 48 (GD-211)
OPENHEIMER
  Simon 29* (CL-41)
ORCHARD
  David 65* (B) (OS-305)
OREAR
  Daniel 54 (MT-12)
  Edwin G. 30* (MT-72)
  Harrison 39 (MT-80)
  Jeremiah C. 68* (MT-81)
  Jeremiah jr. 49 (MT-73)
  John D. 68 (MT-81)
  Newton 39* (MT-21)
  Patsey 35* (B) (MT-5)
  Robert 69* (MT-13)
  Susetta 40 (F-212)
  Tamer 75 (f)* (MT-11)
  Welsley 40 (MT-69)
ORR
  William 46* (F-237)
OSBORN
  Canterberry 24 (CL-59)
  George 70 (CL-59)
  George W. 38 (CL-60)
  Greenup 40 (CL-59)
  Hezikiah? 64* (CL-62)
  Mathew 42 (ES-75)
  Thomas 25 (ES-84)
  Willis 32 (CL-60)
OTTER
  Nancy 14* (MT-67)
  Stephen 92* (MT-64)
OTWELL
  John F. 29 (F-185)

Index

OUTEN
  Mathias 54* (F-185)
OUTON
  Warren 31* (F-129)
OVERSTREET
  Frank 15* (JE-43)
  James 24* (JE-74)
  James sr. 54 (JE-43)
  John 16* (JE-78)
  John P. 15* (JE-33)
  Margaret 20* (F-209)
  Milton 25* (JE-74)
  Nancy 58 (JE-44)
  Sally 48* (GD-228)
  Samuel 23 (JE-29)
  Samuel 38* (B) (JE-54)
  William 33 (JE-44)
  William 40 (B) (JE-54)
  William F. 30 (GD-220)
OVERTON
  Frances 72 (F-197)
  Jane 37* (F-197)
  John W. 59* (F-250)
  Mary S. 42 (F-226)
OWDEN?
  Crepan 23 (m)* (MT-27)
OWEN
  Amanda J. 18* (JE-20)
  Francis T. 34* (CL-27)
  Hezakiah 42* (CL-19)
  Robert 76* (MT-75)
  Thos. 43* (F-233)
  William 45* (CL-20)
OWENS
  Bartheny 67 (f)* (MA-283)
  David 38 (JE-17)
  E. J. 25 (m) (MA-214)
  Eliza 2* (B) (F-144)
  Elizabeth 24* (F-230)
  Elkanah 21* (F-216)
  Fielding 43 (CL-42)
  Grandison? 29 (F-204)
  Horatio 65* (CL-18)
  James W. 48 (MA-276)
  John 51 (MA-295)
  John 56 (MA-285)
  Mastin 42 (MA-320)
  Milton 27* (CL-17)

  Peter 30* (F-198)
  Richard 37* (MT-5)
  Samuel 23* (MA-283)
  Samuel 26* (MA-252)
  W. T. 25 (m)* (F-122)
  Wm. 24* (F-151)
OWINGS
  Ann 15* (MT-6)
  Elizabeth 80* (ES-48)
  Hannah 63* (B) (MT-29)
  John R. 32 (ES-80)
  Joshua 50 (MT-16)
  Samuel 46* (MT-40)
  Samuel J. 34 (JE-53)
  William 65* (B) (MT-40)
OWSLEY
  Ellen 28 (CL-47)
  James R. 21* (CL-47)
  John D. 56 (CL-44)
  Wyatt 47 (CL-44)
PACE
  James 37* (CL-73)
  Joseph 32 (CL-74)
  Nancy 49 (CL-85)
  William 33 (CL-69)
PADEN
  Joseph 2* (MA-268)
PADGETT
  Martha 40* (JE-45)
PADMAN
  Sarah 11/12* (MA-268)
PADON
  James 29 (ES-66)
PAGE
  George 51* (MT-2)
  James 18* (F-146)
PAGGET
  Charlotte 25 (JE-17)
  Harvey 26 (B) (JE-38)
  Mary J. 18* (JE-37)
PAIN
  robert 49 (GD-270)
PALDING
  Jane 60 (B) (GD-288)
PALMER
  Asa W. 45* (MT-2)
  Elizabeth 48 (CL-56)
  Nenion? 44 (m)* (GD-275)

  Robert S. 25 (CL-37)
  Thomas 60* (MA-205)
  Will 47 (GD-274)
  William 24* (CL-2)
  William 65* (CL-76)
PALMERS
  William 22* (CL-82)
PANE
  Elizabeth 8/12* (CL-21)
PAPPUL?
  Lewis 38* (F-128)
PARADORE
  George 36 (CL-31)
PARCAN
  Ephram 22 (MA-276)
PARIDO
  Colby 17* (CL-50)
  John 30* (CL-50)
  William 75 (CL-51)
PARIS
  John 30* (CL-60)
  William 25 (MA-302)
PARISH
  Barnett 59* (CL-55)
  Dabney W. 47* (F-209)
  Edwin 18* (CL-43)
  Frances 17* (MT-82)
  Howard E. 18* (F-233)
  James R. 18* (JE-2)
  John 24* (F-232)
  John W. 26* (JE-4)
  Meredith 27 (CL-56)
  Milton J. 28 (CL-58)
  Paulina 47* (JE-3)
  William 30 (CL-55)
  William M. 27* (CL-53)
PARK
  Asa 70 (ES-86)
  Cora Bell 6* (MT-5)
  Ebenezer 31 (ES-86)
  Ebenezer 74 (ES-99)
  Hezekiah 43 (ES-103)
  Hiram 45* (ES-102)
  Isom 38 (ES-67)
  John 32 (ES-59)
  Jonah 44* (ES-98)
  Polly 75* (ES-60)
  Solomon B. 47* (ES-109)

Index

PARK
  Solomon D. 36 (ES-97)
  William 68 (ES-113)
  Winney 38 (ES-97)
PARKE
  Margaret 57* (F-114)
PARKER
  Catherine 58* (F-118)
  Courtney 35 (f) (MA-272)
  Elizabeth 45* (F-116)
  Howard S. 23 (F-234)
  Jacob 37 (F-180)
  John 53* (F-149)
  John 54 (F-239)
  John T. 50 (F-154)
  Margarett 53* (CL-24)
  Mary 82* (F-144)
  Nancy 29* (F-155)
  Oswell* (F-174)
  Pleasant 25* (MT-4)
  R. B. 54 (m)* (F-123)
  Sarah 75 (CL-56)
  Susan 48 (MA-220)
  W. O. 30 (f) (F-134)
PARKERS
  William 23* (CL-59)
PARKES
  John M. 43 (MA-265)
  Joseph 46* (MA-282)
  Levi 26 (MA-233)
  Louisa 41* (MA-283)
  William 30 (MA-218)
PARKHILL
  Letitia 25* (F-225)
PARKS
  Cortes 35 (m) (MA-299)
  Eli 63 (MA-261)
  George W. 21 (MA-261)
  Harvey 45 (GD-234)
  Hesekiah 37* (MA-283)
  James 59 (MA-301)
  John 46* (F-194)
  John W. 47* (MA-219)
  Johnathan 35 (MA-212)
  Joshua? D. 39 (MA-257)
  Mary 37* (ES-61)
  Rebecca 24* (MA-285)
  Sally A. 21* (GD-261)

  Shipton 66 (MA-302)
PARLEY
  Lewis G. 26 (CL-63)
PARMER
  Lavina 83 (JE-17)
  Nancy 50* (F-177)
PARRIS
  Ezekiel 65 (MA-210)
PARRISH
  Albertis 27 (MA-284)
  Calib 49* (CL-9)
  Dickerson 65 (CL-4)
  Grandison 38* (MT-69)
  Greenberry 26 (CL-30)
  James G. 29* (CL-45)
  John G. 29 (MA-298)
  John G. 62 (MA-296)
  John H. 28 (MA-221)
  Owen 32 (MA-284)
  Paulina 18* (MA-285)
  Samuel 55* (MA-208)
  Sequel 66 (m) (MA-210)
  Temple 48 (CL-7)
  W. D. 22 (m)* (F-189)
  Wesley 55 (MA-283)
  William 58 (MA-285)
PARSONS
  Geo. W. 42* (F-160)
PARTON
  Asher 18* (B) (MT-37)
PASLEY
  James 27 (ES-75)
  Thomas 18* (ES-75)
PASSMORE
  Joseph 59* (MT-29)
PASTLETHWAITE
  G. L. 44 (m) (F-191)
PATERSON
  John 69 (GD-282)
PATRICK
  Alexander 36* (CL-46)
  Benj. 64* (F-128)
  Bryant 48 (CL-36)
  Charles 77 (F-175)
  Hickman 40 (ES-74)
  James 24 (OS-309)
  John W. 21* (CL-36)
  Samuel 25* (ES-81)

  Thomas 52* (ES-54)
  Weeden 25 (CL-59)
  William 40 (OS-314)
  ____ 30 (m)* (JE-78)
PATTEN
  John E. 32 (JE-2)
PATTENT
  John C. 21* (F-190)
PATTERSON
  Clark 37* (MA-288)
  Edward 18* (MT-4)
  Isaac 22* (F-172)
  Jacob S. 47 (MT-11)
  James 40 (GD-244)
  John 63* (JE-54)
  John W. 38* (F-201)
  Joseph 38* (F-235)
  Louisa 24* (F-194)
  Perry 32 (MA-205)
  Samuel 68 (MA-223)
  Thomas 24* (MT-58)
  William 52* (JE-16)
PATTESON
  A. A. 32 (m) (F-238)
PATTON
  Charles 22* (CL-68)
  Elizabeth 81* (CL-87)
  George W. 22 (MT-45)
  Indina? 18* (CL-37)
  John 21 (MT-44)
  Margaret 10* (MT-70)
  Polly Ann 32 (ES-62)
  Rachel 63 (CL-68)
  Sampson 21* (CL-36)
  Thomas 54 (MT-44)
  William 16* (CL-10)
  William 39 (CL-68)
  William M. 20* (CL-68)
PAWL
  John P. 24* (F-203)
PAYNE
  Augustus 34* (F-174)
  Charles F. 28* (JE-19)
  Colby 24 (CL-15)
  Danl. M. D. 52 (F-141)
  Edward 27* (MT-36)
  H. B. 55 (m)* (F-184)
  Henry C. 56 (F-168)

Index

PAYNE
  Isaac 29 (B) (F-151)
  Martha A. 50* (F-215)
  Matilda 61* (F-124)
  Nelly 70* (CL-59)
  O. F. 42 (m) (F-189)
  Richard 30* (F-120)
  Thomas 40* (MT-23)
  William 65 (F-169)
PAYTON
  Amanda 17* (B) (F-152)
  E. 70 (f)* (F-155)
PEACH
  Thomas W. 4* (GD-240)
PEACOCK
  Thomas 32 (GD-287)
PEAK
  James F. 18* (JE-10)
PEANALL?
  John 42 (CL-75)
PEARCE
  E. B. 18 (m)* (MT-5)
  Rachael 41 (GD-252)
PEARL
  Robert 16* (GD-243)
PEARSON
  Eli 38 (ES-86)
  Green 18* (ES-84)
  Henry 29 (ES-112)
  Jemima 2* (ES-72)
  Joseph 25 (ES-85)
  Lourena 6* (ES-110)
  Lucy 65 (ES-110)
  Malinda 14* (ES-59)
  Molly 65 (F-173)
  Robert 34 (ES-92)
  Susan P.? 31* (F-144)
PEBWORTH?
  Stephen 33 (OS-306)
PECK
  A. D. 40 (f)* (F-140)
  A. F. 22 (m)* (F-161)
  Caroline 37* (F-196)
  Julia Ann 5* (F-209)
PEDDICORD
  Dawson 23 (CL-67)
  Nathaniel 60 (CL-66)

PEEBLES
  Margaret 50 (CL-91)
PEEL
  James 29 (F-217)
  Priscilla 39 (F-180)
  Samuel 39 (GD-229)
  Taylor 31* (F-202)
  Thomas 60 (JE-28)
  William 28 (JE-26)
PEERS
  Eliza 26* (F-207)
PEGG
  Lewis 56 (CL-69)
  Martin 23 (CL-69)
PEIRATT
  James 30* (ES-104)
PEIS?
  Blackburn 21* (F-199)
PEMBERTON
  James 20* (CL-94)
PEMBLETON
  Bowlen 58 (F-200)
PENCE
  Henry R. 37 (MT-19)
PENDAGESS
  Adaline 20* (F-208)
PENDLETON
  Dana J. 26 (CL-93)
  Edmond 60* (CL-92)
  Edwd. 23* (F-213)
  John 25 (MT-78)
  Rice 56 (CL-86)
PENELSTON
  Will 18* (GD-289)
PENNINGTON
  Able 53* (OS-284)
  James 51 (OS-318)
  John 23 (OS-285)
  Levi 28* (OS-284)
  Pealy? 33 (m) (ES-52)
  Peter 28 (OS-307)
PENNY
  S. 26 (m) (F-122)
PERKEY
  William 21 (OS-284)
PERKINS
  Ama 45 (B) (GD-284)
  Emanuel 22 (GD-277)

  Gerge T. 33 (MA-202)
  Hardin G. 36 (GD-230)
  Harrison 39* (MA-311)
  Henry 46 (CL-88)
  Isadinda 30 (GD-269)
  James 23* (F-179)
  James 23* (F-235)
  James 64 (GD-269)
  Jefferson 30 (MA-301)
  Jesse 30 (MA-209)
  John 36 (CL-83)
  John 54 (GD-269)
  John F. 32 (MA-202)
  John H. 38 (MA-307)
  Jordon 40 (GD-289)
  Joseph D. 42 (GD-207)
  Madison 40 (MA-305)
  Mary J. 29 (JE-67)
  Mitchel 34 (MA-301)
  Newel 28 (GD-269)
  Plesant 62 (MA-306)
  Richard 23 (MA-211)
  Richard 23 (MA-306)
  Richard 55 (MA-211)
  Sally 61 (MA-209)
  Stacy 45 (GD-269)
  Stephen 62 (MA-313)
  Susan 78* (MA-202)
  Terry 35 (MA-306)
  Wiatte 32 (GD-284)
  William 62 (F-235)
  William H. 45 (MA-207)
  Wm. 31* (F-172)
PERREL
  William S. 47* (GD-226)
PERRIN
  Felix 45* (F-184)
PERRY
  Ellen 25* (F-194)
  Fanny 50 (B) (JE-38)
  George 35 (B) (F-206)
  H. J. 43 (m) (MT-3)
  John 67 (JE-2)
  John jr. 32 (JE-8)
  Oliver 34 (JE-30)
  William 30 (OS-312)
PERRY?
  Ann 22* (F-134)

Index

PERSALL
  Isaac 44 (CL-84)
PERVIS
  Alfred 54 (MA-238)
PETER
  R. 39 (m) (F-144)
PETERS
  Belvard J. 43* (MT-13)
  Elijah 29 (OS-320)
  Elisha 50* (OS-295)
  James 25 (OS-286)
  John 36 (OS-281)
  William 22* (OS-302)
PETITT
  Asa T. 40* (MT-71)
PETRY
  Wm. 70* (F-155)
PETTICORD
  John 25 (OS-307)
  John C. 22* (OS-310)
  Susan 17* (CL-42)
  William 37 (CL-7)
PETTIFORD
  Alfred 38 (B) (MA-298)
  Fanny 65 (B) (MA-298)
  George 27 (B) (MA-298)
PETTIL?
  W. B. 37 (m) (F-166)
PETTIT
  George 11* (F-125)
  Harry 53 (F-253)
  James O. 27 (F-224)
  Rebecca 50* (F-223)
PETTUS
  Will H. 22 (GD-271)
PETTY
  C. 56 (f)* (F-127)
  Garrett S. 40 (GD-236)
  James 17* (CL-57)
  John A. 43 (GD-288)
PEYTON
  Elizabeth 52* (JE-61)
  Griffin 51 (MA-279)
  James T. 25 (MA-279)
  Philip 63* (MT-55)
  Thomas 44* (JE-73)
  Zachariah 38* (JE-1)

PHARRIS
  Mary 15* (OS-287)
PHELPS
  Athony 58* (JE-9)
  Charles G. 35 (MT-61)
  George 30* (JE-2)
  George 45 (MA-284)
  James 55 (MT-29)
  Janett 74 (m)* (MA-302)
  John 44 (MT-22)
  John B. 31* (F-195)
  Jonathan 39 (ES-81)
  Peter T. 26 (MA-300)
  Samuel 62 (MA-299)
  Tabitha 81* (MA-299)
PHERIGO
  Benjamin F. 33 (GD-224)
  James 23 (GD-270)
PHILIPS
  Erasmus 23 (GD-238)
  Garrett 30* (MT-62)
  Harvey 32 (MT-62)
  Isaac 76 (GD-225)
  James 27* (GD-249)
  Lewis 43 (GD-221)
  Madison 15* (GD-228)
  Mary A. 53* (MT-60)
  Sidney S. 42 (m) (GD-227)
  William 50 (GD-238)
PHILLIPS
  Abram 24 (OS-316)
  Asa 24 (OS-302)
  B. F. 44 (m) (OS-309)
  Beverly 33 (m) (ES-72)
  Bright 36 (ES-101)
  Catharine 48* (MA-314)
  Elizabeth 66* (JE-45)
  Hardy 45 (OS-316)
  James 60 (MA-324)
  James M. 34 (GD-289)
  Mason 50 (OS-278)
  Memory 26 (m) (ES-72)
  Persar? 29 (m)* (OS-296)
  Richard 21* (F-167)
  Sallie 16* (B) (F-151)
  Thomas 48 (OS-299)
  Wm. 34 (F-186)

PHILPOT
  Rebecca 39 (GD-283)
PHIPPS
  Abram 40* (MT-80)
PHOENISTER
  E. J. 40 (m) (MA-299)
PIANT
  Cornelia 13* (F-117)
PICKETT
  Alfred 14* (CL-11)
  Courtney 53 (F-198)
  John J. 26* (F-189)
  Mary 72* (F-219)
  Robert 53* (B) (F-250)
PICKLES
  George M. 35* (MA-251)
PIERCALL
  Jane 16* (MT-78)
PIERCE
  Jeremiah 47 (GD-264)
  N. H. 23 (m) (MT-59)
  Thomas W. 45* (MT-27)
PIGG
  Briston 70 (B) (CL-35)
  Henry 45* (F-197)
  James H. 25 (F-121)
  Johnson 34 (ES-93)
  Lewis 29 (F-120)
  M. H. 17 (m)* (ES-60)
  Saml. 37 (F-145)
  Thomas 24 (CL-38)
  Woodford 30 (MT-62)
PIKE
  Elizabeth 18* (F-247)
  Samuel 68* (F-247)
PILANT
  James 56* (MA-318)
PILCHER
  Chas. 53 (F-187)
  David 40 (B) (F-138)
  Frances 27* (F-116)
  Margaret 13* (F-152)
  Sarah 36* (F-130)
PILKINGTON
  J. M. 23 (m)* (F-129)
PINDEGRAS
  Abijah 57* (GD-220)

Index

PINDELL
  Henry C. 27* (F-114)
  R. 37* (F-145)
PINKARD
  M. 17 (f)* (F-124)
PINKSTON
  Allen 39 (MA-247)
  Ann 67 (B) (MA-278)
  John W. 33 (MA-276)
  Thomas M. 33 (ES-84)
PINKSTONE
  Eli 77 (MA-230)
PINMOODY
  Ann M. 11* (MA-222)
PIPER
  William C. 28* (F-230)
PITCHER
  Joshua 50 (ES-62)
PITMAN
  Starling 35* (OS-278)
PITMANN
  Micager 38 (m) (OS-306)
PITT
  Cornelia 21* (MT-71)
PITTITT
  Mary 16* (MT-13)
PITTS
  John L. 31 (GD-207)
  Washington 35 (MT-76)
PLEAK
  James O. 34 (MT-23)
  Jane 54* (MT-84)
PLEAKS
  Amanda 30* (MT-51)
PLEASANTS
  Susan R. 62* (F-185)
PLOWMAN
  Ambrose 16* (ES-99)
  Henry 37 (ES-112)
  James 27 (ES-98)
  Sally 21* (ES-108)
PLUMES
  Samuel 96* (OS-311)
PLUNKETT
  William F. 43* (F-116)
POAG
  J. G. 40 (m)* (F-162)

POAGE
  Samuel 51 (JE-69)
POINDEXTER
  W. 58 (m) (F-208)
  Zach 55 (CL-8)
POINTER
  James 36 (GD-275)
  John 48 (GD-217)
  Matthew 42 (MT-57)
  Squire 40 (GD-217)
  Vincent 29 (GD-274)
  Walker S. 29 (GD-216)
  William 44* (GD-216)
  William H. 20 (GD-217)
POLE
  John 50 (OS-301)
POLE?
  William __* (OS-300)
POLK
  Jmaes 23* (F-184)
POLLARD
  Absolum 50 (GD-276)
  Elizabeth 35* (GD-241)
  Elizabeth 56 (GD-231)
  John 62 (GD-249)
  Mary A. 17* (GD-249)
  Mason 39 (GD-231)
  Thompson 25 (GD-231)
POMPHRY
  A. B. 36 (m)* (F-196)
POND
  Joseph R. 70 (MA-287)
PONDER
  Betsy 26* (OS-318)
  Joseph 18* (OS-309)
  Joseph 45 (OS-278)
  Zadoc 29 (OS-279)
POOL
  Philip 60 (CL-43)
POOR
  Benjamin 48 (ES-74)
  Elizabeth 52 (GD-229)
  John S. 30 (GD-289)
  John W. 28 (GD-220)
  Mary 14* (CL-62)
  Mary W. 20* (JE-18)
  Pricilla 35* (ES-75)
  Robert C. 41 (GD-220)

  Thomas 35 (GD-220)
  William 18* (CL-63)
POPE
  Thomas 39 (GD-277)
POPPAL
  Lewis 38* (F-204)
PORTER
  Clarinda 16* (GD-220)
  Clarinda 17* (GD-238)
  Clarinda 17* (GD-240)
  Eli 43* (OS-287)
  Henrietta 22* (B) (F-228)
  Lyman 31* (MT-73)
  Mary 12* (GD-238)
  Pa__y 10 (m)* (GD-239)
  R. C. 33 (m)* (MT-73)
  Thomas 39 (OS-307)
  Thornton 20* (GD-239)
PORTWOOD
  Ambrose 19 (JE-15)
  Clifton 30 (MA-282)
  Conwell 27* (MA-283)
  Elizabeth 6* (MA-266)
  Ennis 25 (OS-307)
  Fanny 28* (MA-300)
  Hardin 27 (MA-277)
  John 63 (JE-21)
  John P. 22* (MA-260)
  Joseph 45 (MA-259)
  Leonard 20* (MA-278)
  Milton 22* (MA-283)
  Rice 27* (MA-274)
  Silas 48 (MA-259)
  Siquir? 31 (m) (JE-21)
  Solomon 60 (OS-315)
  Thomas 57 (MA-275)
  Zacaria 22* (MA-278)
POSEY
  Harrison 56 (GD-228)
  Thomas 30 (GD-226)
POST
  John 25* (MA-249)
POSTLETHWAIT
  John 17?* (F-130)
  Lewis 42* (JE-68)
POSTON
  Charles 29* (CL-72)
  Edwin 37* (CL-43)

Index

POSTON
  Henry G. 38 (CL-95)
  Mildred 58 (CL-85)
POTTER
  Nancy 53* (F-196)
POTTS
  Alfred 26 (CL-63)
  Ann 69 (JE-20)
  C. A. 32 (f) (JE-43)
  Jefferson 27 (CL-65)
  John F. 32 (ES-57)
  Nancy 50* (MA-265)
  Smith V. 35 (CL-51)
  William 32 (JE-29)
POULTER?
  John 23* (F-134)
POWEL
  Cleveland 37 (MA-236)
  John 32 (MA-236)
  Larkin 21 (MA-236)
  Lorily? 59 (m) (MA-236)
  Manuel 24 (MA-235)
POWELL
  Abram 28 (MA-219)
  Andrew J. 22 (MA-302)
  Benjamin 31 (MA-296)
  E. S. 26 (m) (MT-79)
  Elizabeth 55 (MA-298)
  Elizabeth 56* (MA-296)
  F. M. sr. 31 (m)* (ES-55)
  Jesse 56* (CL-36)
  Joel 35 (MA-276)
  Joel B. 33 (MA-296)
  Joel H. 36 (MA-298)
  John 24* (F-177)
  John 25* (JE-61)
  John 36* (ES-53)
  John B. 58* (ES-60)
  Little B. 67 (MA-296)
  Marcus 44 (MT-46)
  Mary H. 43 (CL-55)
  Michael 48 (MA-220)
  Obediah 56 (MA-295)
  Providence 52* (MT-35)
  Samuel M. 25* (MT-63)
  Samuel S. 38 (MA-296)
  Stephen 31 (MA-296)
  Thomas 70 (MT-46)

Thomas S. 32 (MA-295)
William 22* (MA-206)
POWER
  Lenn 32* (MT-35)
POWERS
  John K. 49 (ES-112)
  Martin 55* (MT-24)
POWLL
  Jeremiah 66 (MA-263)
POYNTER
  James 34* (ES-107)
PRADINGTON
  Mary 4* (OS-295)
PRATER
  Philip 46 (GD-226)
  Willis 41 (GD-226)
PRATHER
  Carroll 30 (m)* (ES-97)
  Freeman 52 (GD-256)
  Hannah 77 (GD-216)
  James B. 38 (GD-244)
  James jr. 20 (GD-216)
  John 65 (F-237)
  John M. 42 (ES-112)
  Lloyd 34 (F-221)
  Nathaniel 51 (MT-64)
  Reuben 56* (F-246)
  Thos. Sr. 73 (F-246)
  Walter 23 (F-246)
  Walter 25 (MT-58)
  William 30* (ES-112)
  Wm. J. 18* (F-246)
PRATT
  W. M. 33 (m) (F-143)
PRESLY
  Enoch 15* (MA-232)
PRESTON
  Alexander M. 36* (CL-45)
  Asbury 18* (JE-31)
  Benjamin F. 1* (JE-45)
  Benjamin R. 33 (CL-28)
  Berryman 30 (JE-31)
  Elias 31 (JE-36)
  Elice 25 (m)* (GD-249)
  Emily 25* (JE-36)
  Enoch 70 (GD-249)
  George W. 38 (GD-240)
  Jilson 28* (JE-21)

Letitia 77 (CL-4)
Lewis 62 (JE-31)
Lucy 63 (B) (CL-4)
Milton 33 (JE-31)
Richard 34 (JE-21)
Rosanna 15* (JE-36)
Samuel 27* (JE-45)
Tabien? 5 (m)* (JE-32)
Toliver 71 (JE-36)
William 55 (GD-249)
William jr. 22 (GD-222)
PREWETT
  David 38 (MA-316)
  Elizabeth 55* (MA-317)
  Henry 32 (MA-317)
  James 26 (MA-316)
  Wiley 43 (MA-317)
  William 25* (MA-318)
  William 30 (MA-316)
PREWIT
  Johnithan 22 (MA-315)
PREWITT
  Alexander 34 (F-239)
  B. A. 28 (m)* (F-241)
  James 49 (MT-9)
  Levi 30 (F-225)
  Nelson 43 (MT-9)
  Solomon 45 (MA-321)
  William C. 62* (F-230)
  William F. 25 (CL-57)
  Willis 53* (MT-7)
PRICE
  Adam 52* (OS-295)
  Andrew B. 45 (CL-60)
  Anna 73 (CL-4)
  Cassa 42* (JE-46)
  Charles 23 (OS-319)
  Cosby 67 (F-170)
  D. L. 36 (m)* (F-169)
  Daniel B. 61* (JE-26)
  David 29 (ES-78)
  Dillard 18* (MT-6)
  Elenor 37 (m) (F-177)
  Elias 31 (OS-295)
  Ellen 24* (F-120)
  Harrell 29* (B) (F-124)
  Henry 52 (B) (F-126)
  Ida 1* (CL-3)

Index

PRICE
  Jacob 41 (ES-78)
  James 50* (CL-91)
  James C. 22 (JE-3)
  Jennings 43 (GD-264)
  John 17* (F-171)
  Klebar F. 43 (m) (JE-9)
  Littleton T. 37 (JE-33)
  Morton M. 45 (ES-88)
  N. B. 36 (m) (GD-268)
  Reben 45 (GD-209)
  Samuel W. 31* (F-203)
  Sanford 28 (F-150)
  Susan 73* (F-191)
  Thomas S. 42 (ES-84)
  William 73 (JE-33)
  Willis 72* (F-173)
PRICE?
  Fedrick 25 (GD-272)
PRIEST
  Daniel 55 (MT-18)
  Mary 20* (F-200)
PRIESTLEY
  Michael 45* (JE-34)
PRINCE
  Arthur 42 (MT-65)
  Mary 15* (F-225)
PRITCHET
  Elizabeth 27* (OS-277)
PRITCHETT
  Edward 65 (ES-108)
  Milly 56 (MT-22)
PROBEIT
  Tho. 25* (F-200)
PROCTOR
  George Ann 16* (GD-271)
  John 21* (GD-270)
  L. H. 39 (m) (JE-64)
  Washington 40* (MT-80)
PROFFIT
  Eli 24 (OS-294)
  Jerry 59 (OS-311)
  John 25 (OS-311)
  Stephen 26* (OS-294)
  Stephen 43 (OS-311)
PROFUT
  Nancy 26* (F-194)

PRONELL?
  J. W. 30 (m) (F-199)
PROUT?
  Dyna 65* (B) (F-173)
PROVINCE?
  Wiley 21* (CL-47)
PRUETT
  James 36 (MA-316)
  Joseph 24 (MA-249)
  Solomon 65* (GD-215)
  Tamor? 69 (f)* (JE-25)
PRUITT
  Mariam 50 (f) (JE-76)
  Sarah 56* (JE-69)
PRUNTY
  Thomas 40 (MA-248)
PRYOR
  Angelina 38* (GD-227)
  George R. 10* (JE-57)
  John 26 (GD-227)
  Jourdon 50 (GD-255)
  Will 22 (GD-255)
PU
  Parker 51 (B) (F-151)
PUCKETT
  James 26 (ES-47)
  Leroy 37 (ES-82)
  Nelson 34 (ES-47)
  William 26 (ES-48)
PULLEN
  Agnes 58* (F-196)
  William 47 (F-133)
PULLEY
  Robert J. 31 (MA-278)
PULLIAM
  Busrod 43* (GD-206)
  John B. 30 (GD-213)
  Stephen 25 (GD-232)
  William sr. 27 (GD-212)
PULLIAMS
  Alvah 31 (m) (GD-253)
PULLINS
  William 28 (MA-314)
PULLUM
  Major 70 (B) (F-237)
  W. A. 40 (m)* (F-230)
PULLY
  Jesse 30* (F-195)

PUMPHREY
  Harrison 36 (GD-208)
PUNCEON?
  Mathew 34 (F-200)
PURSELL
  Cyrus 38 (MA-253)
  Daniel 70* (MA-253)
QEESTER?
  Michael 30* (MT-35)
QUARLES
  Roger 78* (F-173)
QUERTEMOUSE
  Sarah 20* (F-197)
QUEST
  Charles 17* (JE-73)
  George 63 (JE-39)
QUIMBEY
  Daniel 28 (JE-35)
  George 61 (JE-31)
QUINN
  A. W. 57 (m)* (ES-94)
  Ann 25* (F-194)
  Elizabeth 54 (MA-230)
  Hiram 25 (MA-231)
  James W. 23 (MA-231)
  John B. 34 (GD-268)
  Leanny N. 33 (m) (MA-231)
  Susan 5* (MA-262)
  Susan 58* (MA-208)
  William R. 30 (MA-262)
QUISENBERRY
  Achillis 32* (CL-32)
  Cloe 61* (CL-11)
  Colby B. 61* (CL-15)
  Fielding 31* (CL-12)
  James 44 (CL-57)
  James F. 26 (CL-12)
  James T. 30 (MT-39)
  Jas. H. 30 (CL-20)
  Loyed? 25* (CL-22)
  Margaret 9* (CL-52)
  Mills 22* (CL-13)
  P. J. 37 (m) (CL-14)
  P. J. B. 38 (m)* (CL-13)
  Philip 12* (CL-46)
  Roger 57* (CL-12)
  Stephen Q. 28 (CL-40)
  Tandy 59 (m) (CL-15)

Index

QUISENBERRY
  Thacker 32* (CL-13)
  Thomas P. 27 (CL-17)
  William F. 52* (CL-20)
  Wm. J. 26* (CL-22)
QUISENBERY
  C. P. 20 (m)* (CL-1)
  John H. 36 (CL-78)
QUISENBURY
  Jane 6* (CL-14)
  Nicholas 35 (CL-52)
QUISHENBERY
  Joseph 37 (MA-255)
QUISON?
  Patric 16* (F-130)
RADENS
  Thomas 38 (CL-9)
RADER
  George 45 (OS-315)
  Henry 41* (OS-318)
  Jane 78* (OS-297)
  John 37 (OS-318)
RADFORD
  Nancy 29 (OS-317)
  Nathaniel 37 (OS-318)
  Richard 58 (OS-317)
  Sally 30 (OS-318)
RADKIN
  Patrick 40* (F-225)
RADNER
  Claboum 26 (OS-320)
RAGAN
  Alfred 42 (MT-10)
  Dennis 27* (CL-89)
  Mary 51 (F-180)
  Thomas 47 (MT-12)
  William 50 (MT-9)
RAGGANA
  Nathaniel 49 (CL-31)
RAGLAND
  Amand 25* (CL-11)
  Drusilla 26* (MT-25)
  Isaac N. 43* (MT-27)
  John 55 (CL-55)
  Nathaniel T. 25* (CL-31)
  Nathaniel sr. 74 (CL-14)
  Thomas S. 46 (CL-14)
  William 37 (CL-13)

RAGSDALE
  Ann E. 21* (F-146)
  Clifton 24 (JE-16)
  Thomas 48 (MA-290)
RAIBORN
  James 34 (CL-72)
RAIBOURN
  James 50 (MA-255)
  John 30 (MA-208)
  Milton 39* (MA-229)
RAIBOURNE
  Harrison 35 (MA-280)
  Miranda 28* (MA-282)
RAILSBACK
  Daniel 26* (CL-23)
  David 29 (CL-21)
  David 42* (ES-105)
RAIN?
  James K. 19* (F-148)
RAINEY
  Andrew J. 33 (ES-88)
  Elihu 26 (ES-105)
  James 50 (CL-31)
  James sr. 81 (CL-1)
  John 28 (CL-29)
  John 46 (ES-62)
  Lewis 56 (CL-29)
  Squire 22* (CL-60)
  Thomas 68* (CL-29)
  W. H. 56 (m)* (F-138)
RAINS
  W. 21 (m)* (B) (F-140)
RAINY
  John W. 19* (CL-36)
RAKER
  Jacob 37 (CL-52)
  Sarah E. 13* (CL-40)
  William 30 (CL-52)
RALSTON
  Thos. N. 44 (F-217)
RAMEY
  Bartlett 30* (B) (MT-7)
  David 17* (MT-64)
  Elizabeth 18* (B) (MT-20)
  Franklin H. 30 (CL-53)
  Harry 55* (B) (MT-28)
  Randall 40* (B) (MT-82)
  Robert 36 (MT-81)

  Thomas 22* (B) (MT-82)
RAMSDEN
  Jas. 30* (F-196)
RAMSEY
  Alexander 65 (GD-268)
  Andrew 70* (CL-84)
  Burdett 23 (m) (GD-242)
  David 43 (MT-16)
  Eliza A. 6* (CL-88)
  Frances 51* (CL-82)
  Garret 41* (OS-315)
  Hannah 58 (B) (MT-77)
  Jacob 75* (MT-80)
  James 18* (JE-53)
  James 61 (CL-85)
  Jonson 37 (GD-280)
  Joseph 32 (CL-83)
  Lewis 32* (F-172)
  Nancy 30 (CL-85)
  Rachel 58* (CL-76)
  Samuel A. 37 (CL-79)
  Sarah 13* (MT-21)
  Thomas 30 (GD-269)
  Thomas 75 (GD-241)
  Varner 28* (CL-83)
  William U. 36* (MA-256)
RAMY
  Benjamin 40* (B) (MT-71)
RANDALL
  S. C. 48 (m) (F-215)
  Samuel jr. 61 (MT-45)
  Thomas G. 36* (F-215)
  W. R. 58 (m) (F-143)
  William 27 (MT-44)
RANDALLY
  Samuel 26 (MT-45)
RANDELL
  Mary 80* (F-155)
RANDOLPH
  Evelyn B. 19* (JE-57)
  John H. 34* (F-176)
  Judith 52 (B) (CL-89)
  Moses 74* (F-178)
  Robert 30 (MT-60)
RANEY
  Benjamin L. 24 (CL-29)
  George 36 (GD-237)
  John 16* (F-188)

Index

RANEY
- John 45 (GD-233)
- John H. 29 (CL-29)
- Ruhama 48 (MT-5)
- Salley 66 (GD-243)
- William 44 (GD-243)

RANKIN
- John 31* (CL-18)
- Maria 15* (F-223)
- Robert 39? (CL-39)

RANKINS
- A. G. 48 (m) (ES-55)
- Bluford 39* (CL-58)
- Hiram B. 36 (CL-63)
- James 13* (MT-16)
- John 80 (CL-66)

RANSDALE
- Margaret 19* (F-185)

RANSOM
- R. R. 22 (m)* (F-144)

RASEY
- Joel 31 (GD-237)

RASH
- Lewis 33 (CL-94)
- Thomas W. 44 (CL-80)
- William 67 (CL-2)

RATCLIFF
- James 50* (MT-74)
- William 26 (MT-74)

RATCLIFFE
- Francis 57* (F-240)

RATHBURN
- James? 25* (F-114)

RATHNAY
- John A. 30* (F-122)

RATLIFF
- Peter 20 (OS-294)
- Reubin 28 (OS-279)
- William 21* (ES-81)

RATLIFFE
- Wm. D. 24* (F-241)

RATSEL
- W. 32 (m)* (F-204)

RATTELL
- Mary 58* (F-214)

RAULEY
- James 58 (OS-292)

RAVER
- Hezekiah 41 (MT-48)

RAWLINGS
- Robert 26 (ES-59)

RAWLINS
- Andrew 30 (ES-87)
- Benjamin H. 54 (ES-99)
- James 43 (F-125)

RAY
- Alexander 35 (GD-234)
- Daniel 60 (GD-227)
- George 30 (GD-235)
- Hampton 38 (GD-277)
- Harrison 38 (GD-255)
- Hezekiah 48 (GD-210)
- John 68 (GD-254)
- Michael 58* (GD-214)
- Oliver J. 30 (GD-277)
- Robert C. 37 (GD-223)
- Susan 40* (MA-319)

RAYBOURN
- Thomas 56 (MT-8)
- William 28 (MT-8)

RAYEN
- Eli How 16* (F-139)

RAYMON
- Mrs. 78* (F-197)

RAYMOND
- J. K. 22 (m)* (JE-52)

RAYNTS?
- W. R. 3 (m)* (F-149)

READ
- A. O. 42 (m) (F-169)
- Ellen 68* (F-183)
- James 8* (F-217)
- Peter 38?* (B) (F-170)
- R. W. 46 (f) (F-182)
- Thomas S. 42* (F-167)

READEN
- Margaret 18* (F-130)

READMAN
- Loyd 45 (F-157)

READY
- Theresa 35 (GD-275)

REAGAN
- Elizabeth 49* (MA-309)

REARD
- William 55 (OS-304)

REBELIN
- William 59 (MT-20)

RECMAN
- Thomas W. 36 (MT-58)

RECTOR
- Eli 31 (OS-297)
- Phillip 26 (OS-298)
- Thomas 23* (OS-297)

REDD
- Saml. 71* (F-222)

REDMAN
- Garret 21* (MT-78)
- John W. 50* (CL-76)
- Lloyd 24* (JE-44)
- Robert 55 (CL-85)
- Sarah 11* (JE-70)
- Squire P. 34* (MT-22)
- William F. 51 (MT-83)

REDMON
- William 24 (CL-85)

REDVINE?
- William 22 (OS-307)

REECE
- Ann 25* (F-128)
- Sarah 44 (F-126)
- Sidney 17 (f)* (F-142)
- Susanna 61* (CL-26)

REED
- A. J. 33 (m)* (F-125)
- Anda 41 (m) (GD-280)
- Arustus 35 (MT-33)
- Barbara 70 (GD-252)
- Caroline 5* (B) (MT-40)
- Daniel 60 (MT-46)
- Elizabeth 55 (GD-284)
- George 67 (CL-15)
- Henry P. 40 (MT-27)
- James 27 (ES-56)
- James 70* (F-158)
- James M. 37 (GD-284)
- James R. 3* (JE-41)
- John 26 (JE-41)
- John 33* (MA-263)
- John 54* (MA-296)
- John 65* (MA-263)
- John J. 33 (MA-281)
- John W. 27 (JE-55)
- Joseph 71 (MT-8)

Index

REED
Lucy 46 (F-214)
Margaret 54 (B) (MA-263)
Martha L. 56* (CL-35)
Mary 51* (F-196)
Mary B. 45* (F-123)
Nathan 26 (ES-53)
Newton 50 (MT-32)
Paul W. 32* (MT-10)
Rebecca 60* (F-129)
Sarah C. 12* (CL-19)
Sophia 28 (B) (MT-3)
Thomas 30* (CL-49)
Thomas 44 (ES-54)
Thomas 52 (ES-51)
W. L. 32 (m) (F-125)
William 28 (ES-53)
William 34 (CL-76)
William 62 (ES-53)
REESE
David* (OS-278)
Granville 22* (GD-230)
John 28 (OS-284)
Joseph 23 (OS-297)
Lavinia 33 (F-214)
Marion 24 (m) (OS-303)
Mary 34* (MA-320)
William 24* (OS-295)
William 39* (CL-28)
REEVES
James 35 (MA-296)
Jefferson 37 (MA-261)
John 50 (MA-293)
Stephen 40 (MA-258)
Willia S. 44 (MA-200)
REFFETT
Levi 27 (MT-65)
REFFIT
Derret 34 (m) (MT-74)
James 66 (MT-76)
REFFITT
James jr. 25 (MT-75)
REID
James 30* (F-152)
Susan G. 15* (MA-248)
REILBERT
James? 36 (MA-313)

REILEY
Chas. M. 25* (F-206)
REMBLE
David 34* (GD-246)
REMINGTON
B. F. 19 (m)* (F-129)
RENFRO
James 35 (GD-239)
John 27 (GD-241)
Wilson 12* (B) (GD-265)
RENFROE
Isaac 35 (GD-279)
James W. 27 (MA-211)
John 48 (MA-312)
Joseph 70 (MA-211)
Lydia 45 (GD-281)
Peter 62 (MA-312)
Thomas 35 (GD-282)
Thomas J. 40 (MA-227)
RENNOCK
Abram 47 (CL-89)
RETHERFORD
Jesse 77* (F-249)
W. 19 (m)* (F-153)
REYNOLDS
Barney 51 (GD-212)
Catharine 69* (JE-24)
Elizabeth 50* (JE-15)
George T. 33 (MA-318)
H. H. 54 (m)* (MT-46)
Henry 31 (GD-224)
Henry 31 (MT-45)
Henry 50 (JE-25)
Henry 76 (JE-25)
Isom 32* (CL-74)
James 19* (MT-32)
James W. 29 (MA-271)
Jeremiah? 25 (F-135)
John 25* (OS-307)
John 43 (JE-24)
John M. 43 (JE-16)
John W. 37 (JE-28)
John W. 56* (ES-108)
Joseph 24* (OS-296)
Joseph 27 (JE-77)
Joseph 32 (JE-27)
Levi 31 (GD-225)
Levi 53 (MA-319)

Lewis 28 (ES-95)
Lucy 40* (CL-12)
Margaret 86* (JE-47)
Mary W. 48* (JE-73)
Moses 36 (OS-284)
Moses 41 (JE-25)
Moses 66* (GD-214)
Nancy 30* (MT-27)
Nancy 59* (JE-29)
O. P. 34 (m) (GD-261)
Oliver 42 (GD-273)
Plesant 59* (OS-283)
Richard 30 (OS-277)
Richard sr. 48 (OS-278)
Russell 30* (F-205)
Susan 40 (JE-44)
Thomas 38* (MA-319)
Thomas 41* (JE-24)
Tobias 57* (ES-48)
Tom 70* (B) (JE-38)
Wesley 34 (OS-284)
William 24* (OS-295)
William 29 (ES-103)
William 37 (JE-25)
William 48 (JE-24)
William 48 (MT-20)
Williamson 30 (ES-60)
RHIRNENS?
Gilla 16* (JE-27)
RHODES
Elizabeth 30* (F-115)
Isaac 43 (ES-62)
James W. 30 (MA-221)
RHODUS
Abner 23 (MA-259)
Burrel 35 (MA-260)
Douglas 24* (MA-257)
Joseph 69 (MA-259)
William 39 (MA-228)
RHOMBURG
John 18* (CL-57)
RIAL
John 27* (JE-59)
RICE
Abraham 53* (F-183)
Benja. C. 26 (CL-56)
Catharine 66 (CL-38)
Charles 18* (JE-5)

Index

RICE
  Clarke 45* (CL-59)
  Daniel 48* (JE-51)
  Elizabeth 64* (JE-61)
  Elizabeth 76* (JE-58)
  Emeline 38* (F-205)
  Fountain 34 (MA-255)
  Frances 44 (ES-95)
  Isaac 50 (JE-58)
  Isaac J. 35 (ES-70)
  Jacob 60 (GD-246)
  James 62 (MA-201)
  James H. 37 (CL-38)
  James L. 36* (F-150)
  Jasper D. 64 (JE-61)
  John 39 (F-178)
  John C. 40 (CL-60)
  Labina 70* (F-123)
  Lewis C. 30* (F-197)
  Margaret 24* (MA-283)
  Martin 28 (F-183)
  Michael 28* (JE-58)
  Nancy 8* (CL-38)
  Sarah 17* (F-225)
  Soloman 43 (F-190)
  Thomas 30* (MA-251)
  Thomas 30* (MA-283)
RICE?
  Ta? A. 48 (f)* (F-122)
RICHARDS
  Bartlett 30* (CL-10)
  C. N. 13 (f)* (F-138)
  Edwin 26* (F-129)
  M. H. 7 (f)* (F-139)
  Sarah 56* (MT-60)
RICHARDSON
  Aaron 30 (ES-93)
  Absolom 28 (ES-83)
  Ann 50 (F-154)
  Benjamin 37 (ES-90)
  Bradley 24 (ES-100)
  Bradley 68 (ES-100)
  Conrad 21 (ES-85)
  Dudley 28 (ES-67)
  Dudley P. 26 (ES-72)
  Edward 25* (JE-78)
  Elcanah 32 (ES-76)
  Elenor 17* (F-114)
  Eliza 14* (MT-71)
  Elliot 30 (MA-254)
  George P. 52 (F-219)
  Henry 32 (ES-86)
  Isaac 23 (F-132)
  James 13* (OS-285)
  James 27* (MA-242)
  James 30 (ES-92)
  James 30* (MT-84)
  James 34 (ES-86)
  James 40 (ES-84)
  Jesse 14* (MT-63)
  Jesse 39 (ES-84)
  John 21* (JE-44)
  John 22* (CL-55)
  John 22 (ES-73)
  John 32 (ES-100)
  John 38 (CL-71)
  John 42* (MT-70)
  John 58 (ES-98)
  John C. 66 (F-222)
  John H. 34 (ES-96)
  John H. 40 (F-228)
  Joseph 31 (GD-233)
  Joseph 39 (ES-99)
  Kesiah 56 (ES-82)
  L.? M. 38 (f) (F-203)
  Levi 22 (ES-74)
  Luraney 4 (f)* (GD-232)
  Marcus 82* (MT-21)
  Margaret 50* (F-121)
  Moses 50 (JE-41)
  Nancy 17* (CL-36)
  Peyton 58* (CL-60)
  Robert 50* (CL-59)
  Ryon 50 (ES-111)
  Sally 26 (ES-90)
  Sam Q. 34 (F-243)
  Solomon 34 (CL-34)
  Thomas 24 (F-228)
  Thomas 25* (MA-236)
  Thomas 52* (JE-55)
  Thomas 59 (MA-253)
  W. H. 56 (m) (F-159)
  Will jr. 38 (GD-268)
  Will sr. 62 (GD-268)
  William 26 (JE-48)
  William 34 (ES-93)
  William 35 (ES-109)
  William 65 (ES-109)
  Woodson P. 33 (ES-102)
  Zachary 22 (ES-100)
RICHERSON
  Bailey 68 (JE-35)
  James 26* (JE-11)
  James 28* (JE-2)
  James 32 (JE-35)
  Moses 17* (JE-30)
  Moses 20* (JE-16)
RICHIE
  William 55 (CL-31)
RICKET
  Thomas J. 12* (CL-35)
RICKETTS
  H.? 50 (m)* (MT-82)
RICKITS
  Martha 90* (JE-11)
RIDDELL
  Adam 47 (ES-109)
  John H. 42 (ES-87)
  Nancy 70* (F-181)
  Robert 36 (ES-109)
  Sally 42 (ES-109)
  Sally 88* (ES-50)
RIDDLE
  Isaac 62 (B) (JE-72)
RIDEN
  Nancy 61* (CL-5)
RIDGELY
  Jane B. 55 (JE-75)
RIDGEWAY
  Mary 22* (CL-88)
RIFFE
  John M. 27 (CL-44)
RIGGING
  Mary 29 (MT-4)
RIGGOLD
  Maria 37* (B) (F-211)
RIGGS
  Greenberry 52 (MT-27)
  John D. 46* (MT-27)
RIGSBY
  Betsey 70* (CL-10)
  David 26* (GD-270)
  Lucy 43 (GD-268)
  Will 27 (GD-270)

Index

RIGSBY
 Will 69* (GD-269)
RIKER
 Ann 40* (F-194)
RILEY
 Elizabeth 57* (JE-72)
 Emaline 28 (ES-91)
 George S. 43 (MA-259)
 James 30 (OS-320)
 John 49* (MT-35)
 Lidia 46* (F-196)
 William 40 (MA-302)
 William 64 (MA-302)
 William J. 36 (JE-71)
RILLY
 Rachael 20* (OS-306)
RILSY?
 Jackson 29 (MA-207)
RINDER
 Reuben 32* (GD-244)
RINGO
 Elizabeth 86 (MA-267)
 Philip 43 (CL-59)
 Solomon 32 (MT-70)
 Zerilda 14* (MT-75)
RIORDAN
 William 39* (F-130)
RIPPEY
 Gelkerson 32 (CL-49)
 Sarah 67 (CL-30)
RISEN
 Clorah 10* (CL-31)
 James 33 (CL-32)
RISK
 Cynthia 34 (CL-74)
 Joseph 52 (CL-75)
 Margaret 40* (MT-8)
 William 76* (CL-74)
RISPOON
 Robert 32 (GD-257)
RITCHEY
 Saml. 73 (F-170)
RITCHIE
 Samuel 37* (CL-81)
RITTER
 John 34* (JE-51)
 Valentine 29* (F-182)

RIVERS?
 Jeremiah 50 (MA-297)
RIX
 George J. 61* (MA-250)
RIYM?
 William 42 (ES-71)
ROACH
 David 27* (F-235)
 F. 52 (m) (F-157)
 James 35 (MA-305)
 Sally 45 (OS-309)
 Squire 26 (MA-211)
 Thomas 25* (OS-313)
 William 37 (MA-325)
ROBARDS
 James 58 (B) (JE-57)
 Otho 66* (JE-57)
 William O. 20* (JE-75)
ROBARDSON
 William 23 (MA-262)
ROBB
 Ellen 74 (F-219)
 J. H. __ (m)* (F-138)
 John 56 (JE-53)
 Joseph 28 (F-175)
 Joseph 44 (JE-36)
ROBBINS
 Haman 49 (MT-64)
 John 30 (B) (F-203)
 John L. 34 (JE-69)
 W. H. 40 (m) (F-200)
ROBENSON
 Peyton 21* (CL-1)
ROBERDS?
 L. C. 32 (m)* (F-184)
ROBERSON
 Butler 43* (MA-280)
 Elizabeth 50 (MA-243)
 Emily 48 (CL-18)
 Jane 11* (OS-310)
 John 21* (MA-237)
 Mary J. 12* (MA-215)
 Robert 30* (MA-203)
ROBERT
 Jane V. 60* (F-147)
ROBERTS
 Absolum 28 (MA-323)
 Agness A. 30* (F-177)

 Allen 34 (OS-312)
 Amanda 19* (F-173)
 B. F. 29 (m) (F-175)
 Charles T. 26* (JE-23)
 Coler 42 (m) (MA-233)
 D. 43 (m)* (F-127)
 Daniel 30 (MA-307)
 Edward 32* (MT-23)
 Elihu 40 (MA-309)
 Elisha 39* (MA-251)
 Emma 13* (F-114)
 Francis 47 (MA-304)
 Frank 80* (B) (F-234)
 George 42 (ES-95)
 George 66* (CL-36)
 H. S. 14 (m)* (F-122)
 Jackson 35* (MA-221)
 James 23* (JE-16)
 James 25 (GD-258)
 James 33 (MA-216)
 James 35 (MA-311)
 James 49* (OS-287)
 James M. 34 (MA-231)
 James Y. 32* (MT-14)
 Jane 12* (MA-250)
 Jane 65 (F-143)
 Jefferson 43* (GD-219)
 Joel 36 (MA-311)
 John 23 (ES-59)
 John 38 (MT-38)
 John 49 (JE-24)
 Joseph 22* (OS-294)
 Lucindia 16* (OS-289)
 Lucy 49* (JE-47)
 Mar 58 (MA-304)
 Margaret 10* (B) (JE-68)
 Mary 36* (JE-46)
 Mary A. 4* (B) (JE-63)
 Merrel 28 (MA-305)
 Nathan 38 (MA-209)
 Nathaniel 50 (GD-283)
 Rankin 52 (JE-32)
 Samuel 18* (JE-30)
 Sarah 80* (B) (JE-38)
 Shadrich 53 (MA-298)
 Sidney 16 ()* (F-139)
 Talton 28* (MA-206)
 Thomas 23 (JE-21)

Index

ROBERTS
  Thos. 27* (F-195)
  Wiley? 20 (MA-240)
  William 28 (MT-42)
  William 36 (OS-296)
  William 50 (MA-309)
  Willis 41 (MT-12)
  Woodford 38* (MT-38)
ROBERTSON
  Emma 3* (MT-13)
  Geo. 59* (F-210)
  George 21* (JE-26)
  James 11* (MT-75)
  Jno. E. 47* (F-203)
  John 15* (MT-73)
  John 24* (OS-302)
  Mary E. 2* (CL-76)
  Solomon 33 (F-231)
  William 77* (CL-37)
ROBES
  William 56* (MA-276)
ROBINS
  James 33* (F-151)
ROBINSON
  Allen 30 (JE-2)
  Arrin 42 (CL-36)
  Benj. F. 24 (GD-208)
  Benjamin 45* (MT-21)
  Benjamine 34 (JE-4)
  Calvin C. 40* (CL-37)
  Catharine 26* (OS-313)
  Cordilia 22* (B) (F-192)
  David 50 (OS-315)
  DeWit C. 11* (JE-64)
  Eliza 22?* (F-241)
  F. 28 (m)* (B) (F-193)
  George 56 (GD-233)
  Henry 14* (F-121)
  Hugh L. 37 (ES-97)
  Isaac 39 (B) (F-138)
  Isom? 47* (JE-47)
  Jacob 52 (GD-247)
  James S.? 40* (JE-2)
  Jefferson S. 43 (MT-32)
  Jeremiah T. 26* (JE-2)
  Joab 70* (CL-91)
  John 69* (CL-35)
  John 70* (JE-2)
  John 71 (F-238)
  John F. 68* (ES-109)
  Jonas 32 (CL-89)
  Laura 11* (MT-9)
  Martha 57* (F-209)
  Michael 44 (GD-205)
  Milly 65* (B) (F-233)
  Moses 60 (B) (CL-94)
  Priscilla 42* (F-216)
  Priscilla 45* (F-138)
  Richard M. 33 (GD-208)
  Roger 60 (F-231)
  S. J. 42 (m) (OS-318)
  Sarah 50* (MA-290)
  Thomas 70* (CL-50)
  Thomas A. 25* (CL-82)
  Thos. 35 (F-247)
  Will B. 35 (GD-237)
  William 22* (F-203)
  William 32 (GD-232)
  William G. 28* (JE-3)
RODES
  Mary W. 38* (F-222)
  Waller 50 (F-148)
  William 58 (F-238)
RODGERS
  Eliza 12* (MT-2)
  George M. 31 (MT-46)
  Granville S. 28 (MT-31)
  Horace 61 (MT-29)
  James T. 42* (MT-31)
  John 67 (MT-34)
  Joseph 25 (GD-281)
RODINE
  Mary 70* (GD-251)
ROGERS
  Adam 64 (MA-269)
  Berry 29 (ES-48)
  C. C. 31 (m) (F-189)
  C. F. 36 (m) (F-234)
  C. W. 43 (f) (F-139)
  Chas. 55* (F-196)
  Clifton R. 33* (F-233)
  David E. 1* (F-232)
  Dorithy 53* (F-114)
  Edward 75* (B) (F-116)
  Frances H. 65* (F-242)
  Isaac 24 (ES-54)
  J. 21 (m)* (F-204)
  Jacob 46* (F-196)
  James 25 (ES-51)
  James 35* (CL-5)
  Jas. 33* (F-196)
  John 36 (ES-54)
  John D. 37* (F-196)
  Joseph 10* (F-234)
  Joseph 25* (MA-269)
  Joseph M. 10* (F-133)
  Julius 49 (ES-81)
  Lazarus M. 41 (F-117)
  Madison 24* (F-174)
  Milly 51 (ES-54)
  Nathaniel 30 (MA-314)
  Nelson 30 (ES-53)
  Rachel 75* (CL-8)
  Robert C. 41 (CL-6)
  Samuel 31 (MA-215)
  Thomas H. 62* (F-211)
  William 53 (ES-95)
  _____ 52 (m)* (F-197)
ROGURS
  Ellen 24 (MA-289)
ROHRER
  Jacob 54 (JE-43)
  Jonas 43* (JE-57)
  Samuel 51 (JE-46)
ROLAND
  P. B. 26 (m) (GD-235)
ROLLINS
  Moses 23* (MA-224)
  Will W. 28* (GD-283)
ROLSTIN
  John 19* (MA-222)
ROMANS
  Will jr. 36 (GD-260)
  William sr. 65* (GD-248)
RONALDS
  Margaret 55* (F-194)
RONAN
  James 50 (ES-90)
ROSE
  A. J. 28 (m) (JE-66)
  Edward 33 (ES-92)
  Ezekiel 50* (MT-19)
  George W. 32 (GD-276)
  Isreal 50 (MA-241)

Index

ROSE
J. W. 31 (m) (F-155)
James B. 32 (OS-277)
John 22 (OS-300)
John 27 (MA-241)
John 31 (ES-73)
John 45* (MT-84)
Josiah C. 35* (MT-51)
Nathaniel 36 (ES-86)
Powell 48 (MT-51)
Robert jr. 26* (OS-302)
Robert sr. 70* (OS-300)
Samuel 59* (MA-241)
Thomas 52 (JE-58)
William 23 (MA-240)
William 29 (ES-91)
ROSELL
F. 50 (m) (F-156)
ROSETY
Jane 85* (F-206)
ROSS
Alexander 56* (MA-314)
Danl. 30 (F-134)
David 41 (GD-276)
David R. 40* (MA-314)
Emily 18* (B) (OS-305)
Filmore 42 (MA-315)
Gabriel 65 (MA-289)
George 30* (B) (OS-300)
George 7* (MT-11)
George M. 40* (MA-222)
George N. 53 (f) (F-148)
Herod 43 (B) (OS-309)
James 24 (GD-214)
Jane 15* (MT-60)
John W. 17* (F-220)
Joseph 8* (MT-62)
Julian 38 (B) (F-139)
Levi 34 (B)* (OS-301)
Liberty 30* (B) (F-208)
Lucy 52 (F-209)
Morris 35* (MA-289)
Nicholas 28 (MA-314)
Riceton 31 (MA-314)
Sanford 15* (B) (OS-303)
Stephen 33* (MA-289)
Stortling? 12* (B) (F-135)
Susan 66 (MA-222)

Thomas K. 50 (GD-271)
Wm. 74* (F-183)
ROSSEL
Anthony 45 (MA-208)
James 26 (MA-208)
ROSSELL
Fielding 14* (F-227)
ROSSER
William 40 (GD-215)
ROTHWELL
Fountain 51 (GD-254)
Thomas 36 (GD-282)
Will 42 (GD-271)
ROUT
Benjamin 50 (CL-25)
Daniel 82 (CL-26)
Robert L. 30 (GD-231)
ROUTE
Walker 7* (F-224)
ROW
William 74 (GD-225)
ROWARK
Carter 26 (OS-311)
ROWELL
S. B. 39 (m)* (JE-47)
ROWLAND
Christopher 45 (JE-78)
David J. 47* (MA-250)
Henry 46* (JE-48)
James 52 (MA-208)
Jemima 65 (JE-43)
Jeremiah 48* (JE-39)
John 42 (JE-43)
Melissa 40* (MT-66)
Robert G. 39* (JE-54)
Thomas 13* (MA-286)
Thomas 45* (JE-43)
ROWZES
Samuel 41* (CL-94)
ROY
John 24 (CL-89)
Sarah 35* (CL-9)
ROYSTN
Thomas 60* (MA-264)
ROYSTON
Ann 40 (GD-258)
John W. 30 (F-210)
Lytle 55 (GD-278)

Willia 27 (GD-234)
RUBER?
Stanley 36 (CL-18)
RUBITHON
W. 31 (m)* (F-147)
RUBLES
George 60 (ES-71)
Henry 28 (JE-45)
John 26* (ES-71)
William 28 (ES-95)
RUCKELL
Henry 52* (F-129)
RUCKER
Ben 47* (F-195)
Gideon 24* (JE-30)
John 39* (CL-38)
Minty 61* (JE-53)
Nancy 68* (F-203)
Reuben 46 (CL-53)
William 20* (CL-32)
Willis A. 50* (F-195)
RUE
Joseph 36 (JE-27)
Juliann 25* (JE-33)
William 40 (JE-27)
RUFFMAN
Benj. 22* (F-187)
RUFFNER
Samuel 54 (JE-40)
RUGG
Orwell 24* (F-206)
RUMSEY
Martha 54* (F-163)
RUNALDS
Vincent 41* (F-197)
RUNNELS
George 15* (GD-243)
RUNNELS?
Thomas 83* (MA-318)
RUNSDALL
W. R. 24 (m)* (F-149)
RUNYON
Abslum 67 (MA-263)
Asa G. 46 (GD-223)
Benja. 28* (MT-6)
John 26 (MT-2)
Mary 21* (MA-241)
Matilda 47* (MA-285)

Index

RUNYON
 Richard 31* (MA-251)
 S. A. 7 (f)* (F-167)
RUPARD
 Daniel 28* (CL-81)
 Eveline 36 (CL-81)
 Joseph 58 (CL-51)
 Samuel 45 (CL-75)
 Willis 44 (CL-75)
RUPELL
 Samuel 22* (CL-15)
RUPEND
 William 25 (CL-74)
RUPERD
 Louisa 15* (MT-7)
RUPURD
 William 56 (CL-74)
RURDEN?
 Patrick 26* (F-205)
RUSK
 W. J. 22 (m)* (F-169)
RUSSEL
 S. L. 40 (f) (F-192)
 richard 45 (MA-203)
RUSSELL
 Chilton 47* (MT-82)
 Ephariam 23 (GD-287)
 Hezekiah 60* (JE-72)
 J. C. 14 (m)* (F-123)
 James 18* (MT-3)
 Joseph 60 (MT-21)
 William H. 28 (ES-51)
RUST
 Jacob 20* (MA-251)
 Lewis P. 35* (F-195)
RUTER?
 P. J. 33 (m) (F-144)
RUTHERFORD
 Clayborn 37 (JE-1)
 James 57 (JE-1)
 Joseph 28 (JE-1)
 Zerilda 28* (F-116)
RUTLEDGE
 Catharine 38 (CL-19)
 James 40* (CL-21)
 John P. 26* (CL-30)
 Nancy 5* (CL-28)
 Thomas 23* (CL-25)

RUTLEY
 Phillip 77* (JE-20)
RUTNER
 William 50 (MA-304)
RUTOFF
 John 65 (F-133)
RYAL
 Frances 30* (F-154)
RYAN
 E. 18 (f)* (F-126)
 Elisha 42* (CL-19)
 George W. 13* (F-115)
 Isabella 18* (GD-212)
 Jeremiah 22* (F-205)
 John B. 51* (CL-18)
 Philip A. 76 (MT-24)
 Sarah S. 28* (F-136)
 T. P. 32 (m) (MA-229)
RYANT
 Will 22* (GD-265)
RYLAND
 Edwin 12* (JE-5)
RYMAN
 Robt. 51 (F-193)
RYMERS
 John 46 (MT-57)
RYMUS?
 Sarah 50* (B) (MT-71)
RYNE
 Michael 23* (MT-35)
RYNER
 Jane 45* (F-216)
RYON
 Polly 56* (CL-11)
SABASTIAN
 Saml. 21* (F-157)
SACREY
 John? 49 (JE-31)
SADDLER
 John R. 29 (MT-83)
SADE
 James 23* (MT-26)
SADLER
 Edmund 26 (GD-214)
 Mary 60* (GD-277)
 Reuben 31 (GD-228)
 asa 53* (GD-213)

SADORE
 Elizabeth 36* (JE-35)
SAFFOON
 Richard 45 (JE-5)
SAFFRON
 A. B. 40 (m)* (F-249)
SAGACY
 Daniel 60 (JE-35)
 Federick 74* (JE-21)
 Henry 46 (JE-21)
 Jacob 50 (JE-21)
 James 25 (JE-35)
 Jefferson 37* (JE-21)
SAILS
 Anderson 23* (ES-47)
 Samuel 61 (ES-51)
SALBEY
 Archibald 25 (OS-291)
 James 55 (OS-290)
 William 32 (OS-291)
SALE
 Ann 40* (JE-51)
 John 36* (JE-16)
SALLE
 Alvin? A. 49 (MA-288)
 James E. 20* (F-253)
 John 56 (MA-325)
 John F. 24 (MA-287)
 Stephen 39* (MA-287)
 Stephen 86 (MA-287)
SALLEE
 Eliz. 74 (JE-65)
 Henry M. 25 (JE-7)
 Jacob B. 52 (JE-62)
 William A. 40* (JE-63)
SALLER
 Daniel 53 (F-164)
 Geo. M. 25 (F-163)
 Jas. 50 (F-165)
 Joseph 48 (F-165)
SALLYERS
 Mary 52 (F-157)
 Mitcher 27 (F-157)
SALMONDS?
 Louisa 25* (F-136)
SALMONS
 Gilson 33 (CL-87)

Index

SALTER
 Elijah Hiatte 79* (GD-259)
 Gabrael Y. 41 (GD-259)
 Osa 68* (GD-264)
 Susan 35 (GD-234)
 Thomas R. 36 (GD-237)
SALYERS
 Robt. C. 36 (F-178)
 S. P. 30 (m)* (F-175)
SAMME?
 Lewis 33 (GD-219)
SAMMON
 James 26* (MT-35)
SAMMONS
 Aquilla 25* (CL-85)
 John 56 (GD-278)
SAMPSON
 James 36 (F-176)
SAMS
 David 22* (ES-74)
 Edward 32 (ES-62)
 Jesse 21* (GD-208)
 Lervy? 43 (m) (ES-93)
 Sally A. 31* (MA-259)
 Wilson 44 (ES-67)
SAMUEL
 Henry D. 53 (GD-276)
 Reuben sr. 85 (GD-276)
SAMUELS
 James M. 37* (MA-209)
 Sarah 19* (CL-41)
SANDERS
 Allen 14* (F-162)
 C. 60 (f)* (B) (F-125)
 Charles 22* (JE-15)
 Charles 22* (JE-76)
 Cobb J. 57 (F-191)
 David 46 (JE-14)
 Elijah 32 (GD-257)
 Giles 40* (GD-215)
 James 64 (GD-224)
 James M. 25 (GD-252)
 Mary 34 (JE-26)
 Osbern 40 (MA-311)
 S. B. 38 (m)* (JE-9)
 Sarah 39* (F-116)
 Sarah E. 2* (GD-251)
 Siras 28 (m) (GD-257)

Wm. 16* (F-165)
SANDIFER
 James 23* (GD-265)
 Nicholas 33 (GD-265)
SANDLES
 Hiram 50 (OS-311)
SANDLIN
 Ezekiel 34* (OS-278)
 James 52 (OS-282)
 Lewis 25 (OS-282)
SANDRUM
 Silas 25 (CL-62)
SANE
 George 33* (F-196)
SANFORD
 Frances 45* (F-149)
 Mary 46 (JE-68)
SAPPINGTON
 John 59* (MT-69)
SARTAIN
 George F. 24* (GD-266)
SARY
 William B. 11* (MT-6)
SATTERFIELD
 Wm. 30* (F-194)
SATTERWHITE
 Mary S. 17* (F-225)
SAUL
 Micha 44 (m)* (MT-15)
 Susan 64 (MT-15)
 Thomas 30* (MT-17)
 Willey J. 30* (MT-27)
SAUNDERS
 Alex 21* (F-194)
SAUSEY?
 Saml. 75?* (B) (F-130)
SAUTER
 Alexander 50* (MA-267)
SAVARY
 Henry 43* (CL-1)
SAWYERS
 Wiley 60* (B) (F-158)
SAXTON
 Henry A. 30* (F-115)
SAYRE
 A. 20 (f) (F-164)
 Andrew J. 30 (F-198)
 C. C. 19 (m) (F-252)

David A. 57 (F-184)
David T. 18* (F-204)
E. K. 40 (m) (F-215)
James 29* (F-164)
James 33* (F-154)
James 49 (F-164)
John 13* (F-211)
Lucy 50* (F-148)
SCANLAND
 Matilda 22* (JE-15)
SCARBO
 Harvey 42 (GD-279)
SCARBRO
 Jacob 24* (GD-260)
SCHENK
 John C. 39* (F-196)
SCHOEMAKER
 Anna 3* (F-140)
SCHOLL
 Daniel B. 31 (ES-59)
 Joseph 58 (CL-71)
 Peter D. 29 (ES-59)
 William 25 (CL-71)
SCHOOLCRAFT
 Michial 59* (OS-296)
SCHOOLER
 Benjamin 63 (GD-276)
 James 45 (GD-206)
 Lewis 39* (CL-5)
 William 30 (GD-227)
SCHOOLY
 Joseph 24 (F-126)
SCHROCK
 Mary D. 50* (F-246)
SCIDDER?
 William 55* (MA-285)
SCOBEE
 Catharine 66* (CL-87)
 James 29 (CL-72)
 Robert 33 (CL-86)
SCOBY
 Robert 24 (MT-28)
 William 47 (MT-25)
SCOFIELD
 Coleman 35* (F-194)
SCOOLEY
 James 58* (F-151)

Index

SCOTT
 Andrew 72* (F-236)
 Andrew T. 45 (F-236)
 Benjamin 22 (GD-208)
 David 43 (GD-206)
 David 43 (GD-236)
 Docia 1* (B) (F-144)
 Edward 48* (CL-66)
 Elijah 19* (JE-33)
 Eliza 15* (B) (MT-71)
 Elizabeth 21* (JE-32)
 Frances 16* (MT-4)
 Francis 43 (F-188)
 George 46 (JE-35)
 Green 26 (MT-17)
 Harvey 46 (JE-18)
 Isaac W. 35 (F-201)
 J. P. 32 (m) (F-210)
 James 39 (GD-286)
 James 46* (CL-78)
 Jenny 50* (GD-250)
 John 40 (MA-205)
 John 52 (GD-220)
 John 55 (MA-286)
 Jorden 48* (JE-18)
 Joseph 50 (GD-273)
 Joseph 52 (GD-208)
 Lucy C. 49* (F-213)
 M. T. 45? (m)* (F-141)
 Margaret 40* (F-232)
 Martin 25* (CL-92)
 Mary 64* (JE-45)
 Matilda 45* (F-115)
 McEbeny 25 (CL-71)
 Nancy 49* (F-196)
 Newton 40 (JE-47)
 R. 40 (m) (F-147)
 R. S. 33 (m)* (JE-46)
 Rachel 48 (GD-219)
 Richard 25* (JE-15)
 Robert 52 (CL-94)
 Robt. 70 (B) (F-157)
 Salley 39 (GD-283)
 Saml. 24* (F-124)
 Samuel 44 (GD-230)
 Susan 55 (MA-223)
 Telitha 44* (F-178)
 Thomas R. 9* (CL-25)

Thos. J. 49* (F-252)
Tillis 19 (B) (F-142)
Timothy 15* (B) (GD-265)
Will 26 (GD-283)
William 28* (GD-208)
William 46 (CL-82)
William 50 (MT-25)
William S. 42* (JE-74)
SCRIVNER
 Amelia 46 (ES-99)
 James 73 (ES-94)
 Jemima 13* (ES-94)
 John 68 (ES-99)
 John L. 37 (ES-97)
 Joseph 63 (ES-99)
 Joseph Q. 29 (ES-100)
 Joseph jr. 34 (ES-99)
 Morgan J. 35 (ES-98)
 Silas 35* (ES-67)
 William 31* (ES-99)
SCROGGIN
 Geo. 30* (B) (F-210)
 Jas. 34 (F-218)
SCROGGINS
 Louisa 35 (B) (F-218)
 Seana 25* (B) (F-206)
SCROGIN
 John A. 30* (JE-74)
SCRUGGS
 Ann 4* (CL-95)
 E. O.? 25 (m)* (CL-45)
SCRUGHAM
 Clabourn 47 (JE-11)
 Joseph 73 (F-220)
SCULLY
 James 39* (F-151)
SEA
 Almanza 22* (MT-50)
 Joseph M. 16* (JE-69)
 L. M. 28 (m)* (JE-68)
 Nimrod 42* (MT-49)
SEAL
 John K. 41* (OS-295)
 Joseph W. 32 (OS-286)
SEALS
 Dennis 66 (B) (F-206)
SEARCEY
 Anderson 49 (CL-11)

Bryant 40 (MA-254)
Charles 36 (MA-258)
Joseph 52 (MA-247)
SEARCY
 Francis 23? (MA-298)
 Nancy E. 10* (F-240)
 P. M. 45 (f) (F-243)
 Samuel 55* (MA-282)
SEARLES
 James 63* (F-146)
SEAWART
 Robert 28* (OS-304)
SEBASTIAN
 Alexander 30 (GD-257)
 Howard 28 (GD-257)
 Nelly 31 (OS-311)
 Washington 32 (GD-257)
 Wiley 23 (GD-256)
 William 40 (GD-257)
 Wylie sr. 58 (GD-247)
SECHREST?
 John 14* (F-211)
SECRET?
 Jacob 39* (F-166)
SECRIST
 Martha 68 (F-253)
SEDNER?
 W. 22 (m)* (F-149)
SEE
 John 25 (ES-77)
 Nancy 55 (CL-64)
SELBY
 Charles 40 (ES-78)
SELF
 Henry A. 27 (F-115)
 James 21* (F-154)
 Patsey 30* (F-254)
 William Jr. 24 (F-115)
SELLER
 Mary 37* (F-197)
SELLERS
 Nancy 50 (GD-239)
SERGACY
 Henry 34 (GD-265)
SESSIONS
 Susannah 37* (F-195)
SETTELS
 Josephene 12* (F-184)

Index

SETTLE
  Thomas J. 27 (JE-61)
SEWEL
  Sally Ann 30* (JE-21)
  Sarah 50 (JE-36)
  Sarah A. 30 (JE-36)
SEWELL
  George A. 38 (MT-10)
  James 53 (CL-67)
  John 28 (CL-74)
  Samuel 74* (CL-80)
  Sandford 37* (CL-27)
SHACKELFORD
  Edmund 48 (MA-250)
  James 38* (MA-251)
  T. M. 23 (m)* (CL-6)
  William 40 (B) (MA-204)
  Zachery 58* (MA-207)
SHACKIN
  M. 13 (f)* (F-131)
SHAMBLIN
  Ambrose 80* (B) (CL-12)
SHANK
  Greenbury 30* (CL-19)
SHANKLIN
  Ephraim 26* (JE-66)
  George S. 39 (JE-76)
  Jesse 28* (JE-78)
  John 25* (F-253)
  Sarah 60* (JE-57)
  William 66* (JE-76)
SHANKS
  Charles 50 (MA-209)
  David 38 (CL-21)
  James 34 (MA-300)
  Joseph A. 34 (CL-86)
SHAPARD
  John 30* (MA-251)
SHARER
  Albert 25 (OS-305)
SHARES
  William I? 51* (F-147)
SHARP
  Alexander 22 (JE-21)
  Allenton B. 31* (F-239)
  Benjamin 40 (CL-5)
  Benjamin jr. 25* (CL-5)
  Ezekiel 30* (JE-32)

Frances 61* (F-130)
James 35* (F-239)
K. P. 44 (m)* (F-126)
Louisa 14* (JE-45)
Martha 25 (OS-314)
Moses 62 (ES-79)
Nancy 54 (CL-7)
Robert M. 40* (F-114)
Stephen 28 (CL-19)
Temperance 64 (GD-258)
Thomas 48* (JE-27)
Tilman B. 41* (ES-78)
William 19* (F-122)
William A.L.B. 32 (ES-113)
William R. 29* (CL-22)
SHASTEEN
  Eliz. 93* (JE-63)
SHAW
  Alex 55* (F-192)
  Emma 37* (F-130)
  Hiram 41* (F-152)
  Nancy 18* (F-242)
SHAWLEY
  Allen 30* (OS-311)
  David 53* (MT-51)
  John B. 26 (MT-51)
  William 23 (OS-311)
SHAY
  Henry 25* (F-203)
  Murtey 22 (m)* (F-173)
  Patrick 35* (CL-89)
SHEARER
  Benjamin 37 (MA-295)
  James 50* (ES-50)
  Lammion? 29 (m) (MA-289)
  Martha 65* (GD-249)
  Martha 82 (MA-295)
  Michael 42* (MA-208)
  Nicholas 60 (MA-289)
  Perten 42 (m) (MA-294)
  S. B. 40 (m)* (CL-24)
  Samuel 50 (MA-295)
  William 26 (MA-289)
  Zackariah 24* (ES-77)
SHEARRER
  Thomas 44 (MA-272)
SHEDELL
  John J. 35 (F-137)

SHEELY
  Katharine H. 41* (JE-52)
SHEENY
  Eliz. 17* (F-199)
SHEFFER
  J. Howard 42* (F-231)
SHEFFIELD
  George 40 (OS-291)
SHELBY
  Edward 77 (B) (MA-206)
  Evan 26* (F-244)
  Isaac 35* (F-244)
  Isaac 55 (F-193)
  Isaac P. 28 (F-244)
  Jas. 40* (F-195)
  Joseph C. 19 (F-141)
  Thomas 63* (F-244)
  Thomas 70 (B) (F-225)
SHELLY
  Susan P. 20* (F-152)
SHELTON
  Frances 80* (MT-34)
SHELY
  Nancy 40* (JE-15)
SHEOPORD?
  William 37 (MA-205)
SHEPHARD
  J. N. 35 (m)* (F-138)
SHEPHERD
  Ansil D. 24* (ES-50)
  Azariah 24 (CL-74)
  James 38* (CL-36)
  John 26 (ES-48)
  Juretta 50* (F-207)
  Martin 22* (CL-24)
  Mary F. 13* (CL-47)
  Nancy 12* (ES-81)
  ____ 60 (m) (B) (JE-42)
SHEPPARD
  Ann 28* (F-136)
  David 26* (F-122)
  Genevieve 9* (F-207)
  M. A. 17 (f)* (F-134)
SHEPPHERD
  Aquilla 13* (ES-60)
SHERALL
  Charles 25 (F-136)

Index

SHERLEY
Elijah 39 (JE-6)
SHERMAN
Ann 16* (F-126)
Daniel 58 (ES-62)
SHERROW
Henry 26 (JE-36)
Isaac 53* (JE-21)
James 38* (JE-36)
Jefferson 23 (JE-21)
SHERROW?
NAncy A. 24* (GD-222)
SHEVAT?
John 40 (MA-296)
SHEVATTER
Jackson 26* (F-190)
SHICK
Peter 6* (F-210)
SHIDDELL
Susana 54* (F-125)
W. F. 27 (m) (F-168)
SHIELDS
Hugh 35 (JE-67)
James 69 (JE-50)
Mary A. 46 (F-139)
Thomas 37* (JE-56)
SHIFFLET
Fountain 50 (MA-233)
Thomas 41 (MA-233)
SHIFFLETT
Allen 35 (MA-256)
Dudley 35 (MA-267)
Hillery 26 (m) (MA-260)
Margaret 53* (MA-261)
Sidny 26 (m) (MA-246)
SHINDLEBOROUN
Tho. 17* (F-199)
SHINDLEBOUR?
Thomas 50 (F-132)
SHINFESTLE?
Peter 65* (ES-57)
SHINGLES
Jacob 60* (MA-210)
SHINGLETON
David 19* (F-186)
Thos. 90* (F-186)
SHIP
Mary E. 10* (MA-265)

SHIPMAN
John 37 (GD-237)
SHIPP
Dudley 62 (F-231)
SHIPTON
Green 40 (MA-281)
Jesse 75* (MA-281)
SHIRLEY
Magdaloney 51 (F-178)
SHIVEL?
Edwin 24* (F-124)
SHIVERS
Reubin 65* (MA-266)
SHIVERY
G. W. 57 (m) (F-224)
SHIVETT
Maria 18* (F-201)
SHOEMAKER
Andy 24* (OS-311)
Jacob 34 (OS-288)
James 40 (OS-293)
Marion 17 (m)* (MA-229)
Pheba? 60 (OS-310)
William 38 (OS-310)
SHOLL
James 34 (CL-76)
SHOMAN
Patric 30 (F-134)
SHOOMAN
F. 22 (m) (F-139)
SHORROW
William 24 (JE-20)
SHORT
James 22 (JE-29)
James M. 22 (JE-33)
Joel 45 (GD-235)
John 24* (OS-304)
John 58* (CL-6)
Nat 50 (B) (CL-90)
Susan 70* (GD-215)
Wm. 31 (F-205)
SHORTRIDGE
W. J. 27 (m) (F-154)
SHOUSE
Andrew 47 (MT-19)
Caroline 8* (MT-19)
Jacob 77 (MT-18)
M. M. 29 (m) (MT-80)

Obediah 19* (MT-59)
Robert 41 (CL-73)
William 43 (MT-8)
SHOUTS
William 33 (MT-59)
SHOVER
James 37* (F-183)
SHREVE
John M. 39 (JE-14)
SHREWSBERRY
Amelia 14* (F-154)
Penelope 21* (MA-321)
W. S. 23 (m)* (F-128)
SHREWSBERRY?
Cynthia 60* (F-138)
SHRITES
William P. 16* (CL-1)
SHROCK
John G. 28 (MT-80)
SHROPSHIER
N. J. 31 (m) (GD-270)
SHROPSHIRE
Asa 46 (GD-230)
SHRYOCK
John F. 87 (F-232)
S. 32 (m) (F-139)
SHUBART
John N. 28 (MT-73)
Lewis 57 (MT-54)
William C. 32 (MT-56)
SHUBERT
R. J. 23 (MT-78)
SHUCK
David 50* (ES-110)
Valentine 45* (F-185)
SHULER
Tabitha 27 (F-125)
SHULEY
H. J. 3 (f)* (F-124)
SHULTZ
Samuel 45 (CL-72)
SHUMAKE
Elizabeth 23* (F-132)
Mary 47 (F-117)
Thomas 28* (F-123)
SHUMATE
Champ 25* (GD-282)
Daniel 80 (GD-253)

Index

SHUMATE
  Mitchell jr. 23 (GD-253)
  Mitchell sr. 58 (GD-253)
SHUTER
  James 26* (MA-204)
  John 26 (MA-205)
SHUVLY
  Fred. 31* (F-195)
SHY
  James 58 (F-225)
  Saml. 38 (F-223)
SIBASTIAN
  L. 17 (m)* (F-149)
SIDENER
  J. H. 33 (m) (MT-14)
  John A. 35 (MT-33)
  Martin 68 (CL-90)
SIDNER
  Andrew 33 (F-185)
  Daniel 51 (F-186)
  G. P. 41 (m) (F-167)
  Jacob 62 (F-187)
  John 38 (F-133)
  Wm. 49 (F-187)
SIDNER?
  Sarah 32* (F-187)
SIKES
  Jane 50* (B) (F-116)
SILLMAN
  S. 32 (m) (F-127)
SIMMONS
  Benjamin 50 (JE-13)
  J. T. 50 (m) (JE-39)
  John 57 (MA-264)
  Josiah P. 42* (MA-202)
  Susan 25* (MA-264)
  William 33* (MA-278)
SIMMS
  Margaret 3* (F-183)
  Nathaniel 74* (MA-221)
  Sarah 14* (F-225)
  Solomon 21* (F-159)
SIMONS
  Mary 28* (OS-313)
SIMPKINS
  Robert 66 (MT-55)
SIMPSON
  Aly 57 (f) (GD-277)
  Anna 29* (B) (F-192)
  Benjamin 26* (JE-77)
  Benjamin 39 (MA-262)
  Charles 48 (GD-234)
  Delila 49 (B) (GD-288)
  Delpha 50* (B) (CL-42)
  Edward 32 (CL-20)
  Eleanor 41 (CL-7)
  Elijah 40 (GD-235)
  Gabriel 40* (CL-23)
  George 38 (GD-216)
  George 69* (F-199)
  George jr. 28 (GD-223)
  Gilbert 56 (F-193)
  James 53* (CL-45)
  John 29 (F-123)
  John 36 (OS-318)
  Josph 26 (GD-236)
  Martha 3/12* (GD-223)
  Mary 16* (F-225)
  Mary 32* (GD-244)
  Richard B. 66* (MA-262)
  Robert 46 (F-248)
  Saml. 35 (F-187)
  Samuel 60 (JE-8)
  Thos. 31* (F-179)
  Will 31 (GD-275)
  William 53 (JE-76)
  Willis 26 (GD-235)
SIMRALL
  John G. 40 (F-182)
SIMS
  Edna 28 (GD-280)
  Elvira 70 (GD-273)
  James 23* (MA-224)
  James 41 (GD-273)
  John G. 39 (JE-62)
  Levina 35 (GD-274)
  William 50 (MA-215)
SINCLAIR
  Amanda 12* (JE-11)
  Eliza 7* (JE-17)
  William 31* (F-119)
SINGER
  Ephraim 45 (GD-257)
SINGLETON
  Agatha 63 (B) (JE-75)
  C. 7 (f)* (F-143)
  E. S. 19 (m)* (F-163)
  Elijah 54* (JE-66)
  James 19* (F-227)
  James 34 (GD-281)
  Mason 44* (JE-68)
  Merret 34 (MA-281)
  S. E. 15 (f)* (JE-64)
SINNIS
  William 54 (MA-305)
SIOMAY?
  Mary J. 8* (F-124)
SISSEN
  Lucy 73 (B) (F-208)
SISSON
  Charles 35 (JE-68)
SIZEMORE
  Anderson 24 (OS-303)
  Smith 36 (OS-281)
SKERRY
  John 26* (MT-35)
SKILLMAN
  A. T. 60 (m)* (F-141)
  Elizabeth 64* (F-221)
  Thomas _. 29 (MT-21)
SKILMAN
  W. G. 51 (m)* (F-168)
SKINKER
  Marshall 45 (B) (F-234)
SKINNER
  Alfred 41* (CL-52)
  Cato 40 (B) (CL-44)
  Clark 56 (GD-279)
  Elizabeth 60* (ES-110)
  Henry 54 (CL-67)
  Joseph 88* (ES-66)
  Joseph D. 19* (F-144)
  Mary Ann 17* (ES-56)
  Midad? 45 (m) (MA-235)
  Thomas 18* (F-231)
  William 22 (ES-49)
  William 58* (ES-65)
  Willis 43* (CL-68)
SKINNERS
  Isaac C. 45 (CL-85)
SLAUGHTER
  Charles 55 (B) (F-237)
  Edward 50* (JE-35)
  James L. 27* (OS-295)

Index

SLAUGHTER
  John 21 (JE-35)
  Thomas 26* (B) (F-237)
  William 40 (B) (F-220)
SLAVINE
  James G. 49 (GD-258)
  John 94 (GD-258)
SLOAN
  J. R. 31 (m)* (F-145)
SLUTHER
  M. 30 (m)* (F-124)
SMALLWOOD
  Abraham 32 (F-240)
  James 41 (OS-287)
  Randolph 70 (OS-309)
  William 34 (OS-305)
SMAWLEY?
  Josh__d 39 (m)* (MT-18)
SMEADLEY
  Mary 62* (F-147)
SMEDLEY
  Morgan 53 (F-160)
SMEDLY
  Biddy 43* (F-196)
SMEE
  James 25 (F-174)
SMILEY
  John __ (CL-33)
  Marce 50 (GD-206)
SMITH
  Aaron 22* (JE-75)
  Alexaner 39 (OS-280)
  Alice 6* (JE-60)
  Andrew 33 (JE-5)
  Andrew 53* (JE-49)
  Asa 30 (OS-287)
  Asa 46 (MA-232)
  Auston 72* (GD-277)
  B. Franklin 22* (JE-40)
  Benagy 35 (m) (MA-224)
  Benj. 36 (F-187)
  Benjamin 59 (MA-320)
  Benjamin 80* (F-118)
  Beverly 27 (m) (B) (F-220)
  Brady 40 (GD-207)
  Charles 28 (OS-318)
  Charles F. 37 (JE-49)
  Charles H. 39 (MT-4)
  Charles R. 16* (F-202)
  Chas. M. 37 (F-188)
  Clem 24 (JE-39)
  D. 45 (m) (JE-41)
  D. K. 23 (m) (MA-238)
  Daniel 35* (MT-12)
  Daniel 47* (CL-2)
  Daniel 50 (B) (CL-69)
  David 49* (JE-49)
  David F. 28 (GD-262)
  E. R. 33 (m)* (F-185)
  Edmond 71 (GD-262)
  Eleander 46 (f)* (MA-297)
  Eleazer 39 (F-218)
  Eli O. 40* (F-174)
  Elias 21 (OS-284)
  Elijah H. 31* (MT-18)
  Elira A. 24* (JE-10)
  Elisha 25 (MA-269)
  Elizabeth 39 (ES-68)
  Elizabeth 69 (GD-209)
  Elizabeth 77 (CL-33)
  Enoch 54 (MT-14)
  Fleetwood 48* (F-251)
  Francis 53 (CL-33)
  Frank 34 (OS-303)
  G. A. 40 (m)* (F-151)
  G. P. 50 (m) (JE-62)
  Geo. W. 40 (F-152)
  George 47* (CL-42)
  George R. 31 (GD-231)
  George W. 38 (GD-265)
  Grandison 20* (F-165)
  Granville 43* (F-225)
  Green Berry 88 (F-245)
  Hannah 33 (JE-5)
  Harold F. 46 (GD-219)
  Harriet 53 (MT-13)
  Harvey 36 (F-207)
  Henry 41* (MT-26)
  Henry 46 (MT-67)
  Hiram 36 (GD-210)
  Isaac 38 (B) (CL-87)
  Isaac D. 30* (MA-251)
  J. B. 25 (m)* (F-129)
  J. B. 44 (m)* (F-176)
  J. Y. 40 (m)* (F-153)
  Jacob 58 (MA-279)
  James 13* (GD-253)
  James 17* (OS-296)
  James 19 (MA-269)
  James 21* (MT-70)
  James 37 (MT-61)
  James 46 (MA-254)
  James 59 (MA-287)
  James H. 44 (JE-73)
  James J. 30* (GD-288)
  James M. 44 (F-191)
  James sr. 64 (JE-69)
  Jas. 4* (F-160)
  Jasper 70* (F-254)
  Jessee R. 57 (MA-269)
  John 30* (F-194)
  John 34* (CL-94)
  John 38* (MA-254)
  John 38* (OS-303)
  John 41* (F-216)
  John 48 (MT-23)
  John 6* (MA-277)
  John 60* (CL-94)
  John 65 (MT-5)
  John 73 (GD-210)
  John 77 (MA-299)
  John A. 54 (MT-19)
  John B. 33 (MA-205)
  John L. 29 (GD-209)
  John Lynn? 57 (MA-200)
  John M. 42* (MT-14)
  John R. 30* (MA-279)
  John R. 40 (F-210)
  John T. 44* (F-170)
  Josa? 12 (m)* (OS-306)
  Joseph 23* (OS-284)
  Joseph 30* (MT-77)
  Joseph 55 (MT-83)
  Joseph 74* (MT-47)
  Joseph S. 20 (CL-11)
  Joseph? 60* (B) (CL-1)
  Joshua 38 (F-126)
  L. B. 63 (m) (F-146)
  Lorenzo? 36* (GD-265)
  Louisa 49* (F-220)
  Lucy 70* (F-185)
  Margaret 26* (F-209)
  Mark A. 38 (JE-20)
  Martha 48* (JE-4)

Index

SMITH
  Mary 15* (F-225)
  Mary 50 (MA-277)
  Mary 65 (GD-288)
  Mary A. 46* (F-196)
  Mary E. 10* (MT-19)
  Mary Elizabeth 20* (F-226)
  Maslam 53 (F-223)
  Merrill 40 (GD-220)
  Morison A. 8* (F-174)
  Moses 35* (JE-33)
  Nancy 1* (MA-279)
  Nancy A. 17* (GD-261)
  Obadiah 26 (F-155)
  Obediah 47* (MT-59)
  Ophelia 24* (F-255)
  Peter M. 44 (MA-204)
  Peyton W. 24* (GD-210)
  Pleasant 18* (OS-307)
  Polley 13* (OS-287)
  Polly 52* (F-234)
  Quintrella 22* (JE-50)
  R. 31 (m) (JE-39)
  R. F. 20 (m)* (MT-2)
  Reuben 28 (ES-68)
  Richard 24* (JE-48)
  Richard 32 (OS-314)
  Richard 8* (OS-277)
  Richd. 21* (F-211)
  Robert 25 (MA-321)
  Robert 47 (JE-6)
  Robert 49 (OS-286)
  Robert W. 32 (ES-87)
  Robert W. 54 (CL-77)
  Sally 60 (B) (F-119)
  Sarah C. 4* (F-186)
  Sarah F. 36* (MT-52)
  Sarah J. 18* (ES-105)
  Shelton 53 (MA-325)
  Solomon 40 (MA-203)
  Susan 50* (GD-257)
  Thomas 30* (OS-295)
  Thomas 32* (CL-21)
  Thomas 33 (MA-230)
  Thomas 53 (F-135)
  Thomas 65* (F-148)
  W. M. 44 (m) (F-121)
  Will L. 38 (GD-215)

  William 15* (MT-4)
  William 24* (OS-306)
  William 28 (MA-321)
  William 45* (MA-219)
  William B. 23* (MT-3)
  William L. 50 (CL-11)
  William P. 43* (MT-10)
  William S. 41 (MA-290)
  Willis R. 60* (CL-1)
  william 49 (MA-287)
SMITH?
  James 35 (OS-316)
SMITHEA
  Granvith 25* (CL-6)
SMITHER
  E. W. 18 (f)* (F-162)
SMITHERS
  Alexander 30* (MT-4)
  Rebecca 27* (F-195)
SMITHEY
  Austin 36* (JE-71)
SMITHSON
  Wesley 38* (CL-84)
SMOOT
  William 29* (F-218)
SMOTHERS
  Daniel 8* (ES-75)
SMYTH
  Edward 39 (ES-52)
  Tobias 47 (ES-52)
  William 29 (ES-51)
SNEEDER
  H. 44 (m) (F-131)
SNODDY
  Jane 75* (MA-215)
SNOOKS
  R. P. 19 (m)* (MA-215)
SNOWDEN
  Archibald 27 (ES-59)
  Charles C. 25* (CL-57)
  David 14* (CL-63)
  David 21* (CL-56)
  James 10* (CL-39)
  James H. 51 (ES-57)
  John 57 (ES-76)
  John D. 32* (F-190)
  Mary 52 (CL-70)
  Thomas W. 23 (F-145)

  William 35 (CL-71)
SNOWDIN
  David 63 (OS-294)
  Greenbury 25 (OS-289)
  James 29 (OS-288)
SNYDER
  Andrew 18* (CL-41)
  David 10* (CL-25)
SOAPER
  James 47 (MA-216)
SOCHRIST
  Joshua 26* (JE-1)
SODOWSKY
  Ann E. 27 (JE-61)
  Ephraim Sr. 69 (JE-61)
  John E. 32* (JE-61)
  Jonathan 31 (JE-61)
  Malina 13* (JE-62)
SOLOMON
  William 69* (F-117)
SOMMERSALE
  F. M. 49 (f)* (MT-1)
SONS
  Matthew 40 (MT-69)
SOPER
  Dennis 35 (GD-226)
  James __ (JE-13)
  John H. 59* (F-248)
SOULSON
  Stephen? 33 (OS-291)
SOUTEN?
  Mary 12* (F-211)
SOUTHERLY
  Augustus 55* (MA-268)
SPANNER?
  Nancy 75* (B) (F-206)
SPARKS
  Barnett 35 (ES-101)
  Elizabeth 55 (ES-88)
  Ephraim jr. 30 (OS-292)
  Ephraim sr. 68 (OS-292)
  Frances 49 (ES-100)
  Harvey 26 (OS-292)
  Humphry 48* (F-196)
  Isaac 44 (JE-7)
  Isaac 50* (OS-312)
  J. B. 42 (m) (JE-40)
  John 21* (OS-294)

Index

SPARKS
John 23 (ES-92)
Joseph 24 (ES-97)
Mary 20* (JE-13)
Moroe 10 (m)* (JE-7)
Nancy M. 7* (ES-112)
Paulina 43 (JE-40)
Polly 39 (F-117)
Robert 28 (OS-318)
Sally A. 13* (ES-107)
Samuel 37 (ES-69)
Thomas 25 (F-208)
Thomas 45 (ES-61)
Tobias 20* (OS-292)
W. C. 33 (m) (F-251)
William 17* (ES-107)
William 26 (ES-69)
William 34 (OS-306)
William 38 (ES-101)
Wm. 56 (F-222)
SPATIS
Levi 45 (F-177)
Noah 42 (F-178)
SPAULDING
Harrison 34 (JE-43)
Sally A. 25* (MA-246)
SPAYINGHOWER
Henry 41 (GD-277)
SPEAK?
George 24* (JE-4)
SPEAKE
John O. 24* (F-183)
Thos. C. 61 (F-183)
W. F. 26 (m)* (F-178)
SPEAR
A. J. 30 (m) (OS-320)
SPEARS
Elizabeth 41* (F-195)
George C. 52* (JE-11)
John 14* (JE-52)
John 80 (F-248)
SPEGLE
George Ann 24* (F-114)
SPENCER
Alexander 25 (OS-294)
Allen 26 (OS-293)
E. R. 37 (f)* (F-122)
Elijah 30 (OS-293)

Geo. G. 50 (F-159)
Gulman 26 (OS-289)
Hiram 26 (OS-293)
John 16* (OS-292)
John 35 (OS-291)
John 37 (CL-3)
John D. 42* (OS-292)
Joseph 38 (OS-293)
Joseph sr. 48* (OS-291)
Masus 44 (B) (F-131)
Moses jr. 28* (OS-294)
Moses sr. 64* (OS-294)
Samuel 34 (ES-78)
Strong 24 (OS-294)
William 37 (OS-293)
William T. 36* (OS-290)
SPENKS
James 32 (F-211)
SPHAR
James M. _7* (CL-3)
Willis 36 (CL-3)
SPHARS
Daniel 77* (CL-89)
SPILLER
Mildred 56* (MT-21)
SPILLMAN
Hardin 20* (MA-216)
SPILMAN
Charles T. 30 (GD-258)
James 57 (CL-46)
James H. 42* (GD-258)
Pamelia 50 (GD-239)
SPINGEN
David 71 (CL-76)
SPIRES
G. P. 45 (m)* (JE-14)
Jeremiah 51 (F-211)
Mary Ann 19* (F-211)
SPIVEY
Charles 39 (OS-298)
James 41 (OS-279)
SPOONEMORE
Henry 34 (GD-271)
SPRAGGINS
Margaret 31 (JE-7)
SPRAKE
John O. 54* (F-211)

SPRATT
Alexis _. 27 (MT-61)
Charles 29 (GD-218)
Mary 73* (MT-59)
Mary E. 18* (MT-69)
Solomon 45* (MT-61)
William 26* (GD-238)
SPRAUL
Julia 28* (F-250)
SPRING
Amos 34 (F-206)
SPRINGATE
Almoore 22* (F-160)
SPRINGER
Rice 34* (JE-12)
SPRINKLE
Mary 52* (F-168)
SPROWL
Alex 47 (F-143)
William 39 (JE-48)
SPRUCE
John M. 9* (JE-45)
SPRY
Enoch 19 (ES-74)
James 38 (MT-19)
John 45 (ES-75)
Lucy 50* (CL-36)
SPUR
Mary Jane 10* (F-202)
SPURGIN
D. M. 37 (m) (CL-40)
Samuel 22* (MT-72)
Samuel S. 27 (MT-12)
SPURR
B. A. 50 (m)* (F-239)
Estelle 16* (F-225)
James 48* (CL-5)
James 50 (F-243)
Jasper N. 22* (CL-5)
John C. 46* (CL-5)
R. J. 42 (m)* (F-172)
Richard 41* (F-239)
Ruth 65* (GD-233)
Sarah E. 50?* (F-173)
William 32 (F-241)
William H. 41* (CL-4)
SPURRS (SPEARS)
Lee W. 46 (F-247)

Index

SRASLER
  Mary 25* (F-194)
SRELEY?
  B. W. D. 26 (m)* (F-162)
SSBURY
  Miriam 15* (GD-253)
ST CLAIR
  Nancy 26* (JE-41)
ST. CLAIR
  W. P. 23 (m)* (F-246)
STACK
  Robert 30* (JE-78)
STACY
  James 24 (ES-88)
STAFFORD
  Isabella 78 (JE-10)
  John W. 18* (JE-11)
  Mary 40 (F-125)
  William 33* (JE-10)
STAGGS
  Ulfred 50 (CL-75)
STAGNER
  Abner 26* (MA-283)
  Barnett 36 (GD-258)
  David 17* (MA-271)
  John S. 21* (MA-278)
  Joseph 60 (MA-280)
  Mary 75 (MA-320)
  Nancy 21* (MA-263)
  Thomas 19* (MA-270)
  Thomas 57 (MA-278)
STAIRS?
  Robert N. 1/12* (F-117)
STALEY
  John 40 (F-118)
STALL
  Henry 21* (F-200)
STAMPER
  James 29 (OS-290)
  Joel 23 (OS-294)
  Joel 64 (OS-290)
  John 12* (OS-299)
  John A. 42 (OS-290)
  John C. 12* (MT-50)
  Larkin 37 (OS-290)
  William 15* (OS-290)
  William 19* (OS-300)
  William 50 (MA-283)

STANFORD
  E. D. 54 (m)* (F-196)
STANHOPE
  Arthur 38 (CL-58)
  W. F. 36 (m)* (F-162)
STANLEY
  Luke 56* (JE-31)
STANLY
  Nancy 56* (JE-17)
STANTON
  Cyntha A. 44 (GD-274)
  Fleming 60 (GD-273)
  Merela 45 (GD-272)
STAPLES
  Andrew J. 20* (MT-13)
  John 15* (MT-16)
  Joshua 17* (MT-6)
  Richard 14* (CL-76)
  Thomas 26 (CL-83)
STAPLETON
  Edward 42 (OS-283)
  Edward sr. 65* (OS-280)
  Mason 22 (OS-280)
  Plesant 28* (OS-280)
  William 42 (OS-280)
  William 63* (OS-281)
STAPP
  J. Speed 29 (m) (MA-310)
  Thomas 48 (MA-307)
STARK
  Benja. F. 25* (MT-83)
STARNES
  James 12* (MT-63)
  James 34 (MT-48)
  Joseph 76* (MT-53)
  Lucinda 40* (MT-49)
STARNS
  James O. 15* (MT-48)
STAYLY
  Rebecca 55 (MA-300)
STEEL
  Andrew 30* (F-149)
  Andrew 49 (OS-287)
  Henry 16* (F-151)
  John 66* (F-149)
  Mary 13* (B) (F-192)
  Thomas 47* (F-117)

STEELE
  Albert R. 24* (CL-90)
  Gavin 49 (JE-41)
  Jacob 42 (MT-28)
  Mary 34* (F-199)
  Samel Mc. 8* (JE-65)
STEP
  George Jr. 24* (F-245)
STEPHENS
  Allain? 30 (F-125)
  Catharine 53* (MT-55)
  David 63 (MA-235)
  Emily 18 (ES-100)
  Emily 25* (ES-110)
  Frances J. 19* (GD-251)
  Garner 40 (JE-70)
  H. H. 53 (m)* (F-134)
  Harrison 37 (GD-261)
  Huldah 25* (JE-4)
  James Q. 19 (MT-54)
  Jane 52* (ES-70)
  Jehu 91* (MT-81)
  Jesse 46 (MT-73)
  Joel 35 (MT-80)
  John 27 (ES-69)
  John 31* (MT-73)
  John L. 38 (MT-79)
  John M. 32* (MT-78)
  L. 7 (f)* (F-127)
  Mary 38 (ES-100)
  Mary 60 (MT-78)
  Mary 64* (F-117)
  Mary A. 18* (JE-59)
  Mary A. 24 (MT-77)
  Milton P. 30 (MT-78)
  Narcissa 15* (MT-73)
  Richard 29 (MA-268)
  Richard 82 (ES-69)
  Sarah 30 (F-122)
  Sarah 47* (F-165)
  Sarilda J. 21* (GD-251)
  Susan 33* (F-117)
  Taltn 30* (MA-257)
  Thornton 50 (MA-268)
  William 23 (MA-269)
  William 31* (F-125)
  William 42* (MT-82)
  William 64 (ES-61)

Index

STEPHENS
William P. 45 (MA-266)
STEPHENSON
Jane 36 (GD-266)
Mary A. 23* (MA-224)
Mary J. 7* (MA-289)
Sarah 8* (MA-316)
STEPP
Frederick 73 (CL-94)
Jesse 22 (MA-310)
John 49 (MA-311)
Maglin? 74 (f) (MA-311)
Robert 52 (MA-310)
Washington 25 (MA-313)
STEUBAN
Baron 67 (B) (F-126)
STEVANS
J. Y. 62 (m) (MT-56)
STEVENS
A. J. 35 (m)* (MT-1)
Asa 48* (CL-36)
Hiram 47 (CL-39)
James 18* (MT-5)
John 40 (CL-37)
Mary C. 15* (F-232)
Matthias 56 (MT-77)
Sarah P. 27* (F-252)
Walker 40 (MT-85)
William 23* (CL-35)
William 73* (MT-17)
STEVENSON
George 42 (CL-91)
Isaac 48* (MT-21)
James M. C. 49* (MT-58)
Joseph 27 (CL-84)
Lucy 10* (B) (F-152)
Sam 18* (B) (F-151)
Samuel 51* (CL-83)
Samuel M. 24 (MT-28)
Thomas 12* (F-227)
William 17* (ES-86)
William 17* (MT-36)
William 35 (JE-55)
William 55 (CL-84)
William 56* (CL-71)
STEWART
A. C. 22 (m) (MT-33)
Archibald 39* (ES-79)

Benjamin 26 (MA-247)
C. M. 26 (m)* (MT-55)
Daniel 26* (OS-278)
David 48 (MT-57)
Eli 33 (ES-60)
Eli 44* (MT-73)
G. W. 15 (m)* (F-150)
George W. 30 (F-141)
Henrietta 54 (MT-78)
Henry 19* (OS-278)
Isaac 33* (OS-286)
John 22* (MA-267)
John 23* (OS-279)
Joseph 17* (JE-4)
Lewis 56 (GD-286)
Lyttleton 27 (F-249)
Madison 40* (MT-48)
Martin 45 (ES-50)
Mary E. 19* (F-150)
Michael 21* (F-213)
Miller 23?* (MA-303)
Moses 80* (F-249)
Olive 45* (F-196)
Patterson 17* (MT-6)
Rice L. 60* (GD-263)
Robert 57 (JE-4)
Roy 58 (GD-286)
Thomas 70* (MA-308)
Wesley 54* (F-249)
William H. 28* (MT-54)
STIFLER
James M. 38* (F-119)
STILFIELD
Elizabeth 73 (F-123)
John 38 (F-115)
STINNETT
Charles 29 (JE-23)
Jackson 35 (JE-24)
James 26 (GD-233)
John 30* (GD-225)
King A. 40* (JE-23)
Lindsey 25 (m) (JE-24)
Lindsey 56 (m) (JE-23)
Mary T. 4* (JE-24)
Nancy 56 (JE-49)
Reuben 37 (JE-25)
Rubin 31 (JE-25)
William 33* (JE-49)

_____* (JE-39)
STINSON
Edward 38 (MA-223)
Mary 55 (MA-223)
STIP
George 66* (F-237)
STIPE
David 54* (JE-51)
Henry 23 (F-159)
James T. 28* (JE-27)
Margaret 37* (JE-20)
Robert S. 25* (JE-52)
STIPES
Harvey 28 (F-190)
STITH
Harriet E. 7* (MT-14)
Preston 38* (MT-28)
STIVER
George M. 8* (F-244)
STIVERS
Absolem 49 (MA-299)
E. Y. 31 (m) (F-240)
Elizabeth 56* (F-247)
John 19* (F-246)
Robert 14* (F-249)
Sidney 41 (F-244)
STNE
Willia 20* (MA-214)
STOCKDELL
James 19* (F-129)
STOCKER
Hester 22* (MA-324)
Sidney 19 (m) (MA-301)
Sidney 19 (m) (MA-306)
William 21 (MA-301)
STOCKTON
E. D. 31 (m)* (ES-60)
Emily 27* (MT-15)
George F. 342* (MT-1)
Maria T. 48* (MT-5)
Mary 24* (CL-41)
Matilda 60?* (MT-4)
STOFER
John 54 (MT-69)
STOHLS
George 31* (F-199)
STOKELEY
William 28* (CL-21)

Index

STOKELY
  William 25* (MT-84)
STOLL
  Chas. 23* (F-199)
  Christiann 67* (F-196)
STONE
  Berry 46 (ES-74)
  Caleb 65 (MA-279)
  Calvin 35* (F-244)
  Catharine 72* (ES-70)
  Cordelia 32* (F-237)
  David 40 (F-224)
  David 41 (F-242)
  Frances 25* (CL-8)
  Francis 56 (ES-64)
  Francis E. 49 (ES-62)
  George W. 45* (F-123)
  Jacob 65 (F-164)
  James 37 (F-169)
  James 53 (ES-70)
  James M. 33 (MT-13)
  John 25* (ES-63)
  John 71* (F-149)
  John 75 (MA-284)
  John D. 14* (CL-71)
  Joseph 23 (F-170)
  Lerona 25* (ES-81)
  Louis 19* (MA-260)
  M. P. 34 (m) (F-212)
  Martin 23 (MT-74)
  Mary 39* (F-196)
  Oliver 33* (F-174)
  Richard 36 (MT-61)
  Robert H. 29* (MA-276)
  Robert R. 33 (MA-320)
  Samuel 60 (MA-230)
  Smith 62 (GD-240)
  Uriah 34 (F-170)
  William 23 (OS-304)
  William 35* (MA-302)
  William C. 39* (F-234)
  William D. 4* (F-132)
STONER
  Michael L. 33* (MT-34)
STONES
  Frances 13* (MT-6)
STONESTREET
  David 40 (B) (JE-49)

  Edmond 46* (B) (CL-1)
  James 62* (CL-4)
  Jane 18* (B) (JE-54)
STOPP
  William 54 (MA-221)
STORM
  Joel 35 (CL-43)
STORMS
  Asa 48* (JE-73)
  Catharine A. 40 (GD-250)
  E. L. 32 (m)* (GD-225)
  Nathaniel 53* (GD-251)
  Stephen 35 (GD-279)
STOUT
  J. B. 40 (m) (F-132)
  Samuel 40* (CL-19)
STRADER
  Christ 32* (F-196)
STRAFFORD
  Samuel 38 (CL-5)
STRANGE
  Edward 33 (ES-47)
  James 28 (ES-48)
  John 34* (MT-63)
STRATTS
  William 40 (MA-288)
STRAUS
  G. 21 (m) (F-204)
STRAUSS
  Reubene 30 (f)* (B) (F-206)
STRIBLING
  R. A. 40 (f)* (F-214)
STRINGER
  Amy 51 (MT-23)
STRINGFELLEN
  Elizabeth 53* (CL-42)
STRODE
  James 56* (CL-1)
  Nelson 36* (CL-80)
STRONG
  Alexander 62 (OS-302)
  Daniel 36 (OS-281)
  Henry 36 (OS-302)
  Isaac 40 (OS-298)
  Sally 45* (OS-314)
STROP
  Robert 18* (MA-237)

STUART
  Edward W. 44 (CL-57)
  Hezekiah 47 (CL-60)
  James 59* (CL-50)
  John G. 67 (CL-76)
  Joseph 32* (CL-57)
  Margaret 62 (CL-57)
  Roy 64 (CL-76)
  Samuel 28* (CL-80)
  William 76* (CL-55)
  William M. 23* (CL-50)
STUBBLEFIELD
  John P. 59 (CL-43)
STUBBS
  Elizabeth 15* (F-221)
STUGALL
  James 40 (GD-273)
STUGER
  James 50 (GD-268)
STULL
  John 57 (JE-40)
  Lotty 45 (MT-23)
  Mary 21* (JE-76)
STURGEN
  Eli 18* (OS-290)
STURGUS
  John J. 26* (JE-12)
SUDDUTH
  John 41 (CL-85)
SUFFIT
  Elen 23* (B) (JE-38)
SUKER
  James 26 (OS-317)
  Lewis 19* (OS-317)
SULEVAN
  F. 23 (m)* (F-150)
SULEY?
  A. 16 (m)* (F-124)
SULIVAN
  Mary 64 (MA-290)
  Patrick 25* (MA-251)
SULIVANS?
  P. E. 38 (m) (F-207)
SULIVANT
  John 33* (F-132)
SULLIVAN
  Daniel 40* (CL-89)
  Enoch G. 21* (F-217)

Index

SULLIVAN
  Garrett 39* (F-173)
  Jas. W. 43* (F-161)
  John 13* (F-218)
  Maria 42 (F-219)
  Mary 62* (F-161)
  Thomas 27* (MT-35)
SUMATE
  Willis 28 (MA-321)
SUMMERS
  Archibald 72* (MT-38)
  Doel 60 (m)* (MT-61)
  William 22 (MT-61)
  William 59 (MT-10)
SUSBURY
  Sarah 16* (GD-232)
SUTHERLAND
  David 29 (CL-9)
  Frederick 58* (CL-52)
  George 23 (CL-2)
  James 28* (F-250)
  John T. 23* (CL-95)
  Lewis 25 (CL-6)
  Mary 40 (CL-2)
  William 26 (GD-239)
  William 27 (CL-77)
SUTLEY
  Frederick 18* (JE-57)
SUTTEN
  Jos. T. 40* (F-210)
SUTTON
  Benjamin 46 (GD-231)
  D. P. 42 (m) (JE-42)
  Geo. W. 45* (F-190)
  George 19* (F-253)
  Henry O. 33 (GD-231)
  Jane 22* (F-241)
  John 68 (GD-241)
  Julliet 60* (F-166)
  Manuel 70 (B) (JE-38)
  Matilda 48* (F-237)
  Sarah 51* (GD-210)
  Thomas 22* (F-204)
  Walter 34 (GD-241)
  Wm. 22* (F-175)
SWANSON
  C. J. 35 (m) (GD-219)

SWEENY
  Timothy 25* (CL-89)
SWIFT
  Stephen 54 (F-255)
  William 56 (F-140)
SWINNY
  Nancy 40* (CL-42)
SWITZER
  Alexander 20* (JE-21)
  David 22 (JE-21)
  Moses 27 (JE-16)
  Samuel 60 (JE-21)
SWOPE
  Andrew 49* (MT-42)
  Dorcas 54 (GD-221)
  Henry 22* (ES-80)
  John 37 (GD-209)
  John sr. 59* (GD-261)
  William 43 (ES-47)
SYLABAR
  Thomas 25* (OS-305)
SYMONDS
  A. J. 19 (m) (F-204)
SYMPSON
  William C. 51* (CL-40)
TABOUR
  Geo. 33 (F-174)
TACKETT
  Mahalah 14* (ES-53)
  Philip 43 (MT-50)
TADE
  John 26* (MT-74)
  Lucy 11* (MT-11)
  Sarah 19* (MT-80)
TADER
  Hardin 49 (MA-263)
TAILOR
  John 40 (JE-29)
TALBOT
  Chas. 30* (F-117)
  Courtney 46* (F-134)
  Daniel 20* (F-241)
TALBOTT
  Augustus 12* (CL-53)
  Charles 36* (F-197)
  Hampton 33* (B) (F-151)
  Mary A. 72 (JE-58)
TALIAFERRO

John 35* (CL-40)
Thomas 22* (CL-5)
TALIEFARO
  Geo. 32* (F-195)
TANDY
  Elizabeth 12* (F-215)
  George 35 (B) (F-206)
  John 45 (B) (F-118)
  Mary 43* (B) (F-137)
TANKERSLEY
  Danl. 43 (F-122)
  F. 61 (m) (F-143)
  M. 60 (f)* (F-143)
TANKSLEY
  Margaret 20* (JE-39)
TANNER
  Archy 28* (CL-84)
  Branch 65 (CL-84)
  Branch M. 32* (CL-49)
  David 64 (CL-49)
  William 54 (JE-60)
TANNESY
  William 38 (CL-76)
TAPP
  Major 56* (CL-49)
  Mary 84* (MT-82)
  Mildred 70* (JE-12)
  Wilson 56* (F-154)
TAPPS
  P. W. 36 (m) (F-247)
TARBER
  William 50* (ES-57)
TARLTON
  Cabb 46 (F-181)
  L. B. 34 (m) (F-164)
  William Ware 37* (F-133)
  Wm. B. 36 (F-182)
TARPIN
  Abraham 58 (MT-33)
TARRANT
  Charity 85 (GD-232)
  Eastham 50 (GD-240)
TATE
  Casuel 30 (MA-300)
  David 45* (MT-62)
  John 48 (CL-11)
  Waddy 51 (m) (ES-50)
  William sr. 76 (CL-11)

Index

TATE
  Zachariah 37 (CL-11)
TATES
  Loudon 72 (B) (F-213)
TATIM
  George 28 (JE-27)
TATUM
  Jackson 23* (GD-221)
  Margaret 49* (GD-210)
  Mary Ann 16* (MA-202)
  Nicholas S. 67 (GD-224)
  Samuel A. 45 (GD-244)
  Thomas 58 (MA-226)
  William M. 25 (GD-256)
TAUL
  Benjn. M. 48 (F-248)
  John M. 34 (JE-14)
TAUL?
  Andrew J. 35* (CL-94)
TAYLOR
  A. 31 (m)* (F-195)
  A. 39 (m)* (F-122)
  A. B. 37 (m)* (F-160)
  Anarchy 80 (f)* (B) (F-229)
  Andrew 28 (MA-301)
  Andrew J. 28 (MA-306)
  Ann 62* (MA-287)
  B. B. 38 (m) (F-203)
  Barterton 31* (MA-211)
  Bird 39* (F-179)
  C. D. 30 (m) (F-139)
  Calvin C. 30* (CL-32)
  Charlotte 34* (B) (F-198)
  David W. 37 (GD-283)
  Dorotha 37 (CL-1)
  Edmond T. 35* (CL-11)
  Elizabeth 3* (MA-322)
  Elizabeth 37* (MA-256)
  Elizabeth 60* (F-219)
  Elizabeth 67 (JE-28)
  Ellen 13* (F-207)
  Fielding 38* (GD-230)
  Franklin 37 (JE-21)
  Geo. W. 31* (F-162)
  George 85?* (B) (F-114)
  Grooms 40 (MA-306)
  H. M. H. 42 (m) (CL-2)
  Harrison 30 (F-182)
  Harry 36* (B) (F-234)
  Henry 19* (B) (F-207)
  Henry 40 (B) (F-137)
  Henry 73* (B) (F-220)
  Henry S. 25* (CL-1)
  Hiram 45 (MA-260)
  Hubbard D. 38* (F-231)
  Hubbard jr. 30* (CL-41)
  Hubbard sr. 61 (CL-4)
  J. V. 41 (m) (MA-305)
  Jackson 22 (F-141)
  James 30* (MA-319)
  James 32* (MT-34)
  James 37* (B) (MT-19)
  James 46 (JE-28)
  James 79 (GD-233)
  James C. 72 (MA-260)
  James F. 41* (CL-5)
  James L. 18* (MT-28)
  Jesse 40* (GD-222)
  Jesse 47* (MA-211)
  Jesse 48* (MA-301)
  Jesse 48* (MA-306)
  John 27 (B) (F-198)
  John 49 (JE-24)
  John G. 39* (MA-204)
  John J. 54 (GD-234)
  John P. 51 (CL-1)
  John W. 49 (ES-81)
  Jonathan 40* (GD-215)
  Joseph 33* (F-244)
  Leara 50* (B) (F-137)
  Leonard 56* (F-140)
  Louisa 29* (B) (F-140)
  M. 55 (f)* (F-143)
  M. A. 35 (m)* (B) (F-144)
  M. A. 84 (f)* (F-203)
  Malvina 10* (MA-317)
  Mariah 26* (B) (GD-266)
  Mary 17* (GD-222)
  Mary Ann 21* (F-199)
  Mary W. 14* (F-225)
  Matilda 41* (F-211)
  Milky 8 (f)* (F-138)
  Nathaniel 35 (MA-316)
  Parker 54 (JE-6)
  Paten W. 23 (MA-252)
  Robert 23* (B) (JE-68)
  Robert 52 (MA-319)
  Robert S. 30* (CL-4)
  Sally A. 10* (MA-246)
  Samuel 31 (MA-209)
  Samuel M. 65* (CL-42)
  Stark 64 (F-133)
  Talton 67 (MA-211)
  Thomas 29* (F-130)
  Thomas 33 (ES-85)
  Thomas 45* (MA-309)
  Thomas M. 49* (CL-3)
  Thompson 24* (GD-289)
  Thos. 34* (F-194)
  Timier? 26 (m) (JE-6)
  Tom 66* (CL-1)
  Venie 80* (B) (F-120)
  William 52 (MA-211)
  William C. 29 (MA-228)
  Winston 53 (GD-222)
  Zachariah 3* (MT-82)
TEATER
  Fletcher 36 (MA-318)
TEETER
  Alfred 7* (GD-225)
  Nelson H. 30* (GD-252)
  Paris 70* (GD-215)
  Rebecca E. 12* (GD-214)
  Russel H. 36 (GD-215)
  William 50 (GD-234)
TELLYIA
  Alfred 25* (MA-251)
TEMPLE
  William 34 (GD-241)
TEMPY
  Elvira 26* (F-122)
TENNEY
  O. S. 26 (m)* (MT-6)
TEPPER
  Mary L. 15* (F-114)
TERIS?
  Robert M. 20* (MA-255)
TERREL
  Beverly 39 (m) (MA-221)
  William T. 44 (MA-221)
TERRELL
  H. T. 47 (m) (GD-284)
TERRILL
  E. J. 35 (m) (GD-239)

Index

TERRILL
  Martha 49* (GD-259)
  Overton 42 (GD-247)
TERRY
  Enoch 52* (MT-24)
  James 45 (MT-12)
  Joseph 46 (MA-279)
TETER
  John 64* (F-151)
  P. M. C. 30 (m)* (JE-33)
TEVIS
  Elizabeth 40 (MA-302)
  Mar A. 39 (MA-282)
  N. B. 16 (m)* (JE-75)
  William 20* (MA-298)
TEVIS?
  James 14* (MA-254)
THACKER
  William 44 (ES-52)
THARP
  Alexander 55 (MA-248)
  Frances 26* (MA-257)
  George 23 (MA-230)
  Jesse 52* (MT-49)
  Thomas 50* (MA-259)
THEOBALD
  G. P. 58* (F-254)
THERMAN?
  C. 18 (f)* (F-197)
THOMAS
  Andrew 14* (F-206)
  Ann 23 (JE-46)
  Anthony 36 (OS-288)
  Arthurius 63 (MA-248)
  Augustus 24* (CL-35)
  Bary 17* (MT-4)
  Betsey 45 (OS-284)
  Charles B. 25 (F-116)
  Churchill 61 (MA-228)
  Cornelious 50* (OS-300)
  Daniel 13* (JE-45)
  E. A. 3/12 (f)* (B) (F-140)
  Edward A. 28* (MT-6)
  Eleanor 30 (MT-68)
  Elisha 34 (OS-284)
  Elizabeth 47* (F-202)
  Emily A. 13* (MT-1)
  Ennis 30 (CL-56)

Ennis? 21 (CL-68)
Fielder 64* (CL-23)
Fielder jr. 34 (CL-23)
Frances 62* (MT-16)
George H. 18* (MT-1)
George W. 43 (MT-27)
Greenberry 41 (MT-44)
Henry C. 27 (ES-50)
Henry H. 68 (ES-50)
Isaac 24* (ES-49)
Isaac 43* (OS-287)
James 22 (OS-277)
James 40 (OS-287)
James 47 (MA-264)
James 57 (MA-293)
Jesse 34 (OS-281)
Jesse 39 (MA-220)
John 29 (MA-318)
Joseph 27 (OS-288)
Joseph 50 (OS-321)
Josephine 7* (JE-20)
M. C. 14 (f)* (MT-6)
Phebe 70* (B) (JE-77)
Pohma? 45 (m) (CL-2)
Reuben 40 (JE-39)
Robert 68 (MT-82)
Robert H. 50 (CL-34)
Samuel 44* (F-119)
Simeon 50* (JE-46)
William 23 (MA-228)
William N. 25* (CL-38)
William T. 23 (MA-257)
robert 40 (MA-297)
THOMASSON
  Daniel 50 (MA-207)
  Wm. P. 22* (F-233)
THOMISON
  John T. 30 (F-133)
THOMPSON
  A. H. 24 (m) (F-250)
  Abert 17* (MT-36)
  Aggy 50 (B) (F-220)
  Alfred 48 (CL-23)
  Allen 45 (CL-7)
  Almira 30* (F-194)
  Andrew 29 (CL-88)
  Charles 35* (MT-5)
  Chas. R. 26 (F-139)

David 78* (CL-87)
Edgar 26 (MT-23)
Eliza Ann 20* (JE-44)
Emma 20* (F-132)
George 20* (CL-44)
George 27 (GD-281)
Green 38 (MT-20)
Hannah 70* (B) (MT-27)
Harriet 13* (F-225)
Harrison 39 (CL-93)
Haynie 48* (CL-93)
Horatio 67* (MT-23)
J. J. 25 (m)* (F-252)
James 54 (CL-87)
James C. 1* (F-179)
James H. 24 (MA-225)
James K. 34* (F-234)
John 25 (CL-87)
John 36 (F-219)
John 51 (MT-29)
John 76* (CL-87)
John 8* (F-219)
John D. 17* (F-195)
John F. 39* (JE-53)
John H. 52 (JE-56)
Joseph 21* (MA-215)
Josephene 25* (F-195)
Lloyd 60 (MT-34)
Louisa 25 (CL-67)
Lucinda 50* (MT-39)
M. G. 23 (m)* (F-146)
Nancy 28* (CL-86)
Nancy 38 (CL-87)
Nelson 40 (F-137)
P. H. 29 (m)* (F-173)
Q. A. 21 (m)* (F-230)
Sandford 35* (CL-77)
Sarah 64 (JE-72)
Thomas 20* (F-124)
Thomas 37 (CL-40)
Tramon? 45 (m) (MA-237)
Van 35 (MT-27)
William 23 (CL-8)
William 24* (CL-50)
William 30* (CL-83)
William 50 (MT-38)
William 72 (MT-4)
Wm. O. 26 (m)* (F-186)

Index

THOMSEN
- Maria 17* (CL-10)

THOMSON
- Jesse 32 (ES-110)
- John M. 27 (ES-87)

THORNS
- John 39* (F-224)

THORNSBERG
- Mary 15* (CL-3)

THORNSBURG
- John 32 (ES-55)

THORNSBURGH
- Isaac 64 (ES-73)

THORNTON
- Ann 16* (F-216)
- Charles 38 (MT-33)
- Geo. 45* (F-194)
- James 27 (JE-61)
- James B. 27 (GD-277)
- John 24 (GD-268)
- John 57 (GD-243)
- Louisa 16* (GD-273)
- Rebecca 22* (F-237)

THORP
- Dodson 31 (MA-256)
- George 24 (MA-321)
- Lear 8 (f)* (ES-91)

THRASHER
- Sarah 38* (F-196)

THRASHLEY
- M. R. 37 (f)* (F-160)

THURMAN
- Henry 30 (ES-74)
- James 36 (ES-47)
- William 30 (F-244)

THURMON
- John D. 50 (GD-241)

THURNAM?
- John 25 (MA-207)

THWAITS
- Nancy 55 (F-132)

TILERY
- Isaac 81* (MA-240)

TILEY
- Edward 21 (MA-272)
- Joel 8* (MA-272)

TILFORD
- Edward 24 (F-130)

Emily 25* (F-212)
J. B. 38 (m)* (F-130)
John 66* (F-255)

TILLET
- John 24 (MA-320)
- William 20 (F-244)

TILLETT
- E. G. 52 (m) (GD-261)
- Jane 20* (MA-282)
- John 23 (MA-265)
- John G. 22* (GD-289)
- Sarah W. 14* (JE-78)

TILLON
- Sarah F. 15* (F-178)

TILMAN
- John 65* (F-222)

TILY
- Lucy 44 (MA-292)

TIMBERLAKE
- Geo. W. 18* (F-205)

TIMBLE
- David F. 25 (MT-54)

TINCHER
- Rebecca 51 (OS-299)
- William* (CL-91)
- William? 42 (OS-309)

TINDER?
- Anthony 41* (F-196)

TINELL
- William 26* (F-243)

TINGLE
- Amanda 21* (F-142)
- David 25* (F-233)

TINSLEY
- Ransom 37 (CL-7)

TIPTON
- Ann 50 (MA-302)
- Burwell 26 (MT-13)
- Charles 45 (B) (MT-3)
- Christanna 18* (MT-55)
- Davis B. 35 (MA-295)
- Ellen 45* (ES-104)
- Jacob 49 (ES-98)
- Jesse 53 (ES-98)
- Jesse P. 29* (ES-55)
- John 41 (CL-52)
- John 66 (MT-80)
- John J. 50 (ES-108)

Jonathan T. 39 (ES-58)
Joseph 40 (ES-104)
N. P. 41 (m) (MT-69)
Paul 35 (ES-54)
Philadelphia 12* (ES-104)
Reuben S. 54 (ES-104)
Robert L. 24 (CL-51)
Samuel 42 (ES-79)
Samuel 75* (ES-59)
Samuel E. 34* (MT-1)
Shanon 50 (m) (MA-298)
William 36 (MA-292)
William 56 (MT-80)
William H. 26 (ES-104)
William L. 51 (ES-89)

TISDEL
- Thomas 48 (MA-320)

TIVIS
- Elizabeth 37 (MA-290)
- Silas 39 (MA-281)

TODD
- Alvin W. 24 (MA-248)
- Baxter 36 (MA-226)
- Benjamin 69 (MA-268)
- Caleb 56 (MA-320)
- Colemon 28* (MA-205)
- Daniel P. 41 (ES-82)
- Elizabeth 45 (MA-262)
- Haram 33 (MA-274)
- Harvey 32 (ES-107)
- Henry 18* (MA-267)
- Hugh? B. 37* (MT-6)
- Isaac 27* (MA-200)
- Isaac 67 (MA-248)
- Isham F. 31 (MA-236)
- Jane 17* (F-225)
- Jane 76* (F-192)
- Jasper R. 31 (ES-64)
- Joel 50 (MA-226)
- John 25 (MA-226)
- John 45 (MA-215)
- L. O. 32 (m) (F-130)
- Madison 42* (MA-226)
- Madisonia 48* (F-196)
- Mary 50* (MA-221)
- Moses G. 47 (ES-77)
- Newton 29 (MA-264)
- Ninevah 30 (m) (MA-258)

Index

TODD
  Peter 56 (MA-270)
  Peter 75 (MA-264)
  Robt. 34 (F-161)
  Silas 31 (MA-243)
  St. Blair 25* (F-254)
  Thomas 27 (MA-256)
  Thomas 58 (MA-257)
  Thomas C. 51 (MA-247)
  Thomas J. 21* (MA-257)
  Virginia 15* (F-225)
  W. L. 60 (m) (F-161)
  William 28 (MA-243)
  William 60* (MA-256)
TODDHUNTER
  John 28 (F-251)
TODHUNTER
  John 73* (JE-52)
  Parker E. 52* (JE-5)
TOLAND
  James 73 (MT-75)
TOLEN
  Frances 30* (CL-83)
  Morgan 67 (CL-22)
TOLIN
  Jourdan 27 (CL-67)
TOLL
  Jonathan 35* (F-118)
  M. E. 5 (f)* (F-143)
  M. E. 7 (f)* (F-145)
TOMLIN
  Sarah 60 (MA-320)
TOMLINSON
  Chas. 63* (F-155)
  H. 46 (m)* (MT-57)
  Hethy 57* (F-118)
  Joseph 36 (GD-239)
  Lewis C. 45 (MT-25)
TOMPKINS
  Asa 19* (GD-288)
  John M. 27 (GD-256)
  Susan 59* (GD-251)
  Whitfield 36 (F-216)
TOOL
  Michael 48* (F-132)
TOTTEN
  Joseph 59 (GD-255)
  Juan L. 30 (f) (GD-255)

Polly 26* (GD-213)
TOWNSEND
  Eli 26* (ES-53)
  Elizabeth 57 (MT-51)
  Garrett 33 (ES-52)
  James 29 (ES-53)
  James 57 (ES-52)
  John 52 (ES-111)
  Rueben 34 (ES-52)
  William 24 (MT-51)
TRABUE
  C. C. 45 (m)* (JE-69)
TRACEY
  Emaliah 50 (f) (GD-262)
  James 28 (GD-230)
  James B. 45 (GD-230)
  James T. 20 (GD-230)
  Thomas 66* (GD-238)
TRACY
  Asa 54 (CL-72)
  Augustin 61 (MT-43)
  George 32* (CL-58)
  James 30* (CL-73)
  Obed 50 (CL-83)
  Sally 48* (CL-69)
  William 22* (CL-73)
TRAINER
  James 45 (JE-52)
TRAMMELL
  John 57* (CL-40)
TRAVIS
  John 26 (F-116)
  Nancy 65* (B) (F-119)
TRAYLOR
  Jane 86* (GD-260)
TREADAWAY
  Ann 13* (MT-6)
  Edward E. 24 (MT-18)
  John 45 (JE-34)
  John D. 50 (MT-33)
  M. H. 24 (m)* (MT-62)
  Micaga 23* (JE-18)
  Silas 21 (JE-25)
  Stephen 44* (MT-10)
TREADWAY
  Catharine 75* (ES-54)
  E. B. 26 (m)* (OS-305)
  Francis 35* (JE-29)

  Franky 14 (f)* (JE-32)
  Hiram 45* (JE-28)
  Jane 24* (F-209)
  William 50* (OS-305)
TREDAWAY
  Peter 54 (CL-69)
TREDWAY
  Thomas 29 (OS-289)
TRELAURNCEY
  Henry 28 (F-207)
TRIBBLE
  Alexander 40 (MA-214)
  Alfred 14* (CL-93)
  Austin 55 (CL-81)
  Dudley 53 (MA-255)
  Jerusha 66 (MA-263)
  John 17* (CL-93)
  John 59 (MA-249)
TRIGGLE
  James 45 (ES-93)
TRILER
  Lucy A. 32* (JE-48)
TRIMBLE
  David 33 (MT-64)
  Isaac 55 (MT-72)
  James H. 28 (MT-73)
  John 51 (MT-72)
  Sarah 22* (MT-66)
  William 32 (MT-26)
  William 35* (F-125)
  William 48 (CL-92)
TRIPLETT
  John 45 (MT-34)
  Presley 30* (MT-40)
  William 40* (CL-68)
TRISLER
  Elizabeth 30* (JE-78)
  Elizabeth 63* (JE-46)
  James 17* (JE-41)
  Mary 76* (JE-49)
  Nancy 33 (JE-39)
  William 18* (JE-75)
TROBRIDGE
  Jonathan 40* (CL-37)
TROTTER
  Alex 47* (F-130)
  Cordelia 40* (F-190)
  G. R. 34 (m)* (F-199)

Index

TROTTER
  Geo. T. 42* (F-196)
TROUDER?
  John 19* (F-142)
TROUTMAN
  Mercellus 20* (F-210)
TROWBRIDGE
  James 32* (MT-5)
TROWER
  James A. 35 (MA-277)
TROYMAN
  Pleasant B. 21 (CL-32)
TRUE
  Elijah 20* (CL-45)
  Eliza B. 16* (JE-74)
  Ellen 50* (F-231)
  John P. 33 (F-223)
  Robert 35 (F-131)
  Willis 28 (F-252)
  thomas 37* (F-252)
TRUIT
  Reddin 31* (OS-280)
TRUIT?
  William 34 (OS-277)
TRULL
  Sarah Ann 11* (F-230)
TRUMAN
  James 28* (F-126)
TRUMAN?
  Charles W. 6/12* (CL-84)
TRUMBULL
  Jane 43 (F-139)
TRUS
  Phebe 20* (JE-5)
TRUSSELL
  John 40 (CL-32)
  Roberta 40 (CL-37)
TUBBS
  Bartlett 29 (ES-48)
  Mary 70* (ES-99)
TUCKER
  Abraham 70 (B) (F-171)
  Ann 50* (F-171)
  Charles 28* (JE-19)
  David 45 (ES-48)
  F. A. 30 (f)* (F-171)
  John 23* (CL-23)
  John 40 (F-171)
  Margaret 16* (F-200)
  Mathew 65 (B) (F-202)
  Paulina 22* (MA-237)
  Peter G. 43 (MT-3)
  Robt. 44* (F-168)
  Susan 51* (GD-246)
  Willis 32 (MA-272)
TUDDER
  Samuel D. 48 (ES-91)
  Samuel J. 35 (ES-81)
TUDER
  Allen 44 (MA-212)
  Blumer 24 (m) (MA-321)
  Daniel 56 (MA-212)
  Daniel 56 (MA-288)
  Daniel 65 (MA-321)
  John 27 (MA-288)
  John M. 14* (MA-289)
  Josephene 14* (F-154)
  Mark 20 (MA-322)
  Nancy 50 (MA-323)
  Phoeby 55 (MA-322)
  S. 54 (m) (F-153)
  Stephen 36 (MA-288)
  William 15* (MA-308)
  William 29 (GD-256)
  Woodson 30 (MA-288)
TUFTS
  William 26* (F-144)
TUGGLE
  Achillis 44 (CL-19)
  Nancy 93* (CL-18)
  Rebecca 52 (GD-232)
TULLEY
  David O. 43 (MT-36)
TURLEY
  James 38* (MT-82)
  James 43 (MT-24)
  John 31* (MT-20)
  Louisa 27* (MT-39)
  Mitchell 28 (OS-304)
  Willis 29 (MT-20)
TURNBULL
  James R. 51* (CL-46)
TURNER
  Alfred C. 44 (MA-303)
  Amanda 15* (MA-288)
  Barnett 29 (MA-304)
  Benjamin 56* (CL-46)
  Boswell 41 (MA-322)
  Charles 35 (MA-315)
  David 67* (F-181)
  David E. 44 (GD-223)
  Elizabeth 56* (MA-223)
  F. L. 23 (m)* (F-166)
  George 45 (GD-221)
  George 59 (MT-68)
  H. H. 26 (m)* (MT-7)
  Harriett 50 (MA-275)
  James 33* (B) (F-124)
  James B. 31 (MA-307)
  James H. 26 (F-164)
  Jessee 61 (OS-319)
  John 56 (F-162)
  John C. 30 (OS-284)
  Joseph 56 (MA-250)
  Lidany G. 31 (m) (MA-204)
  Lucinda 19* (F-152)
  Marth 12* (MT-28)
  Martha 16* (MA-264)
  Mary 18* (MA-201)
  Mathew 37 (F-191)
  Nelson 68* (F-130)
  Reubin 50 (MA-315)
  Robert 40 (F-217)
  Samuel 43 (GD-215)
  Samuel 75 (MA-307)
  Squire 57 (MA-252)
  Squire 27 (MA-315)
  Susan 62* (GD-243)
  Tempey 54 (OS-284)
  Will 38 (GD-244)
  William 40 (MA-242)
  William 62 (F-208)
  Zeperiah 28 (m)* (OS-299)
TURPIN
  Andrew 17* (MA-275)
  Daniel 52 (JE-48)
  Enoch 29 (JE-49)
  Henry 31* (MA-275)
  Isaac 64* (JE-56)
  James sr. 72 (GD-222)
  John 22 (MA-275)
  John 60 (MA-276)
  M. 74 (f)* (JE-39)
  Martin 30* (ES-82)

Index

TURPIN
  Mary 81 (MA-275)
  Nancy 42 (MA-319)
  Perry 35 (JE-71)
  Sarah 26* (MA-319)
  Solomon 29 (MA-264)
  Solomon 48 (MA-275)
  Talton 42* (MA-297)
  Thomas 35 (JE-34)
  Wilkinson 45* (MT-5)
TUT
  Michial 20* (OS-289)
TUTT
  Adeline 41* (JE-65)
TUTT?
  Margaret 7* (F-201)
TUTTELL?
  Mary 54* (F-132)
TUTTLE
  Benjamin 52 (ES-64)
  Cynthia 27* (CL-36)
  J. C. 25 (m)* (F-122)
  John W. 25* (CL-56)
  William 53* (CL-54)
TUTTLER
  Nelson C. 25 (CL-37)
TWAY
  Patrick 30 (F-238)
TWEEDIE
  William 47 (F-131)
TWYMAN
  David R. 55 (CL-55)
  George 18* (CL-26)
  George 9* (F-243)
  Laura 4* (F-151)
  Simeon 50 (CL-55)
TYLER
  Benj. 65* (F-172)
TYRA
  William 47* (F-115)
TYRE
  George 44 (ES-58)
  Satterwhite 23 (ES-51)
UMBRY
  William 33 (MA-202)
UNDERWOOD
  Emeline 29 (JE-29)
  Gerret 26* (JE-21)
  John 18* (JE-20)
  John 58* (JE-29)
  L. 52 (f) (F-171)
  N. 22 (m)* (F-155)
  Russel 27 (JE-29)
  Thomas 35* (JE-28)
URIETH?
  George K. 58* (B) (MT-79)
URTON
  Henry 53* (GD-208)
USSERY
  James 28* (F-194)
UTINGER
  George 70 (JE-4)
UTLEY
  Alley 75 (f)* (JE-48)
  John 53 (F-216)
  Jordan N. 23* (ES-61)
UTTINGER
  Fred 50 (F-212)
  Samuel 3* (F-227)
VALENTINE
  Elizabeth 19* (F-159)
  John 27* (F-160)
  Rebecca 29* (F-195)
VALLANDINGHAM
  James 47* (F-239)
  Judy 38 (F-242)
VANAKEN
  A. 41 (m)* (F-131)
VANARSDALE
  Abm. 35 (m)* (JE-43)
VANCE
  Eliza 30 (CL-65)
  Harvey 24 (F-183)
  Jacob 70 (GD-212)
  James D. 40 (F-154)
  John 28? (F-178)
  John 65 (ES-57)
  Thomas 23* (CL-22)
VANDERPOOL
  Jacob 25* (OS-312)
  William 9* (JE-36)
VANDERPOOLE
  Abraham 27 (OS-288)
  Joseph 26 (OS-294)
VANDIVER
  Martha 26* (GD-219)
VANMETER
  Abraham 45* (F-172)
  Elizabeth 5* (CL-46)
  Isaac 30* (F-180)
  Isaac 55 (CL-88)
  Lucy 1* (CL-41)
  Solomon 32* (CL-92)
VANORSDAL
  David 40 (MA-314)
VANOY
  Squire 65* (B) (JE-75)
VANPELT
  J. S. 38 (m)* (F-126)
  William 35* (F-208)
  William 65 (F-209)
VANTRICE
  Daniel 45 (JE-18)
VANWINKLE
  Benjamin F. 87 (MA-234)
  James 55 (MA-219)
  John 29 (MA-233)
  Joseph 25 (MA-238)
  Sidney 27 (m) (MA-238)
VARBEL
  Samuel 26 (MA-208)
VARBLE
  Jacob 16* (F-249)
  Mary 23* (JE-5)
  Nancy 45 (F-249)
VARNING?
  William O. 66* (MA-308)
VAUGERSON?
  C. 39 (m)* (F-137)
VAUGH
  Charity 105* (F-209)
  James H. 37* (F-229)
VAUGHAN
  Cornelius 63* (F-158)
  Cornilius 28 (F-158)
  Isabella 1* (JE-2)
VAUGHEN
  Catharine 40 (MA-289)
VAUGHENSTOCK
  V. 23 (m)* (MA-252)
VAUGHN
  Ann 52* (MA-226)
  Arthesa 36* (JE-32)
  Benj. 12* (F-166)

Index

VAUGHN
 Causby 38* (F-134)
 Doretha 68 (ES-58)
 Elijah 31* (ES-47)
 Elijah 74 (ES-58)
 Ellen 34* (F-121)
 Gabriel 26 (ES-93)
 George W. 26 (GD-237)
 George W. 30 (F-119)
 James A. 16* (F-145)
 John 47 (MA-247)
 John B. 45* (F-241)
 Joseph 61 (GD-237)
 Josiah J. 24 (MT-62)
 Julia 53* (MA-270)
 Mary 7* (ES-63)
 Mary J. 36* (F-166)
 Masterson 27* (F-187)
 Nancy 63 (ES-73)
 Rhoda 70* (F-136)
 Ricd. 8* (F-170)
 Samuel J. 43* (ES-58)
 Thomas H. 42 (ES-103)
 William 32* (ES-94)
 William 34* (MA-271)
 William 49* (F-237)
VAUGHTER
 Sarah 70* (F-119)
VEAL
 Dudley 37 (F-224)
VEALE
 Dudley 50 (F-238)
VEATCH
 John W. 57 (JE-67)
VENABLE
 George 33* (F-132)
VERDEN
 Artemisia 26 (F-216)
VERMONT
 Elizabeth 15* (F-120)
VERTNER
 David 78* (F-184)
VESSER
 Melissa 16* (CL-17)
VICE
 John 25 (CL-61)
 Margaret 60 (CL-61)

VICK
 Henry C.? 14* (F-114)
VIGUS
 Susana W. 35 (F-147)
VILLIER
 Peter 40* (F-195)
VINCE
 Abraham 66 (JE-3)
VINSON
 David 58 (MA-323)
VISSER?
 Samuel 16* (ES-63)
VIVION
 Elizabeth 74 (CL-54)
 Flavel 45 (CL-58)
 John 50 (CL-71)
 Milton 45 (CL-58)
 Thomas 73 (CL-12)
VON
 John 29 (OS-279)
VORIS
 John 40* (MT-2)
WACIR?
 Frances 17* (F-225)
WADDLE
 Septimus 76 (F-116)
WADE
 Carter P. 27* (MT-83)
 Charles S. 46* (JE-4)
 Daniel 62 (CL-90)
 Dudly 30 (CL-90)
 George 33 (ES-67)
 John 60* (CL-90)
 Marston W. 29* (F-194)
 Mary 64* (JE-34)
 Nancy 56* (MT-84)
 Robert 37* (MT-84)
 William 63 (JE-33)
WADKINS
 Thomas 48 (MA-277)
WAGEMON
 David 36 (GD-206)
WAGES
 Ambrose 51* (MA-265)
 James 49 (ES-61)
 Judy 85* (B) (ES-111)
 Simpson M. 23 (ES-94)

WAGGEN
 Ann 40 (F-209)
WAGLE
 Lewis 50* (ES-60)
 Thomas 56 (MA-206)
WAIN
 Henry 68* (GD-286)
WAKE
 Celia 51* (JE-18)
WAKEFIELD
 Enoch 43 (ES-83)
WALDEN
 Benjamin 5* (MT-25)
 Elisha 41* (MA-275)
 Elizabeth 68* (GD-284)
 James 56* (ES-104)
 James 6* (MT-16)
 Jemaima 57* (MA-278)
 Thomas 13* (MA-275)
 Tilson 30 (MT-8)
 William 13* (ES-51)
WALDIN
 Elisha 45 (ES-49)
 Stephen 50 (ES-50)
WALDREN
 Silamin 21 (m)* (MA-297)
WALDRIDGE
 John 37 (CL-44)
 Peter jr. 40 (GD-248)
 Peter sr. 70* (GD-251)
 Robert 19* (GD-289)
WALKER
 A. B. 4 (m)* (F-127)
 Calvin 33* (F-221)
 Catharine 21* (GD-287)
 Charles 50 (MA-252)
 Charlott 50* (MT-5)
 Chas. W. 42* (F-196)
 Cupid 75 (B) (JE-38)
 Daniel 60* (MT-26)
 Ed H. 26* (GD-245)
 Elijah M. 6* (GD-249)
 Elizabeth 40* (F-216)
 James 33 (GD-215)
 James 53 (MA-302)
 Jane 70* (MA-203)
 Jinney? 13* (F-159)
 Joel 50* (MA-204)

Index

WALKER
John 48* (GD-287)
John 50 (JE-23)
John 77* (F-148)
Joseph J. 38 (OS-277)
Kemp jr. 28* (GD-249)
Lucy 60 (MA-216)
M. C. 46 (m) (MT-56)
Margaret 52 (F-249)
Maria 39* (F-195)
Mary 38 (MT-72)
Mary A. 23* (JE-44)
Matthew 73 (JE-30)
Nancy 60 (CL-73)
Robert S. 28* (JE-72)
Samuel 19* (JE-60)
Samuel 57 (MA-316)
Stephen 30 (MA-228)
Thomas L. 25* (JE-16)
William 23* (MT-72)
William 31 (OS-305)
William E. 48 (MA-256)
William J. 35* (MA-251)
WALKUP
Samuel 57 (MA-225)
Samuel 93* (MA-227)
William 20* (MA-227)
William 30 (MA-226)
WALL
Michiel 35 (GD-287)
William 60 (GD-213)
WALLACE
Ann J. 61* (MA-281)
Charles 38 (JE-48)
Davidella 20* (F-142)
Enfield 18 (f)* (CL-36)
G? W. 35 (m)* (F-207)
Geo. H. 54 (F-176)
H. B. 44 (m) (F-142)
J. H. 43 (m)* (F-149)
James 38 (JE-39)
James 66* (MA-223)
James H. 37 (CL-77)
James T. 21 (F-149)
Jane 55* (ES-80)
John 52* (ES-107)
John 55 (MA-314)
John 57 (JE-4)

Joseph 71 (JE-39)
Joseph S. 49* (MT-6)
Joseph W. 28 (MT-2)
M. A. 52 (f)* (F-212)
Nancy 66* (F-176)
Rebeca 30* (JE-21)
Richard 46 (F-188)
Susan 33* (MA-223)
Susan 35* (CL-73)
Thomas M. 52 (F-243)
W. K. 32 :(m)* (F-149)
William 34* (JE-20)
Wm. 23 (F-182)
WALLER
Elizabeth 65* (CL-16)
John 30* (MT-51)
John 35 (CL-16)
John 68* (MT-11)
John T. 16* (CL-34)
Joseph H. 34 (JE-75)
Lucy A. 5* (MT-49)
Napoleon B. 24* (JE-67)
Rachel M. 23* (MT-63)
Stephen 38 (JE-9)
William E. 47* (JE-65)
Wm. 65 (F-152)
WALLINGFORD
Cath 25* (F-200)
WALLS
James 17* (F-254)
Joseph L. 16 (JE-54)
Richard 36* (F-191)
Richard 38* (F-141)
Susanna 65 (JE-53)
WALTER
Richard 68* (JE-44)
Stephen 85* (JE-76)
WALTERS
Ann 28* (JE-21)
Baily 46* (OS-303)
David 48 (JE-42)
Eliza 64* (ES-63)
Henry 57 (ES-77)
Jordon 26 (JE-29)
Morton 19* (JE-52)
Owen? 45 (MA-204)
Rebecca 17* (JE-39)
Sampson 58 (ES-60)

Sarah 32* (JE-40)
Thomas 36 (JE-31)
William 32 (ES-64)
William 32* (JE-28)
William 62* (JE-21)
Zelpha 35* (B) (JE-70)
WALTON
David H. 46 (ES-67)
Edward 74 (ES-87)
Elizabeth 63* (MA-230)
John 41 (ES-92)
W. R. 25 (f)* (MA-277)
William 34 (ES-73)
WALTZ?
Frank 81 (F-161)
WAMSLEY
Thomas E. 42 (JE-51)
WARD
Amalza 36 (m)* (CL-41)
Jelson 77* (OS-277)
John 70* (F-150)
John B. 19* (ES-86)
Maria 54 (B) (CL-43)
Mary 44 (MA-258)
Peggy 80* (B) (CL-42)
Rebecca 50* (OS-307)
Sarah 46* (F-196)
Thomas 14* (MT-69)
Voluntine 38* (ES-89)
WARDER
Horace 32 (MT-21)
WARE
Abraham 64* (F-133)
Harvey 30 (CL-26)
James T. 34 (F-232)
Jas. H. 35* (F-166)
John 60 (MT-59)
John E. 28 (CL-60)
Joseph S. 17* (F-224)
Madison 28* (CL-68)
N. W. 69 (m)* (F-154)
Richard 11* (CL-78)
Robert E. 65 (MT-59)
Squire 30 (GD-248)
William 25* (GD-248)
WARES
Robert 28 (CL-66)

Index

WARFIELD
  Benj. 60 (F-215)
  Elisha 39* (F-154)
  Elisha 70 (F-234)
  Nicholas 65* (F-237)
  Ruth 17* (F-225)
  William 23 (F-215)
  Wm. 53* (B) (F-152)
WARFORD
  Abraham 77 (ES-111)
  Camron? 66 (MA-231)
  James 21* (MT-6)
  Joel 50 (ES-111)
  Mitchell 22 (ES-111)
WARMOTH
  Bright B. 30 (MA-316)
  Green B. 32 (MA-316)
  Madison 27 (GD-259)
  Sidney 21 (m) (MA-315)
  Thomas 50 (MA-316)
WARMOUTH
  Philip 23 (GD-228)
  Thomas S. 29 (GD-253)
WARMSLEY
  John 63 (MT-55)
  M. 33 (m) (MT-78)
WARNER
  Anderson 26 (ES-107)
  Daniel 29 (ES-107)
  Derrick 50 (F-211)
  Edward 20 (ES-63)
  Henry H. 35 (MT-21)
  John 53* (ES-63)
  Joseph 44* (MT-26)
  O. S. 27 (m) (F-216)
  William 33 (MA-264)
  Willis 35 (MT-15)
WARNOCK
  John 35* (F-226)
  John R. 28* (F-126)
WARREN
  Alexander 43 (MA-324)
  Athur 22 (GD-236)
  Catharine 26* (GD-289)
  Danica 44 (f) (GD-256)
  Drury 51 (GD-224)
  Elizabeth 26 (F-131)
  Harvey 22* (GD-257)

  Henry 44 (MA-324)
  J. F. 28 (m)* (F-129)
  Jacob 50 (MA-316)
  James 33 (GD-236)
  John 22 (MA-316)
  John 37 (GD-223)
  John 65 (GD-256)
  John T. 24 (ES-59)
  John jr. 29 (GD-223)
  Nancy 21* (GD-247)
  O. S. 26 (m) (F-204)
  Thomas 57* (CL-93)
  Thomas 58 (GD-223)
  Thomas C. 26* (GD-258)
  Thompson 41* (CL-53)
  William 16* (GD-215)
  Wm. H. 7* (F-175)
WARRING
  John 21 (MA-316)
  William 30 (MA-319)
WARSON
  William W. 22 (ES-58)
WASHBUK
  A. H. 26 (m)* (F-140)
WASHINGTON
  C. 30 (f)* (B) (F-128)
  Jane 25* (F-139)
WASON
  Elizabeth 60* (F-158)
WATERS
  Andrew 22 (JE-32)
  Buford 23 (JE-27)
  Harry 43 (JE-8)
  Hetta 20* (JE-26)
  John sr. 52 (GD-211)
  Larkin B. 29 (MA-272)
  Singleton 34 (MA-320)
  Tho. H. 58 (F-206)
  Thomas 26* (JE-27)
  Thomas 27 (MA-270)
  Thomas 29* (JE-32)
  Thomas 30 (JE-32)
  Thomas 75 (JE-32)
WATKINS
  Edward 13* (F-223)
  Marion S. 30 (m) (CL-58)
  Phil J.? 84* (B) (JE-70)
  Sharlotte 58 (B) (JE-75)

WATNER
  William 8* (F-202)
WATRONS
  Warren P. 28?* (MT-6)
WATSON
  Betsy 77* (F-249)
  D. P. (Capt.) 45 (JE-55)
  Daniel 20 (ES-107)
  Drury 43* (F-241)
  Elender 30* (MA-272)
  Elizabeth 38* (ES-99)
  Isaac T. 31 (ES-104)
  Jeptha 29 (m) (ES-104)
  John 22* (F-199)
  John 50 (MA-257)
  John C. 27* (F-138)
  Joseph 21 (JE-40)
  Joseph 55* (F-150)
  Joseph 56* (F-142)
  Sally 60 (MA-216)
  William 20* (JE-11)
  William 43 (MA-271)
  William 47 (MA-262)
  William H. 18* (JE-59)
  Zerilda 14* (MA-257)
WATT
  Henry 64?* (F-130)
WATTERS
  James 47 (ES-50)
WATTON
  Mily G. 39 (m) (ES-56)
WATTS
  Barnett 35 (MA-294)
  Beverly B. __ (CL-63)
  Charles S. 48* (MA-203)
  David P. 18* (MA-202)
  David T. 18 (F-243)
  Elizabeth 22* (CL-63)
  Fielding 24 (CL-84)
  Frances 39* (MA-208)
  Frances C. 39* (F-242)
  George 23* (JE-21)
  Howard 29 (CL-33)
  John 59 (CL-82)
  John B. 39* (F-115)
  John S. 63* (CL-30)
  John W. 21* (ES-61)
  Johnson 43* (CL-28)

Index

WATTS
  Larrett? 43* (F-243)
  Oscar 7* (F-241)
  Oschar F. 24* (CL-41)
  Richard 45 (CL-79)
  Robert 27 (MA-276)
  Susanna 49* (JE-51)
  Vicky 75 (f)* (B) (JE-38)
  William 23* (MA-257)
  William 25 (CL-34)
  William 29* (JE-19)
  Winceton 30 (CL-67)
WATTY
  D. H. 41 (m)* (F-150)
WAYMAN
  James 34 (CL-4)
WEATHERHEAD
  P.? 47 (f)* (F-131)
WEATHERS
  Albert 27* (F-232)
  James 41 (ES-91)
  James 48* (CL-1)
  Lucinda 28* (F-232)
  Polly 50 (F-231)
WEAVER
  Andrew J. 12* (GD-251)
  Betcy J. 23* (JE-19)
  Catharine 55? (JE-21)
  E. L. 27 (m) (F-132)
  Francis 55* (F-218)
  Francis T. 24* (F-219)
  John D. 51 (CL-49)
  Matilda 35 (B) (JE-62)
  Polly 16* (JE-49)
  Thomas 14* (GD-215)
  Thomas 49 (F-148)
  Thomas 56 (F-218)
  William 42 (GD-214)
WEBB
  Allen 30 (F-248)
  Elisha 39 (ES-85)
  Eliz. 8* (F-199)
  Garland 40* (F-190)
  George M. 25 (MA-259)
  Hugh 28* (F-168)
  Isaiah 47* (CL-41)
  Jefferson 45* (CL-27)
  Jesse 27 (ES-84)
  John 23* (F-184)
  John 28 (F-252)
  John 31 (F-156)
  John T. 37 (CL-42)
  Joseph 37 (MA-273)
  Joshua 60 (F-190)
  Lucy 70* (B) (F-124)
  Mary T. 79* (F-189)
  Milly 104* (MA-267)
  Richard 45 (ES-108)
  S. W. 19 (m) (F-141)
  Susan 30 (MA-298)
  Susan 53* (CL-9)
  William 28 (ES-65)
  William 30* (F-245)
  William 69 (ES-90)
  Windfield D. 23* (CL-9)
WEBBER
  Ann W. 33* (F-195)
  Elizabeth 44 (MA-232)
  Jones 37 (ES-65)
  Jones 68* (ES-65)
  Sally 42 (ES-70)
  Sandford 39 (ES-65)
WEBSTER
  Amanda 25 (F-220)
  America 33 (F-234)
  Benjamin 27 (MA-251)
  David 33* (CL-43)
  Dudley 63* (MA-251)
  Eli 21* (CL-44)
  Elizabeth 40* (F-153)
  George 30 (CL-44)
  Hannah 96 (JE-71)
  James W. 26 (CL-44)
  John 27 (MT-34)
  Laura 5* (F-235)
  Lauson 38* (F-255)
  Lawson 22* (F-202)
  Leslie 27 (m)* (CL-41)
  Margaret 13* (JE-77)
  Mary 55* (F-213)
  Peter 60* (CL-89)
  Ruth 34 (F-218)
  Spencer 34* (F-117)
  Thomas 49* (MT-16)
  Thomas J. 9* (JE-26)
  Volentine 36 (MT-33)
  Weall? 36 (m) (F-156)
  William 26* (JE-67)
WEDDLE
  Geo. 42* (F-195)
WEIGART
  George 32 (F-131)
WEIGART?
  William 26 (F-120)
WEIL
  Patrick 30* (F-199)
WEIR
  James 45* (F-218)
WELCH
  A. W. 45 (m) (MT-52)
  Elizabeth 35 (F-219)
  Elizabeth 64* (F-221)
  Francis 31 (MT-82)
  Garrett 28* (CL-18)
  George W. 30 (JE-15)
  Henry 53 (MA-296)
  James 21* (CL-77)
  James 25* (CL-89)
  James 63 (CL-25)
  James M. 39 (JE-75)
  John C. 27* (JE-15)
  Matilda 22* (JE-7)
  Nathaniel 68 (JE-15)
  Patrick 25* (CL-47)
  Robert Y. 44 (MT-58)
  S. D. 25 (m)* (JE-45)
  Sally A. 38* (GD-261)
  Samuel R. 31* (JE-15)
  Thomas 32* (JE-30)
  Thomas 37 (JE-63)
  Tilford 27 (MT-48)
  William 54 (MT-43)
WELDEN
  Margaret 37* (F-205)
  William D. 18* (CL-80)
WELEFORD
  Charles 35* (GD-253)
WELGUS
  Garrard 23* (F-145)
WELLER
  Ann 36* (F-195)
WELLINGTON
  Wm. 16* (B) (F-193)

Index

WELLS
  Amie 34 (GD-238)
  Austin B. 37 (CL-81)
  Benjamin 24* (CL-82)
  Fielding 49 (CL-72)
  Isaac 66 (CL-81)
  John 35 (ES-53)
  John J. 55* (ES-57)
  John P. 47 (CL-78)
  Joseph 35* (MT-6)
  Joshua 48* (CL-89)
  Mary 38 (CL-8)
  N. B. 23 (m)* (MT-6)
  Nancy 63 (MT-59)
  Richard 43 (MA-275)
  Thomas J. 40 (CL-77)
  Thornton 69 (CL-82)
  Tilman T. 37 (CL-81)
  Washington 24* (CL-90)
WELSOA?
  Charles S. 28 (GD-276)
WENDIVER
  Susan M. 26* (JE-37)
WENDOVER
  R. H. 30 (m)* (F-179)
WERNE?
  John 39* (F-196)
WERTMAN
  John 21* (OS-289)
WESSELS
  H. A. 25 (m) (F-205)
WEST
  Buford 32 (OS-297)
  Charles jr. 45* (JE-44)
  Charles sr. 56 (JE-70)
  Charlotte 7* (B) (F-229)
  Dolly 70* (B) (F-124)
  George 46 (MA-227)
  Harriet E. 20* (F-199)
  Herman 18* (F-129)
  James B. 65 (MA-221)
  James W. 26* (F-178)
  John 43 (MA-258)
  John 64 (F-147)
  John M. 32 (MA-274)
  Lysander 30* (GD-241)
  Martha 57* (MA-296)
  Mary 17* (CL-55)

  Milton 29 (JE-70)
  Perry 24 (MA-317)
  Peyton 53 (GD-231)
  Richard 46 (MA-248)
  Richard S. 41 (GD-209)
  Robert 32 (MA-220)
  Sarah 36 (GD-209)
  Simeon 53 (GD-240)
  Thomas E. 62 (JE-76)
  Tinsley 42 (ES-51)
  Turpin 34 (MA-319)
  Tyre 29 (m) (GD-225)
  Walker 68 (GD-236)
  Westly 40 (GD-220)
  William 16* (MA-274)
  William 38 (GD-223)
  William W. 14* (ES-107)
  Wilson H. 38 (JE-6)
  Woodford 26 (JE-44)
  Wright N. S. 25* (CL-42)
WESTBROOK
  James 28 (MT-61)
  Thomas 60 (CL-69)
WESTERFIELD
  Lucasley 23 (f)* (GD-240)
WETHINGTON
  Richard 25 (F-137)
WHANKS
  Mary 80* (MA-300)
WHEATLEY
  Albert 34* (MT-2)
WHEATLY
  Chas. 32 (F-222)
  Ignatius 33* (F-194)
WHEELEN
  Mary 16* (B) (F-200)
WHEELER
  Abel 34 (GD-257)
  Basil 51* (B) (F-138)
  Danl. 18* (B) (F-143)
  Geo. 57 (F-170)
  Geo. W. 31 (F-191)
  James 29 (JE-26)
  James 46 (GD-257)
  John 30* (F-244)
  L. 50 (m) (B) (F-127)
  Leonard 61 (F-152)
  Mary 60 (MA-319)

  Nathaniel 25 (GD-257)
  Samuel 48* (CL-40)
  Susan 18* (B) (F-199)
  Thomas 32 (JE-26)
  William 26 (MA-319)
WHEELOCK
  Sarah J. 47* (F-142)
WHENEY
  Elizabeth 14* (F-139)
WHICK
  Elizabeth 41 (GD-255)
WHICKER?
  Zachariah 21* (OS-302)
WHIRETT
  Samuel 51 (MA-204)
  Will H. 21* (GD-287)
WHITAKER
  Betsy 31* (F-196)
  Irvine 28 (MA-322)
  James 37 (MA-286)
  John 35 (MA-201)
  John 35 (MA-249)
  Vincent 39* (F-117)
  Zacheria 25* (MA-288)
WHITAMORE
  Wm. 20* (F-225)
WHITATON
  Marcus 37* (MA-286)
WHITE
  Abner 27 (ES-86)
  Adderson 26 (MA-203)
  Albert 23* (F-228)
  Allen 44 (MT-65)
  America 5* (ES-89)
  Ann 60 (MT-61)
  Aqquilla 58? (OS-301)
  Aquilla 35* (ES-88)
  Austin 28* (MA-292)
  Austin 55 (F-231)
  Bassel 52 (m) (MA-261)
  Benjamin 26 (MA-273)
  Caswell 26* (F-236)
  Catharine 70* (ES-64)
  Claiborn 54 (MA-203)
  Corella 18* (F-147)
  David 50 (CL-59)
  Durrett 20* (MA-203)
  Edward 51 (ES-91)

Index

WHITE
- Elias 22 (MA-247)
- Elijah 24* (F-158)
- Eliza 40* (F-228)
- Elizabeth __* (F-121)
- Francis 36 (MA-296)
- Francis 65 (CL-25)
- George 28 (GD-210)
- George W. 28 (F-129)
- Henry F. 22 (ES-109)
- Jacob 44 (F-217)
- Jacob S. 50* (MA-252)
- James 24* (ES-59)
- James 35 (F-202)
- James 42 (ES-48)
- James 45* (JE-32)
- James 50 (CL-69)
- James 56* (MA-205)
- James A. 47 (MT-39)
- Jane 39* (JE-32)
- Jeremaih 25* (MA-289)
- Jeremiah 43 (MT-9)
- Joel 46* (JE-78)
- John 22 (MA-267)
- John 24 (MT-66)
- John 33 (OS-306)
- John 38* (MT-11)
- John 41* (JE-66)
- John 41 (MA-323)
- John 77 (JE-67)
- John B. 40 (MA-241)
- John J. 14* (CL-57)
- John P. 39 (F-236)
- Jonathan 47 (ES-97)
- L. 39 (f)* (MT-42)
- Lewis 40* (JE-45)
- Lucinda 25* (MT-20)
- Lucinda 26* (MA-265)
- Margaret 41* (MT-47)
- Martha 16* (GD-264)
- Marue? 26 (m)* (OS-292)
- Mary 19* (F-142)
- Mary E. 8* (F-202)
- Mary Jane 16* (ES-55)
- Milton 47 (MA-250)
- Phillip 60* (B) (F-159)
- R. P. 28 (m) (MA-252)
- Richard 28* (CL-42)
- Richard 40 (F-232)
- Richard 55* (MA-213)
- Richard 57 (CL-23)
- Richard J. 22* (MA-256)
- Rutha 46 (ES-111)
- Shelton 16* (OS-288)
- Stephen 16* (MA-243)
- Stephen 32 (ES-85)
- T. C. S. 45 (m)* (F-194)
- Thomas 26* (F-129)
- Thomas 29 (F-240)
- Thomas 35 (ES-97)
- Thomas 53 (MT-40)
- Thomas 66* (MT-42)
- Vina J. 13* (MT-63)
- Whitfield 66* (OS-289)
- Will 24* (GD-252)
- Will 40 (GD-268)
- William 18* (MA-257)
- William 24* (MA-215)
- William 25* (MT-30)
- William 26* (MA-251)
- William 39 (CL-69)
- William 47 (MT-23)
- William F. 49 (MT-22)
- William W. 41* (JE-70)

WHITE?
- Sally 50 (MA-243)

WHITEHEAD
- Charles P. 2* (CL-72)
- James N. 45 (CL-45)

WHITESELL
- Lewis 30* (JE-68)

WHITESIDE
- Pembroke 30* (F-230)

WHITESIDES
- John 80* (CL-92)
- Louisa 53* (CL-94)

WHITICO
- Charles 33 (GD-217)
- James 42 (GD-277)
- James jr. 20 (GD-286)

WHITING
- Chas. 60* (F-194)

WHITLOCK
- Albert 25 (MA-289)
- James 24* (MA-290)
- Richard 21 (MA-289)

WHITNEY
- Emily 13, Mary 10* (F-116)
- Sarah Ann 52* (F-250)

WHITSETT
- Elizabeth 65 (MT-8)
- Jilson S. 32 (m) (MT-8)

WHITT
- Ann E. 21* (F-176)
- E. A. 38 (f)* (F-147)
- Mason 34 (F-119)

WHITTEN
- Hester 5* (JE-3)

WHITTINGTON
- James H. 10* (CL-5)

WHITTMANN
- Sarah Ann 14* (MT-4)

WHORTON
- Susan M. 51 (JE-68)

WIATE
- John 70 (OS-293)

WIATT
- Green B. 22 (GD-228)

WICKER
- Z. J. 21 (m) (OS-318)

WICKLIFF
- Robt. 30 (F-167)
- Robt. 76 (F-167)

WICKLIFFE
- Charles H. 48 (F-219)
- D. C. 40 (m)* (F-221)
- Fanny W. 45* (F-145)
- R. N. 40 (m)* (F-204)

WIDDLE
- George 56 (MA-273)

WIEGART
- Mary A. 15* (F-142)

WIENICK?
- Michal 39* (OS-290)

WIER
- Lavinia 15* (F-225)

WIERMAN
- John 32 (OS-291)

WIGART
- Alex 27* (F-120)

WILCOX
- Catharine 60* (MT-60)
- Rodolphus 35 (GD-242)
- Squire 35 (MA-273)

Index

WILCOXEN
  Israel 27 (CL-23)
  Margarett E. 8* (CL-19)
  Rachel 57* (CL-22)
  Sarah 66 (CL-22)
WILDER
  Ebenezer 39* (CL-67)
  R. E. 40 (m)* (JE-74)
  William 40 (OS-298)
WILDS
  Benjamin F. 35 (GD-219)
  John R. 50 (GD-230)
WILER
  Samuel 30* (OS-305)
WILES
  Eli 17* (CL-75)
  Leroy 39 (CL-52)
  Washington 74* (CL-88)
WILEY
  Adam 27* (F-169)
  Alexander 76 (MA-324)
  Benjamin 57 (GD-232)
  Carey A. 45 (m) (GD-278)
  D. J. 27 (m) (GD-275)
  David 46 (GD-285)
  Harvey 41 (GD-276)
  Henry 25 (JE-25)
  Jesse 21 (GD-285)
  John 53* (MA-324)
  Mathew 71 (JE-12)
  Salley 37 (GD-283)
  William 26* (GD-232)
  William 44* (MA-324)
WILFON
  Horatio 46 (GD-211)
  Will 20 (GD-211)
WILGUS
  J. B. 26 (m) (F-135)
WILISFORD
  Samuel 66* (MA-224)
WILKERSN
  Bartlett 18 (MA-266)
  Plesant 36 (MA-280)
WILKERSON
  Agnus 38* (MA-251)
  Charles 30 (CL-79)
  Foster 1* (MA-252)
  John W. 41 (F-251)

  Mary 56 (MA-262)
  Patsy H. 1/12* (MA-252)
  William 69* (MA-207)
WILKINS
  Cison? 64 (m)* (B) (F-129)
WILKINSON
  Aberam 58* (MT-6)
  Nimrod A. 48 (MT-14)
WILL
  E. W. 15 (m)* (MA-252)
WILLCOX
  James 23 (ES-71)
WILLIAM
  Henry 14* (B) (MT-16)
WILLIAMS
  A. W. 16 (f)* (F-122)
  Abner 34 (MA-239)
  Abraham 50 (MA-219)
  Abram 25* (CL-2)
  Alfred 30* (CL-38)
  Alfred 30* (OS-309)
  Amos 60 (MT-80)
  Caleb 74 (F-127)
  Caleb jr 24* (F-140)
  Charles B. 24* (CL-3)
  Charles S. 50* (MT-7)
  David 51 (GD-244)
  Delila 45* (B) (CL-31)
  Dennis 49 (ES-99)
  E. 19 (m)* (B) (F-126)
  E. 38 (m) (F-185)
  Edward 38 (B) (F-208)
  Eliz. A. 49* (JE-52)
  Eveline 27* (B) (MT-5)
  George 56 (CL-62)
  George S. 33* (OS-306)
  Hanson 78* (F-169)
  Henry 25 (CL-65)
  Heram S. 39 (CL-70)
  J. B. 32 (m)* (F-126)
  J. H. 36 (m) (F-155)
  Jacob 21* (OS-287)
  James 22* (CL-3)
  James 25* (B) (F-116)
  James 28* (MA-203)
  James 32* (OS-283)
  James 47 (ES-55)
  James 56 (OS-304)

  James C. 30* (ES-68)
  Jefferson 48* (MA-215)
  John 37 (F-174)
  John 40* (F-175)
  John 51* (CL-46)
  John 62* (MA-259)
  John 62* (MT-14)
  John S. 31* (CL-95)
  John W. 31* (CL-71)
  John W. 60 (CL-38)
  Joseph 26 (CL-38)
  Joseph 33 (MA-220)
  Judy 70* (B) (F-125)
  Lemuel 39 (MA-207)
  Louisa 14* (B) (MT-1)
  Louisa 18* (OS-279)
  Louisa 44 (MT-48)
  Lutticia 27* (MA-260)
  M. 50 (f)* (B) (F-140)
  M. L. 3 (f)* (F-169)
  Malinda 50 (B) (F-170)
  Maria 45 (MT-4)
  Marshall 40 (F-207)
  Martha 14* (B) (F-138)
  Mary 16* (B) (MT-6)
  Mary 5* (B) (MT-38)
  Mason 30 (OS-309)
  Milly 16* (GD-243)
  Minerva 20* (MT-74)
  Moses 47 (MA-322)
  Moses 50 (OS-297)
  Nancy 27* (OS-283)
  Nathan 20* (OS-302)
  Nathan 26* (MT-55)
  Nathan 52 (MA-285)
  Nathan 52* (MA-322)
  O. H. 28 (m)* (F-244)
  Oliver B. 44 (MT-29)
  Ongmore? R. 47 (CL-56)
  Original 52 (ES-64)
  Oscar 27* (CL-45)
  Patrick 30 (B) (F-147)
  Philip 30* (B) (F-255)
  Rachel 12* (B) (CL-27)
  Robert 24* (MA-279)
  Sally 25* (CL-87)
  Sam 73* (B) (JE-38)
  Samuel 23 (JE-37)

Index

WILLIAMS
  Samuel 26* (MA-203)
  Samuel 58* (MA-303)
  Samuel 62 (CL-64)
  Samuel L. 68 (MT-38)
  Shadrack 32* (ES-82)
  Shipton 23 (GD-228)
  Susan 50 (CL-70)
  Susan 65* (F-196)
  Tom 40* (F-255)
  Uriah 32 (MT-22)
  W. W. 50 (m) (F-148)
  William 25 (MA-316)
  William 27 (MA-316)
  William 28 (MA-307)
  William 29 (MA-285)
  William 29 (MA-322)
  William 29 (OS-304)
  William 36 (MA-235)
  William 50 (ES-70)
  William 53* (OS-277)
  William 54 (MT-15)
  William 81* (CL-55)
  Z. B. 29 (m)* (F-204)
  Zedekiah 29* (MT-58)
WILLIAMSON
  Dudley 21* (F-160)
  Eunice 49 (F-157)
  John 39 (GD-246)
  John 40* (GD-258)
  Thomas B. 30 (JE-19)
WILLIFORD
  Mary 65*·(CL-6)
WILLIS
  Alex W. 6* (JE-52)
  Alfred 30* (MT-14)
  Benjamin 50* (JE-27)
  Edward 28 (ES-72)
  Elizabeth 16* (JE-14)
  Green B. 39 (JE-13)
  Henry 23 (JE-34)
  Hezekiah 32 (JE-25)
  John 38 (MA-305)
  John 53 (MA-284)
  John 56 (MT-52)
  John A. 27* (JE-47)
  John A. 40 (F-118)
  Leaty 82 (f)* (JE-28)

  Lettie 55 (f)* (MA-319)
  Mary 47 (MA-315)
  McKinsey 51 (ES-110)
  Merrill 21 (ES-112)
  Moses 51* (MA-201)
  Thomas 50* (MA-280)
  William 39 (GD-232)
WILLMORE
  O. A. 32 (m)* (JE-15)
WILLOUGHBY
  Ben J. 39 (MT-64)
  James 31 (MT-8)
  James W. 52* (MT-67)
  Mayland 30 (m) (MT-55)
  Wade 33 (MT-56)
  William 45 (MT-54)
WILLS
  Alexander 31 (ES-64)
  Andrew 20* (MT-68)
  Andrew 55* (MT-19)
  Andrew H. 21 (MT-65)
  Cyrus S. 5* (CL-50)
  Eli B. 38 (CL-84)
  Elijah 43 (ES-71)
  Henry 45 (MA-268)
  James 48 (MT-74)
  James S. 23 (MT-52)
  Malinda 67 (ES-64)
  Martin 32 (MT-47)
  Michael 32 (ES-66)
  Nimrod A. 30* (MT-76)
WILLSON
  John 44* (F-130)
  Joseph 25* (F-122)
  Rebecca 12* (F-129)
WILLUBY
  Silvester 25 (MA-292)
WILLY
  Mary 47 (MA-223)
WILMORE
  Elizabeth 7* (JE-15)
  Jacob 57 (JE-78)
  Jacob W. 30 (GD-220)
  James 6* (JE-41)
  James 66 (JE-14)
  James C. 40* (JE-15)
  John W. 39* (JE-15)
  John sr. 63 (JE-48)
  Thomas D. 37 (JE-15)

WILMOT
  Benjamin 32* (GD-266)
  James 26* (GD-211)
  John L. 32 (F-163)
  Mary T. 56* (F-141)
  S. T.? __ (m)* (F-138)
WILMUT
  Nathaniel 23 (GD-273)
WILSON
  Abner 30 (F-224)
  Abner 31* (F-239)
  Alford 21 (OS-286)
  Alford 25 (OS-319)
  Anderson 33 (ES-66)
  B. R. 37 (m) (F-252)
  Bazel D. 35 (JE-5)
  Carolina 18* (F-137)
  Catharine 48 (ES-88)
  David 55 (MT-32)
  David A. 62 (MT-60)
  Davis 49 (OS-286)
  Dillard 23* (CL-6)
  Ebenezer 55* (ES-96)
  Edmund 28* (MA-251)
  Edwin 25 (OS-301)
  Elihu 24 (ES-66)
  Eliz. 16* (F-200)
  Elizabeth 18* (MA-274)
  Gaberell 23* (OS-285)
  George S. 32 (CL-3)
  Harvey 55 (MT-12)
  Henrietta C. 22* (MT-27)
  Jacob 32 (CL-60)
  James 28* (MA-233)
  James 42 (JE-71)
  James 50 (F-203)
  James 65* (F-177)
  James R. 44 (MT-28)
  Jesse C. 30 (ES-113)
  Jesse M. 30* (MT-61)
  Jessee 32* (OS-297)
  John 19* (OS-302)
  John 28* (ES-94)
  John 28* (MT-2)
  John 37 (OS-319)
  John 77 (MT-36)
  John H. 56 (F-252)
  John J. 38 (F-199)

Index

WILSON
John jr. 26 (OS-286)
Johnson 32 (MT-32)
Jonas 26 (F-248)
Joshua 65 (B) (MT-82)
L. D. 34 (m)* (MT-69)
Lemuel 53 (OS-283)
Lewis M. 32 (ES-88)
M. J. 11 (f)* (F-154)
Mary 32 (CL-60)
Mary E. 12* (F-180)
Mary E. 21* (F-200)
Moses 62 (F-232)
Nancy 58 (F-232)
Nancy 80 (CL-85)
Neal 22* (JE-75)
Phillip 30 (OS-319)
Phillip 40 (OS-283)
Polley 27 (OS-278)
R. J. 33 (m) (F-168)
R. Spaulding 336* (F-207)
Rachal 55 (OS-319)
Robert 33* (OS-296)
Robert 49* (MA-292)
Robert 48 (MA-297)
Roda 44 (JE-10)
Sally 72 (OS-296)
Samuel 54* (MT-79)
Samuel 56 (MT-24)
Samuel 69 (F-185)
Samuel S. 30 (F-251)
Sarah 20* (F-254)
Simeon 27 (MT-83)
Sophia 60* (JE-73)
Susan 35* (F-153)
Thomas 23* (JE-11)
Thomas 26* (JE-41)
Thos. 38* (F-232)
Valentine H. 27 (JE-76)
W. 27 (m)* (F-137)
William 44 (MA-217)
William 46* (GD-238)
William 90 (MA-297)
William D. 30* (ES-97)
William H. 39 (CL-6)
William H. 58 (ES-66)
William S. 51* (MT-57)
William T. 68 (JE-42)

William W. 25 (MT-27)
WIMSCOTT
M. D. 33 (m)* (MA-204)
WINBURN
Jeptha 45* (ES-81)
Rhodes 27 (ES-89)
Sidney 21* (ES-66)
Thomas 22 (ES-90)
William 42 (ES-62)
WINCHESTER
Ann E. 27* (F-186)
Josephine 6* (F-142)
Martha 25* (F-142)
WINFIELD
Elisha N.? 27 (F-210)
WINFREED
Samuel 50 (B) (F-202)
WINGATE
Debra 43* (F-202)
WININS
Alexr. 23* (F-217)
WINKLER
Anderson 22* (ES-97)
Jackson 29 (ES-110)
Jacob 24 (GD-279)
John 31* (ES-97)
Lewis 25 (ES-110)
Lewis 56 (ES-108)
William 52 (ES-83)
WINKLES
JAmes 46 (ES-108)
Levi 23 (ES-106)
William 26 (ES-106)
WINN
Jerry 70 (B) (F-243)
Jesse D. 39* (F-232)
John A. 31* (CL-25)
Joshua N. 28 (CL-88)
Larrey 18* (MT-35)
Minor H. 59 (CL-25)
Nancy 65* (CL-12)
Owen D. 44* (F-243)
Philip B. 64* (CL-88)
Robert N. 33* (CL-25)
Ruth 70 (CL-45)
Sarah 64* (F-217)
William 33* (CL-41)

WINSLOW
Hallitt? M. 76* (F-116)
WINSTERNLY
Mrs. 37* (F-195)
WINT
Susan 4* (F-155)
WINTER
Jane 10* (F-223)
John 37 (F-132)
Julia 2* (F-151)
Walter 46* (F-196)
WINTERS
George 10* (GD-240)
WIRT
J. C. 26 (m)* (F-215)
WISE
David 15* (CL-59)
John 28 (ES-68)
John 80* (JE-3)
WISEMAN
Abner 47* (ES-89)
Isaac 40 (ES-103)
JAcob B. 39 (ES-112)
Mary Jane 12* (ES-54)
William 68 (F-223)
WISMAN
Michial 34 (OS-293)
WITHROW
Jane 40* (F-194)
WITT
Allen 35 (ES-85)
Charles 64* (ES-89)
David 50 (ES-108)
Elisha 56 (ES-87)
Garland 35 (ES-89)
George 39 (ES-63)
James 32* (ES-55)
John M. 25* (CL-38)
Littleberry 38 (MA-230)
Lucy 63 (ES-89)
Mary J. 16* (ES-81)
Mitchael 14* (ES-88)
Robert 25* (MA-271)
Sandy 37 (m) (ES-75)
Silas 47 (ES-88)
William 63 (MA-217)
WOLFORK
Sawyel D. 60 (F-162)

Index

WOLVERTON
  Silas 39* (F-151)
WOOD
  Alexander 20* (F-183)
  Ameter 29 (m) (GD-236)
  Anderson 39 (MA-321)
  B. B. 32 (m) (F-183)
  B. B. 59 (m) (F-187)
  Benj. C. 48 (F-189)
  Charles 30* (CL-62)
  Fielden 29 (ES-64)
  George 33* (MT-21)
  Greene C. 25* (F-230)
  James 26 (GD-231)
  James 41 (ES-70)
  James 54 (F-141)
  Jas. B. 45 (F-182)
  John 48* (ES-66)
  John G. 32 (MA-280)
  John J. 32 (F-168)
  Joseph 40* (MT-35)
  Mary 24* (CL-91)
  Sarah 38* (JE-13)
  Simpson 25 (MA-272)
  Thomas 52 (F-205)
  W. F. 56 (m)* (F-210)
  William 25* (MT-68)
  William H. 33 (CL-47)
  Wm. 27* (F-186)
WOODALL
  James R. 37 (CL-76)
  John 83 (GD-272)
  Sarah 73* (CL-89)
WOODARD
  David 19* (JE-19)
  Heelery 50 (m) (JE-17)
  Joseph 45 (MT-63)
  Judith 50 (MT-80)
  Lavina 72 (JE-18)
  Lucy 70* (B) (MA-207)
  William 39 (JE-33)
  William 7* (JE-33)
WOODFORD
  Edwin T. 33* (CL-35)
  Eliza B. 15* (F-114)
  John 12?* (CL-3)
  Samuel A. B. 35* (CL-9)
  Sarah A. 32* (MT-10)

WOODFORK
  Julius 77* (B) (JE-38)
  Thomas 36 (GD-256)
WOODGATE
  Jackson B. 35 (F-232)
WOODHOUSE
  Frances 9* (B) (F-213)
  Margaret 44* (F-184)
WOODROUGH
  James 24* (F-145)
WOODRUFF
  Benjamin 75* (MA-263)
  Harvey 30 (MA-285)
  Jesse 32* (F-201)
WOODS
  Archibald 64 (JE-72)
  C. C. 38 (m)* (JE-36)
  David 24* (F-210)
  Dudley 50 (MA-306)
  Frances 50 (MA-282)
  Frances E. 29* (CL-45)
  George 45 (MA-254)
  Ibby 18 (f)* (OS-280)
  James 30* (MA-251)
  James 39* (B) (F-151)
  James R. 35 (GD-282)
  John 34 (OS-280)
  John 65 (OS-297)
  John 76 (GD-233)
  Joseph 34 (OS-318)
  Louisa 36 (MA-278)
  Margaret 15* (JE-36)
  Mary 25* (F-148)
  Mary 50 (F-198)
  Merit 31 (JE-65)
  Morton 29* (JE-65)
  Rebecca 53* (OS-280)
  Rice G. 36* (GD-282)
  Richard 63 (JE-65)
  Samuel 25 (OS-297)
  Sarah 36* (CL-51)
  Schuyler 35* (F-230)
  Susan 55* (MA-308)
  Urban 53 (GD-229)
  Wiley 79* (MA-215)
  Will 65 (GD-282)
  William 35 (OS-317)
  William 50 (JE-72)

WOODSON
  Ayrael? 37 (m)* (ES-110)
  Elizabeth 39 (ES-110)
  Francis 17* (MA-283)
  R. e. 33 (m)* (JE-74)
  Sarah T. 22* (JE-57)
  Tarleton 70 (ES-110)
  Tucker 45* (JE-57)
WOODWARD
  Allen 23* (JE-43)
  Oliver 19* (JE-78)
WOOLERY
  Isaac 54* (MA-261)
WOOLEY
  John 62 (F-126)
  Mary C. 13* (GD-226)
  Roberet 14 (m)* (ES-48)
WOOLFOLK
  Absalom 40* (B) (JE-54)
WOOLLEY
  Sallie 43 (F-189)
WOOLNY
  James 49 (MA-246)
WOOLS
  John 31 (MT-24)
WOOLSY
  James 31 (MA-294)
WOOLWINE?
  John 32 (MA-243)
WOOL___
  George G. 68 (MA-237)
WOOMER
  Daniel 20* (MA-264)
WOOSLEY
  Chilton A. 21 (ES-107)
  Peter 27 (CL-24)
  Thomas 30 (ES-99)
  Thomas 68* (CL-24)
  William 42 (CL-24)
WORD
  Eliza 18* (MT-5)
  Fredric 32* (F-196)
  James 27* (GD-215)
  James 32 (GD-223)
  John 41 (OS-298)
  Thomas 50 (GD-214)
  William 52* (GD-223)

Index

WORE
  Samuel C. 39 (MA-204)
WORLAND
  James 42 (MA-280)
  Thos. L. 44* (F-191)
WORLD
  Elijah 35 (GD-272)
WORLEY
  C. T. 32 (m) (JE-71)
  Jane 52* (F-159)
WORNALL?
  Matilda 40 (B) (CL-93)
WORNER
  John 43 (GD-209)
WORSHAM
  Elizabeth 6/12* (F-137)
  Mary 5* (F-127)
  Susan 40* (B) (F-144)
  W. S. 25 (m)* (F-136)
WREN
  Eleanor Ann 60 (MT-34)
  Enoch S. 42* (MT-40)
  George S. 30 (MT-34)
  Hugh B. 50* (MT-27)
  James W. 69* (MT-16)
  Jane 73 (F-202)
  Nelly 80* (B) (MT-27)
  Thomas 40 (MT-39)
WRIGHT
  Alsey 45 (F-157)
  Edwin 10* (MT-2)
  Elias 18* (F-199)
  Elish 50* (OS-291)
  Elisha 33 (GD-272)
  Elizabeth 11* (JE-50)
  Flensy? W. 26 (m) (MA-277)
  Gabriel J. 37 (JE-67)
  George T. 22* (F-127)
  Henry 34 (MA-302)
  Hiram 34 (OS-311)
  Jackson 29 (MA-211)
  James 52* (F-131)
  James B. 35 (MA-201)
  Jeptha 37 (CL-35)
  John 27 (F-157)
  John 45 (MA-298)
  Joseph P. 30 (ES-89)
  Joshua 45 (MT-50)
  Katurah 49 (MA-298)
  M. A. 23 (f) (F-132)
  Mary 34?* (MT-57)
  Mary 65* (CL-35)
  McArthur 32 (CL-15)
  Meredith 45 (MT-81)
  Morgan 40 (F-176)
  Patsey 38* (CL-17)
  Robert G. 35 (JE-67)
  Sally 42 (MA-224)
  Solomon 65* (MT-44)
  Thomas 84 (CL-88)
  Thomas J. 20* (ES-97)
  W. H. H. 38 (m)* (CL-88)
  William 35* (ES-58)
  William 80 (MA-303)
  William B. 23 (MA-298)
  William B. 25 (MA-312)
  William H. 4* (MT-15)
  William T. 27 (CL-14)
WYATT
  Haden 47 (MT-79)
  Margaret 70* (ES-106)
  Thomas J. 40* (JE-4)
  William 37 (ES-81)
WYCKOFF
  J. 52 (m) (MT-61)
WYLIE
  James B. 23* (ES-60)
  Tuman? 23 (m)* (ES-88)
WYMER
  David 27* (MT-67)
  Lucinda 33* (MT-77)
  Lucinda 50* (MT-66)
  Peter 27 (MT-67)
  Peter 30* (MT-57)
WYMORE
  Martin 77* (F-158)
WYNE
  Elkaney 32 (m)* (OS-296)
WYNNE
  Lewis 28* (F-186)
YANCY
  Thomas G. 37 (MA-287)
YANTIS
  James H. 42 (GD-266)
  Jesse 53 (m) (GD-267)
  John 32 (GD-289)
  John Q. 32 (GD-267)
  Robert P. 29 (GD-205)
YARNALL
  Isaac W. 31* (F-173)
YATES
  A. 23* (F-194)
  Abner 57 (F-236)
  Anderson 41 (MA-228)
  C. 21 (f)* (F-195)
  Elijah 54* (MA-243)
  Frances 15* (MT-6)
  George 49* (F-236)
  James 42 (MA-229)
  James M. 18* (F-204)
  James W. 40* (JE-56)
  Jesse 55 (MT-23)
  John 15* (F-160)
  John 80 (MA-229)
  Robert 30 (MA-256)
  Sarah 19* (F-143)
  Thomas jr. 23 (GD-260)
  William 30* (F-236)
  William 85 (MT-38)
  Wm. 23* (F-159)
YEAKEY
  John 26 (GD-282)
YEARING
  Dennis 40* (F-235)
YEATER
  Henry 20* (GD-253)
  Matilda 45 (GD-253)
  Thomas sr. 43 (GD-254)
YEATES
  Benjamin 25* (CL-47)
  Elizabeth A. 11* (GD-277)
  Mary A. 5* (GD-275)
YELMAN
  John Geo. 29* (F-153)
YIREY
  John 50 (OS-301)
YOCUM
  Abel 42 (MT-64)
  Franklin 31* (MT-66)
  Jesse 35 (MT-56)
  Jesse 36* (MT-67)
  Jinsey 40 (f) (MT-67)
  John M. 26 (MT-64)
  Levi 42 (MT-72)

Index

YOCUM
  Melvina 11* (MT-76)
  Nancy E. 4* (MT-13)
  Sylvester 9* (MT-55)
  William 50 (MT-64)
YORK
  Alferd 35 (OS-313)
  Elenor 10* (OS-281)
  William 38 (OS-280)
YOST
  George J. 44* (JE-51)
  Sarah 60 (CL-86)
YOUNG
  A. M. 33 (m) (JE-4)
  Acquilla 57* (MT-1)
  Alfred 23 (F-208)
  Amon 29 (MT-10)
  Andrew M. 28* (JE-60)
  Archibald 58 (JE-72)
  Brown 27* (JE-72)
  Catharine 29* (CL-92)
  Charity 36 (B) (F-214)
  Charles 41 (F-219)
  E. A. 34 (f)* (F-161)
  E. A. 35 (f)* (F-150)
  E. S. 23 (m)* (F-126)
  Edward 19* (F-136)
  Ephraim 31* (JE-59)
  Ephraim 83* (MT-28)
  Frances 59 (GD-266)
  George 20* (MT-8)
  George P. 29* (JE-59)
  Georgean 15 (f)* (MT-6)
  James 31 (CL-9)
  John 48 (OS-315)
  John C. 30 (F-119)
  John C. 50 (MA-276)
  L. K. 37 (m) (F-146)
  Lidia 76* (JE-9)
  Margarett 39* (CL-46)
  Martha P. 35* (MT-59)
  Mary 75* (JE-4)
  Moses 42* (F-249)
  Nancy 62* (MT-26)
  Richd. B. 44* (F-211)
  Robert 46 (JE-75)
  Roland 40* (F-249)
  Sally A. 13* (JE-8)
  Walter C. 42 (JE-4)
  William D. 53* (JE-6)
YOUNG?
  Susan 87 (F-143)
  William 54 (F-142)
YOWELL
  Conner 41 (F-185)
ZEISER?
  R. E. 40 (m)* (F-124)
ZIEGLER
  John 30* (F-135)
ZIKE
  Joseph 50* (JE-40)
ZIMERMAN
  Martin 23 (JE-6)
ZIMMERMAN
  David 40* (F-188)
ZONNY
  Danl. Y. 28* (F-139)

Bryant 45* (B) (F-154)
Caroline 17* (B) (F-130)
Hannah 56 (B) (JE-41)
Henry 25 (B) (F-198)
Isaac 17* (B) (F-164)
Jane 75* (B) (F-163)
Judith 50 (B) (F-193)
Kitty 30* (B) (JE-66)

Fanny 65* (B) (F-149)
Hanah 22* (B) (F-149)
Mary 23* (B) (F-159)